M. PURBHOO

Using Simply Accounting® by Sage 2006

Pro and Basic Versions for Windows®

PEARSON
Addison Wesley
Toronto

LIBRARY AND ARCHIVES CANADA CATALOGUING IN PUBLICATION

Purbhoo, Mary, 1949–
Using Simply Accounting by Sage Pro and Basic versions for Windows / M. Purbhoo. – 2006 ed.

Issued also as trade ed. under title: Teach yourself Simply Accounting by Sage Pro and Basic versions for Windows. The title of trade ed. is found on separate bellyband on monograph.

Includes index.

ISBN-13: 978-0-321-44153-9 (college ed.); ISBN-10: 0-321-44153-2 (college ed.)
ISBN-13: 978-0-321-45595-6 (trade ed.); ISBN-10: 0-321-45595-9 (trade ed.)

1. Simply Accounting for Windows (Computer file)
2. Accounting–Computer programs. I. Title. II. Title: Teach yourself
Simply Accounting Basic and Pro versions for Windows.

HF5679.P896 2007 657'.0285'536 C2006-901560-0

This edition is also published as Teach Yourself Simply Accounting® by Sage 2006: Pro and Basic Versions for Windows®.

ISBN-10: 0-321-44153-2 (college ed.)
ISBN-13: 978-0-321-44153-9 (college ed.)
ISBN-10: 0-321-45595-9 (trade ed.)
ISBN-13: 978-0-321-45595-6 (trade ed.)

Editor-in-Chief, Business & Economics: Gary Bennett
Executive Acquisitions Editor: Samantha Scully
Executive Marketing Manager: Cas Shields
Associate Editor: Rema Celio
Production Editor: Jen Handel
Copy Editor: Nicole Mellow
Proofreader: Lu Cormier
Production Coordinator: Andrea Falkenberg
Page Layout: Mary Purbhoo
Permissions and Photo Research: Sandy Cooke
Art Director: Julia Hall
Interior and Cover Design: Anthony Leung
Cover Image: Will Crocker/Gettyimages

Credits:
Photo of the body fat scale used in the data files on the Student CD-ROM: Photo courtesy of Tanita.
Page 263, screenshot from Canada Revenue Agency website: Reproduced with permission of the Minister of Public Works and Government Services Canada, 2006.

3 4 5 11 10 09 08 07 Printed and bound in Canada.

PEARSON
Addison Wesley

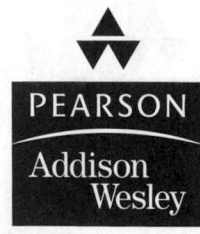

CONTENTS

Part 3: Advanced Pro Features

Part 4: Appendices

Appendices on the Student CD-ROM

PREFACE

Using Simply Accounting® by Sage 2006: Pro and Basic Versions for Windows® is an update of our Version 2005 text and is again based on the Pro version. As usual, however, the book is fully compatible with both Pro and Basic versions and covers both versions completely. Once again, we include the Simply Accounting by Sage 2006 Student Pro (Release A) program with the text. Therefore, even users of the Basic version can examine and learn the features that are specific to Pro. Although we do not address the Premier version of Simply Accounting, the book is also compatible with this version.

In this edition, the new features of the program that we cover include creating an accountant's copy of the data set, importing accountant's journal entries and using the streamlined options screens for settings and payroll information. For reference, we also added a chart of keyboard shortcuts that can be used in Simply Accounting.

We have also added some resources to the Student CD-ROM with Data Files:

- review questions and cases for each chapter; these are placed in an appendix on the Student CD-ROM
- the interactive Accounting Cycle Tutorial that introduces basic accounting terms and concepts
- an Upgrade program to update the 2006 Student Pro (or another 2006 version Release A) program to Release B. Instructions for installing the update can be found in Appendix A, pages A11–A13.

We have also modified the bookmark by adding a ruler marked edge to help you and your instructor refer to specific lines on a page. We realize that page flipping is inevitable in a keystroke text, so you should continue to use the bookmark to mark a source document page as you work through keystrokes or to mark a keystroke page as you work through source documents.

But, we have not changed the basic format and features of the book, including the following:

- comprehensive coverage of all Basic and Pro features of Simply Accounting
- ready-to-use data files for both Pro and Basic versions
- the diversity of companies and business situations, including non-profit, service and inventory businesses
- comprehensive tax coverage for different provinces including remittances
- the realistic approach
- the easy-to-follow, step-by-step keystroke instructions accompanied by many screen illustrations
- the currency of our information (As this book is going to print, the GST rate will be reduced to 6 percent. Government approval for this change came too late to apply in our text. Thousands of numbers are affected, requiring recalculation, rewriting and checking in the text, data files and solutions. Had we made the changes, we would not have had time to ensure the level of accuracy we expect of ourselves and still meet our goal of publication before September. Instead, we built in the tax change as a source document memo throughout the text and apply the updated tax rate in the final chapter of the text.)

We have also kept the organization of our earlier workbooks. Part One provides an overview and introduction to Simply Accounting and sales taxes. Data applications that can be completed with both Basic and Pro versions are located in Part Two. We introduce each ledger of the Simply Accounting program (General, Payables, Receivables, Payroll, Inventory and Project) in six separate applications. Budgeting and account reconciliation procedures are covered in two more applications. Advanced Receivables and Payables features (orders and quotes, credit cards, discounts, tax remittances, sales to foreign customers and Internet linkages) are demonstrated in two separate chapters. Online banking is included again, too, with a simulation that allows you to download a bank statement that integrates with data from the text. The required data files for all these chapters are set up in advance, and for each new type of transaction we provide detailed keystrokes and matching screens.

Three applications provide a comprehensive introduction to setting up a computerized accounting system using Simply Accounting. Again, detailed instructions with screen illustrations are given for each setup as you learn to convert, design and implement a complete accounting system.

- The first setup introduces a new non-profit organization that uses only the General Ledger.
- The second setup is for a service organization using the General, Payables and Receivables Ledgers.
- The third setup describes a comprehensive retail organization and covers the General, Payables, Receivables, Payroll and Inventory Ledgers.

In the final application in Part Two, you set up a computerized accounting system on your own and complete descriptive and realistic source documents that give you the "feel" of actual company transactions.

Time & Billing and Departmental Accounting, advanced features available only in the Pro version, are covered in Part Three. Separate chapters and data files are prepared for these. All Part Three pages are edged with a blue stripe so that you can find them quickly.

Ten appendices are provided for reference or further study — four in Part Four of the text and six on the Student CD-ROM. The text includes the following:

- A: Installing Simply Accounting (also includes instructions for upgrading to Release B)
- B: Windows Basics, Shortcuts & Terms (includes chart of Simply Accounting keyboard shortcuts; accounting vs. non-accounting terms)
- C: Correcting Errors after Posting (descriptions and screen displays for reversing entries)
- D: Working in Multi-user Mode

The remaining appendices in PDF format on the Student CD-ROM are available for you to read or print:

- E: Review Questions and Cases
- F: Customizing Sales Invoices
- G: Setting Security and Passwords (entering and removing users, access rights and passwords)
- H: Integration with Other Software (linking with MS Office documents, exporting GIFI financial reports and payroll T4s to Canada Revenue Agency, importing customer or vendor data, accounts and transactions)
- I: Online Banking
- J: Review of Basic Accounting

USING THIS BOOK

The accounting applications in this text were prepared using the Pro 2006 (Release B) and Basic 2006 (Release B) versions of the Simply Accounting for Windows software published by The Sage Group PLC.

You must have a hard disk and CD-ROM drive, or a network system with Windows installed. If you do not have your own copy of the Simply Accounting program, you can use the Student Pro software included with this text. Network system users should work with the site administrator to ensure complete data access.

In addition, you should have a standard accounting text for reviewing accounting principles. The text provides some accounting principles and procedures, and the Review of Basic Accounting in Appendix J and the Accounting Cycle Tutorial on the Student CD-ROM also provide an introduction. However, these are not intended to replace the breadth and depth of most standard accounting texts. You should also consult the built-in Help features and the Simply Accounting manuals on the program CD.

The text is as simple and straightforward as we could make it, but you will still need some familiarity with computers before you work through it. Your life will be easier still if you have acquired some of the fundamentals of troubleshooting.

Instructors can order an Instructor's Resource CD-ROM that includes Simply Accounting solutions for each application after all transactions are completed, an Instructor's Resource Manual with answers for all the cases in the text and a Test Item File. Instructor packages to accompany this text should be ordered from your Pearson Education Canada sales representative.

The Student CD-ROM with Data Files

Because the text is used with the Basic version as well as Pro, we have tried to make version differences as clear as possible in the text by using Basic Version margin notes. In addition, we provide separate Pro and Basic data sets for the two versions of the software. All data files are ready to use without conversions or passwords.

The Student CD-ROM has an autorun feature that should open the Student CD-ROM home window automatically when you insert the CD into your CD drive. From this home window you can choose to install data files, view the supplementary appendices in PDF format, run the Accounting Cycle Tutorial, upgrade your Student Pro program to Release B, open the ReadMe file or browse the CD. The Student CD-ROM home window will remain open for you to make another selection until you close it.

If the Student CD-ROM does not start automatically,

Choose the **Start menu** and click Run. In the filename window,

Type `d:\start.exe` (where d: is the drive letter for your CD drive). **Click OK**.

Click **Exit** to close the Student CD-ROM.

The separate installation programs for the data sets will help you install the right data set for your program. To choose the correct data set for your program installation, you must know what version you are using. You can get this information from the program package, from the program CD or from the Select Company window in the program. PRO and BASIC also appear in the Home window of the program for all data files. The Simply Accounting welcome screen will tell you what version you have installed.

Use the following chart to help you install the data set you need.

FOR PROGRAM VERSION	CLICK INSTALL BUTTON	DATA SET (FOLDER ON CD)
Basic Version 2006	Install Basic Data	Basic
Student Pro Version 2006	Install Pro Data	Pro
Pro Version 2006	Install Pro Data	Pro
Premier Version 2006	Install Pro Data	Pro

Both installation programs create a data folder named Simdata on drive C. If you need to work with another location for your data files, refer to page 7 in this text. You can install the data files as often as you need to.

If you are using the Premier version, the Simply Accounting data conversion wizard will convert the data files when you open them. You can reinstall the files from the original Student CD-ROM if you need to start over later or if you want to work with the Student Pro version included with the text.

Passwords

We have not added any passwords to the data files on the Student CD-ROM to ensure maximum accessibility. However, if you are using the Pro version in a multi-user or network environment that includes users and passwords, you will need to enter your user name and password before you can open the data files. Ask your instructor or site administrator for the user name and password that you should use. Refer to Appendix G on the Student CD-ROM for instructions on working with passwords.

If you try to open the data files directly from the Student CD-ROM, you will see an error message about access rights. This is different from the password protection message. Refer to the instructions for installing and accessing data files in Chapter 1.

Working with Different Versions of Simply Accounting

You can use the Student CD-ROM data files with the 2006 Basic, Pro, Premier and Pro Student versions of Simply Accounting, Release B or later.

The Student version is a fully functional Pro version that you can use for 14 months after installation. You can install only one version of Simply Accounting 2006 on your computer. If you are using the Basic version and want to install the Student Pro version, you must uninstall the Basic program before installing the other version.

If you try to open the data files with earlier versions of Simply Accounting (2005 and earlier) or with 2006 Release A, Simply Accounting displays an error message. Users who install the Student program accompanying the text or have Release A installed can upgrade to Release B with the Upgrade program on the Student

CD-ROM. Refer to Appendix A, pages A11–A13. This Upgrade program has been included with the permission of The Sage Group PLC.

Although the data files can be used with later versions of the software, you may see changes in screens, keystrokes and payroll tax amounts. Before you open a data file with a later version, the Simply Accounting conversion wizard will update the data file to match the program version you are using. Always refer to the manuals and update notices for later versions.

Working Through the Applications

Keystroke Instruction Style

We have incorporated different paragraph styles for different kinds of statements in the text to help you identify the instructions that you must follow to complete the transactions correctly and see the screens that we present. These different styles are illustrated below:

Press enter or **press** the **Add button** to start the Add Account wizard (Keystroke command line — command word is in bold and the object of the command, what you press, is in colour. Lines are indented and spaced apart. Additional text or information for the line is shown in plain text.)

Type `West Carbide Tools (net 30)` (Command line with text you type in a special font.)

Or you can click the Comment field to advance the cursor. (Alternative keystroke sequence that you may want to use later. Paragraph is indented in block style and plain text style is used.)

Regular text is presented in normal paragraphs like this one. **Key words** are shown in colour to make it easy to identify the topics covered in the text. Names of icons, fields, text and tool buttons that you will see on-screen in the program have all initial letters capitalized in our text (for example, Adjust A Previously Posted Invoice tool or Display A Reminder If Exchange Rate Is One Day Old). The text also uses Notes and Warnings that contain additional important information and cautions.

Account names included in regular text paragraphs are italicized (for example, *Revenue from Sales* or *Cost of Goods Sold*).

Order of Applications

Setup applications are introduced early in the text. Advanced users should have no difficulty working through the applications in the order given and may even choose to skip some applications. However, at a minimum, we recommend working through all keystroke transactions (the ones with a ✓ beside them) so that you become familiar with all the journals before starting the more comprehensive applications.

There are alternatives if the text is used at an introductory level in one course and then at an advanced level for a different course. In this case, the students can complete all the General, Payables and Receivables applications (Chapters 3–9) in the introductory course and the remaining chapters later; complete the source documents for setup applications (except Stratford Country Inn) before starting the setups and Stratford Country Inn — setting up an application that is already familiar from source documents; or complete the chapters in a different sequence as follows:

1. Read and work through the two Getting Started chapters in Part 1.

2A. Complete the ledger applications in order: Missoni Marbleworks (General), Chai Tea Room (basic Payables), Air Care Services (basic Receivables), Andersson Chiropractic Clinic and Maple Leaf Rags (advanced features of the first three ledgers), Lime Light Laundry (Payroll), Adrienne Aesthetics (Inventory) and Truman Tires* (Project).

2B. (Pro version only) Complete Flabuless Fitness — Time and Billing.

3. Complete the account reconciliation (Tesses Tresses) and budgeting (Village Galleries) applications.
4. Complete the three setup applications in order: Toss for Tots (General), Dorfmann Design (three ledgers) and Flabuless Fitness (six ledgers).
5. Complete the Stratford Country Inn setup application with realistic source documents. Users may want to attempt this setup with the help of the setup wizard from the Setup menu in the Home window.

* Truman Tires (Project Ledger, Chapter 12) may be completed after all other chapters because it does not introduce keystrokes required for any other application.

This order is shown graphically in the following chart:

AN ALTERNATIVE SEQUENCE FOR WORKING THROUGH THE APPLICATIONS

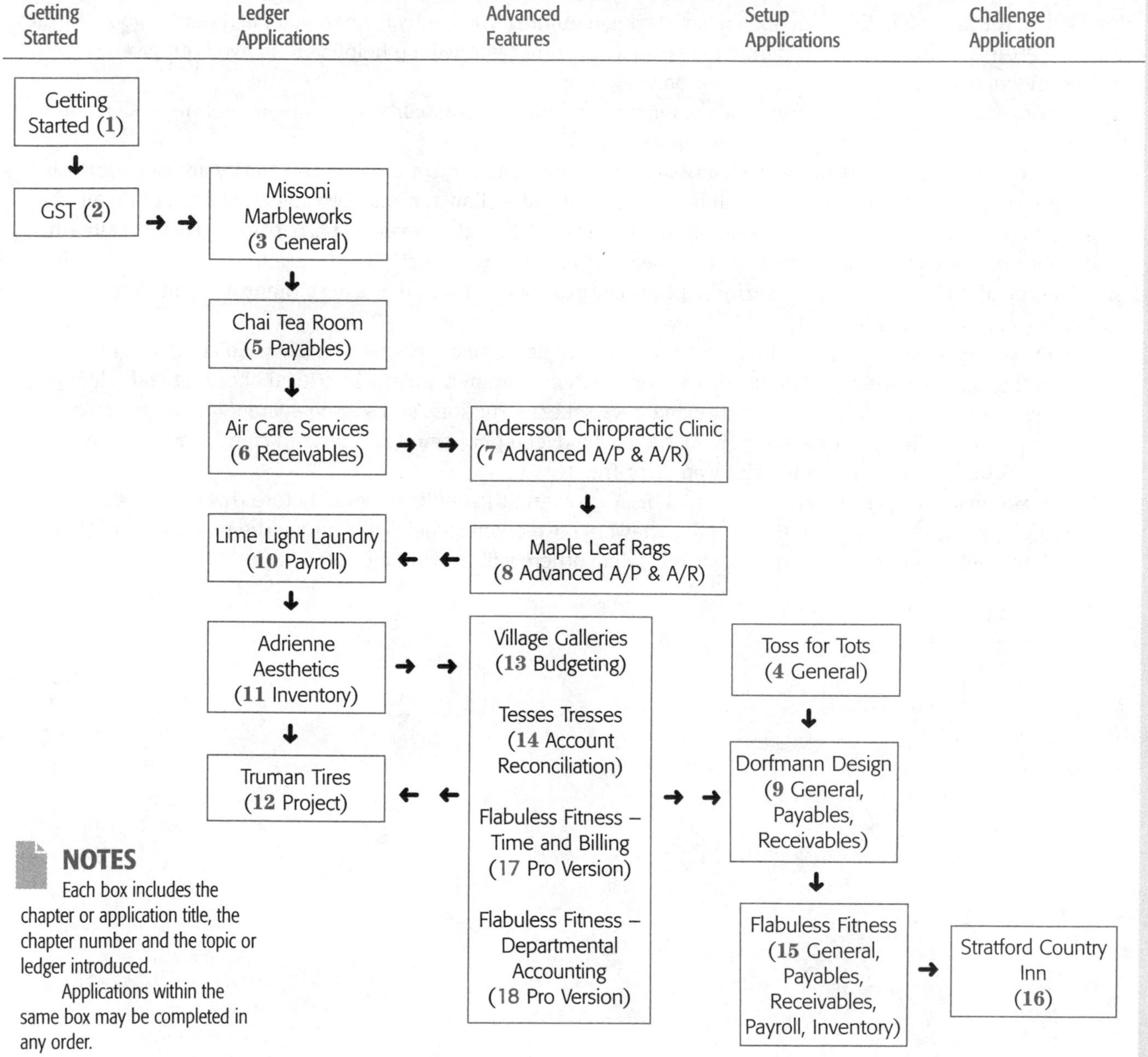

NOTES

Each box includes the chapter or application title, the chapter number and the topic or ledger introduced.

Applications within the same box may be completed in any order.

ACKNOWLEDGEMENTS

A team that works well together has more benefits than just a better product. With deadlines that always seem impossible to meet at the start, the work seems to get done faster with less stress and generally more positive feelings. When the team members are familiar, these benefits are even greater. We were fortunate to have a good team in place for this project. Everyone played their part, whether they occupied a main role or remained behind the scenes.

It has been a pleasure to work with Samantha Scully, Jennifer Handel and Rema Celio again. This trio provided a measure of calm productivity that we feel privileged to experience. Thank you for sharing this aura.

Two key people at Sage have also been invaluable members of the team. Thank you Chris Heaney and Jim Collins for making making my job easier. Having a number you can call when you need help is good, but it is even better when you are confident the person at the other end will be helpful. You have both given me that confidence and I truly appreciate your ongoing support.

Every year Anthony Leung continues to impress us with the originality and suitability of his designs. It is hard to imagine our texts designed by anyone else.

Copy editing material in which the consistency of style, accuracy of content and clarity are as important as grammar, spelling and punctuation cannot be easy. Nicole Mellow not only provides that level of detailed examination but also continues to polish our rough work, adding gloss even to parts that we thought already shone. Our usual reaction to her editorial changes is, "Yes, that is better!" Thanks again, Nicole. And then by proofing the already proofed manuscript, Lu Cormier provided yet another layer of improvement that contributes to our high standards.

After writing several of these texts, it is important to get a fresh perspective. This can come from different sources — feedback from users and non-users or from new people in critical checking and editing roles. This year the painstaking job of checking keystroke instructions and source documents for accuracy and clarity was handled by someone new. Marianne Trudgeon performed this task efficiently and effectively, helping us towards our goal of publishing an error-free text.

User surveys always provoke thought and discussion and the one completed before this edition was no different. We are grateful for the time these reviewers have taken to help us improve the text. Some of their suggestions could be implemented immediately while others will provide input for future editions.

Part 1
Getting Started

CHAPTER ONE

Getting Started

OBJECTIVES

After completing this chapter, you should be able to

- ***access*** the Simply Accounting program
- ***access*** the data files for a business
- ***understand*** Simply Accounting's help features
- ***save*** your work
- ***back up*** your data files
- ***finish*** your session
- ***change*** default date format settings

NOTES

The instructions in this chapter for starting the program and copying files refer to Windows XP procedures. If you are using a different version of Windows, please refer to Windows and Simply Accounting Help and manuals for assistance with these procedures.

WARNING!

You will be unable to open the data files with Simply 2006 Release A or earlier versions.

If you have Release A of the program, you can install the update to Release B from the Student CD-ROM with Data Files. Refer to page 11 and page A-11 in Appendix A.

The Student CD-ROM with Data Files will be referred to as the Student CD-ROM throughout the text.

GETTING STARTED

Data Files and Abbreviations

The applications in this workbook were prepared using Windows XP and the Simply Accounting 2006 Pro and Basic (Release B) software packages produced by Sage Software. You will be unable to open the data files with Simply 2006 Release A or earlier versions. Later versions of the software may have changes in screens or keystrokes. Income tax tables change regularly; the most recent ones will be used in later versions of the software.

The instructions in this workbook have been written for a stand-alone PC, with a hard disk drive and a CD-ROM disk drive. Windows should be correctly installed on your hard drive. Your printers should be installed and accessible through the Windows program. Refer to Windows Help and manuals for assistance with these procedures.

This workbook reflects the author's approach to working with Simply Accounting. There are alternative approaches to setting up company accounts and to working with the software. Refer to Simply Accounting and Windows Help and manuals for further details.

DATA APPLICATION FILES

Company	Folder\File Name	Chapter
Getting started	Start\start.sdb	1
Missoni Marbleworks	Missoni\missoni.sdb	3
Toss for Tots	Setup\Toss\toss.sdb	4
Chai Tea Room	Chai\chai.sdb	5
Air Care Services	Aircare\aircare.sdb	6
Andersson Chiropractic Clinic	Anderson\anderson.sdb	7
Maple Leaf Rags	Maple\maple.sdb	8
Dorfmann Design	Setup\Dorfmann\dorfmann.sdb	9
Lime Light Laundry	Limelite\limelite.sdb	10
Adrienne Aesthetics	Adrienne\adrienne.sdb	11
Truman Tires	Truman\truman.sdb	12
Village Galleries	Village\village.sdb	13
Tesses Tresses	Tess\tess.sdb	14
Flabuless Fitness	Setup\Flab\flab-apr.sdb	15
	Setup\Flab\flab-may.sdb	15
	Setup\Flab\flab-jun.sdb	15
Stratford Country Inn	user setup	16
Flabuless Fitness (Pro version only)	Time\flab-time.sdb	17
Flabuless Fitness (Pro version only)	Depart\flab-dept.sdb	18

The applications increase in complexity, with each one introducing new ledgers, setups or features as shown in the following chart.

DATA APPLICATION	LEDGER USED						OTHER
	GL	AP	AR	PAY	INV	PROJ	
Missoni Marbleworks	*						1
Toss for Tots	*						2
Chai Tea Room	*	*					
Air Care Services	*	*	*				
Andersson Chiropractic Clinic	*	*	*				
Maple Leaf Rags	*	*	*				3, 4, 7
Dorfmann Design	*	*	*				2, 3, 7
Lime Light Laundry	*	*	*	*			
Adrienne Aesthetics	*	*	*	*	*		3, 7
Truman Tires	*	*	*	*	*	*	3, 7
Village Galleries	*	*	*	*	*		3, 5, 7
Tesses Tresses	*	*	*		*		6
Flabuless Fitness (Chapter 15)	*	*	*	*	*		2, 3, 4, 7
Stratford Country Inn	*	*	*	*			1, 3, 8
Flabuless Fitness (Chapter 17)	*	*	*	*	*		PRO 1
Flabuless Fitness (Chapter 18)	*	*	*	*	*		PRO 2

LEDGERS

GL = General Ledger
AP = Accounts Payable
AR = Accounts Receivable
PAY = Payroll
INV = Inventory
PROJ = Project (Jobcosting)

Other:

1 Realistic source documents
2 Setup application with keystrokes
3 Credit cards
4 Internet links
5 Budgeting
6 Account reconciliation
7 Foreign currency transactions
8 Setup application without keystrokes

PRO 1 Time and Billing and Build from Bill of Materials
PRO 2 Departmental Accounting

These additional features are available only in the Pro version.

WARNING!

Before using your data files, you should make backup copies of all the files. Always work with this working backup copy, so that you can use the original to restore the files later if you have data errors. Refer to page 6 and your Windows manuals for complete instructions.

NOTES

The Stratford Country Inn file is not set up in advance for you. You must create that file on your own.

The Student CD-ROM also includes a copy of the Skeleton template file for Chapter 4 and data files for bank reconciliation for Chapter 14, Case 6 for Chapter 15 in Appendix E, and online banking in Appendix I (Appendices E and I are also on the Student CD-ROM.)

NOTES
For an introduction to basic Windows terminology used in this text, refer to Appendix B. This appendix also includes a chart of keyboard shortcuts for the Simply Accounting program.

The Simply Accounting Program

Simply Accounting is an integrated accounting program with many features that are suitable for small- and medium-sized businesses. It includes several ledgers and journals that work together so that data entered in one part of the program will be linked and available in other parts of the program. Thus ledgers are automatically updated from journal entries, and reports always include the most recent transactions and ledger changes. A business can use one or more of the accounting modules: General, Payables, Receivables, Payroll, Inventory, Project and Time and Billing (Pro version). Only the features used are set up. Thus, if payroll is not used, there is no need to set up the Payroll module, and it can be hidden from view. A more complete description of the program and its features is presented in Chapter 15, pages 562–563.

NOTES
For assistance with installing the Simply Accounting program, refer to Appendix A.

Simply Accounting Program Components

When you select the Typical Installation option, several components will be installed:

- **Simply Accounting Program**: the Simply Accounting software you will need to perform the accounting transactions for your company. It will be placed in the main Winsim folder under the Program Files folder or the folder location you selected.
- **Samples**: complete company records for both accrual-basis and cash-basis accounting methods for two sample companies — Universal Construction and Universal Crustacean Farm. They will be placed in a folder under Winsim called Samdata.
- **Templates**: predefined charts of accounts and settings for a large number of business types. These files will be stored in a folder under Winsim called Template. Two starter files with only charts of accounts also appear in this folder.
- **Crystal Reports Print Engine**, **Forms** and **Management Reports**: a variety of commonly used business forms and reports that you can customize to suit your own business needs as well as the program to access and print them. They will be placed in a folder under Winsim called Forms.
- **Customizable Forms** and **Customized Reports**: a variety of MS Office documents designed for integrated use with Simply Accounting. They will be placed in a Reports folder under Winsim.
- **New Business Guide**: a number of checklists showing the steps to follow when setting up a new business, customized for a variety of business types in different provinces. This guide includes addresses and phone numbers as well as Web addresses that you can access for further information.
- **Manuals**: documentation that will help you learn how to use Simply Accounting.

NOTES
Access the business guides from the Start menu on the desktop (choose Start, then point to Programs and Simply Accounting and click New Business Guide). You can also access the business guides from Simply Accounting's Home window (choose the Business Assistant menu and click New Business Guide). Choose your province and type of business.

WARNING!
Unless you have experience working with Windows folders and file attributes, we recommend using the autoinstall option on the Student CD-ROM to install your data set and remove all read-only file properties.

Backing Up Your Data Files

Before you begin the applications, you must copy the data files to your hard disk drive. You cannot work from the CD because Simply Accounting will not open read-only files, and all CD-ROM files are read-only files. Next, you should make a working backup copy of all the files. Keep the original for future use to begin again without returning to the CD. The following instructions will copy all the files to your hard disk drive, create the necessary new folders and remove the read-only file attributes or properties.

Installing Your Data Files

The Student CD-ROM contains Basic and Pro versions of the data files and several supplementary files for the book. It also has programs that will automatically copy the data files to a new SimData folder on your hard drive (drive C:). If you want to use a different location for your data files, proceed to page 7.

You must work with the correct version of the data set. You cannot open Pro version files with the Basic program. If you are working with Basic version, install the Basic data files. If you are working with Pro version, install the Pro data files.

If you are using the **Basic version**, refer to sidebar notes for the differences between the Basic 2006 and Pro 2006 versions.

Insert the **Student CD-ROM** into your CD drive. The home window appears:

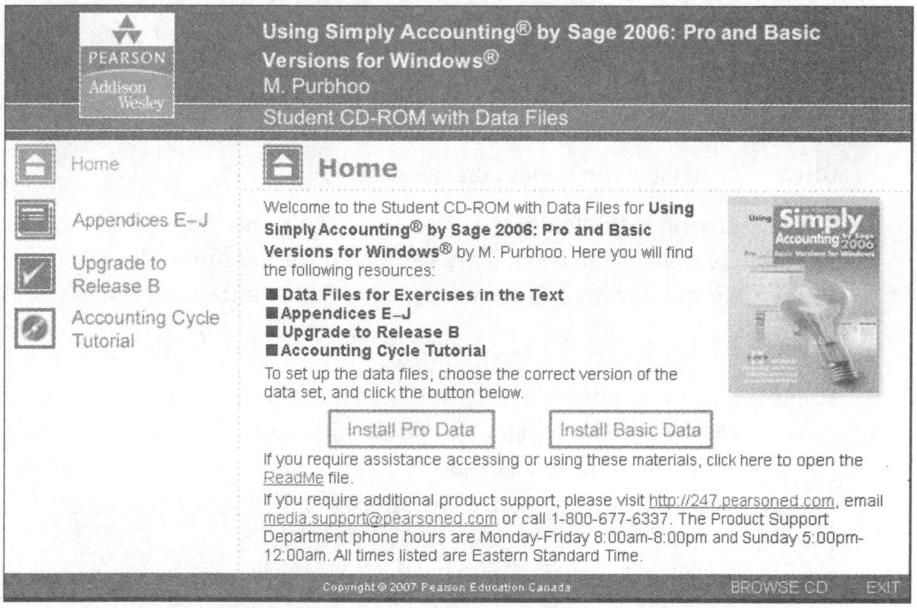

Click **Install Basic Data** (to copy the data set for Basic 2006), or

Click **Install Pro Data** (to copy the data for Pro 2006 and Student versions).

When all the files have been copied, you will see the following message:

Click **OK**. The data files have been copied to C:\SimData.

If the Student CD-ROM home window does not open automatically,

Choose the **Start menu** on the desktop and **click Run** to open the Run window.

Type d:\start.exe (where D: is the drive letter for your CD drive.)

Click **OK**.

You can also view the supplementary files on the CD. You can save these files to your hard drive or print them if you want.

Click **Appendices E–J** and then **click** the **file** you want.

Close the **PDF file** when you have finished viewing or printing it.

NOTES
Keystroke instructions that you must use are shown with highlighted text in indented paragraphs like the ones on this page, starting with **Insert**, **Click**, **Choose** and **Type**.
The command words are in **bold black** type and the object of the command is shown in **colour**.

NOTES
The Student CD-ROM includes an appendix that reviews accounting principles and an interactive Accounting Tutorial that introduces basic accounting procedures for manual accounting.

Click **Exit** to close the Student CD-ROM window.

All the data files for the book are now located in the new SimData folder in drive C:. You should now copy or back up the files to your working folder.

> **NOTES**
> If you need to create a new data folder, refer to page 22.

Copying Data Files on the Hard Disk

To copy the data files to another folder on your hard disk, we will use the Windows Explorer program.

We will copy the data files from the SimData folder (created with the autoinstall feature) to the Data folder under Winsim in the Program Files folder, the default location for the program's installation.

> **NOTES**
> In earlier versions of Windows, Explorer is located directly under Programs.

Click **Start** (on the desktop task bar).

Choose (point to) **Programs**, then **choose** **Accessories** and **click** **Windows Explorer**.

Click **My Computer** in the Folders list.

Click **C:** to view the folders on the hard drive.

> **WARNING!**
> Simply Accounting writes directly to the file you are using throughout your working session. If you do not back up your original data files before using them, you may be unable to access them if you make an unrecoverable error.
> You will need to reinstall the files from the Student CD-ROM.

Click **SimData**, the folder you just created, on the Folders side so that the contents — all the folders — appear on the Name side of the window. (Scroll down if necessary to include SimData in the list of Folders.)

Click **Adrienne**, the first folder in the Contents list. Scroll down.

Press *shift* and **click** **Village**, the last folder in the Contents list. Or, you can **choose** the **Edit menu** and **click** **Select All**. This will highlight all the folders in SimData as shown:

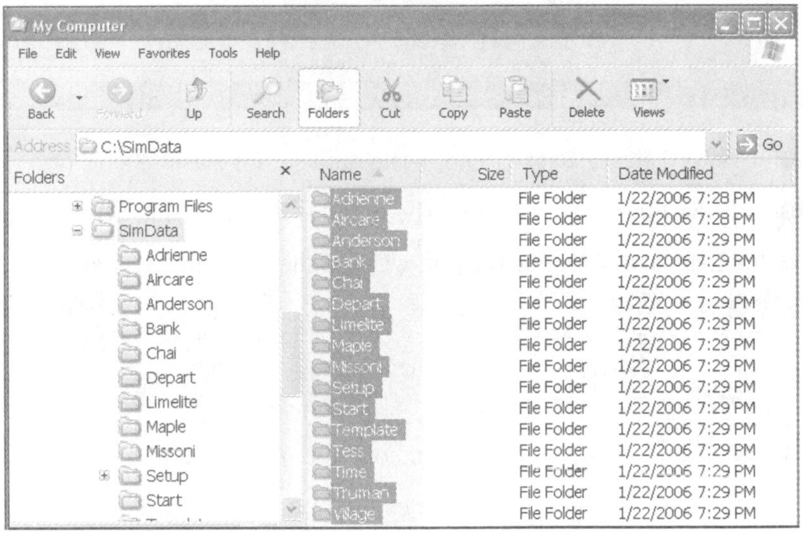

> **NOTES**
> Your screen may look different if you have selected different viewing options such as displaying the folders as icons. We show folders and files listed with details rather than by icon. This selection is changed from the Explorer View menu.

> **NOTES**
> To select all the files, you can also click on one folder and then choose the Edit menu and click Select All.

Choose the **Edit menu** and **click** **Copy** or **click** the **Copy tool** Copy.

Click to scroll up the Folders list to the Program Files folder in drive C:.

Click the ⊞ **beside** the **folder** to see the folders under Program Files.

Click the ⊞ **beside** the **Winsim** folder to list the folders under Winsim. The Data folder should be visible.

Click the **Data folder** so that it is open. The Contents or Name side of the Explorer window should be empty because the folder is empty.

> **NOTES**
> You can also copy from the My Computer screen (double click the My Computer icon) but you will not see the folders and file names at the same time.

You can choose a different destination folder for your data files if you want.

Choose the **Edit menu** and **click Paste** or **click** the **Paste tool** Paste.

Your screen will show the files being copied. When the copying is complete, all the folders and files from SimData will be copied to the Data folder under Winsim that was created during installation. When you click the new ⊞ icon beside Data, you will see the new list of data folders.

Click ☒ to close Windows Explorer.

If you want to copy only the files for a single application, click the folder for the application you want (e.g., Missoni) under SimData to highlight it. Complete the copy as you would for the entire set of folders — use the copy command, open the destination folder and then paste the folder.

WARNING!
Each application has more than one file containing different parts of the accounting information. All files must be contained in the same folder. If any file is missing, you will be unable to access the information. By copying folders and not individual files, you will keep the necessary files together.

Working with Other File Locations

You can copy the files to a different location by copying data folders from the CD just as you would copy other files to your hard disk drive. Choose the correct version of the data set (Basic or Pro) and always copy complete folders.

NOTES
Alternative instructions or commands that you may need to use are shown in indented paragraphs without highlighting, like the paragraph beside this note, beginning with "You can copy the files..."

After copying the folders and files, you must remove the Read Only attribute from all the data files before you can open them with Simply Accounting. If you do not change the attribute or if you try to open the data file from the Student CD-ROM, you will receive an error message about access rights when you try to open the file.

If you see an error message like this one about rights:

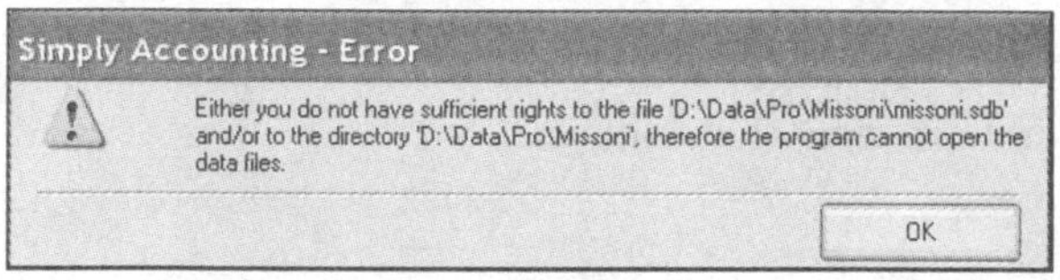

Click **OK** to return to the opening Welcome screen.

If you tried to open the files from the Student CD-ROM, copy the data to your hard disk drive and then remove the Read Only attributes if necessary.

Removing Read-Only Attributes

File attributes must be changed for the files in one folder at a time. You must change the attributes for each data application individually because each application is in a separate folder. Changing the attributes of a folder does not change the attributes for the files inside the folder, but all files in an open folder can be changed at once.

You can change the file properties in Windows Explorer.

WARNING!
If you are working on a network, the site administrator should change the attributes of the master copy before copying the files to individual workstations. Some networks do not allow individual users to change attributes for security reasons.

Open **Windows Explorer** and **find** the **folder** that contains your **data set**.

Double click **Adrienne**, the first data folder, to open it.

Click the **first file** in the folder, **press** shift and **click** the **last file** in the folder to select all the Simply Accounting data files. Some data folders contain only two files, others may have more.

Choose the **File menu** and **click Properties** or **right-click** (click the right mouse button) and **choose Properties** from the pop-up menu.

NOTES
Windows XP Pro removes the read-only attributes from files when you copy from a CD to your hard drive.

NOTES
The files remain selected while the Properties window is open.

The Properties window for the files opens:

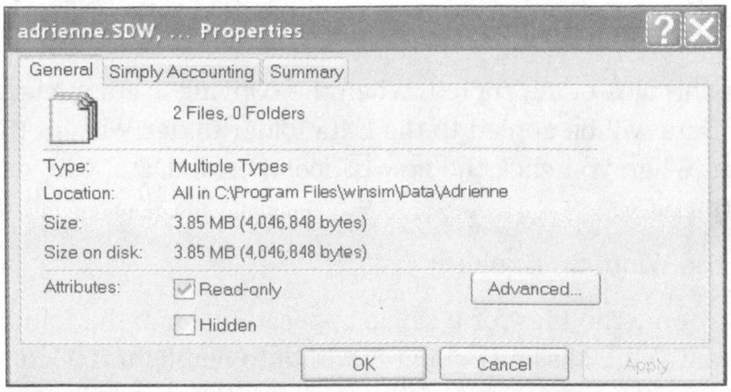

Click Read-Only to remove the ✓. **Click** OK.

Repeat this procedure for the remaining folders and files.

Starting Simply Accounting and Accessing Data Files

NOTES
If you added a desktop shortcut when you installed the program, you can double click it to open the Simply Accounting program.

NOTES
If you used a different name for the program when you installed it, choose that name.

From your Windows desktop,

Click Start (on the task bar) so the pop-up menu appears.

Point to Programs. Hold the mouse on Programs until the list of programs appears.

Point to Simply Accounting by Sage. Hold the mouse on Simply Accounting until its cascading menu list of programs appears.

Click Simply Accounting by Sage. You should follow the path illustrated in the Classic Windows view that follows:

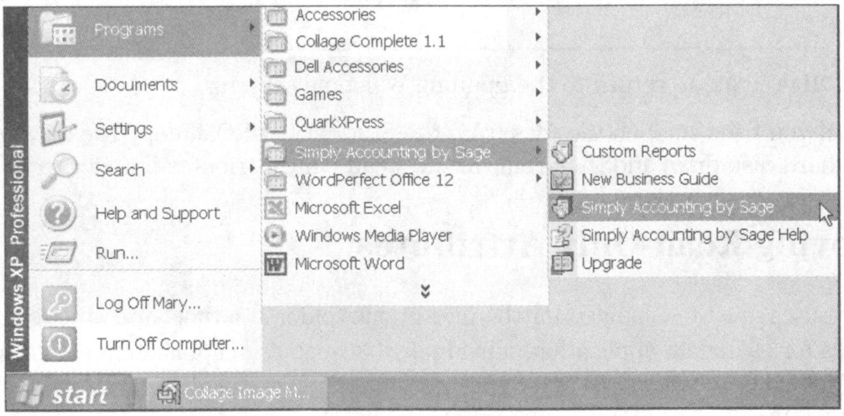

If you are using the Windows XP view,

Click Start. **Point to** All Programs and then **point to** Simply Accounting by Sage as shown in the following screen:

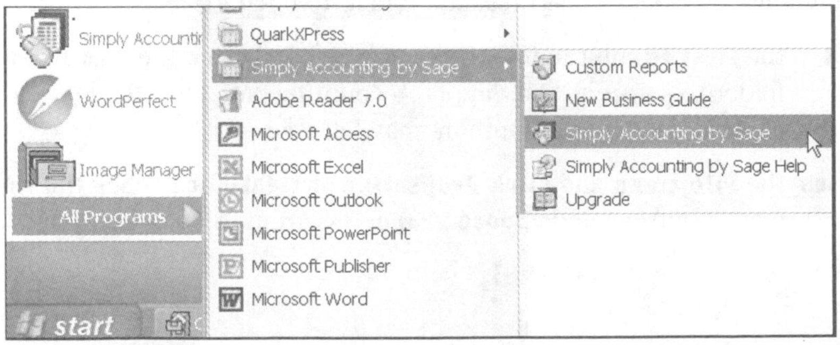

You will open the registration screen the first time you use the program. Otherwise, you will see the Simply Accounting Select Company screen below.

If you have not yet registered the program refer to Appendix A, page A-8 in the text. Until you register and activate the program, you will be allowed to use the program only for a limited time.

Opening a Data File

You will now see the Simply Accounting Select Company Welcome screen:

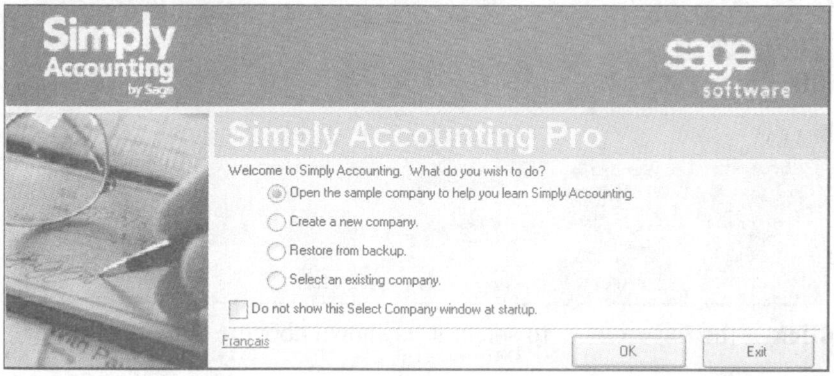

The opening window gives you several options: working with the sample company files, creating new company files, restoring backup files or working with existing data files. If you have worked with the program before, the option to Open The Last Company You Worked On appears last with the name of the file you used. If you use this option when you use the same data set for several work sessions, you will bypass the Open Company window (shown below).

Click **Select An Existing Company**.

Click **OK**.

The Simply Accounting Open File window appears next. The most recently used file will be selected if you have previously used the program. Therefore, the File name you see on your screen may be different from the ones we show.

The next time you start the Simply Accounting program, the name of the file that you used most recently will be selected for you to accept or to change.

Click the **Look In field list arrow** to see the folder path for the file selected:

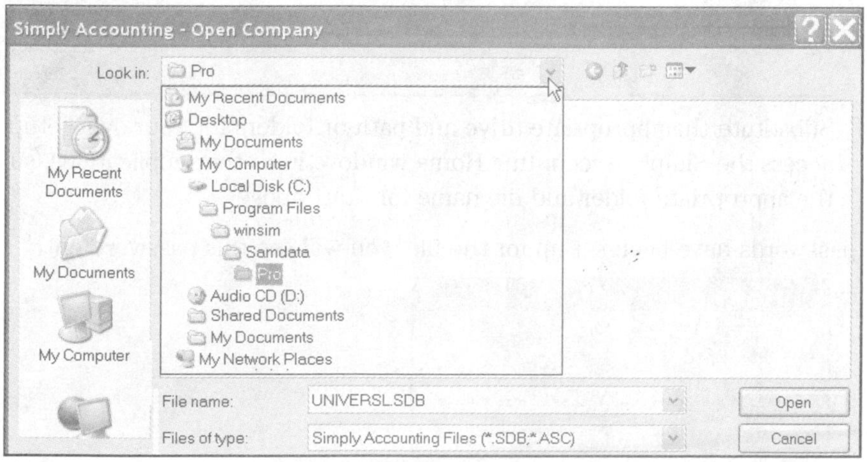

The path shown here is for the sample company, Universal, in Program Files\Winsim\Samdata\Pro in drive (C:).

WARNING!
You will be allowed to use the program only for a limited time before entering the registration validation codes. You must have a payroll ID code in order to use the Payroll features of the program.

The Student Version does not require payroll activation.

NOTES
The Select Company window shows the version you are using. This window has Pro added to the screen.

In Chapter 4, we explain how to restore the Select Company window if it has been turned off.

The following instructions will access data stored in the Winsim\Data folder.

If your starting point is different from the one shown here, click drive (C:) in the Look In field list. Then in the folders/files section, double click the Program Files folder to open it, and then double click the Winsim folder to display the folders.

Double click the **Winsim folder** to list the folders under Winsim in the large files/folders list in the centre of the window. The Look In field now displays Winsim as the folder name:

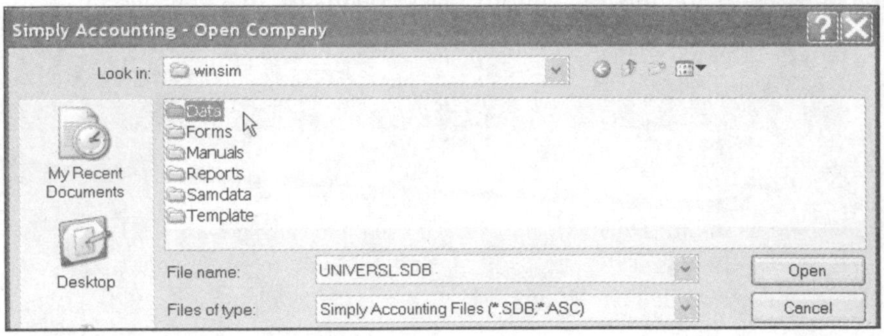

Click the **Data folder** to select it as shown above.

Click **Open** to list the folders containing your workbook data. The folder name Data now appears in the Look In field.

Click the **Start folder** to select it.

Click **Open** to list the Simply Accounting data files contained in this folder and to display the folder name Start in the Look In field. There should be just one file listed, Start (or Start.sdb if you chose to show file name extensions).

You can gain access to the company records through the *.sdb file. Simply Accounting recognizes this file extension as a Simply Accounting format file. Other files that are part of the data set must be located in the same folder.

Click **Start** to select it and add its name to the File Name field as shown:

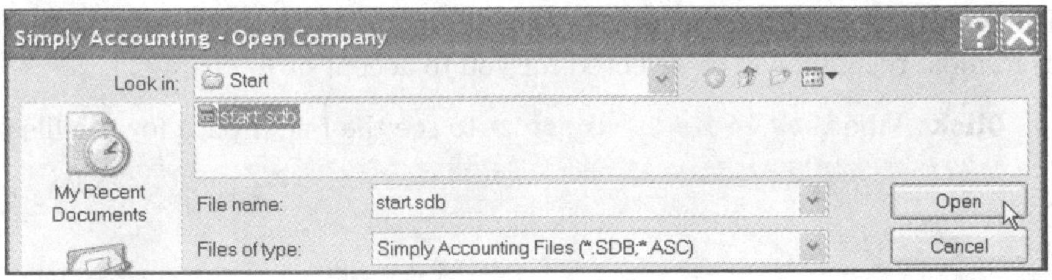

Substitute the appropriate drive and path or folders for your own setup to access the Simply Accounting Home window. For other applications, substitute the appropriate folder and file name for Start above.

If passwords have been set up for the file, you will see this password entry screen:

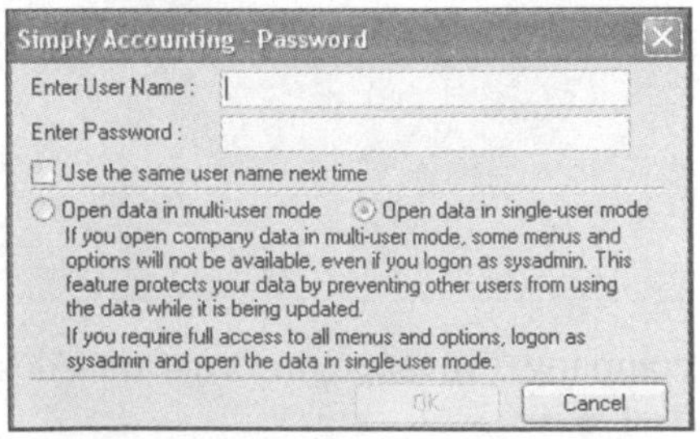

NOTES

The other files will be listed in the Windows Explorer program when you open the Data folder.

NOTES

We have not set passwords for any data files in this text, but your site administrator for the network may have done so.

If you try to open a read-only file or have not updated to Release B, you will see the error messages on page 7 and page 11, respectively, instead of the password screen.

Ask your instructor or site administrator for the name and password you should use (see Appendix G on the Student CD-ROM).Enter your user name and password. Click OK to open the session date screen.

If you see a screen advising that the data has been used in a newer version of the program, your program may be an earlier version of Release B. You will be asked if you wish to proceed; click Yes to open the file. If your version of the program is even earlier (Release A), you will be unable to open the data file. In this case, you must install the update to Release B (See Updating Simply Accounting to Release B below).

Click **Open** to see the following screen prompting you for the session date:

All date fields in Simply Accounting include a calendar that shows the range of dates you can enter for the data file. The program restricts you from moving to a month beyond the range that is allowed. The list arrow beside the Date field offers a list of dates to choose from. Refer to page 18 for more information on dates in Simply Accounting.

NOTES
The session date is explained in the Missoni Marbleworks application, where you will also learn how to change the session date.
The session date list includes the current session date, the end of the fiscal period and the start of the next fiscal period. The list for any date field includes the dates commonly selected.

Click **OK** to accept the date shown.

The first time you use the program, you will see a message about automatic program updates. If you choose to have automatic updates, updates to the program will be installed automatically when you are connected to the Internet. Decide whether you want automatic updates. You can also download updates periodically when needed.

basic BASIC VERSION
You will see an additional message about upgrading to the Pro or Premier version of Simply Accounting.

Make your selection, and **click OK** to open the data file at the Home window.

Remember to activate the Payroll features. Go to page A-9 in Appendix A in the text for help with this step.

Updating Simply Accounting to Release B

If your Simply Accounting program is a Release A version, you will see the following message instead of the Session date dialogue box shown above:

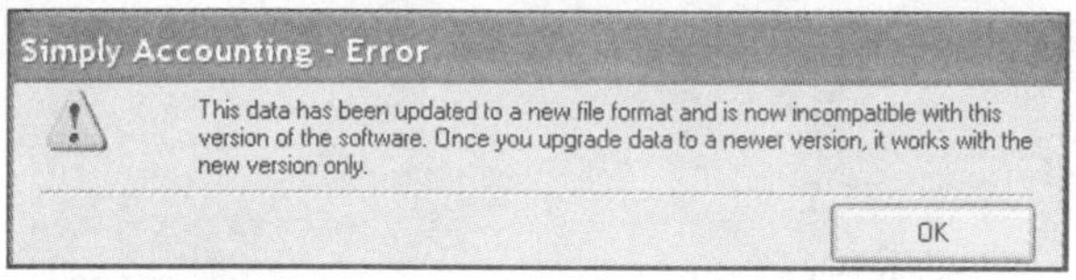

Click **OK**.

Do not turn on the automatic update feature for the program until you have completed the applications in this text.

The automatic updates will upgrade your program to a later version than Release B and your payroll amounts will be different from the ones we show. There may also be other program changes that result in screens and keystrokes that are different from the ones in this text.

You must update the program to Release B to open the data files on the Student CD-ROM. A copy of the update program is located on the Student CD-ROM. For detailed instructions on updating the program, including screen images, refer to Appendix A, page A-11.

Insert the **Student CD-ROM** into your disk drive.

You should see the CD home window with the options to install data files, update your program, or view the additional appendix material.

Click **Update Program To Release B** to begin the update wizard.

Click **Next** to open the Licence Agreement screen.

Click **Yes** to proceed.

The update program will locate your program files and show their location as the destination for the update.

Click **Next** to see the warning about overwriting existing files.

If you have customized forms, click No and copy these to another location.

Click **Yes** to continue to the final information screen.

Click **Next** to continue, unless you still need to back up customized forms.

The program update will begin. When it has finished, you will see the confirmation screen. At this stage, you can start the Simply Accounting program, view the ReadMe files or exit.

Click **Finish** to open the ReadMe file.

Close the **ReadMe file** after reading the information.

Your program is now ready to use the data files for this text.

Follow the **instructions** for accessing a data file on page 8.

Simply Accounting Home Window

The Simply Accounting Home window should be open:

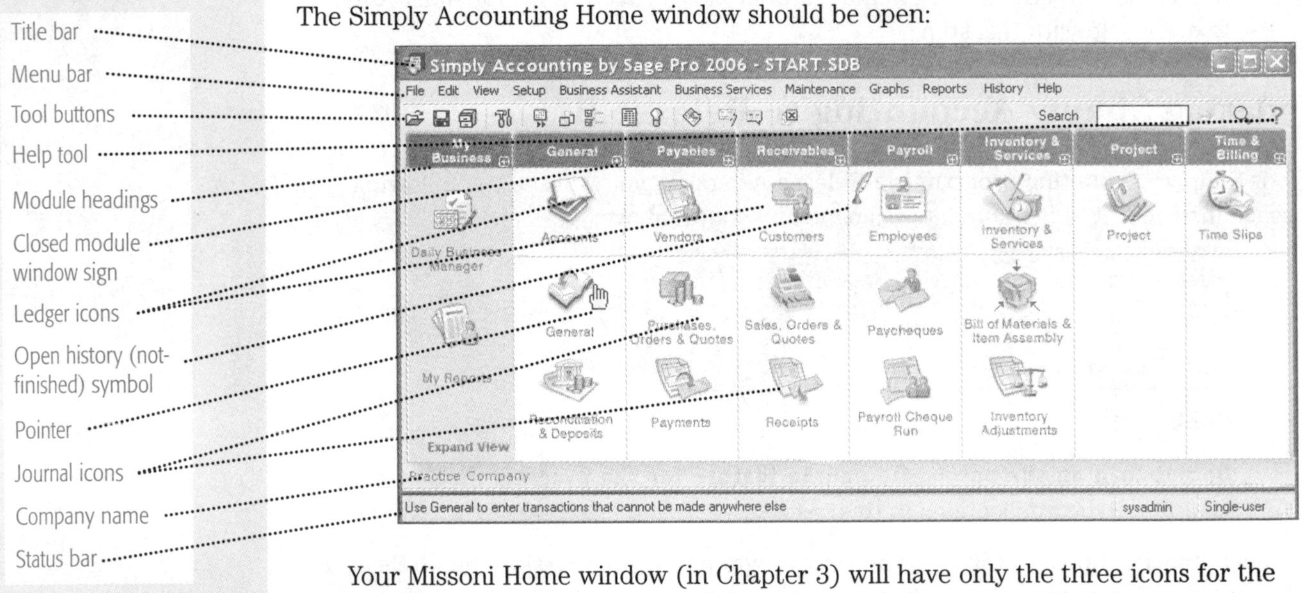

Your Missoni Home window (in Chapter 3) will have only the three icons for the General Ledger — Accounts, General and Reconciliation & Deposits. Unused ledgers will be hidden because they are not set up. In this illustration, the Payroll Ledger is not finished. We show it here to illustrate the Open History symbol and the remaining Home window icons.

basic **BASIC VERSION**
The program name in the title bar is Simply Accounting by Sage Basic 2006 and you will not see the Time Slips icon.

The Home window is organized as follows: the **title bar** is on top with the program name, Simply Accounting Pro, the file name, START.SDB, Control Menu icon and size buttons; the **main menu bar** comes next with the **tool bar buttons** below. Tool buttons provide quick access to commonly used menu items. Different Simply Accounting windows have different buttons on the tool bar. The **ledger** or module names come next with their respective icons filling up the major part of the window — ledgers in the top row below the ledger or module name and **journal icons** under their respective ledgers in the last two icon rows of the window. Below the journal icons are two more information lines: the company name and the **status bar**. The status bar describes the purpose of the General Journal because the pointer is on the General icon.

The **My Business tab** on the left can be customized to include the icons you use most frequently. You can hide this column if you do not use this feature.

The Pro version also has a **Search field** to look up information in any journal or ledger. In the Basic version, you can access the Search function from the Edit menu.

Hold the mouse pointer on a tool button for a few seconds to see the name or function of the tool button and the keyboard shortcut if there is one. Hold the mouse over an icon to see its description or function in the status bar at the bottom of the window.

NOTES
In Windows XP, showing the shortcuts for tool buttons is an optional setting, so you may not see them.

NOTES
Many Simply Accounting windows include a Home window button that brings the Home window to the front without closing the other windows.

Simply Accounting on the Windows Desktop

Click the **General Journal icon** in the journal part of the window.

Click the **Edit menu**. Your desktop should now look like the one that follows:

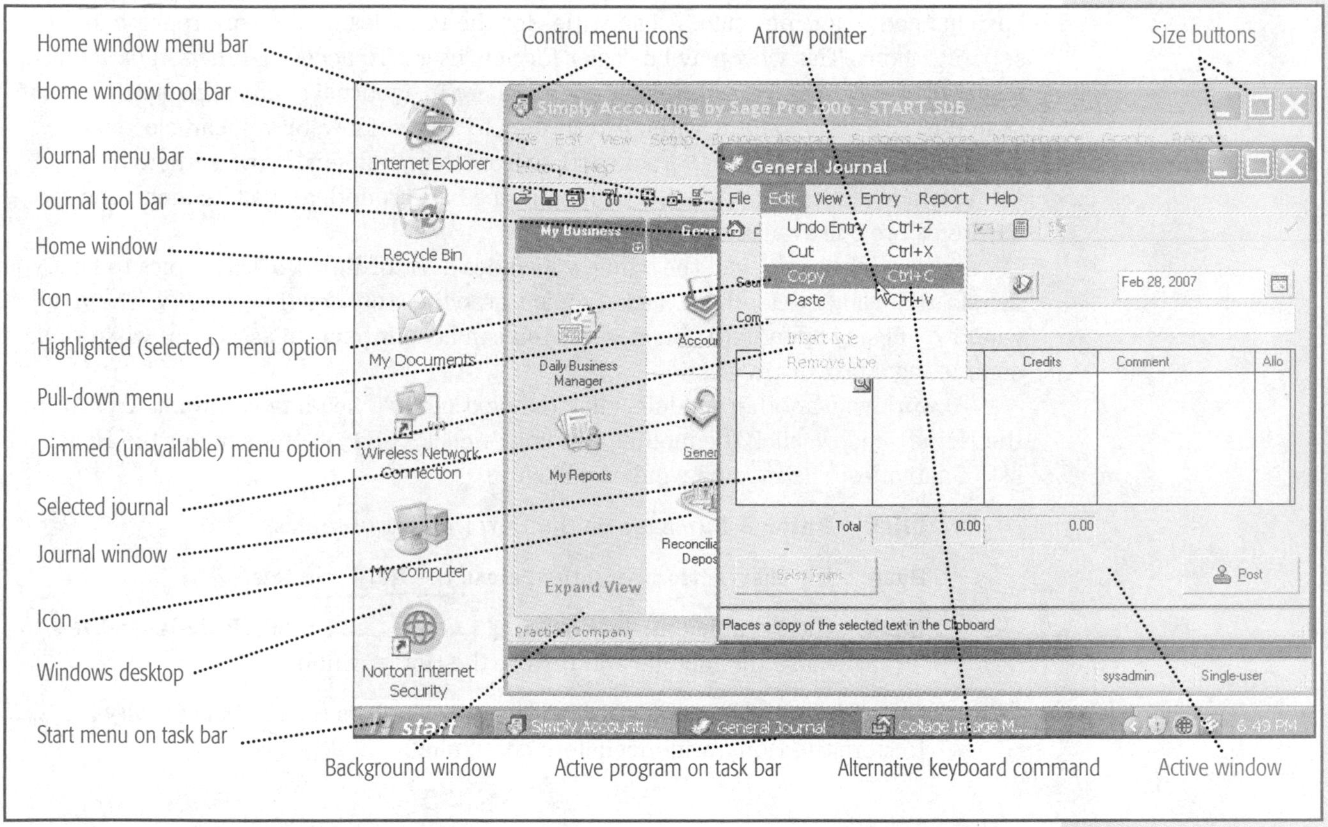

If you need an explanation of terms in this illustration, please refer to Appendix B.

Click ☒ to close the journal window and return to the Home window.

Simply Accounting Module Window

Each module or ledger can be expanded so that its icons are the only ones displayed. The module heading or module name is used to open the module window or close it if it is open.

Click the **Payables module heading** Payables .

You will open the Payables module window:

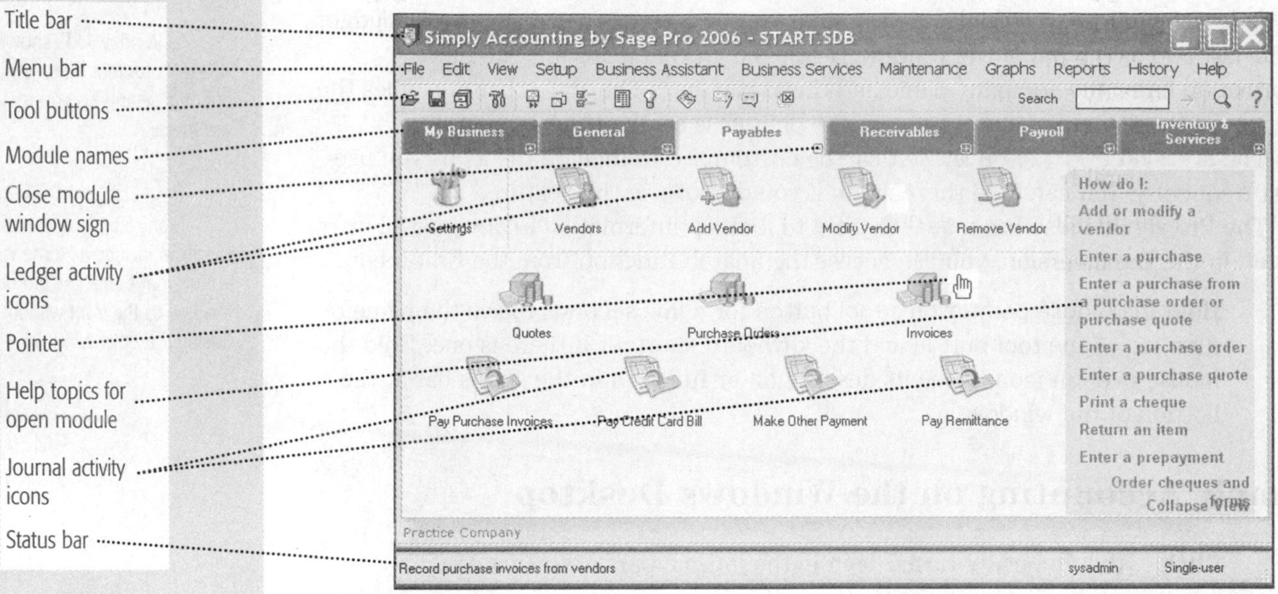

The heading for the open module has the colours reversed, and the boxed plus sign has changed to a minus sign. All activities for the Payables module are represented by separate icons. This view may be easier for new users. To access a function or activity, just click the related icon. However, once you are in a journal such as Invoices, you can switch to Orders or Quotes without returning to this window, or you can close one journal and open the other journal window from the module window. Although the Home window does not appear, it is open in the background, and all its menu and tool bar items are still available.

On the right-hand side, the window includes a list of **How Do I ...** topics to help you get started using the module. Click a topic to see the steps for that activity. The Help window will stay open until you close it. You can keep it open to assist you while you are completing a task or transaction.

To work with another module, click the next module heading you want. To restore the Home window, click the module heading or click **Collapse View** under the How Do I list of activities. The module window will close.

Click **Enter A Purchase** on the How Do I list of topics.

Read the **instructions** and then **close** the **Help window**.

Click the **Payables module heading** [Payables] or **click Collapse View** to close the module and restore the Home window.

Open and close some of the other module windows to see their activity icons. Restore the Home window before continuing.

Simply Accounting Help Features

Simply Accounting provides program assistance in several different ways. You can display or print Help information on many topics. General accounting information, advice topics and Simply Accounting software assistance are included. You can access Help from the menu bar in the Home window, from the Help tool button [?] in the Home window or by pressing [f1].

The most immediate form of help comes from the **status bar** at the bottom of many program windows. It offers a one-line description of the icon or field that the mouse is pointing to. As you move the mouse around the screen, the status bar information changes accordingly. The message in the status bar is connected to the mouse position only. This may not be the same as the position of the cursor or insertion point, which is located wherever the mouse was when you last clicked the mouse button.

We have already seen that each module window includes a **How Do I list** for activities related to that module.

The general help menu can be accessed in several ways: press (f1), choose the Help menu and click Contents, or click the Help button [?].

Close the message about Simply Accounting Courses if it appears.

Click the **Help tool** [?]. The Contents tab "book" menu is shown here:

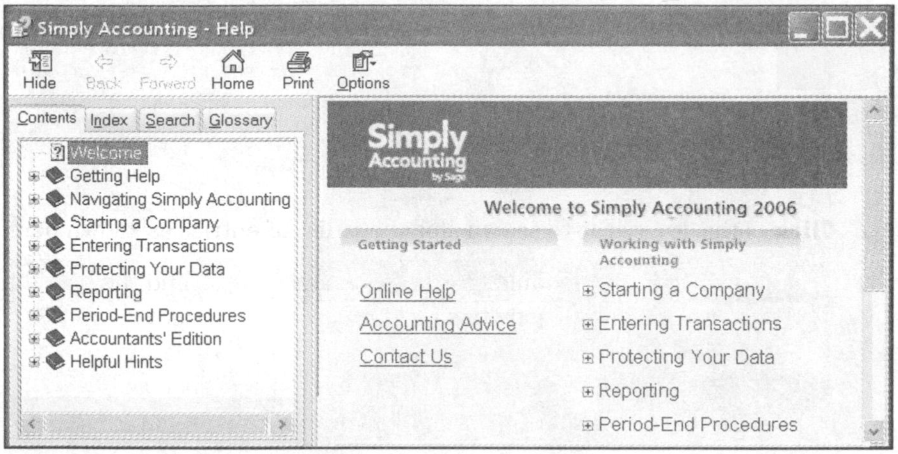

Major topics have a book symbol beside them.

Click [+] beside a topic to see the list of subtopics under that heading (or double click the topic).

When a topic has a question mark beside it [?], there is detailed help on that subject. Click the topic or the question mark symbol to display information on that subject in the right-hand side of the Help window.

The topic "Getting Help" is a good place to begin if you have not previously used the Help features in Windows programs.

Welcome, with a question mark [?] beside it, is selected, so this topic is displayed.

Click any underlined text in the right-hand side display area to get further information on that topic.

Double click a book title or click [−], the boxed minus sign beside it to close the book and hide the list of subtopics.

Double click **Entering Transactions**. The list expands with several subtopics.

Double click **Buying** to view the second list of subtopics.

Click **Making Payments** to see the help information on this topic:

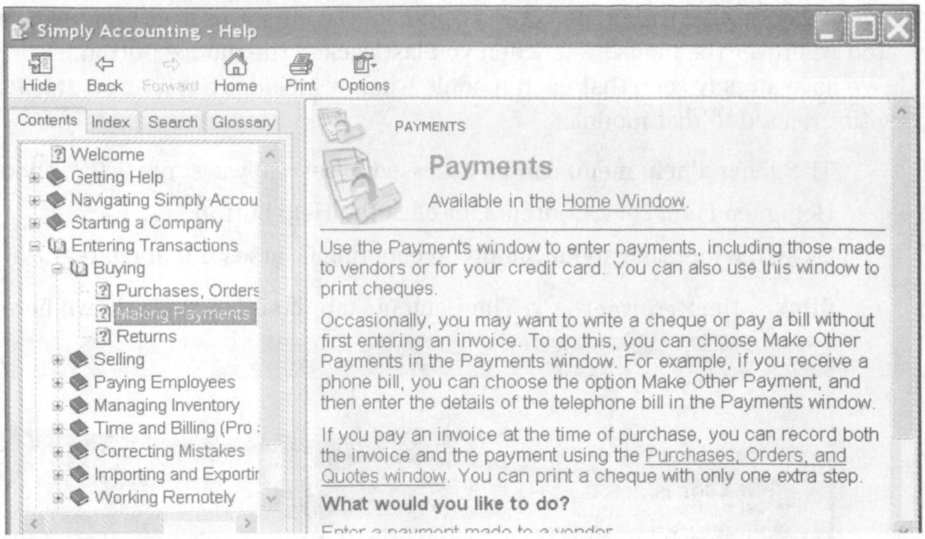

Click the **Index tab** to see an alphabetic list of entries as shown here:

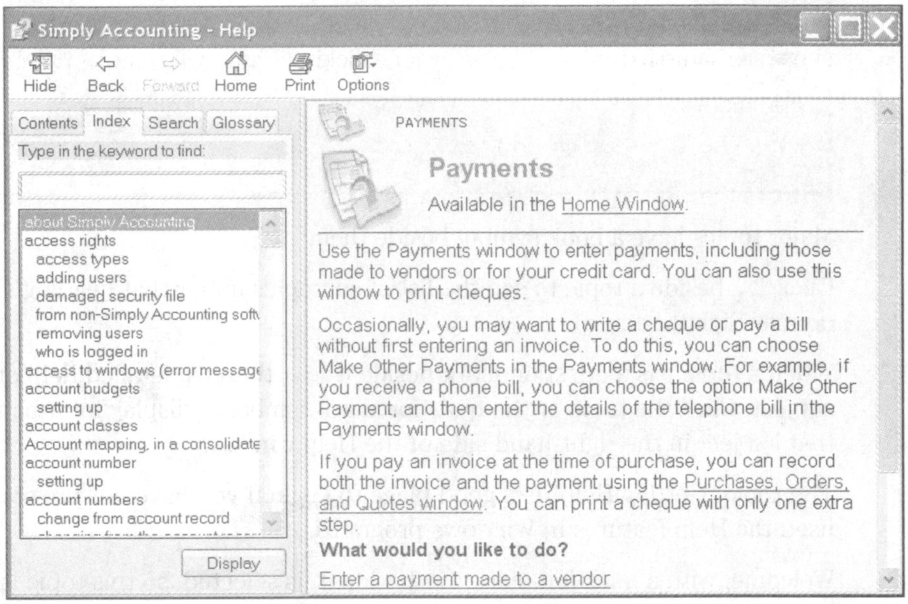

Notice that the previous topic remains on display until you select a new topic.

Click a topic to read the help information on the selected topic. Type a letter in the field above the list to advance the alphabetic list quickly.

Click the **Search tab** to open the Search function:

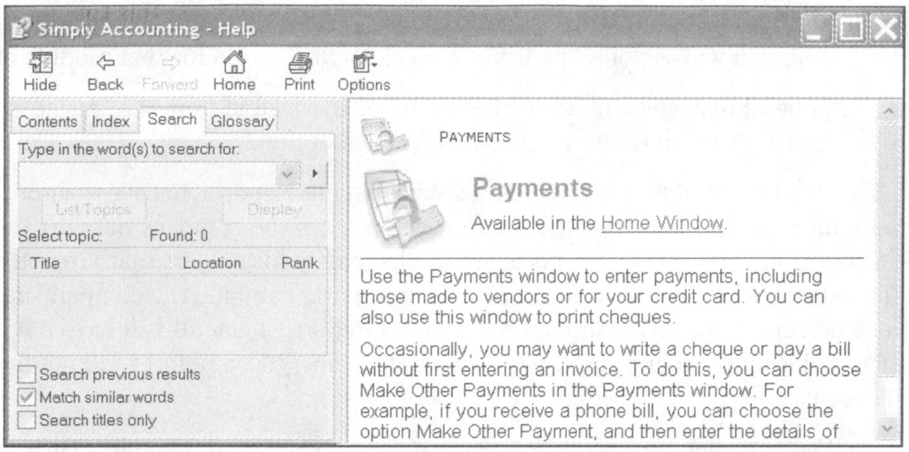

Again, the previous topic remains displayed until you select a new one. The last item you searched for is listed in the Type In... field.

You can search for a topic that you define by typing it in the **Topic** field. Click the **List Topics** button to see the entries that include the topic you typed. The topics are shown in order of likely relevance — their **Rank**. Clicking **Title** will show the same list in alphabetic order. Clicking Rank will restore the rank order of topics.

Click the **Topic field** and **type** Delete

Click the **List Topics button** below the Topic field.

Click **Deleting A Vendor** and then **click** **Display** to see the information.

Also available from the Help window on any topic is an extensive **glossary** of general accounting and Simply Accounting terms. The Help windows on the previous pages include the Glossary tab to access the glossary.

Click the **Glossary tab** and then **click** a glossary **topic** to see the explanation or definition. Continue by exploring other topics and features.

Close the **Help windows** when you have finished.

Another form of help comes from the **Help button** in many Simply Accounting windows. The button provides help related to that specific ledger or window.

The Simply Accounting program also includes **Advice** on a number of topics.

Click the **Advice tool button** in Simply Accounting's Home window to access the main Advice menu shown here:

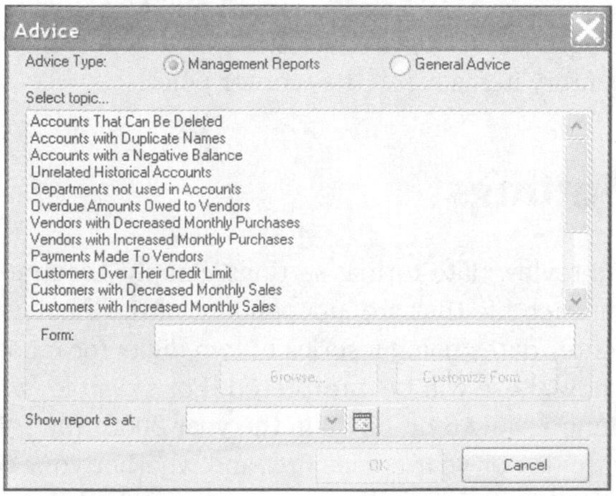

If a Home window ledger or journal icon is selected when you click the Advice tool, you will see only the list of Management Reports for that module or ledger.

General management advice topics are also available from the Business Assistant menu under the Business Advice option.

The default list of topics is the list of Management Reports. Rather than providing general information, these reports relate specifically to the company data set that is in use at the time. Management reports are available only for ledgers that are not hidden, so the list you see is not always complete. The reports combine the company data with forms and reports provided through the Crystal Report Engine. If you have not installed the Crystal Report Engine and the customizable forms, these reports will not be available.

You can click the report or advice topic you want, and then click OK to see the report (or double click the topic).

Click **General Advice** to see the list of topics that provide suggestions about general accounting practices. **Click** the **topic** you want and then **click** **OK**. **Close** the **advice report windows** when finished.

A final source of general assistance is available as **automatic advice**. This feature can be turned off from the Setup menu (User Preferences, View tab) in the Home window if it is not needed. We recommend leaving it on. When it is turned on, the Simply Accounting program will provide warning statements as, for example, when you choose a customer who has exceeded their credit limit:

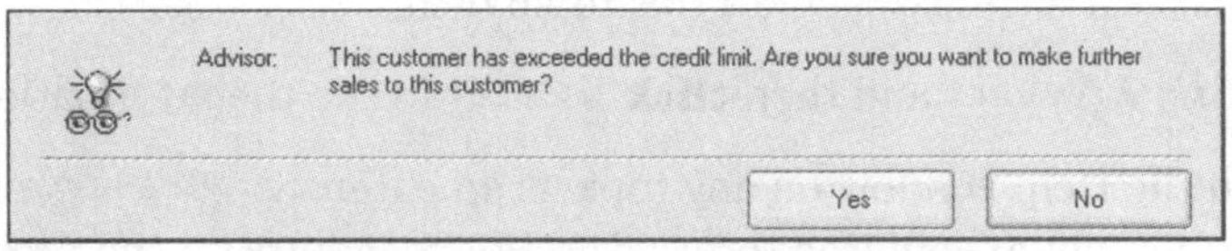

To proceed, you must close the advice screen. In the example shown here, you can click Yes if you want to proceed with the sale, or No if you want to make a change (perhaps by asking for a deposit).

The following warning about an overdrawn chequing account appears when you make a payment from a bank account that exceeds the account balance:

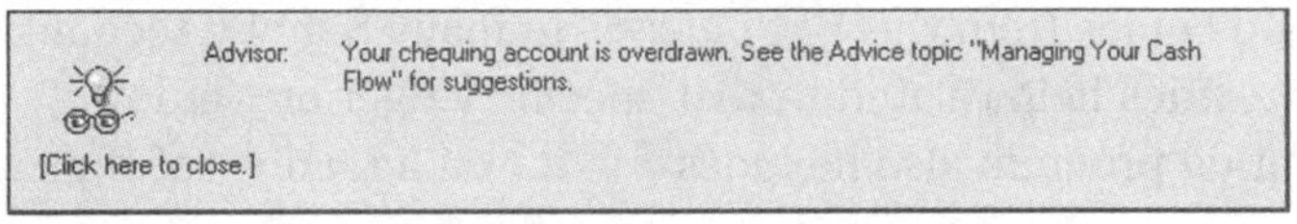

Close this type of message by clicking the advisor icon as indicated [Click Here To Close].

The program also warns when year-end is approaching and it is time to complete year-end adjustments or when inventory items reach the reorder point.

NOTES
Simply Accounting allows you to enter earlier session dates but warns you first. If you have advanced the date incorrectly, you can reverse the decision as long as you have not moved to a new fiscal year. Warnings are also given when you advance the date by more than one week or when you try to move to a new fiscal period. These warnings should serve as signals that you may have made a mistake.

Date Formats and Settings

Before closing the program we will review date format settings. Simply Accounting has date format control settings within each file that are independent of the display date settings for Windows. When you enter dates using a series of two digits for month, day and year, it is important to know how these will be interpreted. For example, when you type 06-07-05, this date may be June 7, July 6 or July 5 in the year 2005, 1905, 1906 or 2006, depending on whether month, day or year comes first and whether your computer defaults to 1900 dates or is preset for 2000 dates. We always use month, day and year as the order for presenting dates in this text.

Fortunately, Simply Accounting allows you to enter and display dates as text. Thus, you may type June 7, 2006, in a date field. And if you want, you can display this date as Jun 7, 2006, even if you enter numbers in the date field.

All date fields also have a Calendar icon that you can click to access a month-by-month calendar from which you can select a date. These two options will help you avoid making date errors from incorrect orders. To access the date settings,

Choose the **Setup menu**, then **choose System Settings** and **click Settings** as shown:

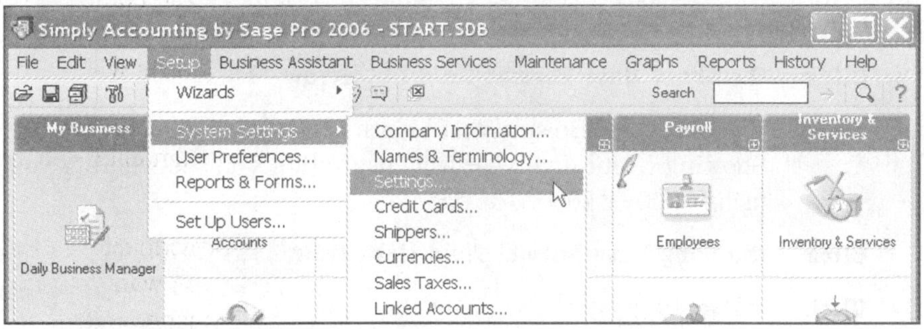

The Settings control window opens:

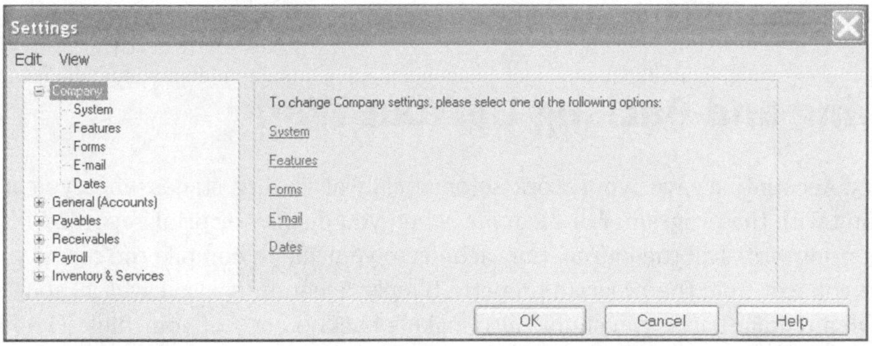

Each entry in the list opens the settings screen for a different part of the program. We want the dates settings.

Click **Dates** (the entry under Company or from the list on the right) to open the Settings window for Dates:

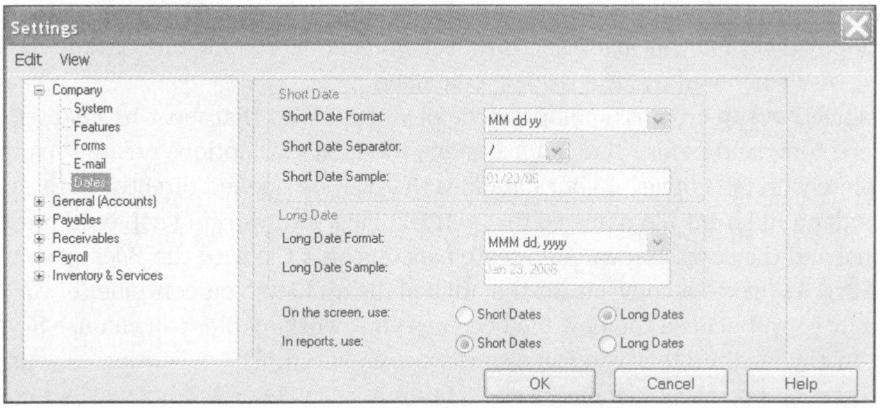

Each field has a drop-down list of format options. The **Short Date Format** uses two digits each for month and day. For the year, you can choose a two-digit or four-digit format. You can choose to begin with month, day or year — the Short Date Format shows which comes first. The **Short Date Separator** character may be a slash, dash or period. This is the character that will appear on the screen regardless of how you

NOTES

Simply Accounting displays only the first three letters of a month when you choose the long or text date format. Therefore Jun is displayed for June.

entered the date. The sample shows the appearance that you can expect from your selections.

The **Long Date Format** shows the month as a three-letter text abbreviation. Either the month or the day can be the first character in the long date style. The sample shows the result of your selection.

The final section allows you to select the short or long date styles for your screen and reports. You can select different date styles for your reports and screen displays.

We will use the same date format settings for all files to avoid any confusion about dates when the numeric entry might be ambiguous. For reports you can use long or short date formats.

Click the **Short Date Format field list arrow**.

Click **MM/dd/yyyy**. Be sure that Month (MM) is the first part of the entry. Showing a four-digit year will ensure that you see whether you are using 1900 or 2000 year dates.

Click the **Long Date Format field list arrow**.

Click **MMM dd, yyyy**.

Click **Long Dates** beside the option On The Screen, Use.

Click **OK** to save the settings.

Saving and Backing Up Your Work

NOTES

To save several backups on a single floppy disk, first back up to your hard disk drive, then copy the backups to a floppy disk. You can restore the files from the floppy disk. Up to four backup files will fit on a single floppy.

You can use removable memory sticks for your backups or for your working copies of data files.

NOTES

You can also use the Windows Copy command to make CD copies of your data, but you must close the Simply Accounting data file before you start to copy. Remember to copy the data folders when you copy from Windows to ensure that you keep the necessary files together.

You cannot open the data files from the CD. You must first copy them back to your hard disk drive and remove the read-only property.

Simply Accounting saves your work automatically at various stages when you are working with the program. For example, when you display or print reports, Simply Accounting writes all the journal transactions to your file to compile the report you want. When you exit from the program properly, Simply Accounting also saves all your work.

On a regular basis, you should also make a backup copy of your files. The Backup command is described in detail in Chapter 3.

Click the **Backup tool** or **choose** the **File menu** and **click Backup** to start the Backup wizard.

The wizard will create a separate backup folder inside your current working folder so that the backup will remain separate from your working copy. If you prefer, you can use floppy disks for your backups. However, you can store only one backup file on a floppy disk when you use the Backup command.

While **Backup** creates a compressed copy of the files that must be restored with the Restore command before you can use them, the next two options create separate complete working copies of your data files that can be opened directly. Both save the file under a different file name so that you will have two working copies of the files, the original and the copy. You cannot create backups on a CD with the Backup command.

Save As makes a copy, closes the original file and lets you continue to work with the new copy. Because the new file becomes your working file, you can use Save As to copy to any medium that you can also work from in Simply Accounting — your hard disk drive or a removable memory stick, but not a CD. **Save A Copy** makes a copy of the file and then allows you to continue working with the original file. You can use Save A Copy to save your files to a CD. You must copy the CD files back to your hard disk drive and remove the read-only property before working with these files.

Because the data files are very large, we recommend using the Backup procedure described in Chapter 3 rather than Save As or Save A Copy for regular backups.

Choose the **File menu** and **click Save A Copy** to open the file name window:

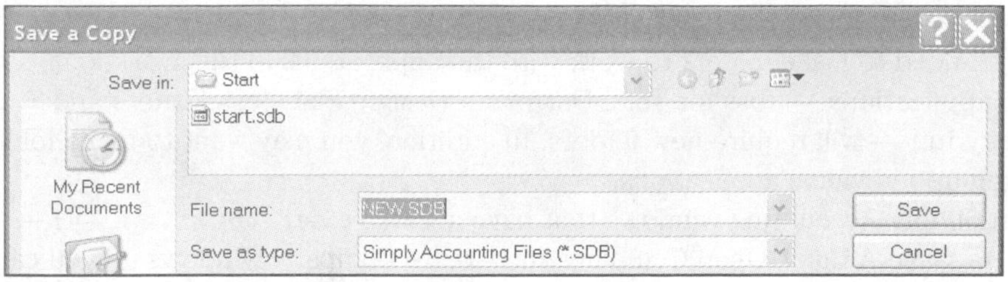

You can save the copy in the same folder as the original or use a different folder. We recommend using different folders. To change to a different folder,

NOTES
You may want to use the Save A Copy or Save As command when you are unsure how a journal entry will be posted and you want to experiment with different methods of entering the same transactions.

Click the **Save In field list arrow** and **choose** a different **folder**.

Double click the **folder** to open it. To create a new folder inside the one that you have open,

Click the **New Folder icon**.

Type the **new folder name** to replace New Folder, the selected text.

Click **Open**.

Double click the file name **NEW** or **NEW.SDB** if you show file extensions.

Type the **new file name**.

Click **Save**.

You will return to your original file and you can continue working.

To save the file under a different name and continue working with the new file, use the Save As command.

Choose the **File menu** and **click Save As** to open the file name window.

The remaining steps are the same as Save A Copy, as shown above.

Change folders, create a new folder, rename the folder, open the new folder, type a file name for the copy and click Save. Remember to return to your original working copy before entering any transactions if you use the Save As command.

WARNING!
Remember to copy all the files for a company when you use the Copy and Paste commands. Copying the folder will ensure you copy all the necessary files.

You can also back up all your data files at the same time by using Windows Explorer Copy and Paste commands as described earlier in this chapter. In this way, you can save the files to a different folder on your hard drive.

Finishing a Session

Choose the **Control Menu icon** and **click Close** or **click** [X] to close the journal input form or display window you are working in.

You will return to the main Home window.

Choose the **Control Menu icon** and **click Close**, or **click** [X] or **choose** the **File menu** and **click Exit** to close the Home window.

Your work will be saved again automatically when you complete this step. You should now be in the Windows desktop.

Creating New Folders

> **NOTES**
> In any Simply Accounting window that has the New Folder tool, you can right-click the mouse and choose New and Folder from the pop-up menu.

You will need to make folders to work with the applications in this workbook. The four setup applications — Toss for Tots, Dorfmann Design, Flabuless Fitness and Stratford Country Inn — will require new folders. In addition, you may want to make folders for backing up individual applications.

In Simply Accounting windows that have a **New Folder tool button** — the Save As, Save A Copy, Open Company and Create Company windows — you can make folders. The method for creating new folders in Simply Accounting is the same in all Simply Accounting windows and is described on page 20 for the Save A Copy method and in Chapter 4 using the Save As option.

We will describe the Windows Explorer approach here.

Double click the **My Computer icon** on the desktop.

Double click the **drive** you want to use and then **double click** the **folder** in the drive where you want to place the new folder (or create the folder at the root of the disk drive, e.g., at C:\).

Choose the **File menu**, then **choose New** and **click Folder** (or **right-click** the mouse and **choose New** and **Folder** from the pop-up menu).

The file menu path should look like the one shown here:

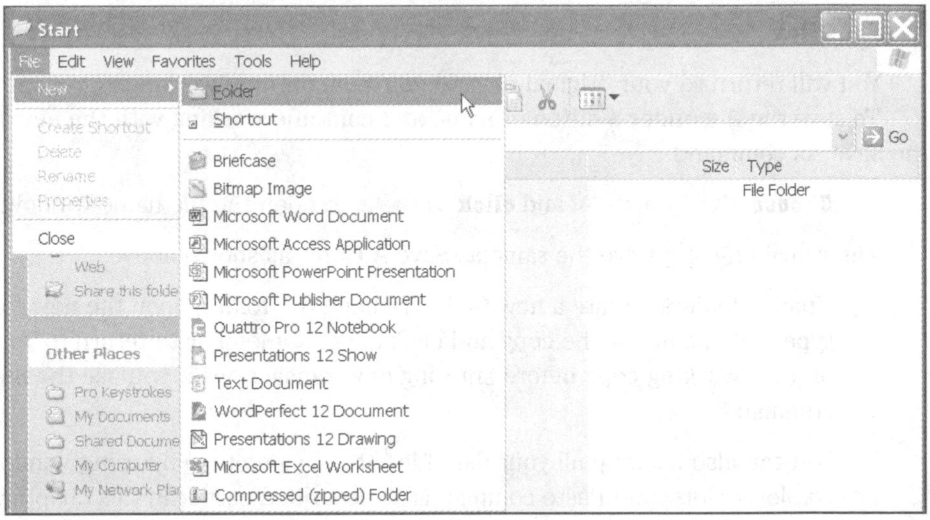

The new folder is placed inside the folder or drive that is open. Its name, New Folder, will be selected so you can type a new folder name immediately.

Enter a **new name** and then **click somewhere else** on the screen to save the name change.

You can create several folders in the same session by repeating these steps.

Close the **My Computer window** when you have finished.

REVIEW

The Student CD-ROM with Data Files includes Review Questions for this chapter.

CHAPTER TWO

The GST and PST

OBJECTIVES

After completing this chapter, you should be able to

- ***understand*** the terms relevant to the federal Goods and Services Tax (GST)
- ***understand*** the different methods of calculating the GST
- ***understand*** how to file for a remittance or refund
- ***understand*** Harmonized Sales Tax and other provincial taxes in relation to the GST

GENERAL TAX INFORMATION

Definition of GST

NOTES

In April 2006, the federal budget proposed a GST rate reduction from 7 percent to 6 percent. The budget approval came too late to be incorporated into all the applications in the text without significantly delaying its publication date.

The Goods and Services Tax is a compulsory tax levied by the federal government on most goods and services in Canada. The tax rate of 7 percent applies at all levels of sales. Retailers pay the GST to wholesalers and other vendors but are allowed to deduct any GST they pay from the GST they collect from customers. Retailers remit the difference, GST owing, to the Receiver General for Canada or claim a refund on a monthly or quarterly basis. Provinces may or may not include GST in the price on which they calculate provincial sales tax (PST). Provincial tax rates vary from province to province.

GST Registration

A business with annual sales exceeding $30 000 per year must register for GST collection and must collect GST on all applicable sales. Registration is optional for businesses whose annual sales are less than $30 000. Businesses that are not registered for GST do not charge GST on sales to their customers, but they also cannot recover the GST they pay on business-related purchases.

Collecting the GST

The business must collect GST for those goods and services sold that are not zero rated or tax exempt. GST collected on sales is reduced by the GST on sales returns. The business must remit GST at regular intervals, filing GST returns monthly, quarterly or annually with quarterly instalments paid, depending on annual income and GST owing.

Zero Rated Goods and Services

Zero rated goods and services are those on which the tax rate is zero. These goods include basic groceries, prescribed medical devices, prescribed drugs, exported goods and services, agricultural products and fish products. A business selling only zero rated goods and services does not collect GST from customers, but it can still claim a refund for GST paid for any purchases made for selling these zero rated goods and services.

Tax Exempt Goods and Services

Tax exempt goods and services are those on which tax is not collected. These goods and services include health care, dental care, daycare services and rents on residences. Most educational and financial services are also included in this group. These businesses are not able to claim refunds for GST paid for business purchases related to selling tax exempt goods and services.

Paying the GST

A business must pay GST for purchases made specifically for business purposes, unless the goods or services purchased are zero rated or tax exempt. The business can use the GST paid as an input tax credit by subtracting the amount of GST paid from the amount of GST collected and remitting GST owing or claiming a refund. The input tax credit is reduced by the amount of GST for purchases returned. GST paid on purchases for personal use do not qualify as input tax credits.

Bank and Financial Institution Services

Most bank products and services are not taxable. Exceptions include safety deposit box rentals, custodial and safekeeping services, personalized cheques, self-administrated registered savings plan fees, payroll services, rentals of night depository, rentals of credit card imprinters and reconciliation of cheques. Banks remit the full amount of GST they collect from customers. Because most bank services are not taxable, banks cannot claim input tax credits for GST they pay on business-related purchases.

GST on Imported and Exported Goods

NOTES
Visitors to Canada can request a GST refund for GST paid on goods purchased in Canada that they are taking home with them. They cannot claim a refund for goods and services they consumed in Canada, such as entertainment and dining.

GST is not charged on exported goods. Customers in other countries who import goods from Canada do not pay GST.

Businesses in Canada must pay GST on the items they import or purchase from other countries. The GST is collected by Canada Revenue Agency (CRA) when the goods enter Canada based on the purchase price (plus import duty) and current exchange rates. Businesses must pay this GST and other import duties before the goods are released to them.

Administering the GST

The federal government has approved different methods of administering the GST; the regular method is most commonly used.

The Regular Method

The regular method of administering the GST requires the business to keep track of GST paid for all goods and services purchased from vendors (less returns) and of GST collected for all goods and services sold to customers (less returns). It then deducts the GST paid from the GST collected and files for a refund or remits the balance owing to the Receiver General on a monthly or quarterly basis.

Accounting Examples Using the Regular Method (without PST)

SALES INVOICE

Sold goods to customer for $200 plus $14 GST collected (7 %). Invoice total, $214.

Date	Particulars	Debit	Credit
xx/xx	Accounts Receivable	214.00	
	GST Charged on Sales		14.00
	Revenue from Sales		200.00

PURCHASE INVOICE

Purchased supplies from vendor for $300 plus $21 GST paid (7 %). Invoice total, $321.

Date	Particulars	Debit	Credit
xx/xx	Supplies	300.00	
	GST Paid on Purchases	21.00	
	Accounts Payable		321.00

NOTES

GST Paid on Purchases is a contra-liability account because it normally has a debit balance while most liability accounts have a credit balance. Therefore, GST Paid on Purchases reduces the total GST liability to the Receiver General.

The GST owing is further reduced by any GST adjustments — for example, GST that applies to bad debts that are written off. If the debt is later recovered, the GST liability is also restored as an input tax credit adjustment.

Other Methods of Calculating GST

Certain small businesses may be eligible to use simpler methods of calculating their GST refunds and remittances that do not require them to keep a separate record for GST on each individual purchase or sale. The simplified accounting method, the streamlined accounting method and the quick method are examples of these alternatives.

NOTES

These alternative methods of calculating GST are not used in the applications in this workbook.

Calculating GST Refunds or Remittances

The following example uses the regular method for a retailer who is filing quarterly.

Quarterly Total Sales (excluding GST)	$50 000.00	
Quarterly Total Purchases	29 700.00	
7% GST Charged on Sales		$3 500.00
Less: 7% GST Paid on Purchases		
Cash Register (cost $1 000)	70.00	
Inventory (cost $25 000)	1 750.00	
Supplies (cost $500)	35.00	
Payroll Services (cost $200)	14.00	
Store Lease (cost $3 000)	210.00	
Total GST Paid		– 2 079.00
GST Remittance		$1 421.00

GST Remittances and Refunds

The business must file a statement periodically that summarizes the amount of GST it has collected and the amount of GST it has paid. CRA may require reports monthly, quarterly or yearly, depending on total sales. Yearly reports usually require quarterly instalments.

GST Collected on Sales	>	GST Paid on Purchases	=	GST Owing
GST Collected on Sales	<	GST Paid on Purchases	=	GST Refund

Accounting Examples for Remittances and Refunds

NOTES
The rules concerning the GST may change periodically, as in the 2006 federal budget. Always refer to current guidelines.

Remittances

Usually a business will make GST remittances since sales usually exceed expenses — the business operates at a profit. The following example shows how the GST accounts are cleared and a liability (*Accounts Payable*) is set up to remit GST owing to the Receiver General for Canada. In this case, the usual one, the Receiver General becomes a vendor for the business so that the liability can be entered and the payment made.

Date	Particulars	Debit	Credit
03/31	GST Charged on Sales	2 500.00	
	GST Paid on Purchases		700.00
	A/P - Receiver General		1 800.00
03/31	A/P - Receiver General	1 800.00	
	Cash in Bank		1 800.00

Refunds

The example below shows how the GST accounts are cleared and a current asset account (*Accounts Receivable*) is set up for a GST refund from the Receiver General for Canada. In this case, the Receiver General owes money to the business; that is, it acts like a customer. A customer record is set up for the Receiver General to record and collect the amount receivable.

Date	Particulars	Debit	Credit
03/31	GST Charged on Sales	1 500.00	
	A/R - Receiver General	500.00	
	GST Paid on Purchases		2 000.00
04/15	Cash in Bank	500.00	
	A/R - Receiver General		500.00

GST and Provincial Sales Taxes

NOTES
If a business purchases inventory for resale but later uses the inventory within the business instead, it must remit PST on this internal transaction. The business has become the final consumer of the products.

The rules governing provincial sales taxes vary from province to province in terms of the rates of taxation, the goods and services that are taxed and whether Provincial Sales Tax (PST) is applied to the GST as well as to the base purchase price, that is, GST is taxable. The following examples assume that the item sold has both GST and PST applied.

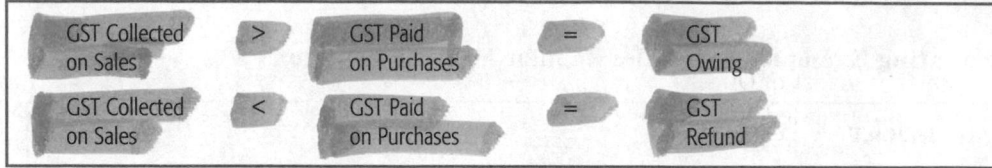

Although GST is applied at each level of sale, resale and manufacturing, PST is paid only by the final consumer of a product or service. Thus, a business purchasing inventory to sell to customers will not pay PST on these purchases. When the same business buys supplies or services for its use in conducting business, it must pay PST because it has become the final consumer of these goods or services.

PST applies only to sales within a province, not to sales to customers in a different province or in a different country.

Alberta has no provincial sales tax. Thus, the examples provided above without PST illustrate the application of GST for Alberta.

PST in Ontario, Manitoba, Saskatchewan and British Columbia

The provinces west of Quebec apply PST to the base price of the sale, the amount without GST included. The following example illustrates the application in Ontario.

Ontario business sold goods on account for $500. GST charged is 7% and PST charged is 8%.

GST = (0.07 × 500) = $35
PST in Ontario = (0.08 × 500) = $40
Total amount of invoice = $500 + $35 + $40 = $575

Date	Particulars	Debit	Credit
xx/xx	Accounts Receivable	575.00	
	GST Charged on Sales		35.00
	PST Payable		40.00
	Revenue from Sales		500.00

The full amount of PST collected on sales is remitted to the provincial Minister of Finance (less any applicable sales tax compensation).

Harmonized Sales Tax — Nova Scotia, New Brunswick and Newfoundland and Labrador

NOTES
The Harmonized Sales Tax is covered in Chapter 5.

In these Atlantic provinces, GST and PST are harmonized at a single rate of 15 percent. The full 15 percent Harmonized Sales Tax (HST) operates much like the basic GST, with HST remittances equal to HST collected on sales less HST paid on purchases. Prices shown to customers may have the HST included (tax-inclusive pricing), but they must show either the amount of HST included in the price or the HST rate. The following example illustrates the application in New Brunswick.

New Brunswick business sold goods on account for $575, including HST at 15% ($500 base price).

HST = (0.15 × 500) = $75
Total amount of invoice = $575

Date	Particulars	Debit	Credit
xx/xx	Accounts Receivable	575.00	
	HST Charged on Sales		75.00
	Revenue from Sales		500.00

A single remittance for the full 15 percent is made to the Receiver General; the provincial portion of the HST is not remitted separately. The administration of the HST may be taken over by the provincial governments in the future.

NOTES
Quebec was the first province to introduce a Harmonized Sales Tax. It differs from the model in the Atlantic provinces in that the GST and QST components are administered separately by the federal and provincial governments respectively. QST is covered in Chapter 13.

Quebec Sales Tax (QST)

Provincial sales tax in Quebec (QST) is also combined with the GST. The provincial tax rate is applied to a broader base of goods and services than PST in Ontario, like the base that has GST applied. The QST is calculated on the base amount of the sale plus the GST. That is, QST is applied to GST — a piggy-backed tax or a tax on a tax.

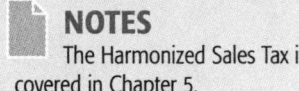

Quebec business sold goods on account for $500. GST charged is 7% and QST charged is 7.5%.

GST = (0.07 × 500) = $35
QST = (0.075 × 535) = $40.13
Total amount of invoice = $500.00 + $35.00 + $40.13 = $575.13

Date	Particulars	Debit	Credit
xx/xx	Accounts Receivable	575.13	
	GST Charged on Sales		35.00
	QST Charged on Sales		40.13
	Revenue from Sales		500.00

QST is remitted to the ministre du Revenu du Québec, separately from GST. However, the QST is refundable and businesses can deduct the QST they pay on their purchases from the QST they collect on sales. The QST paid on a few items or services — QST on some telecommunication services and insurance — is not refundable. Therefore, QST paid must be designated as refundable or non-refundable at the time of the purchase and when the purchase is recorded.

PST in Prince Edward Island

Provincial sales tax in PEI (PST) is applied to the base sale price plus GST. However, unlike Quebec, and like Ontario, some items have only GST applied, and some have both GST and PST applied.

PEI business sold goods on account for $500. GST charged is 7% and PST charged is 10%.

GST = (0.07 × 500) = $35
PST = (0.10 × 535) = $53.50
Total amount of invoice = $500.00 + $35.00 + $53.50 = $588.50

Date	Particulars	Debit	Credit
xx/xx	Accounts Receivable	588.50	
	GST Charged on Sales		35.00
	PST Payable		53.50
	Revenue from Sales		500.00

The full amount of PST collected on sales is remitted to the provincial Minister of Finance (less 3 percent sales tax compensation).

Part 2
Applications

CHAPTER THREE

Missoni Marbleworks

OBJECTIVES

After completing this chapter, you should be able to

- ***access*** the data files for the business
- ***open*** the General Journal
- ***enter*** transactions in the General Journal
- ***edit*** and ***review*** General Journal transactions
- ***post*** transactions
- ***create*** new General Ledger accounts
- ***adjust*** journal entries after posting
- ***display*** and ***print*** General Ledger and General Journal reports
- ***graph*** General Ledger reports
- ***display*** and ***print*** comparative financial reports
- ***customize*** reports and ***create*** report templates
- ***back up*** your data files
- ***advance*** the session date
- ***finish*** an accounting session

COMPANY INFORMATION

Company Profile

NOTES
Missoni Marbleworks
66 Allies Avenue
Edmonton, Alberta T3P 4C2
Tel 1: (403) 763-4127
Tel 2: (800) 455-4127
Fax: (403) 765-4842
Business No.: 743 647 397

Missoni Marbleworks in Edmonton, Alberta is owned and operated by Maria Missoni who opened the business after graduating from college and training in Italy with Renaissance Marble Works. She builds stone fireplaces and chimneys, stone porches, patios and stairs and installs ceramic and marble tile floors in homes and fountains in shopping malls. Her love of Italian architecture has led her to repairing old marble in museums, galleries and homes. She hopes to include more art restoration in her work in the future. Missoni also has considerable artistic and creative talents. The marble stands that she carves for statues, masks and vases are sold from her home studio, at local craft shows and to individual customers who commission special pieces.

Some of her customers have set up accounts with Missoni, and she has set up accounts with her regular vendors and suppliers.

To convert her accounting records to Simply Accounting in April, she has used:

- Chart of Accounts
- Trial Balance
- Accounting Procedures

CHART OF POSTABLE ACCOUNTS

MISSONI MARBLEWORKS

ASSETS
1080 Cash in Bank
1200 A/R - St. Albert Museum
1220 A/R - Jasper Gallery
1240 A/R - Stoney Plain Plaza
1320 Prepaid Insurance
1360 Marble Inventory
1540 Computer Equipment
1550 Power Marble Tools
1560 Power Marble Equipment
1570 Van ▶

▶LIABILITIES
2100 A/P - West Carbide Tools
2120 A/P - Marblehead Suppliers
2140 A/P - Alberta Hydro
2160 A/P - Alberta Telephone
2180 A/P - Chinook Promotions
2650 GST Charged on Sales
2670 GST Paid on Purchases ▶

▶EQUITY
3100 Missoni, Capital
3150 Missoni, Drawings
3600 Net Income

REVENUE
4100 Revenue from Contracts
4150 Revenue from Repairs
4200 Interest Revenue ▶

▶EXPENSE
5020 Advertising & Promotion
5040 Bank Charges
5060 Hydro Expense
5080 Interest Expense
5100 Maintenance & Repairs
5120 Rental Expenses
5140 Telephone Expenses
5160 Wages Expenses

NOTES: The Chart of Accounts includes only postable accounts and the Net Income or Current Earnings account. Simply Accounting uses the Net Income account for the Income Statement to calculate the difference between revenue and expenses before closing the books.

TRIAL BALANCE

MISSONI MARBLEWORKS

April 1, 2008		Debits	Credits
1080	Cash in Bank	$ 24 000	
1200	A/R - St. Albert Museum	2 400	
1220	A/R - Jasper Gallery	3 600	
1240	A/R - Stoney Plain Plaza	1 600	
1320	Prepaid Insurance	1 000	
1360	Marble Inventory	2 050	
1540	Computer Equipment	2 500	
1550	Power Marble Tools	4 500	
1560	Power Marble Equipment	28 000	
1570	Van	32 000	
2100	A/P - West Carbide Tools		$ 1 200
2120	A/P - Marblehead Suppliers		2 400
2650	GST Charged on Sales		1 400
2670	GST Paid on Purchases	840	
3100	Missoni, Capital		83 310
3150	Missoni, Drawings	300	
4100	Revenue from Contracts		18 000
4150	Revenue from Repairs		2 000
5020	Advertising & Promotion	200	
5040	Bank Charges	60	
5060	Hydro Expense	300	
5100	Maintenance & Repairs	400	
5120	Rental Expenses	600	
5140	Telephone Expenses	360	
5160	Wages Expenses	3 600	
		$108 310	$108 310

Accounting Procedures

GST

> **NOTES**
> Most bank and financial institution services used in this application are exempt from GST charges.
> Alberta does not levy a provincial sales tax.

Missoni has chosen the regular method for remittance of the Goods and Services Tax (GST). She records the GST collected from customers as a liability (credit) in the *GST Charged on Sales* account. She records GST that she pays to vendors in the *GST Paid on Purchases* account as a decrease (debit) to her liability to Canada Revenue Agency. Her GST remittance or refund is calculated automatically in the *GST Owing (Refund)* subtotal. You can see these accounts when you display or print the Balance Sheet. Missoni files her GST remittances or requests for refunds with the Receiver General for Canada on the last day of each fiscal quarter. (For details, please read Chapter 2 on the Goods and Services Tax.)

INSTRUCTIONS

1. **Enter** the **source documents for April** in the General Journal in Simply Accounting using the Chart of Accounts and Trial Balance for Missoni Marbleworks. The procedures for entering each new type of transaction for this application are outlined step by step in the Keystrokes section following the source documents. These transactions have a ✓ in the check box and, immediately below the check box, the page number on which the relevant keystrokes begin. Put your own checkmark in each transaction box after you finish entering the transaction to show that you have completed it.

2. **Print** the **reports and graphs** indicated on the printing form below after you have completed your entries. Keystrokes for reports begin on page 49.

REPORTS

Lists
- ☐ Chart of Accounts
- ☐ Account List

Journals
- ☑ General: By Date from April 1 to April 14

Financials
- ☑ Comparative Balance Sheet dates: April 1 and April 14 with difference in percentage
- ☑ Income Statement from April 1 to April 14
- ☑ Trial Balance date: April 14
- ☑ General Ledger accounts: 1080 2650 3100 4100 from April 1 to April 14

Management Reports
- ☐ General

GRAPHS
- ☐ Revenues by Account
- ☐ Expenses by Account
- ☑ Expenses and Net Profit as % of Revenue

SOURCE DOCUMENTS

SESSION DATE – APRIL 7, 2008

> **NOTES**
> Remember that the ✓ in the check box and the number beneath it indicate that keystroke instructions for this entry begin on page 34.

☑ 34 **Purchase Invoice WCT-161** **Dated April 2, 2008**

From West Carbide Tools, $880 plus $61.60 GST paid for diamond-tip drill and drill bits. Purchase invoice total $941.60. Terms: net 30 days.

> **NOTES**
> ☑ 41 Create new Group account 2300 Bank Loan. (See keystrokes on page 41.)

☑ 41 **Bank Credit Memo #AT-C3104** **Dated April 3, 2008**

From Alberta Trust Company, $10 000 bank loan secured for purchase of new marble equipment. Loan deposited into bank account. Create new Group account 2300 Bank Loan.

☐ **Sales Invoice #MM-40** **Dated April 3, 2008**

To St. Albert Museum, $3 200 plus $224 GST charged to build marble display stands for statues as per contract. Sales invoice total $3 424. Terms: net 30 days.

☐ **Sales Invoice #MM-41** **Dated April 4, 2008**

To Stoney Plain Plaza, $800 plus $56 GST charged for repair work on plaza marble fountain. Sales invoice total $856. Terms: net 30 days.

☑ **Memo #1** **Dated April 4, 2008**

43 From Owner: The invoice from West Carbide Tools was entered incorrectly. The cost of the drill was $900 plus $63 GST paid. The revised purchase invoice total is $963. Adjust the posted invoice to make the correction.

☐ **Cheque Copy #48** **Dated April 5, 2008**

To West Carbide Tools, $1 200 in payment of invoice #WCT-129.

☐ **Cash Receipt #20** **Dated April 5, 2008**

From St. Albert Museum, cheque #828 for $2 400 in payment of invoice #MM-37.

☐ **Cash Sales Invoice #MM-42** **Dated April 6, 2008**

To Rolf Kleinje, $1 500 plus $105 GST charged for replacement of marble kitchen counter and repair work. Sales invoice total $1 605. Received certified cheque #AT-603 in full payment of account.

☐ **Purchase Invoice #MS-611** **Dated April 6, 2008**

From Marblehead Suppliers, $6 000 plus $420 GST paid for marble pieces (inventory) of different sizes to complete contracted work. Purchase invoice total $6 420. Terms: net 30 days.

☐ **Cash Receipt #21** **Dated April 7, 2008**

From Stoney Plain Plaza, cheque #4011 for $1 600 in payment of invoice #MM-39.

☐ **Bank Debit Memo #AT-D3691** **Dated April 7, 2008**

From Alberta Trust Company, $24 for bank service charges.

SESSION DATE – APRIL 14, 2008

NOTES

☑ 45 See keystrokes on Advancing the Session Date, page 45.

☐ **Purchase Invoice #WMM-4499** **Dated April 8, 2008**

From West Mall Mechanical, $300 plus $21 GST paid for repairs and maintenance work on equipment. Purchase invoice total $321. Terms: pay on receipt. Create new Group account 2190 A/P - West Mall Mechanical.

☐ **Cheque Copy #49** **Dated April 8, 2008**

To West Mall Mechanical, $321 in full payment of account. Reference invoice #WMM-4499.

☐ **Purchase Invoice #AH-44371** **Dated April 9, 2008**

From Alberta Hydro, $90 plus $6.30 GST paid for hydro services for one month. Purchase invoice total $96.30. Terms: cash on receipt of invoice.

☑ **Cheque Copy #50** **Dated April 10, 2008**

To Alberta Hydro, $96.30 in full payment of account. Reference invoice #AH-44371.

Sales Invoice #MM-43 **Dated April 11, 2008**

To Sherwood Park Estates (new customer), $3 000 plus $210 GST charged for contracted new marble tile kitchen floor and walls. Sales invoice total $3 210. Terms: net 10 days. Create new Group account 1260 A/R - Sherwood Park Estates.

Bank Credit Memo #AT-C3421 **Dated April 11, 2008**

From Alberta Trust Company, $500 semi-annual interest earned on bank account.

Cash Receipt #22 **Dated April 12, 2008**

From Jasper Gallery, cheque #58821 for $3 600 in full payment of invoice #MM-38.

Purchase Invoice #AT-11421 **Dated April 13, 2008**

From Alberta Telephone, $80 plus $5.60 GST paid for cellular telephone service. Purchase invoice total $85.60. Terms: cash on receipt of invoice.

Cheque Copy #51 **Dated April 14, 2008**

To Alberta Telephone, $85.60 in full payment of account. Reference invoice #AT-11421.

Sales Invoice #MM-44 **Dated April 14, 2008**

To Jasper Gallery, $2 000 plus $140 GST charged for building of marble pedestals and base units as per contract. Sales invoice total $2 140. Terms: net 30 days.

KEYSTROKES

Opening Data Files

Choose **Start** then **choose Programs** (or **All Programs**) and **Simply Accounting by Sage**. **Click Simply Accounting by Sage**.

Click **Select An Existing Company** and **click OK**.

Click the **Up One Level icon** to return to the Data folder level.

Double click the **Missoni folder** to open it.

Double click **missoni** or **missoni.sdb**, the data file for Missoni Marbleworks. Refer to Chapter 1, page 9 if you need further assistance.

NOTES
In these instructions, our starting point for opening the file is the Start file in Chapter 1.

The following screen appears, asking (prompting) you to enter the session date for this work session:

NOTES
Many screens include a Cancel button. If you click Cancel, you will return to your previous screen without entering any changes.
The Advancing the Session Date section on page 45 will explain how to work with later dates.
Refer to Chapter 1, page 18, and Windows Help for further information on date formats.

The date format on your screen is controlled by the Dates Settings options in Simply Accounting, not by the format you use to enter the date.

The session date is the date of your work session, the date on which you are recording the accounting transactions on the computer. A business with a large number of transactions may record these transactions at the end of each day. One with fewer transactions may enter them once a week. In this workbook, transactions are entered once a week for most applications so the session date is updated by one week at a time.

The session date may or may not be the same as the date on which the transaction actually took place.

The session date for your first session is April 7, 2008. Since this is not the default shown on the screen, you must change the date. Every date field has a Calendar icon.

Click the **Calendar icon** to open the calendar:

The calendar has the current session date highlighted with a blue background. The calendar for any date field also shows the range of dates that will be accepted based on the settings chosen for the company files. The arrows allow you to move forward to a later month or back to a previous month. The calendar stops at the dates that indicate the range you may use. Click a date on the calendar to enter it or use one of the following alternative formats. Note that they all use the same order of month, day and year. Entering the year is optional.

- use different characters to separate numbers: 04-07-08 or 04/07/08
- omit leading zeros: 4/7/8 or 4-7-8
- leave spaces between numbers: 04 07 08 or 4 7 8
- type lower- or upper-case text: April 7, 2008 or APRIL 7, 2008
- use three-letter abbreviations for the month: Apr 7 8 or apr 7 8
- other non-alpha or non-numeric separating characters may also be used
- you may also enter dates without the year

We will use a variety of date formats throughout this workbook but we always show the dates on-screen in the text format. Using the calendar to choose a date or using a text version to enter a date will also prevent an incorrect date entry.

Click **7** on the April date calendar or

Type `april 7, 2008`

Click **OK**.

Your screen shows the following Home window:

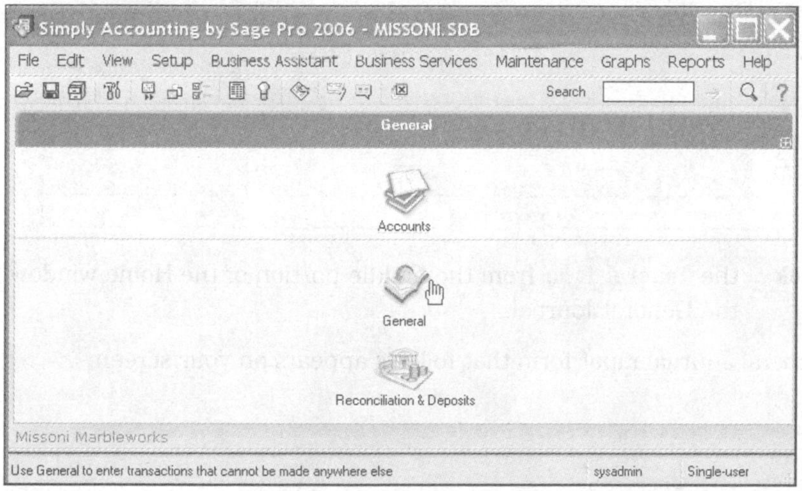

Only the General Ledger and Journal can be accessed for this file. When ledger icons are hidden, all main menu options related to those ledgers are also hidden or unavailable. (Click to maximize the window if necessary.) The Home window is

NOTES
Company settings are discussed in Chapter 4.

NOTES
Refer to Chapter 1, page 18, and Chapter 4, page 86 for instructions on changing date format settings.

NOTES
Keystrokes that you must use are shown in command statements like these:

Type `april 7` or
Click **OK**

Instruction lines are indented; command words are in boldface; text you type is shown in a special font (Courier) and things that you must click on or select are in colour and bold. This format makes it easy to find the instruction statements in the text.

basic **BASIC VERSION**
The program name in the title bar will be Simply Accounting by Sage Basic 2006.
There is no Search field. Search is accessed from the Edit menu.

NOTES
Maximize the Home window if necessary. Refer to Chapter 1 for a more detailed description of the Home window.

divided as follows: the title bar is on top with the program and file names, control menu icon and size buttons; the main menu bar comes next; the tool bar follows. Tool buttons permit alternative and quick access to commonly used menu items. The Home window tools from left to right (with their alternative pull-down menu locations) are Open Company, Save and Backup (File menu), Setup (Setup menu), Change Session Date (Maintenance menu), Daily Business Manager and Checklists (Business Assistant menu), Display Reports (Reports menu) and Advice (Help menu). Form Designer and Upload Direct Deposit have no menu alternative. The last two tools are Switch To French when you are working in English (or from French to English when you are working in French) and Close All Other Simply Accounting Windows (View menu). The Search tool (Edit menu) and Help tool (Help menu) are located on the far right for easy access.

The ledger names with their respective icons occupy the major part of the window — ledgers in the top row below the ledger or module name and journal icons below the line under their respective ledgers in the next two icon rows of the window. Ledgers contain the records for accounts, customers, vendors, employees, inventory items and their balances. Journals are used to enter accounting transactions. Only the General or Accounts Ledger is set up for Missoni Marbleworks, so it is the only ledger displayed. The remaining ledgers are hidden.

NOTES
Account reconciliation is also not set up.

Below the journal icons, the status bar describes the purpose of the General Journal because the hand-shaped pointer is on the General icon. Point to different parts of the Home window to observe the changes in the status bar message.

Entering General Journal Transactions

All transactions for Missoni Marbleworks are entered in the General Journal, indicated by the pointer in the following screen:

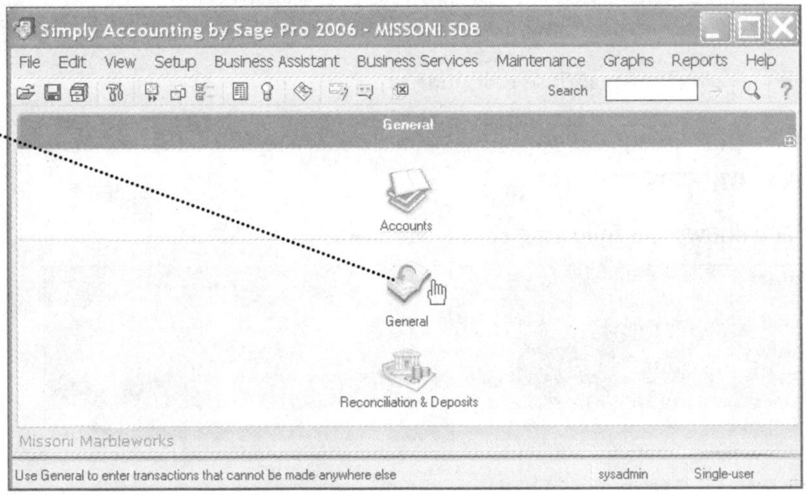

BASIC VERSION
The program name in the title bar will be Simply Accounting by Sage Basic 2006.

Click the **General icon** from the middle portion of the Home window to open the General Journal.

The General Journal input form that follows appears on your screen:

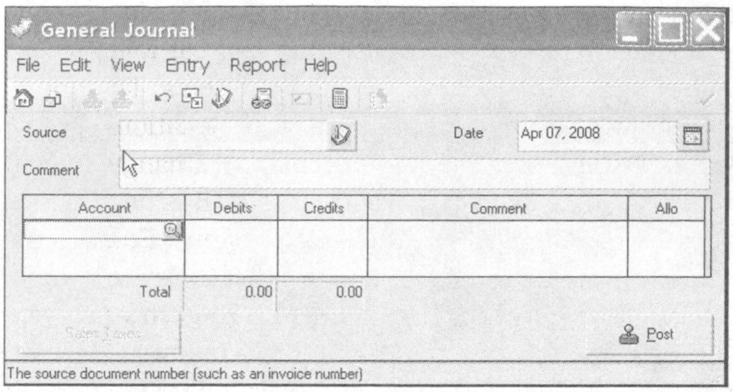

You are now ready to enter the first transaction in the General Journal input screen. The cursor, a flashing vertical line, is blinking in the Source field, ready to receive information. The Source field identifies the reference document from which you obtain the information for a transaction, in this case, the invoice number.

Type `WCT-161`

Press *tab* to advance to the Adjust Journal Entry icon. **Press** *tab* again.

The cursor advances to the next field, the Date field. You should enter the transaction date here. The program enters the session date by default. It is highlighted, ready to be accepted or changed. Because the work was completed on April 2, 2008, the session date of April 7 is incorrect and must be changed.

Type `04-02`

Press *tab* to move to the Calendar icon. Notice that the text form of the date is displayed, even though we entered the date as numbers.

Press *tab* again to accept the date and advance to the Comment field.

If you click the Calendar icon in the Date field now, the session date has a red frame around it. The current transaction date has a solid blue background.

The year is added to the date. In the Comment field, you should enter a description of the transaction to make the permanent record more meaningful. You may enter up to 39 characters, including spaces.

Type `West Carbide Tools`

Press *tab*.

The cursor moves forward to the first line of the Account field, creating a dotted box for the first account.

Simply Accounting organizes accounts into sections or categories using the following boundaries for numbering:

- 1000–1999 Assets
- 2000–2999 Liabilities
- 3000–3999 Equity
- 4000–4999 Revenue
- 5000–5999 Expense

This system makes it easy to remember the first digit of an account. Double clicking the Account field will display the list of accounts. If you type the first digit of an account number then double click or press *enter* while the cursor is flashing in any account field, the program will advance the list to accounts beginning with that digit.

Click the **List icon** , or **double click** the dotted box in the **Account column** to list the accounts.

NOTES
The Refresh tool applies to multi-user use of the program. This feature is not available in Basic or in the Student versions.

NOTES
Source codes can contain up to 13 characters, including spaces.

WARNING!
Unless you change the date, the session date will become the posting date for the entry.
Remember that you can use any date format listed on page 35 and you may also omit the year.

NOTES
Command statements that are indented but do not have the boldfaced command words show alternative keystrokes or optional instructions.

NOTES
When you press *tab* after typing a date in the Date field, you will advance to the Calendar icon. You must press *tab* again to advance to the next input field. That is, you must press *tab* twice. If you choose a date from the calendar, pressing *tab* once will move the cursor to the next input field.

NOTES
If you click the Account field first, you can also press *enter* to open the Select Account list.

NOTES
Many fields that allow you to select an account or other information from a list have the Select or List icon to provide quick access to the list. Showing the List icon is an option that you select in the company settings.

Other fields have list arrows that provide a drop-down or pop-up list.

The following list of accounts appears on your journal screen:

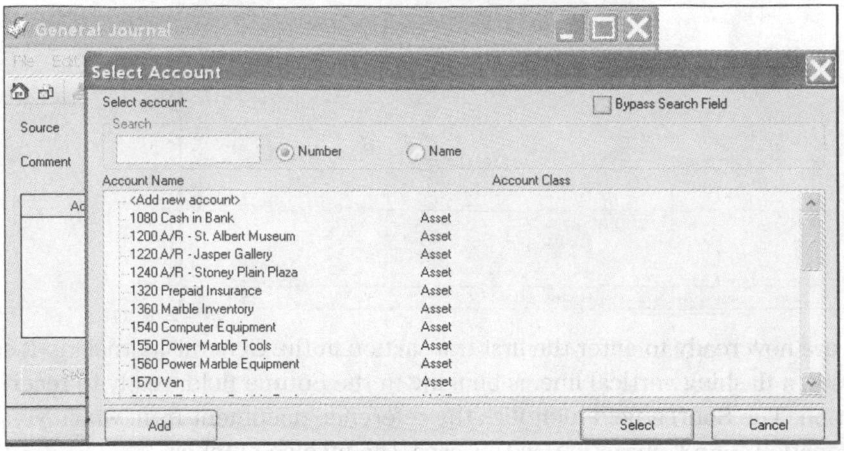

The beginning of the account list is displayed. The list includes only postable accounts, those that can be debited or credited in journal entries. The cursor is in the Search field. If you want to place the cursor in the account list directly from the Account field, you can choose **Bypass Search Field**. We will not select this option. Typing a number in the Search field also places the cursor directly in the list. Following usual accounting practice, we enter the account to be debited first.

Click **1550 Power Marble Tools** to select this asset account.

Click the **Select button**. (A darker frame or an inner dotted box shows that a button is selected.)

You can also double click a selected account or press *enter* to add it directly to your journal entry form. Instead of using the selection list, you can find the number in the Chart of Accounts, type it in and press *tab*.

NOTES
This is another example of an alternative command statement.

Notice that the account number and name have been added to your input form, so you can easily see whether you have selected the correct account. If the screen does not display the entire account title, you can see the rest of the account title by clicking anywhere on the part that is showing.

Your cursor is now positioned in the Debits field. The amount is selected, ready to be changed. All journals include a **Windows Calculator tool** that opens the calculator directly for easy calculation of amounts if needed.

Click the Display The Windows Calculator tool to open the calculator. You can leave it open in the background for easy access.

Type amounts without dollar signs. You do not need to type decimals when you enter whole numbers. The Simply Accounting program ignores any non-numeric characters that you type in an amount field.

Type `880`

Press *tab*.

The cursor moves to the Comment field. You can add a comment for each account line in the journal. Account line comments are optional. You can add a comment for each line, for some lines or for none of the lines, but the extra details can be included in the journal report and will give you more information about the transaction.

Type `diamond tip drill and drill bits`

Press *tab*.

Your input form should now appear as follows:

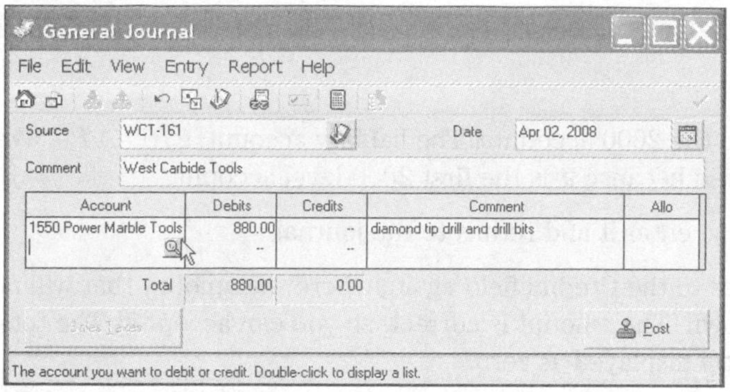

The cursor has advanced to the next line of the Account field, creating a new dotted box so you can enter the next account for this transaction — the liability account *GST Paid on Purchases*. Remember, liability accounts start with 2. However, we will type 3 to advance to the end of the 2000 level accounts.

Type 3

Click the **List icon** to advance your list to the 3000 accounts as shown:

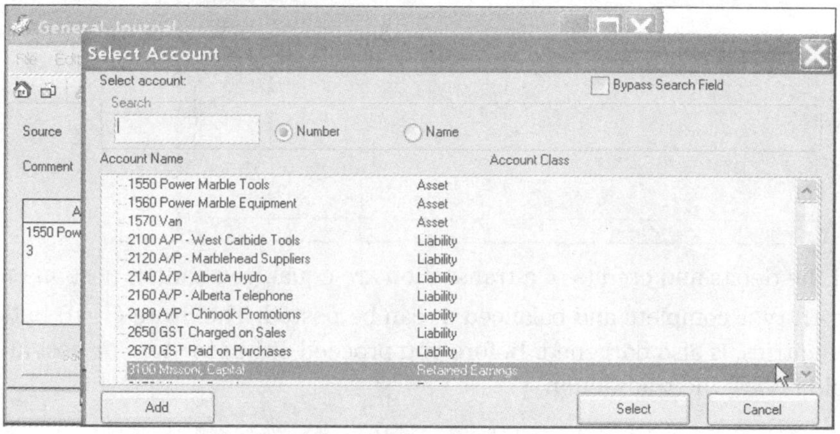

We have bypassed the Search field and selected the first account with the number we typed. This method quickly moves you to a later position in the list.

Click **2670 GST Paid on Purchases** from the displayed list to highlight it. If necessary, click a scroll arrow (or) to move through the account list to include *2670* in the display.

Press *enter*.

Again, the account number and name have been added to your transaction form. The cursor has advanced to the Credits field, which shows 880.00 as the default amount because this amount will balance the entry. The amount is highlighted to indicate that you may edit it. This is a compound entry. You must change the amount to separate the GST, and you must delete the credit entry because the GST account is debited.

Press *del* to delete the credit entry.

Click the **Debits field** on the second journal line below 880.00 to move the cursor.

Type 61.60

Press *tab* to advance to the optional Comment field.

Type GST @ 7%

Press *tab*. The cursor moves to the next line in the Account field.

NOTES

If you know that the account you need is closer to the end of its numbered section, typing the next higher number advances you to the end of the section you want. For example, typing 3 advances to 3100 and includes 2670 in the display. In this way, your account is more likely to be included in the display. Typing 2 will show the list with 2100 at the end and you will have to scroll down to include 2670.

NOTES

Typing a negative number (adding a minus sign) in the Credits field will move the number to the Debits field. Typing a negative number in the Debits field will create a Credit entry.

Press *enter* to open the Select Account list. The cursor is in the Search field.

Type 2

The list advances to the 2000 accounts. The liability account, *2100 A/P - West Carbide Tools*, is selected because it is the first 2000-level account.

Click **Select** to enter it and return to the journal.

The cursor advances to the Credits field again, where the amount that will now balance the entry is shown. The amount is correct, so you can accept it. The total for the Credits column is still displayed as zero.

Press *tab* to update the totals and advance to the Comment field.

Type `terms: net 30`

Your completed input form should appear as follows:

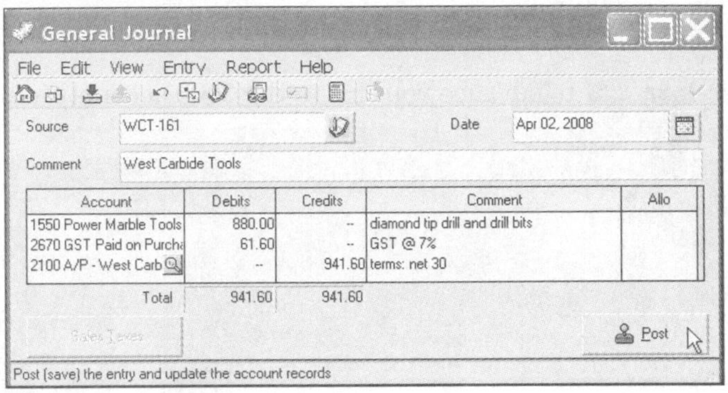

Until the debits and credits of a transaction are equal, you cannot post an entry. Once the entry is complete and balanced, it can be posted. The Store ( ) button, for recurring entries, is also darkened. Before you proceed either to store or post an entry, you should review the transaction.

Reviewing the General Journal Entry

Choose the **Report menu** and then **click** **Display General Journal Entry** as shown:

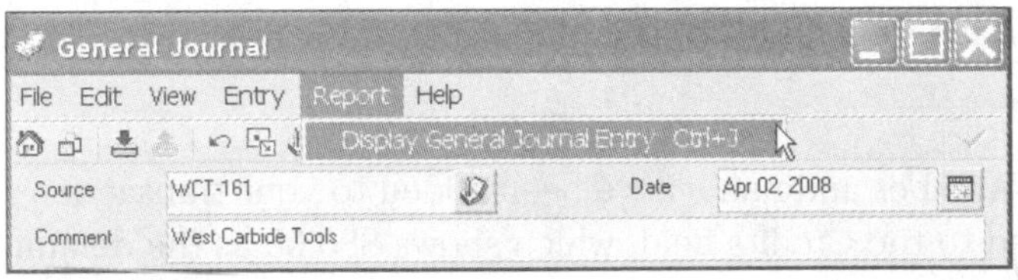

The journal entry for the transaction is displayed as follows:

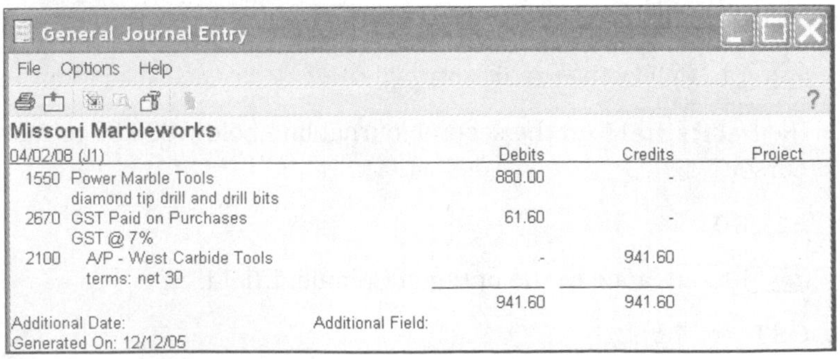

NOTES
The Sales Taxes button will be covered in Chapter 5. Sales Taxes are not set up for Missoni Marbleworks so the button remains dimmed.

NOTES
We will use the Store button in the Chai Tea Room application (Chapter 5).

NOTES
Pressing *ctrl* + J will also display the journal entry in any journal. Refer to Appendix B for a complete list of Simply Accounting keyboard shortcuts.

basic **BASIC VERSION**
The Refresh tool does not apply to the single-user Basic version.

NOTES
The Additional Date and Field can be used to add more information to a journal entry. The Additional Information feature is available in all journals and will be introduced in Chapter 7.

Click the **Maximize button** ▢ to change your display to full screen size or use the scroll arrows to see more of the display if your transaction does not fit on the screen.

To return to your input form,

Click ☒ or **choose** the **Control Menu icon** and **click Close**.

CORRECTING THE GENERAL JOURNAL ENTRY BEFORE POSTING

Press ⌨*tab* to advance to the field that has the error. To move to a previous field, **press** ⌨*shift* and ⌨*tab* together (that is, while holding down ⌨*shift*, **press** ⌨*tab*). The field will be highlighted, ready for editing. **Type** the **correct information** and **press** ⌨*tab* to enter it.

You can also use the mouse to **point** to a field and **drag** through the **incorrect information** to highlight it. You can highlight a single number or letter, or the entire field. **Type** the **correct information** and **press** ⌨*tab* to enter it.

To correct an account number, **click** the **incorrect account number** (or **name**) to select the field. **Press** ⌨*enter* to display the list of accounts. **Click** the **correct account**. **Click Select**. **Press** ⌨*tab* to advance to the next line and enter the correction.

Click an **incorrect amount** to highlight it. **Type** the **correct amount** and **press** ⌨*tab*.

You can insert a line or remove a line by clicking the line that will be moved down or removed and **choosing** the **Edit menu** and **clicking Insert Line** or **Remove Line**.

To discard the entry and begin again, **click** ☒ (Close) to close the journal or **click** ↶ (Undo on the tool bar) to open a blank Journal window. When Simply Accounting asks whether you want to discard the entry, **click Yes** to confirm your decision.

Posting

Once you are sure that all the information is correct, you are ready to post the entry.

Click the **Post button** ⟨🅿 Post⟩ in the lower right corner of the General Journal (the one that looks like a stamp) or **choose** the **Entry menu** and then **click Post**.

A new General Journal input form appears for you to enter the next transaction for this session date.

Adding a New Account

The bank credit memo on April 3 uses an account that is not listed in your Chart of Accounts. Often a company will need to create new accounts as it expands or changes direction. These future needs are not always foreseen when the accounts are first set up. You must add the account *2300 Bank Loan* to enter the bank credit memo transaction. You can add accounts in the Accounts Ledger. The Accounts Ledger is explained in Chapter 4. You can also add accounts directly from the Account field in any journal. First, enter the Source.

Type AT-C3104

Press ⌨*tab* **twice** to advance to the Date field.

Click the **Calendar icon** 📅 and then **click 3**.

Press ⌨*tab* to advance to the Comment field.

Type Alberta Trust - new loan

NOTES
Refer to page 43 and Appendix C for assistance with correcting errors after posting.

⚠ WARNING!
Don't post the transaction until you make sure that it is correct. Always review a transaction before posting it.

NOTES
The date of the previous journal entry becomes the default date until you close the journal. Then the session date becomes the default again.

Double click the **Account field**.

Double click the **Cash in Bank** account. **Type** `10000`, the amount of the loan, as the debit part of the transaction.

Press *tab* to advance to the Comment field for the account.

Type `loan for marble equipment`

Press *tab* to advance to the Account field on the second journal line.

Click the **List icon** or **press** *enter* to see the Select Account list.

Click the **Add button** or **double click Add New Account**, the first entry in the list, to begin the wizard for adding a General Ledger account:

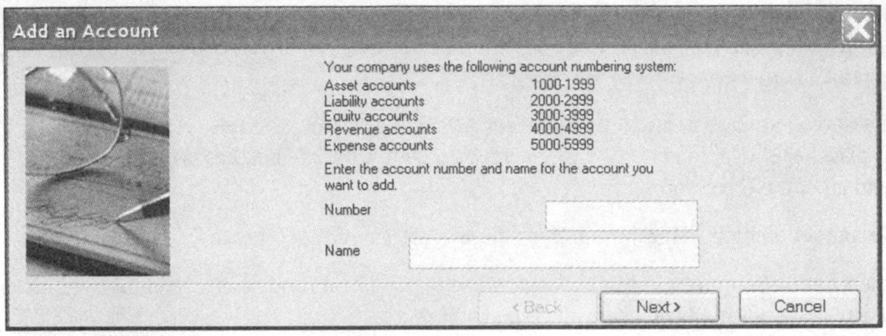

The first screen prompts you for the account number and name. The cursor is in the Number field.

Type `2300`

Press *tab*.

Type `Bank Loan`

Click **Next** or **press** *enter* to continue.

NOTES

Next is selected so you can press *enter* repeatedly to advance through the wizard screens that you do not need to change.

The next screen asks for the **GIFI code**. This is the four-digit account number assigned by Canada Revenue Agency for this category of account for use with electronically filed business returns. GIFI codes are not used in this workbook. They are described in Appendix H.

Click **Next** to skip this screen and continue.

WARNING!

Account types must be set correctly or you will get the error message that accounts are not in logical order when you display financial reports. If you see one of these messages, you can edit the account type. See Chapter 4, page 95 for help with creating and editing accounts.

The next screen asks whether this account is to be used as a **Heading** or **Total** in the financial statements. *Bank Loan* is an ordinary postable account that has a balance so the default selection, No, is correct. A partial balance sheet illustrates account types.

Click **Next** to accept the default and continue.

The following screen deals with another aspect of the **account type**. Accounts may be **subtotalled** within their group of accounts. For example, if you have several bank accounts, you will want your Balance Sheet report to include the total cash deposited in all of them together. Different account types will be explained fully in the Toss for Tots application (Chapter 4), where you will set up the accounting records for a new company.

Bank Loan is a Group account. It is not subtotalled with any other account so the default selection, No, is correct.

Click **Next** to continue.

The next wizard screen refers to the **account class**. Account classes are explained in Chapter 9. The default selection is the name of the section. Therefore, for account

2300, Liability is the section and the default class. Generally, you can accept the default selection.

Click **Next** to continue.

Now you are being asked whether you want to **allocate** the balance of the account to different projects. Projects are not set up for Missoni Marbleworks, so the default selection, set at No for Balance Sheet accounts, is correct.

Click **Next** to continue.

The next setting screen asks whether you want to include or **omit** this account **from financial statements** when it has a zero balance. Choosing Yes means that if the balance in this account is zero, the account will not be included in your financial statements. If you choose No, the account will be printed even if it has a balance of zero. Some accounts, such as *Cash in Bank*, should always be printed in financial statements. In Chapter 4 we explain this setting. The default setting, to include accounts (not to omit), is never wrong.

Click **Next** to continue.

Your final screen should look like the one shown here:

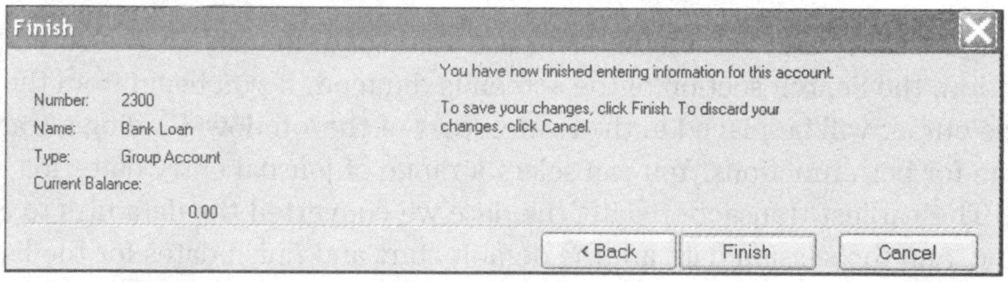

This final screen shows the selections you have made.

Check your **work**. **Click Back** until you reach the screen with the error. **Make** the **correction** and **click Next** until you reach this final screen again.

When all the information is correct, you must save the new account information.

Click **Finish**.

You will return to the General Journal window with the new account added to the account field. Notice that the cursor has not yet advanced, so you can change your account selection if you need to.

Click the **Credits field**.

Press *tab* again to accept the amount and advance to the Comment field.

Type `Alberta Trust loan`

Display the **journal entry** to see whether it is correct.

Close the **display**. **Make corrections** if you find errors.

Click **Post** Post to save the information.

Enter the next two sales transactions.

NOTES

You can use the wizard in any account field to create a new account at any time. You do not need to use the account after creating it when you return to the journal.

Adjusting a Posted Entry

Sometimes you discover after posting a journal entry that it had an error. You can make corrections directly in the General Journal by adjusting the previously posted transaction. Simply Accounting allows you to make the correction by adjusting the entry without completing a reversing entry. The program creates the reversing and correcting journal entries after you post the correction so that the audit trail is complete. The purchase from West Carbide Tools on April 2 was posted with an incorrect amount.

The General Journal should still be open.

Click the **Adjust A Previously Posted Entry tool** or **click** , the **Adjust An Entry button** beside the Source field, or **choose** the **Entry menu** and **click Adjusting Entry** to open the Search screen:

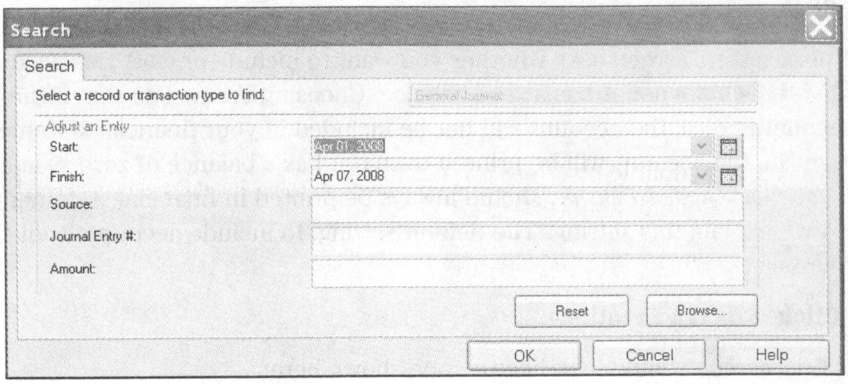

The Adjust Entry and Search functions are combined. Because we selected the Adjust option, the Search section of the screen is dimmed. If you begin from the Search option, the cursor will be placed in the Search part of the window. Finding a transaction is the same for both functions. You can select a range of journal entry dates for browsing. The earliest transaction date, the date we converted the data files to Simply Accounting, and the session date are the default start and finish dates for the list. If you know the Source number for the entry, you can enter it in the Source field and access the journal entry directly by clicking OK. The Reset button will restore the default search parameters that you see in the screen above.

We can accept the default dates because they include the transaction we need.

Click **Browse** to list the journal entries:

NOTES

You should choose the order that makes it easiest to find your entry. That will depend on what information you entered and what you remember as well as how many entries you have.

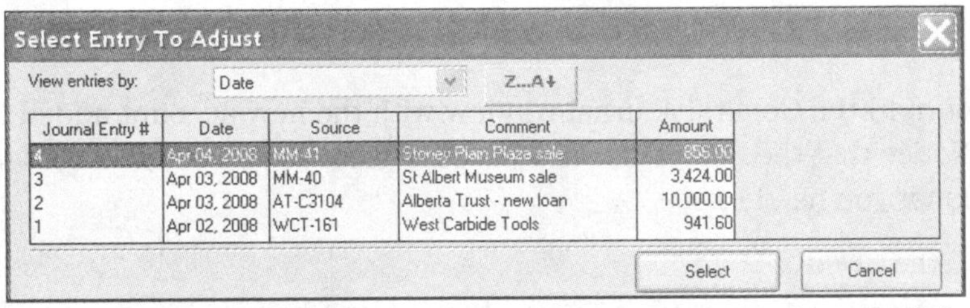

All journal entries are listed with the most recent one at the top of the list (Z...A order). You can choose the way the journal entries are sorted.

Click the **list arrow** beside the Date entry for **View Entries By**:

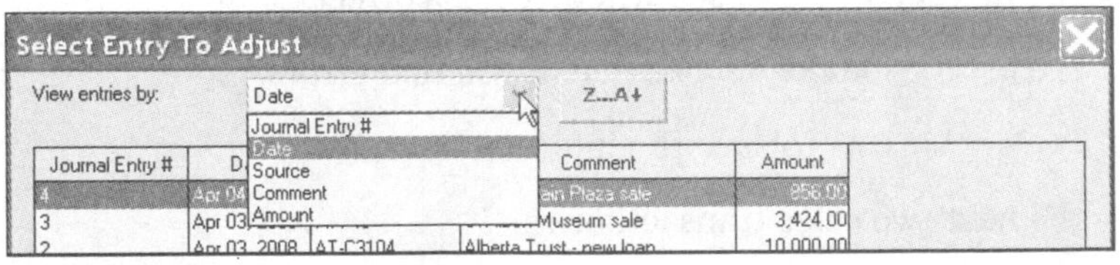

You can organize the list of entries by journal entry number, date, source number, comment or amount. The Z...A button lets you choose ascending or descending order.

Click **Journal Entry #**.

Click **Z...A** to change the order and place the one we want first in the list.

Click **Journal Entry #1**, **WCT-161** to select it.

Click **Select** or **press** (enter) to open the journal entry as it was posted:

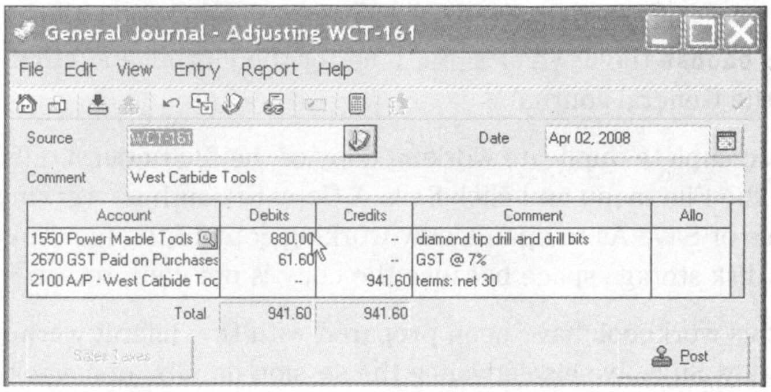

You can also double click anywhere on the line for a journal entry to open the Adjusting General Journal screen.

All fields may now be edited, just as if you had not yet posted the transaction.

Click **880.00**, the amount in the Debit column for *Power Marble Tools*, to select it for editing.

Type 900

Click **61.60** or **press** (↓) to select the Debit column amount for *GST Paid on Purchases*.

Type 63

Click **941.60**, the Credit column amount for *AP - West Carbide Tools*.

Type 963

Press (tab) to update the totals with the correct amounts.

We will also modify the source to show that this entry is the correction for the memo.

Click the **Source field** before the current entry (**before W**).

Type (COR)

Review the **entry** to see the correct transaction and **close** the **display**. **Make corrections** if necessary.

Click **Post** [Post]. **Continue** with the **journal entries**.

When you display the General Journal Report (refer to page 54) with Corrections selected, you will see three entries for the purchase invoice — the original incorrect entry, a reversing adjusting entry created by the program (ADJWCT-161) and the correct entry (COR) WCT-161 — providing a complete audit trail for the transaction and correction.

Advancing the Session Date

When you have finished all the entries for the April 7 session date, the date for the next transaction is later than April 7. Therefore, you must advance the session date before you can continue. If you do not advance the date before posting the April 8 transaction, you will receive an error message.

Before advancing the date, however, save and back up your work because you have already completed one week of transactions.

Although Simply Accounting saves automatically each time you display a report or exit the program, it is important to know how to save and back up your work directly to

NOTES
Usually clicking a number in a field will select the entire number. Sometimes, however, depending on exactly where you click, only part of the number is selected or an insertion point is added. Double clicking will always select the entire number in the field so that you can edit it.

NOTES
The adjusting and correcting entries are posted with the same date – the date you used for the adjusting entry. If you want, you can change the date for the adjusting entry but not for the reversing entry.

NOTES
We have set up the data files for Missoni so that future dated transactions are not allowed.

a separate file and location or disk because your working files may become damaged and unusable.

Click [X] or **choose** the **control menu icon** for the journal and **click Close** to close the General Journal.

You can save a complete duplicate working copy of the file under a different file name. Choose the File menu and click Save A Copy to continue working with the original files or Save As to open a new working copy of the file. This option requires more disk storage space because the copy is not compressed.

NOTES
Refer to pages 20 and 79 for information on the Save As and Save A Copy commands.

The data files for this workbook have been prepared with the default warning to back up your work weekly. Since we also advance the session date by one week at a time, you will be reminded to back up each time you advance the session date. You are now ready to advance the session date to April 14.

Click the **Change Session Date tool** or **choose** the **Maintenance menu** and **click Change Session Date** as shown:

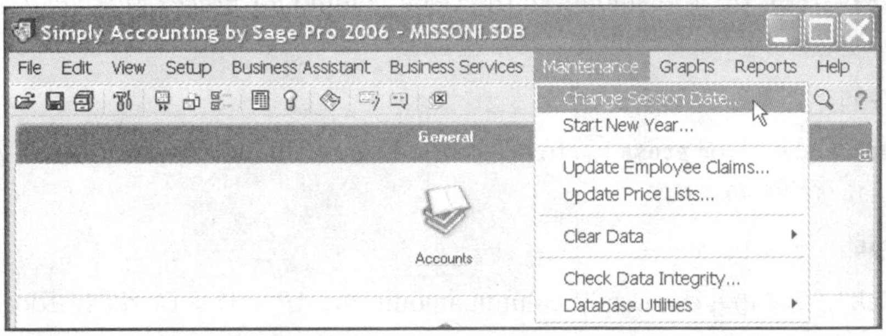

The following message advises you that you have not yet backed up your work:

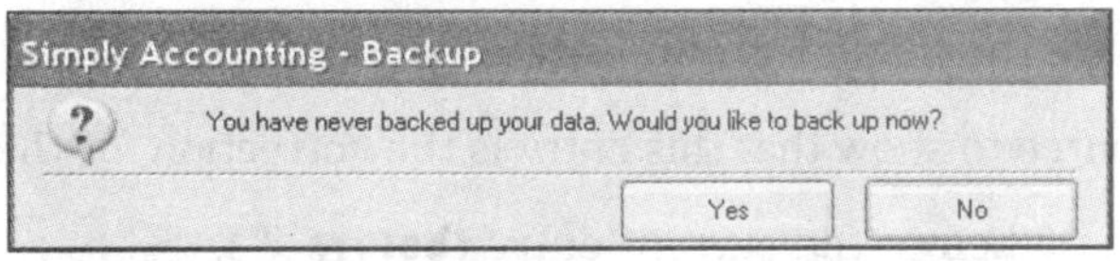

Click **Yes** to proceed with the backup.

WARNING!
Be sure to back up each time you are prompted to do so or each time you advance the session date. If your files are damaged, your work will be lost unless you have a backup.

The next screen asks for a file name for the backup:

NOTES
You cannot create backups when working in multi-user mode.

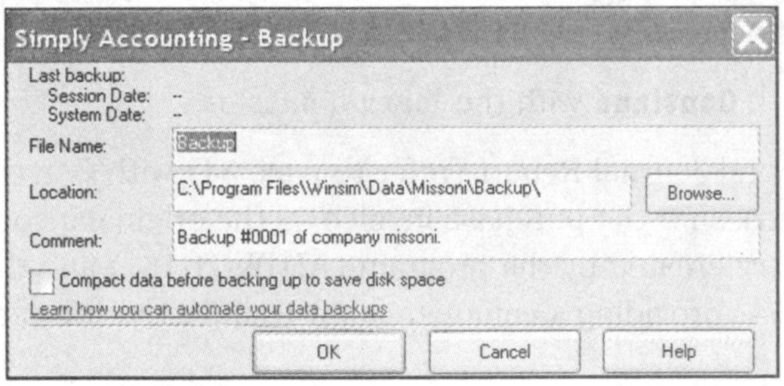

Simply Accounting will create a file named Backup1 inside the folder that contains your working data files.

You can edit the file name and comment. If you want to change the location of the backup, click Browse, select a folder and file name and click Save.

Click **OK** to proceed.

When you name a new folder, you will see the following advisory message:

The program recognizes that the name is new and offers to create the folder. If you have typed the correct location,

Click **Yes** to accept the information and continue.

The backup file is different from the one you create by copying or using the Save A Copy or Save As command. The Copy, Save A Copy and Save As commands create a complete working copy of your data that you can access with the Simply Accounting program directly. Backup creates a compressed file that must first be restored before you can use it to enter transactions.

After a brief interval, you will see the message that the backup is complete:

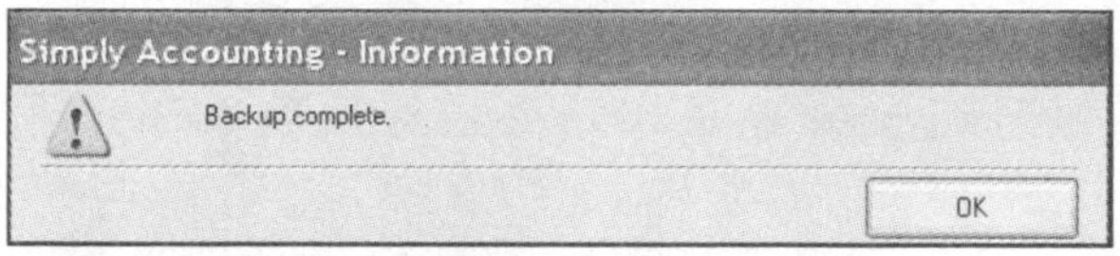

Click **OK** to proceed to the Change Session Date dialogue box with the current session date highlighted:

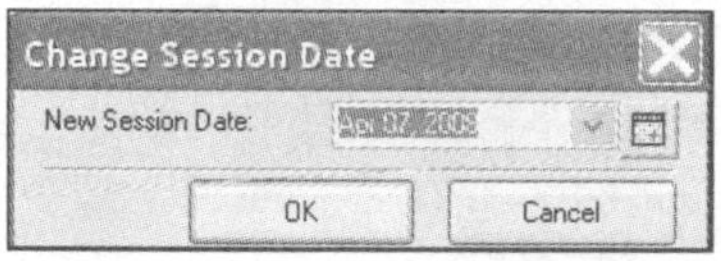

Type 04-14-08 (or click the date calendar and click 14)

Click **OK** to accept the new date.

You may now enter the remaining transactions for this exercise.

The next time you back up your files, Simply Accounting will tell you the date of your most recent backup and will provide the same file name and location that you used for your most recent backup. The backup number in the Comment field will be updated.

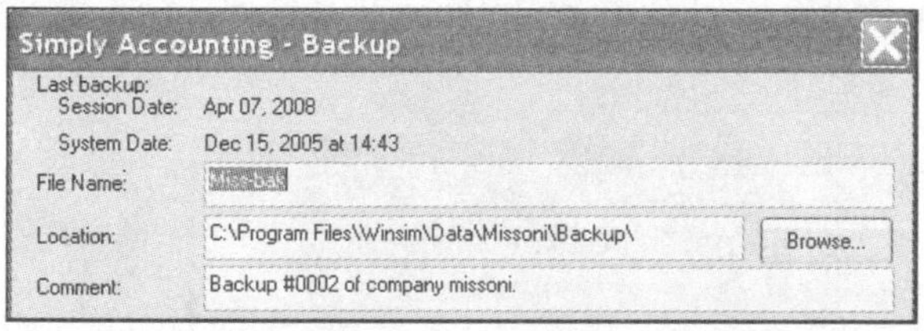

If you use the same backup file name, you will be asked to replace the previous file:

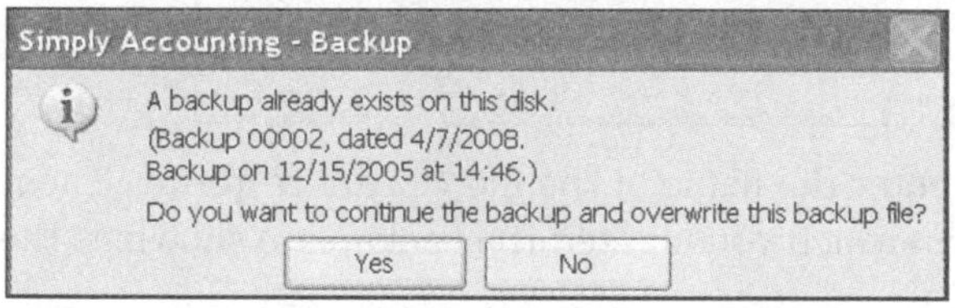

Click Yes to continue with the replacement or click No to return to the previous screen so you can enter a different file name.

Restoring Backup Files

If your working files are lost or damaged, you should restore the backup files.

You can restore files from the File menu in the Home window of any data file. If the data file you need cannot be opened, you can open a Sample Company file to access the File menu.

NOTES

When you change the session date again, the prompt to back up the file will include the session date and calendar date and time of the previous backup.

Choose the **File menu** and **click Restore** to start the wizard:

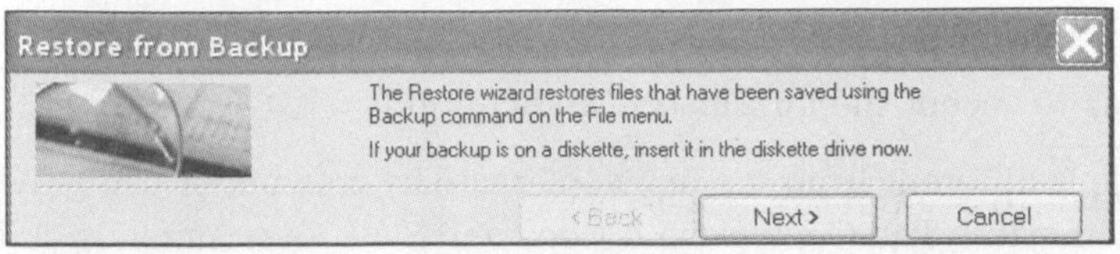

Click **Next** to continue to the backup file location screen:

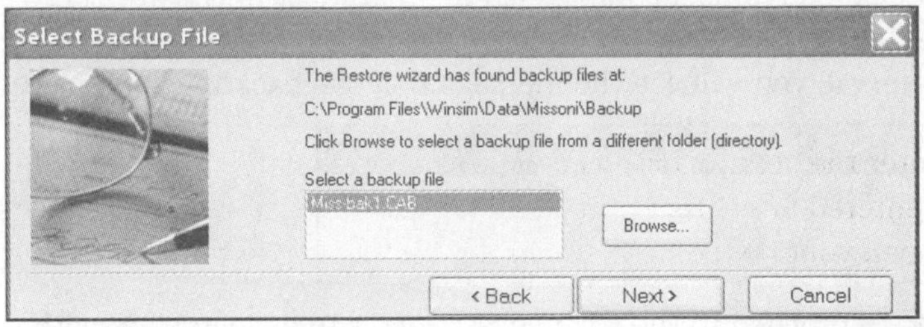

If the file you want is not shown, click Browse to find the file you need.

Click **Next** to see the screen that confirms your file choice:

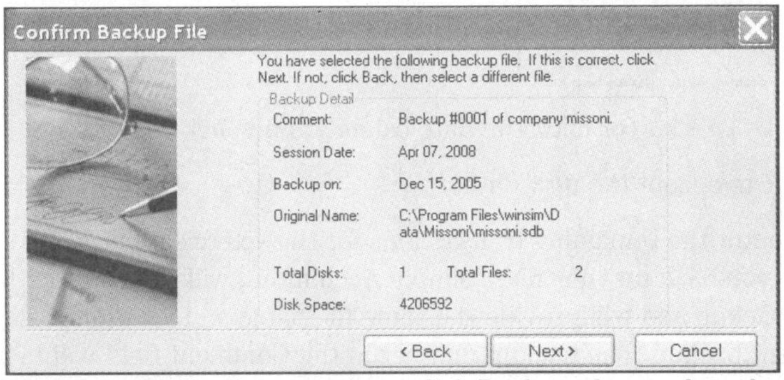

If this information is not correct, click Back to change the selection.

Click **Next**:

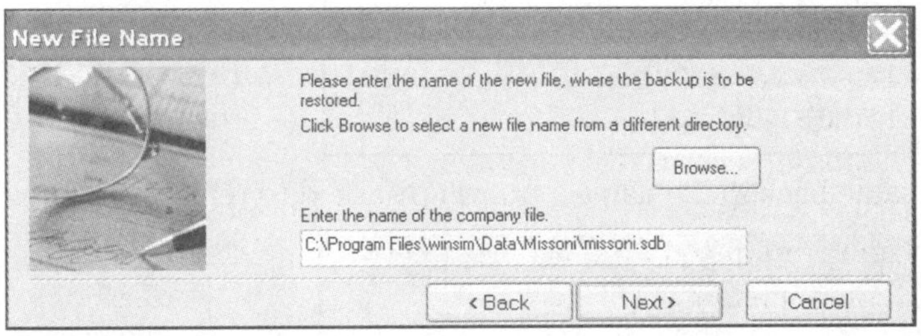

At this stage, you should enter the name of the file you are restoring. The name and location of the original file from which you created the backup are shown as the default.

You can choose a different location and file name by clicking Browse to access your folders. Enter the location and file name you want to use.

Click **Next**. If you used the original file name and location you will see this warning:

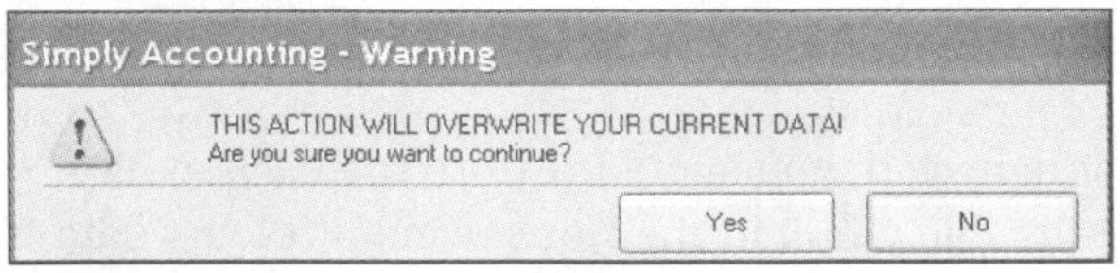

Click **Yes** to continue. If the original file is corrupt, you should replace it.

At this stage, Simply Accounting is ready to restore the file but it has not yet done so:

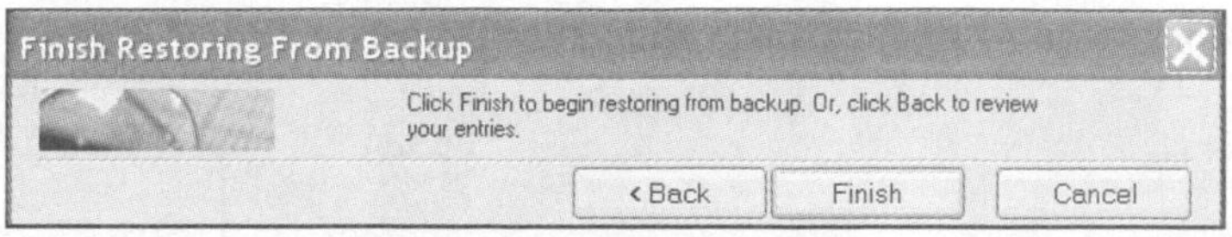

Click **Finish** to begin restoring the file.

After completing the restoration, the Session Date window appears:

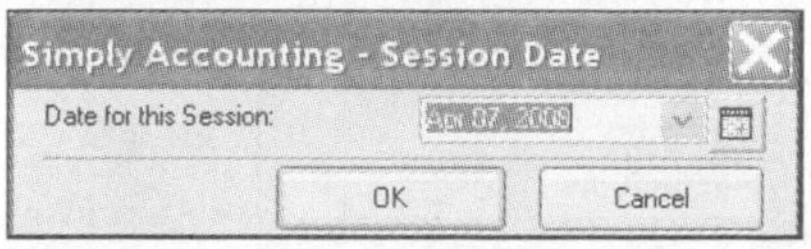

You can now enter the session date you want and work with your file in the usual way. Any data you entered after the backup will be lost but your previous file is intact.

If you cannot open your own data file, you can restore a file from the Select Company window:

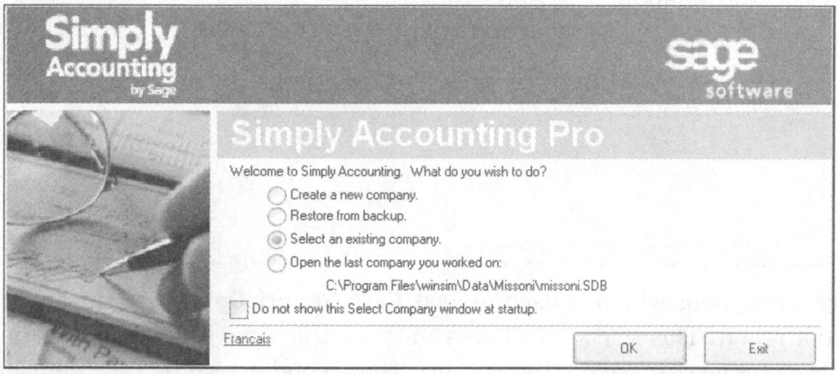

Choose **Restore From Backup** from the Select Company opening window.

Displaying General Reports

A key advantage to using Simply Accounting rather than a manual system is the ability to produce financial reports quickly for any date or time period. Reports that are provided for a specific date, such as the Balance Sheet, can be produced for any date from the time the accounting records were converted to the computerized system up to the most recent journal entry. Reports that summarize a financial period, such as the Income Statement, can be produced for any period between the beginning of the fiscal period and the latest journal entry.

NOTES

If you have data for more than one fiscal period, you can display and print reports for the previous fiscal period as well as for the current period.

The Pro version allows comparison of more than two fiscal periods.

When the Accounts window is open, all General Ledger reports are available from the Reports menu. Click the Accounts icon in the Home window to open the Accounts window.

Displaying the Balance Sheet

The Balance Sheet shows the financial position of the business on the date you select for the report. You can display the Balance Sheet at any time. In the Home window,

Choose the **Reports menu**, then **choose** (point to) **Financials** and **click** **Balance Sheet**.

> **BASIC VERSION**
> Multi-period reports are not available in the Basic version.

The report options window opens as shown:

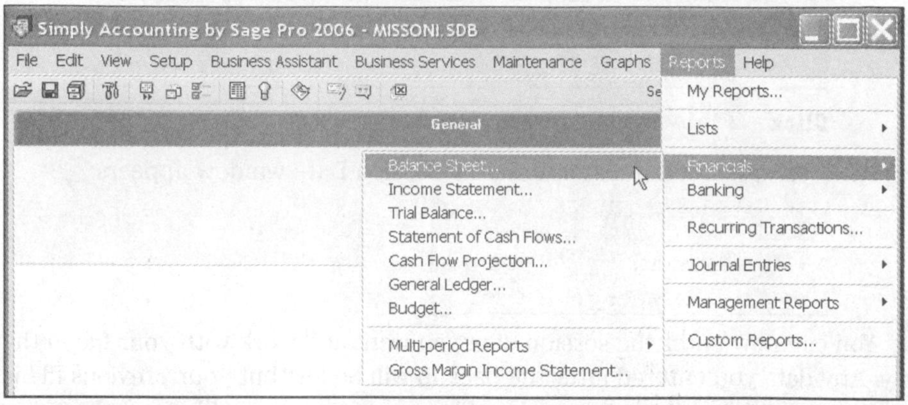

The Home window Reports menu shows only the General Ledger reports because the other ledgers are hidden.

Your screen now includes the following Balance Sheet Options window:

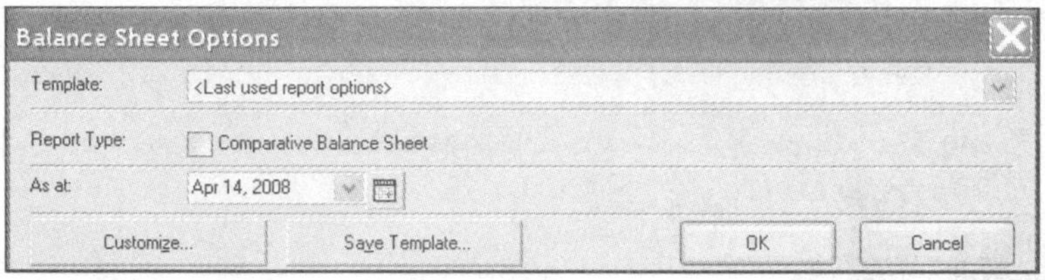

All report options windows use the **Last Used Report Options** as the template for the current report. This selection allows you to see the same report the next time without re-entering dates and other options. The second choice on the Template drop-down list uses the **Default Report Options** to restore the default settings. The Last Used Report Options is the default selection.

> **NOTES**
> Later applications use comparative statements for analysis purposes.

If you want to show the Balance Sheet for two different dates at the same time, you can use the Comparative Balance Sheet.

> **NOTES**
> If you want a single Balance Sheet only, do not click Comparative Balance Sheet (the check box does not have a ✓ in it). Your most recent session date is displayed by default and highlighted. Choose from the calendar, choose from the date field list or type in the date you want. Click OK to display the Balance Sheet.
> If you have accounting data for more than one fiscal period, you can display reports for the previous period as well as for the current period.

Click **Comparative Balance Sheet** to select this style of report and expand the report options as follows:

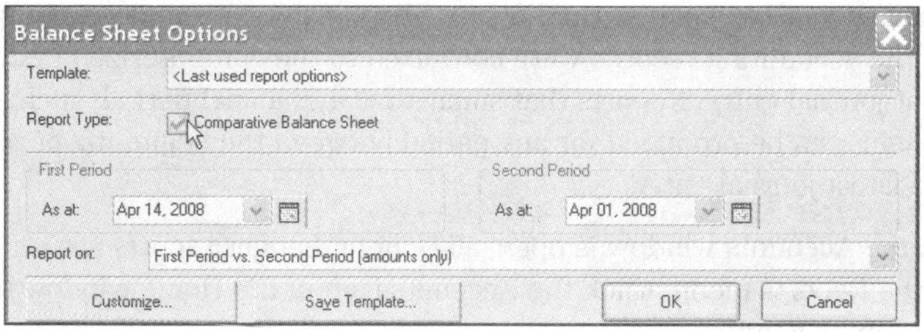

Your most recent session date is displayed in the first date field. The second date is the date on which the files were converted to Simply Accounting, the earliest transaction date.

> **NOTES**
> The date list provided by the list arrow includes the earliest transaction date and the latest session date or latest transaction date. The earliest transaction date is a frequent choice for the starting date in reports.

Press *tab* to highlight the first date if you want to change it.

Click the **Calendar icon** to the right of the date (As At) field. To select a date, click and select a date from the list or type the date you want using one of the accepted formats given earlier.

Press *tab* or **press** *tab* **twice** if you type the date.

Type the **second date** or choose from the calendar.

Click the **Report On field** to display the report types in the drop-down list:

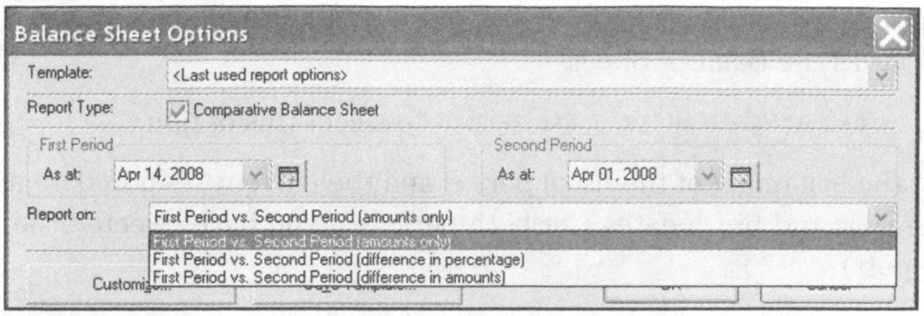

Choose **Amounts Only** if you want only the dollar balances for both dates. Choose **Difference In Percentage** if you want the dollar balances as well as the percentage increase from the second, earlier period amount to the first period amount. Choose **Difference In Amounts** if you want the dollar balances together with the difference between them in dollars. The second, earlier period amount is subtracted from the first to calculate the difference.

Click the report **contents** you want.

Click **OK** to display the Balance Sheet.

You can change the report options at this stage to create a different report.

Click the **Redo Report tool** or **choose** the **Options menu** and **click Redo Report** to access the report options screen again.

Click [X] when you have finished to return to the screen or window you were last working with.

NOTES
All reports include the option to redo them.

Displaying the Trial Balance

The Trial Balance shows account balances for all postable accounts in debit and credit columns. You can display the Trial Balance at any time while working with the software.

Choose the **Reports menu**, then **choose Financials** and **click Trial Balance**.

Click the **default date** and **enter** the **date** for which you want the Trial Balance or choose from the calendar.

Click **OK** to display the Trial Balance.

Click [X] to leave the display and return to the previous screen or window.

NOTES
The Trial Balance is also available as a comparative report with the same options as the Balance Sheet. Click Comparative Trial Balance, enter the first and second dates, choose the report contents from the Report On list and click OK.

Displaying the Income Statement

The Income Statement is a summary of the how much a business has earned in the interval you select for the statement. You can view the Income Statement at any time.

Choose the **Reports menu**, then **choose Financials** and **click Income Statement** to display the Income Statement Options window with Start and Finish dates:

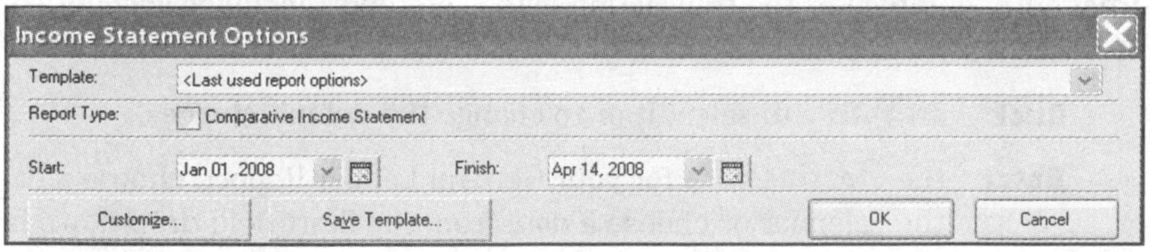

The Income Statement also has a comparative report option, allowing comparisons between two different periods. You might want to compare the income for two months,

NOTES
If you have data for two fiscal periods, the dates for these two periods will be the defaults for comparative income statements.

quarters or years. For the comparative report, you have the same amount and difference options as the Balance Sheet.

Click **Comparative Income Statement** to select this option.

By default, the beginning of the fiscal period and the current session date are provided as the start and finish dates (for both periods if you have selected the comparative report).

You must enter the beginning and ending dates for the period (or periods) you want your Income Statement to cover. Again, you may choose a date from the calendar, choose from the date field list or type in the dates.

Click the **Start date** and **enter** the **date** on which your Income Statement period begins.

Press tab (**twice** if you type the date).

Enter the **date** on which your Income Statement period ends.

Enter the **Start** and **Finish dates** for the second period and **choose** the report **content** if your report is comparative.

Click **OK**.

Click ☒ to close the display window when you have finished.

Displaying the General Ledger Report

The General Ledger Report lists all transactions for one or more accounts in the selected interval. You can display the General Ledger at any time.

Choose the **Reports menu**, then **choose** **Financials** and **click** **General Ledger** to display the following report options:

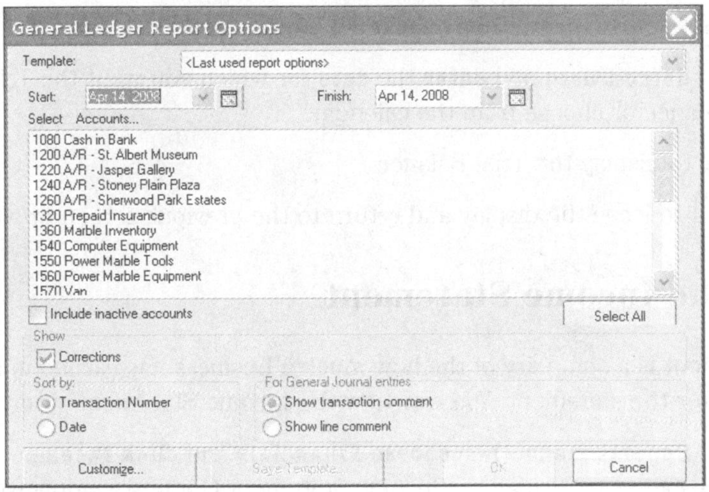

The General Ledger Report can be sorted in order of the transaction number (journal entry number) or the transaction date. The report includes account balances and transaction or account line comments.

Click an **option** to select it or to change the default choices.

Enter the **starting date** for your General Ledger Report, choose a date from the calendar or choose a date from the Start field drop-down list.

Press tab (**twice** if you type the date).

Enter the **ending date** for your General Ledger Report.

Click the **account** or **press** and **hold** ctrl and **click** the **accounts** you want to display. To include all the accounts in the display, **click Select All**.

Use the scroll arrows to see more accounts if the one you want is not visible. Click a selected item or Select All again to turn off the selection.

To select several accounts in a row, click the first one and then press shift and click the last one you want to include in the list.

You can choose to include the comment for the transaction or for individual account lines in your report. You can also choose to sort the report by date or transaction (journal entry) number.

Click **OK** to view the report.

Click ☒ to close the **display window** after viewing it.

Tool Bar Display Tool Button

The Display button on the tool bar provides a shortcut to displaying reports that are related directly to the ledger and journal icons in the Home window. These include lists related to the ledgers such as the Chart of Accounts and customer, vendor and employee lists as well as all journal reports. The Display button works in three different ways.

1. If a ledger or journal icon is highlighted or selected but not open, the options window for that report is displayed immediately when you click the Display button. The label for the Display button changes to name the report for a selected icon.
2. If no icon is highlighted, clicking the Display button produces the Select Report window that lists all journal reports and ledger lists. Click the list arrow and choose a report from this list. Click Select to display the report options window.
3. When the Accounts window is open, clicking the Display button provides a Select A Report window that lists all the reports for the General Ledger. Click the list arrow, choose from this list and click Select to display the report or its options window. In other ledger windows, the report list will include the reports related to that ledger.

Displaying the Chart of Accounts

The Chart of Accounts is a list of all accounts that shows the account number, name and account type and class.

Right-click the **Accounts icon** to select it.

NOTES
Right-click an icon in the Home window (click the right mouse button) to select it without opening the ledger or journal. Click the left mouse button to open the journal or ledger.

Click the **Display tool** on the tool bar or **choose** the **Reports menu**, then **choose Lists** and **click Chart Of Accounts**:

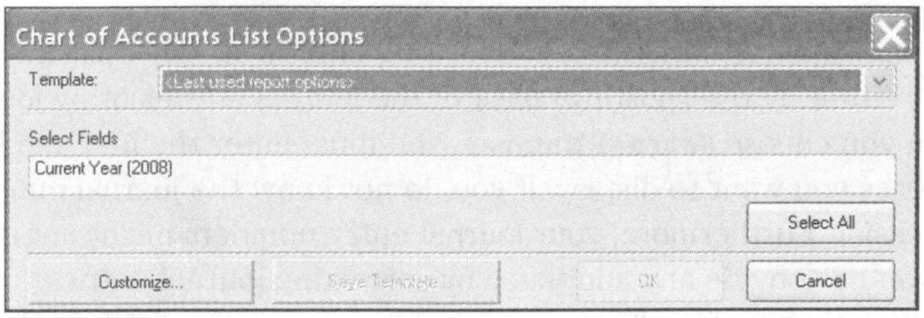

Choose the **Template** and the **year** (in the Select Fields list).

Click **OK** to see the chart.

Close the **display** when you have finished.

BASIC VERSION
The Related Historical Accounts field is not available in Basic.

Displaying the Account List

If you want to print the Chart Of Accounts and include other selected details, you can use the Account List.

Choose the **Reports menu**, then **choose Lists** and **click Accounts** to see the report options:

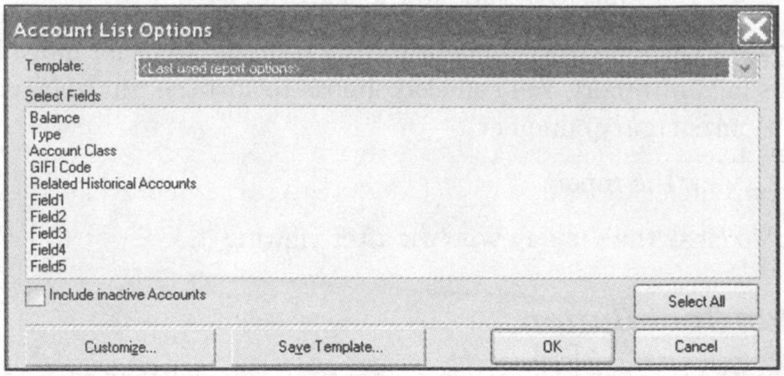

All reports will include the account name and number. For example, you could create an account list with only GIFI numbers (the numbers used for reporting to Canada Revenue Agency) or account balances as the additional information.

Click the **account field** or **press** and **hold** *ctrl* and **click** the **account fields** you want to report on or **click Select All** to include all details.

Click **OK** to view the report with the account name and number and the details you selected.

Click ☒ to close the **display window** after viewing it.

Displaying the General Journal

Right-click the **General icon** to select it.

Click the **Display tool** on the tool bar or **choose** the **Reports menu**, then **choose Journal Entries** and **click General** to display the report options:

WARNING!
If you do not choose Show Corrections, the journal report will include only the latest corrected version of all entries. Showing the corrections will include the original incorrect entry, the reversing entry and the final correct one, thus providing a complete audit trail.

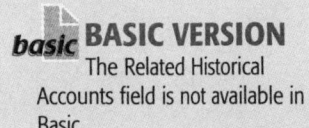

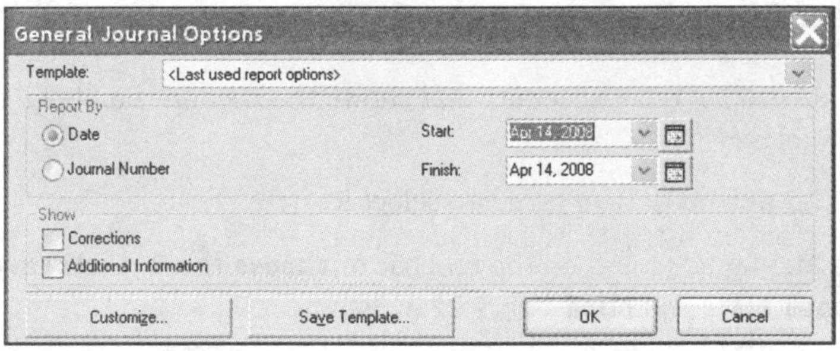

Journal reports may include correcting or adjusting entries or may omit them. You may display journals either by the (posting) **Date** of the journal entries or by journal entry number. When you choose **Journal Number**, you must enter the first and last numbers for the entries you want to display. If you do not know the journal numbers, the date method is easier. Furthermore, your journal entry numbers might not match the ones we use if you have made any additional or correcting journal entries. Therefore, all reports in this workbook are requested by date — the default setting.

The latest session date is given by default for the period of the report because normally a business will print journal reports each day as part of the audit trail.

Click **Corrections** to include the adjusting entries.

Click the **Start date list arrow.**

Click **Apr 1, 2008.**

You can choose any dates for the Journal Report between the fiscal start and the last journal entry, including postdated entries.

Accept **April 14** as the ending date for your journal report.

Customizing Reports

All report options windows include a Customize button, although not all reports can be customized. You can change the columns or fields in the report, sort reports and filter them. Sorting reports changes the order in which data are presented, while filtering reports selects the records to include according to the data fields used as selection criteria. Journal reports may be customized by selecting columns, filtering and sorting.

Click the **Customize button** to open the Customize Report Columns tab:

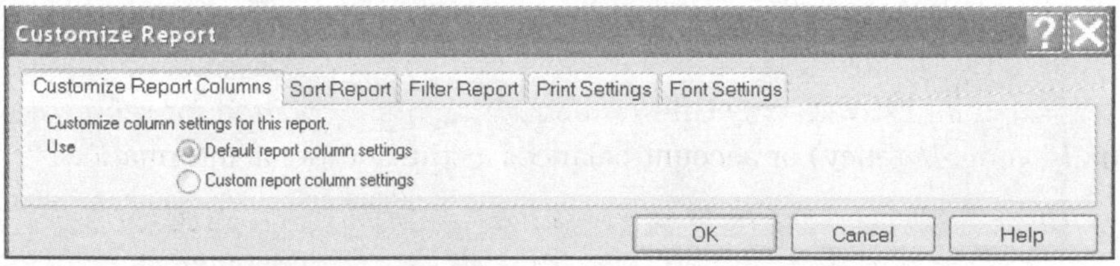

Click **Custom Report Column Settings** to see the column options:

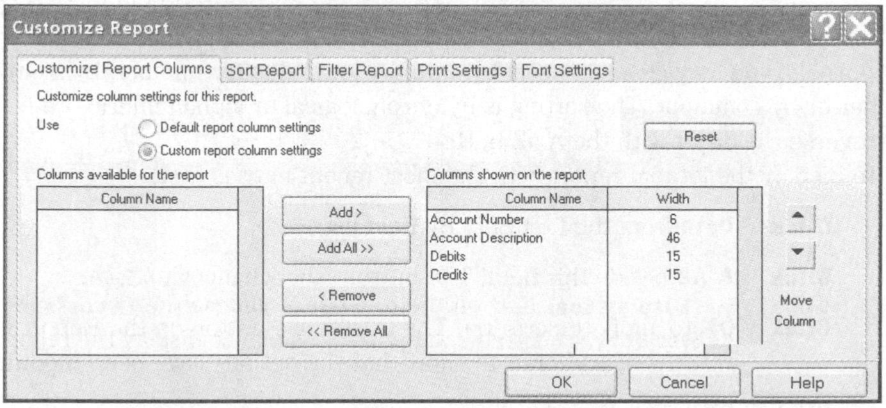

The list on the right of the screen shows the columns included in the report. The width of each column is also included.

To remove one of the default columns, click it to select it. Then click Remove to place it in the list on the left. To move all columns, click Remove All. To add a column from the Removed list to the report, click it and then click Add. To change the column width, click the default size and type the new number. To save the changes, click OK. To restore all default settings, click Reset.

We will not change the columns for this report, but we will sort the journal according to the transaction date.

Click the **Reset button** to cancel any selections you made.

NOTES

If your journal report is on display, you can choose the Customize Report tool and add the criteria you want.

Sorting Reports

Click the **Sort Report tab** to open the Sort Report window:

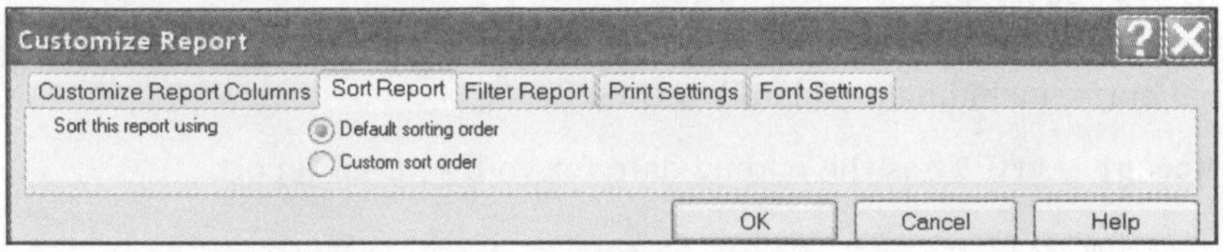

When a report is displayed, click the Customize Report tool to sort or filter a report, or choose Customize Report from the Options menu.

NOTES
If you have made many corrections, sorting the journal report by date and then by journal number will keep the related entries together in a report.

Click **Custom Sort Order** to expand the window and see the options:

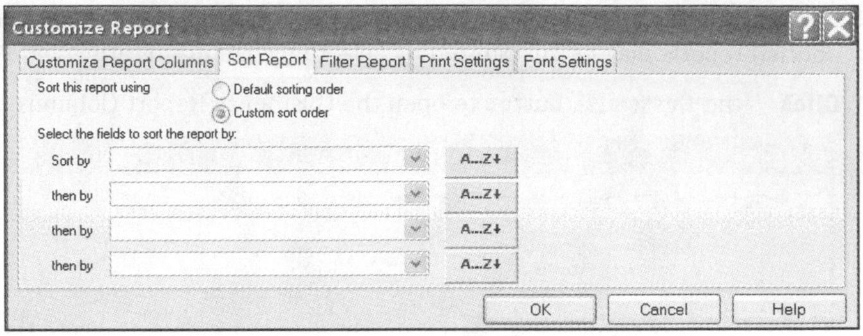

Click the **first Sort By field list arrow** to see the criteria you may use.

You can sort each journal report by up to four criteria, applying each one in order. For journals, you may choose to sort by date, by journal entry number, by source number or by comment. The sorting is by chronological or alphanumeric order. You can also reverse the order with the A...Z button.

To display the journal report with the most recent entries first,

Click **Date** from the first Sort By field list.

Click **A...Z** beside this field. The button label changes to Z...A.

Click **OK** to apply the criteria. The Customize button on the Report Options screen has a ✓ on it to show that the options have been modified.

Click **OK** to see the report.

You will see the report with the new order. The April 14 transactions are listed first and the April 2 transactions are at the end of the report. The sorting criteria remain in effect until you remove or change them. They will apply to the Last Used Report Options template.

To remove the criteria, click the Redo Report tool to display the report options screen again. Choose Default Report Options as the Template. Or you can choose Default Sort Order on the Sort Report tab screen. Click OK to see the standard Journal Report.

To restore the default order and save the sorting criteria you must save the report options as a new template (see page 57).

Close the **display** or the options screen when you have finished.

Filtering Reports

The General Journal icon should still be selected. To filter the report,

Click the **Display tool** to see the General Journal Options window.

Click **Customize** and then **click** the **Filter Report tab** to access the Filter Report screen:

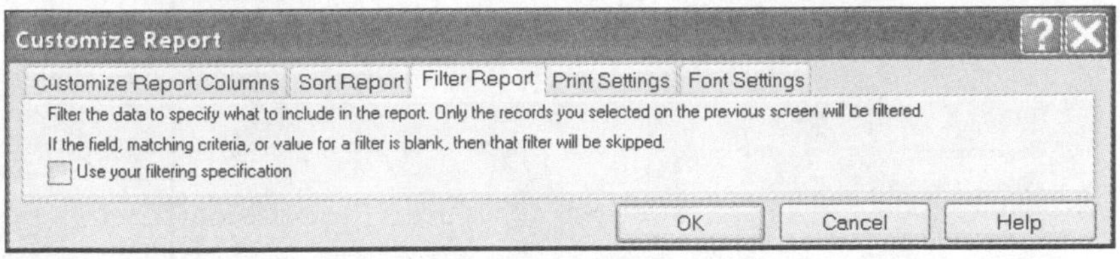

Click **Use Your Filtering Specification** to access the filter options:

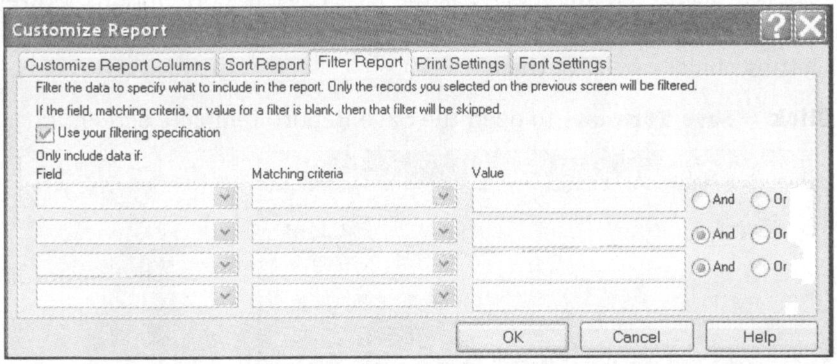

Journal reports may be filtered by the same criteria or fields you use for sorting. For each criterion, you must enter the matching criteria (greater than, equal to, less than, starting character, etc.) and a value for comparison. You can add three more criteria for the report, selecting **And** if you want the data to meet all criteria at the same time. Choose **Or** if you want to include data that meet any one of the criteria. For example, the following steps will generate a report with only sales invoices (if you began the Source with MM... for these entries). We need to apply two criteria — greater than MM and less than MN.

Click the **first Field list arrow** and **choose Source**.

Choose **Is Greater Than** from the Matching Criteria drop-down list.

Click the **Value field**.

Type MM

Leave the joining criterion at **And** so that both will apply.

Click the **second Field list arrow** and **choose Source**.

Choose **Is Less Than** from the Matching Criteria drop-down list.

Click the **Value field**.

Type MN

Click **OK**.

Enter the **Start** and **Finish dates** for the report. **Click OK** to see the report of sales entries.

NOTES

If any other source documents begin with MM, they will also be included in the filtered report.

Saving the New Report Template

When you create new criteria for a report, you can save them as a template. Then you can choose the template later without re-entering the criteria. The report should still be on display.

Click the **Redo Report tool**  to open the report options screen:

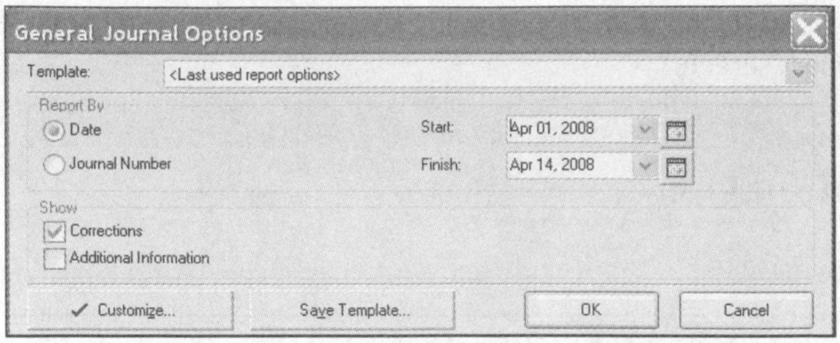

The criteria we entered are applied as the Last Used Report Options. However, when we return to the default or enter a different set of options, we will lose the previous settings unless we save them.

Click **Save Template** to open the Save Report Template screen:

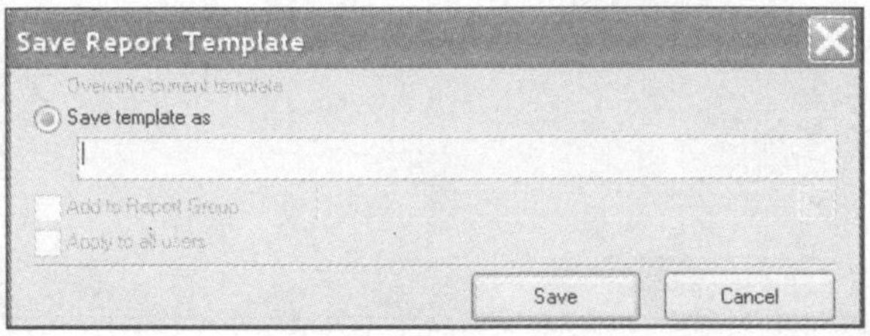

You can save the template as part of a report group, if you have created these, or with the templates for the type of report currently in use. We will save the template with the General Journal report options. The cursor is in the Save Template As name field.

Type `Sales Transactions`

Click **Save** to return to the report options.

Click the **Template list arrow** to see the revised list:

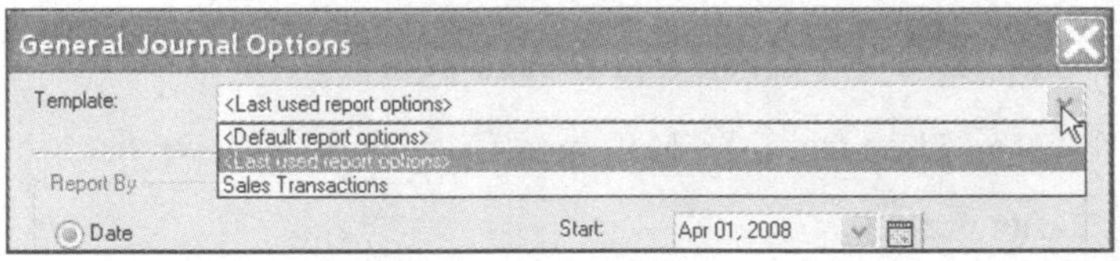

You can also access saved reports from the Home window Reports menu. Choose the Reports menu, then choose My Reports:

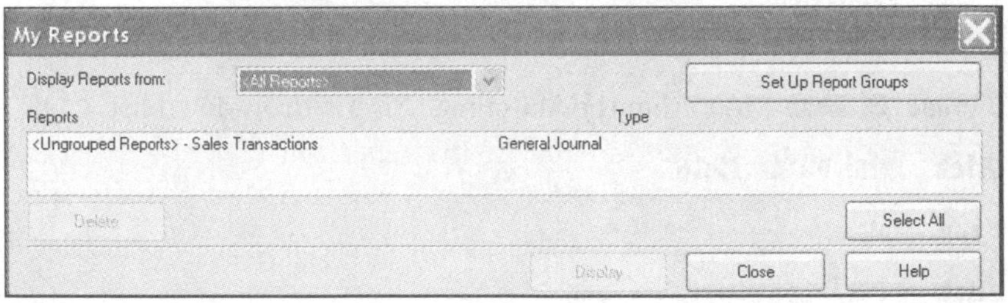

Click Sales Transactions and then click Display to open the modified report.

Removing Filtering Criteria

The filters will remain in effect so you should remove them. The filters will apply to the Last Used Report Options selection. You can remove them from the report while it is displayed or from the journal options screen.

If the report is displayed, click  (the Customize Report tool).

From the General Journal Options screen, click the Customize button.

Click the Filter Report tab. Click Use Your Filtering Specification to remove the ✓. Click OK to return to the options screen. Click OK to see the unfiltered report.

Close the **display** when you have finished.

NOTES
You can also choose Default Options in the Template list to remove the filtering criteria. This will not change the template you saved.

Displaying Management Reports

Management reports provide accounting information that is specific to the company data file. When the other ledgers are used, the menu also includes management reports for these ledgers.

Choose the **Reports menu**, then **choose Management Reports** and **click General** to see the display of available reports:

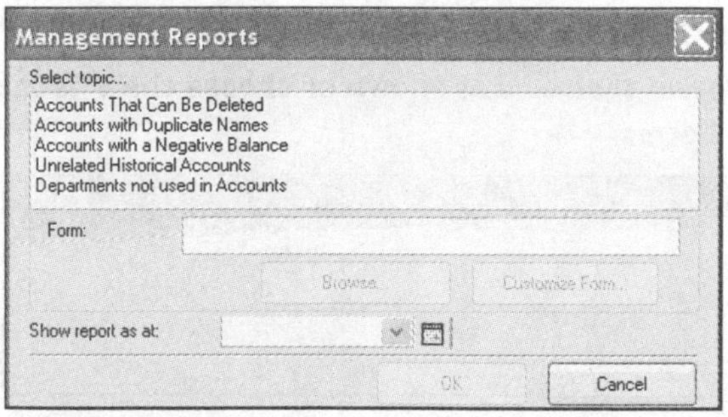

NOTES
Accounts that can be deleted are those that have zero balances and have not been used in journal transactions.

To see a report, click a topic to select it. The date field may de dimmed, depending on the topic selected. If it is not, type the date for the report in the Show Report As At field. The program will select a default report form from the ones you installed with the program. Generally the default is the best choice. You can click Browse to see other report forms available and select the one you need. If you have the appropriate software program, you may customize the report form. Click OK to display the report.

For example, click the advice topic Accounts With A Negative Balance. Click OK. Your report should include *GST Paid on Purchases* and *Missoni, Drawings* because these contra-accounts normally have negative balances.

Close the **display** when you have finished.

Drill-Down Reports

Some reports can be accessed from other reports that you have opened or displayed, except the Management reports. These are cross-referenced or drill-down reports.

Whenever the pointer changes to 🔍 (a magnifying glass icon with a plus sign inside it) the additional reports can be displayed. When the other ledgers are used, detailed customer, vendor and employee reports are also available from the General Ledger Report and from the General Journal.

Move the **mouse pointer** over various items in the first report. The type of second report available may change. The name of the second report will appear in the status bar.

Double click while the magnifying glass icon is visible to display the second report immediately. The first report stays open in the background.

The General Ledger Report is named Transactions By Account in the status bar drill-down message. The General Ledger Report for a specific account can be accessed from the Balance Sheet, Income Statement, Trial Balance, Chart of Accounts or General Journal when you double click an account number, name or balance amount. The General Ledger record for an account can be accessed from the General Ledger Report.

While you have the additional drill-down report displayed, you may print it or drill down to other reports. (See Printing General Reports below.)

Close the **second report** and then **close** the **first report** when you have finished viewing them.

> **NOTES**
> Transactions by Account is the non-accounting term for the General Ledger Report. Refer to Appendix B for a complete list of non-accounting terms.

> **NOTES**
> From the Balance Sheet, Trial Balance, Income Statement and Journal Report, you can drill down to the General Ledger Report for the selected account. The drill-down report will use the same dates as the original report.
> From the General Ledger Report, you can drill down to the journal entry for a line or to the General Ledger record for the account.

Printing General Reports

Display the **report** you want to print by following the instructions in the preceding pages on displaying reports.

If you want to change the appearance of the report, you can do so at this stage.

Click the **Reports & Forms tool** as shown or **choose** the **File menu** and **click Reports & Forms**:

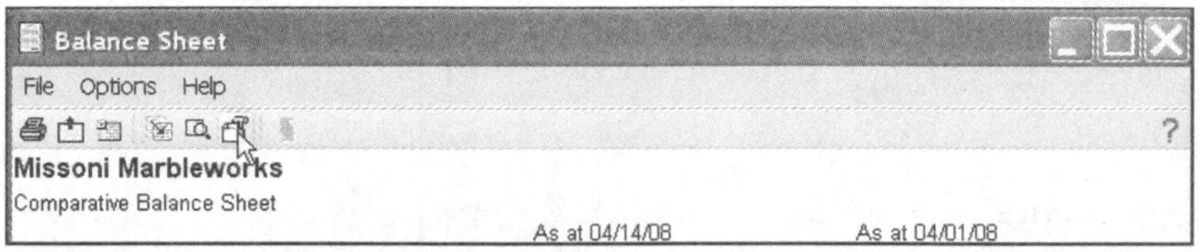

> **WARNING!**
> Always check that the correct printer is selected before printing reports. The printer selection is saved with the data file and may be incorrect for your setup.

The Report & Form Options screen opens:

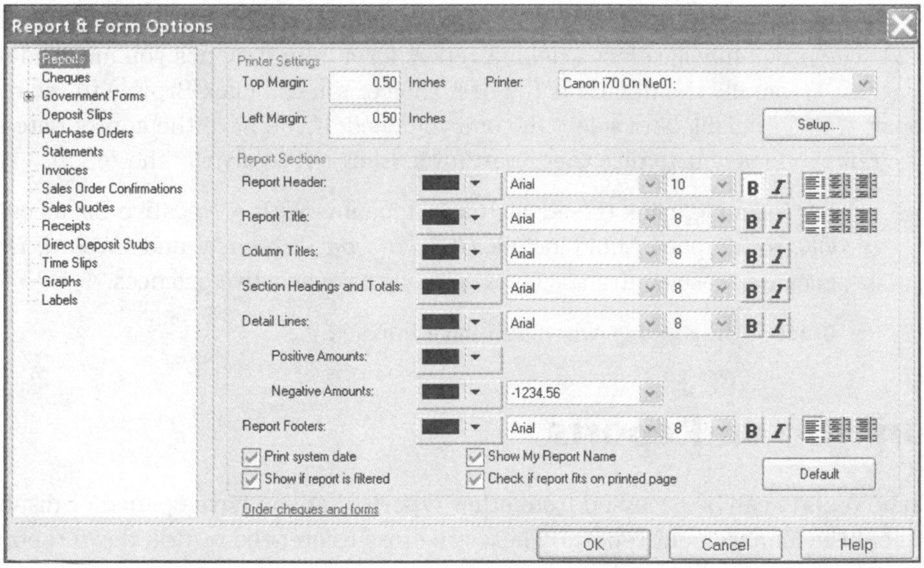

You can select a printer, set the margins, and choose the style for different parts of the report. You can also add the computer system date to the report and indicate whether the report is filtered. The Default button will restore the original default settings for the report.

> **NOTES**
> From the Setup or other option buttons, you can choose advanced settings for the report and printer.

Choose your **printer** from the drop-down list in the Printer field.

Click **OK** to save your changes and return to the display or **click Cancel** if you do not want to save the changes you made.

Click the **Print tool** or **choose** the **File menu** in the report window then **click Print**. Printing begins immediately.

Wait for the displayed printing information to clear from the screen.

Close the displayed **report**.

Graphing General Reports

Graphs are available only from the Home window.

Note that the following graphs were created after completing the additional transactions for April 15 to April 30.

Expenses and Net Profit as % of Revenue

Choose the **Graphs menu**, then **click Expenses And Net Profit As % Of Revenue** to display the following report options:

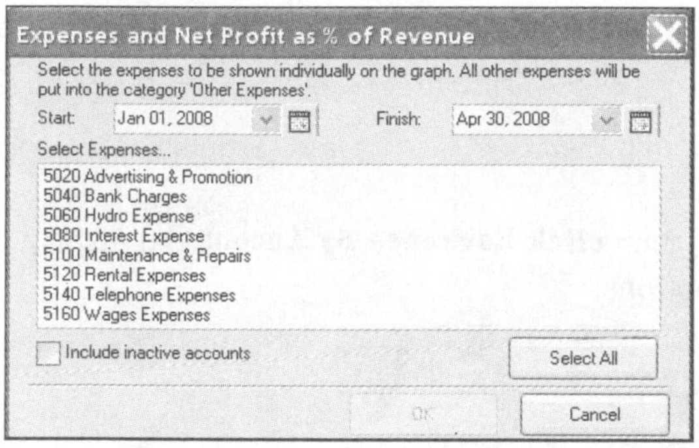

Double click the **default Start date** and **enter** the **beginning date** of the period for your graph.

Press *tab* (**twice** if you type the date).

Type the **ending date** of the period for your graph.

Press and **hold** *ctrl* and **click each expense account you want** included in the graph or **click Select All** to include all accounts.

Click **OK** to display the graph.

The pie chart shown here includes all expense accounts for the period from January 1 to April 30, and is a form of the Income Statement:

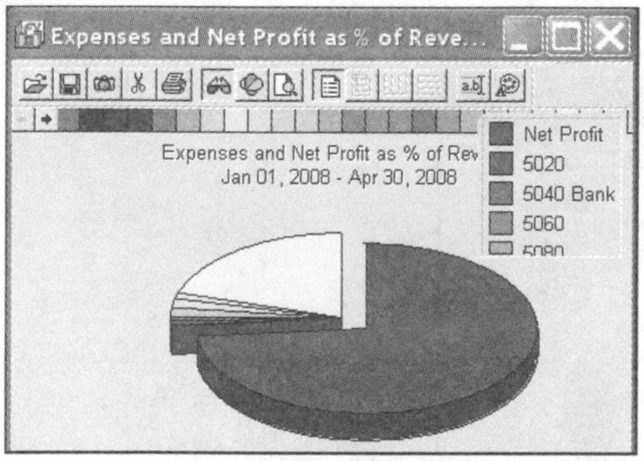

You have several options regarding the graph at this stage. The tool bar options are the same for all graphs. By selecting the appropriate button on the tool bar, you can import a graph, export the displayed graph, copy it to the clipboard as a bitmap or a text file, print the graph, change the view from 3-D to 2-D, hide the legend, edit or add titles, etc. Hold the mouse pointer over a tool button for a few seconds to see a brief description of the tool's purpose. Most tool buttons lead to an additional option or control window requiring your input.

In addition, you can change colours by dragging the colour you want to the pie section you want to change; expand or shrink the legend by dragging its bottom border

NOTES
The graphs in this section were created after completing the additional realistic source documents. If you display the graphs before entering these transactions, your Finish date will display as April 14, and you will be unable to go past this date.

NOTES
The default dates for the graph are the fiscal start date and the session date.

NOTES
You can copy the graph into the Paint program and have full editing capabilities.

down or up respectively; or pull out a section of the pie chart by dragging it away from the rest of the chart. The graph displayed has the Net Profit portion pulled out for emphasis. You cannot separate or pull out the expense sections individually.

Double click a portion of the graph to see the name of the account, the dollar amount and the percentage of the total.

Double click the legend to make it larger and to add the account names. Double click the expanded legend to reduce it.

Right-click the legend title to view a set of options for positioning the legend on the graph page. To move the legend to the new position, click the new legend position option. Double click the legend to restore the original size and position.

Close the **graph** when you have finished.

Revenues by Account

Choose the **Graphs menu**, then **click Revenues By Account** to display the following report options:

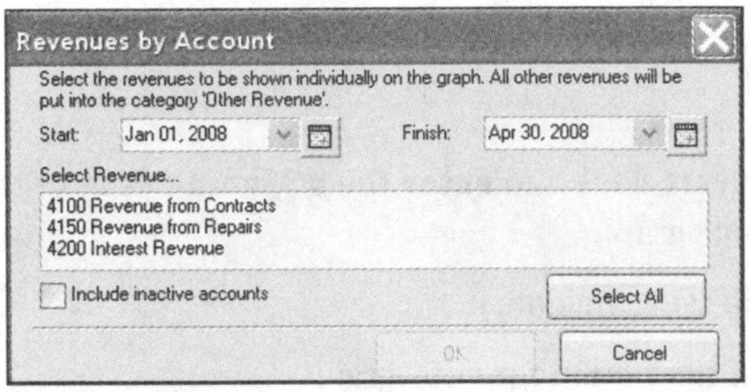

Enter the **beginning date** of the period for your graph.

Press *tab* (**twice** if you typed the date).

Enter the **ending date** of the period for your graph.

Press *ctrl* and **click each revenue account you want** included in the graph or **click Select All** to include all accounts in the graph.

Click **OK** to display the pie chart as shown:

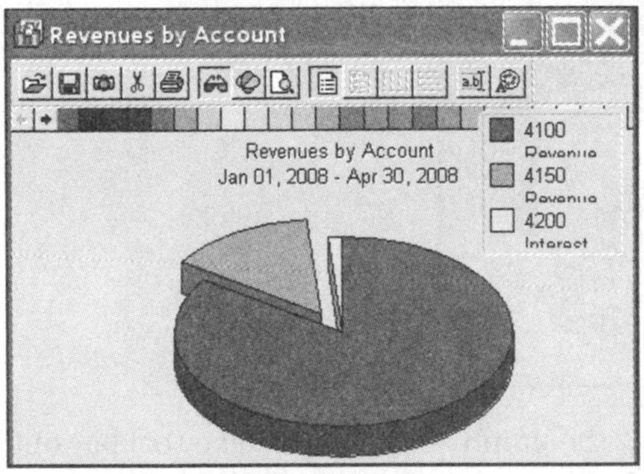

The pie chart has each revenue account represented by a different piece of the pie. You can see that most of the revenue comes from contracts. If you double click a section of the pie, the amount and percentage for that account are shown in a bubble.

You have the same options for this graph as you do for the Expenses and Net Profit as % of Revenue graph.

Double click a **pie section** to show its amount and percentage.

Close the **graph** when you have finished.

Expenses by Account

Choose the **Graphs menu**, then **click Expenses By Account** to display the following report options:

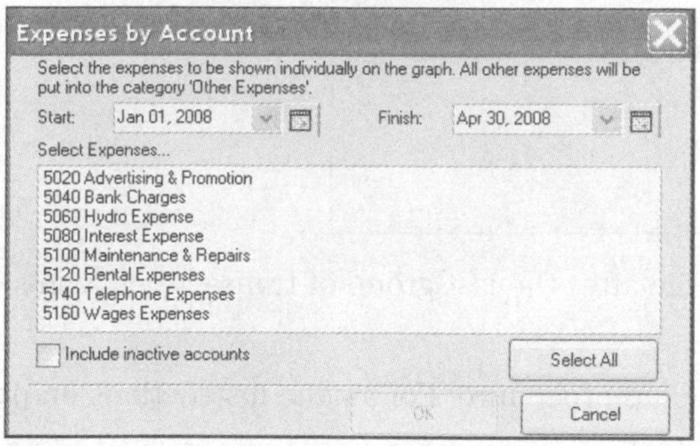

Enter the **beginning date** of the period for your graph.

Press *tab* (**twice** if you typed the date).

Enter the **ending date** of the period for your graph.

Press *ctrl* and **click each expense account you want** included in the graph or **click Select All** to include all accounts in the graph.

Click **OK** to see the pie chart:

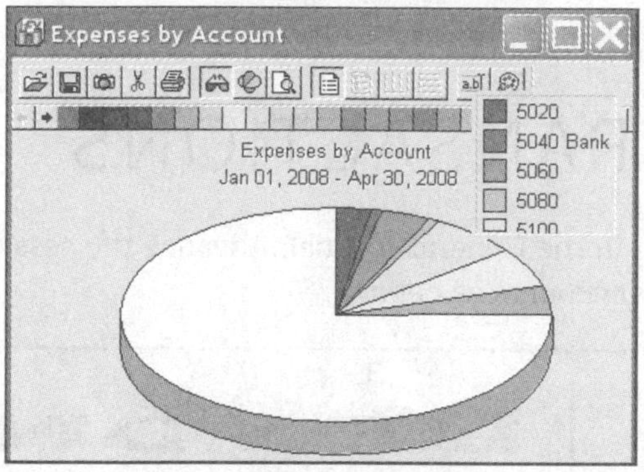

Each expense account that was selected is represented as a separate piece of the pie. The accounts not selected are grouped together in the **Other** category. The expenses graph makes it easy to identify at a glance the items that make up the largest share of expenses — wages in this example.

Close the **graph** when finished.

Finishing a Session

Finish the last transaction you are working on for this session.

Click ☒ to close the transaction window (such as journal input or display) to return to the Home window.

If you have more than one open window, you can use the Close All Windows tool button in the Home window. To restore the Home window,

Click the **Home window tool** in an open journal window. Or,

Click the **Simply Accounting by Sage button** on the desktop task bar.

Click the **Close All Windows tool** in the Home window.

Click [X] to close the program. Alternatively, **choose** the **File menu** and **click Exit** to close the program.

You will see the following message about backing up the data file:

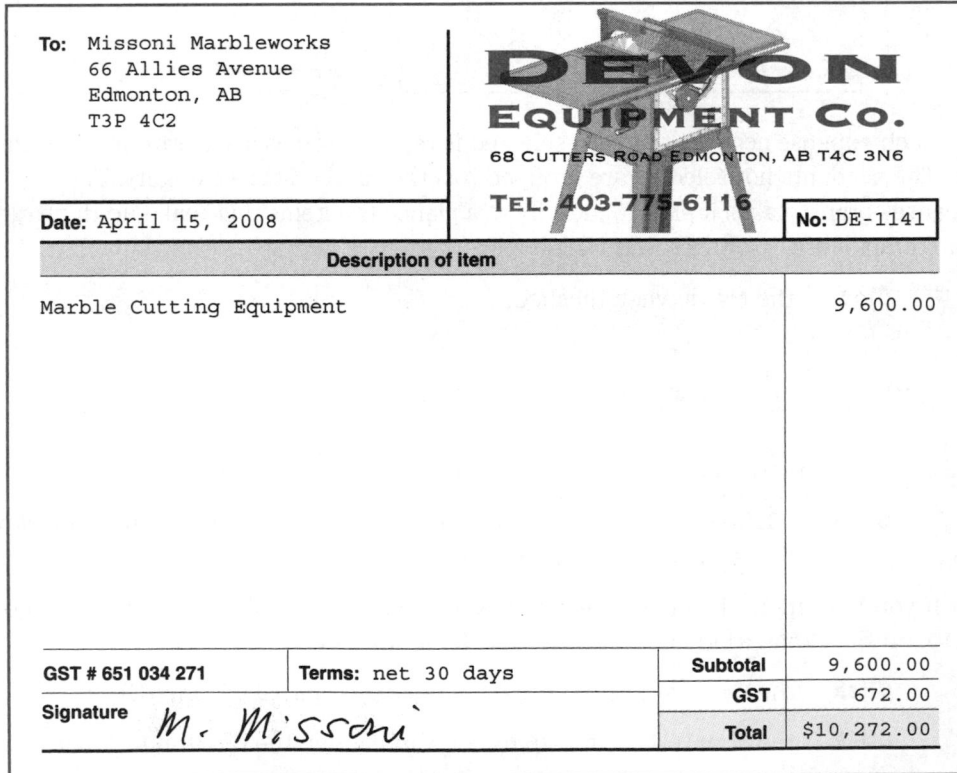

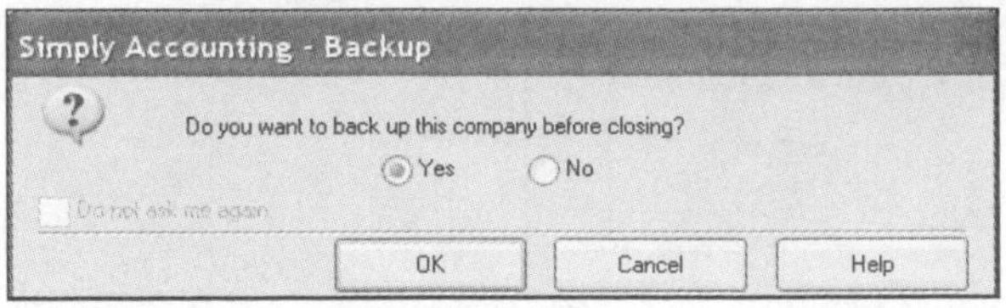

If you have not backed up the file after the last group of transactions, you should do so now.

Click **OK** to start the backup procedure. Follow the instructions on page 46 to complete the backup.

After the backup is complete, the file will close.

The Simply Accounting program will automatically save your work when you finish your session and exit properly.

Click **Start** in the Windows desktop opening screen.

Click **Turn Off Computer**.

Click **Turn Off** to confirm your intention to turn off the computer.

NOTES
The instructions for other versions of Windows may be different.

ADDITIONAL TRANSACTIONS

Enter the following source documents in the General Journal. Advance the session date by one week at a time and create new accounts as needed.

NOTES
The following new Group accounts will be required for completing the additional transactions:
- 2210 A/P - Devon Equipment
- 1280 A/R - Lindbrook Estates
- 2220 A/P - Beaumont Tekstore
- 2230 A/P - Bon Accord Advertising

☐

To: Missoni Marbleworks
66 Allies Avenue
Edmonton, AB
T3P 4C2

DEVON EQUIPMENT Co.
68 Cutters Road Edmonton, AB T4C 3N6
Tel: 403-775-6116

Date: April 15, 2008

No: DE-1141

Description of item	
Marble Cutting Equipment	9,600.00

GST # 651 034 271	**Terms:** net 30 days	**Subtotal**	9,600.00
		GST	672.00
Signature M. Missoni		**Total**	$10,272.00

☐

Missoni Marbleworks
66 Allies Avenue
Edmonton AB
T3P 4C2

No: 52

Date 16042008
D D M M Y Y Y Y

Pay to the order of Marblehead Suppliers $ 2,400.00

Two Thousand Four Hundred 00 /100 Dollars

Alberta Trust
121 Money Way
Edmonton, AB T3C 4N6

M. Missoni

⑈—⑆—— 40361 ⑉⑆ 052

Re: Reference Invoice # MS-594 No: 52
$2,400.00 April 16, 2008

☐

Missoni Marbleworks
66 Allies Avenue
Edmonton AB.
T3P 4C2
Tel.: 403-763-4127
Fax: 403-765-4842

Sold to:
Lindbrook Estates
319 Brookdale Avenue
Edmonton, AB
T5P 3B2

Date: April 16, 2008

MM – 45

Description of Work Completed	Charges
Repairs to fireplace mantel	1,200.00
Terms: net 10 days — Subtotal	1,200.00
GST # 743 647 397 — GST	84.00
Customer Signature Mary Lindbrook — Total	$1,284.00

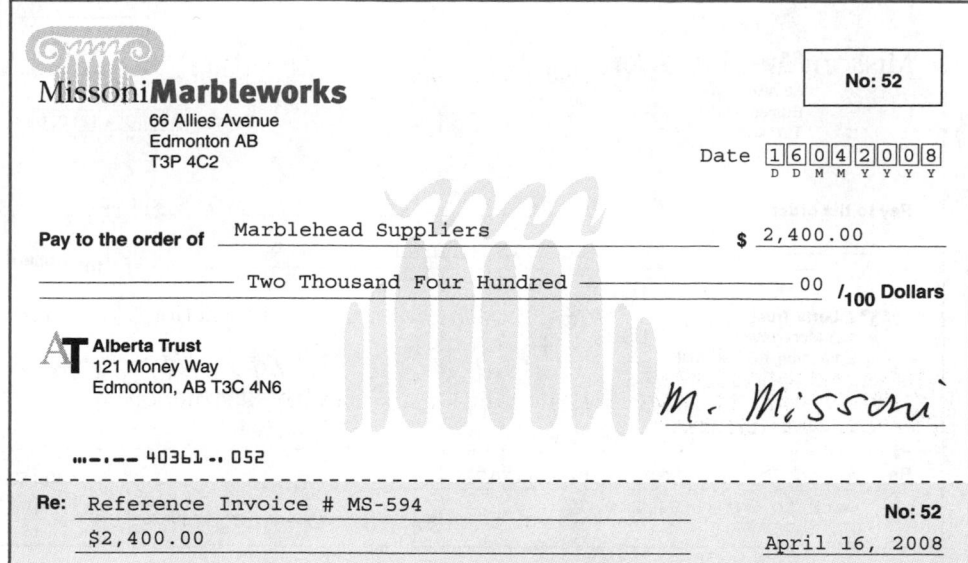

☐

Missoni Marbleworks
66 Allies Avenue
Edmonton AB
T3P 4C2

No: 53

Date 1 8 0 4 2 0 0 8
D D M M Y Y Y Y

Pay to the order of Giovanni Assuri $ 4,200.00

Four Thousand, Two Hundred 00 /100 **Dollars**

Alberta Trust
121 Money Way
Edmonton, AB T3C 4N6

M. Missoni

⑈—⑆—— 40361 ⑉ 053

Re: Wages to assistant for contracted work to date, $4,200.00

No: 53
April 18, 2008

☐

Sherwood Park Estates
900 Sherwood Park Rd.
Edmonton, AB
T4J 4S6

No: 23

Date 1 9 0 4 2 0 0 8
D D M M Y Y Y Y

Pay to the order of Missoni Marbleworks $ 3,210.00

Three Thousand, two hundred and ten 00 /100 **Dollars**

Royal Bank
69 Royalty Avenue
Edmonton, AB T3P 7C6

Robin Sherwood
Signature

⑈——— 393214 ⑉ 023

Re: Reference Invoice #MM-43, $3,210.00
In full payment of account.

$3,210.00

No: 23
April 19, 2008

Missoni Marbleworks
66 Allies Avenue
Edmonton AB.
T3P 4C2
Tel.: 403-763-4127
Fax: 403-765-4842

Sold to:
Stoney Plain Plaza
3 Stoney Plain Avenue,
Edmonton, AB
T4N 3X6

Date: April 21, 2008

MM – 46

Description of Work Completed	Charges
Installation of new marble floor in public washroom as per contract	3,600.00

Terms: net 30 days	**Subtotal**	3,600.00
GST # 743 647 397	**GST**	252.00
Customer Signature C. Ciconi	**Total**	$3,852.00

Marblehead Suppliers
138 Granite Road, Edmonton, AB T5N 4C4
Telephone: (403) 771-8213

No: MS-647

Date: April 21, 2008

To: Missoni Marbleworks
66 Allies Avenue
Edmonton, AB
T3P 4C2

Deliver to: SAME

Transaction	Price
Marble tiles for contract to be completed in May	1,000.00

Terms: net 30 days	**GST # 673 214 672**	**GST**	70.00
Customer: M. Missoni		**Amount owing**	$1,070.00

☐

Lindbrook Estates
319 Brookdale Avenue
Edmonton, AB
T5P 3B2

No: 189

Date 2 1 0 4 2 0 0 8
D D M M Y Y Y Y

Pay to the order of Missoni Marbleworks $ 1,284.00

One Thousand, two hundred and eighty-four 00 /100 **Dollars**

CIBC
CIBC
300 Broadway Rd.
Edmonton, AB T5M 4K6

Mary Lindbrook

⑈--- 379351-⑈914-⑈189

Re: Reference Invoice MM-45, $1284.00
Payment in full.

No: 189

$1,284.00 April 21, 2008

☐

Missoni Marbleworks
66 Allies Avenue
Edmonton, AB
T3P 4C2

BEAUMONT TEKSTORE
661 Technology Road
Edmonton, AB T3B 2N5
Phone: (403) 892-9753

Billing Date: April 24, 2008 **CUSTOMER COPY** BT-2194

Code	Item	Price	Amount
DVD-G30	1 DVD Read/Write Drive	400.00	400.00

GST # 845 894 231

Terms: net 10 days

Signature: M. Missoni

Paid by: Cash | VISA | MasterCard | Cheque | On Account ✓

Subtotal	400.00
Goods & Services	28.00
Amount owing	$428.00

☐

MissoniMarbleworks
66 Allies Avenue
Edmonton AB.
T3P 4C2
Tel.: 403-763-4127
Fax: 403-765-4842

Sold to:
Bruno Scinto
89 Northern Avenue,
Edmonton, AB
T3C 4P6

Date: April 25, 2008

MM – 47

Description of Work Completed	Charges
Installation of new bathroom floor and marble top vanity as per contract	2,400.00

PAID IN FULL
Cheque #38

Terms: Cash Sale	**Subtotal**	2,400.00
GST # 743 647 397	**GST**	168.00
Customer Signature Bruno Scinto	**Total**	$2,568.00

☐

Bon Accord Advertising

99 Benoni Road, Edmonton, AB T4C 5M1

BA

Phone: (403) 775-2141
Fax: (403) 775-2142

Name: Missoni Marbleworks
Address: 66 Allies Avenue
Edmonton, AB
T3P 4C2

BAA- 719

Date	Transaction	Price
April 28 2008	Advertising flyers Ref: Quote #61	80.00

Terms: Cash on Receipt	**Tax**	5.60
GST # 643 214 321 **Customer:** M. Missoni	**Total**	$85.60

Missoni Marbleworks
66 Allies Avenue
Edmonton AB
T3P 4C2

No: 54

Date 29042008 (DDMMYYYY)

Pay to the order of Bon Accord Advertising $ 85.60

Eighty-five 60/100 Dollars

Alberta Trust
121 Money Way
Edmonton, AB T3C 4N6

M. Missoni

---:--- 40361 :: 054

Re: Reference Invoice # BAA-719, $85.60

No: 54

April 29, 2008

April 30, 2008

Account No.	40361	ADVICE TO ACCOUNT HOLDER	DEBIT MEMO
Code:	15		AT-D4341

Particulars:	
Interest charged on outstanding loan	$70.00
Issued by: MP Verified by: JR	

Missoni Marbleworks
66 Allies Avenue
Edmonton AB
T3P 4C2

Alberta Trust
121 Money Way
Edmonton, AB T3C 4N6

MissoniMarbleworks
66 Allies Avenue
Edmonton AB
T3P 4C2

No: 55

Date 30042008
D D M M Y Y Y Y

Pay to the order of Fonteyn Dance Studio $ 120.00

One Hundred and Twenty 00/100 Dollars

Alberta Trust
121 Money Way
Edmonton, AB T3C 4N6

M. Missoni

40361 055

Re: Ballet Lesson for Marla Missoni, $120
Drawings

No: 55
April 30, 2008

R E V I E W

The Student CD-ROM with Data Files includes Review Questions and Supplementary Cases for this chapter.

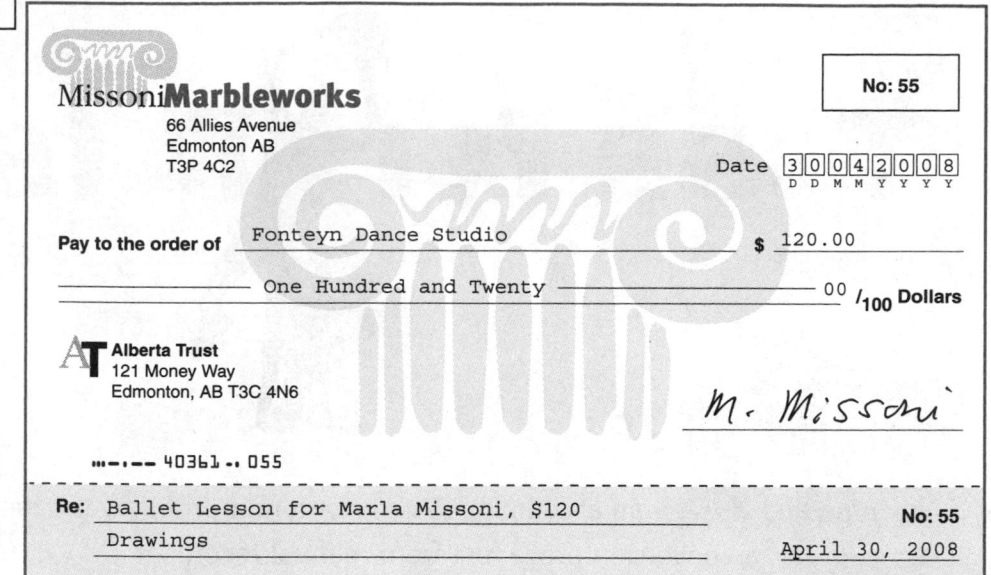

CHAPTER FOUR

OBJECTIVES

After completing this chapter, you should be able to

- ***plan*** and ***design*** an accounting system for a non-profit organization
- ***prepare*** a conversion procedure from manual records
- ***understand*** the objectives of a computerized accounting system
- ***create*** company files using the skeleton starter file
- ***set up*** the organization's accounts
- ***enter*** historical account information
- ***finish*** entering accounting history to prepare for transactions
- ***enter*** fiscal end adjusting transactions
- ***close*** the books and start a new fiscal period
- ***enter*** transactions for a previous fiscal period

COMPANY INFORMATION

Company Profile

NOTES
Toss for Tots
North Toronto PO Box 42665
Toronto, Ontario M5N 3A8
Tel: (416) 489-2734
Fax: (416) 489-6277
Business No.: 127 362 644

Toss for Tots is a charitable organization created to raise awareness and to support research on cancer in children. One salaried event manager, assisted by a large group of volunteers, organizes a basketball free-throw tournament to raise money for children's cancer research and family support. The tournament uses a ladder-style elimination to determine the championship. During the first two weekends, a first round of 20 free throws determines the basic skill level of each participant for the initial pairing. The subsequent one-on-one free-throw elimination rounds take place over the next two weekends. Two basketball courts are rented, allowing eight participants to play at the same time for the early rounds — two at a time at each end of the two courts. One thousand people are expected to participate in the initial rounds. Professional basketball players are not permitted to compete.

Funds are raised in several ways during the event: each participant pays an entry fee of $50 and receives a $30 tax receipt; each participant is expected to get sponsors who can donate a fixed amount or an amount for each successful basketball throw; spectators pay an admission fee to watch the tournament — $10 for one day, $15 for one weekend or $25 for both weekends; snacks and drinks are sold to spectators and participants; surprise bags are sold for $10 each; and photos of participants on the court are sold for $10 each. Prizes, donated by various corporations, are offered to participants who collect large donation amounts, and a cash prize of $1 000 is awarded to the tournament champion.

Volunteers handle all the registrations, monitor the contest and determine placements or pairings for successive rounds on the ladder. Costs are also minimized by the large number of merchandise donations for the surprise packages and prizes. The organization does incur some expenses, including an event manager's salary, rental of the basketball courts, a computer to record all registrations, donations and ladder sequence, office supplies, promotional materials, telephones, drinks, snacks and so on.

At the start of the tournament, many of the participants have already paid their registration fees and most of the merchandise has been purchased or received. The organization has been operating for several months to prepare for the tournament.

The bank account has been set up for the early cash donations and registrations and to write cheques for pre-tournament expenses. Some cash is also kept on hand at the tournament to make change for on-site sales and for immediate purchases. Most of the cash and cheques received from registrations and admissions are deposited immediately for security purposes.

Toss for Tots has decided to use Simply Accounting to keep the accounting records for the tournament in July 2008, part way through their current fiscal year. The charity requires only General Ledger accounts. The following information is available to set up the accounts using the General Ledger:

- Chart of Accounts
- Income Statement
- Balance Sheet
- Trial Balance
- Accounting Procedures

NOTES

Spectators and players can pay $10 for a surprise bag that contains a variety of donated items such as gift certificates, magazines, books and games. The items are hidden from view, and the value of each package is never less than $10.

CHART OF ACCOUNTS

TOSS FOR TOTS

ASSETS

1000 CURRENT ASSETS [H]
1020 Bank: Toss for Tots [A]
1100 Cash on Hand [A]
1150 Total Cash [S]
1200 Surprise Bag Supplies
1300 Food Supplies
1320 Office Supplies
1360 T-shirts
1390 TOTAL CURRENT ASSETS [T]

1400 FIXED ASSETS [H]
1420 Fax/Telephone
1450 Computer
1500 Digital Camera
1590 TOTAL FIXED ASSETS [T] ▶

▶LIABILITIES

2000 CURRENT LIABILITIES [H]
2100 Bank Loan
2200 A/P - Designs U Wear
2300 A/P - Quiq Kopy
2350 A/P - Central College
2400 A/P - Snack City
2670 GST Paid on Purchases
2690 TOTAL CURRENT LIABILITIES [T]

EQUITY

3000 EQUITY [H]
3560 Surplus Funds
3600 Net Income [X]
3690 TOTAL EQUITY [T] ▶

▶REVENUE

4000 REVENUE [H]
4020 Revenue: Registrations
4040 Revenue: Sponsors
4080 Revenue: Surprise Bags
4100 Revenue: Admissions
4120 Revenue: Food Sales
4390 TOTAL REVENUE [T]

EXPENSE

5000 ADMIN EXPENSES [H]
5020 Court Rental Expense
5200 Office Supplies Used
5220 Non-refundable GST
5240 Postage Expense
5280 Printing & Copying ▶

▶5300 Publicity & Promotion
5320 Telephone Expense
5400 Wages - Manager
5420 Miscellaneous Expenses
5440 TOTAL ADMIN EXPENSES [T]

5450 MERCHANDISE & FOOD EXPENSES [H]
5500 Cost of T-shirts
5520 Cost of Surprise Bags
5550 Cost of Food
5690 TOTAL MERCHANDISE & FOOD EXPENSES [T]

NOTES: The Chart of Accounts is based on the current expenses and accounts. Account types are marked in brackets for subgroup Accounts [A], Subgroup totals [S], Headings [H], Totals [T] and Current Earnings [X]. All unmarked accounts are postable Group [G] accounts. The explanation of account types begins on page 91.

INCOME STATEMENT

TOSS FOR TOTS

For the Nine Months Ending June 30, 2008

Revenue		
4000	REVENUE	
4020	Revenue: Registrations	$20 000.00
4040	Revenue: Sponsors	2 000.00
4390	TOTAL REVENUE	$22 000.00
TOTAL REVENUE		$22 000.00
Expense		
5000	ADMIN EXPENSES	
5020	Court Rental Expense	$15 000.00
5200	Office Supplies Used	640.00
5240	Postage Expense	450.00
5280	Printing & Copying	2 000.00
5300	Publicity & Promotion	4 000.00
5320	Telephone Expense	360.00
5400	Wages - Manager	6 000.00
5440	TOTAL ADMIN EXPENSES	$28 450.00
TOTAL EXPENSE		$28 450.00
NET INCOME (LOSS)		($6 450.00)

NOTES: Because the event has not yet started, most expenses are still at zero. Because most of the funds have not yet come in, the Income Statement shows a net loss.

BALANCE SHEET

TOSS FOR TOTS

July 1, 2008

Assets			
1000	CURRENT ASSETS		
1020	Bank: Toss for Tots	$18 550.00	
1100	Cash on Hand	1 000.00	
1150	Total Cash		$19 550.00
1200	Surprise Bag Supplies		500.00
1300	Food Supplies		1 200.00
1320	Office Supplies		750.00
1360	T-shirts		800.00
1390	TOTAL CURRENT ASSETS		$22 800.00
1400	FIXED ASSETS		
1420	Fax/Telephone		500.00
1450	Computer		2 400.00
1500	Digital Camera		900.00
1590	TOTAL FIXED ASSETS		$ 3 800.00
TOTAL ASSETS			$26 600.00

Liabilities		
2000	CURRENT LIABILITIES	
2100	Bank Loan	$ 15 000.00
2200	A/P - Designs U Wear	800.00
2300	A/P - Quiq Kopy	150.00
2350	A/P - Central College	10 700.00
2400	A/P - Snack City	900.00
2670	GST Paid on Purchases	–1 950.00
2690	TOTAL CURRENT LIABILITIES	$25 600.00
TOTAL LIABILITIES		$25 600.00
Equity		
3000	EQUITY	
3560	Surplus Funds	$ 7 450.00
3600	Net Income	–6 450.00
3690	TOTAL EQUITY	$ 1 000.00
TOTAL EQUITY		$ 1 000.00
LIABILITIES AND EQUITY		$26 600.00

TRIAL BALANCE

TOSS FOR TOTS

July 1, 2008		Debits	Credits
1020	Bank: Toss for Tots	$18 550.00	
1100	Cash on Hand	1 000.00	
1200	Surprise Bag Supplies	500.00	
1300	Food Supplies	1 200.00	
1320	Office Supplies	750.00	
1360	T-shirts	800.00	
1420	Fax/Telephone	500.00	
1450	Computer	2 400.00	
1500	Digital Camera	900.00	
2100	Bank Loan		$15 000.00
2200	A/P - Designs U Wear		800.00
2300	A/P - Quiq Kopy		150.00
2350	A/P - Central College		10 700.00
2400	A/P - Snack City		900.00
2670	GST Paid on Purchases	1 950.00	
3560	Surplus Funds		7 450.00
4020	Revenue: Registrations		20 000.00
4040	Revenue: Sponsors		2 000.00
5020	Court Rental Expense	15 000.00	
5200	Office Supplies Used	640.00	
5240	Postage Expense	450.00	
5280	Printing & Copying	2 000.00	
5300	Publicity & Promotion	4 000.00	
5320	Telephone Expense	360.00	
5400	Wages - Manager	6 000.00	
		$57 000.00	$57 000.00

Accounting Procedures

GST

Registered charities have two options with respect to the GST. Like regular for-profit businesses, they can register to apply the GST, charge GST on all sales and membership fees and claim all GST paid as input tax credits to reduce the liability to the Receiver General. The second option, used by Toss for Tots, does not require registration or collection of GST but permits a partial rebate of GST paid. Periodically the charity submits an application for refunds, listing the total of all GST paid toward its operating expenses. Fifty percent of this amount is eligible for the rebate. Therefore, Toss for Tots records all purchases as compound General Journal entries, separating the amount paid for GST from the total and debiting this amount to *GST Paid on Purchases*. This account is cleared with a credit entry as the application for a rebate is submitted. The debit entries to the *GST Refund Receivable* and the *Non-refundable GST* expense accounts (50 percent each) will balance the journal entry.

Bank Accounts

The proceeds from the registrations and from the sale of merchandise are entered into the bank account. The account is used for all cheques to suppliers and to cover operating and administrative expenses and merchandise — drinks, snacks, T-shirts and surprise bag items. During the tournament, a *Cash on Hand* account is set up for day-to-day expenses incurred by the volunteer staff. Regular transfers are made from the

Bank: Toss for Tots account to *Cash on Hand* by writing cheques to the Event Manager.

INSTRUCTIONS

1. **Set up** the **company accounts for Toss for Tots** in the General Ledger in Simply Accounting using all the information provided in this application. Detailed keystroke instructions follow the instructions.
2. **Back up your work frequently** when working through this application to keep your backups updated.

   You may finish your session at any time while completing the setup. Simply open the Toss for Tots data file again, accept the session date and continue from where you left off.

   If you are using a different location for your data files, substitute the appropriate data path, including the drive and folder for your data setup.
3. **Enter** the **source documents** that begin on page 103 in the General Journal in Simply Accounting using the Chart of Accounts and other information provided.
4. **Print** the **following reports** after you have completed your entries:
   a. General Journal from July 1 to September 30
   b. Comparative Balance Sheet at September 30 and October 1 (amounts)
   c. Income Statement for the period October 1, 2007, to September 30, 2008

KEYSTROKES FOR SETUP

The following are the five key stages in preparing the Simply Accounting program for use by a company:

1. creating company files
2. preparing the system
3. preparing the ledgers
4. printing reports to check your work
5. backing up your files and finishing the company history

NOTES
Using subsequent versions of the Simply Accounting program may result in different screens and keystrokes from those described in this application.

The following keystroke instructions are written for a stand-alone PC with a hard disk drive. The keystroke instructions provided in this application demonstrate one approach to setting up company accounts. Always refer to the Simply Accounting and Windows manuals and Help for further details.

Creating Company Files

The following instructions assume that you have the Simply Accounting program correctly installed on your hard disk in drive C: in the Program Files\Winsim folder.

Simply Accounting provides both templates and starter files to make it easier to create files for a new company. These files contain different sets of accounts that match the needs of different kinds of businesses. By starting with one of these files, you eliminate the need to create all the accounts for your business from scratch.

There are many templates that work with the setup wizards to define not only accounts, but also a number of settings for the different ledgers. These settings and accounts are suited to the type of business named by the files.

In addition, Simply Accounting includes two starter files — inteplus.sdb (Integration Plus) and skeleton.sdb. The starter files contain only a set of basic accounts. Starter files are opened like any other company file. You should work with a copy of these files so that you can use the original files for future applications.

The Skeleton starter has only General Ledger accounts, whereas the Integration Plus starter is suitable for a variety of business types because it has the basic linked accounts for all the ledgers.

You will have to customize any of these starter files to your particular company. Rarely are accounts identical for any two businesses. The files that are best suited to the Chart of Accounts for Toss for Tots are the Skeleton starter files (skeleton.sdb). These files contain only a few General Ledger accounts, headings and totals. They contain no linked accounts that link General Ledger accounts to the subsidiary ledgers. This is appropriate for Toss for Tots, which uses only the General Ledger.

The starter files are located in the folder named Template in the Winsim folder — the folder that contains your Simply Accounting program. If you accepted the default installation location, the Skeleton starter file has the path C:\Program Files\Winsim\Template\Skeleton.sdb. The starter files were created when you installed the program. (See the margin note about the Student CD-ROM.)

Start the **Simply Accounting program** to access the Select Company window.

Choose **Select An Existing Company** to access the Open Company window.

If you were previously working with files in the Missoni folder under Winsim\Data, it will be the active or selected folder.

Click the **Up One Level icon** beside the Look In field to go to the Data folder level.

Click the **Up One Level icon** again to see the folders under Winsim:

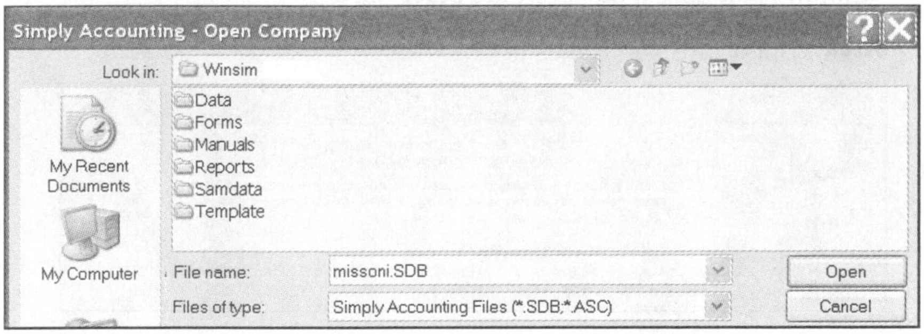

Double click **Template** to open it or **click Template** to highlight it and **click Open** to see the list of starter files as shown:

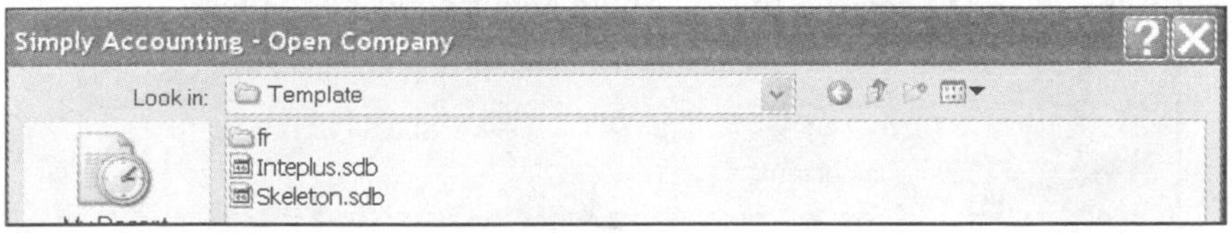

Click **Skeleton** (or Skeleton.sdb).

NOTES

We want to illustrate different ways of creating company files. Therefore, the method of creating your company files from scratch is described in the Dorfmann Design setup application, Chapter 9.

NOTES

If you prefer to enter the source documents before setting up the data files, you can use the Toss \toss.sdb file in the Setup folder inside your Data folder. In this way, the setup may be easier to complete because you are already familiar with the account structure.

NOTES

We have included a copy of the Skeleton starter file on the Student CD-ROM in the Template folder. It will be installed on your hard drive with the other data files. If you have difficulty locating the Skeleton files in the program folder, you can use the Student CD-ROM copy of the file instead.

NOTES

You must work in single-user mode to set up new company files. Access to most settings is restricted in multi-user mode.

NOTES

If you were working with files in another drive, directory or folder, you would use the following steps to switch to the Template folder:

- Click the drop-down list arrow beside the Look In field to see your data path.
- Click (C:).
- Double click Program Files.
- Double click Winsim.
- Double click Template.
- Depending on your starting location, you may skip one or more of the above steps.

Click **Open** to access the files to begin the Upgrade Company Wizard:

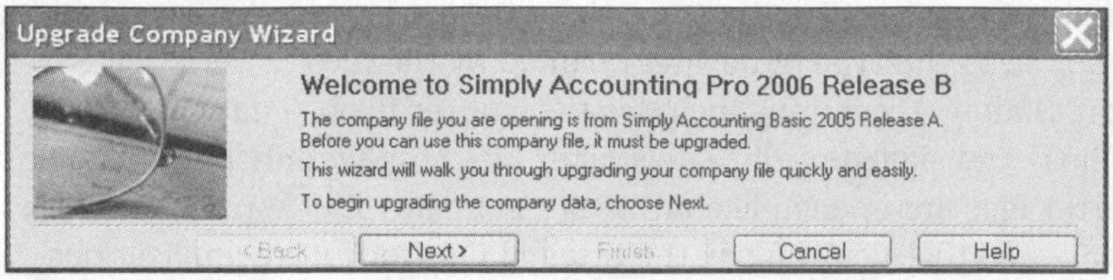

The skeleton starter file is a Basic version file (Release A) so it must be converted to Pro Release B.

Read the **introduction** to the wizard and **click Next** to continue:

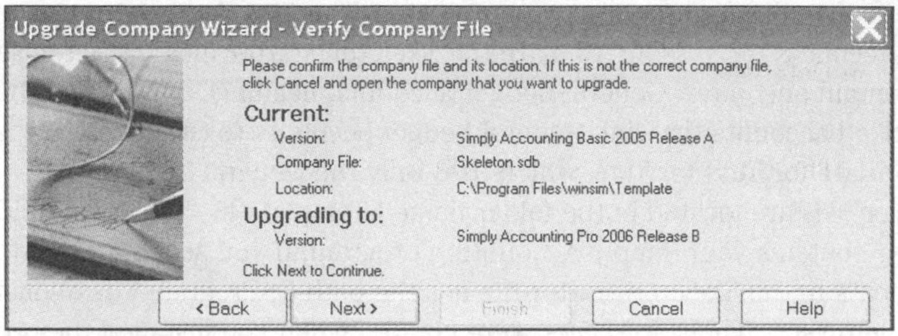

This screen shows the name and location of the working file and the version changes that will be made if you proceed.

Click **Next**:

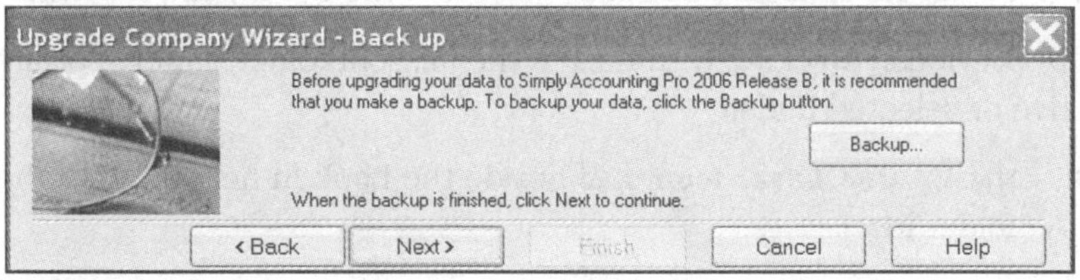

You can now back up the Skeleton file before proceeding.

Click **Next**:

Simply Accounting will check your data file for problems and repair them if you choose this option.

Click **Next** to see the final warning about converting files:

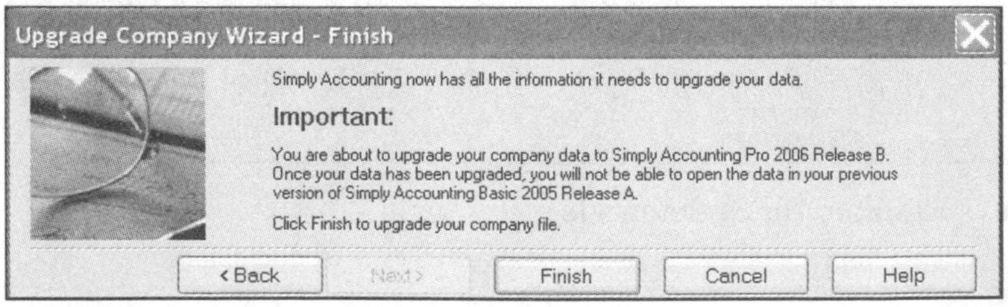

This final screen warns you of the changes you are making. After this step you cannot cancel the conversion. File conversions cannot be reversed — once you convert a file you will be unable to open it in the earlier version.

BASIC VERSION

The file will be converted from Release A to Release B.

WARNING!

If you make a backup at this stage, it will be a Release B backup. To keep the original file without converting it, work from the Data\Template\skeleton version of the starter file.

Click **Finish** to begin the conversion. An information screen opens when the conversion is complete:

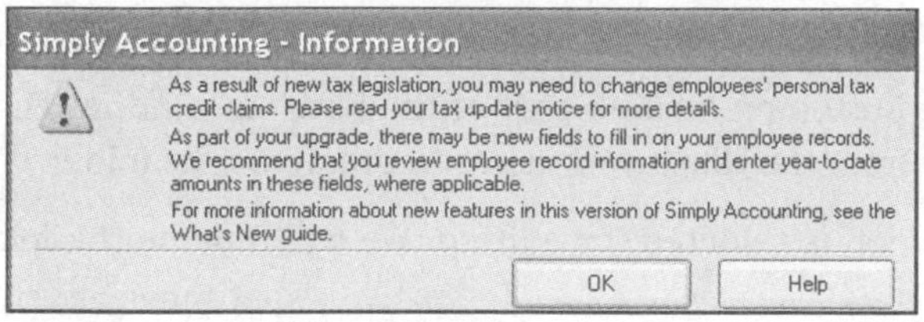

This message advises you that tax legislation changes may require you to update the tax information for employees.

Click **OK** to close the message after reading it.

The Session Date window appears with January 1, 2000, as the session date.

Click **OK** to accept the date and open the Daily Business Manager window. The Home window is open in the background.

Click ☒ to close the Daily Business Manager window:

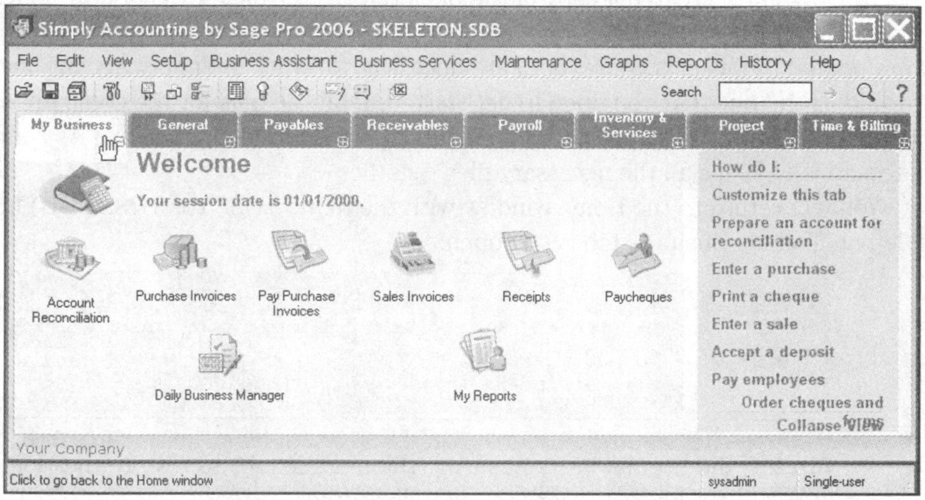

BASIC VERSION
Simply Accounting by Sage Basic 2006 is displayed as the program name in the title bar.

The My Business tab window opens. The file name Skeleton appears in the title bar. Before making any changes to this template, we will make a copy.

Copying the Starter File

We will make a copy of these files to store the records for Toss for Tots. Always work with a backup copy of the starter files so that you will have the original to use when creating other company records. We will use the Save As command because we want to work with the new renamed file and keep the original Skeleton file unchanged.

Choose the **File menu** and **click** **Save As** to open the Save As window:

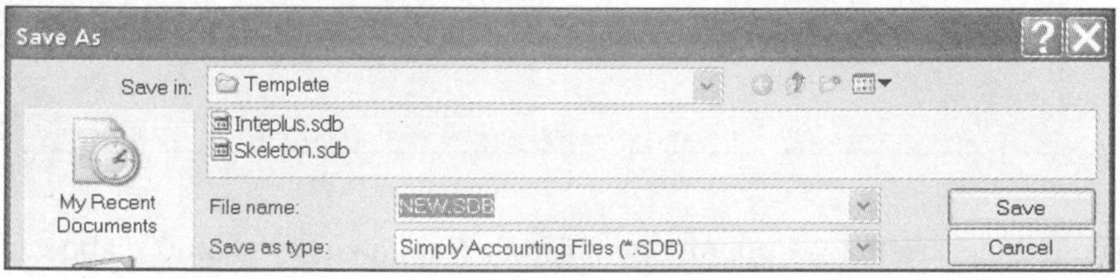

Click the **Up One Level icon** to return to the Winsim folder level.

NOTES
Substitute the appropriate data path, including the drive and folder where your data files are stored (e.g., E:\simplydata\toss\toss.sdb). Refer to Chapter 1, page 22, for more help with making folders.

NOTES
The program will add the .sdb file extension because the correct file type is contained in the Save As Type field.
The .sdb extension for the file name may not appear on the screen, depending on your Windows version and preferences.
Alternative methods of copying files are described in Chapter 1.

basic BASIC VERSION
Simply Accounting by Sage Basic 2006 is displayed as the program name in the title bar.
The Time & Billing module is not available in the Basic version so you will not see the Time Slips icon.

Double click the **Data folder** to open it (or the folder on the hard drive that you are using for your data).

Click the **New Folder icon** , or

Click the right mouse button on a blank part of the Save As window, choose New and then Folder from the displayed menu to create a new folder.

The folder name, New Folder, is selected for editing. We will rename the folder.

Type TOSS

Double click the **TOSS folder** to open it. TOSS should appear in the Save In field.

Double click **NEW** (or **NEW.SDB**), the file name, to prepare the field for entering the new file name.

Type toss

Click **Save**.

You have now created a copy of the Skeleton starter files within a new folder and under a new name in the Data folder where you stored your other data files. Two files were copied in this procedure; both are necessary to work in Simply Accounting. The .sdb file is the one that you open to get started. If all the files for the company are not in the same folder, you will not be able to access your data. Using the Save As command automatically keeps all the necessary files together.

You will return to the Home window with the name TOSS (or TOSS.SDB) in the title bar. The My Business tab is still open:

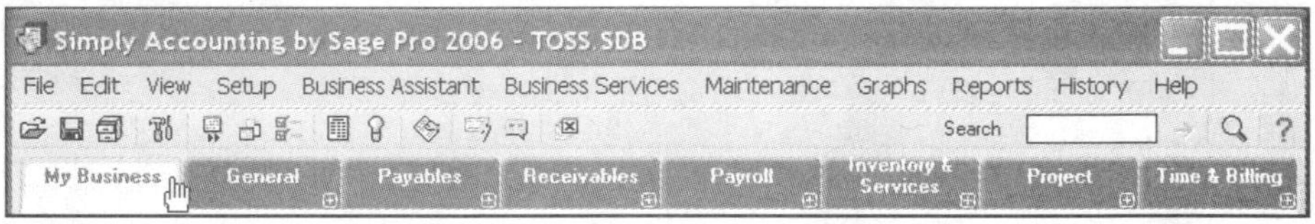

Click the **My Business heading** (the module tab) to restore the Home window with icons for all the modules:

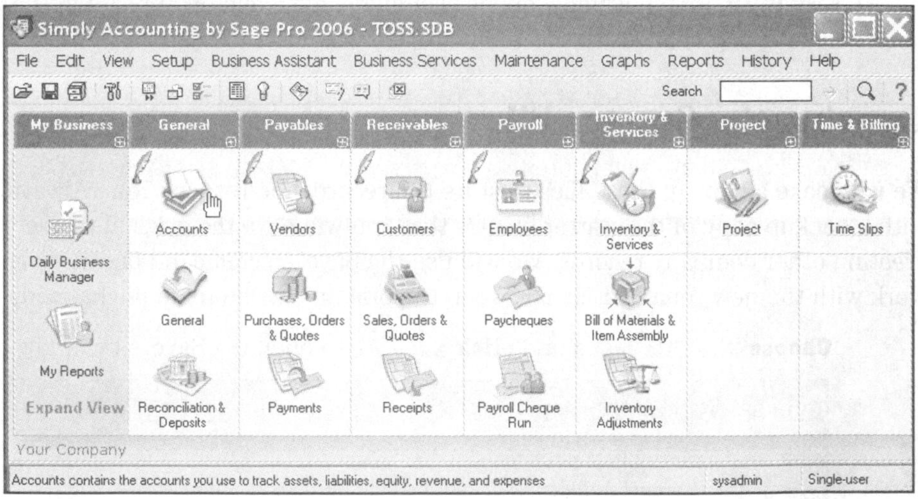

The ledgers are not set up. An open history (quill pen) symbol  appears with each ledger icon, indicating that you can enter historical data for the ledger. Although you can make journal entries at this stage, you should enter all the necessary company information and finish entering the history first.

Preparing the System

Before entering financial records for a new company, you must prepare the system for operation. This involves changing the default settings to reflect the Toss for Tots company information. For the General Ledger, these defaults include the company name and address, fiscal dates, screen display preferences and the Chart of Accounts. When you set up other ledgers, there will be additional default information. Some of the initial defaults will not be suitable for Toss for Tots. You must also provide other information, such as the printer(s) that you will be using and the printing formats. This process of adding, deleting and modifying information is called customizing the system.

NOTES
Simply Accounting includes a Setup wizard that guides you through the company setup step by step with instructions. The wizard is not used in this application. To access the Setup wizard, choose the Setup menu then choose Wizards and click Settings.

Changing Company Default Settings

Entering Company Information

Choose the **Setup menu**, then **choose System Settings** and **click Company Information** to see the following information screen:

NOTES
You cannot complete the setup in multi-user mode.

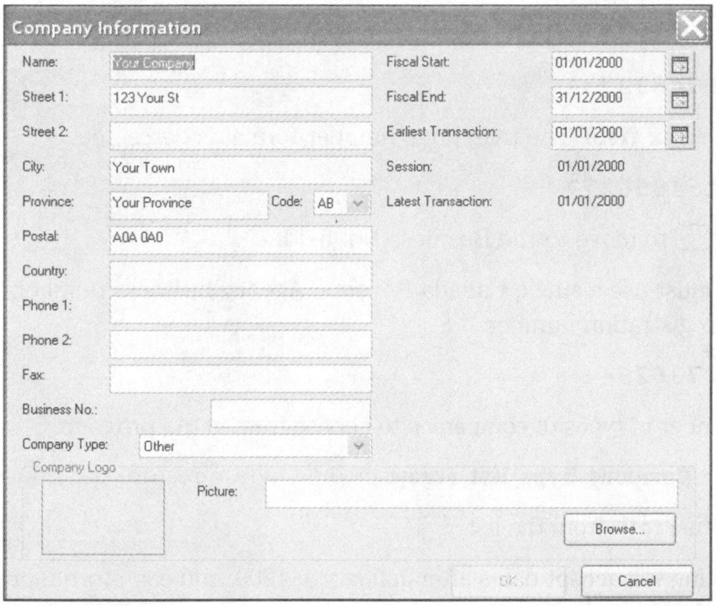

The cursor is in the Name field. This field contains the information "Your Company" to let you know that this is where you should enter the name of your company. The contents of the field are highlighted so that you can enter the name of the business.

If Your Company is not highlighted, drag through the text to select it.

Type `Toss for Tots` (add your own name)

Press *tab*.

NOTES
You can personalize your files by adding your own name to this field (e.g., Toss for Tots - Purbhoo) so that all reports printed will include your name for easy identification.

The cursor moves to the Street 1 field, the first address field. You can enter the address immediately because the current contents are already highlighted.

Type `North Toronto`

Press *tab* to advance to the second street address line (Street 2 field).

Type `PO Box 42665`

Press *tab*.

The cursor advances to and highlights the contents of the City field.

Type Toronto

Press *tab*.

The cursor advances to the Province field. It, too, is ready for editing.

Type Ontario **Press** *tab* to advanced to the province code field.

Choose **ON** as the province code from the drop-down list and **press** *tab*.

The cursor is now placed at the highlighted Postal (postal code) field. You do not have to type the capitals or spaces in postal codes. The program automatically corrects the postal code format when you enter a Canadian postal code pattern.

Type m5n3a8

In this case, all addresses will be in Canada, so we can leave the Country field blank. Now enter the telephone and fax numbers for the business. There is only one phone number so the Phone 2 field will remain blank. You do not need to type brackets or hyphens for phone numbers. Simply Accounting will correct the format when you enter a seven- or ten-digit phone number.

Click the **Phone 1 field**. The postal code format is corrected.

Type 4164892734

Click the **Fax field**. The telephone number format is corrected.

Type 4164896277

Press *tab* to move to the Business No. field.

All companies must use a single Canada Revenue Agency business number that also serves as the GST registration number.

Type 127362644

There are a number of types of companies to choose from in the program.

Click the **Company Type list arrow**.

Choose **Non-Profit** from the list.

Simply Accounting will accept dates after January 1, 1900. You can store more than one year of accounting records. The Basic version stores two years of complete data.

The **Fiscal Start** field contains the date at which the current fiscal year begins. This is usually the date used to define the beginning of the fiscal year for income tax purposes.

The **Fiscal End** is the date at which the company closes its books, usually one year after the fiscal start, and the end of the fiscal year used for income tax reporting purposes. For Toss for Tots, the fiscal end is two months after the tournament, when all the accounting information for the event has been entered.

The **Earliest Transaction** date is the date on which the company converts its manual accounting records to the computerized system. Entries before this date are historical entries. The earliest transaction date must not be earlier than the fiscal start and not later than the fiscal end. The earliest transaction date will be the first session date when you are ready to enter journal transactions. Simply Accounting automatically advances the earliest transaction date when you start a new fiscal year.

The default date format for this file is day-month-year. We will enter these dates in text form and change the date format for the file when we change the other settings. By entering four digits for the year initially, we will ensure that we enter it correctly.

Press *tab* to advance to the Fiscal Start field.

NOTES
All provinces and territories in Canada have a two-letter abbreviation code.

NOTES
All postal codes in Canada use the following pattern: Letter, Number, Letter, Number, Letter, Number. Any other sequence, as for other countries, will not be corrected by the program, and you should enter the correct format.

NOTES
For reporting purposes, business numbers are followed by RT with a four-digit number that identifies the business area, such as payroll.

NOTES
When we entered various dates, the program accepted dates between 1900 and 2400 without an error message. There appear to be no practical restrictions on the dates you can use.

NOTES
Companies may use a fiscal period shorter than one year for reporting purposes and close their books more frequently, but the most common period is one year.

Type oct 1 2007

Press tab **twice**. The cursor moves to the Fiscal End field.

Type sep 30 2008

Press tab **twice**. The cursor is now in the Earliest Transaction field.

Type jul 1 2008

Check your work.

The session date and the latest transaction date will change as you complete journal entries and advance the session date from the Home window. The latest transaction date shows if you have any postdated journal transactions.

You cannot change the earliest transaction date after finishing the history and making journal entries. The company name, address and fiscal end date can be edited at any time. Return to any field with errors to correct mistakes.

Click **Browse** and **click** the **Up One Level icon**. Then **double click Data**, **Setup** and **Logo** to locate the folder with company logos.

Click **toss.bmp** and **click Save** to return to the Company Information window.

Click **OK** to save the new company information.

Changing the Printer Defaults

You may select a different printer for customized forms or you may want to change the format of the printed reports. The following instructions should assist you.

Choose the **Setup menu** and **click Reports & Forms** to see the settings screen:

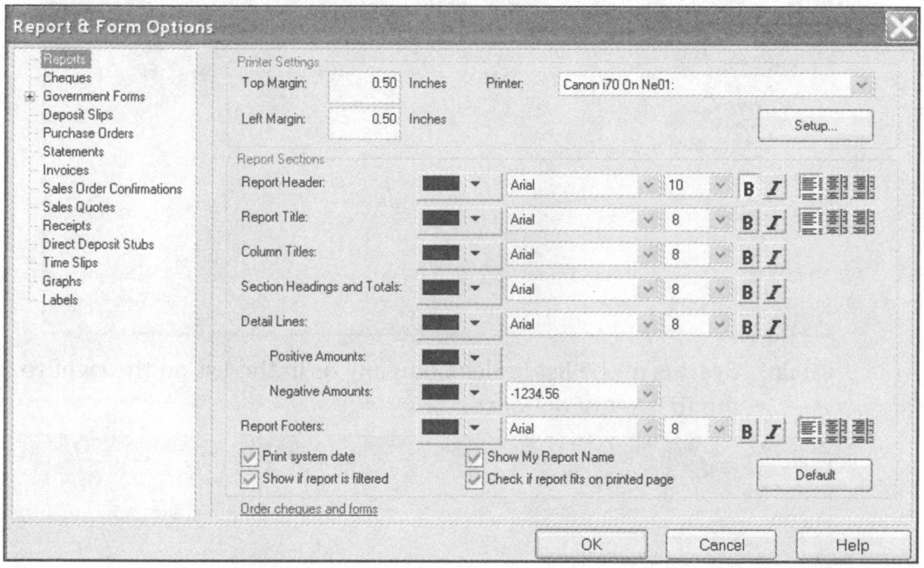

The printer selections are specific to this data file and they are saved with the file, even when you use the file with a different computer system. Therefore, they may be incorrect. You can see that Simply Accounting allows you to set up different printers and settings for reports, graphs, cheques, invoices, labels, purchase orders, T4 slips and so on. Many companies use one printer for their reports and another for various preprinted forms and invoices. Even if you use one printer, you may want to adjust fonts, margins and form selections for each type of printed report or statement.

Choose the printer you will be using for reports from the list provided using the arrow beside the field. All printers that are installed on your computer should

NOTES

Once you have entered the fiscal start, fiscal end and earliest transaction dates, the program will correctly fill in the year when you type only the last two digits or omit the year, because the date must fall between the earliest transaction and fiscal end dates.

NOTES

When you view the Company Information again, the session and latest transaction dates will have been updated to match the new fiscal dates.

basic BASIC VERSION

You will not see the Time Slips entry.

WARNING!

You need to choose a printer for reports and for each form listed. The default may be incorrect if you have changed your computer setup after installing the program.

Printer settings may also be incorrect if you use a data file that was created on a different computer.

be on the list. Change the page margins if necessary. For each part of the report, choose font, type size and how to display positive and negative numbers from the lists available when you click the arrows beside these fields. You can experiment to find the combination that will fit the reports neatly on the page. By default, reports include the computer system date and a message indicating whether filtering is applied.

To modify the printer setup for other outputs, click the relevant form in the list. You can modify printer setup information any time by returning to this screen.

WARNING!
You should view the additional printer control screens but do not change the settings. The printer control screens will vary from one printer to another. Usually the default settings are correct.
Notice that the printer instructions are given as optional command statements.

Click Setup to display additional printer settings if there are any.

At this stage, you may be able to modify the source of the paper, the paper size and orientation. Additional control over your printed copy may be available from this screen by clicking different tabs. Each tab will give you additional printing options. The sequence of screens, options and tabs will vary from printer to printer.

Click OK to leave each dialogue box and save the changes, or

Click **Cancel** to exit without making changes and return to the Home window.

Changing Ledger Default Settings

Setting System Defaults

Choose the **Setup menu**, then **choose System Settings** and **click Settings**.

The settings for all ledgers are available from the Settings screen:

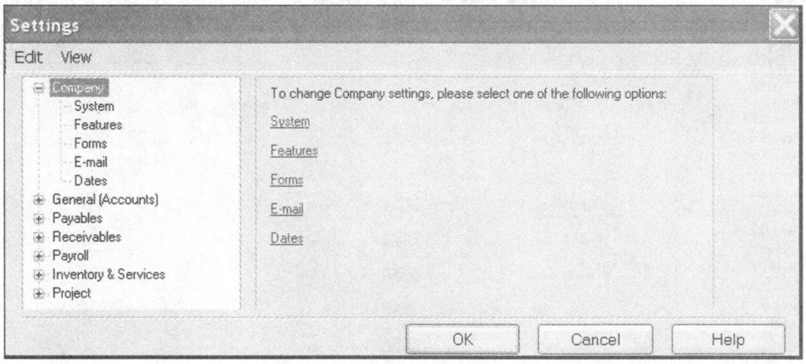

NOTES
If a Home window ledger icon is selected when you choose Settings, you will see the settings for that ledger. Click Company and then click System to see the System Settings.
The Names & Terminology option in the Setup menu applies to other ledgers. It will be introduced in Chapter 15.

Click **System** in the list under Company or in the list on the right to access the first set of options:

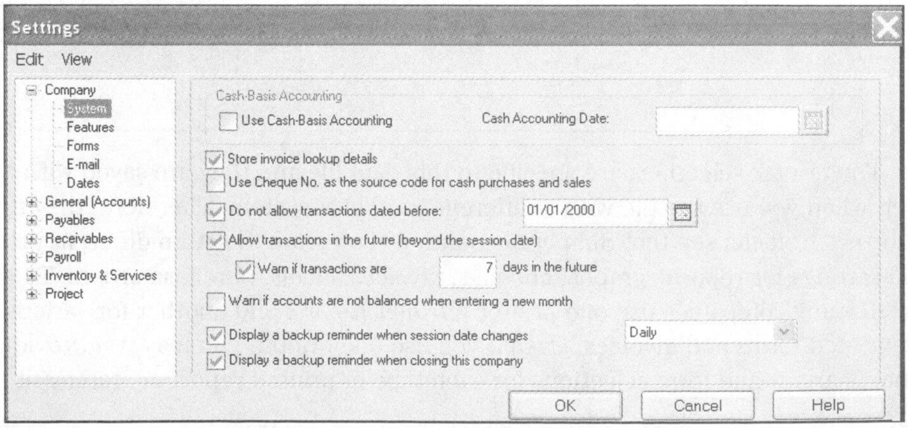

The Company System settings apply to all modules of the program.

There are several important switches and settings in this screen. The first refers to whether the business is using **cash-basis accounting** instead of the default, **accrual-basis accounting**. The cash basis of accounting records revenues and expenses on the date the money is paid or received. In the accrual method, revenues and expenses are recorded on the transaction date (matching principle). To change to the cash basis method, click the check box and enter the date on which the change is to take effect. This workbook uses the accrual basis. Do not change this setting.

The option to **Store Invoice Lookup Details** allows you to display, print, store and adjust invoices that have already been posted. The option is turned on, or selected, when the ✓ appears in the check box. Toss for Tots does not need these features because they refer to Sales and Purchases Journal invoices.

Click **Store Invoice Lookup Details** to turn off this option.

The next option relates to the use of the **Cheque Number As The Source Code For Cash Purchases And Sales** in account reconciliation. Since Toss for Tots uses only the General Ledger, this option does not apply. When you are using the Payables and Receivables Ledgers, you should turn on the option.

The next option, **Do Not Allow Transactions Dated Before**, permits you to lock out any transactions for a previous period by entering the date. You can post transactions to earlier dates by removing the checkmark or entering an earlier date in this field. The feature should be turned off only for specific transactions and then turned on again so that you do not post in error with an incorrect date. Similarly, you should not generally allow posting to future periods, beyond the session date, unless you are entering a series of postdated transactions. You can activate the feature for specific transactions when needed so that you do not post with incorrect future dates. You can add a warning for dates beyond a certain period as well. We will restrict transactions before the starting date for now and not allow postdated transactions.

Remember that the date format is still day-month-year.

Double click the date **01/01/2000**.

Type `Jul 1`

Click **Allow Transactions In The Future** to remove the ✓ and not allow postdating.

Since Simply Accounting allows journal entries before the company setup details are completed, you can add a reminder **warning** as you continue to work with an incomplete and **unbalanced account history**. If you choose to post journal entries before completing the history, you should turn on the warning.

The next option refers to the **frequency** with which you **back up** your data. Since we usually advance the session date weekly, we will choose Weekly as the backup frequency as well. The program prompts you to back up according to this entry.

Click the **Backup Frequency field list arrow** and **choose Weekly**.

If you want, you can choose a specific number of days as the interval between backups by choosing Other and typing the number in the Number Of Days field that opens with this choice.

The final option will show a reminder to back up the file each time you close the company file. Leave the option selected because you should back up data files regularly.

Click **Features** in the list below Company in the left-hand side panel.

NOTES

Refer to Appendix J on the Student CD-ROM for more information on accrual- and cash-basis accounting.

Invoice Lookup is used in the Maple Leaf Rags application, Chapter 8.

WARNING!

The date you enter for Do Not Allow Transactions Dated Before must not be earlier than the Earliest Transaction Date on the Company Information screen.

If the check box is not checked, you can leave the date field blank.

NOTES

Refer to page 110 for details on allowing transactions in a previous year.

You will see a warning that invoice details will be removed:

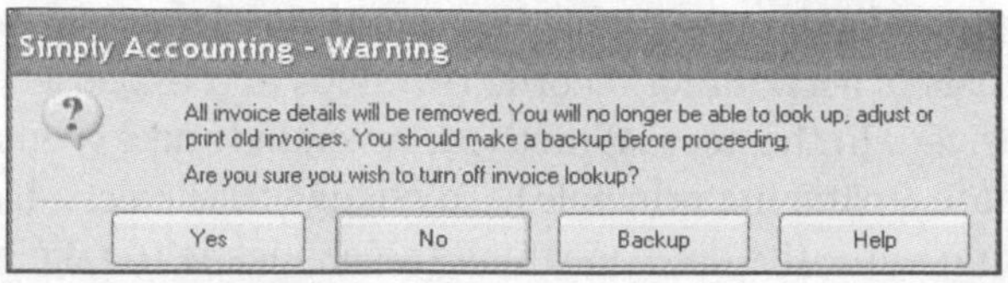

We do not need these details because we are not using the sales and purchases journals to record invoices.

Click **Yes** to continue to the next group of Company settings:

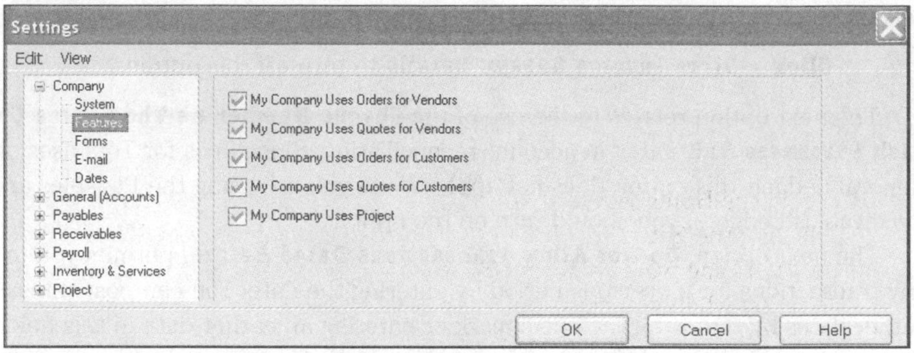

These features apply to the Payables and Receivables ledgers. They do not apply to General Ledger transactions so we can remove them.

Click **each line** to remove all checkmarks.

Form numbers, such as for invoices, cheques, quotes and so on, also do not apply to the General Journal transactions entered by Toss for Tots. We will skip these screens.

Changing Date Formats

The date formats for the starter file are different from the formats we used for other files. To avoid entering incorrect dates, we will choose the same format that we used for our other data files. We need to change the default setting so that month appears first. You can choose any separator character you want.

Click **Dates** in the list below Company in the left-hand side panel:

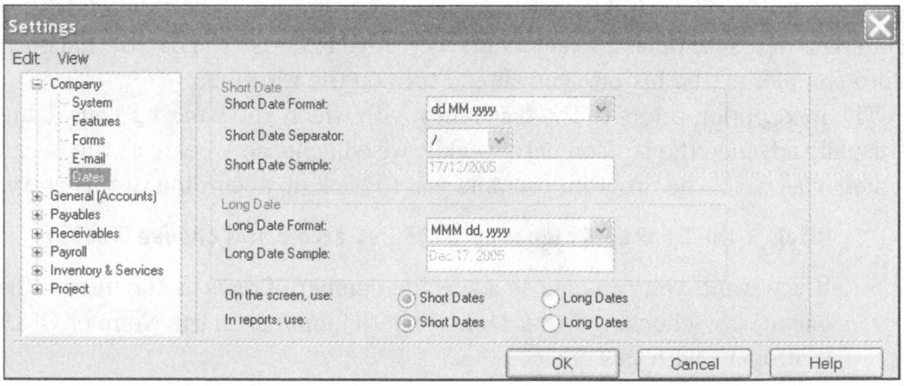

Choose **MM/dd/yyyy** from the Short Date Format drop-down list.

Choose another separator symbol from the Short Date Separator list, if you want.

On the screen we will show dates in the long form to make them as clear as possible. You can choose long or short dates for reports.

Click **Long Dates** beside the option for On The Screen, Use.

Setting General Defaults

To change the settings for the General Ledger for Toss for Tots,

Click **General (Accounts)** in the list on the left:

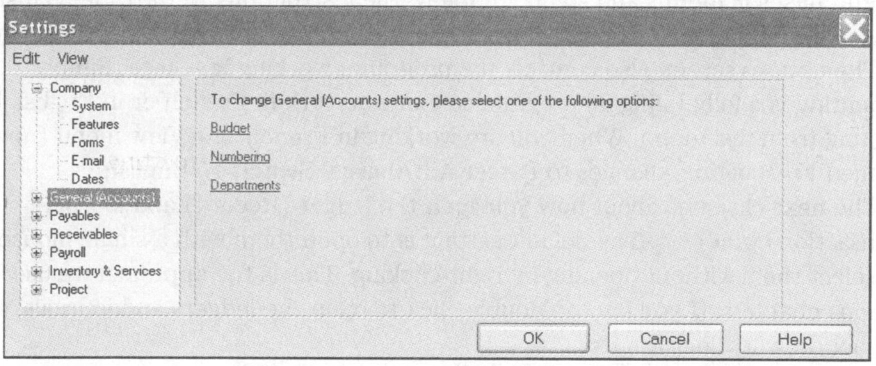

From the Home window you can access the General Settings window by clicking the Setup tool bar button and selecting Accounts. If the Accounts icon in the Home window is already selected, you will access the General Settings directly when you click the Setup button.

If you want the Simply Accounting program to prepare **budget** reports, click Budget to open the Budget setup options. Then click Budget Revenue And Expense Accounts and choose the budget period from the drop-down list. Each revenue and expense ledger account window will include a Budget tab. Click this tab and then enter budget amounts for the account to include the account automatically in budget reports. You can activate budgeting at any time.

From the **Numbering** option, you can choose not to use account numbers in your reports and journal transactions when the account names are unique, that is, there is no duplication of names. We use account numbers in all the applications in this text.

Toss for Tots does not have different **Departments** to track expenses, so we do not need to turn on this option.

Since the other ledgers are not used by Toss for Tots, you do not need to change their settings.

Click **OK** to save all the changes and return to the Home window.

NOTES
The budgeting feature is explained in the Village Galleries application, Chapter 13.
Departments are illustrated in Chapter 18.

Changing User Preference Settings

Choose the **Setup menu**, then **click** **User Preferences** to see the options:

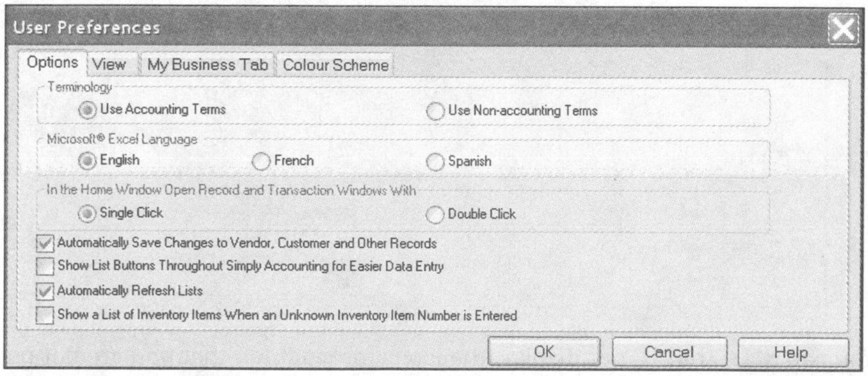

User preferences define the way an individual user wants to work with the program. They do not affect the accounting processes.

NOTES
An additional option, Always Apply Allocation To Entire Transaction, will be included when you use the Project feature.

basic **BASIC VERSION**
You will not see the option Automatically Refresh Lists.

NOTES
Appendix B lists all equivalent accounting and non-accounting terms.

NOTES
The Excel language option will apply only if you have installed a non-English language version of the Excel program.

The first feature refers to the language used by the program. We use **accounting terms** throughout this workbook because most people who use accounting programs are familiar with that language. If you choose non-accounting terms, the General Journal will be labelled Miscellaneous Transactions, the Payables Ledger will be named Vendors and Purchases in menus and so on. To follow the instructions we provide, you should **Use Accounting Terms**. You can also choose the **language** of your **Excel** program.

The options screen also controls the program's working **language**. Simply Accounting is a fully bilingual program so you can work in French or in English by selecting from this menu. When you are working in French, the View menu (now renamed *Vue*) option changes to Passer A L'Anglais/ Switch To English.

The next choice is about how you **open** the ledger (Record) and journal (Transaction) **windows**. The default setting is to open them with a single mouse click and select them without opening by right-clicking. This is the approach we used in previous chapters. If you choose double click to open the ledgers and journals, a single click action will select the icon.

If you choose not to **automatically save changes** to ledger records when you close a record window, the program will prompt you to save if you close the ledger record after making changes and give you the option of always saving changes automatically. **Including the list selection button** in all account fields to select account numbers, vendors, customers, tax codes, employees, inventory items, etc. is the option we use in this text. The **refresh lists automatically** option applies when working in multi-user mode. You can select to **show inventory item lists** whenever a new item is entered in the item field. When you use the Project feature you can always **apply allocations** to the entire transaction. Inventory and allocations are covered in Chapters 11 and 12.

NOTES
The Refresh Lists option applies only to the multi-user version of Simply Accounting Pro.

Click **Show List Buttons Throughout Simply Accounting For Easier Data Entry**.

NOTES
Many account input fields have list buttons or icons like the Account field that you saw in the General Journal in Chapter 3. Other fields have list arrows that provide a drop-down or pop-up list to select from.

The remaining default settings are correct. These settings can be changed at any time by clicking the option.

Changing the View Settings

Several important display or appearance options are controlled from the View tab.

Click the **View tab**:

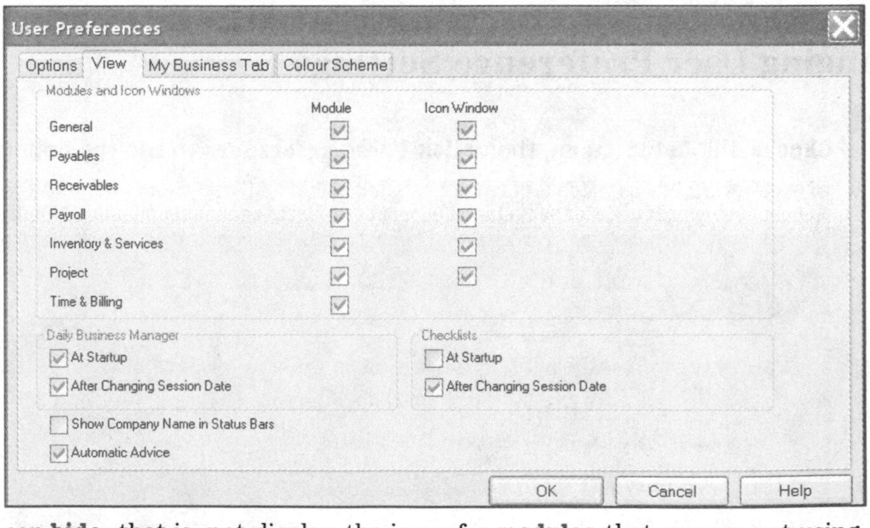

WARNING!
If you do not hide the remaining modules, you will be unable to complete the final setup step of finishing the history because essential information for those modules is missing.

You can **hide**, that is, not display, the icons for **modules** that you are not using. We must hide the modules that are not used.

The **Icon Window** checkboxes allow you to hide the accounts icon window for one or more ledgers. If you select the Home window Accounts icon (or other ledger icon) with this option turned on, account information for the first account will be displayed instead of the list of accounts. Icon windows can be hidden separately only if the module windows are not hidden.

Click the **Module checkbox for Payables** to remove the ✓. The ✓ for Icon Window is also removed.

Repeat this step for **Receivables, Payroll, Inventory, Project** and **Time & Billing** so that all these ✓ are removed.

Do not remove the ✓ for **General**.

WARNING!
Do not choose to hide the Accounts icon window before completing the company setup because you need to see which accounts you have already created.

basic BASIC VERSION
There is no Time & Billing module in the Basic version.

Simply Accounting has reminders about upcoming activities such as payments that are due, discounts available and recurring entries. You can choose to be reminded of these activities through the **Checklists** and the **Daily Business Manager** each time you start the program, each time you advance the session date or both. Toss for Tots does not use these lists.

Click **At Startup** for **Daily Business Manager** to **remove** the ✓.

Click **After Changing Session Date** for **Daily Business Manager**.

Click **After Changing Session Date** for **Checklists** to **remove** the ✓.

You can **Show the Company Name In the Status Bar** or omit this detail.

Automatic Advice shows advisory messages automatically while you are entering transactions, as, for example, when customers exceed credit limits or the chequing account is overdrawn. Clicking removes the ✓ and the feature. Leave Advice turned on.

You can change the design and colour of Simply Accounting windows from the **Colour Scheme** tab. You can choose backgrounds from a variety of colours and patterns for the different journal windows.

Changing the Business Tab Settings

The My Business Tab adds a Home window column with frequently used icons.

Click **My Business Tab** to see the options:

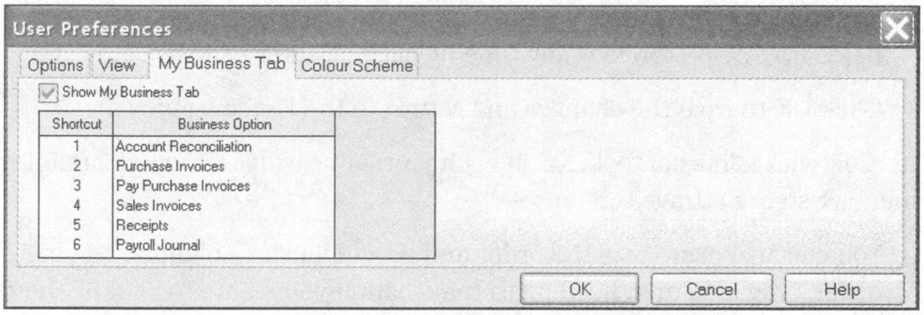

You can show or hide the tab by clicking the check box. If you show the tab, you can select the icons you want in the Business Tab window. You can select specific icons, such as Modify Account or Sales Order, to customize the tab window.

Click an entry and then click the list icon to list the ledgers and journals. Click the ⊞ beside an entry to expand the list of available icons. Click an item on the list and then click Select to add it to the My Business Tab window.

NOTES
The order of icons in the My Business Tab window is the order in the User Preferences list – the Shortcut number. To place an icon first in the window, click the first entry in the list and its list icon to begin customizing.

Toss for Tots uses only the General Journal so My Business Tab is not needed. You can browse through the options by clicking different journals and their List icons.

Click the **Show My Business Tab** to remove the ✓.

Click **OK** to save the settings and return to the Home window.

You may see a message about removing about icon position information:

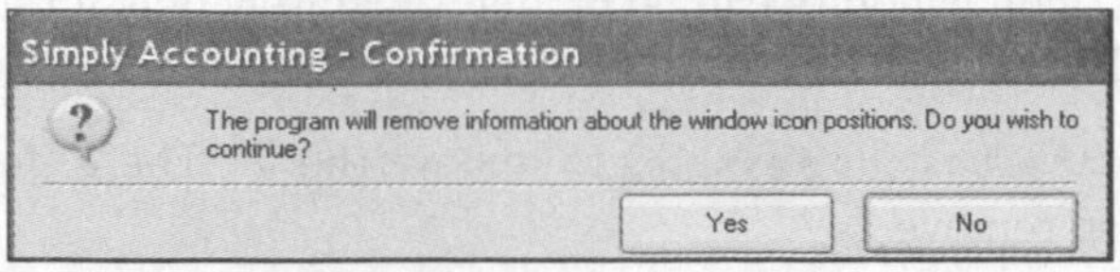

The icon windows we are not showing refer to the unused modules, so we do not need to save any information about them.

Click **Yes** to continue.

Your Home window now looks like this:

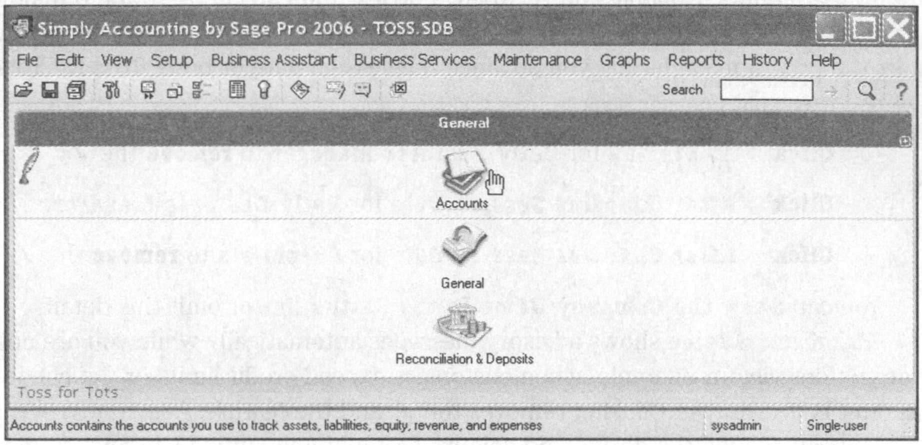

Changing View Menu Settings

Each journal has optional fields that can be hidden if they are not required by the program and the business. You can **customize all journals** from this menu or you can use the customize option within individual journals. To customize a journal,

Choose the View menu and click Customize Journals. Click the tab for the journal you want and click the columns or details you want to remove. Hidden fields may be restored at any time by clicking their names again.

Click OK to save the changes and return to the Home window.

The Customize Journal tool in each journal provides the same options as the View menu System Settings screen.

You can also customize the order and size of journal columns. To change the order, drag a column heading to the location you want. To change the column size, point to the edge of the column heading; when the pointer changes to a double headed arrow, drag the column margin to its new size.

NOTES

We have not hidden any fields in any journals used in the applications in this text, so you can see the full range of input options for each journal.

We show how to customize journals in Chapter 5 and invoices in Appendix F on the Student CD-ROM.

The next choice on the main View menu refers to the **Select Company window** that appears when you first start Simply Accounting. There are advantages to showing this window. If you regularly use the same data file, you can bypass the Open Company file window, and open your data file with a single step. Similarly, you can restore a backup file from this window without first opening another data file. The setting acts as a toggle switch, and you can change it at any time.

NOTES

You can also switch program languages from the View menu in the Home window.

The final View menu options allow you to **switch the program language** to French if you are working in English or to English when you are working in French and to **close all Simply Accounting windows** in a single step, leaving only the Home window open.

You are now ready to make the necessary changes in the General Ledger.

Preparing the Ledgers

The third stage in setting up an accounting system involves preparing each ledger for operation. For Toss for Tots, this stage involves the following steps:

1. organizing all accounting reports and records (this step has been completed)
2. modifying some existing accounts (you will not need to delete any accounts)
3. creating new accounts
4. entering historical account balance information

Defining the Skeleton Starter Files

When you created the company files for Toss for Tots in stage one, Creating Company Files (page 76), the preset startup accounts were provided.

Print the **Chart of Accounts** for the current year. The initial Skeleton Chart of Accounts is shown here:

Toss for Tots Chart of Accounts - Current Year (2008)		Account Class
Chart of Accounts - Current Year (2008)		
ASSETS		
1000 CURRENT ASSETS	H	
1020 Bank	G	Asset
1200 Accounts Receivable	G	Asset
1390 TOTAL CURRENT ASSETS	T	
LIABILITIES		
2000 CURRENT LIABILITIES	H	
2200 Accounts Payable	G	Liability
2690 TOTAL CURRENT LIABILITIES	T	
EQUITY		
3000 EARNINGS	H	
3560 Retained Earnings	G	Retained Earnings
3600 Current Earnings	X	Current Earnings
3690 TOTAL EARNINGS	T	
REVENUE		
4000 REVENUE	H	
4020 General Revenue	G	Revenue
4390 TOTAL REVENUE	T	
EXPENSE		
5000 EXPENSES	H	
5020 General Expense	G	Expense
5390 TOTAL EXPENSES	T	

Accounts are organized by **section**: Assets, Liabilities, Equity, Revenue and Expense. The chart also shows the **account type** — such as Heading (H), Subgroup total (S), Total (T), subgroup Account (A), Group account (G) and Current Earnings (X) — and the Account Class. Account type is a method of classifying and organizing accounts within a section or subsection of a report.

Initial account numbers for each account are also shown on the Chart of Accounts. The accounts in this chart follow the sectional boundaries as follows:

- 1000–1999 Assets
- 2000–2999 Liabilities
- 3000–3999 Equity
- 4000–4999 Revenue
- 5000–5999 Expense

NOTES
Print the Chart of Accounts before you begin and compare it to the Chart of Accounts for Toss for Tots. Refer to page 53 for help with printing the Chart of Accounts if necessary.

NOTES
Account classes will be explained in Chapter 9 when you set up the files for Dorfmann Design. For now you can accept the default class settings.

The Format of Financial Statements

When setting up the complete Chart of Accounts for Toss for Tots, it is important that you understand the composition and format of financial statements in Simply Accounting.

The Balance Sheet is divided into three sections, each with headings: Assets, Liabilities and Equity. The Income Statement is divided into two sections with headings: Revenue and Expense.

Each section of the financial statements can be subdivided into groups. Assets can be divided into groups such as CURRENT ASSETS, INVENTORY ASSETS and PLANT AND EQUIPMENT. Liabilities can be divided into groups titled CURRENT LIABILITIES and LONG TERM DEBT. Equity, Revenue and Expense sections can also be divided. Groups may be further divided by creating subgroups.

Simply Accounting requires that all accounts, including group headings, subgroup totals and group totals, be assigned numbers even if you do not use account numbers in transactions or reports. This is quite different from a manual accounting system, in which numbers are assigned only to postable accounts. Predefined section headings and section totals (e.g., ASSETS, TOTAL ASSETS and LIABILITIES), however, are not assigned numbers by the program.

The following chart illustrates the Simply Accounting rules for organizing accounts.

ORGANIZATION OF ACCOUNTS

BALANCE SHEET

Type	Account Description	Amount	Amount
	ASSETS [section heading]		
H	**CURRENT ASSETS**		
A	Bank: Toss for Tots	xxx	
A	Cash on Hand	xxx	
S	Total Cash		xxx
G	Surprise Bag Supplies		xxx
G	Food Supplies		xxx
	–		
	–		
T	**TOTAL CURRENT ASSETS**		**xxx**
H	**FIXED ASSETS**		
G	Fax/Telephone		xxx
G	Computer		xxx
	–		
T	**TOTAL FIXED ASSETS**		**xxx**
	TOTAL ASSETS [section total]		xxx
	LIABILITIES [section heading]		
H	**CURRENT LIABILITIES**		
G	Bank Loan		xxx
G	A/P – Designs U Wear		xxx
	–		
	–		
T	**TOTAL CURRENT LIABILITIES**		**xxx**
	TOTAL LIABILITIES [section total]		xxx
	EQUITY [section heading]		
H	**EQUITY**		
G	Surplus Funds		xxx
X	Net Income		xxx
	–		
T	**TOTAL EQUITY**		**xxx**
	TOTAL EQUITY [section total]		xxx
	LIABILITIES & EQUITY		xxx

INCOME STATEMENT

Type	Account Description	Amount	Amount
	REVENUE [section heading]		
H	**REVENUE**		
G	Revenue: Registrations		xxx
G	Revenue: Sponsors		xxx
	–		
	–		
T	**TOTAL REVENUE**		**xxx**
	TOTAL REVENUE [section total]		xxx
	EXPENSE [section heading]		
H	**ADMIN EXPENSES**		
G	Court Rental Expense		xxx
G	Office Supplies Used		xxx
	–		
	–		
T	**TOTAL ADMIN EXPENSES**		**xxx**
H	**MERCHANDISE & FOOD EXPENSES**		
G	Cost of T-shirts		xxx
G	Cost of Surprise Bags		xxx
	–		
	–		
T	**TOTAL MERCHANDISE & FOOD EXPENSES**		**xxx**
	TOTAL EXPENSE [section total]		xxx
	NET INCOME		xxx

Financial Statement Sections

The following rules apply to financial statement sections in Simply Accounting:

1. Each financial statement section described above has a **section heading** and a **section total**. You cannot change the titles for these headings and totals.

2. A **section total** is the total of the individual group totals within that section. The program will calculate section totals automatically and print them in the financial statement reports. The five section totals are

   - TOTAL ASSETS
   - TOTAL LIABILITIES
   - TOTAL EQUITY
   - TOTAL REVENUE
   - TOTAL EXPENSE

3. The Liabilities and Equity section totals are also automatically added together. **LIABILITIES AND EQUITY** is the sum of TOTAL LIABILITIES and TOTAL EQUITY.

4. In the Income Statement, **NET INCOME**, the difference between TOTAL REVENUE and TOTAL EXPENSE is automatically calculated and listed under TOTAL EXPENSE.

Financial Statement Account Groups

Financial statement sections are further divided into account groups that are made up of different types of accounts. The following rules apply to account groups in Simply Accounting:

1. Each group must start with a **group Heading (H)**, which will be printed in boldface type. A heading is not considered a postable account, cannot be debited or credited through transaction entries and cannot have an amount assigned to it.

2. Each group must contain at least one **postable account** and can contain more. Postable accounts are those that can be debited or credited through journal transaction entries. Postable accounts may have an opening balance.

3. Postable accounts may be **subgroup Accounts (A)** or **Group accounts (G)**. Subgroup account balances appear in a separate column to the left of the group account balances, which are in the right column.

4. Postable subgroup accounts must be followed by a **Subgroup total (S)** account. A subgroup total is not a postable account and cannot be given an opening balance. The program automatically calculates a subgroup total by adding all preceding subgroup postable account balances that follow the last group, subgroup total or heading account. Subgroup total balances always appear in the right column. For example, in the previous application, *GST Charged on Sales* and *GST Paid on Purchases* are subgroup accounts followed by the subgroup total *GST Owing (Refund)*. For Toss for Tots, the two cash accounts are subtotalled.

5. Each group must end with a **group Total (T)**. All accounts in the right column, both postable and subgroup total accounts, are added together to form the group total. A group total is not a postable account. The program automatically calculates this total and prints it in boldface type.

The Current Earnings (X) Account

There are two linked accounts for the General Ledger — **Retained Earnings** and **Current Earnings**. Both accounts appear under the EQUITY section in the Balance Sheet. You do not need to change the links for these accounts. Their titles will be modified later (see Editing Accounts in the General Ledger, page 96).

It is easy to identify the *Current Earnings* account because it is the only account in the Chart of Accounts whose type is X. This account is calculated as follows:

Current Earnings = Total Revenue – Total Expense

Current Earnings is not a postable account, but it appears in the right column with the group accounts. It cannot be removed, but its title and number can be modified. *Current Earnings* is updated from any transactions that change revenue and expense account balances. At the end of the fiscal period when closing routines are performed, the balance of this account is added to *Retained Earnings* (or a renamed account for *Retained Earnings*) and then reset to zero.

For Toss for Tots, a charitable organization, the *Retained Earnings* account will be renamed *Surplus Funds*. The *Current Earnings* account will be renamed *Net Income*.

Preparing the General Ledger

Compare the Skeleton Chart of Accounts you printed with the Toss for Tots Chart of Accounts, Balance Sheet and Income Statement provided in this application. You will see that some accounts are the same, and some accounts you need are not yet in the program. You have to customize the accounts specifically for Toss for Tots.

Changing the Skeleton Accounts

NOTES
You will not need to delete any of the preset accounts for Toss for Tots.

The first step, that of identifying the changes needed in the Skeleton preset accounts to match the accounts needed for Toss for Tots, is a very important one. The changes that must be made to these preset accounts are outlined below:

1. Some starter accounts provided by the program require no changes. The account title, the initial account number and the account type are the same as those in the financial statements. Those accounts not requiring changes follow:

CURRENT ASSETS	1000	Type H
TOTAL CURRENT ASSETS	1390	Type T
CURRENT LIABILITIES	2000	Type H
TOTAL CURRENT LIABILITIES	2690	Type T
REVENUE	4000	Type H
TOTAL REVENUE	4390	Type T

2. The following accounts have account titles that need to be changed. You must also change the account type for *Bank 1020*. (Account numbers are correct.)

FROM (SKELETON ACCOUNTS)			TO (TOSS FOR TOTS ACCOUNTS)
Account Name	Number	Type	Account Name (Type)
Bank	1020	Type G	Bank: Toss for Tots (Type A)
Accounts Receivable	1200	Type G	Surprise Bag Supplies
Accounts Payable	2200	Type G	A/P - Designs U Wear
EARNINGS	3000	Type H	EQUITY
Retained Earnings	3560	Type G	Surplus Funds
Current Earnings	3600	Type X	Net Income
TOTAL EARNINGS	3690	Type T	TOTAL EQUITY
General Revenue	4020	Type G	Revenue: Registrations
EXPENSES	5000	Type H	ADMIN EXPENSES
General Expense	5020	Type G	Court Rental Expense

3. The following account requires changes in both the account title and the number:

FROM (SKELETON ACCOUNTS)			TO (TOSS FOR TOTS ACCOUNTS)	
Account Name	Number	Type	Account Name	Number
TOTAL EXPENSES	5390	Type T	TOTAL ADMIN EXPENSES	5440

Creating the Chart of Accounts

After identifying the modifications that must be made to the Skeleton accounts, the next step is to identify the accounts that you need to create or add to the preset accounts. Again, you should refer to the company Chart of Accounts on page 73 to complete this step.

The chart that follows shows the accounts that you will need to create. The chart includes account titles, account numbers, account types and the option to omit printing zero balances. It lists both postable (group and subgroup) and non-postable accounts (subgroup totals, group headings and group totals).

CHART OF ACCOUNTS TO BE CREATED

Account: Number	Description	Type	Omit	GIFI	Allocate
1100	Cash on Hand	A	No	NA	No
1150	Total Cash	S			
1300	Food Supplies	G	Yes	NA	No
1320	Office Supplies	G	Yes	NA	No
1360	T-shirts	G	Yes	NA	No
1400	FIXED ASSETS	H			
1420	Fax/Telephone	G	Yes	NA	No
1450	Computer	G	No	NA	No
1500	Digital Camera	G	No	NA	No
1590	TOTAL FIXED ASSETS	T			
2100	Bank Loan	G	Yes	NA	No
2300	A/P - Quiq Kopy	G	Yes	NA	No
2350	A/P - Central College	G	Yes	NA	No
2400	A/P - Snack City	G	Yes	NA	No
2670	GST Paid on Purchases	G	Yes	NA	No
4040	Revenue: Sponsors	G	No	NA	No
4080	Revenue: Surprise Bags	G	No	NA	No
4100	Revenue: Admissions	G	No	NA	No
4120	Revenue: Food Sales	G	No	NA	No
5200	Office Supplies Used	G	Yes	NA	No
5220	Non-refundable GST	G	Yes	NA	No
5240	Postage Expense	G	Yes	NA	No
5280	Printing & Copying	G	Yes	NA	No
5300	Publicity & Promotion	G	Yes	NA	No
5320	Telephone Expense	G	Yes	NA	No
5400	Wages - Manager	G	Yes	NA	No
5420	Miscellaneous Expenses	G	Yes	NA	No
5450	MERCHANDISE & FOOD EXPENSES	H			
5500	Cost of T-shirts	G	Yes	NA	No
5520	Cost of Surprise Bags	G	Yes	NA	No
5550	Cost of Food	G	Yes	NA	No
5690	TOTAL MERCHANDISE & FOOD EXPENSES	T			

Account Types: A = Subgroup Account S = Subgroup Total G = Group Account H = Heading T = Group Total

You are now ready to enter the account information into the Toss for Tots files.

Entering General Ledger Accounts

We can make all ledger account record–related changes from the Accounts 

icon or we can expand the General Module to display icons for each activity separately.

The module heading, 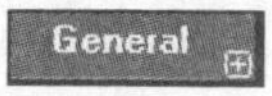

, as shown here, is used to expand the module:

Click the **General Module heading** 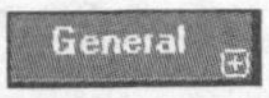

to open the module window:

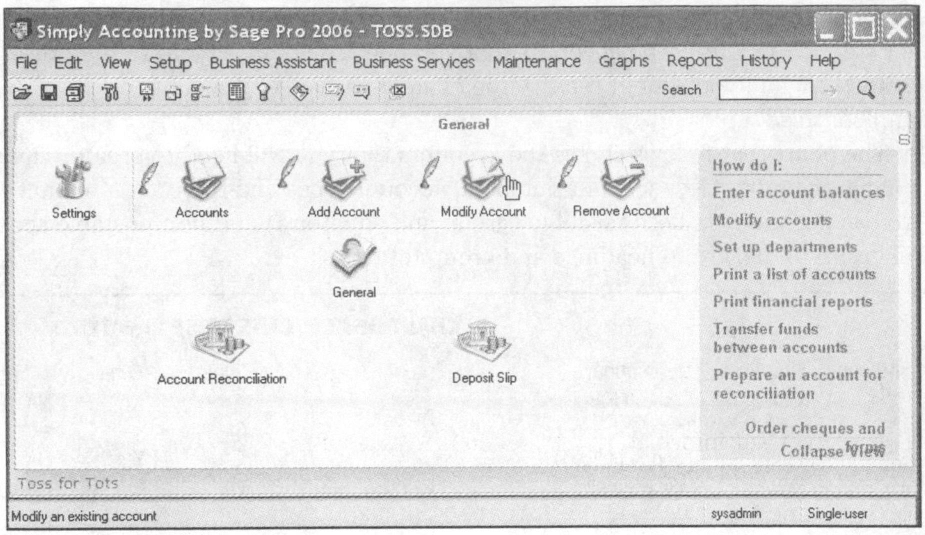

The boxed sign in the module heading changes from + to – and the heading bar changes colour. Clicking the heading again will restore the Home window view.

You can see that there are now several ledger icons as well as the two journal icons. Each one serves a specific purpose as described by its label.

Editing Accounts in the General Ledger

We will change the first account that requires editing, *1020 Bank*. To modify accounts, use the Modify Account icon.

Click the **Modify Account icon** 

to open the Search window:

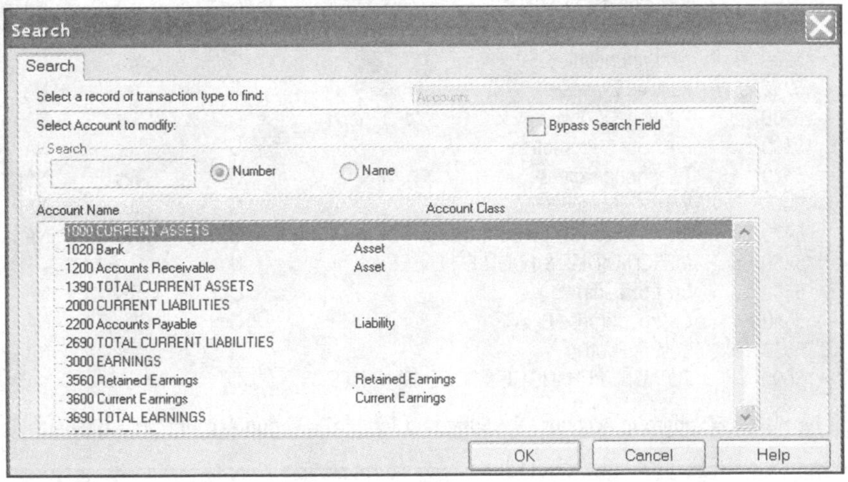

NOTES

You can advance to a later part of the account list by typing the first number in the Search field. You can also search by Description, the name of the account, by choosing this option.

This Search screen is like the one in the General Journal that opens the Adjust Entry feature.

Click **1020 Bank** to highlight or select it.

Click **OK** or double click the account's name to open the account and display its information as shown:

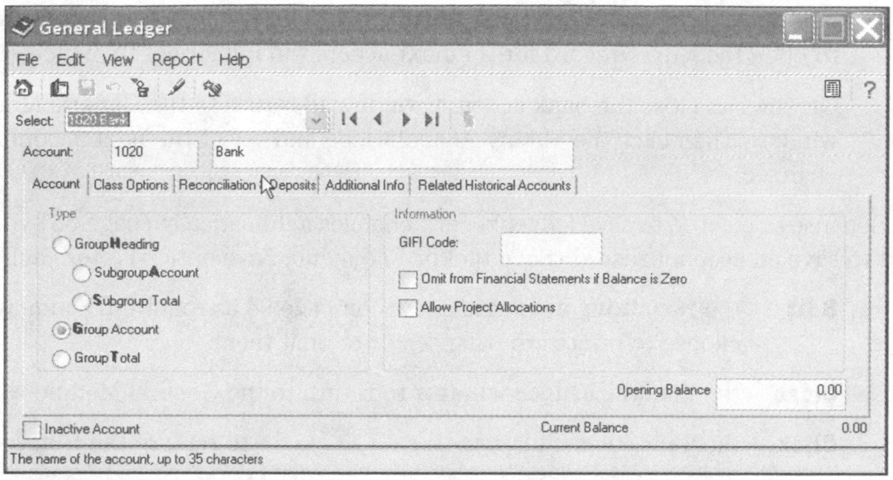

The Account information tab screen is displayed. We use this screen to edit the account name and type. For the bank account, the account number is correct.

Sometimes, it may be appropriate to print an account with a zero balance, although zero balance accounts usually do not need to be printed. In Simply Accounting, you have the option to omit accounts with zero balances from financial statements. You may select this option in the General Ledger.

The balance of bank accounts should always be displayed, so do not select Omit From Financial Statements If Balance Is Zero.

Press tab **twice** to advance to the name of the account and highlight it.

Type `Bank: Toss for Tots`

We are not using GIFI codes (Canada Revenue Agency's account numbering system for electronic report filing) or project allocations, so we can leave these fields empty. The current balance is displayed, but you cannot edit it. It is updated when you enter an opening balance and journal entries. The opening account balance will be added later (see Entering Historical Account Balances). There is no additional account information. We are not using Account Reconciliation, and we do not need to change the account class, so we can skip these tab screens. On the Related Historical Accounts tab screen you can enter the relationship between different account numbers that are used for the same account in multiple fiscal periods. They do not apply here.

Click **Subgroup Account** to change the account type.

The two cash accounts together will be subtotalled. You can now advance to the next account for editing. There are different ways to do this.

Click the **Select field list arrow** to show the list of all accounts as shown:

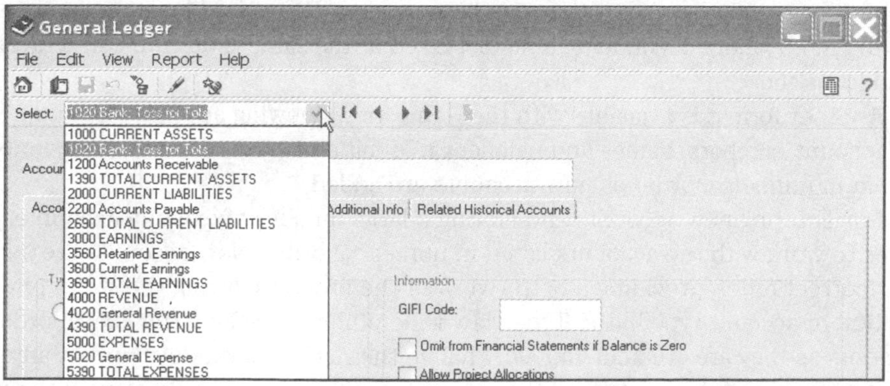

Click **1200 Accounts Receivable** to display the ledger record.

basic BASIC VERSION

The Basic version does not have the Related Historical Accounts tab or the Refresh tool.

NOTES

If you choose to skip the Accounts icon window from the View menu, you will see the General Ledger window for CURRENT ASSETS, the first account, when you click the Home window Accounts icon. You can use the Select field drop-down list of accounts to find the Bank account.

To open a different ledger record, you can also click the Next Account tool to open the ledger record for the next account in numerical sequence.

Or, you can close the bank account window to return to the General Module window. Then click the Modify Account icon and select the next account to be changed.

NOTES
If you close the bank account ledger window, you will return to the General Module window.

Because you chose to save ledger record changes automatically (page 88) you do not need to save an account record (Save tool or File menu, Save option) after each change.

Edit the **remaining accounts** shown on page 94 as required. You may choose to print zero balances or to omit them.

Close the **General Ledger window** to return to the General Module window.

Click the **General Module heading** General to restore the Home window.

The Accounts Window

Click the **Accounts icon** Accounts under the General heading in the Home window to open the main Accounts window:

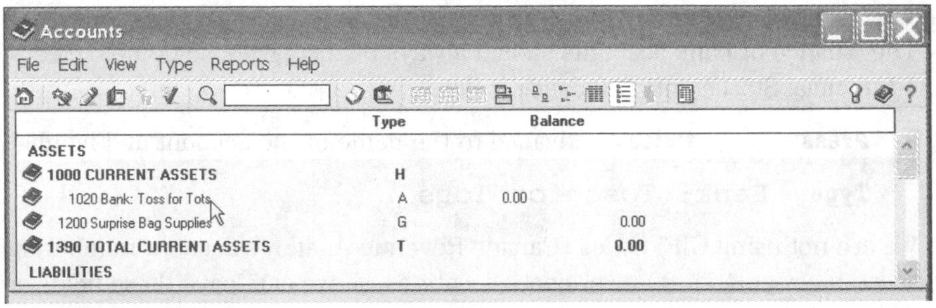

From this window, you can perform all ledger account–related activities as well. The tool buttons and menu options give access to the individual ledger records, and you can modify, delete, add records and so on.

Click the Maximize button so that the Accounts window fills the screen. This will allow you to display more accounts and keep the Accounts window in view in the background while you are creating or editing accounts. To return the window to normal size, click , the Restore button.

The preset accounts should be displayed in the **Type** format shown above. You can also show the Accounts window in the **Icon** format with icons representing each account. In the Icon view, you can rearrange icons by dragging so that frequently used accounts appear at the top for easier access. New accounts are automatically added at the bottom of the screen, but they can be moved to the desired location. In small icon viewing mode, more accounts can be displayed at the same time. You can rearrange the small icons too.

Another format is available with the **Name** view. Viewing accounts by name shows the account numbers, names and balances in debit and credit columns. Accounts remain in numerical order as new accounts are added.

NOTES
To edit an account from the Accounts window, double click the account you want to change; or click the account to select it and then click the Edit tool or choose the Edit menu and click Edit.

For entering new accounts and editing a large number of existing accounts, it is easier to work with the accounts listed in numerical order. New accounts are inserted in their correct order, providing a better view of the progress during the setup phase. The addition of account type in the Type view is helpful for checking the logical order of accounts as they are created. You can change the Accounts window view at any time.

If your screen does not show the accounts by Type, you should change the way accounts are displayed.

Click the **Display By Type button** or **choose** the **View menu** and **click Type**.

When others are using the same data file, you can click the **Refresh tool** to update your data file with changes that other users have made to accounts.

We can also check that the accounts are in proper sequence, that is, they follow the rules outlined on pages 92–93.

Click the **Check Validity Of Accounts tool** or **choose** the **Edit menu** and **click Check The Validity Of Accounts** to see the message:

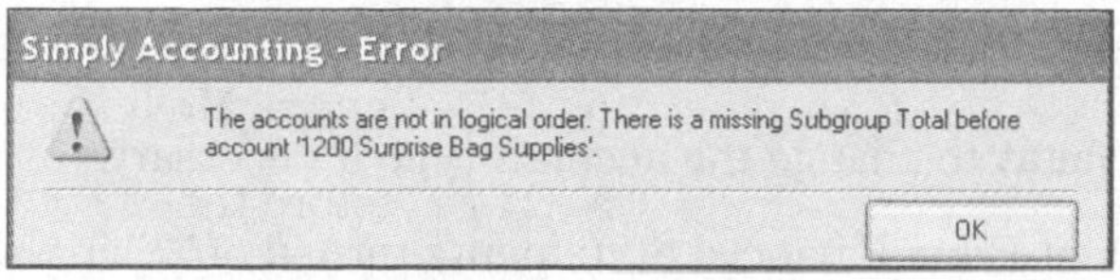

Simply Accounting - Error
The accounts are not in logical order. There is a missing Subgroup Total before account '1200 Surprise Bag Supplies'.
OK

Without the second subgroup account and subgroup total, we have not followed the rules for Groups (page 93, rule 4). The accounts are not in logical order. You can periodically check the validity of accounts while you are adding accounts to see whether you have made errors in your account type sequence that will prevent you from finishing the account history. When we add the remaining accounts, the accounts should be in logical order and the error will be corrected.

Click **OK** to return to the Accounts window.

***basic* BASIC VERSION**
You will not see the Refresh tool.

NOTES
Only one error is listed, the first one encountered in checking the Chart of Accounts for validity of account order. After you correct the first error, the second error will be listed, if there is one.

Creating New Accounts in the General Ledger

You are now ready to enter the information for the first new account, *Cash on Hand*, using the chart on page 95 as your reference. The following keystrokes will enter the account title, number, type and option to include or omit zero balance accounts.

We are entering new accounts from the Accounts window, and it should still be open.

Click the **Create tool** on the Accounts window tool bar or **choose** the **File menu** and **click Create** to display the new account window:

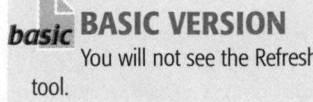

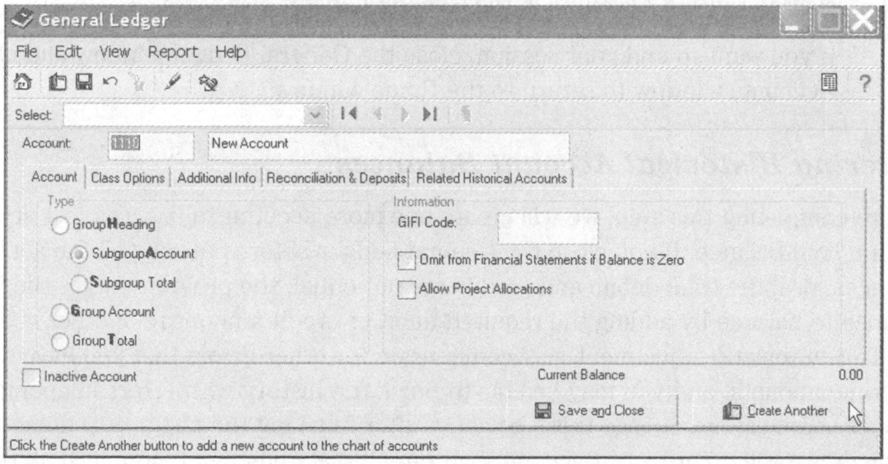

NOTES
You can also press ctrl + N to open a new account ledger form from the Accounts window or from any account's General Ledger window.

The tabs that appear in the ledger depend on the account section as defined by the account number. If no number is entered initially, only the tabs that apply to all accounts appear. We will create the first account that was not in the Skeleton Chart of Accounts, *Cash on Hand*. The account type is selected as the most likely option for logical account order. The default account type depends on the account record you used most recently. For example, group total accounts are often followed by a group

NOTES
Because an Asset account number is entered initially, the Reconciliation & Deposits tab is added.

account. The cursor is in the Account number field. The Simply Accounting program will not allow duplicate account numbers.

Simply Accounting may enter an account number and type that is the most likely next entry based on the previous selection. After the error message, account 1200 is selected in the Accounts window so that you can correct the error. Its preceding account is a Subgroup account so it is most likely that another Subgroup account will follow it. The account number will be selected for editing.

NOTES
Depending on your previous step or cursor position, your initial account number and type may be different from the ones we show.

Type 1100

Press tab to advance to the Account name field and highlight the selection.

Type Cash on Hand

Click **Subgroup Account** to change the account type if necessary.

Leave the option to Omit From Financial Statements turned off. Skip the GIFI field and the Project Allocations check box.

Check your work. **Make** any necessary **corrections** by pressing tab to return to the incorrect field, typing the correct information and pressing tab if necessary.

When the information has been entered correctly, save your work.

NOTES
Simply Accounting enters an Account Class automatically (Class Options tab screen). For most accounts, the section heading is used (Assets, Liabilities and so on). For Expense accounts, the default class is Cost of Goods Sold. This selection will not affect the financial statements for Toss for Tots so you can leave it. If you want, you can change the class on the Class Options screen by choosing Expense for these accounts.
Account class will be introduced in Chapter 9.

Click **Create Another** [Create Another] to save the new account and to advance to another new account information window.

Create the **remaining accounts** from page 95.

Remember that subgroup totals, group headings and group totals — the non-postable accounts — will have the Balance fields removed when you choose these account types.

Click **Save And Close** [Save and Close] to save the final account.

Display or **print** the **Chart of Accounts** to check the accuracy of your work.

If you find mistakes, edit the account information as described above in the section Editing Accounts in the General Ledger.

If you want to end your session, close the General Ledger window and close the Accounts window to return to the Home window.

Entering Historical Account Balances

Before completing this step, we will create one more account to use as a test account for our Trial Balance. If you close the General Ledger before entering all the account balances, or if the total debits and credits are not equal, the program forces the Trial Balance to balance by adding the required debit or credit amount to another account.

This automatic adjustment may compensate for other errors that you have made in entering amounts, and you may be able to finish the history with errors in opening balances. You cannot change these balances after finishing the history. To detect this problem, we will create a test account and put all the adjustments into it. If all the balances are entered correctly, the test account will have a zero balance and we can remove the account.

Create the new Group account **1005 Test Account**.

You are now ready to enter the opening historical account balances for all postable (type G or A) accounts. The opening balances for Toss for Tots can be found in the Trial

Balance on page 75. Accounts with zero balances are not included in the Trial Balance. You should skip these accounts when entering account balances.

Click the **Select field** list arrow and **choose 1020 Bank: Toss for Tots**. The ledger window opens:

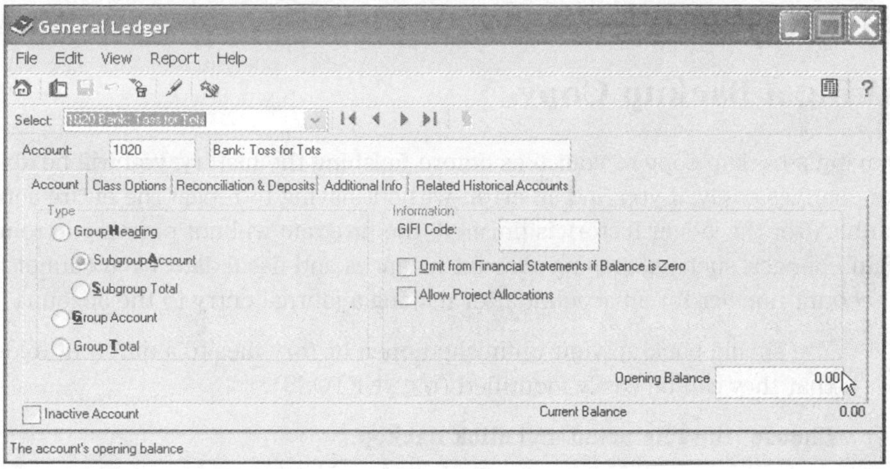

Click the **Opening Balance field** to highlight it.

Type 18550

The Current Balance field is updated but it remains dimmed. Simply Accounting updates this balance automatically from journal entries.

Click the **Next tool** ▶ to advance to the next ledger account window.

Enter the **balances** for the remaining accounts. Remember that *GST Paid on Purchases* has a debit balance (add a minus sign).

If you close the General Ledger window before entering all the account balances, you will see a screen like the following:

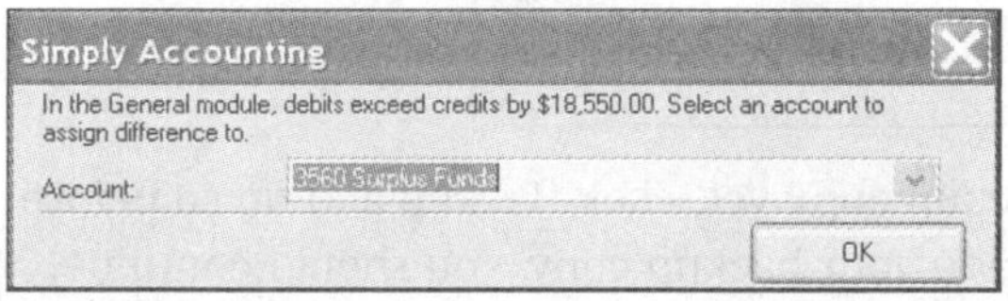

The message asks you to choose an account for the difference — an adjusting, balancing entry that will place the Trial Balance in balance. Choose *Test Account* from the drop-down list of accounts. You can choose any account from the drop-down list or accept the default. If you see this warning,

Choose account 1005 Test Account from the drop-down list.

Click OK to continue.

After entering all the accounts and balances,

Close the **Ledger window** to return to the Accounts window.

Display or **print** the **Trial Balance**, **Balance Sheet** and **Income Statement** to check the accuracy of your work.

Choose the **Reports menu** in the Accounts window and **click Trial Balance** (or Balance Sheet or Income Statement).

Check all your **opening balances** carefully before finishing the history.

Close the **Accounts window** to return to the Home window.

WARNING!
Before you finish the history, the opening balance can be edited. The Current Balance has no data input field because you cannot edit it. Initially, it is the same as the opening balance but it changes when you add journal entries. Because you can enter journal transactions before finishing the history, this distinction is very important. The balance in the Accounts window is the current balance, which may not be the same as the opening balance.

WARNING!
Remember to enter the amount for GST Paid on Purchases with a minus sign to create a debit entry.

Compare your reports with the information on pages 73–75 to be sure that all account numbers, names and balances are correct. The balance for *Test Account* should be zero. Make corrections if necessary.

Finishing the General Ledger History

Making a Backup Copy

WARNING! Back up the not-finished Toss for Tots files before proceeding. See Chapter 3 if you need further assistance.

WARNING! You can change account numbers only after two fiscal periods have passed if the account was used in journal entries.

By having a backup copy of your files before finishing the history, you will be able to make changes easily, if you find an error, without having to repeat the entire setup from scratch. After the ledger history is finished, the program will not permit you to make certain changes, such as opening account balances and fiscal dates. You cannot change the account number for an account after making a journal entry to the account.

You should back up your unfinished open history files to a different folder so that they can be easily identified (e.g., NFTOSS).

Choose the **File menu** and **click Backup**.

Create a **backup copy** by following the instructions. Refer to pages 20 and 46 if you need help.

Finishing the General Ledger History

WARNING! You can finish entering the history when the Trial Balance is in balance. Afterwards, you cannot change opening balances, even if they are incorrect. You will need to make adjusting entries. Simply Accounting always keeps the Trial Balance balanced. Therefore, checking for a zero balance in the Test Account can stop you from proceeding with incorrect account balances.

You should be in the Home window.

Choose the **History menu** and **click Finish Entering History**.

The following caution appears:

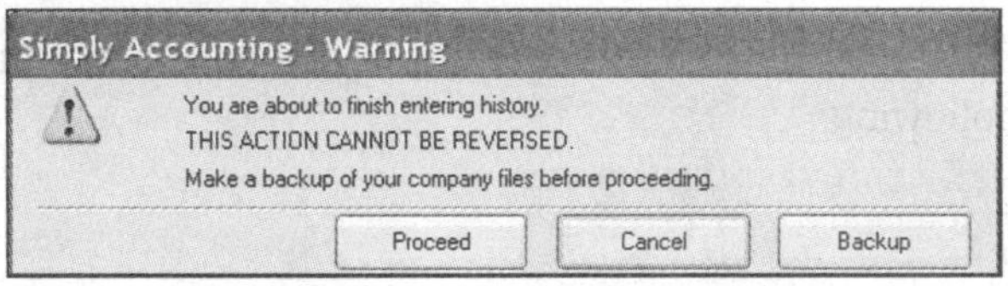

If you have not made a backup copy yet, click Backup and do so before proceeding. If you have made your backup copy, you should continue.

Click Proceed.

If you see a different screen at this stage, like the following one, you have errors that must be corrected before you can continue:

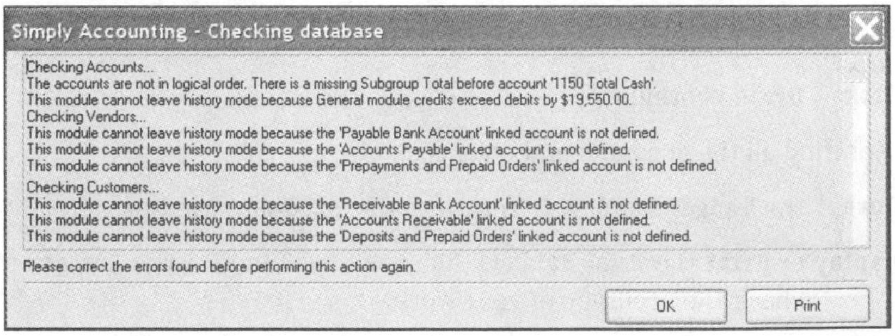

The message describes the mistakes you must correct.

Print the message and read it carefully so you can make corrections. Click OK to return to the Home window. Make the necessary corrections and then try again to finish the history.

If your accounts are out of order, you cannot finish entering the history. If you did not hide the unused modules, you cannot finish entering the history because some essential linked accounts for these modules are not defined. Read the error description carefully, make corrections and try again.

Notice that the open or not-finished history symbol, the quill pen, has been removed from the General Ledger Accounts icon.

You can now exit the program or continue by entering the source documents. Remember to advance the Session Date. Enter all transactions for Toss for Tots in the General Journal.

SOURCE DOCUMENTS

SESSION DATE – JULY 7, 2008

Purchase Invoice #QK-2252 **Dated July 2/08**

From Quiq Kopy, $216 (including PST) plus $14 GST for photocopying registration and donation forms. Invoice total $230. Terms: net 25 days.

Purchase Invoice #BC-10116 **Dated July 2/08**

From Bell Canada, $324 (including PST) plus $21 GST for rental of cellular telephone equipment. Invoice total $345. Deposit required and balance due at end of month or rental period. Create new Group account 2140 A/P - Bell Canada.

Cheque Copy #167 **Dated July 2/08**

To Bell Canada, $100 deposit on rental of telephone equipment. Reference invoice #BC-10116.

Memo #1 **Dated July 2/08**

From Event Manager: Give T-shirts to volunteers. Cost of T-shirts given out is $120. Reduce T-shirt asset account and increase Cost of T-shirts expense account.

Memo #2 **Dated July 4/08**

From Event Manager: Issue cheque #168 for $1 500 to transfer funds to Cash on Hand for snack purchases for the first weekend.

Cash Purchase Invoice #SC-2168 **Dated July 4/08**

From Snack City, $2 160 (including PST) plus $140 GST for drinks and snacks for participants. Invoice total $2 300 paid from Cash on Hand.

Funds Raised Form #FR-08-7 **Dated July 6/08**

Cash and cheques received on first weekend of event. Create new revenue account 4160 Revenue: T-shirt Sales.

Participant registrations	$18 000
Sale of snack foods and drinks	1 250
Sale of T-shirts	580

Total $19 830 deposited in Bank: Toss for Tots.

NOTES

You can now unhide the unused modules, but you do not need to do so. If you want to set them up later, you must first unhide them.

NOTES

You do not enter PST paid as a separate amount because PST is not refundable. Therefore, we have already included it in the asset or expense amounts.

NOTES

In most businesses, the Cash on Hand balance is usually small and is used only for paying small amounts. In this application, we are using the Cash on Hand account to pay for any purchases that normally would require cash or credit card payments. The Event Manager receives cash advances to cover these costs.

SESSION DATE – JULY 14, 2008

Purchase Invoice #DW-9493 **Dated July 8/08**

From Designs U Wear, $1 188 (including PST) plus $77 GST for T-shirts to sell to spectators at tournament. Invoice total $1 265. Terms: net 20 days.

Memo #3 **Dated July 11/08**

From Event Manager: Issue cheque #169 for $1 800 to transfer funds to Cash on Hand for food purchases and other expenses for the weekend.

Cheque Copy #170 **Dated July 13/08**

To Central College, $10 700 in full payment of account for the balance owing on court rental. Reference invoice #CC-47221.

Funds Raised Form #FR-08-8 **Dated July 13/08**

Cash and cheques received on second weekend of event.

Participant registrations	$12 000
Sale of snack foods and drinks	2 250
Sale of T-shirts	420
Sale of surprise bags	560

Total $15 230 deposited in Bank: Toss for Tots.

Cash Purchase Invoice #QAS-4632 **Dated July 14/08**

From Quarts Arts Supplies, $108 (including PST) plus $7 GST for bristol board and paint supplies to make signs in gymnasiums. Invoice total $115. Paid from Cash on Hand. (Debit Office Supplies account.)

SESSION DATE – JULY 21, 2008

Cheque Copy #171 **Dated July 15/08**

To Designs U Wear, $800 in payment of account. Reference invoice #DW-6299.

Cash Purchase Invoice #SC-5217 **Dated July 16/08**

From Snack City, $972 (including PST) plus $63 GST paid for snacks to sell at tournament. Invoice total $1 035 paid from Cash on Hand.

Purchase Invoice #QK-5306 **Dated July 18/08**

From Quiq Kopy, $540 (including PST) plus $35 GST for printing cancer information leaflets for participants and spectators. Invoice total $575. Terms: net 25 days.

Funds Raised Form #FR-08-9 **Dated July 20/08**

Cash and cheques received on third weekend of event, the first weekend of the tournament. Create new revenue account 4180 Revenue: Photos.

Spectator admissions	$4 330
Sale of snack foods and drinks	2 340
Sale of T-shirts	830
Sale of surprise bags	780
Sale of participant photos	1 540

Total $9 820 deposited in Bank: Toss for Tots.

Funds Raised Form #FR-08-10 **Dated July 20/08**

Record $30 200 in pledges to sponsor participants from sponsor forms submitted. Create new asset account 1180 Donations Receivable. (Credit Revenue: Sponsors.)

Cash Purchase Invoice #PH-34982 **Dated July 20/08**

From Pizza House, $270 (including PST) plus $17.50 GST for pizza and soft drinks for volunteers. Invoice total $287.50. Paid from Cash on Hand.

NOTES
Charge pizza expense to Miscellaneous Expenses.

SESSION DATE – JULY 28, 2008

Funds Raised Form #FR-08-11 **Dated July 27/08**

Cash and cheques received on final weekend of tournament.

Spectator admissions	$6 830
Sale of snack foods and drinks	4 340
Sale of T-shirts	1 670
Sale of surprise bags	970
Sale of participant photos	2 360

Total $16 170 deposited in Bank: Toss for Tots.

Funds Raised Form #FR-08-12 **Dated July 27/08**

Record $80 500 in pledges to sponsor participants from sponsor forms submitted by participants. (Debit Donations Receivable.)

Cash Purchase Invoice #PH-39168 **Dated July 27/08**

From Pizza House, $345.60 (including PST) plus $22.40 GST for pizza and soft drinks for volunteers to celebrate successful tournament. Invoice total $368. Paid from Cash on Hand.

Memo #4 **Dated July 27/08**

From Event Manager: Enter adjustments for merchandise sold at tournament. Reduce the appropriate asset account and increase the related expense account for the following amounts:

Cost of the T-shirts sold	$1 750
Cost of snack food items sold	4 230
Cost of surprise bag items sold	500

NOTES
The cost of donated items is not included in these costs.

Cheque Copy #172 **Dated July 28/08**

To Marcie Gillcrest, manager, $2 000 for wages for month.

Cheque Copy #173 **Dated July 28/08**

To Sunni Husein, $1 000 for winning tournament. Create new Group account 5430 Tournament Prizes.

SESSION DATE – JULY 31, 2008

Cheque Copy #174 **Dated July 29/08**

To Designs U Wear $1 265 in payment of account. Reference invoice #DW-9493.

Cheque Copy #175 **Dated July 31/08**

To Quiq Kopy, $955 in full payment of account. Reference invoices #QK-5306, QK-2252 and previous balance owing.

Cheque Copy #176 **Dated July 31/08**

To Bell Canada, $245 in full payment of account. Reference invoice #BC-10116 and cheque #167.

☑ **Cheque Copy #177** **Dated July 31/08**

To Snack City, $900 in full payment of account. Reference invoice #SC-1005.

☑ **Memo #5** **Dated July 31/08**

From Manager: Issue cheque #178 for $500 to transfer funds to Cash on Hand to purchase postage for mailing charitable donation receipts.

☑ **Bank Debit Memo #TDCT-3881** **Dated July 31/08**

From TD-Canada Trust, $21.50 in bank charges for cheques and statement preparation. Create new Group account 5010 Bank Charges.

☑ **Memo #6** **Dated July 31/08**

From Event Manager: Apply for GST rebate of $1 173.45. Record 50% of GST Paid on Purchases as GST Refund Receivable, and 50% as the Non-refundable GST expense. Create new Group account 1190 GST Refund Receivable. (Refer to Accounting Procedures on page 75.)

☑ **Funds Raised Form #FR-08-13** **Dated July 31/08**

Received $92 300 from sponsors for pledges previously recorded. Amount deposited in bank account. (Credit 1180 Donations Receivable.)

SESSION DATE – AUGUST 31, 2008

☑ **Funds Received Form FR-08-14** **Dated August 31/08**

107 Received $18 400 from sponsors for pledges previously recorded. Amount deposited in bank account.

☑ **Cash Purchase Invoice #CP-2** **Dated August 31/08**

From Canada Post, $500 plus $35 GST for postage to mail receipts. Invoice total $535. Paid from Cash on Hand.

☑ **Memo #7** **Dated August 31/08**

From Event Manager: Deposit $159.50, balance of Cash on Hand to bank.

☑ **Bank Debit Memo #TDCT-5218** **Dated August 31/08**

From TD-Canada Trust, withdraw $15 400 from chequing account to repay loan for $15 000 plus $400 interest. Create new Group account 5100 Interest Expense.

SESSION DATE – SEPTEMBER 30, 2008

☑ **Memo #8** **Dated September 30/08**

107 From Event Manager: Small quantities of supplies were left at the end of the tournament. Leftover food supplies and T-shirts have been donated to homeless shelters; craft and some office supplies have been donated to the College's Day Care Centre. Reduce the following asset accounts and increase the corresponding expense accounts to reflect supplies used during tournament:

- Reduce T-shirts and increase Cost of T-shirts by $118
- Reduce Food Supplies and increase Cost of Food by $102
- Reduce Office Supplies and increase Office Supplies Used by $580

☑ **Cash Purchase Invoice #BC-32423** **Dated September 30/08**

From Bell Canada, $129.60 including PST plus $8.40 GST for telephone service for two months. Invoice total $138 paid in full by cheque #179.

☑ **Memo #9** **Dated September 30/08**

108 All accounts for the event are settled so the books can be closed. Make a backup of the data files. Start a new fiscal period to close the books. (See Keystrokes following the next source document.)

☑ **Memo #10** **Dated September 30/08**

110 Received cheque #488129 for $1 173.45 from the Receiver General for GST rebate. We forgot to make the entry before closing the books.

KEYSTROKES FOR CLOSING

Ending a Fiscal Period

When you change the session date to August 31, you will see the following warning:

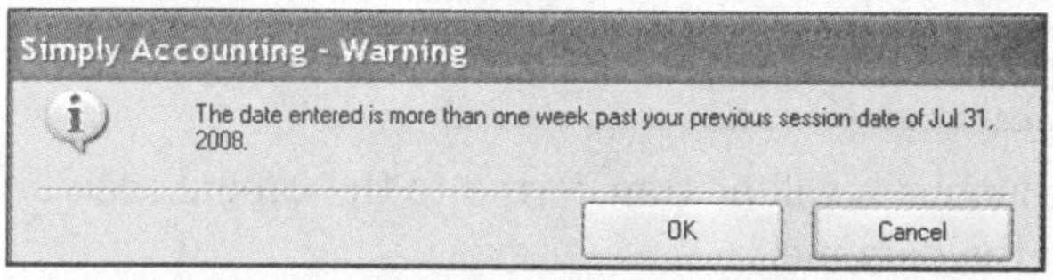

Normally a business would advance the session date by a shorter period so the warning helps you to avoid entering the wrong session date.

Click **OK** to confirm that you entered the date you intended.

You will see another warning that Simply Accounting displays about one month before the end of the fiscal period:

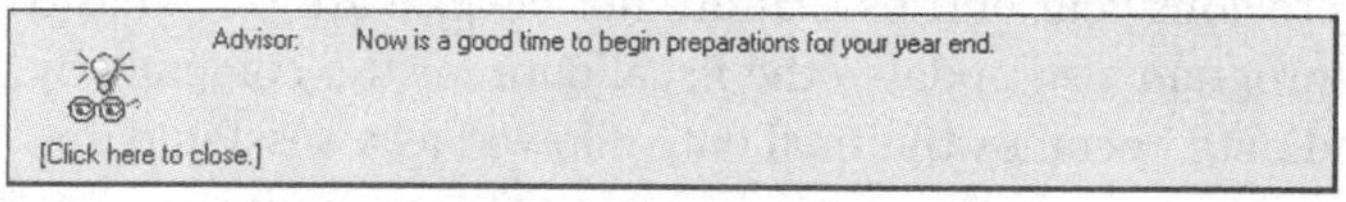

Close the **advisor** to continue with the transactions for August 31.

Closing Adjusting Entries

When you advance the session date further to a date very close to the end of the fiscal period, September 30 in this case, you receive another warning about the types of adjusting entries required at the end of the year:

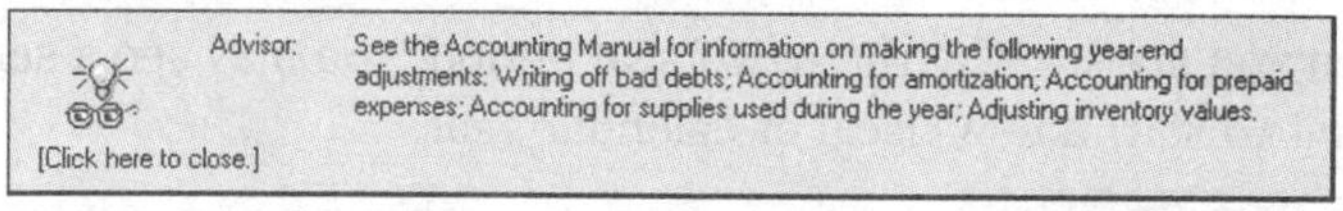

Close the **advisor window**. Continue with the transactions for September 30.

The required adjusting entries are listed for September 30 with the source documents. For Toss for Tots, these are the adjustments for remaining supplies. For other businesses, adjusting entries include depreciation entries, inventory adjustments, adjustments for prepaid expenses that have expired, accrued wages and so on. Most adjusting entries do not have an external source document that reminds you to complete them, and most of them are General Journal entries.

Print all the **financial reports** for Toss for Tots for September 30, 2008.

WARNING! You should advance to the new fiscal period in two steps. First advance to the last day of the current fiscal period and then advance to the first day of the new fiscal period. This control feature prevents you from advancing by mistake and losing important data or forgetting year-end adjusting entries.

> **NOTES**
> If the history is not finished when you choose to start a new fiscal year, the program will ask if you have finished entering the history and give you a chance to do so. You must finish the history before you can start a new fiscal period.

> **NOTES**
> You cannot start a new fiscal period in multi-user mode.

> **WARNING!**
> Initially, from the last day of the fiscal period, you cannot advance the session date past October 1, the first day of the new fiscal period.

Starting a New Fiscal Period

There are two methods for beginning a new fiscal year. The first is the method we have been using to change the session date.

Choose the **Maintenance menu** and **click Change Session Date**.

The first date of the new fiscal period is always on the drop-down list of dates in the Session Date window. The program will not accept any dates later than October 1, 2008.

Type `October 1, 2008` or choose this date from the date field list.

Click **OK**.

Because this step is not reversible, you will see a warning:

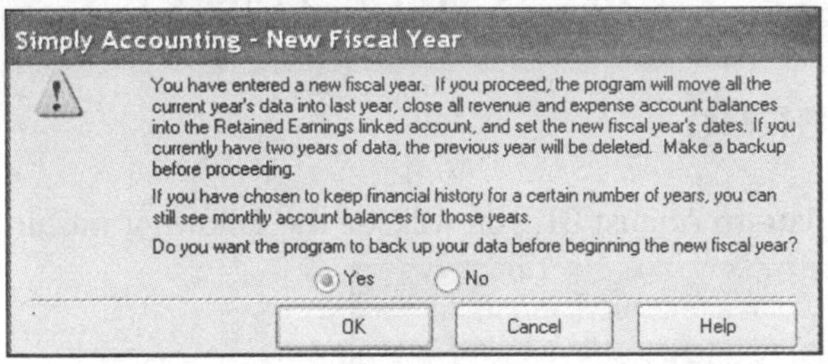

The expense and revenue amounts will be transferred to the capital account but historical data will be saved in the data file.

Read the **warning** carefully.

The warning describes the changes about to take place in the data set. All revenue and expense accounts are reset to zero at the start of the new fiscal year. Their balances are closed out to the linked *Surplus Funds (Retained Earnings)* account, and the linked *Net Income (Current Earnings)* account is reset to zero to begin a new income statement. All previous year entries that are not cleared are stored as data for the previous year. The program also updates the fiscal date for the company by one year. The new fiscal end date becomes the final date allowed as a session date.

At this stage you can choose to back up the data files, continue with the date change or cancel the date change by clicking No.

Click **Cancel** to return to the Session Date window and then **click Cancel** again to close the Change Session Date screen. We will use the second method to change to a new fiscal year.

Choose the **Maintenance menu** and **click Start New Year**.

Depending on when you are starting the new fiscal period, you may see a screen asking whether you want to start a new fiscal or calendar year:

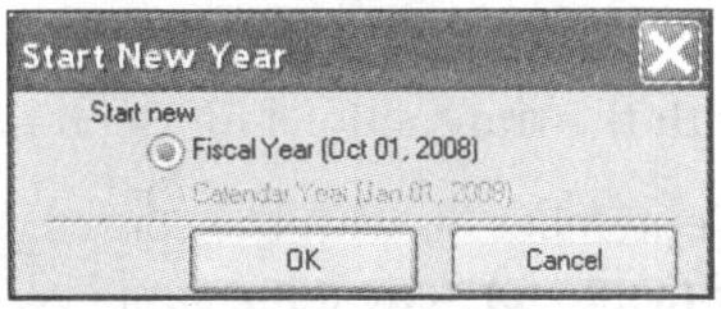

The default will be the period that starts first. Make your choice and click OK to continue. Start New Fiscal Year is correctly selected.

Click **OK** to continue.

You will see a warning similar to the one near the top of this page:

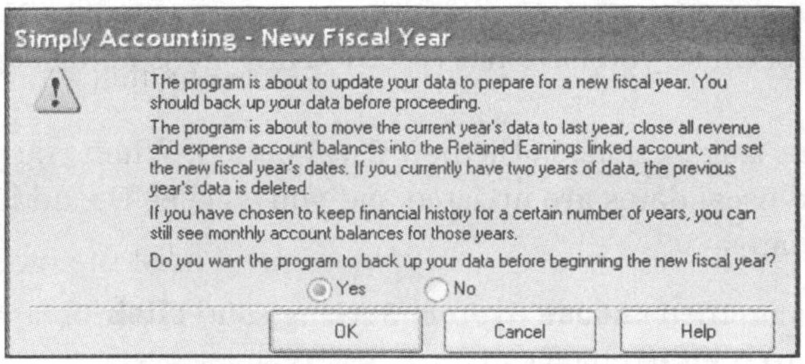

The default setting is to make a backup before continuing. If you have not yet made a backup, do so now. If you do not want to begin a new year, you can click Cancel and the old dates will remain in effect.

Click **No** because you have already backed up your files.

Click **OK** to begin the new fiscal period.

You will now see another warning:

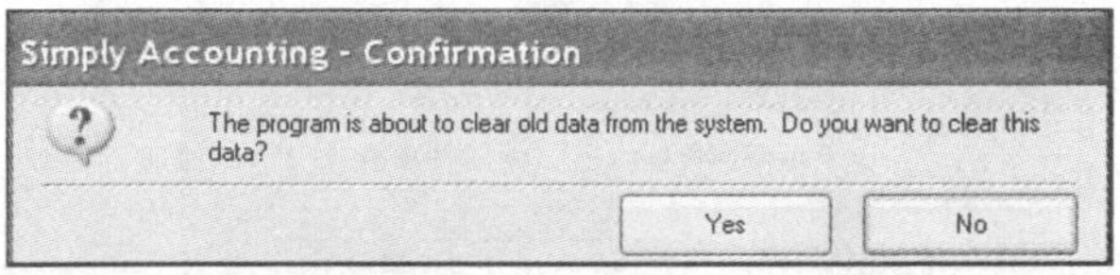

You have the option of retaining the old data or clearing it. Journal entries from the previous year are never cleared and Income Statement and Balance Sheet details for the previous year are also retained.

NOTES
We describe how to clear data from company files in Chapter 14.

Click **Yes** because Toss for Tots has no other data. If in doubt, choose No.

Another message now appears:

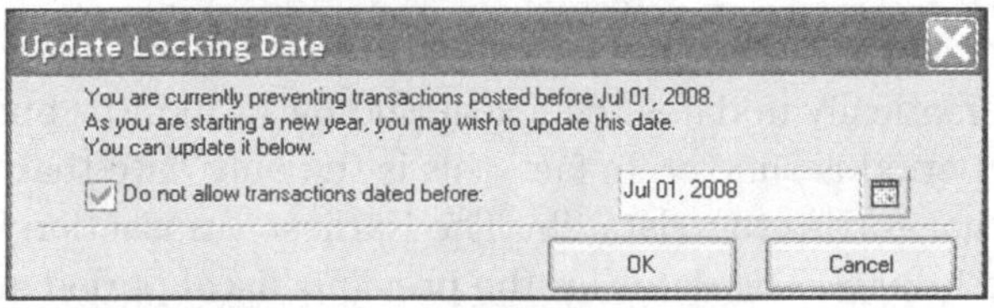

You must now change the earliest date that you will allow transactions for. We should not allow any transactions to the previous fiscal period so that the historical records cannot be altered in error.

Drag through **Jul 1, 2008**, the date entered.

Type 10/01

Click **OK** to continue.

NOTES
Most reports offer comparisons with the previous year as an option.
A fiscal year of one year is assumed so the fiscal end will be advanced by 12 months.

Journal reports are available for both periods, and other financial reports are now available as comparative reports for the two fiscal periods.

WARNING!
If you have cleared paid invoices, these details will be unavailable for reports. Comparative Income Statements and Balance Sheets are always available for the two fiscal periods.

Print the **Comparative Trial Balance** and **Balance Sheet** for September 30 and October 1.

Notice the changes in the capital accounts on the Balance Sheet. The *Net Income* balance for September 30 has been added to the *Surplus Funds* account to create the October 1 balance in the *Surplus Funds* account.

Print the **Comparative Income Statement for the previous year** (Oct. 1, 2007, to Sep. 30, 2008) and the **current fiscal year to date** (Oct. 1, 2008, to Oct. 1, 2008).

The Income Statement for the current year shows no income or revenue. All accounts have a zero balance because you have not recorded any transactions for the new fiscal year.

The files are now ready for transactions in the new fiscal period. When you check the Company Information, the fiscal dates are updated and you will see the additional information about last year's dates.

Choose the **Setup menu**, then **choose System Settings** and **click Company Information** to see the changes:

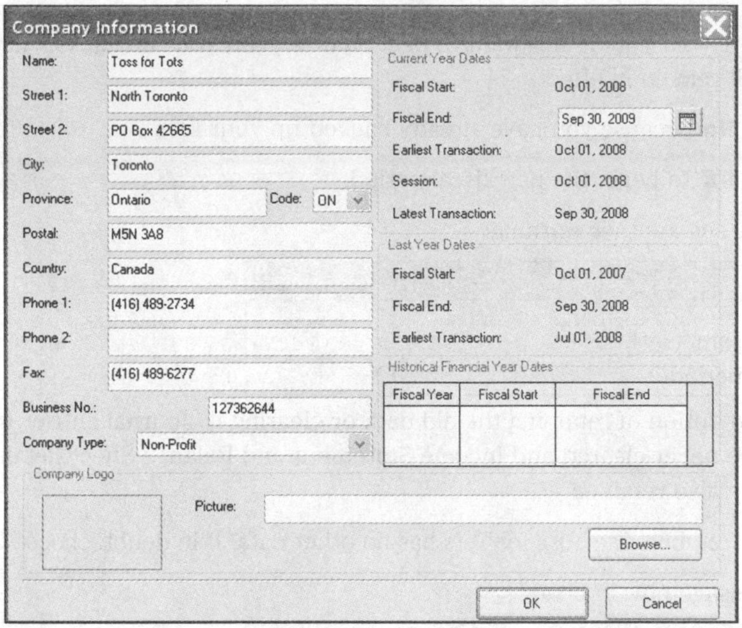

BASIC VERSION
The Historical Financial Year Dates section is not displayed in the Basic version because only one year of historical data is saved.

The new Fiscal Start is October 1, 2008 and the new Fiscal End is September 30, 2009. Simply Accounting automatically updates the Fiscal End by 12 months but you can edit this date if the fiscal period is shorter. In fact, this is the only date that you can edit after you have made journal entries to a data file. The Earliest Transaction Date has also been updated to October 1, 2008. The dates for the previous fiscal period are provided for reference.

Click **Cancel** to close the Company Information window.

Entering Transactions for an Earlier Fiscal Period

Sometimes not all the information required is available before the books are closed for the fiscal period. However, it may be necessary to close the books (start a new fiscal period) so that transactions in the new year may be entered. The details of the adjusting entries may be calculated by an accountant who does not have the information until after a business has started entering transactions for a new year. Simply Accounting allows you to post transactions to the previous year so that the financial statements for both the previous year and the current year will be correct.

Enter **Memo #10**, the GST rebate receipt, with the **September 30** date after starting the new fiscal period.

When you post the entry, you will see the following message:

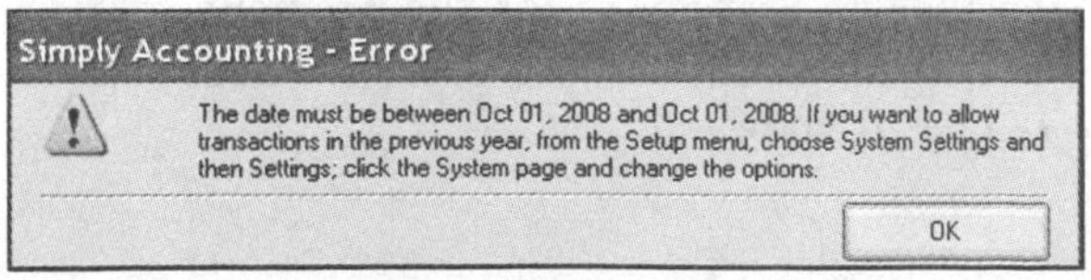

Before the program allows the entry, we must change the System Settings. We indicated that transactions earlier than Oct. 1, 2008 should not be allowed.

Click **OK** to close the message. **Close** the **journal** to discard the entry.

Choose the **Setup menu**, then **choose System Settings** and **click Settings**. **Click System** if necessary to access the field we need:

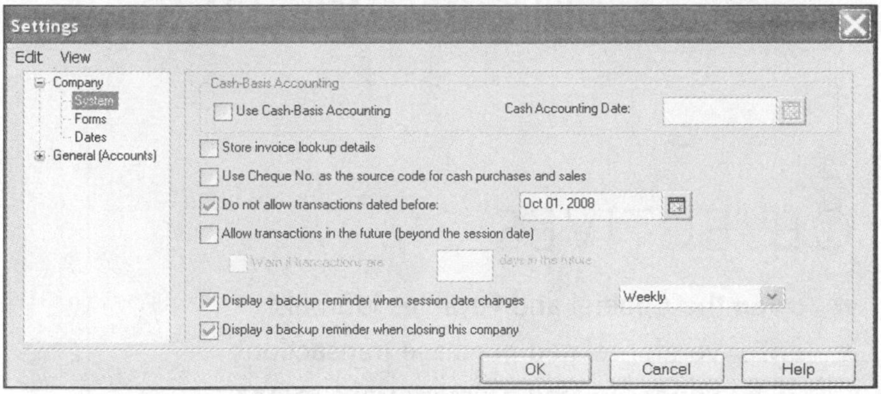

This is the same settings screen we saw earlier but now we must allow transactions in the previous period.

Click **Do Not Allow Transactions Dated Before** to **remove** the ✓.

Click **OK**.

Enter the **transaction** again. **Review** and then **post** it.

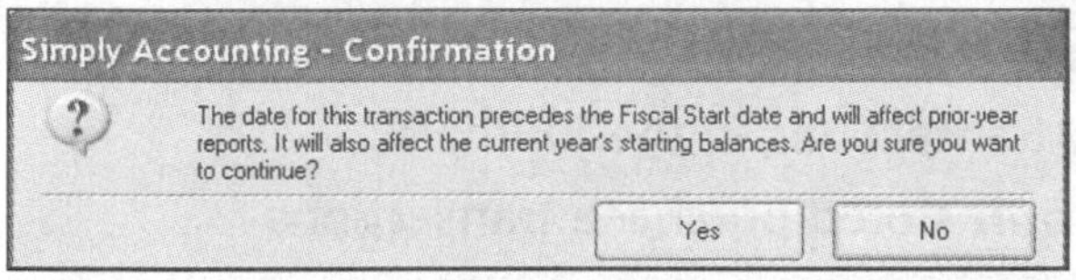

> **NOTES**
> The warnings in Simply Accounting make it difficult to post to the wrong year by mistake.

This time you will see a different warning, that prior period reports may be affected by the transaction. The warning gives you a chance to correct the date if it was incorrect. But we want to proceed. After completing the transaction, we will change the System Settings option again to avoid mistakenly posting to the previous year.

Click **Yes** to continue with posting.

Close the **General Journal**.

Choose the **Setup menu**, then **choose System Settings** and **click Settings**.

Click **Do Not Allow Transactions Dated Before** to **add** the ✓.

Enter **Oct 1** as the date and **click OK**.

Finish your **session** by closing the files for Toss for Tots.

REVIEW

The Student CD-ROM with Data Files includes Review Questions and Supplementary Cases for this chapter.

CHAPTER FIVE

Chai Tea Room

OBJECTIVES

After completing this chapter, you should be able to

- ***open*** the General and Payables journals
- ***enter*** vendor-related purchase transactions
- ***enter*** vendor-related payment transactions
- ***enter*** partial payments to vendors
- ***enter*** cash purchase transactions
- ***enter*** sales taxes in the General Journal
- ***store*** recurring purchase transactions
- ***add*** new vendor accounts
- ***edit*** vendor accounts
- ***edit*** and ***review*** transactions in the journals
- ***recall***, ***use*** and ***edit*** stored purchase transactions
- ***post*** transactions in each of the journals
- ***adjust*** purchase invoices and payments after posting
- ***understand*** Payables Ledger linked accounts
- ***display*** and ***print*** payables transactions and reports
- ***graph*** payables reports

COMPANY INFORMATION

Company Profile

NOTES
Chai Tea Room
125 King St.
Fredericton
New Brunswick E3B 2P4
Tel 1: (506) 454-6111
Tel 2: (800) 454-6000
Fax: (506) 454-6990
Business No.: 186 522 333

Chai Tea Room, located in Fredericton, New Brunswick, is owned by Sarah Quinte. Originally, Quinte wanted to name her business Quintessentials but after an extended tour of the Far East, where she acquired a taste for exotic blends of tea, she chose the name Chai instead. Canadians are becoming more familiar with the name Chai, an East Indian word for tea that is often used for spiced Indian tea.

The downtown tea room, near the New Brunswick Parliament House, Art Gallery and other historic sites, with its scenic lookout over the Saint John River and railroad walking bridge is very popular with professional women. Adjacent to a women's fitness and recreational centre, the tea room provides a comfortable atmosphere for customers to discuss finance, careers, or social or political issues after working out. The tea room boasts refinements such as a fireplace, comfortable living-room-styled cushioned sofas and chairs and very personal care and service from the owner and staff.

Chai Tea Room, essentially a tea room serving specialty teas from all around the world, also provides light lunches and superb desserts. Coffees and other beverages — both alcoholic and non-alcoholic — are available too. Quinte sells gift sets as well, packaged variety teas and tea service sets consisting of teacups, teaspoons, a teapot and a tea cozy. The tea service set items can also be purchased separately.

Sarah Quinte manages the day-to-day activities of the store. An assistant manager and kitchen staff handle business during her absence. The payroll is managed by the bank for a small fee. She has set up accounts with regular vendors, such as the suppliers of food and beverages as well as the utility companies. Cleaning and maintenance of the premises is done professionally once a week by Sunbury Cleaning; they wash and wax floors and steam clean the carpets and furniture. They also clean and check all equipment and complete minor repairs. On a day-to-day basis, the tea room staff do the regular cleaning.

No HST (sales tax) is paid on food purchases but other purchases are subject to HST. HST at 15 percent is charged to customers on all food products consumed in the tea room and the gift sets.

Quinte currently manages all the accounting records for the tea room and has just finished converting the manual records to Simply Accounting using the following:

- Chart of Accounts
- Post-Closing Trial Balance
- Vendor Information
- Accounting Procedures

NOTES

HST, Harmonized Sales Tax, is charged instead of GST and PST in New Brunswick. HST at 15 percent includes both GST at 7 percent and PST at 8 percent. Refer to Accounting Procedures and Chapter 2 for further details.

CHART OF POSTABLE ACCOUNTS

CHAI TEA ROOM

ASSETS
1080 Cash in Bank
1300 Beverage Inventory
1320 Beer, Wine and Liquor
1340 Food Inventory
1360 Gift Set Inventory
1500 Cash Register and Computer
1520 Cutlery and Dishes
1540 Furniture and Fixtures
1560 Equipment
1580 Tea Room Premises ▶

▶LIABILITIES
2100 Bank Loan
2200 Accounts Payable
2650 HST Charged on Sales
2670 HST Paid on Purchases
2850 Mortgage Payable

EQUITY
3100 S. Quinte, Capital
3150 S. Quinte, Drawings
3600 Net Income ▶

▶REVENUE
4100 Customer Service and Sales

EXPENSE
5020 Advertising and Promotion
5040 Bank Charges
5060 Cleaning and Maintenance
5080 Cost of Goods Sold
5100 General Expense
5120 Hydro Expense
5140 Interest Expense ▶
▶ 5160 Licences and Permits
5180 Payroll Services
5220 Telephone Expense
5240 Wages

NOTES: The Chart of Accounts includes only postable accounts and the Net Income or Current Earnings account. Simply Accounting uses the Net Income account for the Income Statement to calculate the difference between revenue and expenses before closing the books.

POST-CLOSING TRIAL BALANCE

CHAI TEA ROOM

August 1, 2008

1080	Cash in Bank	$ 11 155	
1300	Beverage Inventory	1 500	
1320	Beer, Wine and Liquor	2 500	
1340	Food Inventory	500	
1360	Gift Set Inventory	4 000	
1500	Cash Register and Computer	5 000	
1520	Cutlery and Dishes	5 000	
1540	Furniture and Fixtures	15 000	
1560	Equipment	25 000	
1580	Tea Room Premises	150 000	
2100	Bank Loan		$ 12 000
2200	Accounts Payable		2 945
2650	HST Charged on Sales		4 845
2670	HST Paid on Purchases	345	
2850	Mortgage Payable		120 000
3100	S. Quinte, Capital		80 210
		$220 000	$220 000

VENDOR INFORMATION

CHAI TEA ROOM

Vendor Name (Contact)	Address	Phone No. Fax No.	E-mail Web Site	Terms Tax ID
Atlantic Tea Company (Boise Chai)	20 Oceanview Dr. Halifax, NS B3K 2L2	Tel 1: (902) 777-2346 Tel 2: (888) 337-4599	bchai@atcc.com www.atcc.com	net 10 288 411 755
Bathurst Food Supplies (C. Ricotte)	56 Cheddar St. Oromocto, NB E2V 1M8	Tel: (506) 544-6292 Fax: (506) 544-5217	cricotte@bfoods.com www.bfoods.com	net 15 385 345 865
Fundy Gift House (Red Rose)	71 Ridge Way Hopewell Cape, NB E0A 1Y0	Tel: (506) 499-3481 Fax: (506) 499-3482	rrose@fundygifts.com www.fundygifts.com	net 30 124 653 779
Minto Beverages (Earl Gray)	910 Lemone Ave. Bathurst, NB E2A 4X3	Tel 1: (506) 622-3188 Tel 2: (800) 622-2881	eg@mintobev.com www.mintobev.com	net 30 901 200 862
Moncton Kitchenwares (Tiff Flaun)	4 Pottery Rd. Moncton, NB E1C 8J6	Tel: (506) 721-5121 Fax: (506) 721-5522	tflaun@monctonkitchens.com www.monctonkitchens.com	net 30 567 321 447
NB Gas (N. Bridge)	355 Pipeline Road Fredericton, NB E3A 5B1	Tel: (506) 454-8110	nbridge@naturalgas.com www.naturalgas.com	net 7
NB Hydro (N. Ergie)	83 Water Street Fredericton, NB E3B 2M6	Tel: (506) 455-5120	n.ergie@nbhydro.nb.ca www.nbhydro.nb.ca	net 7
NB Liquor Control Board (Darke Beere)	4 Spirits Rd. Fredericton, NB E3B 1C5	Tel: (506) 456-1182	dbeere@lcb.gov.nb.ca www.lcb.gov.nb.ca	net 1
NB Tel (Les Chatter)	2 Communicate Rd. Fredericton, NB E3A 2K4	Tel: (506) 456-2355	chatter@nbtel.ca www.nbtel.ca	net 1
Sunbury Cleaning Company (Dee Tergent)	49 Scrub St. Gagetown, NB E0G 1V0	Tel: (506) 454-6611 Fax: (506) 454-3216	dtergent@sunburyclean.com www.sunburyclean.com	net 15 481 532 556
Vermont Coffee Wholesalers (Java Jean)	60 Columbia Lane Saint John, NB E2M 6R9	Tel 1: (506) 366-1551 Tel 2: (877) 366-1500	java@vermontcoffee.com www.vermontcoffee.com	net 1 345 667 211

OUTSTANDING VENDOR INVOICES

CHAI TEA ROOM

Vendor Name	Terms	Date	Inv/Chq No.	Amount	Total
Bathurst Food Supplies	n/15	Jul. 26/08	BB-1044	$ 800	$ 800
Fundy Gift House	n/30	Jul. 6/08	FG-361	$ 920	$ 920
Moncton Kitchenwares	n/30	Jul. 25/08	MK-1341	$1 725	
		Jul. 25/08	Chq #167	500	
			Balance owing		$1 225
			Grand Total		$2 945

Accounting Procedures

The Harmonized Sales Tax (Provincial Sales Tax, and Goods and Services Tax)

In New Brunswick, federal and provincial taxes are replaced by the Harmonized Sales Tax or HST, a single tax at the rate of 15 percent. The HST is applied to most goods and services. Like the GST, HST may be included in the price or added at the time of the sale. Chai Tea Room uses the regular method for calculating and remitting the HST. All items sold in the tea room have HST added to them. At the end of each quarter, the HST liability to the Receiver General is reduced by any HST paid to vendors on purchases. Beverage and food supplies are zero rated for HST purposes. Chai's *HST Owing (Refund)* subgroup total account shows the amount of HST that is to be remitted to the Receiver General for Canada on the last day of each quarter. (For details please read Chapter 2 on the Goods and Services Tax.)

NOTES

Beverages and food items are zero rated goods, that is, the HST rate is 0 percent. Prepared food, as sold in restaurants, is taxed at 15%.

Most bank services and other financial institution services are exempt from HST charges. Bank payroll services are subject to HST charges.

Provincial sales tax is not levied as a separate tax in New Brunswick. It will be introduced in a later application.

Open-Invoice Accounting for Payables

The open-invoice method of accounting for invoices issued to a business allows a business to keep track of each individual invoice and partial payment made against the invoice. This is in contrast to methods that keep track only of the outstanding balance by combining all invoice balances owed to a vendor. Simply Accounting uses the open-invoice method. When an invoice is fully paid, you can either retain the invoice or remove (clear) it.

Purchase of Inventory Items

Inventory items purchased are immediately recorded in the appropriate inventory or supplies asset account. The items in stock are also manually recorded on inventory cards for periodic updating.

Cost of Goods Sold

Periodically, the food inventory on hand is counted to determine the cost price of the inventory or food supplies sold. The manager then issues a memo to reduce the inventory or supplies asset account and to charge the cost price to the corresponding expense account. For example, at the end of each month, the *Beverage Inventory* asset account (*1300*) is reduced (credited) and the *Cost of Goods Sold* expense account (*5080*) is increased (debited) by the cost price of the amount sold.

INSTRUCTIONS

1. **Enter** the **source documents for August** in Simply Accounting using the Chart of Accounts, Trial Balance, Vendor Information and Accounting Procedures for Chai Tea Room. The procedures for entering each new type of transaction for this application are outlined step by step in the Keystrokes section following the source documents. These transactions have a ✓ in the check box, and below the box is the page number where the related keystrokes begin.
2. **Print** the **reports and graphs** indicated on the printing form below after you have completed your entries. Instructions for reports begin on page 147.

REPORTS

Lists
- ☐ Chart of Accounts
- ☐ Account List
- ☐ Vendors

Journals
- ☐ All Journals
- ☐ General
- ☑ Purchases (by date) from Aug. 1 to Aug. 31
- ☑ Payments (by date) from Aug. 1 to Aug. 31

Financials
- ☑ Comparative Balance Sheet dates: Aug. 1 and Aug. 31 with difference in percentage
- ☑ Income Statement from Aug. 1 to Aug. 31
- ☑ Trial Balance date: Aug. 31
- ☑ General Ledger accounts: 1340 4100 5080 from Aug. 1 to Aug. 31

Banking
- ☐ Cheque Log Report

Payables
- ☑ Vendor Aged Detail for all vendors Aug. 31
- ☐ Aged Overdue Payables

Mailing Labels
- ☐ Labels

Management Reports
- ☐ Ledger

GRAPHS
- ☐ Payables by Aging Period
- ☑ Payables by Vendor
- ☐ Revenues by Account
- ☐ Expenses by Account
- ☑ Expenses and Net Profit as % of Revenue

SOURCE DOCUMENTS

SESSION DATE – AUGUST 7, 2008

☑ **Purchase Invoice #FG-642** **Dated Aug. 1/08**

120 From Fundy Gift House, $800 plus $120 HST for eight tea service sets. Invoice total, $920. Terms: net 30.

☑ **Purchase Invoice #BB-1243** **Dated Aug. 1/08**

125 From Bathurst Food Supplies, $800 for pastries, breads, condiments and other foods. There is no HST on food products. Terms: net 15 days. Store as weekly recurring entry.

☑ **Cheque Copy #171** **Dated Aug. 2/08**

127 To Fundy Gift House, $700 in payment of account. Reference invoice #FG-361.

☑ **Cash Purchase Invoice #Fton-08** **Dated Aug. 2/08**

130 From City Treasurer (use Quick Add for the new vendor), $250 for licensing fees. Paid by cheque #172.

☑ **Cash Purchase Invoice #ACA-3492** **Dated Aug. 3/08**

132 From All Campus Ads (add a complete record for the new vendor), $200 plus $30 HST for advertising brochures. Terms: cash on receipt. Invoice total $230 paid in full by cheque #173.

NOTES

All Campus Ads
☑ (contact Pierre Boaster)
132 447 Slick St.
Fredericton, NB E3B 8J5
Tel: (506) 564-8907
E-mail: pboaster@acads.ca
Terms: net 1
Expense account: 5020
Tax code: H - HST @ 15%

Memo #13 **Dated Aug. 5/08**

138 From Owner: Adjust invoice #FG-642. The order received from Fundy Gift House was for 10 tea service sets for $900 plus $135 HST. The corrected invoice total is $1 035.

Cash Purchase Invoice #BT-100 **Dated Aug. 7/08**

140 From Bette Tomailik (choose Continue for the new vendor), $25 as compensation to cover cost of dry cleaning for wine spilled by waiter. Issue cheque #174. Charge to General Expense account. No tax is applied on this transaction.

Purchase Invoice #SC-701 **Dated Aug. 7/08**

From Sunbury Cleaning Company, $250 plus $37.50 HST for weekly cleaning of store premises. Purchase invoice total $287.50. Terms: net 15 days. Store as weekly recurring transaction.

Cash Sales Receipt #34 **Dated Aug. 7/08**

141 From tea room customers (tapes #5001–5380), $7 600 plus $1 140 HST for tea room sales and services. Total receipts $8 740 deposited in bank.

NOTES
Use the General Journal for sales in this application.

SESSION DATE – AUGUST 14, 2008

Purchase Invoice #BB-2100 **Dated Aug. 8/08**

143 From Bathurst Food Supplies, $800 (no HST) for pastries, breads, condiments and other foods. Terms: net 15 days. Recall stored entry.

Cash Purchase Invoice #NBG-559932 **Dated Aug. 9/08**

From NB Gas, $200 plus $30 HST for monthly supply of natural gas on equal billing method. Invoice total $230 paid in full by cheque #175. Because equal billing applies, store as monthly recurring entry. Create a new Group account 5110 Heating Expense.

Memo #14 **Dated Aug. 9/08**

144 From Owner: Edit the vendor record for NB Gas to include the Heating Expense account as the default expense account selection.

Memo #15 **Dated Aug. 9/08**

145 From Owner: Adjust cheque #171 to Fundy Gift House. The cheque amount was $600 in partial payment of invoice #FG-361.

Cash Purchase Invoice #NBH-45321 **Dated Aug. 9/08**

From NB Hydro, $120 plus $18 HST for one month of hydro service. Invoice total $138 paid in full by cheque #176.

Cheque Copy #177 **Dated Aug. 11/08**

To Bathurst Food Supplies, $800 in payment of account. Reference invoice #BB-1044.

Bank Debit Memo #AT-53186 **Dated Aug. 14/08**

From Atlantic Trust, withdrawals from bank account for bi-weekly payroll:

Wages, including payroll taxes	$3 200
Payroll services	40
HST Paid on Purchases (payroll services)	6

NOTES
Use the General Journal for the payroll transaction in this application.
Remember to enter the sales tax code for the purchase.

Purchase Invoice #MB-6111 **Dated Aug. 14/08**

From Minto Beverages, $600 for bottled spring and mineral water and natural fruit beverages. Terms: net 30.

Purchase Invoice #SC-1219 **Dated Aug. 14/08**

From Sunbury Cleaning Company, $250 plus $37.50 HST for weekly cleaning of store premises. Purchase invoice total $287.50. Terms: net 15. Recall stored transaction.

Cash Sales Receipt #35 **Dated Aug. 14/08**

From tea room customers (tapes #5381–5750), $7 400 plus $1 110 HST for tea room sales and services. Total receipts $8 510 deposited in bank.

SESSION DATE – AUGUST 21, 2008

Purchase Invoice #BB-2987 **Dated Aug. 15/08**

From Bathurst Food Supplies, $800 for pastries, breads, condiments and other foods. Terms: net 15 days. Recall stored entry.

Cash Purchase Invoice #NBT-557121 **Dated Aug. 16/08**

From NB Tel, $100 plus $15 HST for monthly telephone service. Invoice total $115 paid by cheque #178.

Cheque Copy #179 **Dated Aug. 17/08**

To Bathurst Food Supplies, $800 in payment of account. Reference invoice #BB-1243.

Cash Purchase Invoice #VCW-345 **Dated Aug. 19/08**

From Vermont Coffee Wholesalers, $400 for specialty coffees. Invoice paid in full by cheque #180.

Cash Purchase Invoice #NBLCB-776 **Dated Aug. 20/08**

From NB Liquor Control Board, $1 600 including HST and other taxes for beer, wine and liquor. Terms: COD. Invoice paid in full by cheque #181.

NOTES

Use HST code HI, taxes included, for purchases from the NB Liquor Control Board. This is the default tax code setting for this vendor.

Purchase Invoice #SC-1790 **Dated Aug. 21/08**

146 From Sunbury Cleaning Company, $300 plus $45 HST for weekly cleaning of store premises. Purchase invoice total $345. Terms: net 15. Recall and edit the stored transaction. Store the changed entry.

Cash Sales Receipt #36 **Dated Aug. 21/08**

From tea room customers (tapes #5751–6149), $7 750 plus $1 162.50 HST for tea room sales and services. Total receipts $8 912.50 deposited in bank.

SESSION DATE – AUGUST 28, 2008

Purchase Invoice #BB-3778 **Dated Aug. 22/08**

From Bathurst Food Supplies, $850 for pastries, breads, condiments and other foods. Terms: net 15 days. Recall and edit the stored entry. Store the changed entry.

Cheque Copy #182 **Dated Aug. 23/08**

To Bathurst Food Supplies, $800 in payment of account. Reference invoice #BB-2100.

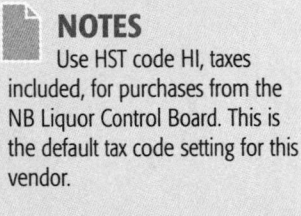

Cash Purchase Invoice #SK-6110 **Dated Aug. 23/08**

From Sweeney's Kitchenwares (use Full Add for the new vendor), $180 plus $27 HST for pots, pans and kitchen utensils. Invoice total $207 paid in full by cheque #183.

Purchase Invoice #ATC-3468 **Dated Aug. 27/08**

From Atlantic Tea Co., $500 for a variety of herbal, black and green teas as specified on order form. Terms: net 10 days.

Cash Purchase Invoice #Party **Dated Aug. 28/08**

From The Little Party Shop (choose Continue), $30 plus $4.50 HST for party favours and decorations to decorate tea room for special event (General Expense). Invoice total $34.50 paid in full by cheque #184.

Bank Debit Memo #AT-99553 **Dated Aug. 28/08**

From Atlantic Trust, withdrawals from bank account for bi-weekly payroll:

Wages, including payroll taxes	$3 200.00
Salaries	8 000.00
Payroll services	70.00
HST Paid on Purchases (payroll services)	10.50

Create new Group account 5250 Salaries.

Purchase Invoice #SC-2987 **Dated Aug. 28/08**

From Sunbury Cleaning Company, $300 plus $45 HST for weekly cleaning of store premises. Purchase invoice total $345. Terms: net 15 days. Recall stored transaction.

Cash Sales Receipt #37 **Dated Aug. 28/08**

From tea room customers (#6150–6499), $7 250 plus $1 087.50 HST for tea room sales and services. Total receipts $8 337.50 deposited in bank.

SESSION DATE – AUGUST 31, 2008

Purchase Invoice #BB-4633 **Dated Aug. 29/08**

From Bathurst Food Supplies, $850 for pastries, breads, condiments and other foods. Terms: net 15 days. Recall stored entry.

Cheque Copy #185 **Dated Aug. 31/08**

To Sunbury Cleaning Company, $1 265 in full payment of account. Reference invoices #SC-701, SC-1219, SC-1790 and SC-2987.

Bank Debit Memo #AT-10023 **Dated Aug. 31/08**

From Atlantic Trust, withdrawals for bank charges, and loan and mortgage payments:

Bank charges	$ 30
Mortgage payment (including $2 250 interest and $250 principal)	2 500
Loan payment (including $80 interest and $2 000 principal)	2 080

Purchase Invoice #MK-8995 **Dated Aug. 31/08**

From Moncton Kitchenwares, $600 plus $90 HST for new gas burners for tea room kitchen. Invoice total $690. Terms: net 30.

NOTES

Sweeney's Kitchenwares
(contact Tracey Potts)
44 Panning Ave.
Grand Sault, NB E3Y 1E1
Tel: (800) 566-7521
Web: www.sweeneys.com
Terms: net 1
Expense account: 1560
Tax code: H - HST @ 15%

Cheque Copy #186 **Dated Aug. 31/08**

To Bathurst Food Supplies, $800 in payment of account. Reference invoice #BB-2987.

Memo #16 **Dated Aug. 31/08**

From Owner: Make adjusting entries to reflect inventory used in the tea room during August. The end-of-month inventory count indicates the following inventory was used or sold:

Beverage inventory	$2 200
Beer, wine and liquor	1 700
Food inventory	3 100
Gift set inventory	1 000

All used inventory is charged to Cost of Goods Sold.

KEYSTROKES

Opening Data Files

Using the instructions for accessing data files in Chapter 1, page 8, open the data files for Chai Tea Room. You are prompted to enter the session date, which is August 7, 2008, for the first group of transactions in this application.

Type `Aug 7 08`

Click **OK** to enter the first session date for this application.

The Home window appears.

Accounting for Purchases

Purchases from vendors can be entered in the Purchases Journal, indicated by the Purchases, Orders & Quotes icon as shown here:

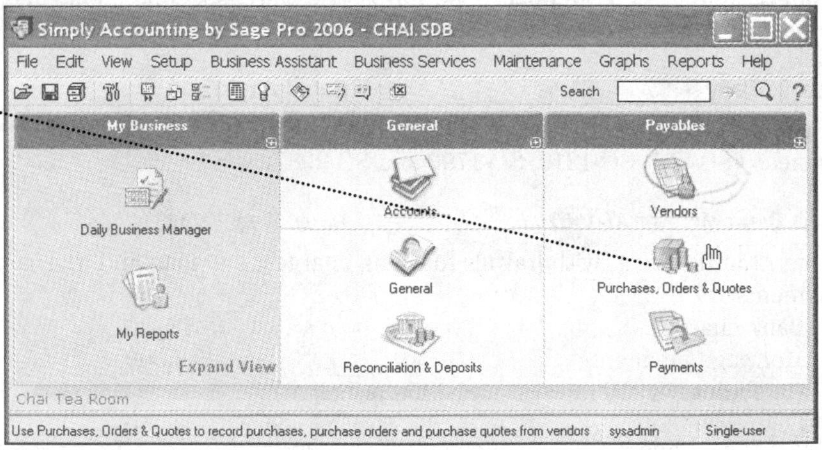

NOTES
Icons for the Receivables, Payroll, Inventory and Project ledgers are hidden because these ledgers are not set up or ready to use.

All vendor-related transactions can also be entered from the Payables module window.

Click the **Payables module heading** 

as shown:

The Payables window opens:

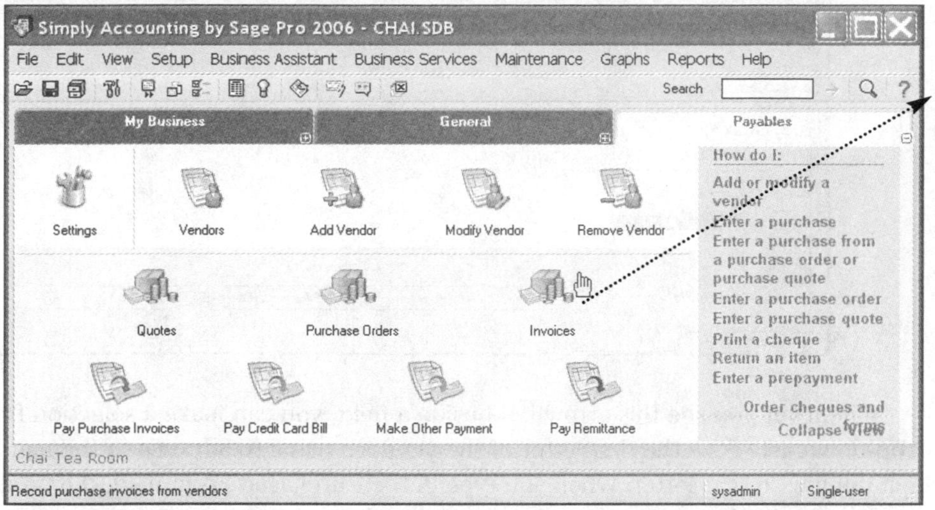

From this window, you can complete all vendor-related transactions. Separate icons are used for each type of activity. The first transaction is a normal purchase invoice.

Click the **Invoices icon** to open the Purchases Journal input form:

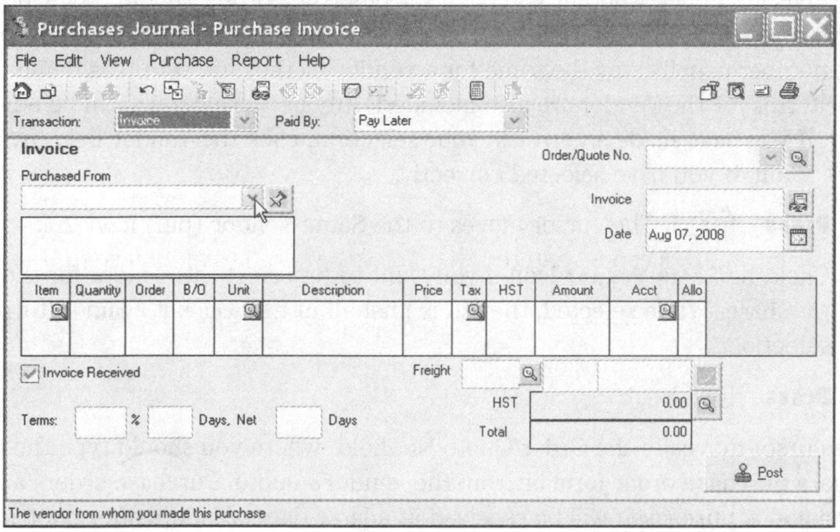

Move the mouse pointer across the various tool buttons and input fields and observe the status bar messages.

Invoice is selected as the Transaction because we selected the Invoices icon. The option to Pay Later is correct because this is a credit purchase. Transaction types also include quotes and purchase orders. Payment methods include cheque, cash and credit cards (when these are set up). When more than one bank account is set up, a drop-down list of bank accounts is available for cheque transactions. These topics are covered in later chapters.

Most tool buttons should already be familiar. Notice that the Calculator button appears again in the tool bar. Several tool buttons have been added to the Purchases Journal window: Remove Quote Or Order, Look Up An Invoice, Look Up Previous and

NOTES

The separate icons in the module windows make it easier for new users to learn the program. Experienced users may prefer to work from the Home window directly, especially if they are using all modules of the program. From the Home window, you can move from a journal in one module to a journal in another in a single step.

basic **BASIC VERSION**

The Refresh Lists tool applies to multi-user mode and does not appear in the Basic version.

NOTES

The different transaction types may be selected from the Transaction drop-down list in the invoice, quote or order windows or from the Payables module window.

WARNING!
You must click the list arrow to see the vendor list. Clicking the field will place an insertion point to prepare for typing a name.

Next Invoice, Track Shipments, Fill Backordered Quantities, Cancel Backordered Quantities, E-mail and Print. Each tool will be discussed when used.

Click the **Purchased From** (Vendor) **field list arrow** to obtain the list of vendors as shown:

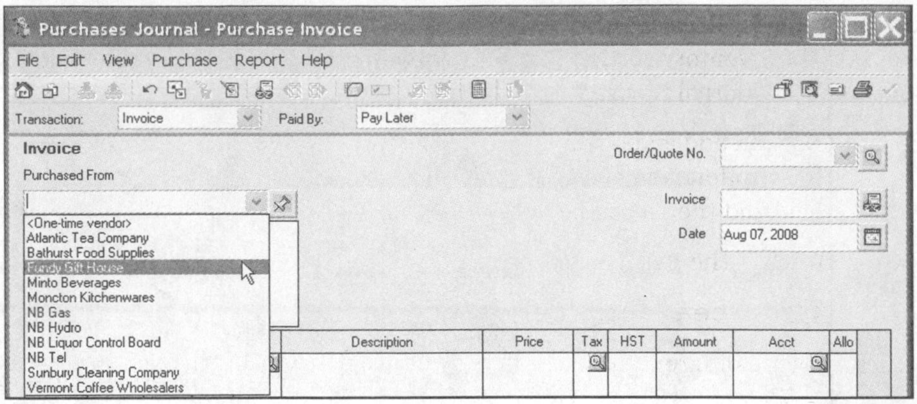

Whenever you see this arrow beside a field, you can make a selection from a drop-down list. Type the first letter of the vendor's name to advance to the names beginning with that letter. When you type in the Purchased From field, the program fills in a name from the vendor list by trying to match the letters you type.

Click **Fundy Gift House**, the vendor for this purchase, to select and enter it.

Notice that the vendor's name and address have been added to your input form, making it easy to check whether you have selected the correct vendor. Many other details have also been added by default from the vendor's record. The tax code and the account number usually stay the same for a vendor so they are set up as defaults. The payment terms for the vendor are also included. Any of these details can be edited if required. If you have made an error in your selection, click the Vendor field list arrow and start again. If you have selected correctly,

NOTES
If you use the same vendor for most purchases, preselecting the vendor can save data entry time. You can still select a different vendor from the list.

Press tab. The cursor moves to the Same Vendor (pin) icon.

Click the **Same Vendor** icon if you want to preselect this vendor for the next purchase. When selected, the pin is pushed in. Click it again to turn off the selection.

Press tab.

The cursor moves to the Order/Quote No. field, where you should type the number from Chai's purchase order form or from the vendor's quote. Purchase orders are used when the goods purchased will be received at a later date. Vendors offer quotes to guarantee purchase prices for a limited time. This field does not apply to invoices, so you should skip it.

NOTES
Orders and quotes are covered in Chapter 7.
Inventory is introduced in Chapter 11.
Invoice Lookup is introduced in Chapter 8.

Press tab to select the List icon for the Order/Quote No. field.

Press tab again to move to the Invoice field where you should type the alphanumeric invoice number.

You can also click the Invoice field directly to move the cursor.

Type `FG-642`

Press tab to select the Invoice Lookup icon.

Press tab again to advance to the Date field.

Enter the date the transaction took place, August 1, 2008. The session date appears by default. It is highlighted, ready to be accepted or changed. You need to change the date.

Type `aug 1`

Many of the invoice fields (Item, Units, Description and Price) pertain mainly to inventory items. Because we are not using the Inventory Ledger for this application, you can skip the inventory-related fields. Any information you type in these fields does not appear in the journal report.

You can add additional details to the invoice if you want. For example, click the Description field and type a description. Or add the quantity (8) in the Quantity field and the unit price in the Price field.

Click the **Description field**.

Type `tea service sets`

To select a different tax code, or to see the codes set up and available,

Click the **Tax field List icon** to see the tax codes for Chai Tea Room:

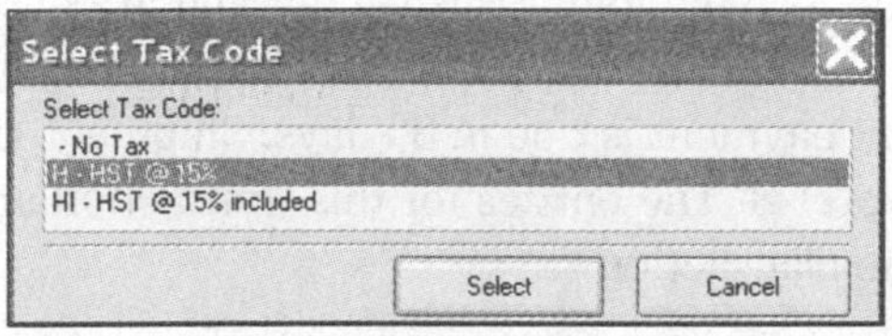

The selected tax code is H, that is, HST is charged on the purchase at 15 percent, and the tax is not included in the price. You can select a different code if needed, but in this case, the tax code is correct.

Click **Cancel** so that the selection remains unchanged.

Click the **first line of the Amount field**, where you will enter the total amount for this purchase.

Type `800`

Press tab.

The cursor moves to the Account field. The Account field for this purchase refers to the debit part of the journal entry, normally the acquisition of an asset or the incurring of an expense. It could also be used to decrease a liability or to decrease equity if the purchase were made for the owner's personal use. When you work in the subsidiary Payables journal, Simply Accounting will automatically credit your *Accounts Payable* control account in the General Ledger for the purchase. In fact, you cannot access *Accounts Payable* directly when the Payables Ledger is set up and linked.

In this example, the business has acquired an asset, and the correct account, *Gift Set Inventory,* is selected as the default for this vendor.

To select a different account, click the List icon for the Account field, double click the Account field or press enter. Each of these approaches will show the Select Account screen. You can also add a new account from the Select Account screen.

Press tab to advance the cursor to the next invoice line. You can now enter additional purchases from this vendor if there are any.

The tax amount is calculated and entered automatically in the HST field when you enter the tax code and the amount.

NOTES

For this application, the sales tax rate is set to 15 percent, the harmonized single tax rate for New Brunswick. For non-Atlantic provinces, the rate is 7 percent and tax codes will display as GST @ 7%.

Since the provincial and federal retail sales taxes are harmonized, there is no separate amount for PST. When PST is applicable and is set up in the defaults for the company, the program will calculate PST as well, based on the tax rates and codes entered for PST.

NOTES

Typing negative amounts will generate a credit entry with a debit for Accounts Payable.

Your screen should now resemble the following:

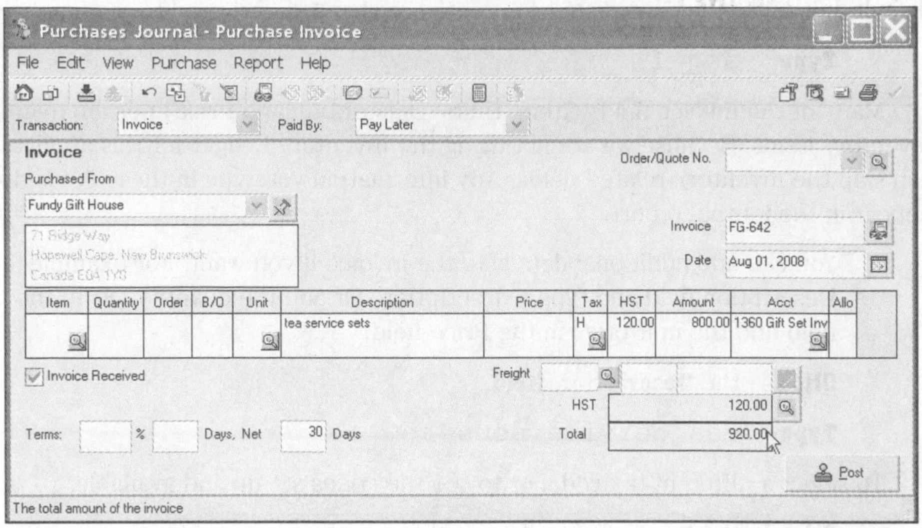

The payment terms have been set up as defaults for this vendor and are entered automatically. They can be edited if needed for specific purchases, but in this case they are correct. There is no discount and full payment is due in 30 days. Shipment tracking is not used by Chai; it is covered in Chapter 8. The entries for this transaction are complete, so you are ready to review the transaction.

Reviewing the Purchases Journal Entry

Choose the **Report menu** and **click Display Purchases Journal Entry** to display the transaction you have entered on the screen:

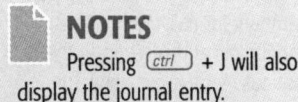

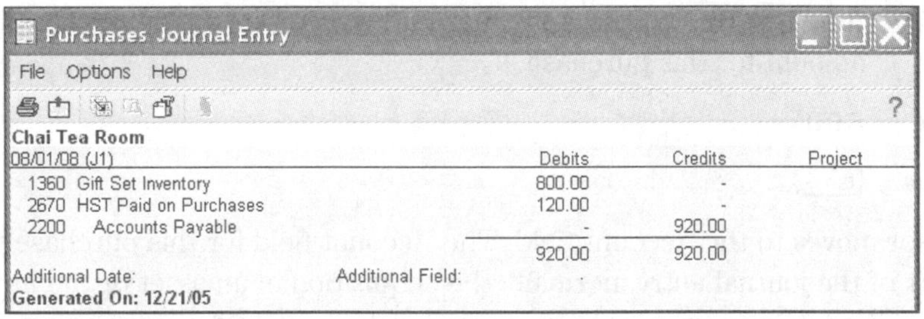

By reviewing the journal entry, you can check for mistakes. Note that the Simply Accounting program automatically updates the *Accounts Payable* control account because the Payables and General Ledgers are linked or fully integrated. Even though you did not enter account *2200*, Simply Accounting uses it because it is defined as the linked account to which all purchases should be credited. *HST Paid on Purchases*, the linked tax account, is also automatically updated. Using the Purchases Journal instead of the General Journal to enter purchases is faster because you need to enter only half the journal entry. The program provides a credit directly to the account of the selected vendor, and it prevents you from choosing an incorrect payables account. The automatic selection of tax codes and accounts makes the transaction even simpler to enter.

Close the **display** to return to the Purchases Journal input screen.

NOTES
The account name may not fit in the account column if the column is very narrow. To change the width of a column, point to the line beside the column title. When the pointer changes to a double-sided arrow, drag the line to the new location. Make a journal window wider by dragging the side frame. You can also maximize a journal window to occupy the entire screen.

NOTES
Pressing ctrl + J will also display the journal entry.

basic BASIC VERSION
The Refresh Report tool applies to multi-user mode and does not appear in the Basic version.

NOTES
Other linked accounts for the Payables Ledger include a bank account, a freight expense account and a purchase discounts account. Each linked account will be explained when it is used in this workbook.

CORRECTING THE PURCHASES JOURNAL ENTRY BEFORE POSTING

Move to the field that has the error. **Press** tab to move forward through the fields or **press** shift and tab together to move back to a previous field. This will highlight the field information so you can change it. **Type** the **correct information** and **press** tab to enter it.

You can also use the mouse to **point** to a field and **drag through** the **incorrect information** to highlight it. **Type** the **correct information** and **press** tab to enter it.

If the vendor is incorrect, reselect from the vendor list by **clicking** the **Vendor field list arrow**. **Click** the name of the **correct vendor**.

Click an **incorrect amount** to highlight it. Then **type** the **correct amount** and **press** tab to enter the change.

To select a different account, **click** the **Account List icon** to display the list of accounts. **Click** the **correct account** number to highlight it, then **click Select** and **press** tab to enter the change.

To insert a line or remove a line, **click** the **line** that should be moved. **Choose** the **Edit menu** and **click Insert Line** or **Remove Line** to make the change.

To discard the entry and begin again, **click** [X] (**Close**) to close the Journal or **click** [↶] (**Undo**) on the tool bar to open a blank journal window. When Simply Accounting asks whether you want to discard the entry, **click Yes** to confirm your decision.

> **NOTES**
> To correct a Purchases Journal entry after posting, refer to page 138 and Appendix C.

Posting

When you are certain that you have entered all the information correctly, you must post the transcation to save it.

Click the **Post button** [Post] or **choose** the **Purchase menu** and **click Post** to save your transaction.

A new blank Purchases Journal form appears on the screen.

> **NOTES**
> You can press alt + P to post the journal entry.

Storing a Recurring Journal Entry

The second transaction is the recurring purchase of food inventory.

Businesses often have transactions that are repeated on a regular basis. For example, loan payments, bank charges and rent payments usually occur on the same day each month; supplies may be ordered more frequently; insurance payments may occur less frequently but nonetheless regularly. Chai Tea Room has food supplies delivered on a regular basis. By storing the entry, and indicating the frequency, the entry can be recalled the next time it is needed without re-entering all the information.

The Purchases Journal should still be open with the transaction type, payment method and date correct from the previous entry.

Choose **Bathurst Food Supplies** from the vendor list, or

Click the **Vendor field** and **type** B

Press tab **repeatedly** to move to the Invoice field.

Type BB-1243

Enter a **description** for the purchase.

> **NOTES**
> Typing the first letter of a vendor name in the Vendor field will add the first vendor name beginning with that letter. Since Bathurst Foods is the first vendor name starting with "B," it will be entered.

The tax code is correct, there is no tax charged on the purchase of food. The payment terms and account are also correct by default.

Click the **Amount field**, **type** 800 and **press** tab to complete the transaction.

NOTES
The procedure for storing entries is the same for all journals when the option is available. Choose Store, assign a name to the entry, then choose a frequency and click OK to save it.

Choose the **Report menu** and **click Display Purchases Journal Entry** to review the entry.

Close the **display** and **make corrections** if necessary.

Click the **Store tool** on the tool bar (or **choose** the **Purchase menu** and **click Store**) to open the following Store Recurring Transaction screen:

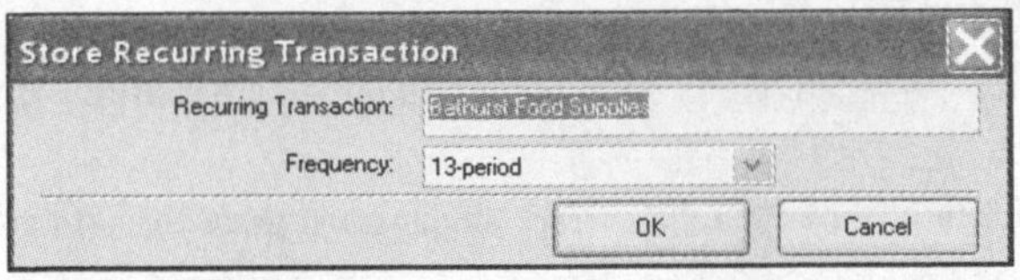

Simply Accounting enters the vendor and 13-period (every four weeks) as the default name and frequency for the entry. The name is highlighted, so it can be changed by typing another descriptive name. Be sure to use one that you will recognize easily as belonging to this entry. The default frequency is incorrect since the food items are purchased weekly.

Click **13-period** to display the list of choices for the recurring frequency:

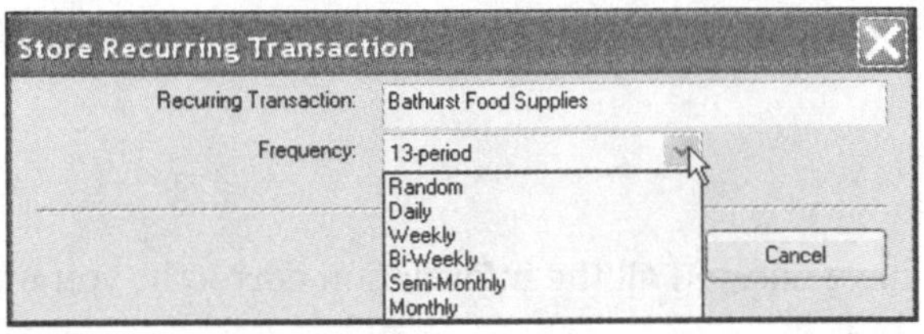

The frequency options are Random (for irregular purchases), Daily, Weekly, Bi-Weekly, Semi-Monthly, Monthly, 13 times per year, Bi-Monthly, Quarterly, Semi-Annually and Annually.

Click **Weekly**.

Simply Accounting will advance the default journal date when you recall the stored entry according to the frequency selected. The session date is entered if the Random frequency is chosen.

Click **OK** to return to the Purchases Journal window.

Notice that (the **Recall tool**) is now darkened and can be selected because you have stored a journal entry. The journal title bar label has also changed. It now shows Using Recurring Transaction Bathurst Food Supplies.

CORRECTING A STORED JOURNAL ENTRY

If you notice an error in the stored journal entry before posting, you must first **correct** the **journal entry** in the Purchases Journal window, then **click Store**. When asked to confirm that you want to overwrite or replace the previous version, **click Yes**.

If you edit the journal entry after storing it, Simply Accounting will warn you that the entry has changed. **Click Yes** to proceed.

Posting

When you are sure that you have entered all the information correctly, and you have stored the entry, you must post the transaction to save it.

Click the **Post button** or **choose** the **Purchase menu** and **click Post** to save your transaction.

A new blank Purchases Journal form appears on the screen. Our next transaction is a payment, however, not a purchase.

Close the **Purchases Journal window** to return to the Payables window.

Accounting for Payments

Payments are made in the Pay Purchase Invoices Journal indicated by the hand pointer in the following screen:

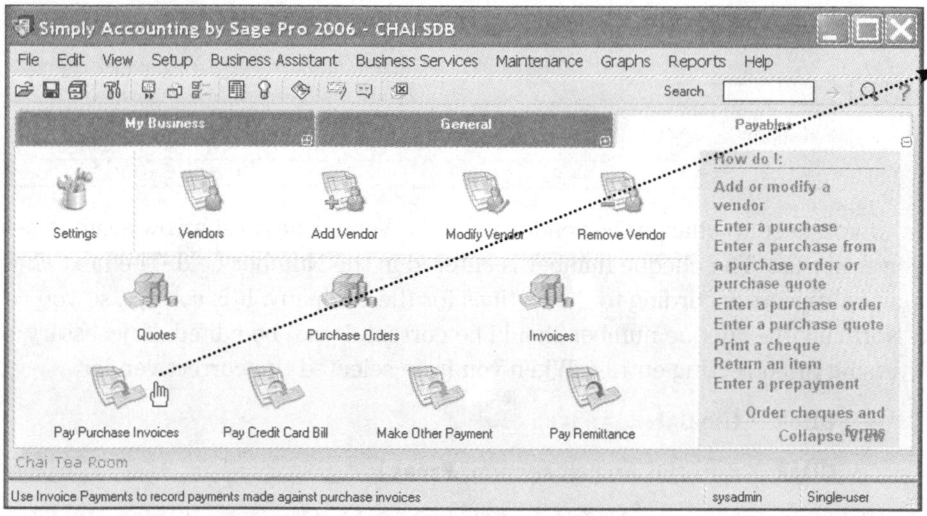

Click the **Pay Purchase Invoices icon** to open the journal and display the following blank Payments Journal input screen:

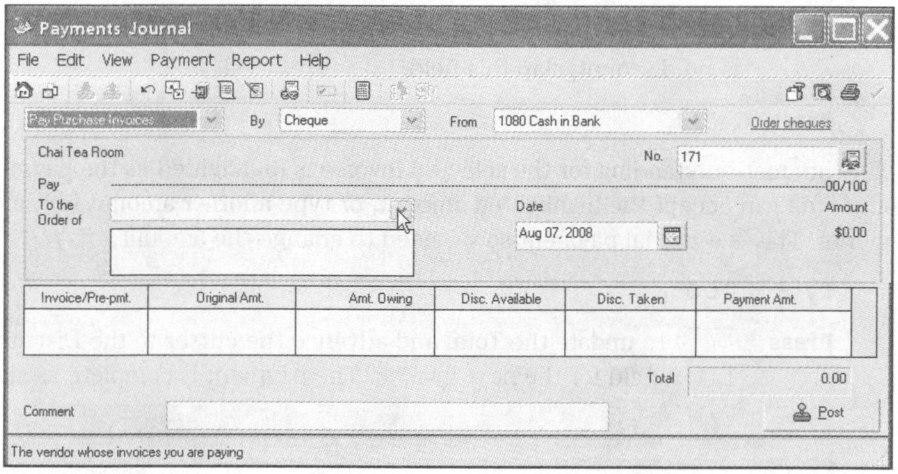

Pay Purchase Invoices is selected as the type of payment in the Pay field, and Cheque appears as the method of payment in the By field. The defaults are correct.

From the Home window, click the Payments icon to open the Payments Journal. Pay Purchase Invoices will be selected as the default type of transaction.

Click the **To The Order Of** (Vendor) **field list arrow** to see the familiar list of vendors displayed in alphabetical order.

Click **Fundy Gift House** (or **type** F) to choose and enter the vendor to whom the payment is made.

The journal input form is updated with the vendor's name, address and outstanding invoice(s), making it easy to see whether you have selected correctly.

basic **BASIC VERSION**
The icon label is Pay Vendor Invoices instead of Pay Purchase Invoices.

basic **BASIC VERSION**
The Refresh tools do not appear in the Basic version.

NOTES
When more than one bank account is set up, you can select the bank from the drop-down list beside From. In Chapters 7 and 8, you will use these upper fields to work with credit card payments and multiple bank accounts.

NOTES
From the Pay drop-down list, you can select the other kinds of transactions for this journal, or you can choose the transaction type from the Payables module window.

NOTES
You can type F in the Vendor field to enter Fundy Gift House because this is the only vendor beginning with "F".

NOTES

Click the Include Fully Paid Invoices tool if you need to make a reversing entry for a payment. The Payments Journal will then display all paid and unpaid invoices for the selected vendor (see page 145).

The updated journal is shown here:

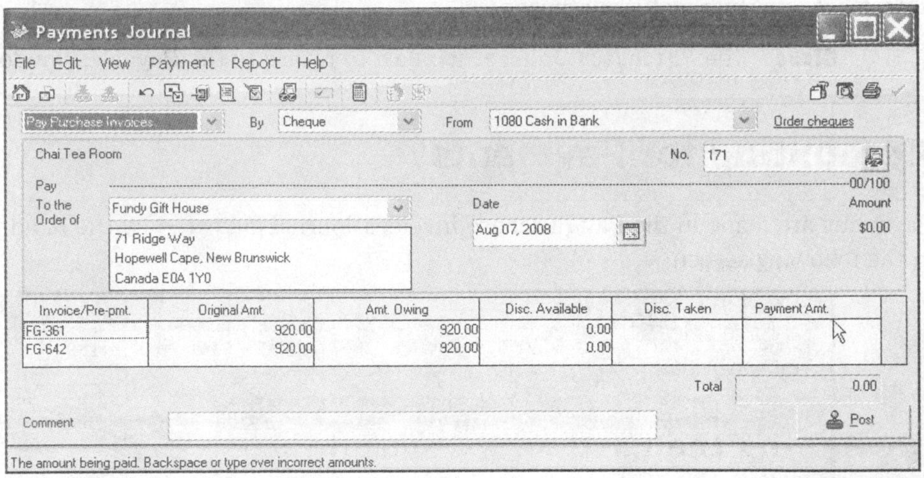

Notes

The Lookup icon appears beside the cheque number so you can look up previous invoices.

If you need to change the vendor, click the Vendor field list arrow again to select from the vendor list. The cheque number is entered in the Number field. The next cheque number appears according to the settings for the company. It is correct, so you can accept it. Normally the cheque number should be correct. It can be edited, if necessary, for reversing or correcting entries. When you have selected the correct vendor,

Click the **Calendar icon**.

Click **2** in the August section. **Press** tab.

The cursor moves to the Invoice/Pre-pmt. field. All outstanding invoices, including both the amount of the original invoice and the balance owing for the selected vendor, are listed on the screen.

Press tab to advance to the Disc. Taken (Discount Taken) field. Since there is no discount, skip this field.

Press tab.

The amount outstanding for the selected invoice is highlighted as the payment amount. You can accept the highlighted amount, or type another amount for partial payments. This is a partial payment so we need to change the amount.

Type 700

Press tab to update the Total and advance the cursor to the Discount Taken field for the next invoice. The payment is complete as shown:

WARNING!

The amount for the next invoice should not be highlighted since this invoice is not being paid. If its amount is highlighted or entered, you must delete it by pressing del and then tab to correct the total cheque amount.

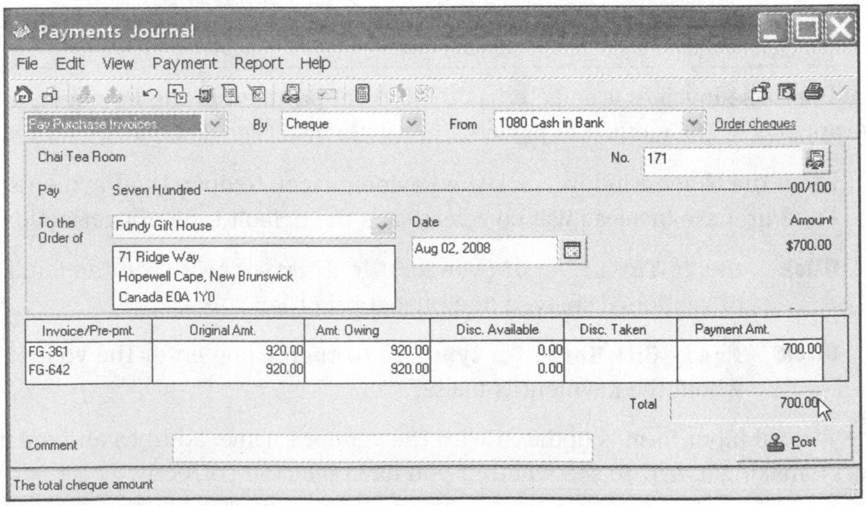

Notice that the upper cheque portion of the form is also complete. Notice too that there is no field for account numbers in the Payments Journal. You only need to enter the amount of the payment on the appropriate invoice line.

As you pay invoices in the subsidiary Payments Journal, you do not enter any accounts. Simply Accounting chooses the default linked accounts defined for the Payables Ledger to create the journal entry.

The entries for this transaction are complete, so you are ready to review and post your transaction.

If you want to print the cheque, you must do so before posting the Payments Journal entry. Be sure that the information is correct before you print and that you have selected the correct printer and forms for printing cheques (see Chapter 4, page 83). Turn on the printer and then click the Print tool.

Reviewing the Payments Journal Entry

Choose the **Report menu** and **click Display Payments Journal Entry** to display the transaction you have entered:

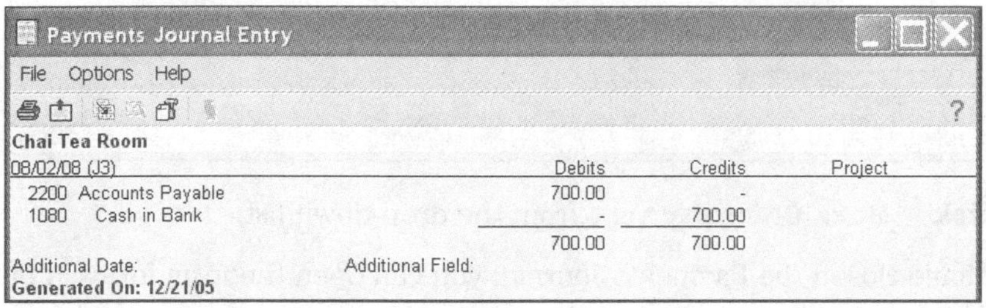

You can see that the Simply Accounting program automatically creates a related journal entry when you complete a Payments Journal entry. The program updates *Accounts Payable* and *Cash in Bank* because the Payables and General Ledgers are fully linked. *Cash in Bank* has been defined as the default Payables linked account to which payments are credited. The payment is also recorded to the vendor's account to reduce the balance owing.

Close the **display** to return to the Payments Journal input screen.

CORRECTING THE PAYMENTS JOURNAL ENTRY BEFORE POSTING

Move to the field that has the error. **Press** tab to move forward through the fields or **press** shift and tab together to move back to a previous field. This will highlight the field information so you can change it. **Type** the **correct information** and **press** tab to enter it.

You can also use the mouse to **point** to a field and **drag through** the **incorrect information** to highlight it. **Type** the **correct information** and **press** tab to enter it.

If the vendor is incorrect, **click** **to** undo the entry or **reselect** from the **Vendor** list by **clicking** the **Vendor list arrow**. **Click** the name of the **correct vendor**. You will be asked to confirm that you want to discard the current transaction. **Click Yes** to discard the incorrect vendor entry and display the outstanding invoices for the correct vendor. **Re-enter** the **payment** information for this vendor.

NOTES

To reverse a payment after posting, refer to Appendix C. Or refer to the section on NSF cheques on page 181.

NOTES

You can correct payment amounts after posting by clicking the Adjust Payment tool. Select the payment to adjust, just as you select a purchase invoice or General Journal entry for editing. Make the correction and post the revised payment. See page 145.

Posting

When you are certain that you have entered all the information correctly, you must post the transaction to save it.

Click the **Post button** Post (or **choose** the **Payment menu** and **click Post**) to save your transaction.

Entering Cash Purchases

The licence fees statement on August 2 is to be paid immediately on receipt of the invoice. Instead of recording the purchase and payment separately, you can record the payment with the purchase in the Payments Journal. This transaction also involves a company that is not listed as a vendor, so you must add the City Treasurer to the vendor list in order to record the transaction.

Vendors can be added directly from the Payables Ledger or from the vendor field in the Purchases Journal or the Payments Journal. We will add the new vendor from the Payments Journal. The Payments Journal should still be open.

The date and the cheque number are correct. The date is unchanged from the previous Payments Journal transaction. The next available cheque number is entered by default, and the bank account is selected for the payment. Cheque numbers are updated in sequence for both payment journal entries and cash purchases.

Click **Pay Purchase Invoices** to see the options for payment transactions:

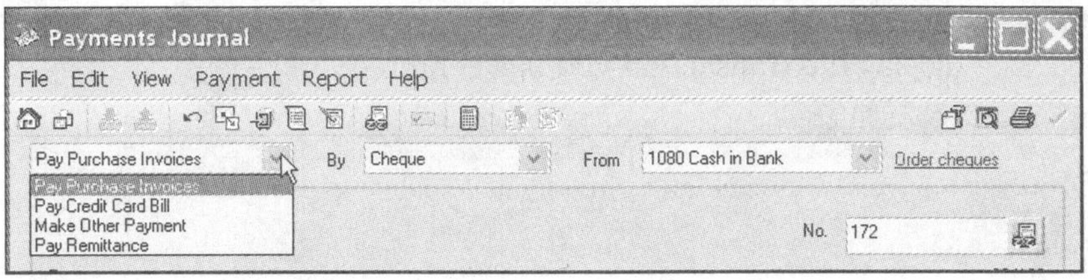

Click **Make Other Payment** from the drop-down list.

If you have closed the Payments Journal, you can open the form for cash purchases from the Payables module window.

NOTES
If you have closed the Payments Journal, the session date will be displayed and you must change it to August 2.

Click the **Make Other Payment icon** 

to add journal input fields to the payment form:

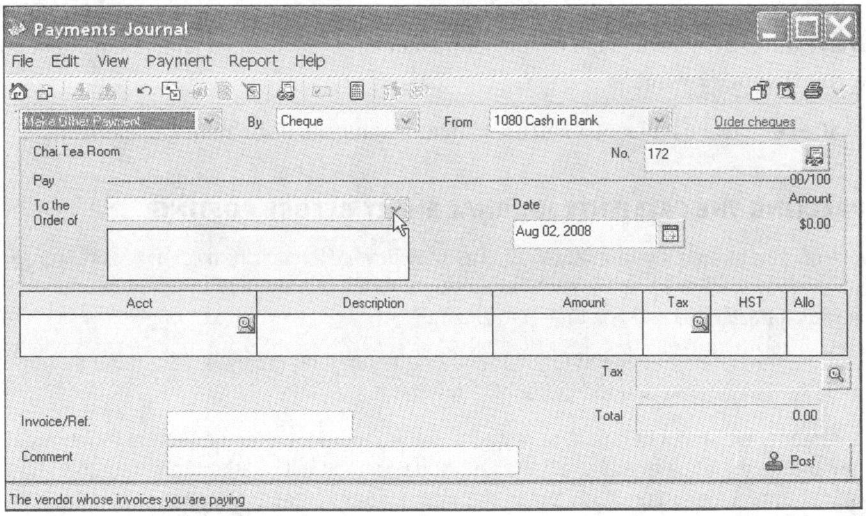

Click the **To The Order Of field** to move the cursor.

Type `City Treasurer` and then **press** *tab* to display the message:

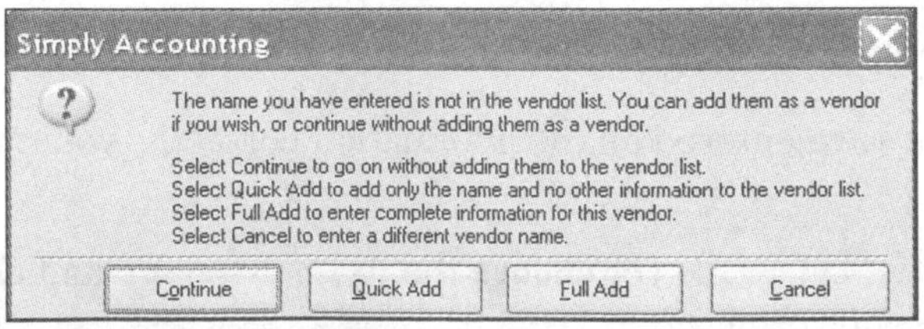

The program recognizes that the name is new and gives you several options: **Continue** — add the name to the journal and the journal report and apply the default settings for the ledger but do not create a vendor record or include the name in the vendor list; **Quick Add** — create a partial record with only the vendor's name, and apply the default settings for the ledger; **Full Add** — open a new ledger record for the vendor and add complete details; or **Cancel** — return to the journal and type or choose another name if the one you typed was incorrect.

If you are making a cash purchase and you will not be making additional purchases from this vendor, you can choose **One-time Vendor** from the Vendor list. Type the vendor's name and address on the invoice in the text box area below the To The Order Of field. The default settings for the ledger will apply to the invoice. The transaction will be included in the GST/HST report but the vendor's name will not appear in vendor lists or in the journal reports.

We want to add a partial record for the new vendor.

Click **Quick Add**.

You will return to the Payments Journal. The Vendor name is added to the journal. Because the account is not set up in the vendor's ledger record, you must enter the asset or expense account that is debited for the transaction.

Enter **Aug 2** as the date if necessary.

Click the **Account field List icon** to see the Select Account list.

Click **Suggested Accounts** to modify the list as shown:

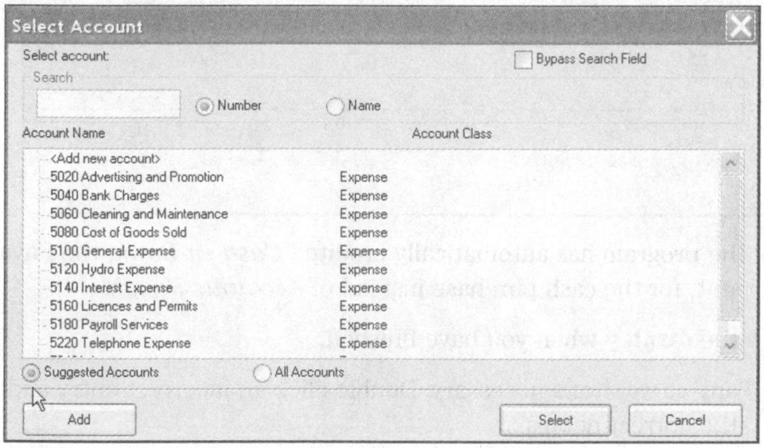

The list now shows only the expense accounts. Because expense accounts are most often used for purchases, they are the suggested accounts. This list is easier to work with because it is shorter. When you enter sales in the Sales Journal, the suggested accounts will list only revenue accounts.

Click **5160 Licences and Permits**.

Click **Select** to add the account and advance to the Description field.

Type `licensing fees`

Press *tab* to advance to the Amount field.

Type `250` **Press** *tab*.

Since no tax is charged on the fees, the default entry of No Tax is correct.

Click the **Invoice/Ref. field**.

Type `Fton-08` **Press** *tab* to advance to the Comment field.

NOTES

If you create a partial vendor record with Quick Add, you can add more vendor details later by editing the record.

NOTES

When we tested the keystrokes, the Invoice/Ref. field contents were not included in journal reports and the Comment was included. Therefore, we repeat the invoice number in the Comment field to be sure that it will be included in the journal reports.

The comment will become part of the journal record so you should include it.

Type `Fton-08, licensing fees`

Your completed payment form should now look like the one shown here:

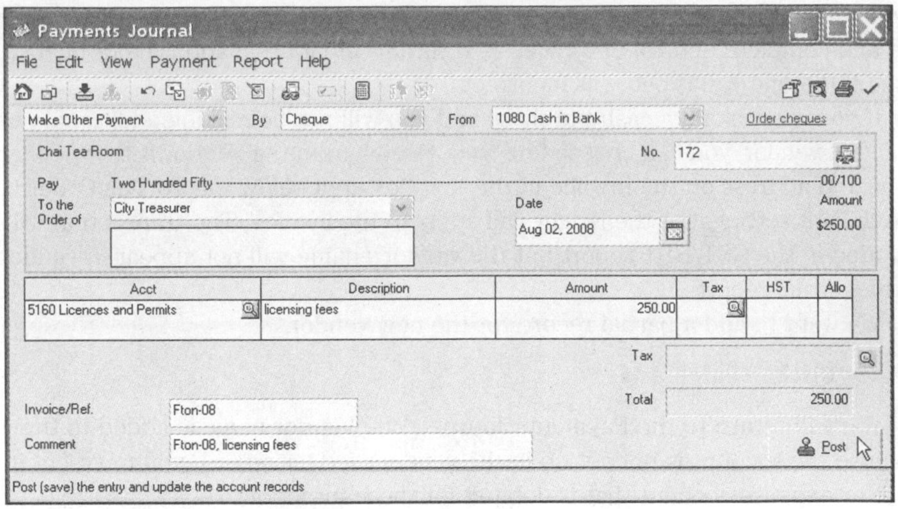

When you have finished, review the entry before posting it.

Choose the **Report menu** and **click Display Payments Journal Entry**. Your display should look like the following:

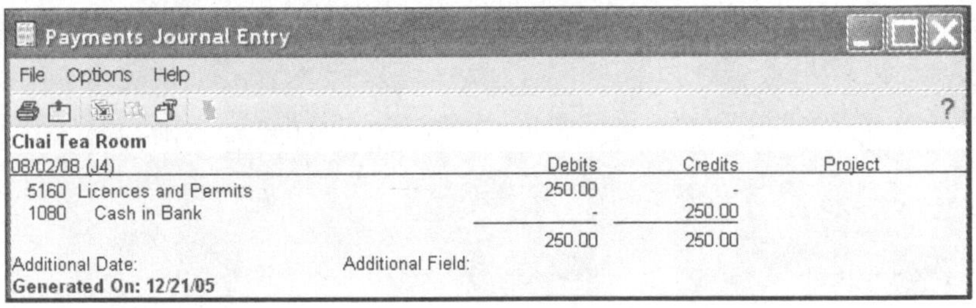

Notice that the program has automatically credited *Cash in Bank*, the Payables linked bank account, for the cash purchase instead of *Accounts Payable*.

Close the **display** when you have finished.

Make any **corrections** necessary. Double click an incorrect entry and type the correct details.

Click the **Post button**  to save the **entry** when you are certain that it is correct.

Close the **Payments Journal**.

Adding a New Vendor Record

Cash purchases and new vendors may be recorded in the Payments Journal or the Purchases Journal. We will record the next cash purchase in the Purchases Journal after we add a full record for the vendor. You can create a new vendor record on the fly, as we did in the previous transaction, or you can add the vendor record from the Payables window using the Add Vendor icon. For this transaction, we will use the ledger option in the Payables module window.

Click the **Add Vendor icon** in the ledger row of the Payables window as shown in the following screen:

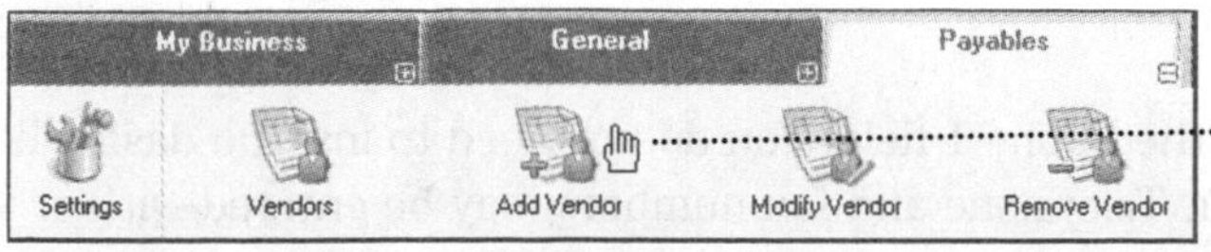

The Payables Ledger input form opens at the Address tab screen:

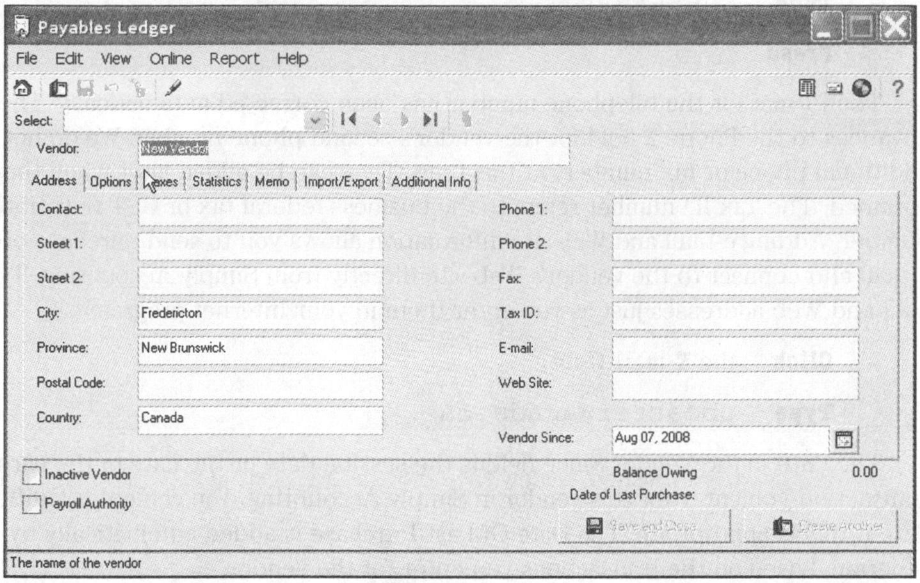

NOTES
If you are missing any information for a vendor, you can leave the field blank and enter the details later by editing the record. See page 144.

***basic* BASIC VERSION**
The Refresh tool does not appear in the Basic version.

You are ready to enter the new vendor. The Vendor Address tab information screen appears first. New Vendor appears in the Vendor field and this name is highlighted so you can edit it immediately.

Type `All Campus Ads` **Press** (tab).

The cursor advances to the Contact field, where you enter the name of Chai Tea Room's contact person at All Campus Ads. This field can also be used to enter a third address line if two street lines are insufficient. This field or any other may be left blank by pressing (tab).

Type `Pierre Boaster`

Press (tab). The cursor moves to the Street 1 field.

Type `447 Slick St.`

The Street 2 field can be used for a second address line, if there is one. By default, the program has entered the name of the city, province and country in which Chai Tea Room is located. You can accept the defaults because they are correct.

NOTES
The default address information is taken from the Company Information settings (see Chapter 4, page 81).

If the vendor is in a different city, province or country, type the correct information before continuing. Press (tab) to advance to a field and highlight the contents to prepare it for editing.

Click the **Postal Code field** to move the cursor.

When you enter a Canadian postal code, you do not need to use capital letters, nor do you need to leave a space within the postal code. The program will make these adjustments for you.

Type `e3b8j5`

Press (tab).

Notice that the format of the postal code has been corrected automatically. The cursor moves to the Country field and the entry is correct.

Press tab.

The cursor moves to the Phone 1 field. You do not need to insert a dash when you enter a telephone number. Telephone and fax numbers may be entered with or without the area code.

Type 5065648907

Press tab.

The format for the telephone number has been corrected automatically. The cursor advances to the Phone 2 field for the vendor's second phone number. We do not have additional phone or fax numbers at this time. They can be added later when they are obtained. The Tax ID number refers to the business federal tax or GST registration number. Adding e-mail and Web site information allows you to send purchase orders by e-mail and connect to the vendor's Web site directly from Simply Accounting. Type e-mail and Web addresses just as you enter them in your Internet program.

Click the **E-mail field**.

Type pboaster@acads.ca

The date in the Vendor Since field is the session date or the date of the earliest transaction you enter for this vendor in Simply Accounting. You can enter a different date if this is appropriate. The Date Of Last Purchase is added automatically by the program, based on the transactions you enter for the vendor.

Click the **Vendor Since date field**.

Type Aug 3

The last two options concern the vendor's status. You can make the vendor inactive and remove the name from the selection lists and reports. Vendors that you will not use again can be made inactive. You can also designate the vendor as a Payroll Authority so that the vendor can be selected for payroll remittances.

NOTES
Payroll authorities and payroll remittances are covered in Chapter 10.

Click the **Options tab** to open the next vendor information screen:

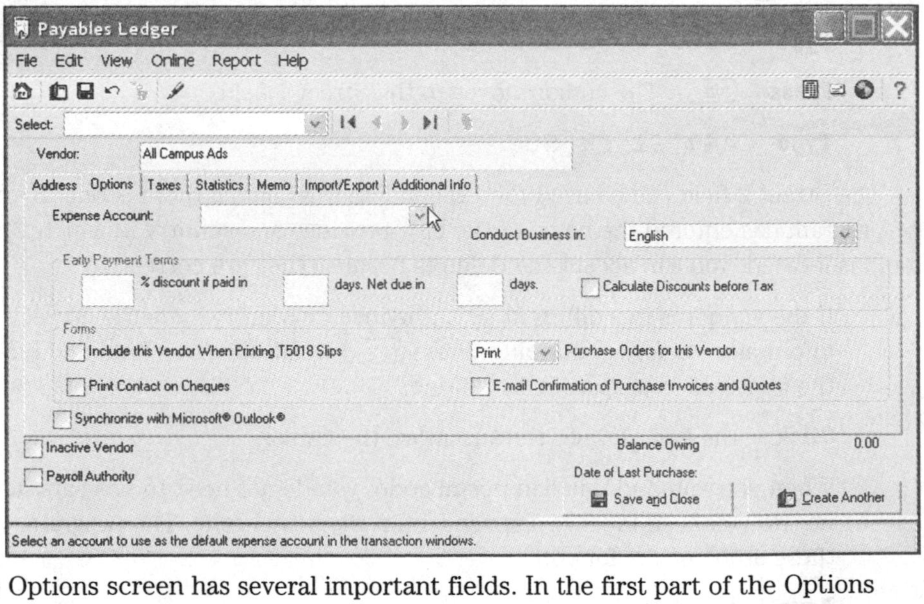

NOTES
Any account can be used as the default expense account, including capital accounts. This allows you to set up the owner as a vendor and link the transactions to the Drawings account.

The Options screen has several important fields. In the first part of the Options screen, you can choose the default account and preferred language (English or French) for the vendor. Forms you send to that vendor will be in the selected language, although your own screens will not change. Usually an expense or asset account is the default account. Even though the field is named Expense Account, you may select any postable account. If you usually buy the same kinds of goods from a vendor, entering the account as the default saves time and prevents errors when completing journal entries. All Campus Ads provides promotional materials.

Click the **Expense Account list arrow** to see the accounts available.

Scroll down and **click 5020 Advertising and Promotion**.

NOTES

If you need to create a new account for this vendor, type the new account number in the Expense Account field and press *tab*. Click Add to confirm that you want to create the account. The Add An Account wizard will open.

In the Early Payment Terms section of the ledger, you can enter the discount for early settlement of accounts and the term for full payment. According to the source document, immediate payment is expected.

Click the **Net Due In ____ Days field** (Early Payment Terms section).

Type 1

NOTES

Typing 0 (zero) in the Net Days field will leave the payment terms fields on the invoice blank. Therefore, we enter net 1 (one) when payment is due immediately.

The next fields appear as check boxes. There are no discounts from this vendor. Leave the check box for Calculate Discounts Before Tax blank.

Include This Vendor When Printing T5018 Slips applies to amounts paid to subcontractors for construction services and does not apply to Chai Tea Room. Selecting Print Contact On Cheques will add the name of the contact person to the cheque written to the vendor. If the Contact field contains address information, check this box; otherwise, leave it unchecked.

The next option allows you to choose Print or E-mail Purchase Orders For This Vendor as the default setting, but you can change the selection for individual purchase orders if necessary. If you choose to e-mail the orders, you should check the E-mail Confirmation Of Purchase Invoices And Quotes option by clicking it.

If you want to synchronize lists in Simply Accounting with Microsoft Outlook, click the Synchronize With Microsoft Outlook check box.

BASIC VERSION

The option to Synchronize With MS Outlook is not available in the Basic version.

The next input screen defines the tax options for this vendor.

Click the **Taxes tab** to open the screen:

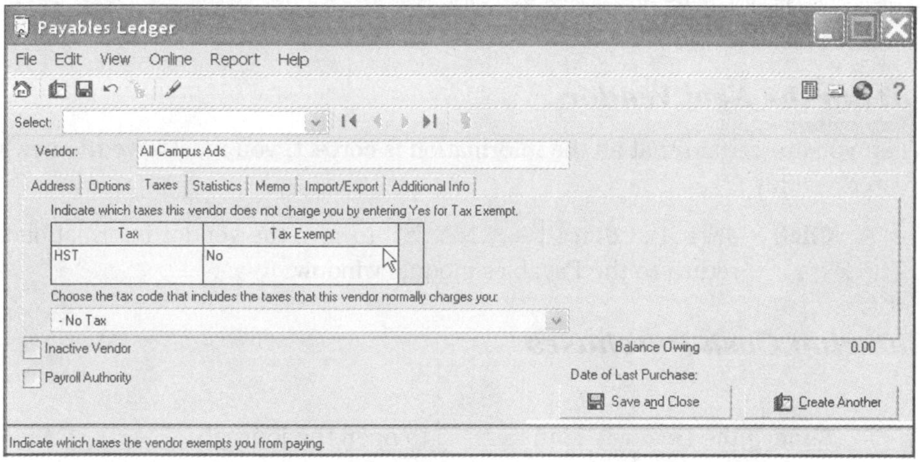

All the taxes that Chai Tea Room usually pays are set up for the company and appear on the list. HST is the only applicable tax. The default option is to pay the tax. The option under Tax Exempt is set at No, that is, Chai is not exempt from taxes on purchases from this vendor. Clicking No will change the tax exemption setting to Yes. This change would be appropriate for vendors, such as the Receiver General, that do not supply goods or services. Refer to Chapter 2 for further information about taxes and discounts.

WARNING!

The tax exempt option Yes should be selected only if all purchases from the vendor are tax exempt because this setting prevents taxes from being calculated on any purchases from the vendor.

To enter a default tax code for purchases from the vendor, we can choose a code from the drop-down list in the next field. The default setting, No Tax, is incorrect for All Campus Ads.

NOTES

When the tax exempt settings are correct, you can change the tax codes in the journals and the tax calculations will be correct. If the tax exempt settings are incorrect, you can change the codes but no taxes will be calculated.

Click **No Tax** to see the codes available:

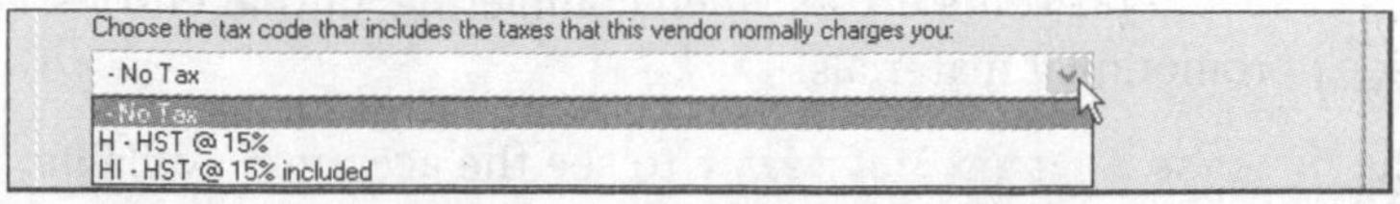

Three codes are defined for Chai Tea Room: **No Tax** for vendors who do not charge any tax such as Bathurst Foods; **H** for suppliers of normal taxable goods or services when HST is not included in the price; and **HI** for suppliers of taxable goods such as gasoline or liquor when the tax is included in the purchase price.

All Campus Ads charges HST but does not include it in the price.

Click **H - HST @ 15%**.

The remaining input screens are not needed; they will be introduced in a later application. The Statistics tab screen stores cumulative historical purchases and payments, the Memo tab screen allows you to add messages to the Daily Business Manager and the Import/Export tab allows you to specify corresponding inventory item codes for your business and your suppliers. The Additional Info tab screen has other vendor information fields that can be customized for the company.

Check your work carefully before saving the information because the options you select will affect the invoices directly.

CORRECTING A NEW VENDOR ACCOUNT

Move to the field that has the error by **pressing** (tab) to move forward through the fields or **pressing** (shift) and (tab) together to move back to a previous field. **Type** the **correct information**.

You can also highlight the incorrect information by **dragging** the cursor through it. You can now **type** the **correct information**.

After a field has been corrected, **press** (tab) to enter the correction.

To open a different tab screen, **click** the **tab** you want.

Saving the New Vendor

When you are certain that all the information is correct, you must save the newly created vendor.

Click **Save And Close** [Save and Close] to save the vendor information and return to the Payables module window.

Entering Cash Purchases

Click the **Invoices icon**  to open the journal.

If you need to create a full vendor record from the Vendor field:

Type the new vendor's name in the Purchased From field. Press (tab). The program will recognize the name is new and give you the option to add a record.

Click Full Add to open a Payables Ledger record at the Address tab screen with the new vendor name already entered as you typed it in the Vendor field.

Enter all the details for the vendor as described above.

Click the Save And Close button to return to the invoice. The vendor's address, tax code and expense account will be added to the invoice form.

Choose **All Campus Ads** from the Purchased From drop-down list. **Press** (tab).

We can now enter the transaction details as we did for previous purchases. We need to change the payment method because this is a cash purchase. Remember that we use the term *cash purchase* for purchases with payment by cheque.

Click **Pay Later** in the Paid By field to see the payment options:

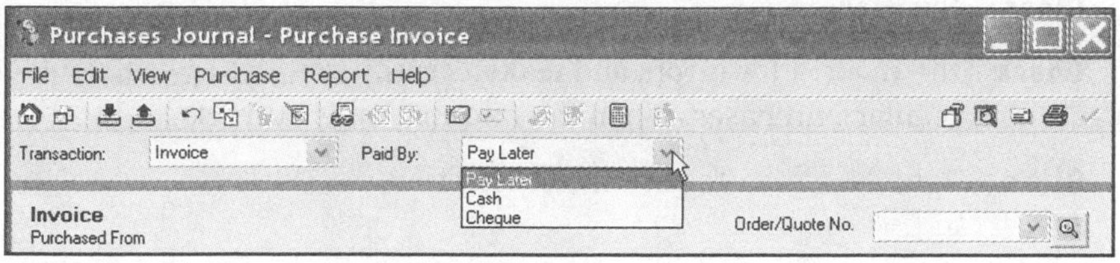

The payment options are the same as those in the Payments Journal for Other Payments, with the addition of Pay Later.

Click **Cheque**.

A cheque number field is added to the invoice with the next cheque number in the lower left corner of the journal. The cheque number is updated automatically. You need to add the invoice number, transaction date and amount.

Click the **Invoice field** and **type** ACA-3492

Click the **Calendar icon** and **choose August 3**.

Click the **Amount field**.

Type 200 **Press** tab. You can add a description if you want.

The invoice is now complete and should look like the one shown:

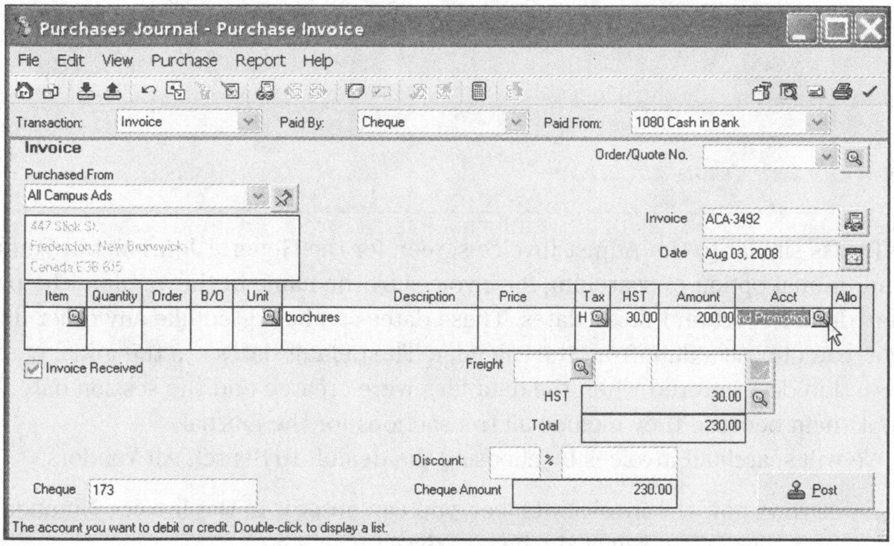

You should review the journal entry before posting it.

Choose the **Report menu** and **click Display Purchases Journal Entry**:

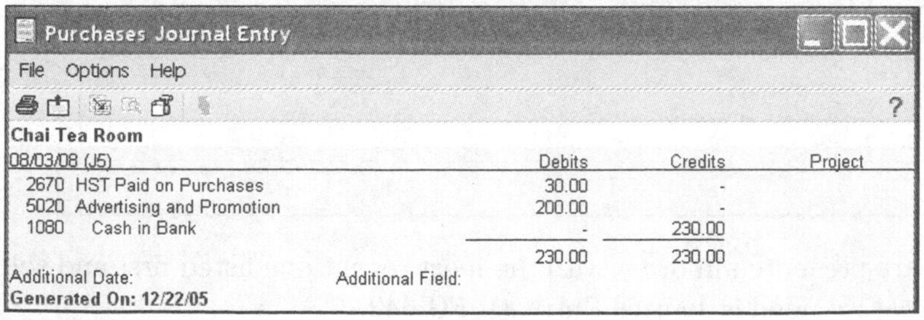

NOTES

Sometimes a business uses more than one bank account. If multiple accounts are set up, all bank accounts will be listed in the Paid From drop-down list. You can choose the appropriate bank account from the list for purchases by cheque and for payments. Credit cards and multiple bank accounts are used in later applications.

You can see that the journal entry is the same as the one from the Payments Journal when we chose Make Other Payment. *Cash in Bank* is credited instead of *Accounts Payable*. The vendor record is updated for the transaction by including both an invoice and a payment for the same date.

Close the **display**.

Check the **invoice** for errors and **make corrections** just as you would for regular purchases. When the information is correct,

Click **Post** [Post] to save the transaction.

Adjusting a Posted Invoice

> **NOTES**
> You must choose the System Settings option to Store Invoice Lookup Details to be able to adjust posted invoices (see page 84).

> **NOTES**
> You can also press ctrl + A to open the Adjust An Invoice window from any journal. See Appendix B for a list of keyboard shortcuts.

In the same way that you can correct or adjust a previously posted entry in the General Journal, you can edit a Purchases Journal invoice after posting. Simply Accounting will create the necessary reversing entry when you post the revised invoice.

The Purchases Journal should still be open.

Click the **Adjust Invoice tool** or **choose** the **Purchase menu** and **click Adjust Invoice** to open the Adjust An Invoice screen:

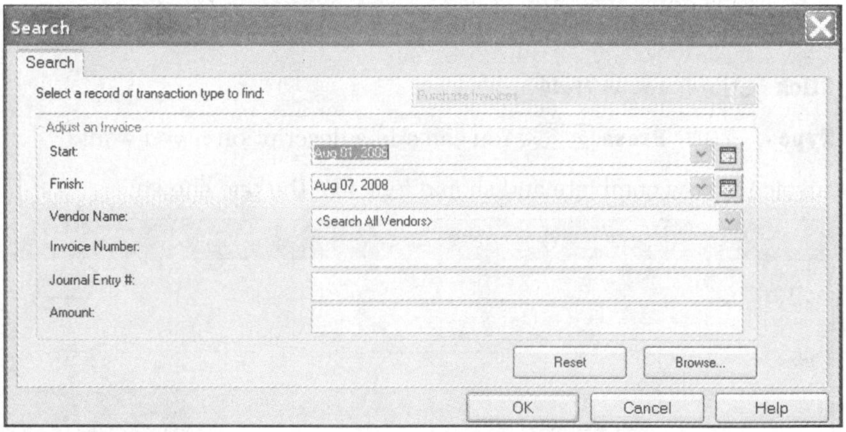

This is similar to the Adjust Invoice screen for the General Journal, but you have the additional option of searching for invoices by the name of the vendor. The program enters default start and finish dates. These dates can be edited like any other date fields or you can choose a date from the calendar. The default dates are the initial earliest transaction date entered when the data files were created and the session date. We can accept them because they include all transactions for the journal.

We will search all invoices by choosing the default to Search All Vendors.

If you know the invoice number, you can enter it in the Invoice Number field and click OK to select the invoice directly.

Click **Browse** to see the requested list of Purchases Journal invoices:

> **NOTES**
> Notice that cash purchases entered in the Payments Journal are not included in this list. You can adjust these transactions from the Payments Journal after you select Make Other Payment (see page 140).

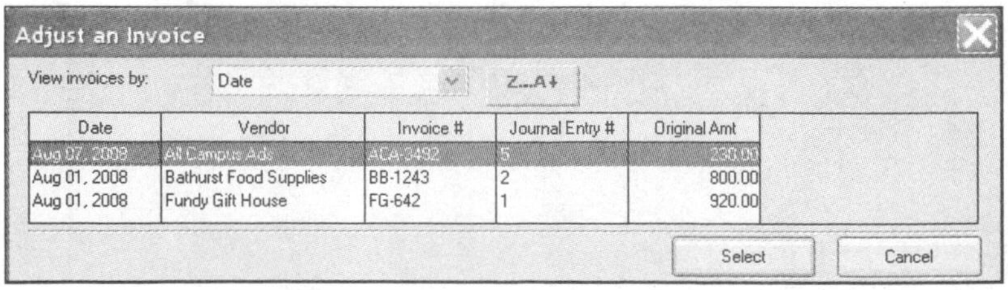

Invoices are presented in order with the most recent one listed first and selected. The invoice that we need is Journal Entry #1, FG-642.

Click **FG-642**. (Click anywhere on the line to highlight the invoice.)

Click **Select** or **press** enter to recall the selected transaction:

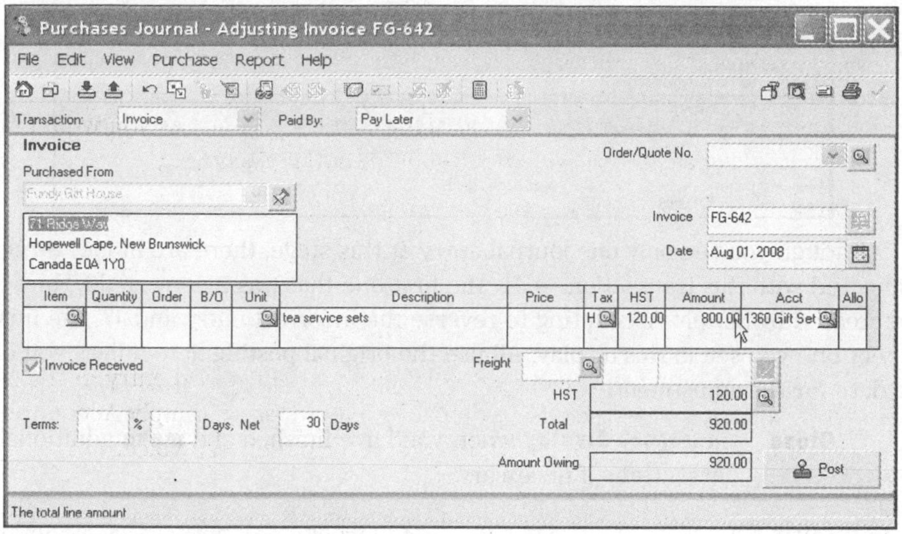

All fields are available for editing, except the vendor. To correct a vendor, you must complete a reversing entry (see Appendix C). We need to edit the amount.

Click **800.00** in the Amount field.

Type 900

Press tab to update the tax amount and totals.

You can add R- to the invoice number if you want to indicate that this is the revised invoice.

Your completed entry should now resemble the following:

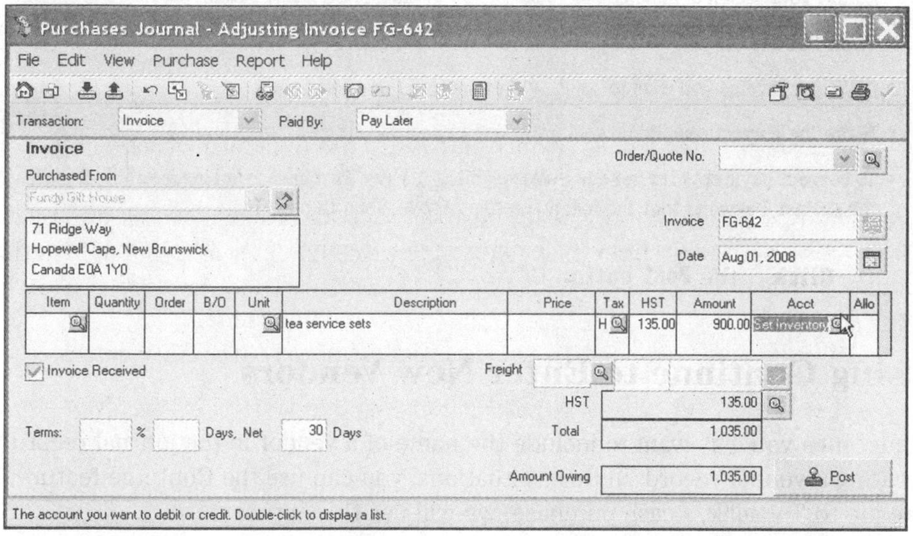

Before posting the revised transaction, review it for accuracy.

> **NOTES**
> If you edit the date, the reversing and correcting entries will be posted with the same revised date. To see all three entries in the journal report, Corrections must be selected (see page 150).

Choose the **Report menu** and **click Display Purchases Journal Entry**:

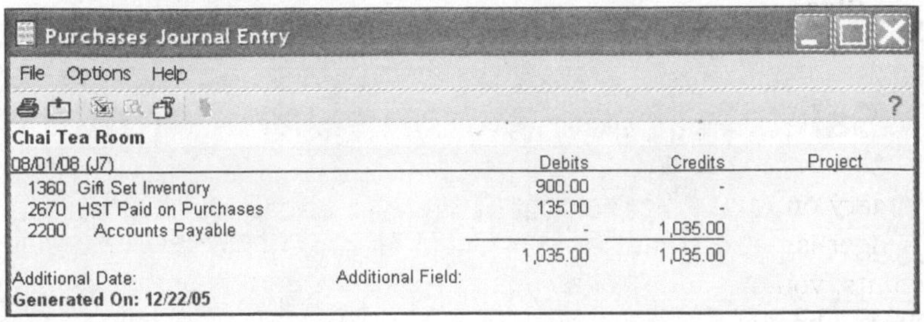

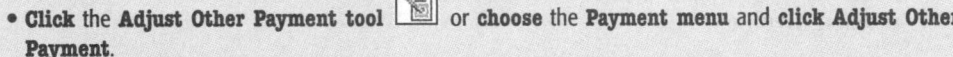

Although you see only one journal entry at this stage, there are in fact three entries connected with this transaction — J1, the first one that was incorrect, J6, the second one created by Simply Accounting to reverse the incorrect entry and J7, the final correct one you see in this display. All use the original posting date unless you change the date for the adjustment.

Close the **report display** when you have finished and **make** additional **corrections** if necessary.

> **CORRECTING CASH PURCHASES AND PAYMENTS FROM THE PAYMENTS JOURNAL**
> Purchases entered as Other Payments in the Payments Journal do not appear on the Adjust An Invoice list from the Purchases Journal. You can, however, adjust these other payments from the Payments Journal as follows:
>
> - **Click** the **Payments Journal icon**  to open the journal.
> - **Click Make Other Payment** from the transaction list.
> - Or from the Payables module window, **click** the **Make Other Payment icon** .
> - **Click** the **Adjust Other Payment tool**  or **choose** the **Payment menu** and **click Adjust Other Payment**.
> - **Select** your search parameters: the **date range**, **vendor** or **cheque number**.
> - **Click Browse** (or **click OK** if you entered the cheque number).
> - **Click** the **invoice** you want to adjust and **press** *enter* or **click Select**.
> - **Make** the **corrections**. **Review** your **entry** and **post** the revised transaction.
> - To **correct payments for vendor invoices**, **click** the **Pay Purchase Invoices icon** , **click** the **Adjust Payment tool** and follow the steps above. Refer to page 145.

Click the **Post button** .

Using Continue to Enter New Vendors

> **NOTES**
> For one-time vendors, type the vendor's name in the Address field. The vendor's name will not be included in journal reports.

Sometimes you may want to include the name of a vendor in the journal record without creating a vendor record. In these situations, you can use the Continue feature. For the cheque to Tomailik, a cash purchase, we will use this approach.

Click the **To The Order Of field**.

Type `Bette Tomailik`

Press *tab* to open the message about a new vendor name.

Click **Continue** to return to the journal.

Enter the **remaining details** of the cash purchase as usual.

Review and **post** the **transaction**.

Enter the **purchase** from **Sunbury Cleaning** for August 7 and **store** the **entry**. **Close** the **Purchases Journal**.

Entering Sales Taxes in the General Journal

The sales summary on August 7 is entered in the General Journal because the Receivables Ledger is not used by Chai Tea Room. When you have set up and linked sales tax accounts, you can add General Journal sales tax entries to the tax reports. A Sales Taxes button becomes available when you use one of these linked tax accounts in the General Journal. Chai has two linked tax accounts, *HST Charged on Sales* and *HST Paid on Purchases*.

To access the General Journal, you must close the Payables window.

Click the **Payables module heading** as shown:

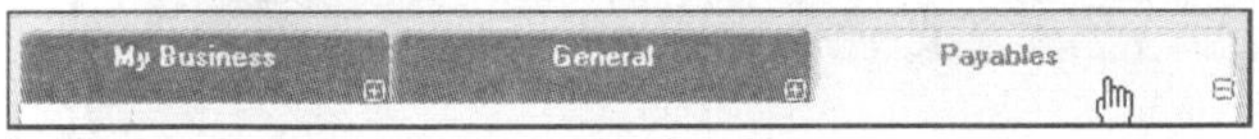

Click the **General icon**  to open the General Journal.

Enter the **Source** and **Comment** for the sales summary. The session date is correct.

Choose **Cash in Bank** as the account to be debited and **type** 8740 as the amount. **Enter** an appropriate **Comment** for the account.

Choose **HST Charged on Sales** as the next account. Advance to the credit column.

Type 1140 as the amount to be credited. **Press** (tab). Your screen should now resemble the one that follows:

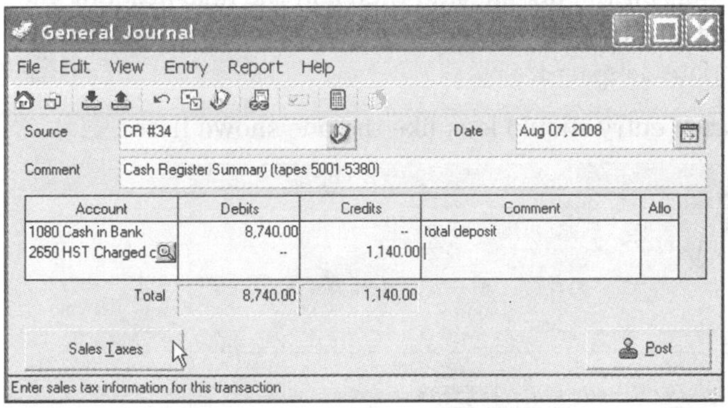

Notice that the Sales Taxes button became available, or highlighted, as soon as you entered the tax amount.

Click the **Sales Taxes button** to open the tax detail screen:

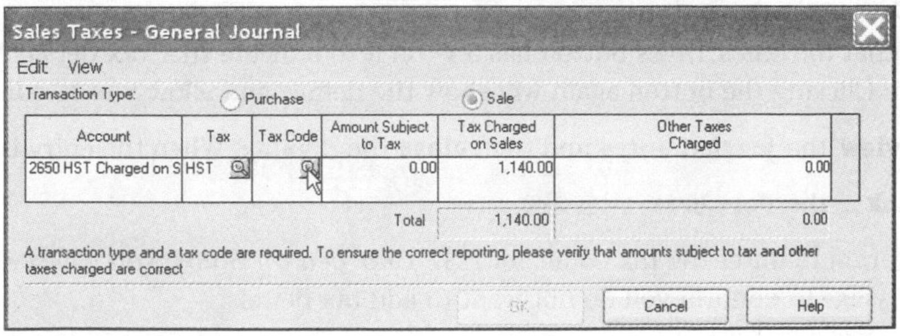

NOTES
To complete transactions involving the General Journal, you must close the Payables window and exit to the Home window. Follow the keystroke instructions for the General Journal from the Missoni Marbleworks application.

NOTES
Notice that the Payables module heading has a minus sign when the ledger window is open and a plus sign when it is closed.

NOTES
When you enter HST Paid on Purchases as the account, Purchase is selected as the default transaction type because this account is linked to the Payables module.

Because you entered *HST Charged on Sales* as the account, the transaction is recognized as a sale. You can change the transaction type if it is not correct. The account and tax amount are already entered on the form. We need to add the tax code.

Click the **List icon** in the Tax Code field to open the tax code list:

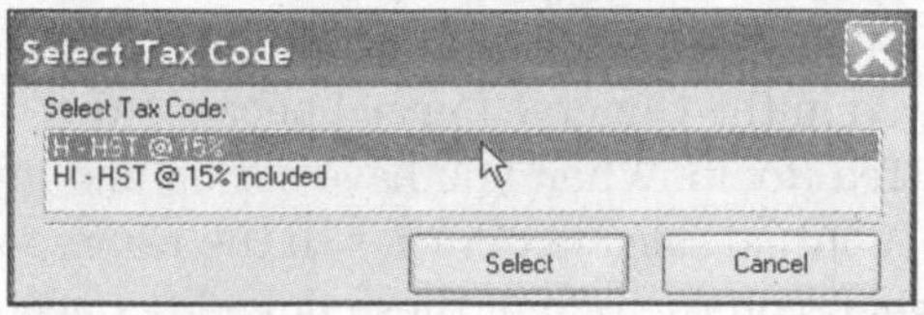

This is the same list that we saw in the Purchases and Payments journals in the tax code fields. Sales have HST at 15 percent added to the price so the correct code is H.

Click **Select** because code H is already highlighted. You will return to the tax detail screen:

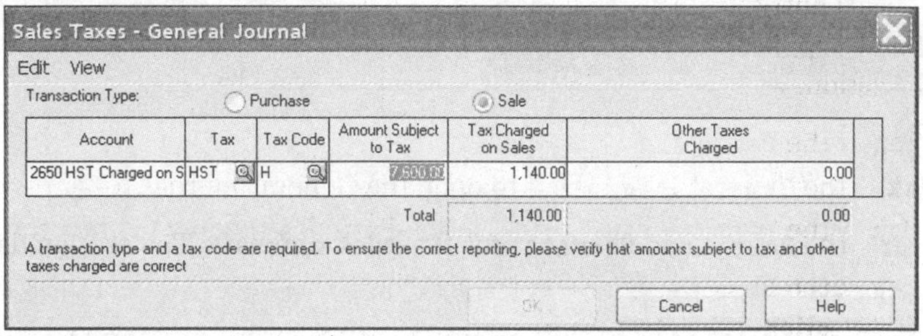

Because the tax amount was already entered, the sales amount — the Amount Subject To Tax — is calculated as soon as you select the tax code. The sales amount is correct so we can continue. If the amount is not correct because there are other taxes included, you can edit the default amount and enter an amount for Other Taxes Charged.

Click **OK**.

Enter a **Comment** for the tax line and then add the final account line by **choosing** account **4100**, accepting the amount and **adding** an appropriate **comment**.

Your completed journal entry should look like the one shown here:

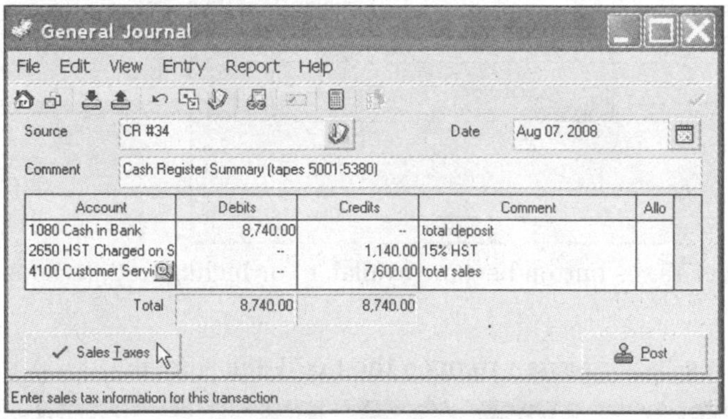

Notice that the Sales Taxes button has a ✔ on it to indicate that tax details have been added. Clicking the button again will show the details and allow you to edit them.

Review the **journal entry** and then **close** the **display**. When the entry is correct,

Click the **Post button** Post.

If you forgot to enter the tax codes for *HST Charged on Sales*, you will see the warning message to confirm you do not want to add tax details:

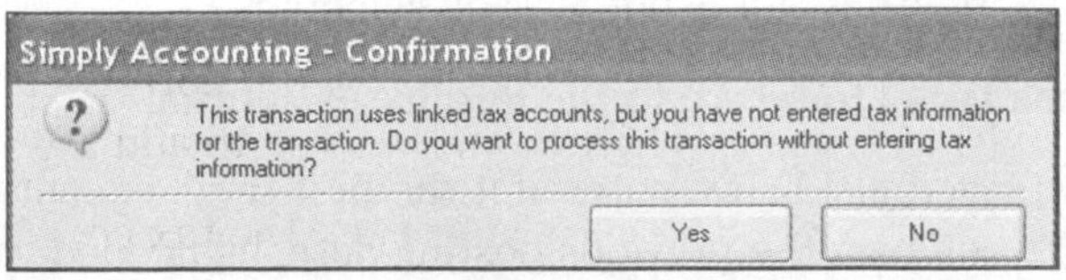

If you forgot to add the tax details, click No to open the Sales Taxes window. Add the missing details and then post the journal entry.

Close the **General Journal** to return to the Home window.

Back up your **data file**. **Advance** the **session date** to **August 14**.

Recalling a Stored Entry

The first journal entry for the August 14 session date is the recurring purchase from Bathurst Food Supplies. Since we have stored this purchase, we do not need to re-enter all the information.

Open the **Payables module window**.

> **NOTES**
> Click the Payables heading bar to open the Payables module window.

Click the **Invoices icon**  in the Payables window to open the Journal.

Click the **Recall tool**  in the tool bar (or **choose** the **Purchase menu** and **click Recall**) to display the Recall Recurring Transaction dialogue box as shown here:

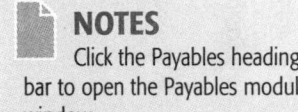

> **NOTES**
> You can press ctrl + R to recall a stored entry.

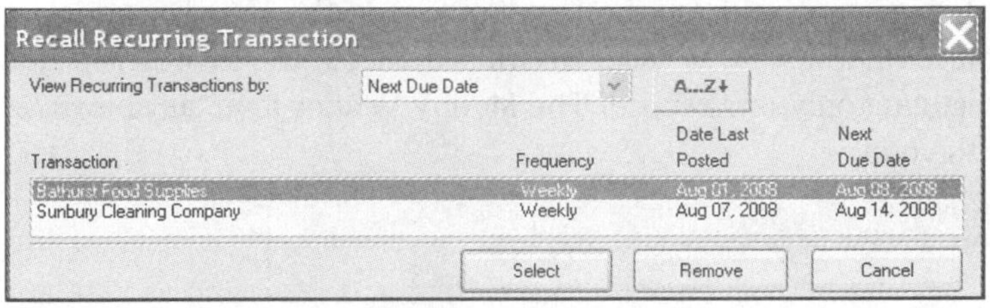

The stored entries are listed in order according to the next date that they will be repeated. If you want, you can display the stored entries in a different order.

Click the **View Recurring Transactions By list arrow** to see the options:

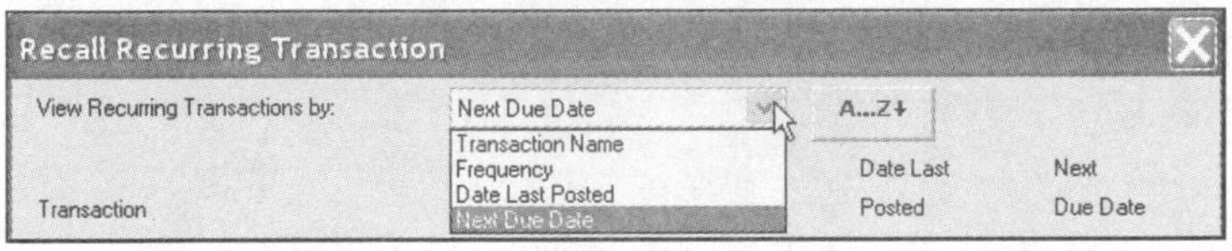

You can choose to view the stored entries in order by Transaction Name (which is the vendor's name if you did not change the default), by Frequency (how often the transaction is repeated), by the Date Last Processed (the posting date) or by the Next Due Date. If you have a large number of stored entries, it may be easier to find the one you need with a different order. You can also reverse the order for any of the order selections with the A...Z button. Since we have only two stored entries, the default order, Next Due Date, placed the one we want first. Do not change the default.

From the Recall Stored Entry dialogue box, you can remove an entry that is incorrect or no longer needed. Click an entry to select it. Click Remove and then click Yes to confirm that you want to delete the entry. (See page 237.)

Bathurst Food Supplies, the name of the entry we want to use, should be selected because it is the recurring entry that is due next.

Click **Bathurst Food Supplies** if it is not already selected.

Click **Select** or **press** *enter* to return to the Purchases Journal.

The entry we stored is displayed just as we entered it the first time, except that the date has been changed to one week past the previous posting date, as needed, and the Invoice field is blank so we can enter the new invoice number. Remember that Simply Accounting does not accept duplicate invoice numbers.

Click the **Invoice field** to move the cursor.

Type `BB-2100`

The entry is now complete. You should review it before posting.

Choose the **Report menu** and **click** **Display Purchases Journal Entry**.

Close the **display** when finished and **make** any necessary **corrections**.

Click the **Post button** .

Close the **Purchases Journal**.

Editing a Vendor Record

Sometimes a vendor record must be revised after it is saved because the initial information has changed or because information that was not available initially is now known. We need to edit the record for NB Gas to add the default expense account.

Vendor records are accessed from the Vendors icon in the Home window or from the Payables module window. In this case, we will start from the module window because we are changing only one record. The Modify Vendor icon, as shown, is the starting point for the edit:

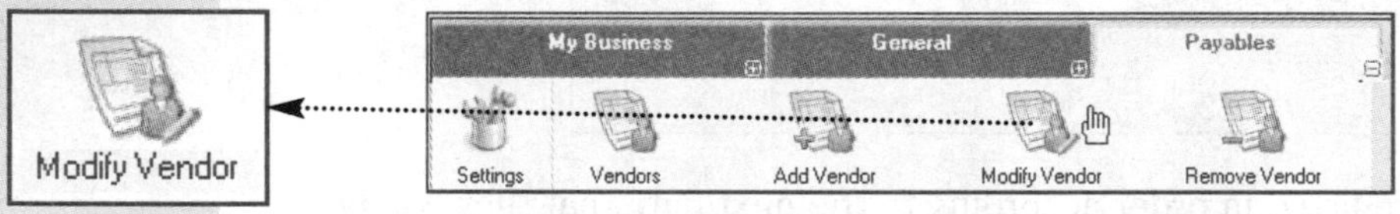

Click the **Modify Vendor icon** to open the Search Vendor window:

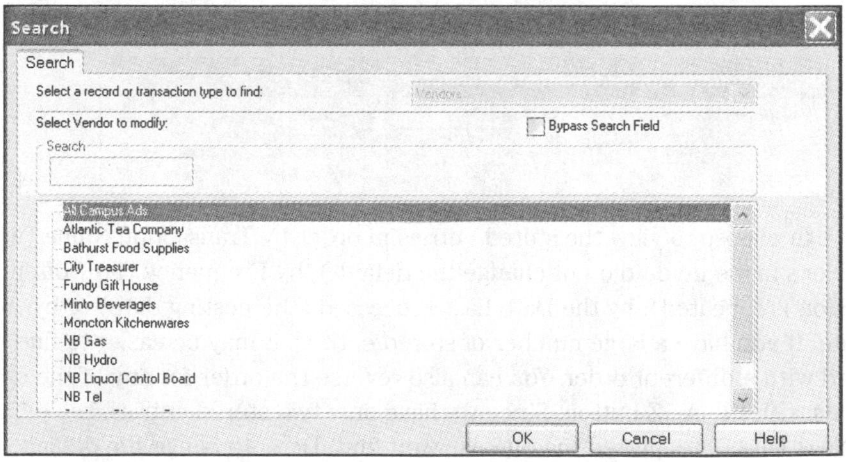

Each vendor on record is listed on the Search vendor selection window. Notice that Bette Tomailik is not listed. Notice too that this window is similar to the Search windows that start the Adjust entry procedure in journals.

Double click **NB Gas** to open its record at the Address tab information screen.

Click the **Options tab** to access the Expense Account field:

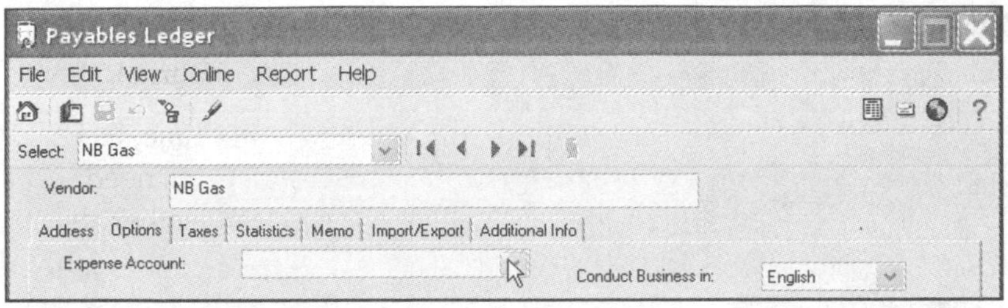

Click the **Expense Account field**.

Type `5110` **Press** *tab* to complete the entry. You can also choose the account from the list provided by the list arrow.

Close the **Payables Ledger** (vendor record) window to return to the Payables module window. Changes are saved automatically.

The next time you enter a transaction for NB Gas, the account will appear automatically.

NOTES
Remember that although the field is named Expense Account, you can choose any postable account as the default for the vendor. You can also select a different account in the journal if necessary.

Adjusting a Posted Payment

Just as you can correct a purchase invoice after posting, you can correct a cheque that has been posted.

Click the **Pay Purchase Invoices icon** [Pay Purchase Invoices] to open the Payments Journal.

Click the **Adjust Payment tool** or **choose** the **Payment menu** and **click Adjust Payment** to open the Search screen for Adjust Payments:

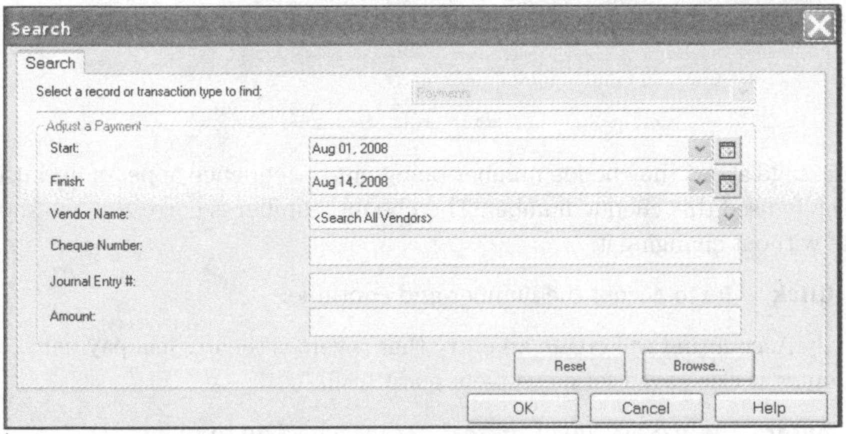

Again we see the familiar Search window for the selected journal.

Click **Browse** to see the list of cheques already posted for this date range:

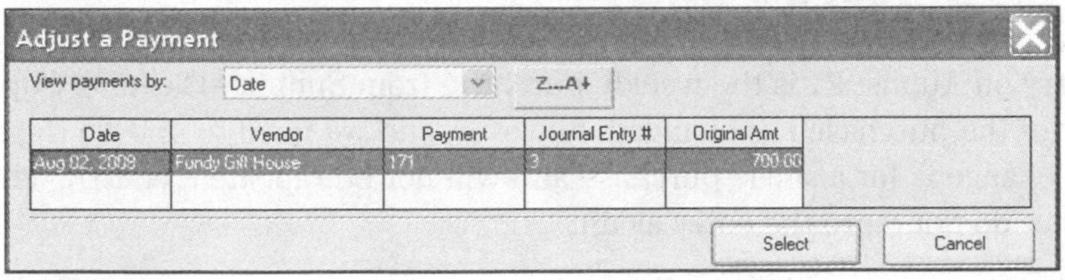

The single cheque used to pay invoices is listed and selected. It is the one we need to correct. Only cheques used to pay invoices are listed.

basic BASIC VERSION
Click the Pay Vendor Invoices icon instead of Pay Purchase Invoices.

NOTES
Pressing *ctrl* + A will also open the Search window to begin the adjusting procedure.

NOTES
To see the cash purchases entered as Make Other Payment, click the Make Other Payment icon in the module window, or choose Make Other Payment from the Pay list to modify the payment form. Then click the Adjust Payment tool.

Click **Select** to see the cheque we posted:

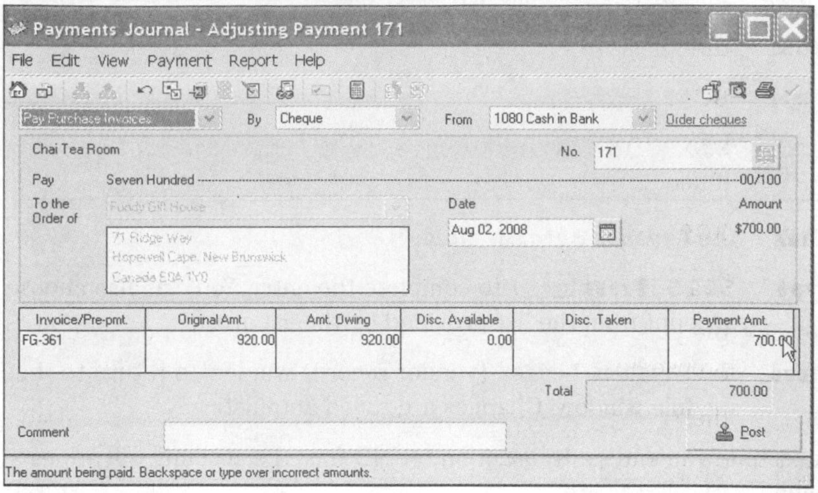

The cheque appears as it was completed. You can edit all the details except the vendor.

Click **700.00** in the Payment Amt field.

Type `600`

Click the **Comment field**.

Type `previous chq amount incorrectly entered`

Check your **work** carefully.

Click **Post** to save the changes:

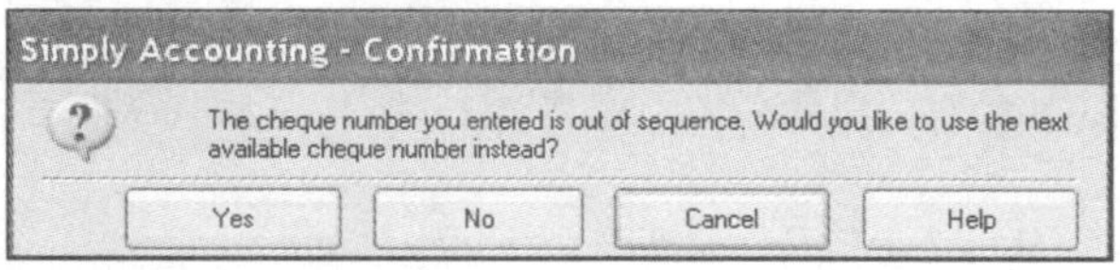

A message about the cheque number being out of sequence appears because we have already used this cheque number. The cheque number is correct so we should continue without changing it.

Click **No** to accept the number and continue.

Simply Accounting will create an entry that reverses the original payment, and the original entry is also saved for a complete audit trail.

Enter the **next** group of **journal transactions** up to August 21.

Changing a Stored Entry

The first entry on August 21 is the weekly purchase from Sunbury Cleaning Supplies. The amount of the purchase has changed, however, and we need to update the stored entry. If the change is for a single purchase and will not be repeated, edit the entry after recalling it but do not store the entry again.

Click the **Invoices icon** 

in the Payables window to open the Journal.

Click the **Recall tool**  on the tool bar, or **choose** the **Purchase menu** and **click** **Recall** to display the Recall Recurring Transaction dialogue box.

Double click **Sunbury Cleaning Supplies**, the entry we want to use to display the purchase entry with the new date.

Click the **Invoice field** so you can add the invoice number.

Type SC-1790

Click **250.00**, the Amount, to highlight it so that you can edit it. Double click if necessary to select the amount.

Type 300

Press tab to enter the change.

Review the **journal entry** as usual to make sure that it is correct before proceeding.

Click the **Store button**, or **choose** the **Purchase menu** and **click Store**.

Click **OK** to accept the name and frequency without changes.

The following warning appears:

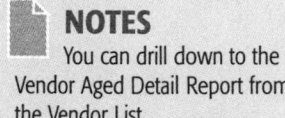

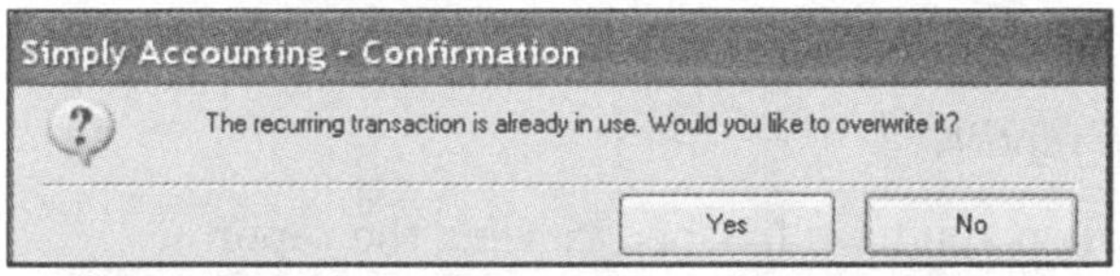
Simply Accounting - Confirmation
The recurring transaction is already in use. Would you like to overwrite it?
Yes
No

Click **Yes** to confirm that you want to replace the previous stored version and return to the Purchases Journal.

Click the **Post button** Post to save the entry. **Close** the **Journal**.

Enter the **remaining journal transactions** for August.

Displaying Vendor Reports

All vendor-related reports can be displayed or printed from the Vendors window.

Click the **Vendors icon** Vendors in the Home window to open the Vendors window.

The Reports menu now lists only vendor reports. You can select the report you want from this list and follow the instructions below to choose report options.

Close the **Vendors window**.

NOTES
The Vendor Purchases Report deals mainly with inventory. It will be introduced in a later application.

Displaying Vendor Lists

Right-click the **Vendors icon** Vendors in the Home window. (Clicking the left mouse button will open the ledger.)

The Display button label changes to the name of the report for the selected icon.

Click the **Display tool** on the tool bar or **choose** the **Reports menu**, then **choose Lists** and **click Vendors**.

NOTES
You can drill down to the Vendor Aged Detail Report from the Vendor List.

You will see the report options:

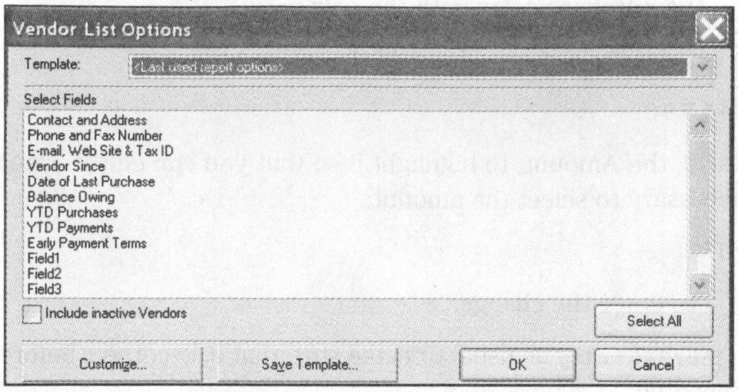

You can select the vendor details that you want in your list. All regular fields are selected initially.

Click the **first field** you want in the report to begin the new selection.

Press and **hold** ctrl and **click** the **remaining fields** you want in the report or **click Select All** to add all the fields.

Click **OK** to see the report.

Close the **display** when you have finished viewing the report.

Displaying Vendor Aged Reports

You can display Vendor Aged reports at any time.

Choose the **Reports menu** in the Home window, then **choose Payables** and **click Vendor Aged** to see the report options window:

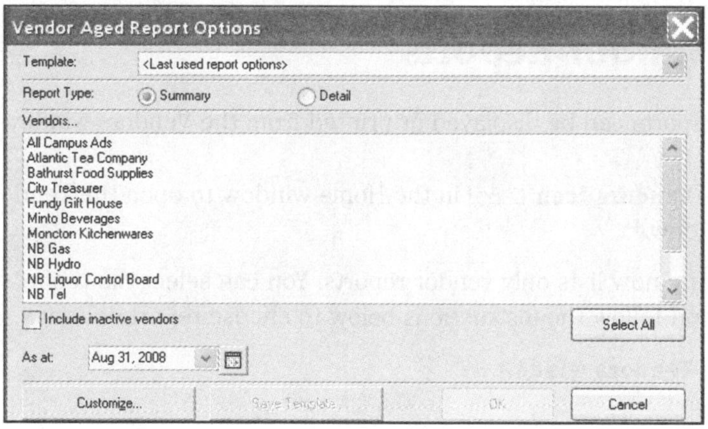

NOTES
From the Vendor Aged Detail Report, you can drill down to look up invoices and to vendor ledgers. From the Summary Report, you can drill down to the Detail Report.

If you chose either One-Time Vendor or Continue for Bette Tomailik, she will not be included by name in the list of vendors for reports and graphs. If you used Quick Add, her name will be included.

The **Summary** option provides the total balance owing to each vendor. It displays an alphabetic list of vendors with outstanding total balances organized into aged columns. By default, the program selects this option.

Select the **Detail** option if you want to see individual outstanding invoices and payments made to vendors. This more descriptive report is also aged. Management can use it to make payment decisions. With the Detail option, you can also add vendor payment terms by clicking Include Terms.

You can sort and filter the reports by vendor name or by the balance owing. You can select or omit any of the columns to customize the report.

Click **Detail** if you want the Detail Report.

Click the **name** or **press** and **hold** ctrl and **click** the **names** in the Vendors list to select the vendors you want in the report. If you want the report to include all vendors, **click Select All**.

Enter the **date** you want for the report or accept the session date given by default. After you have indicated all the options,

Click **OK** to see the report.

Close the **displayed report** when you have finished.

Displaying Aged Overdue Payables Reports

You can display Aged Overdue Payables reports at any time.

Choose the **Reports menu** in the Home window, then **choose Payables** and **click Aged Overdue Payables** to see the report options:

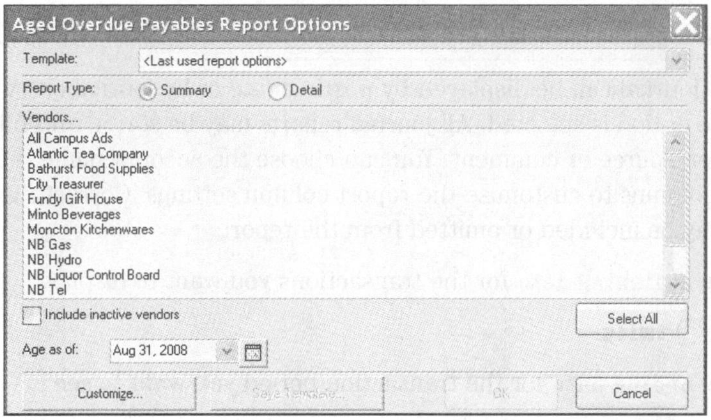

The Aged Overdue Payables Report includes the same information as the Vendor Aged Report but it adds a column for the invoice amounts that are overdue. Vendor name and balance owing may be selected as the criteria for sorting and filtering. The Summary Report shows totals for each vendor while the Detail Report includes details for each invoice.

You can sort and filter the reports by vendor name or by the balance owing. You can select or omit any of the columns to customize the report.

Choose **Summary** or **Detail**.

Press and **hold** ctrl and then **click** the **names** in the Vendors list to select the vendors that you want to see in the report. **Click Select All** to include all vendors.

Enter the **date** you want for the report, or accept the session date given by default. After you have indicated all the options,

Click **OK** to see the report. One invoice from Moncton Kitchenwares and the balance on the first invoice from Fundy Gift House are overdue.

Close the **displayed report** when you have finished.

NOTES

You can drill down to look up invoices and to the Vendor Aged Report from the Aged Overdue Payables Report. From the Summary Report, you can drill down to the Detail Report.

Displaying the Purchases Journal

NOTES
To view the entries for all journals in a single report, choose the Reports menu, then choose Journal Entries and click All.

Right-click the **Purchases icon** in the Home window to select it.

Click the **Display tool** on the tool bar (or **choose** the **Reports menu**, then **choose Journal Entries** and **click Purchases**).

If no icons are selected in the Home window, Purchases and Payments Journal reports are available from the list when you click the Display tool.

NOTES
You can also access the Purchases Journal Report from the Payables module window. Right-click the Invoices, Purchase Orders or Quotes icon and then click the Display tool button.

You will see the report options screen:

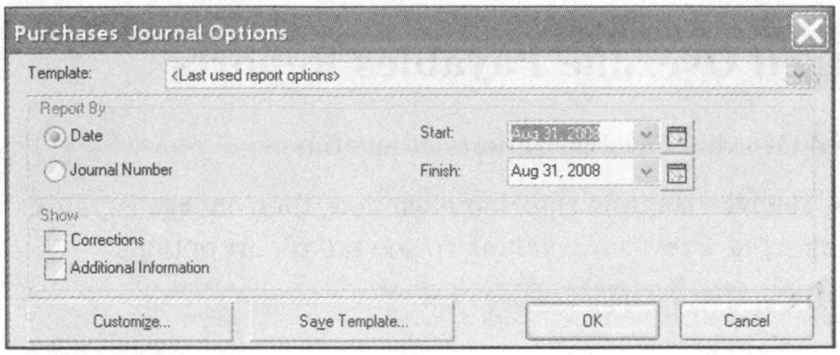

NOTES
If you omit corrections, the journal reports will appear to be out of sequence because the journal entry numbers for the incorrect transactions and their reversing entries will be omitted from the report.

The Purchases Journal can be displayed by posting date or by journal entry number. By default, the Date option is selected. All journal reports may be sorted and filtered by date, journal number, source or comment. You can choose the account name, number, debits and credits columns to customize the report column settings. Correcting or adjusting entries may be included or omitted from the report.

NOTES
You can choose August 1 as the start date from the Start field drop-down list.

Type the **beginning date** for the transactions you want to display.

Press *tab* **twice**.

Type the **ending date** for the transaction period you want to see.

Click **Corrections**.

Click **OK** to see the report.

Close the **display** when you have finished.

Displaying the Payments Journal

NOTES
You can drill down to look up invoices, to the Vendor Aged Report and to the General Ledger Report from the Purchases Journal or the Payments Journal Report.

Right-click the **Payments icon** in the Home window to select it.

Click the **Display tool** or **choose** the **Reports menu**, then **choose Journal Entries** and **click Payments** to see the report options:

NOTES
You can also access the Payments Journal Report options from the Payables module window. Right-click the Pay Vendor Invoices, Pay Credit Card Bill, Make Other Payment or Pay Remittances icon. Then click the Display tool button.

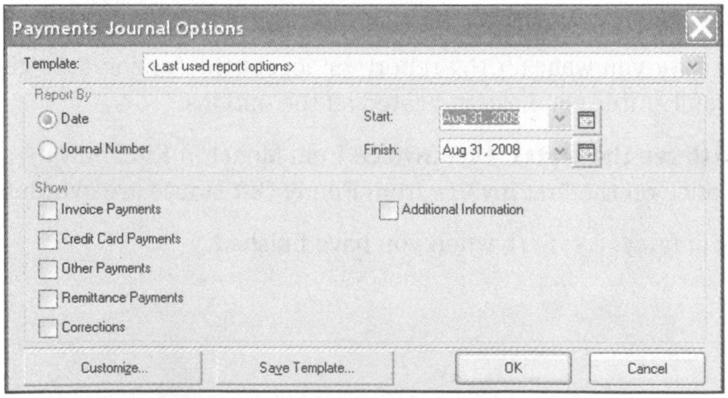

The Payments Journal, like other journal reports, can be displayed by posting date, the default setting, or by journal entry number. In addition, you can choose the type of payment for the report — invoice payments, credit card payments, other payments (cash purchases) and remittance payments. Corrections or adjustments may be included or omitted. None are selected initially and clicking any one will select it for the report. Clicking again will remove the selection.

Type the **beginning date** for the transactions you want to display.

Press tab **twice**.

Type the **ending date** for the transaction period you want to see.

Click **Corrections**.

Click **Invoice Payments** and **Make Other Payments** to include both types of payments in the report.

Click **OK** to see the report.

Close the **display** when you have finished.

Displaying Cheque Log Reports

If you regularly print cheques through Simply Accounting from the Payables journals or the Payroll journals, you can display and print a summary of these printed cheques in the Cheque Log Report.

Choose the **Reports menu** in the Home window, then **choose Banking** and **click Cheque Log**. The report options window appears:

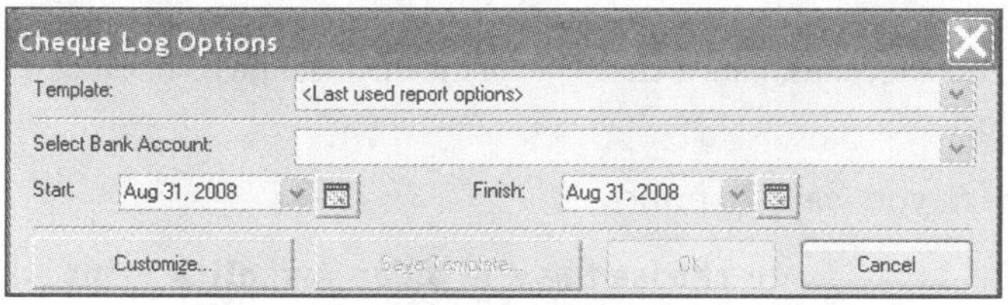

The report will include details for all cheques that you printed including whether or not the journal entry was posted and the number of times the cheque was printed. If you do not print cheques through the program, these payments are listed with a 0 (zero) for the number of times printed. Adjusted cheques are identified as Reversed.

To customize the report, you can choose any of the column headings to sort or filter the report and you can choose to include or omit any of these columns.

Choose the **bank account** from the Select Bank Account drop-down list.

Enter the **Start** and **Finish dates** for the report.

Click **OK** to see the report.

Close the **display** when you have finished.

Displaying Management Reports

Management reports are available for each ledger.

Choose the **Reports menu** in the Home window, then **choose Management Reports** and **click Payables**.

> **NOTES**
> In the management report for overdue payments, negative numbers indicate current invoices and positive numbers show the number of days that the payment is overdue.

The report options window appears:

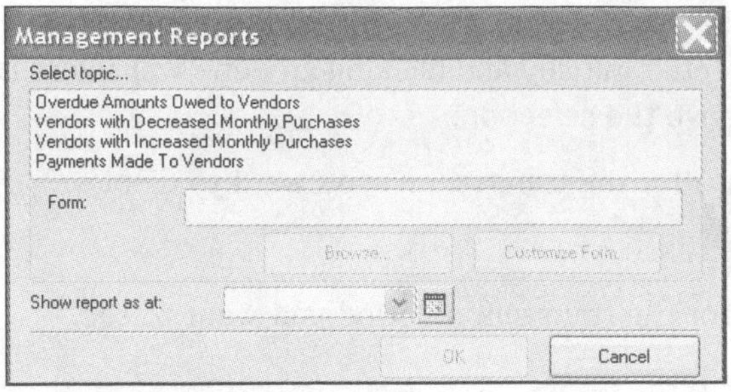

Sometimes management reports can reveal patterns in the business more clearly than the regular financial reports. For example, the report for overdue accounts lists invoices that are outstanding, with vendor contact and invoice details and the number of days remaining until payment is due. The reports for increased or decreased monthly purchases show changes in purchase patterns over the previous year that an aged detail report may not.

When you click a topic, the appropriate form will be selected from those installed with the program. Unless you have the programs required to customize forms, accept the default. If appropriate, enter a date for the report.

Click **OK** to see the report. **Print** the **report** and then **close** the **display**.

Printing Vendor Reports

Before printing vendor reports, make sure that the print options have been set correctly. To print a report,

Display the **report** you want to print.

Click the **Print tool** or **choose** the **File menu** and **click** **Print**.

Printing Mailing Labels

> **NOTES**
> For practice, you can print the labels on plain paper.

To print labels, you should first make sure that the print options have been set correctly and that your printer is turned on and has the correct labels paper. To set the program to use your printing labels,

Choose the Setup menu in the Home window and click Reports & Forms.
Click Labels in the list under Reports.
Enter the appropriate details for the labels you are using.
Click OK to return to the Home window.

Choose the **Reports menu** in the Home window, then **choose** **Mailing Labels** and **click** **Vendors**:

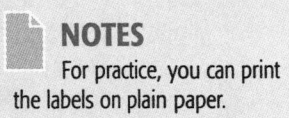

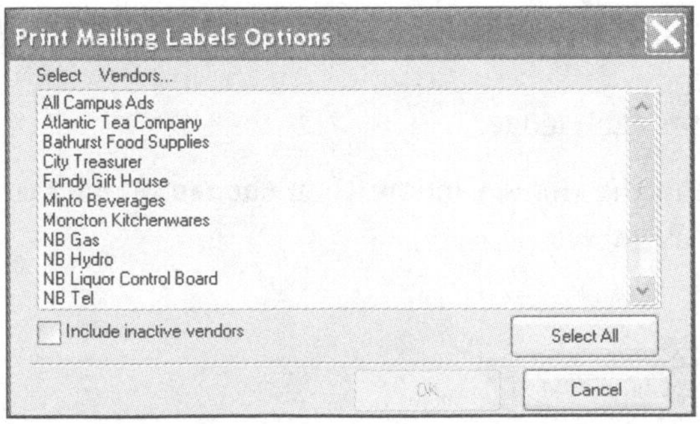

Press and **hold** ctrl and then **click** the **names** of the vendors for whom you want labels, or **click Select All** to include all vendors.

Click **OK**.

Graphing Vendor Reports

Payables by Aging Period Charts

Choose the **Graphs menu** in the Home window, then **click Payables By Aging Period** to display the date entry screen:

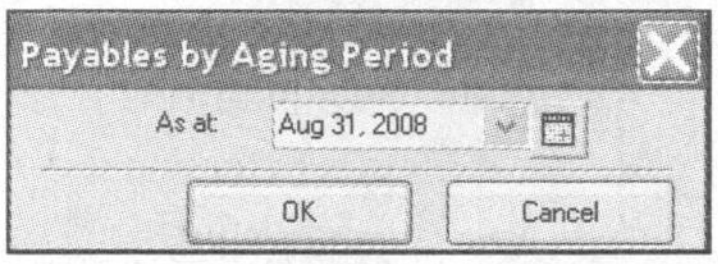

Type the **date** for the graph or accept the default session date.

Click **OK** to display the pie chart:

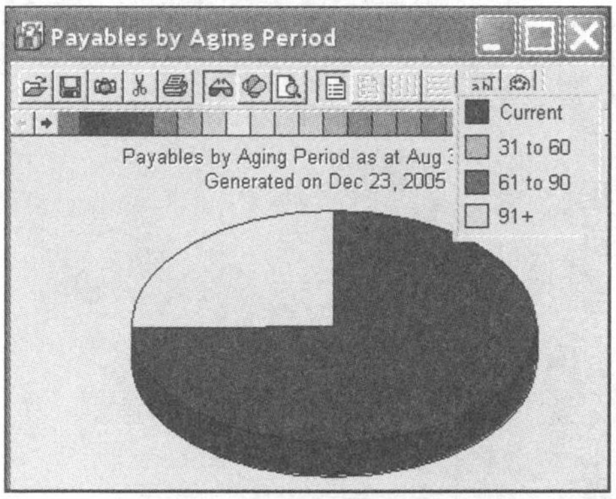

NOTES
The tool bar options, and the control of the colour and the legend, are the same for all graphs. Refer to page 61 for a review of these features.

Your graph provides a quick visual reference of amounts due to all vendors combined in each of the aging periods selected in the company setup options. Most of the payments due are current but about 25 percent are overdue — the amounts owing to Moncton Kitchenwares and Fundy Gift House.

Double click a portion of a graph to see the aging period, the dollar amount and the percentage of the total. Double click the legend to make it larger and add the aging periods if they are not included already. Double click the expanded legend to reduce it.

Close the **graph** when you have finished.

Payables by Vendor Charts

Choose the **Graphs menu** in the Home window, then **click Payables By Vendor** to display the pie chart options:

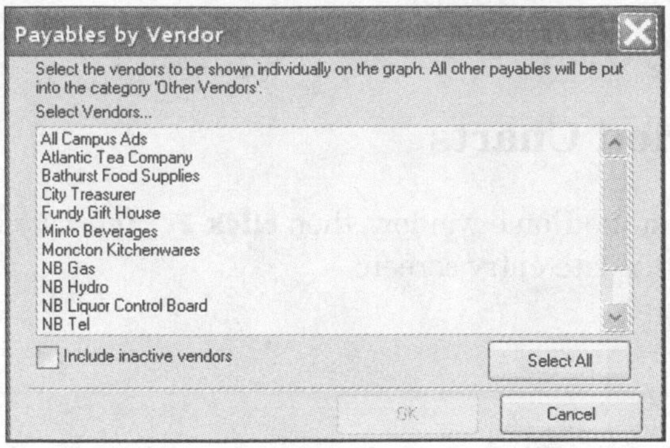

Press and **hold** ctrl and then **click** the **names** of the vendors to include in your pie chart, or **click Select All** to include all the vendors.

Click **OK** to display the pie chart:

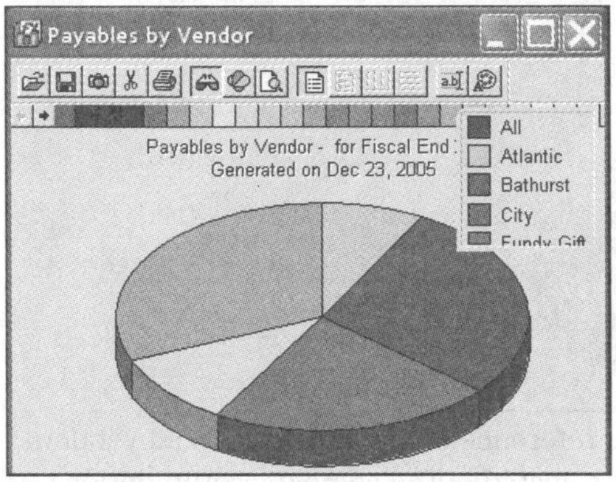

The graph shows the proportion of the total payables that is owed to each selected vendor. The tool bar options, and the control of the colour and the legend, are the same as for the other graphs.

Close the **graph** when you have finished.

R E V I E W

The Student CD-ROM with Data Files includes Review Questions and Supplementary Cases for this chapter.

CHAPTER SIX

AirCare Services

OBJECTIVES

After completing this chapter, you should be able to

- ***enter*** transactions in the General, Payables and Receivables journals
- ***enter*** transactions from the My Business Tab window
- ***enter*** and ***post*** cash and account sale transactions
- ***enter*** and ***post*** customer payment transactions
- ***customize*** the sales journal and invoices
- ***enter*** transactions including GST and PST
- ***store*** and ***recall*** recurring entries
- ***enter*** partial payments made by customers
- ***add*** and ***edit*** customer accounts
- ***handle*** an NSF cheque from a customer
- ***edit*** and ***review*** customer-related transactions
- ***display***, ***print*** and ***graph*** customer reports
- ***understand*** linked accounts for the Receivables Ledger

COMPANY INFORMATION

Company Profile

NOTES
Air Care Services
100 Belair Avenue, Unit 25
Winnipeg, Manitoba R3T 0S3
Tel 1: (204) 456-1299
Tel 2: (888) 455-7194
Fax: (204) 456-3188
Business No.: 533 766 455

Air Care Services, located in Winnipeg, Manitoba, has been operating successfully for the past five years under the ownership and management of Simon Arturro. The company's range of services, related to heating equipment and air-conditioning units, draws on Arturro's experience with electrical wiring, boilers, plumbing and chimney work. He has two occasional assistants.

Revenue comes from four sources: installation, repairs, service contracts and subcontracting. Air Care installs air-conditioning units, heating equipment, electronic thermostats, gas fireplaces and portable air-conditioning units in customers' homes through arrangements with companies that handle only the sales of these units. Installation work may include adding air filtration and air-cleaning units to existing heating systems and installing gas fireplaces in private homes, offices, clubs and funeral homes. Upgrades for old furnaces and fireplaces often require replacing chimney liners and installing direct venting. Product manufacturers pay Air Care for repairing equipment under warranty, and individual customers rely on Air Care for other repairs. Arturro also sells service contracts to homeowners and small businesses. And finally, Arturro handles installation subcontracts for large contractors for work in schools, office buildings and apartment buildings.

Some customers — homeowners, owners of office buildings and companies that sell furnaces and air conditioners — have accounts set up with Air Care. Regular account customers are asked to settle their accounts in 10 days. Payment is by cash or by cheque. PST and GST apply to all service work done by Arturro.

Accounts have been set up with a local hardware store, suppliers of chimney liners and parts for furnaces and air conditioners, and other regular vendors.

After remitting all taxes before the end of April 2008, Arturro converted the accounts for Air Care using the following information:

- Chart of Accounts
- Post-Closing Trial Balance
- Vendor Information
- Customer Information
- Accounting Procedures

CHART OF POSTABLE ACCOUNTS

AIR CARE SERVICES

ASSETS
1080 Cash in Bank
1200 Accounts Receivable
1300 Air Conditioning Parts
1320 Furnace Parts
1340 Office Supplies
1420 Cash Register
1440 Computer System
1460 Service Equipment
1480 Tools ▶

▶1500 Van
1550 Shop

LIABILITIES
2100 Bank Loan
2200 Accounts Payable
2640 PST Payable
2650 GST Charged on Services
2670 GST Paid on Purchases
2850 Mortgage Payable ▶

▶**EQUITY**
3560 S. Arturro, Capital
3600 Net Income

REVENUE
4100 Installation Revenue
4120 Repairs Revenue
4140 Service Contract Revenue ▶

▶**EXPENSE**
5100 Advertising and Promotion
5120 Bank Charges
5140 Interest Expense
5160 Hydro Expense
5180 Payroll Service Charges
5220 Telephone Expense
5240 Vehicle Expenses
5300 Wages

NOTES: The Chart of Accounts includes only postable accounts and the Net Income or Current Earnings account.

POST-CLOSING TRIAL BALANCE

AIR CARE SERVICES

April 30, 2008		Debits	Credits
1080	Cash in Bank	$ 15 660	
1200	Accounts Receivable	4 140	
1300	Air Conditioning Parts	1 200	
1320	Furnace Parts	600	
1340	Office Supplies	400	
1420	Cash Register	500	
1440	Computer System	2 500	
1460	Service Equipment	10 000	
1480	Tools	3 000	
1500	Van	25 000	
1550	Shop	100 000	
2100	Bank Loan		$ 10 000
2200	Accounts Payable		4 200
2850	Mortgage Payable		80 000
3560	S. Arturro, Capital		68 800
		$163 000	$163 000

VENDOR INFORMATION

AIR CARE SERVICES

Vendor Name (Contact)	Address	Phone No. Fax No.	E-mail Web Site	Terms Tax ID
Beausejour Chimney Products (Janine Beausejour)	50 Fireplace Rd. Winnipeg, Manitoba R3F 2T2	Tel: (204) 476-5282 Fax: (204) 476-5110	jb@beausejour.com www.beausejour.com	net 30 444 276 534
Brandon Hardware (Nutley Bolter)	72 Hammer St. Winnipeg, Manitoba R4P 1B8	Tel: (204) 369-0808 Fax: (204) 369-6222	nbolter@yahoo.com	net 15 385 416 822
Killarney Furnace Equipment (Kieper Warme)	91 Radiator St. Winnipeg, Manitoba R1B 4F4	Tel: (204) 363-0210 Fax: (204) 363-2000	kwarme@heatexchange.com	net 10 571 277 631
Manitoba Hydro (Kira Strong)	1 Power Station Rd. Winnipeg, Manitoba R6G 2C1	Tel: (204) 479-2999	kira.strong@mnhydro.man.ca www.mnhydro.man.ca	net 1
Manitoba Telephone (Sotto Voce)	4 Speakers Corners Winnipeg, Manitoba R1E 2K2	Tel: (204) 361-3255	www.manitobatel.ca	net 1
Starbuck Advertising Agency (Pam Fletts)	300 Flyer St. Winnipeg, Manitoba R3V 6S3	Tel: (204) 361-1727 Fax: (204) 361-8229	pfletts@saa.com www.saa.com	net 1 610 728 365
Steinbach Airconditioning Inc. (Ezra Steinbach)	2 Ventilate St. Winnipeg, Manitoba R2H 9J9	Tel: (204) 475-6432 Fax: (204) 475-8600	esteinb@steinair.com www.steinair.com	net 30 177 235 441
UPS Delivery (Bea Carrier)	8 Freight St. Winnipeg, Manitoba R3A 7B2	Tel 1: (204) 479-1UPS (1877) Tel 2: (800) 477-1UPS Fax: (204) 477-6000	www.ups.com	net 1 522 534 677
Willow Garage (Axel Rodd)	699 Willow St. Winnipeg, Manitoba R2P 1B3	Tel: (204) 368-6444 Fax: (204) 368-6000	axel@wefixcars.com www.wefixcars.com	net 30 129 732 010

OUTSTANDING VENDOR INVOICES

AIR CARE SERVICES

Vendor Name	Terms	Date	Invoice No.	Amount	Total
Beausejour Chimney Products	net 30	Apr. 8/08	B-894	$1 600	$1 600
Steinbach Airconditioning Inc.	net 30	Apr. 16/08	SA-2141	$1 500	$1 500
Willow Garage	net 30	Apr. 10/08	W-1142	$1 100	$1 100
			Grand Total		$4 200

CUSTOMER INFORMATION

AIR CARE SERVICES

Customer Name (Contact)	Address	Phone No. Fax No.	E-mail Web Site	Terms Credit Limit
Brandon School Board (Ed Ducate)	49 Trainer St. Winnipeg, Manitoba R3P 2T5	Tel 1: (204) 466-5000 Tel 2: (204) 466-1123 Fax: (204) 466-2000	Ed.D@bsb.com www.bsb.com	net 10 $2 500
Grande Pointe Towers (Sophie Grande)	77 LaPointe Cr. Winnipeg, Manitoba R2G 4D1	Tel: (204) 322-7500 Fax: (204) 322-7436	sgrande@GPTowers.com www.GPTowers.com	net 10 $3 000
Midwestern Funeral Home (N. Mourning)	8 Quiet St. Winnipeg, Manitoba R7B 1E1	Tel: (204) 763-WAKE (9253) Fax: (204) 762-9301	nm@midwestfh.com www.midwestfh.com	C.O.D. (net 1) $2 000

▶

Customer Name (Contact)	Address	Phone No. Fax No.	E-mail Web Site	Terms Credit Limit
Oak Bluff Banquet Hall (Ann Oakley)	4 Celebration Ave. Winnipeg, Manitoba R8V 3H7	Tel: (204) 622-7391 Fax: (204) 622-7900	annie@OBBH.com www.OBBH.com	net 10 $5 000
Selkirk Furnaces Inc. (Elsa Selkirk)	588 Heater St. Winnipeg, Manitoba R3T 8N1	Tel: (204) 368-4575 Fax: (204) 368-2198	elsas@selkirk.com www.selkirk.com	net 10 $5 000

OUTSTANDING CUSTOMER INVOICES

AIR CARE SERVICES

Customer Name	Terms	Date	Inv/Chq No.	Amount	Total
Grande Pointe Towers	net 10	Apr. 25/08	A-696	$1 380	
		Apr. 25/08	Chq #3166	700	
		Apr. 26/08	A-698	700	
			Balance owing		$1 380
Oak Bluff Banquet Hall	net 10	Apr. 28/08	A-700	$1 140	
		Apr. 30/08	A-702	1 620	
			Balance owing		$2 760
			Grand Total		$4 140

Accounting Procedures

Open-Invoice Accounting for Receivables

The open-invoice method of accounting for invoices issued by a business allows the business to keep track of each individual invoice and of any partial payments made against it. In contrast, other methods keep track only of the outstanding balance by combining all invoice balances owed by a customer. Simply Accounting uses the open-invoice method. When an invoice is fully paid, you can either retain the invoice or remove (clear) it.

NSF Cheques

If a cheque is deposited from an account that does not have enough money to cover it, the bank may return it to the depositor as NSF (non-sufficient funds). The treatment of an NSF cheque from a customer requires a reversing entry in the Receipts Journal. (See Keystrokes, page 181.) In most companies, the accounting department notifies the customer who wrote the NSF cheque to explain that the debt remains unpaid. Many companies charge an additional fee to the customer to recover their bank charges for the NSF cheque. A separate sales invoice should be prepared for the additional charge. NSF cheques to vendors are handled in the same way, through reversing entries in the Payments Journal.

Taxes (GST and PST)

Air Care Services is a service business using the regular method of calculating GST. GST, at the rate of 7 percent, charged and collected from customers will be recorded as a liability in *GST Charged on Services*. GST paid to vendors will be recorded in *GST Paid on Purchases* as a decrease in tax liability. The balance owing is the difference between the GST charged and GST paid. The balance to be remitted or the request for a refund will be sent to the Receiver General for Canada by the last day of the month for the previous quarterly period.

Air Care charges customers 7 percent PST on all sales and pays PST on some goods. Air Care is exempt from PST for purchases of items that are sold or used in service work because the customer pays PST on these products.

Cash Sales of Services

Cash transactions are a normal occurrence in most businesses. Simply Accounting has Paid By options to handle cash transactions. (See Keystrokes, page 175.) When you choose Paid By Cash or Cheque, the program will debit *Cash in Bank* instead of the *Accounts Receivable* control account. All other accounts for the transaction will be debited or credited in the same way as credit sales.

INSTRUCTIONS

1. **Record entries for the source documents** in Simply Accounting using the Chart of Accounts, Vendor Information, Customer Information and Accounting Procedures for Air Care Services. The procedures for entering each new type of transaction in this application are outlined step by step in the Keystrokes section following the source documents. These transactions are indicated with a ✓ in the completion box beside the source document. The page on which the relevant keystrokes begin is printed immediately below the check box.
2. **Print** the **reports and graphs** indicated on the following printing form after you have finished making your entries. Instructions for reports begin on page 187.

REPORTS

Lists
- ☐ Chart of Accounts
- ☐ Account List
- ☐ Vendors
- ☐ Customers

Journals
- ☑ All Journals (by date) May 1 to May 31
- ☐ General
- ☐ Purchases
- ☐ Payments
- ☑ Sales (by date) May 1 to May 31
- ☑ Receipts (by date) May 1 to May 31

Financials
- ☑ Balance Sheet: May 31
- ☑ Income Statement from May 1 to May 31
- ☑ Trial Balance date: May 31
- ☑ General Ledger accounts: 1300 4120 4140 from May 1 to May 31
- ☐ Statement of Cash Flows
- ☑ Cash Flow Projection Detail Report for account 1080 for 30 days

Taxes
- ☑ GST Report May 31
- ☑ PST Report May 31

Banking
- ☐ Cheque Log Report

Payables
- ☐ Vendor Aged
- ☐ Aged Overdue Payables

Receivables
- ☑ Customer Aged Detail for all customers
- ☐ Aged Overdue Receivables
- ☐ Customer Statements

Mailing Labels
- ☐ Labels

Management Reports
- ☐ Ledger

GRAPHS
- ☐ Payables by Aging Period
- ☐ Payables by Vendor
- ☐ Receivables by Aging Period
- ☐ Receivables by Customer
- ☑ Sales vs Receivables
- ☑ Receivables Due vs Payables Due
- ☑ Revenues by Account
- ☐ Expenses by Account
- ☑ Expenses and Net Profit as % of Revenue

SOURCE DOCUMENTS

WARNING!
Do not include A- in the sales invoice number in the journal. The numeric portion will then be correctly updated by the program.

SESSION DATE – MAY 8, 2008

☑ **Sales Invoice #A-710** **Dated May 1/08**

164 To Selkirk Furnaces Inc., $800 plus $56 GST and $56 PST for subcontracting work on apartment air-conditioning system. Invoice total, $912. Terms: net 10. Create new Group account 4160 Subcontracting Revenue. Customize the sales invoice by removing the columns that are not used by Air Care Services.

☑ **Cash Receipt #20** **Dated May 2/08**

171 From Grande Pointe Towers, cheque #3499 for $880, including $680 in full payment of invoice #A-696 and $200 in partial payment of invoice #A-698.

☑ **Cash Sales Invoice #A-711** **Dated May 3/08**

175 To Midwestern Funeral Home, $900 plus $63 GST and $63 PST for installation of air-conditioning equipment. Terms: Cash on completion of work. Received cheque #394 for $1 026 in full payment.

☑ **Sales Invoice #A-712** **Dated May 3/08**

177 To Hazel Estates (use Full Add for the new customer), $1 600 plus $112 GST and $112 PST for installation of new furnace equipment. Invoice total $1 824. Terms: net 10.

NOTES
Hazel Estates
☑ (contact Joelle Beausoleil)
177 488 Sunshine St., Ste 1200
West St. Paul, MB R4G 5H3
Tel 1: (204) 367-7611
Tel 2: (877) 367-9000
Fax: (204) 369-2191
E-mail: JB@hazelestates.com
Web: www.hazelestates.com
Terms: net 10
Revenue account: 4100
Tax code: GP
Credit limit: $4 000

☑ **Bank Debit Memo #14321** **Dated May 4/08**

181 From Flatlands Credit Union, cheque #3499 for $880 from Grand Pointe Towers has been returned because of non-sufficient funds. Reverse the payment and notify the customer of the outstanding charges.

☑ **Memo #1** **Dated May 5/08**

183 From Owner: Edit the ledger record for Grande Pointe Towers to change the payment terms to net 1. Certified cheques will be requested in the future. Edit the records for all other customers to set the credit limit at $4 000.

☑ **Cash Sales Invoice #A-713** **Dated May 5/08**

184 Cash Sales Summary
To various one-time customers

Repairs Revenue	$ 600
Service Contract Revenue	800
GST charged	98
PST charged	98
Total cash received and deposited	$1 596

NOTES
Choose One-Time Customer and enter Cash Sales Summary in the Address field.
Use tax code GP for the Cash Sales.
If you want, you can store the cash sale as a weekly transaction. When you recall it, you can edit the amounts and accounts. Refer to page 146 and page 184.

☑ **Memo #2** **Dated May 5/08**

185 From Owner: The work done for Hazel Estates included $800 plus $56 GST and $56 PST for repairs to the heating system. The revised and correct invoice total is $2 736. Adjust the posted entry (reference invoice #A-712) and then print it.

☑ **Cheque Copy #101** **Dated May 5/08**

To Beausejour Chimney Products, $1 600 in payment of account. Reference invoice #B-894.

☑ **Purchase Invoice #W-1993** **Dated May 6/08**

From Willow Garage, $60 for gasoline, including taxes (use tax code IN) for weekly fill-up of van. Store the transaction as a weekly recurring entry. Terms: net 30.

NOTES
Enter payments from the Pay Invoices icon.
Enter purchase invoices from the Purchase Invoices icon.

Purchase Invoice #SA-2309 **Dated May 6/08**

From Steinbach Airconditioning, $400 plus $28 GST. Invoice total $428 for air-conditioning parts, filters, coils, etc. Terms: net 30. Store as bi-weekly recurring transaction.

Sales Invoice #A-714 **Dated May 7/08**

To Brandon School Board, $500 plus $35 GST and $35 PST for installation of new pipes on school furnace. Invoice total $570. Terms: net 10.

Cheque Copy #102 **Dated May 8/08**

To Willow Garage, $1 100 in payment of account. Reference invoice #W-1142.

Purchase Invoice #BH-42001 **Dated May 8/08**

From Brandon Hardware, $500 plus $35 GST and $35 PST for new ladders and tools. Invoice total $570. Terms: net 15.

Sales Invoice #A-715 **Dated May 8/08**

To Vinod Residence (use Full Add for the new customer), $400 plus $28 GST and $28 PST for repairs. Invoice total $456. Terms: net 10.

NOTES

Vinod Residence
(contact Virin Vinod)
56 House St.
Winnipeg, MB R2P 8K1
Tel: (204) 761-8114
E-mail: v.vinod@interlog.com
Terms: net 10
Revenue account: 4120
Tax code: GP
Credit limit: $2 000

SESSION DATE – MAY 15, 2008

Bank Credit Memo #21432 **Dated May 9/08**

From Flatlands Credit Union, $3 000 loan for new service equipment approved and deposited to bank account. Principal of six-month loan and interest at 7.5% to be paid in full at the end of six months.

Cash Receipt #22 **Dated May 9/08**

From Oak Bluff Banquet Hall, cheque #2995 for $1 900, including $1 140 in full payment of invoice #A-700 and $760 in partial payment of invoice #A-702.

Sales Invoice #A-716 **Dated May 9/08**

To Selkirk Furnaces Inc., $1 200 plus $84 GST and $84 PST for subcontracting work. Invoice total $1 368. Terms: net 10.

Cash Receipt #23 **Dated May 10/08**

From Selkirk Furnaces Inc., cheque #533 for $912 in payment of account. Reference invoice #A-710.

Cash Sales Invoice #A-717 **Dated May 12/08**

Cash Sales Summary
To various one-time customers

Repairs Revenue	$ 500
Installation Revenue	600
GST charged	77
PST charged	77
Total cash received and deposited	$1 254

Purchase Invoice #W-2356 **Dated May 13/08**

From Willow Garage, $60 for gasoline, including taxes (use tax code IN) for weekly fill-up of van. Terms: net 30 days. Recall stored entry.

Cash Receipt #24 **Dated May 14/08**

From Hazel Estates, cheque #230 for $2 736 in full payment of account. Reference invoice #A-712.

NOTES
Refer to page 144 if you need help with editing a vendor record.

Cash Purchase Invoice #UPS-3467 Dated May 14/08

From UPS Delivery, $60 for special delivery of air-conditioner parts plus $4.20 GST. Invoice total $64.20. Issued cheque #103 in full payment. Create new Group account 5130 Delivery Expenses. Edit the vendor record to add the new expense account as the default expense account.

Cheque Copy #104 Dated May 14/08

To Steinbach Airconditioning, $1 500 in payment of account. Reference invoice #SA-2141.

Cash Receipt #25 Dated May 15/08

From Vinod Residence, cheque #432 for $456 in payment of account. Reference invoice #A-715.

Cash Receipt #26 Dated May 15/08

From Grande Pointe Towers, certified cheque #3682 for $1 380 in payment of account. Reference invoices #A-696 and A-698.

SESSION DATE – MAY 22, 2008

Sales Invoice #A-718 Dated May 18/08

To Oak Bluff Banquet Hall, $2 000 for air-conditioning installation and $1 000 for repair to furnaces, plus $210 GST and $210 PST. Invoice total $3 420. Terms: net 10. Allow customers to exceed credit limits.

Bank Debit Memo #37191 Dated May 18/08

From Flatlands Credit Union, cheque #432 for $456 from Vinod Residence has been returned because of non-sufficient funds. Reverse the payment and notify the customer of the outstanding charges.

Memo #3 Dated May 18/08

Edit the ledger record for Vinod Residence to set the credit limit to zero and terms to net 1. The customer will be placed on cash-only terms.

Cash Receipt #28 Dated May 19/08

From Selkirk Furnaces Inc., cheque #586 for $1 368 in payment of account. Reference invoice #A-716.

Cash Sales Invoice #A-719 Dated May 19/08

Cash Sales Summary
To various one-time customers

Repairs Revenue	$ 600
Service Contract Revenue	400
GST charged	70
PST charged	70
Total cash received and deposited	$1 140

Purchase Invoice #W-2893 Dated May 20/08

From Willow Garage, $75 for gasoline, including taxes for weekly fill-up of van. Terms: net 30 days. Recall the stored entry, edit the amount and save the changed entry.

Purchase Invoice #SA-2579 Dated May 20/08

From Steinbach Airconditioning, $400 plus $28 GST for air-conditioning parts and filters, etc. Invoice total $428. Terms: net 30. Recall stored entry.

Cash Receipt #29 Dated May 20/08

From Vinod Residence, certified cheque #CC-432 for $456 in payment of account. Reference invoice #A-715, cash receipt #24 and bank debit memo #37191.

Purchase Invoice #KE-679 Dated May 20/08

From Killarney Furnace Equipment, $3 000 plus $210 GST and $210 PST for new service equipment. Invoice total, $3 420. Terms: net 10.

Cheque Copy #105 Dated May 21/08

To Brandon Hardware, $570 in payment of account. Reference invoice #BH-42001.

Cash Purchase Invoice #SAA-1098 Dated May 22/08

From Starbuck Advertising Agency, $1 100 plus $77 GST and $77 PST for brochures and flyers. Invoice total, $1 254. Paid by cheque #106.

Cash Purchase Invoice #BD-4821 Dated May 22/08

From Staples Business Depot (use Full Add for the new vendor), $140 plus $9.80 GST and $9.80 PST for stationery and office supplies. Invoice total, $159.60. Paid by cheque #107.

NOTES
Staples Business Depot
Expense account: 1340
Tax code: GP
Leave the remaining fields blank.

Sales Invoice #A-720 Dated May 22/08

To Grande Pointe Towers, $2 400 plus $168 GST and $168 PST for installation of new furnace and air-conditioning unit. Invoice total, $2 736. Terms: net 1.

Cash Purchase Invoice #MH-44371 Dated May 22/08

From Manitoba Hydro, $400 plus $28 GST for one month of hydro service. Invoice total, $428. Paid by cheque #108.

SESSION DATE – MAY 31, 2008

Cash Receipt #30 Dated May 24/08

From Grande Pointe Towers, certified cheque #4543 for $2 736 in payment of account. Reference invoice #A-720.

Cash Purchase Invoice #BD-6113 Dated May 25/08

From Staples Business Depot, $40 plus $2.80 GST and $2.80 PST for stationery and other office supplies. Invoice total, $45.60. Paid by cheque #109.

Cash Purchase Invoice #MT-36128 Dated May 25/08

From Manitoba Telephone, $130 plus $9.10 GST and $9.10 PST for telephone and Internet service. Invoice total, $148.20. Paid by cheque #110.

Sales Invoice #A-721 Dated May 26/08

To Felicia Mountbatten (use Quick Add for the new customer), $1 600 plus $112 GST and $112 PST for installation services. Invoice total $1 824. Terms: net 1.

NOTES
When you use Quick Add, you can type the address in the Ship To field so that it will appear on the printed invoice. The new customer's name appears in the Sold To and Ship To fields.

Cash Sales Invoice #A-722 Dated May 26/08

Cash Sales Summary
To various one-time customers

Repairs Revenue	$400
Installation Revenue	400
GST charged	56
PST charged	56
Total cash received and deposited	$912

Sales Invoice #A-723 **Dated May 26/08**

To Midwestern Funeral Home, $1 000 plus $70 GST and $70 PST for repair work on furnace and heating system. Invoice total $1 140. Terms: net 10. Remember to edit the terms for the invoice.

Cheque Copy #111 **Dated May 28/08**

To Killarney Furnace Equipment, $3 420 in payment of account. Reference invoice #KE-679.

Bank Debit Memo #55131 **Dated May 30/08**

From Flatlands Credit Union, pre-authorized monthly payroll for employees

Wages and payroll expenses	$4 000
Payroll services fee	100
GST paid on payroll service	7
Total withdrawal	$4 107

NOTES

Enter the payroll transaction in the General Journal.

Remember to add the sales tax details for GST Paid on Purchases.

Memo #4 **Dated May 31/08**

From Owner: Create three new Group expense accounts for supplies used during the month: 5125 Air Conditioning Parts Used
5135 Furnace Parts Used
5165 Office Supplies Used

Enter adjustments for supplies used:

Air Conditioning Parts	$600
Furnace Parts	350
Office Supplies	200

Bank Debit Memo #56159 **Dated May 31/08**

From Flatlands Credit Union, pre-authorized withdrawals for service charges, mortgage and loan payments

Bank charges, including NSF cheques	$ 80
Interest expense	900
Loan principal repayment	1 000
Mortgage principal repayment	200

KEYSTROKES

Opening Data Files

Using the instructions for accessing data files in Chapter 1, page 8 open the data files for Air Care Services. Enter the first session date, May 8, 2008, for this application.

Type `May 8 2008`

Click **OK** to see the following warning statement:

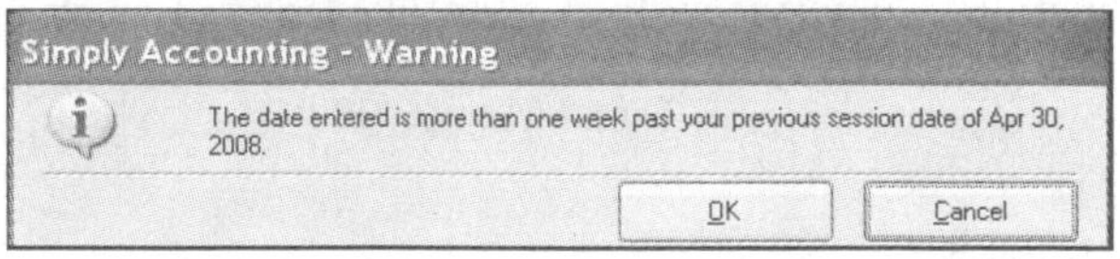

This warning appears whenever you advance the session date by more than one week. Normally a business would update its accounting records more frequently. If you have entered the correct date,

Click **OK** to accept the date entered and display the Home window.

The icons for the Payroll, Inventory and Project ledgers are hidden because these ledgers are not set up.

Accounting for Sales

Sales are entered in the Sales Journal indicated by the Sales, Orders & Quotes icon in the Receivables column:

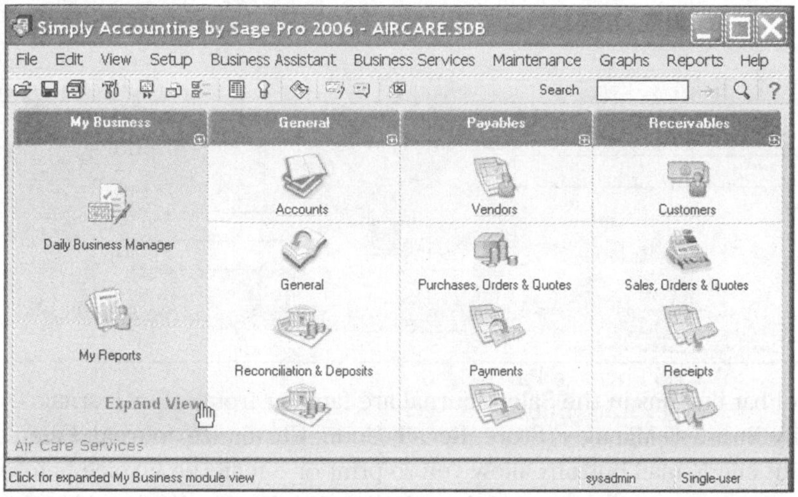

You can enter sales from the Sales, Orders & Quotes icon in the Home window. In this chapter, however, we will use the My Business tab window to enter all journal transactions. We have customized this window to include all the journals we need for Air Care Services.

Click the **My Business tab heading** :

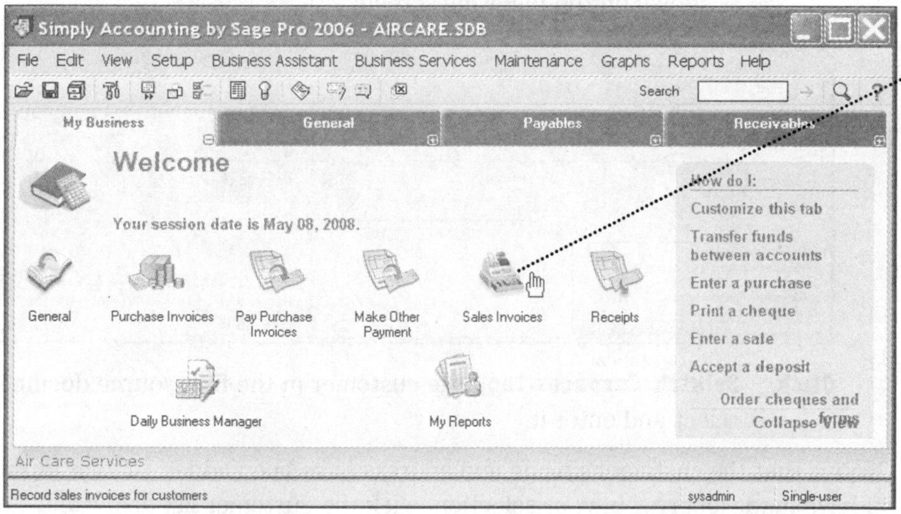

basic BASIC VERSION
Pay Vendor Invoices replaces the icon label Pay Purchase Invoices in the Basic version.

All the journals appear as separate icons as they do in individual module windows. Thus, the Pay Purchase Invoices icon appears as well as the Make Other Payment icon, but we do not show the icons for purchase or sales orders and quotes. None of the ledger icons are part of this window. The order of the journal icons is determined when you customize the window and choose the journals (see page 89).

Click the **Sales Invoices icon.**

The Sales Journal input form appears on the screen as follows:

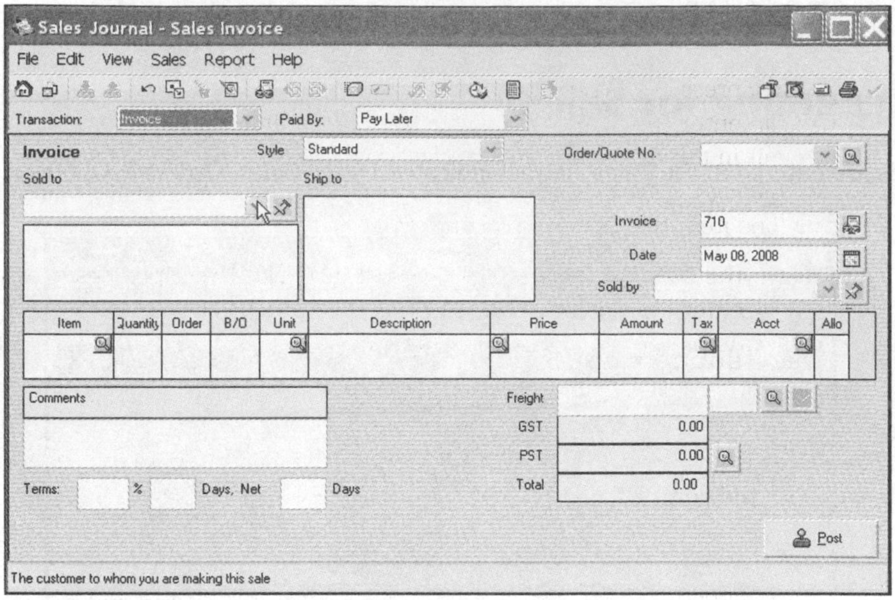

BASIC VERSION
The Time Slips and Refresh tools and the Invoice Style field do not appear in the Basic version.

Most tool bar buttons in the Sales Journal are familiar from other journals — Home window, Daily Business Manager, Store, Recall, Undo, Customize Journal, Calculator and Allocate. Print and E-mail buttons allow you to print or e-mail the invoice before posting to provide a customer or store copy of the sales invoice. You can use tool buttons to remove, fill or cancel an order and to adjust a posted invoice. Invoice Lookup, Track Shipments and Add Time Slip Activities will be explained in later applications.

The Invoice option is selected as the default Transaction type and Pay Later as the payment option. Since this is a regular sale, leave the selections unchanged.

WARNING!
You must click the list arrow to see the customer list. Clicking the field will place an insertion point to prepare for typing a name.

Click the **Sold To** (Customer) **field list arrow** to obtain the list of customers as shown on the following screen:

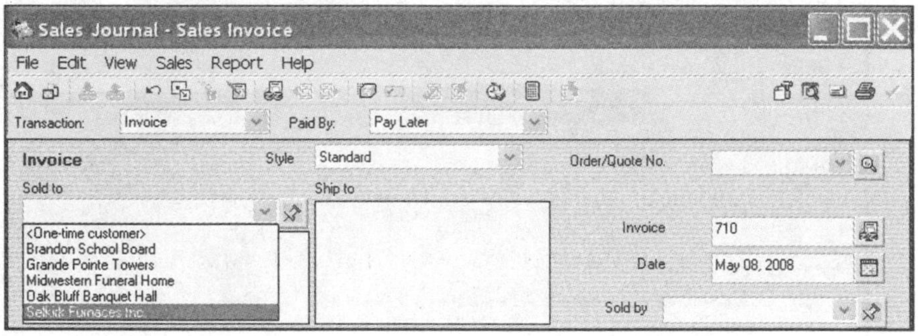

Click **Selkirk Furnaces Inc.**, the customer in the first source document, to select and enter it.

Notice that the customer's name and address have been added to your input form. If you have made an error in your selection, click the customer list arrow and start again. By default, the Sold To and the Ship To fields are completed from the customer's ledger record. You can edit the shipping address if necessary. If you have selected the correct customer, you can skip over the shipping information.

The invoice number, 710, the numeric portion, is entered and correct. It is updated automatically by the program. The payment terms and tax code for the customer have also been entered. When a default revenue account is entered in the customer's record, it will also be included on the invoice form.

The session date appears by default so you need to change it. Enter the date on which the transaction took place, May 1, 2008.

Click the **Date field Calendar icon** .

Click **1**

You can press (tab) repeatedly to move to the field you need next. If you want, you can enter the quantity (one for the service, in this case), enter the price per unit in the Price field and let the program calculate the amount by multiplying the two together. You can use this method if you are selling more than one item that is not an inventory item.

Click the **Description field** on the first line. The Description field is used to enter a description or comment concerning the sale.

Type `subcontracting - apartment building`

Press (tab).

NOTES

When you use the long date format, the parts of the date appear as separate words. Double clicking will select only one part of the date, either the month, the day or the year.

NOTES

Remember that you can always choose the date from the pop-up calendar in the Date field.

The cursor is now in the Price field. The Price field also refers to unit prices; it is not needed for the contract.

Press (tab).

The cursor should now be positioned in the Amount field, where you will enter the amount for this invoice before taxes.

Type `800` **Press** (tab).

The cursor is now positioned in the Tax field. The default tax code for the customer, GP, is entered from the customer record details in the data files and it is correct. Customers pay both GST and PST on services.

Press (enter) to see the tax code descriptions set up for Air Care Services:

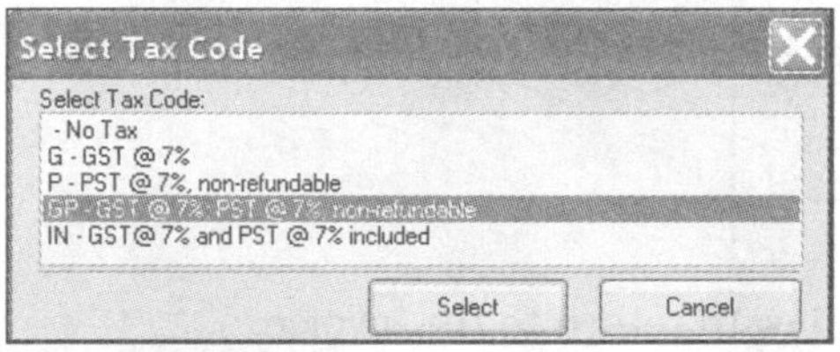

The tax code options are charge **No Tax** on the sale; code **G**, charge GST only; code **P**, charge PST only; code **GP**, charge both GST and PST; and code **IN**, both GST and PST are charged and included in the price. Notice that PST is described as not refundable.

You can select a different tax code from this list if the default is incorrect. Click the correct code and then click Select. You will return to the Sales Journal with the cursor in the Account field.

NOTES

When you select a tax code from the selection list, the cursor advances to the next invoice field. When you choose Cancel, the cursor does not move to the next field.

Click **Cancel** to return to the journal.

Press (tab) to advance to the Account field.

The Account field in a sales invoice refers to the credit portion of the journal entry, usually a revenue account. Again, you cannot access *Accounts Receivable*, the linked account, directly. The software will automatically debit the *Accounts Receivable* control account in the General Ledger when you enter positive amounts.

You may set up a default revenue account for customers, just as you set up default expense accounts for vendors. Because each customer uses more than one revenue account, we have not entered these default accounts for most customers. In the Account field, you can choose an account from the list of accounts or create a new account, just like any other account field. We need to create a new revenue account for this sale.

NOTES

Entering a negative amount in the Amount field will generate a debit entry for the sale with a credit to Accounts Receivable.

NOTES

You can choose any postable account as the default revenue account for customers just as you can use any account as the default expense account for vendors.

Type `4160`

Press *enter*.

> **NOTES**
> Because the Add button is already selected, pressing *enter* will choose it.

Click the **Add button** or **press** *enter* to open the Add An Account wizard.

Press *tab*.

Type `Subcontracting Revenue` as the **account name** and **accept** the remaining **defaults**. **Click Finish** to return to the journal. The account number is added to the journal.

Press *tab* to advance the cursor to line 2 in the Item field, ready for additional sale items if necessary.

The Comments field can be used in two ways: you can set up a default comment for the business that appears on all invoices, or you can enter a comment at the time of the sale. You can add to or change a default comment if you want. We will add a comment.

Click the **Comments field**.

Type `We guarantee our work.`

The payment terms have been set up as defaults for customers as net 10 days with no discount. You can change terms for individual customers or sales invoices.

> **NOTES**
> Payment terms can be modified for individual customers in the Receivables Ledger. You can also edit the terms for individual sales in the Sales Journal.
> If you set up shippers and enter tracking numbers, you can access the shipper's Web site to trace goods shipped to customers.

Click the **List icon beside the PST amount field** to see the detailed summary of taxes included in the sale:

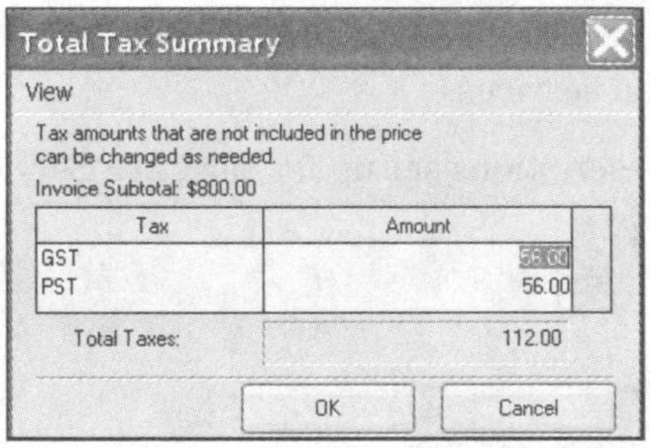

> **NOTES**
> If necessary, you can edit the tax amounts on the Tax Summary screen.

Close the **Tax Summary window** to return to the invoice.

The transaction is now complete, and your invoice should resemble the following:

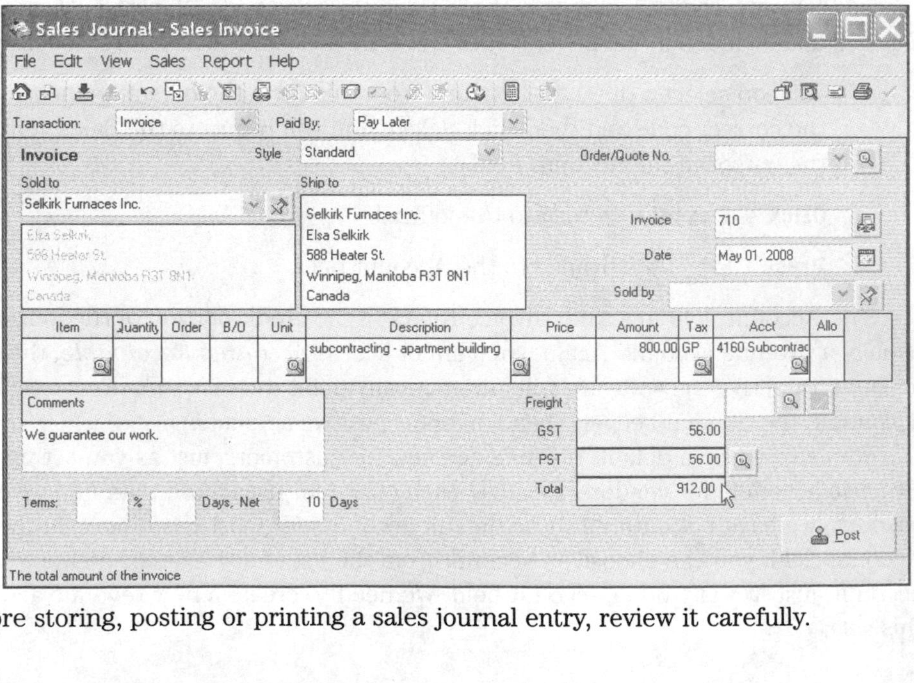

Before storing, posting or printing a sales journal entry, review it carefully.

Reviewing the Sales Journal Entry

Choose the **Report menu** and **click Display Sales Journal Entry** to display the transaction you have entered as shown:

```
Sales Journal Entry Display                              _ □ X
File  Options  Help

                                                            ?
Air Care Services
05/01/08 (J1)                          Debits     Credits       Project
  1200  Accounts Receivable            912.00        -
  2640  PST Payable                       -        56.00
  2650  GST Charged on Services           -        56.00
  4160  Subcontracting Revenue            -       800.00
                                       912.00     912.00
Additional Date:          Additional Field:
Generated On: 01/12/06
```

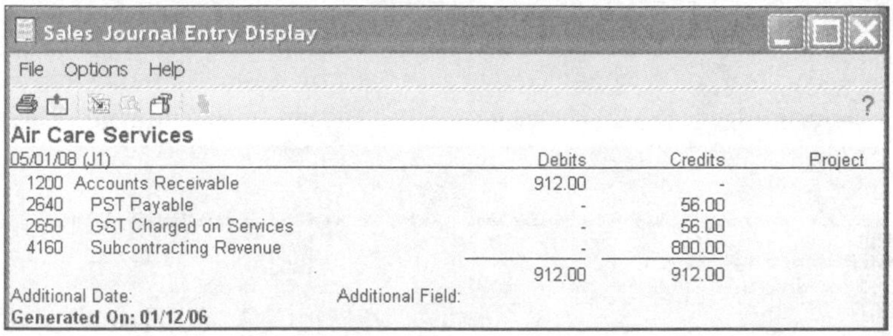

Review the **journal entry** to check for mistakes.

You can see that *Accounts Receivable*, the control account, has been updated automatically by the Simply Accounting program because the Receivables and General ledgers are fully integrated. All credit sales are debited to *Accounts Receivable*, the default linked account for the Receivables Ledger. *GST Charged on Services* has also been updated correctly because of the tax code you entered and because *GST Charged on Services* was defined as the GST linked account for sales. Similarly, *PST Payable* is defined as the linked account for PST collected from customers and it too is updated correctly because of the tax code. You did not need to enter any of these accounts directly in the Sales Journal. The balance owing by this customer is also directly updated as a result of the Sales Journal entry.

Close the **display** to return to the Sales Journal input screen.

NOTES
Other Receivables Ledger linked accounts will be used and explained later. These are the Receivables bank account, freight revenue account and sales discount account.

NOTES
To correct Sales Journal entries after posting, refer to page 185 and Appendix C.

CORRECTING THE SALES JOURNAL ENTRY BEFORE POSTING

Move to the field that has the error. **Press** (tab) to move forward through the fields or **press** (shift) and (tab) together to move back to a previous field. This will highlight the field information so you can change it. **Type** the **correct information** and **press** (tab) to enter it.

You can also use the mouse to **point** to a field and **drag** through the **incorrect information** to highlight it. **Type** the **correct information** and **press** (tab) to enter it.

If the customer is incorrect, **reselect** from the **Customer** list by **clicking** the **Customer list arrow**. **Click** the name of the **correct customer**.

Click an **incorrect amount** or description to highlight it. Then **type** the **correct information** and **press** (tab) to enter the change.

To correct an account number or tax code, **click** the **Account List icon** to display the selection list. **Click** the **correct entry** to highlight it, then **click Select** and **press** (tab) to enter the change.

To insert a line or remove a line, **click** the **line** that you need to move. **Choose** the **Edit menu** and **click Insert Line** and **type** the new line or **click Remove Line** to delete a line.

To discard the entry and begin again, **click** ☒ (**Close**) to close the journal or **click** ↶ (**Undo**) on the tool bar to open a blank journal window. When Simply Accounting asks whether you want to discard the entry, **click Yes** to confirm your decision.

Customizing the Sales Invoice

The sales invoice includes a number of fields/columns that we do not need. Before saving the invoice, we will customize it to remove the unnecessary columns.

Click the **Customize Journal tool** 🖼 or **choose** the **View menu** and **click Customize Journal**.

The customization options window opens:

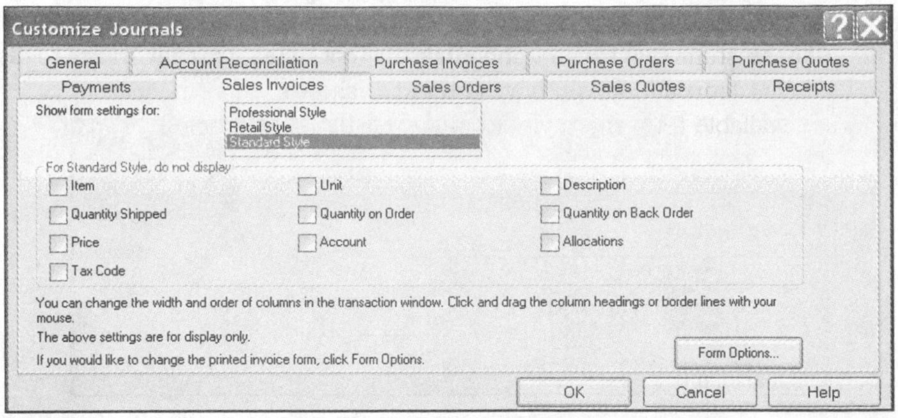

There are three pre-defined invoice styles for different business types. Each style displays a different combination of columns. The Standard Style, the default, includes all columns. The columns we can remove are listed under the For Standard Style, Do Not Display heading. We can remove columns by clicking the check boxes. The Form Options button accesses printer setup options for the forms.

First we will select the style that more closely matches our needs. Both the Standard and Retail styles include columns for inventory and orders. Air Care does not use these features so we will choose the Professional Style, which is better suited to service companies.

Click **Professional Style** in the Show Form Settings For list:

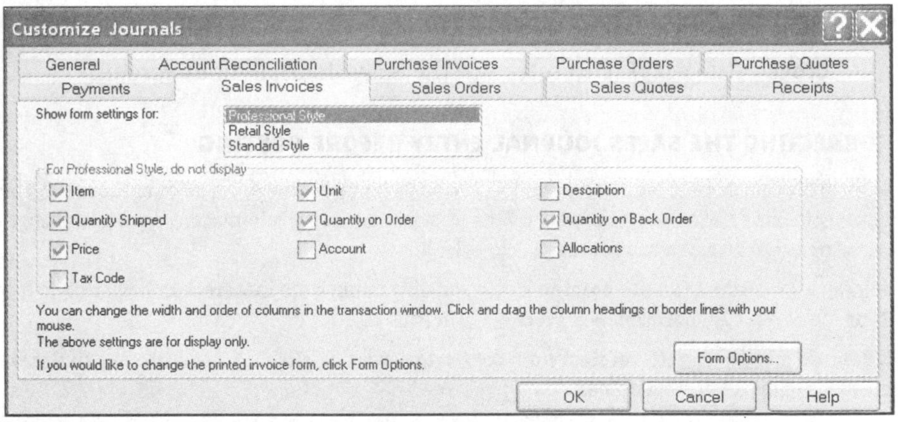

In the modified options screen, most of the fields we want to hide are removed. Air Care does not allocate to projects so we can also remove the Allocations column.

Click the **check box** for **Allocations**.

Click **OK** to return to the modified journal:

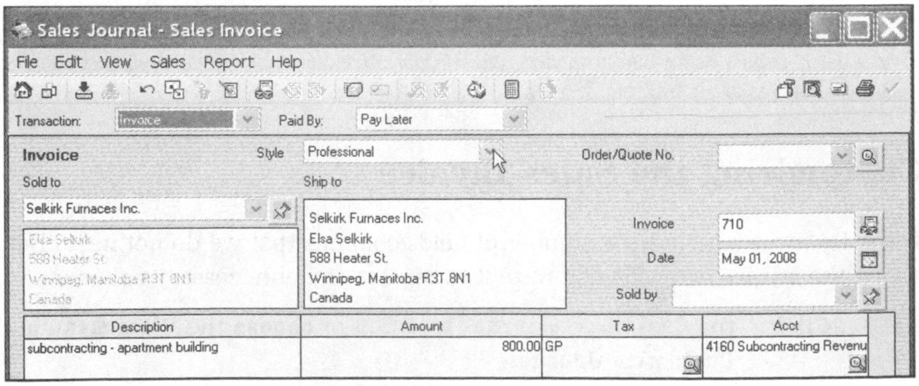

basic **BASIC VERSION**

Different invoice styles are not available in the Basic version. The Standard Style is the only one used. You can still hide or show any of the columns by clicking them.

basic **BASIC VERSION**

In the Basic version, a single tab is used for purchases, purchase orders and purchase quotes. Another single tab represents sales, sales orders and sales quotes. These forms cannot be individually customized in the Basic version as they can in the Pro version.

basic **BASIC VERSION**

All check boxes will be blank. You must click the check boxes for Item, Quantity Shipped, Price, Unit, Quantity On Order, Quantity On Back Order and Allocations to create the form we show here.

NOTES

You can also customize journals by dragging the column headings to change the size of columns. Point to the column heading margin. When the arrow changes to a double-headed arrow, drag the margin to its new location or size. Dragging the right column margin to the left until it overlaps the next column will remove that column. You can restore missing columns from the Customize Journal window.

Now when we press the *tab* key, the cursor will advance to the next field, and it will be one we use for the sale.

Instead of customizing the journal, you can select one of the predefined forms within the Sales Journal. The same three styles we saw in the Customize Journals window are available from the Style drop-down list as shown below:

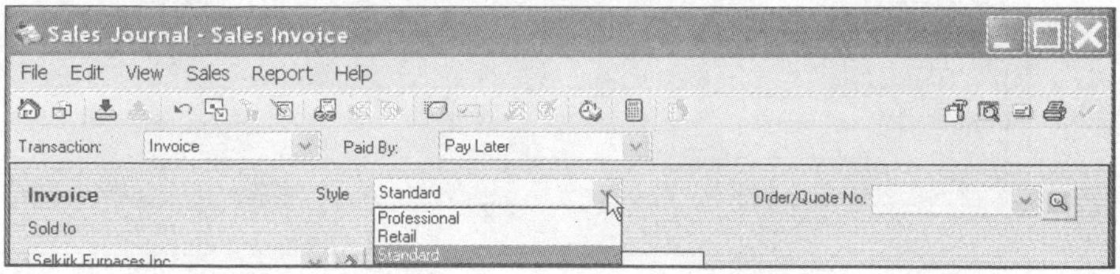

Posting

When you are certain that you have entered all the information correctly, you must post the transaction to save it.

Click the **Post button** [Post] or **choose** the **Sales menu** and **click Post** to save your transaction.

A new blank Sales Journal form appears on the screen. The next transaction is a receipt so we must exit from the Sales Journal.

Close the **Sales Journal** input form to return to the My Business window.

Accounting for Receipts

Receipts from customers are entered in much the same way as payments to vendors. After you choose the customer, outstanding invoices appear automatically and you can enter the payment amounts. No accounts are entered.

Receipts are entered in the Receipts Journal indicated by the hand pointer:

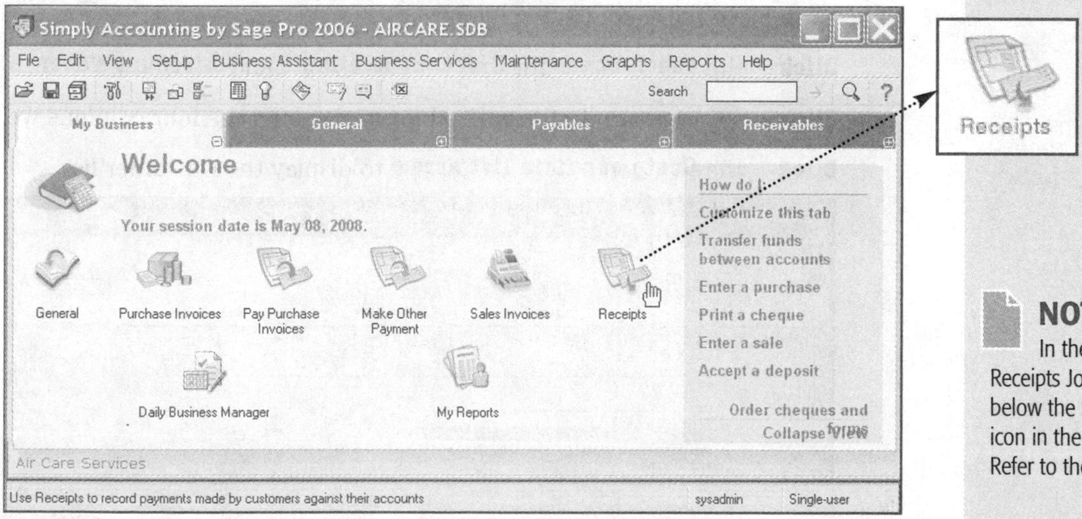

Click the **Receipts icon** to open the Receipts Journal.

NOTES

In the Home window, the Receipts Journal icon is located below the Sales, Orders & Quotes icon in the Receivables column. Refer to the screen on page 165.

basic BASIC VERSION
The Refresh tools do not appear in the Basic version.

The following blank Receipts Journal input screen appears:

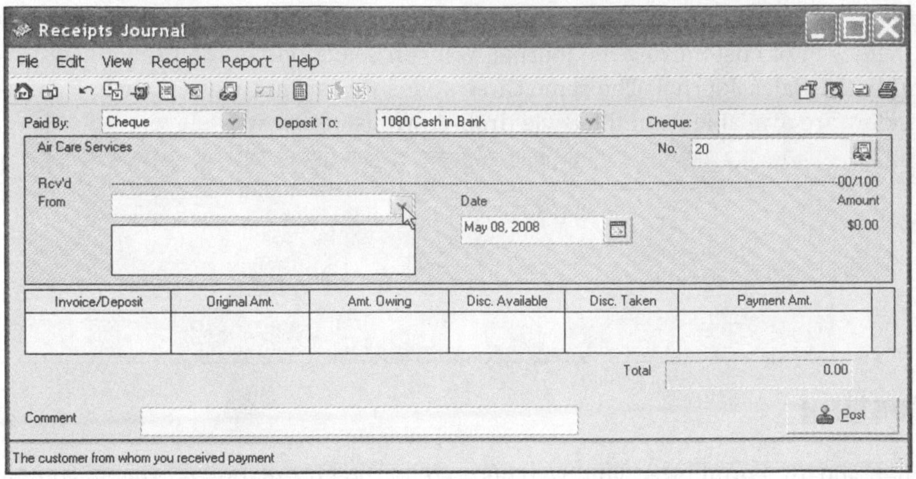

NOTES
The Refresh tools will update the journal with changes made by other users, such as the addition of new invoices.

As with payments to vendors, you cannot enter account numbers in the Receipts Journal. You need to enter only the amount paid on the appropriate invoice line. The program automatically creates the journal entry.

As with the Sales Invoice, there are fields that do not apply to Air Care and we can customize the form to remove them.

Click the **Customize Journal tool** or **choose** the **View menu** and **click Customize Journal** to open the customization options:

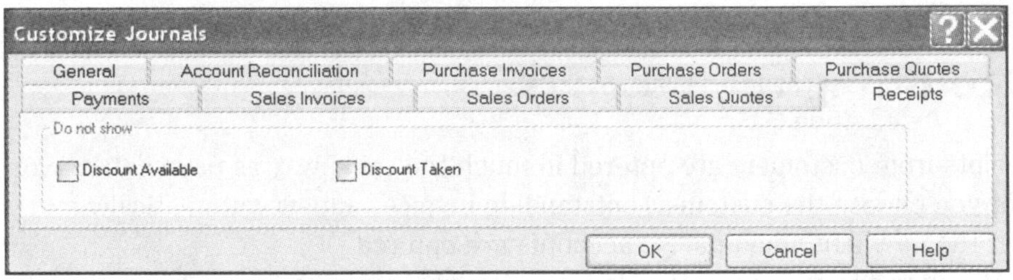

basic BASIC VERSION
In the Basic version, a single tab is used for purchases, purchase orders and purchase quotes. Another single tab represents sales, sales orders and sales quotes. These forms cannot be customized individually in the Basic version as they can in the Pro version.

We can remove both Discount columns.

Click the **check boxes** for **Discount Available** and **Discount Taken**.

Click **OK** to return to the revised form with only the four columns we need.

Click the **Customer field list arrow** to display the Customer list:

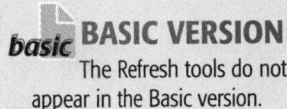

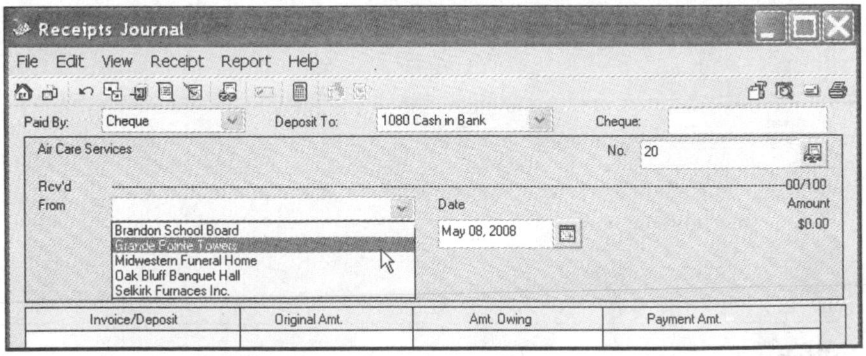

Click **Grande Pointe Towers** to choose this customer.

The customer information is added to the form:

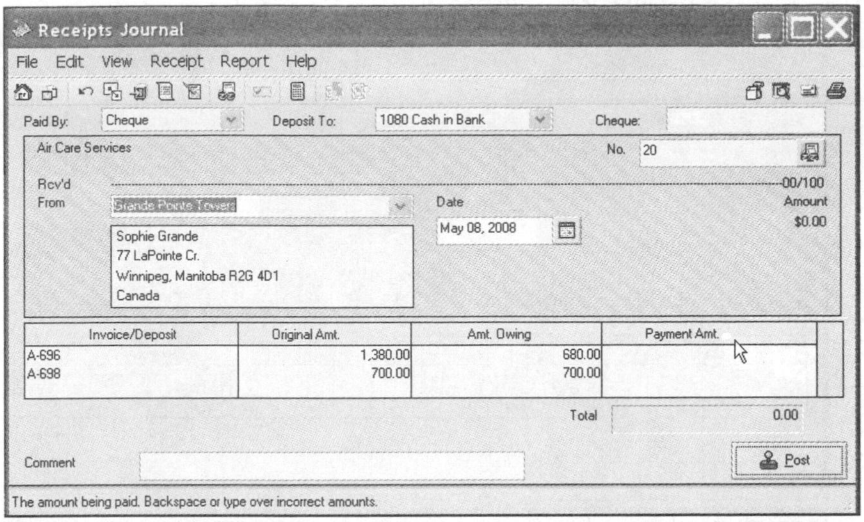

The customer's name and address have been added to your input form, together with all outstanding invoices for the customer.

Air Care has a single bank account so it is correctly selected in the Deposit To field. If you have chosen the wrong customer, display the list again and click the correct customer. If you have selected correctly,

Click the **Cheque field** to enter the customer's cheque number.

Type 3499

The No. field records the receipt number that increases automatically. There is a Lookup icon beside the No. field

We need to replace the session date with the date for this transaction.

Choose May 2 from the Date field pop-up calendar.

Press tab .

The cursor moves to the Invoice/Deposit field.

Press tab to advance to the Payment Amt. field.

You can accept a highlighted amount, or type an exact amount for a partial payment.

By default, the amount owing on the first invoice is shown and highlighted. All outstanding invoices are listed on the screen. For this invoice, the full amount is being paid so you can accept the default.

Press tab to accept the amount in the Payment Amt. field.

The cursor will advance to the Payment Amt. field for the next invoice. To replace the highlighted default amount,

Type 200 **Press** tab to enter the new amount.

NOTES
Simply Accounting allows you to set up more than one bank account. If more than one bank account is set up, choose the account from the Deposit To drop-down list.

NOTES
Invoice Lookup is covered in Chapter 8.

NOTES
When you do not remove any columns, the cursor moves to the Disc. Taken field from the Invoice/Deposit field and from the Payment Amt. field.

WARNING!

When an invoice amount is highlighted and it is not being paid, press del to remove the amount from the total, and press tab to update the total.

The completed Receipts form should now appear as follows:

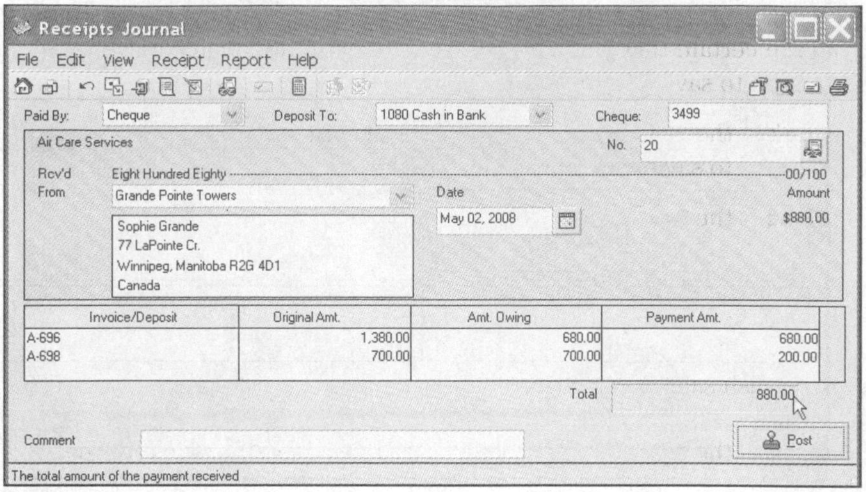

Notice that the upper cheque portion of the form has also been completed. In making Receipts Journal entries, you do not need to enter any accounts because Simply Accounting chooses the linked bank and receivable accounts defined for the Receivables Ledger to create the journal entry.

You have made all the entries for this transaction, so you are ready to review before posting your transaction.

Reviewing the Receipts Journal Entry

Choose the **Report menu** and **click Display Receipts Journal Entry** to display the transaction you have entered as follows:

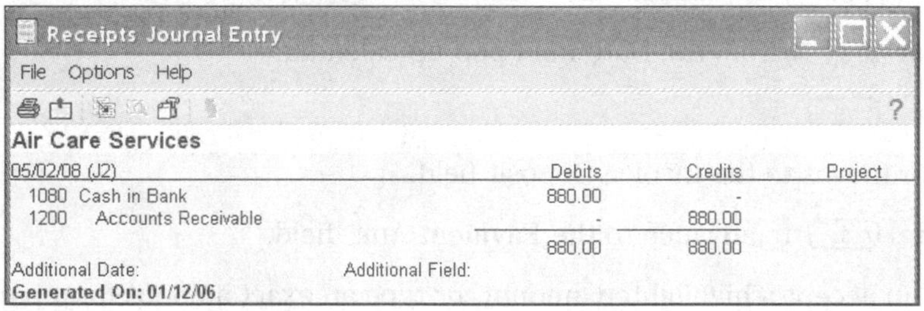

Here you can see the related journal entry created by Simply Accounting when you complete a Receipts Journal transaction. The program updates the *Accounts Receivable* control account in the General Ledger and *Cash in Bank* because the Receivables and General ledgers are fully integrated. *Cash in Bank* is defined as the default linked bank account for the Receivables Ledger as well as for the Payables Ledger because Air Care has only one bank account. The receipt will also be credited directly to the customer's account in the Receivables Ledger to reduce the balance owing.

Close the **display** to return to the Receipts Journal input screen.

CORRECTING THE RECEIPTS JOURNAL ENTRY BEFORE POSTING

Move to the field with the error. **Press** tab to move forward or shift and tab together to move back to a previous field. This will highlight the field contents. **Type** the **correct information** and **press** tab to enter it.

You can also use the mouse to **point** to a field and **drag** through the **incorrect information** to highlight it. **Type** the **correct information** and **press** tab to enter it.

If the customer is incorrect, **reselect** from the **Customer** list by **clicking** the **Customer list arrow**. **Click** the name of the correct **customer**. To confirm that you want to discard the current transaction, **click Yes** to display the outstanding invoices for the correct customer. **Type** the **correct** receipt **information**.

You can also discard the entry. **Click** ☒ or ↶ and then **click Yes** to confirm.

Posting

When you are certain that you have entered all the information correctly, you must post the transaction to save it.

Click the **Post button**  or **choose** the **Receipt menu** and **click Post** to save your transaction.

Close the **Receipts Journal**.

Entering Cash Sales

To enter the cash sale on May 3,

Click the **Sales Invoices icon**  to open the Sales Journal.

Click the **Paid By list arrow** to view the payment options — Pay Later, Cash and Cheque:

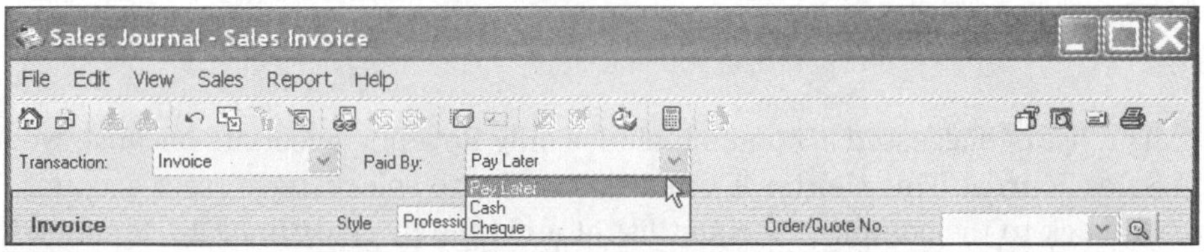

Click **Cheque** as the method of payment to change the invoice screen as shown here:

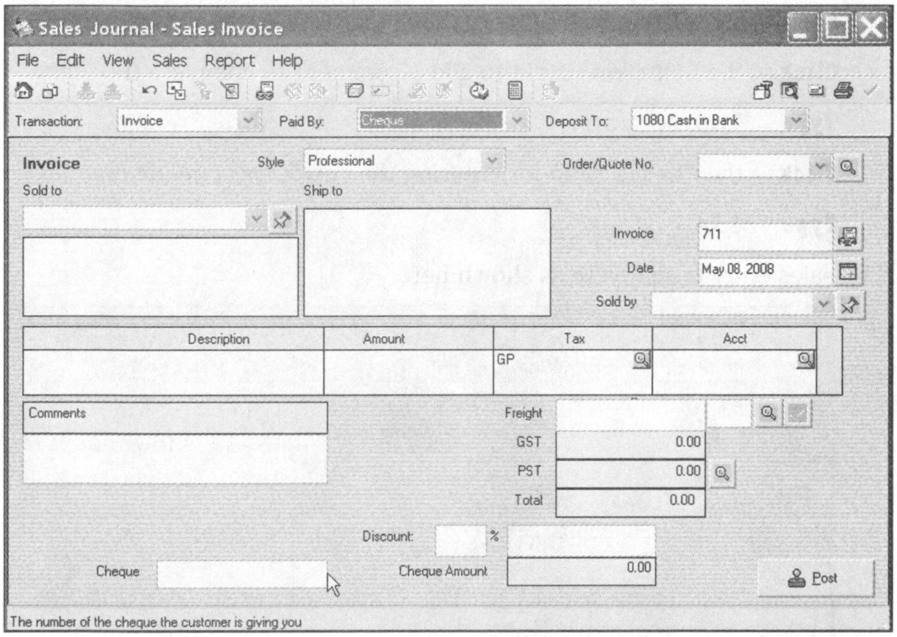

When you choose Cheque as the method of payment, a cheque number field is added at the bottom of the invoice so that you can add the customer's cheque number. When you choose Cash, the cheque number field is not included.

Notice that the invoice number has also been increased automatically.

In the payment terms section, the Net Days field has been removed and a Cheque Amount field has been added.

Click the **Sold To field** to place the cursor in the Customer field.

Type M

NOTES
When credit cards are set up, they will also appear on the Paid By drop-down list.

Midwestern Funeral Home is added to the Sold To field because it is the first customer entry beginning with M. The rest of the name is still highlighted in case you want to continue typing another name.

Enter **May 3** in the Date field as the transaction date.

Click the **Amount field**.

Type 900

Double click the **Account field**.

Click **Suggested Accounts** to modify the Select Account list as shown:

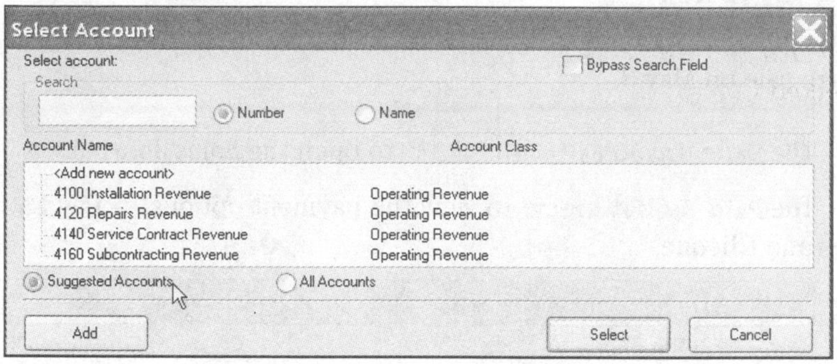

The list of suggested accounts includes only Revenue accounts because we are in the Sales Journal. This shorter list makes it easier to select the correct account. You can switch back to the complete account list at any time by selecting All Accounts. The Suggested Accounts button remains selected when we close the journal until we change the selection again.

Select **4100 Installation Revenue**.

Click the **Comments field** to add a comment to complete the entry.

Type Thank you.

Click the **Cheque field** for entering the customer's cheque number.

Type 394

The sales entry is complete as shown here:

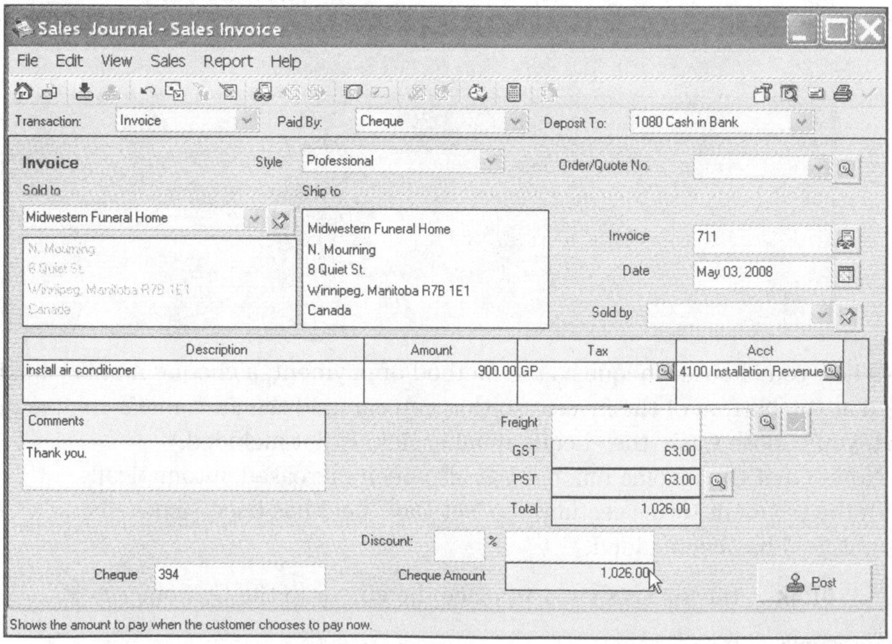

> **NOTES**
> When you open the Purchases Journal, the list of suggested accounts will show only the Expense accounts. You will need to choose All Accounts to include Asset accounts in the list.

As usual you should review the entry.

Choose the **Report menu** and **click Display Sales Journal Entry**. Your display should look like the one shown here:

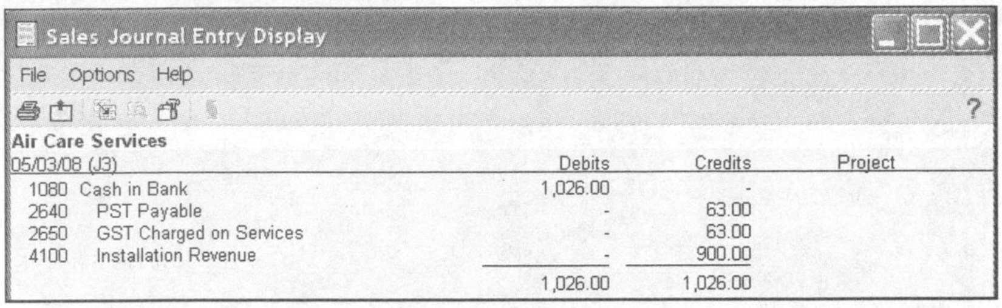

Notice that *Cash in Bank* is debited automatically instead of *Accounts Receivable* because we selected Cheque as the method of payment.

Close the **display** when you have finished. **Make corrections** if necessary.

Click **Post** [Post] to save the entry. Leave the journal open.

Adding a New Customer

The next sale is to a new customer who should be added to your files. We will add the customer directly from the Sales Journal.

Click the **Paid By field** and **choose Pay Later** as the method of payment. The date is correct.

Click the **Sold To** (Customer) **field**.

Type `Hazel Estates`

Press [tab] to display the warning that you have typed a name that is not on the list and the option to add a ledger record:

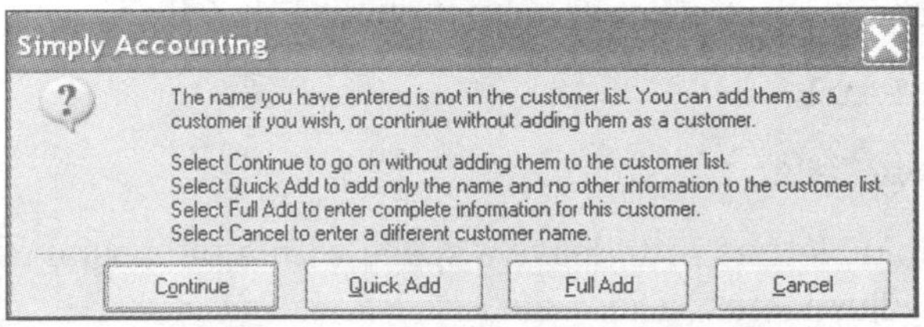

The options are the same as for new vendors. If you typed an incorrect name, click **Cancel** to return to the journal and start again. If you typed the name correctly, you can choose to add the customer's name only — **Quick Add** — or to add a full customer record with the **Full Add** option. If you need to change any defaults, you must choose the Full Add option. You can still skip customer fields that you do not need. The remaining option, **Continue**, will add the customer's name to the journal entry but will not create a ledger record for the customer or add the customer to the other Receivables Ledger reports.

NOTES

If you need to change the payment terms, revenue account or the tax options for a new customer, you must choose Full Add so that you can enter these fields in the ledger.

You can use the Full Add option and create an incomplete customer record. For example, you can enter the customer's name, tax code, payment terms, revenue account and credit limit and then add the remaining details later.

Click **Full Add** to open the Customer Ledger at the Address information screen:

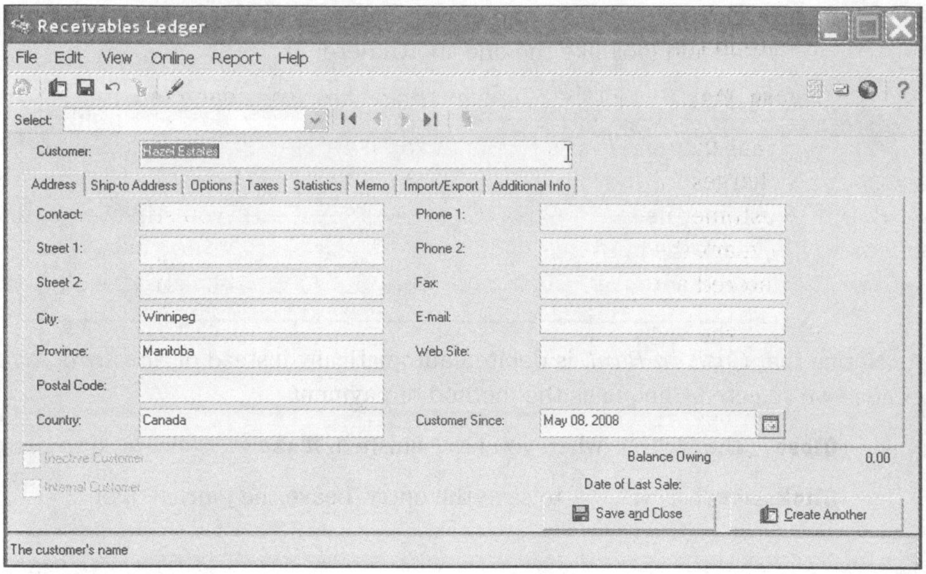

basic BASIC VERSION
The Internal Customer option and the Refresh tool do not apply to the Basic version.

You are ready to enter your new customer. The Customer field is completed with the new name highlighted for editing if necessary. The field we need next is the Contact field. Enter the name of the particular individual Air Care normally deals with.

Click the **Contact field**.

Type `Joelle Beausoleil`

Press *tab* to move the cursor to the Street 1 field.

Type `488 Sunshine St.` **Press** *tab*.

Type `Suite 1200` **Press** *tab* to move to and select the City field.

Notice that the city, province and country in which Air Care is located have been entered by default. The province is correct but you must change the city.

Type `West St. Paul`

Click the **Postal Code field**.

You do not need to use capital letters or to leave a space within the postal code. The program will make these adjustments.

Type `r4g5h3`

Click the **Phone 1 field**. The postal code format is corrected automatically.

You do not need to add dashes or brackets for telephone numbers. Telephone and fax numbers may be entered with or without the area code.

Type `2043677611` **Press** *tab*.

Type `8773679000` **Press** *tab* to move to the Fax field.

Type `2043692191` **Press** *tab* to advance to the E-mail field.

Notice that the format for telephone and fax numbers is corrected automatically.

E-mail and Web addresses are typed exactly as you would type them in your regular Internet and e-mail access programs. You can also add these details later when you actually want to use them. When you click the Web or E-mail buttons, you will be prompted to enter the addresses if they are not part of the customer's record already.

Type `JB@hazelestates.com` **Press** *tab*.

Type www.hazelestates.com

Hazel Estates is completing its first sale on May 3 but the session date is entered as the default date in the Customer Since field.

Choose May 3 from the Customer Since field calendar icon.

The **Internal Customer** option applies when one department supplies services to another and charges for these services. The option is available when time and billing is used. If the customer no longer buys from the company, but you still want to keep the record on file, mark the customer as **Inactive**. The **Balance Owing** and **Date Of Last Sale** will be entered automatically by the program based on the customer's transactions.

Click the **Ship-to Address tab**:

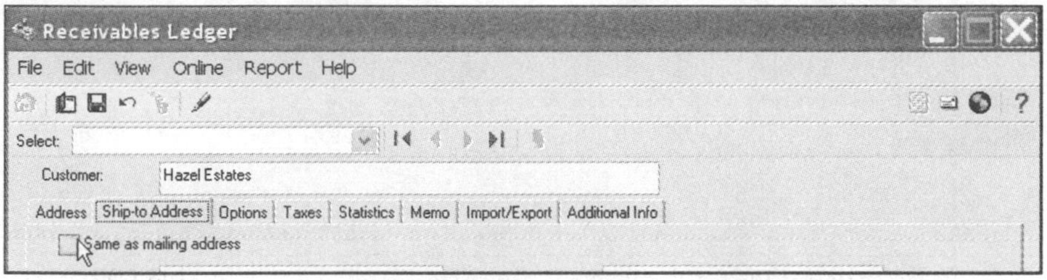

The shipping address is the same as the business address for this customer so the customer's address should be entered as the shipping location on all invoices.

Click Same As Mailing Address.

Click the **Options tab**:

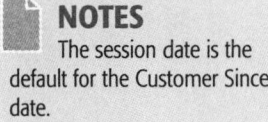

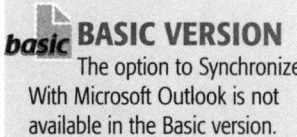

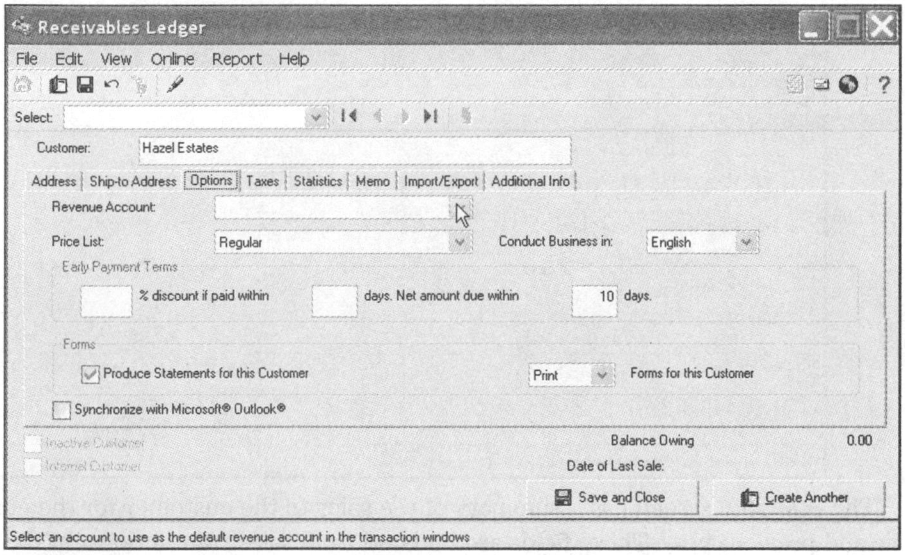

The first option is to add a default revenue account for the customer.

Click the **Revenue Account list arrow**.

Click 4100.

The Options tab contains payment terms details. The **Price List** — Regular, Preferred or Web Price — refers to the prices customers pay for inventory items and will be introduced in Chapter 11. For Air Care, all customers are Regular. You can select French or English as the customer's preferred **language for conducting business**. Sales invoices and other forms you prepare for customers will be printed in the language you select here. Your own program screens will not change.

The payment terms for Hazel Estates are the same as those for other customers and are entered by default.

NOTES

The session date is the default for the Customer Since date.

BASIC VERSION

The option to Synchronize With Microsoft Outlook is not available in the Basic version.

You may also choose to **Produce Statements For This Customer**, and you may print or e-mail invoices and quotes. You should use the correct forms, but you can also print statements on ordinary printer paper.

You can change these settings at any time.

Click the **Taxes tab**:

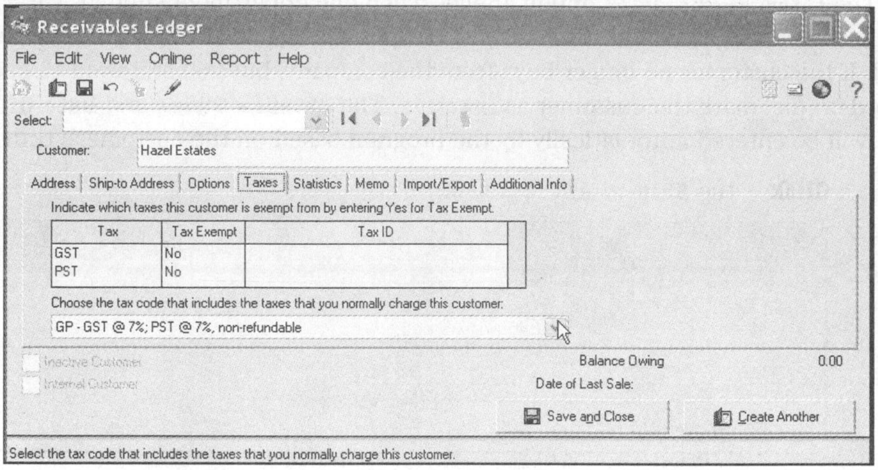

WARNING!
Unless you have indicated that the customer is not exempt from taxes, the taxes will not be calculated in the Sales Journal for that customer, even if you select the correct tax code.

The customer is correctly described as not **Tax Exempt** for PST and GST by default, allowing accurate tax calculations for sales transactions to be included in Tax reports. The default tax code is also correct from the ledger settings.

Click **GP - GST @7%; PST @7%, non-refundable** to see the codes available.

Click the **Statistics tab** to open the next screen we need:

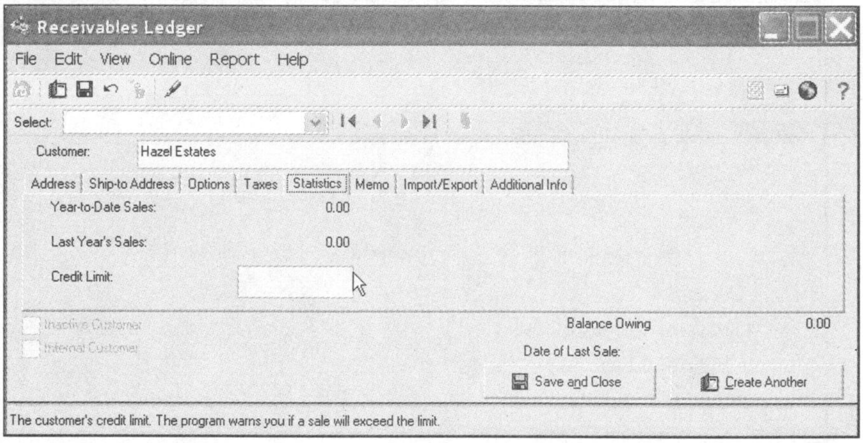

The Statistics screen has a summary of the sales to the customer for the current year and previous year. These fields are updated from sales transactions. In the **Credit Limit** field, you can enter the upper credit limit for a particular customer to help minimize bad debts. When a customer exceeds the credit limit, the program will warn you before you can post the sale. You can accept the over-the-limit sale, or ask for a deposit to avoid exceeding the credit limit. Customers should be notified of changes in credit policies. Customers who have previously defaulted on making their payments can be placed on a cash-only basis by setting their credit limits at zero. Air Care is presently analyzing customer payment trends to add this feature. The limit is set at $4 000 on a trial basis.

Click the **Credit Limit field** to position the cursor.

Type 4000

Saving a New Customer Account

When you are certain that all the information is correct, you must save the newly created customer account and add it to the current list.

Click **Save And Close** [Save and Close] to save the new customer information and return to the Sales Journal.

Notice that the tax code, revenue account and payment terms are added to the journal. Any of these fields can be edited for an individual invoice.

Enter the **sale** for the new customer by following the procedures outlined earlier.

Review the **journal entry**. **Close** the **display** and **make corrections**.

Click **Post** [Post] and then **close** the **Sales Journal**.

Reversing a Payment (NSF Cheques)

When a cheque is returned by the bank as NSF, you need to record the fact that the invoice is still outstanding. You can do this in the Receipts Journal by entering a negative payment to reverse the cheque.

Click the **Receipts icon** [Receipts] to open the Receipts Journal.

Choose **Grande Pointe Towers** from the customer list to display the unpaid invoices:

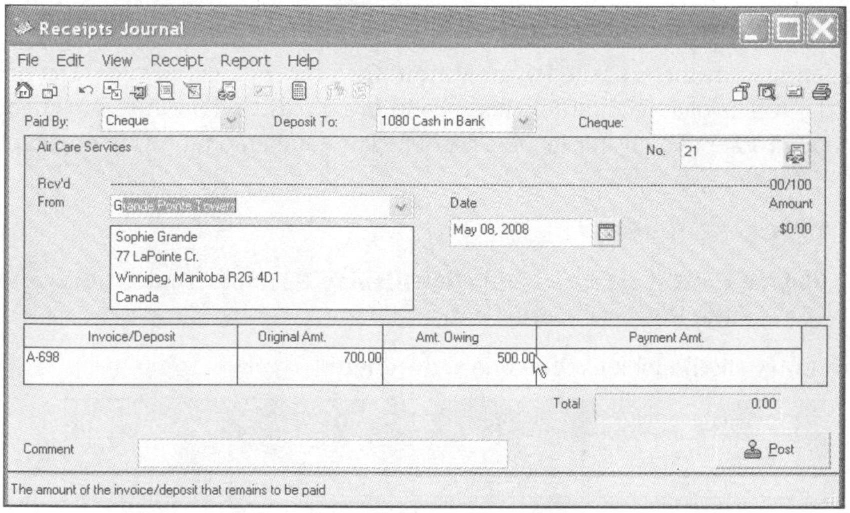

Only the unpaid balance for invoice #A-698 is displayed.

Click the **Cheque field** so you can enter the cheque number.

To indicate that the original cheque is NSF and is being reversed, add NSF to the cheque number, or enter the bank memo number for reference.

Type `NSF-3499`

Click the **Date field** so you can enter the date of the bank memo.

Type `May 4`

Click the **Include Fully Paid Invoices/Deposits tool** or **choose** the **Receipt menu** and **click** **Include Fully Paid Invoices/Deposits**.

NOTES

If you recorded a receipt incorrectly, and do not need to reverse it, you can choose the Adjust Receipt tool to access the posted receipt and make the correction. See page 183.

The invoice that was paid is now included, with 0.00 as the amount owing, as shown:

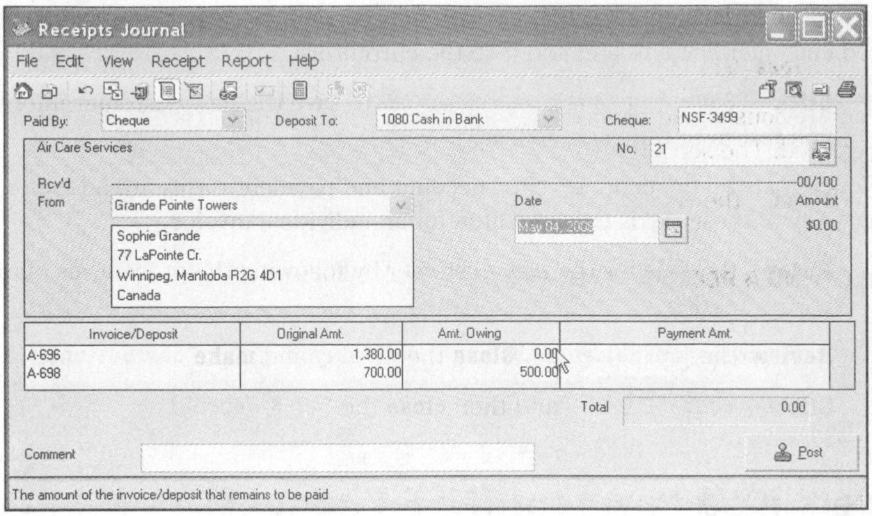

Click **invoice number A-696**, the one that the NSF cheque was issued against. This ensures you will select the right invoice line.

Press (tab) to advance to the Payment Amt. field for this invoice.

Or, you can click the Payment Amt. field on the line for invoice A-696.

NOTES
You can add the bank debit memo number in the Comment field if you want. The comment will appear in the Journal Report.

Notice that the Payment Amount field is still blank because no balance is owing. Enter negative amounts to reverse the original payments ($680 of the cheque amount was used to pay invoice #A-696 and $200 was for #A-698).

Type -680 **Press** (tab).

The cursor advances to the Payment Amt. field for the next invoice. You need to restore the full invoice amount for this second invoice as well because the cheque included a partial payment for invoice #A-698. The total amount owing appears as the default entry and is selected.

Type -200 **Press** (tab).

Choose the **Report menu** and **click Display Receipts Journal Entry** to review the Receipts Journal entry.

Your entry should look like the one shown here:

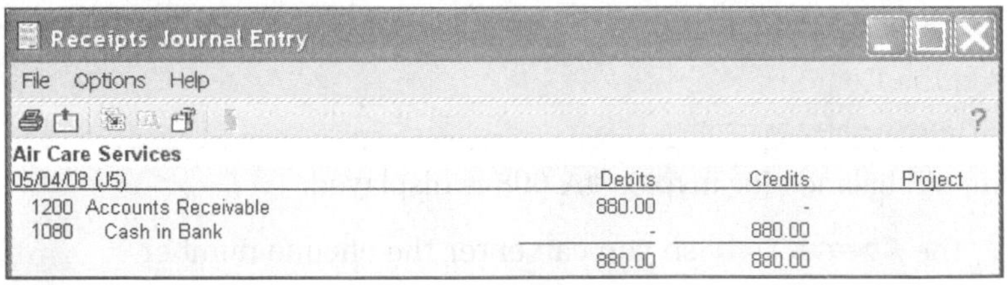

Notice that the same two linked accounts are used to create the reversing journal entry as the regular Receipts Journal entry. However, this time, *Cash in Bank* is credited and *Accounts Receivable* is debited because we entered negative amounts instead of positive amounts for the payment. This is a reversing entry of the payment.

Close the **display** when you have finished and **make corrections** if necessary.

Click the **Post button** (Post) to display a blank Payments Journal.

Including paid invoices in the journal can make it more difficult to find the invoice that you are paying, so you should not normally include paid invoices unless you need to reverse them. This option will be deselected when we save the transaction.

Choose **Grande Pointe Towers** from the Customer list.

The previously paid invoice is added to the outstanding invoices because now it is not fully paid. The second invoice balance owing is also fully restored.

Close the **Receipts Journal**.

ADJUSTING A RECEIPT AFTER POSTING

If you recorded a receipt or payment incorrectly, you can edit it in the same way that you adjust a General Journal entry, purchase or sale after posting.

- **Click** the **Adjust tool,** and **enter** the **search parameters** (or choose to Browse through all receipts).
- **Click** the **receipt** in the list and **click Select** to bring the posted receipt to the screen.
- **Make** the **correction** and then **post** the corrected **receipt**.

When you post the corrected entry, Simply Accounting will create the reversing entry automatically. You can see the complete audit trail by choosing Corrections in the Journal Reports.

NOTES
You must choose the System Settings option to Store Invoice Lookup Details to be able to adjust posted invoices (see page 84).

Editing a Customer Record

Most fields in the customer record can be changed at any time. Only the current balance owing, which is updated from sale and payment transactions, cannot be changed. To modify a customer's record, you should be in the Home window. Therefore, we must close the My Business Tab window.

Click the open **My Business tab heading** .

Click the **Customers icon**  as shown:

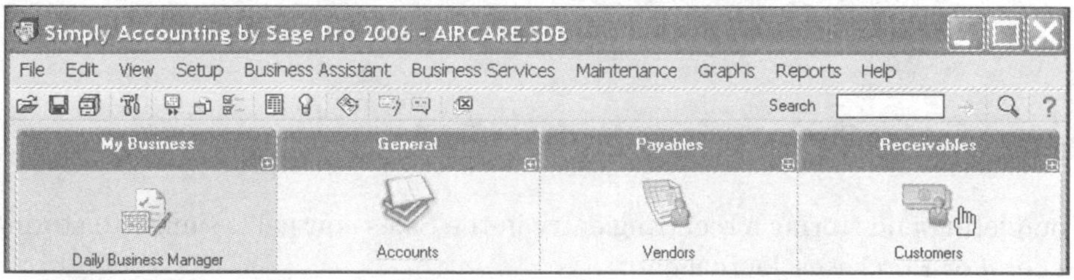

You will open the Customers window:

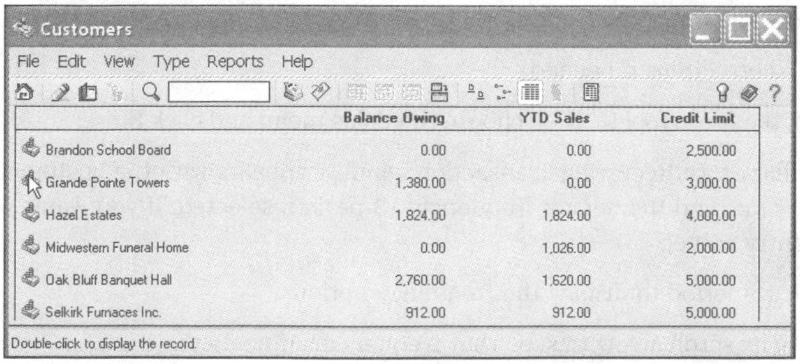

Click **Grande Pointe Towers** to select it.

Click the **Edit tool**  or **choose** the **Edit menu** and **click Edit**.

NOTES
When the My Business window is not open and you have opened a journal from the Home window, you can return to the Home window directly from the open journal.

Click the Home Window icon  in the open journal to access the Home window.

You can also restore the Home window by clicking the Simply Accounting button or icon on the task bar of the desktop, or right-clicking this button and choosing Restore.

The Receivables Ledger record for Grande Pointe Towers opens at the Address screen. We need to modify the Terms, which appear on the Options tab.

Click the **Options tab** to access the payment terms information:

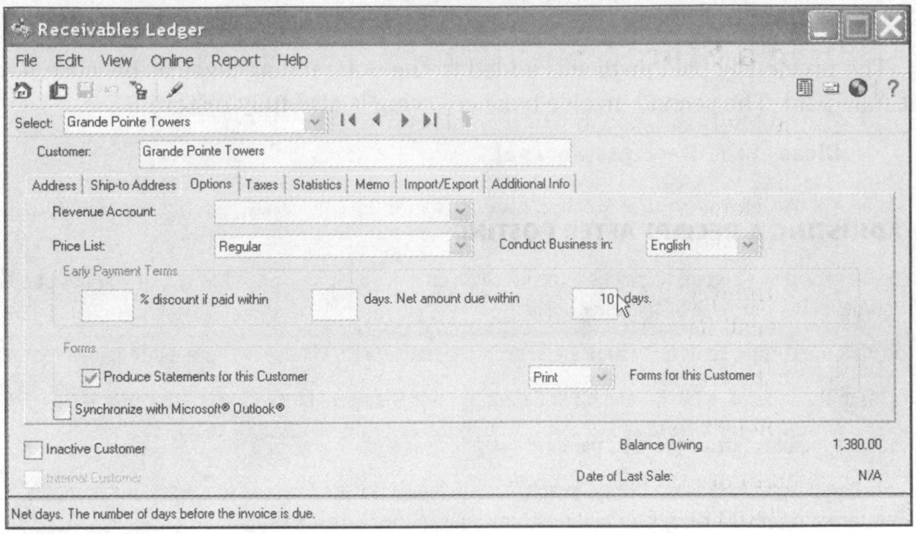

Click **10** in the Net Days field of the Early Payment Terms section.

Type 1

To modify other customer records, click Next or Previous to move to a different record or choose the customer you need from the Select drop-down list.

Click the **Statistics tab** to change credit limits.

Close the **Receivables Ledger** and **close** the **Customers window**.

Click the **My Business tab heading** to open the window so you can continue with the journal entries.

If you started from an open journal, click the Minimize button in the Home window to restore the journal window as the active window.

Storing a Recurring Sales Entry

Completing and storing a recurring entry in the Sales Journal is similar to storing a General or Purchases Journal entry.

Enter the transaction details in the journal.

Review the entry to be sure that it is correct.

Make corrections if needed.

Click the Store tool or choose the Sales menu and click Store.

The familiar Store Recurring Transaction window appears with the customer name as the entry name, and the default frequency, 13-period, selected. If you want, you can change the entry name.

Click 13-period to display the frequency options.

Click the scroll arrow to see other frequencies if needed.

Click the frequency.

Click OK to save the entry and return to the Sales Journal. The Recall button will be available.

Click Post to save the journal entry.

Recalling a Stored Sales Entry

In the My Business tab window click the Sales Invoices icon, or

In the Home window, click the Sales Orders & Quotes icon to open the Sales Journal.

Click the Recall tool or choose the Sales menu and click Recall to display the Recall Recurring Transaction window.

Click the transaction you want to use to select it.

Click Select to display a copy of the entry previously posted.

The default date is entered according to the frequency selected. The invoice number is updated automatically so the entry is complete.

Review the entry to be certain that it is correct.

Click the Post button to save the entry.

If you have made any changes to the entry, Simply Accounting may warn that posting the entry may affect the next due date. This warning will appear if you have made any changes to the entry before posting, although the message is a generic one referring only to the date.

Click Yes to accept the change and post the entry.

Adjusting a Posted Sales Journal Entry

If you discover an error in a Sales Journal entry after posting it, you can adjust or correct the posted transaction in the same way that you can adjust a purchase invoice after posting. You can edit any field in the invoice except the customer.

The entry for Hazel Estates was missing the second invoice line to record the revenue from repair work.

Click the **Sales Invoices icon** to open the Sales Journal.

Click the **Adjust Invoice tool** to open the Search window:

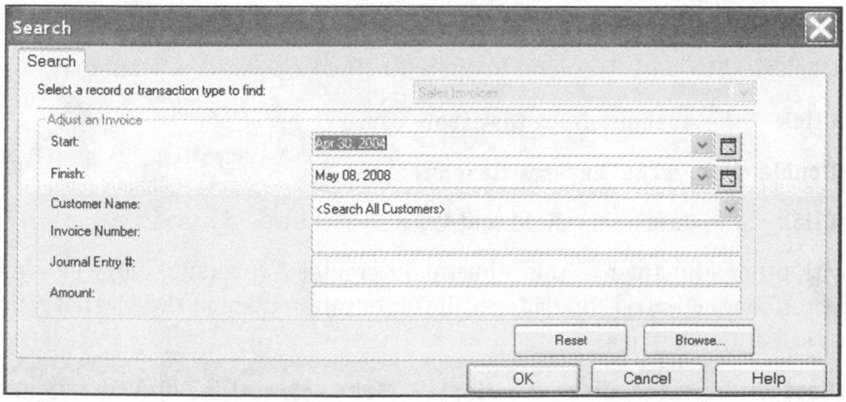

The default date and customer selections will include all invoices.

NOTES
You must choose the System Settings option to Store Invoice Lookup Details to be able to adjust posted invoices (see page 84).

NOTES
Just as you can choose a specific vendor for purchase invoice adjustments, you can choose a specific customer and click Browse to see a reduced list of invoices for the selected customer. You can also enter a specific invoice number and click OK to access the invoice directly.

Click **Browse** to open the Adjust An Invoice screen:

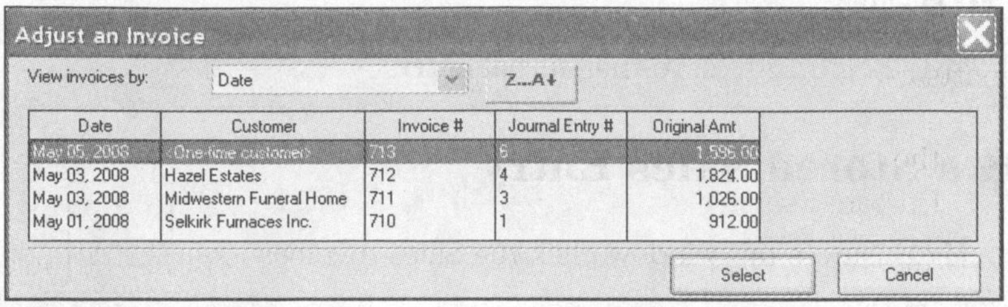

NOTES

If you have chosen the wrong customer, you must complete a reversing entry to correct it. Refer to Appendix C.

All Sales Journal entries for the selected customers and within the selected date range are listed. You can **view** the list of transactions in order by date, the default selection, customer, invoice number, journal entry number or amount. For each one you can switch between descending and ascending order with the **Z...A button**.

Journal Entry #4 for Hazel Estates is the one we need to edit.

Click **Hazel Estates**.

To choose an invoice for adjusting, you can click on any part of the line for that invoice to highlight it, then press *enter*, or click Select or you can double click the entry to open the journal immediately.

Click **Select** or **press** *enter* to open the invoice. It is ready for editing:

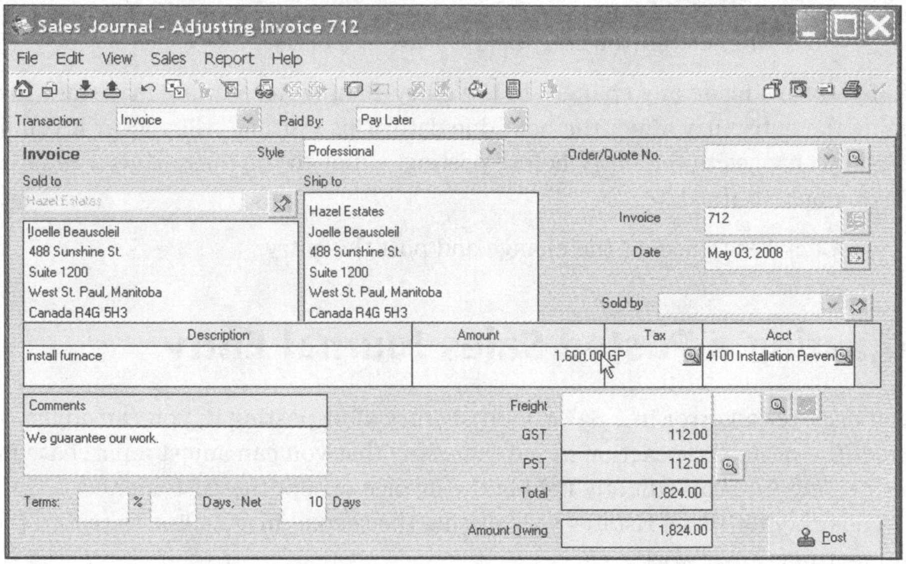

Click the **Description field** on the second line, below the first description.

Type `repair work` **Press** *tab* to advance to the Amount field.

Type `800` **Press** *tab*.

The tax code GP should be entered. You can select or change the code if needed. Click the Tax code List icon to open the Tax Code screen. Double click GP.

Click the **Account field List icon**.

Double click **4120 Repairs Revenue**.

Click the **Comments field** and **type** `Revised invoice`

NOTES

You can change the invoice number if you want to make the audit trail clearer. For example, you can enter 712-R as the invoice number to identify it as a revised invoice.

If you change the date, the reversing and corrected entry will have the same revised date.

As with other adjustments, this adjustment creates a reversing entry in addition to the corrected journal entry. You will see all three transactions in the journal reports when you select Corrections.

Review the **entry**. **Close** the **display**. **Make corrections** if necessary and **Post**.

Enter the **remaining transactions** and then **restore** the **Home window**.

Displaying Customer Reports

Customer reports can be accessed any time from the Home or the Customers window.

Click the **Customers icon** in the Home window to open the Customers window.

The Reports menu now contains only customer reports. You can select the report that you want from this list and follow the instructions below to choose report options. Customer-related graphs are not available from the Customers window.

Displaying Customer Lists

You should be in the Home window.

Right-click the **Customers icon** to select it.

Click the **Display tool** on the tool bar, or **choose** the **Reports menu**, then **choose Lists** and **click Customers** to see the options:

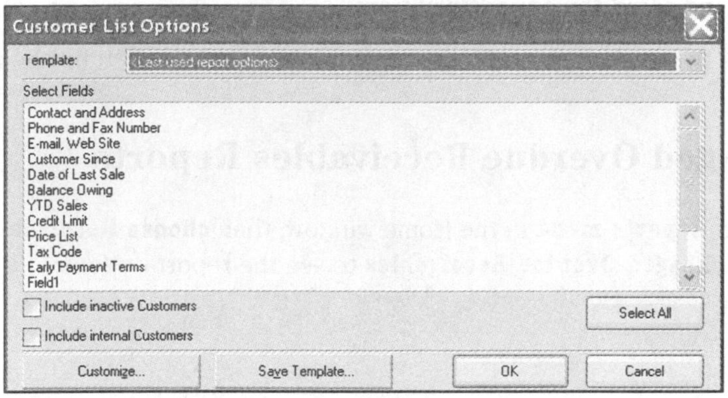

All the regular customer fields are selected initially. You can sort and filter Customer Lists by any of the fields selected for the report.

Click the **first field you want** in the report.

Press and **hold** *ctrl* and **click** the **names** of the fields you want in the list, or **click Select All** to include all the details.

Click **OK**. **Close** the **display** when you have finished viewing it.

NOTES
You can drill down to the Customer Aged Report from the Customer List.

BASIC VERSION
The option to Include Internal Customers is not available.

Displaying Customer Aged Reports

Choose the **Reports menu** in the Home window, then **choose Receivables** and **click Customer Aged** to see the following Report Options window:

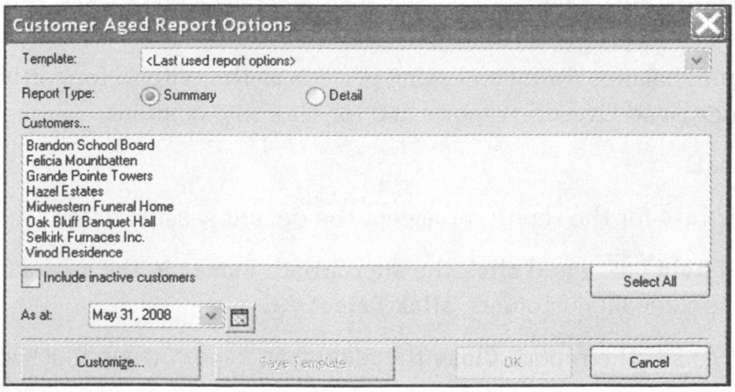

NOTES
You can drill down to look up invoices and to the Customer Ledger from the Customer Aged Report. From the Summary Report, you can drill down to the Detail Report.

NOTES
If you want to list customers in order according to the amount they owe with the largest balance reported first, you could sort by balance and click A...Z to reverse the order.

New customers you entered using Quick Add will appear on the list of customers in the report options windows. Sales for one-time customers and customers for whom you chose the Continue option will not appear because these cash transactions did not create an entry for Accounts Receivable.

The **Summary** option will display an alphabetic list of the selected customers with outstanding total balances owing, organized into aging period columns, according to the defaults set up for the company. By default, the program selects this option. The **Detail** option shows all the invoices and payments made by customers and the balance owing. This more descriptive report is also aged. Management can use it to make credit decisions. You can add payment terms to the Detail Report.

You can customize the Customer Aged and Aged Overdue reports (that is, choose columns, sort and filter) by name, balance owing and aging periods.

Click **Detail**.

Enter the **date** for the report, or accept the default session date.

Press and **hold** ctrl and **click** the appropriate **names** in the customer list. To include all customers, **click Select All**.

After you have indicated the options you want,

Click **OK** to see the report. **Close** the **displayed report** when finished.

Displaying Aged Overdue Receivables Reports

NOTES
You can drill down to look up invoices and to the Customer Aged Report from the Aged Overdue Receivables Report. From the Summary Report you can drill down to the Detail Report.

Choose the **Reports menu** in the Home window, then **choose Receivables** and **click Aged Overdue Receivables** to see the report options:

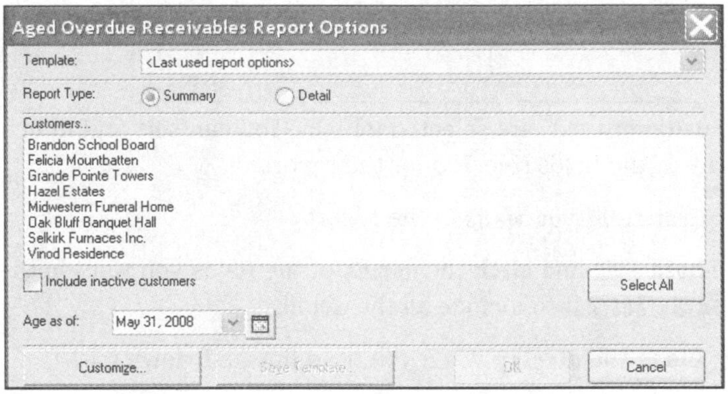

Enter the **date** for the report, or accept the default session date.

NOTES
Three customers currently have overdue accounts.

The **Summary** option will display an alphabetic list of the selected customers with outstanding total balances owing, organized into aging period columns, with an additional column for the overdue amount. Individual invoices, due dates, payments, overdue amounts and the balance owing for the selected customers are added when you choose the **Detail** Report.

You can use name, balance owing and aging periods as the criteria for sorting and filtering the Customer Aged Overdue reports and for choosing columns.

Click **Detail**.

Enter the **date** for the report, or accept the default session date.

Press and **hold** ctrl and **click** the appropriate **names** in the customer list. To include all customers, **click Select All**.

Click **OK** to see the report. **Close** the **displayed report** when finished.

Displaying the Sales Journal

Right-click the **Sales icon** 

in the Home window.

Click the **Display tool**  or **choose** the **Reports menu**, then **choose Journal Entries** and **click Sales** to see the report options:

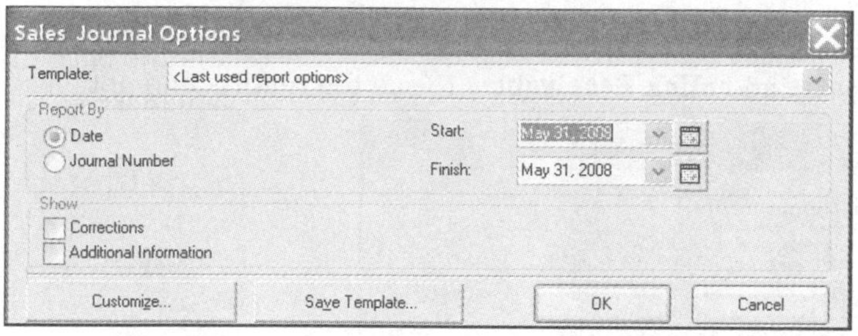

Sales and Receipts Journal reports are also available from the Select Report list when you click the Display tool button if no icon is selected in the Home window.

You can display the Sales Journal by posting date or by journal entry number. You can include corrections (adjusting entries) or omit them. The default setting, by Date, is the option used for all reports in this workbook, so leave the selection unchanged.

You can sort and filter journal reports by Date, Journal No., Source and Comment. You can choose account, description, debits and credits columns for the reports.

Enter the **beginning date** for the journal transactions you want. Or choose a date from the list arrow selections.

Press *tab* **twice**. **Enter** the **ending date** for the transaction period.

Click **Corrections**.

Click **OK** to view the report. **Close** the **display** when you have finished.

NOTES
You can drill down to an invoice, to the Customer Aged Report and to the General Ledger Report from the Sales and the Receipts Journal reports.

Displaying the Receipts Journal

Right-click the **Receipts icon** 

in the Home window.

Click the **Display tool**  or **choose** the **Reports menu**, then **choose Journal Entries** and **click Receipts** to see the report options:

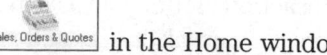

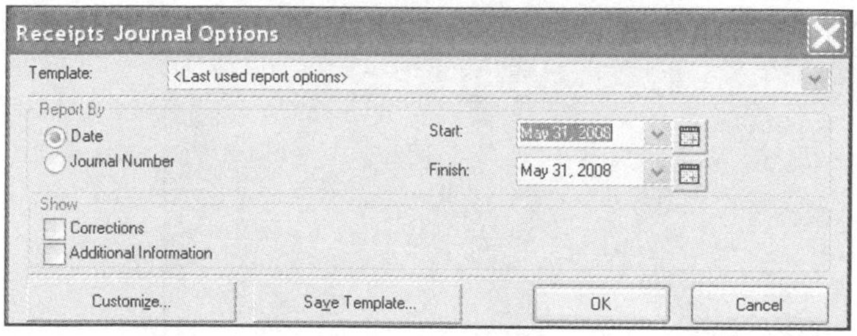

The Receipts Journal, like the other journals, can be displayed by date or by journal number. Leave the default Date selection unchanged.

Enter the **beginning date** for the journal transactions you want.

Press *tab* **twice** and **enter** the **ending date** for the transaction period you want to see.

Click **Corrections**.

NOTES
To include all journal entries in a single report, choose the Reports menu, then choose Journals and click All. Choose May 1 from the list arrow selections in the Start date field and May 31 as the Finish date.

Click **OK** to view the report. **Close** the **display** when you have finished.

To see the transactions for all journals in a single report, choose the Reports menu, then choose Journal Entries and click All.

Displaying Management Reports

Choose the **Reports menu** in the Home window, then **choose Management Reports** and **click Receivables** to see the reports and options:

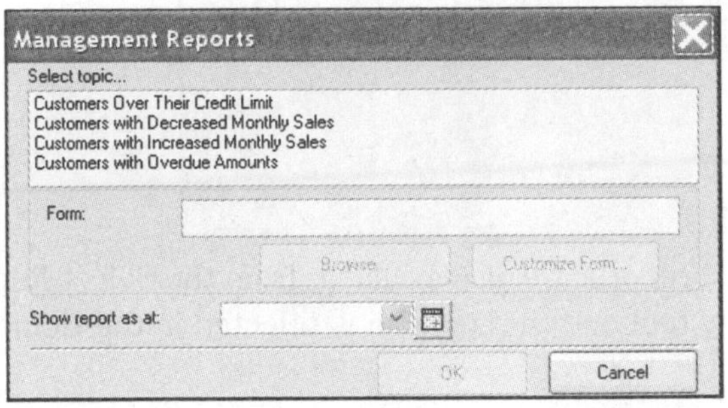

You can produce four different reports for the Receivables Ledger: a list of all customers who have exceeded their credit limits, sales amounts for customers who have decreased their purchases since the previous year, amounts for customers who have increased purchases and customers with overdue payments. The Overdue Accounts Report is helpful for making a list of customers to remind about settling their accounts because it includes customer contact details.

Click the **topic** for the report.

The program will add a date, if appropriate, and a form for the report. Change the date if you need to, but leave the default report form unless you have the programs required to modify these forms.

Click **OK** to display the report and print it if you want. **Close** the **display**.

NOTES

You cannot customize columns for the tax report.

You can sort and filter tax reports by name, invoice number, date, taxable purchases/sales excluding or including taxes, taxes paid/charged, other taxes paid/charged and total purchases/sales including taxes.

Displaying the Tax Report

Tax reports show the taxable purchases and sales with and without tax amounts included and the taxes paid or charged on each transaction or the total.

Choose the **Reports menu** in the Home window and **click Tax** to display the Tax Report Options window:

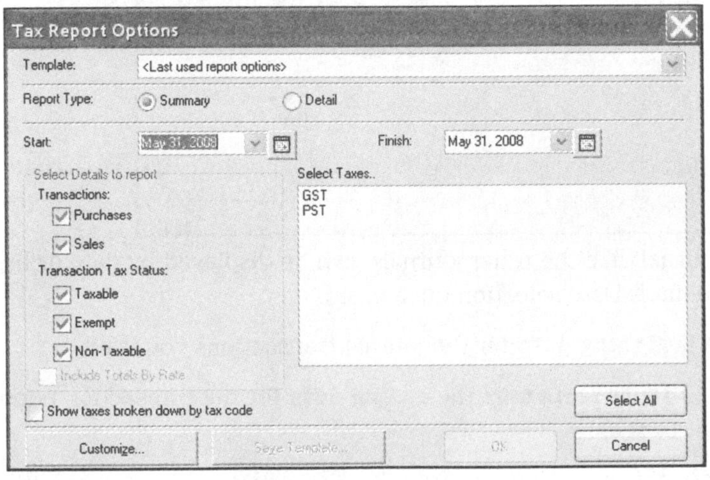

All taxes that were defined for the company and included the option to report on them are listed in the Select Taxes field.

The session date is selected as the default start and finish dates. You can include either sales or purchase transactions that include tax or both. Both purchases and sales are reported by default. In addition, the report can include taxable, exempt and non-taxable transactions. By default all are selected. You can also organize the report by tax codes.

The **Summary** Report has only the totals for each category selected while the **Detail** Report lists individual transactions for each category. You can include the total tax amounts by the tax rate as well.

Click **Detail** to select the more detailed level for the report.

Enter or **choose** the **dates** for which you want the report to start and finish.

Click a **tax name** in the Select Tax list to select it or **click Select All** to report on all the taxes listed.

Click the **transactions** (Purchases or Sales) to remove a ✓ or to add one if it is not there to include the transaction in the report.

Click a **transaction tax status** (Taxable, Exempt or Non-Taxable) to remove a ✓ or to add one if it is not there.

Click **Include Totals By Rate** if you have selected more than one tax.

Once you have selected the options you want,

Click **OK** to view the report.

Close the **display** when you have finished.

Displaying the Statement of Cash Flows

NOTES
You cannot customize the Statement of Cash Flows or the Cash Flow Projection Report.

The Cash Flow Statement summarizes sources (income, investments, etc.) and uses of cash (purchase of assets, etc.) and changes in liabilities during the designated period.

Choose the **Reports menu** in the Home window, then **choose Financials** and **click Statement Of Cash Flows** to see the report options:

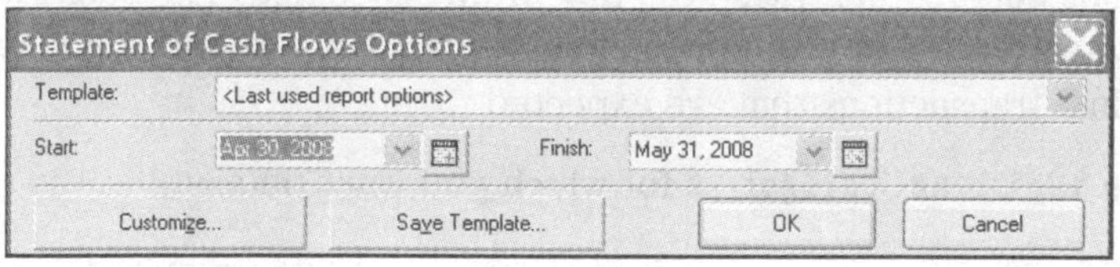

Enter the **Start** and **Finish dates** for the report. The fiscal start and session dates are the defaults.

Click **OK** to view the report.

By organizing the transactions involving cash, net changes in cash positions, as well as changes in liabilities, the statement allows the owner to judge how efficiently cash is being used for the business. The owner can also see potential problems resulting from increases in liabilities or decreases in the collection of receivables.

Close the **display** when you have finished.

Displaying Cash Flow Projection Reports

Cash Flow Projection reports predict the flow of cash in and out of an account — usually a bank account — over a specific future period based on current information.

Choose the **Reports menu** in the Home window, then **choose Financials** and **click Cash Flow Projection** to see the report options:

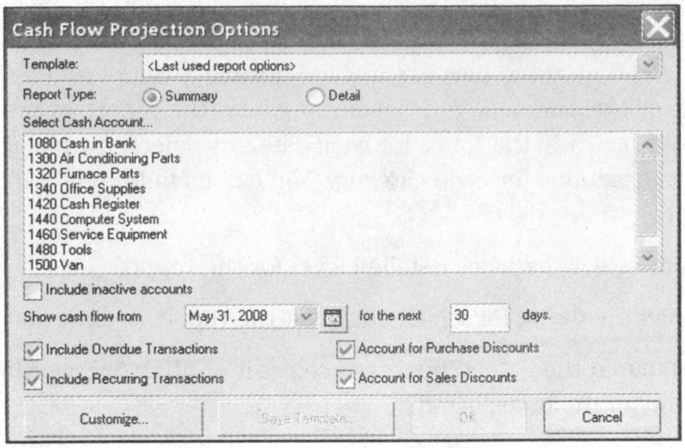

Click **1080 Cash in Bank**, the account for which you want the report.

Click the **Date field**.

Type the **date** at which you want the projection to start.

Press tab **twice**.

Enter the **number of days** in the future for which the report should project the cash flow.

NOTES

You might want to compare projection reports prepared with and without some of these extra details.

Usually you will include only the number of days for which you have reasonable information, such as the number of days in which net payment is due. The session date and 30 days are useful periods, so you can accept the defaults.

In the report, you may choose to include discounts in the amounts you expect to receive or pay, and you may include overdue transactions, or omit them if you expect them to remain unpaid. By default, all details are included. Clicking a detail will remove it from the report. The Projection Report assumes all amounts are paid on the invoice due date.

The report projects the account balance based on receivables and payables due and recurring transactions coming due within the time frame specified. The **Summary** Report shows the totals for the specified report period while the **Detail** Report shows, by date, the individual transactions that are expected.

Select the **additional categories** for which you want details.

Click **Detail**.

Click **OK** to view the report.

Close the **display**.

Printing Customer Reports

Display the **report**.

Click the **Print tool** or **choose** the **File menu** in the report window, and then **click Print**.

Close the **display** when you have finished.

Printing Customer Statements

You can e-mail all customer statements or print them, or you can choose e-mail and print on a customer-by-customer basis according to the setting (preference) in the customer's ledger record.

Be sure your printer is set up with the correct forms before you begin because statements are printed immediately when you click OK after selecting your options.

Choose the **Reports menu** in the Home window, then **choose Receivables** and **click Customer Statements** to see the following options:

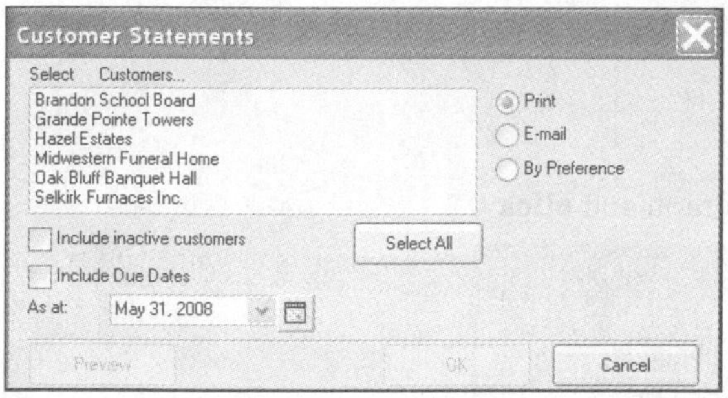

You should preview statements before printing them. To preview statements, you must select Custom Simply Form. Choose the Setup menu and click Reports & Forms. Click Statements. Choose Custom Form and then Custom Simply Form. If you also want to customize the statements, choose User Defined Form in the Printed Form Description field. Click the Customize button to open the Simply Form Designer. Save the new form when finished.

Press and **hold** ctrl and **click** the **customers** for whom you want to print statements, or **click Select All** to include all customers.

Click **Include Due Dates** if you want to add the payment due dates for invoices, and **click OK**.

NOTES
Customizing statements is similar to customizing invoices. Refer to Appendix F for assistance with previewing and customizing forms.

Printing Customer Mailing Labels

You should turn on the printer, insert labels paper and set the program for printing labels before choosing the options for the labels because printing begins immediately.

Choose the Setup menu in the Home window and click Reports & Forms. Click Labels. Enter the details for the labels. Click OK.

Choose the **Reports menu** in the Home window, then **choose Mailing Labels** and **click Customers** to see the following options:

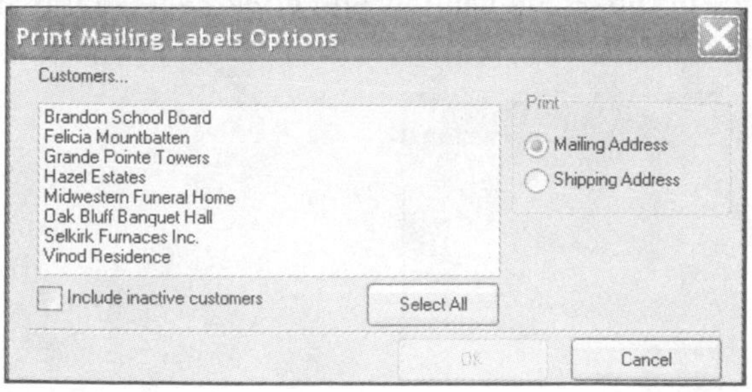

You can print labels for business mailing addresses or for shipping addresses.

Press and **hold** ctrl and **click** the **customers** for whom you want to print the labels, or **click Select All** to include all customers. **Click OK.**

NOTES
Refer to Chapter 4, page 83, and to Chapter 5, page 152, for details on setting up printers for different forms, reports and labels.

NOTES
You can customize customer statements but not mailing labels.

Graphing Customer Reports

The customer-related graphs are available from the Home window. You cannot view them from the Customers window.

Receivables by Aging Period Graph

Choose the **Graphs menu** in the Home window and **click Receivables By Aging Period** to see the options screen:

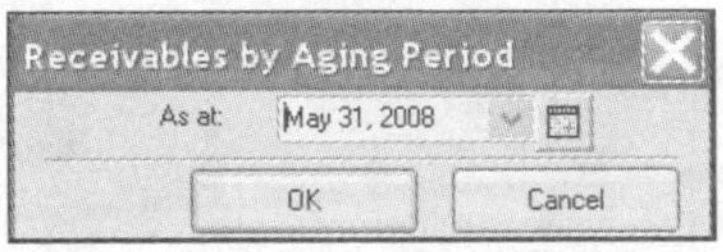

Enter a **date** for the graph and **click OK**.

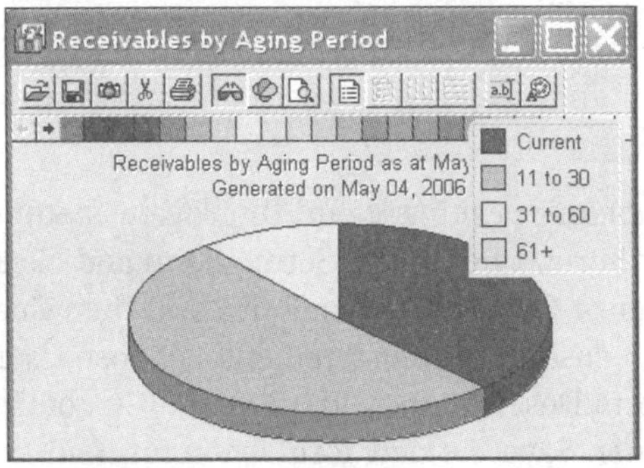

The pie chart shows the total receivables divided according to the aging intervals set up in the company defaults. The chart is the customer equivalent of the Payables By Aging Period Graph and shows the timeliness of account collections. You have the same tool bar options and colour and legend control choices that you have for the other graphs. Refer to page 61 for a review of these features if you need further assistance.

Double click a portion of a graph to see the aging period, the dollar amount and the percentage of the total.

Double click the legend to make it larger. Double click the expanded legend to reduce it.

Close the **graph** when you have finished.

Receivables by Customer Graph

Choose the **Graphs menu** in the Home window and **click Receivables By Customer** to see the following options:

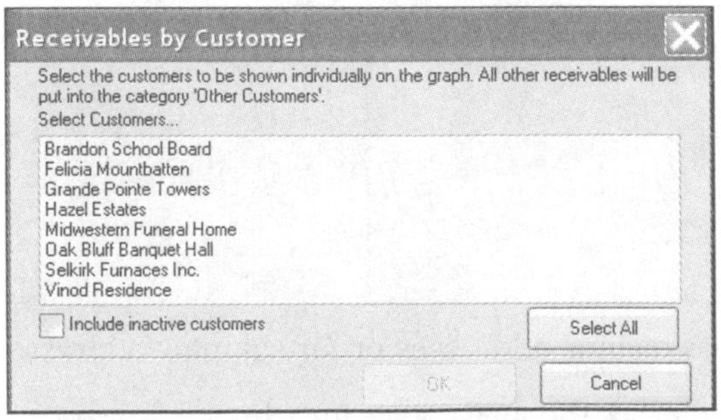

Press and **hold** ctrl and **click** the individual **customers** you want on the chart, or **click Select All** to include all customers.

Click OK to display the chart:

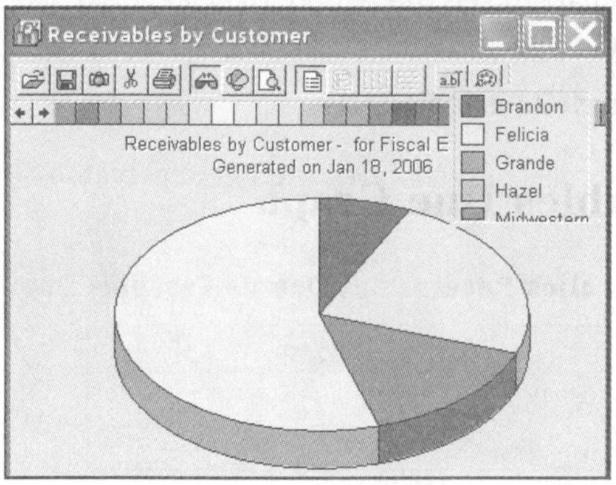

The amount owed by each customer, represented by different colours in the pie chart, is shown as a proportion of the total receivables. The options for displaying, editing, printing and exporting the graph are the same for all graphs.

Double click a portion of a graph to see the customer, the dollar amount and the percentage of the total.

Double click the legend to make it large and add the customer names. Double click the expanded legend to reduce it.

Close the **graph** when you have finished.

Sales vs Receivables Graph

Choose the **Graphs menu** and **click Sales Vs Receivables** to see the options:

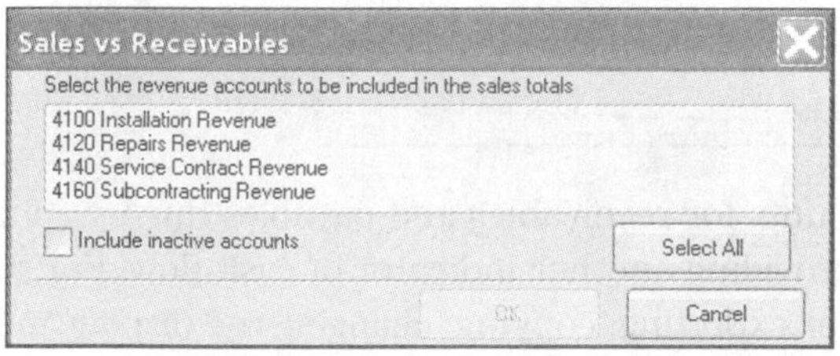

Press and **hold** ctrl and **click** the **revenue accounts** that you want in the graph. **Click Select All** to include all revenue accounts.

Click OK to display the following bar chart for the end of May:

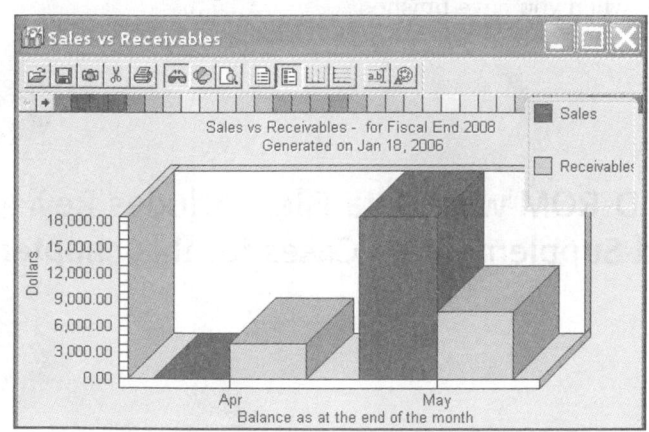

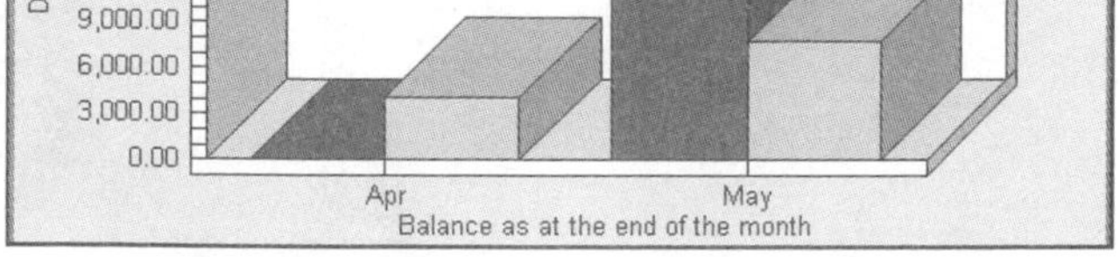

NOTES

The sales for April show as zero because we have not entered any transactions for April. The April receivables balance was the historical amount outstanding when we set up the data file.

Although this is not a pie chart, you have the same options for exporting, copying, changing the display and so on that you do for other graphs. The graph indicates cash flow by showing how much of the sales are not yet collected.

Double click a portion of the chart to see the period, the category (Sales or Receivables) and the dollar amount.

Close the **graph** when you have finished.

Receivables Due vs Payables Due Graph

Choose the **Graphs menu** and **click Receivables Due Vs Payables Due**:

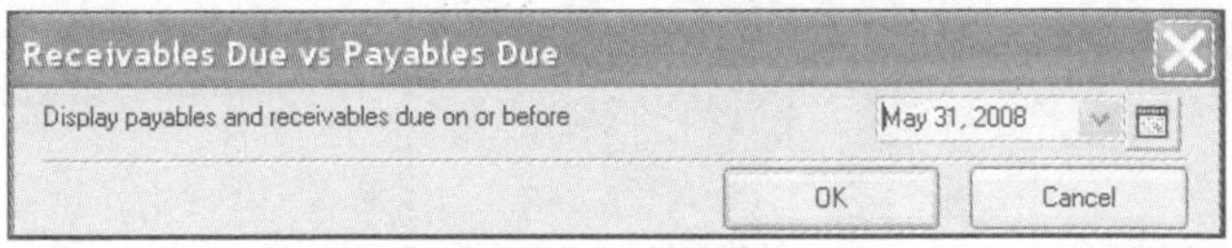

All receivables and payables due by the date displayed will be included.

Enter the **date** that you want the graph to include.

Click **OK** to display the bar chart:

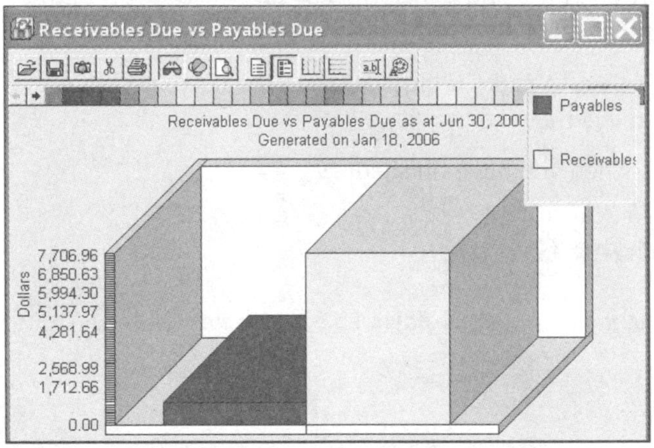

The graph shows the total amounts for receivables and payables due by June 30, 30 days beyond the session date, providing another indicator of cash flow. For this bar chart, you have the same options for exporting, copying, changing the display and so on that you do for other graphs.

Double click a portion of the graph to see the period, the category (Payables or Receivables) and the dollar amount.

Close the **graph** when you have finished.

REVIEW

The Student CD-ROM with Data Files includes Review Questions and Supplementary Cases for this chapter.

CHAPTER SEVEN

Andersson Chiropractic Clinic

OBJECTIVES

After completing this chapter, you should be able to

- ***enter*** receipts and payments with discounts
- ***track*** additional information for receipts, sales and purchases
- ***understand*** linked accounts for discounts
- ***place*** and ***fill*** purchase orders and quotes
- ***enter*** and ***fill*** sales quotes and orders
- ***convert*** sales and purchase quotes to orders
- ***adjust*** orders and quotes
- ***enter*** debit card sale transactions
- ***make*** payments and deposits using multiple bank accounts and a line of credit
- ***enter*** deposits from customers and prepayments to vendors
- ***delete*** a stored transaction
- ***remove*** quotes

COMPANY INFORMATION

Company Profile

NOTES
Andersson Chiropractic Clinic
4500 Rae St.
Regina, Saskatchewan S4S 3B4
Tel 1: (306) 577-1900
Tel 2: (306) 577-2199
Fax: (306) 577-1925
Business No.: 459 556 291

Andersson Chiropractic Clinic is a private clinic owned by Maria Andersson, who practises her profession in Regina, Saskatchewan. This is her second year in private practice after graduating as D.C. (Doctor of Chiropractic) and D.Ac. (Doctor of Acupuncture). She used some bank loans and her line of credit to consolidate her student loans and set up the clinic.

Andersson specializes in sports injuries and has some sports teams as clients. To treat patients, she uses chiropractic treatments and adjustments for back pain, and physiotherapy, massage, ultrasound, laser treatments, electrical stimulation and acupuncture for other joint and soft tissue injuries. Individual regular patients usually come two or three times per week, although some come daily. These patients settle their accounts bi-weekly. Sports teams have contracts and are billed monthly. Contract customers are offered a discount if they settle their accounts within 10 days. Cash, cheques and debit cards are accepted in payment.

A single assistant in the clinic divides her time between reception, administration and some basic treatments such as laser and ultrasound under the chiropractor's supervision. Andersson designates the precise area to be treated and the time and intensity settings for the equipment.

The office space that Andersson rents has a reception area and four treatment rooms with tables. The monthly rent includes heat but not hydro or telephone. One of the four treatment rooms doubles as Andersson's office and another room has the potential to accommodate a whirlpool. She is considering adding a whirlpool for hydrotherapy and deep water massage treatments because some sports injuries respond well to hydrotherapy.

For new sports team contracts, Andersson prepares sales quotes. When new customers accept a contract, they pay a deposit that is applied to the first month's payment.

Andersson has two bank accounts and a line of credit she uses to pay her bills. The limit on her line of credit is $50 000, and she has already borrowed $15 000 against it. A third bank account is used exclusively for debit card transactions.

Accounts for regular vendors and suppliers of treatment equipment, linens, laundry services, office maintenance and so on, are set up. Some of these vendors also offer discounts for early payments and some require Andersson to make prepayments with purchase orders.

No taxes are charged for medical treatment and supplies. Andersson pays both PST and GST for other goods and services. The business is not eligible for a GST refund since GST is not charged to customers and no taxes are recorded.

To convert her accounting records to Simply Accounting on October 1, 2008, she used the following information:

- Chart of Accounts
- Trial Balance
- Vendor Information
- Customer Information
- Accounting Procedures

CHART OF POSTABLE ACCOUNTS

ANDERSSON CHIROPRACTIC CLINIC

ASSETS
- 1060 Bank: Regina Chequing
- 1080 Bank: Eastside Chequing
- 1100 Bank: Interac
- 1200 Accounts Receivable
- 1220 Prepaid Insurance
- 1240 Prepaid Subscriptions
- 1280 Purchase Prepayments
- 1300 Linen Supplies
- 1320 Office Supplies
- 1340 Other Supplies
- 1420 Computer Equipment
- 1430 Accum Deprec: Computers
- 1450 Treatment Equipment
- 1460 Accum Deprec: Equipment
- 1520 Office Furniture ▶
- ▶1530 Accum Deprec: Furniture
- 1550 Treatment Tables
- 1560 Accum Deprec: Tables
- 1580 Vehicle
- 1590 Accum Deprec: Vehicle

LIABILITIES
- 2100 Loans Payable
- 2200 Accounts Payable
- 2250 Prepaid Sales and Deposits
- 2300 Line of Credit Payable

EQUITY
- 3400 M. A. Capital
- 3450 M. A. Drawings
- 3600 Net Income ▶

▶REVENUE
- 4100 Revenue from Services
- 4150 Sales Discounts
- 4200 Interest Income

EXPENSE
- 5010 Bank Charges and Interac Fees
- 5030 Purchase Discounts
- 5050 Office Supplies Used
- 5060 Other Supplies Used
- 5080 Subscriptions and Books
- 5090 Insurance Expense
- 5100 Interest Expense
- 5110 Freight Expense
- 5120 Clinic Maintenance ▶
- ▶5140 Laundry Services
- 5150 Professional Dues
- 5180 Depreciation Expenses
- 5200 Hydro Expense
- 5240 Telephone Expense
- 5260 Rent
- 5300 Vehicle Expenses
- 5500 Wages Expense
- 5520 Payroll Services

NOTES: The Chart of Accounts includes only postable accounts and the Net Income or Current Earnings account.

TRIAL BALANCE

ANDERSSON CHIROPRACTIC CLINIC

September 30, 2008		Debits	Credits			Debits	Credits
1060	Bank: Regina Chequing	$33 530		▶ 3450	M. A. Drawings	18 000	
1080	Bank: Eastside Chequing	19 100		4100	Revenue from Services		114 000
1100	Bank: Interac	3 430		4150	Sales Discounts	140	
1200	Accounts Receivable	12 500		4200	Interest Income		160
1220	Prepaid Insurance	1 600		5010	Bank Charges and Interac Fees	390	
1240	Prepaid Subscriptions	480		5030	Purchase Discounts		210
1300	Linen Supplies	1 300		5050	Office Supplies Used	350	
1320	Office Supplies	270		5060	Other Supplies Used	1 130	
1340	Other Supplies	530		5080	Subscriptions and Books	2 400	
1420	Computer Equipment	4 200		5090	Insurance Expense	8 000	
1430	Accum Deprec: Computers		$ 1 050	5100	Interest Expense	2 500	
1450	Treatment Equipment	12 600		5110	Freight Expense	120	
1460	Accum Deprec: Equipment		2 100	5120	Clinic Maintenance	2 100	
1520	Office Furniture	9 600		5140	Laundry Services	1 800	
1530	Accum Deprec: Furniture		800	5150	Professional Dues	495	
1550	Treatment Tables	8 400		5180	Depreciation Expenses	10 850	
1560	Accum Deprec: Tables		1 400	5200	Hydro Expense	1 200	
1580	Vehicle	22 000		5240	Telephone Expense	1 100	
1590	Accum Deprec: Vehicle		5 500	5260	Rent	23 000	
2100	Loans Payable		45 000	5300	Vehicle Expenses	1 300	
2200	Accounts Payable		7 290	5500	Wages Expense	21 000	
2300	Line of Credit Payable		15 000	5520	Payroll Services	450	
3400	M. A. Capital		33 355 ▶			$225 865	$225 865

VENDOR INFORMATION

ANDERSSON CHIROPRACTIC CLINIC

Vendor Name (Contact)	Address	Phone No. Fax No.	E-mail Web Site	Terms
Canadian Chiropractic Association (O. Fisshal)	33 Backer Road Toronto, Ontario M4T 5B2	Tel 1: (416) 488-3713 Tel 2: (888) 488-3713	www.cca.ca	net 10
Cleanol and Laundry Services (Bessie Sweeps)	19 Duster Road Regina, Saskatchewan S4R 4L4	Tel: (306) 398-0908 Fax: (306) 398-8211	bsweeps@cls.com www.cls.com	net 30
Grasslands Fuel				net 1 (cash)
Medical Linen Supplies (Oll Whyte)	500 Agar St. Saskatoon, Saskatchewan S7L 6B9	Tel: (306) 662-6192 Fax: (306) 662-4399	owhyte@medsupplies.com www.medsupplies.com	2/10, n/30
OnLine Books			www.onlinebooks.com	net 1 (cheque)
Prairie Power Corp. (M. Jouls)	48 Powers Bay Regina, Saskatchewan S4X 1N2	Tel: (306) 395-1125	www.prairiepower.ca	net 1
Pro Suites Inc. (Kendra Walls)	19 Tenant Cr. Regina, Saskatchewan S4N 2B1	Tel: (306) 396-6646 Fax: (306) 396-5397	walls@prosuites.com www.prosuites.com	net 1 (first of month)
Sonartek Ltd. (T. Waver)	390 Retallack St. Regina, Saskatchewan S4R 3N3	Tel: (306) 579-7923 Fax: (306) 579-8003	twaver@sonartek.com www.sonartek.com	2/15, n/30
The Papery				net 15
Thera-Tables Inc. (Li Flatte)	60 Flatlands Cr. Saskatoon, Saskatchewan S7K 5B1	Tel: (306) 662-6486 Fax: (306) 662-7910	www.theratables.com	2/5, n/30
Western Communications (V. Du Parler)	99 Listener St. Regina, Saskatchewan S4R 5C9	Tel: (306) 395-5533	www.westcom.ca	net 1

OUTSTANDING VENDOR INVOICES

ANDERSSON CHIROPRACTIC CLINIC

Vendor Name	Terms	Date	Invoice No.	Amount	Total
Cleanol and Laundry Services	net 30	Sep. 14/08	CLS-2419	$90	
	net 30	Sep. 28/08	CLS-2683	90	
			Balance owing		$180
Medical Linen Supplies	2/10, n/30	Sep. 24/08	MLS-102		$690
Sonartek Ltd.	2/15, n/30	Sep. 19/08	SL-3456		$6 420
			Grand Total		$7 290

CUSTOMER INFORMATION

ANDERSSON CHIROPRACTIC CLINIC

Customer Name (Contact)	Address	Phone No. Fax No.	E-mail Web Site	Terms Credit Limit
Albert Blackfoot	16 Prairie Bay Regina, Saskatchewan S4N 6V3	Tel: (306) 582-1919	ablackfoot@shaw.ca	net 15 $500
Canadian Royals (K. Player)	1910 Buckingham St. Regina, Saskatchewan S4S 2P3	Tel: (306) 578-4567 Fax: (306) 578-7382	kplayer@canroyals.com www.canroyals.com	1/10, n/30 $5 000
Interplay Ballet School (S. Lightly)	2755 Flamenco St. Regina, Saskatchewan S4V 8C1	Tel: (306) 396-6190 Fax: (306) 396-8186	lightly@lighterthanair.com www.lighterthanair.com	1/10, n/30 $5 000
Roughrider Argos (B. Ball)	2935 Fowler St. Regina, Saskatchewan S4V 1N5	Tel: (306) 399-8000 Fax: (306) 399-8115	www.proball.com/ra	1/10, n/30 $5 000
Suzanne Lejeune	301 Pasqua St. Regina, Saskatchewan S4R 4M8	Tel: (306) 573-6296	slejeune@hotmail.com	net 15 $500

OUTSTANDING CUSTOMER INVOICES

ANDERSSON CHIROPRACTIC CLINIC

Customer Name	Terms	Date	Invoice No.	Amount	Total
Canadian Royals	1/10, n/30	Sep. 28/08	#638	$4 500	$4 500
Interplay Ballet School	1/10, n/30	Sep. 25/08	#632	$3 100	$3 100
Roughrider Argos	1/10, n/30	Sep. 28/08	#639	$4 900	$4 900
			Grand Total		$12 500

Accounting Procedures

Taxes

Since medical services are not taxable, customers do not pay GST or PST on the treatments and GST paid is not refundable. Therefore, no taxes have been set up in the data files, and no tax options are available in the journal Tax fields. Andersson pays provincial tax at the rate of 6 percent and GST at 7 percent on normal purchases — medical equipment is not taxed. All prices are shown with taxes included but taxes are not recorded separately.

Cash and Debit Card Sales

Andersson's individual customers frequently pay by Interac or debit card. Sales invoice amounts are deposited directly to the linked bank account. For this service, Andersson pays a small fee to the bank for each transaction, as well as a monthly rental fee for the terminal. These fees are deducted from the account periodically and are not deducted from deposits for individual transactions. Rather than create a large number of small invoices, debit card transactions are summarized every two weeks.

Payroll

Andersson's assistant is paid a monthly salary through arrangements with the bank. In lieu of a salary, Andersson draws $2 500 per month.

Discounts

Customers who have contracts with Andersson are offered a 1 percent discount if they pay their accounts in full within 10 days. Full payment is requested within 30 days. Individual patients are asked to pay their accounts every two weeks. Some vendors also offer discounts for early payments.

All discount terms are set up in the customer and vendor records.

NOTES
All discounts are calculated on the full invoice amounts. For purchases, these amounts include taxes.

Deposits

When sports team managers sign new contracts for regular monthly billing for treating the team members, they pay a deposit to Andersson. Similarly, some vendors ask for a deposit or prepayment when Andersson places a large order.

Revenue and Expense Accounts

The customer records for Andersson Chiropractic Clinic are set up with *Revenue from Services* as the default account. For vendors, the account most often associated with purchases for a vendor has been entered as the default for that vendor.

Bank Accounts and Line of Credit

Andersson has two chequing accounts for deposits and payments. A third bank account is used for all Interac or debit card payments.

Andersson also uses her line of credit when making payments by cheque. At the end of each month Andersson makes a payment for the interest owing on the line of credit used. When she has the funds, she also pays down the principal owing.

All cheque numbers are updated automatically when the correct account is selected.

NOTES
The line of credit is set up as a liability account (the money is owed to the bank), but it is also a bank account that can be used to write cheques. The amount of credit available does not appear on the Balance Sheet or Trial Balance. It is usually added as a Note to the financial statements.

INSTRUCTIONS

1. **Record entries for the source documents** in Simply Accounting using the Chart of Accounts, Vendor Information, Customer Information and Accounting Procedures for Andersson Chiropractic Clinic. The procedures for entering each new type of transaction in this application are outlined step by step in the Keystrokes section following the source documents. These transactions are indicated with a ✓ in the completion box beside the source document. The page on which the relevant keystrokes begin is printed immediately below the check box.
2. **Print** the **reports and graphs** indicated on the following printing form after you have finished making your entries.

REPORTS

Lists
- ☐ Chart of Accounts
- ☐ Account List
- ☐ Vendors
- ☐ Customers

Journals
- ☑ All Journals (by date) Oct. 1 to Nov. 30
- ☐ General
- ☐ Purchases
- ☐ Payments
- ☐ Sales
- ☐ Receipts

Financials
- ☑ Comparative Balance Sheet: amounts only for Oct. 31, 2008 and Nov. 30, 2008
- ☑ Income Statement from Dec. 1, 2007 to Nov. 30, 2008
- ☑ Comparative Trial Balance: amounts only for Nov. 30 and Dec. 1, 2008
- ☐ General Ledger
- ☑ Statement of Cash Flows from Oct. 1 to Nov. 30
- ☑ Cash Flow Projection Detail Report for accounts 1060 and 1080 for 30 days

Taxes
- ☐ Tax

Banking
- ☐ Cheque Log Report

Payables
- ☑ Vendor Aged Detail for all vendors
- ☐ Aged Overdue Payables
- ☑ Pending Purchase Orders as at Jan. 15, 2009

Receivables
- ☑ Customer Aged Detail for all customers
- ☐ Aged Overdue Receivables
- ☐ Customer Statements
- ☑ Pending Sales Orders as at Jan. 15, 2009

Mailing Labels
- ☐ Labels

Management Reports
- ☐ Ledger

GRAPHS
- ☐ Payables by Aging Period
- ☐ Payables by Vendor
- ☐ Receivables by Aging Period
- ☐ Receivables by Customer
- ☑ Sales vs Receivables
- ☑ Receivables Due vs Payables Due
- ☑ Revenues by Account
- ☐ Expenses by Account
- ☑ Expenses and Net Profit as % of Revenue

SOURCE DOCUMENTS

SESSION DATE – OCTOBER 7, 2008

WARNING!
Two bank accounts and the line of credit are available for receipts and payments. Before posting a transaction, check carefully that you have selected the right account.

☑ **Cash Receipt #58** **Dated October 1, 2008**

210 From Interplay Ballet, cheque #447 for $3 069 in payment of account including $31 discount for early payment. Reference invoice #632. Deposited to Eastside Chequing account.

☑ **Cheque Copy #103** **Dated October 2, 2008**

212 To Sonartek Ltd., $6 291.60 from the line of credit in payment of account including $128.40 discount for early payment. Reference invoice #SL-3456.

☑ **Cash Purchase R2008-10** **Dated October 2, 2008**

To Pro Suites Inc., cheque #121 for $2 300 to pay rent for October. Store the transaction as a monthly recurring entry. Pay from Eastside Chequing.

☑ **Purchase Quote #TT-44** **Dated October 2, 2008**

214 Delivery date October 10, 2008
From Thera-Tables Inc., $4 000 including taxes for custom-built adjustable height treatment table with drop ends. Terms: 2/5, n/30. Deposit of 10 percent required on accepting quote.

☑ **Purchase Quote #MT-511** **Dated October 2, 2008**

Delivery date October 20, 2008
From Medi-Tables (use Quick Add for the new vendor), $4 550 including all taxes for custom-built treatment table. Terms: net 20. Deposit of 20 percent required on accepting quote.

☑ **Purchase Order #TT-44** **Dated October 3, 2008**

217 Delivery date October 10, 2008
To Thera-Tables Inc., $4 000 including taxes for custom-built treatment table. Terms: 2/5, n/30. Convert quote #TT-44 to purchase order #TT-44.

☑ **Cheque Copy #122** **Dated October 4, 2008**

218 To Thera-Tables Inc., $400 from Eastside Chequing account as prepayment in acceptance of quote #TT-44 and to confirm order #TT-44.

☑ **Cheque Copy #567** **Dated October 4, 2008**

To Medical Linen Supplies, $676.20 from Regina Chequing account in payment of account including $13.80 discount for early payment. Reference invoice #MLS-102.

☑ **Sales Quote #51** **Dated October 4, 2008**

220 Starting date October 15, 2008
To Giant Raptors (use Full Add for the new customer), a local basketball team, $3 500 per month for unlimited chiropractic services during the regular six-month training and playing season. Andersson will attend or be on call for all home games. If the team enters the playoffs, the contract may be extended for $1 200 per week. Terms: 1/10, n/30. A deposit of $2 000 is required on acceptance of the contract. Enter 6 as the number ordered.

NOTES
Each month, the sales invoice for Giant Raptors will be entered as partially filling the order.

NOTES
☐ Giant Raptors
(contact Rex Saurus)
550 Tyrannus Dr.,
Regina, SK S4R 5T1
Tel 1: (306) 398-8753
Tel 2: (306) 398-5339
Fax: (306) 398-5339
E-mail: rex@raptors.com
Web: www.raptors.com
Terms: 1/10, n/30
Revenue account: 4100
Credit limit: $5 000

☑ **Memo #1** **Dated October 5, 2008**

222 After some negotiations with the Giant Raptors, Andersson agreed to reduce the contract price to $3 300 per month for the playing season. Playoff games will be billed at $1 100 per week. Adjust the sales quote to change the price.

☑ **Sales Order #51** **Dated October 5, 2008**

223 Starting date October 15, 2008
The Giant Raptors have accepted the modified sales quote #51. Convert the quote to a sales order. All terms and dates are unchanged from the revised quote for $3 300 per month.

☑ **Cash Receipt #59** **Dated October 6, 2008**

224 From the Giant Raptors, cheque #838 for $2 000 as deposit #14 to confirm sales order #51. Deposited to Eastside Chequing account.

☑ **Cash Receipt #60** **Dated October 7, 2008**

From Roughrider Argos, cheque #1122 for $4 851 in payment of account including $49 discount for early payment. Reference sales invoice #639. Deposited to Eastside Chequing account.

SESSION DATE – OCTOBER 14, 2008

☑ **Cash Receipt #61** **Dated October 8, 2008**

From Canadian Royals, cheque #3822 for $4 455 in payment of account including $45 discount for early payment. Reference sales invoice #638. Deposited to Regina Chequing account.

☑ **Purchase Order #44** **Dated October 9, 2008**

226 Delivery date October 19, 2008
From Sonartek Ltd., $6 000 including taxes for ultrasound machine with multiple frequencies and interchangeable wands. Terms: 2/15, n/30. Deposit of 25 percent required to confirm order.

Purchase Invoice #TT-4599 **Dated October 10, 2008**

227 From Thera-Tables Inc., to fill purchase order #TT-44 for $4 000 including taxes for custom-built treatment table. Terms: 2/5, n/30.

Sales Invoice #649 **Dated October 10, 2008**

229 To Giant Raptors, to fill the first month of sales order #51 for $3 300 for the first month of the contract. Terms: 1/10, n/30.

Cash Receipt #62 **Dated October 13, 2008**

230 From the Giant Raptors, cheque #939 for $1 267 in full payment of account including $33 discount for early payment. Reference sales invoice #649 and deposit #14. Deposited to Eastside Chequing account.

NOTES

Veronica Kain School of Dance
(contact Veronica Kain)
35 Lady Slipper Rd.
Regina, SK S3V 4H7
Tel: (306) 376-3218
E-mail: vkain@dancestudio.ca
Terms: 1/10, n/30
Revenue account: 4100
Credit limit: $4 000

Sales Quote #52 **Dated October 13, 2008**

Starting date October 25, 2008
To Veronica Kain School of Dance (use Full Add for the new customer), $2 500 per month for unlimited contracted chiropractic services for the school year. Fees will be higher during the summer months when the school operates full time. Terms: 1/10, n/30. A deposit of $1 000 is required on acceptance of the contract. Enter 1 as the quantity ordered.

Sales Order #52 and Deposit #15 **Dated October 14, 2008**

232 Starting date October 25, 2008
From Veronica Kain School of Dance, acceptance of quote #52. Convert the quote to a sales order leaving all terms, amounts and dates unchanged. Received cheque #865 for $1 000 as deposit #15 to confirm sales order #52. Deposited to Eastside Chequing account.

Debit Card Sales Summary Invoice #650 **Dated October 14, 2008**

233 To various one-time customers, $260 for initial assessments for new patients and $450 for follow-up treatment sessions. Total amount deposited in Interac bank account, $710. Store as a recurring bi-weekly transaction.

Cheque Copy #568 **Dated October 14, 2008**

To Sonartek Ltd., $1 500 from Regina Chequing account as prepayment to confirm purchase order #44.

Cheque Copy #123 **Dated October 14, 2008**

To Cleanol and Laundry Services, $90 from Eastside Chequing in payment of account. Reference invoice #CLS-2419.

Cheque Copy #124 **Dated October 14, 2008**

To Thera-Tables Inc., $3 520 from Eastside Chequing account in full payment of account including $80 discount for early payment. Reference invoice #TT-4599 and cheque #122. Remember to "pay" the prepayment.

Purchase Invoice #CLS-3926 **Dated October 14, 2008**

From Cleanol and Laundry Services, $90 for contracted twice weekly laundry service. Terms: net 30. Store the transaction as a bi-weekly recurring entry.

SESSION DATE – OCTOBER 21, 2008

Purchase Invoice #SL-4622 **Dated October 17, 2008**

From Sonartek Ltd., to fill purchase order #44, $6 000 including taxes for multi-frequency ultrasound machine. Terms: 2/15, n/30.

Cash Purchase GF-2641 **Dated October 18, 2008**

From Grasslands Fuel, $62 for gasoline for business vehicle and $35 for tire repairs. Invoice total $97 paid in full by cheque #569 from Regina Chequing account.

Cash Sales Invoice #651 **Dated October 20, 2008**

To Albert Blackfoot, $315 for seven treatment sessions. Invoice total paid in full by cheque #43 and deposited to Regina Chequing account.

SESSION DATE – OCTOBER 31, 2008

NOTES

When you advance the session date to Oct. 31, you will see an advice statement that it is time to prepare for year-end. Read and then close the advisory statement to proceed.

Sales Invoice #652 **Dated October 25, 2008**

235 To Veronica Kain School of Dance, to fill sales order #52, $2 500 for contracted services for one month. Terms: 1/10, n/30. Store as recurring monthly entry.

Sales Invoice #653 **Dated October 25, 2008**

To Interplay Ballet School, $3 100 for contracted services for one month. Terms: 1/10, n/30. Store transaction as recurring monthly entry.

Debit Card Sales Summary Invoice #654 **Dated October 28, 2008**

To various one-time customers, $130 for initial assessments and $630 for follow-up treatment sessions. Total amount deposited in Interac bank account, $760. Recall the stored transaction and edit the amounts. Do not store the changed transaction.

Purchase Invoice #CLS-4723 **Dated October 28, 2008**

From Cleanol and Laundry Services, $90 for contracted laundry service. Terms: net 30. Recall stored transaction.

Cash Purchase Invoice #WC-83835 **Dated October 28, 2008**

From Western Communications, $125 including taxes for one month of telephone and Internet service. Invoice total paid by cheque #125 from Eastside Chequing account.

Sales Invoice #655 **Dated October 28, 2008**

To Canadian Royals, $4 500 for contracted services for one month. Terms: 1/10, n/30. Store transaction as recurring monthly entry.

Sales Invoice #656 **Dated October 28, 2008**

To Roughrider Argos, $4 900 for contracted services for one month. Terms: 1/10, n/30. Store transaction as recurring monthly entry.

Cheque Copy #570 **Dated October 29, 2008**

To Cleanol and Laundry Services, $180 from Regina Chequing in payment of account. Reference invoices #CLS-2683 and #CLS-3926.

Bank Debit Memo #477211 **Dated October 29, 2008**

From Eastside Trust, $2 100 for monthly payroll and $45 payroll service fee withdrawn from chequing account. Store payroll transaction as monthly recurring entry.

Cash Receipt #63 **Dated October 29, 2008**

236 From Veronica Kain School of Dance, cheque #878 for $1 475 in payment of account including $25 discount for early payment. Reference sales invoice #652 and deposit #15. Deposited to Regina Chequing account.

☑ **Cash Receipt #64** **Dated October 29, 2008**

From Interplay Ballet, cheque #501 for $3 069 in payment of account including $31 discount for early payment. Reference sales invoice #653. Deposited to Regina Chequing account.

☑ **Purchase Quote #45** **Dated October 30, 2008**

Starting date November 1, 2008
From Cleanol and Laundry Services, $210 every two weeks to increase service from twice per week to daily laundry service. Terms: net 30.

☑ **Purchase Quote #FS-644** **Dated October 30, 2008**

Starting date November 1, 2008
From Fresh Spaces (use Quick Add for the new vendor), $125 per week for daily laundry service. Terms: net 30.

☑ **Memo #2** **Dated October 31, 2008**

Transfer $1 060 from the Regina Trust Chequing account to pay down the line of credit. This amount includes $60 for one month of interest on the amount of credit used.

NOTES
To transfer the funds, you should debit the Line of Credit Payable and Interest Expense and credit the bank account.

SESSION DATE – NOVEMBER 7, 2008

☑ **Purchase Order #45** **Dated November 1, 2008**

Starting date November 1, 2008
From Cleanol and Laundry Services, $210 bi-weekly for daily laundry service. Terms: net 30. Convert purchase quote #45 to a purchase order.

☑ **Cheque Copy #571** **Dated November 1, 2008**

To Sonartek Ltd., $4 380 from Regina Chequing account in full payment of account including $120 discount for early payment. Reference purchase invoice #SL-4622 and cheque #568 (prepayment).

☑ **Cash Purchase R2008-11** **Dated November 2, 2008**

To Pro Suites Inc., cheque #126 for $2 300 from Eastside Chequing account to pay rent for November. Recall stored entry.

☑ **Cash Receipt #65** **Dated November 5, 2008**

From Canadian Royals, cheque #4011 for $4 455 in payment of account including $45 discount for early payment. Reference sales invoice #655. Deposited to Regina Chequing account.

☑ **Purchase Order #46** **Dated November 6, 2008**

Delivery date December 28, 2008
From Get Better Whirlpools (use Full Add for new vendor), $24 000 including taxes for therapeutic whirlpool. Terms: net 20. Deposit of $2 000 required to confirm order. Create new Group account 1480 Whirlpool.

NOTES
☐ Get Better Whirlpools
(contact Ira Spinner)
35 Eddy Circle
Saskatoon, SK S7K 6E3
Tel 1: (306) 665-7210
Tel 2: (877) 699-1270
Fax: (306) 663-6281
Web: www.gbw.com
Terms: net 20
Expense acct: 1480 (Start the Add Account wizard by typing the new account number in the Expense Account field.)

☑ **Cash Receipt #66** **Dated November 7, 2008**

From Roughrider Argos, cheque #1636 for $4 851 in payment of account including $49 discount for early payment. Reference sales invoice #656. Deposited to Eastside Chequing account.

SESSION DATE – NOVEMBER 14, 2008

Sales Invoice #657 **Dated November 9, 2008**

To Giant Raptors, to fill one month of the contract in sales order #51 for $3 300. Terms: 1/10, n/30.

Purchase Invoice #CLS-5884 **Dated November 11, 2008**

237 From Cleanol and Laundry Services, to fill purchase order #45, $210 for contracted daily laundry service. Terms: net 30. Store as bi-weekly recurring entry. (Remove the old stored entry then store new one.)

Debit Card Sales Summary Invoice #658 **Dated November 11, 2008**

To various one-time customers, $195 for initial assessments and $495 for follow-up treatment sessions. Total amount deposited in Interac bank account, $690. Recall the stored transaction and edit the amounts. Do not save the changes.

Cash Purchase Invoice #TP-1188 **Dated November 12, 2008**

From The Papery, $230 for paper supplies for treatment rooms and $60 for office paper supplies. Invoice total $290 paid in full from Eastside Chequing account by cheque #127.

Cash Receipt #67 **Dated November 14, 2008**

From the Giant Raptors, cheque #1334 for $3 267 in full payment of account including $33 discount for early payment. Reference sales invoice #657. Deposited to Eastside Chequing account.

Cash Purchase Invoice #GF-3677 **Dated November 14, 2008**

From Grasslands Fuel, $84 for gasoline for business vehicle. Invoice total paid in full from Regina Chequing account by cheque #572.

SESSION DATE – NOVEMBER 21, 2008

Purchase Quote #SU-5532 **Dated November 19, 2008**

Starting date December 1, 2008
From Space Unlimited (use Quick Add), $2 250 per month for rent of office space for the next 12 months. Rent does not include heat or hydro. Terms: net 1. Rent payment is due on the first of each month. Security deposit of one month's rent required in advance. Postdated cheques will be accepted.

Cheque Copy #573 **Dated November 19, 2008**

To Get Better Whirlpools, $2 000 as prepayment to confirm purchase order #46. Paid from Regina Chequing account.

Purchase Order #47 **Dated November 19, 2008**

Starting date January 1, 2009
From HydraTub Care (use Full Add for new vendor), $200 per month, including all taxes for one-year service contract. The contract includes weekly maintenance of whirlpool and repairs. Parts required for repairs will be billed separately. Terms: net 20. Create new Group account 5220 Whirlpool Maintenance. Use this as the default expense account for the vendor.

Purchase Quote #48 **Dated November 19, 2008**

Starting date December 1, 2008
From Pro Suites Inc., $2 350 per month for rent of office space for the next 12 months. Rent includes heat but does not include hydro. Rent payment is due on the first of each month. A series of postdated cheques will be accepted.

NOTES

HydraTub Care
550 Splash St.
Regina, SK S4T 7H5
Tel: (306) 578-2996
Terms: net 20
Expense acct: 5220 (Start the Add Account wizard by typing the new account number in the Expense Account field.)

Purchase Order #48 **Dated November 20, 2008**

Starting date December 1, 2008
From Pro Suites Inc., $2 350 per month for rent of office space for the next 12 months. Convert purchase quote #48 to a purchase order.

NOTES
The year-end advisor appears when you advance the session date. Read the message and close the advisor.

SESSION DATE – NOVEMBER 28, 2008

Debit Card Sales Summary Invoice #659 **Dated November 25, 2008**

To various one-time customers, $260 for initial assessments and $630 for follow-up treatment sessions. Total amount deposited in Interac bank account, $890. Recall the stored transaction and edit the amounts. Do not save the changes.

Purchase Invoice #CLS-6543 **Dated November 25, 2008**

From Cleanol and Laundry Services, $210 for contracted laundry service. Terms: net 30. Recall stored transaction.

Sales Invoice #660 **Dated November 25, 2008**

To Interplay Ballet School, $3 100 for contracted services for one month. Terms: 1/10, n/30. Recall stored transaction.

Sales Invoice #661 **Dated November 25, 2008**

To Veronica Kain School of Dance, $2 500 for contracted services for one month. Terms: 1/10, n/30. Recall stored transaction.

Sales Invoice #662 **Dated November 28, 2008**

To Canadian Royals, $4 500 for contracted services for one month. Terms: 1/10, n/30. Recall stored transaction.

Sales Invoice #663 **Dated November 28, 2008**

To Roughrider Argos, $4 900 for contracted services for one month. Terms: 1/10, n/30. Recall stored transaction.

Cash Purchase Invoice #PPC-76511 **Dated November 28, 2008**

From Prairie Power Corp., $380 including taxes for two months of hydro service. Invoice total paid from Eastside Chequing account by cheque #128.

Cheque Copy #574 **Dated November 28, 2008**

To Cleanol and Laundry Services, $300 from Regina Chequing account in payment of account. Reference invoices #CLS-4723 and CLS-5884.

Cash Purchase Invoice #WC-122002 **Dated November 28, 2008**

From Western Communications, $115 including taxes for telephone and Internet service. Invoice total paid from Eastside Chequing account by cheque #129.

SESSION DATE – NOVEMBER 30, 2008

Cash Receipt #68 **Dated November 29, 2008**

From Interplay Ballet, cheque #553 for $3 069 in payment of account including $31 discount for early payment. Reference invoice #660. Deposited to Eastside Chequing account.

Bank Debit Memo #747721 **Dated November 29, 2008**

From Eastside Trust, $2 100 for monthly payroll and $45 payroll service fee withdrawn from chequing account 1080. Recall stored transaction.

Bank Debit Memo #747937 **Dated November 29, 2008**

From Eastside Trust, pre-authorized withdrawals from chequing account:
For bi-monthly loan repayment, $1 370 principal and $230 interest
For bank service charges and debit card fees, $108

Memo #3 **Dated November 30, 2008**

Transfer $1 060 from the Regina Trust Chequing account to pay down the line of credit. This amount includes $60 for one month of interest on the amount of credit used.

Bank Debit Memo #120022 **Dated November 30, 2008**

From Regina Trust, $36 withdrawn from account for service charges.

Memo #4 **Dated November 30, 2008**

From Manager: Record the accumulated depreciation for the two-month period for all fixed assets as follows:

Computer Equipment	$ 230
Treatment Equipment	420
Office Furniture	160
Treatment Tables	280
Vehicle	1 100

Memo #5 **Dated November 30, 2008**

From Manager: Record the adjusting entries for supplies used in the previous two months:

Office Supplies	$105
Paper and Other Supplies	260

Cheque Copy #130 **Dated November 30, 2008**

To M. Andersson (use Quick Add), $5 000 from Eastside Chequing for drawings to cover personal expenses.

Memo #6 **Dated November 30, 2008**

238 From Manager: Three purchase quotes that are on file are no longer valid. Remove quote #MT-511 from Medi-Tables, quote #FS-644 from Fresh Spaces and quote #SU-5532 from Space Unlimited.

Memo #7 **Dated November 30, 2008**

From Manager: Close out the M. A. Drawings account by transferring the balance to M. A. Capital.

Memo #8 **Dated November 30, 2008**

From Manager: Print all financial reports. Back up the data files and start a new fiscal period on December 1, 2008.

NOTES
To close the Drawings account, credit Drawings and debit Capital. You can find the amount in the Trial Balance, Balance Sheet or General Ledger.

NOTES
Refer to page 108 for assistance with starting a new fiscal period if needed.

KEYSTROKES

Opening Data Files

Open the **Andersson data files**. **Enter** **Oct. 7, 2008** as the Session date.

Entering Discounts for Customers

NOTES
A discount of 1 percent for paying within 10 days is comparable to an interest penalty of over 18 percent per year.

Discounts for early payments are an incentive to encourage prompt payments because the real rate of interest for forgoing the discount is higher than normal interest penalties for late payments.

We will work from the Home window for the first group of transactions. Customer Receipts are entered from the Receipts icon, the same one we used in the My Business tab window in the previous chapter.

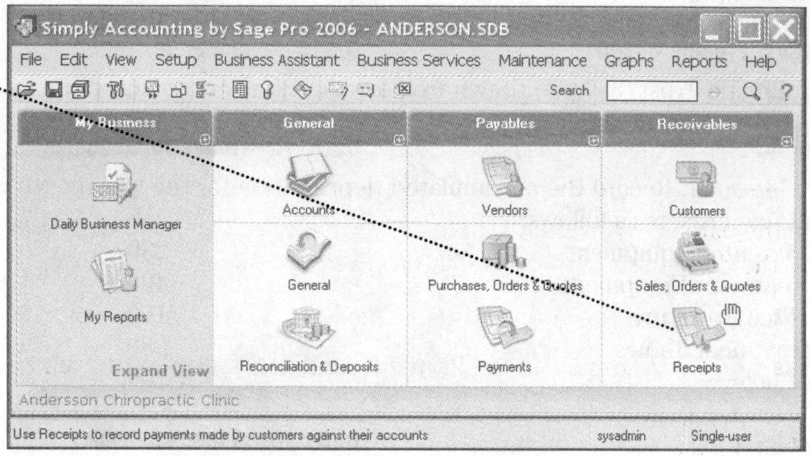

NOTES
The icons for the Payroll, Inventory and Project ledgers are hidden because these ledgers are not used and are not set up.

Click the **Receipts icon** to open the Receipts Journal.

Choose **Interplay Ballet School** from the customer list to display the outstanding invoices for this customer:

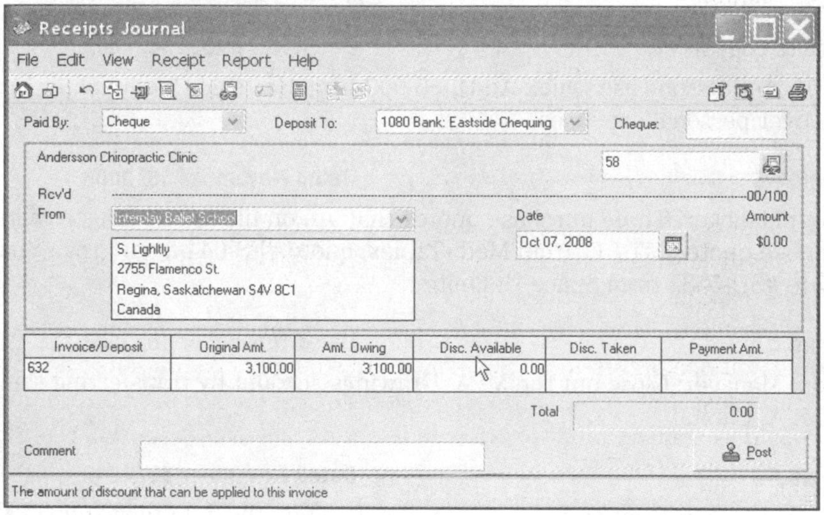

No discount is available because the session date is more than 10 days past the invoice date. The discount period has elapsed and the discount is no longer available. The default bank account, Eastside Chequing, is correct for this deposit.

Click the Cheque field.

Type **447**

Click the **Date field Calendar icon**.

Choose **October 1**.

Press *tab* to advance to the Invoice field and update the journal as shown:

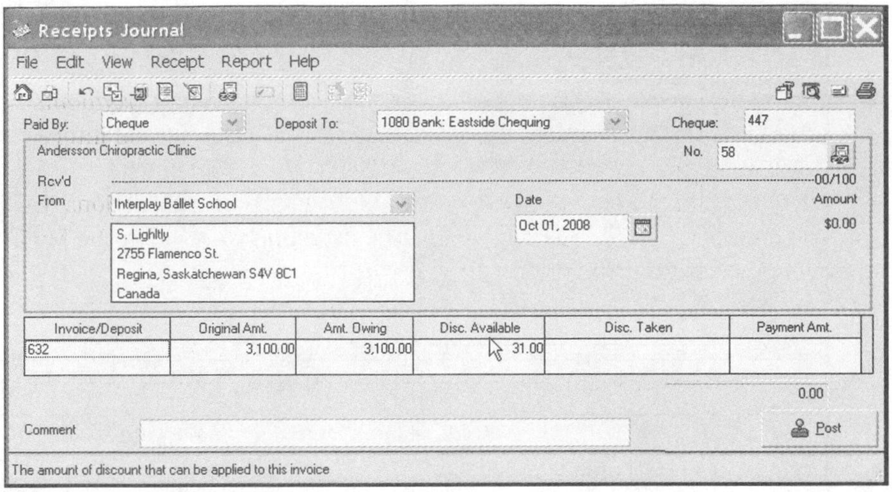

Because the date is now within the 10-day discount period, calculated from the invoice date, the discount is available and appears in the Disc. Available field.

Press tab to advance to and enter the Disc. Taken amount.

Press tab to advance to the Payment Amt. field and enter the amount.

Notice that the discount has been subtracted from the invoice amount. The cheque amount and total are still zero.

Press tab to accept the amount in the Payment Amt. field and update the total and the cheque portion of the journal.

No discount is allowed for partial payments. To omit a discount from an invoice, click the Payment Amt. field directly without tabbing across or clicking the Disc. Taken field. Once a discount amount shows in the Disc. Taken field, you can remove it by clicking the amount and then pressing del to remove it. Then press tab to update the totals. Review the journal entry to be sure that you have made the change correctly.

The discount is calculated on the amount — 1 percent of $3 100 — according to the settings for the Receivables Ledger. We are now ready to enter the invoice number as additional information.

The tool bar has an icon for the option of adding information to a journal report. This Additional Information tool allows tracking of one additional date and one other field for transactions in all journals. Andersson has chosen to enter the number of the invoice paid as additional information so it can be included in journal reports.

Click the **Enter Additional Information tool** or **choose** the **Receipt menu** and **click Enter Additional Information**:

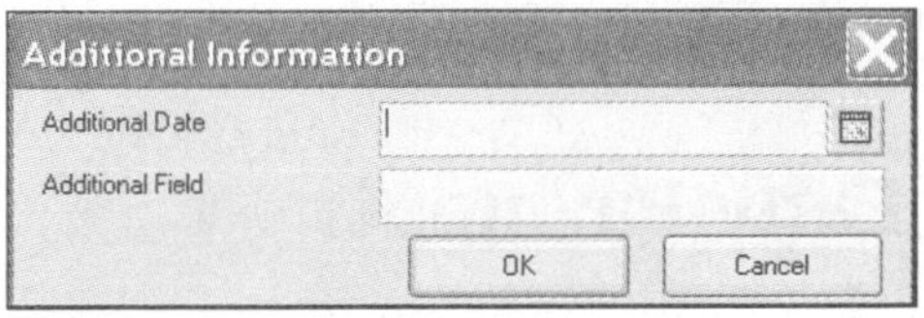

You can enter one additional date for the transaction and additional text. Both will be available for journal reports.

Click the **Additional Field** text box.

Type `Ref: inv #632`

NOTES

Discounts in Simply Accounting may be calculated on before-tax or after-tax amounts. The choice is entered as the default setting so the program makes the correct calculations automatically.

Since Andersson does not record taxes, these different calculations do not apply. Later chapters include both after-tax and before-tax discounts.

NOTES

You can enter discount amounts manually as well. Type the discount before you enter the payment amount and then press tab.

If you change an amount, delete the discount taken amount and the payment amount. Click the invoice number and press tab to reset the default amounts, or click the Undo tool to start again.

WARNING!

Because the additional field information is optional, the program does not warn you if you forget to enter it.

Click **OK** to return to the journal to see the completed receipt as follows:

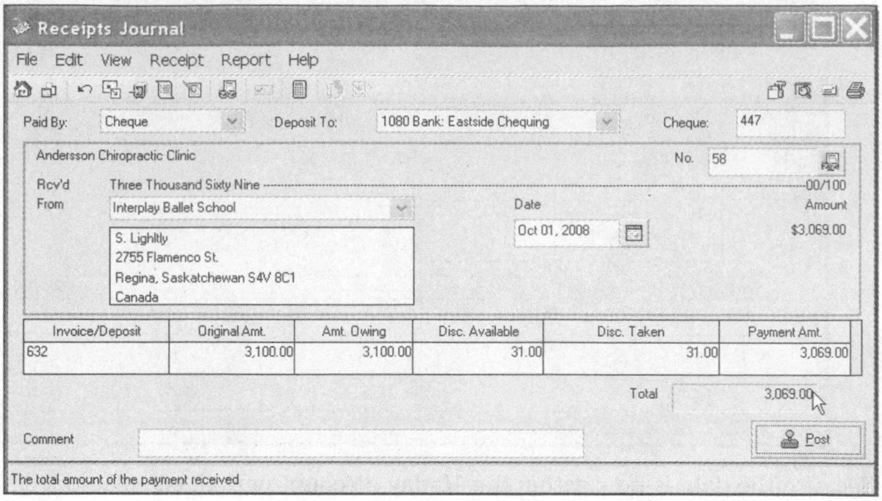

Adding the additional details does not change the appearance of the journal. You are ready to review the transaction before posting it.

Choose the **Report menu** and **click Display Receipts Journal Entry** to display the transaction you have entered as follows:

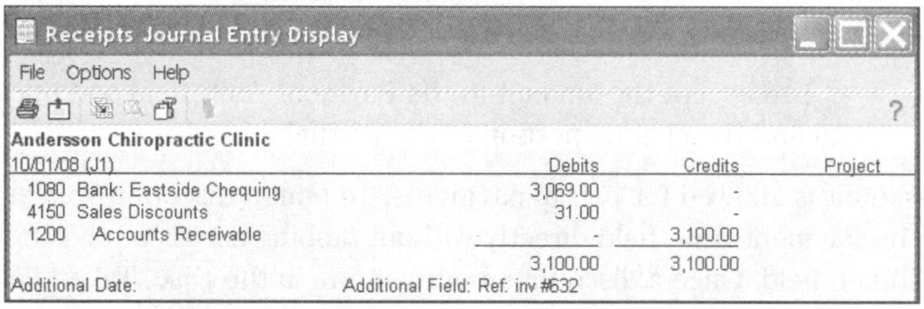

Receipts Journal Entry Display
File Options Help
Andersson Chiropractic Clinic
10/01/08 (J1)
Debits
Credits
Project
1080 Bank: Eastside Chequing 3,069.00 -
4150 Sales Discounts 31.00 -
1200 Accounts Receivable - 3,100.00
3,100.00 3,100.00
Additional Date:
Additional Field: Ref: inv #632

In the related journal entry, the program has updated the General Ledger *Accounts Receivable* control account for the full amount of the invoice and reduced the customer's balance owing by the same amount. The amount deposited to *Bank: Eastside Chequing* is the actual amount of the payment, taking the discount into consideration. The discount amount is automatically debited to the linked *Sales Discounts* account. *Sales Discounts* is a contra-revenue account. It has a debit balance and reduces total revenue. The invoice number entered as additional information is included in the display so that you can check it as well.

Close the **display** to return to the Receipts Journal input screen and **correct** your **work** if necessary. (Refer to page 174 for assistance.)

Click **Post** 

.

Close the **Receipts Journal** to return to the Home window.

Entering Discounts for Early Payments

Entering discounts for early payments is very much like entering discounts for early receipts. Andersson will not track any additional details for payments although the option is available for the journal and can be accessed from the tool bar or from the Payment menu.

The next group of transactions involve the Payables module journals so we will work from the module window.

Click the **Payables module heading** 

.

Click the **Pay Purchase Invoices icon** 

to open the Payments Journal.

Choose **Sonartek Ltd.** from the vendor list to display outstanding invoices:

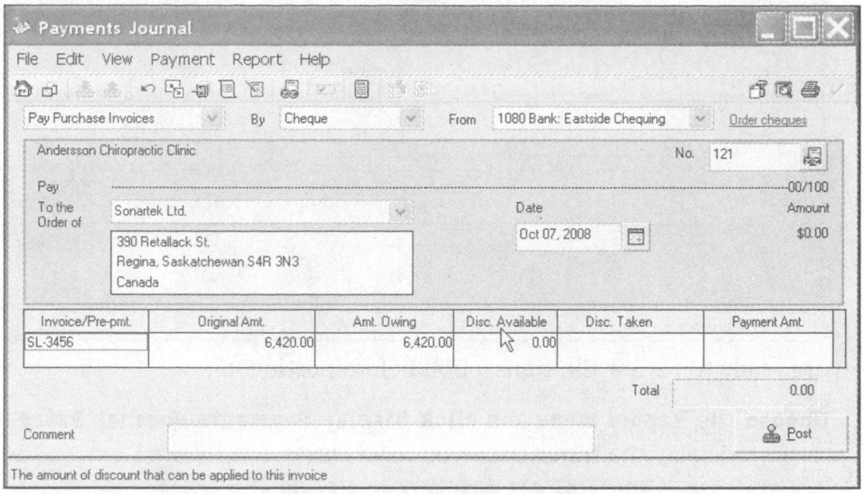

Initially, no discount is entered because the session date is beyond the discount period, that is, more than 15 days past the September 19 invoice date.

Enter **October 2** as the date of the payment. **Press** *tab*.

The discount is now available because the payment date falls within the 15-day discount period. However, the payment is being made from the Regina Chequing account so the cheque number and bank are not correct.

Click the **From list arrow** as shown in the following screen:

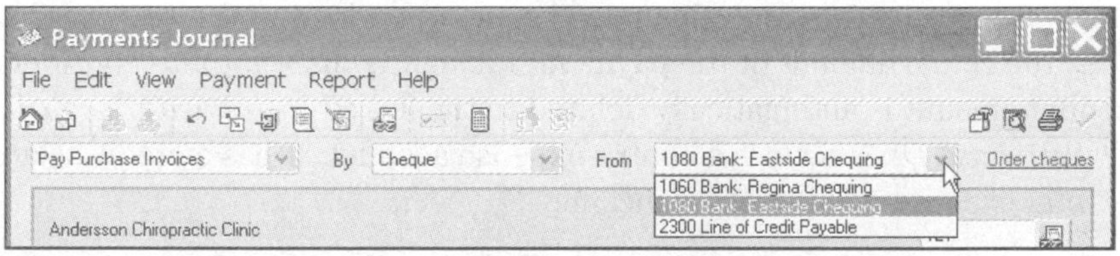

All accounts defined as bank accounts for the company files are listed.

Click **2300 Line of Credit Payable** to change bank selections.

The cheque number changes to 103, the next cheque available for this account, and it is correct. We can now proceed to accept the default amounts.

Click the **Disc. Taken field** to enter the discount amount.

Press *tab* to advance to the Payment Amt. field and enter the amount.

Notice that the discount has been subtracted from the invoice amount.

Press *tab* to accept the amount in the Payment Amt. field and update the total and the cheque portion of the journal.

basic BASIC VERSION

Click the Pay Vendor Invoices icon instead of the Pay Purchase Invoices icon.

NOTES

The line of credit is a liability account that operates like a bank account with a credit balance. By defining it as a Bank class account, it can be used to write cheques in the Payments Journal.

The Credit Card account class is assigned to Bank: Interac so it does not appear with the list of banks.

Bank is an account class that is available for all Balance Sheet accounts from the Options tab in the General Ledger. Account classes are introduced in Chapter 9.

The completed payment form should now appear as follows:

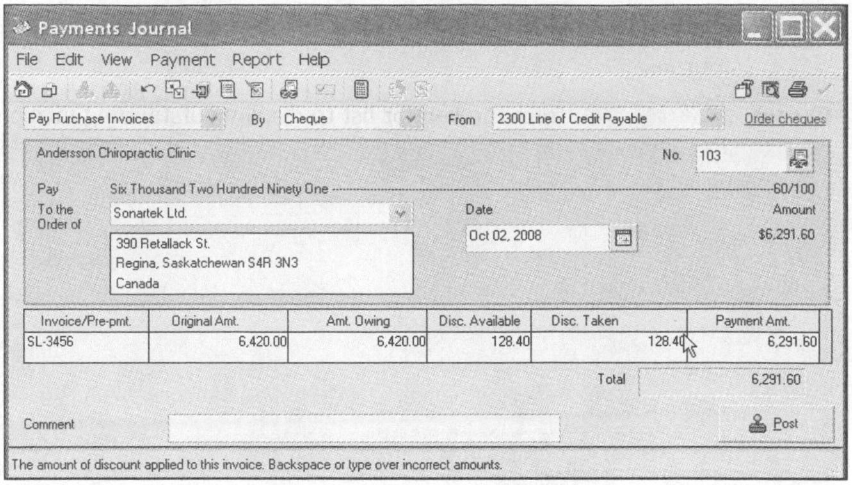

You are ready to review the transaction before posting it.

Choose the **Report menu** and **click Display Payments Journal Entry** to display the transaction you have entered as follows:

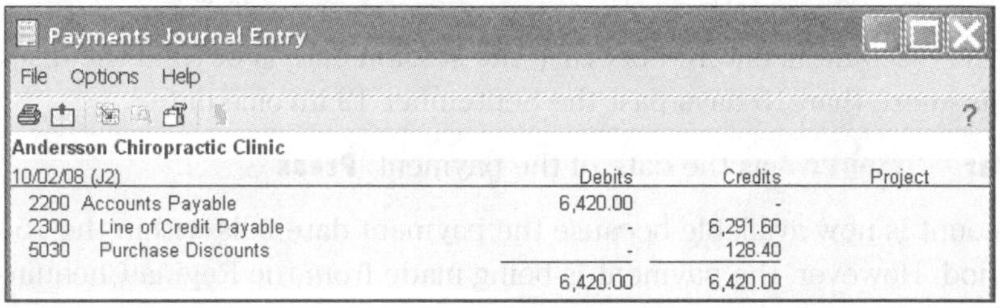

In the related journal entry, the program has updated the General Ledger *Accounts Payable* control account for the full amount of the invoice and reduced the balance owing to the vendor by the same amount. The amount added to the *Line of Credit Payable* is the actual amount of the payment, taking the discount into consideration. The discount amount is automatically debited to the linked *Purchase Discounts* account. *Purchase Discounts* is a contra-expense account. It has a credit balance and reduces total expense and increases income.

Close the **display** to return to the Payments Journal input screen and **correct** your **work** if necessary. (Refer to page 129 for assistance).

Click **Post** . **Close** the **journal**.

Click the **Make Other Payment icon** .

Enter the **cash purchase**. Remember to check the bank account selection.

Close the **Payments Journal** after entering the cash purchase.

NOTES

As for sales, no discount is allowed for partial payments. To omit a discount from an invoice, click the Payment Amt. field directly without tabbing across or clicking the Disc. Taken field. Once a discount amount shows in the Disc. Taken field, you can remove it by clicking the amount and then pressing del to remove it. Then press tab to update the totals. Review the journal entry to be sure that you have made the change correctly.

NOTES

Refer to page 130 for assistance with entering cash purchases in the Payments Journal.

Instead of closing the Pay Invoices journal, you can choose Make Other Payment from the Pay transaction drop-down list to open the Make Other Payment Journal.

If you do not close the journal, the previously selected bank account remains selected.

Entering a Purchase Quote

On October 2, Andersson received two purchase quotes for a treatment table that will be delivered later in the month. A quote usually provides a fixed price for some work or products. Often the offer is limited to a stated time period. If the business chooses to accept the offer, the quote may be filled as a purchase for immediate delivery or converted to a purchase order for future delivery. When the goods are received, or the work is completed, the quote is filled and the purchase is completed. Purchase quotes are entered and filled in the Purchases Journal.

Click the **Quotes icon**  shown in the following screen:

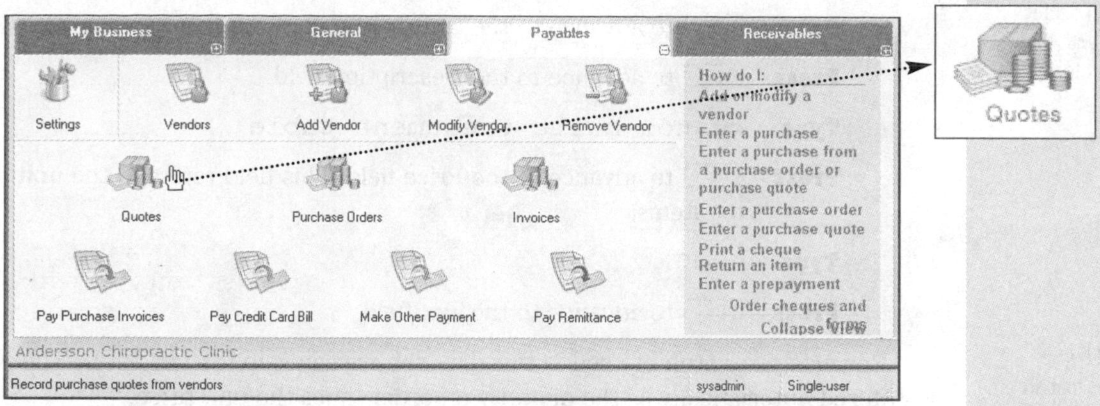

The Purchase Quote window opens.

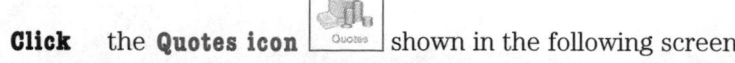

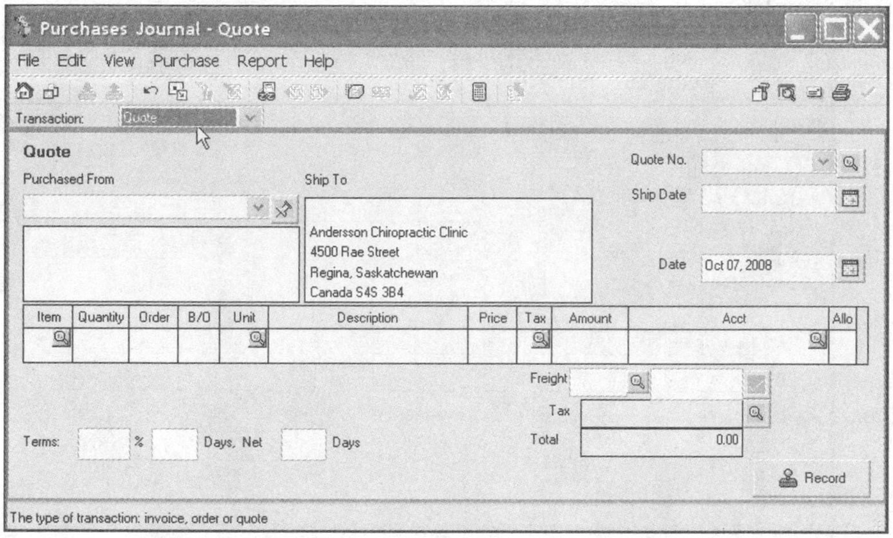

Quote is selected in the Transaction field.

Click the **Purchased From field** and **select Thera-Tables Inc.**

Click the **Quote No. field** to advance the cursor and skip the address fields.

Type TT-44

Press *tab* **twice** to advance to the Ship Date field and skip the Lookup icon.

This is the date on which the order is to be received or the work is to be completed. Sometimes, instead of shipping date, we use the term delivery date for services or starting date for a contract because these terms are more appropriate for quotes and orders for services.

Type 10-10

Press *tab* **twice** to advance to the Date field where you should enter the date that the quote was received.

Type 10-2

The Item field refers to the code for inventory items and the Quantity (quantity received with this purchase) field can also be skipped because this is not a purchase and no goods are received. However, you must enter the number of units that are ordered. You cannot leave the Order field blank. One table is being ordered.

NOTES
You can open the Purchase Quote screen from the Home window. Click the Purchases, Orders & Quotes icon and choose Quote from the Transaction drop-down list.

NOTES
Additional fields are not available for quotes and orders.

NOTES
You must choose the vendor before entering the quote number because the vendor issues the quote number.

> **NOTES**
> In a purchase order, the B/O (backordered quantity) field is filled in automatically with the order quantity. In a quote, this field remains blank.

Click the **Order field**.

Type `1`

Press *tab* to advance to the Unit field that also applies to inventory.

Press *tab* to advance to the Description field.

Type `custom-built treatment table`

Press *tab* to advance to the Price field. This field refers to the unit price of the items.

Type `4000`

Press *tab* to advance to the Tax field.

> **NOTES**
> If you want, you can customize the journal by removing the columns that are not required. Refer to page 169.
> You can remove (do not show) the Item, Unit and Allo fields because they are not needed.

Because taxes are not used in this data set, we can skip the tax fields. The Amount is entered automatically as the quantity on order times the unit price.

The account is also entered automatically from the vendor's ledger record, so the quote is complete as shown:

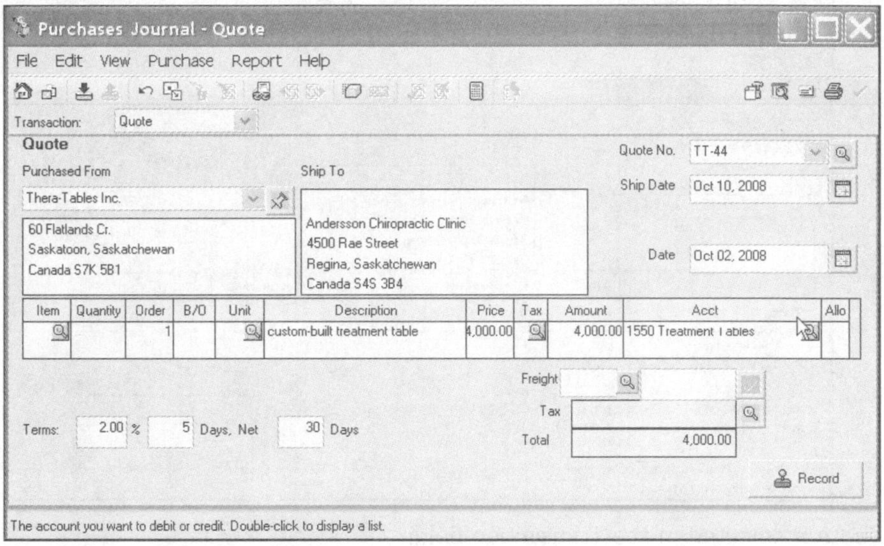

Check your **work** carefully and **make** any **corrections** necessary just as you do for other Purchases Journal entries. Refer to page 125 if you need help correcting the entry.

If you try to display the Purchases Journal entry, you will see that there is no journal entry associated with the quote. The related journal entry will be completed when the quote is filled and the purchase is completed. When you are sure that the entry is correct,

> **NOTES**
> The Post button label changes to Record for quotes and orders because no journal entry is posted.

Click the **Record button**  or **choose** the **Purchase menu** and **click Record** to save your transaction.

If you forgot to enter the quantity ordered, you will see the following warning:

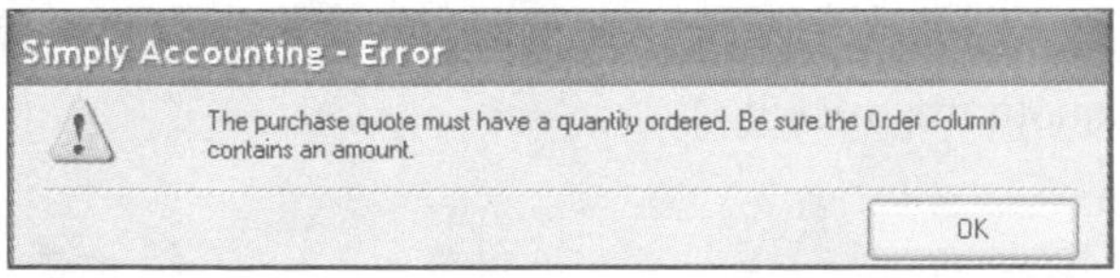

Click OK and enter the quantity in the Order field and try again to record.

Enter the **second purchase quote** from a new vendor. Remember to add the account number and payment terms to the quote.

Placing a Purchase Order from a Quote

Sometimes purchase orders are entered without a quote and sometimes they are converted from a purchase quote. Entering a purchase order directly, without the quote, is the same as entering a purchase quote except that you choose Purchase Order as the type of transaction.

The purchase order to Thera-Tables Inc. is a quote converted to an order. The Purchases Journal should still be open and Quote is selected as the Transaction type.

Click the **Quote No. field** as shown:

The drop-down list includes all unfilled purchase quotes and purchase orders. The two quotes entered above are listed.

Click **TT-44** to select it.

Press *tab* to select the quote and place it on-screen.

Click the **Transaction list arrow** to see the transaction types as shown:

Click **Purchase Order** as the transaction type. The quote screen changes to a purchase order. Order No. replaces Quote No. as the field label:

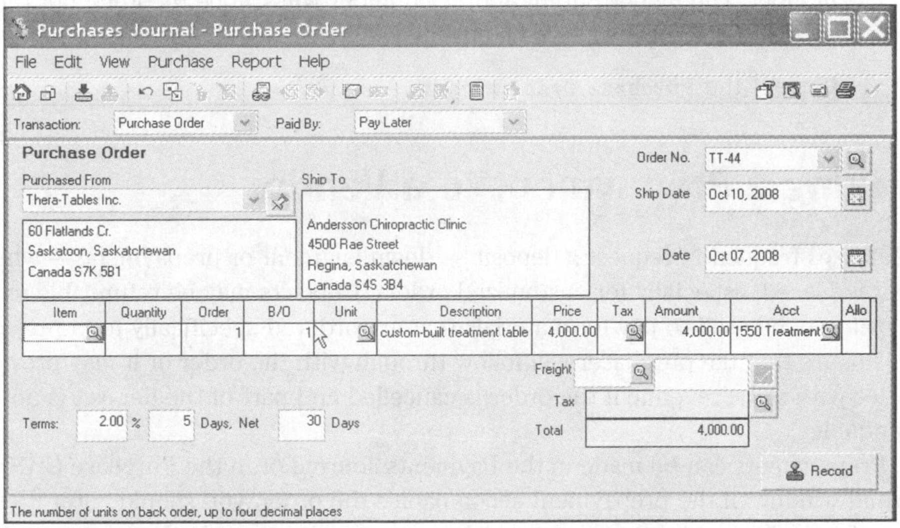

The session date is entered so we need to change the date of the order. If you try to change the quote number, you will see the warning (see margin note):

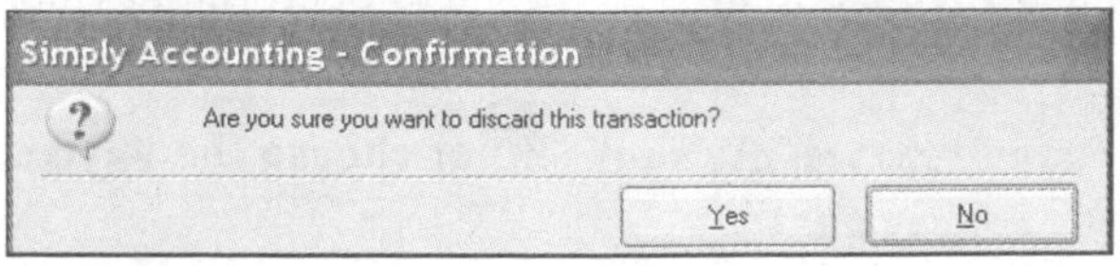

NOTES

To change the number of a purchase order to match the number sequence on preprinted forms, you should

- Recall the quote
- Choose the Adjust Quote tool (adjust purchase quotes in the same way as sales quotes – see page 222)
- Change the quote number
- Record the revised quote
- Choose Purchase Order
- Recall the quote
- Record the purchase order
- Confirm the conversion
- Check that the order sequence number is correct and update the next order number if necessary

Click No to save the quote information.

Click the **Date field Calendar icon** .

Choose **October 3. Press** tab .

Click the **Record button** Record .

The program displays the warning message:

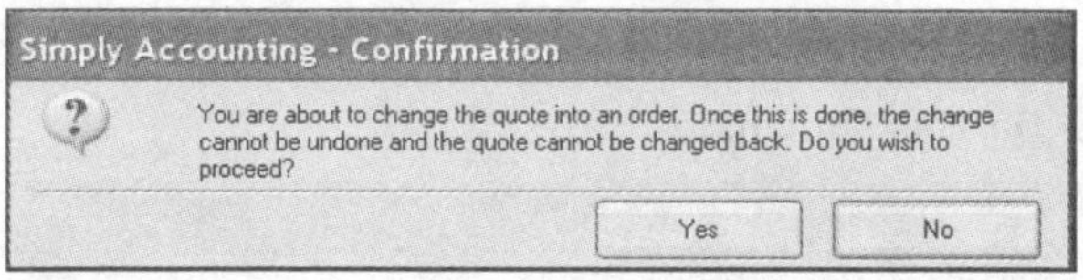

Since we want to convert the quote to an order, you should proceed. The order will replace the quote.

Click **Yes**.

Purchase order numbers are updated automatically by the program, just like sales invoice and cheque numbers. If the number for the quote that you are converting is larger than the next purchase order sequence number, a second warning will appear when you record the order because the number is out of sequence. When the number is larger than the next automatic sequence number for purchase orders, Simply Accounting asks if you want to update your sequence starting number:

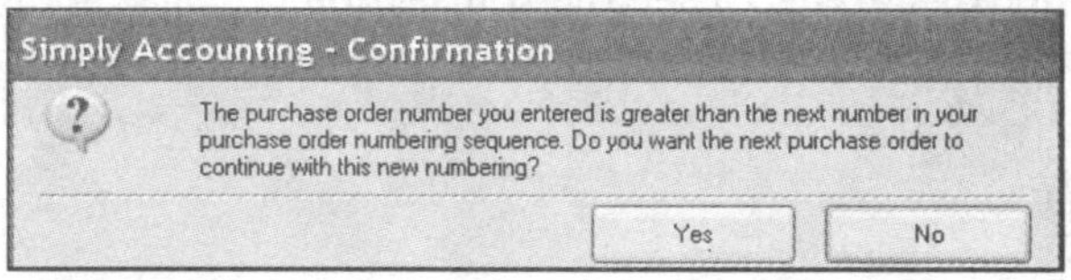

This does not apply to the alpha-numeric number we used.

Click Yes if you want to reset the numbering sequence for future purchase orders. Click No to avoid resetting the automatic sequence to the higher number. The higher purchase order number will still be recorded but the automatic counter will not be changed.

Close the **Purchase Order window**.

Making a Prepayment to a Vendor

NOTES
Entering a prepayment on the Purchase Order form is the same as entering a prepayment on a Sales Order form (see page 232). When you fill the purchase order, you will need to change the payment method for the invoice.

Businesses frequently request a deposit — down payment or prepayment — when an order is placed, especially for customized orders. Deposits may be refundable or not. A deposit may be used to pay for materials that are ordered specifically for a project; it may ensure that the purchaser will follow through with the order or it may provide the vendor with some revenue if the order is cancelled and part of the deposit is not refundable.

Prepayments can be made in the Payments Journal or in the Purchase Order Journal window. If the prepayment accompanies the order, you should enter it on the Order form. This prepayment is made later, so we will enter it in the Payments Journal.

basic BASIC VERSION
Click the Pay Vendor Invoices icon instead of the Pay Purchase Invoices icon.

Click the **Pay Purchase Invoices icon** Pay Purchase Invoices to open the Payments Journal.

Click the **Enter Vendor Prepayments tool** or **choose** the **Payment menu** and **click** **Enter Prepayments**.

This tool button/menu option acts as a switch that opens the fields for deposits:

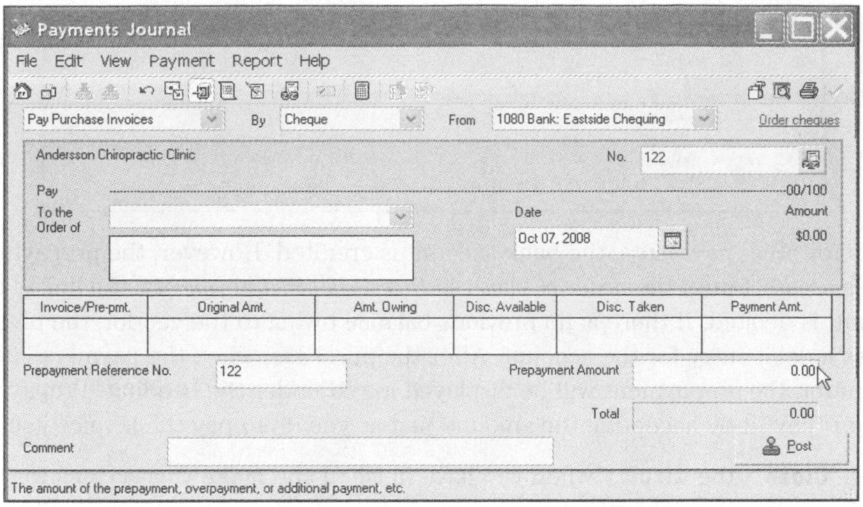

Two new fields are added to the journal: one for the prepayment reference number and one for the amount. The reference number is the next cheque number in sequence for the selected bank account and is updated automatically by the program. The rest of the journal is the same as before, but the invoice payment lines are not used. Outstanding invoices, if there are any, will be included in the journal. The bank account and cheque number are correct.

If an outstanding invoice is paid with the same cheque, enter the invoice payment in the usual way in addition to the deposit amount.

Choose **Thera-Tables Inc.** as the vendor from the drop-down list.

Enter **October 3** as the date of the cheque.

Click the **Prepayment Amount field**.

Type `400`

Click the **Comment field**. Advancing the cursor updates the Total.

Type `Prepayment for order #TT-44`

The entry is complete and the journal looks like the one shown here:

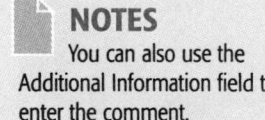

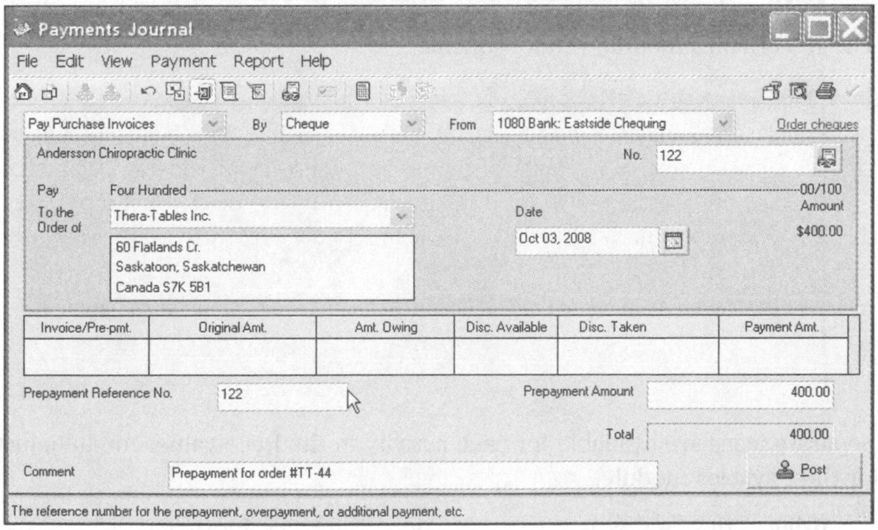

You are ready to review the journal entry.

NOTES
You can also use the Additional Information field to enter the comment.

Choose the **Report menu** and **click Display Payments Journal Entry**:

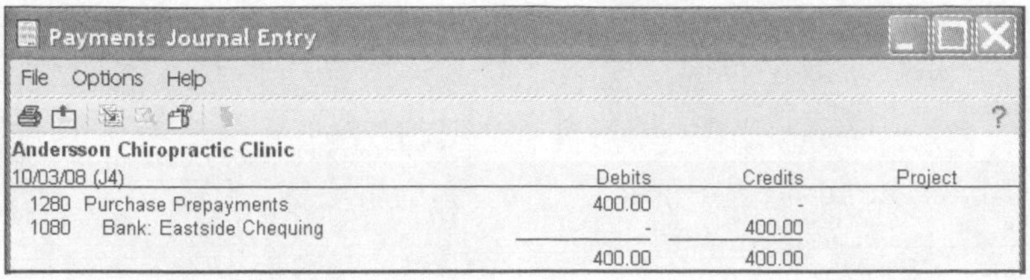

> **NOTES**
> Notice that the journal entry number (J4) has not increased because of the quotes and orders.

As for other payments, the bank account is credited. However, the prepayment creates an asset until the order is filled, so *Purchase Prepayments*, the linked asset account, is debited. If there is no previous balance owing to the vendor, the prepayment creates a debit entry for the account. After the purchase, when the payment is made to the vendor, the prepayment will be displayed in red under the heading "Prepayments" and you "pay" it by accepting the amount, just as you do to pay the invoice itself.

Close the **display** when you have finished and **make corrections** to the journal entry if necessary.

Click **Post** to save the transaction.

Click the **Enter Vendor Prepayments tool** again to close the prepayment fields.

Enter the **payment** to Medical Linen Supplies. Remember to change the selected bank account.

Close the **Payments Journal**.

> **NOTES**
> For corrections to deposits or prepayments after posting, use the Adjust tool or refer to Appendix C.

Entering a Sales Quote

Sales quotes are like purchase quotes. They offer a customer a guaranteed price for a limited time for merchandise or for work to be completed. The customer may choose to accept or reject the offer. First we will expand the Receivables module the way we expanded the Payables module earlier.

When you click a module heading, that module opens, and the module window previously open will close.

Click the **Receivables module heading**.

The Receivables module window opens:

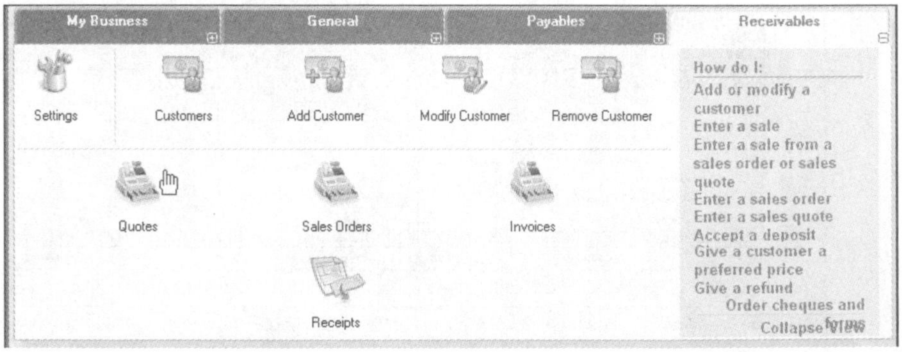

Separate icons are available for each activity in the Receivables module, just as they are for the Payables module.

Click the **Quotes icon** to open the Sales Journal.

The invoice screen changes to the form for a sales quote:

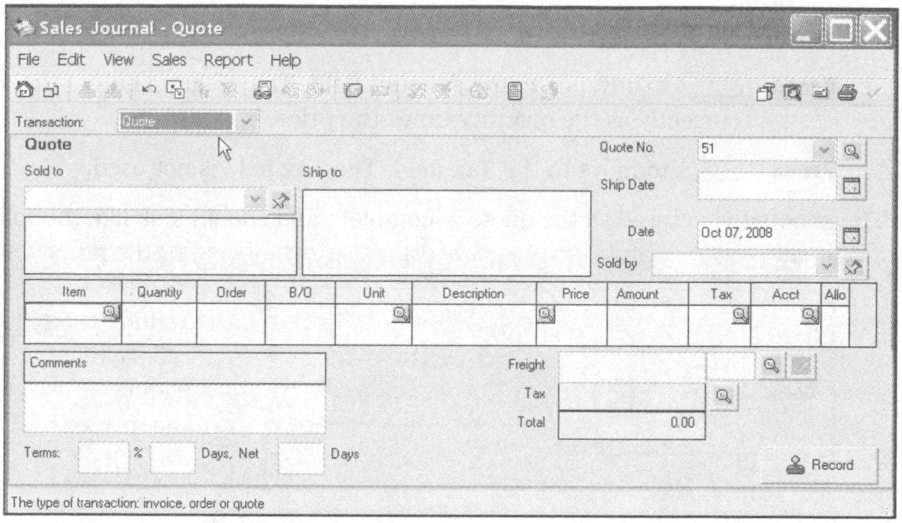

The quote is completed in much the same way as the sales invoice. However, you must enter a quantity in the Order field, just as you did for purchase quotes and orders. The quote number is entered and updated automatically from the defaults for the Receivables Ledger.

Click the **Customer field**.

Type `Giant Raptors` in the Customer field and **press** (tab).

Notice that you cannot choose Continue for new customers when entering quotes.

Choose **Full Add** and add the customer record.

> **NOTES**
> You must choose Quote as the Transaction type before entering the customer. Otherwise, a blank quote screen replaces the previous one and you must re-enter the customer.

Customer Name (Contact)	Address	Phone No. Fax No.	E-mail Web Site	Revenue Account	Terms Credit Limit
Giant Raptors (Rex Saurus)	550 Tyrannus Dr. Regina, Saskatchewan S4R 5T1	Tel 1: (306) 398-8753 Tel 2: (306) 398-5339 Fax: (306) 398-5339	rex@raptors.com www.raptors.com	4100	1/10, n/30 (change default terms) $5 000

Click **Save And Close** [Save and Close] after entering all the customer details.

You will return to the quote screen with the account and payment terms added.

Click the **Ship Date field** to move the cursor because the shipping address and quote number are correct.

Type `10 15`

Drag through the **date in the Date field**.

Type `10 4`

Click the **Order field**.

> **NOTES**
> For services such as those provided by Andersson, the term Shipping Date is not appropriate so we have used Starting Date instead.

Instead of entering the quote as the monthly rate and filling it in the first month, we will enter it as a six-month contract with monthly unit prices. After each month of service, the quote will be partially filled with one month of service.

Type `6`

Click the **Description field**.

Type `6 months of service`

WARNING!
If you do not enter a price in the Price field, you cannot fill the quote or order – when you choose this option, the form will remain incomplete.

Press tab to move to the Price field. You must compete the Price field.

Type 3500

Press tab to advance to the Amount field. The program enters the amount correctly as the quantity times the price.

Press tab to move to the Tax field. The Tax field is not used.

The account is entered so the quote is complete and should look like the following:

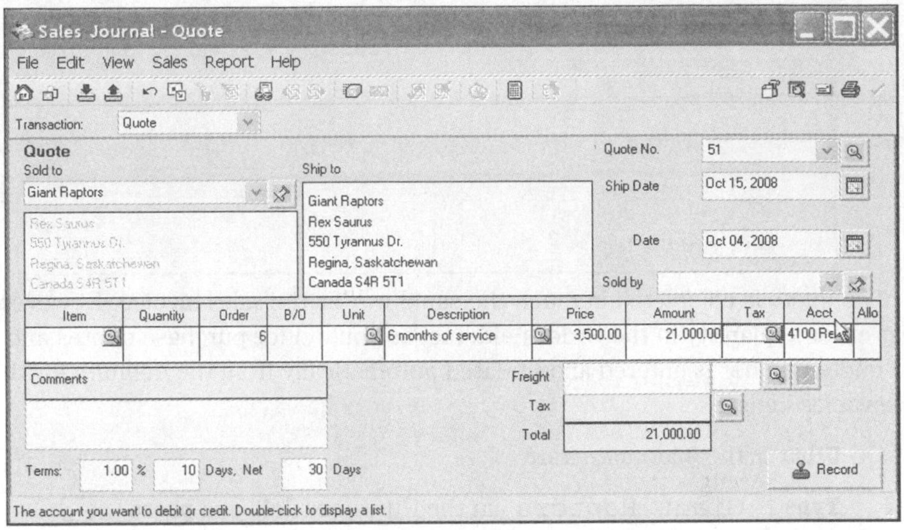

Check the **quote** carefully and **correct mistakes** just as you do in sales invoices. Refer to page 169 for assistance if needed.

There is no journal entry to display. When a quote is filled by making a sale, the journal entry will be created.

Click **Record**  to save the quote.

Leave the **Sales Journal open** to adjust the quote.

Adjusting a Sales Quote

Sometimes a quote contains an error or must be changed if prices are renegotiated. You can adjust sales and purchase quotes and orders after recording them just as you can adjust sales and purchase invoices after posting.

The Sales Quote screen should still be open.

WARNING!
If Quote is not selected as the Transaction type, you will convert the quote to a sales order, or fill the quote when you bring the quote on to the screen.

Click the **Quote No. field** to see the list of quotes on file.

Click **51** to select the quote you just entered.

Press tab to add the quote to the screen:

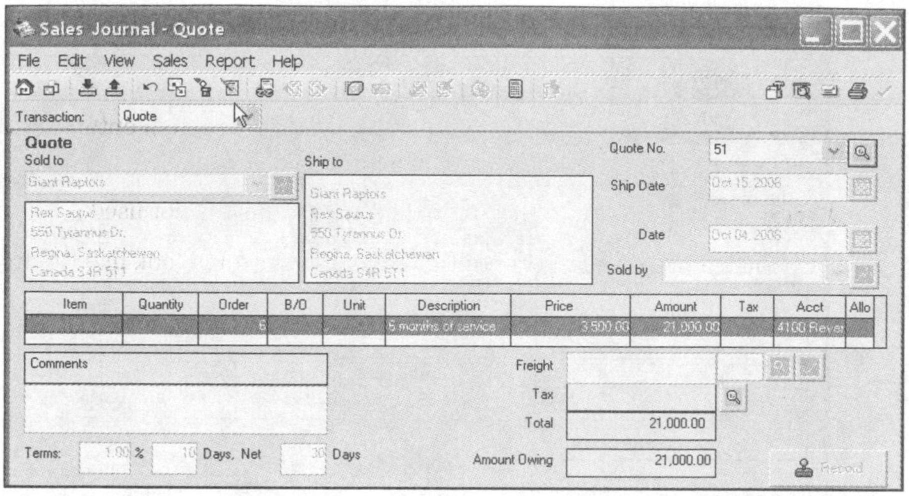

At this stage, you cannot edit the quote.

Click the **Adjust Quote tool** or **choose** the **Sales menu** and **click Adjust Quote** to open the fields for editing.

Click **3,500.00** in the Price field.

Type 3300 **Press** *tab* to update the totals.

Drag through the **date in the Date field**.

Type 10-5 to type the date for the revised quote.

Check your **work** carefully.

Click **Record** [Record] to save the revised quote. Keep the journal open.

Converting a Sales Quote to a Sales Order

Sales quotes can be converted to orders just as purchase quotes can be converted to purchase orders.

The Sales Journal should be open with Quote selected as the transaction type.

Click **Quote** in the Transaction field and then **click Sales Order** as shown:

Click the **Quote No. field** and **click 51**, the quote number we want.

NOTES

To view and adjust orders and quotes, you do not need to use the lookup or search features we used to adjust purchase and sales invoices after posting. Orders and quotes are available directly from the Order/Quote No. field.

NOTES

All fields in a quote can be edited, except the name and address details. To change the name, you must remove the quote and re-enter it for the correct customer. However, you cannot use the same quote number twice.

NOTES

Pressing *ctrl* + A will open the quote fields for editing. In other journals, pressing *ctrl* + A opens the Adjust An Invoice window.

Press tab to place the revised quote on-screen as a sales order:

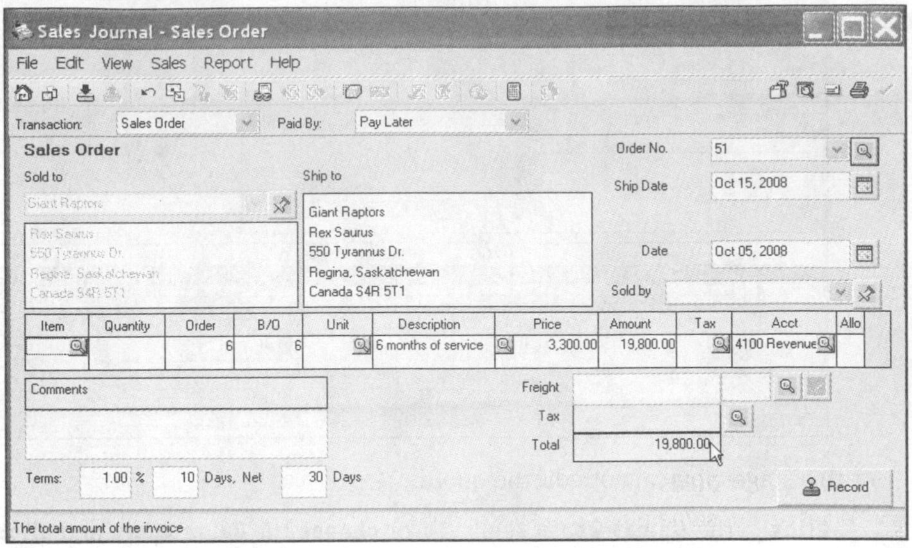

Enter **October 5** as the sales order date if necessary.

Check all the **details** carefully because there is no journal entry to review. All other details should be correct for the order because they have not changed. The order can be edited at this stage if needed.

Click **Record** [Record] to save the sales order and see the warning:

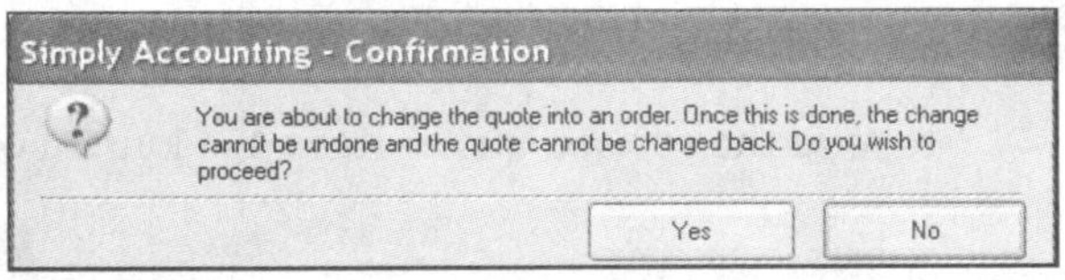

Simply Accounting - Confirmation
You are about to change the quote into an order. Once this is done, the change cannot be undone and the quote cannot be changed back. Do you wish to proceed?
Yes
No

Since we want to change the quote to an order, we should proceed.

Click **Yes**.

Close the **Sales Journal** so that you can enter the customer's deposit.

Entering Customer Deposits

Customer deposits are entered in the Receipts Journal in the same way as vendor prepayments are entered in the Payments Journal. The customer deposit tool opens fields for a reference number and an amount.

Click the **Receipts icon** to open the Receipts Journal.

Click the **Enter Customer Deposits tool** or **choose** the **Receipt menu** and **click** **Enter Deposits**.

This tool button/menu option acts as a switch that opens the fields for deposits:

NOTES

The second customer deposit accompanies the sales order, and on page 232, we show how to enter the deposit in the Sales Order window.

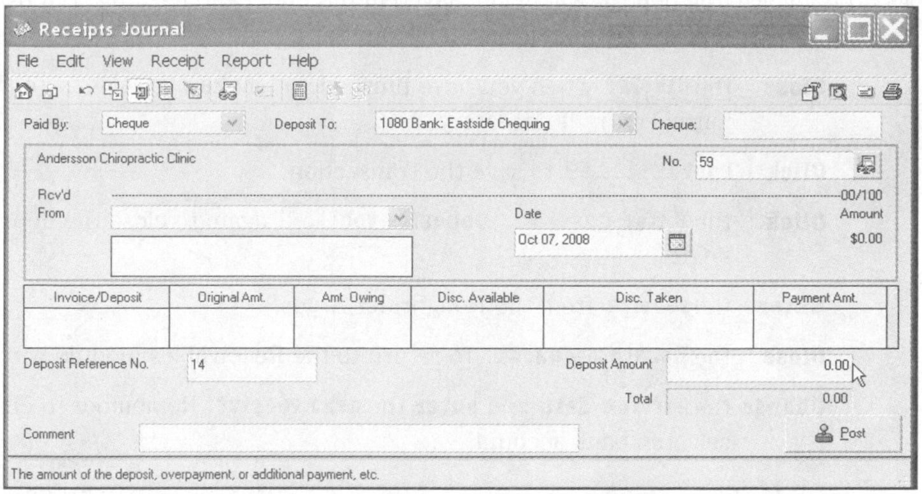

The two new fields added to the journal for the reference number and for the amount serve the same purpose as they do for vendor prepayments. The reference number is the deposit number and is updated automatically by the program. The invoice lines are not used for the deposit. Outstanding invoices, if there are any, will be included in the journal. If they are being paid with the same customer cheque, enter the receipt in the usual way in addition to the deposit amount.

The bank account is correct and the receipt number is updated.

Choose **Giant Raptors** from the customer drop-down list.

Click the **Cheque field**.

Type 838

Enter **October 6** as the date of the cheque.

Click the **Deposit Amount field**.

Type 2000 **Press** tab.

Click the **Enter Additional Information tool**  or **choose** the **Receipt menu** and **click** **Enter Additional Information**.

Click the **Additional Field** text box.

Type Deposit for SO #51

Click **OK** to return to the journal.

The journal entry is complete and you are ready to review it.

Choose the **Report menu** and **click** **Display Receipts Journal Entry**:

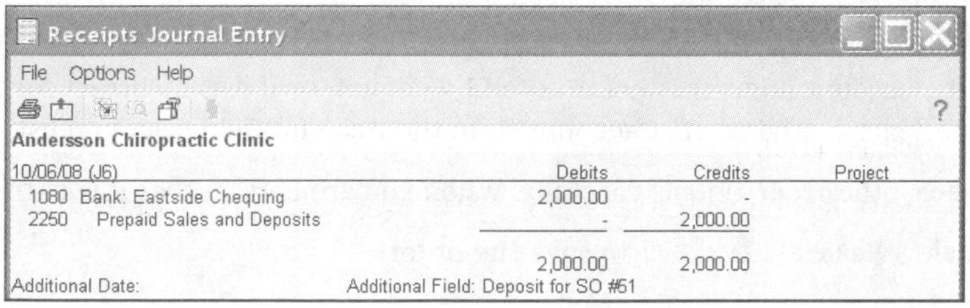

As for other receipts, the bank account is debited. The account credited is *Prepaid Sales and Deposits*, a liability account linked to the customer deposits field. If the customer has no previous outstanding balance, the deposit creates a credit entry for the account. Until the sale is completed, the deposit creates a liability — we owe the customer this amount until the order is filled. After the purchase, when the customer pays the invoice, the deposit will be displayed in red under the heading "Deposits" and it is "paid" by accepting its amount, just as you enter receipts for the invoice itself.

Close the **display** when you have finished and **make corrections** to the journal entry if necessary.

Click **Post** [Post] to save the transaction.

Click the **Enter Customer Deposits tool** again to close the deposit fields.

Enter the **receipt** from the Roughrider Argos.

Close the **Receipts Journal** to return to the Receivables module window.

Change the **session date** and **enter** the **next receipt**. Remember to change the selected bank account.

Placing a Purchase Order

> **NOTES**
> You must choose the type of transaction before selecting the vendor or customer. If you do not, the vendor or customer field will be cleared when you select a different type of transaction.

Placing a purchase order directly without the quote is similar to entering a purchase quote.

Click the **Payables module heading** [Payables] to open the Payables module window.

Click the **Purchase Orders icon** [Purchase Orders] to open the Purchases Journal with Purchase Order selected as the transaction type.

Or you can click the Purchases Orders & Quotes icon in the Home window to open the Purchases Journal. Invoice is selected as the type of transaction. Click Invoice and choose Purchase Order from the Transaction drop-down list.

Choose **Sonartek Ltd.** from the vendor list.

Enter **Oct. 19** as the shipping date.

Enter **Oct. 9** as the order date.

Click the **Order field**.

Type 1 **Press** tab.

The program automatically completes the backordered quantity (B/O) field with the quantity on order. The entire order quantity is considered as backordered.

Click the **Description field**.

Type `ultrasound machine` **Press** tab to move to the Price field.

Type `6000` **Press** tab.

If the account number is not entered by default, or if it is incorrect for this order, choose the correct account from the Account field selection list.

Check the **order** details carefully. When you are certain that it is correct,

Click **Record** [Record] to save the order.

Entering a Sales Order

> **NOTES**
> Sales order numbers are generated by the customer so they are not entered or updated by the program.

Sales orders are entered in the same way as sales quotes, except that you start with the Sales Order form instead of the Sales Quote form.

From the Home window, click the Receivables module heading arrow and then click the Sales Orders icon. Or click the Sales Orders & Quotes in the Home window. The Sales Journal opens with Invoice as the Transaction type. Click Invoice and choose Sales Order from the Transaction list. Then choose the customer and complete the order details. The Order field cannot be left blank.

Filling a Purchase Order

When an ordered item is received, or work is completed, you must complete a purchase invoice entry to record the transaction. Andersson will record the purchase order number in the Additional Field for the journal reports.

The Purchases Journal should still be open. Purchase Order is selected as the Transaction type and must be changed.

Choose Invoice from the Transaction list as shown:

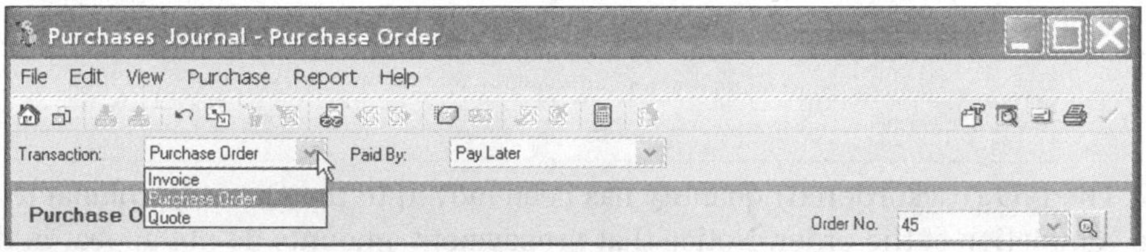

The default selection in the Paid By field, Pay Later, is correct because this is a credit purchase.

Click the **Order/Quote No. list arrow** to display the numbers for all unfilled quotes and orders.

Click TT-44.

Press *tab* to see the purchase order that was placed on October 3:

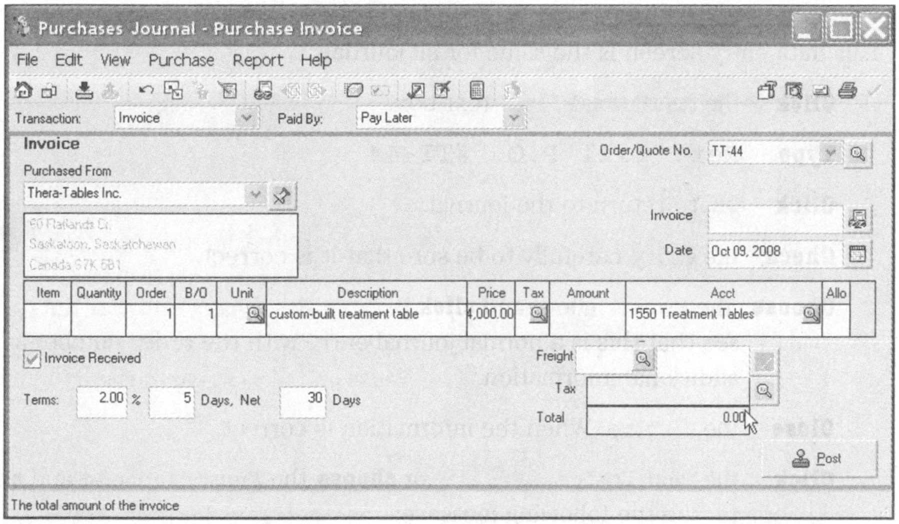

Notice that the prepayment does not show on the invoice and that the full amount is invoiced. The cursor is in the Invoice field.

Type TT-4599

Press *tab* **twice** to advance to the Date field.

Type 10-10

The invoice is still incomplete because the quantity displays as backordered and the invoice amount is zero. We need to "fill" the order.

NOTES

After you choose the purchase order number, the order does not appear until after you press *tab* or advance to the next field.

> **NOTES**
> If you did not enter the price for the order, you must edit the invoice to add the missing details.

Click the **Fill Backordered Quantities tool** in the tool bar or **choose** the **Purchase menu** and **click Fill Purchase Order**.

Your invoice should now look like the one shown below:

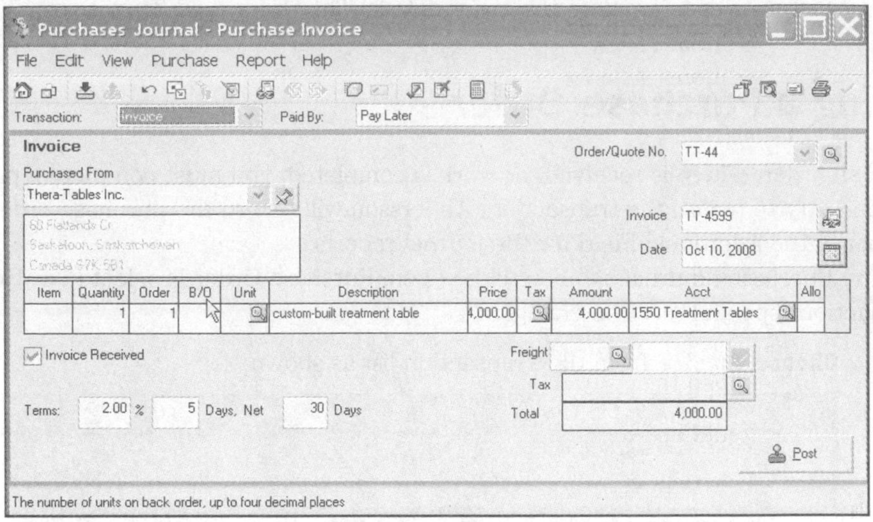

> **NOTES**
> If the order is partially filled, the backordered quantity will be reduced.

The B/O (backordered) quantity has been moved to the Quantity column to reflect the completion of the order. Notice that prepayment amounts do not appear in the journal.

Click the **Enter Additional Information tool** or **choose** the **Purchase menu** and **click Enter Additional Information**:

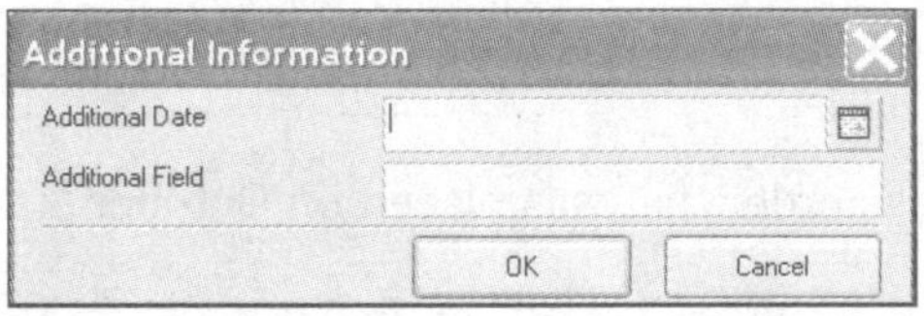

This data entry screen is the same for all journals.

Click the **Additional Field** text box.

Type `Ref: fill P.O. #TT-44`

Click **OK** to return to the journal.

Check the **entry** carefully to be sure that it is correct.

Choose the **Report menu** and **click Display Purchases Journal Entry**. You can see that this is a normal journal entry with the order number as additional information.

Close the **display**. When the information is correct,

Click the **Post button** or **choose** the **Purchase menu** and **click Post** to see the following message:

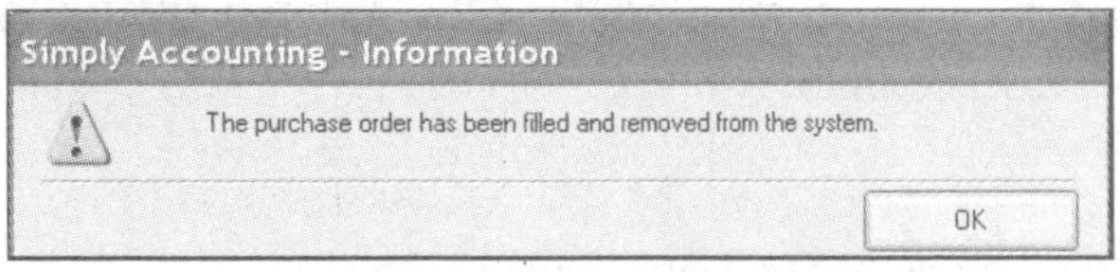

Filled orders and quotes are not saved but their numbers cannot be used again.

Click **OK** to display a new Purchases Journal invoice form.

Close the **Purchases Journal** and **close** the **Payables module window**.

Filling a Purchase Quote

Filling a purchase quote is similar to filling an order. Choose Invoice, select the quote number and press *tab* to place the quote on-screen as an invoice. The quantity automatically moves to the Quantity column and the total Amount is added. You do not need to choose Fill Backordered Quantities for quotes. Again, you can record the quote number as an additional field for the journal.

Filling a Sales Order

Filling a sales order is similar to filling a purchase order. Sometimes only part of the order is received and the order is not completely filled at once.

Click the **Sales Orders & Quotes icon** 

in the Home window to open the Sales Journal.

Pay Later should be selected as the payment option and Invoice as the transaction.

Click the **Quote/Order No. list arrow** to see the available quotes.

Click **51**.

Press *tab* to display the sales order on the invoice screen as shown:

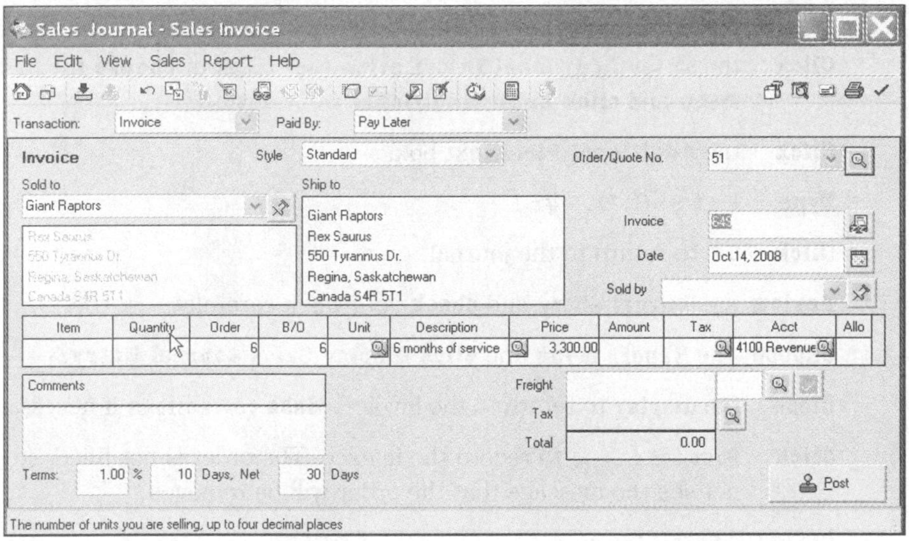

Enter **October 10** as the transaction date.

Click the **Quantity field**. Only one month is being charged at this time.

Type 1 **Press** *tab*.

NOTES

You could also fill the invoice and then edit the number in the Ship field from 6 to 1.

The updated invoice now looks like the following one:

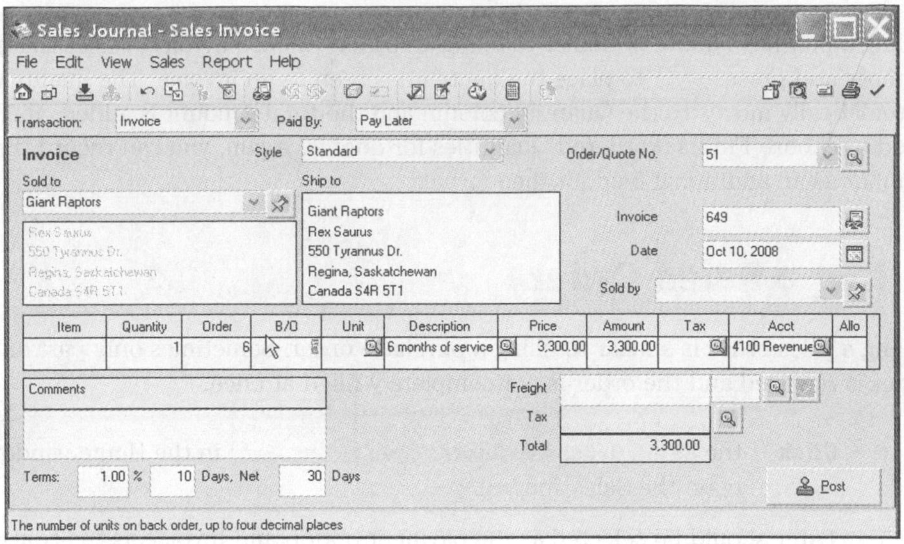

The Amount entered is the fee for one month of service and the backordered quantity (B/O) is reduced to five. When the sixth and final month is completed, the order will be filled and removed.

Type an appropriate **comment** in the Comments field to complete the invoice.

Click the **Enter Additional Information tool** or **choose** the **Sales menu** and **click Enter Additional Information**.

Click the **Additional Field** text box.

Type `Ref: S.O. #51`

Click **OK** to return to the journal.

Review the **journal entry** and **check** your **work** carefully.

Choose the **Report menu** and **click Display Sales Journal Entry**.

Close the **display** to return to the invoice. **Make corrections** if necessary.

Click **Post** [Post] to record the invoice. The order is not filled, so you do not see the message that the order will be removed.

Close the **Sales Journal**.

Filling a Sales Quote

Filling a sales quote is similar to filling an order. Choose Invoice, select the quote number and press (tab) to place the quote on-screen as an invoice. The quantity automatically moves to the Quantity column and the total Amount is added. You do not need to choose Fill Backordered Quantities for quotes.

Entering Receipts on Accounts with Deposits

The next receipt will pay the balance of an account when the customer has made a deposit.

Click the **Receipts icon** to open the Receipts Journal.

Choose Giant Raptors from the Received From customer drop-down list:

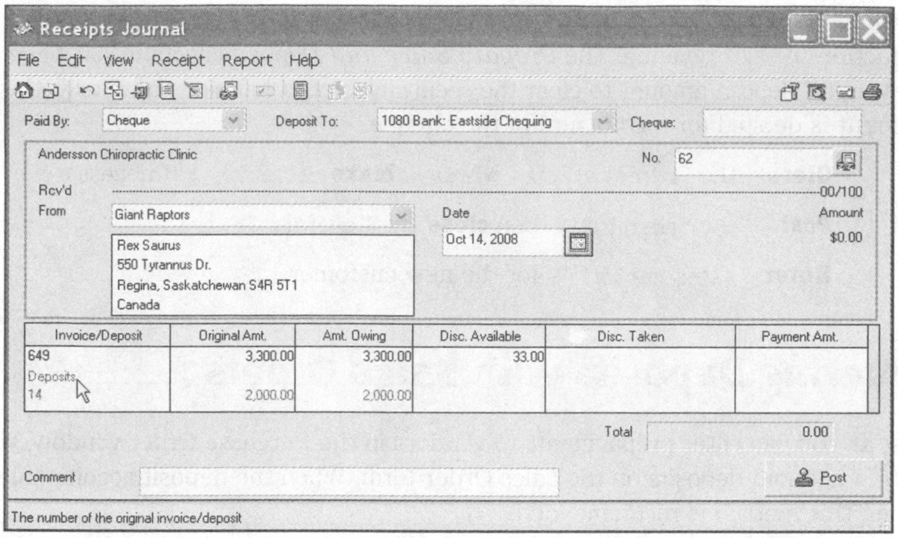

Customer deposits are displayed in red below the outstanding invoices. The colour indicates that they are negative invoices that reduce the balance owing. The invoice is shown with the full amount.

Enter 939 as the Cheque number field and **enter Oct 13** in the Date field.

Click the **Disc. Taken field** for invoice #649 to accept the discount.

Press *tab* to accept the Payment Amount.

Press *tab* again to accept the Deposit amount and update the receipt:

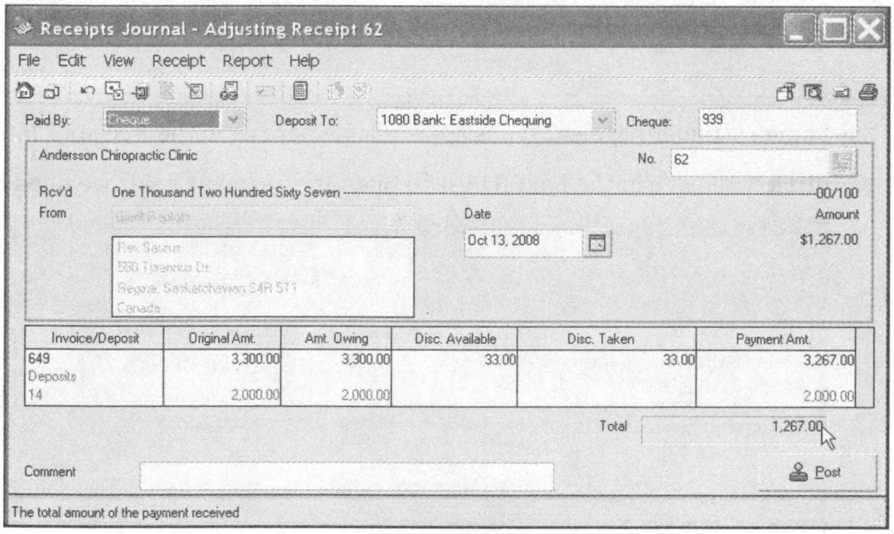

The discount and deposit are subtracted from the full invoice amount so that the total amount now matches the cheque amount.

Choose the **Report menu** and **click Display Receipts Journal Entry**:

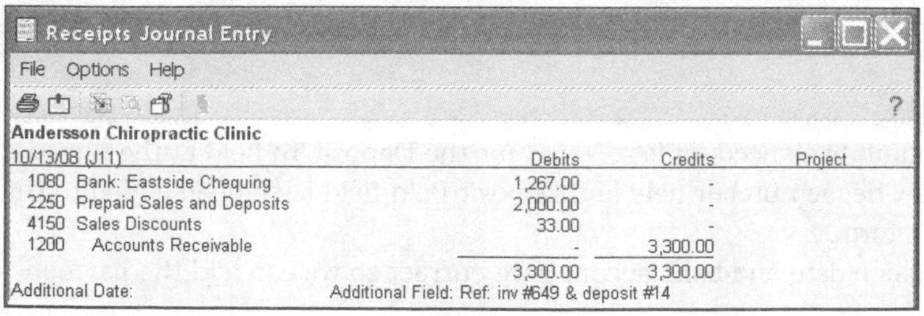

Receipts Journal Entry
File Options Help
Andersson Chiropractic Clinic
10/13/08 (J11)
Debits
Credits
Project
1080 Bank: Eastside Chequing 1,267.00
2250 Prepaid Sales and Deposits 2,000.00
4150 Sales Discounts 33.00
1200 Accounts Receivable - 3,300.00
3,300.00 3,300.00
Additional Date:
Additional Field: Ref: inv #649 & deposit #14

Accounts Receivable has been credited for the full invoice amount to clear the invoice. The *Sales Discounts* contra-revenue account has been debited to record the reduction to sales revenue. The *Prepaid Sales and Deposits* account has been debited for the full deposit amount to clear the receivable credit balance and finally, the bank account is debited for the amount of the cheque.

Close the **journal display window**. **Make corrections** if necessary.

Post the **receipt** and then **close** the **Receipts Journal**.

Enter **sales quote #52** for the new customer.

Entering Deposits with Sales Orders

Just as you can enter prepayments to vendors in the Purchase Order window, you can enter customer deposits on the Sales Order form. When the deposit accompanies the order, this method is recommended.

The Sales Journal should still be open with Quote selected as the transaction type.

Choose **52** from the Quote No. field list and **press** tab.

Choose **Sales Order** as the transaction type from the drop-down list to convert the quote to an order.

Click the **Paid By list arrow** to see the payment options:

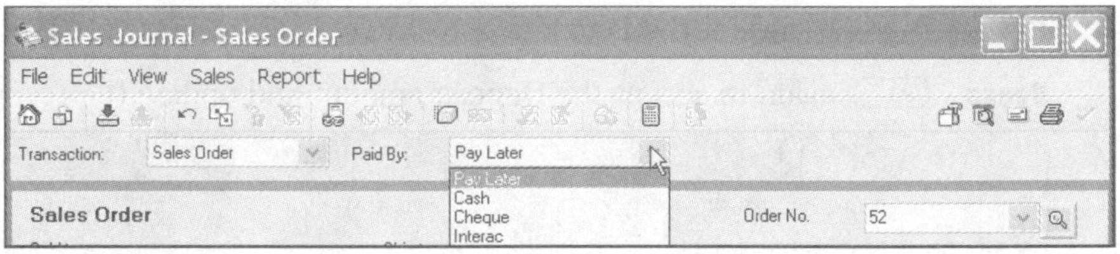

The same customer payment types are available here as in the Receipts Journal.

Click **Cheque** in the Paid By list to open the payment fields we need :

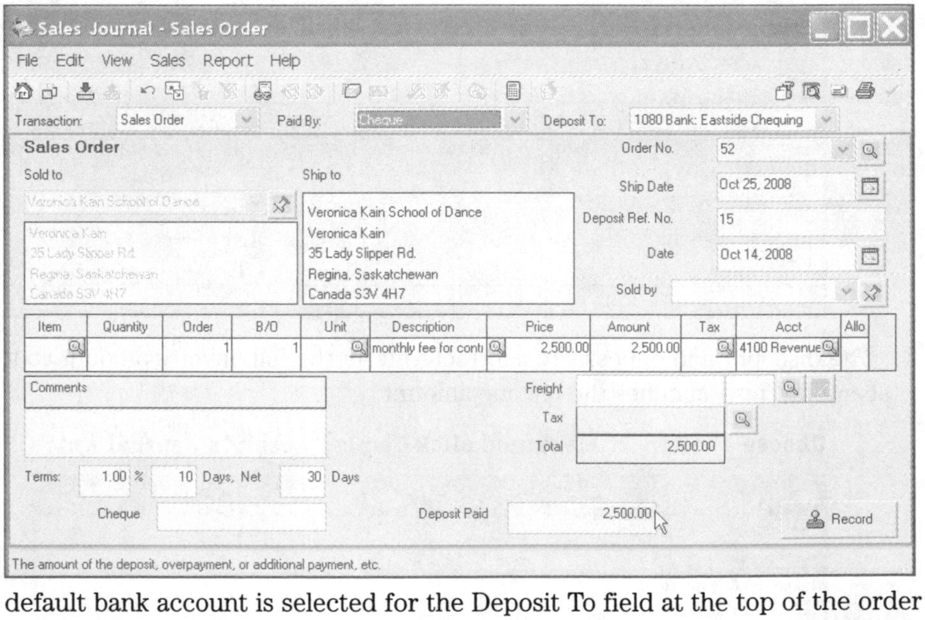

The default bank account is selected for the Deposit To field at the top of the order form, and a Cheque number field and Deposit Paid field have been added to the bottom of the order form.

The session date and bank account are correct so we can add the payment details.

Click the **Cheque field**.

Type 865

Press tab to advance to the Deposit Paid field. The full amount of the order is entered as the default amount.

Type 1000

Press tab to update and complete the form. The deposit part of the order is shown here:

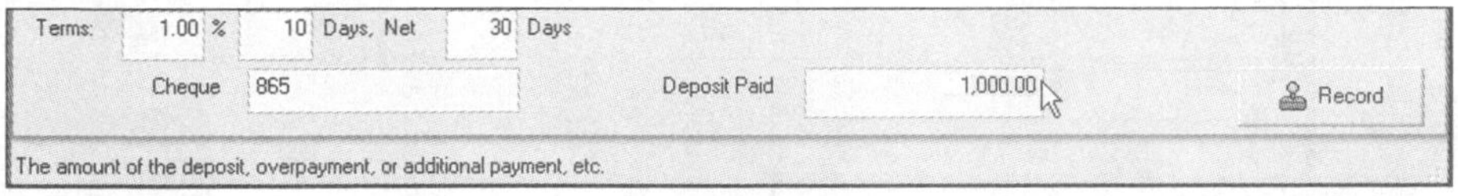

Choose the **Report menu** and **click Display Sales Journal Entry**:

Andersson Chiropractic Clinic			
10/14/08 (J12)	Debits	Credits	Project
1080 Bank: Eastside Chequing	1,000.00	-	
2250 Prepaid Sales and Deposits	-	1,000.00	
	1,000.00	1,000.00	

You can see that this journal entry is identical to the journal entry for deposits entered in the Receipts Journal. The prepayment or deposit with the sales order does create a journal entry although the sales order itself does not.

Close the **display** and **click Record** Record to save the transaction.

Click **Yes** to confirm that you are changing the quote to an order.

Entering Debit Card Sale Transactions

Customers pay for purchases using cash, cheques, credit cards or debit cards. Debit and credit card purchases are similar for a store — the payment is deposited immediately to the linked bank account. The difference is that debit card transactions withdraw the money from the customer's bank account immediately while credit cards advance a loan that is to be repaid on receipt of the credit card bill. The store pays a percentage discount or transaction fee to credit card companies for the service. For debit card transactions, the store pays a flat fee for each transaction. Both involve a setup fee and a monthly service charge for renting the terminal that communicates directly with the card-issuing company. Andersson uses the name Interac for all debit card transactions.

The Sales Journal should be open from the previous transaction. If it is not, open it by clicking the Sales icon. The session date is correct as the invoice date.

Choose **Invoice** from the Transaction list.

Choose **One-Time Customer** from the Sold To list and **press** tab.

For One-Time Customers, Cash replaces the Pay Later option. The Net Days field is removed to match the immediate payment option and the default bank account is selected. The terms for new customers offer no discount so the discount fields are blank.

Click the **Paid By list arrow** as shown to see the payment options:

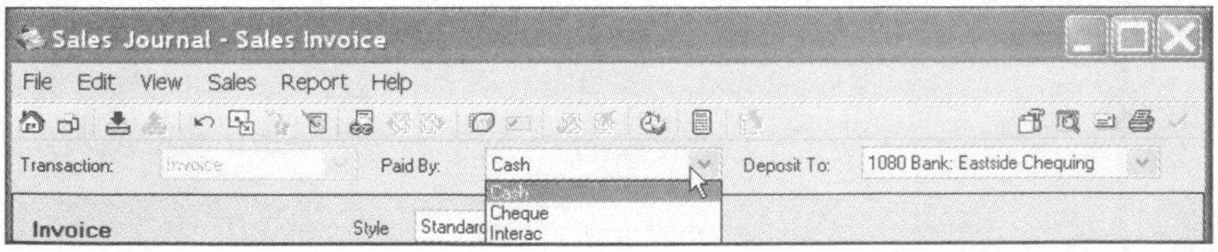

NOTES
Pay Later is not an option for one-time customers so the Cash Amount (amount received) field is added automatically.

Click **Interac** as the method of payment to see the modified invoice:

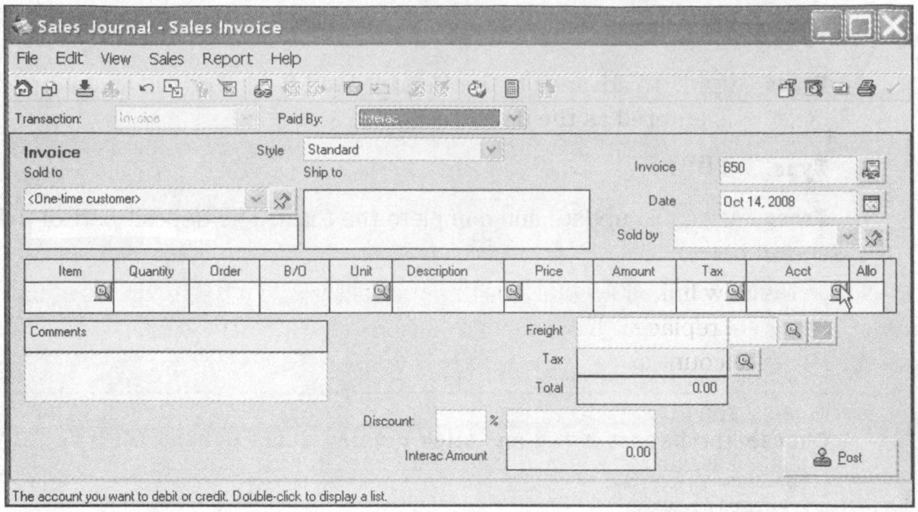

There is no bank account field or cheque number field as there is when the payment is made by cheque. Interac is linked automatically to a dedicated bank account as part of the company file setup. Interac Amount replaces Cash Amount as the label for the amount received.

Type `Debit Card Sales Summary` (in the Address field).

Complete the rest of the **invoice** in the same way as account or cash sales.

Click the **Description field** and **type** `Initial assessments`

Click the **Amount field** and **type** `260`

Click the **List icon** in the Account field to display the Account list.

Double click **4100 Revenue from Services** to add it to the invoice.

Click the **Description field** on the second line of the invoice.

Type `Follow-up treatments`

Click the **Amount field**.

Type `450`

Click the **List icon** in the Account field to display the Account list.

Double click **4100 Revenue from Services** to complete the invoice:

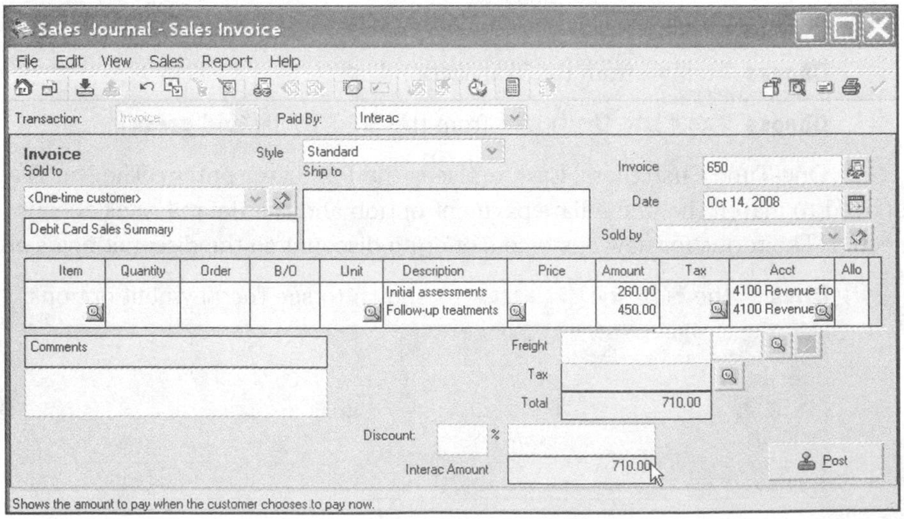

Choose the **Report menu** and **click Display Sales Journal Entry** to review the entry before posting:

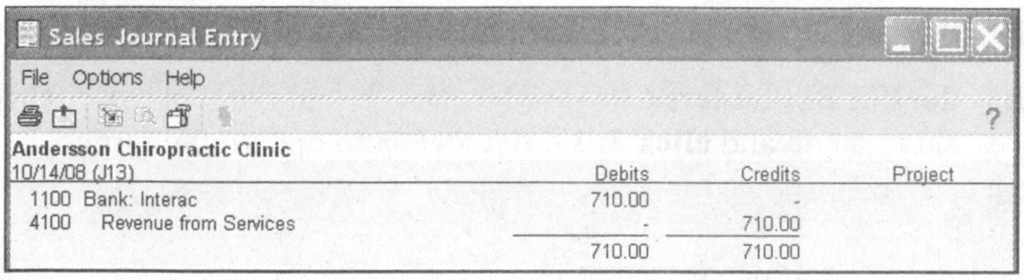

Notice the new linked account for this transaction. The debit card account — *Bank: Interac* — replaces the usual bank account for other cash sales and *Accounts Receivable* for account sales.

Close the **display** to return to the Sales Journal input screen.

Make corrections if necessary, referring to page 169 for assistance.

We can store the entry and use it to enter the debit card summaries each week. When you recall the transaction, you can edit the amounts. You will not need to save the changes and store the transaction again.

Click the **Store tool** to save the transaction for repeated entries.

Choose Biweekly as the frequency and **click OK** to save the stored entry.

Click the **Post button** Post.

Close the **Sales Journal** so that you can enter the payment transactions.

Filling Sales Orders with Deposits

When you advance the session date to October 31, you will see an advisor message:

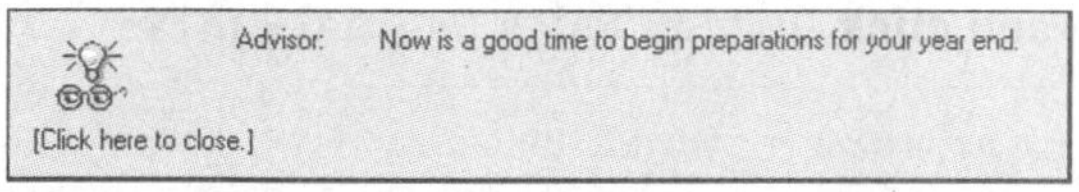

Advisor: Now is a good time to begin preparations for your year end.
[Click here to close.]

Click to close the message about year-end preparation.

Open the **Sales Journal**. Invoice should be selected as the transaction.

Select Sales Order #52 from the Order/Quote No. list and **press** tab to recall the order:

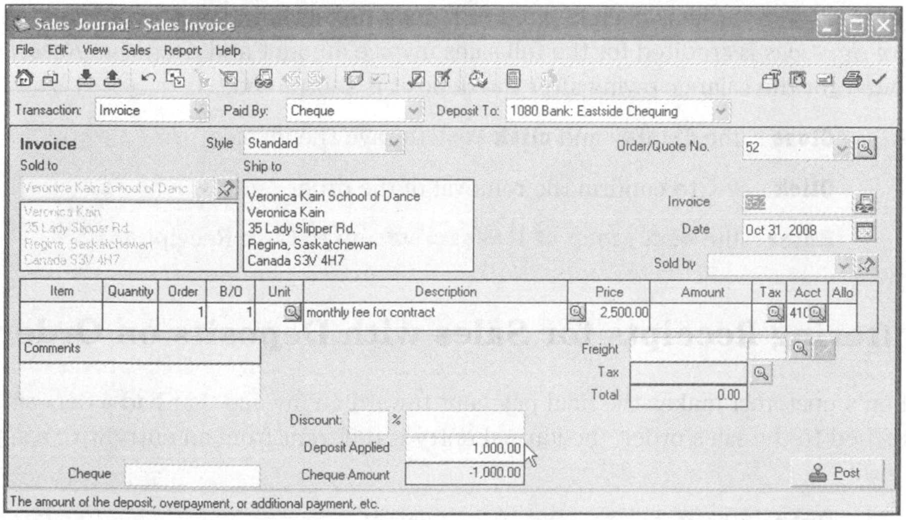

Information about the deposit is included in the invoice. Since the deposit was paid by cheque, this is the default payment method, and we need to change it.

Click the **Paid By list arrow** and **choose Pay Later** to modify the form.

Click the **Fill Backordered Quantities tool** in the tool bar or **choose** the **Sales menu** and **click Fill Sales Order** to update the form:

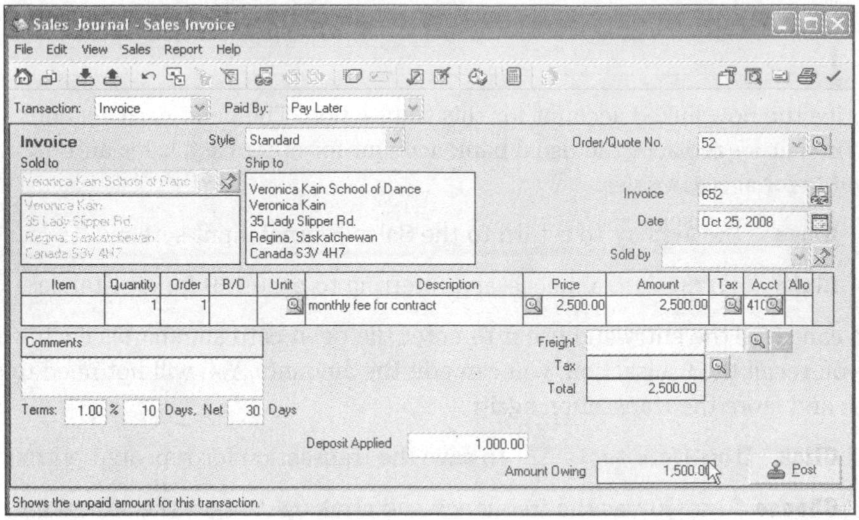

The Cheque Amount field has been removed but the Deposit Applied details remain. The Amount Owing is reduced by the $1 000 deposit.

Click the **Enter Additional Information tool** or **choose** the **Sales menu** and **click Enter Additional Information**.

Enter `Ref SO #52 and deposit #15` in the Additional Field.

Click **OK** to return to the journal.

Choose the **Report menu** and **click Display Sales Journal Entry**:

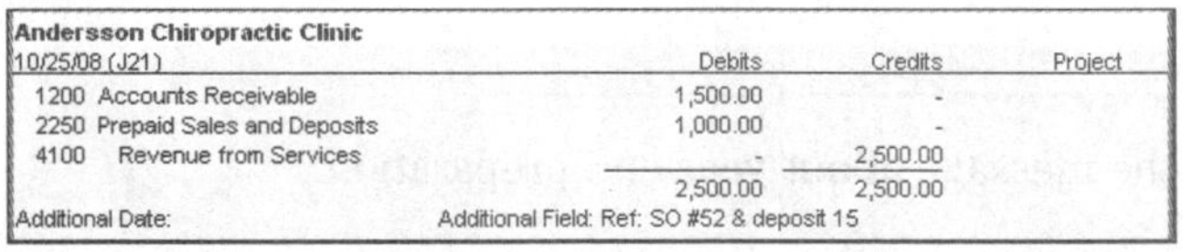

Andersson Chiropractic Clinic

10/25/08 (J21)	Debits	Credits	Project
1200 Accounts Receivable	1,500.00	-	
2250 Prepaid Sales and Deposits	1,000.00	-	
4100 Revenue from Services	-	2,500.00	
	2,500.00	2,500.00	

Additional Date: Additional Field: Ref: SO #52 & deposit 15

> **NOTES**
> When the deposit for a sales order is entered as a receipt separately from the sales order, the deposit amount does not appear in the sales journal entry that fills the order.

The entry is different from the standard journal entry because of the amount for *Prepaid Sales and Deposits*. Because the sale is complete, the liability is removed and the prepayment is treated like a partial payment toward the invoice. Thus *Prepaid Sales and Deposits* has been debited to reduce the account balance to zero, *Revenue from Services* is credited for the full sales invoice amount and *Accounts Receivable* is debited for the balance owing after the deposit is subtracted.

Close the **display** and **click Post** to save the invoice.

Click **OK** to confirm the removal of the order.

Enter the **next group of transactions** up to Cash Receipt #64.

Entering Receipts for Sales with Deposits on Orders

When a customer makes the final payment toward an invoice that had a deposit attached to the sales order, the journal entry is different from an entry with a separate deposit.

Open the **Receipts Journal** and **select Veronica Kain School of Dance**:

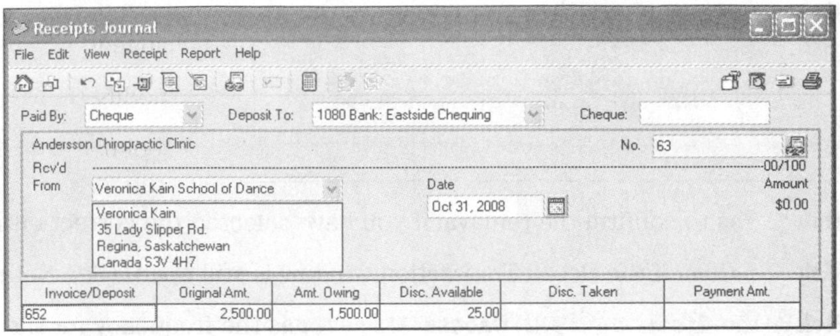

Because the prepayment was cleared at the time of the sale, it does not appear in the Receipts Journal. Instead, the Amount Owing has been reduced so this is a standard receipt entry. The discount is based on the full invoice amount, or 1 percent of $2 500.

Enter the **remaining transaction details** to complete the entry. Remember to change the bank account.

Review the **transaction** and then **post** it.

Removing Recurring Transactions

Sometimes a recurring transaction is no longer required, or it needs to be replaced. If you try to store the new purchase invoice from Cleanol and Laundry Services before removing the old entry, Simply Accounting will not allow you to continue because the name duplicates the entry on file.

Fill the **purchase order** from Cleanol and Laundry Services.

Click the **Store tool** .

Choose **Biweekly** as the frequency for the transaction and **click OK**.

You will see the Duplicate Entry warning:

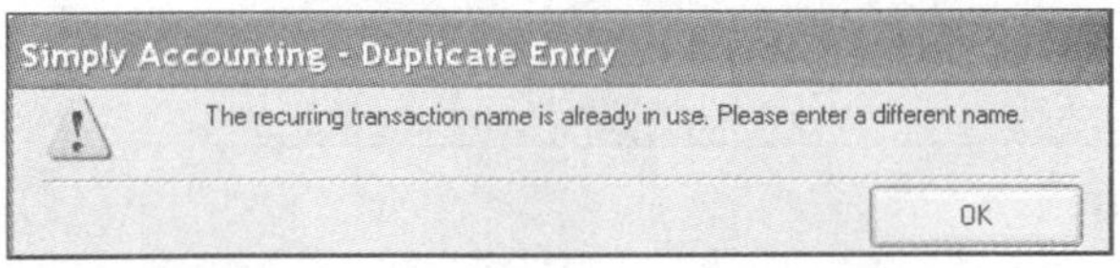

Click **OK** to return to the Store Recurring Transaction screen.

Click **Cancel** to return to the journal.

We need to remove the old stored transaction first.

Click the **Recall tool** to open the Recall Recurring Transaction list:

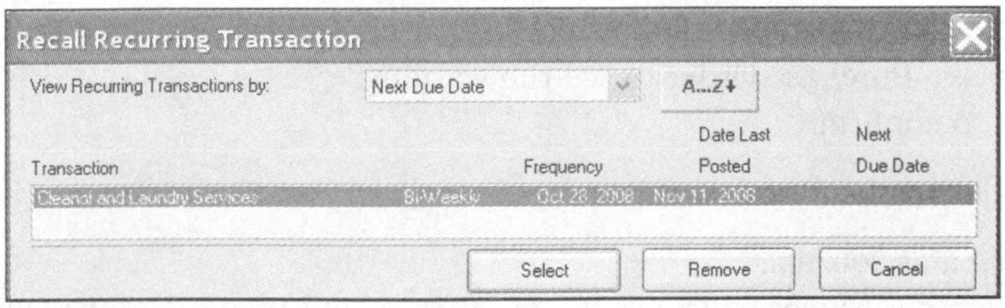

Cleanol and Laundry Services should be selected. If you entered the rental payment to Pro Suites in the Purchases Journal instead of the Payments Journal as an Other Payment, it will be listed in this window as well. The entry for Cleanol should still be selected because it is the next entry that is due. If it is not selected, click to select it.

Click **Remove** to see the confirmation warning:

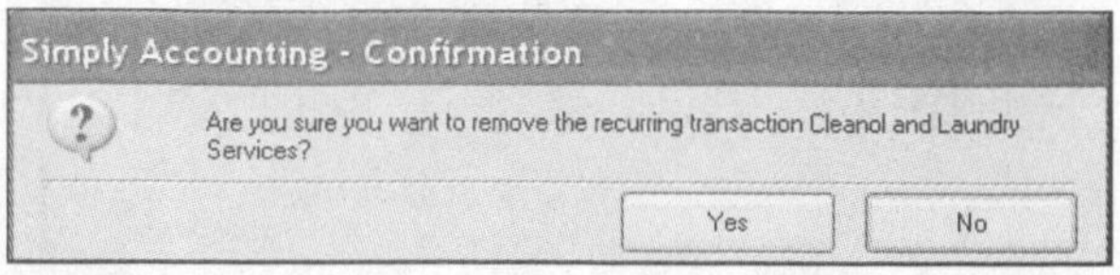

Click **Yes** to confirm the removal if you have selected the correct entry.

Click **Cancel** if the Recall Transaction window is still open. (See Notes.)

Click the **Store tool**. **Choose** **Biweekly** as the frequency for the new recurring invoice. **Click** **OK**.

Post the **purchase transaction** and **click** **OK** to confirm that the order will be removed.

Close the **Purchases Journal**.

NOTES

If you have only one recurring transaction, the window closes after you remove it. If there are more transactions, the window stays open and you must click Cancel to close it.

Removing Quotes and Orders

Quotes and orders that will not be filled should be removed so that they are not confused with active quotes and orders. To remove purchase quotes,

Open the **Purchases Journal**.

Choose **Quote** from the Transaction list.

Choose **quote #MT-511** and **press** *tab* to place the quote on-screen.

Click the **Remove Quote tool** or **choose** the **Purchase menu** and **click** **Remove Quote**.

As usual, Simply Accounting warns you before making the deletion:

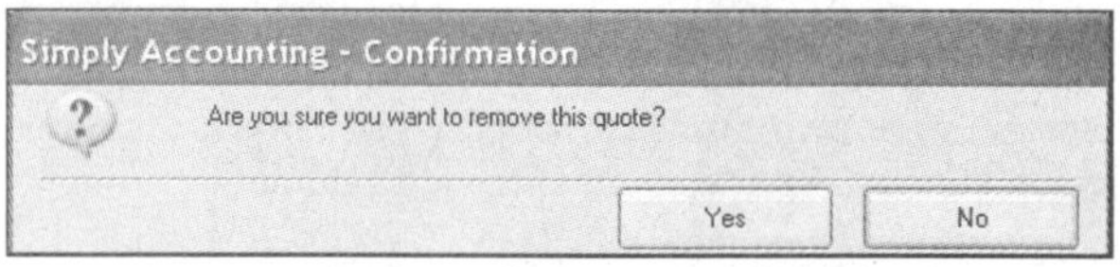

Click **Yes** to confirm.

Remove the **other two quotes** that are not needed and then **close** the **journal**.

To remove purchase orders,

Open the Purchases Journal.
Choose Purchase Order from the Transaction list. Choose the purchase order number and press *tab* to put the order on-screen.
Click the Remove Purchase Order tool or choose the Purchase menu and click Remove Purchase Order to see the warning.
Click Yes to confirm.

To remove sales quotes or sales orders,

Open the Sales Journal.
Choose Quote (or Sales Order) as the transaction and then select the Quote or Order No. from the list. Press *tab* to bring the sales quote or order onto the screen.
Click the Remove Quote (or Sales Order) tool or choose the Sales menu and click Remove Quote (or Sales Order).
Click Yes to confirm that you want to delete the quote or order.

Displaying Reports

Displaying Pending Purchase Orders

Any purchase orders that are not yet filled can be displayed in a report. You can also use this report to check for orders that are delayed or should be removed.

Choose the **Reports menu**, then **choose Payables** and **Pending Purchase Orders** and **click By Vendor** to see the report options:

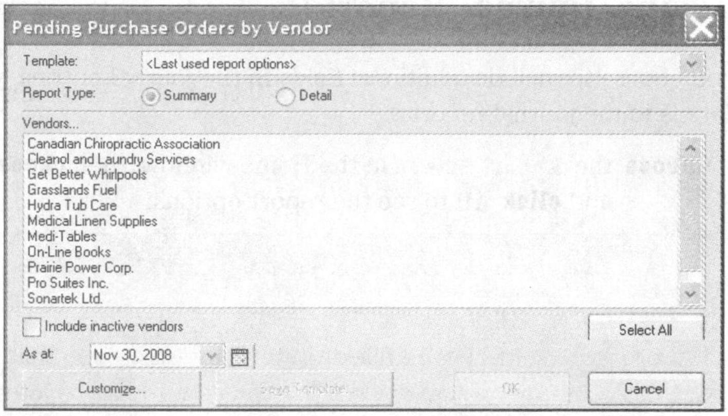

Press and **hold** ctrl and **click** the appropriate **names** in the vendor list, or **click Select All** to select all vendors.

Enter **Dec. 31** as the date for the report.

Click **OK** to view the report.

All orders due in the next month should be included in the report. The purchase order with HydraTub Care is not included because its starting date is January 1.

Click the **Redo Report tool** .

Display the **report** again using January 15 as the date to see the outstanding order.

Close the **display** when you have finished.

NOTES
The Pending Purchase/Sales Orders reports can be sorted and filtered by Order No., Order Date, Ship Date and Amount.

NOTES
From the Pending Purchase/ Sales Orders reports, you can drill down to the Vendor/Customer Aged Report and to the order form.

If you drill down to the order, you can fill the order directly by choosing Invoice as the type of transaction and then filling the order as usual. Confirm your intention to change the order to an invoice.

Displaying Pending Sales Orders

Any sales orders that are not yet filled can be displayed in the Pending Sales Orders Report. You can also use this report to check for orders that should be removed.

Choose the **Reports menu**, then **choose Receivables** and **Pending Sales Orders** and **click By Customer** to view the report options:

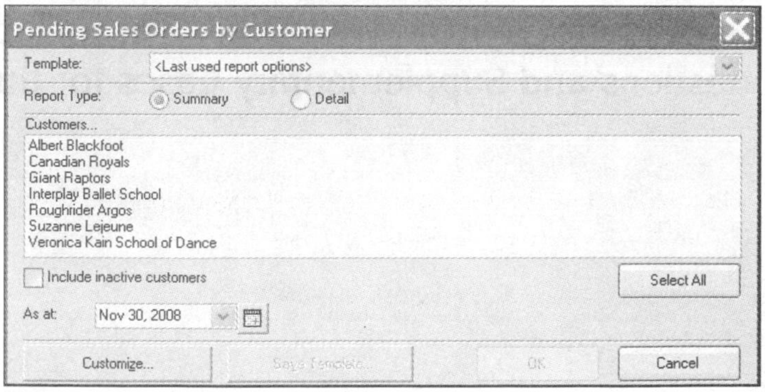

Press and **hold** ctrl and **click** the appropriate **names** in the customer list, or **click Select All** to select all customers.

Enter **Dec. 31** as the report date to see orders for the next month.

Click **OK** to view the report. One sales order is listed, the partially filled order for the Giant Raptors' contract.

Close the **display** when you have finished.

Displaying Journal Reports

When you choose to include additional fields in the journal entries, you can also include these details in the journal reports.

Choose the **Reports menu** in the Home window, then **choose Journal Entries** and **click All** to see the report options:

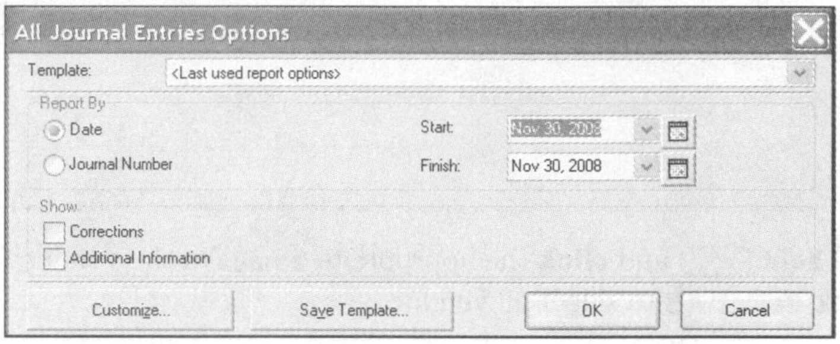

A check box is used for the Additional Information. If you do not want to include these details in the report, you can leave the check box blank.

Click **Additional Information** to add a ✓.

Click **Corrections**.

Enter the **Start date** for the report. You can type the date or choose from the list or the calendar.

Enter the **Finish date** for the report.

Click **Customize** and **enter Sort** and **Filter** and **column selections** if you want.

Click **OK** to see the Journal Report.

Close the **display** when you have finished.

R E V I E W

The Student CD-ROM with Data Files includes Review Questions and Supplementary Cases for this chapter.

CHAPTER EIGHT

OBJECTIVES

After completing this chapter, you should be able to

- ***enter*** credit card sales and purchases
- ***make*** payments toward credit card accounts
- ***make*** GST and PST remittances
- ***apply*** sales taxes to interprovincial sales
- ***enter*** sales and receipts for foreign customers
- ***enter*** purchases and payments for foreign vendors
- ***access*** vendor or customer Web sites
- ***e-mail*** invoices to customers
- ***look up*** invoices after posting them
- ***track*** shipments to customers
- ***transfer*** funds between different currency bank accounts
- ***monitor*** business routines with the Daily Business Manager
- ***create*** an Accountant's Copy of data for adjustments
- ***import*** Accountant's Copy journal entries

COMPANY INFORMATION

Company Profile

NOTES
Maple Leaf Rags Inc.
2642 Goldstream Avenue
Victoria
British Columbia V9B 2X2
Tel 1: (250) 63M-USIC
Tel 2: (888) 63M-USIC
Fax: (250) 633-4888
Business No.: 128 488 632
Rag is a style of music set in ragtime. Many of Scott Joplin's tunes, including "Maple Leaf Rag," are examples of ragtime music.

Maple Leaf Rags Inc. is a privately held corporation operated by Jaz Bands out of a small office in Victoria, British Columbia. While studying fine arts at Concordia University, Bands worked part time in local music stores. Customers frequently asked about Canadian performing artists in general and were sometimes frustrated that they had to look in every department to find a variety of types of music by Canadians. After completing an MBA at Queen's University, and based on his knowledge of and contacts in the music industry and some careful business research, Bands opened his own business, Maple Leaf Rags Inc., a store specializing in Canadian recording artists.

Maple Leaf Rags Inc. sells CDs by Canadian artists over the Internet to individuals. It also sells to music stores throughout Canada and the United States, usually to American stores that serve a large Canadian resident and tourist clientele. These stores rely on Bands as a convenient source of Canadian artists' recordings, including native and ethnic music produced by A.B. Original Sounds, which is Bands' recording company. Bands hopes to expand the business to other countries where pockets of Canadian populations can be found, such as countries with Canadian Armed Forces bases.

Bands is fortunate to be able to rely on the advice of his friend Dave Manga whose Outset Media board-game business distributes its products in a similar way to Maple Leaf Rags. His friend also shares information about vendors who might be able to provide some of Bands' supplies.

Maple Leaf Rags has expanded rapidly, though Bands is still able to operate out of his own home because the demands for inventory storage space are small. He pays himself rent for use of his home office space.

Bands buys CDs from various recording studios. He buys CD masters from A.B. Original Sounds, and vendors across Canada copy and package the CDs for his company at competitive prices. He has accounts set up for all his regular suppliers, many of whom offer discounts for early payments. Bands also has set up accounts for his wholesale customers, with discounts for early payment.

At the end of each fiscal year, Bands creates a copy of the data files for the accountant who checks the accuracy of the accounting records and adds the outstanding adjusting entries.

Bands converted his accounting records to Simply Accounting after completing a brief course at the community college. The following company information summarizes the conversion after the first nine months of the current fiscal period:

- Chart of Accounts
- Trial Balance
- Vendor Information
- Customer Information
- Accounting Procedures

CHART OF POSTABLE ACCOUNTS

MAPLE LEAF RAGS INC.

ASSETS
1020 Bank: Savings Account
1040 Bank: Chequing Account
1060 Bank: Visa
1080 Bank: MasterCard
1100 Bank: Amex
1140 Bank: USD
1200 Accounts Receivable
1240 Purchase Prepayments
1280 Office Supplies
1300 CD Inventory
1340 Prepaid Expenses
1410 Computers
1420 Accum Deprec: Computers
1450 Furniture & Equipment
1480 Accum Deprec: Furn & Equip ▶

▶1500 Automobile
1520 Accum Deprec: Automobile

LIABILITIES
2100 Bank Loan
2180 Prepaid Sales and Deposits
2200 Accounts Payable
2250 Amex Payable
2260 Visa Payable
2460 PST Payable
2650 GST Charged on Sales
2660 HST Charged on Sales
2670 GST Paid on Purchases
2680 HST Paid on Purchases
2850 Long Term Loan ▶

▶EQUITY
3560 Common Stock
3600 Retained Earnings
3800 Current Earnings

REVENUE
4100 Revenue from Sales
4180 Sales Discounts
4200 Freight Revenue
4250 Interest Revenue
4280 Sales Tax Compensation
4300 Exchange Rate Differences

EXPENSE
5100 Advertising & Publicity
5150 Bank Charges & Card Fees
5200 Depreciation Expense ▶

▶5220 Freight & Shipping Expenses
5260 Purchase Discounts
5280 Interest Expense
5300 Internet & Web Site Expenses
5360 CD Assembly Materials Costs
5380 Cost of CDs Sold
5400 Office Rent
5500 Office Supplies Used
5520 Research Expenses
5560 Telephone Expenses
5580 Travel Expenses

NOTES: The Chart of Accounts includes only postable accounts and the Net Income or Current Earnings account.

TRIAL BALANCE

MAPLE LEAF RAGS INC.

June 30, 2008		Debits	Credits			Debits	Credits
1020	Bank: Savings Account	$ 46 000		▶ 2670	GST Paid on Purchases	2 300	
1040	Bank: Chequing Account	31 000		2850	Long Term Loan		6 000
1060	Bank: Visa	1 800		3560	Common Stock		160 000
1080	Bank: MasterCard	2 350		3600	Retained Earnings		12 640
1100	Bank: Amex	840		4100	Revenue from Sales		321 000
1120	Bank: USD ($550 USD)	760		4180	Sales Discounts	6 840	
1200	Accounts Receivable	68 480		4200	Freight Revenue		5 460
1280	Office Supplies	600		4250	Interest Revenue		2 150
1300	CD Inventory	194 350		4280	Sales Tax Compensation		45
1340	Prepaid Expenses	3 900		5100	Advertising & Publicity	18 800	
1410	Computers	8 200		5150	Bank Charges & Card Fees	1 980	
1420	Accum Deprec: Computers		$ 1 100	5220	Freight & Shipping Expenses	4 810	
1450	Office Furniture & Equipment	9 100		5260	Purchase Discounts		850
1480	Accum Deprec: Furn & Equip		1 500	5280	Interest Expense	9 960	
1500	Automobile	16 800		5300	Internet & Web Site Expenses	540	
1520	Accum Deprec: Automobile		9 800	5360	CD Assembly Materials Costs	1 800	
2100	Bank Loan		12 000	5380	Cost of CDs Sold	150 650	
2200	Accounts Payable		1 600	5400	Office Rent	7 200	
2250	Amex Payable		390	5500	Office Supplies Used	800	
2260	Visa Payable		860	5520	Research Expenses	1 200	
2460	PST Payable		450	5560	Telephone Expenses	905	
2650	GST Charged on Sales		3 650	5580	Travel Expenses	1 950	
2660	HST Charged on Sales		420 ▶			$593 915	$593 915

VENDOR INFORMATION

MAPLE LEAF RAGS INC.

Vendor Name (Contact)	Address	Phone No. Fax No.	E-mail Web Site	Terms Tax ID
A.B. Original Sounds (Marie Raven)	380 Abbey Rd. Vancouver, BC V3P 5N6	Tel: (604) 882-6252 Fax: (604) 882-1100		1/10, n/30 (before tax) 129 646 733
BC Tel (Manny Voyses)	45 Nexus Ave. Victoria, BC V7R 3D1	Tel: (250) 679-1011 Fax: (250) 679-1000	www.bell.ca	n/1
Federal Express (DayLee Runner)	59 Effex Road Victoria, BC V7F 6X2	Tel: (800) 488-9000 Fax: (250) 488-1230	www.fedex.com	n/1
Grandeur Graphics (Kathy Grandeur)	26 Drawing Way Halifax, NS B5T 3D1	Tel: (902) 665-3998 Fax: (902) 665-3900	www.wedesignit.com	2/20, n/30 (before tax) 459 112 341
Let 'm Know (Jabber Jaws Lowder)	599 Broadcast Rd. Vancouver, BC V2F 7J8	Tel: (604) 604-6040 Fax: (604) 604-4660	www.wetellit.com	2/20, n/30 (before tax) 453 925 376
Miles 'R on Us (N. Gins)	522 Drivers St. Victoria, BC V6T 5E3	Tel: (800) 592-5239 Fax: (250) 591-4929		n/1
Minister of Finance	55 Munificence St. Victoria, BC V7P 2B5	Tel: (250) 529-7292	www.fin.gov.bc.ca	n/1
Purolator (Speedy Carriere)	46 Shipping Mews Victoria, BC V7H 6S2	Tel: (800) 355-7447 Fax: (250) 355-7000	www.purolator.com	n/1
Receiver General for Canada	Summerside Tax Centre Summerside, PE C1N 6L2	Tel: (902) 821-8186	www.cra-arc.gc.ca	n/1
Wrap It (Able Boxer)	80 Cubit Road Richmond Hill, ON L5R 6B2	Tel: (905) 881-7739 Fax: (905) 881-7000		1/5, n/30 (before tax) 634 529 125

OUTSTANDING VENDOR INVOICES

MAPLE LEAF RAGS INC.

Vendor Name	Terms	Date	Invoice No.	Amount	Tax	Total
Grandeur Graphics	2/20, n/30 (before tax)	6/28/08	GG-1304	$ 400	$ 60	$ 460
Let 'm Know	2/20, n/30 (before tax)	6/29/08	LK-692	$1 000	$140	$1 140
			Grand Total			$1 600

CUSTOMER INFORMATION

MAPLE LEAF RAGS INC.

Customer Name (Contact)	Address	Phone No. Fax No.	E-mail Web Site	Terms Credit Limit
Canadian Sounds (X. Pats)	46 Ontario St. Tampa, Florida 33607 USA	Tel: (813) 930-4589 Fax: (813) 930-7330	XPats@cansounds.com www.cansounds.com	3/30, n/60 (before tax) $20 000 USD
CDN Music (Michelle Strings)	230 Nightingale Pl. Scarborough, ON M2R 9K4	Tel: (416) 288-6189 Fax: (416) 288-6000	mstrings@upbeat.com www.cdn.music.ca	3/30, n/60 (before tax) $20 000
Entertainment House (Rob Blinde)	101 Booker St. Toronto, ON M4F 3J8	Tel: (416) 484-9123 Fax: (416) 488-8182	www.ent.house.com	3/30, n/60 (before tax) $150 000
It's All Canadian (Leaf Mapleston)	39 Federation Ave. Victoria, BC V8W 7T7	Tel: (250) 598-1123 Fax: (250) 598-1000	www.canstuff.com	3/30, n/60 (before tax) $20 000
Music Music Music (M. Porter)	10 Red Rock Canyon Sedona, Arizona 86336 USA	Tel: (520) 678-4523 Fax: (520) 678-4500	mporter@music3.com www.music3.com	3/30, n/60 (before tax) $10 000 USD
Total Music (Goode Sounds)	93 Waterside Rd. Fredericton, NB E3B 4F4	Tel: (506) 455-7746 Fax: (506) 455-7000	goode@totalmusic.com www.totalmusic.com	3/30, n/60 (before tax) $50 000
Treble & Bass (Bea Flatte)	399 Chord Blvd. Vancouver, BC V4E 5T6	Tel: (604) 557-5438 Fax: (604) 557-5550	bflatte@t&b.com www.t&b.com	3/30, n/60 (before tax) $30 000
Web Store Customers				Prepaid by Credit Card

OUTSTANDING CUSTOMER INVOICES

MAPLE LEAF RAGS INC.

Customer Name	Terms	Date	Invoice No.	Amount	Tax	Total
CDN Music	3/30, n/60 (before tax)	6/25/08	591	$ 4 500	$ 315	$ 4 815
Entertainment House	3/30, n/60 (before tax)	1/4/08	233	$56 000	$3 920	$59 920
It's All Canadian	3/30, n/60 (before tax)	6/6/08	589	$ 3 500	$ 245	$ 3 745
			Grand Total			$68 480

Accounting Procedures

GST

Maple Leaf Rags Inc. uses the regular method of calculating GST. The GST charged and collected from customers is recorded as a liability in *GST Charged on Sales*. Customers in Nova Scotia, New Brunswick, and Newfoundland and Labrador (participating provinces) pay HST at the rate of 15 percent instead of GST, and these amounts are recorded in *HST Charged on Sales*. Bands has set up both GST and HST as taxes with appropriate codes. GST paid to vendors is recorded in *GST Paid on Purchases* (or *HST Paid on Purchases* if the vendor is in a participating province) as a decrease in tax liability. The balance owing is the difference between the GST plus HST charged and GST plus HST paid.

Cash Sales of Services

Cash transactions for Bands are limited to credit card sales since most of his business is with wholesale customers who have accounts. He has merchant Visa, MasterCard and American Express (Amex) arrangements with three different financial institutions. Maple Leaf Rags pays a percentage of each sale directly to the credit card companies (the fee is withheld from the sale amount). To simplify the transaction entries, we provide summaries of these credit card sales as if they were to a single customer called Web Store Customers.

Bands uses a Visa gold card and an American Express card for some business purchases and pays annual user fees for these cards.

Discounts

Discounts are calculated automatically by the program when the discount terms are entered as part of the invoices. If the payments are made before the discount terms have expired, the discount appears in the Payments and Receipts journals automatically. All discounts are calculated on before-tax amounts. Bands offers a 3 percent discount to wholesale customers to encourage them to pay their accounts on time. Web store customers pay by credit card and do not receive discounts.

Some vendors offer before-tax discounts to Maple Leaf Rags as well. These discount terms are set up in the vendor and customer records.

> **NOTES**
> The sales tax rules for discounts are complex and may vary from province to province. Rules for federal taxes may also be different from those for provincial taxes. Simply Accounting calculates sales discounts as before or after tax but applies the same formula to GST and retail sales taxes. Adjusting General Journal entries may be required to adjust the amount of tax owing and calculate the tax remittance. We have omitted the tax adjustments for sales discounts.

PST

Wholesale customers do not pay PST on merchandise they buy for resale. Thus when Bands sells directly to stores, he charges only GST. He does not charge PST to stores because they are not the final consumers of the product. When individual customers buy directly from Bands, he charges PST at 7 percent to customers in British Columbia but not to customers in other provinces. All customers pay GST at 7 percent or HST at 15 percent. PST and GST are also paid on all freight or shipping charges in British Columbia. When Maple Leaf Rags makes the PST remittance, it reduces the amount of the remittance by 3.3 percent, the amount of the sales tax compensation.

Freight

Customers who order through the Internet pay a shipping rate of $5 for the first CD and $2 for each additional CD. Wholesale customers pay the actual shipping costs. GST and PST are charged on freight in British Columbia. Bands has accounts set up with his three regular shippers so that he can track shipments online. Their Web site addresses are included in the shipping setup data.

Sales Orders and Deposits

When a customer places a sales order, Bands requests a deposit as confirmation of the order. Deposits are entered on the Sales Order form (see page 232).

Foreign Customers and Vendors

Customers outside Canada do not pay GST or PST on goods imported from Canada. Therefore, sales outside the country do not have taxes applied to them. These customers also do not pay GST or PST on shipping charges.

Purchases from vendors outside of Canada are subject to GST when the goods are used in Canada. No import duties are charged on goods coming from the United States.

INSTRUCTIONS

1. **Record entries for the source documents** in Simply Accounting using the Chart of Accounts, Vendor Information, Customer Information and Accounting Procedures for Maple Leaf Rags. The procedures for entering each new type of transaction in this application are outlined step by step in the Keystrokes section following the source documents. These transactions are indicated with a ✓ in the completion box beside the source document. The number for the page on which the relevant keystrokes begin is printed immediately below the check box.
2. **Print** the **reports for the end of the fiscal period** suggested by the Simply Accounting checklists after you have finished making your entries. Refer to the Keystrokes section, page 280.

SOURCE DOCUMENTS

SESSION DATE – JULY 15, 2008

NOTES
In the data files, PBC is the tax name we use for PST in BC (British Columbia) so that it can be distinguished from PST applied in other provinces. PST applied in Ontario is named PO in the data files.

☑ **Visa Credit Card Sales Invoice #593** **Dated July 2/08**

253 To various Web Store customers, for CDs sold during previous three months

Sales to BC customers	$1 200	plus 7% GST and 7% PST
Sales to Ontario customers	1 400	plus 7% GST
Sales to HST provinces	600	plus 15% HST
Shipping	480	plus 7% GST and 7% PST

(Shipped by Purolator #PCU773XT)
Invoice total $4 103.20. Paid by Visa.

NOTES
Remember to select the correct credit card name.
You do not need to enter shipping information for the remaining Web store sales.

☑ **MasterCard Credit Card Sales Invoice #594** **Dated July 2/08**

To various Web Store customers, for CDs sold during previous three months

Sales to BC customers	$2 300	plus 7% GST and 7% PST
Sales to HST provinces	900	plus 15% HST
Sales to other provinces	2 800	plus 7% GST
Shipping	780	plus 7% GST and 7% PST

Invoice total $7 542.20. Paid by MasterCard.

Amex Credit Card Sales Invoice #595 **Dated July 2/08**

To various Web Store customers, for CDs sold during previous three months

Sales to BC customers	$ 700	plus 7% GST and 7% PST
Sales to HST provinces	200	plus 15% HST
Sales to other provinces	1 300	plus 7% GST
Shipping	280	plus 7% GST and 7% PST

Invoice total $2 738.20. Paid by Amex.

Visa Purchase Invoice #MR-1699 **Dated July 2/08**

257 To Miles 'R on Us, $520 plus 7% GST and 8% PST for two-week car rental while attending Trade Show in Toronto. Invoice total $598. Paid by Visa.

Cheque #761 **Dated July 2/08**

258 To Visa, $723.50 in payment of credit card account, including $609 for purchases charged from May 16 to June 15, $105 for annual renewal fee and $9.50 in interest charges on unpaid balance from previous statement.

Memo #43 **Dated July 3/08**

261 From J. Bands: Access the Web site for Canada Revenue Agency to see whether any recent announcements about GST affect the business.

Memo #44 **Dated July 5/08**

264 From J. Bands: Refer to June 30 General Ledger balances to remit GST and HST to the Receiver General. Issue cheque #762 for $1 770 from Chequing Account.

Memo #45 **Dated July 5/08**

266 From J. Bands: Refer to the June 30 General Ledger balance to remit PST Payable to the Minister of Finance. Reduce the payment by the sales tax compensation of 3.3% of the balance owing. Issue cheque #763 for $435.15 from Chequing Account.

Sales Invoice #596 **Dated July 5/08**

266 To Canadian Sounds, $2 190 USD for CDs. Shipped by Federal Express (#F19YTR563) for $120. Invoice total $2 310 USD. Terms 3/30, n/60. The exchange rate is 1.215.

Cash Receipt #125 **Dated July 5/08**

From It's All Canadian, cheque #884 for $3 640 in payment of account including $105 discount taken for early payment. Reference invoice #589.

Sales Order #TB-04 & Deposit #14 **Dated July 5/08**

Shipping date July 10/08

From Treble & Bass, $10 300 plus 7% GST for CDs. Enter one (1) as the order quantity. Shipping by Purolator for $110 plus GST and PST. Invoice total $11 146.40. Terms 3/30, n/60. Received cheque #911 for $2 000 as deposit #14 to confirm the order. Refer to page 232.

Sales Invoice #597 **Dated July 10/08**

To Treble & Bass, to fill sales order #TB-04, $10 300 plus 7% GST for CDs. Shipped by Purolator (#PCU899XT) for $110 plus GST and PST. Invoice total $11 146.40. Terms 3/30, n/60. Enter the shipper so you can track the shipment.

Sales Invoice #598 **Dated July 11/08**

To Music Music Music, $1 630 USD for CDs. Shipped by Federal Express (#F27CGB786) for $100. Invoice total $1 730 USD. Terms 3/30, n/60. The exchange rate is 1.210.

NOTES

Because the car rental is purchased and used in Ontario, the Ontario Provincial Sales Tax rate applies. Use tax code GO (GST plus Ontario PST).

NOTES

You can use the Additional Field for the invoice number.

Use the bank account 1040 for receipts from Canadian customers.

NOTES

Wholesale customers who will be selling the product to their own customers do not pay PST, except on shipping charges.

WARNING!

Remember to change the payment method to Pay Later for invoice #597. Cheque remains selected from the Sales Order.

☑ **Cash Receipt #126** **Dated July 15/08**

268 From Canadian Sounds, cheque #2397 for $2 240.70 USD in payment of account less $69.30 discount for early payment. Reference invoice #596. The exchange rate for July 15 is 1.205.

☑ **Memo #46** **Dated July 15/08**

270 From J. Bands: Treble & Bass called to inform you that they have not received their shipment of CDs. Look up invoice #597, e-mail a copy of the invoice to the customer and check the delivery status.

SESSION DATE – JULY 31, 2008

NOTES

Use Full Add so you can enter the correct currency

☑ Design Anything
(contact Joy Pikchur)
900 Park St., Unit 5
Seattle, Washington 98195
USA
Tel: (800) 639-8710
Fax: (206) 755-8852
Currency: USD
Terms: net 30
Expense account: 5360
Tax code: G

☑ **Purchase Invoice #DA-722** **Dated July 16/08**

274 From Design Anything (use Full Add for new USD vendor), $3 000 plus 7% GST for design of labels and CD case inserts for new CDs. Invoice total $3 210 USD. Terms: net 30. The exchange rate is 1.208.

☑ **Cheque Copy #764** **Dated July 16/08**

To Amex, $335 in payment of credit card account, including $290 for purchases charged from May 25 to June 25 and $45 for annual renewal fee.

☑ **Cheque Copy #765** **Dated July 18/08**

To Grandeur Graphics, $452 in full payment of account, including $8 discount for early payment. Reference invoice #GG-1304.

☑ **Cheque Copy #766** **Dated July 18/08**

To Let 'm Know, $1 120 in full payment of account, including $20 discount for early payment. Reference invoice #LK-692.

☑ **Cash Receipt #127** **Dated July 20/08**

From CDN Music, cheque #28563 for $4 680 in payment of account including $135 discount taken for early payment. Reference invoice #591.

☑ **Cheque Copy #284** **Dated July 30/08**

276 To Design Anything, $3 210 USD in full payment of account. Reference invoice #DA-722. The exchange rate is 1.204.

☑ **Memo #47** **Dated July 30/08**

278 From J. Bands, transfer $1 000 USD from Bank: Chequing Account to Bank: USD. The exchange rate is 1.204.

☑ **Purchase Order #204 & Cheque #767** **Dated July 31/08**

Shipping date Aug. 15/08
To A.B. Original Sounds, $50 000 plus 7% GST for master copies of new CDs. Invoice total $53 500. Enter 1 as the order quantity. Terms: 1/10, n/30. Use CD Assembly Materials Costs account.
Paid $10 000 as prepayment on order with cheque #767.

NOTES

Super Dupers
☐ 777 Copiers Ave.
Richmond Hill, ON L4T 6V2
Terms: 1/10, n/30 before tax (Remember to click Calculate Discount Before Tax.)
Expense account: 5360
Tax code: G (PST is not charged on freight in Ontario.)

☑ **Purchase Order #205 & Cheque #768** **Dated July 31/08**

Shipping date Aug. 15/08
To Super Dupers (use Full Add for the new vendor), $12 000 plus 7% GST for duplicating CDs, labels and case inserts. Invoice total $12 840. Terms: 1/10, n/30. Use CD Assembly Materials Costs account.
Paid $2 000 as prepayment on order with cheque #768.

Purchase Order #206 & Cheque #769 **Dated July 31/08**

Shipping date Aug. 15/08
To Wrap It, $6 300 plus 7% GST for CD preparation for sales (includes CD cases, adding labels and inserts). Shipped by Canada Post for $120 plus 7% GST (tax code G). Invoice total $6 869.40. Terms: 1/5, n/30. Use CD Assembly Materials Costs account.
Paid $2 000 as prepayment on order with cheque #769.

Purchase Invoice #LK-2303 **Dated July 31/08**

From Let 'm Know, $1 500 plus 7% GST and 7% PST for series of ads to run for the next five months (prepaid expense). Invoice total $1 710. Terms: 2/20, n/30.

NOTES
Change the default account to Prepaid Expenses for the invoice from Let 'm Know.

Cash Purchase Invoice #BCT-6632 **Dated July 31/08**

From BC Tel, $165 plus 7% GST and 7% PST for telephone services for two months. Invoice total $188.10. Terms: payment on receipt of invoice. Paid by cheque #770.

Cash Purchase Invoice #PE-49006 **Dated July 31/08**

From Purolator, $1 400 plus 7% GST and 7% PST for shipping services used from May 25 to July 25. Invoice total $1 596. Terms: payment on receipt of invoice. Paid by cheque #771.

Visa Purchase Invoice #PC-34992 **Dated July 31/08**

From Petro-Canada (use Quick Add), $50 plus 7% GST and 7% PST for gasoline for business use. Invoice total $57 paid by Visa.

NOTES
Use Quick Add for new vendor. Include gasoline costs with Travel Expenses. Use tax code GP – GST and PBC (PST in BC) apply.

SESSION DATE – AUGUST 15, 2008

Cheque Copy #772 **Dated Aug. 2/08**

To Visa, $849 in payment of balance shown on Visa account statement for purchases before July 15, 2008.

Cheque Copy #773 **Dated Aug. 8/08**

To Let 'm Know, $1 680 in full payment of account, including $30 discount for early payment. Reference invoice #LK-2303.

Cash Receipt #128 **Dated Aug. 9/08**

From Music Music Music, cheque #8531 for $1 678.10 USD in payment of account less $51.90 discount for early payment. Reference invoice #598. The exchange rate for Aug. 9 is 1.2065. Deposit to Bank: USD account.

Cash Receipt #129 **Dated Aug. 9/08**

From Treble & Bass, cheque #1144 for $8 834.10 in payment of account including $312.30 discount taken for early payment. Reference invoice #597 and deposit #14. Deposit to Bank: Chequing Account.

NOTES
For the receipt from Treble & Bass, remember to change the bank account for the deposit.
Also remember to mark Deposit #14 as paid.

Sales Invoice #599 **Dated Aug. 9/08**

To Total Music, $4 000 plus 15% HST for CDs. Shipping charges $210 plus GST and PST. Invoice total $4 839.40. Terms 3/30, n/60.

Sales Order #FA-05 **Dated Aug. 9/08**

Shipping date Aug. 22/08
To Fiddler & Associates (use Full Add for the new customer), $24 000 plus 7% GST for CDs purchased by major music store chains. Shipping charges $200 plus GST and PST. Invoice total $25 908. Terms 3/30, n/60.

NOTES
Fiddler & Associates
(contact Ken Fiddler)
50 Rue des Bagatelles
Montreal, QC H4S 9B3
Tel: (514) 487-2936
Fax: (514) 488-1500
E-mail: kfiddler@istar.ca
Terms: 3/30, n/60
Revenue account: 4100
Tax code: G - GST @ 7%
Credit limit: $70 000

Cheque Copy #774 **Dated Aug. 10/08**

To Amex, $100 in payment of account, for purchases charged from June 25 to July 25.

Cash Receipt #130 **Dated Aug. 11/08**

From Fiddler & Associates, cheque #502 for $5 000 as down payment, deposit #15, to confirm sales order #FA-05.

Purchase Invoice #CA-7998 **Dated Aug. 12/08**

To Cars for All (use Quick Add for new vendor), $20 000 plus 7% GST and 7% PST for new automobile less $5 000 as a trade-in allowance on old car. Invoice total $17 100. The entry to write off the old car will be made by the accountant at year-end.

WARNING!
Remember to change the payment method to Pay Later for invoices that fill purchase orders with prepayments.

Purchase Invoice #ABO-8823 **Dated Aug. 13/08**

From A.B. Original Sounds, to fill purchase order #204, $50 000 plus 7% GST for CD masters. Invoice total $53 500. Terms: 1/10, n/30.

SESSION DATE – AUGUST 31, 2008

NOTES
When you advance the session date to Aug. 31, you should see an advice statement that it is time to prepare for year-end. Read and then close the advisory statement to proceed.

Purchase Invoice #SD-9124 **Dated Aug. 18/08**

From Super Dupers, to fill purchase order #205, $12 000 plus 7% GST for duplicating CDs, labels and case inserts. Invoice total $12 840. Terms: 1/10, n/30.

Purchase Invoice #WI-3719 **Dated Aug. 18/08**

From Wrap It, to fill purchase order #206, $6 300 plus 7% GST for CD preparation for sales. Shipped by Canada Post (#75 553 789 249) for $120 plus 7% GST (tax code G). Invoice total $6 869.40. Terms: 1/5, n/30.

Memo #48 **Dated Aug. 20/08**

From J. Bands: Owner invests $50 000 personal capital to finance production of new CDs. Amount deposited to Bank: Savings Account and credited to Common Stock.

Sales Invoice #600 **Dated Aug. 21/08**

To Fiddler & Associates, to fill sales order #FA-05, $24 000 plus 7% GST for CDs purchased by major music store chains. Shipping charges $200 plus GST and PST. Invoice total $25 908. Terms 3/30, n/60.

NOTES
Close the advisor warning about the overdrawn chequing account. The funds transfer in Memo #49 will cover the cheques.

Cheque Copy #775 **Dated Aug. 23/08**

To A.B. Original Sounds, $43 000 in full payment of account, including $500 discount for early payment. Reference invoice #ABO-8823 and prepayment by cheque #767.

Cheque Copy #776 **Dated Aug. 23/08**

To Wrap It, $4 805.20 in full payment of account, including $64.20 discount for early payment. Reference invoice #WI-3719 and prepayment by cheque #769.

Cheque Copy #777 **Dated Aug. 23/08**

To Super Dupers, $10 720 in full payment of account, including $120 discount for early payment. Reference invoice #SD-9124 and prepayment by cheque #768.

Memo #49 **Dated Aug. 23/08**

From J. Bands: Transfer $60 000 CAD from Bank: Savings Account to Bank: Chequing Account to cover cheques because the chequing account is overdrawn.

Purchase Invoice #JH-0875 **Dated Aug. 23/08**

To J. Henry & Associates (use Quick Add), $1 500 plus $105 GST for legal fees to recover money owed by Entertainment House. Invoice total $1 605. Terms: net 30. Create new Group account 5240 Legal Fees.

Visa Purchase Invoice #PC-49986 **Dated Aug. 30/08**

From Petro-Canada, $50 plus 7% GST and 7% PST for gasoline for business use. Invoice total $57 paid by Visa.

SESSION DATE – SEPTEMBER 15, 2008

Memo #50 **Dated Sep. 2/08**

When his Visa bill arrived, Bands realized that he had entered the purchase from Cars for All as a Pay Later invoice instead of a Visa payment. Adjust invoice #CA-7998 from Cars for All. Change the method of payment to Visa.

Cheque Copy #778 **Dated Sep. 2/08**

To Visa, $17 157 in payment of account for purchases from July 16 to August 15, 2008.

Sales Invoice #601 **Dated Sep. 5/08**

To Canadian Sounds, $4 500 USD for CDs. Shipped by Federal Express (#F36FYT863) for $220. Invoice total $4 720 USD. Terms 3/30, n/60. The exchange rate is 1.2005.

Cash Receipt #131 **Dated Sep. 5/08**

From Total Music, cheque #2491 for $4 713.10 in payment of account including $126.30 discount taken for early payment. Reference invoice #599. Deposit to Bank: Chequing Account.

Sales Invoice #602 **Dated Sep. 10/08**

To Music Music Music, $1 500 USD for CDs. Shipped by Federal Express (#F97HRP632) for $120. Invoice total $1 620 USD. Terms 3/30, n/60. The exchange rate is 1.209.

SESSION DATE – SEPTEMBER 29, 2008

Cash Receipt #132 **Dated Sep. 18/08**

From Fiddler & Associates, cheque #574 for $20 182 in payment of account including $726 discount taken for early payment. Reference invoice #600 and deposit #15. Deposit to Bank: Chequing Account.

Visa Purchase Invoice #PC-59128 **Dated Sep. 29/08**

From Petro-Canada, $50 plus 7% GST and 7% PST for gasoline for business use. Invoice total $57 paid by Visa.

Visa Credit Card Sales Invoice #603 **Dated Sep. 29/08**

To various Web Store customers, for CDs sold during previous three months

BC	$1 100	plus 7% GST and 7% PST
HST provinces	200	plus 15% HST
Other provinces	2 100	plus 7% GST
Shipping charges	350	plus 7% GST and 7% PST

Invoice total $4 130. Paid by Visa.

NOTES

If you do not change the date for the purchase invoice adjustment, you will see a warning that the transaction date precedes the session date because the transaction was dated in a previous month. Click Yes to proceed.

NOTES

When you advance the session date to Sep. 29, you may see an advice statement about the year-end adjustments required. Read and then close the advisory statement to proceed.

Amex Credit Card Sales Invoice #604 **Dated Sep. 29/08**

To various Web Store customers, for CDs sold during previous three months

BC	$600	plus 7% GST and 7% PST
HST provinces	150	plus 15% HST
Other provinces	880	plus 7% GST
Shipping charges	210	plus 7% GST and 7% PST

Invoice total $2 037.50. Paid by Amex.

MasterCard Credit Card Sales Invoice #605 **Dated Sep. 29/08**

To various Web Store customers, for CDs sold during previous three months

BC	$1 400	plus 7% GST and 7% PST
HST provinces	500	plus 15% HST
Other provinces	1 900	plus 7% GST
Shipping charges	360	plus 7% GST and 7% PST

Invoice total $4 614.40. Paid by MasterCard.

Cash Purchase Invoice #BCT-9810 **Dated Sep. 29/08**

From BC Tel, $180 plus 7% GST and 7% PST for telephone services for two months. Invoice total $205.20. Terms: payment on receipt of invoice. Paid by cheque #779.

Cash Purchase Invoice #PE-62331 **Dated Sep. 29/08**

From Purolator, $1 200 plus 7% GST and 7% PST for shipping services. Invoice total $1 368. Terms: payment on receipt of invoice. Paid by cheque #780.

Cash Purchase Invoice #FE-46678 **Dated Sep. 29/08**

From Federal Express, $2 100 plus 7% GST and 7% PST for shipping services. Invoice total $2 394. Terms: payment on receipt of invoice. Paid by cheque #781.

SESSION DATE – SEPTEMBER 30, 2008

Memo #51 **Dated Sep. 30/08**

From J. Bands: Refer to the Sep. 30 General Ledger balance to remit PST Payable to the Minister of Finance. Reduce the $719.60 payment by the sales tax compensation of 3.3% of the balance owing. Issue cheque #782 for $695.85 from Bank: Chequing Account.

Memo #52 **Dated Sep. 30/08**

From J. Bands: Prepare for closing the books by completing adjusting entries for prepaid expenses and supplies used:

Office Supplies	$ 280
Prepaid Internet Expenses (3 months)	135
Prepaid Rent (3 months of 6)	2 400
Prepaid Advertising (2 months of 5)	642

Memo #53 **Dated Sep. 30/08**

From J. Bands: Complete an adjusting entry for $36 500 of inventory sold during the quarter. Reduce the CD Inventory asset account and increase Cost of CDs Sold expense.

Memo #54 **Dated Sep. 30/08**

From J. Bands: Complete an adjusting entry to transfer $73 724 in completed CDs from production and assembly to CDs inventory. Debit CD Inventory and credit CD Assembly Materials Costs.

✓ **Memo #55** **Dated Sep. 30/08**

From J. Bands: Received debit memo from Western Trust regarding preauthorized withdrawals from Bank: Chequing Account for quarterly interest payments on loans. Complete adjusting entries for interest paid during the quarter:

On bank loan	$ 200
On long term loan	4 000

✓ **Memo #56** **Dated Sep. 30/08**

From J. Bands: The following transfers of funds were completed.

$15 000 from Bank: Chequing Account to Bank: Savings Account
$7 000 from Bank: Visa to Bank: Savings Account
$12 000 from Bank: MasterCard to Bank: Savings Account
$3 000 from Bank: Amex to Bank: Savings Account

✓ **Memo #57** **Dated Sep. 30/08**

From J. Bands: Record Interest Revenue as follows:

Bank: Savings Account	$300
Bank: Chequing Account	70

✓ **Memo #58** **Dated Sep. 30/08**

279 From J. Bands: Create an Accountant's Copy of the data files so the accountant can review the accounting entries and add the final adjustments for depreciation and the trade-in on the automobiles.

✓ **Memo #59** **Dated Sep. 30/08**

280 From J. Bands: Review the year-end checklists. Print all reports for the fiscal period ended. Back up the data files. Check data integrity. Advance the session date to October 1, the first day of the next fiscal period.

✓ **Memo #60** **Dated Oct. 1/08**

282 From J. Bands: Import the adjusting entries completed by the accountant.

NOTES
Bands pays only interest on the loans. Both amounts are deducted from the Bank: Chequing Account.

KEYSTROKES

Opening Data Files

Using the instructions for accessing data files in Chapter 1, page 9, open the data files for Maple Leaf Rags Inc. Session dates are advanced two weeks at a time for Maple Leaf Rags, and the backup frequency is set at two-week intervals.

Enter **July 15, 2008** as the session date for this application to open the Home window.

Click **OK** and then **click** **OK** to bypass the session date warning.

NOTES
The icons for the Payroll, Inventory and Project ledgers are hidden because these ledgers are not set up.

Accounting for Credit Card Sales

Most businesses accept credit cards from customers in lieu of cash and cheques. Customers expect this convenience, and although businesses benefit by avoiding NSF cheques, they do incur a cost for this service. Credit card companies charge the business a transaction fee: a percentage of each sale is withheld by the card company.

Click the **Sales Journal icon** (Sales, Orders & Quotes) to open the Sales Journal.

Choose **Web Store Customers** from the Sold To list. Leave the transaction type as Invoice.

> **NOTES**
> Some customers may have accounts set up and pay later for Internet purchases.

Web store purchases are usually paid by credit card.

Click the **Paid By list arrow** as shown to see the payment options:

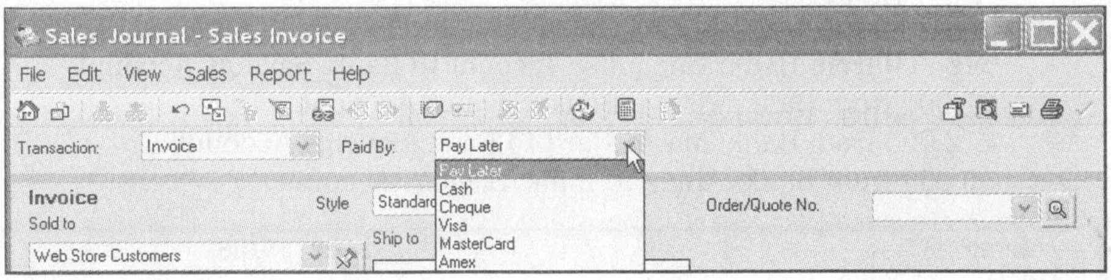

Click **Visa** as the method of payment.

The Net Days field is removed to match the immediate payment selection. Internet customers have been set up without discounts so the discount fields are blank.

Type `July 2` (as the transaction date).

Click the **Description field**.

Type `BC sales`

Click the **Amount field**.

Type `1200` **Press** *tab* to advance to the Tax field.

> **NOTES**
> We have used the tax name PBC for provincial sales tax in BC and PO for the Ontario sales tax.

Press *enter* to see the Tax codes, or **click** the **List icon**:

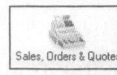

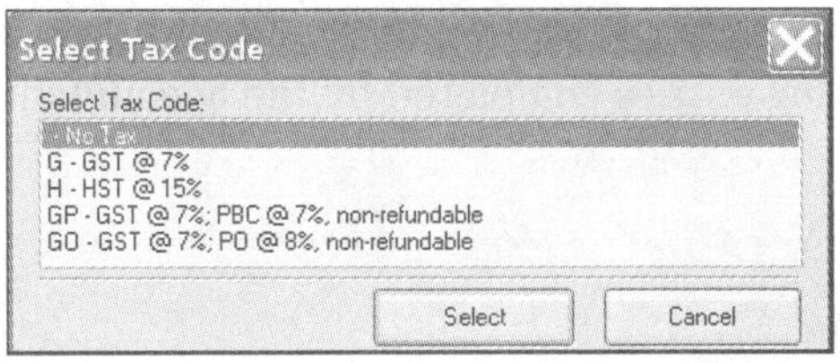

We have created tax codes to accommodate interprovincial sales to customers in the participating Atlantic provinces who pay HST (**code H**) and to customers in other provinces who do not pay PST (**code G**). The **code GO** is used for purchases in Ontario because Bands frequently makes purchases in Ontario on his business trips. He pays the Ontario PST rate at 8% on these purchases. The first sale is to BC customers, so the **code GP** is used — the GST rate is 7% and the PST rate is 7%.

> **NOTES**
> If the entire contents of a field do not fit inside a narrow column, you can change the width of a column by dragging its border in the title line of the column. You can customize the journal by removing the Item, Unit and Allo columns.

Click **GP - GST @ 7%, PBC @ 7% non-refundable**.

Click **Select** to return to the sales invoice and advance to the Account field. Account 4100 is correctly entered as the default revenue account.

Click the **Description field** on the second invoice line.

Type `Ontario sales`

Click the **Amount field**.

Type `1400` **Press** *tab*.

> **NOTES**
> Usually the same tax code would apply for all invoice lines for a single customer.

The tax code GP is entered as the default from the previous invoice line. PST is charged to BC customers only and customers outside the province do not pay this tax. These customers pay only GST so code G is needed.

Press enter or **click** the **List icon** to see the Tax Code list.

Double click **G - GST @ 7%** to add the code and advance to the Account field. The default account is entered only for the first invoice line.

Type 4100

Click the **Description field** on the next invoice line.

Type HST province sales

Click the **Amount field**.

Type 600 **Press** tab.

Tax code G is now entered as the default from the previous line. Again PST is not applied to these sales because it is harmonized with the GST. The HST rate at 15% applies to these sales.

Press enter or **click** the **List icon** to see the Tax Code list.

Double click **H - HST @ 15%** to add the code and advance to the Account field.

Type 4100

There are two freight fields in the Sales Journal, directly above the tax and total amount lines:

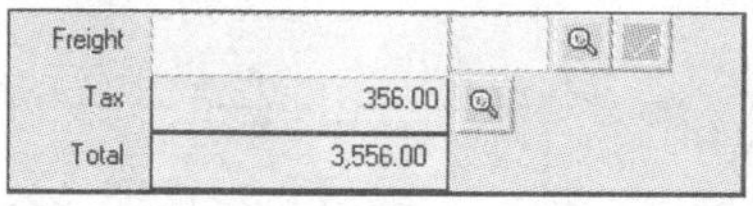

The first field is for the freight amount and the second is for the tax code. Because taxes are paid on freight you must enter a tax code if the customer pays freight. In British Columbia, both PST and GST apply to freight so code GP is required.

Click the **first Freight field**.

Type 480 **Press** tab to advance to the tax code field for Freight.

Tax code H, the last code used, is entered as the default.

Press enter or **click** the **List icon** to display the list of tax codes.

Double click **GP - GST @ 7%, PBC @ 7% non-refundable** to add the tax code.

The tax amount is calculated as soon as you enter the amount of freight charged and the tax code. This amount is added to the Tax total.

We will now enter the shipping information so that the shipments can be traced if they are not delivered within the expected time. To track a shipment, you must have the tracking number for the package. To arrange for tracking shipments online, a business must have an account with the shipper and a PIN (personal identification number) to access the account. When an invoice for these shipments is received from the shipper, it will be entered as a purchase to record the expense to Maple Leaf Rags.

Click the **Track Shipments tool** or **choose** the **Sales menu** and **click** **Track Shipments** to open the shipping data entry window:

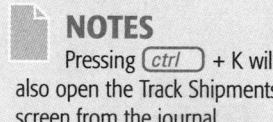

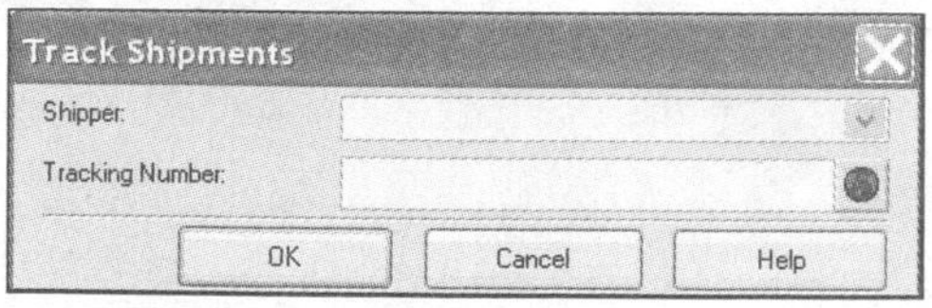

NOTES

Pressing ctrl + K will also open the Track Shipments screen from the journal.

Click the **Shipper field list arrow** to see the list of shippers:

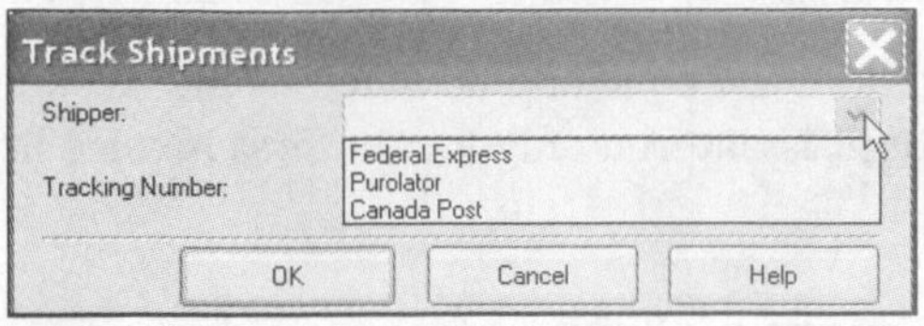

Click **Purolator**.

Press *tab* to advance to the Tracking Number field.

Type PCU773XT

Click **OK** to return to the completed invoice:

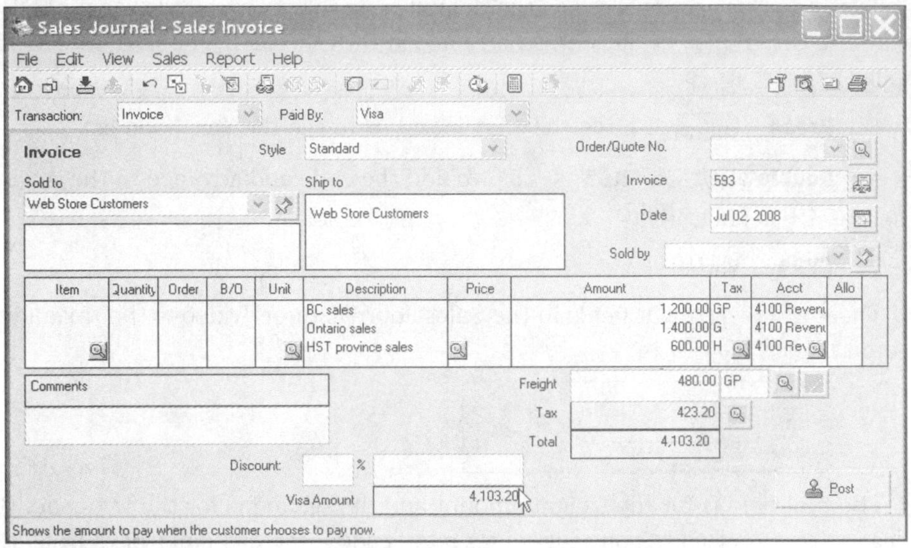

All taxes are combined on the invoice as a single entry in the Tax field. To see the breakdown of individual taxes paid by the customer,

Click the **List icon** beside the Tax field to see the detailed list:

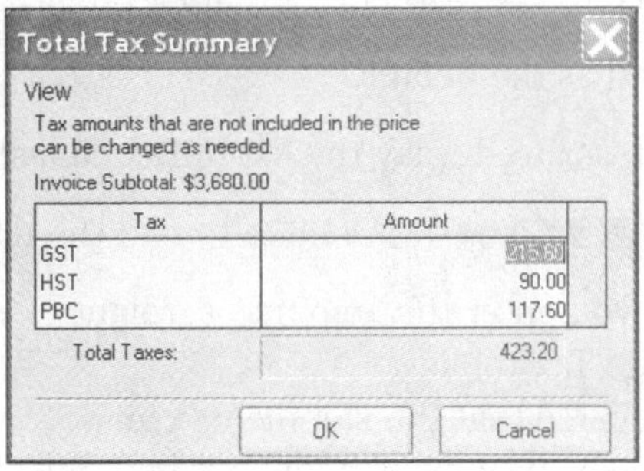

You can edit these tax amounts if they are incorrect.

Click **OK** to return to the Sales Journal.

Before posting the entry, you should review it.

Choose the **Report menu** and **click** **Display Sales Journal Entry**:

Maple Leaf Rags Inc.

07/02/08 (J1)	Debits	Credits	Project
1060 Bank: Visa	3,959.59	-	
5150 Bank Charges & Card Fees	143.61	-	
2460 PST Payable	-	117.60	
2650 GST Charged on Sales	-	215.60	
2660 HST Charged on Sales	-	90.00	
4100 Revenue from Sales	-	3,200.00	
4200 Freight Revenue	-	480.00	
	4,103.20	4,103.20	

Notice the additional linked accounts used for this transaction. The credit card account — *Bank: Visa* — is debited for the total invoice amount minus the transaction discount fees withheld by the credit card company. These fees are debited to the linked fees expense account — *Bank Charges & Card Fees.* Both the *GST* and *HST Charged on Sales* accounts are credited to show the increase in the tax liability to the Receiver General. PST collected from customers is credited to the *PST Payable* account to show the increased liability to the Minister of Finance for British Columbia. Freight charged to customers is credited automatically to the linked *Freight Revenue* account.

Close the **display** to return to the Sales Journal input screen. **Make corrections** if necessary, referring to page 169 for assistance.

The next two transactions are also summary sales to Web Store customers. We can choose to use the same customer next time so that the customer is selected automatically.

Click the **Use The Same Customer Next Time tool** beside the customer name.

The Use The Same Customer Next Time tool has changed shape to indicate it is selected. Clicking the tool again will turn off the selection.

Click the **Post button** Post.

Enter the next two credit card sale transactions. Remember to select the correct credit card from the Paid By list.

Close the **Sales Journal** to return to the Home window.

NOTES

When you close the Sales Journal, the Use The Same Customer Next Time tool is automatically turned off or deselected.

Entering Credit Card Purchases

Credit card purchases can be entered in the Purchases Journal or as Other Payments in the Payments Journal. Credit card purchases are similar to other purchases paid by cash or by cheque.

Open the **Payables module window**.

Click the **Invoices icon** to open the Purchases Journal.

Invoice is the correct transaction type.

Click the **Paid By list arrow** to see the payment options:

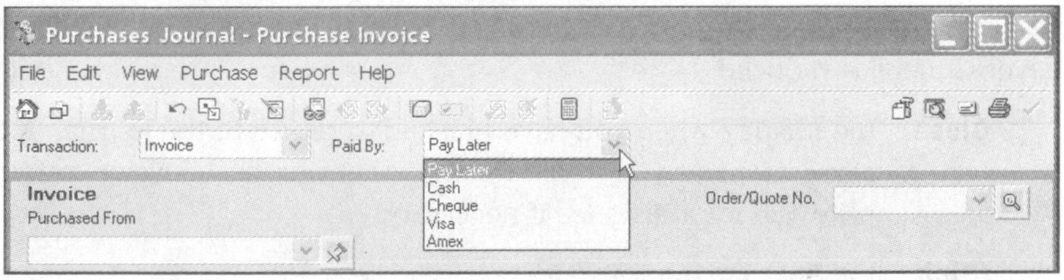

NOTES

If you want to customize the Purchases Journal, you can remove the Item, Unit and Allo columns.

Click **Visa** as the method of payment.

The rest of the entry is the same as other purchase transactions.

Choose **Miles 'R on Us** as the vendor.

The default account number and tax code are added to the journal.

Click the **Invoice field**.

Type `MR-1699` **Press** *tab*.

NOTES

Because the rental took place in Ontario, the 8% PST rate for Ontario applies. Therefore, you should use tax code GO. The List icon button hides part of the tax code. When you advance to the next invoice line, you will see the code.

Choose **July 2** from the pop-up calendar to enter the transaction date.

Click the **Description field**.

Type car rental

Click the **Amount field**.

Type 520 **Press** tab to update the totals.

Your completed journal entry should look like the following:

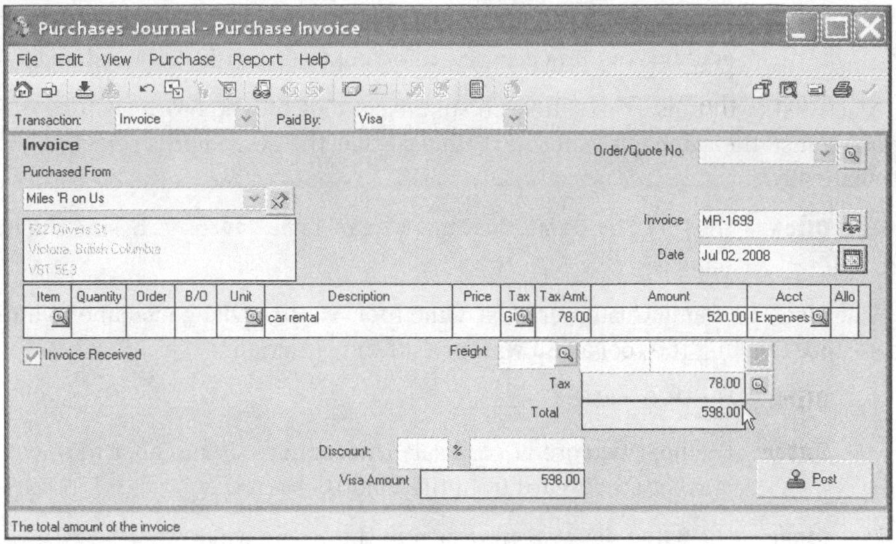

You should review the journal entry before posting it.

Choose the **Report menu** and **click Display Purchases Journal Entry** to see the transaction:

Maple Leaf Rags Inc.			
07/02/08 (J4)	Debits	Credits	Project
2670 GST Paid on Purchases	36.40	-	
5580 Travel Expenses	561.60	-	
2260 Visa Payable	-	598.00	
	598.00	598.00	

The only difference between the Visa purchase transaction and other cash transactions is that *Visa Payable* is credited instead of the bank account. *Visa Payable* is defined as the linked account for the Visa card used for purchases rather than for the Payables Ledger as a whole because Maple Leaf Rags has more than one credit card with separate linked accounts. As usual, PST paid is added to the expense part of the journal entry, and *GST Paid on Purchases* is debited to show that the liability to the Receiver General is reduced.

Close the **display** when you have finished to return to the journal. **Make corrections** as you would for any other purchase invoice, referring to page 125 for assistance if necessary.

Click the **Post button** Post.

Close the **Purchases Journal** to return to the Payables module window.

Entering Credit Card Bill Payments

Credit card payments are entered in the Payments Journal. You can access the bill payment window from the Pay Credit Card Bill icon in the Payables module window as shown:

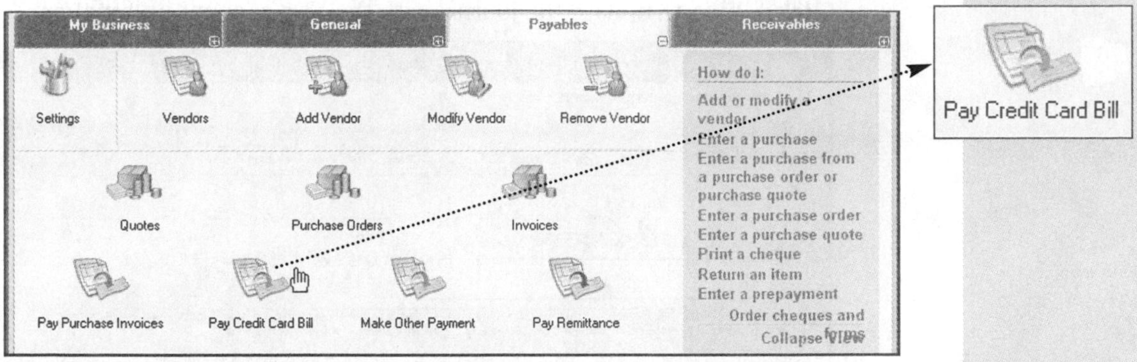

Click the **Pay Credit Card Bill icon** to open the Payments Journal:

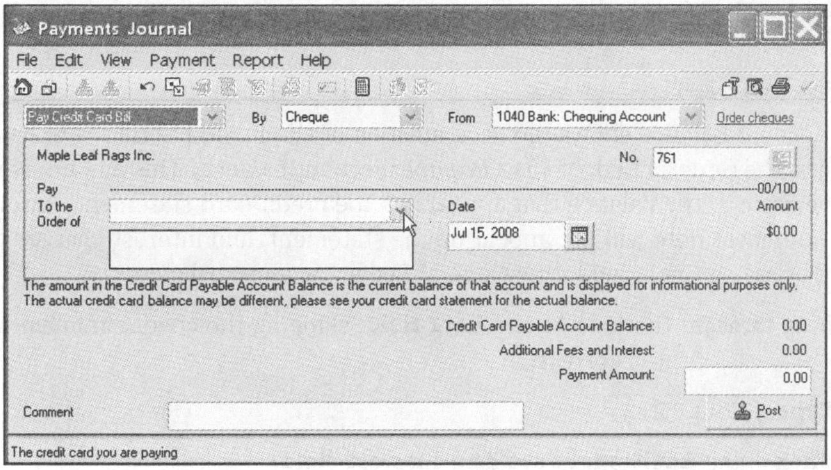

You can also access this form by clicking the Payments icon in the Home window and selecting Pay Credit Card Bill from the transaction (Pay) drop-down list.

Pay Credit Card Bill is selected as the transaction type in the Pay field.

The Pay list allows you to choose between paying vendors, paying credit card bills, making cash purchases (other payments) and making payroll remittances. The By field (method of payment) has the same options as the Purchases Journal — payment by cash, cheque or by any of the credit cards set up. The From field allows you to select a bank account from which to pay because more than one bank account is defined as a Bank class account.

The default payment is by cheque. The bank account is correct and the cheque number is the next one in the sequence for this bank account. The From list has three bank accounts. The default account is correct for this payment.

Click the **To The Order Of field list arrow** to access the list of credit cards set up for purchases:

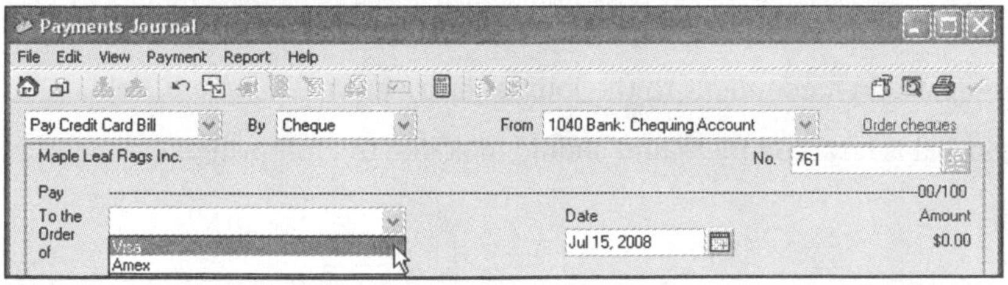

Credit card accounts are set up for Visa and Amex (American Express).

NOTES

All accounts defined as Bank class accounts are on the From list. Bank class is explained in Chapter 9.

Credit Card accounts are not Bank class accounts.

When you choose a different Bank class account from the From list, the cheque number changes to match the numbering sequence set up for that account.

Click **Visa** to update the journal with the Visa account information:

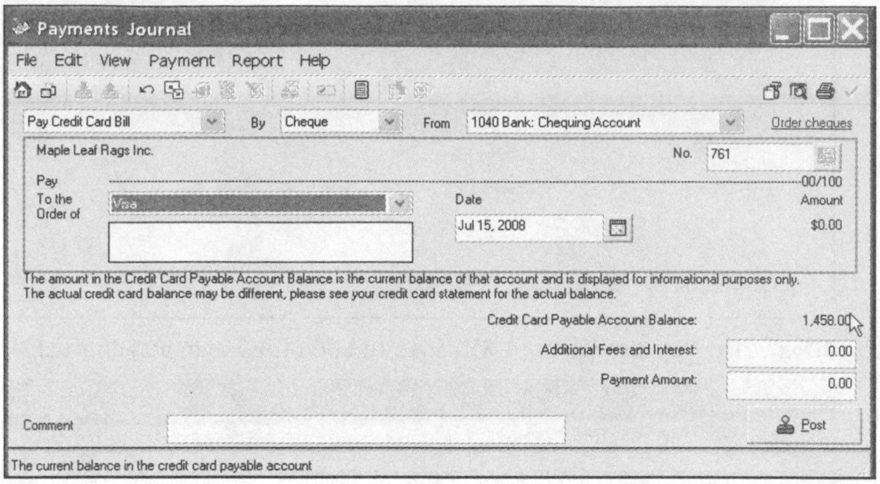

The Account Balance shows the accumulation of all unpaid purchases to date according to the General Ledger *Visa Payable* account balance. This amount is not usually the same as the balance that appears on the credit card statement. Purchases after the statement date will not appear on the statement, and interest charges or renewal fees are not included in the General Ledger account balance.

Drag through the **date in the Date field**, skipping the cheque number because it is correct.

Type `Jul 2`

Click the **Additional Fees And Interest field**.

This field is used to record interest charges on previous unpaid amounts as well as other fees associated with the use of the card. These amounts usually appear on the statement. You must add these amounts together and enter the total in the Additional Fees And Interest field. Maple Leaf Rags owes $105 for the annual card renewal fee and $9.50 in accumulated interest for a total of $114.50.

Type `114.50` **Press** *tab* to advance to the Payment Amount field.

In this field you should enter the total amount of the cheque that is written in payment, including interest, fees and purchases. This will match the balance owing on the statement if the full amount is being paid, or some other amount if this is a partial payment. The remaining balance in the General Ledger *Visa Payable* account reflects current charges or purchases that will be included in the balance owing on the next statement and paid at that time.

NOTES

When a partial payment is made to a credit card bill, the payment is applied first to interest and additional fees before reducing the outstanding balance from purchases.

Type `723.50`

Press *tab* to update the journal and complete the cheque amount in the upper portion of the journal.

You can add a comment to the journal entry in the Comment field.

The journal is now complete and should look like the following:

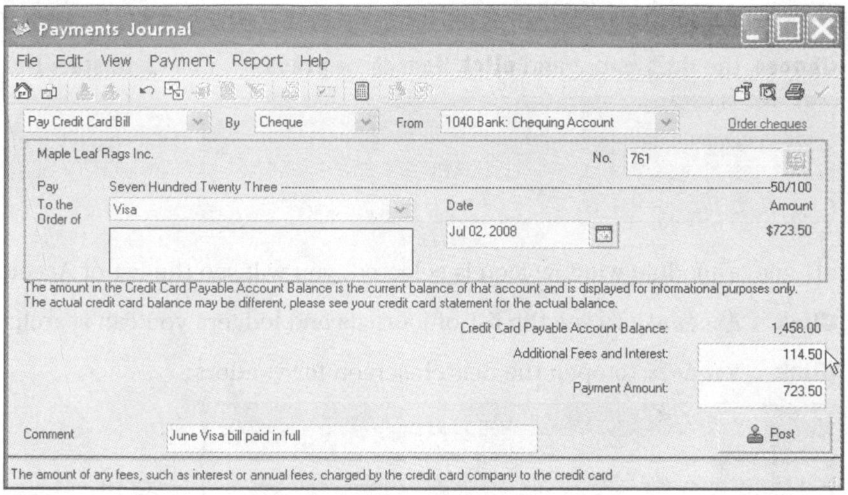

You should review the journal entry before proceeding.

Choose the **Report menu** and **click Display Payments Journal Entry** to display the transaction:

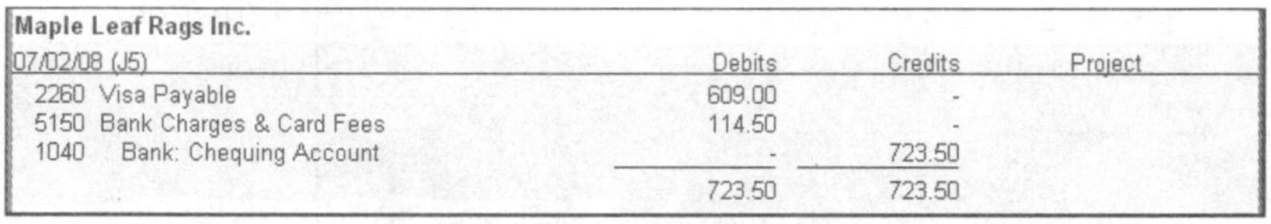

Maple Leaf Rags Inc.

07/02/08 (J5)	Debits	Credits	Project
2260 Visa Payable	609.00	-	
5150 Bank Charges & Card Fees	114.50	-	
1040 Bank: Chequing Account	-	723.50	
	723.50	723.50	

Notice that the linked Payables bank account is credited for the full amount of the payment. The payment amount is divided between the debit to *Visa Payable* to reduce the liability and the debit to *Bank Charges & Card Fees*, the linked expense account for credit card expenses.

Close the **display** when you have finished reviewing it to return to the Payments Journal.

Make **corrections** by reselecting from a drop-down list or by highlighting an incorrect entry and typing the correct amount. Press tab after changing an amount to update the totals.

Click the **Post button** Post. A message appears about the cheque number:

> **NOTES**
> This message appears only for credit card bill payments.

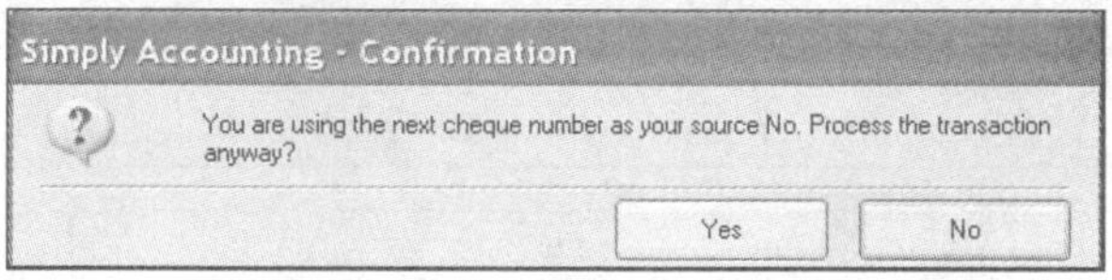

Click **Yes** to continue processing the payment.

Close the **Payments Journal** and then **restore** the **Home window**.

Accessing a Vendor's Web Site

Before making the GST remittance, we will search the Canada Revenue Agency Web site to see whether there are any recent tax changes that affect this business.

There are a number of ways to access a vendor record.

> **NOTES**
> You can also access the vendor record from the Modify Vendor icon in the Payables module or from the Vendors icon in the Home window.

In the Pro version, you can type Receiver in the Search field and press —> to open the list of all transactions and records that include this text. Double click Receiver General to open the record.

In all versions, you can begin the search from the Edit menu.

Choose the **Edit menu** and **click Search** or **press** ctrl + **F** to start the search:

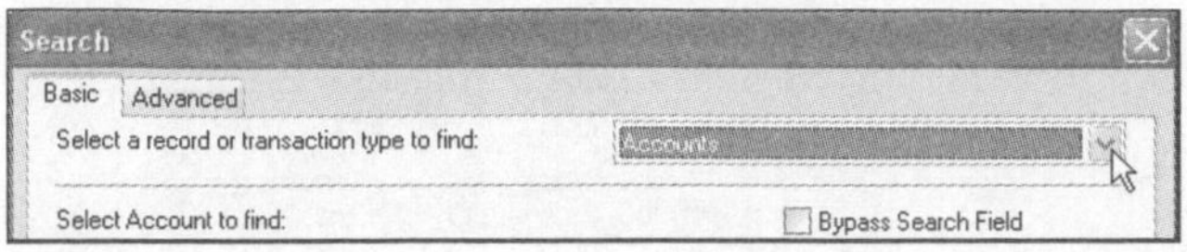

If no Home or module window icon is selected, you will see the list of Accounts.

Click **Accounts** to see the list of journals and ledgers you can search.

Click **Vendors** to open the Search screen for vendors:

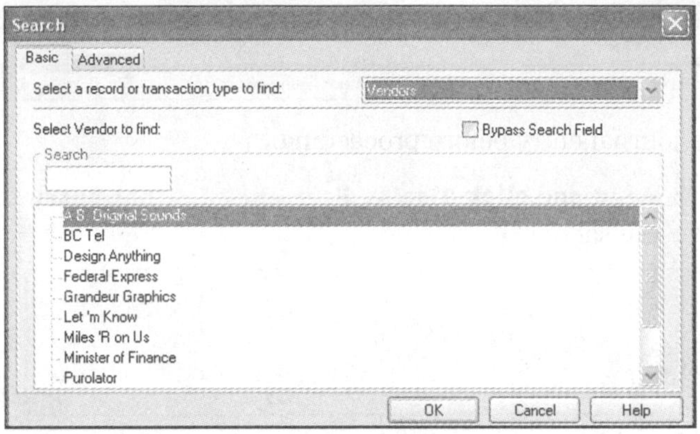

NOTES

You can type a letter in the Search field to advance the list if you have many vendors.

The Advanced Search feature allows you to define specific search parameters.

basic BASIC VERSION

The Advanced Search option is not available in the Basic version.

Click the **Search field** and **type** R

Receiver General for Canada should be selected because it is the first record beginning with R.

Click **OK** or **double click Receiver General for Canada** to open the ledger. (See screen at the top of next page.)

Clicking the Modify Vendor icon  in the Payables module window will also open the Vendor Search list.

To access the ledger from the Home window, click the Vendors icon  to open the Vendors window:

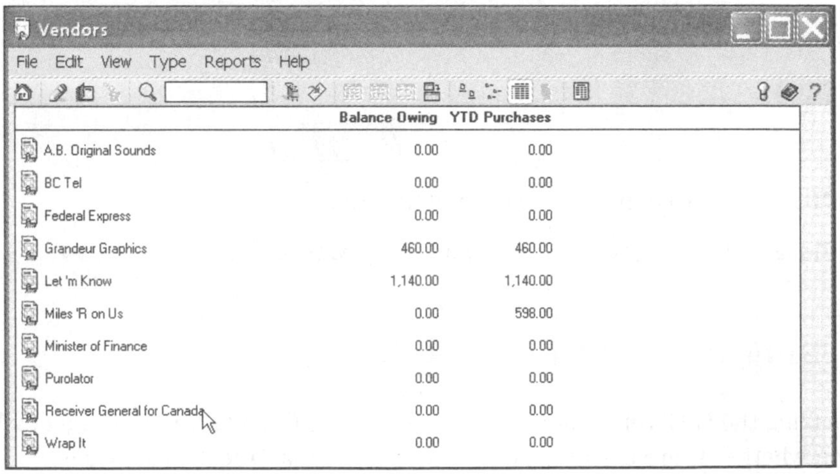

Each vendor record is represented by name in the list, along with their balances and total year-to-date purchases.

Double click the **Receiver General for Canada** to open the vendor's ledger:

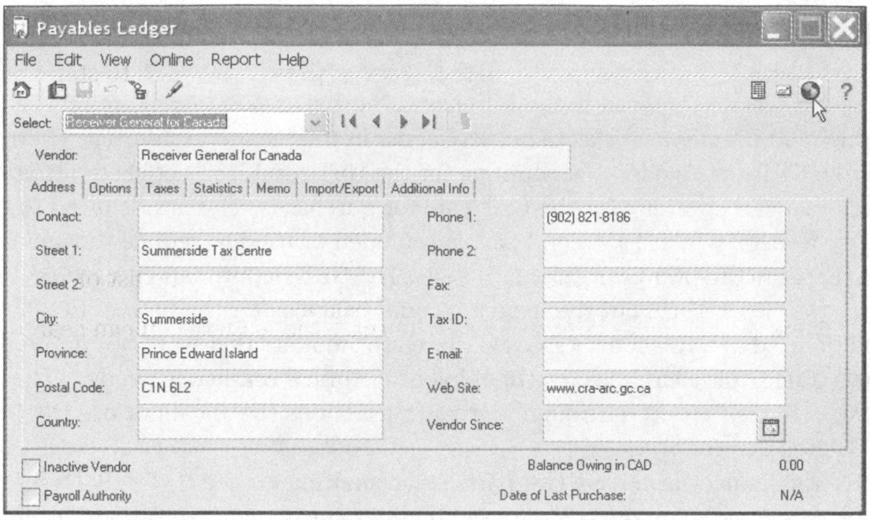

You can access the Web site directly from this vendor ledger page.

Click the **Web tool** or **choose** the **Online menu** and **click Web Site**:

Depending on how your Internet connection is set up, you may access the Web site directly or you may see a screen asking you to connect at this stage. You may need to enter the user ID and password for your Internet provider (if they are not set up to be saved and allow automatic connection). Again, your setup may be different.

You should see the Home page for the Canada Revenue Agency.

Choose your language preference.

Click the **Forms And Publications** option.

Click the **Document Type** option.

You should see a list of types of publications. There are several types of GST publications listed. Select one to list the items for that type.

You can also click Search, enter "GST publications" in the Search The CRA Web Site field and click the Search button.

Close your **Internet connection** when you have found the information you need or when you have finished. You will return to the vendor's ledger.

Close the **Ledger window** to return to the Payables module window.

WARNING!
If you have a network connection to access the Internet, such as for high-speed access, you must start your Internet connection before clicking the Web tool in the Payables Ledger window.

NOTES
Web sites are continually updated so the screens and sequence of steps may be different from the ones we provide.

NOTES
If you started from the Home window instead of the Payables module window, close the Ledger window, then close the Vendors window.

Tax Remittances

Tax remittances are entered in the Purchases Journal as non-taxable purchase invoices with payment by cheque, or as Other Payments in the Payments Journal. There are two parts to a GST remittance — accounting for the GST (and HST) collected from customers and accounting for the GST paid for purchases. The first is owed to the Receiver General while the second part is refunded or used to reduce the amount owing. Refer to Chapter 2 for further details. The GST Report can be used to help prepare the GST return, but the ledger account balances for the date of the filing period should be used as a final check in case there are amounts that were not entered in the journals. For Maple Leaf Rags, the opening or historical balance is needed. These amounts were not entered through journal transactions so we cannot use the GST or the PST Report.

NOTES
Tax amounts that you enter on the Sales Taxes screen in the General Journal are included in the tax reports.

PST remittances also have two parts — accounting for the PST collected from customers and reducing the tax remitted by the sales tax compensation for filing the return on time. Again, you can refer to the PST Report to help you.

Display or **print** the **General Ledger Report** for the following tax accounts for June 30, 2008, to see the amounts you must enter. (See page 52 if you need assistance.)

- 2460 PST Payable
- 2650 GST Charged on Sales
- 2660 HST Charged on Sales
- 2670 GST Paid on Purchases
- 2680 HST Paid on Purchases

The General Ledger balances you need are the GST and PST amounts in the Trial Balance on page 243. You can also display or print the Trial Balance or Balance Sheet for June 30 to see the amounts for the tax accounts.

Making GST Remittances

Click the **Make Other Payment icon** [Make Other Payment] to open the Payments Journal.

From the Home window, click the Payments icon and select Make Other Payment from the Pay drop-down list.

Choose **Receiver General for Canada** as the vendor.

Choose **July 5** from the pop-up calendar as the transaction date.

Click the **Account field List icon** to display the account list.

NOTES
No default account was entered for the Receiver General because four different accounts are required.

Choose **2650 GST Charged on Sales** to advance to the Description field.

Type `Debiting GST Charged on Sales`

Press *tab* to advance to the Amount field.

Type `3650`

No Tax is correctly selected as the default tax code.

Click the **Account field List icon** on the next journal line.

Choose **2660 HST Charged on Sales** and advance to the Description field.

Type `Debiting HST Charged on Sales`

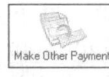

Press tab to advance to the Amount field.

Type `420`

Click the **Account field List icon** on the next journal line.

Choose **2670 GST Paid on Purchases**. In the Description field,

Type `Crediting GST Paid`

Press tab to advance to the Amount field.

Type `–2300` (Use a **minus sign** or hyphen. The minus sign is necessary to create a credit for the liability account.)

The balance in the *HST Paid on Purchases* account is zero so we do not need to include an invoice line for it.

Click the **Invoice/Ref. field**.

Type `Memo 44` **Press** tab.

Type `Memo 44, GST remittance for June`

This completes your entry as shown here:

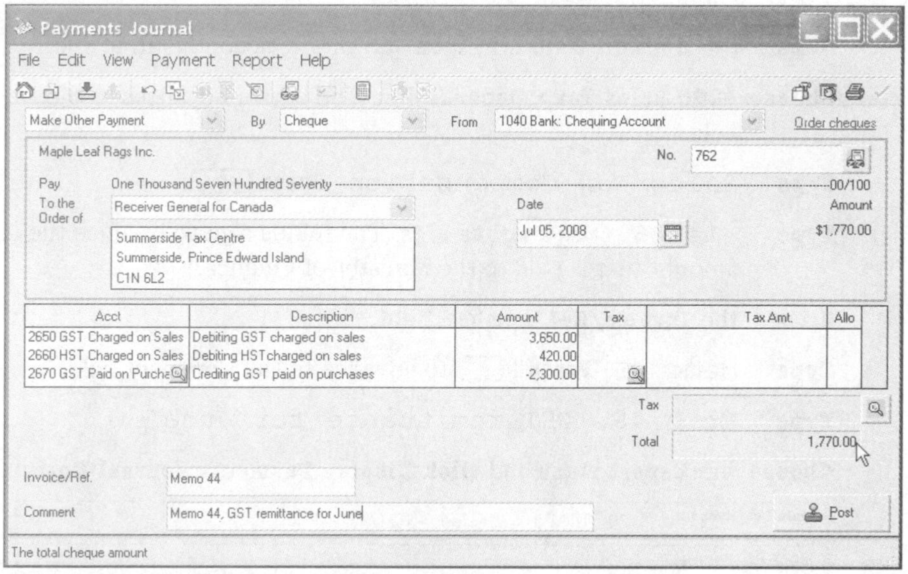

A review of the journal entry will help to clarify the transaction.

Choose the **Report menu** and **click Display Payments Journal Entry**:

Maple Leaf Rags Inc.			
07/05/08 (J6)	Debits	Credits	Project
2650 GST Charged on Sales	3,650.00	-	
2660 HST Charged on Sales	420.00	-	
1040 Bank: Chequing Account	-	1,770.00	
2670 GST Paid on Purchases	-	2,300.00	
	4,070.00	4,070.00	

Normally a positive amount will create a debit entry in the Payments Journal for an expense or an asset purchase. *GST/HST Charged on Sales* are GST payable accounts with a credit balance. Therefore, entering a positive amount will reduce the GST payable balance by debiting the accounts, as we did for the GST and HST collected from customers. The negative entry or credit for *GST Paid on Purchases* will offset the debit balance in the ledger and will reduce the total amount that is paid to the Receiver General. *HST Paid on Purchases* would also be entered as a negative amount because this amount is also refundable.

Close the **display** window when you have finished. **Make corrections** if necessary.

Click **Post** Post. You are now ready to make the PST remittance.

Making PST Remittances

You should still be in the Payments Journal with Make Other Payment selected as the type of transaction.

Choose **Minister of Finance** as the vendor. Accept the default bank account.

Accept **July 5** as the date and **accept** the default **account**, *2460 PST Payable*.

Click the **Description field**.

Type `Debiting PST Payable`

Press tab to move the cursor to the Amount field.

Type `450`

You are now ready to enter the revenue from sales tax compensation, 3.3 percent of the *PST Payable* amount.

Click the **Account field List icon** on the second journal line.

Choose **4280 Sales Tax Compensation**. The cursor advances to the Description field.

> **NOTES**
> Click the Calculator tool to access the calculator if you need to calculate the sales tax compensation amount.

Type `Sales Tax Compensation` **Press** tab.

Type `-14.85` (Use a **minus sign**. The minus sign will reduce the total amount that is paid to the Minister of Finance.)

Click the **Invoice/Ref. number field.**

Type `Memo 45` **Press** tab to advance to the Comment field.

Type `Memo 45, PST remittance for June`

Choose the **Report menu** and **click** **Display Payments Journal Entry**:

Maple Leaf Rags Inc.

07/05/08 (J7)	Debits	Credits	Project
2460 PST Payable	450.00	-	
1040 Bank: Chequing Account	-	435.15	
4280 Sales Tax Compensation	-	14.85	
	450.00	450.00	

The full *PST Payable* amount is debited to reduce the liability by crediting the bank account for the amount of the cheque and the *Sales Tax Compensation* revenue account for the amount of the tax reduction.

Close the **display** when you have finished. **Make corrections** if needed.

Click **Post** Post. **Close** the **Payments Journal**.

Close the **Payables module**.

Entering Sales to Foreign Customers

Click the **Sales icon** Sales, Orders & Quotes to open the Sales Journal. Invoice and Pay Later, the default selections, are correct.

Choose Canadian Sounds as the customer from the Sold To drop-down list.

The invoice is modified for the foreign customer:

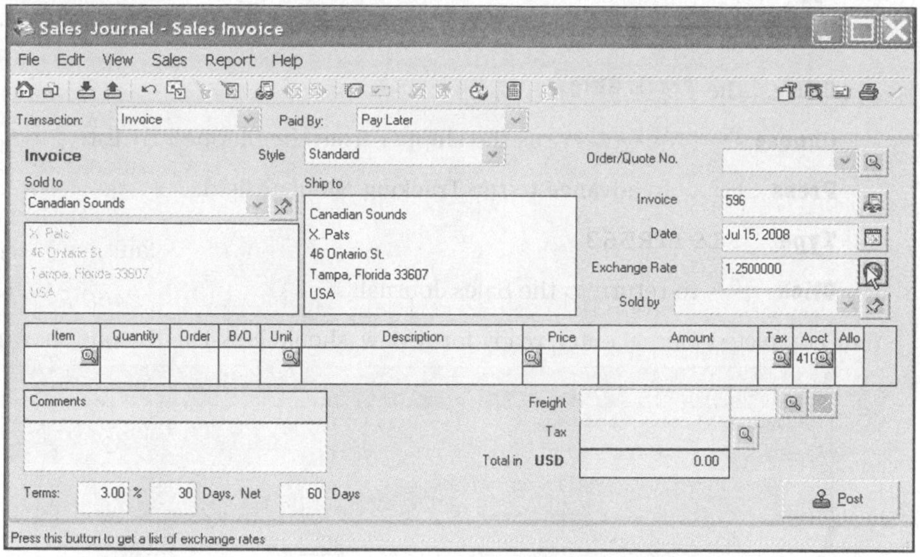

A field for the exchange rate appears below the Date, and the Total is expressed in USD (United States dollars) rather than in Canadian dollars. An exchange rate button provides a list of exchange rates already entered for various dates. There is no rate for July 5.

Choose July 5 from the Date field calendar.

The Exchange Rate screen opens because the exchange rate on record is more than one day old and no rate has been recorded for this date:

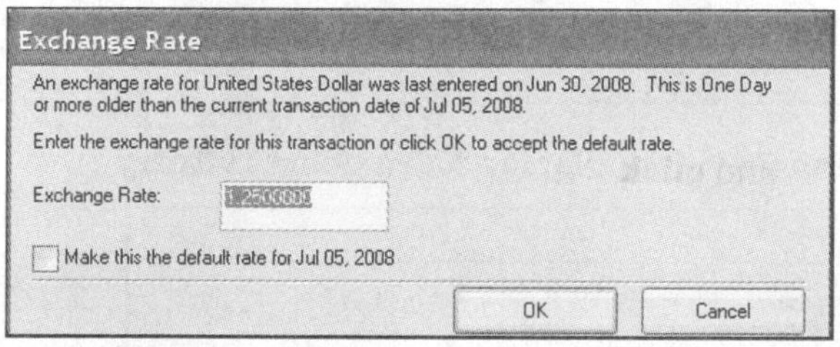

WARNING!

If you click the Date field before clicking the calendar, the Exchange Rate screen pops up. Then when you enter the transaction date, the Exchange Rate screen pops up again.

If you click the calendar first, the Exchange Rate screen will not open until after you choose the date.

The Exchange Rate setting for the company file warns when the exchange rate on record is more than one day old so that an incorrect old rate is not accepted in error. The most recent exchange rate is entered and selected for editing. You can also edit the exchange rate directly in the journal screen just as you enter information in any other field.

Type 1.215

Click **Make This The Default Rate For Jul 05, 2008**.

Click **OK** to return to the Sales Journal.

Click the **Description field**.

Type CDs

Click the **Amount field**.

Type 2190

Exported goods are not taxable because they are "consumed" outside of Canada. The No Tax code (blank) is entered as the default and it is correct. The default revenue account is also correct.

Click the **Freight field**.

Type 120

No taxes are applied to freight on exported goods.

Click the **Track Shipments tool**.

Choose **Federal Express** as the shipper from the Shipped By list.

Press *tab* to advance to the Tracking Number field.

Type F19YTR563

Click **OK** to return to the Sales Journal.

Your completed journal entry, ready for review, should look like the one shown:

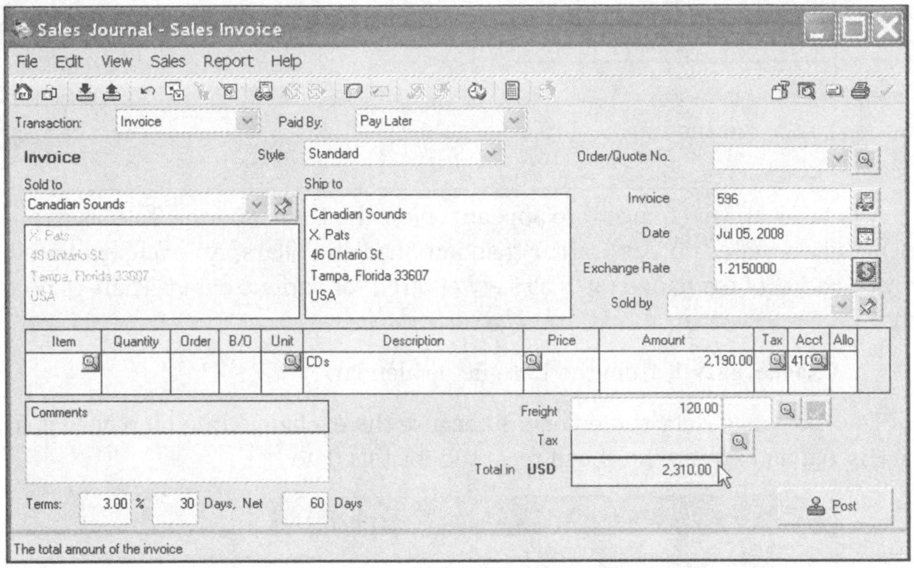

basic **BASIC VERSION**

In the Basic version, the USD amounts are shown under the heading USD Amount because this version allows only two currencies, the home currency and one foreign currency.

Choose the **Report menu** and **click** **Display Sales Journal Entry**:

Maple Leaf Rags Inc.

07/05/08 (J8)	Foreign Amt.	Debits	Credits	Project
1200 Accounts Receivable	US$2,310.00	2,806.65	-	
4100 Revenue from Sales	US$2,190.00	-	2,660.85	
4200 Freight Revenue	US$120.00	-	145.80	
		2,806.65	2,806.65	

1 United States Dollar equals 1.2150000 Canadian Dollars

Although the journal itself shows the amounts only in US dollars, the journal entry has both the Canadian amounts and the US amounts as well as the exchange rate applied to the transaction. The remainder of the entry is the same as it would be for sales to Canadian customers.

Close the **display** when finished and **make** **corrections** if necessary.

Click **Post** [Post] to save the transaction. **Close** the **Sales Journal**.

Enter the **next group of transactions** up to the receipt from Canadian Sounds.

Entering Foreign Customer Receipts

Click the **Receipts icon** [Receipts] to open the Receipts Journal.

Choose **Canadian Sounds** from the customer list:

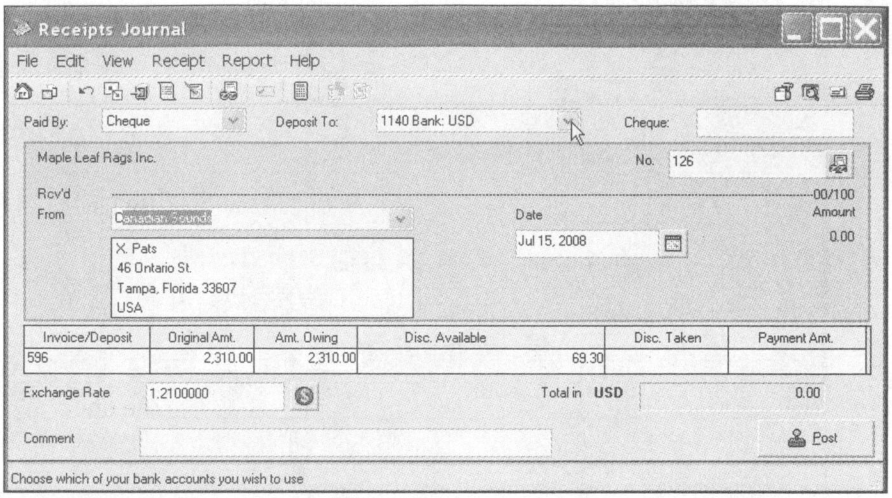

The journal is modified for the foreign customer. The outstanding invoice appears on the screen and the currency is marked as USD. An Exchange Rate field also becomes available.

Deposits from US customers are made to the USD bank account. This account is set up as the default bank account for foreign currency transactions.

NOTES
If the correct bank account is not selected by default, you can choose it from the Deposit To drop-down list of bank accounts.

Click the **Cheque field**.

Type `2397`

Click the **Date field**. The session date is correct as the transaction date.

Press *tab* to open the Exchange Rate screen.

If the rate has not changed, you can accept it by clicking Make This The Default Rate For Jul 15, 2008 and click OK.

NOTES
If the Exchange Rate screen does not open when you enter a date, you can type the exchange rate directly in the Exchange Rate field.

Again, because the last exchange rate we entered was for July 10, the rate is out of date, and we must enter a new one. The previous rate is highlighted.

Type `1.205`

Click **Make This The Default Rate For Jul 15, 2008**.

Click **OK** to return to the Receipts Journal. The cursor is on the calendar icon.

Click the **Disc. Taken field**.

Press *tab* to accept the discount because the full invoice is being paid. The cursor advances to the Payment Amt. field.

Click the **Enter Additional Information tool** 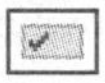.

The Total and cheque amount fields are updated in the background journal window.

Click the **Additional Field text box** to move the cursor.

Type `Ref: inv #596`

Click **OK** to return to the completed journal entry:

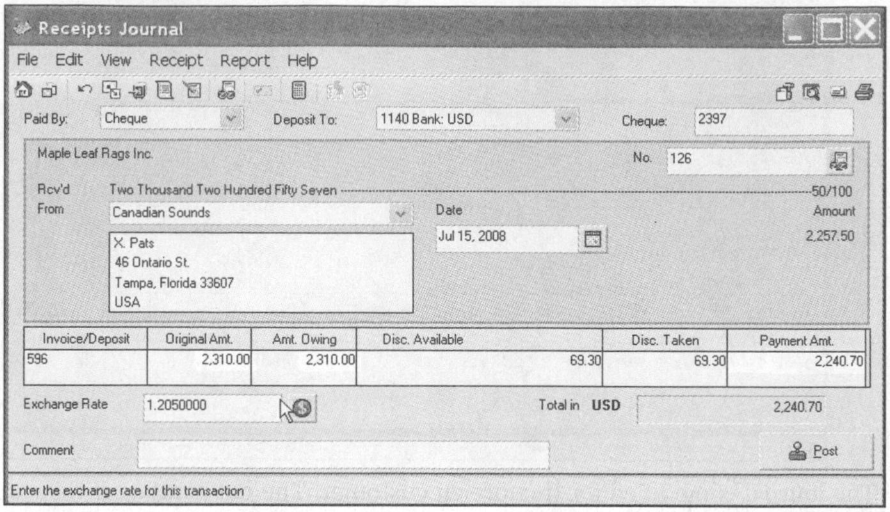

You should review the journal entry.

Choose the **Report menu** and **click** **Display Receipts Journal Entry**:

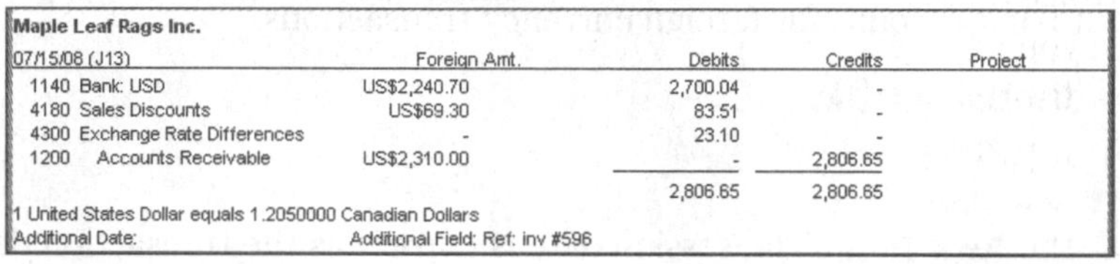

Maple Leaf Rags Inc.

07/15/08 (J13)	Foreign Amt.	Debits	Credits	Project
1140 Bank: USD	US$2,240.70	2,700.04	-	
4180 Sales Discounts	US$69.30	83.51	-	
4300 Exchange Rate Differences	-	23.10	-	
1200 Accounts Receivable	US$2,310.00	-	2,806.65	
		2,806.65	2,806.65	

1 United States Dollar equals 1.2050000 Canadian Dollars
Additional Date: Additional Field: Ref: inv #596

NOTES

The gain/loss situation is reversed for payments to foreign vendors..When the rate increases, the purchase costs more and money is lost. A decrease in exchange rate creates a loss.

In addition to the usual linked accounts for receipts, an entry for *Exchange Rate Differences* appears. Because the exchange rate was higher on the day of the sale, the date the revenue was recorded, than on the day of the receipt, there has been a debit to the account. Maple Leaf Rags has lost money on the lag in payment — fewer Canadian dollars are received for the same US dollar amount when the exchange rate is higher. When the rate increases, there is a gain. As for foreign customer sales, amounts are given in both currencies along with the exchange rate.

Close the **display** to return to the journal and **make corrections** if necessary.

Click **Post** [Post] to save the transaction.

Close the **Receipts Journal**.

Looking Up Invoices to Track Shipments

Lookup provides an exact copy of the posted invoice that you can store, print or e-mail if you have forgotten to do so before posting. This feature can be useful if a customer has an inquiry about a purchase or needs a copy of the invoice. Once a sales or purchase invoice is posted with details about the shipping company, you can look up the invoice to track the shipment to see when delivery is expected.

NOTES

You must choose the System Settings option to Store Invoice Lookup Details to be able to look up posted invoices. (See page 84.)

Click the **Sales icon** [Sales, Orders & Quotes] to open the Sales Journal.

Click the **Look Up An Invoice tool** on the tool bar or beside the Invoice field, or **choose** the **Sales menu** and **click** **Look Up Invoice**.

You will open the following Search dialogue box:

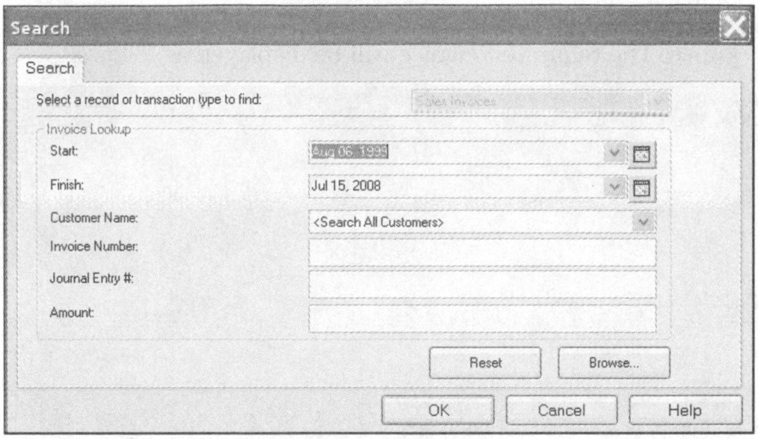

The lookup screen options are like those for adjusting an invoice. You can search through all invoices for the fiscal year to date (or for the previous year if you have not cleared the transactions and lookup data) or enter a narrower range of dates; you can search through invoices for all customers or for a specific customer; or you can search for a specific invoice number. Your search strategy will depend on how much information you have before you begin the search and how many invoices there are altogether.

The default displayed Start date may be the start of the fiscal period, the calendar date or the date you created the company files. The Finish date is the most recent session date. You can change these dates to narrow the search, just as you would edit any other date fields, or you can choose dates from the drop-down list or calendar. We want to include all invoices in the search, beginning with the earliest transaction date in the data file, the fiscal start date.

Click the **Start date**.

Type 7 1

The Customer Name option allows you to Search All Customers, the default setting, or a specific customer's invoices. You can also look up the invoices for one-time customers.

To display the list of customers, click the Customer Name field or its drop-down list arrow and click the name you need to select a specific customer.

If you know the invoice number, enter it in the Invoice Number field and click OK.

In this case we will look at all invoices by choosing the default to Search All Customers.

Click **Browse** to display the list of invoices that meet the search conditions of date and customers:

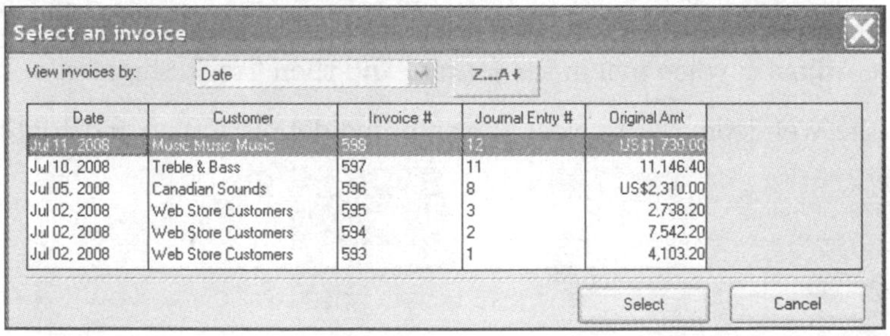

You can sort the list by order of posting date, customer, journal entry number, invoice number and amount. You can also reverse the order of the entries in the list by clicking the A...Z button.

Click **Treble & Bass, Invoice Number 597** for $11 146.40 to select it. Click anywhere on the line.

Click **Select** The requested invoice will be displayed as follows:

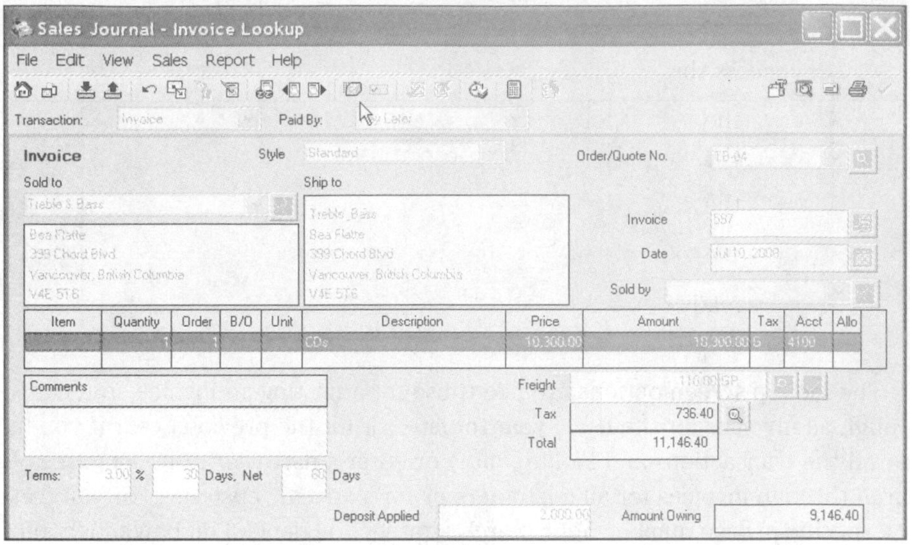

Notice that this is an exact copy of the original invoice, except that you cannot edit or post it. You can, however, store, e-mail or print it. Although you cannot adjust an invoice from the Lookup window directly, the Adjust Invoice button is available. When you click Adjust Invoice, the journal screen changes to the Adjust Invoice form. You can use the lookup method to locate the invoice you need to adjust.

If you have selected the wrong invoice, or if you want to view other invoices from this one, you can access them from any Lookup window. If there are no invoices in one or both directions, the corresponding button or buttons will be dimmed.

Click Look Up Next Invoice or Look Up Previous Invoice or choose Previous or Next Invoice from the Sales menu to display other invoices. You can browse through the invoices in this way until you find the one you need. You should practise viewing other invoices by clicking the Look Up Next and Previous Invoice buttons.

WARNING!
If you have a network connection, such as high-speed access, you must start the Internet connection before clicking the Track Shipments tool.

Click the **Track Shipments tool** or **choose** the **Sales menu** and **click** **Track Shipments** to see the shipping details for the sale.

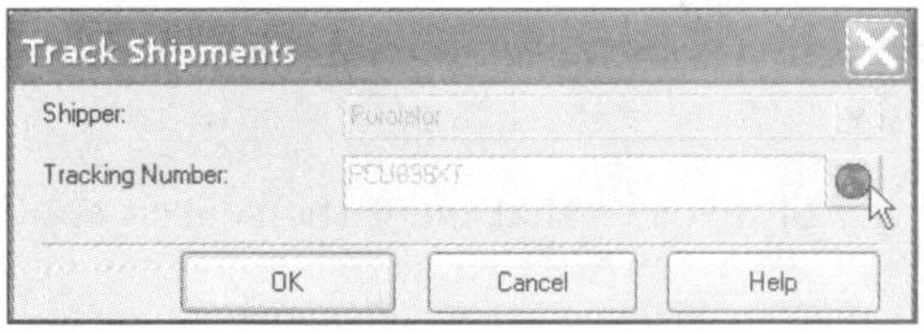

If you need to add or edit the information, click Cancel to close the tracking details window. Click the Adjust Invoice tool in the journal and then Track Shipments.

Click the Web icon to close the shipping details screen and continue:

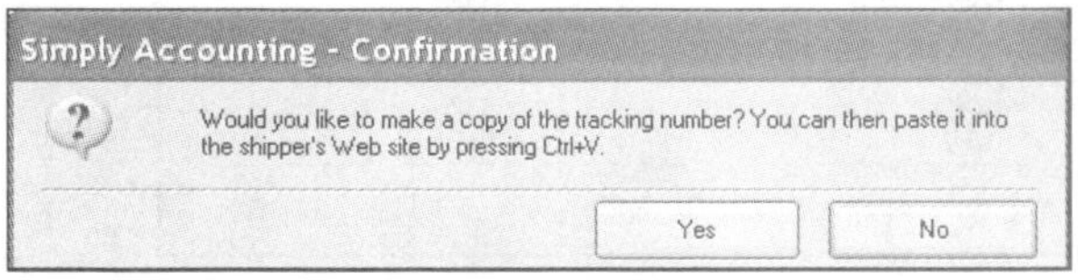

If you have set up a shipping account and have entered the actual number, you can choose Yes and save the number for entering on the Web site tracking page. However, we do not have an account with Purolator.

Click **No** to continue to the Internet connection.

Your screen at this stage will depend on your Internet setup — you may connect and access the Web site directly, or you may need to enter your account and password first.

Continue as you would for your usual Internet connection.

You will access the Web site for Purolator.

Click the **Track Shipment field**, **enter** the **PIN Number**, **press** **-->** and follow the instructions provided to proceed with tracking the shipment.

Close the **Web Site screen** when finished to return to the Lookup screen.

Click **OK** to close the Track Shipments screen.

NOTES
Web sites are continually updated so the screens and sequence of steps may be different from the ones we provide.

We are now ready to e-mail a copy of the invoice to the customer as notice of the shipping date and carrier.

NOTES
The E-mail feature in Simply Accounting works best when Microsoft Outlook Express is set up as your default e-mail program.

Click the **E-mail tool** or **choose** the **File menu** and **click** **E-mail**.

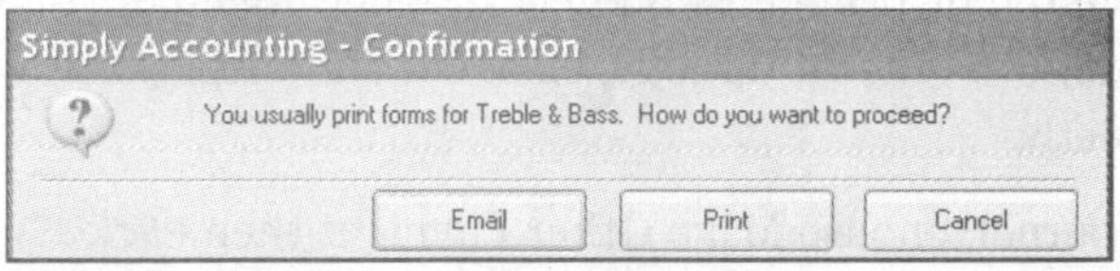

Since printing invoices is the default setting in the customer's ledger record, you are asked if you want to continue, just in case you clicked the wrong button by mistake.

Click **E-mail** to continue to the E-mail Information screen:

NOTES
If you are using a program other than Outlook Express as your default e-mail program, you may be asked to choose a profile and enter the settings before you can e-mail the invoice.

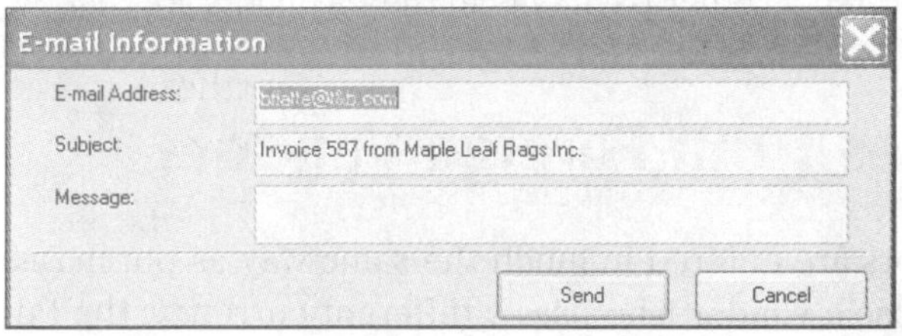

If there is no e-mail address in the ledger record, you can enter it here. You could also edit the default ledger record entry if needed. The E-mail Address field should be selected. You can replace it with your own address to test the e-mail feature.

Type (Type your own e-mail address in this field, or that of a classmate.)

You can add a message in the Message field about the shipment tracking details to inform the customer of the expected delivery date.

Click **Send**.

You will see another advisory screen asking whether you want to update the e-mail address in the ledger record.

Click **Yes** to proceed.

At this stage, your screens will depend on your e-mail and Internet setups. You should be connected to your Internet provider. Depending on the e-mail program you are using, you may see a message that the program is trying to send a message:

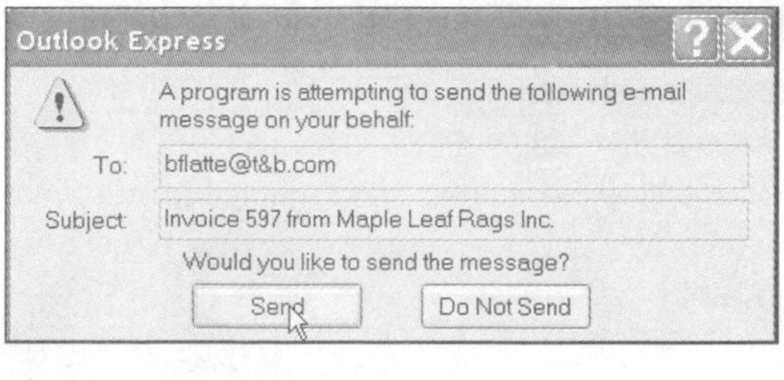

Click **Send**.

You may have to enter your ID and password before your e-mail program starts.

Close your **e-mail** and **Internet connections** to return to the Sales Journal - Invoice Lookup window.

Close the **Lookup window** to return to the Home window.

Looking Up and Tracking Purchases

You can look up purchase invoices in the same way as you look up sales invoices. You can look up purchase invoices from the Purchases Journal and from the Payments Journal.

Open the Purchases or Payments Journal, click Look Up An Invoice, decide whether you want to restrict the search dates or vendors and click Browse. Choose an invoice from the displayed list and click Select. Again, if you know the invoice number, you can enter it directly, click OK and display the requested invoice directly.

From the Payments Journal, choose Make Other Payment then click (Look Up An Invoice) to see cash invoices posted in the Purchases Journal.

Once you look up a purchase invoice, you can track shipments and look up other invoices in the same way as you do for Sales. You can also adjust the invoice. Tracking is not available for cash purchases entered as other payments in the Payments Journal.

Entering Purchases from Foreign Vendors

Purchases from foreign vendors are entered in much the same way as purchases from other vendors. Once you choose a vendor who uses a different currency, the Purchases Journal changes to add the appropriate fields.

Click the **Purchases icon** Purchases, Orders & Quotes to open the Purchases Journal. Invoice and Pay Later are correctly selected.

Click the **Vendor field**.

Type `Design Anything` **Press** tab.

Entering a Foreign Vendor Record

WARNING!
You must choose Full Add for the new vendor so that you can choose USD as the currency.

Click **Full Add** to open the Payables Ledger vendor input screen.

Type the vendor address details.

Enter **July 16** as the date for the Vendor Since field.

Click the **Options tab**. Notice the additional field for currency.

Choose **5360 CD Assembly Materials Costs** as the default expense account.

Click the **Currency list arrow** as shown:

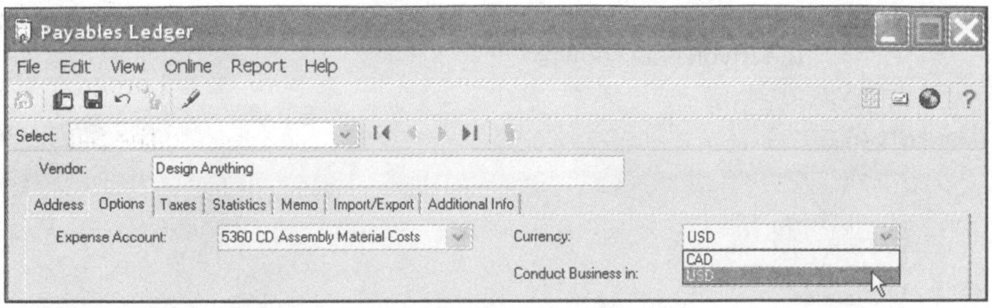

Choose **USD**. A Balance Owing in USD amount is added to the record.

Enter **net 30 days** as the payment terms.

Click the **Taxes tab** to see the default settings.

Click the **Tax Code list arrow** to see the options:

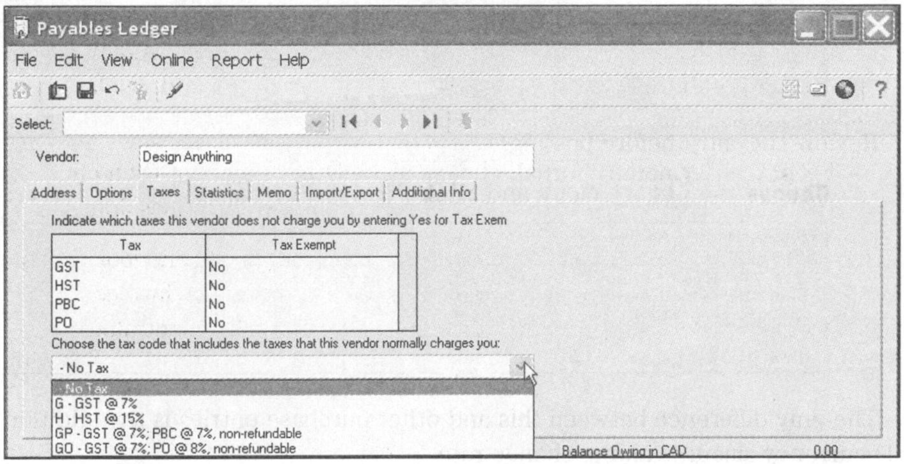

Maple Leaf Rags is not exempt from paying taxes on purchases from Design Anything, and that is the default selection. All tax codes will be available. Most purchases from US vendors are subject to GST so we should choose G - GST @ 7% as the default tax code. Maple pays GST on imported goods.

Click **Code G - GST @ 7%**.

Click **Save And Close** [Save and Close] to return to the modified invoice:

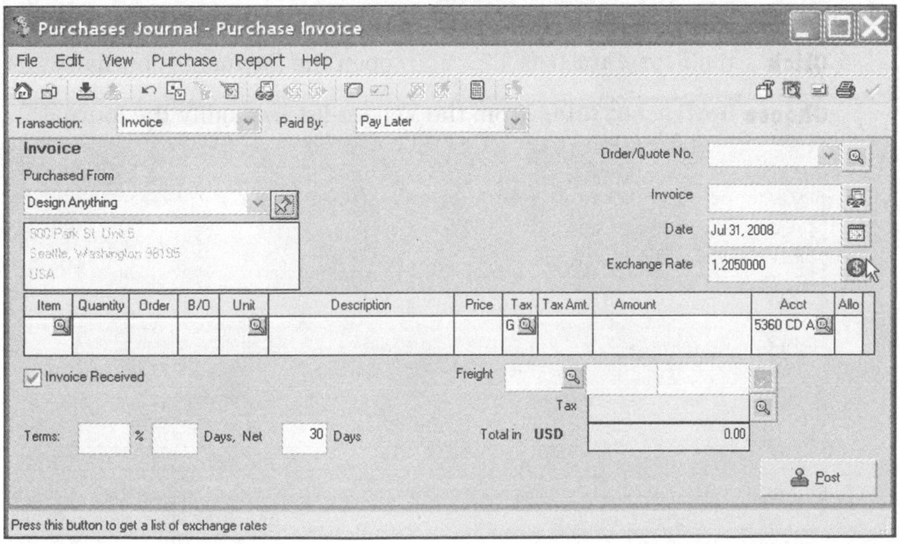

The invoice currency is now shown as USD and exchange rate fields are added. The default terms, expense account and tax code are also on the invoice.

NOTES

Leave all Tax Exempt settings at No in case other tax codes are required for taxes on other purchases or on freight.

NOTES

GST is paid directly to the Receiver General at the time the goods arrive in Canada. The foreign vendor does not collect these taxes.

To keep the exercises more basic, we do not show this aspect of the tax collection and instead include the GST on foreign purchases with the invoices.

Enter the **Invoice number**, **Date**, **Exchange Rate** and **Amount** to complete the invoice as shown:

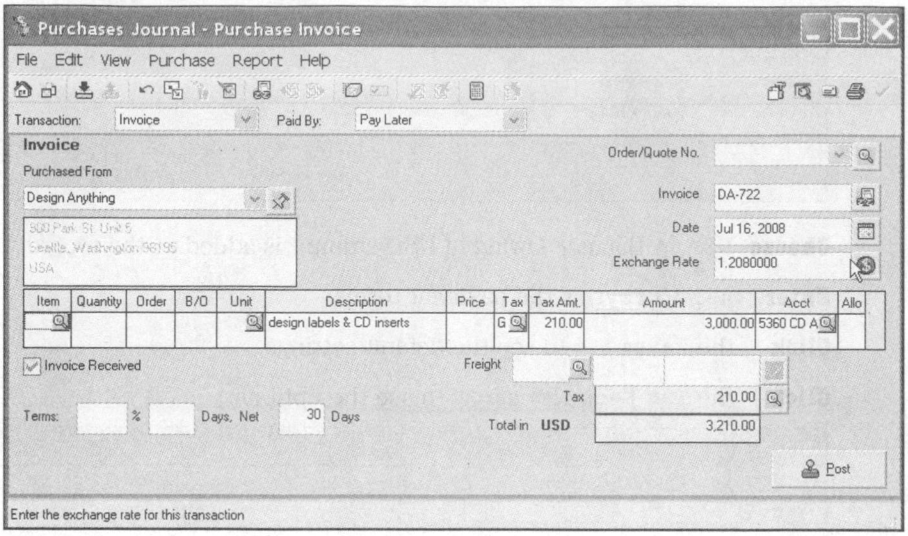

Review the entry before posting.

Choose the **Report menu** and **click Display Purchases Journal Entry**:

Maple Leaf Rags Inc.

07/16/08 (J14)	Foreign Amt.	Debits	Credits	Project
2670 GST Paid on Purchases	US$210.00	253.68	-	
5360 CD Assembly Material Costs	US$3,000.00	3,624.00	-	
2200 Accounts Payable	US$3,210.00	-	3,877.68	
		3,877.68	3,877.68	

1 United States Dollar equals 1.2080000 Canadian Dollars

BASIC VERSION
In the Basic version, you will see foreign amounts in a column with the heading USD Amount.

The only difference between this and other purchase entries is the addition of the USD currency amounts and exchange rate.

Close the **display** to return to the journal and **make corrections** if necessary.

Click **Post** [Post]. **Close** the **Purchases Journal**.

Return to the source documents and **enter** the **next group of transactions**.

Entering Payments to Foreign Vendors

Click the **Payments icon**  to open the Payments Journal.

Choose **Design Anything** from the Vendor list to modify the journal:

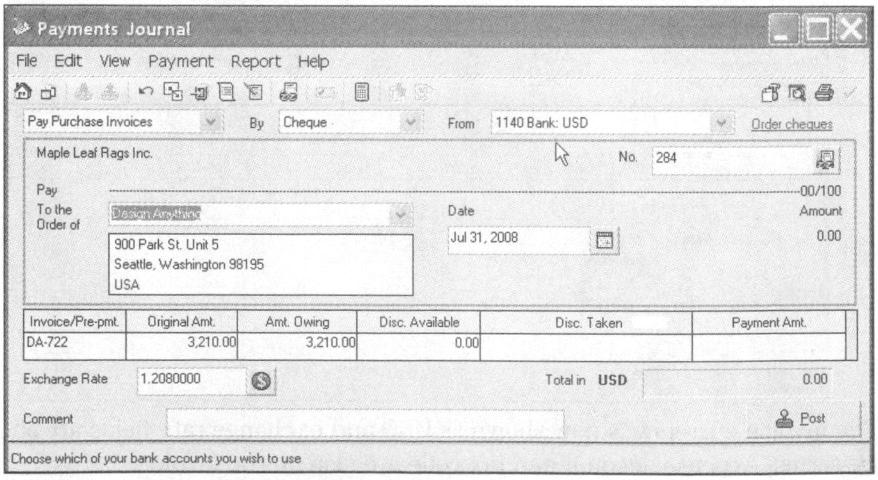

The outstanding invoice appears on the screen and the currency is marked as USD. An Exchange Rate field also becomes available.

Payments to US vendors are made from the USD bank account. This account is set up as the default bank account for foreign currency transactions. The cheque number is the next in sequence for this account.

Click the **Calendar icon** and **choose July 30** as the transaction date.

The Exchange Rate screen should open automatically because the exchange rate is out of date.

Type 1.204

Click **Make This The Default Rate For Jul 30, 2008**.

Click **OK** to return to the Payments Journal. The cursor is on the calendar icon.

Click the **Payment Amt. field**.

Press *tab* to accept the amount and complete the entry as shown:

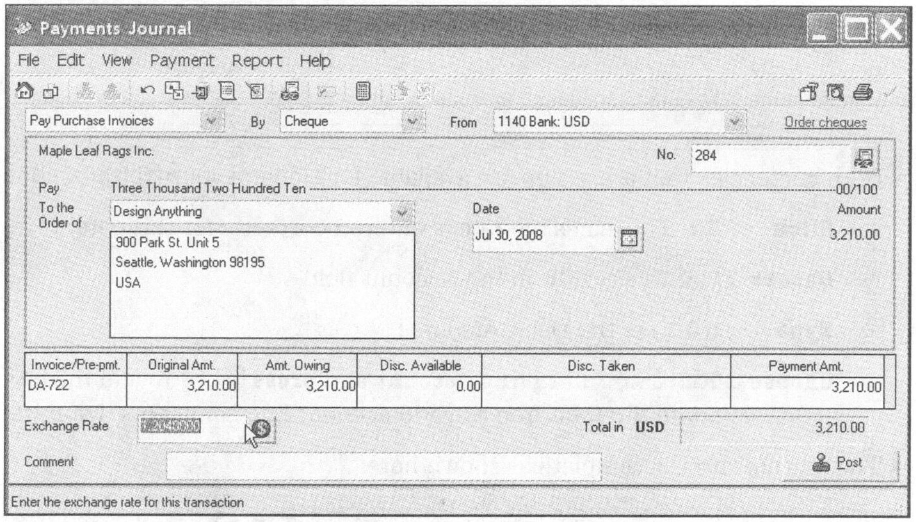

You should review the journal entry.

Choose the **Report menu** and **click Display Payments Journal Entry**:

Maple Leaf Rags Inc.					
07/30/08 (J19)		Foreign Amt.	Debits	Credits	Project
2200	Accounts Payable	US$3,210.00	3,877.68	-	
1140	Bank: USD	US$3,210.00	-	3,864.84	
4300	Exchange Rate Differences	-	-	12.84	
			3,877.68	3,877.68	
1 United States Dollar equals 1.2040000 Canadian Dollars					

A credit entry for *Exchange Rate Differences* appears because the exchange rate was higher on the day of the purchase, the date the purchase was recorded, than on the day of the payment. However, because this is a payment, Maple Leaf Rags has gained on the lag as shown by the credit entry — fewer Canadian dollars are needed to pay the same US dollar amount. As for other foreign currency transactions, amounts are given in both currencies, and the exchange rate is included.

Close the **display** to return to the journal. **Make corrections** if necessary.

Click **Post** Post. A message appears that the bank account is overdrawn:

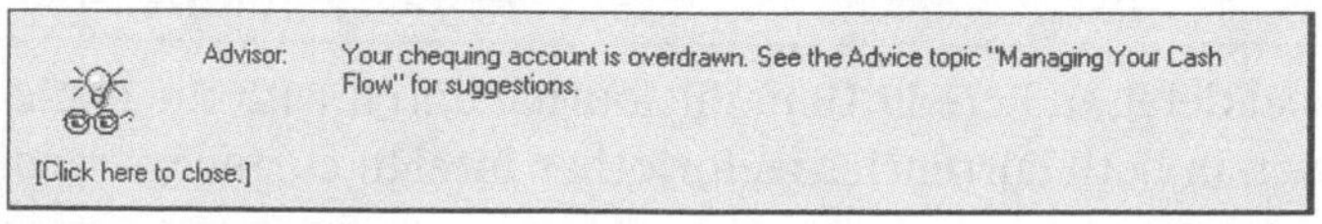

We will transfer funds to the USD account to cover the cheque before the vendor has a chance to cash it.

Click the **Advisor icon** to close the message and **close** the **Payments Journal**.

Transferring Foreign Funds

Click the **General Journal icon** to open the General Journal.

Type `Memo 47` (as the Source).

Type `July 30` (as the Date).

Type `Transfer $1000 USD to cover cheque` (as the Comment).

Click the **Currency list arrow** to see the currency options as shown:

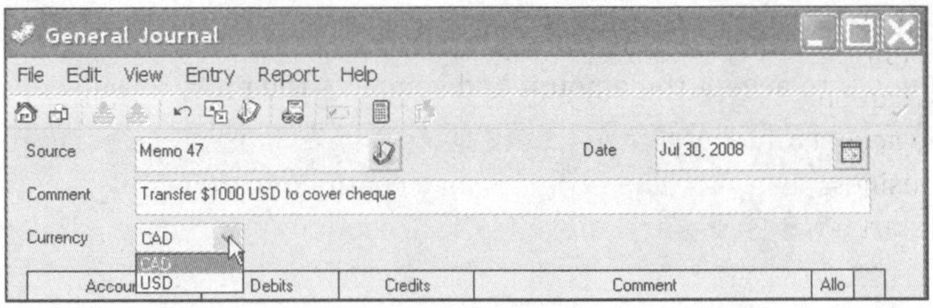

Both currencies that are set up are available for General Journal transactions.

Click **USD**. The exchange rate is entered correctly for this date.

Choose **1140 Bank: USD** in the Account field.

Type `1000` (as the Debit Amount).

Choose **1040 Bank: Chequing Account** and **press** *tab* to add the credit and update the total. You can add account line comments if you want.

The journal entry is complete as shown here:

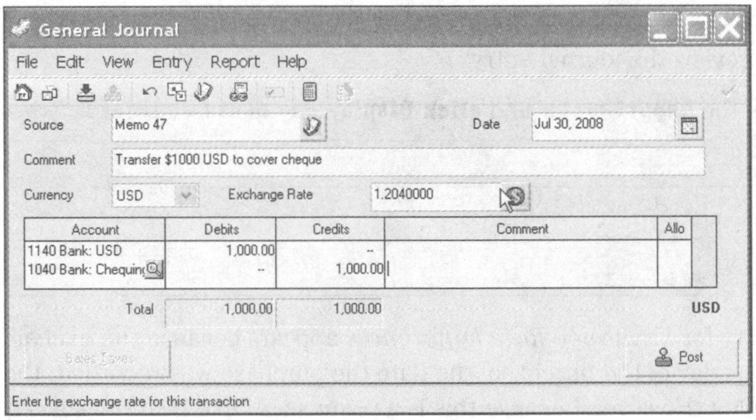

Choose the **Report menu** and **click Display General Journal Entry** to review the entry:

Maple Leaf Rags Inc.				
07/30/08 (J20)	Foreign Amt.	Debits	Credits	Project
1140 Bank: USD	US$1,000.00	1,204.00	-	
1040 Bank: Chequing Account	US$1,000.00	-	1,204.00	
		1,204.00	1,204.00	
1 United States Dollar equals 1.2040000 Canadian Dollars				

The entry is a typical debit and credit General Journal entry, with the exchange rate added and amounts given in both currencies as for other foreign currency transactions.

NOTES
The Exchange Rate window does not open because we have already entered a rate for July 30. You can still change the rate if needed by editing the amount in the Exchange Rate field.

WARNING!
You must choose USD as the currency for the transfer of funds. The CAD bank account will be available for the foreign currency transaction. If you choose CAD as the currency, you cannot access the USD bank account.

Close the **display** to return to the journal. **Make corrections** if needed.

Click **Post**  to save the transaction.

Close the **General Journal**.

Enter the **remaining transactions to September 30**. **Close** all **journals** to return to the Home window.

Creating an Accountant's Copy

Many businesses rely on professional accountants to assist them with their accounting. The accountants will check the data entered by the business for errors and make corrections. They also may add the adjusting entries required at the end of a fiscal period to bring the books up to date and to prepare for filing tax returns. The business then begins the new year with a complete and accurate data file.

Simply Accounting allows a data file to be saved as an accountant's copy. This backup data file can only be restored and opened in the Accountants' Edition of Simply Accounting. The accountant can add journal entries to the file that can be added back to the original business data file. The business may continue with day-to-day journal entry and even start a new fiscal period while the accountant is preparing the additional entries.

To create an accountant's copy,

Choose the File menu, then **choose Accountant's Copy** and **click Create Accountant's Copy** as shown:

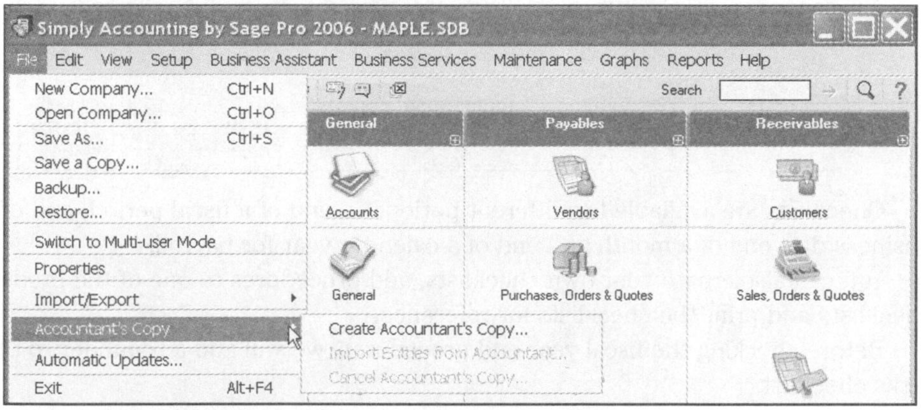

You will be asked to choose a location for the new backup file:

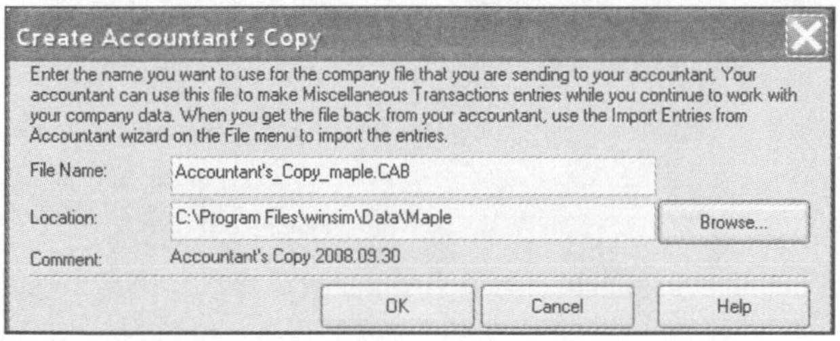

The default name for the file adds Accountant's_Copy_ to the original name so it will not be confused with your other backup files. The default location is the working folder for your current file.

To choose another folder, click Browse and click the folder you want to use. Enter a different name for the file if you want.

Click **OK** to begin making the specialized backup.

When the copy is complete, you will see the following information window:

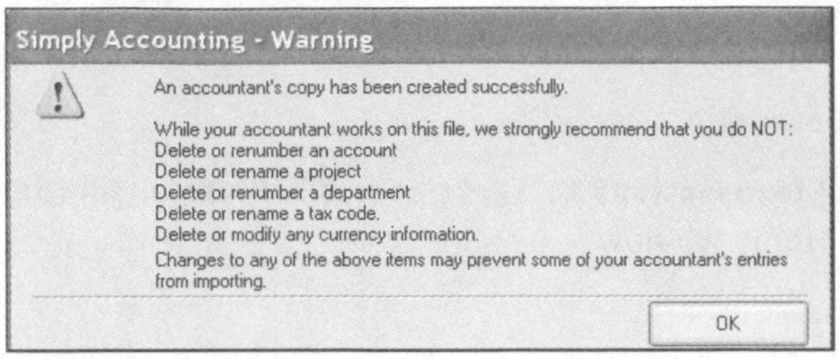

Read this message carefully as it warns you of the things you can and cannot do in your working file while the accountant is working with the accountant's copy of your file.

Click **OK** to return to your data file.

Monitoring Routine Activities

The end of September is the end of Bands' fiscal year. There are a number of steps to complete before beginning the new year. Simply Accounting provides assistance with these steps in its checklists.

Click the **Checklists tool** or **choose** the **Business Assistant menu** (in the Home window) and **click Checklists** to see the lists available:

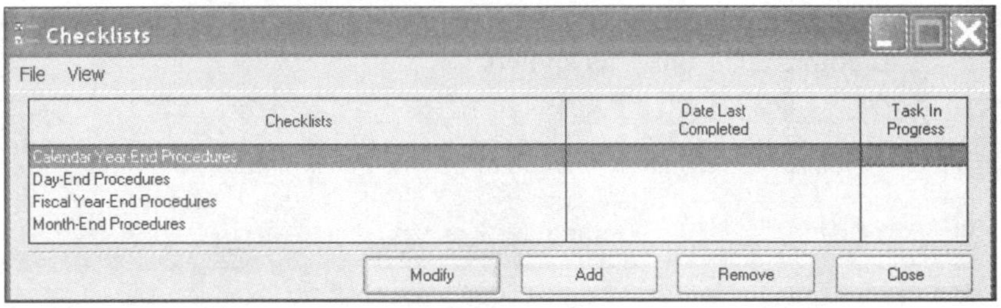

Checklists are available for different periods — end of a fiscal period, end of a business day, end of a month and end of a calendar year for payroll.

You can also create your own checklists, add procedures to one of the predefined checklists and print the checklists for reference.

Before checking the fiscal year-end procedures, we will add a reminder to the daily tasks checklist.

Click **Day-End Procedures** and then **click Modify** to open the list:

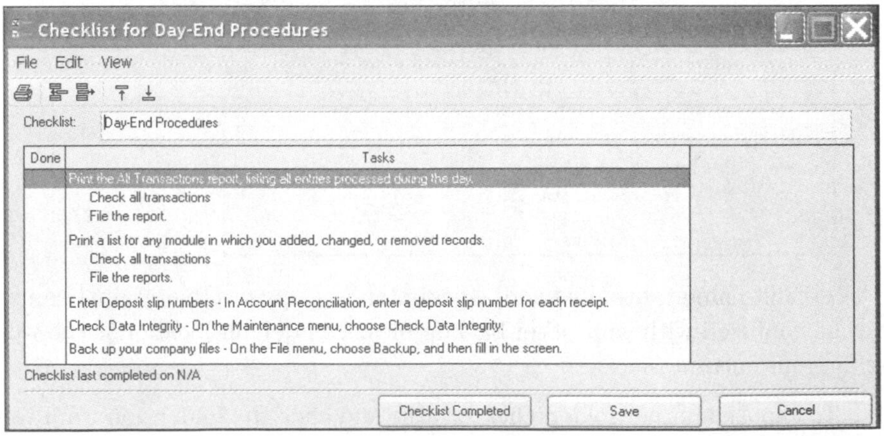

Each checklist can be customized for a company by using the tool buttons or the Edit menu items to insert activities, delete them or rearrange them.

Click the **Insert Item tool** or **choose** the **Edit menu** and **click Insert** to add a blank line at the top of the task list.

Press *tab* to advance to the Tasks field.

Type `Check bank balances for possible overdrafts`

Click **Save** to return to the Checklists window.

Double click **Fiscal Year-End Procedures** to see the checklist we need:

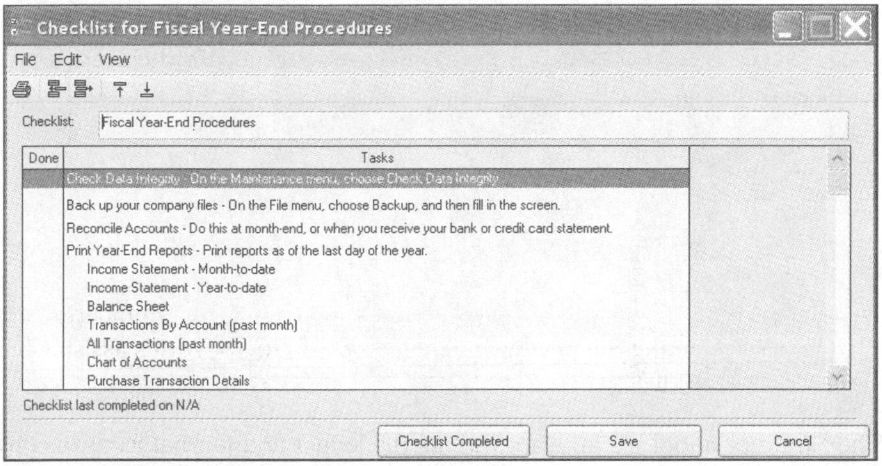

Maple Leaf Rags does not use the budgeting feature of the program so we can remove these tasks from the checklist.

Scroll down and **click Printing Budget Reports**.

Click the **Remove Item tool** or **choose** the **Edit menu** and **click Remove**.

Click **Yes** to confirm that you want to continue with the deletion.

Remove the **second budget-related task (Preparing This Year's Budget)**.

Click the **Print button** to print the checklist for reference.

Back up the **data files** and **print reports**. These are the most important elements on this list. Do not print reports for Payroll, Inventory, Projects or Budgets. You can remove these reports from the list if you want.

Click the **Done column** after completing a task. As you complete each activity a ✓ will be added to the Done column.

Click Save if you want to leave the list and return later. A ✓ will appear in the Task In Progress column on the Checklists screen.

Complete all the **tasks** listed, except printing the reports for the modules that are not used. After finishing all the activities,

Click **Checklist Completed**. The session date will be added to the Date Last Completed column on the Checklists screen.

Open the remaining checklists to see the tasks to be completed at the end of each month and at the start of a new calendar year. Print these lists for reference.

Click **Close** to leave the Checklists window when you have finished.

Start the **new fiscal year** on October 1, 2008.

NOTES
You cannot edit checklists in multi-user mode.

NOTES
Reconciling Accounts will be explained in Chapter 14 and Budgeting is covered in Chapter 13.

NOTES
In Chapter 14, we describe how to clear data from company files.

NOTES
Refer to page 107 for assistance with starting a new fiscal period.

Working with the Accountants' Edition

When the accountant opens the file you sent, it will be restored in the same version of Simply Accounting that you used. Only the General Journal, the one used for adjusting entries, is available to the accountant. The Home window for the Accountant's Copy file is shown here:

NOTES
The Accountants' Edition allows full access to regular data files created in the Basic, Pro and Premium versions. Only the Accountant's Copy data file is restricted.

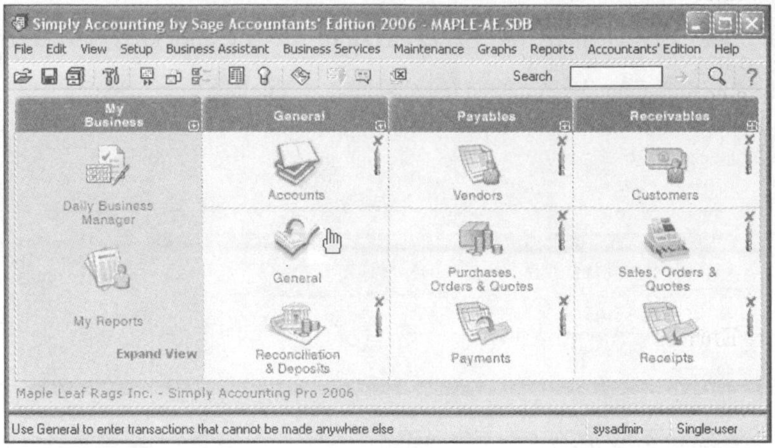

The No Edit symbol  appears with all the ledger and journal icons except for the General Journal. The accountant can view, but not change, the information in the other journals and ledgers.

After adding all the adjustments required, the new journal entries are exported to a text file. This option is available from the Accountants' Edition menu by choosing Accountant's Copy and then Export Entries for Client as shown:

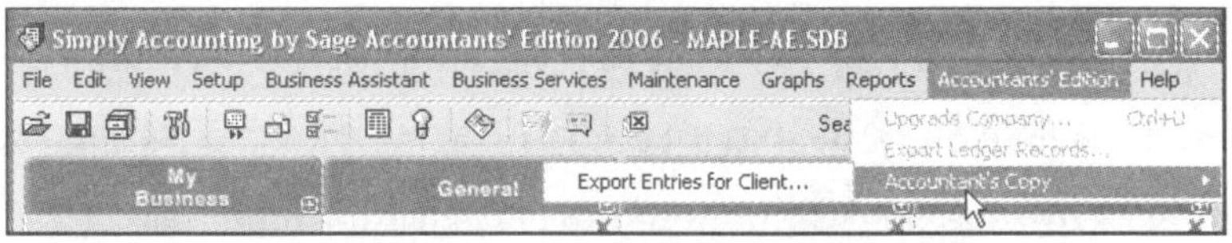

The exported text file is now sent back to you, the client.

Importing the Accountant's Journal Entries

When you receive the file from the accountant, you must import the journal entries to add them to your working file. Use the data file Maple\ACCOUNTANT\AE-maple for this step.

WARNING!
You must use the same file for creating the accountant's copy and importing the accountant's entries. You will not be able to import the accountant's entries to your own working file. You must use the special file we created that matches the imported entries.

Choose the File menu, then **choose Accountant's Copy** and **click Import Entries from Accountant** as shown:

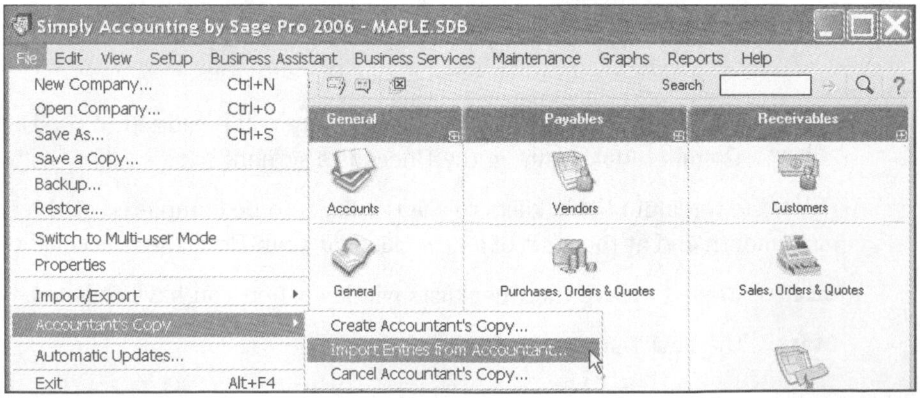

Once you create an accountant's copy, the other submenu options become available. The program stores the information that there is an outstanding accountant's copy for the file so you can import the journal entries later. This menu option remains available until the entries have been imported. You cannot create another accountant's copy while there is one outstanding. If you discover an error after you create the accountant's copy, you can cancel that version and then create a new accountant's copy. The option to Cancel Accountant's Copy is used for this purpose. After cancelling, the option to create becomes available again.

If you try to import the journal entries to a different file from the one used to create the accountant's copy, you will see the following error message:

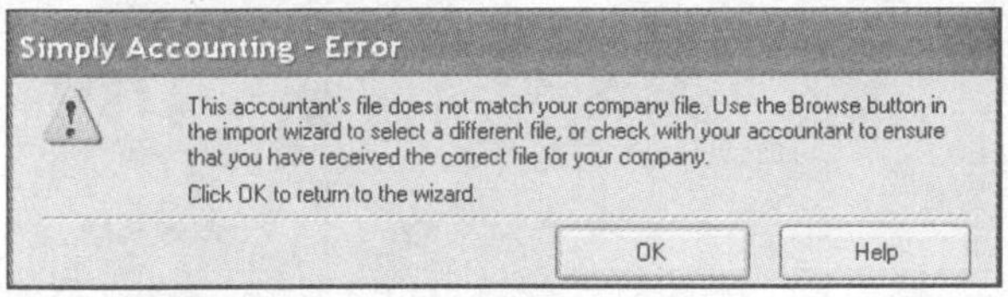

The Import Entries wizard begins:

Click **Next**:

You are asked to make a backup before proceeding. Since the step of importing entries cannot be reversed, you should back up the data file first.

Click **Backup** and follow the steps for creating a backup of the data file.

Click **Next**:

Now you must locate the file the accountant sent. We have added the file you need to the Maple folder where the other Maple data files are stored.

Click **Browse** and **locate** and **click** **Accountant's_Entries_maple-AE.TXT**.

Click **Open** and then **click** **Next**:

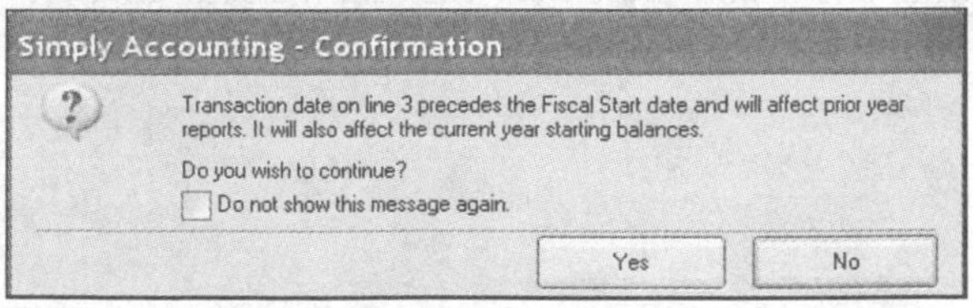

NOTES

The file you need is Accountant's_Entries_maple-AE.TXT. It is located in the ACCOUNTANT folder in the Maple folder that contains the other data files for Maple Leaf Rags.

This warning appears because the entries are dated in the previous fiscal year. We want to accept the dates the accountant used because they are correct and the entries should be added to the financial reports for the previous year. We need to allow all these entries and do not want the message to appear for each one.

NOTES

If your system settings do not allow transactions in the previous year, you must first change this setting. Refer to page 110.

Click **Do Not Show This Message Again**.

Click **Yes**:

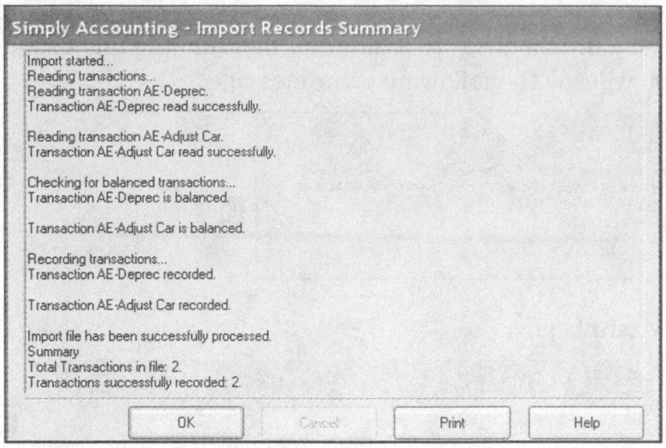

This summary of the imported transactions appears after the entries are added to your file.

Click **OK**:

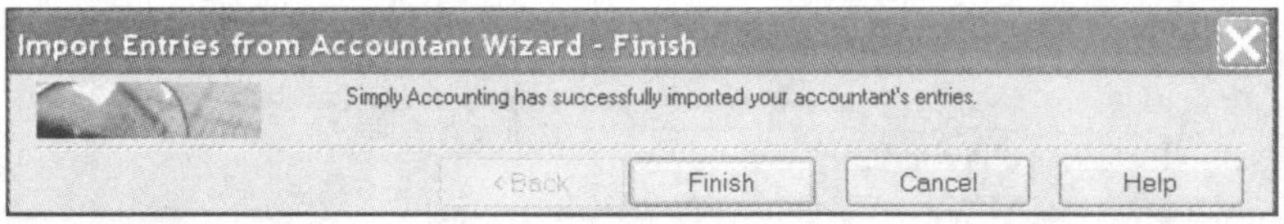

The process is now complete.

Click **Finish**.

If you display the General Journal report for September 30, you will see that the two entries that the accountant created have been added:

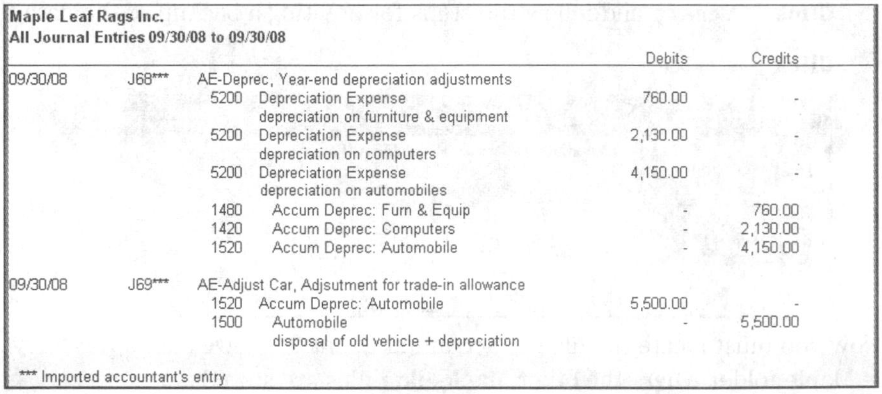

Maple Leaf Rags Inc.
All Journal Entries 09/30/08 to 09/30/08

				Debits	Credits
09/30/08	J68***		AE-Deprec, Year-end depreciation adjustments		
		5200	Depreciation Expense depreciation on furniture & equipment	760.00	-
		5200	Depreciation Expense depreciation on computers	2,130.00	-
		5200	Depreciation Expense depreciation on automobiles	4,150.00	-
		1480	Accum Deprec: Furn & Equip	-	760.00
		1420	Accum Deprec: Computers	-	2,130.00
		1520	Accum Deprec: Automobile	-	4,150.00
09/30/08	J69***		AE-Adjust Car, Adjsutment for trade-in allowance		
		1520	Accum Deprec: Automobile	5,500.00	-
		1500	Automobile disposal of old vehicle + depreciation	-	5,500.00

*** Imported accountant's entry

The journal entry numbers are marked *** to show that they were created outside the regular file by the accountant. The numbers may be out of sequence if you have added transactions yourself while the accountant was working with the file.

Displaying Exchange Rate Reports

When a business has foreign currency transactions, Simply Accounting will generate reports related to exchange rate gains and losses. The first report includes the gains or losses already realized or recorded because the payment has been made or received and the exchange rate difference is known.

> **NOTES**
> You cannot customize the Exchange Rate reports.

Choose the **Reports menu**, then **choose Financials** and **click Realized Exchange Gain/Loss** to see the report options:

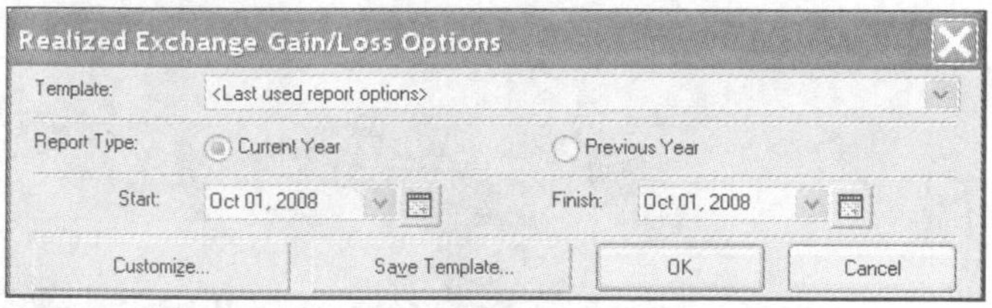

Enter the **dates** for the report and **click OK**.

Close the **display** when finished.

The second report includes the gains or losses that have not yet been realized or recorded because the payment has not yet been made but the exchange rate is known to have changed. When the payment is made or received, the actual gain may be different if the rate has changed again.

The report also revalues existing account balances and previous payments and receipts for the new exchange rate.

Choose the **Reports menu**, then **choose Financials** and **click Unrealized Exchange Gain/Loss** to see the report options:

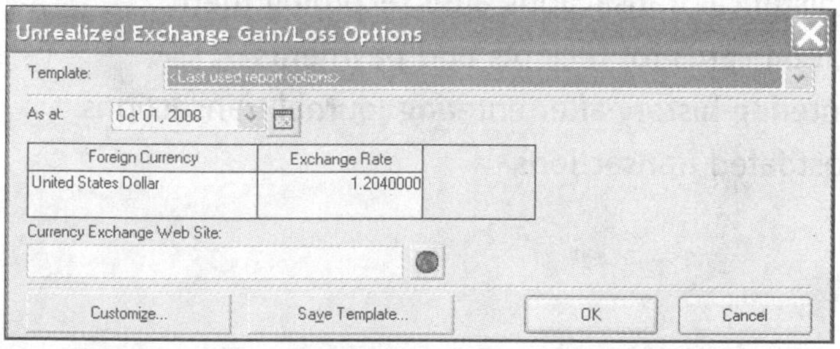

Enter the **date** for the report and an **Exchange Rate** for that date. **Click OK**.

Close the **display** when finished.

REVIEW

The Student CD-ROM with Data Files includes Review Questions and Supplementary Cases for this chapter including a case with stock transactions that can be completed in the General Journal.

CHAPTER NINE

Dorfmann**Design**

OBJECTIVES

After completing this chapter, you should be able to

- ***plan*** and ***design*** an accounting system for a small business
- ***prepare*** procedures for converting from a manual system
- ***understand*** the objectives of a computerized system
- ***create*** company files
- ***observe*** and ***understand*** linked accounts
- ***create*** linked accounts
- ***enter*** settings for foreign currency transactions
- ***set up*** accounts in the General, Payables and Receivables ledgers
- ***enter*** historical information for vendors and customers
- ***correct*** historical transactions after recording them
- ***set up*** credit cards for receipts and payments
- ***finish*** entering history after entering journal transactions
- ***enter*** postdated transactions

COMPANY INFORMATION

Company Profile

NOTES
Dorfmann Design
17 Tapestry Lane
Calgary, Alberta T3B 4U2
Tel: (403) 683-9145
Fax: (403) 685-8210
Business No.: 233 281 244

Dorfmann Design, owned by Desiree Dorfmann, has operated successfully in Calgary, Alberta for several years. As a master of space management, Dorfmann is invited to take on many different work assignments. She has designed boutiques in department stores, cosmetic counters and coffee bars; office space in banks; offices for professionals; countertop display areas in stores; shelving for display items, books or journals; and classroom and auditorium arrangements in colleges, universities and schools. She is frequently asked to convert unpleasant or unused spaces into attractive, inviting places by maximizing the usable space and making it open and comfortable while respecting the need for privacy. Sometimes she employs rich, textured fabrics in classical designs as well as sleek and modern materials to enhance an office or sales area. The end result always attracts attention.

Some clients ask only for her consultation, preferring to do the work themselves. For those clients she generates reports on how to maximize the use of space, or how to create attractive environments that encourage customers to buy. Most clients employ her because they understand the value of good design.

Dorfmann has accounts set up with her regular suppliers, some of whom offer discounts for early payment on a before-tax basis. These vendors provide office and computer supplies and materials for building scale models. An American vendor sells the specialized design software that she uses. She also has a maintenance contract with a local cleaning company. All purchases are subject to GST.

Most of Dorfmann's customers are in the Calgary region. She is negotiating with businesses in Wyoming, but so far none of these leads has led to confirmed contracts. Canadian customers pay GST on all services provided and are offered an after-tax discount of 1 percent if they pay within five days. Overdue accounts are subject to interest charges at the rate of 1.5 percent after 30 days.

On March 31, she gathered the following business information to convert her accounting records to Simply Accounting:

- Business Information
- Chart of Accounts
- Income Statement
- Balance Sheet
- Trial Balance
- Vendor Information
- Customer Information
- Accounting Procedures

BUSINESS INFORMATION

DORFMANN DESIGN

COMPANY INFORMATION

Address: 17 Tapestry Lane
Calgary, Alberta T3B 4U2
Phone: (403) 683-9145
Fax: (403) 685-8210
Business No.: 233 281 244
Fiscal Start: Jan. 1, 2008
Fiscal End: June 30, 2008
Earliest Transaction: April 1, 2008

PRINTERS

Select printer for
Reports:
Other:

SETUP USER PREFERENCES

Use Accounting Terms
Open Ledgers & Journals with Single Click
Automatically Save Changes to Records
Show List Buttons

VIEW SETTINGS

Hide Modules:
Payroll, Inventory & Services, Project
Daily Business Manager: turn off
Checklists: turn off
Show Select Company Window at Startup
My Business Tab: do not show

SYSTEM SETTINGS

Store Invoice Lookup Details
Allow Future Transactions
Warn if more than 7 days in future
Warn if Accounts Not Balanced
Backup Weekly

GENERAL SETTINGS

no changes

PAYABLES SETTINGS

Aging Periods: 15, 30, 45 days
Discounts before Tax: Yes

RECEIVABLES SETTINGS

Aging Periods: 5, 15, 30 days
Interest Charges: 1.5% after 30 days
Statements Include Invoices for 31 days
Payment Terms: 1/5, n/15 after tax
Discounts before Tax: No
Default Tax Code: G

FORMS SETTINGS (NEXT NUMBER)

Sales Invoices No. 44
Sales Quotes No. 41
Receipts No. 25
Customer Deposits No. 12
Purchase Orders No. 16

COMMENTS

Sales Invoice: Interest @ 1.5% per month charged on accounts over 30 days.

FOREIGN CURRENCY

Currency: USD – United States Dollars
Tracking Account: 5030
Exchange Rate on 04/01/08: 1.177

BANK ACCOUNTS: NEXT CHEQUE NO.

Bank: Chequing 65
Bank: USD 104

TAXES

Taxes: GST 7%
Code: G - GST @ 7%

CREDIT CARD INFORMATION

Card Accepted: Visa
Discount Fee: 2.9%
Expense Account: 5020
Asset Account: 1070

Card Accepted: MasterCard
Discount Fee: 2.7%
Expense Account: 5020
Asset Account: 1080

Card Used: Visa
Payable Account: 2160
Expense Account: 5020

CHART OF ACCOUNTS

DORFMANN DESIGN

ASSETS
1000 CURRENT ASSETS [H]
1010 Test Balance Account
1060 Bank: Chequing [A]
1070 Bank: Visa [A]
1080 Bank: MasterCard [A]
1090 Bank: USD [A]
1100 Net Bank [S]
1200 Accounts Receivable
1210 Prepaid Insurance
1220 Model Parts Inventory
1230 Computer Supplies
1240 Office Supplies
1250 Software
1280 Purchase Prepayments
1290 TOTAL CURRENT ASSETS [T]

1400 OFFICE & EQUIPMENT [H]
1410 Computer Equipment
1420 Design Equipment
1430 Furniture & Fixtures ▶
▶1440 Motor Vehicle
1450 Office Condominium
1490 TOTAL OFFICE & EQUIPMENT [T]

LIABILITIES
2000 CURRENT LIABILITIES [H]
2100 Bank Loan
2160 Credit Card Payable
2200 Accounts Payable
2220 Prepaid Sales and Deposits
2650 GST Charged on Services [A]
2670 GST Paid on Purchases [A]
2750 GST Owing (Refund) [S]
2790 TOTAL CURRENT LIABILITIES [T]

2800 LONG TERM LIABILITIES [H]
2850 Mortgage Payable
2890 TOTAL LONG TERM LIABILITIES [T] ▶

▶**EQUITY**
3000 OWNER'S EQUITY [H]
3560 D. Dorfmann, Capital
3650 Current Earnings [X]
3690 UPDATED CAPITAL [T]

REVENUE
4000 GENERAL REVENUE [H]
4020 Revenue from Design
4040 Revenue from Consulting
4060 Sales Discounts
4100 Interest Revenue
4290 TOTAL REVENUE [T]

EXPENSE
5000 OPERATING EXPENSES [H]
5010 Bank Charges
5020 Credit Card Fees ▶
▶5030 Exchange Rate Differences
5040 Purchase Discounts
5050 Delivery Expenses
5060 Hydro Expense
5070 Maintenance Services
5100 Model Parts Used
5110 Computer Supplies Used
5120 Office Supplies Used
5150 Insurance Expense
5160 Telephone Expense
5200 Loan Interest Expense
5210 Mortgage Interest Expense
5990 TOTAL OPERATING EXPENSES [T]

NOTES: The Chart of Accounts includes all accounts. Account types are marked for all subgroup Accounts [A], Subgroup totals [S], Heading accounts [H], Total accounts [T] and the type X account. All other unmarked accounts are postable Group accounts.

INCOME STATEMENT

DORFMANN DESIGN

January 1 to March 31, 2008

Revenue		
4000	GENERAL REVENUE	
4020	Revenue from Design	$38 000
4040	Revenue from Consulting	7 400
4060	Sales Discounts	−400
4100	Interest Revenue	371
4290	TOTAL REVENUE	$45 371
	TOTAL REVENUE	$45 371 ▶

▶ Expenses		
5000	OPERATING EXPENSES	
5010	Bank Charges	$ 225
5020	Credit Card Fees	600
5030	Exchange Rate Differences	−10
5040	Purchase Discounts	−300
5050	Delivery Expenses	180
5060	Hydro Expense	750
5070	Maintenance Services	1 391
5100	Model Parts Used	1 600
5110	Computer Supplies Used	1 200
5120	Office Supplies Used	1 150
5150	Insurance Expense	600
5160	Telephone Expense	400
5200	Loan Interest Expense	625
5210	Mortgage Interest Expense	6 000
5990	TOTAL OPERATING EXPENSES	$ 14 411
	TOTAL EXPENSE	$ 14 411
	NET INCOME (LOSS)	$30 960

BALANCE SHEET

DORFMANN DESIGN

March 31, 2008

Assets			
1000	CURRENT ASSETS		
1060	Bank: Chequing	$ 26 078	
1070	Bank: Visa	1 950	
1080	Bank: MasterCard	1 060	
1090	Bank: USD ($2 720 USD)	3 200	
1100	Net Bank		$ 32 288
1200	Accounts Receivable		3 920
1210	Prepaid Insurance		1 800
1220	Model Parts Inventory		4 000
1230	Computer Supplies		1 500
1240	Office Supplies		1 000
1250	Software		2 000
1290	TOTAL CURRENT ASSETS		$ 46 508
1400	OFFICE & EQUIPMENT		
1410	Computer Equipment		12 000
1420	Design Equipment		8 000
1430	Furniture & Fixtures		4 000
1440	Motor Vehicle		50 000
1450	Office Condominium		100 000
1490	TOTAL OFFICE & EQUIPMENT		$174 000
TOTAL ASSETS			$220 508 ▶

▶ Liabilities			
2000	CURRENT LIABILITIES		
2100	Bank Loan		$ 25 000
2160	Credit Card Payable		1 010
2200	Accounts Payable		9 301
2650	GST Charged on Services	$1 530	
2670	GST Paid on Purchases	–840	
2750	GST Owing (Refund)		690
2790	TOTAL CURRENT LIABILITIES		$ 36 001
2800	LONG TERM LIABILITIES		
2850	Mortgage Payable		75 000
2890	TOTAL LONG TERM LIABILITIES		$ 75 000
TOTAL LIABILITIES			$ 111 001
Equity			
3000	OWNER'S EQUITY		
3560	D. Dorfmann, Capital		$ 78 547
3650	Current Earnings		30 960
3690	UPDATED CAPITAL		$ 109 507
TOTAL EQUITY			$ 109 507
LIABILITIES AND EQUITY			$220 508

TRIAL BALANCE

DORFMANN DESIGN

March 31, 2008

		Debit	Credit
1060	Bank: Chequing	$ 26 078	
1070	Bank: Visa	1 950	
1080	Bank: MasterCard	1 060	
1090	Bank: USD ($2 720 USD)	3 200	
1200	Accounts Receivable	3 920	
1210	Prepaid Insurance	1 800	
1220	Model Parts Inventory	4 000	
1230	Computer Supplies	1 500	
1240	Office Supplies	1 000	
1250	Software	2 000	
1410	Computer Equipment	12 000	
1420	Design Equipment	8 000	
1430	Furniture & Fixtures	4 000	
1440	Motor Vehicle	50 000	
1450	Office Condominium	100 000	
2100	Bank Loan		$ 25 000
2160	Credit Card Payable		1 010
2200	Accounts Payable		9 301
2650	GST Charged on Services		1 530
2670	GST Paid on Purchases	840	
2850	Mortgage Payable		75 000 ▶

		Debit	Credit
▶ 3560	D. Dorfmann, Capital		78 547
4020	Revenue from Design		38 000
4040	Revenue from Consulting		7 400
4060	Sales Discounts	400	
4100	Interest Revenue		371
5010	Bank Charges	225	
5020	Credit Card Fees	600	
5030	Exchange Rate Differences		10
5040	Purchase Discounts		300
5050	Delivery Expenses	180	
5060	Hydro Expense	750	
5070	Maintenance Services	1 391	
5100	Model Parts Used	1 600	
5110	Computer Supplies Used	1 200	
5120	Office Supplies Used	1 150	
5150	Insurance Expense	600	
5160	Telephone Expense	400	
5200	Loan Interest Expense	625	
5210	Mortgage Interest Expense	6 000	
		$236 469	$236 469

VENDOR INFORMATION

DORFMANN DESIGN

Vendor Name (Contact)	Address	Phone No. Fax No.	E-mail Web Site Tax ID	Terms Account	YTD Purchases (YTD Payments) Tax Code
Alberta Energy Corp. (Con Edison)	50 Watts Rd. Suite 800 Calgary, Alberta T3G 5K8	Tel 1: (403) 755-6000 Tel 2: (403) 755-3997 Fax: (403) 754-7201	accounts@aeg.ca www.aeg.ca 459 021 643	net 10 5060	$802 ($802) G
Designers Den (Art Masters)	166 Blackfoot Trail Calgary, Alberta T3P 5P4	Tel: (403) 459-3917 Fax: (403) 459-6200	artm@artful.com www.artful.com 562 553 400	2/10, n/30 (before tax) 1420	 G
DesignMaster Software (Dee Collage)	233 Crowchild Trail Casper, Wyoming 82601 USA	Tel: (561) 566-3754 Fax: (561) 566-5623	deecoll@dms.com www.dms.com	1/5, n/30 (before tax) 1250	 G
Maintenance & More (Rehab Major)	51 Bragg Creek Rd. Calgary, Alberta T3C 4N3	Tel: (403) 762-7622 Fax: (403) 762-9888	RMajor@mandm.com www.mandm.com 712 300 807	net 15 5070	$1 177 ($1 177) G
Models to Scale (Bill Derr)	649 4th Street Calgary, Alberta T4P 5D6	Tel: (403) 477-5997 Fax: (403) 478-8103	billd@models.com www.models.com 923 488 561	2/10, n/30 (before tax)	 G
Purolator Delivery (Cam Carter)	598 Bow River Rd. Calgary, Alberta T4T 2M1	Tel 1: (403) 458-2144 Tel 2: (888) 458-2144	 www.purolator.com 822 012 906	net 1 5050	$193 ($193) G
Receiver General for Canada	Sudbury Tax Services Office PO Box 20004 Sudbury, Ontario P3A 6B4	Tel 1: (800) 561-7761 Tel 2: (800) 959-2221	 www.cra-arc.gc.ca	net 1 2650	 ($790) No tax
Staples Business Depot (Joel)	60 Richmond Rd. Calgary, Alberta T4G 2T2	Tel: (403) 761-6288 Fax: (403) 769-5532	joel@businessdep.com www.businessdep.com	net 10 1240	$1 926 ($1 926) G
Western Bell (Sal Fone)	74 Sounder Ave. Calgary, Alberta T5L 4G2	Tel 1: (403) 755-3255 Tel 2: (403) 755-5721	accounts@bell.ca www.bell.ca 492 304 590	net 1 5160	$428 ($428) G

OUTSTANDING VENDOR INVOICES

DORFMANN DESIGN

Vendor Name	Terms	Date	Inv/Chq No.	Amount	Tax	Total
Designers Den	2/10, n/30 (before tax)	Mar. 26/08	DD-4502	$2 500	$175	$2 675
		Mar. 26/08	Chq 62			2 210
	2/10, n/30 (before tax)	Mar. 28/08	DD-4630	500	35	535
			Balance owing			$1 000
DesignMaster Software	1/5, n/30 (before tax)	Mar. 13/08	DMS-234	USD$1 575	USD$110.25	CAD$1 982
Maintenance & More	net 15	Mar. 24/08	MM-211			$107
	net 15	Mar. 31/08	MM-242			107
			Balance owing			$214
Models to Scale	2/10, n/30 (before tax)	Mar. 25/08	MS-376	$4 000	$280	$4 280
		Mar. 25/08	Chq 59			2 000
	2/10, n/30 (before tax)	Mar. 28/08	MS-453	2 000	140	2 140
			Balance owing			$4 420
				Grand Total		$7 616

CUSTOMER INFORMATION

DORFMANN DESIGN

Customer Name (Contact)	Address	Phone No. Fax No.	E-mail Web Site	Terms Revenue Acct Tax Code	YTD Sales (Credit Limit) Customer Since
Alberta Heritage Bank (A. Spender)	306 Revenue Road Fourth Floor Okotoks, Alberta T0L 1T3	Tel 1: (403) 744-5900 Tel 2: (403) 744-6345 Fax: (403) 744-5821	spender@heritagebank.com www.heritagebank.com	1/5, n/15 (after tax) 4020 G	$3 210 ($5 000) Jan. 1/08
Banff Condominiums (R.T. House)	99 Main Street Banff, Alberta T0L 0C0	Tel: (403) 764-3884 Fax: (403) 764-3917	rthouse@banffcondos.ca www.banffcondos.ca	1/5, n/15 (after tax) 4020 G	($5 000) Jan. 1/08
Calgary Arms Hotel (Enda Lodge)	601 Regiment Road Calgary, Alberta T4G 5H4	Tel 1: (403) 622-4456 Tel 2: (877) 623-9100 Fax: (403) 622-5188	enda@calgarms.com www.calgarms.com	1/5, n/15 (after tax) 4020 G	$7 918 ($5 000) Apr. 1/08
Calgary District School Board (Seconde Grader)	88 Learnex Avenue 8th Floor Calgary, Alberta T3C 4B6	Tel 1: (403) 788-3000 Tel 2: (403) 788-7107 Fax: (403) 788-3327	sg@cdsb.ca www.cdsb.ca	1/5, n/15 (after tax) 4020 G	$8 560 ($5 000) Jul. 1/04
Glitter Jewellers (Di Monde)	60 Ruby Street Calgary, Alberta T4C 2G6	Tel: (403) 745-6181 Fax: (403) 745-6297	di@glitter.com www.glitter.com	1/5, n/15 (after tax) 4020 G	$5 350 ($5 000) Apr. 1/07
Lougheed, Klein & Assoc - Lawyers (Bill Bigger)	121 Advocate Ave. Suite 300 Calgary, Alberta T4D 2P7	Tel 1: (403) 398-4190 Tel 2: (403) 377-2534 Fax: (403) 377-3799	bbigger@LKlawyers.com www.LKlawyers.com	1/5, n/15 (after tax) 4020 G	$10 700 ($5 000) Jul. 1/05
Passions Dept Store (Mann E. Kinn)	44 Highlife Ave. Bragg Creek, Alberta T0L 0K0	Tel: (403) 762-8662 Fax: (403) 763-9115	www.passions.com	1/5, n/15 (after tax) 4020 G	$6 420 ($5 000) Jan. 1/04

OUTSTANDING CUSTOMER INVOICES

DORFMANN DESIGN

Customer Name	Terms	Date	Inv/Chq No.	Amount	Total
Alberta Heritage Bank	1/5, n/15 (after tax)	Mar. 23/08	38	$3 210	
		Mar. 23/08	Chq 6754	1 400	
			Balance owing		$1 810
Banff Condominiums	1/5, n/15 (after tax)	Mar. 28/08	39	$2 140	
		Mar. 28/08	Chq 4388	1 100	
	1/5, n/15 (after tax)	Mar. 31/08	41	1 070	
			Balance owing		$2 110
				Grand Total	$3 920

Accounting Procedures

Open-Invoice Accounting for Payables and Receivables

The open-invoice method of accounting for invoices allows the business to keep track of each individual invoice and any partial payments made against it. This method is in contrast to methods that only keep track of the outstanding balance by combining all invoice balances owed to a vendor or by a customer. Simply Accounting uses the open-

NOTES

Provincial sales taxes are not levied in Alberta.

Most bank services and other financial institution services are exempt from GST collection.

invoice method. When invoices are fully paid, they should be removed periodically after statements are received from the vendor or sent to the customers.

The Goods and Services Tax: Remittances

Dorfmann uses the regular method for GST remittances. GST collected from customers is recorded as a liability in *GST Charged on Services*. GST paid to vendors is recorded in *GST Paid on Purchases* as a decrease in the liability. The balance, or request for refund, is remitted to the Receiver General for Canada by the last day of the month for the previous month.

Sales of Services

Accounts are set up for several customers and sales quotes are prepared and sales orders accepted from regular and new customers on request. Other customers pay for their purchases immediately by cash, cheque or credit card. Separate bank accounts are set up for credit card deposits. You can enter transactions for cash and credit card customers by choosing One-Time Customer and typing the name of the customer in the Address field or by typing the customer's name in the Name field and choosing the Quick Add option.

For cash sales, the program will debit *Bank: Chequing* (or *Bank: Visa* or *MasterCard* for credit card payments) instead of the *Accounts Receivable* control account.

Purchases

Most regular vendors have given Dorfmann credit terms, including some discounts for early payment. Purchase quotes and purchase orders are also a regular part of dealing with these vendors. Some purchases are accompanied by immediate payment, usually by cheque or credit card. Cheque payments are preferred because the cancelled cheques become part of the business records. Enter the cash transaction for purchases from new vendors in the Payments Journal as an Other Payment. Choose the appropriate "paid by" option; choose One-Time Vendor from the Vendor list; type the vendor's name in the Address field. You can also type the name in the Vendor field and choose Quick Add.

For cash purchases paid by cash or cheque, the program will credit *Bank: Chequing* instead of the *Accounts Payable* control account. For credit card purchases, *Credit Card Payable* is credited. All other accounts for this transaction will be appropriately debited and credited. Dorfmann pays her credit card balance in full each month. Refer to Chapter 8, page 258, for further information about credit card payments.

Discounts

Dorfmann Design offers a 1 percent discount to account customers if they settle their accounts within five days. Full payment is requested within 15 days. These payment terms are set up as defaults. When the receipt is entered, if the discount is still available, the program will show the amount of the discount and the net amount owing automatically. Discounts are not allowed on partial payments or on cash purchases paid by cheque or credit card. All sales discounts are calculated on after-tax amounts.

Some vendors also offer discounts, calculated on the amounts before taxes, for early settlement of accounts. Again, when the terms are entered for the vendor and full payment is made before the discount period expires, the program will display the pretax discount as available and automatically calculate a net balance owing. Payment terms vary from vendor to vendor.

INSTRUCTIONS

1. **Set up** the **company accounts** using the Business Information, Chart of Accounts, Balance Sheet, Income Statement, Trial Balance and Vendor and Customer Information provided for March 31, 2008. Detailed instructions to assist you in setting up the company accounts follow. Source documents begin on page 341 after the setup instructions.
2. If you prefer to enter the source documents before setting up the data files, you can use the dorfmann.sdb file in the SETUP\DORFMANN folder (inside the Data folder). In this way, you will become familiar with the account structure, and the setup may be easier to complete.
3. **Enter** the **transactions** beginning on page 341 in Simply Accounting using the Chart of Accounts, Vendor Information, Customer Information and Accounting Procedures.
4. **Print** the **reports and graphs** indicated on the following printing form after you have completed your entries:

REPORTS

Lists
- ☐ Chart of Accounts
- ☐ Account List
- ☐ Vendors
- ☐ Customers

Journals
- ☑ All Journals (by date): April 1 to June 15
- ☐ General
- ☐ Purchases
- ☐ Payments
- ☐ Sales
- ☐ Receipts

Financials
- ☑ Comparative Balance Sheet: April 1 and April 30, difference in percentage
- ☑ Income Statement: January 1 to April 30
- ☑ Trial Balance: April 30
- ☑ General Ledger accounts: 1060 4020 4040 from April 1 to April 30
- ☑ Cash Flow Projection Detail Report for account 1060 for 30 days
- ☐ Statement of Cash Flows

Tax
- ☑ GST Report April 1 to April 30

Banking
- ☐ Cheque Log Report

Payables
- ☐ Vendor Aged
- ☐ Aged Overdue Payables
- ☐ Pending Purchase Orders

Receivables
- ☐ Customer Aged
- ☐ Aged Overdue Receivables
- ☐ Pending Sales Orders
- ☐ Customer Statements

Mailing Labels
- ☐ Labels

Management Reports
- ☐ Ledger

GRAPHS
- ☐ Payables by Aging Period
- ☐ Payables by Vendor
- ☐ Receivables by Aging Period
- ☐ Receivables by Customer
- ☐ Sales vs Receivables
- ☐ Receivables Due vs Payables Due
- ☐ Revenues by Account
- ☐ Expenses by Account
- ☑ Expenses and Net Profit as % of Revenue

NOTES: Include foreign amounts and corrections in reports when these are available.

KEYSTROKES FOR SETUP

Creating Company Files

For Dorfmann Design, we will create the company files from scratch rather than use one of the starter files. Once we create the files and define the defaults, we will add the accounts, define linked accounts for the General, Payables and Receivables ledgers and create vendor and customer records.

Start the **Simply Accounting program**. You should see the Welcome To Simply Accounting, Select Company window:

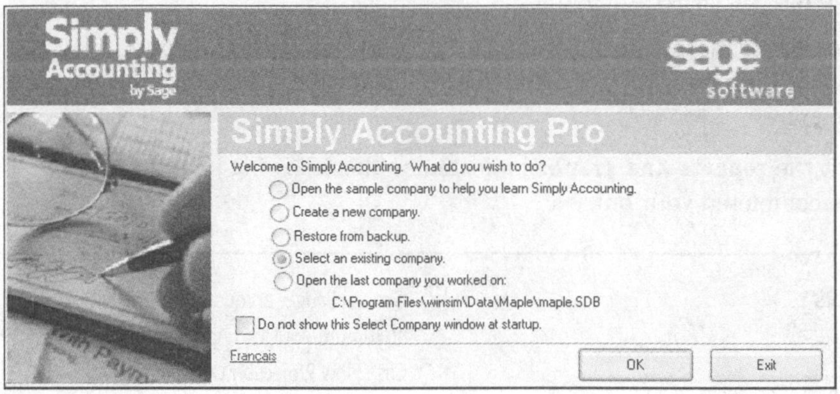

Click **Create A New Company**.

Click **OK**.

You will see the Setup wizard welcome screen:

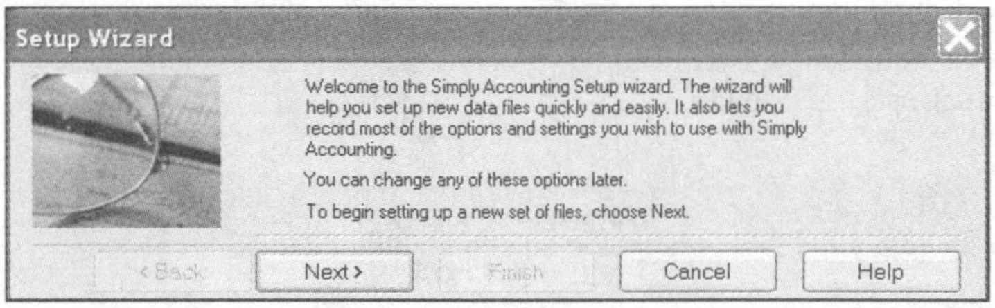

This screen invites you to use the Setup wizard to begin the company setup.

Click **Next** to continue:

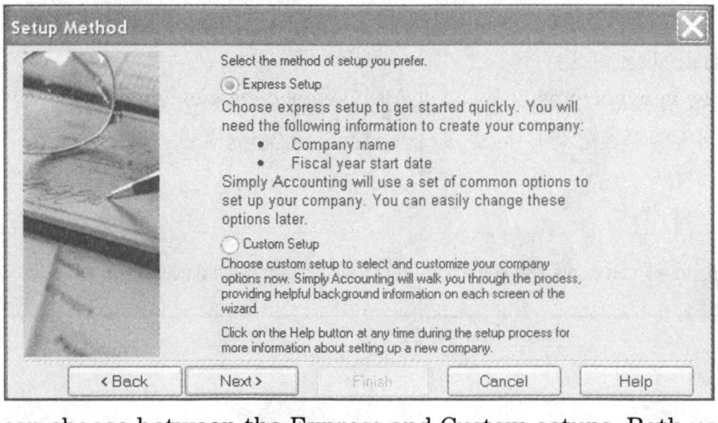

You can choose between the Express and Custom setups. Both use the Setup wizard but the Express Setup has fewer steps, and you must add the remaining details on your own. We will not be using the Setup wizard, and the initial steps are the same for both methods.

Click **Express Setup**. **Click Next** to continue:

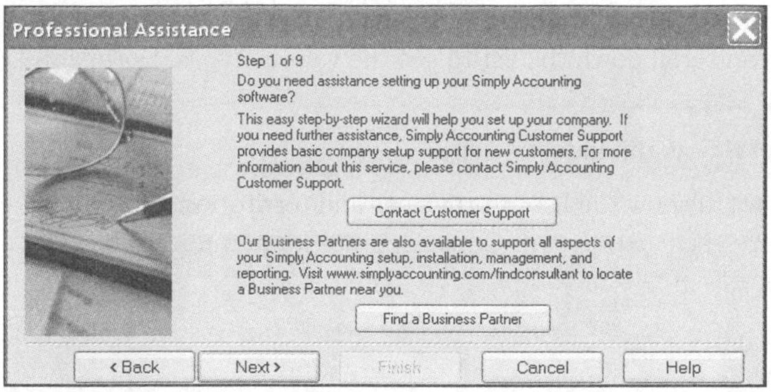

If you want assistance with setting up the data files in Simply Accounting or using the program, the Find A Business Partner button will connect you to a Web site to help locate trained and certified consultants in your region.

Click **Next** to continue:

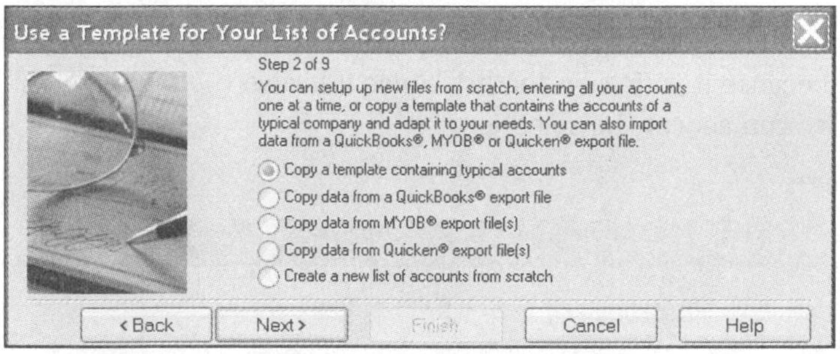

You can use one of the many templates that came with the program, start from scratch to create the data files or copy data from another program. Because our setup is relatively small and we want to show all the stages of the setup, we will start from scratch. This approach allows us to show all the options available for each stage.

Click **Create A New List Of Accounts From Scratch**:

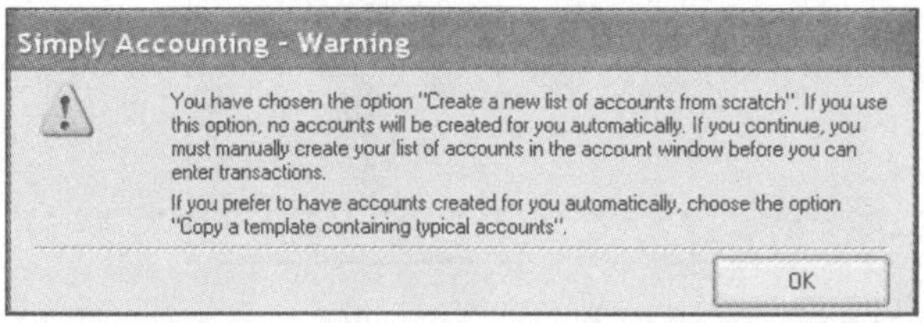

This message reminds you that your selection requires you to create all the accounts on your own.

Click **OK** to return to the template options and then **click Next** to continue:

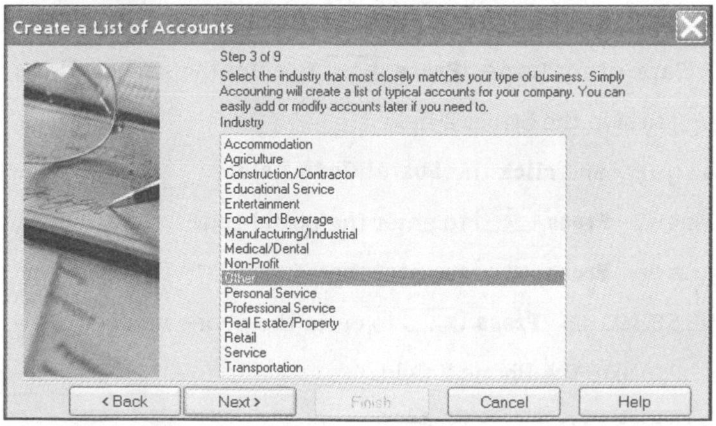

At this stage you should choose the type of business that best describes your company. This selection will determine some of the default settings when you use the Setup wizard. You can scroll down the list to see the various types. Dorfmann Design is a service business.

Click **Service** as the Industry type.

Click **Next** to show the list of provinces and territories:

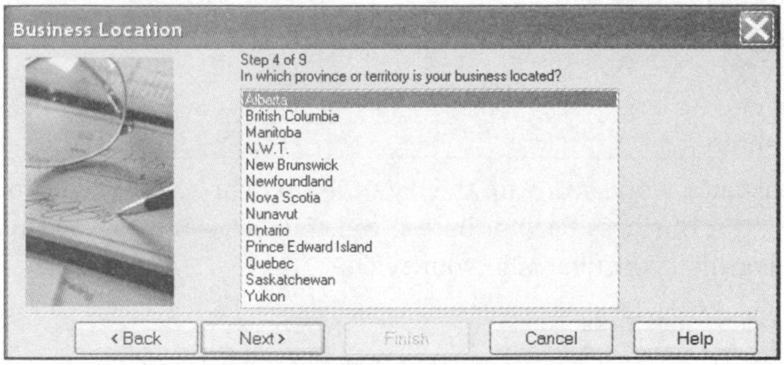

Simply Accounting uses province information to start creating default settings. Alberta is selected because it is first on the list. Since it is also the province for Dorfmann Design, we can accept the selection.

Click **Next**:

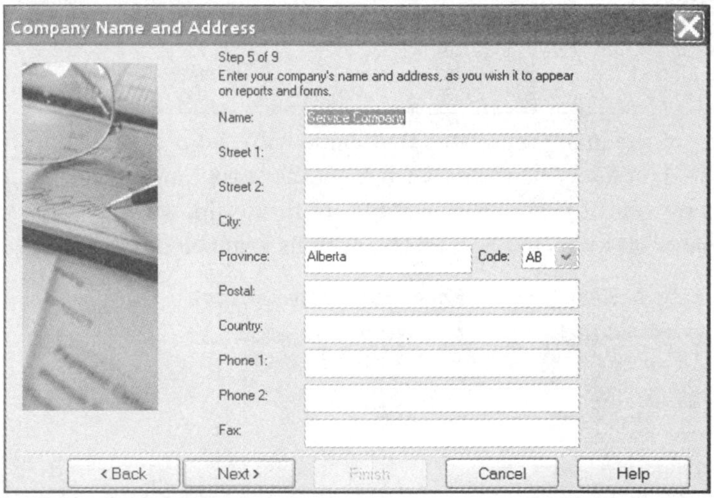

You must now enter company information for the business. The Name field is selected so you can edit the default entry. Alberta and its two-letter abbreviation are entered from the province selection we made earlier. Use the Business Information on page 287 to enter the company name and address details.

NOTES
Remember that you can personalize the data file by adding your own name to the company name.

Type `Dorfmann Design` **Press** *tab* to enter the name.

Type `17 Tapestry Lane` **Press** *tab* to enter the street address.

Press *tab* to skip the Street 2 field.

Type `Calgary` and **click** the **Postal Code field**.

Type `t3b4u2` **Press** *tab* to enter the postal code.

Type `Canada` **Press** *tab* to enter the country.

Type `4036839145` **Press** *tab* to enter the phone number.

Press *tab* to skip the Phone 2 field.

Type `4036858210`

Click **Next** to open the File Name screen:

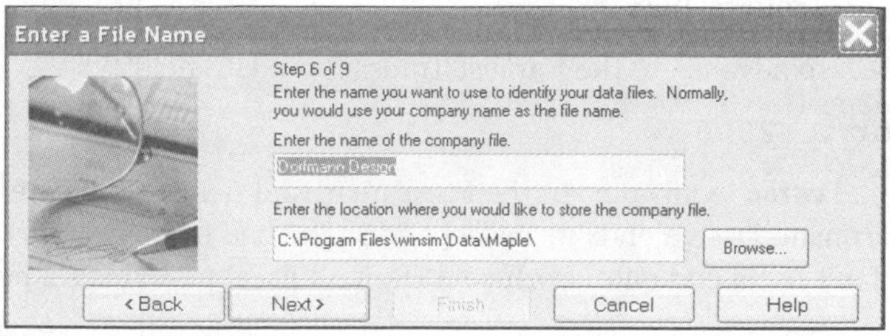

Now you must choose a file name and folder to store the new data set. The company name is entered as the default name for the data file, and it is selected.

Type `dorfmann`

Press *tab* to advance to the location field.

The last folder you used will be the default selection — that is, Maple, if you last worked with the Maple Leaf Rags data set. Change folders if necessary to access the one with your other data files. If you have already created the folder you want to use,

Click **Browse** to open the Browse for Folder screen to select a folder. Otherwise,

Drag through Maple\ in the folder name or the last folder in the location field.

Type DORFMANN\ to replace Maple or the last folder in the name.

Click **Next** to see the confirmation message:

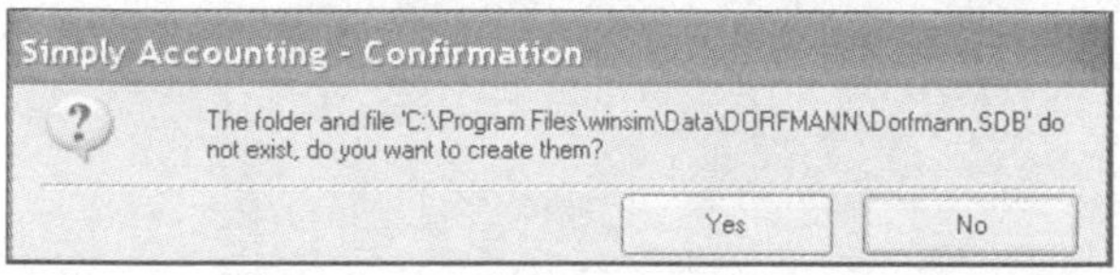

Simply Accounting advises you that you have named a new folder and asks if you want to create it.

Click **Yes** to see the following company Dates window:

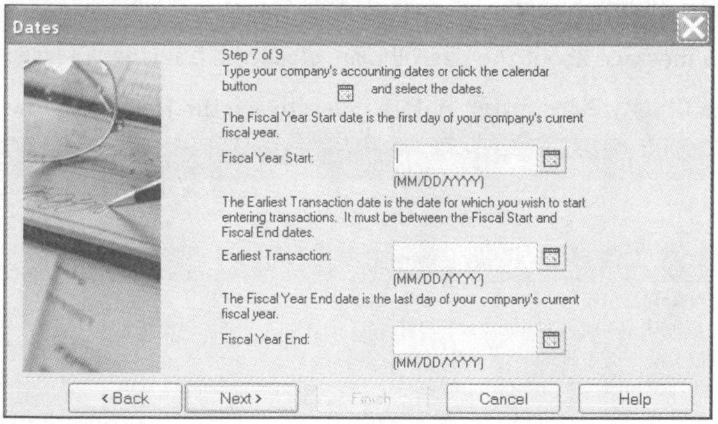

These company fiscal dates are like the ones you entered for Toss for Tots (Chapter 4) as part of the Company Information setup. The cursor is in the Fiscal Year Start field. This is the date on which the business begins its fiscal year. For Dorfmann Design, the fiscal start date is the beginning of the calendar year.

Type `jan 1 2008` **Press** *tab*.

The program enters the fiscal start as the **earliest transaction date**. This is the date on which the business is changing from a manual accounting system to a

NOTES
Refer to Chapter 1, page 22 if you need further assistance with creating and naming new data folders.

NOTES
Simply Accounting will automatically add the correct file extension. You do not need to type it when you are creating a new data set.

NOTES
The Calendar icon shows the current month for your computer system. It is easier to type in the dates than it is to scroll through several months to find the one you need.

Remember that you should type a four-digit year the first time you enter a date in the year 2000 or later to be certain that the year will be 2008 and not 1908.

Typing the date in text format ensures that we enter it correctly.

NOTES
The Earliest Transaction date is also the initial date before which you do not allow transactions.

computerized accounting system — the earliest date for posting journal entries and the latest date for historical information.

Press (tab) to advance to the Earliest Transaction date field.

Type `apr 1 2008`

Press (tab) **twice** to advance to the Fiscal Year End field — the date Dorfmann Design ends its fiscal period. The end of the year is the default fiscal end date. Dorfmann Design's fiscal period is six months.

Type `jun 30 2008`

Click **Next**:

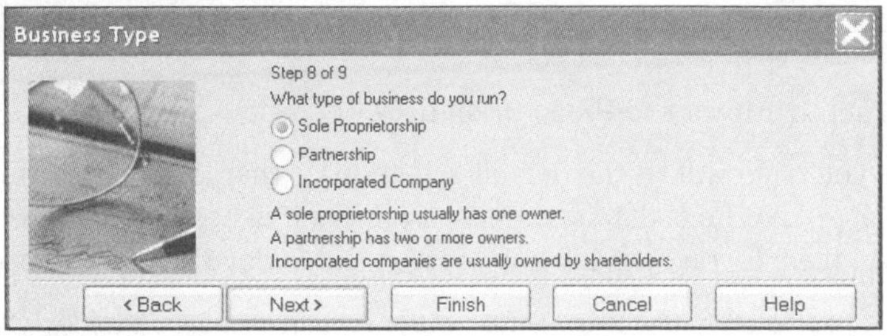

The next selection involves the type of business ownership. The default selection, Sole Proprietorship, is correct.

NOTES
You can click Finish at this stage and then confirm that you are leaving the Setup wizard.

Click **Next** to see the final Setup screen:

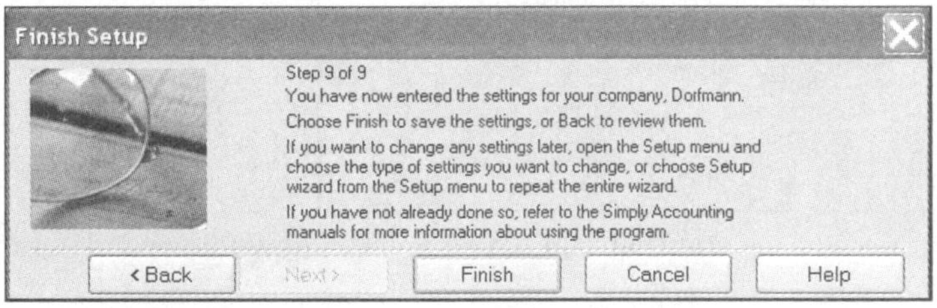

Click **Finish** to complete the file creation stage and start the Simply Accounting program.

If you see a message about the payroll plan, **close** the **advisor message**.

Close the **Simply Accounting Help window** to see the Home window:

BASIC VERSION
basic Pay Vendor Invoices replaces Pay Purchase invoices as the icon label.

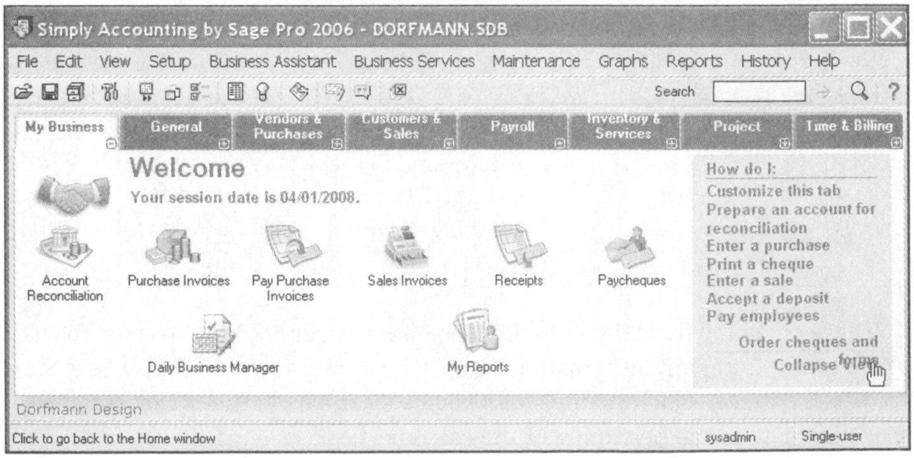

The My Business Tab window is open.

Click **Collapse View** in the How Do I list or **click** the **My Business tab heading** to close the My Business tab and restore the Home window.

The Home window is now open with the name Dorfmann in the title bar. However, non-accounting terms are selected, so the icon names will be different from the ones in previous applications. Miscellaneous Transactions replaces General Journal, Vendors & Purchases replaces Payables, and Customers & Sales replaces Receivables as module headings. We will change these terms as part of the setup.

NOTES
The list of equivalent accounting and non-accounting terms is shown in Appendix B.

All the ledger icons have the open history quill pen icon because the ledgers are still open for entering historical information. No ledgers are hidden.

Display the **Chart of Accounts** for the Current Year.

You will see that the only account provided by default is the type X account, the General Ledger linked account, *Current Earnings*.

Close the **Chart of Accounts**.

Preparing the System

The next step is to enter the company information that customizes the files for Dorfmann Design. You begin by preparing the system and changing the defaults.

You should change the user preference and reports and forms defaults to suit your own work environment.

WARNING!
You cannot complete many of the setup steps in multi-user mode.

Changing Defaults

Use the Business Information on page 287 to enter the defaults for Dorfmann Design.

Changing Company Information

Choose the **Setup menu**, then **choose System Settings** and **click Company Information** to display the Company Information screen.

Most of the fields on this screen are complete from the information we entered earlier. You can edit the information if you made a mistake. We still need to add the business number and the company logo. The logo is located in the DATA\SETUP folder (or the folder you chose) where you copied the other data files.

NOTES
You may want to refer to keystrokes in Chapter 4 to assist you in completing the setup and to the keystrokes in other chapters to assist you with the transactions for this application.

Click the **Business Number field**.

Type 233 281 244

Click **Browse**, then **click Data**, **Setup**, **Dorfmann** and **dorfmann** (or **dorfmann.bmp**).

NOTES
If you are showing file extensions, the picture file will be named dorfmann.bmp.

Click the **Open button** to add the image to the field.

Check the **information** you have just entered and **make** any necessary **corrections**, including corrections to the fiscal dates.

Notice that the earliest transaction date appears as the session date on the Company Information screen. If there are any postdated transactions in the file, the Latest Transaction Date will be later than the session date.

Click **OK** to save the new information and return to the Home window.

You can return to the Company Information screen at any time to make changes. The program will set up defaults for the session date and for the city, province and country fields for customers and vendors based on the information you entered.

Changing the Printer Defaults

Choose the **Setup menu** and **click Reports & Forms**.

The printer setting options for reports are given. Notice that the defaults include adding the computer system (calendar) date to reports and information about whether the report is filtered. You can check to see if the report fits on the page to improve the appearance of your printed reports and you can change reports & forms settings any time. When the settings are correct,

Click **OK** to save the new information, or click Cancel if you have not made any changes, and return to the Home window.

Changing User Preferences

Choose the **Setup menu**, then **click User Preferences**.

If you are working in multi-user mode, decide whether you want to refresh lists automatically so that changes other users make affect your file immediately.

Choose **Use Accounting Terms** so that your on-screen terms will match the ones used in this workbook.

Choose **Automatically Save Changes To Vendor, Customer And Other Records**.

Choose **Show List Buttons Throughout Simply Accounting...**.

Click the **View tab**.

Click **Payroll**, **Inventory**, **Project** and **Time & Billing** to hide the unused modules.

Click **After Changing Session Date** to remove the ✓ for **Daily Business Manager** and **Checklists**.

Click **My Business Tab** to open the My Business Tab options window.

You can customize the My Business Tab window. If your company uses only a few Home window icons regularly, you can place these icons in the My Business Tab window. Then use the open My Business Tab column to enter most transactions.

We are not using the My Business Tab for Dorfmann so we will hide it.

Click **Show My Business Tab** to remove the ✓.

Click **OK** to save the changes and return to the Home window.

You should now see the familiar accounting term labels for the ledger and journal icons. At this stage your Home window should look like the following:

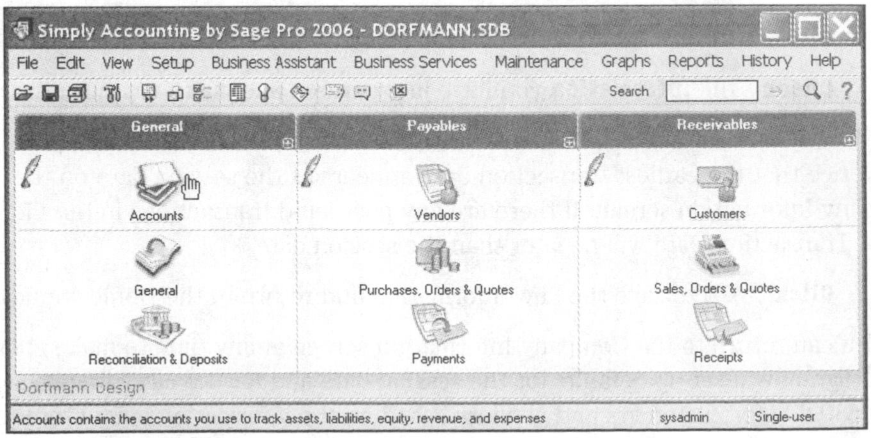

BASIC VERSION
The Automatically Refresh Lists option does not apply to the Basic version.

NOTES
When you automatically save the changes to records, you will not be prompted to save information each time you close a ledger after making a change.

NOTES
The option to show inventory lists does not apply to Dorfmann, so you can remove this checkmark if you want.

BASIC VERSION
The Time & Billing module is not available in Basic so you do not need to hide it.

Changing System Defaults

Choose the **Setup menu**, then **choose System Settings** and **click Settings**.

- If you choose Settings when a ledger icon is selected, you will display the settings for the selected ledger.
- If you click the Setup tool when a ledger icon is selected, you will display the settings for the selected ledger.
- If you click the Setup tool when no ledger or journal icon is selected, you must select a ledger from the list.

Click **System** in the list on the right to access the first set of options.

Most of the default System Settings are correct. Dorfmann uses the accrual basis of accounting, so Use Cash-Basis Accounting should be unchecked. The option to Use Cheque No. as the source code can remain selected because Dorfmann uses cheques and may later choose to use account reconciliation.

The Store Invoice Lookup option is correctly selected for Dorfmann Design. This feature allows us to look up and adjust or correct invoices already posted.

Initially, we will not allow any transactions before April 1, the earliest transaction date. We want to allow posting to future transactions but receive a warning if the dates are more than seven days in the future. The defaults are correct. Since you can enter transactions before completing the history, you should activate the warning about unbalanced accounts to prevent mistakes. The warning makes you aware of errors or omissions before you proceed too far with transactions.

We will back up the files on a weekly basis and leave on the reminder to back up each time we close the data file.

Click **Do Not Allow Transactions Dated Before** to add a ✓. **Press** *tab*.

Type 4-1-8

Click **Warn If Accounts Are Not Balanced When Entering A New Month**.

Choose **Weekly** as the Backup frequency.

Click **Features**. You can hide the icons for orders and quotes if they are not used. Customizing the icons that appear can simplify journal entries.

Changing Forms Default Settings

Click **Forms** to display the Settings for Forms:

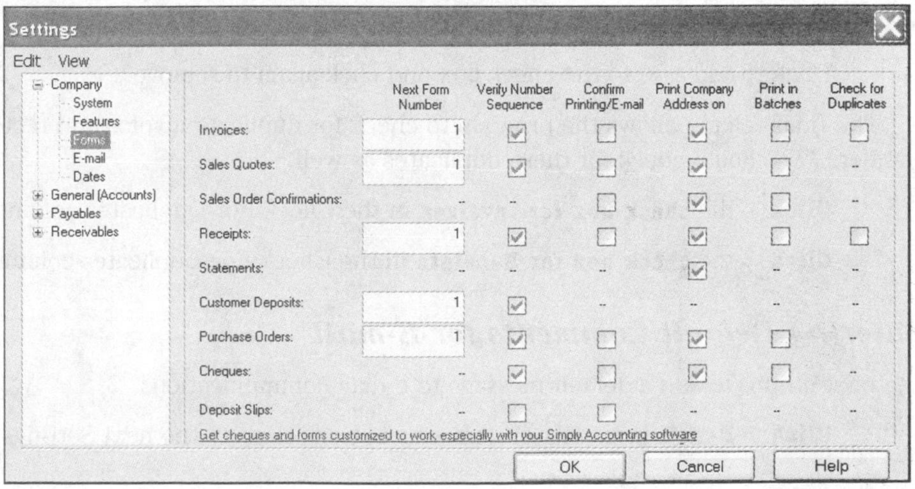

NOTES
Save your work frequently and update your backup copy frequently as you work through the setup.

NOTES
If you click the calendar for the prior transactions field, you will see that the program does not allow you to choose a date before April.

The Forms screen allows us to set up the automatic numbering sequences for business forms and to include warnings if the number you entered is a duplicate or out of sequence. You can set up the numbering sequence for all business forms that are generated internally or within the company.

Some forms that include numbers are not on this list. Because sales orders originate with customers and purchase quotes come from vendors, their numbers are not automatically updated. You can enter a cheque sequence number in the reports and forms settings for each bank account. (See page 312.)

The Invoices number field is ready for editing.

NOTES
Numbers for forms in the modules that are not used are hidden. For Payroll, the Direct Deposit Stubs are numbered and for Time and Billing, the time slips are numbered.

Type 44

Click the **Sales Quotes field** to highlight the contents.

Type 41

Click the **Receipts field**.

Type 25

Click the **Customer Deposits field**. This entry will update the sequence number for deposits or advances from customers.

Type 12

Click the **Purchase Orders** field to highlight the contents.

Type 16

The Deposit Slip number refers to bank deposit slips, and a starting number can be entered for each bank account in its ledger record.

NOTES
The additional options in the columns also apply to Sales Order Confirmations and Cheques, even though we do not have sequence numbers for them on the Forms Settings screen. These should be set correctly for your own setup.

The column checklists on the Forms Settings screen allow you to **verify sequence numbers** and add reminders if you print invoices, quotes, purchase orders and so forth. Verifying sequence numbers will warn you if you skip or duplicate a number and give you a chance to make a correction if necessary before posting. Choosing to **confirm** will set up the program to remind you to print or e-mail the form if you try to post before printing since posting removes the form from the screen. You should add the confirmation if you print or e-mail these forms regularly.

The third column allows you to add the **company address** to various forms. If you have preprinted forms that already include the address, remove the checkmarks to avoid double printing this information. If you are using generic blank forms, leave the checkmarks so that the address is included. The next column refers to **batch printing**. If you want to be able to print the forms on the list in batches, for example, print all the invoices for the day at the end of each day, you should check this option. Batch printing is covered in Chapter 13.

Click to add a ✓ to the check box and click again to remove a ✓.

The final column allows the program to check for duplicate invoice and receipt numbers. We should check for these duplicates as well.

Click the **check box for Invoices** in the Check For Duplicates column.

Click the **check box for Receipts** in the Check For Duplicates column.

Entering Default Comments for E-mail

The next step is to add a default message to e-mail communications.

Click **E-mail** in the list of Company options to open the next Settings screen:

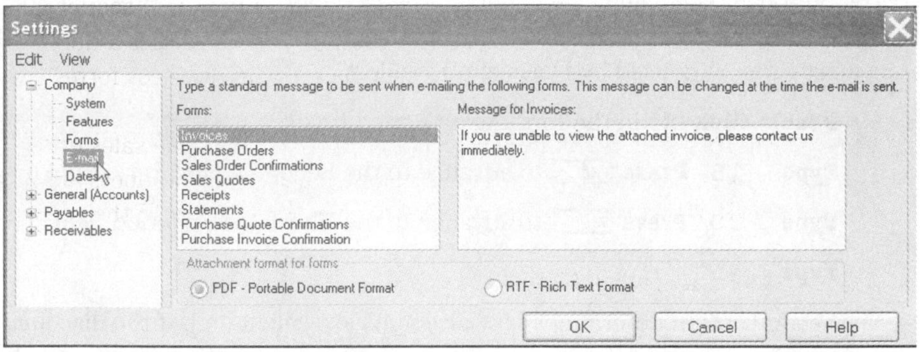

The left-hand list box contains the forms that you can e-mail to vendors or customers. The right-hand box contains the message that will be added to these e-mails. You could add the company phone and fax numbers to the message so that the customer or vendor can contact you more easily. You can also select PDF or RTF as the format for the file you e-mail to your customers and vendors. You do not need to change the default messages for Dorfmann.

Click a form to select it and then type a message in the box beside it.

Entering Defaults for Date Formats

The default date formats use the short form on-screen. We want to use the long form so that the date will always be clear.

Click **Dates** in the list of Company options to open the Dates Settings screen.

Click **Long Dates** beside On The Screen, Use to change the selection.

NOTES
The General Ledger settings are correct for Dorfmann Design. For now, Dorfmann will not use the budgeting feature or departmental accounting so you can skip this screen.

Payables Default Settings

Click **Payables** in the list on the left:

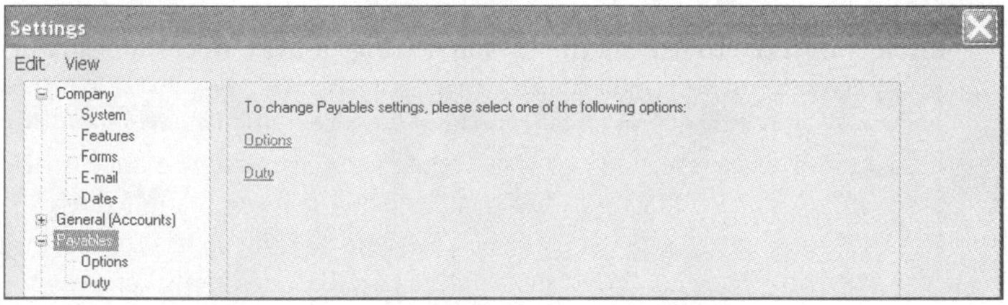

The Payables Ledger has general settings (Options) and settings for imports (Duty). Dorfmann does not import items that have duty applied.

Click **Options** to display the default settings for the Payables Ledger:

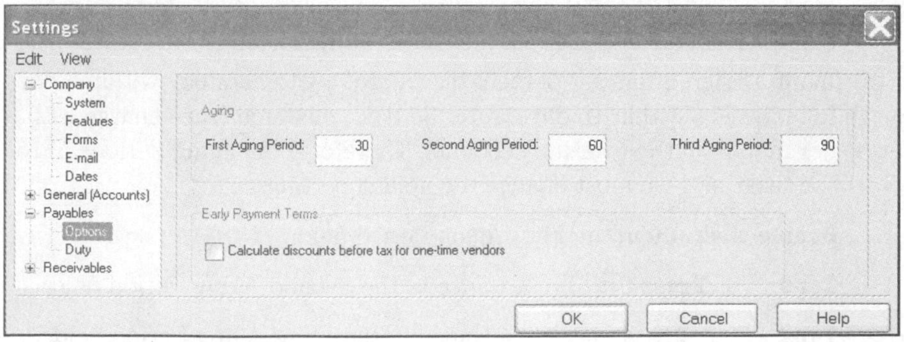

NOTES
Refer to Chapter 2 for further information about taxes and discounts. We will add discount terms to individual vendor records when we set up the Payables Ledger.

NOTES
Usually clicking a number in a field will select the entire number. Sometimes, however, depending on exactly where you click, only part of the number is selected or an insertion point is added. Double clicking will always select the entire number in the field so that you can edit it.

The option for the aging of accounts in the Payables Ledger is preset at 30, 60 and 90 days. We will change these options for Dorfmann to reflect the payment and discount terms most commonly used by Dorfmann's vendors.

Double click **30** in the First Aging Period field.

Type 15 **Press** tab to advance to the Second Aging Period field.

Type 30 **Press** tab to advance to the Third Aging Period field.

Type 45

The second option determines how discounts are calculated. If the discount is taken only on the pretax total of the invoice, the discount is calculated before taxes. If the discount is applied to the entire invoice amount, including taxes, the discount is not calculated before taxes. Dorfmann's vendors calculate discounts before taxes so you must change the setting.

Click **Calculate Discounts Before Tax For One-Time Vendors**.

Receivables Default Settings

Click **Receivables** to display the Receivables Ledger choices:

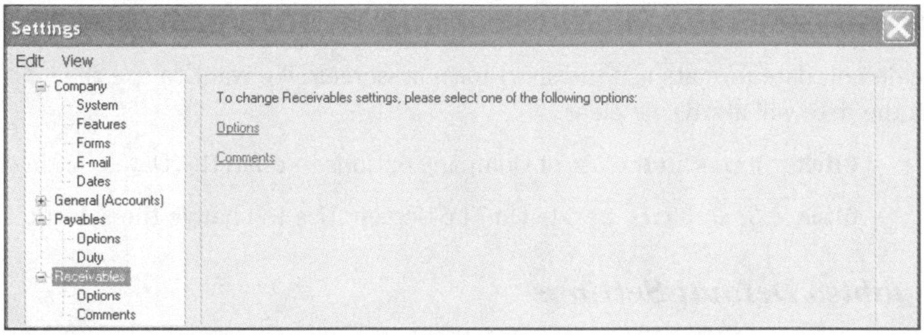

The Receivables Ledger has general settings (Options) and settings for Comments.

Click **Options** to display the default settings for the Receivables Ledger:

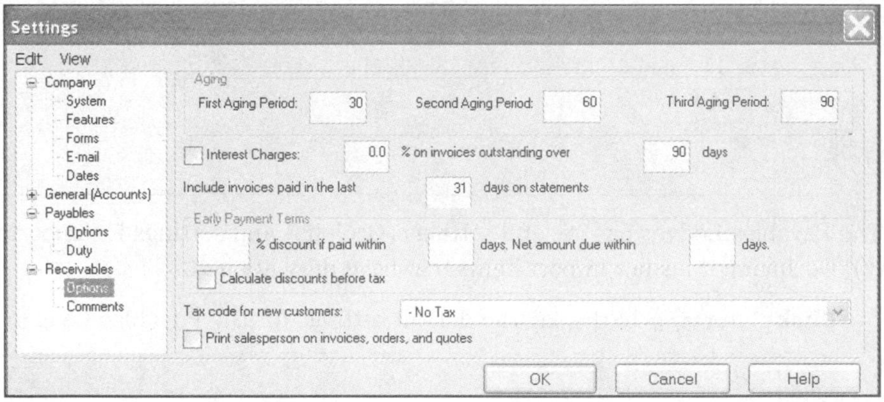

Dorfmann Design offers a 1 percent discount if customers pay within 5 days and expects full payment within 15 days. After 30 days, customers are charged 1.5 percent interest per month on the overdue accounts. Therefore, the aging periods 5, 15 and 30 days will be used, and we must change the default settings.

Double click **30** in the First Aging Period field.

Type 5 **Press** tab to advance to the Second Aging Period field.

Type 15 **Press** tab to advance to the Third Aging Period field.

Type 30

Click **Interest Charges** to add a ✓ and select this feature.

When interest charges are applied on overdue invoices, Simply Accounting calculates interest charges and prints them on the customer statements and management reports. However, the program does not create an invoice for the interest. You must create a Sales Journal entry for the amount of interest charged.

Press tab to advance to and highlight the contents of the Interest Rate field for editing.

Type 1.5 **Press** tab to advance to and highlight the contents of the Days field for editing.

Type 30

The next option relates to printing historical information on invoices. The maximum setting is 999 days. For Dorfmann Design, customer statements are sent every month so the period should be 31 days. Any invoices paid in the past 31 days will be included in the statements and unpaid invoices are always included. The default setting is correct.

Next we must enter the payment terms for account customers: 1 percent discount if the account is paid in the first 5 days and net payment due in 15 days. All customer discounts are calculated on after-tax amounts so the Calculate Discounts Before Tax selection is correctly turned off.

Click the **% field** in the first Early Payment Terms section to advance the cursor.

Type 1.0 **Press** tab to advance to the Days field.

Type 5 **Press** tab to advance to the Net Days field.

Type 15

Simply Accounting adds the customer payment terms you just entered as a default for all customers. Individual customer records or invoices can still be modified if needed.

If all or most customers use the same sales tax code, you can choose a **default tax code** that will be entered when you create new customers or when you choose One-time Customer or Quick Add in a sales invoice. We have not yet created tax codes so they cannot be entered now. We will enter the default code after setting up sales taxes.

When salespersons are set up, you can **print** the name of the **salesperson** on invoices, orders and quotes. Dorfmann does not have sales staff.

Entering Default Comments

Simply Accounting allows you to add a default comment to all customer forms. You can change the default message any time you want, and you can edit it for a particular form when you are completing the invoice, quote or confirmation.

Click **Comments** to open the screen for default comments:

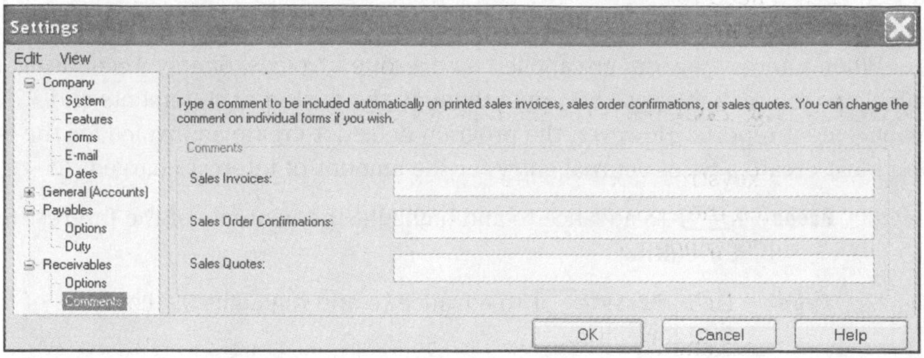

We want to add a comment that will appear on every customer invoice. The comment may include payment terms, company motto, notice of an upcoming sale or a warning about interest charges.

NOTES
For cash sales, you should replace the default comment with a more appropriate comment such as "Thank you."

Click the **Sales Invoices field** to move the cursor.

Type `Interest at 1.5% per month charged on accounts over 30 days.`

You can enter the same comment for all sales forms (invoices, sales order confirmations and quotes) or you can add a unique comment for each. Leave the remaining Comment fields blank.

Click **OK** to return to the Home window and save all the changes.

Preparing the Ledgers

NOTES
If necessary, refer to the Toss for Tots application, pages 81–84, for a review of the financial statement formats, the organization of accounts and the Current Earnings account.

The third stage in setting up an accounting system involves preparing each ledger. This stage involves the following steps:

1. organizing all accounting reports and records (this step has been completed)
2. modifying the *Current Earnings* account
3. creating new accounts
4. defining linked accounts for the ledgers
5. setting up credit cards, currencies, taxes and other features
6. inserting vendor and customer information
7. entering historical account balances, invoices and payments

Preparing the General Ledger

Accounts are organized by section, including Assets, Liabilities, Equity, Revenue and Expense. **Account type**, such as **Heading** (H), **Subgroup total** (S), **Total** (T), **subgroup Account** (A), **Group account** (G) and **Current Earnings** (X), is a method of classifying and organizing accounts within a section or subsection of a report.

The accounts follow the same pattern described previously:

- 1000–1999 Assets
- 2000–2999 Liabilities
- 3000–3999 Equity
- 4000–4999 Revenue
- 5000–5999 Expense

Use the Chart of Accounts, Income Statement and Balance Sheet to enter all the accounts you need to create. Remember to include all group headings, totals and subgroup totals in addition to the postable group and subgroup accounts.

Modifying Accounts in the General Ledger

The following keystrokes will modify the *Current Earnings* account in the General Ledger to match the account number defined in the Chart of Accounts.

In the Home window,

Click the **Accounts icon** Accounts to open the Accounts window.

The accounts should be displayed in Type view — in numerical order, with names, account types and balances. There is only one predefined account.

If necessary, change the view by choosing the Accounts window View menu and clicking Type.

Double click **3600 Current Earnings** to display its ledger form.

You can also open the ledger by clicking the account to select it. Then click the Edit tool button or choose the Edit menu and click Edit.

Press tab to select the Account number field.

Type 3650

The account types are dimmed because the *Current Earnings* account type must remain as type X. Only the account number and account title can be edited. You cannot enter a balance because the program automatically calculates the amount as the net difference between the total revenue and expense account balances for the fiscal period.

Close the **General Ledger account window**.

Close the **Accounts window** to return to the Home window unless you want to continue to the next step, which also involves working in the General Ledger.

NOTES

If you did not choose to save changes automatically (page 300), you will be asked if you want to save the changes and if you want to always save changes without asking. Choose to save changes without asking.

Creating New Accounts in the General Ledger

We will enter account balances as a separate step so that you can enter all balances in a single session. This may help you to avoid leaving the data file with an incorrect Trial Balance.

Open the **Accounts window** or any **account ledger window**.

Click the **Create tool** in the Accounts window or **choose** the **File menu** and **click Create**.

NOTES

Pressing ctrl + N will also open a new ledger record form.

Enter **account information** for all accounts from the Chart of Accounts on page 288. Remember, you cannot use duplicate account numbers.

Type the **account number** and **press** tab.

Type the **account name** or title.

Click the **account Type** for the account.

If this is a postable account, indicate whether you want to omit the account from financial statements if its balance is zero. Leave Allow Project Allocations unchecked.

Skip the **Opening Balance field** for now. We will enter all account balances in the next stage.

When all the information is entered correctly, you must save your account.

Click **Create Another** [Create Another] to save the new account and advance to a new blank ledger account window.

Create the **remaining accounts** from the Chart of Accounts, Balance Sheet and Income Statement.

Click **Save And Close** [Save and Close] to close the General Ledger account window after entering the last account.

Display or **print** your updated **Chart of Accounts** to check for account type errors as well as incorrect numbers and misspelled names. **Make corrections**.

Click the **Check The Validity Of Accounts tool** for descriptions of errors in account type. **Make** the **corrections** required.

Check the **validity** again and repeat the process until you see the message that the accounts are in logical order.

Entering Opening Account Balances

The opening historical balances for Dorfmann Design can be found in the Trial Balance dated March 31, 2008 on page 289. Headings, totals and subgroup totals — the non-postable accounts — have no balances and the Balance field is removed.

Use the *Test Balance Account* for any adjustments that would leave the Trial Balance in a forced balance position before you are finished or if one of the remaining balances is incorrect. After entering all balances, the *Test Balance Account* should have a zero balance, and you can remove it.

The Accounts window should be open.

Open the **General Ledger** account information window for the first account that has a balance, **1060 Bank: Chequing**.

Notice the additional tabs on the ledger screen for the Balance Sheet account.

Click the **Opening Balance field** to highlight its contents.

Type the **balance**.

Accounts that decrease the total in a group or section (i.e., *GST Paid on Purchases*, *Sales Discounts*, *Purchase Discounts* and *Exchange Rate Differences*) must be entered as negative numbers. The balances for these accounts have a (–) minus sign in the Balance Sheet or Income Statement.

WARNING!
Remember that Net Bank and GST Owing (Refund) are subgroup totals, following the subgroup bank and GST accounts respectively.

Correct the **information** if necessary by repeating the above steps.

Click the **Next button** in the Ledger window to advance to the next account ledger record.

Enter the **remaining account balances** as indicated in the Trial Balance by repeating the above procedures.

Close the **General Ledger window** to return to the Accounts window. You can check your work from the Trial Balance.

Choose the **Reports menu** and **click Trial Balance** to display the Trial Balance. **Print** the **report**.

Close the **display**. **Correct** the account **balances** if necessary. Open the Ledger window, click the amount and type the correction.

Close the **Accounts window**.

You may want to save your work and finish your session.

Setting Up Foreign Currencies

Before entering vendor and customer records, we must define the currencies used by the company so that we can choose a currency when we create customers and vendors. Dorfmann has vendors in the United States but no customers at this time. By defining the currencies first, we will also be able to set up the bank account for the foreign currency and then identify it as the linked foreign currency bank account.

You should be in the Home window.

Choose the **Setup menu**, then **choose System Settings** and **click Currencies** to see the Currency Information window:

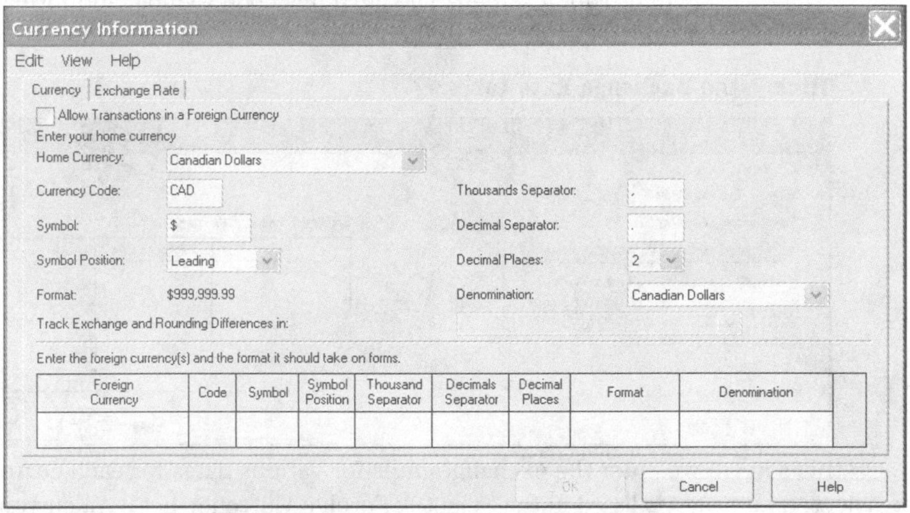

Canadian Dollars is the default in the Home Currency field, and its code, symbol, format and so on are added. You enter the currencies in the columns in the lower half of the screen. First you must turn on the option for other currencies.

Click **Allow Transactions In A Foreign Currency**.

Exchange rates vary from day to day and even within the day. When purchases and payments are made at different times, they are subject to different exchange rates. We have seen these differences in the Maple Leaf Rags chapter. Exchange rate differences may result in a gain — if the exchange rate drops before a payment is made or if the rate increases before a payment is received from a customer — or a loss — if the rate increases before a payment is made or if the rate drops before a customer makes a payment. These differences are tracked in the linked account designated on this screen. Rounding differences may also result in gains and losses because the amounts are recorded with two decimal places and exchange rates usually have several significant digits. The account for these differences may be an expense account or a revenue account. Dorfmann uses an expense account because there are no foreign customers yet, so the gain or loss is linked to business purchases or expenses.

Click the **list arrow** for **Track Exchange And Rounding Differences In**.

Both revenue and expense accounts are available for linking.

Click **5030 Exchange Rate Differences** to enter the linked account.

NOTES

To remove the Test Balance Account, click its icon or name in the Accounts window and click the Remove tool or choose the File menu and click Remove. Check that you have selected the right account. Click Yes to confirm that you want to remove the account.

If the Test Account balance is not zero, you cannot remove the account.

NOTES

The Pro version of Simply Accounting accepts more than one foreign currency. The Basic version of Simply Accounting is a dual currency version, with one home currency and one foreign currency.

basic **BASIC VERSION**

After you click Allow Transactions In A Foreign Currency, the screen expands and the fields you need to add the currency will open. Choose the account for tracking exchange rate differences. Then select United States Dollars from the Foreign Currency field drop-down list. Enter the date and exchange rate in the Date and Exchange Rate columns.

NOTES

You can add a new account at this stage if necessary. Type the new account number and press *tab*. Click Add to start the Add An Account wizard.

The next step is to identify the foreign currency or currencies.

Click the **Foreign Currency field**.

Click the **List icon** for the field to open the list of currencies:

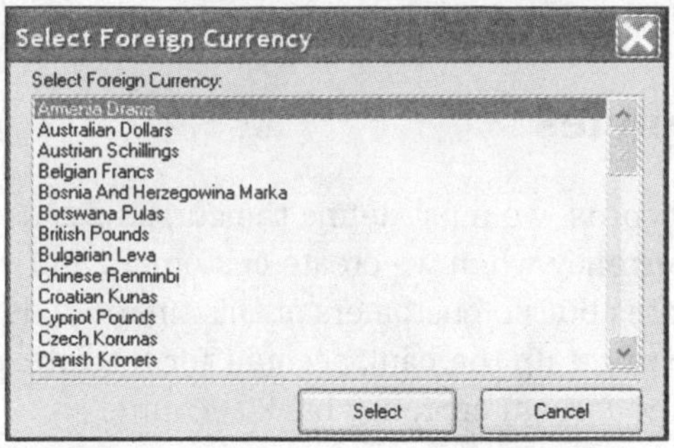

Type U (We want to include currencies beginning with U in the list.)

Scroll down and **double click United States Dollars** to add it to the Currency Information screen. The currency code, symbol and format are added for the selected currency. Accept the defaults.

Click the **Exchange Rate tab**:

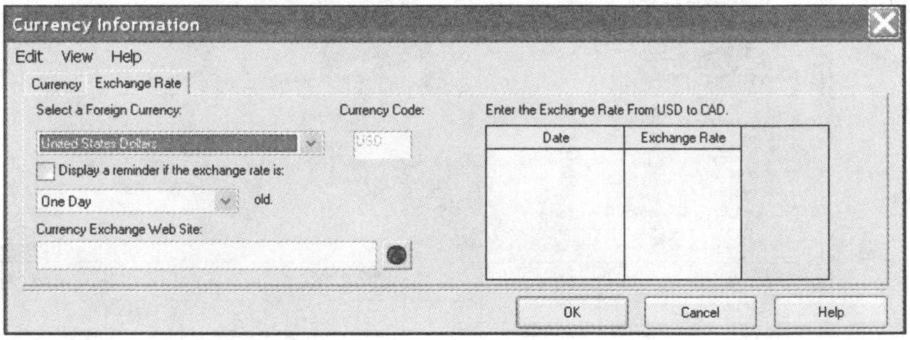

BASIC VERSION

There is no separate screen for exchange rates (no Exchange Rate tab) because only one foreign currency can be identified.

NOTES

If you have a Web site that you use for exchange rate information, you can enter it here as well. Then click the Web tool to access the Web site directly and obtain current rates. The Web tool appears on the Exchange Rate list screen that you access by clicking the Exchange Rate tool beside the Exchange Rate field.

On this screen, we enter the exchange rates for various dates for each currency. The selected currency is listed in the Select A Foreign Currency field. All currencies you created will be listed in the drop-down list for this field.

Click the **Date field**.

Type 04 01 **Press** *tab* to advance to the Exchange Rate field.

Type 1.177

If you know the rates for other dates, you can enter them as well. Otherwise, you can enter current rates in the journals as we did in the previous chapters. These rates will be added to the list on this screen.

To ensure that you do not use an old exchange rate that is no longer accurate, you should turn on the reminder that warns if the rate is out of date. A one-day period for updating should be sufficient.

Click **Display A Reminder If The Exchange Rate Is**.

Accept **One Day Old** as the time interval .

Now every time you change the transaction date to one day past the rate previously used, the program will warn you and give you an opportunity to change the rate. If the rate has not changed, you can accept the old rate.

Click **OK** to save the currency information and return to the Home window.

Entering Bank Class Accounts

Before setting up the Payables and Receivables ledgers, we must change the account class for bank accounts and some other accounts. **Account class** is another way of organizing accounts into related groups. Each section may be divided into various classes. For example, assets may be subdivided into bank accounts, credit card accounts, receivables, inventory and so on. When you create a new account, the program assigns a default class (Asset, Liability, Equity, Operating Revenue or Cost of Goods Sold) according to the first digit of the account number. For most accounts, you can accept this setting and the program will prompt you to change the class for special purpose accounts as needed. Bank accounts are not automatically reassigned by the program. You should also change the class for expense accounts by choosing either Expense or Operating Expense as the account class. Dorfmann does not sell merchandise and has no Cost of Goods Sold accounts.

Chequing bank accounts have additional information that must be entered in the ledger and therefore require that you change the class. You cannot select bank accounts for payments and receipts unless the **Bank class** is assigned. Bank class accounts must also be defined as such before you can select them as the default linked accounts for the Payables, Receivables and Payroll ledgers. Two chequing accounts, *Bank: Chequing* and *Bank: USD*, must be defined as Bank class accounts.

Click the **Accounts icon** 

.

Double click **1060 Bank: Chequing** to open its ledger window. Notice that the currency for the balance is defined as Canadian.

Click the **Class Options tab** to see the current class setting — Asset:

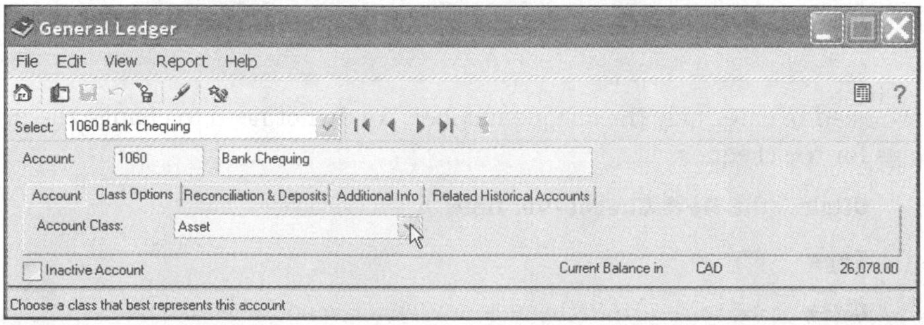

Click the **Account Class list arrow** to see the asset account class options.

Click **Bank** from the list to open the bank-related fields:

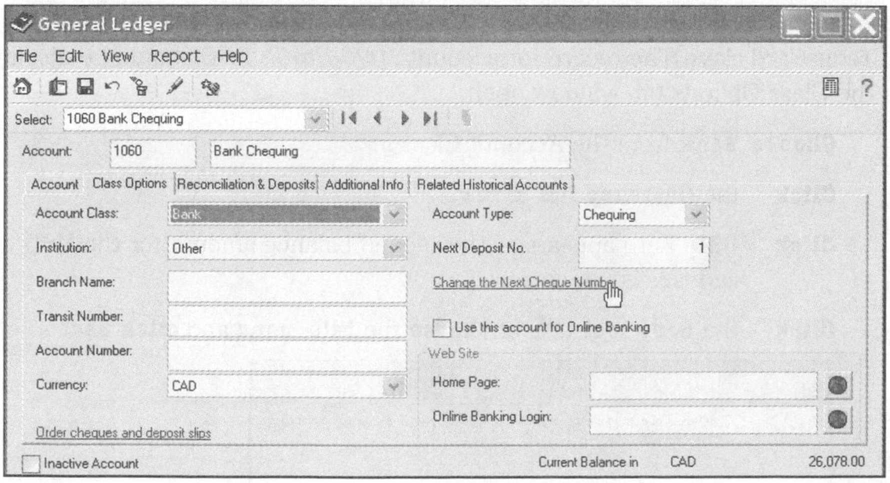

NOTES
The available account classes vary for different account sections. For example, you cannot assign the Bank class to an expense account.

This screen allows you to define the type of bank account, and Chequing, the default, is correct. You can also enter a starting number for the deposit slip sequence and identify the bank for online banking access. We are not using deposit slips in this exercise, so you can skip this field. You can also identify the currency for the account. By setting up the foreign currency before defining bank accounts, we can complete the bank account setup.

NOTES
Until you have saved the record or closed the ledger, the account class change has not been recorded so the cheque fields for the account will not yet be available.

Before entering the cheque number, we need to save the account class change.

Click the **Save tool** or **choose** the **File menu** and **click Save**.

Click **Change The Next Cheque Number** to open the cheque Form settings:

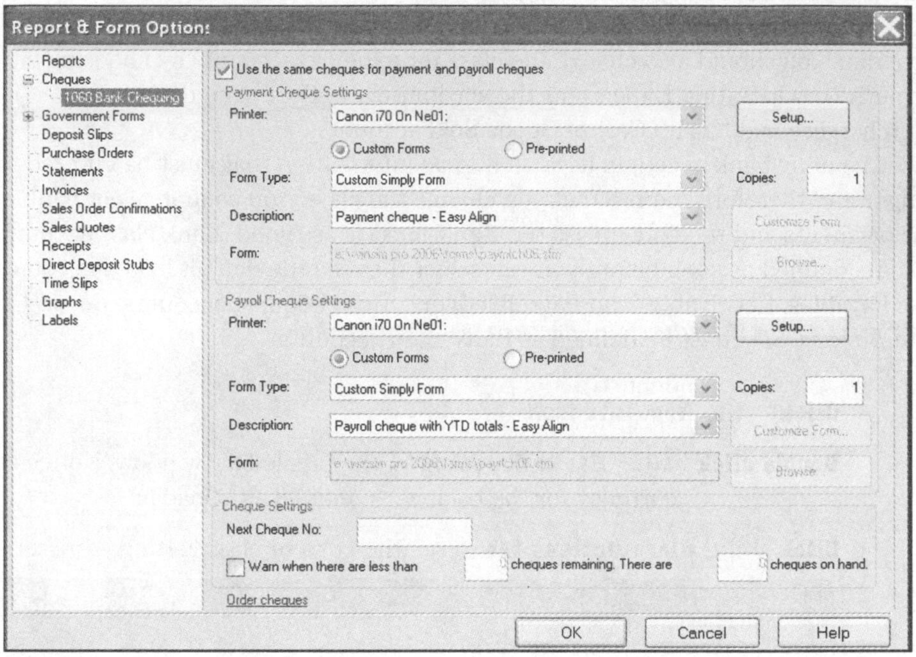

NOTES
Deposit slips are used in Chapter 14 together with account reconciliation.

We need to enter only the cheque number. We do not need to change the printer settings for the cheques.

Click the **Next Cheque No. field**.

Type 65

Click **OK** to return to the account ledger window.

Click the **Next button** **three times** to advance to account 1090.

Although credit card accounts are bank accounts, they cannot be defined as Bank class accounts because they are used as credit card linked accounts and are assigned the Credit Card class. The record for account *1090 Bank: USD* should be displayed with the Class Options tab window open.

Choose **Bank** from the Account Class list.

Click the **Currency list arrow**.

Click **USD**. Zero appears as the second balance amount for the USD currency, and this is not correct.

Click the **Save tool** or **choose** the **File menu** and **click Save**:

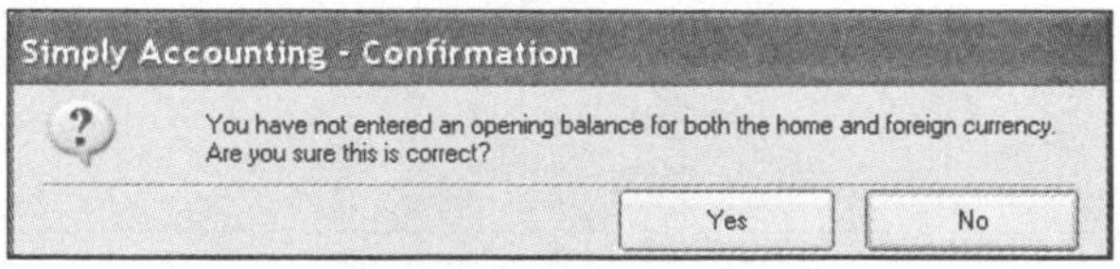

Because we have entered the balance in only the Home currency, we are asked to confirm that this is correct. It is not.

Click **No** to return to the ledger window so we can add the USD balance.

Click the **Account tab** to return to the Opening Balance fields. A second field has been added for the balance in USD.

Click the **Opening Balance In USD field**.

Type 2720

Click the **Save tool** .

Click the **Class Options tab**.

Click **Change The Next Cheque Number** to open the cheque Form settings.

Click the **Next Cheque No. field**.

Type 104

Click **OK** to return to the account ledger window.

Defining the Class for Expense Accounts

Expense accounts are defined as Cost of Goods Sold by default when you create them from the General Ledger new account window. These account classes should be changed unless they refer to inventory cost accounts. When you create expense accounts from an Account field using the Add An Account wizard, the default account class is Operating Expense, so you do not need to change it.

To create the Gross Margin Income Statement Report, you must correctly separate the Cost of Goods Sold accounts from other expenses.

Choose **account 5010** from the Select Account list to open the ledger.

Choose **Operating Expense** (or **Expense**) from the Account Class list.

Click the **Next button** . **Change** the **class** for all Group expense accounts.

Close the **Ledger window**. The Type view in the Accounts window now shows the account balances in both currencies.

Close the **Accounts window** to return to the Home window.

Entering Linked Accounts

Linked accounts are accounts in the General Ledger that are affected by changes resulting from entries in journals for the other ledgers. We have seen some of these linked accounts at work in journal entries in previous chapters. For example, an entry to record a credit sale in the Sales Journal will cause automatic changes in several General Ledger accounts. In the General Ledger, the *Accounts Receivable* [+], *Revenue from Sales* [+], *GST Charged on Services* [+] and *PST Payable* [+] accounts will all be affected by the sale. The type of change, increase [+] or decrease [–], is indicated in the brackets. The program must know which account numbers are to be used for posting journal entries in any of the journals. Often you do not enter account numbers for linked accounts in the journals. It is this interconnection of account numbers and information between ledgers that makes Simply Accounting fully integrated.

Since the only linked account already defined is *Current Earnings*, the linked account for Current Earnings in the General Ledger, we must identify the remaining linked accounts for the General, Payables and Receivables ledgers.

NOTES

The Integration Plus starter files have a full set of linked accounts already defined.

If you want to use this starter file, open the inteplus.sdb file from the Template folder and copy the file as you did for Toss for Tots before changing any of the default information. Then you can delete and modify the linked accounts for the ledgers as needed rather than entering them from scratch.

Setup Tool Button

The Setup tool on the tool bar works very much like the Display tool. Select a journal icon and click the Setup tool to see the Linked Accounts window for the corresponding ledger. If no icon is selected, choose the journal name from the Select Setup list to display the linked accounts for the corresponding ledger. If a ledger icon is selected, clicking the Setup tool displays the Settings window for that ledger.

Defining the General Linked Accounts

We will begin by defining the linked accounts for the three ledgers used by Dorfmann Design.

WARNING!
Do not click (i.e., click the left mouse button) the journal icons because you want to select the icon without opening the journal. Right-clicking will select the icon.

Right-click the **General Journal icon** in the Home window to select it.

Click the **Setup tool**, or **choose** the **Setup menu**, then **choose System Settings** and **Linked Accounts** and **click General** to display the General tab in the Linked Accounts window:

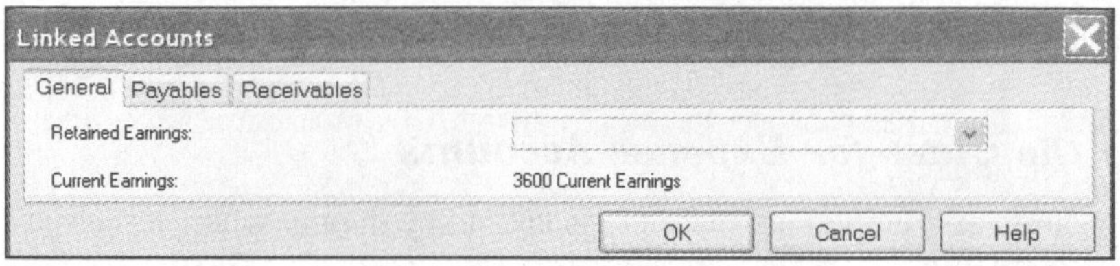

WARNING!
You must define essential linked accounts before you can finish the history for a company and before you can enter sales and purchase transactions.

Dorfmann does not use the Payroll or Inventory ledgers. Because they are hidden, there are no tabs for them and you do not need to define linked accounts for them.

The cursor is in the Retained Earnings field. The Retained Earnings account is the capital (equity) account to which expense and revenue accounts are closed at the end of the fiscal period. You must choose a capital (3000 range) account.

WARNING!
Simply Accounting will not allow you to remove accounts if they are being used as linked accounts. First you must remove the account in the Linked Accounts screen. Then you can remove the account in the General Ledger.

Click the **list arrow** beside the field. All available postable capital accounts are listed.

Click **3560 D. Dorfmann, Capital**.

You can also type account numbers directly in the linked account fields. Then press *tab* to complete the entry and advance to the next field. If you type a new account number, you can create the new account.

The Current Earnings account is correctly defined and cannot be changed, although, as you saw earlier, you can modify the account number and account name.

Defining the Payables Linked Accounts

To enter the Payables Ledger linked accounts,

NOTES
To display the Payables Linked Accounts from the Home window, click the Setup menu, then choose System Settings and Linked Accounts and click the Payables tab. Or you can right-click the Purchases or Payments Journal icon and click the Setup tool.

Click the **Payables tab** to display the Linked Accounts window:

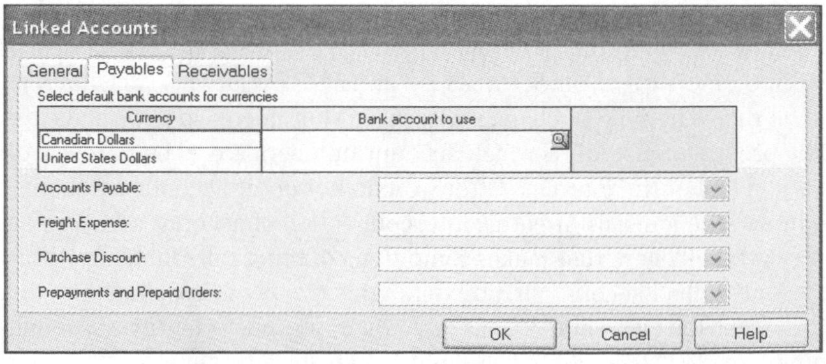

We need to identify the default General Ledger bank accounts used to make payments to vendors. Cash transactions in the Payments Journal will be posted to the bank account you select in the journal window. All Bank class accounts are available in the journals, and the principal linked account defined here will be selected as the default.

You can see the list of accounts available for linking by clicking the drop-down list arrow for any linked account field. Only Bank class accounts may be used in the bank fields. That is why we needed to define the Bank class accounts first.

Dorfmann has two bank accounts for payments. The chequing account is the principal bank account for Canadian currency transactions, and the USD account is used for transactions in United States dollars.

You can choose a separate linked account for each currency, or you may use the Canadian dollar account for more than one currency. You can select a Home currency bank as the linked account for foreign currency transactions, but you cannot select a foreign currency account as the linked account for Home currency transactions.

Click the **List icon** in the Bank Account To Use column for Canadian Dollars.

Click **1060 Bank: Chequing** and **click Select**.

Click **List icon** in the Bank Account To Use column for United States Dollars.

Click **1090 Bank: USD** and **click Select**.

The cursor advances to the Accounts Payable field. This account is used to record the amounts owing to vendors whenever a credit (Pay Later) Purchases Journal entry is completed. The balance in this account reflects the total owing to all vendors. You must use a liability account in this field.

Select **2200 Accounts Payable**, the control account, from the Account list.

Press *tab* to enter the account number.

The cursor advances to the Freight Expense field, used to record the delivery or freight charges associated with purchases. Only freight charged by the vendor should be entered using this account. Since Dorfmann's vendors do not charge for delivery, you should leave this field blank. You can add a linked account for freight later if you need it.

Press *tab* to advance to the Purchase Discount field. This account is used to record any vendor discounts taken for early payments.

Choose **5040 Purchase Discounts** from the drop-down list.

Press *tab* to advance to the Prepayments And Prepaid Orders field.

Prepayments to vendors are normally linked to an asset account because the vendor owes us merchandise for the prepayment.

Choose **1280 Purchase Prepayments** from the drop-down list.

Check the linked accounts carefully. To delete a linked account, click it to highlight it and press *del*. You must complete this step of deleting the linked account before you can remove the account in the General Ledger from the Accounts window.

To select a different account, highlight the one that is incorrect and type the correct number, or select an account from the drop-down list.

NOTES
If you have not yet set up the foreign currency, the linked bank account field will not be available.

NOTES
If you do not enter a linked account for prepayments, you cannot enter prepayments.

> **NOTES**
> To display the Receivables Linked Accounts from the Home window, click the Setup menu, then choose System Settings and Linked Accounts and click the Receivables tab. Or you can right-click the Sales or Receipts Journal icon and click the Setup tool.

Defining the Receivables Linked Accounts

The Receivables Ledger linked accounts parallel those for the Payables Ledger.

Click the **Receivables tab**:

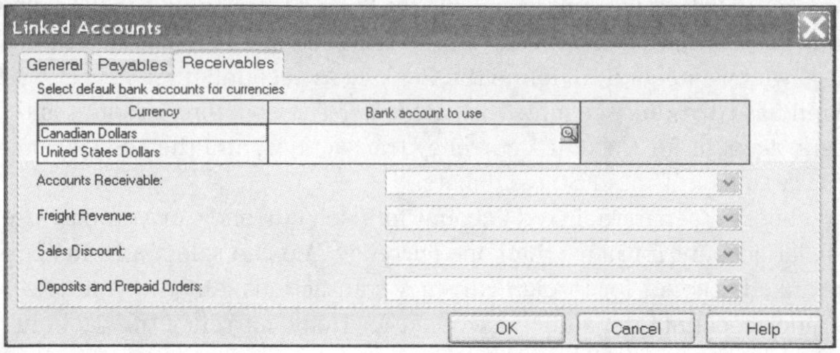

We need to identify the default General Ledger bank account used to receive payments from customers. Cash transactions in the Sales and Receipts journals will be posted to the bank account you select in the journals. The linked account will be the default account but any Bank class account may be selected.

Dorfmann has two bank accounts — *Bank Account: Chequing*, the principal Canadian bank account, and *Bank: USD* for foreign currency customer transactions. Although most linked accounts may be used only once, one bank account can be linked to the Payables, Receivables and Payroll ledgers.

> **NOTES**
> If the foreign currency is not yet set up, the linked bank account field will not be included in the Linked Account screens.

Click the **List icon** in the Bank Account To Use column for Canadian Dollars.

Click **1060 Bank: Chequing** and **click Select**.

Click **List icon** in the Bank Account To Use column for United States Dollars.

Click **1090 Bank: USD** and **click Select**.

The cursor advances to the Accounts Receivable field. This account records the amounts owed to Dorfmann by customers whenever a credit (Pay Later) Sales Journal entry is completed. The balance in this account reflects the total owed by all customers. You must use an asset account in this field.

Select **1200 Accounts Receivable**, the control account, from the drop-down list.

> **NOTES**
> If you do not enter a linked account for deposits, you cannot enter customer deposits.

Dorfmann does not collect freight revenue because it does not charge for deliveries. Leave the Freight Revenue field blank.

Click the **Sales Discount field list arrow**.

This field is used to record the discounts customers receive for early settlement of their accounts.

Choose **4060 Sales Discounts** from the drop-down list. **Press** *tab*.

The cursor advances to the Deposits And Prepaid Orders field. This account is linked to customer deposits. Normally a liability account is selected because the prepayment creates a liability to the customer until the sale is completed.

Choose **2220 Prepaid Sales And Deposits** from the drop-down list.

Click **OK** to see the program's message about account class changes:

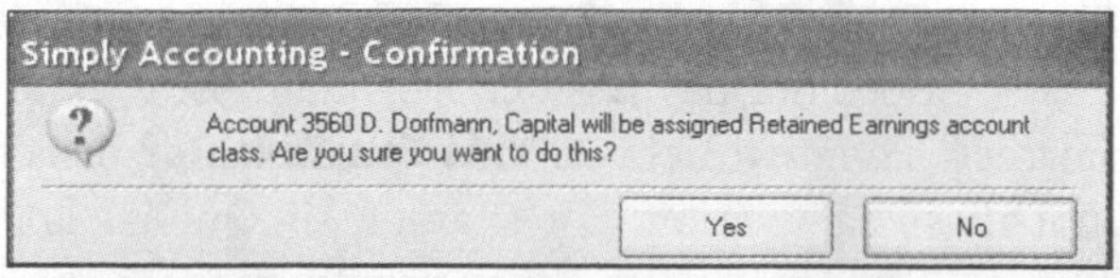

Many linked accounts must have the correct account class to be used as linked accounts. Normally, you can accept the account class definitions and changes assigned by the program. The exception is the Bank class accounts, which you must define before you can use them as linked bank accounts.

Click **Yes** to accept the change and save the linked account setting. You will see a second confirmation message for account 2200:

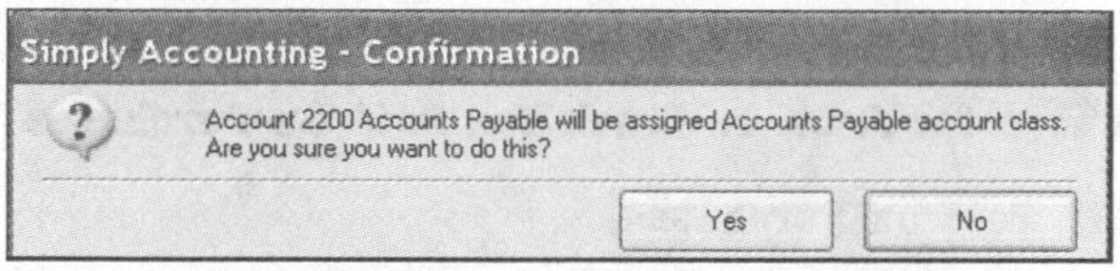

Click **Yes** to accept the class change, save the linked accounts and see the final message about the account class change for account 1200:

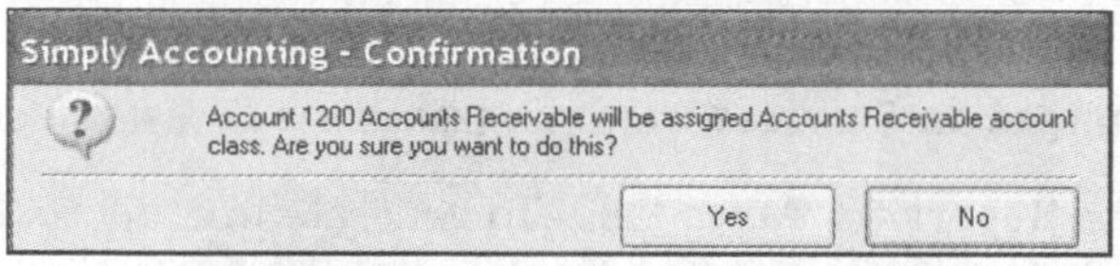

Click **Yes** to accept the change and return to the Home window.

> **NOTES**
> You must choose Yes to confirm the account class changes and to continue. If you choose No, you will return to the Linked Accounts screen.

Setting Up Sales Taxes

Setting up sales taxes before entering vendor and customer records will allow us to choose default tax codes for customers and vendors for automatic entry in journals.

Choose the **Setup menu**, then **choose System Settings** and **click Sales Taxes** to see the Sales Tax Information screen:

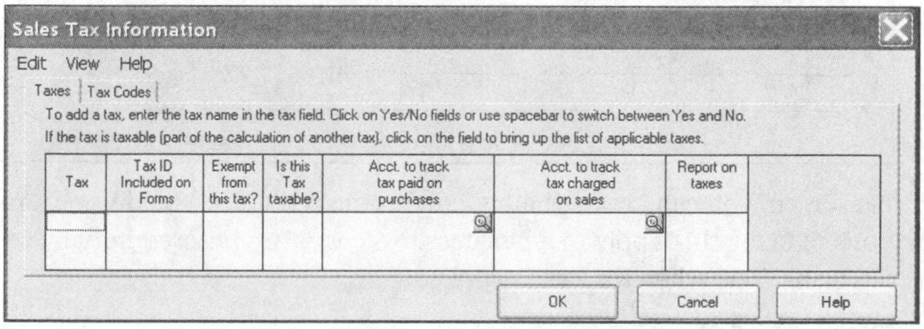

Simply Accounting has no preset tax information. You can customize the taxes to suit any business by entering all the taxes applied and paid by a business and by creating as many tax codes as needed to account for all the possible combinations of taxes. Additional taxes can be added later if they are needed.

The cursor is in the Tax field where you should enter the name of the tax. For Dorfmann, the only tax that applies is the GST.

Type GST **Press** *tab* to advance to the Tax ID field.

If the tax number should be included on invoices, you can enter it in this field. For GST, this is the business number. For PST, it is the provincial registration number that indicates the vendor is licensed to charge PST. GST numbers are normally included on forms because GST is refundable. PST numbers are not normally included on invoices.

Type `233 281 244` **Press** *tab*.

> **NOTES**
> Other taxes and tax codes can be added later if needed. The details for each tax and code can be modified if the tax legislation changes.

NOTES
A PST registration number is required for businesses that charge PST on sales and do not pay PST on purchases of merchandise that they sell to customers (only the final customer pays PST).

NOTES
Sales tax amounts entered in the General Journal are also tracked in these linked accounts.

The cursor moves to the **Exempt From This Tax?** column. Choose Yes if your business — Dorfmann in this case — does not pay the tax. Dorfmann Design pays GST, so the default selection No is correct. The next field, **Is This Tax Taxable?** asks if another tax includes this tax in its base calculation. For example, in Quebec and Prince Edward Island, PST is charged on GST so the GST in those provinces is taxable. For Alberta, where Dorfmann is located, the correct answer is No.

The next two fields define the linked accounts that **track the taxes paid** and the **taxes charged**. The taxes paid account records the total of the amounts entered in the GST field in the Purchases Journal whenever a purchase is made. Although you may choose an asset or a liability account, we use liability accounts because there is normally a balance owing to the Receiver General. If the tax is not refundable, such as PST paid, you can leave the field blank.

Click , the **List icon for Acct. To Track Tax Paid On Purchases**.

Double click **2670 GST Paid on Purchases**.

The cursor advances to the field for the Account To Track Taxes Charged On Sales. This account records the total of the amounts entered in the GST field in the Sales Journal whenever a sale is made. You may use an asset or a liability account.

Choose **2650 GST Charged on Services** from the List icon list of accounts.

The cursor advances to the **Report On Taxes** field. To generate tax reports from Simply Accounting, you should choose Yes. The Yes and No entries on the tax screens act as toggle switches. Clicking will change the entry from one to the other, and you can change these entries at any time.

Click **No** to change the default entry to Yes.

Click the **Tax Codes tab** to open the next information screen:

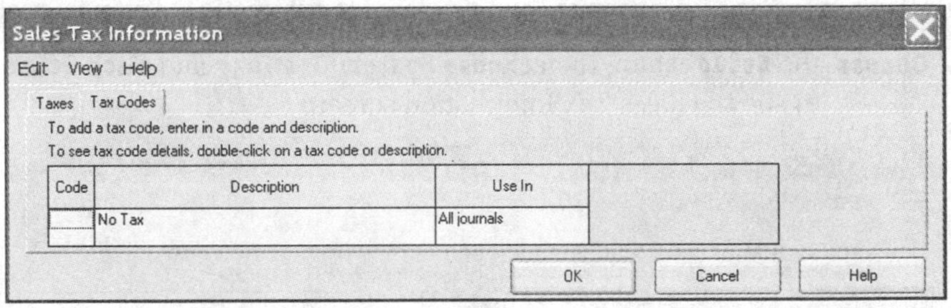

On this screen, you can create the tax codes required for all the different rates and combinations of taxes that apply to a business. No codes are entered initially so the only entry is the blank code when **No Tax** is applied.

Click the **Code column** below the blank on the first line.

Type G **Press** *tab* to move to the Description field.

Press *enter* or **double click** to open the Tax Code Details screen:

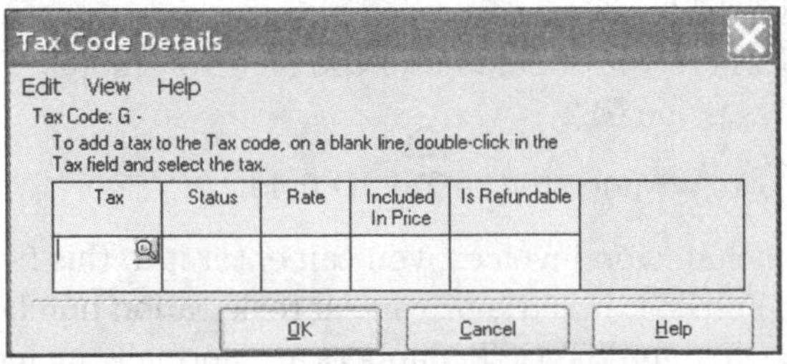

On this screen, you define how the tax is calculated and reported.

Click the **Tax field List icon** to see the list of taxes entered:

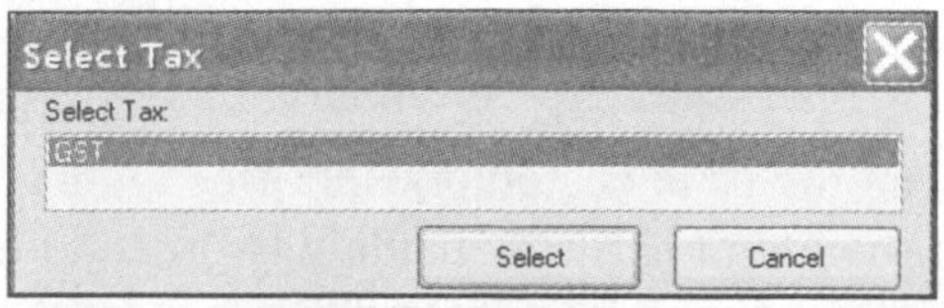

Because only one tax was entered on the taxes list, only one is listed here. At this stage, you are asked to choose the taxes that should be applied (charged or paid) when this code is used in a journal entry.

Click **Select** because GST is already selected and return to the Details.

Defaults are entered for the remaining fields. The tax **Status** is Taxable and this is correct — tax is calculated and charged. Other status options and their explanations can be viewed by clicking the List icon. The Non-taxable Status is used for items that are not taxed but for which the amounts are still included in reports to the Receiver General. Similarly, the Exempt Status is used for items that are exempt from the tax but the amounts are still included in the tax reports filed. For example, although food is zero-rated (no tax is charged), vendors may still claim a GST refund and must report their sales amounts.

NOTES

If at any time the tax regulations change, you can return to this screen and change the settings. For example, in 2004, BC decreased the PST rate from 7.5% to 7%. To make this change in the data files, just edit the Rate in the Tax Code Details screen.

In 2006, the federal budget included a GST rate change to 6 percent. This change was introduced too late to be incorporated in all the applications in this text. Memo #10 in the Source Documents asks you to update the tax rates and codes to apply this change.

The remaining fields are straightforward. **Rate** is the percentage rate for the tax. Taxes may be **included** in the sales and purchase prices or not included. If some vendors include the tax and others do not, create two separate tax codes. And finally, is the tax **refundable** — that is, are the taxes paid on purchases refunded? GST is not included for any of Dorfmann's vendors' or customers' prices and GST is refundable.

Click the **Rate field**.

Type 7

Click **No** in the Is Refundable column to change the entry to Yes.

Click **OK** to return to the Tax Codes screen for additional codes.

The description GST @ 7% appears beside the code G. You can edit the description if you want. If the tax were not refundable, non-refundable would be added to the description automatically.

You can also choose in which journals you want to have the tax codes appear. The default is to have the codes available in all journals and is usually the correct choice.

Click **All Journals** and then **click** the **List icon** to see the options:

NOTES

The List icon does not appear until you click the field.

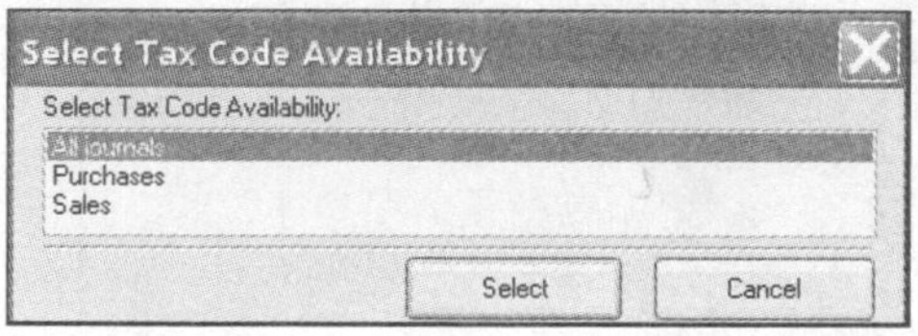

You can choose the Purchases Journal, the Sales Journal or All Journals.

NOTES

Charities that do not charge GST but are eligible for GST refunds may choose to show tax codes only in the Purchases Journal.

Click **Cancel** or **Select** to return to the Tax Codes screen because the default selection is correct.

Click **OK** to save the settings and return to the Home window.

At this stage, you can enter a default tax code for customers. (Refer to page 304.)

Choose the **Setup menu**, then **choose** **System Settings** and **click** **Settings**.

Click **Receivables** and then **click** **Options**.

Choose **tax code G** for new customers and **click** **OK** to save the change.

Setting Up Credit Cards

Since Dorfmann accepts credit card payments from customers and uses credit cards in payment for purchases, we must set up the credit cards by naming them and identifying the linked accounts for deposits, payments and fees associated with the cards. Dorfmann accepts Visa and MasterCard for sales, and uses Visa for credit card payments. You should be in the Home window.

Changing the Account Class for Credit Card Accounts

Before setting up the cards with their linked accounts, we must change the account class for the accounts we need. We will change the linked asset accounts to the Credit Card Receivable class and the payable account to the Credit Card Payable class. If you also make payments from or deposits to these accounts, you should use the Bank class for them so they will be available in the bank account fields in the journals.

WARNING!
You must choose either a Credit Card or Bank class account as the linked asset account for cards accepted. You must choose either a Credit Card Payable or a Bank class account as the linked payable account for credit cards used.

Click the **Accounts icon** to open the Accounts window.

Double click **1070 Bank: Visa** to open the Ledger window.

Click the **Class Options tab**.

Choose **Credit Card Receivable** from the Account Class list to change the class.

Click the **Next button** to open the ledger for 1080 Bank: MasterCard.

Choose **Credit Card Receivable** from the Account Class list.

Click the **Select field list arrow** to see the list of accounts.

Click **2160 Credit Card Payable** to open this account ledger.

Choose **Credit Card Payable** from the Account Class list.

Close the **Ledger window**.

Close the **Accounts window** to return to the Home window.

Entering the Credit Cards

NOTES
Although credit card information is not used in the vendor or customer records, we are setting up the credit cards first because they involve linked accounts.

Choose the **Setup menu**, then **choose System Settings** and **click Credit Cards** to access the Credit Card Information screen:

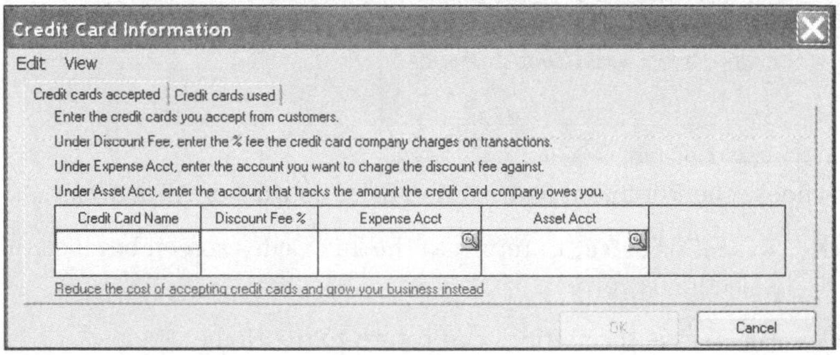

The first tab screen applies to credit cards accepted from customers. The cursor is in the **Name** field. All the cards you name here will appear in the Paid By list for Sales Invoices. Each card accepted should be listed on a separate line.

Type Visa **Press** *tab*.

The cursor advances to the **Discount Fee %** field. The discount fee is the amount that the card company withholds as a merchant transaction fee for use of the card. This expense is withheld from the total invoice amount that the card company deposits to the business bank account for each sale. Fees vary from one credit card company to another and also for the type of business. For example, high-volume businesses pay a lower percentage than businesses with a smaller volume of sales.

NOTES
Debit card transactions are set up as credit cards, but the discount fee is entered as 0.0%.

Type 2.9 **Press** *tab*.

The cursor advances to the **Expense Account** field. This is the linked account that will be debited automatically for the discount fee for a credit card sale. The expense amount or fee is the total invoice amount times the discount fee percentage.

Click the **Account List icon** to see the accounts available for linking.

Click **5020** to choose the account.

Click **Select** to add the account to the Card Information screen.

The cursor is in the **Asset Account** field, the linked account for deposits from the card company. Normally a bank account is set up for credit card deposits.

Click the **Account List icon** to see the list of accounts available for linking.

NOTES
You must choose a Bank, Cash or Credit Card Receivable class account as the linked Asset account.

Click **1070 Bank: Visa** to choose the account.

Click **Select** to add the account and advance to the second line.

Enter **MasterCard** in the Name field and **2.7** in the Discount Fee % field. **Choose** Expense Account **5020** and Asset Account **1080**.

If there are additional credit cards, enter the information for them in the same way.

Cards used for payments to vendors are set up in the same way. The business may use and accept the same cards or different cards.

Click the **Credit Cards Used tab** to open the screen for the cards that the business uses:

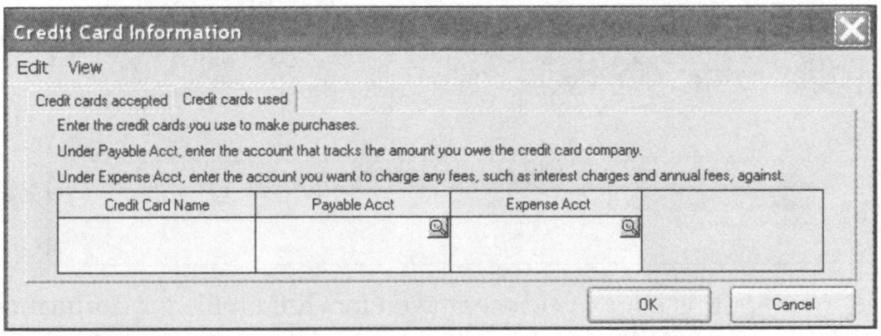

Each card named on this screen will appear in the Purchases Journal in the Paid By list. There is no discount fee associated with individual purchases, although there may be an annual or monthly fee attached to the card. Again, each card is listed on a separate line with its associated linked accounts.

Click the **Credit Card Name field**.

Type Visa **Press** *tab*.

The cursor moves to the **Payable Acct** field. This account is the liability account that records the balance owing to the card company.

NOTES
You must choose a Bank, Cash or Credit Card Payable class account as the linked Payable account.

Click the **Account List icon** to see the list of available accounts.

Click **2160**, the liability account for the card.

Click **Select** to add the account and move to the Expense Acct field.

The **Expense Account** records any monthly or annual fees paid to the card company for the privilege of using the card and interest charges on cash advances or overdue amounts. Not all cards have user fees, but all cards charge interest on cash advances and balances not paid by the due date. These amounts are entered in the Additional Fees And Interest field when you pay credit cards in the Payments Journal. Dorfmann uses the same expense account for all credit card–related expenses.

Click the **Account List icon** to see the account list.

Double click **5020**

Click **OK** to save the setup details.

If you did not change the account class correctly, you will see the following warning message about incorrect account classes:

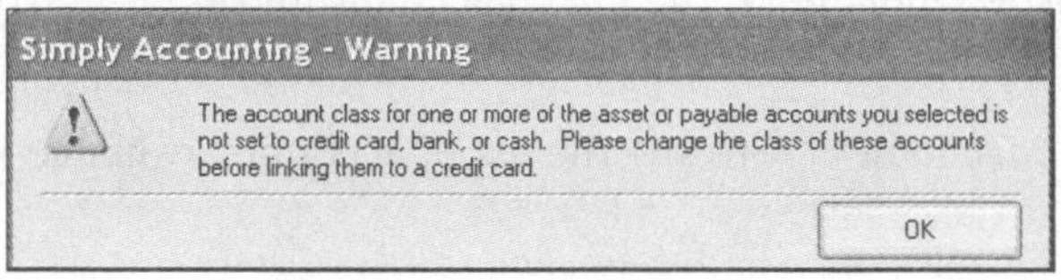

Click OK. Click Cancel to close the Credit Card Information window. Return to the section Changing the Account Class for Credit Card Accounts (page 320). Make the necessary account class changes and re-enter the credit card details.

Entering Vendors in the Payables Ledger

Use the Vendor Information for Dorfmann Design on page 290 to enter vendor details and historical invoices. The following keystrokes will enter the information for Alberta Energy Corp., the first vendor on Dorfmann Design's list.

Click the **Vendors icon** in the Home window.

You will display the empty Vendors window:

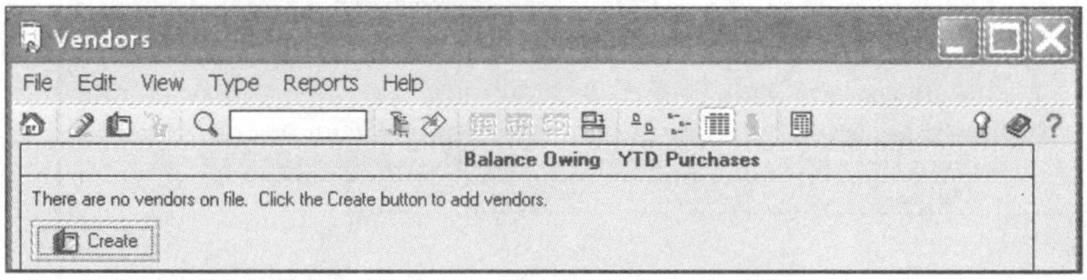

The Vendors window is empty because no vendors are on file for Dorfmann. Once we add the vendor accounts, this window will contain a listing for each vendor that you can use to access the vendor's ledger record. The vendors may be displayed in icon form or by name with balances and year-to-date amounts. The default is the listing by name.

If you prefer to list the vendors by icon in the Vendors window, choose the View menu and click Icon. New vendors will be added at the end of the display but you can drag icons to any position you want so that frequently used icons appear together at the top of the window. You can restore alphabetic order for the icons by choosing the Options menu and clicking Re-sort Icons.

Click the **Create button** or the **Create tool** in the Vendors window, or **choose** the **File menu** and **click Create**.

NOTES
Pressing ctrl + N will also open a new vendor ledger record form.

You will display the vendor Address tab screen:

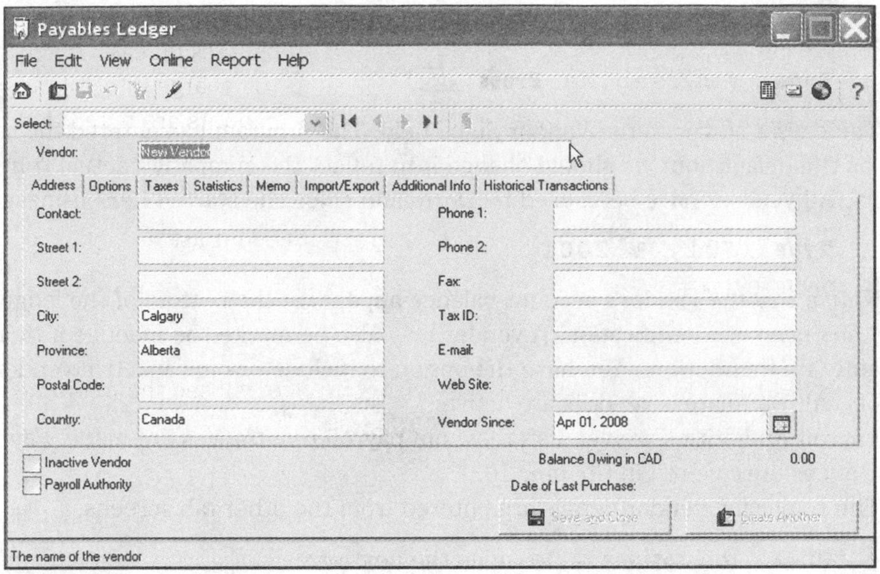

Most of the Vendor input screens should be familiar from entering records for new vendors in previous chapters. The Address tab screen is displayed first and the Vendor field is highlighted, ready for you to enter information.

Type `Alberta Energy Corp.` **Press** tab.

The cursor advances to the Contact field. Here you should enter the name of the person (or department) at Alberta Energy Corp. with whom Dorfmann Design will be dealing. This information enables a company to make inquiries more professionally and effectively. For a small business, the owner's name may appear in this field.

Type `Con Edison` **Press** tab to advance to the Street 1 field.

Type `50 Watts Rd.` **Press** tab to move to the Street 2 field.

Type `Suite 800`

The program uses the Company Information entries as the defaults for the City, Province and Country fields. Therefore, Calgary has been entered in the City field because it is the city in which Dorfmann Design is located. It is correct. The default Province and Country are also correct.

Click the **Postal Code field**.

Type `t3g5k8`

Click the **Phone 1 field**.

The program corrects the format of the postal code. (Only Canadian postal codes are reformatted — those with the specific letter and number sequence.) You can enter phone and fax numbers with or without the area code.

Type `4037556000` **Press** tab to advance to the Phone 2 field.

Type `4037553997` **Press** tab to advance to the Fax field.

Type `4037547201` **Press** tab to advance to the Tax ID field.

The program corrects the format of the phone numbers. The Tax ID field allows you to enter the vendor's tax ID or business number. The following two fields contain the e-mail and Web site addresses for the vendor. Enter them just as you would type them in your Internet and e-mail programs.

NOTES

If you choose to skip the Vendors icon window from the Setup menu (User Preferences, View tab) in the Home window, you will see this Payables Ledger (vendor) Address tab window immediately when you click the Vendors icon.

NOTES

You may skip any of the address tab fields if the information is missing for the vendor. Just click the next field for which you have information to move the cursor. To edit any field, drag to highlight the contents and type the correct information.

NOTES

Remember that the postal code sequence for Canada is letter, number, letter, number, letter and number.

Type 459 021 643 **Press** tab.

Type accounts@aeg.ca **Press** tab.

Type www.aeg.ca **Press** tab.

The cursor moves to the Vendor Since field. The program has entered the session date as the default, but we should change it to reflect the company's actual transaction history. All vendors have been used by Dorfmann since she started her business in 2001.

Type July 1 2001

Notice that the vendor's account balance appears at the bottom of the ledger, along with the currency identification. A vendor may also be marked as Inactive if there are currently no transactions. You have the option to include or omit inactive vendors from reports. All Dorfmann's vendors are active.

Payroll Authorities are vendors to whom payroll remittances are made. Payroll remittances are covered in Chapter 10.

The remaining vendor details are entered from the other tab screens.

Click the **Options tab** to open the next screen:

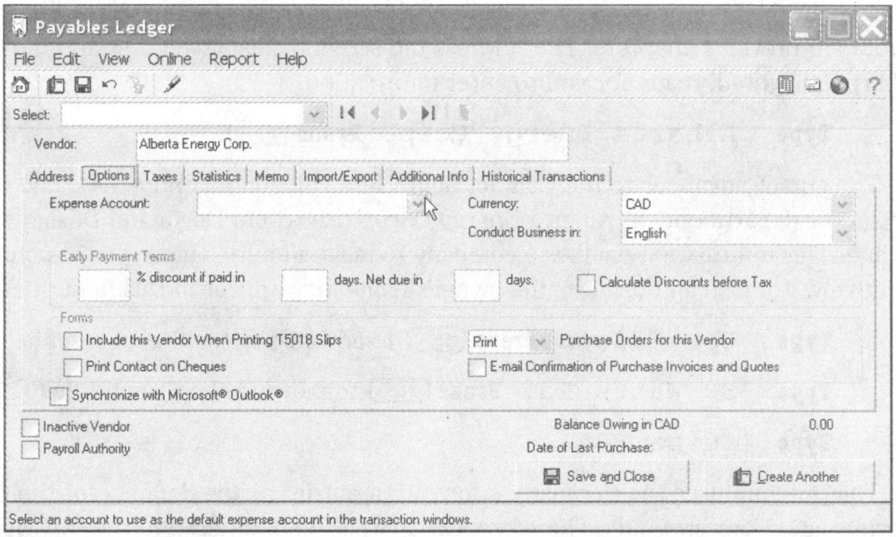

The vendor's name appears at the top of each tab screen for reference. We want to enter the default expense account so that it will automatically appear in journal entries.

Click the **Expense Account list arrow**. All postable accounts are listed.

Click **5060 Hydro Expense** (you will need to scroll down first).

Currency is also defined on the Options tab screen. By default, vendors use the home currency, CAD. The currencies set up in the Currency Information screen are listed in the drop-down list in the Currency field. After you enter historical transactions or journal transactions for a vendor in one currency, you cannot change the currency. Records for foreign vendors will show all amounts in both currencies.

Regardless of the language you use to work in Simply Accounting, you can choose a language for the vendor so that all Simply Accounting forms you send to this vendor will be in the language selected on the Options tab screen.

If the vendor offers a discount for early payment or has a term for the net amount, you can enter these details in this screen. There is no discount, so start in the third Terms field.

Click the **Net Due In ____ Days field**.

Type 10

NOTES
T5018 slips apply to the purchase of construction materials.

NOTES
If you have not yet created the account you want to use as the default account, type the new account number in the Expense Account field and press tab to start the Add An Account wizard. Choose Add when asked if you want to create the account.

WARNING!
Do not forget to choose USD as the currency for DesignMaster Software (see page 330).

NOTES
Remember that all vendor discounts are calculated on before-tax amounts.

Skip the discount before or after tax option because there is no discount.

Do not turn on the option to Print Contact On Cheques because the Contact field does not contain address information.

If you e-mail purchase orders to a vendor, choose this option from the drop-down list to replace the default option to print purchase orders. Click E-mail Confirmation if you choose to e-mail purchase orders to be certain that the order is received. Even if you choose Print as the default, you can still e-mail the order from the Purchases Journal.

Click the **Taxes tab** to access the next input screen:

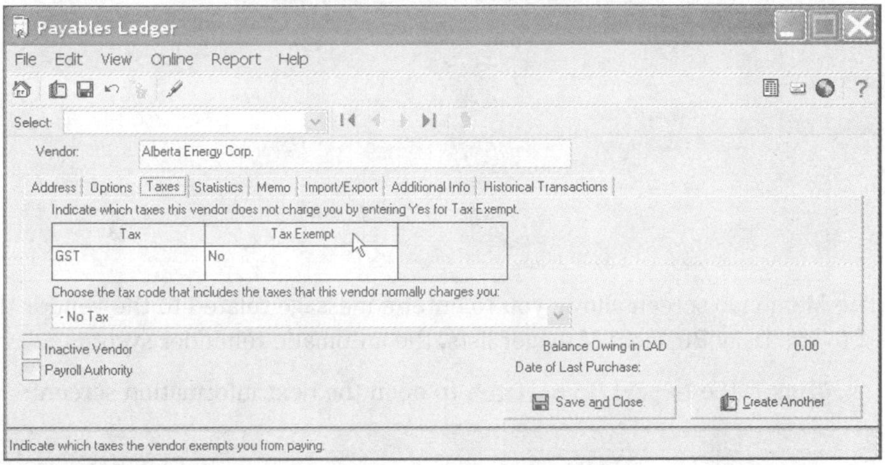

This screen allows you to indicate which taxes the vendor normally charges and the default tax code for journal entries.

All vendors for Dorfmann Design, except the Receiver General, charge GST so the correct entry for the Tax Exempt column is No. Vendors such as the Receiver General for Canada, who do not supply goods or services eligible for input tax credits, should have Yes in the Tax Exempt column to indicate that Dorfmann does not pay tax to them. If you choose Yes, the tax will not be calculated in the Purchases Journal for that vendor, even if you choose a tax code that applies the tax.

Leave the Tax Exempt entry as No to indicate that this vendor charges GST and tax codes are available for purchases. Clicking No changes the entry to Yes.

Click the **list arrow beside No Tax** to choose a default tax code.

Click **G - GST @ 7%** to select the code.

Click the **Statistics tab** to open the next information screen:

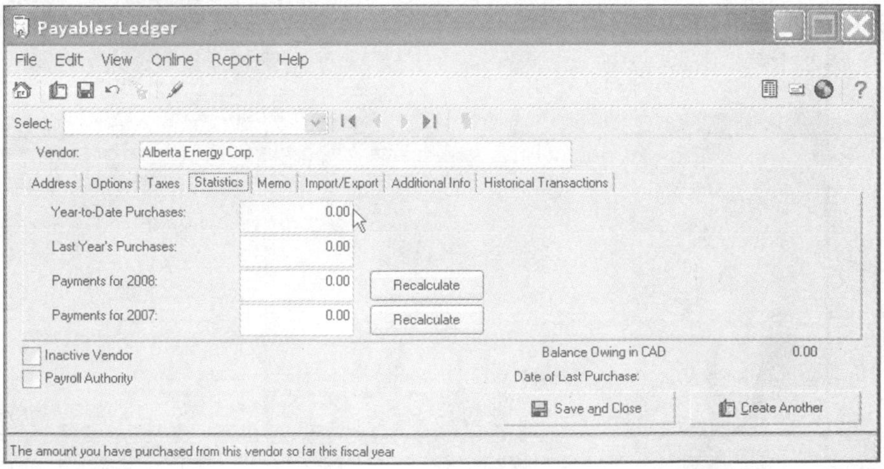

NOTES
For vendors who request payment on receipt, enter 1 in the Net Days field. When you enter zero in the Net Days field, the Terms fields remain blank and invoices will not show as overdue. Payment terms may be changed in the journal for individual invoices.

NOTES
When PST applies, businesses that sell inventory at the retail level do not pay PST on the inventory they purchase for resale. Thus they are exempt from paying PST. If, however, the vendor charges for shipping – and shipping charges are subject to PST charges – you must choose No in the Exempt column for PST so that taxes can be calculated correctly for the shipping charges.

NOTES
When the vendor uses a foreign currency, the statistics summary information is presented for both currencies.

The Statistics fields record the historical purchase and payment totals for two years and are updated automatically from journal entries.

Click the **Year-To-Date Purchases field.**

Type 802

Click **the Payments For 2008 field.**

Type 802

Click the **Memo tab** to advance to the next screen:

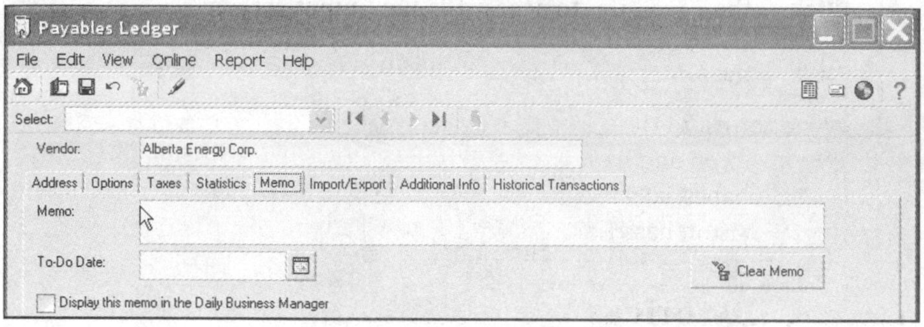

NOTES
The message in the memo may be up to 255 characters in length.

The Memo tab screen allows you to enter a message related to the vendor that is added to the Daily Business Manager lists, the automatic reminder system.

NOTES
The Daily Business Manager is used in Chapter 10.
The Import/Export feature is described in Appendix H on the Data CD.

Click the **Import/Export tab** to open the next information screen:

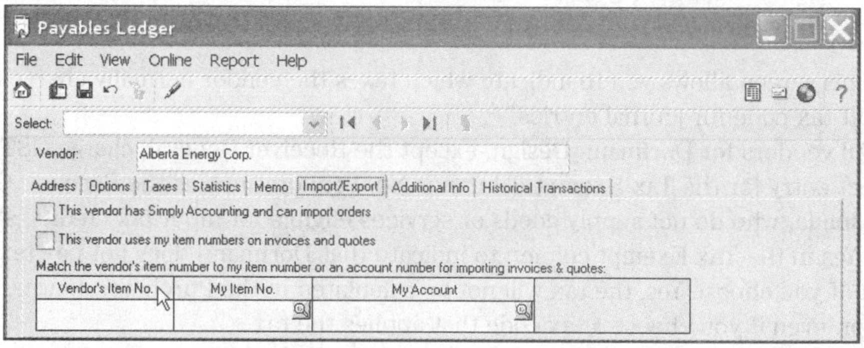

The Import/Export screen refers to inventory items. If the vendor also uses Simply Accounting, you can match the vendor's inventory item codes to your own for electronic transfers of information.

Click the **Additional Info tab**:

NOTES
You can name the additional fields from the Setup menu by choosing System Settings and Names and Terminology.
We will customize records by adding fields in Chapter 15.

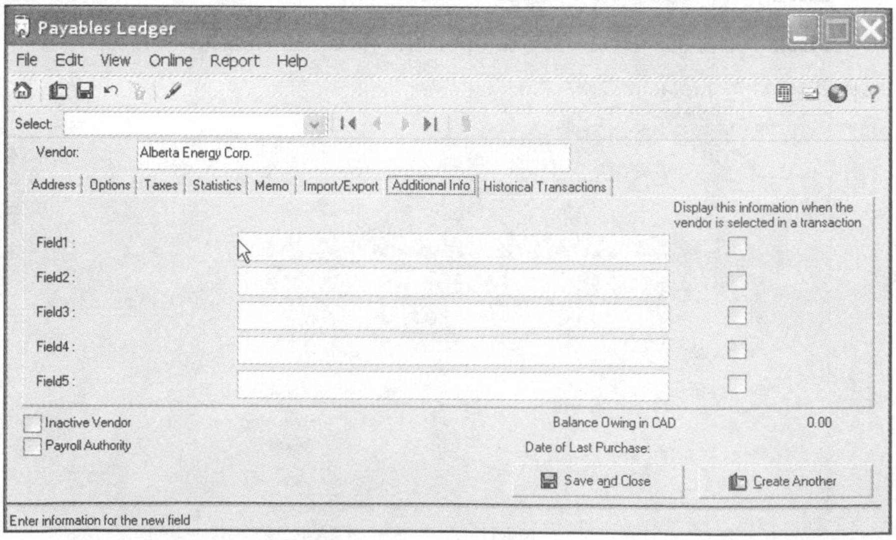

You can customize the records for any ledger by adding up to five fields. The customized names you added will appear on this Additional Info screen. This additional information can be included in journal transaction windows and in Vendor List reports. Dorfmann Design does not use any additional fields and there are no outstanding invoices for Alberta Energy Corp. so we can check the vendor details.

Correct any **errors** by returning to the field with the mistake, **highlighting** the **errors** and **entering** the **correct information**. You can now save the record.

Click **Create Another** [Create Another] to save the vendor information and display a blank New Vendor screen.

Click the **Address tab** to prepare for entering the next vendor record.

When you return to the Vendors window, you will see that Simply Accounting has created a Vendor icon and listing for Alberta Energy Corp. The default view for vendors is to list them alphabetically by name with the balance owing and year-to-date purchases.

The Create button has been removed. The Create tool is still available.

WARNING!
Remember to click Calculate Discounts Before Tax for all vendors who offer discounts.

NOTES
You can also display vendors by icon. Choose the Icon tool or choose the View menu and click Icon. Vendor icons may be moved to a different position by dragging. New vendors are added to the end of the display, regardless of order. To restore the alphabetic order for icons, choose the Options menu and then Re-sort Icons.

Entering Historical Vendor Information

The following keystrokes will enter the historical information from page 290 for Designers Den, the first vendor with outstanding invoices. You should have a blank Payables Ledger Address tab window on-screen.

You can enter all the historical invoices and payments for the fiscal year to date, but you must enter all outstanding invoices and partial payments toward them. Designers Den has outstanding invoices so we must enter historical transaction details.

Finish entering the **Address, Options, Taxes and Statistics details**, remembering to click Calculate Discounts Before Tax.

You can also enter these details for all vendors and then open the ledger to add historical information by clicking the Historical Transactions tab. Open the ledger for any vendor by double clicking the vendor's name in the Vendors window.

Click the **Historical Transactions tab**:

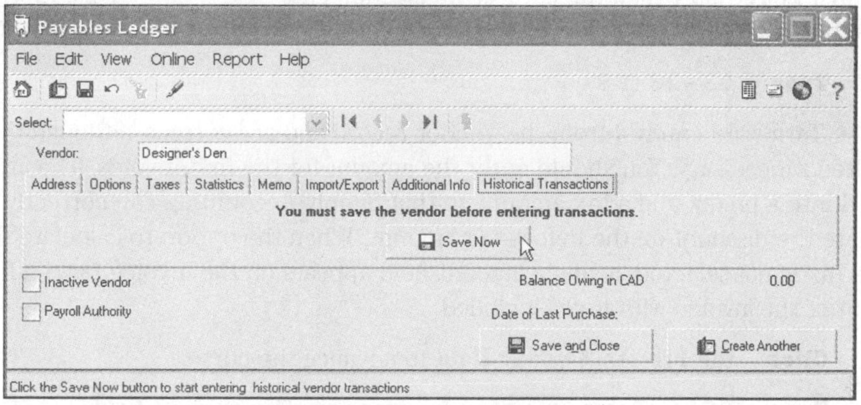

You must save or create the vendor record before adding historical invoices.

NOTES
If you have already created the record, you will not see the Save Now option on the Historical Transactions tab screen. Instead, you will see the next screen asking you to choose Invoices or Payments.

Click the **Save Now button** to modify the ledger screen:

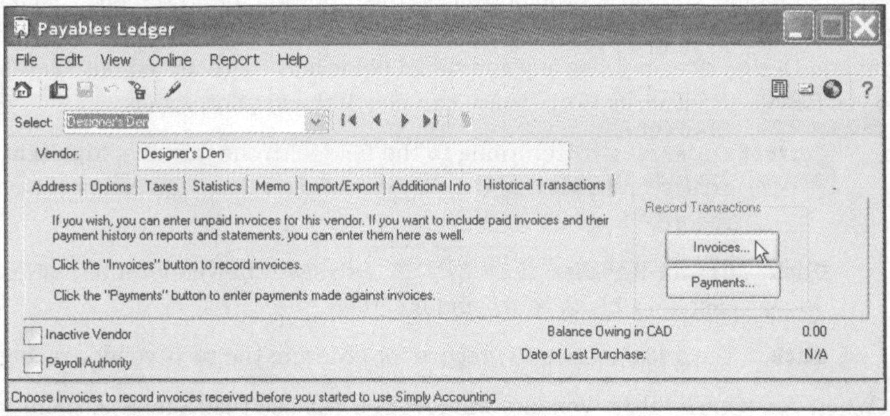

The Create Another and the Save And Close buttons are removed from the form. The screen now has two new buttons: Invoices and Payments. You should select Invoices to record outstanding invoices and Payments to record prior payments that you want to keep on record after entering invoices.

WARNING!
Enter invoice details carefully. To correct a historical invoice amount, you must pay the invoice and clear the paid transactions (Maintenance menu). Then reset the historical payments for the year to zero (Payables Ledger, Statistics tab screen) and re-enter the outstanding invoices. Refer to page 339.

Click **Invoices** to see the following input screen:

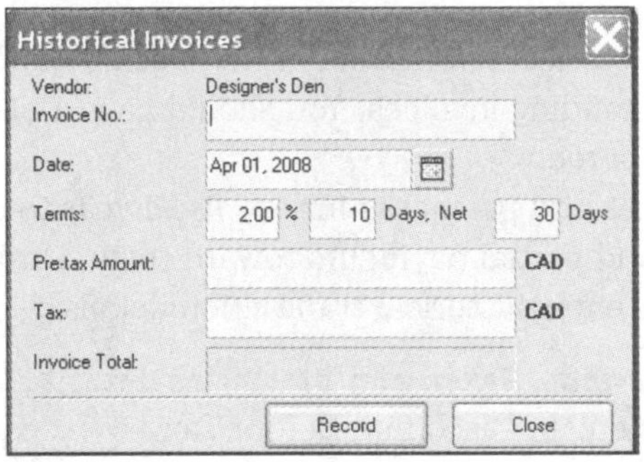

The cursor is in the Invoice No. field so you can enter the first invoice number.

Type DD-4502 **Press** tab to advance to the Date field.

Enter the invoice date to replace the default earliest transaction date. The invoice date must not be later than the earliest transaction date — the date of the first journal transaction after the historical data in the setup.

Type 03-26-08

The Terms are entered from the Vendor record and are correct, although they can be edited if necessary. You should enter the amount for the first invoice. The amount is divided into a pretax and a tax amount so that Simply Accounting can correctly calculate the discount on the before-tax amount. When the option to calculate discounts before tax is not selected, a single amount field appears on the invoice for the full amount of the invoice with taxes included.

Click the **Pre-tax Amount field** to advance the cursor.

Type 2500 **Press** tab to advance to the Tax amount field.

Type 175 **Press** tab to update the Invoice Total.

The totals of all outstanding invoice and payment amounts must match the opening balance in the *Accounts Payable* control account in the General Ledger.

Correct any **errors**. **Press** tab to return to the field with the error and **highlight** the **error**. Then **enter** the **correct information**.

Be sure that all the information is entered correctly before you save your vendor invoice. If you save incorrect invoice information and you want to change it, refer to page 339 for assistance.

Click **Record** to save the information and to display another blank invoice for this vendor.

Enter **invoice DD-4630** (not the payment, Chq #62) for Designers Den by repeating the steps above.

When you have recorded all outstanding invoices for a vendor,

Click **Close** to return to the ledger.

The two invoices have been added to the Balance field at the bottom of the ledger screen. Now you can enter historical payment information for this vendor.

Click **Payments** to display the payments form:

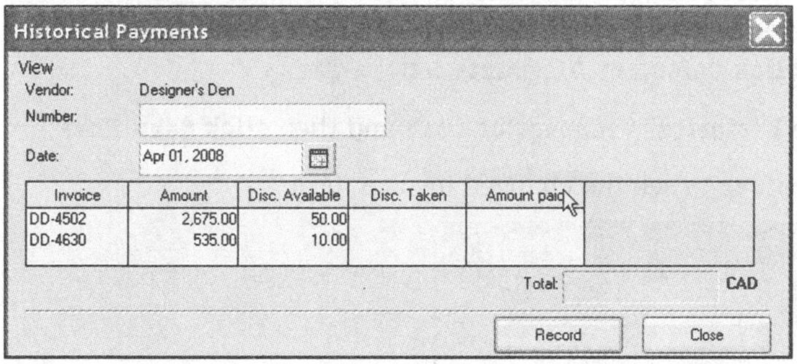

All outstanding invoices that you entered are displayed. Notice that the discount is 2% of the pretax amounts. Entering historical payments is very much like entering current payments in the Payments Journal. You should make separate payment entries for each cheque.

Click the Number field if necessary to move the cursor to the cheque number field.

Type 62 **Press** *tab* to advance to the Date field.

Enter the cheque date for the first payment toward invoice #DD-4502 to replace the default earliest transaction date.

Type 3-26

Click the **Amount Paid column** on the line for Invoice #DD-4502.

Because the full amount is not being paid, the discount does not apply. The full amount of the discount will remain available until the 10 days have passed. If the balance is paid within that time, the full discount will be taken.

The full invoice amount is displayed as the default and is highlighted so you can edit it.

Type 2210 **Press** *tab*. **Press** *del* to delete the Disc. Taken amount.

Check the **information** carefully and **make corrections** before you proceed.

Click **Record** to save the information and display another payment form for this vendor in case there are additional payments to record.

The amount owing for invoice DD-4502 has been updated to include the payment you entered but the full discount amount remains available.

Repeat these procedures to enter any other payments to this vendor.

WARNING!
You must choose Record to save each invoice and payment and then Close the invoice form. If you close the input screen before selecting Record, the information is not saved.

NOTES
The View menu has the option to refresh the invoices from information added by other users. It applies only to the multi-user mode and is not available in the Basic version.

NOTES
The discount amounts are $50 (2% of $2 500) and $10 (2% of $500).

NOTES
Clicking the Amount Paid field directly ensures the discount amount is not entered.

WARNING!
If an amount appears in the Disc. Taken field, delete it before recording the payment.

When you have recorded all outstanding payments to a vendor,

Click **Close** to return to the vendor information form.

When you click the Statistics tab, you will see that the invoices and payment you entered have been included to increase the totals for 2008.

Click the **Create tool** or **press** ctrl + **N** to enter the next vendor.

Click the **Address tab** to prepare for entering the next vendor record.

Entering Foreign Vendor Records

Entering records for foreign vendors is the same as entering home currency vendors except for choosing a different currency and adding some details to the invoices.

WARNING!
You cannot change the currency for a vendor or customer after entering historical invoices so you must set up the currencies first. After you enter historical invoices for a foreign vendor or customer, you cannot change the currency setting for the company. You must pay the invoices, clear paid transactions, remove the vendor and then recreate the vendor record from scratch.

Enter **address details for DesignMaster Software**. **Click** the **Options tab**.

Choose **USD** from the Currency list. The balance owing is shown in both currencies. **Enter** the remaining **options** and **taxes** details. Remember to **click** **Calculate Discounts Before Tax**.

Click the **Historical Transactions tab** and then **click** **Save Now**.

Click **Invoices** to see the changed invoice form:

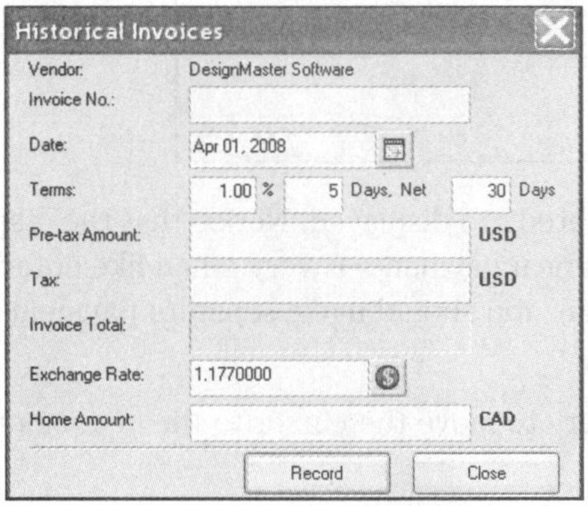

USD vendors have USD as the currency designation as well as a field for the exchange rate and the amount in the home currency.

NOTES
The Exchange Rate screen opens as soon as you enter the date. If you press tab after entering the date, it will open immediately. If you do not press tab and click the USD Amount field, it will open at that point. Click Cancel when it appears.

Enter **DMS-234** as the **Invoice No.** and **Mar 13** as the transaction **Date**.

Click the **USD Pre-tax Amount field**. (See margin notes.)

Click **Cancel** to close the Exchange Rate screen when it opens.

Type `1575` **Press** tab to advance to the USD Tax amount field.

Type `110.25` **Do not press** tab.

Click the **Home Amount field** to select the default amount that is based on the default exchange rate for April 1.

Type `1982` **Press** tab to let the program recalculate the exchange rate.

Click **Record** and then **click** **Close** to return to the ledger.

Click the **Create tool**. **Click** the **Address tab** to enter the next vendor.

NOTES
The Statistics tab screen shows the summary amounts in both Canadian and United States dollars for DesignMaster Software.

Enter the **remaining vendors** and historical transactions. After entering the last vendor record,

Click **Save And Close** (Save and Close) to close the Vendor Ledger. **Close** the **Vendors window** to return to the Home window.

Display or **print** your **Vendor List** to check the address details.

Display or **print** a **Vendor Aged Detail Report**. Include terms and historical differences to check the historical transactions.

Entering Customers in the Receivables Ledger

Use the Customer Information chart for Dorfmann Design on page 291 to complete this step. The following keystrokes will enter the information for Alberta Heritage Bank, the first customer on the list for Dorfmann Design.

Click the **Customers icon** in the Home window to display the Customers window. The Customers window is empty because there are no customers on file yet for Dorfmann.

Click the **Create button** Create or **tool** in the Customers window, or **choose** the **File menu** and **click Create** to open the customer information input screen:

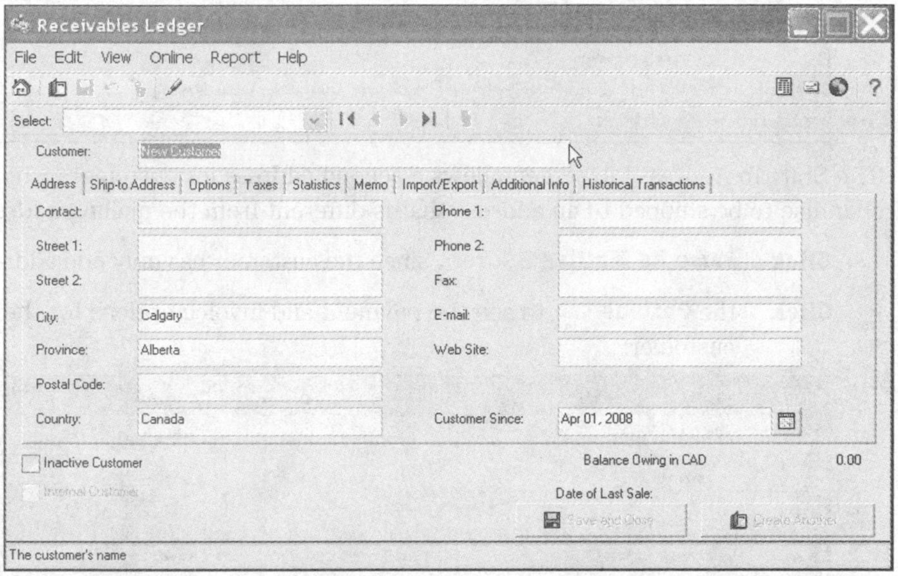

The Address tab screen is displayed initially and the Customer field is highlighted, ready for you to enter information. The default Province and Country are correct.

You may skip any of the address tab fields if information is missing. Just click the next field for which you have information to move the cursor.

Type `Alberta Heritage Bank` **Press** *tab*.

Dorfmann's primary contact about a sale should be entered in the Contact field.

Type `A. Spender` **Press** *tab* to advance to the Street 1 field.

Type `306 Revenue Road` **Press** *tab* to move to the Street 2 field.

Type `Fourth Floor` **Press** *tab* to advance to the City field.

Type `Okotoks`

Click the **Postal Code field**.

Type `t0l1t3` **Press** *tab*.

Click the **Phone 1 field**. The postal code format is corrected.

Type `4037445900` **Press** *tab*. The format is corrected automatically.

NOTES
Even though the historical invoices and payments were entered correctly, you will notice that there is an outstanding historical difference. This is addressed on page 339.

NOTES
If you prefer to list the customers by icon in the Customers window, choose the View menu and then Icon. New customers will be added to the end of the display. To restore alphabetic order, choose the Options menu and click Re-sort Icons.

NOTES
If you choose to skip the Customers icon window from the Home window Setup menu (User Preferences, View tab), you will see this Receivables Ledger window immediately when you click the Customers icon.

BASIC VERSION
The option to define the customer as an Internal Customer does not appear in the Basic version.

NOTES
Remember that the postal code sequence for Canada is letter, number, letter, number, letter and number.

Type 4037446345 **Press** (tab).

Type 4037445821 **Press** (tab) to advance to the E-mail field.

Type spender@heritagebank.com **Press** (tab) to move to the Web Site field.

Type www.heritagebank.com

Press (tab) to move to the Customer Since date field.

Type Jan 1 08

NOTES
The Internal Customers option works with the time and billing feature and is used to identify other departments within the company who use your services. The time and cost for these internal services can be tracked. Time and billing is covered in Chapter 17.

The current balance and currency are noted at the bottom of the Ledger window. Like vendors and accounts, customers may be marked as inactive and omitted from reports if they have not bought merchandise or services for some time.

Click the **Ship-To Address tab**:

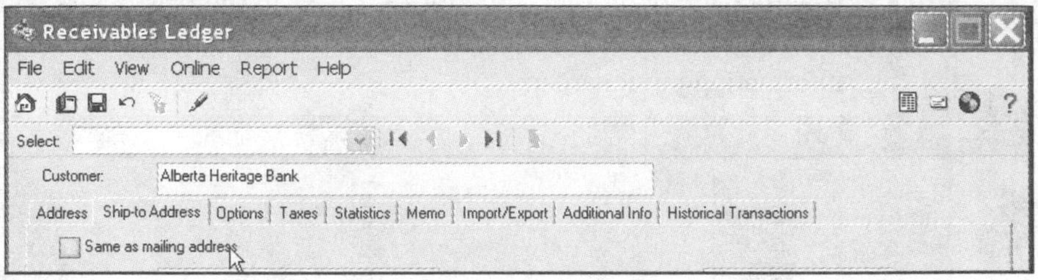

The Ship-To Address tab screen allows a second address for customers who want merchandise to be shipped to an address that is different from the mailing address.

Click **Same As Mailing Address** since the customer has only one address.

Click the **Options tab** to see the payment and invoice options for the customer:

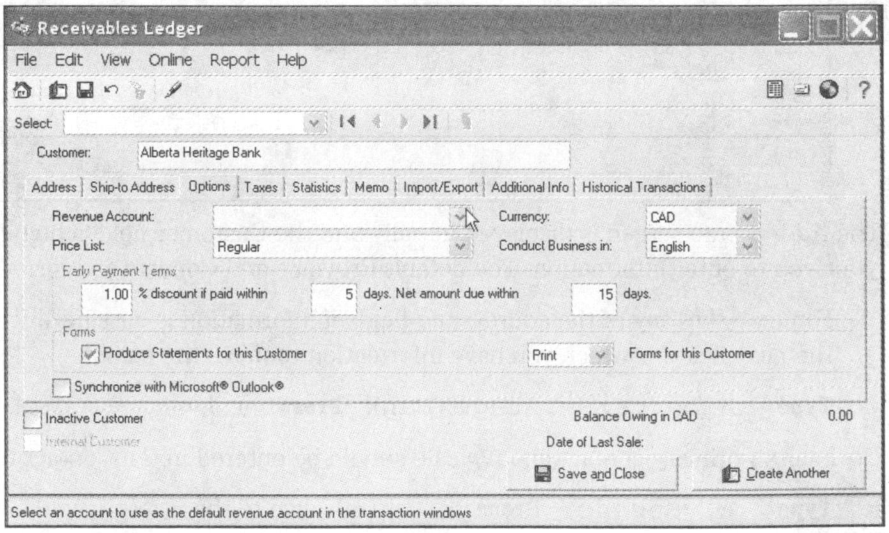

NOTES
The option to calculate discounts before or after tax is selected for the Receivables Ledger as a whole (see page 304). You cannot change the setting for individual customers.

All the default settings, including currency, are correct. You can select English or French as the customer's language — all forms you send to the customer will be prepared in the selected language. The Price List field applies to inventory and services prices that can be set at different rates for different customers. Dorfmann supplies customized services and does not use the Inventory module. The payment terms are entered automatically from the Receivables Settings. Terms can be edited if necessary for individual customers and invoices in the Sales Journal. Dorfmann charges interest on overdue accounts so we need to be able to produce statements, and the currency definition is correct as CAD, the home currency.

You need to add only a default revenue account for the customer. Although there are two revenue accounts that apply to customers, most customers use Dorfmann's design services, so we can choose this as the default. Remember that you can choose a different account in the Sales Journal for any invoice. You may prefer to leave the Revenue Account field blank so that you do not select an incorrect revenue account.

Click the **Revenue Account field list arrow**.

Click **4020 Revenue from Design**.

Click the **Taxes tab**:

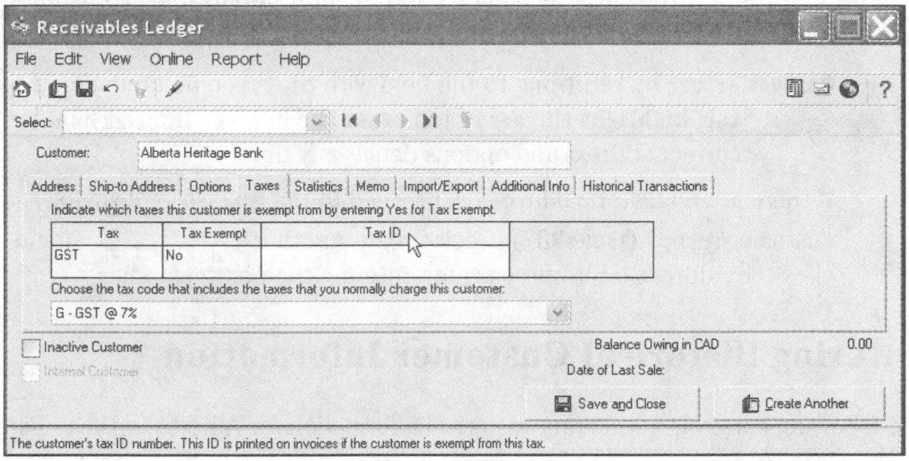

The customer is not exempt from paying GST so the default is correct. If the customer does not pay the tax, enter the tax ID number so that it appears on invoices. For example, retail stores do not pay PST on inventory that they will sell. They must have a tax number to permit the exemption. Some customers are also exempt from GST payments. Taxes will be calculated only if the customer is marked as not tax exempt. The default tax code, G - GST @ 7%, should be entered.

NOTES
The PST number for retailers identifies that they can collect PST from their customers and be exempted from paying the tax on purchases of the items they sell.

NOTES
You can change the default tax code for individual customers if necessary by choosing a different code from the Tax Code list. You can also change the code for individual invoices or accounts on the invoice.

Click the **Statistics tab** to view the next set of customer details:

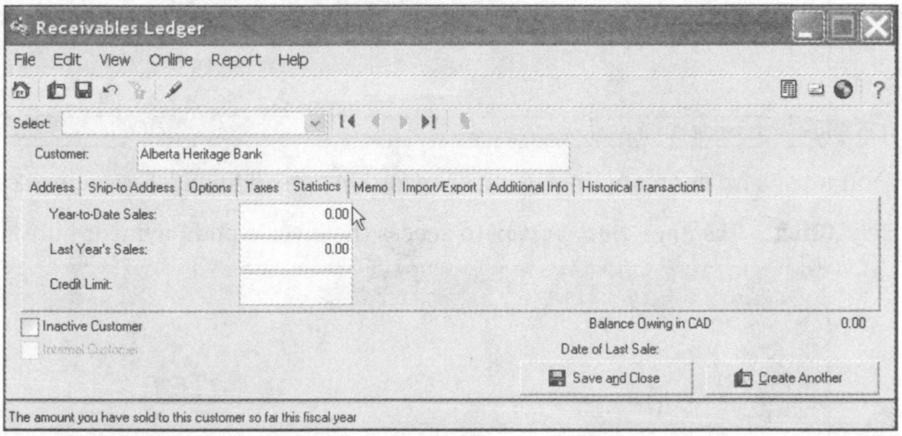

Balances will be included automatically once you provide the outstanding invoice information. **Year-To-Date Sales** are updated from journal entries, but you can add a historical balance as well. When you have two years of data, there will be an amount for last year's sales too. Records for foreign customers will have sales summary amounts and balances in both currencies.

The **Credit Limit** is the amount that the customer can purchase on account before payments are required. If the customer goes beyond this credit limit, the program will issue a warning when you attempt to post the invoice.

Click the **Year-To-Date Sales field**.

Type 3210 **Press** *tab* **twice** to advance to the Credit Limit field.
Type 5000

The **Memo tab** screen for customers is just like the Memo tab screen for vendors. It allows you to enter messages related to the customer. If you enter a reminder date, the program will display the message on the date you provide.

If the customer also uses Simply Accounting, you can match the customer's inventory codes to your own on the **Import/Export tab** screen to allow for electronic data transfers.

The **Additional Info tab** screen allows you to enter details for the custom-defined fields you created for customers, similar to the Additional Info tab fields for vendors.

Correct errors by returning to the field with the error. **Click** the appropriate **tab**, **highlight** the **error** and **enter** the **correct information**. You can correct address and options details any time.

If there are no historical invoices, proceed to the final step of saving the customer record (page 337). Click Create Another [Create Another] and then click the Address tab to prepare for entering the next customer.

Entering Historical Customer Information

The following keystrokes will enter historical information for Alberta Heritage Bank.

Click the **Historical Transactions tab**:

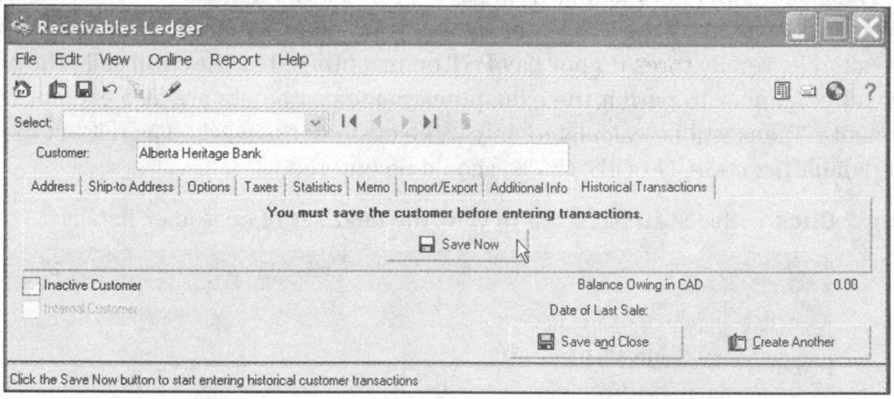

> **NOTES**
> If you have already saved (created) the record, you will not see the Save Now option on the Historical Transactions tab screen. Instead, you will see the next screen asking you to choose Invoices or Payments.

You must save or create the customer record before adding historical invoices.

Click the **Save Now button** to access the invoice and payment buttons:

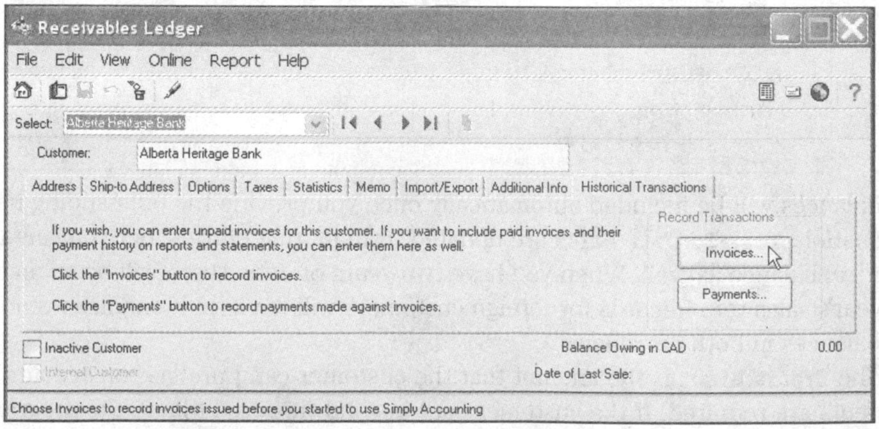

The Create Another and Save buttons are removed because you have already saved the record.

If you prefer, you can enter address, options and credit limit details for all customers and then add the historical invoices and payments from the Historical Transactions tab screen. You can open a customer ledger record by double clicking the customer's name in the Customers window. Then click the Historical Transactions tab.

Just as in the Payables Ledger, you enter invoices and payments separately. You can use the Payments option to record any payments against previous invoices that you want to keep on record. The totals of all outstanding invoices, after payments, must match the opening balance in the *Accounts Receivable* control account in the General Ledger.

Click **Invoices** to display the following input form:

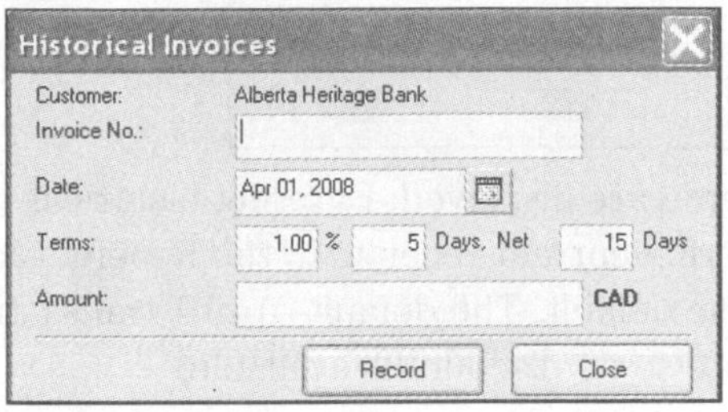

WARNING!
Enter invoice details carefully. To correct a historical invoice amount, you must pay the invoice and then clear paid transactions (Maintenance menu). Then re-enter the outstanding invoices. See page 339.

There is a single Amount field because customer discounts are calculated on after-tax amounts. When discounts are calculated before tax, there is an additional input field so that the sale and the tax amounts can be entered separately as we saw in the Payables Historical Invoices screen. The earliest transaction date is the default invoice date. The cursor is in the Invoice No. field so you can enter the first invoice number.

Type 38 **Press** tab to advance to the Date field.

Type mar 23

Because the payment terms are correctly entered, we can skip them. Discounts are calculated after taxes so only the single after-tax amount is needed.

Click the **Amount field**.

Type 3210

Correct **errors** by returning to the field with the error, **highlighting** the **error** and **entering** the **correct information**.

NOTES
This invoice amount will be added to the Year-To-Date Sales amount on the Statistics tab screen.

For foreign customers, amounts are entered in the foreign currency together with the exchange rate and the amount in the home currency.

Check the **information** carefully before saving the invoice.

Incorrect invoices can be changed only by paying the outstanding invoices, clearing paid transactions (Home window, Maintenance menu, Clear Data, Clear Paid Transactions, Clear Paid Customer Transactions) and then re-entering the invoices (see page 339).

Click **Record** to save the invoice and to display a new blank invoice form for this customer.

Repeat these **procedures** to enter the remaining invoices for this customer, if there are any.

Click **Close** to return to the historical information window after entering all invoices for a customer.

Notice that the program has added the customer's balance to the Ledger window. You are now ready to record the payment made by Alberta Heritage Bank against this invoice.

Click **Payments** to display the customer payments form:

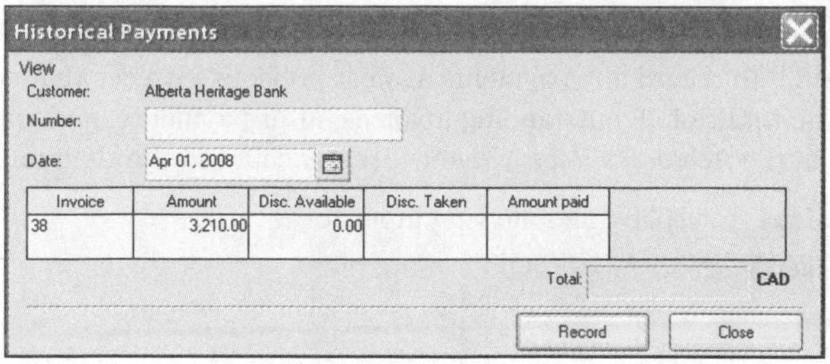

All outstanding invoices that you entered are displayed. Entering historical customer payments is very much like entering current receipts in the Receipts Journal. As usual, the earliest transaction date is the default. The default April 1 transaction date is more than five days after the invoice date so no discount is available.

Click the Number field to move the cursor to the cheque number field if necessary.

WARNING!
If an amount appears in the Disc. Taken field, delete it before recording the payment.

Type 6754 **Press** tab to advance to the Date field.

Type 03-23

The discount is now available. Discounts can be taken only when the full payment is made before the due date, so we must skip the Discount fields. The full discount remains available until the discount period has ended.

Click the Amount Paid column on the line for invoice #38.

The full invoice amount is displayed as the default and highlighted so you can edit it.

Type 1400 **Press** tab.

Check your **information** carefully before you proceed and **make corrections** if necessary.

Click **Record** to save the information and to display another payment form for this customer in case there are additional payments to record. Notice that the full discount remains available after the payment — its amount is not reduced although the balance owing has been reduced.

Repeat these procedures to enter other payments by this customer if there are any.

When you have recorded all outstanding payments by a customer,

Click **Close** to return to the customer information form.

Notice that the amount owing in the ledger has been updated to include the payment entry just completed.

Click the **Address tab** to prepare for entering the next customer.

Click the **Create tool** to open another new customer input screen.

Saving the Customer Record

When all the information is entered correctly, you must save the customer information. If you have not added historical information,

Click **Create Another** to save the information and advance to the next new customer input screen.

Click the **Address tab** to prepare for entering the next customer.

Simply Accounting created a listing for Alberta Heritage Bank in the Customers window.

Repeat these **procedures** to enter the remaining customers and historical transactions. After entering the last customer,

Click **Save And Close** to close the Customer Ledger window. **Close** the **Customers icon window** to return to the Home window.

Display or **print** the **Customer List** to check the accuracy of your address information.

Display or **print** a **Customer Aged Detail Report** including terms and historical differences to check the historical information.

Preparing for Journal Entries

The last stage in setting up the accounting system involves closing off the historical entries and indicates that all historical data have been entered and cannot be changed. You can proceed with journalizing before finishing the history, but you must complete this step before beginning the next fiscal period. Finishing history involves changing the status of each ledger from an open to a finished history state. In the open history state the ledgers are not integrated, so you can add or change historical information in one ledger without affecting any other ledger. It is easier to correct mistakes.

WARNING!
Make a backup copy before proceeding. This way, if you finish entering history and discover an incorrect amount, you can correct the error without re-entering all the information.

Making a Backup of the Company Files

To make a backup of the not-finished files, you can use Save A Copy from the File menu or use the Backup command. Both methods allow you to keep working in your original working data file.

Choose the **File menu** and **click Backup**.

Create a **new folder** called **NF-DORF** in your data folder to store the not-finished version of your data files. In the File name field,

Type `C:\program files\winsim\data\nf-dorf\nf-dorf`

Click **OK**.

Click **Yes** when prompted so that the program will create the new folder and **click OK** when the backup is complete.

The "NF" designates files as not finished or open to distinguish them from the ones you will work with to enter journal transactions. Continue by following the backup instructions on-screen. You can use another name and location for your backup if you want. This will create a backup copy of the files for Dorfmann Design.

WARNING!
You cannot use Backup or Save As with CDs in Simply Accounting. You can use Save A Copy to make CD backups.
Refer to page 20 for more information on backup methods and storage media.

NOTES
Substitute the appropriate drive and folders for the location of your files. You can use a floppy disk for a backup but you can save only one backup on each floppy disk.

NOTES
You can create new accounts
"on the fly" while making journal
entries by using the Add An
Account wizard. You will also be
prompted to add the essential
linked accounts when you try to
open the journals. However, some
linked accounts, such as Sales
Discounts, are not essential and
you can access the journals
without them. However, the
journal entry will not be correct
without the linked account, so
there are some accounts that you
must create before you can use
the journals.

NOTES
If you printed the Vendor
Aged Detail Report with historical
difference, you would also see
that the vendor history was not
correct.

NOTES
Notice that the unused,
hidden ledgers are balanced. If
you view these ledgers and finish
the history, you will be unable to
add historical information for
them later.
If you finish the history
when the unused ledgers are
hidden, they remain in the
unfinished state and you can add
historical information later.

Working with Unfinished History

Simply Accounting allows you to enter current journal transactions before the history is finished and balanced. In this way, you can keep the journal records current and enter the historical details later when there is time available to do so, or the setup may be completed later by a different individual.

There are, however, a number of elements that you must complete before you can make journal entries. You must create the General Ledger accounts and define the essential linked accounts before you can use the journals. You must enter historical customer and vendor invoices before you can enter payments for them, and invoices must have the correct payment terms and dates.

You do not need to enter General Ledger opening account balances. These balances may be added later in the Opening Balance field on the Account tab screen. The General Ledger also shows the current balance that changes as you post new journal entries. Without the opening balances, the current balance is also not correct and you cannot get accurate reports. The Trial Balance and the Accounts window display only current balances, making it more difficult to trace the correct historical amounts.

Some errors may be corrected at any time. For example, after entering journal transactions and after finishing the history, you can correct account, vendor and customer names and address details, but you cannot change historical amounts because their dates precede the earliest transaction date.

From a control point of view, it is preferable to enter all historical information first so that you do not confuse the historical and current data or work with accounts that are not correct in some way. You cannot change account numbers after the accounts are used in journal entries so some corrections may be difficult to make later. After you start journalizing, the balances for *Accounts Receivable* and *Accounts Payable* reflect all the entries made to date. There may be mistakes in current journal entries as well as in the history, making it more difficult to find the historical errors later.

There are a number of checks that you can perform to increase the accuracy of your work. You should compare your reports carefully with the charts given at the beginning of this application and make corrections. Pay particular attention to correct account numbers and historical invoices. Printing Vendor and Customer Aged reports with historical differences can reveal errors in invoices or payments. The Accounts window has an option to check the validity of accounts from the Edit menu or the tool button. The Home window Maintenance menu has an option to check data integrity that looks for differences in balances between the subsidiary ledgers and the corresponding General Ledger control accounts. All these checks help point to mistakes that should be corrected before proceeding.

Choose the **Maintenance menu** and **click Check Data Integrity**:

Integrity Summary			
Total Debits:	$234,919.00	Total Credits:	$234,919.00
A/P Balance:	$9,301.00 *	Unpaid Invoices:	$7,616.00
Prepayment Acct. Bal:	$0.00	Pre. Ord./Prepayment:	$0.00
A/R Balance:	$3,920.00	Unpaid Invoices:	$3,920.00
Deposit Acct. Bal:	$0.00	Pre. Ord./Deposit:	$0.00
Advances Rec'ble:	$0.00	Advances Paid:	$0.00
Vac. Pay Balance:	$0.00	Vac. Pay Owed:	$0.00
Account Reconciliation Files		Matched	
	Data inconsistencies have been detected.		
	Historical Information		
Vendors		Not Balanced	
Customers		Balanced	
Employees		Balanced	
Inventory & Services		Balanced	

OK

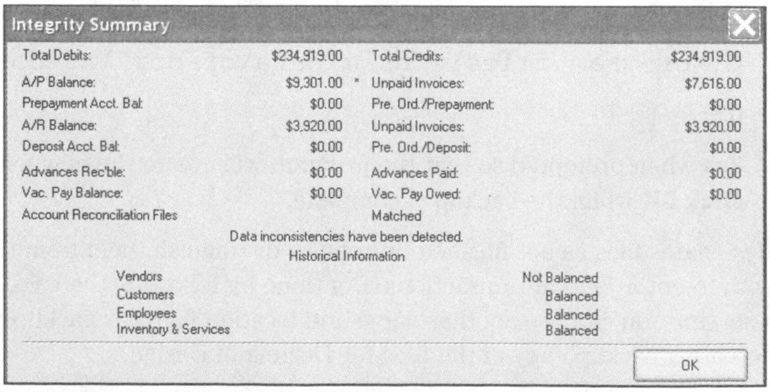

The summary shows that the vendor history is not correct. This error will prevent us from finishing the history as we will see in the following step.

Click **OK** to return to the Home window.

Choose the **History menu** and **click Finish Entering History**:

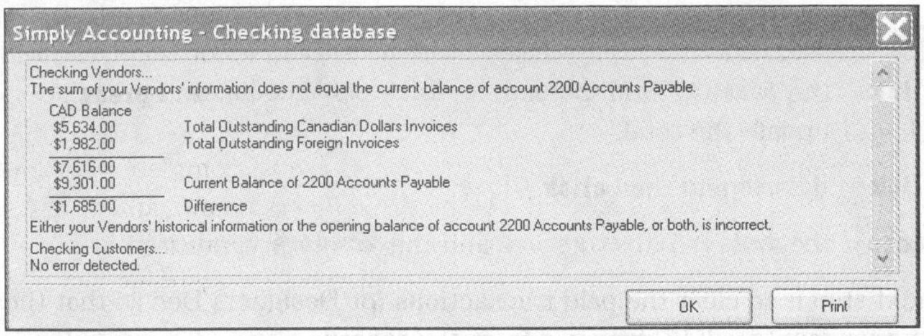

When all your essential linked accounts are defined and all historical amounts balance, you will see the warning that this step cannot be reversed, as in Chapter 4, page 102. Otherwise, Simply Accounting warns you about errors that prevent you from finishing the history. For example, the accounts may be out of order if a subgroup total is missing after a set of subgroup accounts, or the Receivables Ledger balances may not equal the *Accounts Receivable* control account balance. If you have omitted an essential linked account, that information will also be included on this screen.

We see the message that the Vendors or Accounts Payable history is not balanced. Since the Trial Balance is correct, we may be missing a historical Payables Ledger invoice.

Click **Print** to print the message for reference to help you correct mistakes.

Click **OK** to return to the Home window.

We can proceed with entering the source documents and when the missing invoice surfaces, we can enter it and finish the history. You can proceed with journal entries until you start the next fiscal period. At that point, you must finish the history.

WARNING!
Make sure that the Test Account balance is zero. An error in this amount will not prevent you from finishing the history.

Correcting Historical Invoices

In reviewing all the records for the year to date, Dorfmann discovered part of the discrepancy between the Accounts Payable balance and the vendor ledger balances. Invoice #DD-4630 from Designers Den was incorrectly entered. The correct amount was $1 500 plus $105 tax, not $500 and $35. We will correct this error before making journal entries. The first step is to pay the invoices already entered.

NOTES
You must pay the invoices before you can clear them.

Click the **Vendors icon** (Vendors) to open the Vendors window.

Double click **Designers Den** (Designers Den) to open the ledger.

Click the **Historical Transactions tab**.

Click **Payments** to open the Historical Payments form:

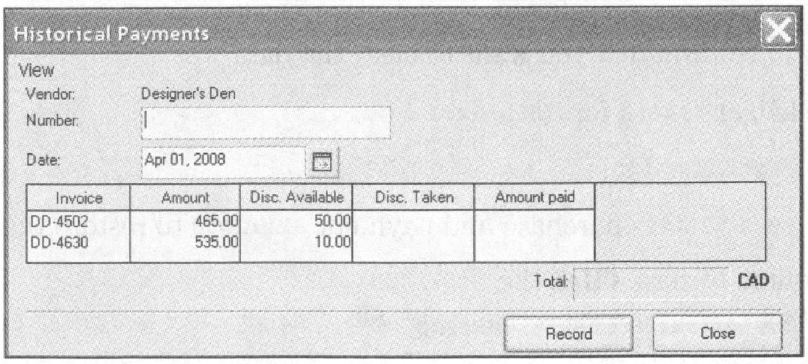

WARNING!
Be certain that the Discount Taken amounts are not selected and included in the amounts paid.

NOTES
You may need to close and then re-open the data file before you can access the Clear Data menu option.

NOTES
If you do not clear the transactions, they will be stored for the vendor and will be included in the Aged Detail Report. By clearing them, you can also use the original invoice and cheque numbers. Duplicate numbers are not allowed but if they are cleared, the numbers are not stored.

NOTES
You must pay and clear all invoices and then re-enter all invoices. Otherwise, the errors will be included in the aged reports and historical amounts will be incorrectly reported.

Type 55 in the Number field.

Type 3-28 in the Date field.

Click the **Amount Paid column for Invoice DD-4502**.

Click the **Amount Paid column for Invoice DD-4630** and **press** tab to update the total.

Click **Record** and then **click** **Close**.

Close the **vendor ledger record** and the **Vendors window**.

The next step is to clear the paid transactions for Designers Den so that these invoices and payments will be removed from the records.

Choose the **Maintenance menu** and then **choose** **Clear Data** and **Clear Paid Transactions** and **click** **Clear Paid Vendor Transactions** as shown:

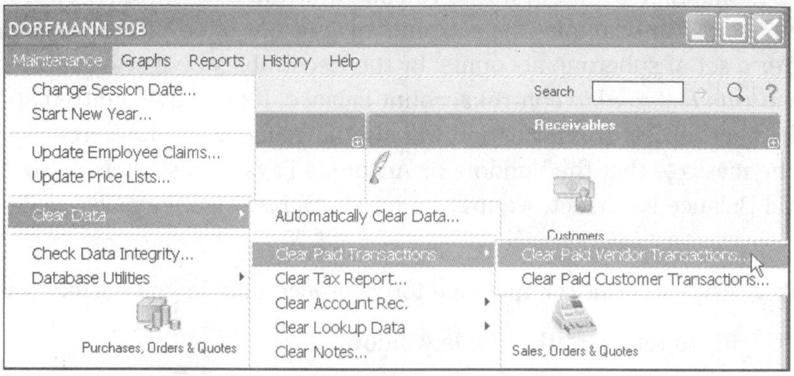

You will see the list of vendors:

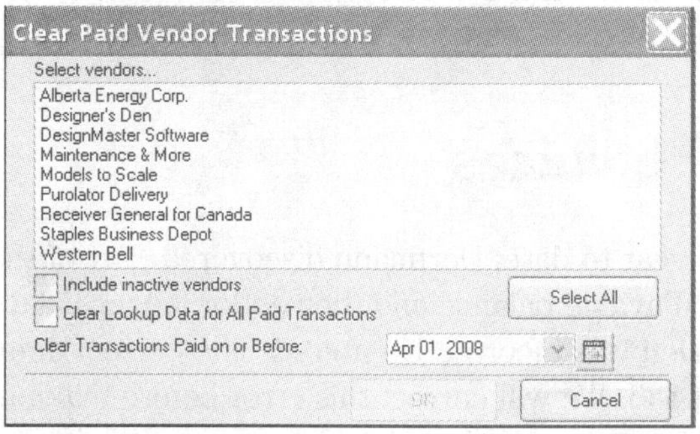

Click **Designers Den** to select the vendor.

Accept the **default date** and the other **settings** and **click** **OK**:

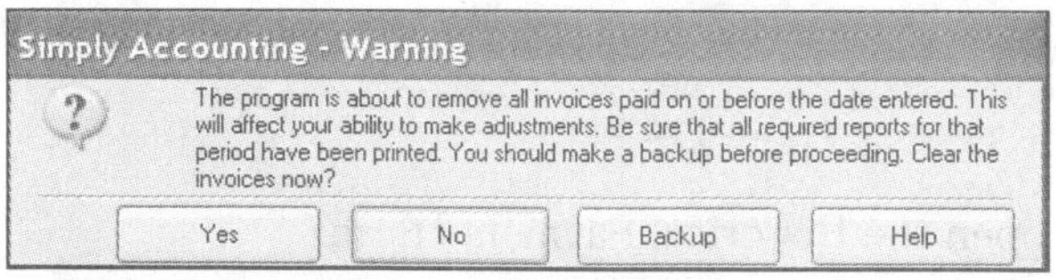

Click **Yes** to confirm that you want to clear the data.

Open the ledger **record** for **Designers Den**.

Click the **Statistics tab**.

Delete the **year-to-date** purchase and payment **amounts** to restore the balance amounts to zero. **Click** the **Save tool** .

Click the **Historical Transactions tab**.

Enter the **correct invoices** and **payments** shown below:

Vendor Name	Terms	Date	Inv/Chq No.	Amount	Tax	Total
Designers Den	2/10, n/30 (before tax)	Mar. 26/08	DD-4502	$2 500	$175	$2 675
		Mar. 26/08	Chq 62			2 210
	2/10, n/30 (before tax)	Mar. 28/08	DD-4630	1 500	105	1 605
			Balance Owing			$2 070

Close the **vendor ledger record** and the **Vendors window**.

There are still one or more invoices outstanding that we will enter later when we find them.

You can now exit the program or continue by entering the transactions that follow. Remember to advance the session date.

SOURCE DOCUMENTS

SESSION DATE – APRIL 7, 2008

☐ **Purchase Order #16** **Dated Apr. 2/08**

Shipping date Apr. 6/08
From Staples Business Depot, $200 for office supplies and $300 for computer supplies, plus $35 GST. Purchase invoice total, $535. Terms: net 10 days.

☐ **Purchase Order #17** **Dated Apr. 2/08**

Shipping date Apr. 6/08
From DesignMaster Software, $750 USD plus $52.50 GST for new design software. Purchase order total, $802.50 USD. Terms: net 1/5, n/30.

☐ **Sales Invoice #44** **Dated Apr. 4/08**

To Glitter Jewellers, $2 000 plus $140 GST for designing a "welcoming" space for customer shopping. Sales invoice total, $2 140. Terms: 1/5, n/15.

☐ **Cash Receipt #25** **Dated Apr. 4/08**

From Alberta Heritage Bank, cheque #7110 for $1 810 in full payment of account. Reference invoice #38.

☐ **Cheque Copy #65** **Dated Apr. 4/08**

To Models to Scale, $4 300 in payment of account including $120 discount for early payment. Reference invoices #MS-376 and MS-453.

☐ **Cheque Copy #66** **Dated Apr. 4/08**

To Designers Den, $1 990 in payment of account including $80 discount for early payment. Reference invoices #DD-4502 and DD-4630.

☐ **Cheque Copy #67** **Dated Apr. 5/08**

To Maintenance & More, $214 in payment of account. Reference invoices #MM-211 and MM-242.

NOTES

You do not need to enter an exchange rate for foreign quotes and orders because no transaction has taken place. You can accept the default rate.

WARNING!

Be sure to select the correct revenue account for sales. You may need to change the default selection.

☐ **Sales Quote #41** **Dated Apr. 5/08**

Delivery date Apr. 14/08
To Passions Department Store, $3 000 for designing display cabinets for cosmetic department and $800 for consultation work and reports, plus $266 GST. Sales quote total, $4 066. Terms: 1/5, n/15.

NOTES

Editing a purchase order is like editing a sales quote. Refer to page 222 if you need help.

- Choose Purchase Order as the Transaction
- Choose Order #17
- Click the Adjust Order tool
- Edit the order
- Record the changed order

☐ **Memo # 1** **Dated Apr. 5/08**

Edit purchase order #17 from DesignMaster Software. The design software was upgraded with new features by the software company and the price was increased to $800 USD, plus $56 GST. New purchase order total, $856 USD. Dorfmann agreed to pay the new price. Change the payment terms for the order to net 30 days. (Read the margin notes for assistance.)

☐ **Sales Quote #42** **Dated Apr. 6/08**

Delivery date Apr. 18/08
To Banff Condominiums, $2 500 for designing foyer with water fountain for condominium complex and $800 for consultation work and reports, plus $231 GST. Sales quote total, $3 531. Terms: 1/5, n/15. Reports and designs to be shipped by Purolator Delivery.

☐ **Purchase Invoice #SBD-643** **Dated Apr. 7/08**

From Staples Business Depot, to fill purchase order #16, $200 for office supplies and $300 for computer supplies, plus $35 GST. Purchase invoice total, $535. Terms: net 10 days.

☐ **Purchase Invoice #DMS-596** **Dated Apr. 7/08**

From DesignMaster Software, to fill purchase order #17 for $800 plus $56 GST for design software. Purchase invoice total, $856. Terms: net 30 days. The exchange rate is 1.171.

☐ **Visa Purchase Invoice #P-61142** **Dated Apr. 7/08**

From Purolator Delivery, $30 plus $2.10 GST for delivery charges for express shipment of designs and reports. Purchase invoice total, $32.10 charged to Visa account.

☐ **Purchase Invoice #MM-263** **Dated Apr. 7/08**

From Maintenance & More, $100 plus $7 GST for regular maintenance of premises. Purchase invoice total, $107. Terms: net 15 days. Store as weekly recurring entry.

NOTES

Although the owner's withdrawal is a cash purchase, you should create a vendor record for the owner because she will make further withdrawals. Enter Yes in the Tax Exempt column and enter 3580 Dorfmann, Drawings as the default expense account. Record the withdrawal as a cash purchase in the Payments Journal or the Purchases Journal.

☐ **Memo #2** **Dated Apr. 7/08**

From Owner: Withdrew $250 from the business to pay for daughter's birthday presents. Issued cheque #68. Use Full Add for the Owner's vendor record. Create new Group account 3580 Dorfmann, Drawings.

SESSION DATE – APRIL 14, 2008

☐ **Cheque Copy #69 – Visa Statement** **Dated Apr. 8/08**

To Visa $390 for new purchases in March and $400 outstanding balance from previous month plus $20 annual fee and $6 interest on previous outstanding balance. Current balance $816 paid in full.

☐ **Cash Receipt #26** **Dated Apr. 8/08**

From Glitter Jewellers, cheque #342 for $2 118.60 in full payment of account including $21.40 discount for early payment. Reference sales invoice #44.

☐ **Sales Order #41** **Dated Apr. 8/08**

Delivery date Apr. 14/08
To Passions Department Store, acceptance of quote #41 for $3 000 for designing display cabinets for cosmetic department and $800 for consultation work and reports, plus $266 GST. Sales order total, $4 066. Terms: 1/5, n/15.

☐ **Sales Order #42** **Dated Apr. 10/08**

Delivery date Apr. 18/08
To Banff Condominiums, acceptance of quote #42 for $2 500 for designing foyer with water fountain for condominium complex and $800 for consultation work and reports, plus $231 GST. Sales order total, $3 531. Terms: 1/5, n/15. Reports and designs to be shipped by Purolator Delivery.

☐ **Memo #3** **Dated Apr. 10/08**

From Owner: A model of store interior was accidentally dropped and destroyed. It was worth $400 in model parts. Charge to new Group account 5025 Damaged Model Parts.

☐ **Purchase Invoice #DD-6431** **Dated Apr. 11/08**

From Designers Den, $800 for Artograph vertical projector and $450 for tracer projector, plus $87.50 GST paid. Purchase invoice $1 337.50. Terms: 2/10, n/30.

☐ **Purchase Quote #PI-417** **Dated Apr. 11/08**

Shipping date Apr. 15/08
From Prairie Insurance (use Quick Add), $170 per month for a one-year car insurance policy with $1 000 000 liability coverage and $500 deductible. Terms: first month payable in advance on acceptance of quote followed by monthly instalments at the end of each month.

NOTES
Use Full Add for the new vendors if you want to add the default expense account (Insurance Expense). GST is not charged on insurance so you do not need to add a tax code.

☐ **Purchase Quote #WI-674** **Dated Apr. 11/08**

Shipping date Apr. 15/08
From Westrock Insurance (use Quick Add), $185 per month for a one-year car insurance policy with $2 000 000 liability coverage and $400 deductible. Terms: first month payable in advance on acceptance of quote followed by monthly instalments at the end of each month.

☐ **Sales Invoice #45** **Dated Apr. 12/08**

To Calgary District School Board, $1 200 plus $84 GST for consultation and reports on redesign and refurbishing atrium at Board's central office. Sales invoice total, $1 284. Terms: 1/5, n/15.

☐ **Bank Debit Memo #642067** **Dated Apr. 13/08**

From Midwestern Trust, $1 500 for reduction of bank loan principal. Since this is a fixed payment, store it as a recurring monthly entry. Interest on the loan was $200. The bank withdrew $1 700 from the chequing account.

☐ **Cheque Copy #70** **Dated Apr. 14/08**

To Staples Business Depot, $535 in full payment of account. Reference invoice #SBD-643.

☐ **Memo #4** **Dated Apr. 14/08**

From Owner: Remit GST payment to the Receiver General for the month of March. Refer to April 1 General Ledger account balances to determine the amount owing and issue cheque #71.

NOTES
You can process the GST remittance as a cash purchase from the Receiver General. Refer to page 264.

☐ **Sales Invoice #46** **Dated Apr. 14/08**

To Passions Department Store, to fill sales order #41 for $3 000 for designing display cabinets for cosmetic department and $800 for consultation work and reports, plus $266 GST. Sales invoice total, $4 066. Terms: 1/5, n/15.

☐ **Purchase Invoice #MM-314** **Dated Apr. 14/08**

From Maintenance & More, $100 plus $7 GST for regular maintenance of premises. Purchase invoice total, $107. Terms: net 15 days. Recall stored entry.

SESSION DATE – APRIL 21, 2008

☐ **Cash Receipt #27** **Dated Apr. 15/08**

From Calgary District School Board, cheque #1437 for $1 271.16 in full payment of account including $12.84 discount for early payment. Reference sales invoice #45.

☐ **Cash Purchase Invoice #WI-6913** **Dated Apr. 15/08**

From Westrock Insurance, acceptance of quote WI-674 for a one-year car insurance policy. Pay first month's premium of $185 in advance. Issue cheque #72. Store as recurring monthly transaction.

NOTES

Use the Purchases Journal for the cash purchase so that you can fill the purchase quote.

☐ **Memo #5** **Dated Apr. 15/08**

Recall the stored entry for car insurance from Westrock Insurance to pay next month's premium of $185. Issue cheque #73 postdated for May 15. After posting, recall the entry again to pay the premium due June 15 with cheque #74. Choose Yes to confirm that the future date is correct.

NOTES

Add A and B to the original purchase invoice numbers for the postdated payment entries.

☐ **Purchase Invoice #MS-850** **Dated Apr. 16/08**

From Models to Scale Co., $500 plus $35 GST for outsourcing on a design. Purchase invoice total, $535. Terms: 2/10, n/30. Create new Group account 5015 Contracted Labour Costs.

☐ **Cheque Copy #104** **Dated Apr. 16/08**

To DesignMaster Software, $1 685.25 USD in payment of account. Reference invoice #DM-234. The exchange rate is 1.165.

☐ **Sales Invoice #47** **Dated Apr. 18/08**

To Banff Condominiums, to fill sales order #42, $2 500 for designing foyer with water fountain for condominium complex and $800 for consultation work and reports, plus $231 GST. Sales invoice total, $3 531. Terms: 1/5, n/15. Reports and designs shipped by Purolator Delivery. Tracking number P70431. Allow customer to exceed credit limit.

☐ **Sales Invoice #48** **Dated Apr. 18/08**

To Lougheed, Klein and Associates, $800 plus $56 GST for consultation on future design work on law office building. Sales invoice total, $856. Terms: 1/5, n/15.

☐ **Cheque Copy #75** **Dated Apr. 20/08**

To Designers Den, $1 312.50 in payment of account including $25 discount for early payment. Reference invoice #DD-6431.

☐ **Purchase Invoice #DD-6896** **Dated Apr. 20/08**

From Designers Den, $1 200 plus $84 GST for new Designtek aluminum drawing table. Purchase invoice total $1 284. Terms: 2/10, n/30.

☐ **Visa Sales Invoice #49** **Dated Apr. 21/08**

To Alliance Party Headquarters (use Quick Add or Continue for the new customer), $500 plus $35 GST for consultation fee to redesign and refurbish party headquarters. Sales invoice total, $535 paid by Visa. There is no discount.

☐ **Purchase Invoice #MM-399** **Dated Apr. 21/08**

From Maintenance & More, $120 plus $8.40 GST for regular maintenance of premises. Purchase invoice total, $128.40. Terms: net 15 days. Recall and edit the stored entry to enter the increased price. Store the entry to save the changes.

☐ **Cash Receipt #28** **Dated Apr. 21/08**

From Lougheed, Klein and Associates, cheque #444 for $847.44 in full payment of account including $8.56 discount for early payment. Reference sales invoice #48.

☐ **Cheque Copy #76** **Dated Apr. 21/08**

To Maintenance & More, $214 in payment of account. Reference invoices #MM-263 and MM-314.

SESSION DATE – APRIL 28, 2008

☐ **Sales Invoice #50** **Dated Apr. 27/08**

To Calgary Arms Hotel, $3 200 for design work and $800 consultation fee, plus $280 GST charged. Sales invoice total, $4 280. Terms: 1/5, n/15.

☐ **Cash Receipt #29** **Dated Apr. 28/08**

From Passions Department Store, cheque #614 for $4 066 in full payment of account. Reference sales invoice #46.

☐ **Cash Purchase Invoice #WB-669943** **Dated Apr. 28/08**

From Western Bell, $125 plus $8.75 GST for telephone services. Purchase invoice total, $133.75. Issue cheque #77 in full payment.

☐ **Cash Purchase Invoice #AE-43214** **Dated Apr. 28/08**

From Alberta Energy Corp., $120 plus $8.40 GST for hydro services. Purchase invoice total, $128.40. Issue cheque #78 in full payment.

☐ **Visa Purchase Invoice #P-70431** **Dated Apr. 28/08**

From Purolator Delivery, $30 plus $2.10 GST for delivery charges for sending reports to Banff Condominiums. Purchase invoice total, $32.10. Full amount charged to Visa credit card.

☐ **Purchase Invoice #MM-464** **Dated Apr. 28/08**

From Maintenance & More, $120 plus $8.40 GST for regular maintenance. Purchase invoice total, $128.40. Terms: net 15 days. Recall the stored entry.

SESSION DATE – APRIL 30, 2008

☐ **Memo #6** **Dated Apr. 30/08**

From Owner: Prepare adjusting entries for the following

Model Parts used	$450
Computer Supplies used	240
Office Supplies used	220
Prepaid Insurance expired	208

☐ **Bank Debit Memo #643214** **Dated Apr. 30/08**

From Midwestern Trust, $30 for monthly bank service charges and $1 320 for monthly mortgage payment withdrawn from chequing account. The mortgage payment includes $1 200 for interest and $120 for reduction of principal.

☐ **Memo #7** **Dated Apr. 30/08**

From Owner: Received monthly statements showing missing historical information. The statement from Staples Business Depot included an overdue amount of $133.50 from invoice #SBD-201 dated March 24, 2008. The statement from Models to Scale included an overdue amount of $450 plus $31.50 GST from invoice #MS-287 dated March 14, 2008.

Add the historical invoices for these two transactions in the vendor ledger records as historical transactions. Refer to page 327.

Pay these two invoices in the Payments Journal as current transactions dated April 30 using cheques #79 and #80.

WARNING!
You must enter these outstanding invoices as historical invoices and the payments as current payments or you will be unable to finish the history.

☐ **Memo #8** **Dated Apr. 30/08**

Check the data integrity (Maintenance menu) after entering the historical invoices. Make a backup copy of the data files and finish entering the history. Choose the History menu in the Home window and click Finish Entering History.

SESSION DATE – MAY 1, 2008

☐ **Memo #9** **Dated May 1/08**

From Owner: Print or preview customer statements. Two invoices for Banff Condominiums are overdue. Complete sales invoice #51 for Banff Condominiums for $31.65, the interest charges on the overdue amount. Terms: net 15 days. Use the No Tax code for the interest charges and choose Interest Revenue as the account. Remember to remove the discount.

☐ **Memo #10** **Dated May 1/08**

The federal government has reduced the GST rate from 7% to 6%. Edit all tax codes and descriptions to make this change effective immediately.

R E V I E W

The Student CD-ROM with Data Files includes Review Questions and Supplementary Cases for this chapter.

CHAPTER TEN

Lime Light Laundry

Laundry Services • Pickup & Deliver

OBJECTIVES

After completing this chapter, you should be able to

- ***open*** the Payroll Journal
- ***enter*** employee-related payroll transactions
- ***understand*** automatic payroll deductions
- ***understand*** Payroll Ledger linked accounts
- ***edit*** and ***review*** payroll transactions
- ***calculate*** and ***enter*** sales commissions
- ***adjust*** Payroll Journal invoices after posting
- ***enter*** employee benefits and entitlements
- ***complete*** payroll runs for a group of employees
- ***release*** vacation pay to employees
- ***remit*** payroll taxes
- ***display*** and ***print*** payroll reports
- ***use*** Daily Business Manager lists to make journal entries

COMPANY INFORMATION

Company Profile

NOTES
Lime Light Laundry
25 Snow White Lane
Vancouver
British Columbia V8G 3B2
Tel: (604) 633-8201
Fax: (604) 633-8396
Business No.: 324 732 911

Lime Light Laundry started in Vancouver, British Columbia in 1994 with a single employee assisting the owner, Charles Chaplin. They provided laundry services to one hotel as a regular customer and to a few individual customers. Now Lime Light provides complete laundry services for a number of large hotels in the Vancouver area and has seven full-time employees. Chaplin himself is no longer involved in daily business operations, and the laundry serves only hotels and no individual clients. Chaplin's goal as entrepreneur is business growth. In fact, two employees have recently been hired. Chaplin is negotiating new contracts with a major hotel chain and considering expansion into adjacent premises that are for sale.

Lime Light's business success has enabled it to establish favourable account terms with regular suppliers, including some discounts for early payments. The discount terms for customers also encourage timely payment of accounts. All discounts are calculated on after-tax amounts. Because there are no individual customers, only hotels, Lime Light does not accept credit card payments. Similarly, most regular vendors do not accept credit cards and Chaplin does not use them in his business.

All laundry services provided by Lime Light are subject to 7 percent GST. Cleaning services are exempt from provincial sales taxes. Lime Light pays the 7 percent PST on non-exempt purchases as well as the 7 percent GST.

After paying all payroll taxes for the year and closing his books, Chaplin converted his accounts on January 1, 2008, using the following information:

- Chart of Accounts
- Post-Closing Trial Balance
- Vendor Information
- Customer Information
- Employee Profiles and Information Sheet
- Accounting Procedures

CHART OF POSTABLE ACCOUNTS

LIME LIGHT LAUNDRY

ASSETS
1080 Cash in Bank
1200 Accounts Receivable
1240 Advances Receivable
1250 Purchase Prepayments
1260 Prepaid Insurance
1280 Cleaning Supplies
1300 Clothes Hangers
1320 Packaging Supplies
1520 Computer System
1540 Delivery Vehicle
1560 Laundry and Cleaning Equipment
1580 Pressing Equipment
1600 Railings and Belts
1620 Laundry Premises ▶

▶**LIABILITIES**
2100 Bank Loan
2200 Accounts Payable
2250 Prepaid Sales and Deposits
2300 Vacation Payable
2310 EI Payable
2320 CPP Payable
2330 Income Tax Payable
2400 Medical Payable
2410 RRSP Payable
2420 Travel Allowances Payable
2430 Tuition Fees Payable
2440 Medical Payable - Employer
2460 WCB Payable
2640 PST Payable
2650 GST Charged on Services ▶

▶2670 GST Paid on Purchases
2920 Mortgage Payable

EQUITY
3560 C. Chaplin, Capital
3600 Net Income

REVENUE
4020 Revenue from Services
4040 Sales Discounts

EXPENSE
5020 Advertising Expenses
5040 Bank Charges
5060 Hydro Expenses
5080 Insurance Expense ▶

▶5100 Cleaning Supplies Used
5120 Clothes Hangers Used
5140 Packaging Supplies Used
5150 Purchase Discounts
5160 Telephone Expenses
5180 Vehicle Expenses
5300 Wages: General
5305 Wages: Cleaning Staff
5310 EI Expense
5320 CPP Expense
5330 WCB Expense
5340 Commissions
5350 Piece Rate Bonuses
5360 Travel Allowances
5380 Tuition Fees Expense
5400 Medical Premium Expense

NOTES: The Chart of Accounts includes only postable accounts and Net Income.

POST-CLOSING TRIAL BALANCE

LIME LIGHT LAUNDRY

January 1, 2008

		Debits	Credits
1080	Cash in Bank	$49 435	
1200	Accounts Receivable	$4 218	
1260	Prepaid Insurance	2 400	
1280	Cleaning Supplies	2 000	
1300	Clothes Hangers	800	
1320	Packaging Supplies	1 200	
1520	Computer System	3 000	
1540	Delivery Vehicle	35 000	
1560	Laundry and Cleaning Equipment	15 000	
1580	Pressing Equipment	25 000	
1600	Railings and Belts	10 000	
1620	Laundry Premises	250 000	
2100	Bank Loan		$ 12 000
2200	Accounts Payable		5 130 ▶
▶ 2300	Vacation Payable		576
2310	EI Payable		1 208
2320	CPP Payable		1 486
2330	Income Tax Payable		3 761
2400	Medical Payable		396
2410	RRSP Payable		200
2440	Medical Payable - Employer		396
2460	WCB Payable		476
2650	GST Charged on Services		1 890
2670	GST Paid on Purchases	630	
2920	Mortgage Payable		200 000
3560	C. Chaplin, Capital		171 164
		$398 683	$398 683

VENDOR INFORMATION

LIME LIGHT LAUNDRY

Vendor Name (Contact)	Address	Phone No. Fax No.	E-mail Web Site	Terms Tax ID
BC Energy Group (Sol R. Heater)	33 Windmill Rd. Vancouver, BC V8K 3C3	Tel: (604) 388-1298	srh@bceg.ca www.bceg.ca	net 1
BC Minister of Finance (M.T. Handed)	7 Fiscal Way Victoria, BC V8V 2K4	Tel: (250) 887-3488 Fax: (250) 887-8109	www.fin.gov.bc.ca	net 1
BC Telephone (Kommue Nicate)	91 Cellular Way Vancouver, BC V8G 8B5	Tel: (604) 348-2355	www.bell.ca	net 1
BC Workers' Compensation Board (N. Jured)	55 Accidental Cr. Victoria, BC V8W 3X6	Tel: (250) 887-7199 Fax: (250) 887-9211	www.worksafebc.com	net 1
Ferndale Paper Products (T. Issue)	43 Ferndale Ave. Vancouver, BC V8F 2S6	Tel: (604) 466-3929 Fax: (604) 466-3935	tissue@ferndalepaper.com www.ferndalepaper.com	1/10, n/30 (after tax) 445 668 714
Langley Service Centre (Otto Fixer)	64 Mechanic St. Langley, BC V2Z 2S4	Tel: (604) 556-7106 Fax: (604) 556-7188	otto@lss.com www.lss.com	net 1 672 910 186
Pacific Laundry Suppliers (Al Washindon)	29 Spotless Dr. Vancouver, BC V8K 1N6	Tel: (604) 782-1618 Fax: (604) 781-5127	aw@pacificlaundry.com www.pacificlaundry.com	net 30 129 554 377
Receiver General for Canada	PO Box 20004 Sudbury, Ontario P3A 6B4	Tel 1: (800) 561-7761 Tel 2: (800) 959-2221	www.cra-arc.gc.ca	net 1
Richmond Equipment Co. (N. U. Dryer)	78 Richmond St. Richmond, BC V7C 3V2	Tel: (604) 699-3601 Fax: (604) 699-1577	Dryer@REC.com www.REC.com	1/10, n/30 (after tax) 366 455 281
Surrey Printers (H.P.L. Jett)	690 Surrey Ave. Surrey, BC V3H 6T1	Tel: (604) 286-9193 Fax: (604) 286-9100	jett@surreyprinters.com www.surreyprinters.com	net 1 125 481 262
Victoria Trust (Victoria Royale)	59 Queen St. Vancouver, BC V8U 1M6	Tel: (604) 388-1825 Fax: (604) 388-2663	www.victoriatrust.ca	net 1

OUTSTANDING VENDOR INVOICES

LIME LIGHT LAUNDRY

Vendor Name	Terms	Date	Invoice No.	Amount	Total
Ferndale Paper Products	1/10, n/30	Dec. 29/07	FP-901	$570	$570
Pacific Laundry Suppliers	net 30	Dec. 3/07	PL-644	$1 140	$1 140
Richmond Equipment Co.	1/10, n/30	Dec. 27/07	RE-4111	$3 420	$3 420
			Grand Total		$5 130

CUSTOMER INFORMATION

LIME LIGHT LAUNDRY

Customer Name (Contact)	Address	Phone No. Fax No.	E-mail Web Site	Terms Credit Limit
Capilano Centre Hotel (Lotte Reste)	3 Stopover Cr. North Vancouver, BC V7H 5D3	Tel 1: (604) 587-2563 Tel 2: (888) 587-3882	lreste@cch.com www.cch.com	1/15, n/30 (after tax) $5 000
Coquitlam Motel (B. & B. Roadside)	56 Sliepers Rd. Vancouver, BC V8K 6F3	Tel 1: (604) 366-7155 Tel 2: (800) 366-9175	bbr@coquitlammotel.com www.coquitlammotel.com	1/15, n/30 (after tax) $5 000

▶

Customer Name (Contact)	Address	Phone No. Fax No.	E-mail Web Site	Terms Credit Limit
Delta Hotel (A. Good-Knight)	86 Holiday St. Richmond, BC V7R 4D9	Tel: (604) 782-5431 Fax: (604) 781-7528	goodknight@deltahotel.com www.deltahotel.com	1/15, n/30 (after tax) $5 000
Kingsway Inn (Abel Traveller)	77 Roomie Dr. Vancouver, BC V8E 2W2	Tel: (604) 566-7188 Fax: (604) 565-4281	at@kingsway.com www.kingsway.com	1/15, n/30 (after tax) $5 000
Port Moody Resort (Kat Napper)	425 Vacation Ave. Port Moody, BC V3H 4S3	Tel: (604) 369-5826 Fax: (604) 369-7993	knapper@pmresort.com www.pmresort.com	1/15, n/30 (after tax) $5 000

OUTSTANDING CUSTOMER INVOICES

LIME LIGHT LAUNDRY

Customer Name	Terms	Date	Invoice No.	Amount	Total
Delta Hotel	1/15, n/30	Dec. 28/07	69	$2 850	$2 850
Kingsway Inn	1/15, n/30	Dec. 30/07	72	$1 368	$1 368
			Grand Total		$4 218

EMPLOYEE INFORMATION SHEET

LIME LIGHT LAUNDRY

	Claire Brumes	Clyne Fretton	Mouver Durtee	Soffte Landings	Iean Sissler	S. Pott Tran	Cryper Houseman
Position	Manager	Senior Cleaner	Cleaner	Senior Presser	Presser	Delivery	Maintenance
Social Insurance No.	726 911 134	218 738 631	552 846 826	422 946 541	931 771 620	638 912 634	822 546 859
Address	11 Sweeper St. Vancouver, BC V7N 2L2	21 Spotter St. Vancouver, BC V3K 4K2	34 Wash Ave. Vancouver, BC V9B 4C1	92 Flat St. Vancouver, BC V8U 1X3	63 Iron Blvd., #2 Vancouver, BC V7N 2L2	2 Kerry St. Richmond, BC V8K 4K2	4 Fixall Cr. Vancouver, BC V9B 4C1
Telephone	(604) 829-6291	(604) 693-7595	(604) 381-8138	(604) 488-6353	(604) 389-2291	(604) 693-7995	(604) 381-2238
Date of Birth (mm-dd-yy)	7-31-72	8-15-78	11-3-75	8-6-65	7-31-72	8-15-78	11-3-75
Federal (BC) Tax Exemption – TD1							
Basic Personal	$9 039 (8 858)	$9 039 (8 858)	$9 039 (8 858)	$9 039 (8 858)	$9 039 (8 858)	$9 039 (8 858)	$9 039 (8 858)
Spouse	–	$7 675 (7 585)	–	$7 675 (7 585)	–	$7 675 (7 585)	$7 675 (7 585)
Other	–	–	–	$7 999 (7 848)	$1 760 (1 280)	–	–
Total Exemptions	$9 039 (8 858)	$16 714 (16 443)	$9 039 (8 858)	$24 713 (24 291)	$10 799 (10 138)	$16 714 (16 443)	$16 714 (16 443)
Employee Earnings							
Regular Wage Rate	–	$18.00	$14.00	$16.00	$14.00	–	–
Overtime Wage Rate	–	$27.00	$21.00	$24.00	$21.00	–	–
Regular Salary	$4 000/mo	–	–	–	–	$1 600	$3 600/mo
Pay Period	monthly	bi-weekly	weekly	bi-weekly	weekly	bi-weekly	monthly
Hours per Period	150	80	40	80	40	80	150
Commission	1% net sales	–	–	–	–	–	–
Piece Rate	–	$0.10	$0.10	$0.10	$0.10	–	–
Vacation	3 weeks	6% retained	4% retained	6% retained	4% retained	3 weeks	3 weeks
Vacation Pay Owed	–	$377.60	$67.20	$64.00	$67.20	–	–
WCB Rate	3.02	3.02	3.02	3.02	3.02	5.00	3.02
Employee Deductions							
Medical	$54.00	$22.15	$6.23	$22.15	$6.23	$24.92	$54.00
RRSP	$50.00	–	–	–	$25.00	–	$50.00
EI, CPP & Income Tax	Calculations built into Simply Accounting program						

NOTES: Medical premiums are deducted every pay period. The amounts are adjusted for the monthly rates.

Employee Profiles and TD1 Information

Employee Benefits and Entitlements All employees are entitled to 10 days per year as sick leave and five days' leave for personal reasons. If the days are not needed, employees can carry these days forward to a new year, to a maximum of 20 and 10 days respectively. Currently all employees have some unused sick leave and personal leave days accrued from the previous year. Salaried employees are allowed to carry forward two of their three weeks' vacation entitlement. That is, they are allowed to accumulate a maximum of 25 unused vacation days at any one time.

To encourage personal development, Lime Light offers to pay 50 percent of the tuition fees for any employee enrolled in college or university programs. Currently only Iean Sissler is taking courses and receiving the tuition fee benefit. This benefit for Sissler is considered an expense for Lime Light Laundry. A second benefit applies to all employees — Lime Light Laundry pays 50 percent of the medical premiums.

Piece Rate Bonuses Lime Light Laundry pays the cleaning staff — the cleaners and pressers — a piece rate bonus of 10 cents per sheet set in excess of the first 500 sets each week. This bonus is added to each paycheque.

Employer Expenses Lime Light Laundry currently has three employer payroll expenses beyond the compulsory CPP, EI and WCB — 50 percent of the employee's medical premiums for the BC Medical Services Plan are paid by Lime Light; Lime Light also pays 50 percent of eligible tuition fees and travel allowances for Brumes' work-related travel expenses. Brumes receives this allowance as compensation for using her own car for business travel.

Claire Brumes As the manager of the laundry, Brumes negotiates deals with customers, schedules work, hires new staff and discusses problems with the owner who does not participate in the day-to-day affairs of the business. She is married and has no children. Since her husband is also fully employed, she uses the single federal and provincial tax claim amounts but she pays the family medical premiums. At the end of each month, she receives her salary of $4 000 per month plus a commission of 1 percent of revenue from services, net of taxes and returns, by cheque. She is recorded as salesperson for all sales for the purpose of calculating the revenue on which the commission is based. In addition, she receives $300 per month in a separate cheque as a travel allowance to cover the expense of her regular client visits and business promotion. This amount is considered an employer expense, not an employee benefit. She makes monthly contributions to her RRSP plan as well. In lieu of vacation pay, she is entitled to take three weeks of paid vacation each year.

Clyne Fretton As the senior cleaner, Fretton performs regular laundry duties, such as cleaning the incoming bed sheets and table linens. She has several years of experience with Lime Light and is helping to train Durtee, the junior cleaner who was recently hired. Her regular pay of $18 per hour is supplemented by the piece rate bonus and by overtime wages at the rate of $27 per hour when she works more than 40 hours per week. In addition, she receives vacation pay at the rate of 6 percent of her total wages, equivalent to about three weeks of pay, but this amount is retained until she chooses to take a vacation. Because she is married and fully supports her husband, she claims a spousal amount for income tax purposes and she also pays medical premiums at the family rate. She has her pay deposited directly to her bank account every two weeks.

Mouver Durtee is the second and junior cleaner. For sharing all the cleaning duties with Fretton, he earns $14 per hour, $21 per hour overtime when he works more than 40 hours in a week and the piece rate bonus. He is paid weekly by cheque and his 4 percent vacation pay is retained. As a single self-supporting person, Durtee claims the basic single amounts for income tax and pays single medical premiums.

Soffte Landings is the senior presser. She operates the clothes pressing equipment, assisted by Sissler. Landings is single but supports her invalid aged mother so she is able to claim the spousal equivalent TD1 amount, the caregiver amounts and her mother's age amount. These claims significantly reduce the income tax she pays on her wages of $16 per hour, $24 for overtime hours and her piece rate bonus. Her medical premium is deducted from her bi-weekly paycheque at the family rate to cover herself and her mother. Her 6 percent vacation pay is retained.

NOTES

Taxable benefits are not paid in cash to the employee. However, they are added to gross pay to determine income tax and then subtracted again to determine the net pay. Spreading the benefit over a larger period will ensure that income taxes are calculated fairly.

Iean Sissler assists Landings with operating the equipment to press the laundry. She is single with no dependents, so she pays single medical premiums and has only the basic single TD1 claim amounts. From her weekly deposited pay, she contributes $50 to an RRSP program. Her pay at $14 per hour and $21 for overtime hours with 4 percent vacation pay, is less than Landings' pay because she has less experience. She also receives the piece rate bonus. Sissler is enrolled in a business program at the local community college. She pays 50 percent of her $800 tuition herself and Lime Light Laundry pays an equal amount. This taxable benefit is entered on Sissler's paycheque at the rate of $25 per week for four months.

S. Pott Tran Tran's main responsibility with Lime Light is delivery. He picks up the dirty laundry from hotels throughout the city and drops off the clean linens. Tran is married and fully supports his wife and one child, so he pays the family medical premiums and has the basic and spousal claim amounts for income taxes. He is paid his bi-weekly salary of $1 600 by cheque, and he can take three weeks of vacation yearly.

Cryper Houseman is responsible for general maintenance at Lime Light — he keeps the machines running and cleans the premises. As a single parent who supports two children, he can claim the spousal amount for income tax purposes. He has worked for Lime Light since the business started. At the end of each month, Houseman has his monthly salary of $3 600 deposited to his bank account. He also makes contributions to his RRSP program with regular payroll deductions. As a salaried employee, he is entitled to take three weeks of paid vacation per year.

Accounting Procedures

Taxes : GST and PST

Lime Light Laundry uses the regular method for remittance of the Goods and Services Tax. It records the GST collected from customers as a liability in *GST Charged on Services*. GST paid by vendors is recorded in *GST Paid on Purchases* as a decrease in the liability to Canada Revenue Agency. The GST quarterly refund or remittance is calculated automatically in the *GST Owing (Refund)* subgroup total account. Lime Light files for a refund or remits the balance owing to the Receiver General for Canada by the last day of the month for the previous quarter.

Provincial Sales Tax is not charged on laundry services in British Columbia. Lime Light does pay PST on most purchases. Tax codes are set up in the defaults for the company so that Simply Accounting will automatically calculate the tax when it is paid.

Discounts

All customers are offered a discount of 1 percent on the after-tax amount of the sale if they pay their accounts in full within 15 days. Full payment is requested in 30 days. Discount terms are set up as the default in the customer records.

Some vendors also offer discounts on after-tax purchase amounts. These discount terms are set up in the vendor records so that Simply Accounting will automatically calculate the discount when full payment is made within the discount period.

Sales Quotes and Deposits

Chaplin prepares sales quotes for new contracts. When clients sign a contract, they pay an advance of 50 percent of the contracted price, usually a bi-weekly or monthly rate.

Direct Payroll Deposits

Chaplin allows employees to have their regular pay deposited directly to their bank accounts or to be paid by cheque. Three employees have selected direct payroll deposits.

Payroll Remittances

Four vendors are identified as payroll authorities with the following remittances: EI, CPP and income tax are remitted to the Receiver General for Canada; medical premiums are remitted to the BC Minister of Finance; Workers' Compensation Board premiums are remitted to the BC Workers' Compensation Board; and RRSP contributions are remitted to Victoria Trust.

INSTRUCTIONS

1. **Enter** the **transactions** in Simply Accounting using the Chart of Accounts and Vendor, Customer and Employee Information. The procedures for entering new transactions for this application are outlined step by step in the Keystrokes section following the source documents. These transactions have a ✓ in the check box, and the page number where the keystrokes begin appears immediately below the check box.
2. **Print** the **reports and graphs** marked on the following printing form after you have finished making your entries. Keystrokes for payroll reports begin on page 391.

REPORTS

Lists
- [ ] Chart of Accounts
- [ ] Account List
- [ ] Vendors
- [ ] Customers
- [ ] Employees

Journals
- [x] All Journals (by date): Jan. 1 to Jan. 31
- [ ] General
- [ ] Purchases
- [ ] Payments
- [ ] Sales
- [ ] Receipts
- [x] Payroll (by date): Jan. 1 to Jan. 31

Financials
- [x] Comparative Balance Sheet: Jan. 1 and Jan. 31 with difference in percentage
- [x] Income Statement: Jan. 1 to Jan. 31
- [x] Trial Balance date: Jan. 31
- [x] General Ledger accounts: Jan. 1 to Jan. 31 4020 5300 5305
- [ ] Statement of Cash Flows
- [x] Cash Flow Projection Detail Report: for 1080 for next 30 days

Tax
- [x] GST Report: Jan. 1 to Jan. 31

Banking
- [ ] Cheque Log Report

Payables
- [ ] Vendor Aged
- [ ] Aged Overdue Payables
- [ ] Pending Purchase Orders

Receivables
- [ ] Customer Aged
- [ ] Aged Overdue Receivables
- [x] Sales by Salesperson Jan. 1 to Jan. 31
- [ ] Pending Sales Orders
- [ ] Customer Statements

Payroll
- [x] Employee Summary for all employees
- [ ] Payroll Remittance Detail Report
- [ ] T4 Slips
- [ ] Record of Employment

Mailing Labels
- [ ] Labels

Management Reports
- [ ] Ledger

GRAPHS
- [ ] Payables by Aging Period
- [ ] Payables by Vendor
- [ ] Receivables by Aging Period
- [ ] Receivables by Customer
- [ ] Sales vs Receivables
- [ ] Receivables Due vs Payables Due
- [ ] Revenues by Account
- [ ] Expenses by Account
- [x] Expenses and Net Profit as % of Revenue

SOURCE DOCUMENTS

SESSION DATE – JANUARY 7, 2008

NOTES
Enter Brumes as the salesperson for all sales.

☑ **Sales Invoice #101** **Dated Jan. 2/08**

359 To Capilano Centre Hotel, $2 900 plus $203 GST for weekly contracted linen laundry service. Invoice total $3 103. Terms: 1/15, n/30. Store as recurring weekly transaction. Enter Brumes as the salesperson.

☐ **Cash Purchase Invoice #LS-504** **Dated Jan. 2/08**

From Langley Service Centre, $300 plus $21 GST and $21 PST for maintenance service and repairs to delivery truck. Invoice total $342. Paid by cheque #74.

☐ **Purchase Invoice #FP-1297** **Dated Jan. 2/08**

From Ferndale Paper Products, $200 plus $14 GST and $14 PST for bags and wrapping paper for clean laundry. Invoice total $228. Terms: 1/10, n/30. Store as bi-weekly recurring entry.

☐ **Cash Receipt #31** **Dated Jan. 3/08**

From Delta Hotel, cheque #4123 for $2 821.50 in payment of account, including $28.50 discount for early payment. Reference invoice #69.

WARNING!
Remember not to include the discount for the second invoice in payments and receipts.

☐ **Cheque Copy #75** **Dated Jan. 5/08**

To Ferndale Paper Products, $564.30 in payment of account, including $5.70 discount for early payment. Reference invoice #FP-901.

☐ **Sales Invoice #102** **Dated Jan. 6/08**

To Coquitlam Motel, $3 400 plus $238 GST for contracted bi-weekly laundry services. Invoice total $3 638. Terms: 1/15, n/30. Store as bi-weekly recurring transaction. Enter Brumes as the salesperson.

☐ **Purchase Invoice #PL-903** **Dated Jan. 6/08**

From Pacific Laundry Suppliers, $300 plus $21 GST and $21 PST for weekly supply of cleaning products. Invoice total $342. Terms: net 30. Store as weekly recurring transaction.

☐ **Sales Invoice #103** **Dated Jan. 7/08**

To Port Moody Resort, $2 600 plus $182 GST for contracted laundry services for two weeks. Invoice total $2 782. Terms: 1/15, n/30. Store as bi-weekly recurring transaction. Enter Brumes as the salesperson.

EMPLOYEE TIME SUMMARY SHEET #1

(pay period ending January 7, 2008)

	Name of Employee	Regular Hours	Overtime Hours	Piece Rate Quantity	Benefits	Advance (Repaid)	Sick Days	Personal Days	Direct Deposit
☑ 360	Durtee, Mouver	40	2	480	$ 6.23	$100	–	–	No
☑ 366	Sissler, Iean	40	–	395	$31.23	–	–	1	Yes

a. Using Employee Time Summary Sheet #1 and the Employee Information Sheet, complete payroll for weekly paid employees. Sissler has been granted a personal leave day to register for her course.
b. Issue $100 advance to Mouver Durtee and recover $25 from each of the following four paycheques.
c. Issue cheque #76 and Direct Deposit (DD) slip #48.

☐ **Cheque Copy #77** **Dated Jan. 7/08**

To Pacific Laundry Suppliers, $1 140 in partial payment of account. Reference invoice #PL-644.

☐ **Cash Purchase Invoice #SP-2991** **Dated Jan. 7/08**

From Surrey Printers, $600 plus $42 GST and $42 PST for copying and mailing advertising brochures outlining new prices to customers. Invoice total $684 paid in full with cheque #78.

☐ **Cash Purchase Invoice #BC-499** **Dated Jan. 7/08**

From Burnaby College (use Quick Add for new vendor), $400 for tuition fees. The cheque covers 50 percent of the fees. Sissler will pay the balance. Invoice total $400 paid in full with cheque #79. Choose Tuition Fees Payable as the account.

SESSION DATE – JANUARY 14, 2008

✓ **Memo #1** **Dated Jan. 8/08**

368 From Manager: Mouver Durtee returned his paycheque for adjustment. He worked 6 hours of overtime during the week but was paid for only 2 hours. Adjust his paycheque and re-issue cheque #76 to make the correction.

☐ **Sales Invoice #104** **Dated Jan. 9/08**

To Capilano Centre Hotel, $2 900 plus $203 GST for weekly contracted linen laundry service. Invoice total $3 103. Terms: 1/15, n/30. Recall stored transaction.

NOTES

Brumes will be entered as the salesperson in the stored transaction.

Allow customers to exceed the credit limit.

☐ **Cheque Copy #80** **Dated Jan. 12/08**

To Richmond Equipment, $3 420 in payment of invoice #RE-4111.

☐ **Cash Receipt #32** **Dated Jan. 12/08**

From Capilano Centre Hotel, cheque #2314 for $3 071.97 in partial payment of account, including $31.03 discount for early payment. Reference invoice #101.

☐ **Purchase Invoice #PL-1213** **Dated Jan. 13/08**

From Pacific Laundry Suppliers, $300 plus $21 GST and $21 PST for weekly supply of cleaning products. Invoice total $342. Terms: net 30. Recall stored transaction.

☐ **Sales Invoice #105** **Dated Jan. 13/08**

To Kingsley Inn (use Full Add for the new customer), $2 800 plus $196 GST for new contract for daily laundry service with bi-weekly invoices. Invoice total $2 996. Terms: 1/15, n/30. Brumes is the salesperson. Store as recurring bi-weekly entry.

NOTES

Kingsley Inn
☐ (contact Rume Kingsley)
302 Sandman Dr.
Vancouver, BC V8H 1P1
Tel: (604) 259-1881
Fax: (604) 259-1893
Terms: 1/15, n/30
Revenue account: 4020
Tax code: G - GST @ 7%
Credit limit: $5 000

☐ **Sales Invoice #106** **Dated Jan. 13/08**

To Delta Hotel, $2 900 plus $203 GST for bi-weekly invoice for contracted laundry services. Invoice total $3 103. Terms: 1/15, n/30. Enter Brumes as the salesperson. Store as bi-weekly recurring transaction.

☐ **Cash Purchase Invoice #BCEG-78522** **Dated Jan. 14/08**

From BC Energy Group, $600 plus $42 GST for one month of hydro services. Invoice total $642 due within five days to avoid interest penalty. Paid in full with cheque #81.

☐ **Cash Purchase #BCT-11229** **Dated Jan. 14/08**

From BC Telephone, $100 plus $7 GST and $7 PST for monthly telephone services. Invoice total $114. Paid in full with cheque #82.

NOTES

Type -25 in the Advance Amount field for Durtee to recover this amount.

EMPLOYEE TIME SUMMARY SHEET #2

(pay period ending January 14, 2008)

	Name of Employee	Regular Hours	Overtime Hours	Piece Rate Quantity	Benefits	Advance (Repaid)	Sick Days	Personal Days	Direct Deposit
✓	Durtee, Mouver	40	–	370	$ 6.23	-$25	1	–	No
✓	Sissler, Iean	40	–	470	31.23	$200	–	–	Yes
✓	Fretton, Clyne	80	–	860	22.15		1	–	Yes
✓	Landings, Soffte	80	2	950	22.15		–	–	No
✓	Tran, S. Pott	80	–	–	24.92		–	–	No

370

a. Using Employee Time Summary Sheet #2 and the Employee Information Sheet, complete payroll for all hourly paid employees.
b. Recover $25 advanced to Mouver Durtee.
c. Issue $200 advance to Sissler and recover $50 from each of the next four paycheques.
d. Issue cheques #83, #84 and #85 and DD slips #49 and #50.

SESSION DATE – JANUARY 21, 2008

☐ **Cash Purchase Invoice #LS-593** **Dated Jan. 15/08**

From Langley Service Centre, $170 plus $11.90 GST and $11.90 PST for oil change and lubrication on delivery truck. Invoice total $193.80 paid in full with cheque #86.

☐ **Purchase Invoice #FP-2635** **Dated Jan. 16/08**

From Ferndale Paper Products, $200 plus $14 GST and $14 PST for wrapping paper and bags. Invoice total $228. Terms: 1/10, n/30. Recall stored entry.

☐ **Sales Invoice #107** **Dated Jan. 16/08**

To Capilano Centre Hotel, $2 900 plus $203 GST for weekly contracted linen laundry service. Invoice total $3 103. Terms: 1/15, n/30. Recall stored transaction.

☐ **Cash Receipt #33** **Dated Jan. 18/08**

From Port Moody Resort, cheque #5120 for $2 754.18 in payment of account, including $27.82 discount for early payment. Reference invoice #103.

☐ **Cash Receipt #34** **Dated Jan. 18/08**

From Capilano Centre Hotel, cheque #2692 for $3 071.97 in partial payment of account, including $31.03 discount for early payment. Reference invoice #104.

☐ **Purchase Invoice #PL-1634** **Dated Jan. 20/08**

From Pacific Laundry Suppliers, $300 plus $21 GST and $21 PST for weekly supply of cleaning products. Invoice total $342. Terms: net 30. Recall stored transaction.

☐ **Sales Invoice #108** **Dated Jan. 20/08**

To Coquitlam Motel, $3 400 plus $238 GST for contracted bi-weekly laundry services. Invoice total $3 638. Terms: 1/15, n/30. Recall stored transaction.

NOTES

Use Quick Add for new cash customers. Remember to enter Brumes as the salesperson.

☐ **Cash Sales Invoice #109** **Dated Jan. 20/08**

To Burnaby Private Hospital (use Quick Add), $800 plus $56 GST for emergency linen and laundry service. Invoice total $856. Terms: C.O.D. Received cheque #561 for $856 in full payment. There is no discount.

☐ **Sales Invoice #110** **Dated Jan. 21/08**

To Port Moody Resort, $2 600 plus $182 GST for contracted laundry services for two weeks. Invoice total $2 782. Terms: 1/15, n/30. Recall stored transaction.

☐ **Cash Receipt #35** **Dated Jan. 21/08**

From Delta Hotel, cheque #4439 for $3 071.97 in payment of account, including $31.03 discount for early payment. Reference invoice #106.

☐ **Purchase Order #22** **Dated Jan. 21/08**

Shipping date Jan. 28/08
From Richmond Equipment, $2 000 plus $140 GST and $140 PST for new presser. Invoice total $2 280. Terms: 1/10, n/30.

EMPLOYEE TIME SUMMARY SHEET #3

(pay period ending January 21, 2008)

	Name of Employee	Regular Hours	Overtime Hours	Piece Rate Quantity	Benefits	Advance (Repaid)	Sick Days	Personal Days	Direct Deposit
☐	Durtee, Mouver	40	2	440	$ 6.23	–$25	1	–	No
☐	Sissler, Iean	40	2	520	$31.23	–$50	–	–	Yes

a. Using Employee Time Summary Sheet #3 and the Employee Information Sheet, complete payroll for the weekly paid employees. Use the Payroll Journal or the Payroll Run Journal.
b. Recover $25 advanced to Mouver Durtee and recover $50 advanced to Iean Sissler.
c. Issue cheque #87 and DD slip #51.

NOTES
Type –25 in the Advance Amount field for Durtee and –50 for Sissler to recover these amounts.
Type 31.23 in the Benefits Amount field for Sissler.

SESSION DATE – JANUARY 28, 2008

NOTES
Use Quick Add for new cash customers. Remember to enter Brumes as the salesperson.

☐ **Cash Sales Invoice #111** **Dated Jan. 23/08**

To Twin Peaks Ski Resort, $1 600 plus $112 GST for laundry services. Invoice total $1 712 (no discount). Received cheque #492 for $1 712 in full payment.

Memo #2 **Dated Jan. 23/08**

Use the Daily Business Manager to complete the following six transactions:

NOTES
Use the Daily Business Manager to enter all Memo #2 transactions (GST Remittance, Recurring Transactions, Sales Due, Payments Due and Purchase Order Due).

☑ **Cheque Copy #88** **Dated Jan. 23/08**

374 To Receiver General, $1 260 to pay GST owing as at December 31, 2007. (This is the January 1, 2008 balance.)

☑ **Recurring Sales Invoice #112** **Dated Jan. 23/08**

376 To Capilano Centre Hotel, $2 900 plus $203 GST for weekly laundry service. Invoice total $3 103. Terms: 1/15, n/30.

☑ **Sales Due: Cash Receipts #36, 37, 38** **Dated Jan. 25/08**

378 From Capilano Centre Hotel, cheque #2974 for $3 071.97 in payment of account, including $31.03 discount for early payment. Reference invoice #107.
From Kingsley Inn, cheque #439 for $1 966 in partial payment of account. Reference invoice #105.
From Coquitlam Motel, cheque #276 for $3 638 in payment of account. Reference invoice #102.

☑ **Payment Due** **Dated Jan. 26/08**

379 To Ferndale Paper Products, cheque #89 for $453.72 in payment of account, including $2.28 discount for early payment. Reference invoices #FP-1297 and #FP-2635.

☑ **Recurring Transactions Due** **Dated Jan. 27/08**

380 From Pacific Laundry Suppliers, purchase #PL-2098 for $300 plus $21 GST and $21 PST for weekly supply of cleaning products. Invoice total $342. Terms: net 30.

To Delta Hotel, sales invoice #113 for $2 900 plus $203 GST for bi-weekly invoice for contracted services. Invoice total $3 103. Terms: 1/15, n/30.
To Kingsley Inn, sales invoice #114 for $2 800 plus $196 GST for bi-weekly billing for daily laundry service. Invoice total $2 996. Terms: 1/15, n/30.

☑ **Purchase Order Due** **Dated Jan. 28/08**

380 From Richmond Equipment, Purchase Invoice #RE-6998 to fill purchase order #22 for $2 000 plus $140 GST and $140 PST for new presser. Invoice total $2 280. Terms: 1/10, n/30.

NOTES
Use the Adjust Receipt tool to make the correction. Simply Accounting will automatically make the reversing entry. Delete the original Payment Amount. You will need to enter the amount of discount taken manually. See page 381 and page 183.

☑ **Memo #3** **Dated Jan. 28/08**

381 From Manager: Receipt #37 from Kingsley Inn for $1 966 was entered incorrectly. On Jan. 25, cheque #439 for $2 966.04 was received from Kingsley Inn in full payment of invoice #105, including $29.96 for early payment. Adjust the original receipt to make the correction.

EMPLOYEE TIME SUMMARY SHEET #4

(pay period ending January 28, 2008)

	Name of Employee	Regular Hours	Overtime Hours	Piece Rate Quantity	Benefits	Advance (Repaid)	Sick Days	Personal Days	Direct Deposit
☐	Durtee, Mouver	40	–	510	$ 6.23	–$25	–	–	No
☐	Sissler, Iean	40	2	510	31.23	–$50	–	–	Yes
☐	Fretton, Clyne	80	2	1 030	22.15	–	–	–	Yes
☐	Landings, Soffte	80	–	930	22.15		1	–	No
☐	Tran, S. Pott	80	–		24.92		–	–	No

a. Using Employee Time Summary Sheet #4 and the Employee Information Sheet, complete payroll for all hourly paid employees. Use the Payroll Journal or the Payroll Run Journal.
b. Recover $25 advanced to Mouver Durtee and recover $50 advanced to Iean Sissler.
c. Issue cheques #90, #91 and #92, and DD #52 and #53.

SESSION DATE – JANUARY 31, 2008

☐ **Purchase Invoice #FP-3129** **Dated Jan. 30/08**

From Ferndale Paper Products, $200 plus $14 GST and $14 PST for wrapping paper and bags for clean laundry. Invoice total $228. Terms: 1/10, n/30. Recall stored entry.

☐ **Sales Invoice #115** **Dated Jan. 30/08**

To Capilano Centre Hotel, $2 900 plus $203 GST for weekly contracted linen laundry service. Invoice total $3 103. Terms: 1/15, n/30. Recall stored transaction.

NOTES
The travel allowance for Brumes is set up in her ledger record so that the amount is included automatically as an employer expense that debits Travel Allowance Expenses and credits Travel Allowances Payable just as tuition fees were set up for Sissler. You do not need to enter the expense separately.
This is not a taxable benefit.
In Chapter 15, we set up travel expenses as a non-taxable reimbursement.

☑ **Memo #4** **Dated Jan. 31/08**

382 Clyne Fretton is taking some vacation time. Clyne asked to receive her vacation pay by cheque. Release her retained vacation pay and issue cheque #93.

☑ **Memo #5** **Dated Jan. 31/08**

385 Complete payroll run for Houseman and Brumes. Claire Brumes earned a sales commission of $292 for the month of January and took five days' vacation (use the Vacation Days Released field, Entitlements tab). Issue cheque #94 and DD slip #54.

☐ **Memo #6** **Dated Jan. 31/08**

Issue cheque #95 for $300 to Claire Brumes (use Quick Add to add Brumes as a new vendor) for travel expenses as a cash purchase in the Payments Journal, Choose Travel Allowances Payable as the account.

☐ **Bank Debit Memo #532281** **Dated Jan. 31/08**

From Mountain Heights Bank, $2 045 was withdrawn from chequing account for the following pre-authorized transactions:

Bank Charges	$ 45
Interest on Bank Loan	120
Reduction of Principal on Bank Loan	880
Interest on Mortgage	900
Reduction of Principal on Mortgage	100

Create two new Group accounts:

5105 Interest on Bank Loan
5110 Interest on Mortgage

☐ **Memo #7** **Dated Jan. 31/08**

Complete month-end adjusting entries for supplies used in January.

Cleaning supplies used	$680
Clothes hangers used	250
Packaging supplies used	350

☐ **Memo #8** **Dated Jan. 31/08**

Complete an adjusting entry for one month of prepaid insurance expired. The one-year insurance policy was purchased on December 31, 2007.

☑ **Memo #9** **Dated Jan. 31/08**

386 Adjust the paycheque for Brumes. She has returned her paycheque because her earned commission was incorrect. Use the Sales By Salesperson Report to verify that the correct amount was $403, not $292.

☑ **Memo #10** **Dated Jan. 31/08**

387 Using the payroll remittance option, remit the following payroll taxes:
To Receiver General: EI Payable, CPP Payable and Income Tax Payable
To BC Minister of Finance: Medical Payable and Medical Payable - Employer
To BC Workers' Compensation Board: WCB Payable
To Victoria Trust: RRSP Payable
Issue cheques #96 through #99 in payment.

☐ **Memo #11** **Dated Jan. 31/08**

Edit all tax codes to reduce the GST rate to 6 percent.

KEYSTROKES

Adding Salespersons to Sales Invoices

When employees receive sales commissions, you can add the salesperson's name to the sales invoice. You can then use the Sales By Salesperson Report to determine the sales revenue amount for calculating the commission. After creating job categories such as Sales and Admin, you can indicate for each category whether its employees are salespersons and then identify the employees in the category.

Open the data file for **Lime Light Laundry**.

Enter **January 7** as the session date.

Open the **Sales Journal**.

Choose **Capilano Centre Hotel** as the customer.

Enter **Jan 2** as the invoice date.

Enter a **Description** for the sale.

Enter **2900** as the invoice amount.

Click the **Sold By list arrow** to see the list of salespersons as shown:

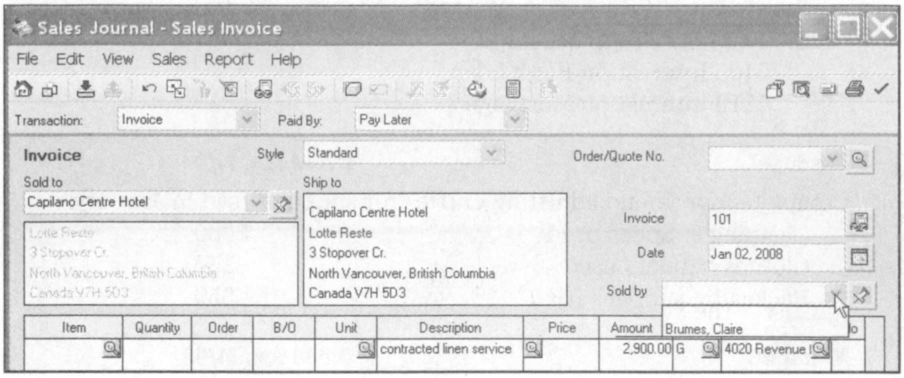

Brumes is the only employee responsible for sales at Lime Light Laundry so she is the only one on the list. Brumes is the only employee in the Sales job category. All other employees are in a second category labelled "Other" which does not have any salespersons.

NOTES
The Use The Same Salesperson pin icon is the same as the Use The Same Customer Next Time and works the same way.

Click **Brumes** to add her name to the invoice.

Click the **Use The Same Salesperson pin icon**.

This will lock in the salesperson's name on the invoice form until we close the Sales Journal. The pin has changed position — it now looks like it has been pushed in:

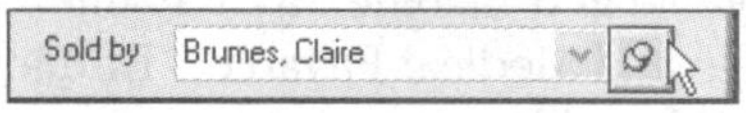

NOTES
You can keep the Sales Journal open throughout the exercise so Brumes will be added automatically when you enter sales. You can keep the journal open until you need to advance the session date.

If you leave the journal open in the background, the salesperson remains selected. If you close the journal, you must reselect the salesperson for each invoice. You must close the journal before advancing the session date.

Review the **journal display**.

Close the **display** when finished.

Check your **work** and **make corrections** if necessary.

Store the **transaction** to recur **weekly**.

Post the **invoice** and **minimize** (or close) the **Sales Journal** (see margin note).

Enter the **remaining transactions** up to the payroll transaction on January 7.

NOTES
Remember that you must have a valid Payroll ID code from Sage Software in order to use the payroll features of the program.
Choose the Business Services menu and click Simply CARE Payroll for more information.

Entering Payroll Transactions

Payroll transactions may be entered in the Payroll Journal or in the Payroll Cheque Run Journal. We will show both methods. If you are preparing paycheques for more than one employee at once, the Payroll Cheque Run Journal is usually faster.

Paycheques are entered in the Payroll Journal indicated by the pointer on the Paycheques icon on the following screen:

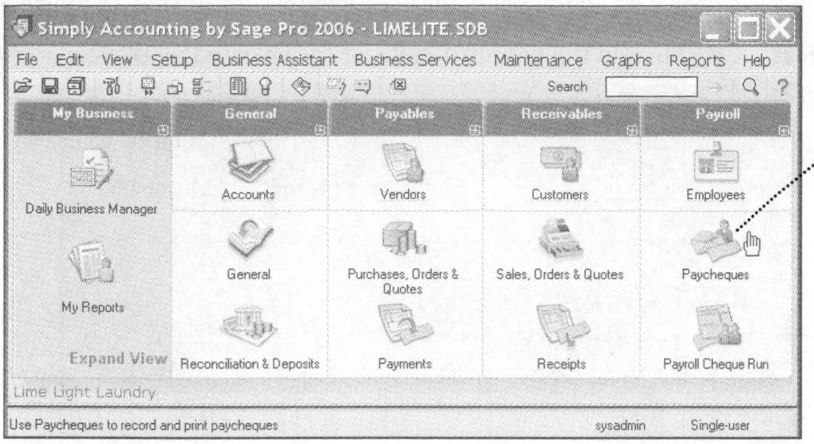

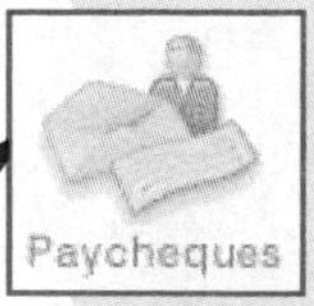

Click the **Paycheques icon** to open and display the Payroll Journal:

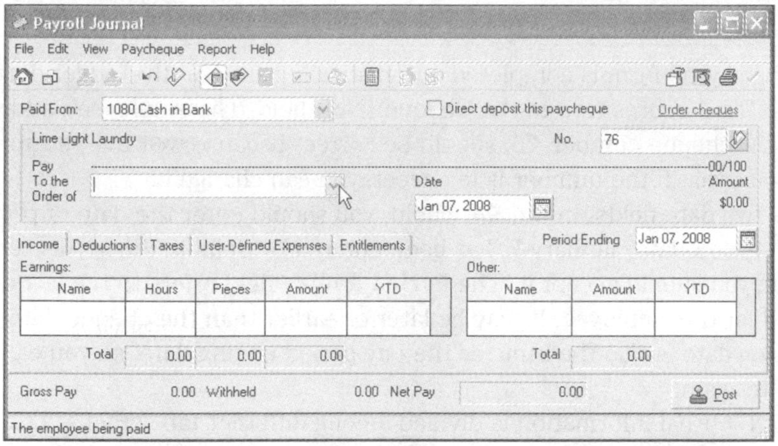

Three tool buttons on the tool bar relate specifically to the Payroll Journal: Calculate Taxes Automatically, Enter Taxes Manually and Recalculate Taxes. The Time Slips tool is used to enter time and billing information for the employee and will be covered in Chapter 17. The remaining tools — Home window, Daily Business Manager, Store, Recall, Undo, Adjust Cheque, Enter Additional Information, Windows Calculator, Refresh, Print and Allocate — are the same as those found in other journals. You can also change report form options and preview the payroll form before printing. Adjust Cheque is the Payroll Journal equivalent of the Adjust tool in other Journals.

The cursor is in the Employee (To The Order Of) field.

Click the **To The Order Of (Employee) field arrow** to see the employee list:

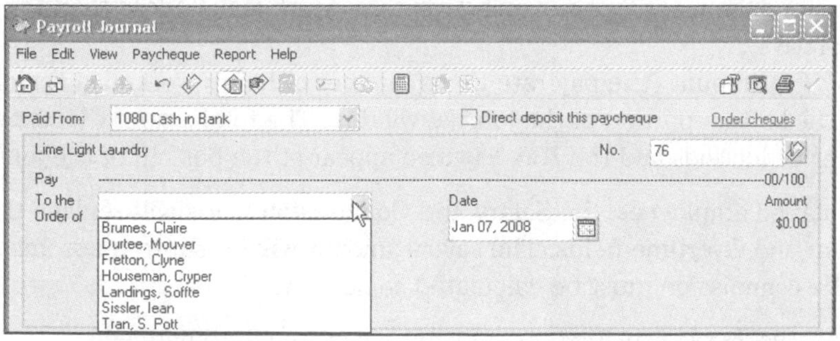

Click **Durtee, Mouver** to select this employee and add his name to the form.

If you have not chosen correctly, return to the employee list and select again.

NOTES

We will not open the Payroll module for Payroll Journal entries because no journal icons are added in this view. You may choose to open the module to see the icons. The same ledger options that we saw for other modules are available for Payroll. That is, the payroll settings, employees window and add, modify or remove an employee.

basic BASIC VERSION

The Refresh and Time Slips tools do not appear in the Basic version.

To add new employees from the Payroll Journal, type the new name in the Name field and press *tab* and click Add. There is no Quick Add option for employees because additional details are required for income tax purposes.

Press *tab* to add the payroll details for the selected employee:

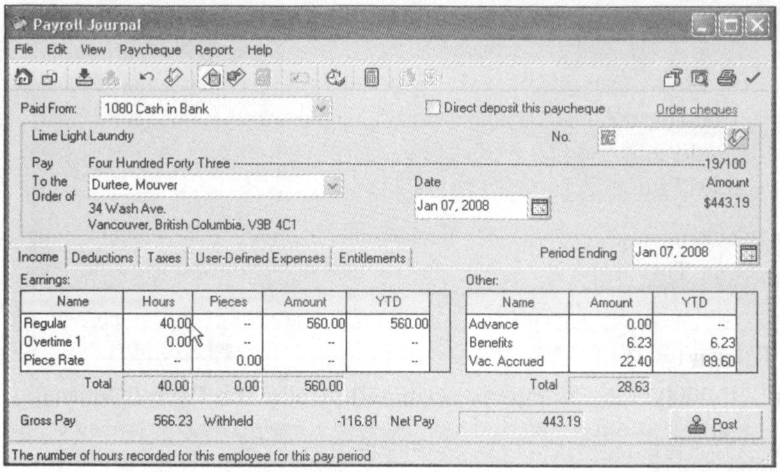

Most of the payroll form is completed automatically based on the ledger details for the employee. The cursor is now in the Cheque (No.) field. The employee's address has been added. The cheque number, 76, should be correct because we have set up automatic numbering. If the number is incorrect, you can change it.

There are two date fields. In the **Date** field, you should enter the date of payment. As usual, the session date, January 7, has been entered by default. Since this session date is correct, you should accept it. The **Period Ending** field refers to the last day of the pay period for the employee. It may be later or earlier than the cheque date. In this case, the session date is also the same as the pay period ending date, so you can accept the default date again.

The Payroll Journal information is divided among different tab screens. The Income tab screen has all the sources of income for the employee divided into two categories: Earnings and Other. **Earnings** include the regular income sources such as Regular and Overtime wages and the Piece Rate for the hourly paid employees. We have set up the employee records so that only their own sources of income appear on the form. **Other** has all the other sources of income, including payroll advances, taxable benefits and vacation pay accrued and paid out. Year-to-date amounts are added for all fields.

The **Regular** hours field contains the number of hours an employee has worked for the regular pay rate during the pay period. You can edit the default entry. The **Overtime** field contains the number of overtime hours an employee has worked during the pay period. No default number of overtime hours is entered because the time varies from week to week. If there are different overtime rates, you can set up a second overtime field and rate. For example, pay for evening overtime work may be less than the pay for Sundays or holidays.

The **Gross Pay** amount (the pay rate times number of hours worked) is calculated and added to the bottom portion of the journal window. The total amount **Withheld** for taxes and other deductions and the **Net Pay** also appear at the bottom of the journal.

For salaried employees, the Salary and Commission fields will replace the Regular and Overtime fields. The salary amount will be entered automatically but the commission must be calculated separately.

Click the **Taxes tab**. Tax amounts are calculated automatically.

Because we have chosen to let the program complete the tax calculations, the tax fields are not available for editing.

NOTES

Lime Light Laundry uses a single chequing account for Payables and Payroll cheques so there is a single sequence of cheque numbers.

NOTES

The Period Ending date is usually earlier than the cheque date for hourly paid employees who must complete the hours and have this summary submitted to the payroll department before a cheque is prepared.

For salaried workers, the Period Ending date may be later than the cheque date because they are paid at the same rate each period. If they are not paid for missed work days, they may have those amounts deducted from later paycheques.

If you need to edit the tax amounts, click the **Enter Taxes Manually tool**.

Click the **Income tab** to continue with the payroll entry.

Click the **Overtime 1 Hours field** to continue.

Type 2 **Press** tab.

Notice that the Gross Pay and Vacation pay are updated to include the additional pay. Notice, too, that the upper cheque portion of your Input Form window is updated continually as you add information. Year-to-date (YTD) amounts are also updated continually as you add information.

If amounts are not updated, click the **Calculate Taxes Automatically tool** on the tool bar. The option to enter taxes manually may be selected, an option that allows you to edit tax amounts but will not update these amounts automatically.

The cursor has advanced to the **Piece Rate** number of **Pieces** field. The rate in this field is entered for each employee in the ledger records. Lime Light pays 10 cents for each sheet set that is laundered beyond the base of 500 sets. When you enter the number of pieces, Simply Accounting calculates the total dollar amount by multiplying the piece rate times the number of pieces. You can define a different rate for each employee. If different rates are paid for different kinds of work, you can define additional piece rate fields.

NOTES
To verify that tax amounts have also changed, click the Taxes tab. Click the Income tab again to continue with the payroll entry.
Click the Piece Rate number of Pieces field to position the cursor.

Type 480 **Press** tab to enter the Amount paid for piece rate.

The cursor now moves to the Advance field in the Other income column. The **Advance** field is used to enter an amount advanced to an employee in addition to his or her normal pay from wages or salary. Advances are approved by management for emergencies or other personal reasons. An advance offered to an employee is shown as a positive amount. An advance recovered is indicated as a negative amount in this same field. An advance of $100 for Mouver Durtee has been approved. Advance amounts owing will appear in the YTD column for Advance.

Press tab again to move to the Amount field for Advances.

Type 100 **Press** tab.

The cheque portion of the journal and the gross pay are updated again. Advances do not affect the tax amounts or vacation pay.

The **Benefits** field is used to enter the total amount of taxable benefits a business offers to its employees, such as health insurance or dental plans. Half of Durtee's medical premium is paid by Lime Light. This contribution to medical expenses is also set up as an automatic entry that appears on the **User-Defined Expenses** tab screen. Employee entitlements and employer expenses (User-Defined Expenses) will be covered later in the chapter for other employees.

Simply Accounting automatically calculates an amount in the **Vac. Accrued Amount** field and displays it as a default. Durtee's default amount is calculated at the vacation pay rate of 4 percent and will be retained by the business (*Vacation Payable* account) until he takes a vacation or leaves the employ of the business. (See the Employee Information Sheet for each employee's vacation pay rate.)

The total accumulated vacation pay owing (withheld since vacation pay was last paid and including this pay) shows as the YTD amount for the Vac. Accrued. This amount appears in the **Vac. Paid** field when you release the accumulated vacation pay retained for an employee. The amount that has been retained and is available for release appears as a default when you turn off the option to retain vacation in the Employee Ledger. (See page 382.)

NOTES
Salaried employees receive their regular pay during their vacations instead of receiving vacation pay. They receive vacation days as an entitlement.

NOTES
If the amount of a deduction is incorrect, and it is not a one-time change, you should edit the employee record in the Payroll Ledger. The next time you open the Payroll Journal for the employee, the edited amount will be entered.

NOTES
If you are using a later version of the Simply Accounting program than 2006 Release B, your tax amounts and amount withheld may be different from those shown because different tax tables are used. Your Gross Pay and Vacation amounts should always be the same as the ones we show.

NOTES
Separate linked wage accounts are set up for the wages of general salaried employees, for cleaning staff (cleaners and pressers) and for commissions, and piece rate bonuses. Vacation pay can also be linked to a separate account if you want to track this amount separately from other wage expenses.

The **Deductions tab screen** has the medical deduction entered automatically because the amounts are stored in the ledger record. For other employees, the RRSP contributions also appear on the Deductions tab screen. If necessary, the deduction amounts can be edited.

As in other journals, you can enter additional information, one date and one other field, for the Payroll Journal by clicking the tool or choosing from the Paycheque menu.

Click each **tab** to see the fields that are on that tab screen.

Click the **Income tab** again to see the complete payroll form as shown below:

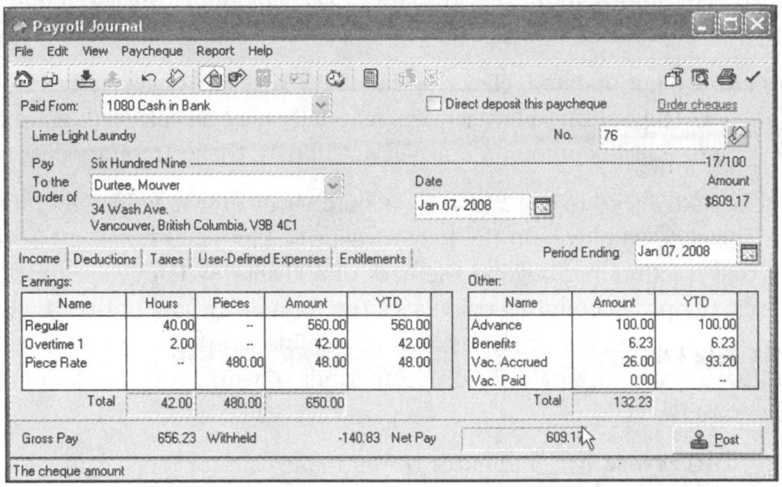

Reviewing the Payroll Journal Transaction

When you have entered all the information, you should review the completed transaction before posting.

Choose the **Report menu** and **click Display Payroll Journal Entry**. The transaction you have just completed appears as follows:

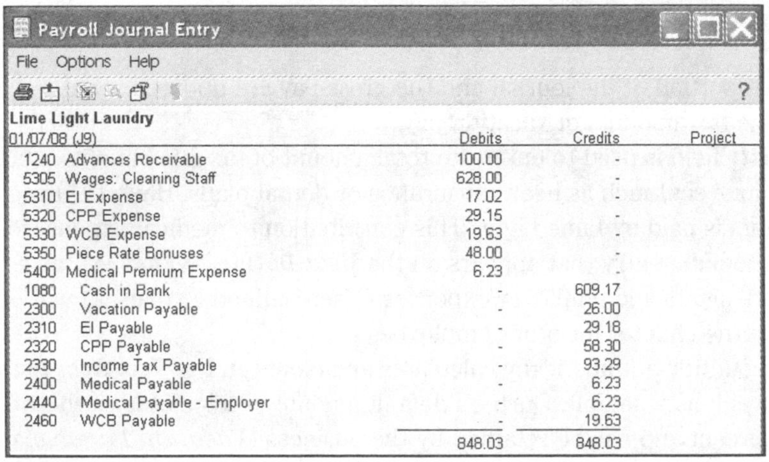

Lime Light Laundry

01/07/08 (J9)	Debits	Credits	Project
1240 Advances Receivable	100.00	-	
5305 Wages: Cleaning Staff	628.00	-	
5310 EI Expense	17.02	-	
5320 CPP Expense	29.15	-	
5330 WCB Expense	19.63	-	
5350 Piece Rate Bonuses	48.00	-	
5400 Medical Premium Expense	6.23	-	
1080 Cash in Bank	-	609.17	
2300 Vacation Payable	-	26.00	
2310 EI Payable	-	29.18	
2320 CPP Payable	-	58.30	
2330 Income Tax Payable	-	93.29	
2400 Medical Payable	-	6.23	
2440 Medical Payable - Employer	-	6.23	
2460 WCB Payable	-	19.63	
	848.03	848.03	

Notice that all the relevant wage expense accounts have been debited. The hourly wages and piece rate bonuses are tracked in separate wage expense accounts. In addition, all the wage-related liability accounts and *Cash in Bank* have been updated automatically because the Payroll Ledger is linked to the General Ledger. All accounts in the journal entry have been defined as linked accounts for the Payroll Ledger so you do not enter any account numbers directly.

Simply Accounting uses the Canada Revenue Agency tax formulas to calculate the deduction amounts for CPP, EI and income tax. These formulas are updated every six months. The remaining deductions are determined from Employee Ledger entries when different rates apply to different employees (WCB, vacation pay rate and Medical), or from Payroll Ledger settings when the same rate applies to all employees (EI factor of 1.4).

Payroll expense accounts reflect the employer's share of payroll tax obligations. The liabilities reflect the amounts that the owner must remit to the appropriate agencies and include both the employer's share of these tax liabilities and the employee's share (deductions withheld). For example, CPP contributions by the employee are matched by the employer. Therefore, the *CPP Expense* (employer's share) is one-half of the *CPP Payable* amount (employee and employer's share). WCB is paid entirely by the employer (the expense amount is the same as the liability amount). Medical contributions by employer and employee are equal but they are represented in different accounts — the employer's share is shown in expense and payable accounts, *Medical Premium Expense* and *Medical Payable - Employer*, while the employee's share appears only in the payable account, *Medical Payable*. For EI, the employer's share is 1.4 times the employee's share. Vacation pay is part of the Wages expense.

NOTES
Both the employer's and the employee's share of the medical premiums are payable to the provincial Minister of Finance.

NOTES
Payroll Journal entries may be stored as recurring entries before posting. Follow the same steps as you do for recurring sales or purchases.

Close the **display** to return to the Payroll Journal input screen.

CORRECTING THE PAYROLL JOURNAL ENTRY BEFORE POSTING

Move the cursor to the field that contains the error. If you need to change screens to access the field you want, **click** the appropriate **tab**. **Press** tab to move forward through the fields or **press** shift and tab together to move back to a previous field. This will highlight the field information so that you can change it. **Type** the **correct information** and **press** tab to enter it.

You can also use the mouse to **point** to a field and **drag** through the **incorrect information** to highlight it. You can highlight a single number or letter or the entire field. **Type** the **correct information** and **press** tab to enter it.

Click an **incorrect amount** to highlight it. **Type** the **correct amount** and **press** tab.

You can discard the entry by **clicking** ☒ **(Close)** or ↶ **(Undo)** or by returning to the Employee list and **clicking** a **different employee** name. **Click** the name of the **correct employee** and **press** tab. When prompted, confirm that you want to discard the incorrect entry. **Click Yes**, and start again.

You can preview the paycheque before printing it if you want. You can also modify the reports and forms settings from the journal. Tool buttons are included for both these functions. You must have selected Custom Forms and Custom Simply Form as the Form Type in the Reports and Forms settings screen.

NOTES
Previewing the paycheque is similar to previewing Sales Invoice forms. Refer to Appendix F on the Student CD-ROM.
The data files include the settings for previewing paycheques. However, if you see an error message about the missing file or form, click the Reports & Forms tool and choose Payment Cheque (or Direct Deposit Stubs) in the Description fields so the file location reference will be dimmed..

Click the **Print Preview tool**. You will see the warning about payroll formulas:

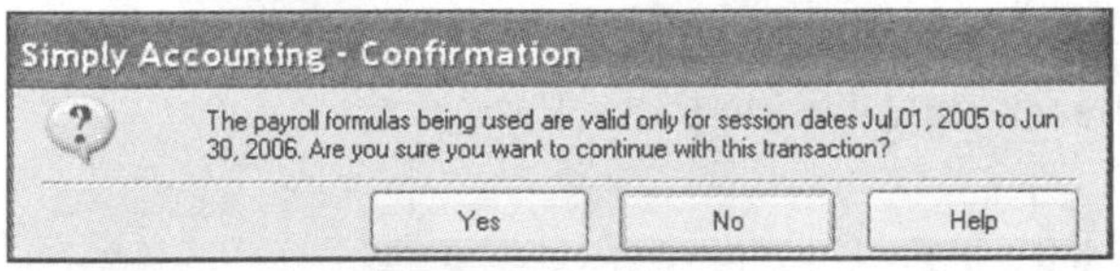

The caution is displayed whenever the dates of the transaction are different from the dates of the tax tables in your Simply Accounting program.

Click **Yes** to continue to the preview. At this point, you have not yet posted the transaction, so you can still make changes if needed.

The preview shows the cheque and cheque stub with payroll summary details.

Click **OK** to close the preview when finished to return to the journal.

NOTES
Of course, a real business should always work with the current payroll tax tables. Sage Software provides payroll updates every six months when you sign up for the payroll update service.

Posting

When all the information in your journal entry is correct,

Click **Post** Post to see the caution about dates and tax tables again.

Click **Yes** to continue, unless you have made a mistake.

A blank Payroll Journal input screen appears for entering the next payroll transaction.

Entering Payroll Entitlements and Benefits

Lime Light Laundry pays 50 percent of the medical premiums for all employees. The company also pays 50 percent of eligible tuition fees for its employees. Both are taxable benefits.

Iean Sissler is currently taking a course and receives the tuition fees benefit. Her paycheques for the next four months will include a benefit of $25 toward her college tuition fees. She has also taken a personal leave day during the week to enroll in her course.

Choose **Sissler, Iean** from the employee list. **Press** tab to add her payroll information to the form as shown:

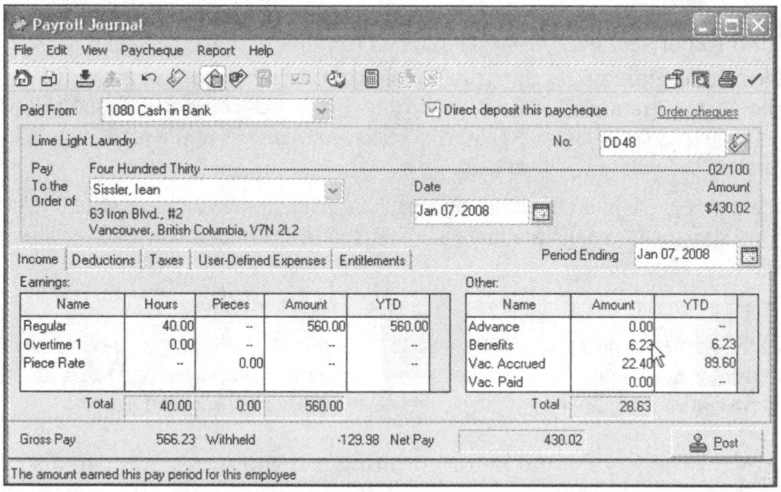

You will notice that instead of a cheque number, the entry DD48 appears on the form because the check box for Direct Deposit This Paycheque is selected. Sissler has chosen to have her pay deposited directly to her account. The bank account deposit details are added to the employee's ledger record.

Sissler has no overtime hours for this week but we need to add the piece rate quantity.

NOTES

For this data set, we chose not to include the benefit amount for tuition in the ledger record, so it will not be included in the journal automatically. In this way, we are able to demonstrate how you enter one-time or periodic entries for benefits. The tuition benefit is also temporary – it will be terminated at the end of the semester once the full amount has been paid.

We also pay the tuition over several paycheques to avoid a one-time large increase in pay that would distort the taxes for that paycheque.

Click **0.00** in the **Pieces field** beside Piece Rate.

Type 395

The $25 weekly tuition fee benefit is not yet added so we need to enter it. It could also be set up in the employee ledger so that it was added automatically until the entire amount was paid. Then it would be removed from the ledger. Instead, we will edit the amount in the journal.

Click **6.23** in the **Benefits field**.

Type 31.23 **Press** tab to update the tax amounts.

Employee benefits are taxable amounts. After adding the benefit, Sissler's total withheld has increased from $140.42 to $146.66. The Gross Pay amount has increased by the $25 benefit, but the Net Pay amount has changed only by the additional taxes withheld, from $459.09 to $452.84. Although the employee does not receive the benefit as cash, the amount is included in the pre-tax total income to arrive at the amount of income tax. The benefit is subtracted again to determine the net pay amount. In most cases, the benefit is an expense to the employer and is entered as such on the User-Defined Expenses tab.

Click the **User-Defined Expenses tab** to open these fields:

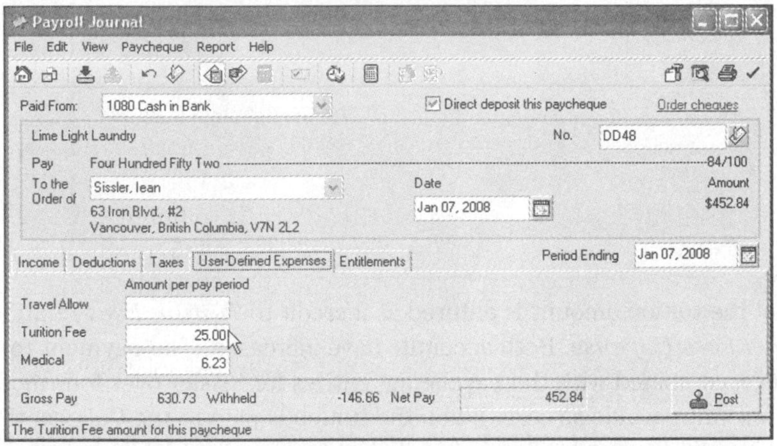

User-defined expenses are employer payroll expenses that are specific to a business, unlike the expenses we saw earlier that apply to all businesses. The expense for Sissler's tuition has been entered in her ledger record so it appears automatically in each paycheque. You can see that the fields can also be accessed directly in the journal for one-time expenses or one-time changes in amounts.

Next we must enter the personal leave day that Sissler has taken.

Click the **Entitlements tab** to open these fields:

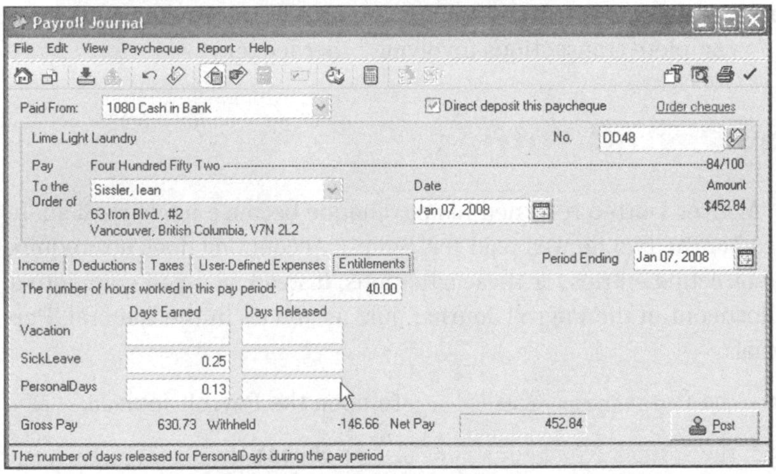

Three entitlements are defined for Lime Light Laundry: vacation days (for salaried employees only), sick leave days and personal leave days. The amounts entered in the Days Earned fields show only the number of days earned for this pay period — one week. Sick leave is accrued at the rate of 5 percent per hour worked and personal days accrue at the rate of 2.5 percent. The total number of days accrued from prior work periods will be recorded and updated in the ledger record. If the number of days released exceeds the number of days accrued, you will see a warning message that asks you if a negative balance is allowed. Entitlements do not affect gross pay, net pay or taxes.

Sissler has taken one personal leave day this week.

Click the **Days Released column beside PersonalDays**.

Type 1 **Press** *tab* to save the entry and update the form.

NOTES
After clearing data, display the relevant reports to see that the information has been cleared. You will be unable to look up and adjust posted invoices if you have removed lookup details for cleared paid transactions.

NOTES
If the User-Defined Expense amount for tuition is omitted from the record, it can be entered in the paycheques journal as needed.

NOTES
For every 20 days of work, the employee is entitled to one day of sick leave (the rate is 5%). Employees are allowed one personal day for every 40 full days worked, for a rate of 2.5%.

For some entitlements, such as vacation days, employers may require the employee to work a minimum number of months before taking any time off.

The total number of days accrued appears only in the ledger record for the employee and does does not appear in the journal.

NOTES
We omitted the space in the name for Personal Days because the entitlement name cannot exceed 12 characters.

You are now ready to review the journal entry.

Choose the **Report menu** and **click Display Payroll Journal Entry**:

Lime Light Laundry
01/07/08 (J10)

		Debits	Credits	Project
5305	Wages: Cleaning Staff	583.98	-	
5310	EI Expense	15.69	-	
5320	CPP Expense	27.89	-	
5330	WCB Expense	18.10	-	
5350	Piece Rate Bonuses	39.50	-	
5380	Tuition Fees Expense	25.00	-	
5400	Medical Premium Expense	6.23	-	
1080	Cash in Bank	-	452.84	
2300	Vacation Payable	-	23.98	
2310	EI Payable	-	26.90	
2320	CPP Payable	-	55.78	
2330	Income Tax Payable	-	76.33	
2400	Medical Payable	-	6.23	
2410	RRSP Payable	-	25.00	
2430	Tuition Fees Payable	-	25.00	
2440	Medical Payable - Employer	-	6.23	
2460	WCB Payable	-	18.10	
		716.39	716.39	

Notice that the tuition amount is entered as a credit to *Tuition Fees Payable* and a debit to *Tuition Fees Expense*. Both accounts have increased. The payment to Burnaby College, combined with the paycheque entries for Sissler over four months, will leave the net amount payable as zero. When the tuition is paid to the College, the *Tuition Fees Payable* account will temporarily have a negative (debit) balance. The expense account balance will of course remain at the end of this period.

Close the **journal entry display** to return to the journal.

Make **corrections** to the journal entry if necessary.

Click **Post** to save your work.

Click **Yes** to bypass the warning about payroll dates.

Close the **Payroll Journal window** to return to the Home window and complete transactions involving other ledgers.

Adjusting Payroll Entries

On January 8, Mouver Durtee returned his paycheque because he worked six hours of overtime instead of the two he was paid for. Simply Accounting does not require reversing and correcting entries for these situations. Instead, you can complete a paycheque adjustment in the Payroll Journal, just as you do in the General, Purchases and Sales journals.

Click the **Paycheques icon** to open the Payroll Journal.

Click the **Adjust Paycheque tool** or **choose** the **Paycheque menu** and **click Adjust Cheque** to open the familiar Search window:

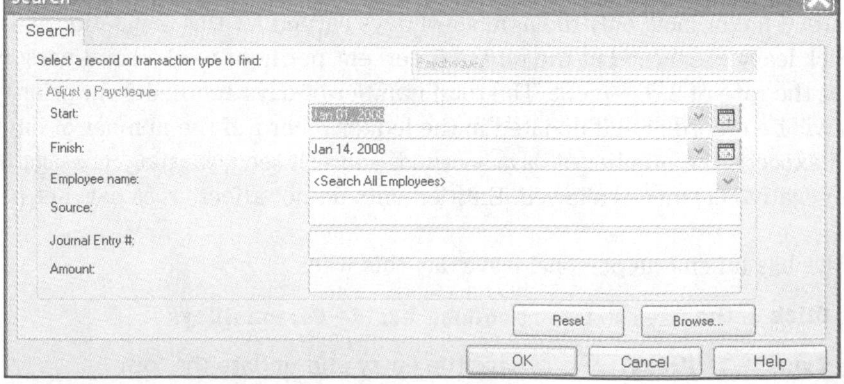

Paycheques is selected as the search area because we started from the Paycheques Journal.

You can select beginning and ending dates to create the list. You can also enter the source (cheque or direct deposit number) or journal entry number and click OK to access the paycheque immediately.

The default dates are the earliest transaction date and the session date for the data file. We can accept the default dates to see all payroll transactions listed.

Click **Browse** to access the list of posted payroll entries:

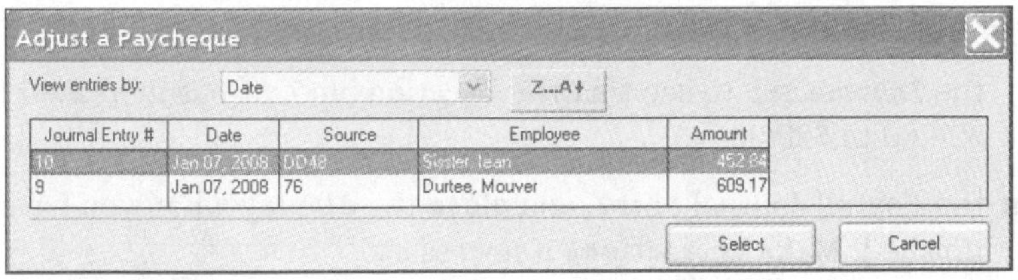

Click **Journal Entry #9 Durtee, Mouver** to select Durtee's journal entry.

Click **Select** to display the entry that was posted.

First, Simply Accounting offers the following reminder about recalculating taxes:

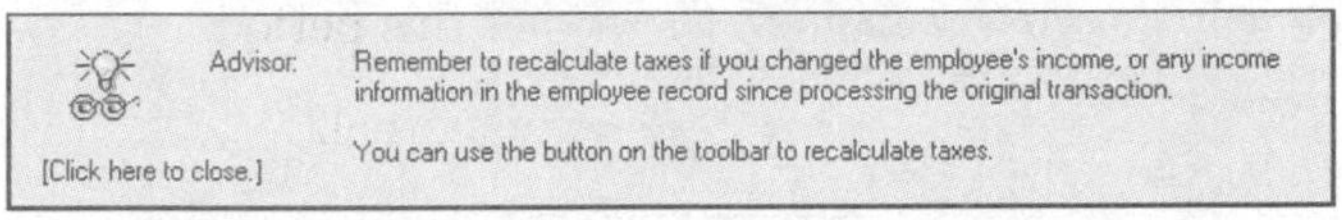

Advisor:
Remember to recalculate taxes if you changed the employee's income, or any income information in the employee record since processing the original transaction.
You can use the button on the toolbar to recalculate taxes.
[Click here to close.]

The program is advising you that the tax recalculation will not be automatic if you change an amount on the payroll entry.

Click the **Advisor icon** to close the warning and display the journal:

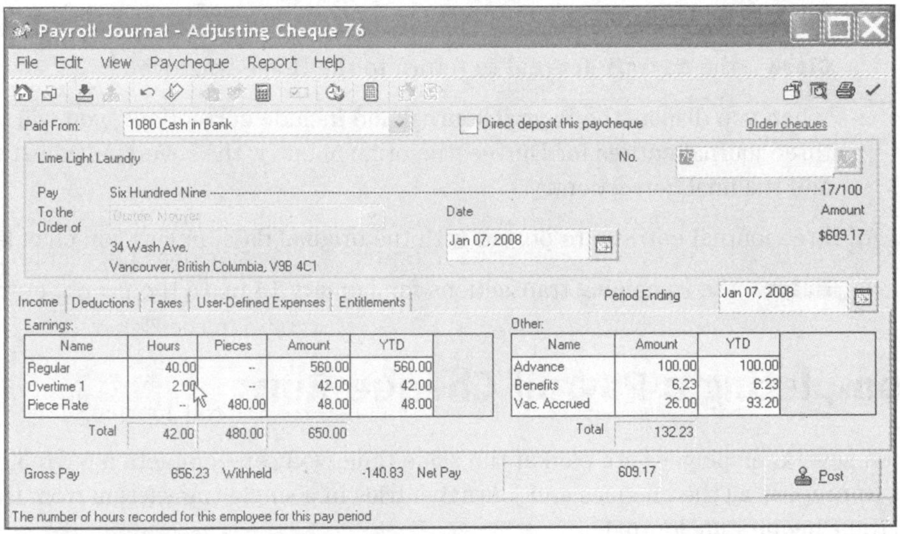

This is a duplicate of the payroll entry. All the fields can be edited with the exception of the employee name. If you want, you may change the date for the new cheque to January 8. The reversing entry will retain the original posting date. The cheque number is highlighted because normally you would prepare a new cheque. However, Durtee has returned the cheque so we can use the same number. We need to change the number of overtime hours.

Click **2.00** in the **Hours column for Overtime 1** to select the current entry.

Type 6 **Press** tab to enter the change and update the gross pay.

NOTES

Your journal entry numbers may be different if you have made other correcting or adjusting entries.

NOTES

To correct an entry when you have selected the wrong employee, you must complete a reversing entry. See Appendix C.

NOTES
The total amount Withheld is still $140.83 and the Vacation Accrued is still $26.00.

WARNING!
Do not confuse the Recalculate Taxes tool with the Window Calculator tool. The Calculator tool is the last one on the left side of the tool bar before the Refresh tools.

The Vacation pay and Withheld amounts have not been updated for the new amount of gross pay. Compare the amounts with those in the journal screen display on page 364.

Click the **Taxes tab**. The deduction amounts have not changed yet and they can be edited.

Click the **Recalculate Taxes button** on the Payroll Journal tool bar or **choose** the **Paycheque menu** and **click Recalculate Taxes**.

All the deduction and vacation pay amounts are updated for the additional wages for the extra overtime hours worked.

Click the **Income tab** to see that the Vacation amount has increased from $26.00 to $29.36.

Review the Payroll Journal **entry**, and **close** the **display** when you have finished. **Make corrections** if necessary.

Click the **Post button** Post to save the adjustment.

NOTES
The program provides the warning about the cheque sequence because we selected to verify number sequences in the Forms Settings window (see page 301).

Simply Accounting displays the following warning when you do not change the cheque number:

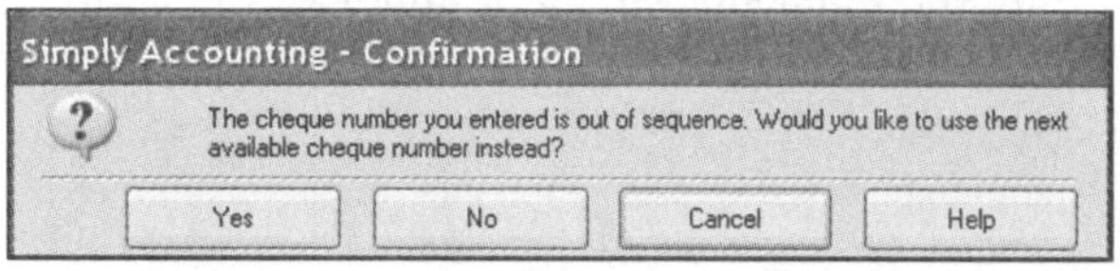

Read the question in the warning carefully. To change the cheque number to the next number in the automatic sequence, click Yes. In this case, you can use the duplicate cheque number because Durtee returned the original cheque.

Click **No** to continue.

Close the **Payroll Journal** to return to the Home window.

When you display the Payroll Journal and include corrections, you will see three journal entries for Durtee: the original entry, the reversing adjusting entry and the final correct entry.

All three journal entries are posted with the original date, unless you changed it.

Enter the remaining transactions for January 14 up to the payroll entry.

Completing a Payroll Cheque Run

When several employees are paid at the same time, you can complete a payroll cheque run to prepare all the cheques and journal entries in a single transaction from the Payroll Cheque Run Journal.

The Payroll Cheque Run Journal is shown with the pointer in the following screen:

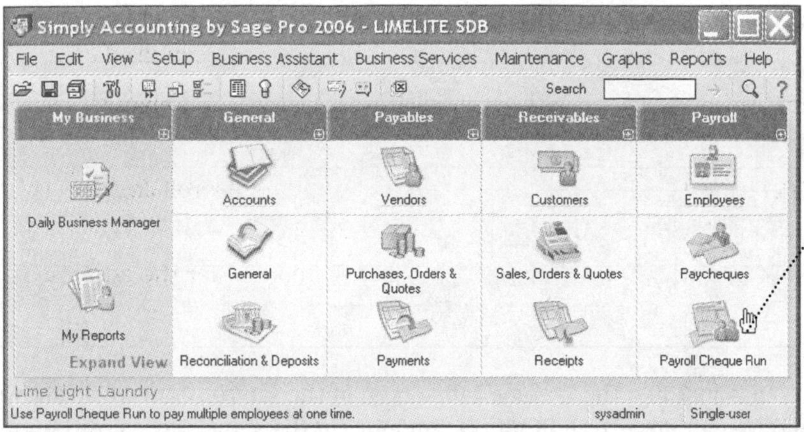

Click the **Payroll Cheque Run** icon to open the Payroll Run Journal:

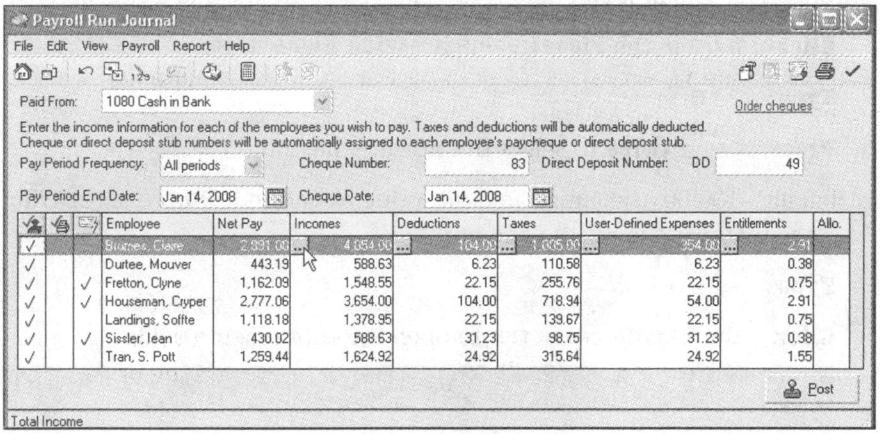

From this screen, you can pay all employees with a single transaction, and you can enter or edit any details that you can enter or edit in the Payroll Journal. Employees are listed in alphabetic order and checkmarks indicate who will be paid in this payroll run and who has selected direct deposits instead of cheques.

Initially, all employees have a ✓ in the **Post column**. The program selects all employees for inclusion if their pay cycle has ended because the default **Pay Period Frequency** option is All Periods. You can select a single pay period frequency for the cheque run from the Pay Period Frequency list or you can choose All periods to include more than one period. If we chose 26 (bi-weekly pay) as the Pay Period Frequency, only the three bi-weekly paid employees would be marked with a ✓ in the Post column. We want to pay all employees except the two monthly paid salaried employees.

The form also includes deposit information in the **Direct Deposit column**. A ✓ in this column indicates that the paycheque will be deposited to the employee's bank account. You can change the preference by clicking the ✓ to remove the selection. Both the next Cheque and Direct Deposit Numbers are on the form.

The pay period ending date and initial cheque number can also be edited if necessary.

The columns mirror the tabs in the Payroll Journal and contain total amounts for all fields in that tab screen. You can open the individual fields for a column heading by clicking the **Detail button** beside an amount.

Click the ✓ **beside Brumes** in the Post column to deselect the employee and remove her ✓ and amounts.

Click the ✓ **beside Houseman, Cryper** to remove his ✓. Durtee, Fretton, Landings, Sissler and Tran should remain selected.

Click **Durtee** to select this employee. Detail buttons are added to the amounts.

basic BASIC VERSION
The Refresh and the Time Slips tools do not appear in the Basic version.

NOTES
You cannot adjust paycheques from the Payroll Run Journal, although paycheques prepared here can be adjusted in the Paycheques Journal.

NOTES
The salaried employees on monthly pay cycles are also selected because no paycheque has been issued for them.

WARNING!
The Cheque Date for the payroll run must be the same as the session date. If you need to use a different date, use the Paycheques Journal.

NOTES
If you have difficulty clicking a column for a line that is selected, click a different line before clicking the ✓ you want to remove (or add).

WARNING!
The Payroll Detail screens do not include the employee name, so choose the employee carefully before you add the details. Clicking the name before opening a detail screen will place the cursor on the right line and help you select correctly.

Click the **Incomes Detail button** to open the Earning fields:

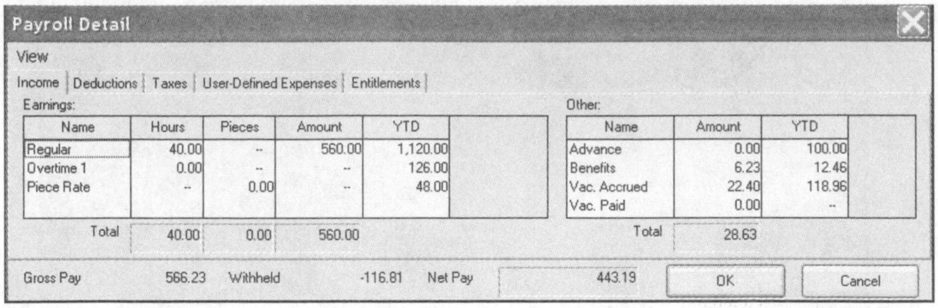

This screen is just like the Income tab screen in the Payroll Journal as shown on page 362, and we can enter or edit all the amounts in the same way as in the journal. For Durtee, we need to add the number of pieces, the advances repayment and the sick leave information. The first two details are entered in the Income Detail screen.

Click **0.00** in the **Pieces column beside Piece Rate**.

Type 370

Press *tab* **twice** to select the Advance amount.

WARNING!
Remember to enter a negative number for advances that are repaid.

By default, –100.00, the entire amount owing, is entered. Durtee is repaying $25 each week so we must change the amount.

Type -25

Click the **Entitlements tab** to open the entitlements fields:

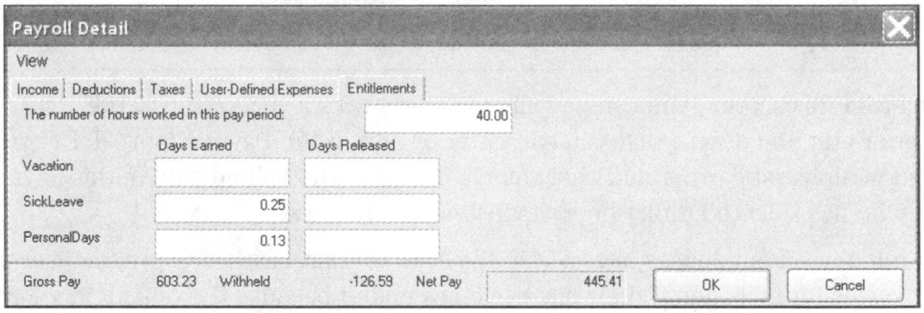

NOTES
Remember that the entry for Days Earned reflects only the amount earned for this pay period based on the number of hours worked in this pay period.

Once again, the fields we see are the same as those in the Payroll Journal Entitlements tab screen (see page 367).

Click the **Days Released field beside SickLeave**.

Type 1

Click **OK** to return to the Payroll Run Journal summary screen.

Click **Sissler** to prepare for entering the additional details for her.

We need to add the number of pieces for the piece rate bonus, edit the Benefits amount and add her advance.

Click the **Incomes Detail button** to open the Earning fields.

Click **0.00** in the **Pieces column beside Piece Rate**.

Type 470

Press *tab* **twice** to select the Advance amount.

Type 200 **Press** *tab* to select the Benefits amount.

Type 31.23

Click the **Deductions tab**:

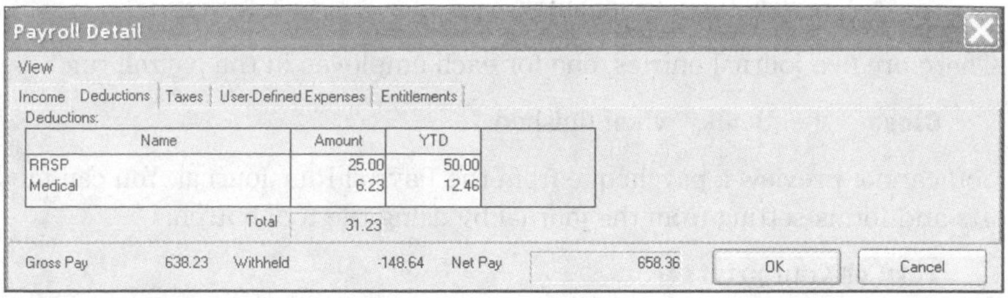

We do not need to change these amounts, but you can see that the deduction amounts are available for editing.

Click **OK** to return to the Payroll Run Journal summary screen.

Click **Fretton** to prepare for entering the additional details for her.

We need to add the number for the piece rate bonus and enter her sick leave.

Click the **Incomes Detail button** [...] to open the Earning fields.

Click **0.00** in the **Pieces column beside Piece Rate**.

Type 860

Click the **Entitlements tab** to open the entitlements fields.

Click the **Days Released field beside SickLeave**.

Type 1

Click **OK** to return to the Payroll Run Journal summary screen.

Click **Landings** to prepare for entering the additional details.

We need to add the overtime hours and the number for the piece rate bonus.

Click the **Incomes Detail button** [...] to open the Earnings fields.

Click **0.00** in the **Hours column beside Overtime 1**.

Type 2 **Press** *tab* to advance to the Pieces entry.

Type 950

Click **OK** to return to the updated Payroll Run Journal summary screen.

No changes are required for Tran's salaried paycheque so the transaction is complete and should look like the one we show here:

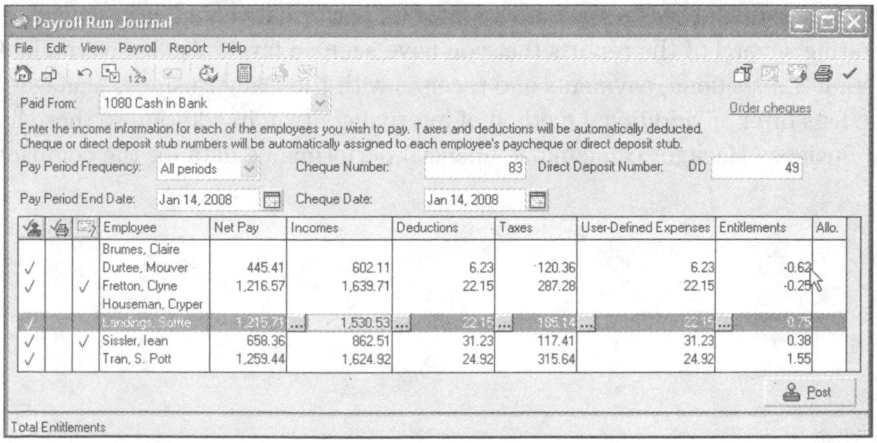

You are now ready to review the journal entry.

Choose the **Report menu** and **click Display Payroll Run Journal Entry** to review the journal entry.

There are five journal entries, one for each employee in the payroll run.

Close the **display** when finished.

You cannot preview a paycheque from the Payroll Run Journal. You can modify the reports and forms setting from the journal by using the tool button.

Turn on your **printer**.

Choose the **Report menu** and **click Payroll Cheque Run Summary** to provide a printed record of the payroll run transactions. You cannot display this summary.

Click Post Post to save the transaction. **Click Yes** to bypass the warning about payroll formula dates.

The Payroll Run Journal remains open with the direct deposit and cheque numbers updated after the five payroll run cheques and direct deposits as shown:

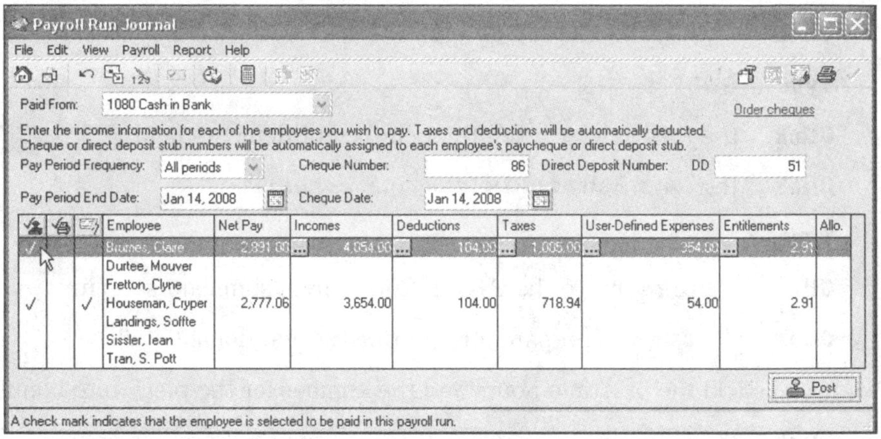

The Journal now selects the remaining two unpaid salaried employees for the next run. They still have a ✓ in the Post column. They will be paid at the end of the month.

Close the **Journal** to return to the Home window.

Enter the **remaining source documents** up to Memo #2 on January 23.

Working from the Daily Business Manager

Simply Accounting helps a business monitor its performance and cash flow by generating several of the reports that you have seen so far. It also keeps track of recurring transactions, payments and receipts with the Daily Business Manager lists. These lists offer an additional method of internal control. In addition to these lists, the Daily Business Manager can compile financial performance data for the company.

When the Home window shows the My Business tab, it includes a Daily Business Manager icon as shown here:

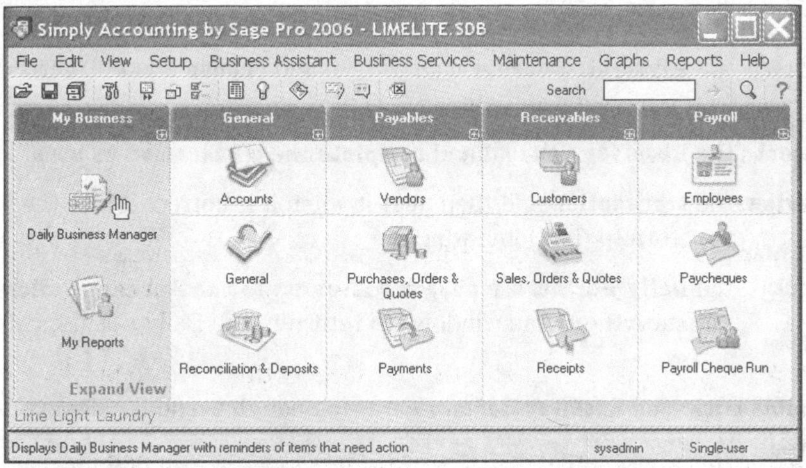

Clicking this icon will open the Daily Business Manager.

Otherwise, from the Home window,

Click the **Daily Business Manager tool** or **choose** the **Business Assistant menu** and **click Daily Business Manager**:

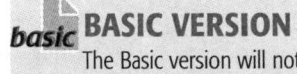

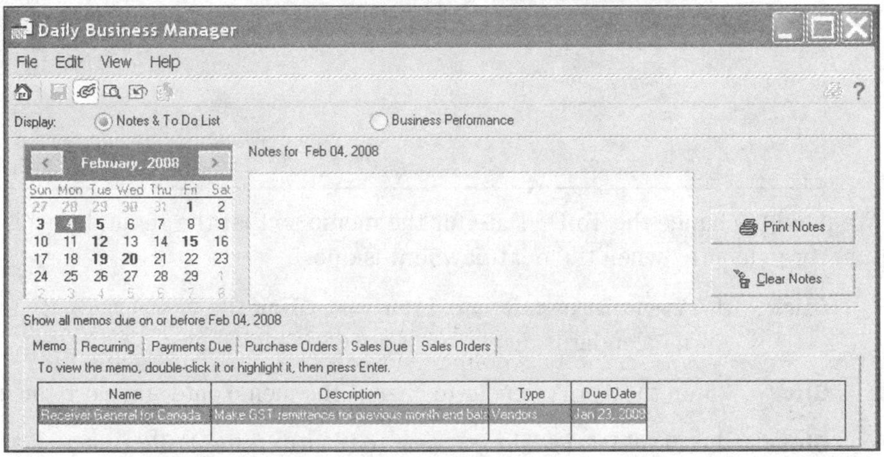

You can also access the Daily Business Manager from any of the journals by clicking the Daily Business Manager tool icon or by choosing the View menu and clicking Daily Business Manager.

You can show Daily Business Manager lists automatically each time you advance the session date, each time you start the program or both. Choose the Setup menu, then choose User Preferences and click the View tab. Click the option At Startup to add the checkmark. Repeat the procedure for After Changing Session Date to add a checkmark for this option. Menu and tool bar access to the lists are always available from the Home window.

By default, Simply Accounting chooses a date that is one week past the current session date for its Daily Business Manager. The date can be changed by clicking a new date on the calendar. The list will be updated to reflect the change in date.

Each tab screen includes instructions for accessing journals or selecting an entry.

You can also type notes for a date directly into the Notes box. They will remain on-screen for that date until you choose Clear Notes. You can print these notes and clear them when they are no longer needed.

The memo on file is a reminder to pay the GST instalment.

basic **BASIC VERSION**

The Basic version will not include the Refresh tool.

NOTES

Calendar numbers in boldface indicate that a transaction is due on that day, that is, the Daily Business Manager has an entry for that day.

NOTES

In the setup for Toss for Tots and Dorfmann Design, we turned off the Daily Business Manager.

Click the **Home window tool** (or **click** the **Simply Accounting program button on the task bar**) to bring forward the Home window.

Click the **Payments Journal icon** and **choose Make Other Payment** as the type of transaction.

NOTES

Use the January 1 General Ledger balances for GST Charged on Services and GST Paid on Purchases to make the remittance. Refer to page 264 for assistance if necessary.

Select the **Receiver General** and **complete** the **transaction** as usual.

Review the **transaction** and then **post** it when it is correct. **Close** the **journal** to return to the Home window.

Click the **Daily Business Manager button on the task bar** (or **click** to minimize the Home window) to return to the Daily Business Manager screen.

Double click the **Receiver General entry** to open the vendor's Memo tab screen:

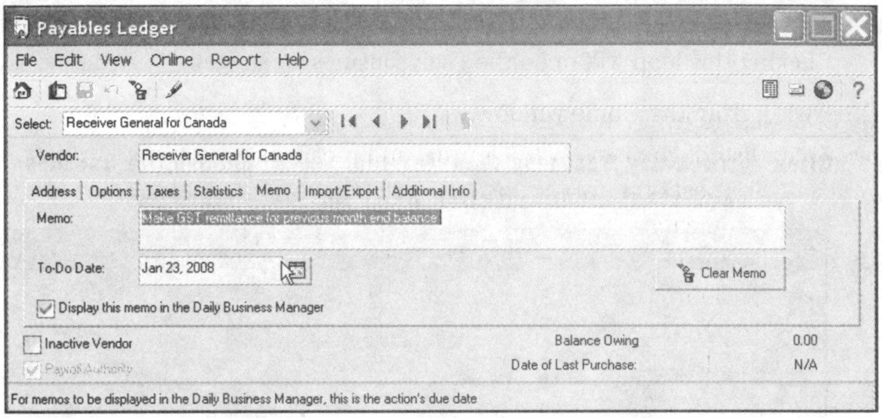

We need to change the To-Do Date for the memo so that the reminder will appear again in three months when the next payment is due.

Click the **To-Do Date calendar icon**. **Click** the **next arrow** until the April calendar is displayed. April 23 is highlighted.

Click **23** on the April calendar to change the memo date and close the calendar.

Close the **Payables Ledger window** to return to the Daily Business Manager.

The memo no longer appears because it is not due within the one-week time frame for the messages in the Daily Business Manager.

Recurring Transactions Due

Click the **Recurring tab** to see the next list of transactions that we can process directly from the Daily Business Manager:

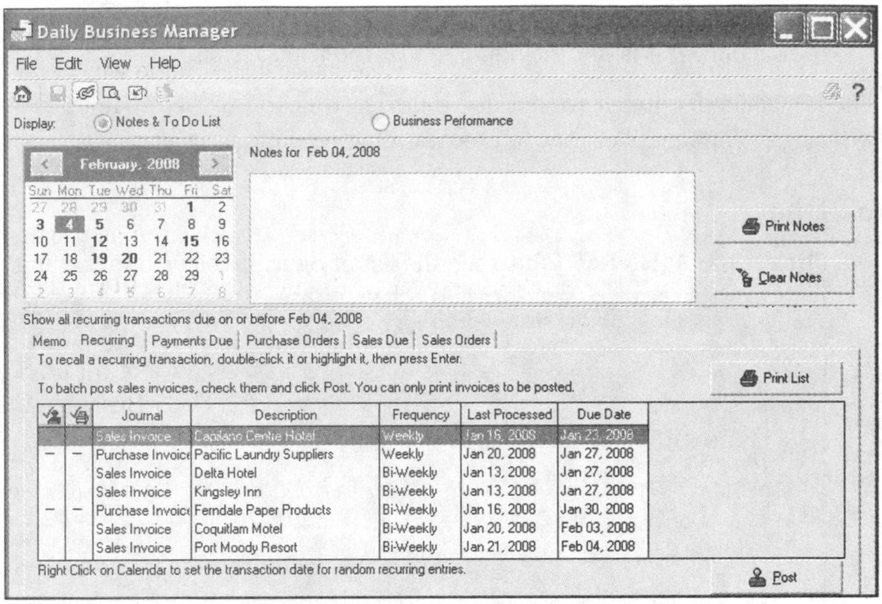

An advantage to using the Daily Business Manager is that the recurring entries for all journals are listed. You can open a journal and recall a stored transaction in a single step. You can also post and print sales invoices, individually or in batches, directly from this screen, but you cannot preview them.

All recurring entries due on or before the date marked on the calendar are listed, together with the Journal used for the original entry, the entry name (Description) and its recurring Frequency. The most recent posting date (Last Processed) and the Due Date are also included. The entries are listed according to the Due Date, with the earliest date at the top of the list.

You can see that the first entry — the sale to Capilano Centre Hotel — is due today, January 23. As indicated by the instructions on the screen, you can post a sale directly from the Daily Business Manager, or you can open the journal first.

Click the **Post column** (the first column) **beside** the sale for **Capilano Centre Hotel.**

Click **Post** Post.

A message appears asking if there is additional information to enter before posting:

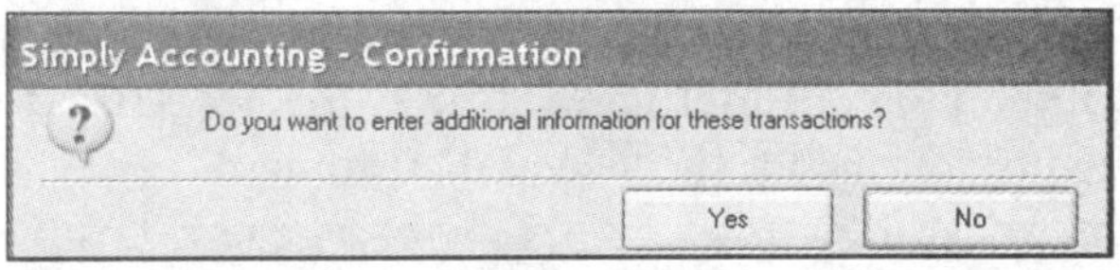

If you want to add details, click Yes to open the Additional Information screen. There are no details to add to the Sales Journal entry so we can continue.

Click **No** to see a message naming the invoice that is currently being processed. When it is finished, you will see the confirmation screen:

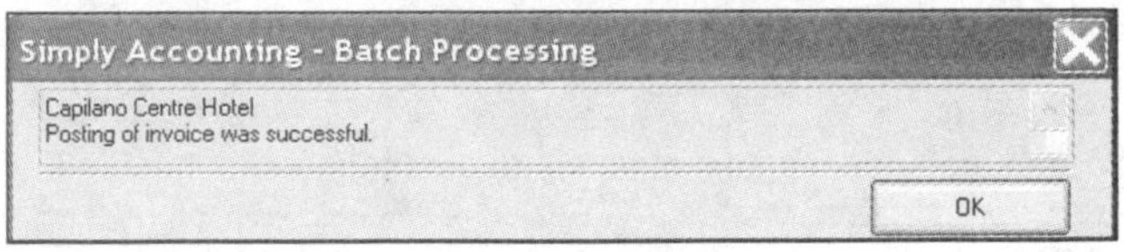

All invoices that were processed will be listed.

Click **OK** to return to the list of recurring entries. The Capilano sales invoice has been removed from the list because the next entry will occur after Feb. 4.

NOTES

You may need to click on another line first to remove the selection and then click the Post column for Capilano.

WARNING!

Remember that when you post directly from the Daily Business Manager, you cannot see or review your journal entry or preview the invoice before posting, so be very careful when you use this approach.

If the entry did not post successfully, check the journal report for the transaction. If it is not included, repeat the transaction.

The remaining list items are not due today, so we can proceed to another list in the Daily Business Manager. We want to process some receipts next.

Sales Due

Click the **Sales Due tab** to see the list of Sales Invoices due within the week:

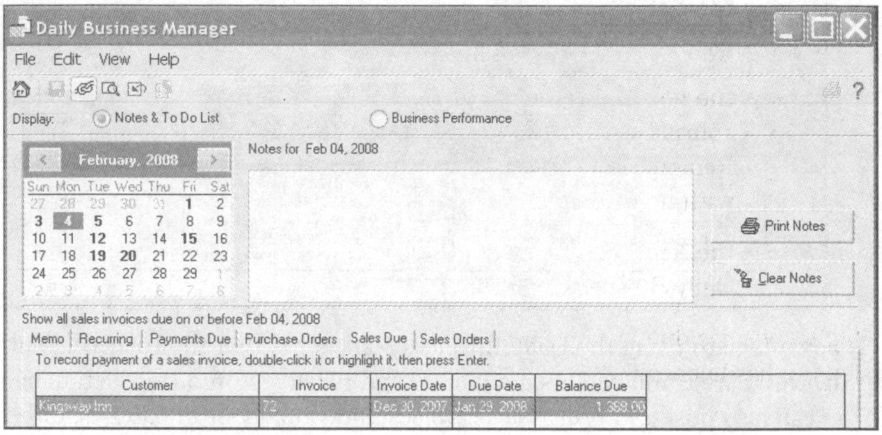

The Sales Due list is user-friendly and can be used to locate customers with outstanding debts. The list shows the Customer's name, Invoice number, Invoice Date, payment Due Date and Balance Due (owing) on the due date without the discount. Invoices displayed can be matched against receipts on hand and you can open the Receipts Journal directly from this window. Only one invoice is listed because the others are not due in the next week. However, no payment has been received from Kingsway Inn. Furthermore, since some of Lime Light's customers take advantage of sales discounts, we should look at sales due over a longer span than one week. We need to enter the payments received from Capilano Centre Hotel, Kingsley Inn and Coquitlam Motel.

WARNING!
Always check that you have the correct month when you are using the calendar because you can postdate entries from the Daily Business Manager.

Click **25** on the February calendar to see invoices due in the next month.

The invoices we need now appear on the list so we can enter receipts for them.

To open the journal, you can double click any part of the line for the entry you want or click the line and press *enter*.

Double click the **Capilano Centre Hotel journal line** (Invoice #107) to open the Receipts Journal for the selected customer:

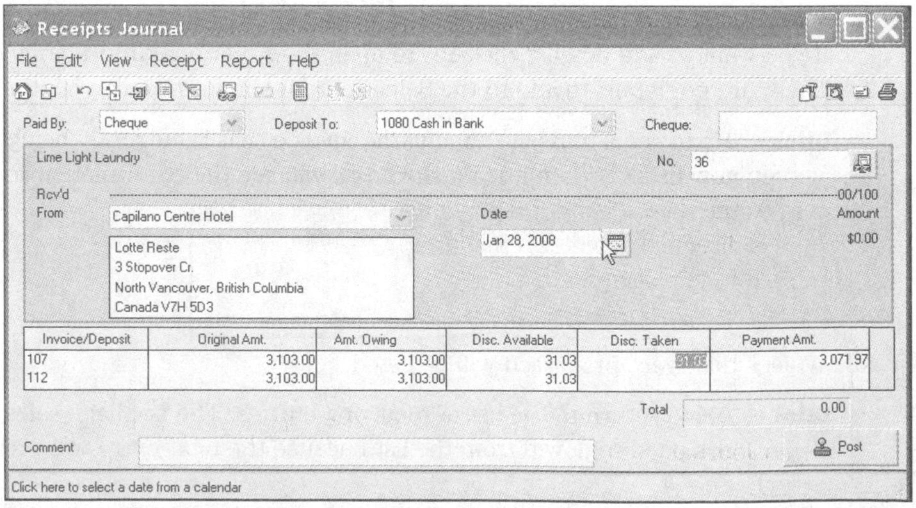

Press tab to accept the discount and amount for the first invoice. The amount should appear in the Total field and the upper cheque portion. Be careful not to select the second invoice that is not paid.

Add the customer's **cheque number** (2974) in the Cheque field.

Change the **date** of the cheque to January 25.

Display the **journal entry** to review your work. **Close** the **display** and **make corrections** if necessary.

Click **Post** [Post] to record the transaction.

Enter the next **two receipts** from the Receipts Journal or close the Receipts Journal to return to the Daily Business Manager window first. Remember to enter the receipt from Kingsley Inn as a partial payment with no discount.

Close the **Receipts Journal** after entering the three cheques to return to the Daily Business Manager.

WARNING!
Remember not to include the second discount for Capilano or the discounts for Kingsley and Coquitlam in the receipts.

The list of sales due has been updated by the three receipts. The amount owed by Kingsley Inn has been reduced by the partial payment.

Payments Due

The next source document describes a cheque issued in payment for outstanding invoices from a vendor. To be certain that all outstanding invoices are paid in a timely fashion, we can use the Daily Business Manager.

Click the **Payments Due tab**:

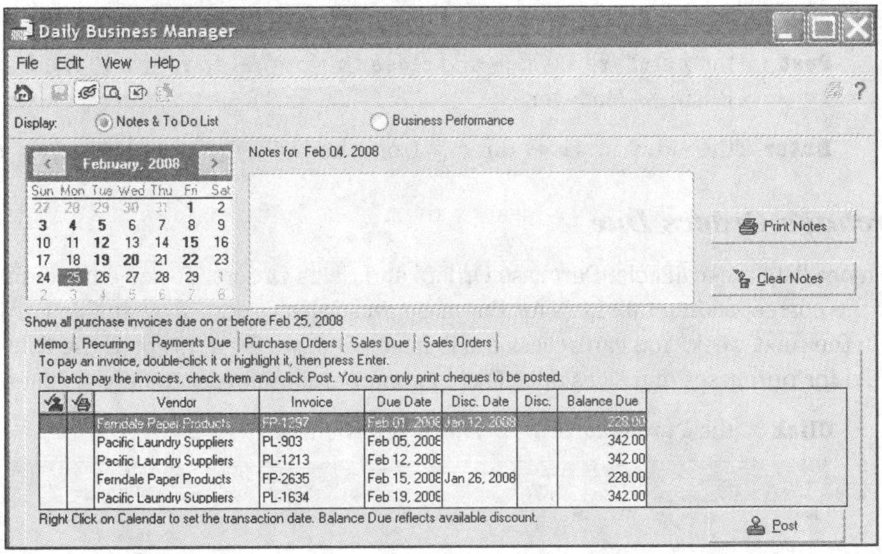

The screen now lists the payments due within one month because February 25 is still selected as the date. This list is the vendor equivalent of the Sales Due list except that it includes discount dates. You might use this list to plan a payment schedule. We want to be able to take advantage of purchase discounts, so we will leave the list selection date for one month past the current transaction date.

The list includes the Vendor name, Invoice number, payment Due Date, Discount Date, Discount availability and the Balance Due (owing). We can pay the invoices directly from this screen because no further information is needed. You can also open the Payments Journal by double clicking an invoice line or by clicking an invoice and pressing enter.

NOTES
Remember that when you post directly from the Daily Business Manager, you cannot see or review your journal entry before posting. Be very careful when you use this approach.

WARNING!
You cannot select a transaction date in a previous month from the Daily Business Manager, so you must move the calendar back to January before selecting January 26 as the cheque date.

NOTES
When you select January 26 as the transaction date, a ✓ will be added to the Disc. column to indicate that the discount is included. The discount amount is subtracted from the Balance Due.

From the list we can see that no invoices are due on January 26. However, the discount period for one invoice from Ferndale has passed but the second invoice from Ferndale is still eligible for the discount on January 26. The Disc. Date shows when the discount period ends. We will pay both of these invoices.

Click **January 31** to move the calendar period to January.

Right-click **26 on the January calendar** to select this as the cheque date.

The discount for invoice #FP-2635 is now deducted from the balance owing.

Click the **Post column** beside the Ferndale entries — invoices #FP-1297 and #FP-2635.

Click the **Post button** Post to save the entry. The confirmation message about the additional information appears.

Click **No** to continue with posting the transaction. The message about the cheque being processed successfully appears.

Click **OK** to confirm the message that the transaction was entered successfully.

The Ferndale Paper Products entries have been removed from the list.

Click **4** on the calendar for **February** to change the list viewing period back to one week.

Click the **Recurring tab**.

Enter the next **three recurring transactions**, the purchase from Pacific Laundry Suppliers and the two sales invoices.

Enter the **purchase** from the Purchases Journal. **Double click** the **Pacific Laundry Suppliers entry** to open the journal. **Add** the **invoice number**.

Post the **purchase invoice** and **close** the **journal** to return to the Daily Business Manager.

Enter the **sales invoices** directly from the Daily Business Manager screen.

Purchase Orders Due

Two more lists are available, Purchase Orders and Sales Orders. To see outstanding items, click the corresponding tab. Lists for Purchase and Sales Orders show unfilled orders due within the next week. You can access the journal windows for items on these lists just as you did for purchases and sales due. There is one purchase order unfilled on January 28.

Click the **Purchase Orders tab** to see the list:

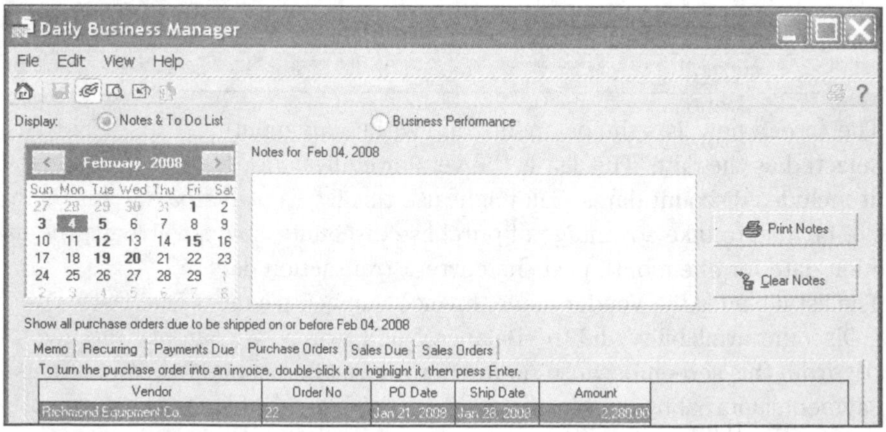

The list displays the vendor, order number, order date, shipping date and amount, making it easy to find orders that you need to track or follow up with the vendor.

Again, you can turn the order into an invoice from the Daily Business Manager by opening the journal with the order on-screen. The presser ordered from Richmond Equipment has been delivered so we should enter the invoice for it.

Double click the **Richmond Equipment Co.** order line to see the journal.

Enter **RE-6988** as the invoice number. The invoice date is correct.

Click the **Fill Backordered Quantities tool** .

Review the **journal entry** and then **make corrections** if needed.

Click **Post** to save the entry.

Click **OK** to confirm that the filled order has been removed.

Close the **Purchases Journal** to return to the Daily Business Manager.

Currently there are no sales orders on record. The Sales Orders list is the same as the Purchase Orders list. The same order information is also provided: customer, order number, order date, shipping date and invoice amount. You can turn the order into an invoice and then fill it just as you do purchase orders.

Before closing the Business Manager, we will look at the key performance indicators.

Business Performance

Click **Business Performance**:

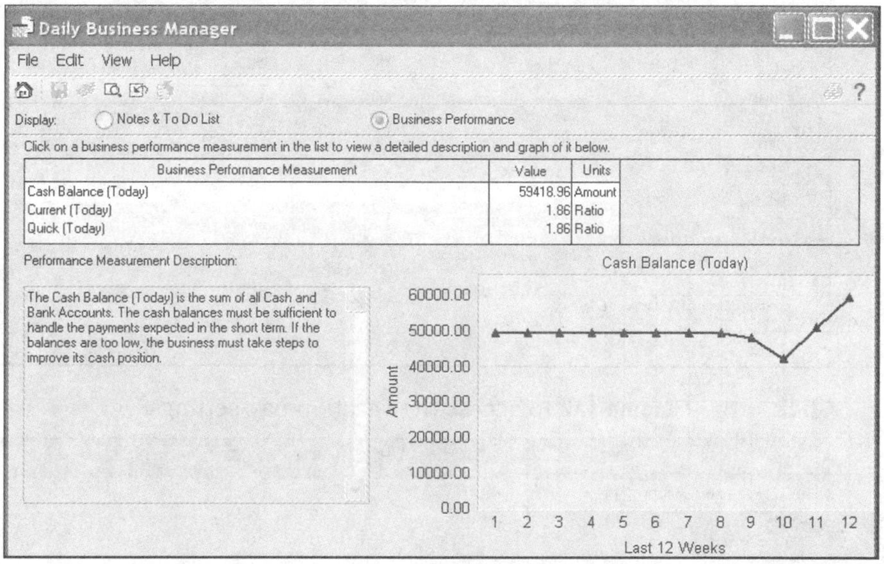

Performance information includes the current bank account balance, the current ratio and the quick ratio at the session date. The information is provided numerically and graphically. Detailed descriptions explain the indicators and guidelines for them. Clicking an indicator will display the results for it.

Click to close the Daily Business Manager and return to the Home window.

Open the **Receipts Journal**. **Choose** the **Adjust Receipt tool** . **Click** **Browse** and then **double click** **Kingsley Inn** (Receipt #37 for $1 966). **Click** **1966.00** and **press** *del* to delete the original payment amount. Enter **29.96** in the Disc. Taken field and **press** *tab*. **Press** *tab* to accept the amount and update the receipt. **Review** and **post** the receipt.

Enter the next group of **transactions**.

NOTES

Use the Receipts Journal to adjust the receipt. Refer to page 183 for assistance.

Releasing Vacation Pay

When Fretton takes a vacation at the end of January, she should receive the retained vacation pay. Before releasing the vacation pay, you must change the setting in the employee ledger so that the vacation pay is not retained.

You should be in the Home window.

Click the **Employees icon** 

to open the Employees window:

BASIC VERSION
The Refresh tool applies to multi-user operation of the program. It does not apply in the single-user Basic version.

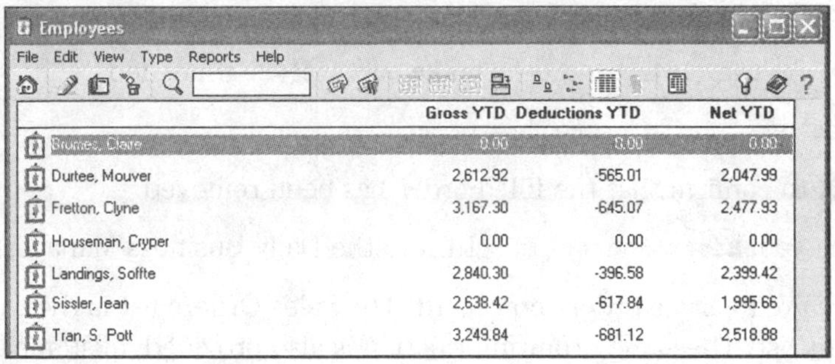

Double click the listing for **Clyne Fretton** to open her ledger record:

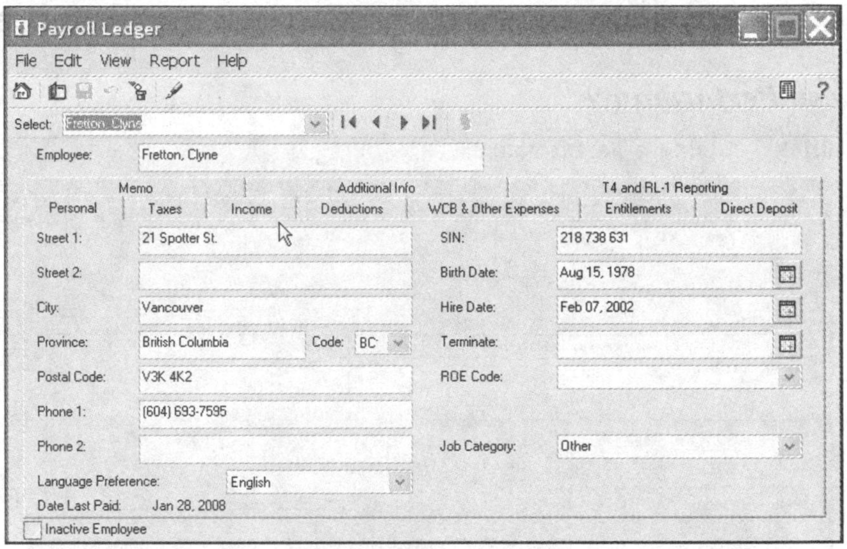

Click the **Income tab** to access the vacation pay settings:

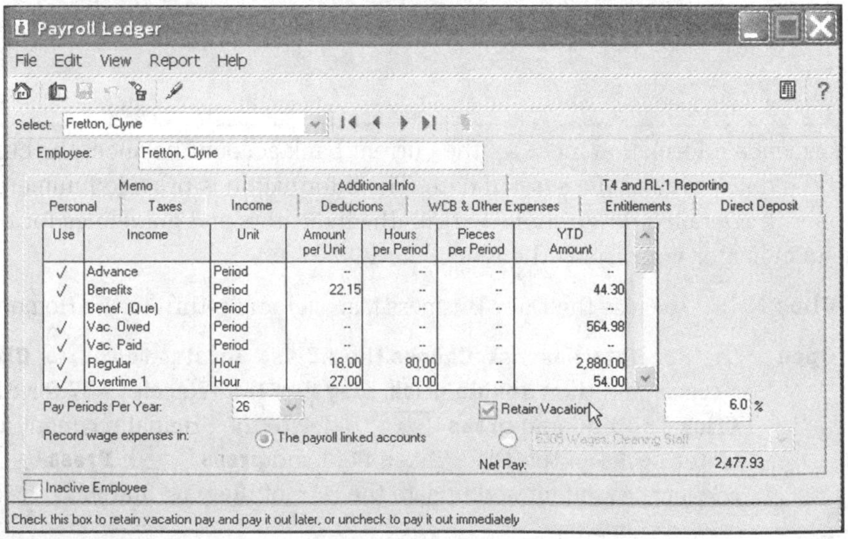

Click **Retain Vacation** to remove the checkmark.

Close the **Ledger window** to return to the Employees window. Fretton's name should still be selected.

Click the **Payroll Journal icon** in the Employees window or **choose** the **Type menu** and **click Payroll Journal** to access the Payroll Journal with Fretton already entered as the employee:

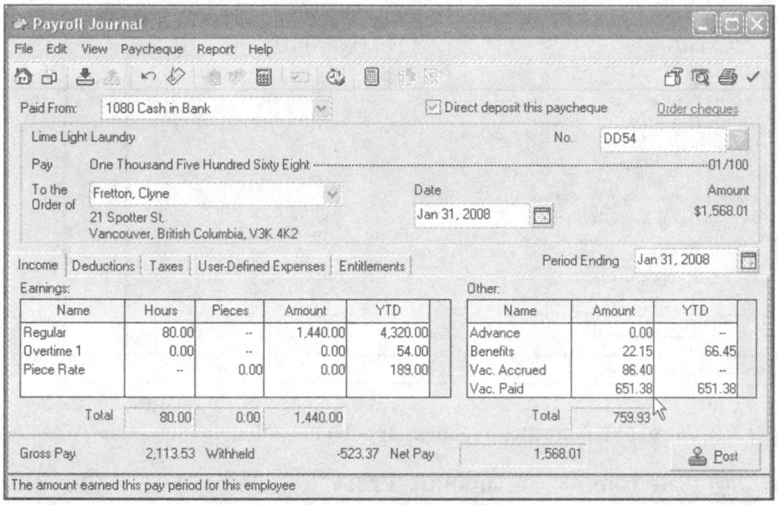

If Fretton's name is not selected when you open the journal, no employee will be selected. Choose Fretton from the employee list and press *tab* to continue.

Notice that the accumulated vacation pay appears in the Vac. Paid Amount field. We need to delete the number of regular hours worked and the benefits.

Click **80.00** in the Regular Hours field. (Double click if the entire amount is not selected.)

Press *del*.

Click **22.15** in the Benefits Amount field.

Press *del*. **Press** *tab* to update the amounts.

Deductions should not be taken from vacation pay so Fretton's medical premium amount should also be deleted before printing the cheque and recording the entry. Since this is a one-time change, it should be made directly in the journal.

Click the **Deductions tab** to open this screen:

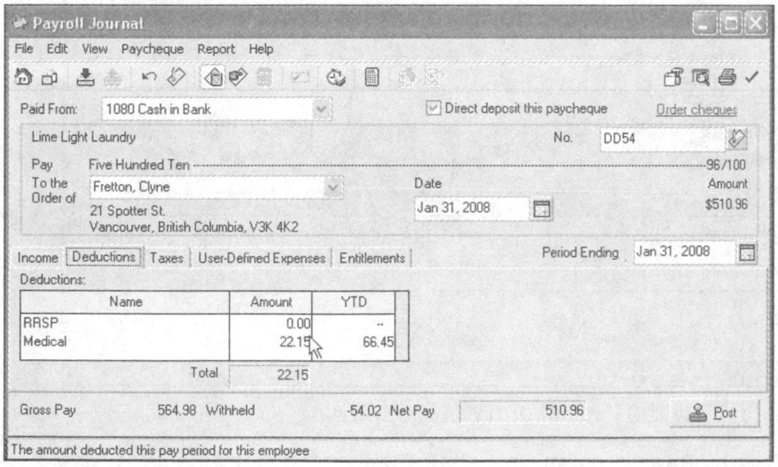

Click the **Medical Amount field entry** to select it.

Press *del* to remove the amount. **Press** *tab* to update the net pay. The Taxes tab screen opens.

Click the **User-Defined Expenses tab**:

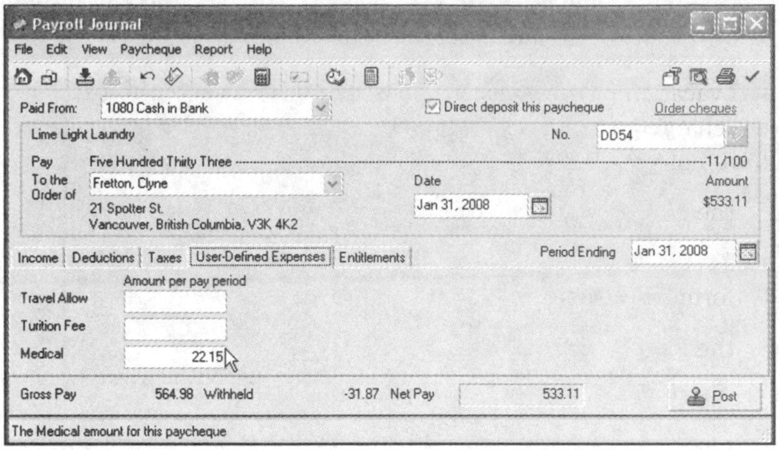

Click the **Medical Amount field entry** to select it.

Press *del* to remove the amount. **Press** *tab* to update the journal.

The Entitlements tab screen opens. No entitlements are earned for the cheque because no hours were worked.

Click **80.00** in the Number Of Hours field.

Press *del* to remove the number of hours and reduce the entries for Days Earned to zero.

Click the **Income tab** to open this screen again.

Clyne has requested her vacation pay as a cheque so we need to change the direct deposit selection.

Click the ✓ for the Direct Deposit This Paycheque option to remove the ✓.

The next cheque number is added. The journal entry is now complete as shown here:

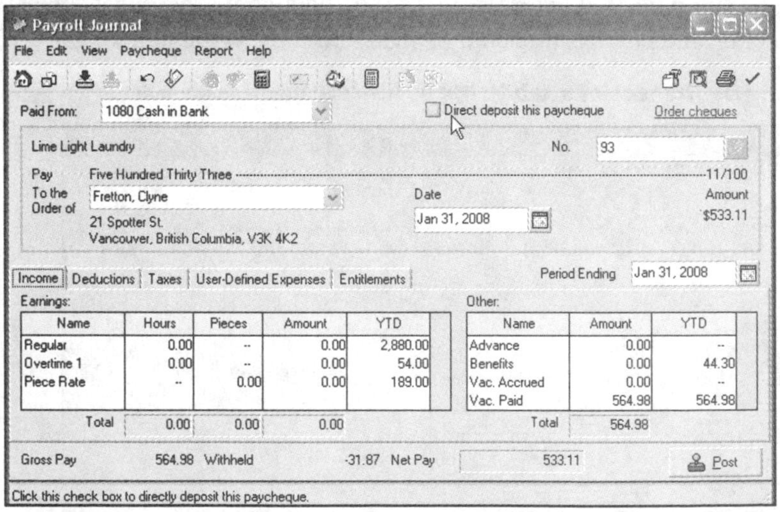

You should review the journal entry before posting.

Choose the **Report menu** and **click Display Payroll Journal Entry**:

NOTES

Taxes are not paid on the vacation pay retained, so they must be paid when the vacation pay is released. Sometimes, however, the amount is too small to generate an automatic income tax deduction.

Lime Light Laundry

01/31/08 (J61)	Debits	Credits	Project
2300 Vacation Payable	564.98	-	
5310 EI Expense	14.80	-	
5320 CPP Expense	21.30	-	
5330 WCB Expense	17.06	-	
1080 Cash in Bank	-	533.11	
2310 EI Payable	-	25.37	
2320 CPP Payable	-	42.60	
2460 WCB Payable	-	17.06	
	618.14	618.14	

The released vacation pay shows as a debit (decrease) to *Vacation Payable*. Payroll taxes are charged on the vacation pay, as they are charged on other wages, because they have not yet been paid on this income.

Close the **display** to return to the journal and **make corrections** if necessary.

Click **Post** [Post] to save the transaction. **Click Yes** to skip the payroll formula warning.

Close the **Payroll Journal**.

Open the **Ledger** for **Fretton** and **click** the **Income tab**.

Click **Retain Vacation** so that her future paycheques will be entered correctly with vacation pay retained.

Close the **Ledger window** and then **close** the **Employees window** to return to the Home window.

NOTES
Notice that the accrued vacation amount is reduced to zero and the Vacation Paid amount has increased by the amount released.

Paying Commissions to Salaried Employees

We will add the sales commissions to Brumes' paycheque from the Payroll Run Journal.

Click the **Payroll Cheque Run icon** [Payroll Cheque Run] to open the Payroll Run Journal.

Click the **Post column beside Durtee and Sissler**, if necessary, to remove their checkmarks, leaving only Brumes and Houseman checked. No changes are needed for Houseman's paycheque.

WARNING!
Check that only Brumes and Houseman are being paid, that is, have checkmarks in the Post column.

Click **Brumes** since she is the only employee who earns a sales commission.

Click the **Incomes Detail button** [...] to open the Earning fields:

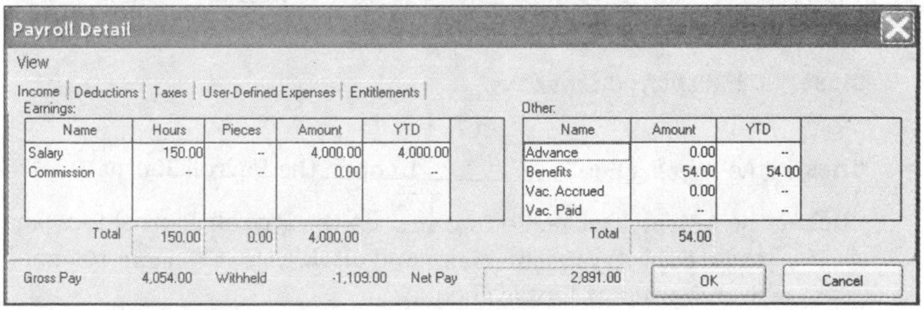
Payroll Detail

View

Income | Deductions | Taxes | User-Defined Expenses | Entitlements

Earnings:

Name	Hours	Pieces	Amount	YTD
Salary	150.00	--	4,000.00	4,000.00
Commission	--	--	0.00	--
Total	150.00	0.00	4,000.00	

Other:

Name	Amount	YTD
Advance	0.00	--
Benefits	54.00	54.00
Vac. Accrued	0.00	--
Vac. Paid	--	--
Total	54.00	

Gross Pay 4,054.00 Withheld -1,109.00 Net Pay 2,891.00 OK Cancel

Click **0.00** in the **Amount column beside Commission**.

Type 292 **Press** tab to update the totals.

Click the **Entitlements tab**.

Click the **Vacation Days Released column**.

Type 5 **Click OK** to return to the updated Payroll Run summary screen.

Review the **transaction** and **post** the **entry**. **Close** the **Journal**.

Adjusting a Payroll Run Entry

We can adjust a Payroll Run Journal entry from the Payroll Journal, just as we edited the transaction for Durtee. Before making the adjustment, we will review the Sales By Salesperson Report to be certain that we have the correct amount this time.

Choose the **Reports menu**, then **choose Receivables** and **click Sales By Salesperson** to open the report options screen:

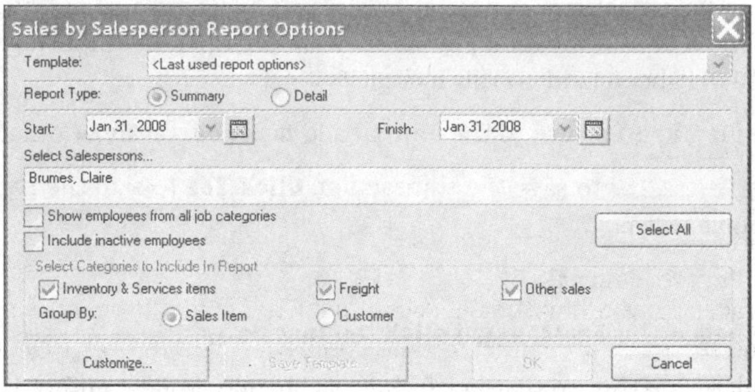

Brumes is the only employee designated as a salesperson so only her name appears on the list. You have the option to show all employees, but we do not need them all — we want Brumes' January sales data. The session date is the default for Start and Finish dates. You can group the sales information by customer or by sales item. You can also include information for freight and other non-inventory sales. For Lime Light, we need to show only the Other sales because inventory and freight do not apply. You can also show the report in detail with a line item for each sale, or in summary form with totals only for each item or customer.

Click the **Start date calendar icon**.

Click **Jan 1** to select this date.

Click **Brumes** to select the employee.

You can exclude Inventory and Freight amounts from the report by clicking them to remove the ✓.

Click **OK** to see the report.

The total sales revenue for January was $40 300, so Brumes' commission amount should be changed to $403.

Close the displayed **report**.

Click the **Paycheques icon**  to open the Payroll Journal.

Click the **Adjust Paycheque tool** on the Payroll Journal tool bar or **choose** the **Paycheque menu** and **click Adjust Cheque** to open the Search window for paycheques.

Click **Browse** to access the list of posted payroll entries.

Click the **Cheque #94** entry for **Brumes, Claire** to select Brumes' paycheque.

Click **Select** to display the posted entry.

Click the **Advisor icon** to close the warning and display the Payroll Journal.

Click **292** in the **Amount field for Commission** to select the current entry.

Type 403 **Press** tab to enter the change and update the gross pay.

Click the **Recalculate Taxes tool** on the Payroll Journal tool bar or **choose** the **Paycheque menu** and **click Recalculate Taxes**.

All amounts are updated for the additional wages.

Review the Payroll Journal **entry**. **Close** the **display** when you have finished. **Make corrections** if necessary.

Click the **Post button** Post to save the adjustment.

Click **No** to bypass the cheque number warning.

Close the **Journal**.

Making Payroll Tax Remittances

Simply Accounting tracks payroll remittances when the vendors are designated as payroll authorities and the taxes are linked to these vendors. Taxes are remitted from the Payments Journal.

You cannot adjust these remittances once they are posted, so you should make a backup copy of your data file before making the payments. Any corrections must be entered as Adjustments in the Payments Journal Pay Remittance form, but it may be difficult to sort out the exact amounts that you need to enter for the correction.

WARNING!
Back up your data file before making the payroll remittances.

Back up your **data file**.

Click the **Payments icon** Payments to open the Payments Journal.

Click **Pay Purchase Invoices** to see the types of payments:

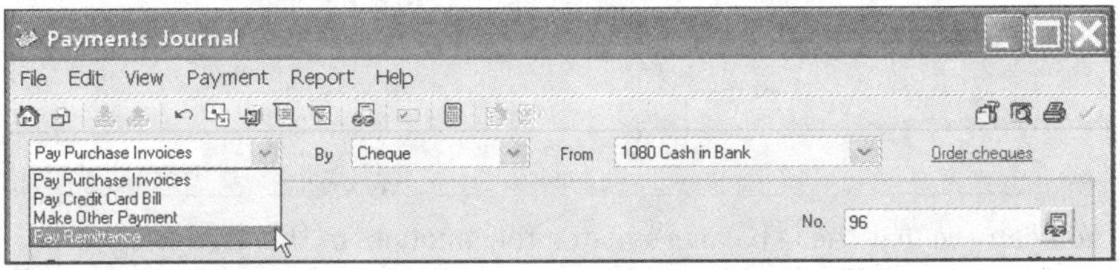

Click **Pay Remittance** to modify the Payments Journal.

Click the **Pay To The Order Of list arrow** to see the payroll authorities:

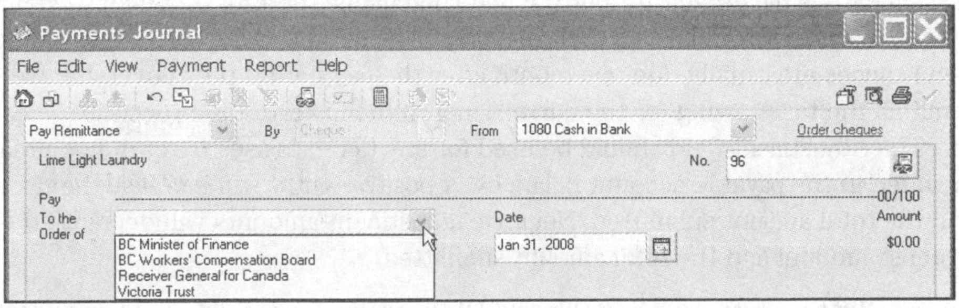

The four vendors to whom payroll deductions and taxes are paid have been identified as payroll authorities in the vendor records so their names appear on the list of vendors.

The first remittance will be to the Receiver General for EI, CPP and income tax.

Click **Receiver General for Canada** to select the vendor.

The Payments Journal is updated with the taxes collected for this vendor:

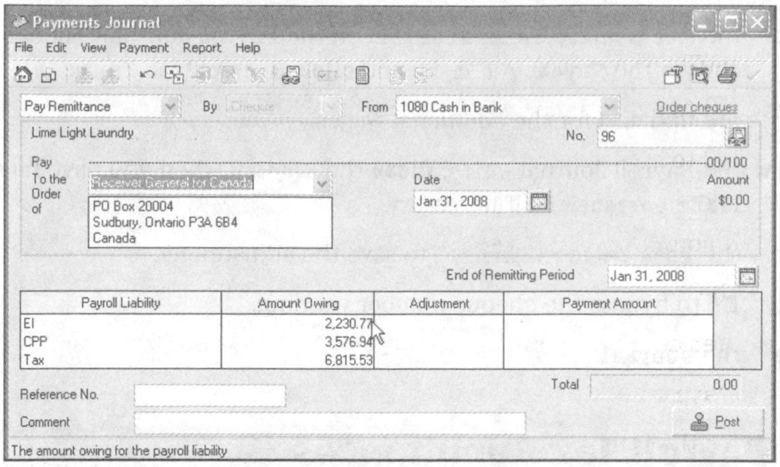

These amounts include only the taxes entered through Payroll Journal entries and any opening balance adjustments. Any amounts that were entered in the General Ledger will not be included. If taxes were not remitted immediately before the files were converted to Simply Accounting, the payroll tax liability accounts will have outstanding balances. For Lime Light Laundry, these opening balances were entered as part of the Payroll Ledger setup. These amounts are shown here:

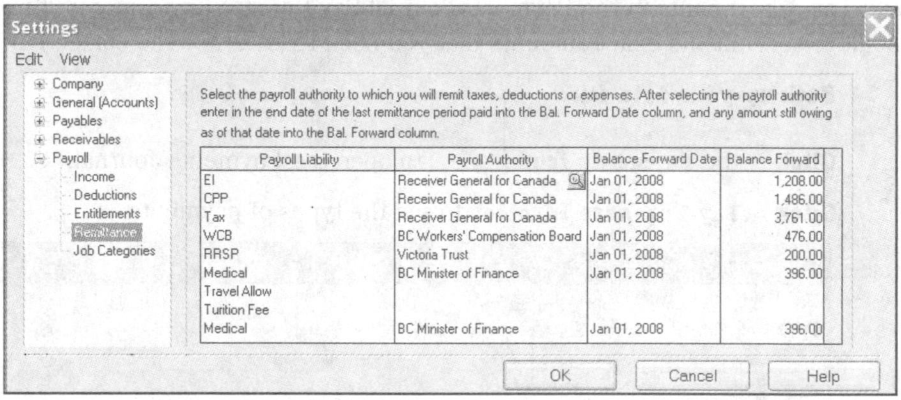

You can see that these balances match the amounts in the Trial Balance for January 1 on page 348.

The Remittance journal has two date fields: one for the date of the cheque and a second below the vendor address for the payroll period covered by the remittance. The session date is the default for both. When you change the **End Of Remitting Period date**, the amounts will be updated to show the General Ledger amounts at that date. Remittances are usually due one month after the pay period they cover, but we will remit all the taxes owing for the current month to illustrate the procedure.

The Adjustment field should be used for any tax expenses that are not already included in the payable account balances. A positive entry will increase the tax expense and the total amount submitted. Negative adjustment amounts will decrease the tax expense amount and the total amount submitted.

Enter **January 15** in the End Of Remitting Period date field and **press** *tab*.

Notice that all the tax amounts have been reduced. If you compare these amounts with the General Ledger balances for January 15, you will see that they match the balances for that date.

Enter **January 31** in the End Of Remitting Period date field and **press** *tab* to restore the previous balances.

NOTES

Your tax amounts may be different if your program uses later payroll tax tables.

Accept the default amounts in your data file, unless you know that you have made an error in the paycheque.

NOTES

In Chapter 15, we show how to enter these opening balances as Payroll Ledger settings.

The Medical liability is entered twice, once for the employees' share and once for the employer's share.

The full amount is being paid for each tax.

Click the **Payment Amount column for EI** to enter the amount owing as the payment amount.

Press (↓) to enter the payment amount for CPP.

Press (↓) to enter the payment amount for Tax.

Press (tab) to accept the final Payment Amount and update the cheque amount.

Click the **Reference field.**

Type `Memo 10A` **Press** (tab) to advance to the comment field.

Type `Payroll Tax remittance for January`

This completes the form as shown:

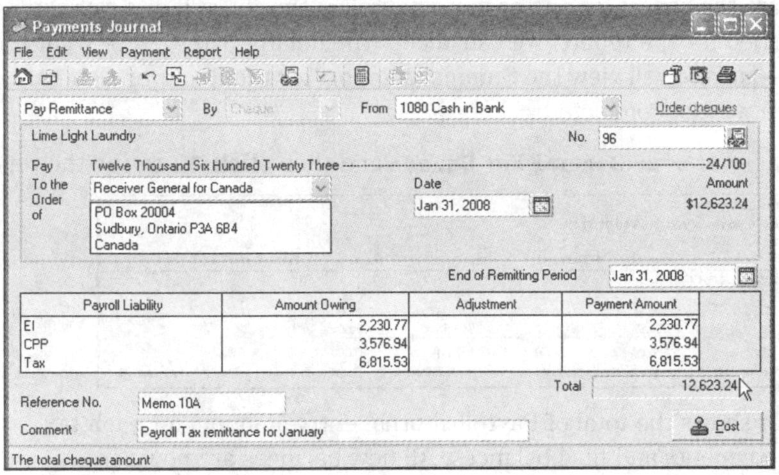

We can now review the journal entry.

Choose the **Report menu** and **click Display Payments Journal Entry**:

Lime Light Laundry

01/31/08 (J70)	Debits	Credits	Project
2310 EI Payable	2,230.77	-	
2320 CPP Payable	3,576.94	-	
2330 Income Tax Payable	6,815.53	-	
1080 Cash in Bank	-	12,623.24	
	12,623.24	12,623.24	

The three liability accounts have been debited to reduce the liability, and the bank account is credited. If you had entered adjustments, those amounts would be debited (for positive adjustments) to the corresponding tax expense account.

From the journal Report menu you can also display the Remittance Report, the same report that you get from the Home window Reports menu. If you display this report before posting the payment, the payment amount will still be zero.

Close the **display** when finished. **Make corrections** if necessary.

Post the **payment**.

Choose the **Report menu** and **click Display Remittance Report**:

Remittance Report Options

Template:	<Last used report options>
Report Type:	◉ Summary ○ Detail

Select year

◉ Year 2008

Select period

Start: Jan 01, 2008

Finish: Jan 31, 2008

Select Payroll Authorities...

BC Minister of Finance
BC Workers' Compensation Board
Receiver General for Canada
Victoria Trust

☐ Include inactive Payroll Authorities Select All

Customize... Save Template OK Cancel

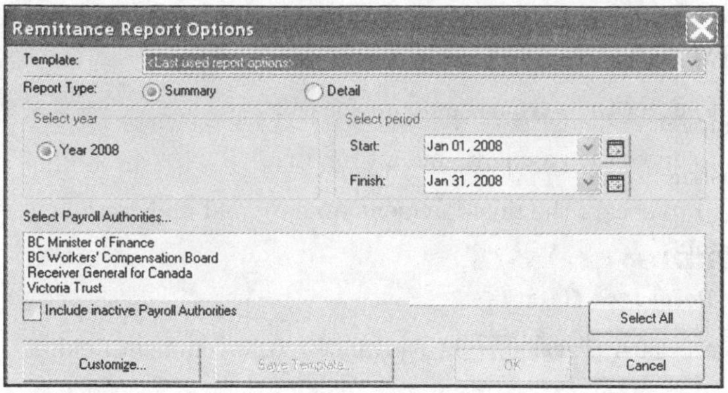

You can display a **Summary Report** with total amounts for each tax, or a **Detail Report** with a line entry for each tax for each payroll transaction in the report period. You can prepare the report for one or more payroll authority, and you can choose a remittance period for the report. We can accept the default dates — we want the report for January — and we will view the Summary Report for the Receiver General to see the remittance we just completed.

Click **Receiver General For Canada** and then **click OK** to see the report:

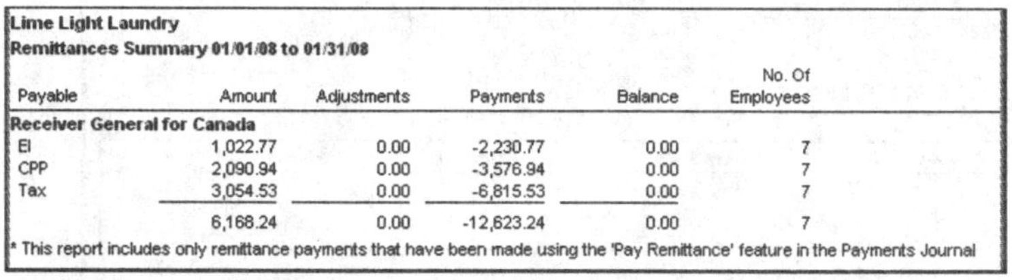

Lime Light Laundry
Remittances Summary 01/01/08 to 01/31/08

Payable	Amount	Adjustments	Payments	Balance	No. Of Employees
Receiver General for Canada					
EI	1,022.77	0.00	-2,230.77	0.00	7
CPP	2,090.94	0.00	-3,576.94	0.00	7
Tax	3,054.53	0.00	-6,815.53	0.00	7
	6,168.24	0.00	-12,623.24	0.00	7

* This report includes only remittance payments that have been made using the 'Pay Remittance' feature in the Payments Journal

The report shows the total of Payroll Journal entry amounts for each tax, adjustments, payments and final balances. All new balances are now zero.

NOTES

The original Amount entries reflect only the amounts from Payroll Journal entries and do not include the opening balance forward amounts.

The note reminds us that the report accounts only for transactions completed with the Pay Remittance feature.

Close the **report** when finished to return to the Payments Journal.

Choose **BC Minister of Finance** as the vendor for the next remittance.

Pay the **two Medical tax amounts**.

Enter **Memo 10B** in the Reference field and **enter** a **comment**.

Review and then **post** the **payment**.

Choose **BC Workers' Compensation Board** as the vendor.

Pay the **WCB amount**.

Enter **Memo 10C** in the Reference field and **enter** a **comment**.

Review and then **post** the **payment**.

Choose **Victoria Trust** as the vendor for the next remittance.

Pay the **RRSP contributions** withheld.

Enter **Memo 10D** in the Reference field and **enter** a **comment**.

Review and then **post** the **payment**. Leave the journal open.

Click the **Accounts icon** [Accounts] to open the Employees window.

Scroll down to the liability accounts. You should see that the ledger account balances for the payroll liabilities are now zero.

Displaying Payroll Reports

You can access all payroll reports from the Reports menu in the Employees window.

Click the Employees icon to open the Employees window.

The following instructions begin from the Home window.

Displaying Employee Lists

You should be in the Home window.

Right-click the **Employees icon** to select it.

Click the **Display tool** or **choose** the **Reports menu**, then **choose Lists** and **click Employees** to see the report options:

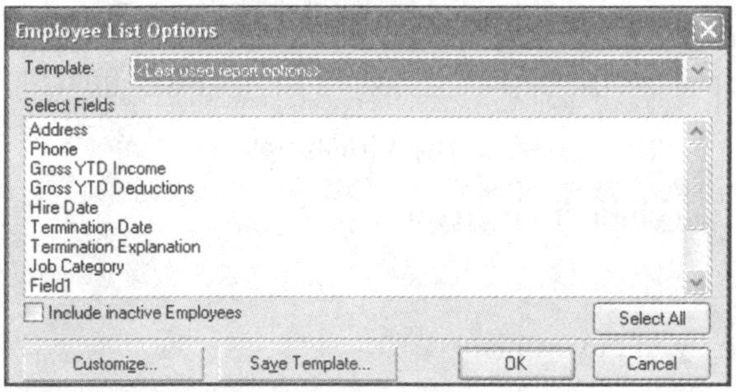

No regular employee fields are selected by default. The list will show only employee names. To add information to the report,

Click the **first field** you want to start a new selection.

Press and **hold** ctrl and **click** the **remaining fields** you want to report on.

Click **Select All** to include all fields in the report.

The report will display a list of all current employees, together with data for all the details you chose.

Close the **display** when you have finished.

Displaying Employee Reports

Choose the **Reports menu**, then **choose Payroll** and **click Employee** to see the following Employee Report Options window:

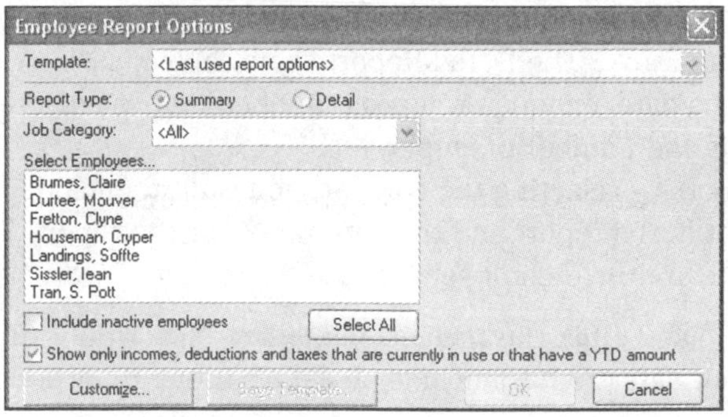

Press and **hold** ctrl and **click** the **employees** for whom you want in the report, or **click Select All** to include all employees in the report.

> **NOTES**
> You can drill down to the Employee Detail Report from the Employee List. Sorting and filtering are not available for employee reports.

NOTES
Since summary reports are available only for the session date, you must use an earlier backup to see the summary for that specific period (i.e., session date) or print a hard copy of the summary output.

The **Summary** option allows you to see the accumulated totals for all deductions and payments, which are updated each pay period. Summary reports are available only for the session date.

If there are employees who are inactive (e.g., taking an unpaid leave of absence) you can include their names on the list by choosing to Include Inactive Employees.

You can also prepare the report for employees in a single job category. A drop-down list of categories is available for the Job Category field. The default includes all categories.

If you want to prepare the report for specific deductions or payments, you can customize the report and select the columns you want to include. You cannot sort or filter the Employee Report.

Click **Detail** if you want to see the individual amounts for each paycheque.

NOTES
You can drill down to the Detail Report from the Summary Report. From the Detail Report you can drill down to the Employee Ledger.

The amount for each detail you choose will be listed for each payroll period in the selected date range for the selected employees, together with the totals for the period selected. The fiscal start and session dates are the default dates for the Detail Report.

Enter the **beginning date** for the report you want in the Start field.

Enter the **ending date** for the report in the Finish field.

Select the **employees** to include in the report.

Click **OK**.

Close the **display** when you have finished.

Displaying Deductions and Expenses Reports

Choose the **Reports menu**, then **choose Payroll** and **click Deductions & Expenses**:

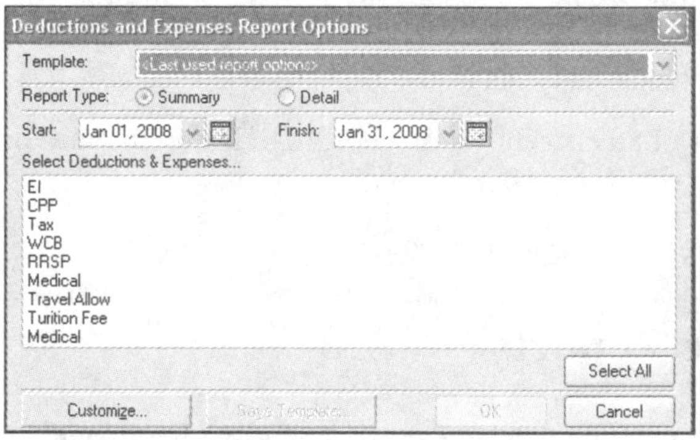

This report provides details for all payroll deductions and expenses. You can choose the Summary Report to see the total amounts and number of employees listed for each payroll item in the selected date range. The Detail Report shows individual entries for each selected item including the date, cheque or deposit number, employee, job category, amount, period totals and number of employees.

You can customize the report by selecting the columns you want to include.

Select the details you want in the report and the date range for the report. The fiscal start and the session date are the default selections.

Press and **hold** *ctrl* and **click** the **Deductions & Expenses** you want in the report, or **click Select All** to include all details in the report.

Enter the **Start date** and the **Finish date** for the report.

Click **OK** to see the report and **close** the **display** when you have finished.

Displaying the Job Category Report

Choose the **Reports menu**, then **choose Payroll** and **click Job Category**:

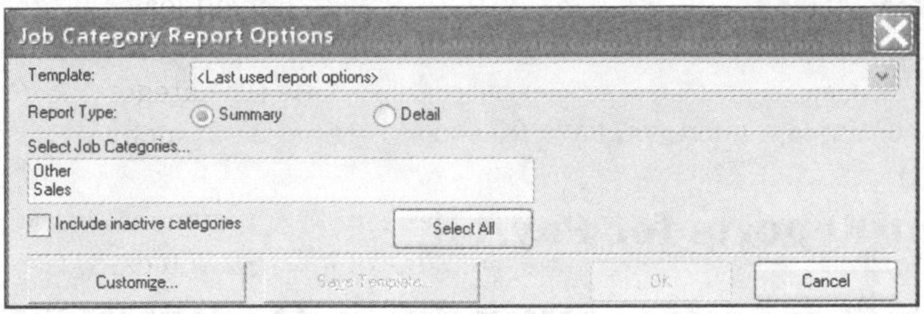

The Job Category Report provides the totals for each income and deduction amount used for payroll for each category. The Detail Report shows the same items with a line for each transaction that included the item. The Summary Report shows year-to-date total amounts and cannot be customized. The Detail Report can be customized by selecting a date range and the columns you want to include.

Press and **hold** ctrl and **click** the **category** you want in the report, or **click Select All** to include all categories in the report.

Click **Detail** to select the Detail Report.

Enter the **Start** and **Finish dates** for the Detail report.

Click **OK** to see the report.

Close the **display** when you have finished.

Displaying the Payroll Remittance Report

The Payroll Remittance Report was described on page 390. To access this report from the Reports menu,

Choose the **Reports menu**, then **choose Payroll** and **click Remittance**.

Displaying the Payroll Journal

The Payroll Journal Report includes all transactions from the Payroll Journal and the Payroll Cheque Run Journal.

Right-click the **Paycheques icon** (or the **Payroll Cheque Run Journal icon**) to select it.

Click the **Display tool** or **choose** the **Reports menu**, then **choose Journal Entries** and **click Payroll** to display the Options window:

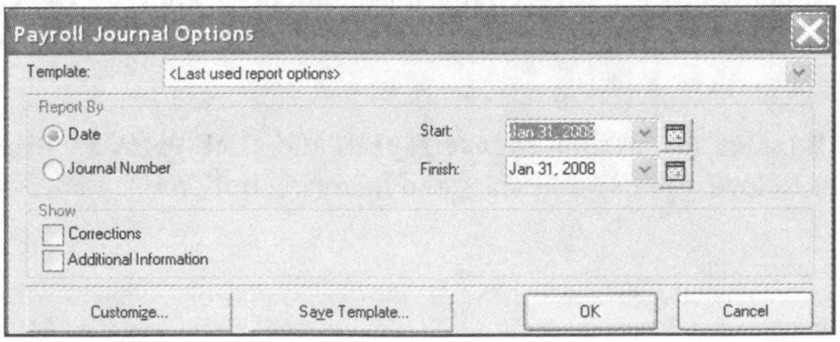

The usual sort and filter journal options are available for the Payroll Journal Report. By default, the Date option that we use is selected. Your latest session date appears as the default Start and Finish dates. The start date is highlighted and ready for editing.

NOTES
You can drill down to the Employee Detail Report and the General Ledger Report from the Payroll Journal.

Type **the beginning date** for the report and **press** tab **twice**.

Type the **ending date** for the report you want to see.

Click **Corrections**.

Click **OK**.

Close the **display** when you have finished.

Management Reports for Payroll

Choose the **Reports menu**, then **choose Management Reports** and **click Payroll**:

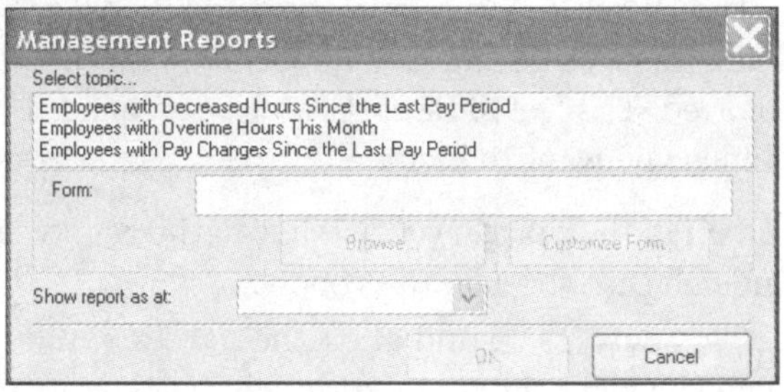

Click the **topic** you want to see. For the report on Employees With Overtime Hours This Month,

Choose a **month** from the list for Show Report As At. Choose a form, if appropriate.

Click **OK** to see the report. **Close** the **display** when you have finished.

Printing Payroll Reports

Display the **report** you want to print. **Click** [print icon] or **choose** the **File menu** from the report window and **click Print**. **Close** the **display** when finished.

Printing T4s

You can also print reports that are not available for display: T4 Slips and Relevé 1 Slips. Relevé 1 slips are used only in Quebec, and the Print Relevé 1 Slips Report options screen will list only employees for whom Quebec is the province of taxation. Relevé 1 options are similar to those for T4 slips. To print T4 slips, which are compulsory for employees filing income tax returns, you should have the proper tax statement forms from Canada Revenue Agency (CRA) to take full advantage of this option. You should retain payroll information for employees who leave during the year so that you can prepare T4 slips to mail to them.

Choose the **Reports menu**, then **choose Payroll** and **click Print T4 Slips** (or Print Relevé 1 Slips) to display the following options:

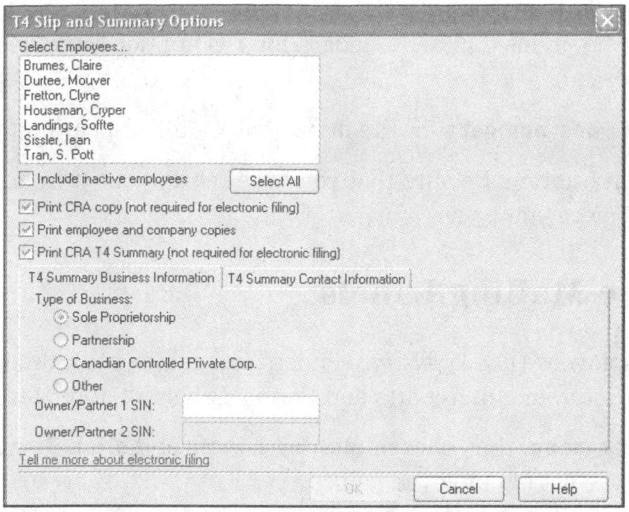

You need to select the employees in order to prepare their T4 slips. You may include inactive employees. You can print copies of the T4s for the employees and the company, or for CRA. You can also print the summary for CRA.

Click **Select All** or **press** and **hold** ctrl and **click** the **names** of the employees for whom you want the report printed.

Enter the type of business and, for sole proprietorship, partnership or private companies, the Social Insurance Number of the owners or partners. You must also enter the contact details for the person completing the forms.

Click the **T4 Summary Contact Information tab** to open the contact fields:

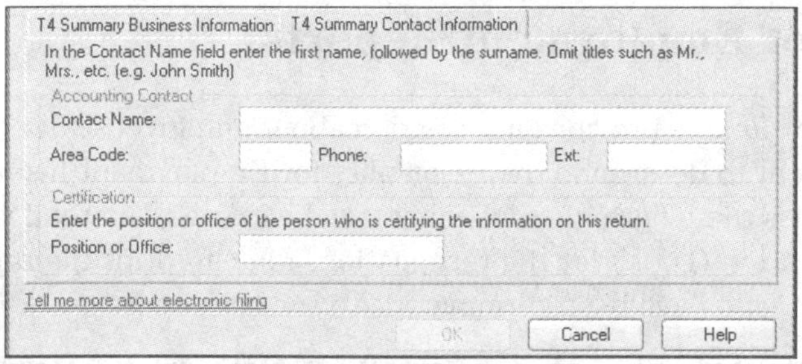

Enter the contact details for the person completing the forms.

Click **OK** to open the T4 Box Options screen:

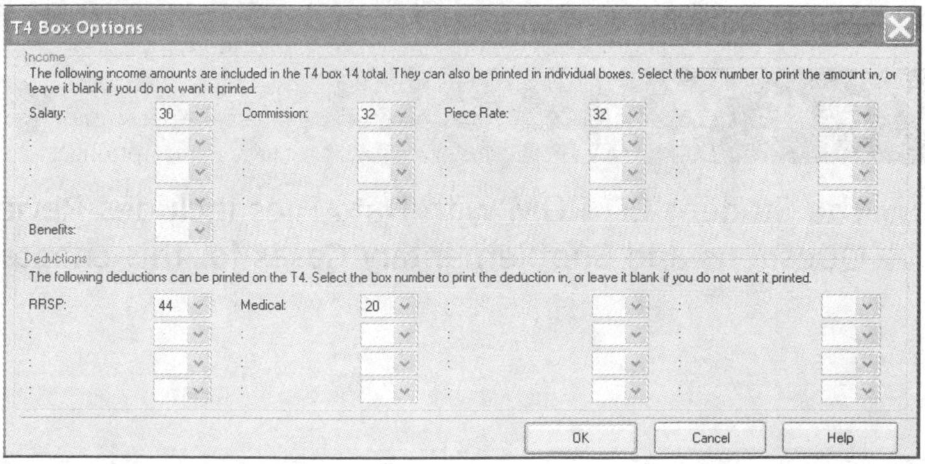

Each box on the T4 slip is numbered and can be designated for a specific deduction or income. You can choose a form box number for these amounts if they are related to

BASIC VERSION

The Type of Company and the Contact Information sections are not included.

You have the option to display the summary as well as print it.

NOTES

If you select all employees, you must also select Inactive Employees, even if no employees are inactive.

NOTES

You cannot display T4 slips or summaries in the Pro version.

income tax and should be included on the T4s. Each item has a list of box numbers that you can select. Income and tax items that are standard for T4s are not listed because their boxes are already assigned.

Choose appropriate **box numbers** for the items that should appear on the T4.

Click **OK** to begin printing. Be sure that you have set up your printer correctly before you begin.

Printing Employee Mailing Labels

You can print labels for employees (like labels for vendors and customers). Set up the printer for printing labels (Setup menu, Reports and Forms, Labels) before starting.

NOTES

You cannot display mailing labels.

Choose the **Reports menu**, then **choose Mailing Labels** and **click Employees** to display the list of employee names:

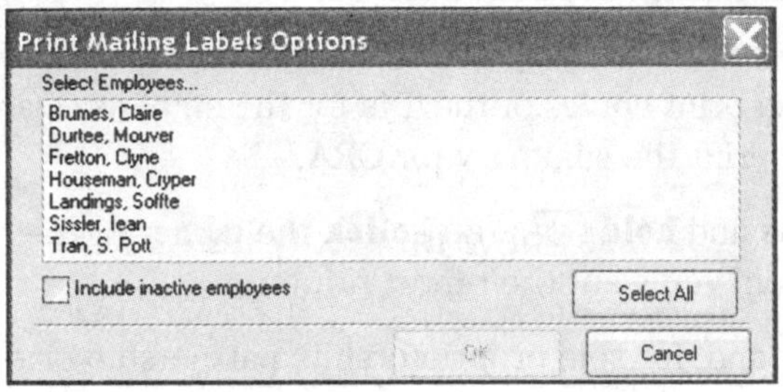

Press and **hold** ctrl and **click** the employees' **names** or **click Select All**.

Click OK to start printing.

Printing Record of Employment Reports

The Record of Employment Report provides information about employees who have terminated their employment to determine their eligibility for Employment Insurance benefits. The report includes the length of employment, the earnings, the total number of hours worked and the reason (code) for the termination. You can print the report only if there are employees who have been terminated. To see the report:

Choose the **Reports menu**, then **choose Payroll** and **click Print Record Of Employment**. To begin printing,

Click **OK** in response to the message about manually adding missing details.

R E V I E W

The Student CD-ROM with Data Files includes Review Questions and Supplementary Cases for this chapter.

CHAPTER ELEVEN

Adrienne Aesthetics

OBJECTIVES

After completing this chapter, you should be able to

- ***enter*** inventory-related purchase transactions
- ***enter*** inventory-related sale transactions of goods and services
- ***make*** inventory adjustments
- ***assemble*** new inventory items from other inventory
- ***enter*** returns on sales and purchases
- ***enter*** sales to preferred customers
- ***record*** import duty on purchases from foreign vendors
- ***understand*** the integration of the Inventory Ledger with the Payables, Receivables and General ledgers
- ***enter*** new inventory items
- ***display*** and ***print*** inventory reports

COMPANY INFORMATION

Company Profile

NOTES
Adrienne Aesthetics
65 Bytown Ave.
Ottawa, Ontario K2C 4R1
Tel 1: (613) 722-9876
Tel 2: (613) 722-8701
Fax: (613) 722-8000
Business No.: 567 643 778

Adrienne Aesthetics Beauty Salon and Spa is located in the Bytown Market area in the heart of downtown Ottawa. Nearby are the Parliament Buildings, galleries, museums and downtown shopping district. Adrienne Aesthetics caters to professional women and the well-to-do clientele of the upwardly mobile community.

Regular products for sale include high-quality cosmetic and beauty products but the salon also provides a variety of services and consultation for clients. For Valentine's Day, the salon offers special packages, which have been popular gifts.

Adrienne Kosh, the owner, is active in the day-to-day sales and management of the salon, assisted by two employees who provide all the services. All are trained cosmeticians. Among the repeat customers, Adrienne serves a local television show and an Austrian film studio that regularly makes films in Canada. This studio uses Adrienne Aesthetics' services while filming in Canada but they also have inventory items shipped to them in Austria. All customers rely on the honest and professional advice and service provided by the staff. The on-site service is also appreciated by the regular customers who receive a 2 percent discount when they settle their accounts within five days. Full payment is requested in 30 days. The Austrian film studio chooses to settle its accounts in euros (EUR or €). Preferred price list customers receive an additional discount of about 10 percent off the regular prices and are eligible for the early payment discount for 15 days.

Adrienne has accounts with most of her regular vendors, including beauty product manufacturers. One of these vendors, located in France, also uses the euro as its currency. Adrienne Aesthetics has set up a foreign currency bank account for these transactions. Adrienne Aesthetics is required to pay import duties on items imported from France, and the duty rates are set up directly in the Inventory Ledger.

At the end of January, Adrienne converted all her business records to Simply Accounting using the following information:

- Chart of Accounts
- Post-Closing Trial Balance
- Vendor Information
- Customer Information
- Employee Profiles and TD1 Information
- Inventory Information
- Accounting Procedures

CHART OF ACCOUNTS

ADRIENNE AESTHETICS

ASSETS

Current Assets
- 1080 Bank Account: Chequing
- 1090 Bank Account: Credit Cards
- 1100 Bank Account: Euros
- 1150 Investments
- 1180 Purchase Prepayments
- 1200 Accounts Receivable
- 1250 Clinical Supplies
- 1260 Packaging Supplies
- 1270 Prepaid Insurance
- 1280 Towels and Capes

Inventory Assets
- 1310 Creams and Lotions
- 1320 Face Care Products
- 1330 Sun Care Products
- 1380 Miscellaneous Inventory Products

Fixed Assets
- 1420 Cash Register
- 1440 Computer Equipment ▶
- ▶1480 Display Cabinets
- 1500 Clinical Equipment
- 1520 Aesthetics Salon

LIABILITIES

Current Liabilities
- 2100 Bank Loan
- 2200 Accounts Payable
- 2220 Credit Card Payable
- 2240 Import Duty Payable
- 2260 Prepaid Sales and Deposits
- 2300 EI Payable
- 2310 CPP Payable
- 2320 Income Tax Payable
- 2390 EHT Payable
- 2400 Group Insurance Payable
- 2420 WSIB Payable
- 2640 PST Payable
- 2650 GST Charged on Sales
- 2670 GST Paid on Purchases ▶

▶Long Term Liabilities
- 2940 Mortgage Payable

EQUITY

Equity
- 3560 Share Capital
- 3600 Current Earnings

REVENUE

Revenue
- 4020 Revenue from Sales
- 4030 Sales Allowances and Discounts
- 4040 Revenue from Services
- 4050 Sales Returns
- 4080 Freight Revenue
- 4100 Sales Tax Compensation

EXPENSE

Operating Expenses
- 5020 Advertising and Promotion ▶
- ▶5030 Bank Charges
- 5040 Credit Card Fees
- 5050 Exchange Rate Differences
- 5060 Cost of Goods Sold
- 5065 Cost of Services
- 5070 Variance Costs
- 5080 Item Assembly Costs
- 5090 Purchases Returns
- 5100 Inventory Losses
- 5200 Freight Expense
- 5220 Interest Expense
- 5240 Hydro Expense
- 5250 Telephone Expense

Payroll Expenses
- 5300 Salaries
- 5310 EI Expense
- 5320 CPP Expense
- 5330 WSIB Expense
- 5360 EHT Expense

NOTES: The Chart of Accounts includes only postable accounts and Current Earnings. WSIB (Workplace Safety and Insurance Board) is the name for WCB (Workers' Compensation Board) in Ontario.

POST-CLOSING TRIAL BALANCE

ADRIENNE AESTHETICS

February 1, 2008

		Debits	Credits
1080	Bank Account: Chequing	$48 915.52	
1090	Bank Account: Credit Cards	2 100.00	
1100	Bank Account: Euros (€2 035)	2 810.00	
1150	Investments	90 000.00	
1200	Accounts Receivable	4 173.00	
1250	Clinical Supplies	600.00	
1260	Packaging Supplies	700.00	
1270	Prepaid Insurance	2 200.00	
1280	Towels and Capes	1 200.00	
1310	Creams and Lotions	2 660.00	
1320	Face Care Products	5 810.00	
1330	Sun Care Products	5 240.00	
1420	Cash Register	1 500.00	
1440	Computer Equipment	2 500.00	
1480	Display Cabinets	4 500.00	
1500	Clinical Equipment	8 400.00 ►	
► 1520	Aesthetics Salon	100 000.00	
2100	Bank Loan		$5 000.00
2200	Accounts Payable		3 210.00
2220	Credit Card Payable		255.00
2300	EI Payable		270.00
2310	CPP Payable		481.26
2320	Income Tax Payable		2 605.26
2390	EHT Payable		117.60
2400	Group Insurance Payable		30.00
2420	WSIB Payable		284.40
2640	PST Payable		2 400.00
2650	GST Charged on Sales		2 100.00
2670	GST Paid on Purchases	875.00	
2940	Mortgage Payable		80 000.00
3560	Share Capital		187 430.00
		$284 183.52	$284 183.52

VENDOR INFORMATION

ADRIENNE AESTHETICS

Vendor Name (Contact)	Address	Phone No. Fax No.	E-mail Web Site	Terms Tax ID
Acqua Viva Cosmetics (Tomi Hillfinger)	466 Ralf Loren Dr. Montreal, Quebec H3B 4C4	Tel: (888) 448-7274 Fax: (514) 447-3726	thill@acquaviva.com www.acquaviva.com	net 10 438 456 120
Bell Canada (Annie Heard)	82 Wireless Alley Ottawa, Ontario K3B 5R9	Tel: (613) 781-2355	heard@bell.ca www.bell.ca	net 1
Biotech Laboratories (Avivah Rubenstein)	75 Klinique St. Markham, Ontario L3K 1P1	Tel: (800) 466-2991 Fax: (905) 471-2494	avivah@biotech.com www.biotech.com	net 10 297 382 266
Derma Laboratories (Masc Karah)	34 Makeover Way Mississauga, Ontario L8H 7V1	Tel: (877) 374-8107 Fax: (905) 722-5491	mk@skindeep.com www.skindeep.com	net 5 178 629 718
Esthetica Incorporated (Ellis Arden)	61 Pumice Rd. 75018 Paris, France	Tel: (33-1) 4380 5399 Fax: (33-1) 4380 2963	ea@superficial.com www.superficial.com	net 30
Minister of Finance, Ontario	49 Pecuniary Rd. Toronto, Ontario M5G 4T1	Tel: (800) 622-5100	www.fin.gov.on.ca	net 1
Ottawa Hydro (Kohl Genrater)	77 Voltage St. Orleans, Ontario K4B 3N7	Tel: (613) 785-9113	www.otthydro.ca	net 1
Sun Lab Products Inc. (Maxine Factor)	59 Botox Cr. Kanata, Ontario K2F 3M8	Tel: (613) 620-5388 Fax: (613) 621-7392	maxine@sunlab.com www.sunlab.com	net 15 724 527 455

OUTSTANDING VENDOR INVOICES

ADRIENNE AESTHETICS

Vendor Name	Terms	Date	Invoice No.	Pretax Amount	Tax	Total
Esthetica Incorporated	net 30	Jan. 8/08	EI-641	€2 175.00	€ 152.25	€2 327.25 EUR
				$3 000.00	$210.00	$3 210.00 CAD

CUSTOMER INFORMATION

ADRIENNE AESTHETICS

Customer Name (Contact)	Address	Phone No. Fax No.	E-mail Web Site	Terms Credit Limit
Ariandanos Residence (Arianne Ariandanos)	29 Revlon Blvd. Ottawa, Ontario K1P 2M2	Tel: (613) 762-8664	arianne@radiantway.com www.radiantway.com	2/5, n/30 $1 500
Botelli & Giroux, Lawyers (Gina Botelli)	30 Court St. Orleans, Ontario K4R 1C7	Tel: (613) 699-2911 Fax: (613) 697-2735	gina@botelli.giroux.com www.botelli.giroux.com	2/5, n/30 $1 500
*Euro Film Corporation (Francine Despardieu)	6 Alpine Way Graz A-8013, Austria	Tel: (43-316) 824 006 Fax: (43-316) 824 622	fdes@eurostars.com www.eurostars.com	2/15, n/30 €3 000
Lavender Estates (Katherine Harris)	9 Lavender Ct. Ottawa, Ontario K1X 3J6	Tel: (613) 782-7300 Fax: (613) 782-8190	harris@lavender.com www.lavender.com	2/5, n/30 $3 000
Montreal Fashions (Leontyne Coutumier)	85 Haute Couture Ave. Kanata, Ontario K2N 5F9	Tel: (613) 622-1711 Fax: (613) 623-8118	leontyne@lookpretty.com www.lookpretty.com	2/5, n/30 $3 000
*Valley TV (CKOV) (Celeb Brittie)	17 Broadcast Ave. Ottawa, Ontario K6B 7F3	Tel: (613) 784-6000 Fax: (613) 784-5234	celebrit@valleystars.com www.valleystars.com	2/15, n/30 $4 000

NOTES: The asterisk (*) indicates preferred price list customers. A record is also set up for Cash Customers.

OUTSTANDING CUSTOMER INVOICES

ADRIENNE AESTHETICS

Customer Name	Terms	Date	Invoice No.	Pretax Amount	Tax	Total
*Euro Film Corporation	2/15, n/30	Jan. 20/08	AA-11	$2 150.00 €1 558.00	$150.50 €109.06	$2 300.50 CAD €1 667.06 EUR
*Valley TV (CKOV)	2/15, n/30	Jan. 24/08	AA-16	$1 750.00	$122.50	$1 872.50 CAD
			Grand Total			$4 173.00 CAD

EMPLOYEE INFORMATION SHEET

ADRIENNE AESTHETICS

	Blossom, Lysis	Hydra, Collagen
Position	Beautician	Beautician
Social Insurance No.	459 562 344	562 391 888
Address	522 Colvin Cline Ct., #22 Ottawa, Ontario K6B 2L8	71 Lipogone St. Ottawa, Ontario K3V 5F2
Telephone	(613) 729-1991	(613) 753-7994
Date of Birth (mm-dd-yy)	02-02-69	02-14-72
Federal (Ontario) Tax Exemption - TD1 Total Exemptions	$9 039 (8 377)	$9 039 (8 377)
Employee Earnings Regular Salary Commission	 $2 000 bi-weekly (75 hours) 2% (sales less returns)	 $2 000 bi-weekly (75 hours) 2% (sales less returns)
WSIB Rate	2.37	2.37
Employee Deductions Group Insurance EI, CPP & Income Tax	 $5 Calculations built into Simply Accounting program	 $5

Employee Profiles and TD1 Information

Lysis Blossom and **Collagen Hydra** both assist with sales in the salon and provide the services to customers. Blossom specializes in facials, pedicures and massages while Hydra handles the waxing and electrolysis services. Both are salaried employees who receive their $2 000 bi-weekly pay by cheque and contribute $5 each period to a group insurance plan. Blossom and Hydra are single and self-supporting with no dependants and no other deductions, so they have the basic claim amounts for income tax. Instead of vacation pay, they take three weeks of vacation with regular pay each year. Neither has received any payroll advances.

Both employees are listed as salespersons. They receive a sales commission of 2 percent of their net sales (sales less returns) with each paycheque.

INVENTORY INFORMATION

ADRIENNE AESTHETICS

Code	Description	Min Stock	Selling Price Reg	(Pref)	Price: EUR Reg	(Pref)	Unit	Qty on Hand	Total (Cost)	Duty (Taxes)
Creams and Lotions (asset account 1310)										
CL01	Cleansing Lotion 225 ml	2	$15	($13)	€11	(€10)	tube	20	$ 120	8.0%
CL02	Cleansing Milk 225 ml	2	25	(22)	18	(16)	tube	20	240	8.0%
CL03	Eye Contour Smoothing Cream 30 ml	2	35	(32)	28	(25)	jar	20	320	8.0%
CL04	Eye Contour Smoothing Gel 30 ml	2	40	(36)	31	(28)	jar	20	360	8.0%
CL05	Masks: herb 100 ml	2	40	(36)	31	(28)	jar	20	360	8.0%
CL06	Masks: sea 100 ml	2	35	(32)	27	(24)	jar	20	320	8.0%
CL07	Night Cream 200 ml	2	45	(41)	33	(30)	jar	20	420	8.0%
CL08	Protection Cream: dbl action 60 ml	2	25	(22)	18	(16)	tube	20	240	8.0%
CL09	Protection Cream: moisturizer 60 ml	2	30	(27)	22	(19)	tube	20	280	8.0%
	Total Creams and Lotions								$2 660	
Face Care Products (asset account 1320)										
FC01	Blush 8 g	3	10	(9)	7	(6)	each	30	120	8.0%
FC02	Concealer 15 ml	3	20	(18)	15	(13)	tube	30	240	8.0%
FC03	Epidermal Cleanser: face+ 300 ml	3	60	(55)	44	(39)	jar	30	750	8.0%
FC04	Epidermal Cleanser: phytogel 300 ml	3	50	(45)	37	(33)	jar	30	660	8.0%
FC05	Eye Shadow duo-pack	3	15	(13)	11	(10)	pair	30	120	8.0%
FC06	Foundation 35 ml	3	25	(22)	18	(16)	jar	30	360	8.0%
FC07	Lipstick 5 g	20	15	(13)	11	(10)	tube	400	2 400	8.0%
FC08	Kohl Pencil	10	15	(13)	11	(10)	each	60	180	8.0%
FC09	Mascara 9 ml	12	10	(9)	7	(6)	tube	80	320	8.0%
FC10	Powder: loose 15 g	3	20	(18)	15	(13)	jar	30	240	8.0%
FC11	Powder: pressed 15 g	3	30	(27)	22	(19)	each	30	420	8.0%
	Total Face Care Products								$5 810	
Sun Care Products (asset account 1330)										
SC01	Sun Care Cream SPF#15 125 ml	4	30	(27)	22	(19)	tube	40	560	8.0%
SC02	Sun Care Cream SPF#30 125 ml	4	45	(41)	32	(29)	tube	40	840	8.0%
SC03	Sun Tan Milk SPF#4 200 ml	4	40	(36)	31	(28)	jar	40	720	8.0%
SC04	Sun Tan Milk SPF#15 200 ml	4	50	(45)	37	(33)	jar	40	840	8.0%
SC05	UV #15 Total Cream 125 ml	4	50	(45)	37	(33)	tube	40	880	8.0%
SC06	UV #30 Total Cream 125 ml	4	75	(68)	55	(50)	tube	40	1 400	8.0%
	Total Sun Care Products								$5 240	
	Total Inventory								$13 710	

NOTES: All inventory products use the same linked Revenue, COGS and Variance accounts: 4020 Revenue from Sales, 5060 Cost of Goods Sold and 5070 Variance Costs. Linked asset accounts are shown in the inventory list with the heading line for each inventory group.

Code	Description	Selling Price Reg	(Pref)	Price: EUR Reg	(Pref)	Unit	Taxes
Aesthetic Services							
AS01	Bridal Makeup/Styling	$ 70	($63)	€51	(€47)	job	no PST
AS02	Cellulite Treatment	80	(72)	62	(56)	job	no PST
AS03	Electrolysis: 45 min treatment	60	(54)	44	(40)	session	no PST
AS04	Electrolysis: 60 min treatment	75	(68)	55	(50)	session	no PST
AS05	European Deep Cleansing Facial	60	(54)	44	(38)	job	no PST
AS06	Hydroptimate Treatment	120	(108)	86	(77)	job	no PST
AS07	Makeup	40	(36)	31	(28)	job	no PST
AS08	Massage: Swedish	75	(68)	55	(50)	job	no PST
AS09	Promotional Pkg: spa treatment	100	(90)	75	(68)	job	no PST
AS10	Package: Super 5 spa treatments	600	(540)	430	(400)	series	no PST
AS11	Package: Deluxe 5 spa treatments	800	(720)	600	(550)	series	no PST
AS12	Skin Treatment	100	(90)	75	(68)	job	no PST
AS13	Manicure/Pedicure	25	(22)	18	(16)	job	no PST
AS14	Waxing: full leg	50	(45)	37	(33)	job	no PST
AS15	Waxing: half leg or bikini	20	(18)	15	(13)	job	no PST

NOTES: All Services are linked to 4040 Revenue from Services for revenue and to the expense account 5065 Cost of Services.

Accounting Procedures

The Goods and Services Tax (GST): Remittances

NOTES
Refer to Chapter 2 and pages 264–266 for further information about GST and PST remittances.

Adrienne Aesthetics uses the regular method for remittance of the Goods and Services Tax. GST collected is recorded as a liability in *GST Charged on Sales*. GST paid, recorded in *GST Paid on Purchases,* decreases the liability. The salon files its return with the Canada Revenue Agency (CRA) quarterly, either requesting a refund or remitting the balance owing.

Provincial Sales Tax (PST)

Provincial Sales Tax of 8 percent is applied to all cash and credit sales of goods in Ontario. Customers do not pay PST on the services provided by Adrienne Aesthetics. PST on goods is remitted monthly to the Minister of Finance. Set up a liability owing to the vendor, Minister of Finance, in the Payments Journal (choose Make Other Payment), using the General Ledger balance in *PST Payable* for the end of the previous month to determine the balance owing. A 5 percent sales tax compensation is earned for prompt payment and reduces the liability to the Minister of Finance.

PST at the rate of 8 percent is also paid on purchases that are not inventory items for resale. Since PST paid is not refundable, it is charged to the asset or expense account associated with the purchase, not to a separate account.

Sales Invoices

Adrienne allows customers to pay on account, or by cash, cheque or credit card. The keystrokes for cash and credit card inventory transactions are similar to those for account sales, except for the method of payment. The program will automatically debit the appropriate bank account instead of *Accounts Receivable*.

Source documents for cash and credit card sales are presented as weekly summaries to avoid a large number of small revenue transactions. Cash Customer and Credit Card Customer records are set up so these sales can be tracked.

NOTES
Printing of invoices will begin immediately, so be sure you have selected the correct printer and forms before you begin.

You can print and e-mail sales invoices through the program. Before posting the Sales Journal transaction, click the Print button or the E-mail button.

Credit Card Sales and Purchases

Adrienne has set up its accounts for credit card sales and purchase transactions.

Freight Expenses and Charges

When a business purchases inventory items, the cost of any freight that cannot be directly allocated to a specific item must be charged to *Freight Expense*. This amount is regarded as an expense rather than a charge to an inventory asset account. Freight or delivery charges to customers are allocated to *Freight Revenue*.

Discounts

To encourage customers to settle their accounts early, Adrienne Aesthetics offers its account customers a 2 percent discount on before-tax amounts if they pay their accounts within five days. For preferred customers, the discount period is 15 days. Discounts are calculated automatically when the payment terms are set up and the customer is eligible for the discount. There are no discounts on cash or credit card sales.

In addition, some customers have preferred price list status that entitles them to reduced prices. Regular and preferred prices in Canadian dollars and euros (€) are set up in the Inventory Ledger so the prices are entered automatically.

NOTES

We use the term cash sales and purchases to apply to payments by cash and by cheque.

Valentine's Day Packages

Each February, Adrienne Aesthetics offers special promotional gift packages that include a variety of popular beauty products and services. When assembled, these packages require some special packaging materials such as boxes, wrappings, foils and ribbons, which incur additional costs.

Returns

Returned goods are a normal part of retail businesses. Customers may not be satisfied with the product for a number of reasons. Adrienne Aesthetics provides full refunds on unopened items returned within 14 days. Some items such as lipstick cannot be returned for hygienic reasons. Returned items are debited to the contra-revenue account, *Sales Returns*, so that the returns can be tracked. Refer to page 433.

Returns on purchases also occur for a variety of reasons, for example, the goods may be damaged or the wrong items may have been shipped. Refer to page 434.

Import Duties

Adrienne Aesthetics pays import duties on all purchases from France. Rates are entered in the Inventory Ledger for inventory items and can be added directly in the Purchases Journal for other purchases. The duty is payable to the CRA at the time the goods are received. The program calculates the amount automatically and credits the linked account, *Import Duty Payable*. Payments are made like other tax remittances, as Other Payments in the Payments Journal.

INSTRUCTIONS

1. **Record entries** for the source documents in Simply Accounting using the Chart of Accounts, Trial Balance, and Vendor, Customer, Employee and Inventory Information provided. The procedures for entering each new type of transaction are outlined step by step in the Keystrokes section that follows the source documents.

These transactions have a ✓ in the check box, and the page number where the keystrokes begin is printed below the check box.

2. **Print** the **reports** indicated on the following printing form after finishing your entries. Instructions for printing inventory reports begin on page 437.

REPORTS

Lists
- ☐ Chart of Accounts
- ☐ Account List
- ☐ Vendors
- ☐ Customers
- ☐ Employees
- ☐ Inventory & Services

Journals
- ☑ All Journals (by date): Feb. 1 to Feb. 14
- ☐ General
- ☐ Purchases
- ☐ Payments
- ☐ Sales
- ☐ Receipts
- ☐ Payroll
- ☑ Item Assembly (by date): Feb. 1 to Feb. 14
- ☑ Adjustments (by date): Feb. 1 to Feb. 14

Financials
- ☑ Balance Sheet date: Feb. 14
- ☑ Income Statement: Feb. 1 to Feb. 14
- ☑ Trial Balance date: Feb. 14
- ☑ General Ledger accounts: 1310 1320 1330 4020 4040 from Feb. 1 to Feb. 14
- ☐ Statement of Cash Flows
- ☐ Cash Flow Projection Detail Report for
- ☑ Gross Margin Income Statement: Feb. 1 to Feb. 14

Tax
- ☐ Report on

Banking
- ☐ Cheque Log Report

Payables
- ☐ Vendor Aged
- ☐ Aged Overdue Payables
- ☐ Vendor Purchases
- ☐ Pending Purchase Orders

Receivables
- ☐ Customer Aged
- ☐ Aged Overdue Receivables
- ☐ Customer Sales
- ☑ Sales by Salesperson: Feb. 1 to Feb. 14
- ☐ Pending Sales Orders
- ☐ Customer Statements

Payroll
- ☐ Employee
- ☐ T4 Slips
- ☐ Record of Employment

Inventory & Services
- ☑ Inventory Synopsis
- ☐ Inventory Quantity
- ☐ Inventory Statistics
- ☑ Inventory Sales Summary for all Services: from Feb. 1 to Feb. 14
- ☑ Inventory Transaction Summary: for FC07 Lipstick, all journals: Feb. 1 to Feb. 14
- ☐ Inventory Price Lists

Mailing Labels
- ☐ Labels for

Management Reports
- ☐ Ledger

GRAPHS
- ☐ Payables by Aging Period
- ☐ Payables by Vendor
- ☐ Receivables by Aging Period
- ☐ Receivables by Customer
- ☐ Sales vs Receivables
- ☐ Receivables Due vs Payables Due
- ☐ Revenues by Account
- ☐ Expenses by Account
- ☑ Expenses and Net Profit as % of Revenue

SOURCE DOCUMENTS

SESSION DATE – FEBRUARY 7, 2008

☑ **Sales Invoice #20** **Dated Feb. 1/08**

411 Sold by Hydra to Montreal Fashions

8	CL04	Eye Contour Smoothing Gel 30 ml	$40 /jar
8	FC02	Concealer 15 ml	20 /tube
4	FC03	Epidermal Cleanser: face+ 300 ml	60 /jar
4	FC04	Epidermal Cleanser: phytogel 300 ml	50 /jar
8	FC05	Eye Shadow duo-pack	15 /pair
5	AS02	Cellulite Treatment	80 /job
8	AS07	Makeup	40 /job
		Goods and Services Tax	7%
		Provincial Sales Tax	8%

Terms: 2/5, n/30.

☑ **Purchase Invoice #AC-1124** **Dated Feb. 1/08**

415 From Acqua Viva Cosmetics

5	SC03	Sun Tan Milk SPF#4 200 ml	$ 90.00
5	SC04	Sun Tan Milk SPF#15 200 ml	105.00
		Freight	10.00
		GST Paid	14.35
Invoice Total			$219.35

Terms: net 10 days.

☑ **Memo #1** **Dated Feb. 2/08**

418 From Owner: Adjust inventory records for Eye Contour Smoothing Gel, item CL04. One jar was dropped and broken. Charge to Inventory Losses.

☑ **Memo #2** **Dated Feb. 3/08**

420 From Owner: Two new inventory items are required for special Valentine's Day gift packages. Create new asset Group account 1350 Gift Packages. Create two new inventory records.

Number	Description	Min.	Selling Price CAD$	(EUR €)	/Unit	Picture
VP01	Valentine Gift: super pkg	1	$100	(€75)	/pkg	VP01.bmp
VP02	Valentine Gift: deluxe pkg	1	150	(105)	/pkg	VP02.bmp

Linked accounts: Asset 1350
Revenue 4020
Expense 5060
Variance not required

☑ **Item Assembly #ItA-1** **Dated Feb. 3/08**

427 Assemble 10 VP01 Valentine Gift: super packages. Transfer 10 of each item as follows:

10	CL01	Cleansing Lotion 225 ml	$ 6 each tube
10	CL07	Night Cream 200 ml	21 each jar
10	FC01	Blush 8 g	4 each
10	FC07	Lipstick 5 g	6 each tube
10	SC01	Sun Care Cream SPF#15 125 ml	14 each tube
Additional Costs			$50

Assembled Items:

10	VP01	Valentine Gift: super pkg	$56 each pkg

☐ **Item Assembly #ItA-2** **Dated Feb. 3/08**

Assemble 10 VP02 Valentine Deluxe Gift Packages. Transfer 10 of each item as follows:

10	CL02	Cleansing Milk 225 ml	$12 each tube
10	CL07	Night Cream 200 ml	21 each jar
10	FC07	Lipstick 5 g	6 each tube
10	FC11	Powder: pressed 15 g	14 each
10	SC06	UV #30 Total Cream 125 ml	35 each tube
Additional Costs			$50

Assembled Items:

10	VP02	Valentine Gift: deluxe pkg	$93 each pkg

☐ **Memo #3** **Dated Feb. 3/08**

From Owner: Adjust purchase invoice #AC-1124 from Acqua Viva Cosmetics. Change the quantity for both items to 10. The unit cost price and freight are unchanged. The revised invoice total is $428.

NOTES

Notice that only inventory items appear on this list because service items do not have quantities in stock.

NOTES

You will see the advisor message that one or more inventory items has dropped below the reorder point. Read and then close the message.

☑ **Sales Invoice #21** **Dated Feb. 4/08**

431 Sold by Hydra to Valley TV (CKOV) preferred customer

5	CL03	Eye Contour Smoothing Cream 30 ml	$ 32.00 /jar
5	CL05	Masks: herb 100 ml	36.00 /jar
5	FC02	Concealer 15 ml	18.00 /tube
5	AS06	Hydroptimate Treatment	108.00 /job
5	AS07	Makeup	36.00 /job
		Goods and Services Tax	7%
		Provincial Sales Tax	8%

Terms: 2/15, n/30.

NOTES

To change a purchase price, click the number in the Amount field to select it. Type the new total amount to replace it, and press (tab) to update the unit price and totals.

☑ **Purchase Order #11** **Dated Feb. 4/08**

432 Shipping date Feb. 8/08

From Biotech Laboratories

5	FC10	Powder: loose 15 g	$ 40.00
15	FC11	Powder: pressed 15 g	210.00
		GST Paid	17.50
		Order Total	$267.50

Terms: net 10 days.

☐ **Cash Receipt #11** **Dated Feb. 4/08**

From Euro Film Corporation, cheque #6732 for €1 635.90 in payment of account including €31.16 discount for early payment. Reference invoice #AA-11. The exchange rate is 1.375.

☐ **Purchase Invoice #DL-518** **Dated Feb. 4/08**

From Derma Laboratories

10	CL01	Cleansing Lotion 225 ml	$ 60.00
10	CL02	Cleansing Milk 225 ml	120.00
20	CL07	Night Cream 200 ml	440.00
		Freight	20.00
		GST Paid	44.80
		Invoice Total	$684.80

Terms: net 5 days. Note price increase for CL07.

☐ **Purchase Invoice #SL-4100** **Dated Feb. 4/08**

From Sun Lab Products Inc.

10	SC01	Sun Care Cream SPF#15 125 ml	$140.00
15	SC06	UV #30 Total Cream 125 ml	525.00
		Freight	10.00
		GST Paid	47.25
		Invoice Total	$722.25

Terms: net 15 days.

☐ **Cheque Copy #392** **Dated Feb. 5/08**

To Esthetica Incorporated, €2 327.25 in full payment of account. Reference invoice #EI-641. The exchange rate is 1.368.

☐ **Cash Receipt #12** **Dated Feb. 5/08**

From Valley TV (CKOV), cheque #29975 for $1 837.50 in payment of account, including $35 discount taken. Reference invoice #AA-16.

☐ **Cheque Copy #205** **Dated Feb. 6/08**

To Derma Laboratories, $684.80 in full payment of account. Reference invoice #DL-518.

☐ **Visa Sales Summary Invoice #22** **Dated Feb. 6/08**

Sold by Blossom to various one-time Cash Customers

5	CL08	Protection Cream: dbl action 60 ml	$ 25 /tube	$ 125.00
3	FC05	Eye Shadow duo-pack	15 /pair	45.00
5	FC10	Powder: loose 15 g	20 /jar	100.00
3	SC05	UV #15 Total Cream 125 ml	50 /tube	150.00
2	AS08	Massage: Swedish	75 /job	150.00
4	AS13	Manicure/Pedicure	25 /job	100.00
4	AS14	Waxing: full leg	50 /job	200.00
2	VP02	Valentine Gift: deluxe pkg	150 /pkg	300.00
		Goods and Services Tax	7%	81.90
		Provincial Sales Tax	8%	57.60
Total paid by Visa				$1 309.50

☐ **MasterCard Sales Summary Invoice #23** **Dated Feb. 6/08**

Sold by Blossom to various one-time Cash Customers

20	FC08	Kohl Pencil	$ 15 each	$ 300.00
10	FC09	Mascara 9 ml	10 /tube	100.00
2	SC03	Sun Tan Milk SPF#4 200 ml	40 /jar	80.00
2	AS12	Skin Treatment	100 /job	200.00
4	AS15	Waxing: half leg or bikini	20 /job	80.00
3	VP02	Valentine Gift: deluxe pkg	150 /pkg	450.00
		Goods and Services Tax	7%	84.70
		Provincial Sales Tax	8%	74.40
Total paid by MasterCard				$1 369.10

☐ **Item Assembly #ItA-3** **Dated Feb. 7/08**

Assemble five VP02 Valentine Deluxe Gift Packages. Transfer five of each item as follows:

5	CL02	Cleansing Milk 225 ml	$12	each tube
5	CL07	Night Cream 200 ml	22	each jar
5	FC07	Lipstick 5 g	6	each tube
5	FC11	Powder: pressed 15 g	14	each
5	SC06	UV #30 Total Cream 125 ml	35	each tube
Additional Costs			$25	

Assembled Items:

5	VP02	Valentine Gift: deluxe pkg	$94	each pkg

☐ **Cash Sales Summary Invoice #24** **Dated Feb. 7/08**

Sold by Hydra to various one-time Cash Customers

2	CL04	Eye Contour Smoothing Gel 30 ml	$ 40 /jar	$ 80.00
5	CL06	Masks: sea 100 ml	35 /jar	175.00
15	FC07	Lipstick 5 g	15 /tube	225.00
3	SC02	Sun Care Cream SPF#30 125 ml	45 /tube	135.00
2	AS01	Bridal Makeup/Styling	70 /job	140.00
5	AS03	Electrolysis: 45 min treatment	60 /session	300.00
2	AS06	Hydroptimate Treatment	120 /job	240.00
2	VP01	Valentine Gift: super pkg	100 /pkg	200.00
		Goods and Services Tax	7%	104.65
		Provincial Sales Tax	8%	65.20
Total cash received				$1 664.85

☐ **Cheque Copy #206** **Dated Feb. 7/08**

To Sun Lab Products, $722.25 in full payment of account. Reference invoice #SL-4100.

NOTES

Choose Cash Customers for the Visa and MasterCard sales summaries.

NOTES

If you recall the stored item assembly transaction, change the total amount for the Assembled Items to $470. Notice that the assembly component price for CL07 is updated from $21 to $22 automatically for the new costs. (See Item Assembly #ItA-2 on page 405.)

NOTES

Choose Cash Customers for the cash sales summary.

SESSION DATE – FEBRUARY 14, 2008

NOTES
The freight charge was not included on the purchase order so it must be added to the invoice.

☐ **Purchase Invoice #BL-669** **Dated Feb. 8/08**

From Biotech Laboratories, to fill purchase order #11

5	FC10	Powder: loose 15 g	$ 40.00
15	FC11	Powder: pressed 15 g	210.00
		Freight	10.00
		GST Paid	18.20
		Invoice Total	$278.20

Terms: net 10 days. Remember to add the freight expense to the order.

NOTES
Foreign customers do not pay Canadian taxes on items shipped to them or on the shipping charges.

☐ **Sales Invoice #25** **Dated Feb. 8/08**

Sold by Blossom to Euro Film Corporation (preferred customer)

4	CL05	Masks: herb 100 ml	€28 /jar
4	CL06	Masks: sea 100 ml	24 /jar
8	FC03	Epidermal Cleanser: face+ 300 ml	39 /jar
8	FC04	Epidermal Cleanser: phytogel 300 ml	33 /jar
3	FC06	Foundation 35 ml	16 /jar
5	SC06	UV #30 Total Cream 125 ml	50 /tube
		Shipping	€20

Terms: 2/15, n/30. The exchange rate is 1.363.

☑ **Visa Sales Return #22-R** **Dated Feb. 8/08**

433 Sold by Blossom to Cash Customer

–1	CL08	Protection Cream: dbl action 60 ml	$25.00
–1	SC05	UV #15 Total Cream 125 ml	50.00
		Goods and Services Tax	5.25
		Provincial Sales Tax	6.00
		Total credited to Visa account	$86.25

☑ **Purchase Return #BL-669R** **Dated Feb. 8/08**

434 Return to Biotech Laboratories because package safety seal was broken.

–5	FC10	Powder: loose 15 g	$40.00
		GST Paid	2.80
		Invoice Total	$42.80

Terms: net 60 days.

NOTES
Remember to edit the purchase prices by changing the numbers in the Amount field.

☑ **Purchase Invoice #EI-933** **Dated Feb. 9/08**

435 From Esthetica Incorporated

				Duty
		Manicure and pedicure preparation products	€ 80.00	6.5%
5	FC02	Concealer 15 ml	30.00	8.0%
5	CL03	Eye Contour Smoothing Cream 30 ml	60.00	8.0%
5	CL04	Eye Contour Smoothing Gel 30 ml	65.00	8.0%
		Freight	30.00	
		GST Paid	18.55	
		Invoice Total	€283.55	
		Import Duty		€17.60

Terms: net 30 days. The exchange rate is 1.365.

☐ **Cheque Copy #207** **Dated Feb. 9/08**

To Acqua Viva Cosmetics, $428 in full payment of account. Reference invoice #AC-1124.

☐ **Memo #4** **Dated Feb. 09/08**

From Owner: Using the Feb. 1 General Ledger balance, pay the PST to the Minister of Finance, Ontario for January. Recognize $120 as the sales tax compensation earned (5% of $2 400). Issue cheque #208 in payment.

☐ **Sales Order #66** **Dated Feb. 10/08**

Delivery date Feb. 13/08
From Ariandanos Residence

1	AS01	Bridal Makeup/Styling	$ 70 /job
1	AS04	Electrolysis: 60 min treatment	75 /session
1	AS05	European Deep Cleansing Facial	60 /job
1	AS06	Hydroptimate Treatment	120 /job
1	AS12	Skin Treatment	100 /job
		Goods and Services Tax	7%

Terms: 2/5, n/30.

NOTES

Only GST applies to the sales order from Ariandanos Residence because it includes only services.

☐ **Sales Invoice #26** **Dated Feb. 10/08**

Sold by Blossom to Lavender Estates

3	CL09	Protection Cream: moisturizer 60 ml	$ 30 /tube
3	SC04	Sun Tan Milk SPF#15 200 ml	50 /jar
2	AS11	Package: Deluxe 5 spa treatments	800 /series
2	VP02	Valentine Gift: deluxe pkg	150 /pkg
		Goods and Services Tax	7%
		Provincial Sales Tax	8%

Terms: 2/5, n/30.

☐ **Sales Invoice #27** **Dated Feb. 11/08**

Sold by Hydra to Botelli & Giroux, Lawyers

3	AS09	Promotional Pkg: spa treatment	$100 /job
3	VP01	Valentine Gift: super pkg	100 /pkg
3	VP02	Valentine Gift: deluxe pkg	150 /pkg
		Goods and Services Tax	7%
		Provincial Sales Tax	8%

Terms: 2/5, n/30.

☐ **Cash Purchase Invoice #HP-125** **Dated Feb. 11/08**

From Hull Promotions (use Quick Add for the new vendor), $200 plus $14 GST and $16 PST for business cards and flyers for promotion. Purchase invoice total $230 paid by cheque #209.

☐ **Purchase Invoice #EI-1303** **Dated Feb. 12/08**

From Esthetica Incorporated				Duty
		Manicure and pedicure preparation products	€ 55.00	6.5%
5	CL05	Masks: herb 100 ml	65.00	8.0%
5	CL06	Masks: sea 100 ml	60.00	8.0%
5	FC03	Epidermal Cleanser: face+ 300 ml	90.00	8.0%
5	FC04	Epidermal Cleanser: phytogel 300 ml	80.00	8.0%
		Freight	30.00	
		GST Paid	26.60	
Invoice Total			€406.60	
Import Duty				€27.18

Terms: net 30 days. The exchange rate is 1.3628.

☐ **Cash Purchase Invoice #OH-42455** **Dated Feb. 13/08**

From Ottawa Hydro, $200 plus $14 GST for hydro services. Purchase invoice total $214 paid by cheque #210.

☐ **Cash Purchase Invoice #BC-16721** **Dated Feb. 13/08**

From Bell Canada, $80 plus $5.60 GST and $6.40 PST for telephone services. Purchase invoice total $92 paid by cheque #211.

☐ **Sales Invoice #28** **Dated Feb. 13/08**

Sold by Blossom to Ariandanos Residence, to fill sales order #66

1	AS01	Bridal Makeup/Styling	$ 70 /job
1	AS04	Electrolysis: 60 min treatment	75 /session
1	AS05	European Deep Cleansing Facial	60 /job
1	AS06	Hydroptimate Treatment	120 /job
1	AS12	Skin Treatment	100 /job
		Goods and Services Tax	7%

Terms: 2/5, n/30.

☐ **Visa Sales Summary Invoice #29** **Dated Feb. 13/08**

Sold by Hydra to various one-time Cash Customers

3	CL02	Cleansing Milk 225 ml	$ 25 /tube	$ 75.00
2	CL07	Night Cream 200 ml	45 /jar	90.00
5	AS09	Promotional Pkg: spa treatment	100 /job	500.00
2	VP01	Valentine Gift: super pkg	100 /pkg	200.00
1	VP02	Valentine Gift: deluxe pkg	150 /pkg	150.00
		Goods and Services Tax	7%	71.05
		Provincial Sales Tax	8%	41.20
Total paid by Visa				$1 127.25

☐ **MasterCard Sales Summary Invoice #30** **Dated Feb. 13/08**

Sold by Blossom to various one-time Cash Customers

2	CL01	Cleansing Lotion 225 ml	$ 15 /tube	$ 30.00
2	CL02	Cleansing Milk 225 ml	25 /tube	50.00
1	AS05	European Deep Cleansing Facial	60 /job	60.00
2	AS11	Package: Deluxe 5 spa treatments	800 /series	1 600.00
2	VP01	Valentine Gift: super pkg	100 /pkg	200.00
		Goods and Services Tax	7%	135.80
		Provincial Sales Tax	8%	22.40
Total paid by MasterCard				$2 098.20

☐ **Cash Sales Summary Invoice #31** **Dated Feb. 14/08**

Sold by Hydra to various one-time Cash Customers

1	CL06	Masks: sea 100 ml	$ 35 /jar	$ 35.00
2	FC01	Blush 8 g	10 each	20.00
2	AS01	Bridal Makeup/Styling	70 /job	140.00
3	AS10	Package: Super 5 spa treatments	600 /series	1 800.00
2	VP02	Valentine Gift: deluxe pkg	150 /pkg	300.00
		Goods and Services Tax	7%	160.65
		Provincial Sales Tax	8%	28.40
Total cash received				$2 484.05

☐ **Cash Receipt #13** **Dated Feb. 14/08**

From Euro Film Corporation, cheque #8091 for €1 079.96 in payment of account including €22.04 discount for early payment. Reference invoice #25. The exchange rate is 1.3688.

☐ **Memo #5** **Dated Feb. 14/08**

From Owner: Complete payroll run to pay salaried employees Blossom and Hydra. Issue cheques #212 and #213. Add the 2 percent sales commissions based on the net sales for each employee from Feb. 1 to Feb. 14.

NOTES
Use the Sales by Salesperson Summary Report (by Customer) to find the net sales for each employee. Do not include freight or other sales in the report.

☐ **Memo #6** **Dated Feb. 14/08**

From Owner: Update all tax settings and tax codes to reduce the GST rate to 6 percent.

KEYSTROKES

Accounting for Inventory Sales

The first transaction involves the sale of inventory items. Many of the steps are identical to those you used for sales in previous applications. You will be using the inventory database and all the Sales Invoice fields to complete this transaction.

Using the instructions for accessing data files in Chapter 1, page 8, open the files for Adrienne Aesthetics.

Type 2 7 08 or **choose Feb. 7** from the calendar and **click OK**.

This will enter the session date February 7, 2008. The familiar Home window appears. The Inventory Ledger icons are added but the Project Ledger is hidden because it is not set up and it is not used. Inventory sales are entered in the Sales Journal.

Click the **Sales Journal icon** 

to open and display the familiar Sales Journal input screen:

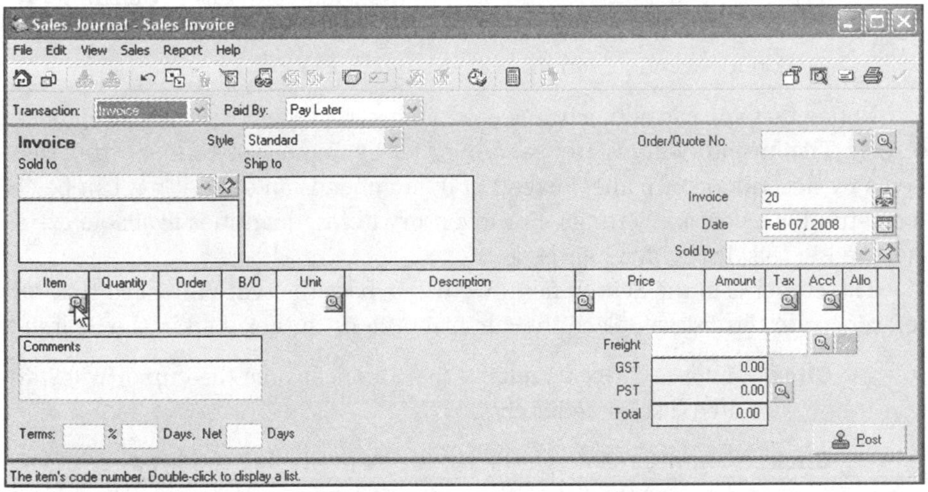

The Sales Journal looks the same as in earlier data files because we did not remove any inventory fields that were not used in those earlier chapters. Invoice is selected as the type of transaction and Pay Later as the payment method. These default choices are correct.

Click the **Sold To** (Customer) **field list arrow** to display the list of customers.

Click **Montreal Fashions** to enter the customer's name and address on the form. If you selected an incorrect customer, return to the customer list and select again.

You can skip the Ship To fields because the default information is correct, and the Order/Quote No. is not used for invoices. The Invoice number is correct because the numeric invoice sequence has been set up in the defaults. If necessary, you can edit the invoice number. Payment terms are also added from the default settings and can be edited if necessary.

Click the **Date field Calendar icon** to advance the cursor. The default session date is incorrect.

Click **1** on the February calendar and **press** tab to advance the cursor to the Sold By field.

Choose **Hydra** as the salesperson.

Press tab twice to skip the Use Same Salesperson icon.

The cursor advances to the first line of the Item field. One line is used for each inventory item or service sold by the business. A separate line would also be used to enter returns and allowances made.

Click the **Item field List icon**, or **press** enter or **double click** the **field** to access the inventory list:

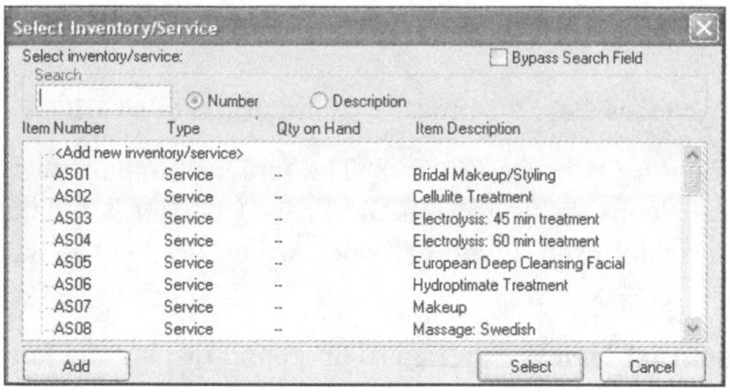

Type C, the first letter or number of the code, in the Item field and press enter to advance to the part of the list beginning with that letter or number, just as you do for account, vendor and customer lists.

Notice that you can add new inventory items from the Select Inventory/Service screen. The inventory items are listed in order by number or code. Sorting the inventory items by description or name, instead of by number, is an option that can be selected in the setup for Inventory Settings. For inventory items, quantities available are also included in this display for reference.

The cursor is in the Search field. We will bypass the search field so that future references to this list will place the cursor in the list rather than in the Search field.

Click **Bypass Search Field** so that the next time the cursor will start in the item list immediately.

Click to scroll down the list. **Click** in the **list** and **type** c if you want to advance the list to the codes beginning with C.

Click **CL04 Eye Contour Smoothing Gel 30 ml** from the list.

Click **Select** to add the inventory item to your form. If you have made an incorrect selection, return to the Item field and reselect from the inventory list.

You can also type the code number in the Item field and press tab, but you must match the case of the code number in the ledger.

The cursor moves to the Quantity sold field. Notice that the program adds information in each field automatically, based on the inventory record information. All the information except quantity and amount is added by default as soon as you enter the inventory item number. If you select a preferred customer, the default price is the preferred customer price instead of the regular selling price.

You should enter the number of units of this item sold in the Quantity field.

Type 8 **Press** tab.

If you enter a quantity greater than the available stock, the program prevents you from continuing, unless your company settings allow inventory levels to go below zero.

Since the remaining default information is correct, you do not need to change it. The default tax code — GP — is the code entered for the customer because the

NOTES

You may need to click the Item field to place the cursor to show the List icon. Or you can access the list by pressing enter or by double clicking.

NOTES

Inventory items can be oversold, but you must change the Inventory Ledger settings to allow the quantity on hand to go below zero. This setting is explained in the setup for Flabuless Fitness.

No quantities are shown for services because they are not held in stock.

NOTES

You may want to continue with the order to oversell the items if the customer is purchasing backordered inventory stock.

customer pays both GST at 7 percent and PST at 8 percent. Services have been set up in the Inventory Ledger so that by default PST is not applied.

The program automatically calculates an amount based on the selling price per unit. This figure appears in the Amount field.

The default revenue account for the item appears but can be accepted or changed. You would change the account for returns and allowances or unusual entries. Accept the default revenue account for this sale.

You can select another tax code from the Tax Code list if necessary. You can also edit the price to change the selling price for a particular item or customer. To change the account, click the Account field List icon, press *enter* or double click in the Account field to obtain a list of accounts.

Press *tab* **repeatedly** to advance to the next invoice line and update the first line because all the default information based on the records is correct.

Or you can click the Item field on the second line, or the third line, if the item description wraps around to the second invoice line.

Press *tab* in the Account field to add a new invoice line in the viewing space of the journal when you reach the last invoice line of the journal.

Enter the **remaining sale items** using the same steps that you used to enter the first item.

As you complete each line and advance to the next, the totals and tax amounts at the bottom of the form are updated to include the last item entered.

The tax code shown on the screen for the service items is GP, the one for the customer, but only GST is added to the invoice total.

To include more invoice lines on your screen, drag the lower frame of the Sales Journal window or maximize the window.

If freight is included in a sale, you can add it just as you do for other non-inventory sales. There are no freight charges for these items.

After entering the final service item for the customer, your completed invoice should look like the one shown here:

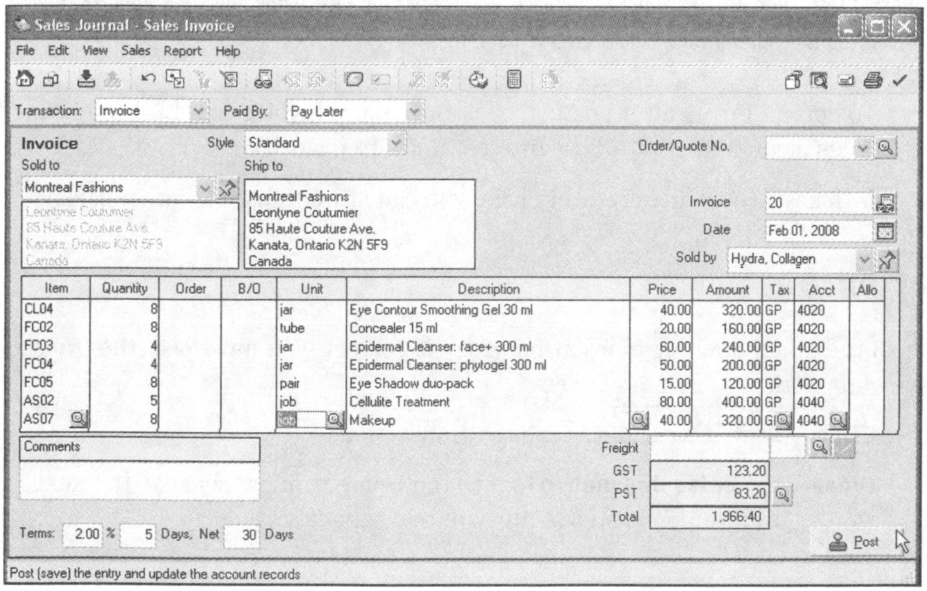

You should review the journal entry before posting it.

NOTES

If you have entered a default revenue account for the customer that is different from the one for the item, the account for the item replaces the customer's revenue account.

WARNING!

If you click the second line and it is used for part of the description for the first item, you will select the first item instead.

You can maximize the journal or drag the side frame to provide wider columns.

Reviewing the Inventory Sales Journal Transaction

NOTES
Pressing ctrl + J will also open the journal display.

Choose the **Report menu** and **click Display Sales Journal Entry**:

Adrienne Aesthetics

02/01/08 (J1)	Debits	Credits	Project
1200 Accounts Receivable	1,966.40	-	
5060 Cost of Goods Sold	428.00	-	
1310 Creams and Lotions	-	144.00	
1320 Face Care Products	-	284.00	
2640 PST Payable	-	83.20	
2650 GST Charged on Sales	-	123.20	
4020 Revenue from Sales	-	1,040.00	
4040 Revenue from Services	-	720.00	
	2,394.40	2,394.40	

From the tax amounts, you can see that PST is charged only on the *Revenue from Sales* amount — 8% × $1 040 = $83.20 — while GST is charged on both sales and services — 7% × ($1 040 + $720) = $123.20. Both taxes are calculated correctly because of the tax codes assigned in the Inventory Ledger records.

NOTES
Adrienne uses a single cost of goods sold account for all inventory items.

Notice that all relevant accounts have been updated automatically because the Inventory and Receivables ledgers are linked to the General Ledger. Therefore, the linked asset, revenue and expense accounts defined for each inventory item have been debited or credited as required. In addition, the linked Receivables accounts we saw earlier are used — *PST Payable*, *GST Charged on Sales* and *Accounts Receivable*. The inventory database and customer record are also updated.

Simply Accounting uses the average cost method to determine the cost of goods sold. If the stock for an inventory item were purchased at different times and prices, the average of these prices would be used as the cost of goods sold.

Close the **display** to return to the journal input screen.

CORRECTING THE INVENTORY SALES ENTRY BEFORE POSTING

To **correct** an **item** on the inventory line, **click** the **incorrect field** to move the cursor and highlight the field contents. **Press** enter to display the list of inventory items, tax codes or accounts. **Click** the **correct selection** to highlight it, then **click Select**, or for the remaining fields, **type** the **correct information**. **Press** tab to enter the change.

If you **change** the **inventory** item, you must **re-enter** the **quantity sold** in the Quantity field, and **press** tab. The totals will be updated correctly if you follow this procedure.

To **insert** a new **line**, if you have forgotten a complete line of the invoice, **click** the **line below** the one you have forgotten. **Choose** the **Edit menu** and **click Insert Line** to add a blank invoice line to your form. To **remove** a **line**, **click** the **line** you want to delete and **choose** the **Edit menu** and **click Remove Line**.

For corrections of other invoice details, refer to page 169.

WARNING!
You cannot adjust invoices to correct for selecting the wrong vendor or customer. For these errors, you must complete a reversing entry. Refer to Appendix C.

To correct errors after posting, click the Adjust Invoice tool or choose the Sales menu and click Adjust Invoice. Refer to page 185.

If this is a recurring inventory sale, you can store it just like other sales.

Posting

When all the information in your journal entry is correct, you must post the transaction to save your work.

Click **Post** Post to save the transaction.

Close the **Sales Journal** to exit to the Home window because the next transaction is an inventory purchase, not a sale.

Accounting for Inventory Purchases

The second transaction involves the purchase of inventory items. Inventory purchases are entered in the Purchases Journal, and many of the steps are the same as those for other credit purchases. Now the inventory database will provide the additional information.

Click the **Purchases Journal icon** 

in the Home window to display the familiar Purchases Journal input form window:

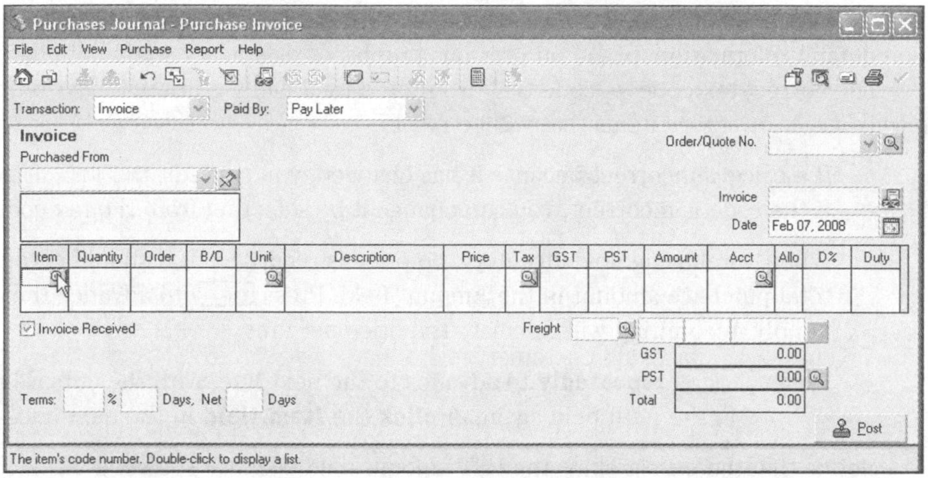

basic BASIC VERSION
You will not see the Duty columns until you select a foreign vendor.

You are now ready to enter the second transaction. Invoice is correctly selected as the type of transaction, and Pay Later as the method of payment. We have set up the company files to apply import duties, so duty fields appear on the form.

Click the **Purchased From** (Vendor) **field list arrow** to display the list of vendors.

Click **Acqua Viva Cosmetics** from the list to add it to your input form.

Check your selection. If you have selected an incorrect vendor, select again from the vendor list. If you have selected correctly, proceed by entering the invoice number.

The duty fields are removed because they do not apply to Canadian vendors.

Click the **Invoice field** to skip the Order/Quote No.

Type `AC-1124` **Press** (tab) **twice**.

The cursor advances to the Date field. Here you should enter the source document date, unless it is the same as the default session date.

Type `February 1`

Press (tab) **twice** to advance the cursor to the Item field. **Press** (tab) **once** if you choose the date from the Date field calendar.

Press (enter) or **click** the **List icon**  to see the list of inventory items.

Notice that you can add new inventory from the Select Inventory/Service window.

Scroll down and **click** **SC03 Sun Tan Milk SPF#4 200 ml** from the list to highlight it.

Press (enter). If you have made an incorrect selection, return to the Item field and select again.

The cursor advances to the Quantity received field. The Description field should now show the name, Sun Tan Milk SPF#4 200 ml. The default price is the most recent purchase price. Now enter the quantity for this item.

Type 5 **Press** tab.

The cursor advances to the Unit field, skipping the Order and B/O (backorder) fields because this is not a purchase order or quote.

The Unit and Description are correct based on Inventory Ledger records.

The Price field records the unit price paid for the purchase of the inventory items. This amount should not include any GST paid that can be used as an input tax credit. The default information, based on previous purchases, is correct so do not change it.

The correct tax code — code G — is entered by default. Adrienne pays only GST on purchases of inventory items that will be resold.

NOTES
PST is not paid on items that are purchased for resale because the store is not the final customer.

If a price is incorrect because it has changed, you can edit the default amount. If the code is incorrect, you can change it by selecting from the tax code list.

When purchasing new inventory, no price is recorded. You should enter the total purchase amount in the Amount field. Press tab to advance the cursor. Simply Accounting will calculate the price per unit.

Press tab **repeatedly** to advance to the next line, with the cursor blinking in the Item field again, or **click** the **Item field** in the next line.

Notice that the cursor skips the PST amount field because the vendor tax code does not include PST. The Account field was also skipped over, because you cannot change the entry for inventory purchases. The Asset account for the inventory purchase is defined in the Inventory Ledger as the linked account for purchases and sales. To change the account, you must edit the Inventory Ledger record. The default account for the vendor does not apply to the inventory purchase.

Enter **the second item** from the source document, using the same steps that you used to record the first item.

The Freight fields are used to enter any freight charges that cannot be allocated to a specific item purchased and to enter the taxes paid on the freight charges. There are four Freight fields: tax code, GST amount, PST amount and finally the base amount of the freight charge. Because GST is paid on freight you must enter a tax code if the vendor charges freight.

Click the **first Freight field**. The tax code for the vendor, code G, may be entered by default. If it is not,

NOTES
PST is not charged on freight in Ontario so the correct tax code for freight is code G - GST @ 7%.

Press enter to see the list of tax codes and **double click G - GST @ 7%**.

You do not need to enter amounts for the taxes on freight; they are calculated as soon as you enter the amount of freight charged.

Click the **final Freight field**, the amount field.

Type 10 **Press** tab.

Simply Accounting calculates the amount of GST (and PST if it is paid) and updates all the totals.

Your input form is complete and should appear as follows:

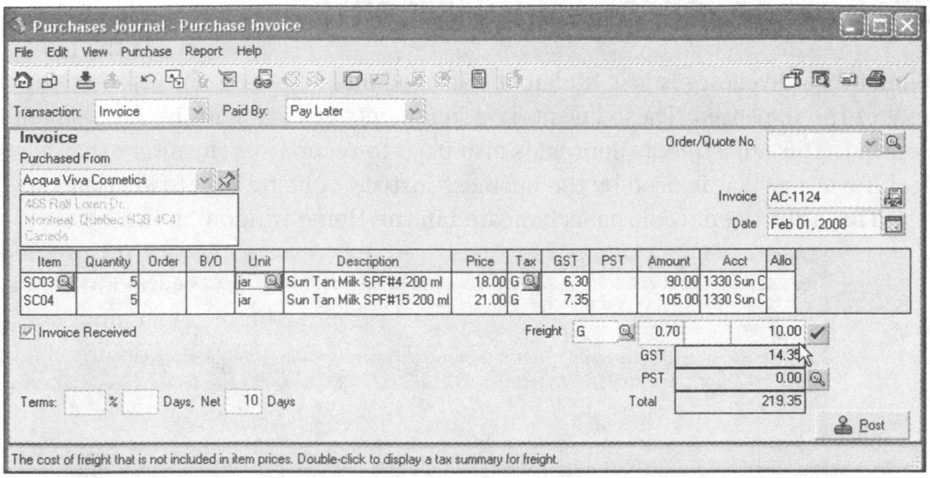

Reviewing the Inventory Purchase Transaction

Choose the **Report menu** and **click Display Purchases Journal Entry** to display the transaction you have entered, as shown:

Adrienne Aesthetics
02/01/08 (J2)

	Debits	Credits	Project
1330 Sun Care Products	195.00	-	
2670 GST Paid on Purchases	14.35	-	
5200 Freight Expense	10.00	-	
2200 Accounts Payable	-	219.35	
	219.35	219.35	

Simply Accounting has automatically updated all accounts relevant to this transaction. The appropriate inventory asset account (*Sun Care Products*), *Accounts Payable*, *GST Paid on Purchases* and *Freight Expense* have been updated as required because the ledgers are linked. The inventory database and the vendor record are also updated.

Close the **display** to return to the Purchases Journal input screen.

> **NOTES**
> Pressing ctrl + J will also open the journal display.

CORRECTING THE INVENTORY PURCHASES JOURNAL ENTRY

If the inventory item is incorrect, **reselect** from the **inventory** list by **pressing** enter while in this field. **Click Select** to add the item to your form. **Type** the **quantity** purchased and **press** tab to update the totals.

Account numbers cannot be changed for inventory items on the purchase invoice. They must be edited in the Inventory Ledger.

To **insert** a new **line**, if you have forgotten a complete line of the invoice, **click** the **line below** the one you have forgotten. **Choose** the **Edit menu** and **click Insert Line** to add a blank invoice line to your form. To **remove** a complete **line**, **click** the **line** you want to delete and **choose** the **Edit menu** and **click Remove Line**.

For assistance with correcting other invoice details, refer to page 125.

To correct an inventory purchase after posting, use the Adjust Invoice tool or choose Adjust Invoice from the Purchase Menu. Refer to page 138.

If this is a recurring purchase, you can store it, just like other recurring purchases.

Posting

When all the information in your journal entry is correct, you must post the transaction to save your work.

Click Post Post. **Close** the **Purchases Journal** to exit to the Home window. The next transaction is an inventory adjustment.

Making Inventory Adjustments

Sometimes inventory is lost, stolen or damaged and adjusting entries are required to reflect the expenses. These inventory adjustments are made in the Adjustments Journal. The Adjustments Journal is also used to record lost inventory that is recovered and inventory that is used by the business instead of being sold to customers.

The Adjustments Journal is indicated in the Home window shown here:

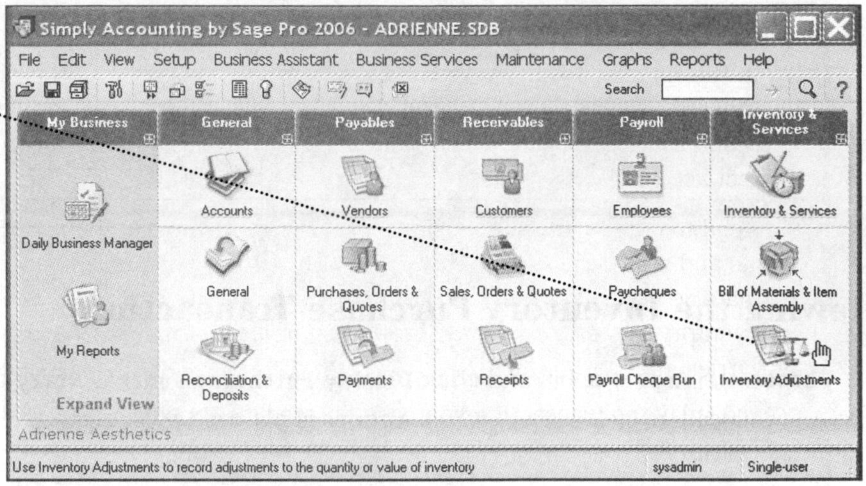

basic BASIC VERSION
The Inventory Ledger icon in the Basic version does not include the clock image.
The Journal icon is named Item Assembly instead of Bill of Materials & Item Assembly.
The Basic icons are:

Click the **Adjustments Journal icon** to display the blank Inventory Adjustments Journal input screen:

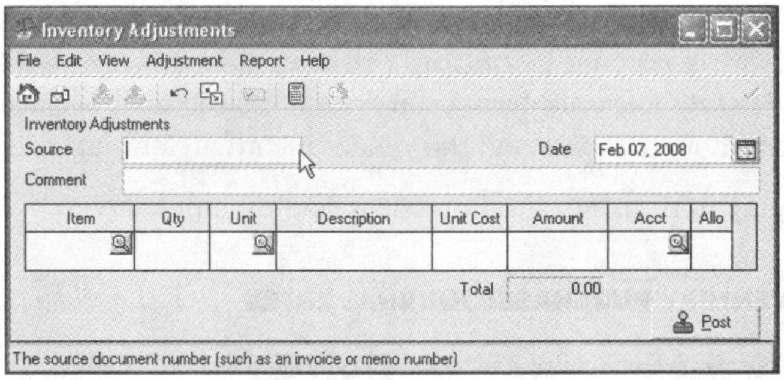

basic BASIC VERSION
The Basic version does not include the Refresh tool.

The cursor is in the Source field. The source for an adjustment will normally be a memo from a manager or owner.

Type `Memo 1` **Press** *tab*.

The cursor is in the Date field, with the session date entered and highlighted.

Type `02-02-08` **Press** *tab* **twice**.

The cursor is now in the Comment field, where you can enter a brief explanation for this transaction.

Type `Jar dropped and broken` **Press** *tab*.

The cursor is now in the Item field.

Press *enter* or **click** [icon] to display the familiar inventory list.

Notice that the quantities on the list have been updated to include the previous sale and purchase. Services are not included in the list because they have no quantities in stock and cannot be lost or damaged.

Double click **CL04 Eye Contour Smoothing Gel** from the list to select it and enter it onto the form.

The item name, Eye Contour Smoothing Gel, the unit, the unit cost and the account have been added automatically. The cursor advances to the Quantity field. You need to indicate that the inventory has been reduced because of the damaged item. You do this by typing a **negative** number in the field. Remember always to enter a negative quantity when there is an inventory loss. If lost inventory is recovered later, enter the adjustment with a positive quantity.

Type -1 **Press** (tab).

The cursor advances to the Unit field. The rest of the journal line is completed automatically. In the Amount field, a negative amount, reflecting the inventory loss, automatically appears as a default based on the average cost. In the Account field, *Inventory Losses*, the default linked account for inventory losses appears for this entry. This is the correct account.

> If you need to choose another account, press (enter) to display the list of accounts and select the account as usual. You can also edit the amount if you know that the price of the unit was different from the default price, the average of all inventory in stock. You can store Adjustments Journal entries just as you store entries in other journals.

The Allo (allocation) field for project allocations is not used by Adrienne Aesthetics, so skip it. We will discuss it in the next application. The Additional Date and one Additional Field are available in the Adjustments Journal just as they are in the other journals, and you access them the same way — from the tool button or the Adjustment menu. In the Adjustments Journal, these fields are not used by Adrienne Aesthetics, so your entry is complete as shown and you are ready to review it:

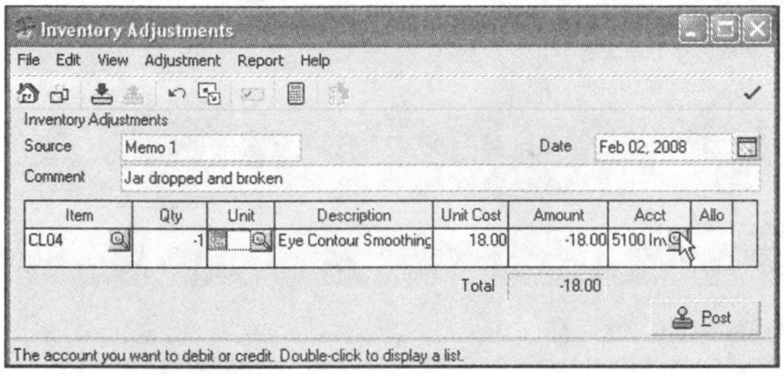

Reviewing the Adjustments Journal Entry

Choose the **Report menu** and **click Display Inventory Adjustments Journal Entry** to display the transaction you have entered as shown here:

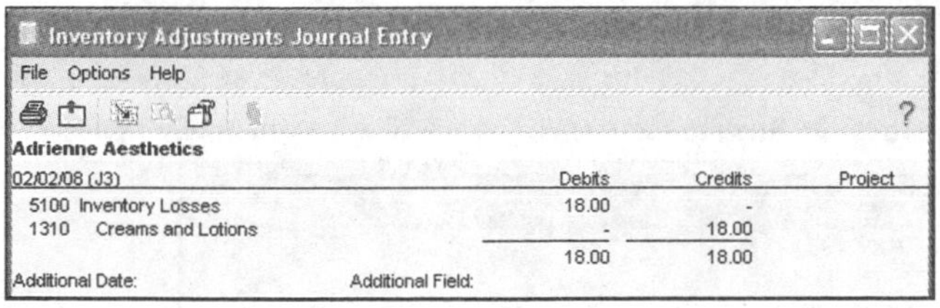

You can see that Simply Accounting has automatically updated all relevant accounts for this transaction. The appropriate inventory asset defined for this inventory item, *Creams and Lotions*, and the inventory database have also been reduced to reflect the loss at the average cost price. *Inventory Losses*, the Inventory linked expense account that was defined for inventory losses or adjustments, has been debited or increased.

Close the **display** to return to the Adjustments Journal input screen.

NOTES

Stores that sell inventory frequently use some inventory stock in the store. Use the Adjustments Journal to record these transfers by choosing the appropriate asset or expense account to replace the default linked account. Enter negative quantities because the inventory stock is reduced. Because the store has become the final customer – it has bought the items from itself – it is responsible for reporting the purchase and paying PST on the cost price of these internal sales.

NOTES

Pressing (ctrl) + J will also open the journal display.

NOTES

The second Inventory Ledger linked account is used for item assembly costs in the Item Assembly Journal. Item assembly is introduced in the next transaction.

CORRECTING THE ADJUSTMENTS JOURNAL ENTRY

Move to the field that has the error. **Press** *tab* to move forward or **press** *shift* and *tab* together to move back to a previous field. This will highlight the field information so you can change it. **Type** the **correct information** and **press** *tab* to enter it.

You can also use the mouse to **point** to a field and **drag** through the **incorrect information** to highlight it. **Type** the **correct information** and **press** *tab* to enter it.

If the inventory item is incorrect, **reselect** from the **inventory** list by **pressing** *enter* while in this field. **Click Select** to add it to the form. **Type** the **quantity** and **press** *tab*. After changing any information on an inventory item line, **press** *tab* to update the totals.

To start over, **click** [X] or [↶] (or **choose** the **Edit menu** and **click Undo Entry**). **Click Yes** when asked to confirm that you want to discard the transaction.

Posting

When all the information in your journal entry is correct, you must save the transaction.

Click **Post** [Post].

Close the **Adjustments Journal** to return to the Home window. The next keystroke transaction is an assembly of new inventory items.

Adding a New Inventory Item

Before entering the next assembly transaction, we will add the new inventory item. Refer to Memo #2 for the inventory item details. Inventory items can be added from any inventory item field in a journal, from the Inventory module window or from the Inventory & Services icon in the Home window as shown:

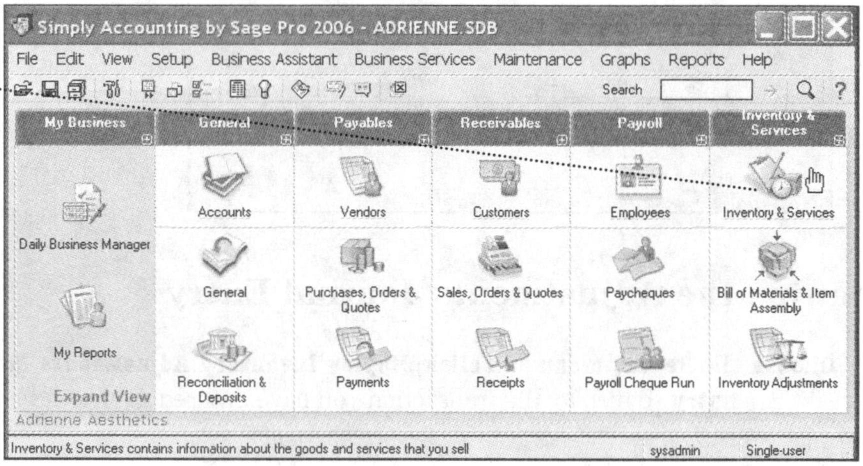

basic **BASIC VERSION**

The Inventory & Services icon is shown here. It does not include the clock.

NOTES

You can add inventory items from any journal inventory field when the selection list is available, that is, in the Sales and Purchases journals and the two inventory journals, Adjustments and Item Assembly. Click the List icon in the Item field to open the selection list. Click Add to open the Inventory Ledger window.

Click the **Inventory & Services icon** to open the Inventory & Services window:

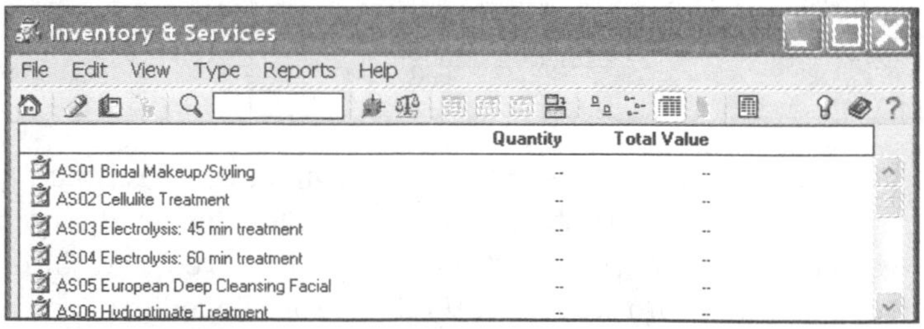

This window is like the Accounts, Vendors, Customers and Employees windows in other modules and it lists all inventory items and services.

Click the **Create tool**, **choose** the **File menu** and **click Create** or **press** *ctrl* + **N** to open the the Inventory Ledger:

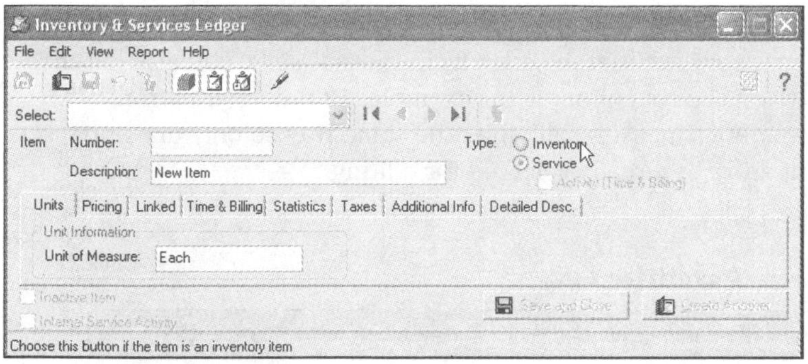

basic **BASIC VERSION**

The Time & Billing tab and function are not available in the Basic version.

The Basic version has only two Show tools – one for inventory items and one for service items. The Refresh tool is also not on the Basic version tool bar.

The Inventory & Services Ledger record has many of the tools that are available in other ledgers, including the Refresh tool. The Show tool icons allow you to limit the Select field list to inventory items, services or activities (for time and billing). If all three tools are selected, the list includes all three kinds of items. All Show tools are selected for Adrienne Aesthetics so all records are included in the Select list.

When you enter a service item, you can designate it as an activity with time and billing information attached. Activities are available for the time and billing features and for selection as internal services — services that are provided by one department to another within the company and can be tracked as expenses. The Time and Billing function is not available in the Basic version. It will be covered in Chapter 17.

NOTES

As in other ledgers and journals, the Refresh tool applies when you work in multi-user mode. Clicking the tool will update the record with changes made by other users who are accessing the data file at the same time.

The Inventory Ledger is set for the entry of services because the last item entered was a service. The gift packages are inventory rather than services.

Click **Inventory** in the Type section of the ledger to change the form:

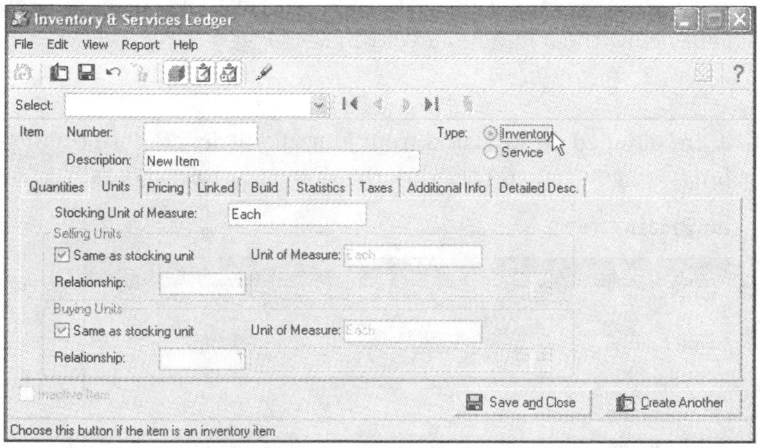

basic **BASIC VERSION**

The Basic version does not have the Build tab. It applies to the Build From Bill Of Materials option we saw in the Bill of Materials & Item Assembly Journal. This feature is not available in Basic.

The fields needed for inventory items are added to the Ledger window. The Units tab information is still displayed because it is the first tab screen for Services and it remains selected.

The setup option we selected for inventory sorts the items by code or number. Therefore, the Number field is the first item field. When you choose to sort by description, the longer Description field will come first. (See Chapter 15, page 596.)

From your source document information, you must enter the item code and description. The first Item field contains the code or number of the inventory item; the second Item field contains the description or item name.

Click the **Item Number field**.

Type `VP01` **Press** *tab* to advance to the Item Description field.

Type `Valentine Gift: super pkg` **Press** *tab* **twice**.

We have already selected the type as inventory, so we want to advance to the Units field. Units show the way in which goods are stored, bought and sold (e.g., by the dozen, by the tonne or by the item). These units may be different if, for example, merchandise is purchased in bulk packages and sold in individual units. When a store buys or stocks inventory in different units from those it sells, you also enter the relationship between the sets of units, for example, 12 units per carton.

Adrienne Aesthetics measures all units the same way so only one entry is needed. Each, the default entry, is already selected for editing.

Type pkg

Click the **Quantities tab**:

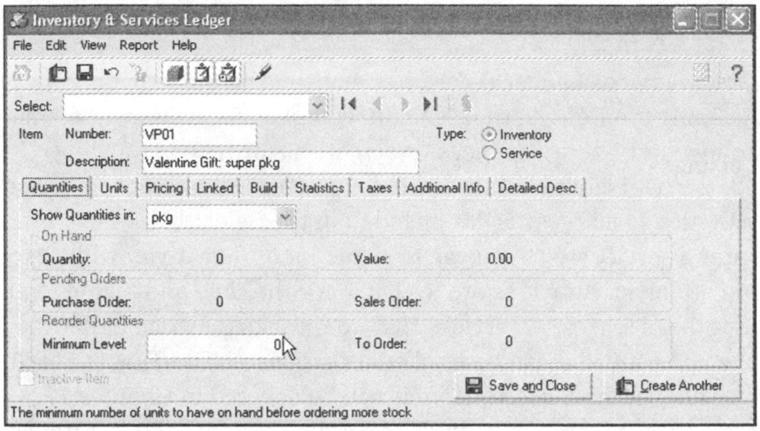

Click the **Minimum Level field** in the Reorder Quantities section.

Here you must enter the stock level at which you want to reorder the item in question, or in this case, assemble more packages. When you print inventory reports, items that have fallen below the minimum level will be flagged.

Type 1

The fields that are dimmed are updated from journal entries. Before the Inventory Ledger history is finished, you can add this information as historical data.

Click the **Pricing tab**:

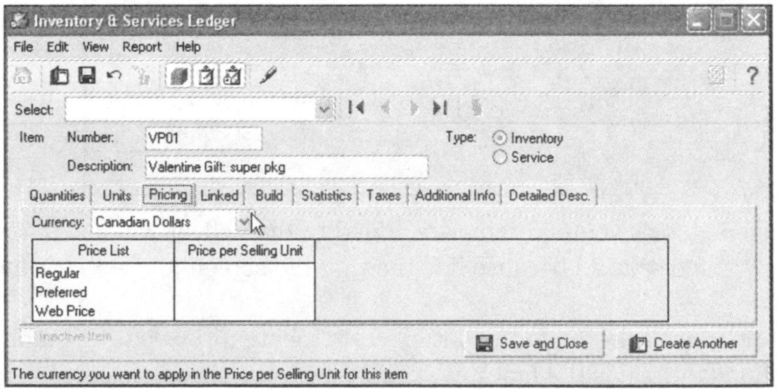

Each item may be assigned a regular price, a preferred selling price for customers who should be given discounted prices and a Web price. Adrienne Aesthetics has two customers with preferred customer status. Regular and preferred selling prices can also be entered for foreign customers in the foreign currencies. Gift packages do not have preferred prices. Web prices can also be added for each currency. Canadian Currency price fields are displayed first — Canadian Dollars is selected in the Currency field.

NOTES

The Pro version allows you to create additional price lists. The Basic version does not include this feature.

NOTES

In the settings for the Inventory Ledger, you have the option of taking foreign currency prices from the ledger or from the exchange rate. If prices are based on the exchange rate, the foreign currency price fields are not included in the Pricing tab screen.

Click the **Price Per Selling Unit column** beside Regular.

Type `100` **Press** (tab).

The regular price is entered as the default Preferred and Web Price. These defaults are correct — there are no preferred customer prices for the gift packages. We can continue to enter the prices in euros.

Choose **Euro** from the Currency list as shown:

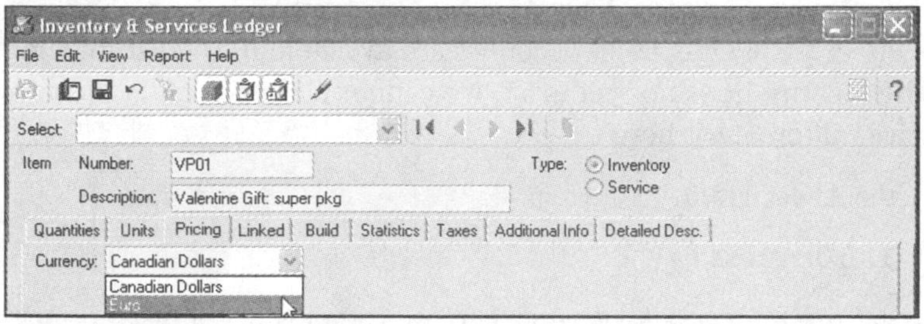

The screen changes to display the input fields for foreign currency prices:

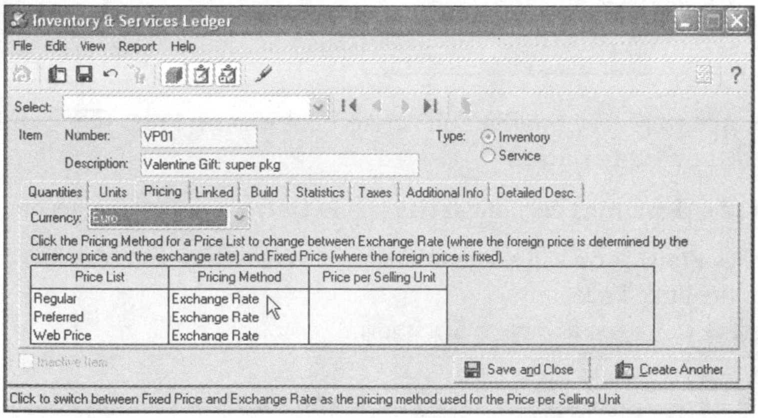

Foreign prices for inventory items may be based on the exchange rate at the time of the sale or on the price and method defined in the ledger record. The default ledger selection calculates the prices based on the exchange rate. We need to change this setting to make the Price field available so we can enter a price.

Click **Exchange Rate** beside Regular. The setting changes to Fixed Price.

Press (tab) to advance to the Price Per Selling Unit field.

Type `75` **Press** (tab) to advance to the Pricing Method for Preferred Prices.

Click **Exchange Rate** to change the setting to Fixed Price. **Press** (tab).

Type `75`

Click the **Linked tab** to access the linked accounts for the inventory item:

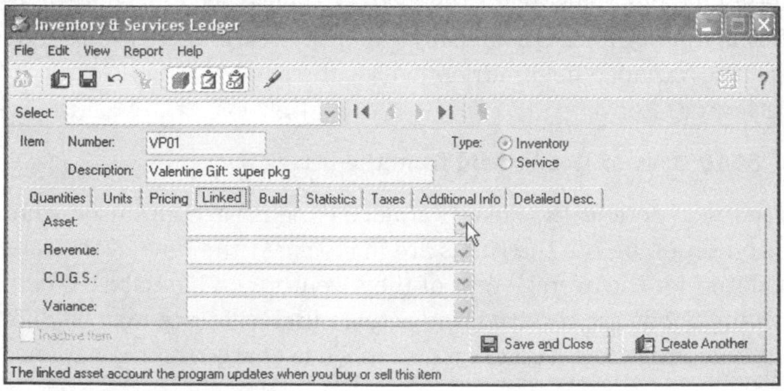

NOTES

If you select the Inventory Ledger setting to take prices from the exchange rate, you will not see this screen.

NOTES

When you take the foreign prices from the Inventory Ledger record, you can select the fixed price or exchange rate method on an item-by-item basis. You can also choose different methods for different price lists for each item.

NOTES

You can also change the Pricing Method setting by pressing the space bar when the cursor is on Exchange Rate.

NOTES
For other ledgers, the linked accounts are defined for the entire ledger. For example, there is only one Accounts Receivable account.

There are two sets of linked accounts for inventory, those that apply to the entire ledger — the default accounts for inventory adjustments and item assembly costs — and those that apply to specific inventory items. The ones in the ledger are item specific and are used as the default accounts whenever inventory items are sold or purchased. Linked accounts are defined for each item in the Inventory Ledger because each inventory item can be related to separate asset, revenue, expense and variance accounts.

In the **Asset** field, you must enter the number of the linked asset account affected by purchases and sales of this item. A list of accounts is available from the drop-down list arrow in the Asset field. Only asset accounts are available in the list for the Asset field. Because the account does not yet exist, we cannot choose it from the account list for the field, so we will create it here.

Click the **Asset field**.

Type `1350` **Press** tab.

You will see the screen that allows you to create the new account:

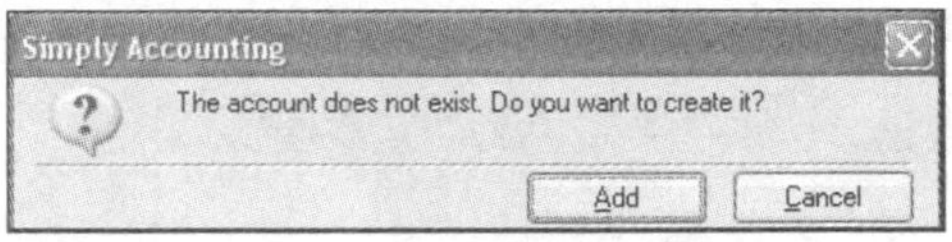

Click **Add** to proceed to the Add An Account wizard. **Press** tab and **type** `Gift Packages`

Accept the **remaining** account **settings** and **finish** creating the account.

After you click Finish, you will see another message advising you of an account class change for the linked account:

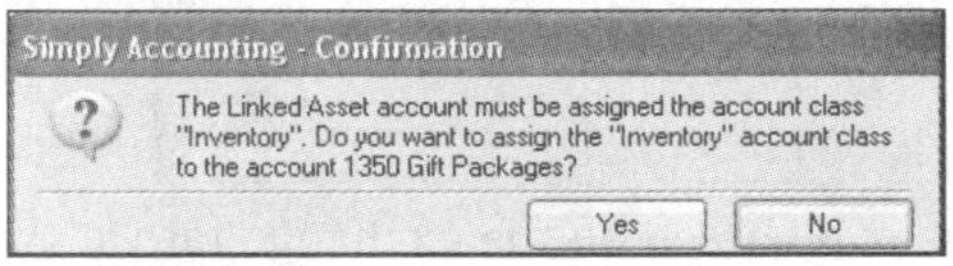

Simply Accounting - Confirmation
The Linked Asset account must be assigned the account class "Inventory". Do you want to assign the "Inventory" account class to the account 1350 Gift Packages?
Yes
No

Click **Yes** to accept the change. Clicking No will return you to the Linked Accounts screen so you can select a different account.

NOTES
If necessary, you can create new linked revenue and expense accounts in the same way you created the new asset account.

In the **Revenue** field, you must enter the linked revenue account that will be credited when this inventory item is sold. You can type the account number or select from the list. Only revenue accounts are available for the Revenue field.

Click the **Revenue field list arrow** to see the revenue accounts available.

Click **4020 Revenue from Sales** to enter it on your form.

Click the **C.O.G.S. field list arrow** (Cost of Goods Sold expense) to see the expense accounts available.

WARNING!
Check the linked account numbers carefully. If they are incorrect, corresponding journal entries will be posted incorrectly. If you discover the error when you are reviewing the journal entry, you should delete the journal entry line and then edit the Inventory Ledger record before posting.

In the **C.O.G.S.** field, you must enter the linked expense account that will be debited when this inventory item is sold. Only expense accounts are available for the C.O.G.S. field and the Variance field. Adrienne uses the single *Cost of Goods Sold* account for all inventory items.

Click **5060 Cost of Goods Sold** from the list.

The **Variance** field contains the linked variance expense account used when the inventory sold is on order, before the goods are in stock. At the time of the sale, *Cost of Goods Sold* is debited for the average cost of the inventory on hand, based on previous purchases. When the goods are received, the actual purchase price may be different from this historical average cost. The price difference is charged to the variance account. Adrienne Aesthetics does not allow inventory to be oversold so you can leave the Variance account field blank.

NOTES
Variance accounts are used in the Truman Tires application.

basic BASIC VERSION
Skip the Build tab screen. Click the Statistics tab at this stage.
The Basic version does not have a Build tab because this screen applies to Build From Bill Of Materials, a function not available in Basic.

Click the **Build tab**:

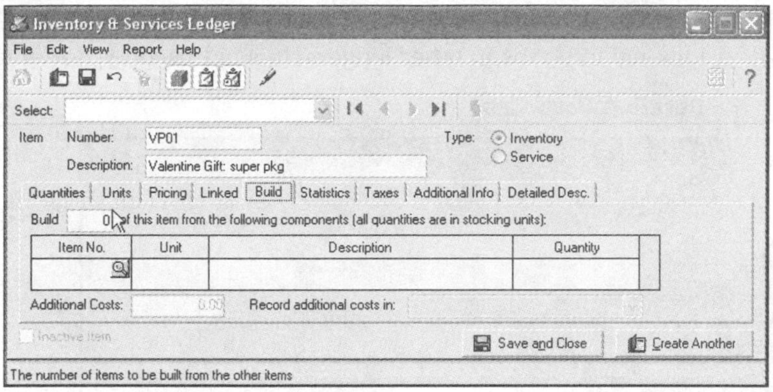

On the Build tab screen, you enter the inventory components that are needed to make the item. You identify the number of items you are building at one time and the required component items. This process is similar to the one found in the Components section of the Item Assembly Journal (see page 428). When it is time to build the item (in the Bill of Materials & Item Assembly Journal), you indicate how may items you are building and the rest of the details are taken from the Build screen of the ledger record. We will use the Build feature in Chapter 17.

NOTES
You can define multiple levels of building – one item may be made from other items that in turn are made from multiple inventory items.

Click the **Statistics tab**.

This screen applies to historical data. Since this is a new inventory item, there are no previous sales, and you should leave all entries at zero. The **Date Of Last Sale** shows the most recent date that this item was sold. The **Year To Date** section refers to historical information for the current fiscal period, and the **Last Year** fields apply to the previous year because Simply Accounting stores two years of transactions. Inventory Statistics are added to inventory tracking reports.

NOTES
You can enter the historical dates using any of the usual date formats.
Simply Accounting continually updates the Statistics tab fields from journal entries.

The **No. (number) Of Transactions** refers to the total number of times the item was sold. For example, if one customer bought the item on three separate dates, there would be three transactions. If four customers bought the item on one day, there would be four transactions. If one customer bought four of the same item at one time, there would be one transaction. The **Units Sold** counts the total number of items that were sold on all occasions to all customers in the relevant period. In the **Amount Sold** field you would enter the total sale price of all items sold in the period, and in the **Cost Of Goods Sold** field, you would enter the total purchase price of all items sold.

Click the **Taxes tab**:

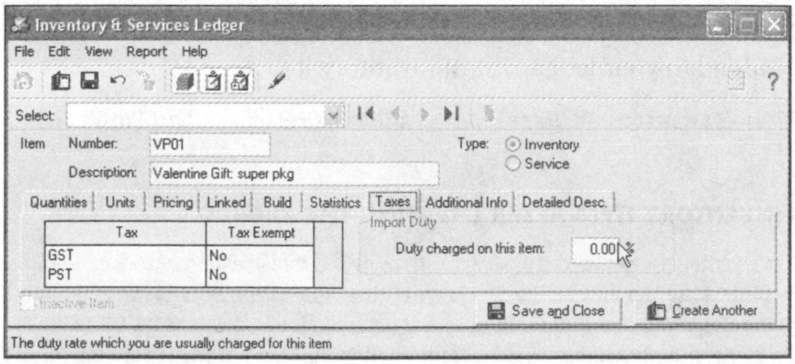

All taxes set up for the company will appear on this screen. PST and GST may be charged or omitted by default. Because most goods have these taxes applied to the sale, the default is to charge them. The **Tax Exempt** entry is a toggle switch. Clicking the current entry changes it. The default settings are correct. The services provided by Adrienne Aesthetics were designated as tax exempt for PST.

Since the gift packages cannot be imported directly, the duty field does not apply. When duty is charged for an item, enter the tax rate in the **Duty** field.

The **Additional Info** tab allows for custom-defined information fields relating to the item, just like the Additional Info tabs in other ledgers. It is not used by Adrienne.

Click the **Detailed Desc. tab**:

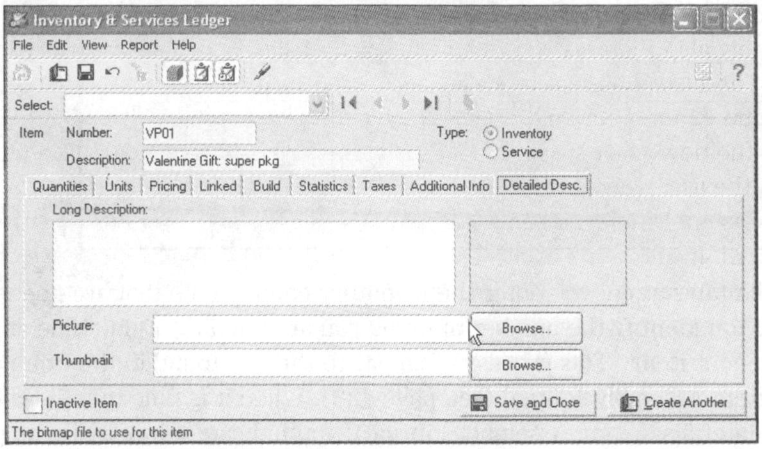

On this screen you can enter a detailed description of the inventory item and the name of a file where an image of the item is stored. The bitmap file for this item is located in the Setup\Logos folder in the Data folder that has your other data files.

Click **Browse** beside the Picture field to open the file location window.

Click the **Up One Level tool** to access the Data folder.

Double click **Setup** and then **double click Logos** to open these folders.

Double click **VP01** (or **VP01.bmp**) to add the image and file name.

CORRECTING THE INVENTORY ITEM BEFORE CREATING THE RECORD

Correct the information if necessary by **clicking** the field that contains the **error**. **Click** the appropriate **tab** to change information screens if necessary. **Highlight** the **error** and **type** the **correct information**. **Press** tab to enter the correction.

When all the information is correct, you must save your information.

Click **Create Another** to save the new record. The ledger remains open so you can add the second new item.

Enter all the details for item **VP02**.

Click **Save And Close** to save the new record. Both items are added to your ledger list of inventory items.

Close the **Inventory & Services window** to return to the Home window.

EDITING AN INVENTORY ITEM AFTER CREATING THE RECORD

You cannot edit an Inventory Ledger record while you are using the item in a journal so you must first **delete** the **journal line containing the item**. **Click** the **journal line**, **choose** the **Edit menu** and **click Remove Line**. Then **click** the **Home window tool** in the journal to return to the Home window. **Click** the **Inventory & Services icon** to open the Inventory window. **Double click** the name of the **inventory item** that you need to change to open the item's ledger record. **Click** the **tab** you need. **Highlight** the **information** that is incorrect, and then **type** the **correct information**. **Close** the **Ledger window** and then **close** the **Inventory & Services window**. **Click Minimize** to minimize the Home window and return to the journal.

Assembling Inventory Items

Inventory item assembly can be used to build new inventory from other inventory items, to create package offers of two or more regular items for sale at a special price or to reserve inventory for a special project or contract. The new inventory item, the special package, is priced at the sale price, and the cost is the sum of the original component costs. Adrienne Aesthetics uses the inventory Bill of Materials & Item Assembly Journal in Simply Accounting to create the special Valentine's Day gift packages.

The assembly also requires you to add the gift packages as new inventory items to the current list and to add a new asset account. This is described in the source document, Memo #2, on February 3. We will add the new inventory items, the gift packages, and the new asset account, *1350 Gift Packages*, directly from the journal while entering the assembly transaction.

Inventory assemblies or transfers are completed in the Bill of Materials & Item Assembly Journal. In the Basic version, we use the Item Assembly Journal.

The Bill of Materials & Item Assembly Journal is show with the pointer:

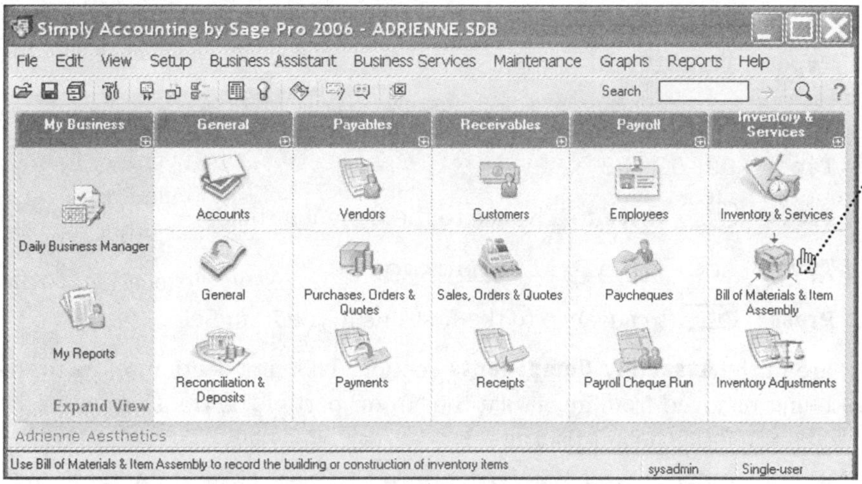

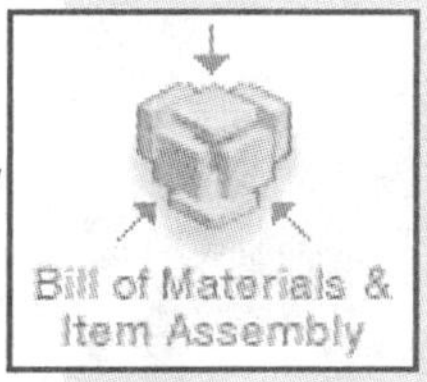

NOTES
We will use the name Item Assembly Journal to refer to the Bill of Materials & Item Assembly Journal.

Click the **Bill of Materials & Item Assembly icon** to open the Journal:

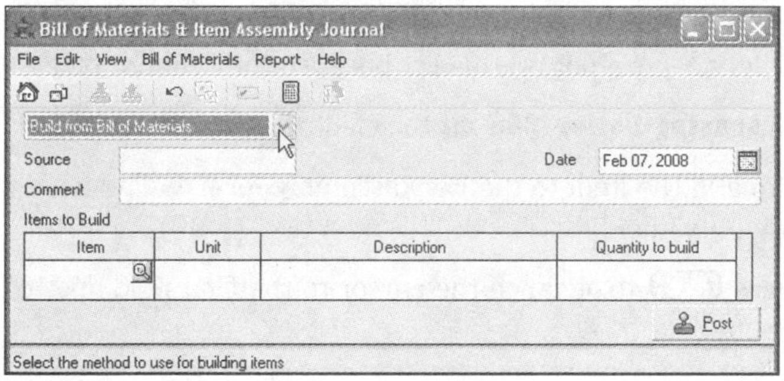

basic BASIC VERSION
Click the Item Assembly Journal icon shown here to open the Item Assembly Journal.

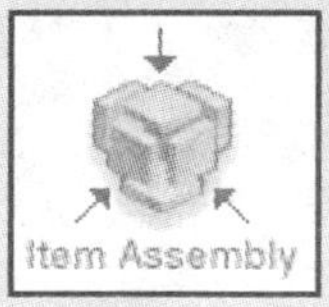

There are two ways to assemble items in the Pro version of Simply Accounting: Item Assembly or Build From The Bill Of Materials defined in the ledger on the Build tab screen (see page 425). The build method will be covered in Chapter 17. We will use the Item Assembly method now.

Click **Build From Bill Of Materials** to see the alternative methods:

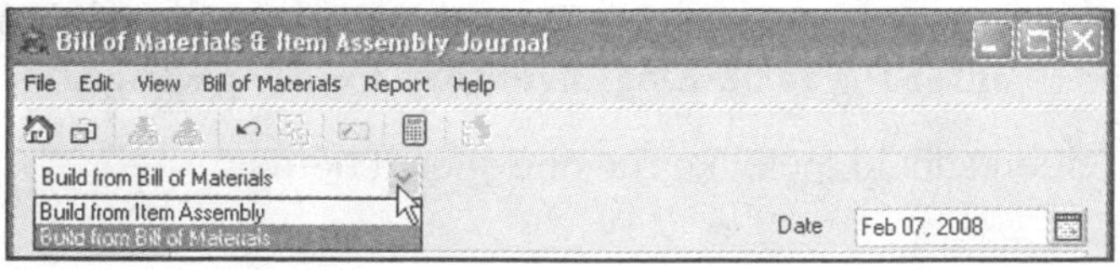

basic BASIC VERSION
You will skip this step in the Basic version. When you click the Item Assembly icon, the journal you need will open because it is the only one available.

The cursor will be in the Source field.

Click **Build From Item Assembly** to modify the journal:

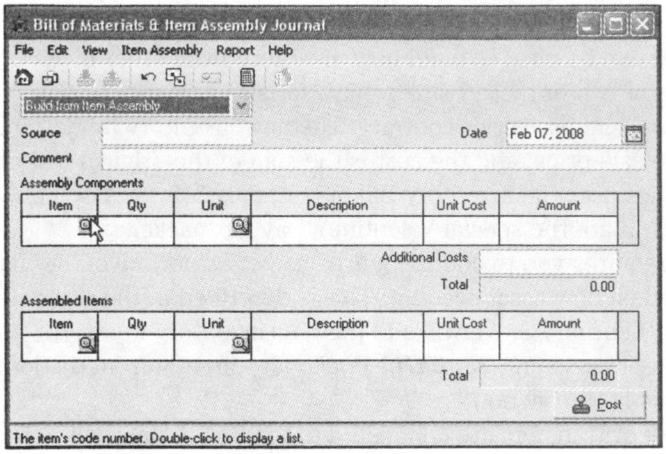

Press `tab` to place the cursor in the Source field, where you should enter the invoice number.

Type `ItA-1`

Press `tab` to advance to the Date field. Enter the date of the transfer.

Type `02-03-08`

Press `tab` **twice** to advance to the Comment field.

Type `Assemble gift packages`

Press `tab` to advance to the first line in the Item field.

You are in the **Assembly Components** section. This first section refers to the items that are being removed from inventory, the "from" part of the transfer or assembly. These items will form the gift package.

Press `enter` or **click** the **List icon** to display the familiar inventory selection list.

Notice that you can add new inventory items from the Select Inventory list in the Item Assembly Journal. Services are not on this list because they cannot be assembled.

Click **CL01 Cleansing Lotion 225 ml** to select the first item needed.

Click **Select** to add the item to the item assembly form and advance to the Quantity (Qty) field.

Type `10` **Press** `tab` to advance the cursor to the Unit field and to update the amount.

> **NOTES**
> The unit cost may be different when the cost of transferred items is lower than the default because older stock is being transferred and it was purchased at a lower price. If you change the unit cost, press `tab` to update the amount.

The unit cost is correct but can be edited if necessary. The unit cost may be incorrect if inventory was purchased at different prices over time.

Drag the **lower frame of the journal window** to have more input lines on the screen and see your entire entry on the screen at once.

Click the **next line** in the Item column.

Select the next **inventory item** to be transferred, **enter** the **quantity** and then continue to **enter** the **remaining inventory** for the package.

At this stage, your screen should look like the one shown here:

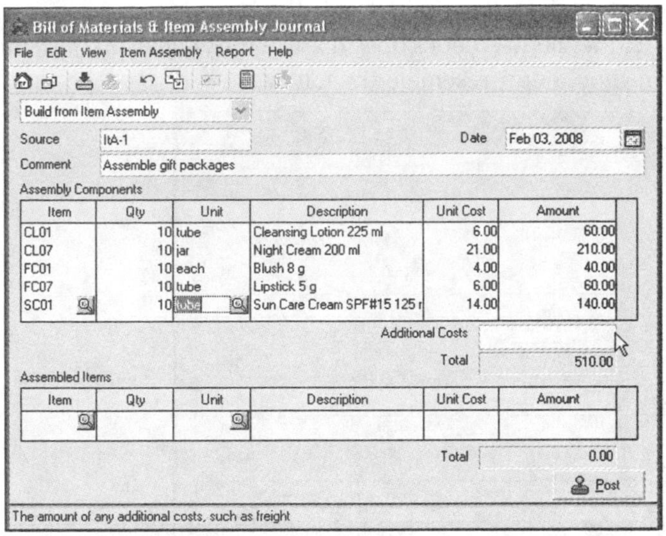

The middle part of the item assembly form contains two fields, Additional Costs and Total. **Additional costs** may come from shipping or packaging involved with assembling, moving or transferring the inventory. Services involved in the package may also be entered as additional costs. The extra costs for all items transferred should be entered into the Additional Costs field. The **Total** is calculated automatically by Simply Accounting to include the individual costs of all items transferred or assembled plus any additional costs. Adrienne Aesthetics has additional costs of $50 ($5 per package) for additional wrapping and boxes.

Click the **Additional Costs field**.

Type 50 **Press** *tab* to update the total.

The cursor advances to the first line in the Item column of the **Assembled Items** section. This section refers to the new or reserved inventory, the item being assembled or the "to" part of the transfer.

Press *enter* or **click** the **List icon** to display the familiar inventory selection list.

Click **VP01 Valentine Gift: super pkg** to select the item we created.

Click **Select** or **press** *enter* to add the item to the item assembly form and advance to the Quantity (Qty) field.

Type 10

The unit cost of the assembled items is the total cost of the assembly components, plus additional costs, divided by the quantity or number of units assembled. When a single type of item is assembled and the quantity is greater than one, it is simpler to enter the quantity and the amount (the Total in the assembly components portion in the top half of the form) and let Simply Accounting calculate the unit cost. You can also enter the individual item cost in the Unit Cost field and allow the program to calculate the Amount (Qty times Unit Cost). We will enter the total from the upper portion of the journal.

Click the **Amount field**.

Type 560 **Press** *tab* to enter the cost and update the unit cost and total. The cursor moves to the Item field on the next line.

The totals in the two parts of the assembly form should be the same. If they are not, you will be unable to post the entry.

NOTES

Because the two totals must be the same, entering the total cost and allowing the program to determine the unit cost ensures this balance.

The additional information fields are available for the Item Assembly Journal as they are for all other journals. Adrienne Aesthetics does not use these fields in this journal.

Your completed form should now resemble the following:

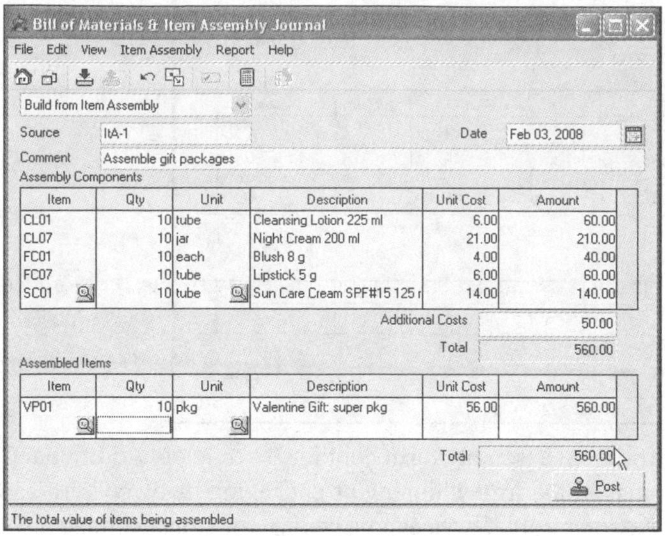

Reviewing the Item Assembly Journal Entry

basic BASIC VERSION

In Basic, you will choose the Report menu and then click Display Item Assembly Journal Entry to see the transaction.

NOTES

Pressing ctrl + J will also open the journal display.

Choose the **Report menu**, then **click Display Bill Of Materials & Item Assembly Journal Entry** to display the transaction you have entered:

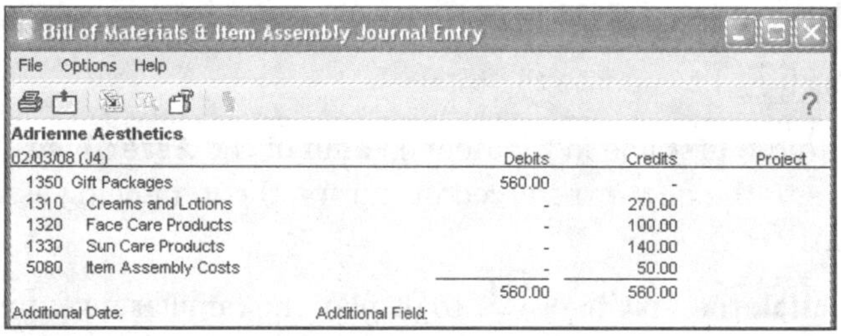

Notice that Simply Accounting has moved the inventory items from their original asset accounts to the newly created inventory account. When you display inventory selection lists or quantity reports, you will see that the quantities for all items involved have been updated. The necessary items are taken out of their regular individual item inventory account and transferred to the new account. Thus the quantities of the original items are reduced because they have been transferred to the new account.

The Additional Costs are assigned to *Item Assembly Costs*, the linked account defined for these costs. This is a contra-expense account because it adds to the inventory value of the assembled inventory asset.

Close the **display** to return to the Item Assembly Journal input screen.

CORRECTING THE ITEM ASSEMBLY JOURNAL ENTRY

Move to the field that has the error. **Press** tab to move forward through the fields or **press** shift and tab together to move back to a previous field. This will highlight the field information so you can change it. **Type** the **correct information** and **press** tab to enter it. You must advance the cursor to the next invoice field to enter a change.

You can also use the mouse to **point** to a field and **drag** through the **incorrect information** to highlight it. **Type** the **correct information** and **press** tab to enter it.

If an inventory item is incorrect, **press** enter while the cursor is in the Item field to **display** the appropriate **list. Double click** the **correct inventory item. Re-enter** the **quantity** and **press** tab to update the totals.

Because the item assembly is a complex transaction, it is very easy to make a mistake, so check your work carefully. You may also want to store the original entry. If you discover later that you have made an error, you can recall the entry and add a minus sign to each quantity and to the Additional Costs amount to create a reversing entry.

Click the **Store button** to display the familiar Store Recurring Transaction screen:

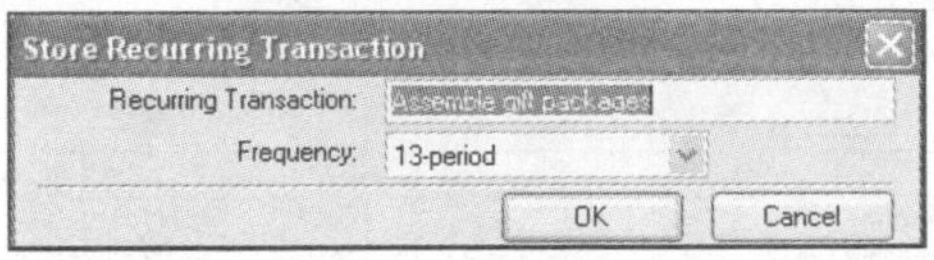

WARNING!

When you recall an Item Assembly transaction, the unit costs and amounts for assembly components may be different from the original entry. The average cost may have changed since you posted the entry if you purchased new components at different prices. The new average cost price will be displayed. The quantities will be correct.

Because this is not a regular recurring transaction, we will use the Random frequency. Choosing the Random frequency for recurring entries enters the session date as the default transaction date when you recall the journal entry.

Click **13-Period** to display the Frequency options.

Click **Random** to select this frequency.

Click **OK** to save the entry and return to the Item Assembly Journal. Notice that the Recall button is now active.

Posting

When you are certain that you have entered all the information correctly,

Click **Post**. **Enter** the next **assembly transaction** and **purchase invoice adjustment**.

Selling to Preferred Customers

NOTES

Customers may also be identified as using Web prices or another user-defined price list.

Simply Accounting allows you to record different inventory prices and to identify customers by the prices they will pay (preferred or regular). Sales for both groups of customers are entered the same way since the program automatically enters the correct price depending on the customer selected. Valley TV is a preferred customer.

Click the **Sales Journal icon** (Sales, Orders & Quotes) to open the Sales Journal.

Invoice and Pay Later are the correct selections for this sale to Valley TV. The Invoice number is also correct by default.

Choose **Valley TV (CKOV)** from the customer list.

Enter **Feb. 4** in the Date field.

Double click the **Item field** to see the inventory list.

Scroll down and then **double click** **CL03 Eye Contour Smoothing Cream 30 ml** to add it and advance to the Quantity field.

This adds the first item sold to the customer at the preferred customer price of $32.00 instead of $35.00, the regular price.

Type 5 **Press** (tab).

Enter the **remaining items** sold to this customer.

Choose **Hydra** as the salesperson in the Sold By field.

This completes the journal entry as shown:

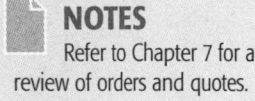

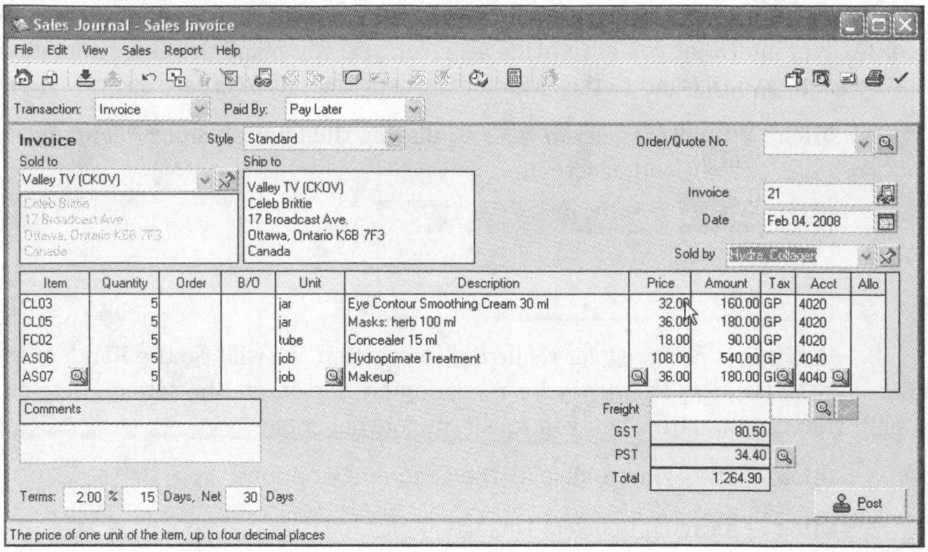

You should review the entry as usual.

Choose the **Report menu** and **click Display Sales Journal Entry**:

Adrienne Aesthetics

02/04/08 (J8)	Debits	Credits	Project
1200 Accounts Receivable	1,264.90	-	
5060 Cost of Goods Sold	210.00	-	
1310 Creams and Lotions	-	170.00	
1320 Face Care Products	-	40.00	
2640 PST Payable	-	34.40	
2650 GST Charged on Sales	-	80.50	
4020 Revenue from Sales	-	430.00	
4040 Revenue from Services	-	720.00	
	1,474.90	1,474.90	

This entry is the same as a regular non-discounted sale. Revenue is reduced because of the change in selling price but this change is not recorded as a discount.

Close the **display** when finished and **make corrections** if necessary.

Post the **entry** and **close** the **Sales Journal**.

Continue with the **journal entries** up to the sales return on February 8.

Orders and Quotes

NOTES
Refer to Chapter 7 for a review of orders and quotes.

NOTES
You can choose Purchase Order or Quote as the type from the transaction list in the journal or you can open the Payables Module and click the Purchase Orders or the Quotes icon.

NOTES
You can choose Sales Order or Quote as the type from the transaction list in the journal or you can open the Receivables Module and click the Sales Orders or the Quotes icon.

Placing a purchase order or quote for inventory items is the same as entering a purchase order or quote for non-inventory items.

Open the Purchases Journal. Choose Purchase Order as the Transaction Type.

Choose the vendor from the Vendor list.

Enter the Order or Quote Number and Shipping Date. Sales quote and purchase order numbers are updated automatically.

Then complete the selection of inventory items as you would for an inventory purchase. Instead of filling in the Quantity field, however, you will complete the Order and B/O fields. As soon as you enter the item, the cursor moves to the Order field instead of the Quantity field.

When the goods are received, fill the purchase order/quote.

Enter and fill sales orders and quotes for inventory items in the same way as non-inventory items, except, of course, for the addition of inventory item details.

Entering Sales Returns

Customers may return purchases for many different reasons. The size, colour or quality may have been other than expected. Stores have different policies with respect to accepting and refunding returns. Most stores place reasonable time limits on the period in which they will give refunds. Some stores offer credit only and some charge a handling fee on goods returned. Adrienne Aesthetics will provide full refunds for purchases within two weeks of the sale if the items have not been opened. Sales returns are entered in the Sales Journal and are very similar to sales. Only the quantity is entered differently. A minus sign is added — a negative quantity is sold.

Open the **Sales Journal** if it is not open from the previous transactions.

Invoice is the correct selection for this sale returned by a Visa customer. The return must use the same customer and payment method as the original sale.

Choose **Visa** from the Paid By list.

Choose **Cash Customers** from the Customer list.

You should use a different invoice number so that the return can be differentiated from a normal sale. Most stores have separate forms for returns with their own separate number sequences.

Click the **Invoice field** and **type** 22-R

Enter **Feb. 8** in the Date field if this is not the date shown already.

Enter **Blossom** as the salesperson.

Double click the **Item field** to see the inventory list.

Scroll down and **double click** **CL08 Protection Cream: dbl action 60 ml** to enter it and move the cursor to the Quantity field.

This adds the first item returned by the customer at the regular price.

Type -1 **Press** tab.

Notice that a positive amount appears in the Price field and a negative amount is added to the Amount field — a positive price times the negative quantity. We should also change the default account so that returns can be tracked separately.

Click the **Account field List icon** and **choose** **4050 Sales Returns**.

Enter the **second item** returned by this customer. Your finished journal entry should look like the following one:

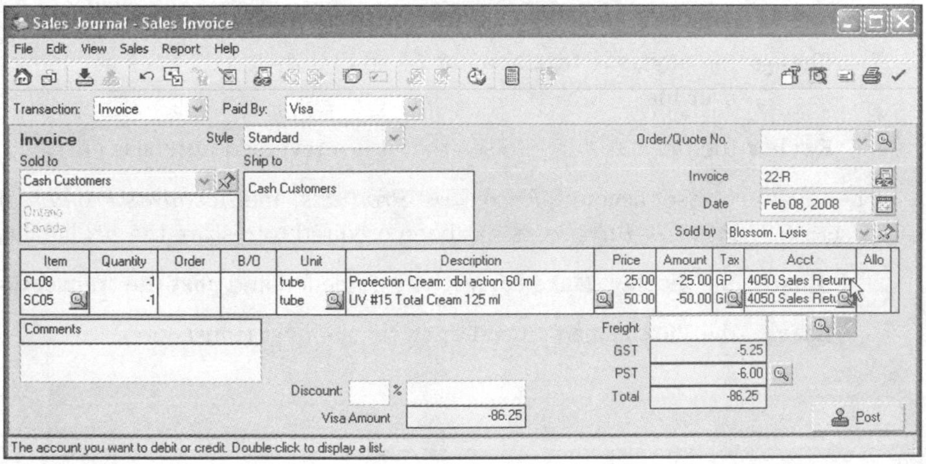

NOTES

The salesperson should be entered for sales returns because commissions are calculated on total sales less returns.

Choose the **Report menu** and **click Display Sales Journal Entry** to review the entry as usual.

Adrienne Aesthetics
02/08/08 (J22)

	Debits	Credits	Project
1310 Creams and Lotions	12.00	-	
1330 Sun Care Products	22.00	-	
2640 PST Payable	6.00	-	
2650 GST Charged on Sales	5.25	-	
4050 Sales Returns	75.00	-	
1090 Bank Account: Credit Cards	-	83.88	
5040 Credit Card Fees	-	2.37	
5060 Cost of Goods Sold	-	34.00	
	120.25	120.25	

Notice that the entry is the reversal of a regular sale. The two asset accounts are debited because inventory is added back. *Sales Returns* — a contra-revenue account — is debited, and *Bank Account: Credit Cards* is credited because money has been returned to the customer's credit card account. Similarly, *PST Payable* and *GST Charged on Sales* are debited because the tax liabilities have decreased and finally, the expense accounts, *Credit Card Fees* and *Cost of Goods Sold* are credited because expenses have gone down.

Close the **display** when finished to return to the journal. **Make corrections** if necessary.

In the Comment field, you could add the reason for the return. The customer's name and address could be added to the Ship To field or the Comment field.

Post the **entry** and **close** the **Sales Journal**.

Entering Purchase Returns

Purchase returns are entered in the same way as sales returns — by adding a minus sign to the quantity so that all the amounts become negative. The vendor and payment method must be the same as the original purchase.

Click the **Purchases Journal icon** 

. Invoice and Pay Later are correct.

Choose **Biotech Laboratories** as the vendor.

Enter **BL-669R** as the invoice number and **Feb. 8** as the date.

Choose **FC10 Powder: loose 15 g** from the inventory selection list and advance to the Quantity field.

Type –5 (the quantity with a minus sign).

You cannot change the default asset account for inventory purchases.

Change the **payment terms** to **net 60** so that the credit does not show as overdue.

Review the **journal entry** to see that it is a reversed purchase entry.

The inventory asset account, *Face Care Products*, and *Accounts Payable* have decreased. *GST Paid on Purchases* has been credited to restore the tax liability.

Close the **display**. **Make corrections** if needed and **post** the **transaction**.

Leave the **Purchases Journal open** for the next transaction.

Entering Import Duties on Purchases

Governments may apply import duties to encourage the local economy by raising the price of imported goods. Duty rates or tariffs vary from one type of item to another. The duty is collected by Canada Revenue Agency when the goods enter Canada before they are released to the buyer.

In Simply Accounting, before you can enter duty amounts with the purchase, you must set up the company files for charging and tracking import duties. You must also indicate in the foreign vendor's record that duty is applied to purchases from that vendor. In the Inventory Ledger records, you can enter the duty applied as a percentage, or you can enter the rates in the Purchases Journal. For non-inventory purchases, you must enter the rate directly in the Purchases Journal.

The purchase invoice from Esthetica has import duties applied because Canada does not have a free trade agreement with France. The company settings and the Vendor and Inventory Ledger records for Adrienne Aesthetics are set up to apply duties.

Choose **Esthetica Incorporated** from the list of vendors. **Press** tab.

Scroll to the **right** to see the additional columns for duty, or **drag** the **right-hand side of the invoice frame** or **click** ☐ to maximize the journal:

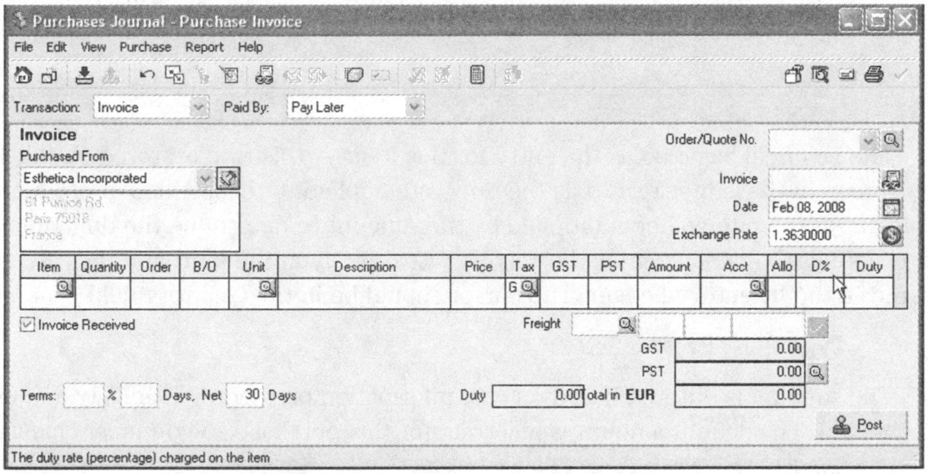

In addition to the Exchange Rate field and the indication that euro (EUR) is the currency for this vendor, the duty fields are not removed because we selected a foreign vendor. The fields are used for the duty percentage and for the duty amount. Duty is charged on all items purchased from Esthetica.

Click the **Invoice field** and **type** `EI-933`

Enter **Feb. 9** in the Date field and **press** tab to open the Exchange Rate screen with the most recent rate highlighted.

Type `1.365` **Click Make This The Default Rate For Feb 09, 2008.**

Click **OK** to return to the journal.

Click the **Description field**.

Type `manicure and pedicure products`

Click the **Amount field**.

Type `80` **Press** tab to advance to the Account field.

Choose **1380 Miscellaneous Inventory Products** from the Account list.

NOTES

GST on imported goods is also collected by CRA at the same time as the import duties. This transaction would require a separate journal entry to record the GST paid (a purchase from the Receiver General for the amount of the GST paid) and then a cash payment to CRA. To reduce the complexity of the transactions, we indicate that the foreign vendors collect the GST.

basic BASIC VERSION

You will not see the Duty columns until you select a foreign vendor.

NOTES

If no duty is charged, you can leave the duty fields blank.

The cursor advances to the D% (duty rate) field where you should enter the rate that the government applies to this type of product.

Type 6.5 **Press** *tab* to enter the duty amount.

Press *tab* again to advance to the next line in the Item field. You can now add the inventory item purchases.

Double click the **Item field** to open the Inventory Selection screen.

Double click **FC02 Concealer 15 ml** to add this item to the invoice:

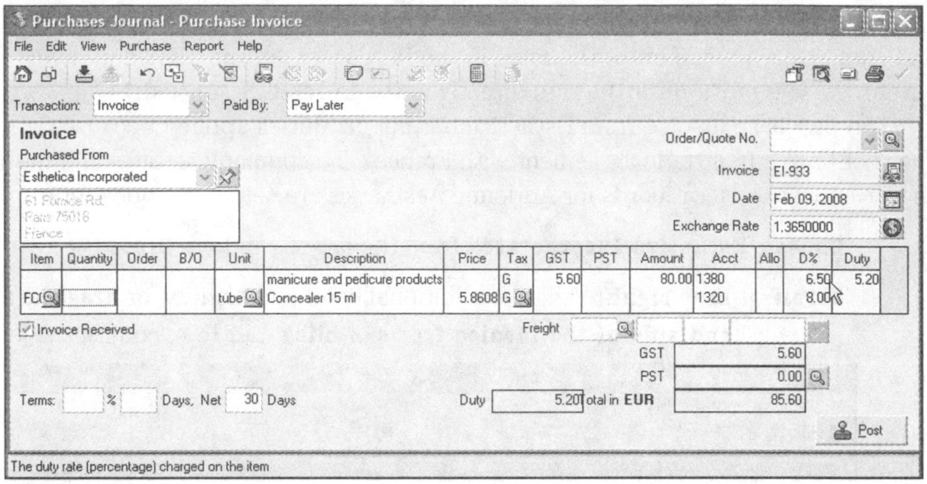

The D% field has 8.00 as the entry for this item — this rate is stored on the Taxes tab screen in the ledger record as the duty rate applied to these kinds of products (see page 425). The rate will be multiplied by the Amount to determine the duty amount. You can edit the rate, or enter the correct rate directly in the journal if the rate is not stored in the Inventory Ledger. The cursor should be in the Quantity field.

Type 5 **Press** *tab*.

The Amount is entered based on cost information on record. The Duty amount is also added. The default amount is incorrect for this purchase so you must change it.

Click the **Amount field**.

Type 30 **Press** *tab* to update the totals and the duty amounts.

Enter the **remaining items** purchased and the **freight**.

After entering all the items, your finished journal should look like the following:

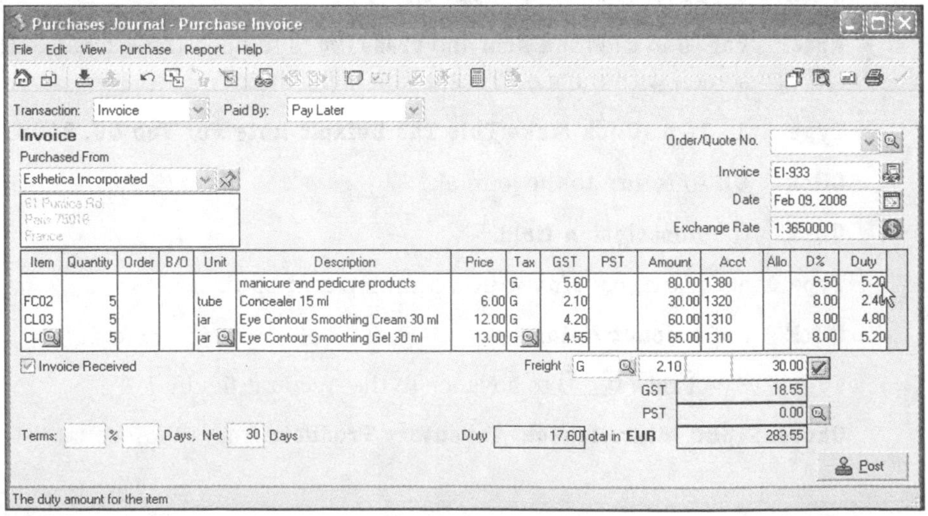

You should review the journal entry before proceeding.

Choose the **Report menu** and **click Display Purchases Journal Entry**:

Adrienne Aesthetics				
02/09/08 (J24)	Foreign Amt.	Debits	Credits	Project
1310 Creams and Lotions	€135.00	184.27	-	
1320 Face Care Products	€32.40	44.23	-	
1380 Miscellaneous Inventory Prod...	€85.20	116.30	-	
2670 GST Paid on Purchases	€18.55	25.32	-	
5050 Exchange Rate Differences	-	0.01	-	
5200 Freight Expense	€30.00	40.95	-	
2200 Accounts Payable	€283.55	-	387.05	
2240 Import Duty Payable	€17.60	-	24.03	
		411.08	411.08	
1 Euro equals 1.3650000 Canadian Dollars				

The journal entry differs from the standard purchase in several important details. The journal shows amounts in both Canadian dollars and euros. The total duty amount for all items is credited to the *Import Duty Payable* linked account. This liability account is credited because the amount of the duty is added (debited) to the inventory asset amount and the duty amount must be paid to the Receiver General. The total of the Amounts on the invoice is €283.55, the *Accounts Payable* amount. The €135 debit to the linked *Creams and Lotions* includes the import duties — €60 plus €65 plus €10. The debits to *Miscellaneous Inventory Products* and *Face Care Products* also include the duty. The amount owing to the vendor and credited to *Accounts Payable* does not include the amount for import duties because duties are collected by CRA and not by the vendor.

Enter payments of import duties to the Receiver General as cash purchases in the Payments Journal in the same way that you enter sales tax remittances. Simply Accounting makes all the calculations for you, so the remittance amounts are easy to determine from the *Import Duty Payable* ledger balance (see page 480).

Close the **display** when you have finished to return to the journal.

Make **corrections** if necessary. **Post** the **entry** and **close** the **journal**.

NOTES

The linked Exchange Rate Differences account may have a balance because of rounding off from the exchange rate's three or more decimals to two for the actual dollar amount. The Exchange Rate Differences linked account tracks rounding errors as well as differences arising from fluctuating exchange rates between the time of purchase and payment. Refer to page 309 to see the screen for defining and setting up the linked account for Exchange Rate Differences.

Displaying Inventory Reports

Most inventory reports can be displayed from the Reports menu in the Inventory & Services window. All the following instructions start from the Home window.

Displaying Inventory Lists

In the Home window,

Right-click the **Inventory & Services icon** 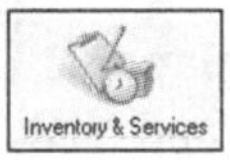

to select it.

Click the **Display tool** or **choose** the **Reports menu** and **choose Lists**, then **click Inventory & Services** to see the report options:

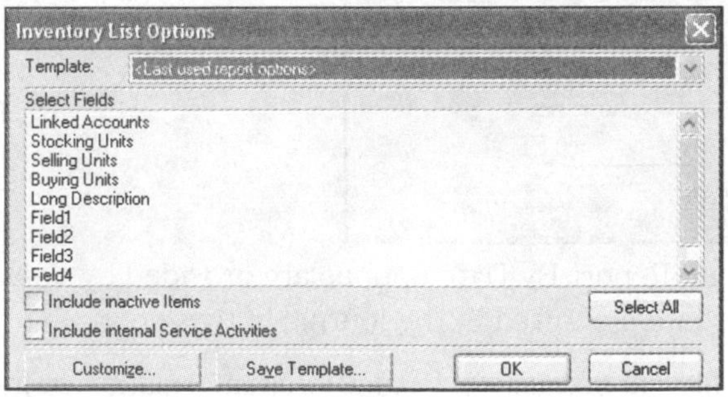

Initially, no fields are selected for the report. You select the fields for the report in the same way as you do for other reports.

BASIC VERSION

The Inventory & Services Ledger icon in the Basic version does not include the clock. See page 418.

NOTES

You can drill down to the Inventory Transaction Report and the General Ledger Report from the Inventory List.

BASIC VERSION

The Basic version does not have the option to Include Internal Service Activities.

Click the **first field** for the report then **press** and **hold** ctrl and **click** the **remaining fields** you want in the report.

Click **OK** to see the list.

Close the **display** when you have finished.

Displaying the Adjustments Journal

NOTES
You can drill down to the General Ledger reports from the Adjustments Journal and from the Item Assembly Journal.

You should be in the Home window.

Right-click the **Adjustments Journal icon** 

to select it.

Click the **Display tool** or **choose** the **Reports menu**, then **choose Journal Entries** and **click Inventory Adjustments** to see the journal options:

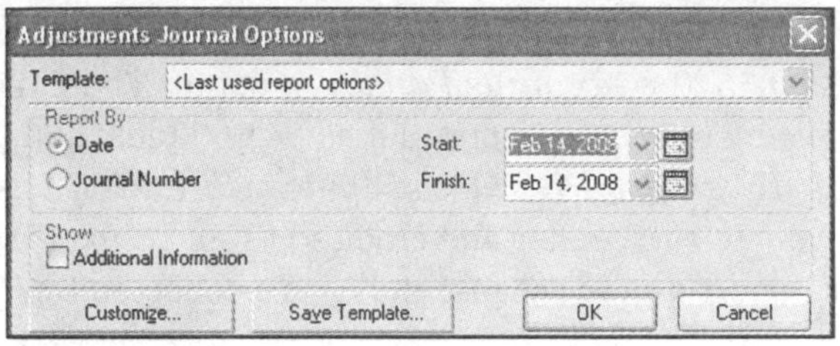

As usual, the session date and the Report By Date option are provided by default.

Enter the **beginning date** for the report you want.

Press tab (**twice** if you type the date).

Enter the **ending date** for the report.

Click Additional Information, if you added it, to include it in the journal report.

Click **OK**.

Close the **display** when you have finished.

Displaying the Item Assembly Journal

basic BASIC VERSION
Right-click the Item Assembly icon, or choose the Report menu, then choose Journal Entries and click Item Assembly. To see this icon, refer to the Basic version note on page 418.

Right-click the **Bill Of Materials & Item Assembly Journal icon** 

to select it.

Click the **Display tool** or **choose** the **Reports menu**, then **choose Journal Entries** and **click Item Assembly**.

You will see the familiar journal options:

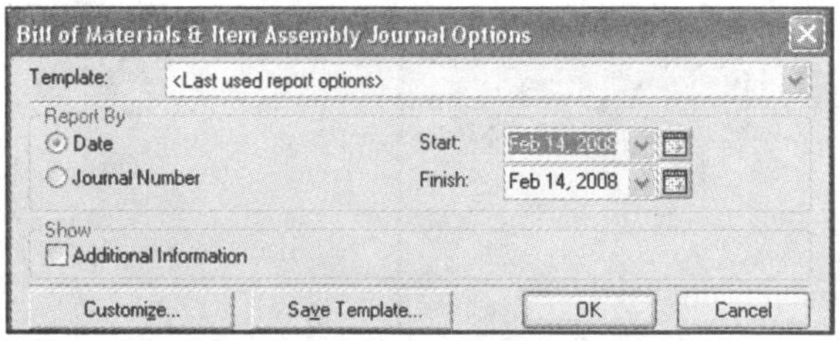

As usual, the session date and Report By Date options are provided by default. You can include any additional information entered in the journal in the report.

If you have entered additional details, click Additional Information to include them in the journal report.

Enter the **beginning date** for the report you want.

Press tab (**twice** if you type the date).

Enter the **ending date** for the report.

Click **OK**.

Close the **display** when you have finished.

Displaying Inventory Synopsis Reports

Choose the **Reports menu**, **choose Inventory & Services** and then **click Synopsis** to display the following report options:

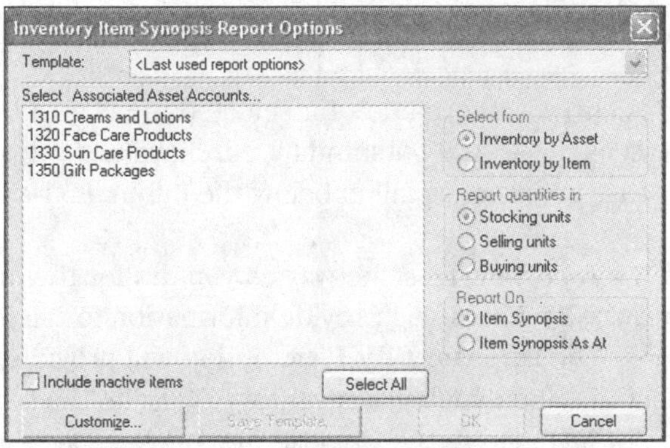

NOTES

For all inventory reports, the sort and filter options include most of the fields that are also included in the reports.

You can customize most inventory reports by selecting any of the columns usually included in the report.

Selecting **Inventory By Asset** will provide information for all inventory items in the asset group(s) chosen. The **Inventory By Item** option will provide information for all the items selected. When you click Inventory By Item, the box lists all inventory items. Services are not included in the Synopsis Report because there is no quantity or cost information for them.

Clicking or selecting a single asset or item will provide a report for that item only. To obtain information for all items, choose Select All. To select multiple items, press and hold ctrl and then click the items you want in the report.

NOTES

You can drill down to the Inventory Transaction Report from the Inventory Synopsis or Quantity reports.

The **Synopsis** Report lists the selling price, the quantity on hand, the unit cost of the inventory, the total value or cost of inventory on hand and the profit margin or markup for the items requested. The total value of the inventory in an asset group is also provided when you select Inventory By Asset. You can view the Synopsis Report for the Session Date or for another date by choosing the **Item Synopsis As At** option. A date field will open for you to enter the date for the report.

You can prepare the report with quantities in any of the units you use for the item if these are different, that is, the stocking, buying or selling units (see page 422).

Choose the **options** you need for your report.

Press and **hold** ctrl and **click** the **names** of all the items or asset groups you want included in the report.

Click **OK**.

Close the **display** when you have finished.

Displaying Inventory Quantity Reports

Choose the **Reports menu**, **choose Inventory & Services** and then **click Quantity** to display the following report options:

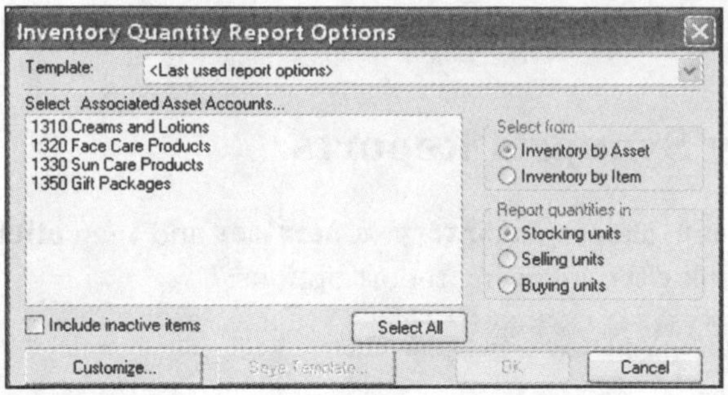

The **Quantity** Report provides current information for selected items about the quantity on hand, the minimum stock levels and outstanding purchase and sales orders. This report can also tell you whether an item has fallen below the minimum level and needs to be re-ordered.

You can select the items for the report in the same way as you did for the Inventory Synopsis Report. Selecting **Inventory By Asset** will provide information for all inventory items in the asset group(s) chosen. The **Inventory By Item** option will provide information for all the items selected. When you click Inventory By Item, the box lists all inventory items. Services are not included in the Quantity Report because there is no quantity or cost information for them.

Clicking or selecting a single asset or item will provide a report for that item only. You can obtain information for all items by choosing Select All. To select multiple items, press and hold *ctrl* and then click the items you want in the report.

You can prepare the report with quantities in any of the units you use for the item if they are different, that is, the stocking, buying or selling units (see page 422).

Choose the **options** you need for your report.

Press and **hold** *ctrl* and **click** the **names** of all the items or asset groups you want to include in the report.

Click **OK** and **close** the **display** when you have finished.

Displaying Inventory Price Lists

All the different inventory prices — regular, preferred, Web and foreign currency prices — are not available in the other inventory reports, but you can see all of these prices together on the Price Lists Report.

Choose the **Reports menu**, **choose Inventory & Services** and then **click Price Lists** to display the following report options:

NOTES

You cannot sort or filter the Price List Report but you can select or omit the Item and Description columns.

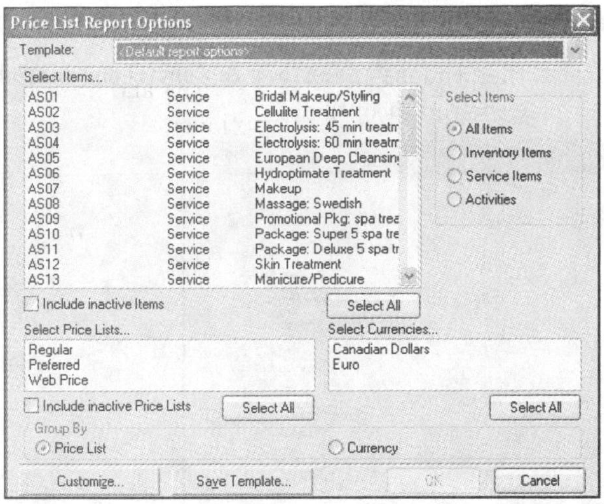

You can select the item or items that you want on the price list by selecting them from the list, just as you select items for other inventory reports. You can include Regular, Preferred and Web prices for one or more currencies. The two grouping options will organize the prices differently. Grouping by **Price List** will show the prices for the two currencies under each type of Price List (Regular, Preferred or Web). The **Currency** option will show the Canadian prices together and the foreign prices together.

> **NOTES**
> If you have created other price lists or use additional currencies, they will be listed in the Report Options screen and you can include them in the report.

Click the **Price List** you want to report on or **click Select All** to include all three.

Click the **Currency** you want in the report or **click Select All** to show both.

Choose the **Grouping** for the report.

Click **OK** to see the price lists and **close** the **display** when you have finished.

Displaying Inventory Management Reports

The management reports for the Inventory Ledger focus on potential problem items, inventory items with low markups or items that are not profitable.

> **NOTES**
> Adrienne currently has no products that meet the Inventory Management Reports' criteria so there will be no data included in these reports.

Choose the **Reports menu**, then **choose Management Reports** and **click Inventory & Services**:

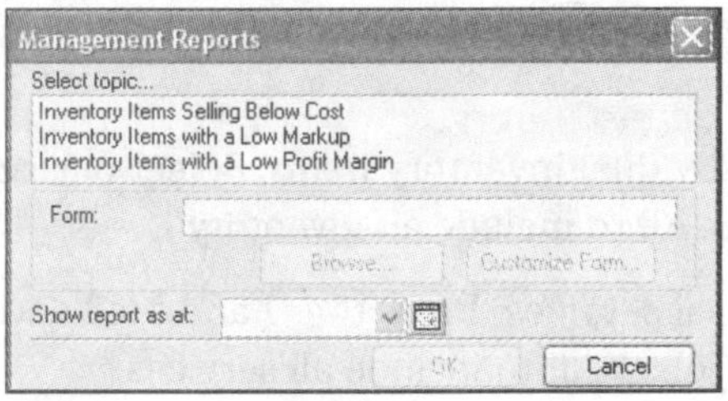

Select a **report** from the list and choose the report form if necessary.

Click **OK** to view the report. **Close** the **display** when finished.

Displaying Inventory Tracking Reports

Several reports provide information about the turnover of inventory products. These reports show whether items are selling well and are profitable and how the sales are distributed over time and customers.

Inventory Statistics Reports

Choose the **Reports menu**, then **choose Inventory & Services** and **click Statistics** to display the report options:

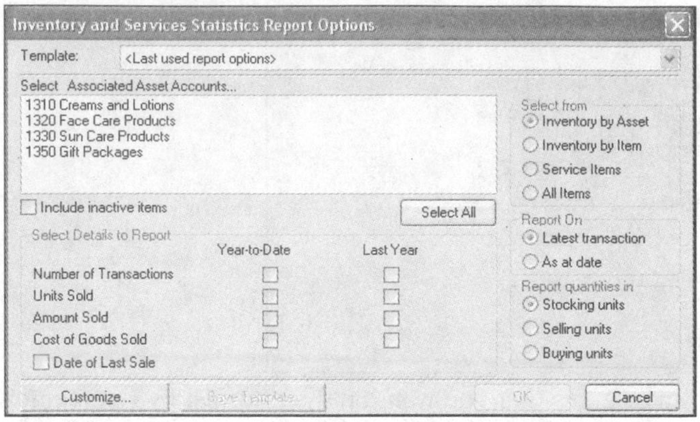

NOTES

You cannot customize the column selection for the Statistics Report. You can sort and filter this report.

NOTES

You can drill down to the Inventory Sales Report from the Inventory Statistics Report.

The Statistics Report summarizes transactions for the year to date and the previous year, the same historical information that is contained in the Inventory Ledger record. You can use the report to determine whether a large volume of sales of an item resulted from a single sale for a large quantity or from a large number of smaller sales.

You can prepare the report for the session date (**Latest Transaction**) or for another date (**As At Date**). When you choose As At Date, a date field will open. The report will show the statistics you request as at the date you enter.

Clicking a detail will include it in the report for each selected item or asset group. There are five details that you can add to the report. The **Number Of Transactions** refers to the number of separate sales invoices that included the inventory item. **Units Sold** reports on the total number of individual items of a kind that were sold in the period. The **Amount Sold** refers to the total sale price for all items sold. The **Cost Of Goods Sold** is the total purchase cost of all the items that were sold. Simply Accounting uses the average cost method to calculate the cost of goods sold. The **Date Of Last Sale**, the date on which the item was most recently sold, can also be included in the report.

Press and hold *ctrl* and click one or more asset groups to include them in the report, or click Select All to include all asset groups in the report. Selecting an asset group will include all the inventory items in that group in the report. To select multiple assets or items, press *ctrl* and then click the items you want to add to the list.

Click **Inventory By Item** to list individual inventory items. Select one or more items for the report, or click Select All to include all inventory items.

Click **Service Items** to list individual services. Press *ctrl* and hold and click services to include them, or click Select All to include all services.

Click **All Items** to include both individual inventory items and individual services in the report. Press *ctrl* and hold and click the items and services to include them in the report, or click Select All to include all items and services in the report.

The list of items will expand according to your selection, and you can choose single or multiple items for inclusion. **Quantities** can be reported in any of the units on record — the units for stocking the inventory, for buying and for selling — if these are different.

Choose the **items** you want in the report.

Choose the **date** for the report (Latest Transaction or As At Date). **Enter** a **date** in the Date field if you chose the As At Date option.

Choose the **details** you want in the report.

Click **OK** to display the report.

Close the **display** when you have finished.

Inventory Sales Reports

Choose the **Reports menu**, then **choose Inventory & Services** and **click Sales** to display the following report options:

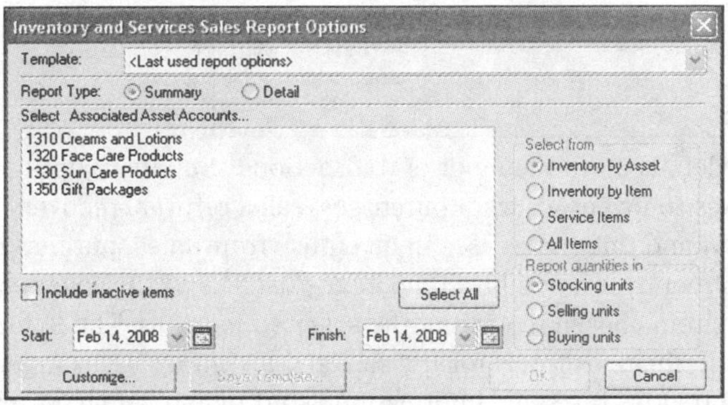

The reports include details on the number of transactions (Summary option only), the quantity of items sold, the revenue per item, the cost of goods sold and the profit on each sale transaction. Non-inventory sales are not included. The **Summary** option, selected by default, shows the total for each detail for the selected inventory items organized by item. The **Detail** option provides the same information listed by individual journal entry, including the source document numbers and journal entry numbers. Click Detail to choose the Detail option. **Quantities** may be reported for stocking, buying or selling units.

As usual, choosing **Select All** provides a report on all items that are in the list, and you can choose to report on inventory items, services or both. To report only on all services, click **Service Items** and then Select All. Click **All Items** to include both inventory and services. The list of items will expand accordingly, and you can choose single or multiple items for inclusion. Select All at this stage will provide a report on all inventory and service items.

Again, quantities may be reported in stocking, buying or selling units.

Type the **starting date** for the report in the Start field and the **ending date** for the report in the Finish field. By default, the latest session date appears in both fields.

Choose the **items** to include in the report.

Choose the **Summary** or **Detail** option.

Click **OK**. **Close** the **display** when you have finished.

Inventory Transaction Reports

The Transaction Report shows the inventory activity summarized according to the journal used to record the transaction.

NOTES
To see the Inventory Sales Summary Report on Services, you must click Select From Service Items or choose All Items. The Inventory By Item and Inventory Asset selections include only inventory items.

NOTES
You can drill down to the Inventory Detail Report from the Inventory Sales Summary Report. You can display the Customer Aged, Inventory Ledger, Journal Report and Invoice Lookup from the Inventory Sales Detail Report.

NOTES
You cannot sort or filter the Sales Report but you can customize the report by selecting the columns you want to include.

Choose the **Reports menu**, then **choose Inventory & Services** and **click Transaction** to display the report options:

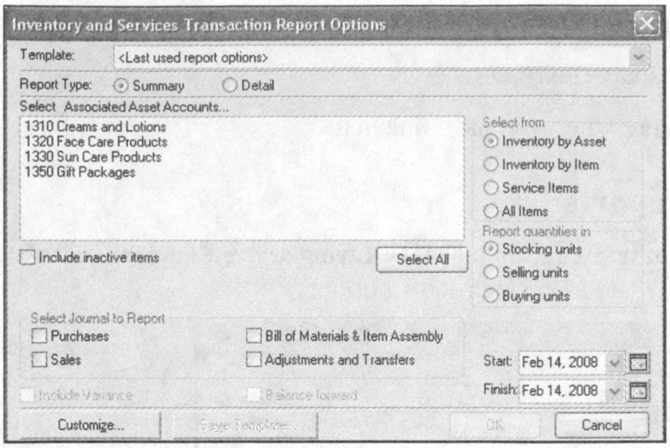

basic BASIC VERSION
Item Assembly is the Journal name in the Basic version instead of Bill of Materials & Item Assembly.

NOTES
You can drill down to the Transaction Detail Report from the Transaction Summary Report. You can display the Inventory Ledger and Journal Report from the Transaction Detail Report. You can also look up invoices from the Detail Report.

The report includes details on the number of transactions (Summary option only), the **Quantity In** (increases to inventory from purchases, sales returns, recovery of lost items or assembled items) and **Out** (decreases in inventory from sales, purchase returns, losses and adjustments or assembly components used) and the **Amount In** and **Out** (cost price) for each item chosen in each of the selected journals. The **Summary** option, selected by default, includes totals for the selected inventory items organized by item. The **Detail** option provides the same information listed by individual journal entry, including the source document numbers and journal entry numbers.

As in the previous report, you can prepare a report for one or more asset groups, one or more inventory items, one or more service items or a combination of services and items (All Items). Clicking the appropriate button in the Select From list will expand the item list accordingly. Select All will automatically include all items that are displayed in the list box.

Quantities may be reported in stocking, buying or selling units. Variances can also be added to the report when they are used.

Click **Detail** to choose the Detail option.

Type the **starting date** for the report in the Start field and the **ending date** for the report in the Finish field. By default, the latest session date appears in both fields.

Click the **journals** to include in the report.

Click **Balance Forward** to include opening balances or **Include Variance** to add cost variances for each item.

Click **OK**. **Close** the **display** when you have finished.

Vendor Purchases Reports

The next two reports combine inventory information with vendor or customer details to show how purchases are spread among vendors and how sales are divided among customers. The Vendor Purchases and Customer Sales reports also allow you to include information for non-inventory purchases or sales.

NOTES
You cannot sort or filter the Vendor Purchases Report, but you can select the columns you want in the report.

The Vendor Purchases report includes details on the number of transactions (Summary option only), the quantity purchased, the unit cost and the total cost of the purchase. Non-inventory purchases, such as telephone services, are listed as **Other**.

Choose the **Reports menu**, then **choose Payables** and **click Vendor Purchases** to display the following report options:

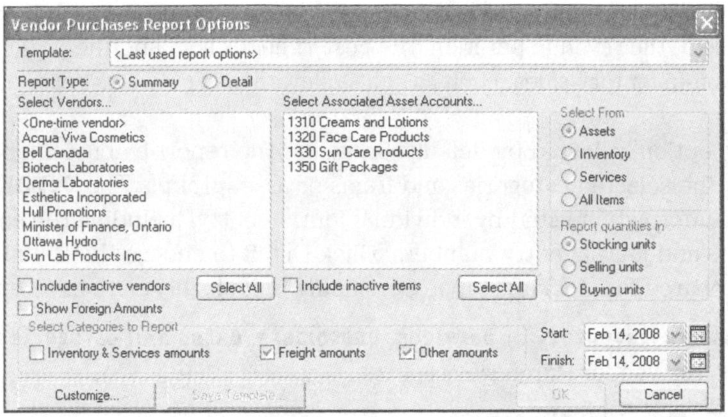

NOTES

As soon as you select an item, Inventory & Services Amounts will be selected so all categories will be included by default.

NOTES

You can drill down to the Inventory Purchases Detail Report from the Purchases Summary Report. You can look up invoices or display the Vendor Aged and Journal Report from the Purchases Detail Report.

The **Summary** option, selected by default, organizes the report by vendor and includes totals for the selected categories and items or asset group. The **Detail** option provides the same information by individual journal entry, including the source document numbers and journal entry numbers. Click Detail to choose the Detail option.

Amounts for foreign vendors may be shown in either the home **currency** or the foreign currency. The selection of inventory, services or asset groups is the same as for the other inventory reports. Reports can be prepared for either stocking, buying or selling units if these are different.

NOTES

To select multiple items, press ctrl and then click the items or vendors you want to add to the report.

Click the **assets**, inventory **items** or **services** to include in the report, or **click Select All** to include all listed items in the report.

Click the **vendor name** to include in the report, or **click Select All** below the Select Vendors list to include all vendors in the report.

NOTES

The date list provided by the list arrow includes the earliest transaction date and the latest session date or latest transaction date. The earliest transaction date is a frequent choice for the starting date in reports.

Enter the **starting date** for the report in the Start field and the **ending date** for the report in the Finish field.

Click a purchase category — Inventory & Services, non-inventory (Other) and Freight charges — to remove the ✓ and deselect it for the selected vendor and item transactions. Click it again to select it.

Click **OK**. **Close** the **display** when finished.

Customer Sales Reports

The Customer Sales Report provides the same details as the Inventory Sales Report, but the Customer Sales Report has the details organized by customer as well as by item. Customer Sales reports also have the option to include non-inventory sales.

NOTES

You can drill down to the Inventory Sales Detail Report from the Customer Sales Summary Report. You can drill down to the Customer Aged, Invoice Lookup and Journal Report from the Customer Sales Detail Report.

Choose the **Reports menu**, then **choose Receivables** and **click Customer Sales** to display the following report options:

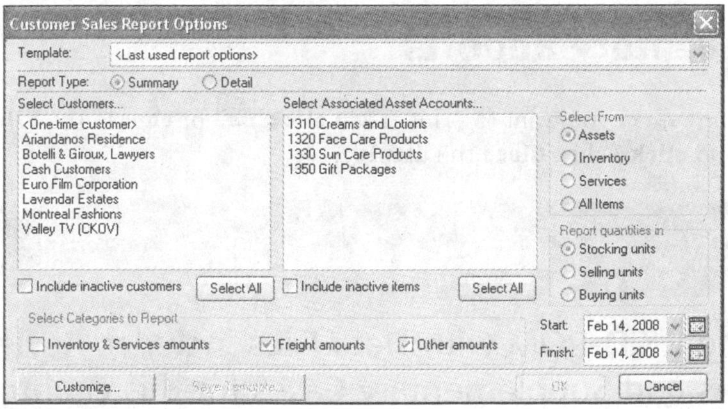

NOTES

As soon as you select an item, Inventory & Services Amounts will be selected so all categories will be included by default.

The report includes the number of transactions (Summary option only), the quantity of items sold, the revenue per item, the cost of goods sold and the profit on each sale transaction. Non-inventory sales, such as sales allowances or non-inventory services, are listed as **Other**.

NOTES
You cannot sort or filter the Customer Sales Report but you can select the columns you want in the report.

The **Summary** option, selected by default, organizes the report by customer and includes totals for the selected categories and items or asset groups. The **Detail** option provides the same information listed by individual journal entry, including the source document numbers and journal entry numbers. Click Detail to choose the Detail option. Reports can be prepared for stocking, buying or selling units if these are different.

Select **assets**, **inventory** or **services**, **customers**, **dates** and **categories** as you do for Vendor Purchases reports.

Click **OK**. **Close** the **display** when you have finished.

Gross Margin Income Statement

This financial report becomes relevant when a business sells inventory. The report shows the income after inventory costs have been deducted from revenue and before operating expenses are included. To see this report,

Choose the **Reports menu**, **choose Financials** and then **click Gross Margin Income Statement** to display the following report options:

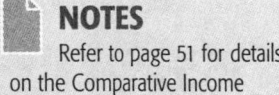

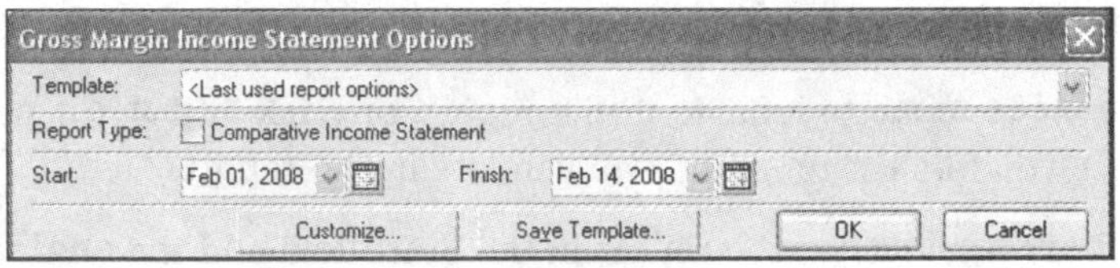

WARNING!
You must assign the correct account classes to expense accounts to generate the Gross Margin Income Statement. Cost of Goods Sold Accounts must be correctly identified and separated from other types of expenses.

The report will include different income amounts. The first income amount is the Gross Margin, revenue minus cost of goods sold, before taking into account the other operating expenses. Next, operating expenses are deducted from the gross margin to determine the income from operations. The final section includes non-operating revenue and expenses, if you have assigned these account classes to any accounts in the General Ledger.

The options for this Income Statement are the same as for regular Income Statements, including the option to generate a Comparative Income Statement.

NOTES
Refer to page 51 for details on the Comparative Income Statement.

Type the **starting date** for the report in the Start field and the **ending date** for the report in the Finish field. By default, the fiscal start and latest session date appear in these fields.

Click **OK**. **Close** the **display** when you have finished.

Printing Inventory Reports

Display the **report** you want to print. Then **click** [print icon] or **choose** the **File menu** and **click Print**. **Close** the **display**.

R E V I E W

The Student CD-ROM with Data Files includes Review Questions and Supplementary Cases for this chapter.

CHAPTER TWELVE

TRUMAN TIRES

OBJECTIVES

After completing this chapter, you should be able to

- ***enter*** transactions in all journals
- ***allocate*** revenues and expenses in the General, Sales, Purchases and Payroll journals
- ***create*** new projects
- ***change*** the Project Ledger name
- ***make*** import duty remittances
- ***enter*** purchases with cost variances
- ***display*** and ***print*** transactions with project details
- ***display*** and ***print*** project reports

COMPANY INFORMATION

Company Profile

NOTES
Truman Tires
600 Westminster St.
London, Ontario N6P 3B1
Tel: (519) 729-3733
Fax: (519) 729-7301
Business No.: 230 192 821

Truman Tires, located in London, Ontario, sells tires and wheels for all types of passenger cars including taxis and service fleets for other businesses. Tyrone Truman completed an auto mechanics program at the local community college and then worked for an auto repair shop in Windsor for several years. He studied business administration part time to prepare him for starting his own business, which he now has operated for several years.

Although he sells all kinds of tires, throughout the year most people buy all-season radial tires. In December, the month in this application, Truman Tires sells mainly winter tires. All tire sales include free installation. The service centre, with its four service bays, also provides a limited range of services for automobiles including oil changes, brake repairs and replacements, shocks replacements and wheel alignments. Four employees work on the cars while a manager and assistant manager handle all customer contacts and schedule appointments.

Truman Tires has a number of regular suppliers of inventory and other parts and supplies. Truman has accounts with most of these suppliers and some offer discounts for early payment. Some of the tires and wheels are imported from Japan and Truman pays import duties on these items.

Regular customers also have accounts with Truman Tires and are offered a 2 percent discount if they settle their accounts within 10 days. Some customers receive additional discounts through the preferred pricing schedule for all inventory sales and services.

In preparation for expanding his business, Tyrone Truman has decided to apply project costing for his two departments, Sales and Service. He hopes to determine which aspect of the company is more profitable.

At the end of November 2008, Truman remitted all the company payroll taxes and deductions and closed his books. To convert his accounting records to Simply Accounting, he used the following:

- Chart of Accounts
- Post-Closing Trial Balance
- Vendor Information
- Customer Information
- Employee Information
- Employee Profiles and TD1 Information
- Inventory Information
- Project Information
- Accounting Procedures

CHART OF ACCOUNTS

TRUMAN TIRES

ASSETS

Current Assets
1050 Bank: Chequing CAD
1060 Bank: Foreign Currency
1070 Bank: Visa
1080 Bank: MasterCard
1090 Bank: Interac
1200 Accounts Receivable
1220 Purchase Prepayments
1240 Brakes & Shocks Parts
1250 Supplies: Garage
1260 Supplies: Office

Inventory Assets
1360 Wheels
1380 Wheel Nuts & Locks
1400 Winter Tires

Plant & Equipment
1650 Cash Register
1660 Computer Equipment
1670 Garage Equipment
1680 Machinery & Tools
1690 Shop & Garage Bays ▶
▶1700 Tow Truck
1710 Yard

LIABILITIES

Current Liabilities
2100 Bank Loan
2150 Prepaid Sales and Deposits
2200 Accounts Payable
2220 Import Duty Payable
2300 Vacation Payable
2310 EI Payable
2320 CPP Payable
2330 Income Tax Payable
2390 EHT Payable
2400 CSB Payable
2410 Union Dues
2460 WSIB Payable
2640 PST Payable
2650 GST Charged on Sales
2670 GST Paid on Purchases

Long Term Liabilities
2850 Mortgage Payable ▶

▶**EQUITY**

Owner's Equity
3560 T. Truman, Capital
3580 T. Truman, Drawings
3600 Net Income

REVENUE

Revenue
4020 Revenue from Sales
4040 Revenue from Services
4100 Other Revenue
4150 Sales Discounts
4160 Sales Tax Compensation

EXPENSE

Operating Expenses
5020 Advertising & Promotion
5030 Bank Charges
5035 Exchange Rate Differences
5040 Credit Card Fees
5045 Assembly Costs
5050 Cost of Goods Sold
5055 Variance Costs ▶
▶5060 Cost of Services
5065 Freight Expense
5070 Hydro Expense
5080 Interest Expense - Loan
5090 Interest Expense - Mortgage
5100 Inventory Adjustment
5110 Tool Rentals
5120 Inventory Parts Used
5130 Purchase Discounts
5140 Repairs & Maintenance
5150 Telephone Expense

Payroll Expenses
5300 Management Wages
5310 General Wages
5320 Piece Rate Wage Expense
5330 Commissions and Bonuses
5410 EI Expense
5420 CPP Expense
5430 WSIB Expense
5460 EHT Expense

NOTES: The Chart of Accounts includes only postable accounts and Net Income. WSIB (Workplace Safety and Insurance Board) is the name for WCB (Workers' Compensation Board) in Ontario.

POST-CLOSING TRIAL BALANCE

TRUMAN TIRES

November 30, 2008

		Debits	Credits			Debits	Credits
1050	Bank: Chequing CAD	$20 549		▶ 1670	Garage Equipment	75 000	
1060	Bank: Foreign Currency (¥203 600)	2 000		1680	Machinery & Tools	25 000	
1070	Bank: Visa	8 000		1690	Shop & Garage Bays	175 000	
1080	Bank: MasterCard	5 000		1700	Tow Truck	40 000	
1090	Bank: Interac	2 500		1710	Yard	25 000	
1200	Accounts Receivable	4 255		2100	Bank Loan		$ 12 000
1240	Brakes & Shocks Parts	6 800		2200	Accounts Payable		5 992
1250	Supplies: Garage	2 400		2300	Vacation Payable		6 943
1260	Supplies: Office	600		2640	PST Payable		3 360
1360	Wheels	9 136		2650	GST Charged on Sales		2 940
1380	Wheel Nuts & Locks	738		2670	GST Paid on Purchases	1 400	
1400	Winter Tires	15 480		2850	Mortgage Payable		140 000
1650	Cash Register	2 500		3560	T. Truman, Capital		252 623
1660	Computer Equipment	2 500 ▶				$423 858	$423 858

VENDOR INFORMATION

TRUMAN TIRES

Vendor Name (Contact)	Address	Phone No. Fax No.	E-mail Web Site	Terms Tax ID
Bell Canada (Louis Gossip)	100 Ring Road London, Ontario N5W 2M3	Tel: (519) 387-2355	www.bell.ca	n/10
CAW Union				n/30
Equity Life				n/30
Gulf Oil Company (Petro Crewd)	30 Refinery Cr. London, Ontario N4R 6F1	Tel: (519) 641-6277	pc@gulfoil.com www.gulfoil.com	n/30
London Hydro (Les Current)	755 Ohm Blvd. London, Ontario N6C 1P9	Tel: (519) 649-8100	lesc@londonhydro.on.ca www.londonhydro.on.ca	n/10
London Tool Rentals (Roto Tiller)	239 Pneumatics Rd. London, Ontario N5X 2S4	Tel: (519) 633-7102 Fax: (519) 635-8191	roto@getitfromus.com www.getitfromus.com	n/20 325 622 934
Minister of Finance	Box 620, 33 King St. W Oshawa, Ontario L1H 8H5	Tel: (905) 443- 8200	www.gov.on.ca/fin	n/30
MoTech Auto Parts (Moe Torrs)	2 Revving Parkway Windsor, Ontario N7T 7C2	Tel: (519) 722-1973 Fax: (519) 725-3664	moe@motech.com www.motech.com	2/10, n/30 (after tax) 163 482 977
Receiver General for Canada	PO Box 20004, Station A Sudbury, Ontario P3A 6B4	Tel: (705) 821-8186	www.cra-arc.gc.ca	n/30
Snowmaster Tire Company (I.C. Winters)	86 Sleet St. Tokyo, Japan 162-0829	Tel: (81-3) 5249 7331 Fax: (81-3) 5261 6492	icw@snowmaster.com www.snowmaster.com	2/15, n/30 (after tax)
Sylverado Wheels (Roy Rimmer)	100 Round Rd., Unit 2 Tokyo, Japan 100-7227	Tel: (81-3) 3643 8459 Fax: (81-3) 3663 5188	royrimmer@sylverado.com www.sylverado.com	n/30
TuffArm Shocks (Sally Shockley)	489 Spring St. Toronto, Ontario M4Z 3G3	Tel: (416) 699-2019 Fax: (416) 699-3854	Sal@tuffarm.shocks.com www.tuffarm.shocks.com	n/30 263 495 687
Western Hydraulic Repairs (Otto Raizer)	109 Lift St. London, Ontario N6F 8A5	Tel: (519) 645-6722 Fax: (519) 646-1145	o_raizer@whydraulics.com www.whydraulics.com	n/30 466 345 291
Workplace Safety & Insurance Board				n/30

OUTSTANDING VENDOR INVOICES

TRUMAN TIRES

Vendor Name	Terms	Date	Invoice No.	Amount CAD	Amount JPY
MoTech Auto Parts	2/10, n/30 (after tax)	Nov. 27/08	MT-1142	$642	
Snowmaster Tire Company	2/15, n/30 (after tax)	Nov. 26/08	ST-842	$2 568	¥261 427
Sylverado Wheels	n/30	Nov. 10/08	SW-724	$1 712	¥174 826
TuffArm Shocks	n/30	Nov. 4/08	TS-699	$1 070	
		Grand Total		$5 992	

CUSTOMER INFORMATION

TRUMAN TIRES

Customer Name (Contact)	Address	Phone No. Fax No.	E-mail Web Site	Terms Credit Limit
*Airport Taxi Service (Jett Plane)	100 Runway Rd. London, Ontario N5G 3J7	Tel: (519) 643-6182 Fax: (519) 645-1772	jett@gofly.com www.gofly.com	2/10, n/30 $4 000
Cash Customers				n/1
City Cab Company (Able Driver)	890 Transport St. London, Ontario N5W 1B3	Tel: (519) 641-7999 Fax: (519) 641-2539	driver@wetakeyou.com www.wetakeyou.com	2/10, n/30 $4 000
*London Car Leasing (Nick Borrow)	44 Fleet St. London, Ontario N6T 7V2	Tel: (519) 788-2538 Fax: (519) 789-3264	borrow@whybuy.com www.whybuy.com	2/10, n/30 $4 000
Lovely U Cosmetics (N.O. Blemish)	450 Phare Skinn Cr. London, Ontario N6B 3H3	Tel: (519) 782-4477 Fax: (519) 781-4372	blemish@lovelyU.com www.lovelyU.com	2/10, n/30 $4 000
*Polly Maid Services (Polly Mayden)	92 Scouring St. London, Ontario N6T 2K6	Tel: (519) 648-3645 Fax: (519) 648-2774	polly@pollymaid.com www.pollymaid.com	2/10, n/30 $4 000
Pronto Pizza & Delivery (Wayte Nott)	52 Marguerite St. London, Ontario N5B 2R5	Tel: (519) 784-7287 Fax: (519) 785-8220	waytenott@pronto.com www.pronto.com	2/10, n/30 $4 000

NOTES: Preferred price list customers are marked with an asterisk (*) beside their names. All discounts are after tax.

OUTSTANDING CUSTOMER INVOICES

TRUMAN TIRES

Customer Name	Terms	Date	Invoice No.	Amount	Total
City Cab Company	2/10, n/30 (after tax)	Nov. 26/08	120	$1 840	$1 840
Lovely U Cosmetics	2/10, n/30 (after tax)	Nov. 24/08	116	$1 380	$1 380
Polly Maid Services	2/10, n/30 (after tax)	Nov. 29/08	124	$1 035	$1 035
		Grand Total			$4 255

EMPLOYEE INFORMATION SHEET

TRUMAN TIRES

	Trish Tridon	Joy Fram	Shockley Monroe	Karlby Holley	Troy Niehoff	Albert C. Delco
Position	Manager	Asst Manager	Auto Worker	Auto Worker	Auto Worker	Auto Worker
Social Insurance No.	464 375 286	572 351 559	398 577 619	821 887 114	618 524 664	404 535 601
Address	59 Pond Mills Rd. London, Ontario N5Z 3X3	8 Rington Cres. London, Ontario N6J 1Y7	36 Artisans Cres. London, Ontario N5V 4S3	44 Lockyer St. London, Ontario N6C 3E5	98 Novello Ave. London, Ontario N6J 2A5	18 Ravenglass Cres. London, Ontario N6G 4K1
Telephone	(519) 645-6238	(519) 738-5188	(519) 784-7195	(519) 648-1916	(519) 641-6773	(519) 788-2826
Date of Birth (mm-dd-yy)	09-28-67	02-03-79	05-21-78	08-08-76	05-28-74	08-19-80
Federal (Ontario) Tax Exemption - TD1						
Basic Personal	$9 039 (8 377)	$9 039 (8 377)	$9 039 (8 377)	$9 039 (8 377)	$9 039 (8 377)	$9 039 (8 377)
Spouse	$7 675 (7 113)	–	–	–	$7 675 (7 113)	–
Other	–	–	–	$7 200 (7 608)	–	–
Total Exemptions	$16 714 (15 490)	$9 039 (8 377)	$9 039 (8 377)	$16 239 (15 985)	$16 714 (15 490)	$9 039 (8 377)
Employee Earnings						
Regular Wage Rate	–	–	$16.00	$16.00	$16.00	$16.00
Overtime Wage Rate	–	–	$24.00	$24.00	$24.00	$24.00
Regular Salary	$3 500/mo	$2 500/mo	–	–	–	–
Pay Period	monthly	monthly	bi-weekly	bi-weekly	bi-weekly	bi-weekly
Hours per Period	150	150	80	80	80	80
Piece Rate	–	–	$10/job	$10/job	$5/job	$5/job
Commission	1% (Sales–Returns)	–	–	–	–	–
Vacation	4 weeks	3 weeks	4% retained	4% retained	4% retained	4% retained
Vacation Pay Owed	–	–	$1 793	$1 486	$1 811	$1 853
WSIB Rate	3.40	3.40	3.40	3.40	3.40	3.40
Employee Deductions						
CSB	$200	$100	$50	$50	–	–
Union Dues	–	–	1%	1%	1%	1%
EI, CPP & Income Tax	Calculations built into Simply Accounting program.					

Employee Profiles and TD1 Information

All Employees All employees are allowed ten days per year for illness and five for personal reasons. All employees have their paycheques deposited directly into their bank accounts. There are no other company benefits. All payroll remittances are due at the end of each month.

Trish Tridon As the manager at Truman Tires, Tridon supervises the other employees, resolves customer problems and assists with sales. Her salary of $3 500 per month is supplemented by a commission of 1 percent of sales, less returns. Tridon is entered as the salesperson on all sales invoices to calculate the commission. She is paid at the end of each month and is allowed four weeks of vacation with pay. Tridon is married with two children under 12, and claims the basic and spousal tax claim amounts. She has $200 deducted from each paycheque to buy Canada Savings Bonds.

Joy Fram As assistant manager, Fram helps Tridon with all her duties and also manages the accounting records for the business. She is paid a monthly salary of $2 500 and is allowed three weeks of vacation with pay. She has only the basic tax claim amount because she is single and self-supporting. She has chosen to buy Canada Savings Bonds by having $100 deducted from each paycheque.

Hourly Paid Employees The four hourly paid employees — Monroe, Holley, Niehoff and Delco — share the work of servicing vehicles. Every two weeks, they are paid $16 per hour for the first 40 hours each week and $24 per hour for additional time for performing the full range of services provided by Truman Tires: installing, repairing and rotating tires, brake work, shocks and oil service. However, each hourly employee has one area of specialization and the piece rate supplement is based on the number of jobs in this area. All receive 4 percent vacation pay that is retained until they take time off. All are union members and pay 1 percent of their wages as union dues.

Shockley Monroe specializes in brake work. He is single and pays $50 from each paycheque toward the purchase of Canada Savings Bonds.

Karlby Holley also buys Canada Savings Bonds through payroll deductions. Her specialty is shocks. As a recent graduate, she has $4 000 tuition and eight months of full-time study to increase her basic single tax claim amount.

Troy Niehoff is married with one child under 12 years of age, so he has the basic and spousal tax claim amounts. He is not enrolled in the Canada Savings Bonds plan. His area of specialization is tire installation and wheel alignment.

Albert C. Delco is single and does not purchase Canada Savings Bonds through payroll. His area of specialization is oil service and winter preparation.

INVENTORY INFORMATION

TRUMAN TIRES

Code	Description	Min Stock	Selling Price Reg	(Pref)	Unit	Qty on Hand	Total (Cost)	Duty	Taxes
Winter Tires (Linked Accounts: Asset 1400; Revenue: 4020; COGS: 5050; Var: 5055)									
T101	P155/80R14 Tires	4	$ 70	($ 65)	each	20	$ 560	7.0%	GST & PST
T102	P175/70R14 Tires	4	85	(80)	each	20	680	7.0%	GST & PST
T103	P195/75R15 Tires	4	95	(88)	each	20	760	7.0%	GST & PST
T104	P205/75R15 Tires	8	100	(92)	each	28	1 120	7.0%	GST & PST
T105	P185/70R15 Tires	4	105	(96)	each	20	840	7.0%	GST & PST
T106	P195/65R15 Tires	4	110	(100)	each	20	880	7.0%	GST & PST
T107	P185/65R15 Tires	4	115	(105)	each	20	920	7.0%	GST & PST
T108	P185/60R15 Tires	4	120	(110)	each	20	960	7.0%	GST & PST
T109	P195/60R16 Tires	8	125	(115)	each	28	1 400	7.0%	GST & PST
T110	P195/65R16 Tires	8	130	(120)	each	28	1 456	7.0%	GST & PST
T111	P205/65R16 Tires	8	135	(124)	each	28	1 512	7.0%	GST & PST
T112	P205/60R16 Tires	8	140	(127)	each	28	1 568	7.0%	GST & PST
T113	P215/60R16 Tires	8	145	(132)	each	28	1 624	7.0%	GST & PST
T114	P225/60R17 Tires	4	150	(136)	each	20	1 200	7.0%	GST & PST
							$15 480		
Wheels (Linked Accounts: Asset 1360; Revenue: 4020; COGS: 5050; Var: 5055)									
W101	Aluminum R14 Wheels	4	180	(165)	each	16	$1 152	6.0%	GST & PST
W102	Aluminum R15 Wheels	4	195	(187)	each	16	1 248	6.0%	GST & PST
W103	Aluminum R16 Wheels	8	210	(190)	each	20	1 680	6.0%	GST & PST
W104	Aluminum R17 Wheels	4	225	(207)	each	16	1 440	6.0%	GST & PST
W105	Chrome-Steel R14 Wheels	4	70	(65)	each	16	448	6.0%	GST & PST
W106	Chrome-Steel R15 Wheels	4	80	(75)	each	16	512	6.0%	GST & PST
W107	Chrome-Steel R16 Wheels	8	90	(83)	each	20	720	6.0%	GST & PST
W108	Chrome-Steel R17 Wheels	4	100	(92)	each	16	640	6.0%	GST & PST
W109	Steel R14 Wheels	4	40	(38)	each	16	256	6.0%	GST & PST
W110	Steel R15 Wheels	4	45	(42)	each	16	288	6.0%	GST & PST
W111	Steel R16 Wheels	8	50	(46)	each	20	400	6.0%	GST & PST
W112	Steel R17 Wheels	4	55	(50)	each	16	352	6.0%	GST & PST
							$9 136		

▶

INVENTORY INFORMATION

TRUMAN TIRES

Code	Description	Min Stock	Selling Price Reg	(Pref)	Unit	Qty on Hand	Total (Cost)	Duty	Taxes
Wheel Nuts & Locks (Linked Accounts: Asset 1380; Revenue: 4020; COGS: 5050; Var: 5055)									
WN01	Chrome Wheel Nuts	4	$ 10	($ 10)	pkg	24	$ 96	6.0%	GST & PST
WN02	Chrome Wheel Locks	4	25	(23)	pkg	24	240	6.0%	GST & PST
WN03	Nickel/Chrome Wheel Nuts	4	10	(10)	pkg	24	114	6.0%	GST & PST
WN04	Nickel/Chrome Wheel Locks	4	30	(28)	pkg	24	288	6.0%	GST & PST
							$738		
Services (Linked Accounts: Revenue: 4040; COGS: 5060)									
SRV01	Alignment - standard		75	(70)	job				GST & PST
SRV02	Alignment - w caster replacement		130	(120)	job				GST & PST
SRV03	Brake Service - standard pkg		140	(130)	job				GST & PST
SRV04	Brake Service - complete pkg		175	(163)	job				GST & PST
SRV05	Oil Service - standard pkg		30	(28)	job				GST & PST
SRV06	Oil Service - premium pkg		40	(37)	job				GST & PST
SRV07	Shocks - economy gas-charged		100	(92)	job				GST & PST
SRV08	Shocks - premium gas-matic		140	(130)	job				GST & PST
SRV09	Tire Repairs		30	(28)	job				GST & PST
SRV10	Tire Rotation		10	(10)	job				GST & PST
SRV11	Winter Prep. Service		60	(55)	job				GST & PST

Project Information

Truman Tires uses two projects — one for sales of tires and wheels and their installation and one for services. Division is used as the ledger name instead of Project. Fram will set up these projects at the beginning of December and Tridon will keep track of the percentage of time each employee works in each division. Because these times vary from one vehicle to another, the percentage allocation is included with each source document. Allocation details for other expenses and revenues are also included with the source documents. Amounts for assets, liabilities and equity accounts are not allocated.

Accounting Procedures

The Employer Health Tax (EHT)

The Employer Health Tax (EHT) is paid by employers in Ontario to cover the costs of health care for all eligible residents in the province. The EHT rate depends on the total annual remuneration paid to employees (gross wage expense). Employers with total payroll less than $400 000 are exempt from paying EHT. For those with higher annual payrolls, the EHT rate is 1.95 percent. Simply Accounting will calculate the employer's liability to the Ontario Minister of Finance automatically once the information is set up correctly in the payroll defaults and linked accounts. A later application, Flabuless Fitness, will show the keystrokes necessary for setting up the EHT information. The EHT can be remitted monthly or annually, depending on the total payroll amount.

NOTES

Although the total payroll for Truman is below the minimum amount at which they must pay the EHT, we have included the tax for teaching purposes.

Taxes: GST and PST

Truman Tires pays GST on all goods and services that it buys, including the imported products, and charges GST on all sales and services. It uses the regular method for remittance of the Goods and Services Tax. GST collected from customers is recorded as a liability in *GST Charged on Sales*. GST paid to vendors is recorded in *GST Paid on Purchases* as a decrease in liability to Canada Revenue Agency. The report is filed with the Receiver General for Canada by the last day of the month for the previous quarter, either including the balance owing or requesting a refund.

In Ontario, PST is calculated on the base amount of the invoice, which does not include the GST. In this application, Provincial Sales Tax of 8 percent is applied to all sales and services offered by Truman Tires.

NSF Cheques

NOTES

The Sales Journal entry will credit Bank: Chequing CAD for the full amount of the sale including taxes and debit Accounts Receivable for the customer.

When a bank returns a customer's cheque because there were insufficient funds in the customer's bank account to cover the cheque, the payment must be reversed. If the payment was processed through the Receipts Journal, the reversal should also be processed through the Receipts Journal by including fully paid invoices on the screen (see page 181). If the sale was a cash sale, the reversal must be processed through the Sales Journal. Create a customer record for the customer and process a credit (Pay Later) sale for the full amount of the NSF cheque. Enter No Tax in the Tax Code field to show that the amount is non-taxable because taxes for the sale were recorded at the time of the original sale. Enter the amount as a **positive** amount in the Amount field and enter *Bank: Chequing CAD* in the Account field. On a separate invoice line, enter the amount of the handling charge for the NSF cheque in the Amount field with *Other Revenue* in the Account field. Again, the handling charge is non-taxable.

NOTES

If you created a customer record by using Quick Add, or used an existing record (e.g., Cash Customers), you can adjust the sales invoice by changing the method of payment from Cheque to Pay Later. You cannot change the payment method for one-time customers.

Returns

When customers return merchandise, they are charged a 20 percent handling charge. In the Sales Journal, enter the quantity returned with a **minus** sign at the regular sale price, add the tax code and enter *Sales Returns & Allowances* in the Account field. The amounts will automatically be negative because of the minus sign in the quantity field, so that *Accounts Receivable* will be credited automatically as well. On a separate invoice line, enter the amount withheld — the handling charge — as a positive amount and credit *Other Revenue*. *Accounts Receivable* will be debited automatically for the amount of the handling charge.

If the original sale was a credit sale, and the account is not yet paid, the return should also be entered as a credit sale so that *Accounts Receivable* will be credited. If the original sale was paid in cash or by credit card, or the account has been paid, the return should be entered as a cash sale or credit card sale so that the appropriate bank account will be credited. (See page 433.)

Reserved Inventory for Projects

When customers sign a contract, the inventory items needed to complete the work are set aside or reserved by transferring them through the Item Assembly Journal to a designated account. In this way, these items cannot be sold to other customers because the inventory quantities are already reduced. The minimum stock level for reserved inventory will be zero. Refer to page 420.

Cash, Credit Card and Debit Card Sales

NOTES

We use the term Cash Sales and Purchases for cash and cheque transactions.

You can also enter the name in the customer field and choose Continue when prompted. The name is then added to the journal report without creating a customer record.

Cash and credit card transactions for goods and services occur normally in most types of businesses. The Simply Accounting program handles these transactions automatically through the Sales Journal when you choose the appropriate method of payment. Choose Cash Customers from the Customer list, and add the new customer's name in the Ship To field if this is not a regular customer. If payment is by cheque, a Cheque Number field opens. Truman Tires accepts Visa, MasterCard and Interac Debit Cards from customers for store sales. Refer to Chapters 7 and 8.

The program will debit the appropriate bank account instead of the *Accounts Receivable* control account. All other accounts for this transaction will be appropriately debited or credited.

Cash Purchases

Similarly, for cash purchases, choose the vendor from the Vendor list or add the vendor using Quick Add. Cash purchases may be entered in the Payments Journal as Other Payments or in the Purchases Journal. Choose the appropriate method of payment from the Paid By list. For cheque payments, a Cheque Number field opens with the next cheque number entered. Complete the remainder of the cash transaction in the same way you would enter other transactions.

The program will debit *Bank: Chequing CAD* instead of *Accounts Payable*, the control account. All other accounts for the transaction will be appropriately debited or credited.

Freight Expense

When a business purchases inventory items, the cost of any freight that cannot be directly allocated to a specific item must be charged to *Freight Expense*. This amount will be regarded as an expense rather than charged to an inventory asset account.

Printing Invoices, Orders and Quotes

If you want to print the invoices, purchase orders or sales quotes through the program, complete the journal transaction as you would otherwise. Before posting the transaction, choose the File menu and then Print or click the Print tool on the tool bar for the invoice form. Printing will begin immediately, so be sure you have the correct forms for your printer before you begin. If you and the customer or vendor have e-mail, click the E-mail tool to send the invoice or order.

Foreign Purchases

Truman Tires imports some inventory items from companies in Japan. The currency for these transactions is Japanese yen (JPY) and the currency symbol is ¥. Truman Tires pays GST and import duties on all these purchases. Duty rates are set up in the Inventory Ledger for the individual items and the amounts are calculated automatically by the program.

INSTRUCTIONS

1. **Record entries** for the source documents for December 2008 in Simply Accounting using the Chart of Accounts, Trial Balance and other information. The procedures for entering each new type of transaction are outlined step by step in the Keystrokes section that follows the source documents. A ✓ in the source document completion check box indicates that keystrokes are provided. The page number immediately below the check box indicates where these specific keystroke instructions begin. Keystroke instructions begin on page 468, after the source documents.
2. **Print** the **reports** and **graphs** indicated on the following printing form after you have finished making your entries.

REPORTS

Lists
- ☐ Chart of Accounts
- ☐ Account List
- ☐ Vendors
- ☐ Customers
- ☐ Employees
- ☐ Inventory & Services
- ☐ Project

Journals
- ☑ All Journals (by date) from Dec. 1 to Dec. 31 with division allocations
- ☐ General
- ☐ Purchases
- ☐ Payments
- ☐ Sales
- ☐ Receipts
- ☐ Payroll
- ☐ Item Assembly
- ☐ Adjustments

Financials
- ☑ Comparative Balance Sheet: Dec. 1 and Dec. 31, difference in percentage
- ☑ Income Statement from Dec. 1 to Dec. 31
- ☑ Trial Balance date: Dec. 31
- ☑ General Ledger accounts: 1400 4020 4040 from Dec. 1 to Dec. 31
- ☐ Statement of Cash Flows
- ☑ Cash Flow Projection Detail Report for account 1050 for 30 days
- ☑ Gross Margin Income Statement from Dec. 1 to Dec. 31

Tax
- ☐ Report on

Banking
- ☐ Cheque Log Report

Payables
- ☐ Vendor Aged
- ☐ Aged Overdue Payables
- ☐ Vendor Purchases
- ☐ Pending Purchase Orders

Receivables
- ☐ Customer Aged
- ☐ Aged Overdue Receivables
- ☐ Customer Sales
- ☑ Sales by Salesperson
- ☐ Pending Sales Orders
- ☐ Customer Statements

Payroll
- ☑ Employee Summary for all employees
- ☑ T4 Slips for all employees
- ☐ Record of Employment

Inventory
- ☐ Inventory Synopsis
- ☐ Inventory Quantity
- ☐ Inventory Statistics
- ☑ Inventory Sales Summary for Winter Tires from Dec. 1 to Dec. 31
- ☑ Inventory Transaction Summary for Wheels, all journals from Dec. 1 to Dec. 31
- ☐ Price Lists

Division (Project)
- ☑ Division Income Summary: all departments, all accounts from Dec. 1 to Dec. 31
- ☐ Division Allocation Report

Mailing Labels
- ☐ Labels

Management Reports
- ☐ Ledger

GRAPHS
- ☐ Payables by Aging Period
- ☐ Payables by Vendor
- ☐ Receivables by Aging Period
- ☐ Receivables by Customer
- ☐ Sales vs Receivables
- ☐ Receivables Due vs Payables Due
- ☐ Revenues by Account
- ☐ Expenses by Account
- ☑ Expenses and Net Profit as % of Revenue

SOURCE DOCUMENTS

SESSION DATE – DECEMBER 7, 2008

☑ **Memo #1** **Dated Dec. 1/08**

468 From Owner: Create the following new departments for the shop to begin on December 1, 2008:
Sales Division
Service Division

☑ **Purchase Invoice #L-4441** **Dated Dec. 1/08**

472 From London Tool Rentals, $280 plus $19.60 GST and $22.40 PST for monthly rental fee for specialty tools according to contract. Purchase invoice total $322. Terms: net 20 days. Charge 20% of the expenses to Sales Division and 80% to Service Division. Store as a monthly recurring entry.

☐ **Cheque Copy #200** **Dated Dec. 2/08**

To TuffArm Shocks, $1 070 in payment of account. Reference invoice #TS-699.

NOTES
There is no allocation in the Payments or the Receipts journals.

☑ **Purchase Invoice #ST-916** **Dated Dec. 2/08**

476 From Snowmaster Tire Company

20 T110 P195/65R16 Tires		¥ 105 200
20 T111 P205/65R16 Tires		109 400
Freight		7 500
GST Paid		15 547
Invoice Total		¥237 647
Import Duty	CAD $147.81	¥ 15 022

The exchange rate is 0.00984.
Terms: 2/15, n/30.
Allocate 100% of the freight expense to the Sales Division.

☐ **Purchase Invoice #SW-876** **Dated Dec. 2/08**

From Sylverado Wheels

20 W103 Aluminum R16 Wheels		¥170 800
20 W107 Chrome-Steel R16 Wheels		73 200
Freight		5 600
GST Paid		17 472
Invoice Total		¥267 072
Import Duty	CAD $144.06	¥14 640

The exchange rate is 0.00984.
Terms: net 30.
Allocate 100% of the freight expense to the Sales Division.

☐ **Cash Receipt #80** **Dated Dec. 3/08**

From Lovely U Cosmetics, cheque #4887 for $1 352.40 in payment of account including $27.60 discount for early payment. Reference invoice #116.

☐ **Cash Receipt #81** **Dated Dec. 3/08**

From City Cab Company, cheque #855 for $1 803.20 in payment of account including $36.80 discount for early payment. Reference invoice #120.

☑ **Visa Sales Invoice #125** **Dated Dec. 4/08**

477 Sold by Tridon to Bruno Scinto

4	T104 P205/75R15 Tires	$100 each	$ 400.00
4	T105 P185/70R15 Tires	105 each	420.00
4	W102 Aluminum R15 Wheels	195 each	780.00
1	SRV06 Oil Service - premium pkg	40 /job	40.00
	Goods and Services Tax	7%	114.80
	Provincial Sales Tax	8%	131.20
	Total paid by Visa #4205 5921 7456 3010		$1 886.00

Allocate 100% of revenue and expenses for inventory items to Sales Division and for service item to Service Division.

☐ **MasterCard Sales Invoice #126** **Dated Dec. 5/08**

Sold by Tridon to Alice Ferante

4	T114 P225/60R17 Tires	$150 each	$ 600.00
4	W104 Aluminum R17 Wheels	225 each	900.00
	Goods and Services Tax	7%	105.00
	Provincial Sales Tax	8%	120.00
	Total paid by MasterCard #5901 8223 6558 6201		$1 725.00

Allocate 100% of revenue to Sales Division.

☐ **Cheque Copy #201** **Dated Dec. 6/08**

To MoTech Auto Parts, $629.16 in payment of account, including $12.84 discount for early payment. Reference invoice #MT-1142.

NOTES

Edit the purchase amounts.

Amounts for Balance Sheet accounts are not allocated so there is no allocation for inventory purchases.

Allocate freight expenses for purchases by clicking the Allocate tool beside the Freight fields.

Remember that GST is charged on freight expenses.

NOTES

For all cash, credit card or debit card sales, you can type the new customer name and choose Continue or choose Cash Customers and use the Additional Field for the customer name or credit card number.

There is no discount for cash, credit card or debit card sales (Visa, MasterCard and Interac).

☐ **Interac Sales Invoice #127** **Dated Dec. 6/08**

Sold by Tridon to Kaaren Dannenmann

1	SRV05	Oil Service - standard package		$30.00
1	SRV09	Tire Repair		30.00
		Goods and Services Tax	7%	4.20
		Provincial Sales Tax	8%	4.80
		Total paid by Debit Card #4500 5901 2365 5862		$69.00

Allocate 100% of revenue and expenses to Service Division.

☐ **Sales Invoice #128** **Dated Dec. 6/08**

Sold by Tridon to London Car Leasing (preferred customer)

8	T101	P155/80R14 Tires	$ 65 each
8	T103	P195/75R15 Tires	88 each
8	T106	P195/65R15 Tires	100 each
8	W106	Chrome-Steel R15 Wheels	75 each
8	W109	Steel R14 Wheels	38 each
8	W110	Steel R15 Wheels	42 each
		Goods and Services Tax	7%
		Provincial Sales Tax	8%

Terms: 2/10, n/30.

Allocate 100% of revenue and expenses to Sales Division.

☐ **Cash Sales Invoice #129** **Dated Dec. 7/08**

Tridon's Sales Summary for one-time Cash Customers

8	T101	P155/80R14 Tires	$ 70 each	$ 560.00
8	T103	P195/75R15 Tires	95 each	760.00
2	W103	Aluminum R16 Wheels	210 each	420.00
4	SRV01	Alignment - standard	75 /job	300.00
3	SRV02	Alignment - w caster replacement	130 /job	390.00
2	SRV03	Brake Service - standard pkg	140 /job	280.00
1	SRV04	Brake Service - complete pkg	175 /job	175.00
8	SRV06	Oil Service - premium pkg	40 /job	320.00
2	SRV08	Shocks - premium gas-matic	140 /job	280.00
		Goods and Services Tax	7%	243.95
		Provincial Sales Tax	8%	278.80
		Total cash received and deposited to bank account		$4 007.75

Allocate 100% of revenue and expenses for inventory items to Sales Division and for service items to Service Division.

☐ **Memo #2** **Dated Dec. 7/08**

From Owner: Two winter specials will be offered. Both packages will include four tires and wheels and a winter preparation service. Alignments are included in one of the packages.

Create new asset Group account 1420 Winter-Holiday Tire Packages.

Create two new inventory records:

No.	Description	Min.	Selling Price/Unit Regular	(Preferred)
WHP1	Tires/Wheels/Winter Pkg	0	$900 /pkg	($850)
WHP2	Tires/Wheels/Alignment/Winter Pkg	0	$1 400 /pkg	($1 300)

Linked accounts: Asset 1420
Revenue 4020
Expense 5050
Variance not required

Taxes: Not exempt for GST and PST
Import Duty Rate: not applicable

☐ **Item Assembly #IA-1** **Dated Dec. 7/08**

Assemble five WHP1 Tires/Wheels/Winter Pkg. Transfer 20 of each component as follows:

20 T110	P195/65R16 Tires	$53.409 each	$1 068.18
20 W107	Chrome-Steel R16 Wheels	37.0878 each	741.76
Additional Costs (for services)			$250.00

Assembled Items:

5 WHP1	Tires/Wheels/Winter Pkg	$411.988 each	$2 059.94

Accept the default prices for assembly components and copy the total to the assembled items total.

☐ **Item Assembly #IA-2** **Dated Dec. 7/08**

Assemble five WHP2 Tires/Wheels/Alignment/Winter Pkg. Transfer 20 of each component as follows:

20 T111	P205/65R16 Tires	$55.4969 each	$1 109.94
20 W103	Aluminum R16 Wheels	86.5376 each	1 730.75
Additional Costs			$500.00

Assembled Items:

5 WHP2	Tires/Wheels/Alignment/Winter Pkg	$668.138 each	$3 340.69

Accept the default prices for assembly components and copy the total to the assembled items total.

NOTES

The services are included as additional costs. You cannot assemble the service items with the inventory to create the package because no purchase costs are associated with the services. Accept the default prices for assembly components and copy the total to the assembled items total. There is no allocation in the Item Assembly Journal.

NOTES

The unit costs change continually as new inventory is purchased at different prices.

SESSION DATE – DECEMBER 14, 2008

☐ **Purchase Order #21** **Dated Dec. 8/08**

Delivery date Dec. 13/08
From Snowmaster Tire Company

16 T101	P155/80R14 Tires	¥ 45 600
16 T103	P195/75R15 Tires	61 920
8 T106	P195/65R15 Tires	35 840
8 T107	P185/65R15 Tires	37 440
	Freight	7 500
	GST Paid	13 181
Invoice Total		¥201 481

Terms: 2/15, n/30.
The exchange rate is 0.00985.

☐ **Purchase Order #22** **Dated Dec. 8/08**

Delivery date Dec. 13/08
From Sylverado Wheels

8 W106	Chrome-Steel R15 Wheels	¥26 000
8 W109	Steel R14 Wheels	12 960
8 W110	Steel R15 Wheels	14 640
	Freight	5 600
	GST Paid	4 144
Invoice Total		¥63 344

Terms: net 30.
The exchange rate is 0.00985.

☐ **Cash Receipt #82** **Dated Dec. 8/08**

From Polly Maid Service, cheque #2189 for $1 014.30 in payment of account including $20.70 discount for early payment. Reference invoice #124.

WARNING!
Do not include the discount for invoices that are not being paid.

NOTES
Close the advisor message about the overdrawn account. The transaction, Memo #3, will transfer funds to cover the overdraft.

☐ **Cheque Copy #330** **Dated Dec. 9/08**

To Snowmaster Tire Company, ¥256 198 in payment of account, including ¥5 229 discount for early payment. Reference invoice #ST-842. The exchange rate is 0.00987.

☐ **Cheque Copy #331** **Dated Dec. 9/08**

To Sylverado Wheels, ¥174 826 in payment of account. Reference invoice #SW-724. The exchange rate is 0.00987.

☐ **Memo #3** **Dated Dec. 9/08**

From Owner: Transfer ¥400 000 from Chequing account to Foreign Currency account to cover cheques. The exchange rate is 0.00987. Remember to change the currency setting to JPY.

☐ **Cash Receipt #83** **Dated Dec. 9/08**

From London Car Leasing, cheque #111 for $3 678.53 in payment of account including $75.07 discount. Reference invoice #128.

☐ **Visa Sales Invoice #130** **Dated Dec. 9/08**

Sold by Tridon to Dee Wollen

4	T113	P215/60R16 Tires	$145 each	$ 580.00
4	W103	Aluminum R16 Wheels	210 each	840.00
4	WN04	Nickel/Chrome Wheel Locks	30 /pkg	120.00
1	SRV04	Brake Service - complete pkg	175 /job	175.00
1	SRV08	Shocks - premium gas-matic	140 /job	140.00
		Goods and Services Tax	7%	129.85
		Provincial Sales Tax	8%	148.40
Total paid by Visa #4520 3591 2745 6300				$2 133.25

Allocate 100% of revenue for inventory items to Sales Division and for service items to Service Division.

☐ **MasterCard Sales Invoice #131** **Dated Dec. 10/08**

Sold by Tridon to Hansa Patel

4	T114	P225/60R17 Tires	$150 each	$ 600.00
4	W104	Aluminum R17 Wheels	225 each	900.00
4	WN04	Nickel/Chrome Wheel Locks	30 /pkg	120.00
1	SRV02	Alignment - w caster replacement	130 /job	130.00
1	SRV04	Brake Service - complete pkg	175 /job	175.00
1	SRV07	Shocks - economy gas-charged	100 /job	100.00
		Goods and Services Tax	7%	141.75
		Provincial Sales Tax	8%	162.00
Total paid by MasterCard #5190 2823 5568 2016				$2 328.75

Allocate 100% of revenue for inventory items to Sales Division and for service items to Service Division.

NOTES
You will see the advisor message that inventory items have dropped below the reorder point. Close the advisor to continue.

☐ **Sales Invoice #132** **Dated Dec. 11/08**

Sold by Tridon to Pronto Pizza & Delivery

8	T108	P185/60R15 Tires	$120 each
8	W106	Chrome-Steel R15 Wheels	80 each
2	SRV03	Brake Service - standard pkg	140 /job
2	SRV07	Shocks - economy gas-charged	100 /job
		Goods and Services Tax	7%
		Provincial Sales Tax	8%

Terms: 2/10, n/30.

Allocate 100% of revenue and expenses for inventory items to Sales Division and for service items to Service Division.

☐ **Sales Invoice #133** **Dated Dec. 13/08**

Sold by Tridon to Airport Taxi Company (preferred customer)

8	T103	P195/75R15 Tires	$ 88 each
8	W102	Aluminum R15 Wheels	187 each
8	WN04	Nickel/Chrome Wheel Locks	28 /pkg
		Goods and Services Tax	7%
		Provincial Sales Tax	8%

Terms: 2/10, n/30.
Allocate 100% of revenue and expenses for inventory items to Sales Division.

☐ **Purchase Invoice #SW-1024** **Dated Dec. 13/08**

From Sylverado Wheels, to fill purchase order #22

8	W106 Chrome-Steel R15 Wheels		¥26 000
8	W109 Steel R14 Wheels		12 960
8	W110 Steel R15 Wheels		14 640
	Freight		5 600
	GST Paid		4 144
	Invoice Total		¥63 344
	Import Duty	CAD $31.71	¥3 216

Terms: net 30. The exchange rate is 0.00986. Allocate the freight to Sales.

☑ **Purchase Invoice #ST-1141** **Dated Dec. 13/08**

479 From Snowmaster Tire Company, to fill purchase order #21

16	T101	P155/80R14 Tires		¥ 45 600
16	T103	P195/75R15 Tires		61 920
8	T106	P195/65R15 Tires		35 840
8	T107	P185/65R15 Tires		37 440
	Freight			7 500
	GST Paid			13 181
	Invoice Total			¥201 481
	Import Duty		CAD $124.78	¥12 656

Terms: 2/15, n/30. The exchange rate is 0.00986. Allocate the freight to Sales.

☐ **Purchase Invoice #MT-1521** **Dated Dec. 13/08**

From MoTech Auto Parts

2 dozen	WN01	Chrome Wheel Nuts	$ 96.00
2 dozen	WN02	Chrome Wheel Locks	240.00
2 dozen	WN03	Nickel/Chrome Wheel Nuts	114.00
2 dozen	WN04	Nickel/Chrome Wheel Locks	288.00
	Freight		20.00
	GST Paid		53.06
Invoice Total			$811.06

Terms: 2/10, n/30. Allocate the freight to Sales.

NOTES

Enter 2 as the quantity for the purchases from MoTech Auto Parts and edit the amount if necessary.

The wheel locks and nuts have different buying and selling units. They are purchased in boxes of one dozen packages and sold as individual packages.

☑ **Memo #4** **Dated Dec. 13/08**

480 From Owner: Pay import duty charged on purchases to date to Receiver General. Issue cheque #202 for $448.36 to pay account balance in full. Reference sales invoices #ST-916, ST-1141, SW-876 and SW-1024.

☐ **Sales Order #12-1** **Dated Dec. 14/08**

Starting date for contract Dec. 21/08
From Lovely U Cosmetics, $5 100 plus $357 GST and $408 PST for tire and wheel contract for five vehicles. Invoice total $5 865. Deposit of 20% payable on acceptance of contract. Terms: 2/10, n/30.
This is a non-inventory sales order. Credit Revenue from Sales.
Sold by Tridon. Received cheque #9754 for $1 020 as deposit #13 with order.

NOTES
Accept the default costs and enter total assembly components cost for assembled items total cost.

☐ **Item Assembly:** **Dated Dec. 14/08**
Reserve Inventory Form #RIF-1001

Reserve inventory required for Lovely U Cosmetics contract.
Create new inventory asset Group account 1440 Reserved Inventory for Workorders.
Create new inventory record in the Inventory Ledger for the project as follows:

No.	Description	Min.	Regular Selling Price/unit
LC1	Lovely U Cosmetics Inventory	0	$5 100/contract

Linked accounts: Asset 1440 Revenue 4020 COGS 5050
Taxes: Not exempt for GST and PST. Duty does not apply.

Assemble the following as reserved inventory at cost price for the project:

20	T111	P205/65R16 Tires	$ 55.4968 each	$1 109.94
20	W107	Chrome-Steel R16 Wheels	37.0875 each	741.75
20	WN04	Nickel/Chrome Wheel Locks	12 /pkg	240.00

Package includes free installation.

Assembled Items:

1	LC1	Lovely U Cosmetics Inventory	$2 091.69 each	$2 091.69

☐ **Cash Sales Invoice #134** **Dated Dec. 14/08**

Tridon's Sales Summary for one-time Cash Customers

5	SRV01	Alignment - standard	$ 75 /job	$ 375.00
5	SRV03	Brake Service - standard pkg	140 /job	700.00
5	SRV05	Oil Service - standard pkg	30 /job	150.00
5	SRV06	Oil Service - premium pkg	40 /job	200.00
10	SRV11	Winter Prep. Service	60 /job	600.00
1	WHP1	Tires/Wheels/Winter Pkg	900 /pkg	900.00
1	WHP2	Tires/Wheels/Alignment/Winter Pkg	1 400 /pkg	1 400.00
		Goods and Services Tax	7%	302.75
		Provincial Sales Tax	8%	346.00
		Total cash received and deposited to bank account		$4 973.75

Allocate 100% of revenue for service items to Service Division.
Allocate 95% of revenue for WHP1 to Sales and 5% to Service.
Allocate 90% of revenue for WHP2 to Sales and 10% to Service.

WARNING!
Updated data files are available for downloading from <www.pearsoned.ca/text/purbhoo 2006>. Zipped files for both Basic and Pro versions are available.

Alternatively, you can make the changes yourself.

Edit the Employee record for Monroe. On the Income tab screen, change his Vacation Rate to 4%. Edit the Employee record for Niehoff. On the Income tab screen, change the regular number of hours from 24 to 80.

NOTES
If you have difficulty accessing the Allo column, you can click an employee name and then click the Allo tool button.

You can apply the allocation to the entire transaction in the Payroll Cheque Run Journal.

EMPLOYEE TIME SUMMARY SHEET #51

(pay period ending December 14, 2008)

	Name of Employee	Week 1	Week 2	Regular Hours	Overtime Hours	No. of Piece Rate Jobs	Sick Days	Personal Days
✓	Delco	40	40	80	0	20	1	–
480								
☐	Holley	40	42	80	2	6	–	1
☐	Monroe	42	40	80	2	12	–	–
☐	Niehoff	40	42	80	2	15	–	–

a. Use Employee Time Summary Sheet #51 and the Employee Information Sheet to complete the payroll run for hourly paid employees.
b. Allocate 100% of the payroll expenses to Service for all employees.
c. Issue deposit slips #112 to #115.

SESSION DATE – DECEMBER 21, 2008

☐ **Visa Sales Invoice #135** **Dated Dec. 16/08**

Sold by Tridon to Peter Manga

1	SRV08	Shocks - premium gas-matic		$ 140.00
1	WHP2	Tires/Wheels/Alignment/Winter Pkg		1 400.00
		Goods and Services Tax	7%	107.80
		Provincial Sales Tax	8%	123.20
		Total paid by Visa #4500 4678 1274 5630		$1 771.00

Allocate 100% of revenue for service items to Service Division.
Allocate 90% of revenue for WHP2 to Sales and 10% to Service Division.

☐ **Cheque Copy #332** **Dated Dec. 16/08**

To Snowmaster Tire Company, ¥232 894 in payment of account, including ¥4 753 discount for early payment. Reference invoice #ST-916. The exchange rate is 0.00983.

☐ **Memo #5** **Dated Dec. 16/08**

From Owner: Transfer ¥400 000 (JPY) from Chequing account to Foreign Currency account to cover cheques. The exchange rate is 0.00983.

☐ **Cash Purchase Invoice #LH-31421** **Dated Dec. 17/08**

From London Hydro, $250 plus $17.50 GST for hydro services. Invoice total $267.50 paid in full with cheque #203. Allocate 30% of expense to Sales and 70% to Service Division.

☐ **Cash Purchase Invoice #BC-64261** **Dated Dec. 17/08**

From Bell Canada, $90 plus $6.30 GST and $7.20 PST for telephone services. Invoice total $103.50 paid in full with cheque #204. Allocate 40% of expense to Sales and 60% to Service Division.

☐ **Cash Purchase Invoice #WH-690** **Dated Dec. 17/08**

From Western Hydraulic Repairs, $400 plus $28 GST and $32 PST for repairs to hydraulic lift in service bay and maintenance of other lifts. Invoice total $460 paid in full with cheque #205. Allocate 10% of expense to Sales and 90% to Service Division.

☐ **Cash Receipt #84** **Dated Dec. 19/08**

From Pronto Pizza & Delivery, cheque #399 for $2 344.16 in payment of account including $47.84 discount for early payment. Reference invoice #132.

☐ **MasterCard Sales Invoice #136** **Dated Dec. 20/08**

Sold by Tridon to Daniel BenDavid

1	WHP1	Tires/Wheels/Winter Pkg		$ 900.00
1	SRV04	Brake Service - complete pkg		175.00
1	SRV08	Shocks - premium gas-matic		140.00
		Goods and Services Tax	7%	85.05
		Provincial Sales Tax	8%	97.20
		Total paid by MasterCard #5809 8213 6238 1601		$1 397.25

Allocate 100% of revenue for service items to Service Division.
Allocate 95% of revenue for WHP1 to Sales and 5% to Service Division.

☐ **Cash Purchase Invoice #MS-40002** **Dated Dec. 21/08**

From Motor Supply Company (use Quick Add for the new vendor), $500 plus $35 GST and $40 PST for cleaning fluids, cleaning cloths and other garage supplies. Invoice total $575 paid in full with cheque #206.

NOTES
You may see a message about the Cost of Goods Sold not being fully allocated. This message results from differences in rounding the amounts.

☐ **Cash Sales Invoice #137** **Dated Dec. 21/08**

Tridon's Sales Summary for one-time Cash Customers

4	WN01	Chrome Wheel Nuts	$ 10 /pkg	$ 40.00
5	SRV05	Oil Service - standard pkg	30 /job	150.00
5	SRV06	Oil Service - premium pkg	40 /job	200.00
1	WHP1	Tires/Wheels/Winter Pkg	900 /pkg	900.00
1	WHP2	Tires/Wheels/Alignment/Winter Pkg	1 400 /pkg	1 400.00
		Goods and Services Tax	7%	188.30
		Provincial Sales Tax	8%	215.20
		Total cash received and deposited to bank account		$3 093.50

Allocate 100% of revenue for inventory items to Sales Division.
Allocate 100% of revenue for service items to Service Division.
Allocate 95% of revenue for WHP1 to Sales and 5% to Service.
Allocate 90% of revenue for WHP2 to Sales and 10% to Service.

NOTES
Remember to enter the quantity returned with a minus sign.
Enter Tridon as the salesperson so that her net sales revenue will be calculated correctly for the sales commission.

☐ **Sales Return #R-137** **Dated Dec. 21/08**

From one-time Cash Customer (sold by Tridon)

–4	WN01	Chrome Wheel Nuts	$10 /pkg	–$40.00
		Handling charge (20% of total sales price)		9.20
		Goods and Services Tax	7%	–2.16
		Provincial Sales Tax	8%	–2.46
		Total cash paid to customer		–$35.42

Customer returned the wheel nuts because they were not required.
Create new Group revenue account: 4130 Sales Returns & Allowances.
The handling charge is credited to Other Revenue. Allocate 100% of the returns and the revenue to Sales.

NOTES
Refer to page 222 for assistance with editing the sales order. Choose Sales Order as the transaction type before choosing the order to adjust. Do not edit the prepayment.

WARNING!
When filling the sales order, change the method of payment to Pay Later.

☐ **Memo #6** **Dated Dec. 21/08**

Edit sales order #12-1 from Lovely U Cosmetics. Change the contract item ordered to the reserved inventory LC1. The quantity ordered remains as one.

☐ **Sales Invoice #138** **Dated Dec. 21/08**

Sold by Tridon to Lovely U Cosmetics, to fill sales order #12-1

1	LC1	Lovely U Cosmetics Inventory	$5 100
		Goods and Services Tax	7%
		Provincial Sales Tax	8%

Terms: 2/10, n/30.
Allocate 100% of sale to Sales Division.

SESSION DATE – DECEMBER 28, 2008

☐ **Interac Sales Invoice #139** **Dated Dec. 22/08**

Sold by Tridon to Cedric Ng

4	T111	P205/65R16 Tires	$135 each	$ 540.00
4	W107	Chrome-Steel R16 Wheels	90 each	360.00
		Goods and Services Tax	7%	63.00
		Provincial Sales Tax	8%	72.00

Total paid in full by debit card #5300 5291 6730 8161 $1 035.00
Allocate 100% of the sale to the Sales Division.

NOTES
Use the Trial Balance on page 449 for the November 30 PST Payable balance.

☐ **Memo #7** **Dated Dec. 22/08**

From Owner: Use the balance for November 30 to record PST payable for November as a liability to the Minister of Finance. Reduce PST payable by 5% for PST compensation. Issue cheque #207 for $3 192. Do not allocate the revenue amount because it applies to the previous month.

☐ **Purchase Invoice #SW-1159** **Dated Dec. 22/08**

From Sylverado Wheels

8	W107 Chrome-Steel R16 Wheels		¥29 280
	Freight		1 200
	GST Paid		2 134
Invoice Total			¥32 614
Import Duty		CAD $17.36	¥1 757

Terms: net 30. The exchange rate is 0.00988. Allocate the freight to Sales.

☐ **Purchase Invoice #TS-817** **Dated Dec. 22/08**

From TuffArm Shocks, $2 000 plus $140 GST for shocks and parts for services. Invoice total $2 140. Terms: net 30.

☐ **Cash Receipt #85** **Dated Dec. 23/08**

From Airport Taxi Company, cheque #9902 for $2 731.85 in payment of account including $55.75 discount for early payment. Reference invoice #133.

☐ **Cheque Copy #208** **Dated Dec. 23/08**

To MoTech Auto Parts, $794.84 in payment of account, including $16.22 discount for early payment. Reference invoice #MT-1521.

☐ **Purchase Invoice #MT-1894** **Dated Dec. 26/08**

From MoTech Auto Parts, $800 plus $56 GST for brake hoses, cables, pads and other brake parts and hardware. Invoice total $856. Terms: 2/10, n/30.

☐ **Visa Sales Invoice #140** **Dated Dec. 26/08**

Sold by Tridon to Sam Gallo

8	T114	P225/60R17 Tires	$150 each	$1 200.00
8	W108	Chrome-Steel R17 Wheels	100 each	800.00
		Goods and Services Tax	7%	140.00
		Provincial Sales Tax	8%	160.00
Total paid by Visa #4500 4678 1274 5630				$2 300.00

Allocate 100% of revenue for sales items to Sales Division.

☐ **Cheque Copy #333** **Dated Dec. 26/08**

To Snowmaster Tire Company, ¥197 451 in payment of account, including ¥4 030 discount for early payment. Reference invoice #ST-1141. The exchange rate is 0.00982.

☐ **MasterCard Sales Invoice #141** **Dated Dec. 26/08**

Sold by Tridon to Russ Campbell

1	WHP2	Tires/Wheels/Alignment/Winter Pkg		$1 400.00
1	SRV04	Brake Service - complete pkg		175.00
		Goods and Services Tax	7%	110.25
		Provincial Sales Tax	8%	126.00
Total paid by MasterCard #5098 2813 2386 0101				$1 811.25

Allocate 100% of revenue for service item to Service Division.
Allocate 90% of revenue for WHP2 to Sales and 10% to Service Division.

☐ **Interac Sales Invoice #142** **Dated Dec. 27/08**

Sold by Tridon to Federica Yuen

1	WHP1	Tires/Wheels/Winter Pkg		$ 900.00
1	SRV03	Brake Service - standard pkg		140.00
		Goods and Services Tax	7%	72.80
		Provincial Sales Tax	8%	83.20
Total paid by Debit Card #2816 3238 6010 1291				$1 196.00

Allocate 100% of revenue for service item to Service Division and allocate 95% of revenue for WHP1 to Sales and 5% to Service Division.

NOTES

You will see another message about Variance Costs not fully allocated.

☐ **Sales Invoice #143** **Dated Dec. 27/08**

Sold by Tridon to City Cab Company

1	WHP1	Tires/Wheels/Winter Pkg	$ 900 /pkg
2	WHP2	Tires/Wheels/Alignment/Winter Pkg	1 400 /pkg
		Goods and Services Tax	7%
		Provincial Sales Tax	8%

Terms: 2/10, n/30.
Allocate 95% of revenue for WHP1 to Sales and 5% to Service Division.
Allocate 90% of revenue for WHP2 to Sales and 10% to Service Division.

NOTES
Accept the default prices for assembly components and copy the Total to the assembled items Amount field.

☐ **Item Assembly #IA-3** **Dated Dec. 27/08**

Assemble three WHP2 Tires/Wheels/Alignment/Winter Pkg. Transfer 12 of each component as follows:

12	T111	P205/65R16 Tires	$55.495 each	$ 665.94
12	W103	Aluminum R16 Wheels	86.5379 each	1 038.45
Additional Costs				$300.00

Assembled Items:

3	WHP2	Tires/Wheels/Alignment/Winter Pkg.		
			$668.13 each	$2 004.39

NOTES
You may see the message about incomplete allocations. Rounding off dollar amounts in the currency conversion can lead to this warning. Check that you have allocated the amount correctly and then accept the incomplete allocation.

☐ **Purchase Invoice #ST-1383** **Dated Dec. 27/08**

From Snowmaster Tire Company

12	T108	P185/60R15 Tires		¥ 58 320
20	T111	P205/65R16 Tires		109 400
8	T112	P205/60R16 Tires		45 440
8	T114	P225/60R17 Tires		48 400
		Freight		7 500
		GST Paid		18 834
		Invoice Total		¥287 894
Import Duty			CAD $180.34	¥18 309

Terms: 2/15, n/30. The exchange rate is 0.00985.
Edit prices if necessary to match those in the invoice. Allocate the freight to Sales.

☐ **Memo #8** **Dated Dec. 28/08**

From Owner: Write off one Chrome-Steel R17 Wheel (W108) that was dented beyond repair by machinery. Allocate 100% of the write-off to Sales.

☐ **Cash Sales Invoice #144** **Dated Dec. 28/08**

Tridon's Sales Summary for one-time Cash Customers

8	T112	P205/60R16 Tires	$140 each	$1 120.00
4	W101	Aluminum R14 Wheels	180 each	720.00
4	W103	Aluminum R16 Wheels	210 each	840.00
4	W105	Chrome-Steel R14 Wheels	70 each	280.00
4	WN02	Chrome Wheel Locks	25 /pkg	100.00
5	SRV01	Alignment - standard	75 /job	375.00
1	SRV03	Brake Service - standard pkg	140 /job	140.00
1	SRV07	Shocks - economy gas-charged	100 /job	100.00
		Goods and Services Tax	7%	257.25
		Provincial Sales Tax	8%	294.00
	Total cash received and deposited to bank account			$4 226.25

Allocate 100% of revenue for inventory items to Sales Division.
Allocate 100% of revenue for service items to Service Division.

☐ **Purchase Invoice #SW-1419** **Dated Dec. 28/08**

From Sylverado Wheels

8	W102 Aluminum R15 Wheels		¥ 63 200
16	W103 Aluminum R16 Wheels		136 640
8	W104 Aluminum R17 Wheels		72 800
8	W106 Chrome-Steel R15 Wheels		26 000
20	W107 Chrome-Steel R16 Wheels		73 200
	Freight		7 000
	GST Paid		26 519
	Invoice Total		¥405 359
	Import Duty	CAD $219.98	¥22 310

Terms: net 30. The exchange rate is 0.00986. Allocate the freight to Sales.

☐ **Visa Sales Invoice #145** **Dated Dec. 28/08**

Sold by Tridon to Louise Binder

4	T114	P225/60R17 Tires	$150 each	$ 600.00
4	W104	Aluminum R17 Wheels	225 each	900.00
4	WN04	Nickel/Chrome Wheel Locks	30 /pkg	120.00
		Goods and Services Tax	7%	113.40
		Provincial Sales Tax	8%	129.60
Total paid by Visa #4515 7827 4563 8900				$1 863.00

Allocate 100% of revenue for sales items to Sales Division.

EMPLOYEE TIME SUMMARY SHEET #52

(pay period ending December 28, 2008)

	Name of Employee	Week 1	Week 2	Regular Hours	Overtime Hours	No. of Piece Rate Jobs	Sick Days	Personal Days
☐	Delco	40	42	80	2	10	–	–
☐	Holley	42	40	80	2	3	–	–
☐	Monroe	42	40	80	2	4	1	–
☐	Niehoff	40	44	80	4	10	–	2

a. Use Employee Time Summary Sheet #52 and the Employee Information Sheet to complete the payroll run for hourly paid employees.
b. Add a holiday bonus of $200 to each employee's paycheque. Use the Bonus field for the bonus.
c. Allocate 100% of the payroll expenses to Service for all employees.
d. Issue deposit slips #116 to #119.

NOTES

If you have difficulty accessing the Allo column, you can click an employee name and then click the Allo tool button.

SESSION DATE – DECEMBER 31, 2008

☐ **Memo #9** **Dated Dec. 30/08**

From Owner: Pay import duty charged on purchases (#SW-1159, ST-1383, SW-1419) to date to Receiver General. Issue cheque #209 for $417.68 to pay balance in full.

☐ **Bank Debit Memo #92564** **Dated Dec. 31/08**

From Universal Bank, authorized withdrawals were made from the chequing account.

Loan payment principal	$1 000
Loan payment interest	200
Mortgage payment interest	910
Mortgage payment principal	90
Bank charges	30

Allocate 50% of the expenses to Sales and 50% to the Service Division.

☐ **Bank Credit Memo #65925** **Dated Dec. 31/08**

From Universal Bank, $515 interest deposited to chequing account. Create new Group account 4200 Revenue from Interest and remember to allow allocation for this account. Allocate 50% of the interest revenue to Sales and 50% to the Service Division.

☐ **Memo #10** **Dated Dec. 31/08**

From Owner: Complete payroll run to pay salaried employees Fram and Tridon. Add a holiday bonus of $300 to Fram's cheque and $500 to Tridon's cheque. Issue deposit slips #120 and 121. Allocate 50% of Tridon's pay to Sales and 50% to Service. Allocate 60% of Fram's pay to Sales and 40% to Service.

Issue cheque #210 to Tridon for $409, her sales commission. Allocate 100% of the commission to Sales. Include 10% income tax for the commission. Use the Sales by Salesperson Report using stocking units or the Income Statement. (Refer to margin note.)

☐ **Memo #11** **Dated Dec. 31/08**

From Owner: Make payroll remittances for the December pay period as follows:
To Receiver General for Canada: EI, CPP and Income Tax
To Minister of Finance: EHT
To Equity Life: CSB Payable
To CAW Union: Union Dues
To Workplace Safety & Insurance Board: WSIB
Issue cheques #211 to #215 in payment. Use Memo11a, 11b, etc. as the source.

☐ **Memo #12** **Dated Dec. 31/08**

From Owner: Prepare an adjusting entry for supplies used.
Create new Group accounts: 5160 Brakes & Shocks Parts Used
5170 Supplies Used: Garage
5180 Supplies Used: Office

Supplies Used: Brakes and Shocks Parts	$4 900
Supplies: Garage	1 820
Supplies: Office	430

Allocate 90% of the Parts and Garage supplies to Service and 10% to Sales.
Allocate 50% of the Office Supplies to Service and 50% to Sales.

☐ **Memo #13** **Dated Dec. 31/08**

From Owner: Update all tax codes and GST rates to apply the tax rate reduction from 7 percent to 6 percent.

NOTES
Use the Bonus field for the bonus amounts.
Issue a separate cheque for Tridon's sales commission. Use the Paycheques Journal so that you can change the tax amounts. Choose the Enter Taxes Manually tool to open the tax fields for editing. Remove the income amounts and enter 40.90 in the Income Tax field. Do not remove the CPP amount. Remove the CSB deduction on the Deductions tab screen and the number of hours worked on the Entitlements tab screen.
The Sales by Salesperson Report using stocking unit reports only on inventory items, and for Truman, selling and stocking units are the same. The general Sales by Salesperson Report includes revenue from services. The sales commission is based only on the sales revenue.

NOTES
Assign the Expense or Operating Expense account class to the new accounts. Operating Expense is the default when you use the Add Account wizard.

KEYSTROKES

Creating New Projects

Simply Accounting allows allocations for all accounts. Each account ledger record has a check box to allow project allocations for the account (refer to page 97). If this box is checked, the allocation option is available for that account in any journal entry. If it is not checked, you cannot allocate an amount for that account. If you are unable to allocate an amount, check the ledger record for the account you are using to be sure that the option to Allow Project Allocations is selected. Truman Tires will allocate amounts for all revenue and expense accounts. The option to allow allocations is already turned on for all these accounts in your file.

NOTES
The option to allow allocations for Balance Sheet accounts is not selected in the files for Truman Tires.

Before entering any transactions with cost or revenue allocations, you should create the projects.

Open the files for **Truman Tires**. **Enter Dec. 7, 2008** as the session date.

Click **OK** to enter the session date. The Home window appears.

Projects are created in the Project Ledger indicated with the pointer as shown:

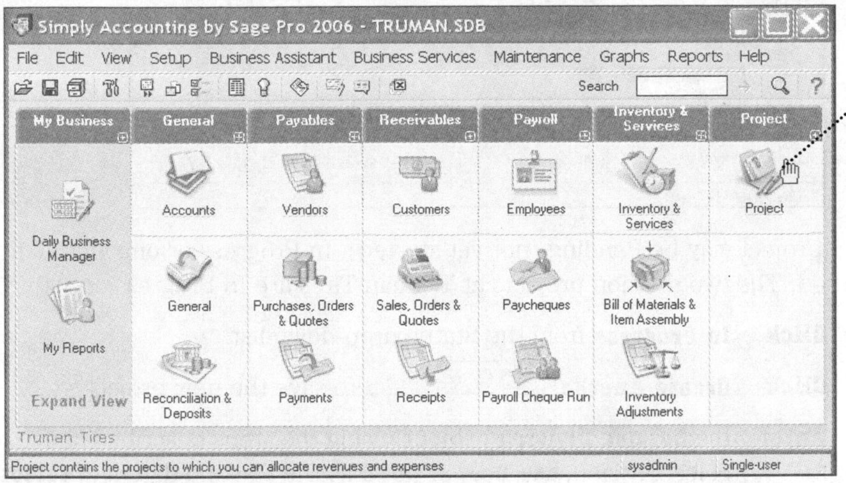

Click the **Project module heading** to open the Project module window:

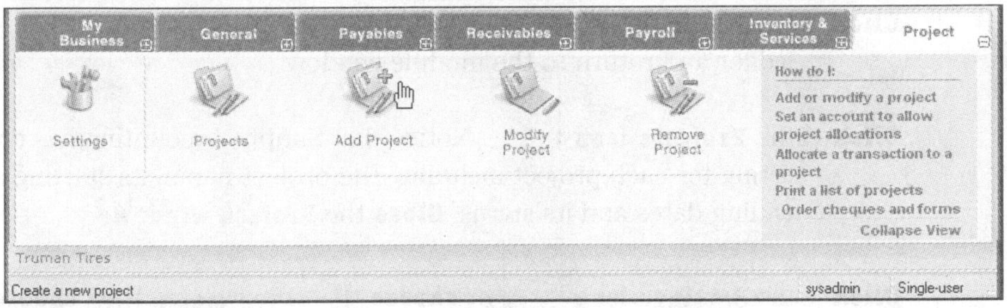

NOTES

You can also click the Project icon in the Home window to open the Project window. Then click the Create button to open the Project Ledger window.

The Project module has no journals.

Click the **Add Project icon** 

. The new Project Ledger screen appears:

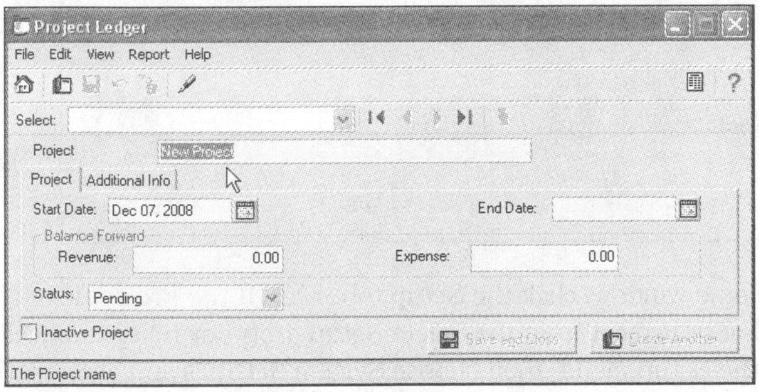

The cursor is in the Project name field with the contents highlighted, ready to be edited. You must enter the name of the first project.

Type `Sales Division` **Press** *tab*.

The cursor moves to the Start Date field. Enter the date on which you want to begin recording project information, December 1, 2008. The session date appears automatically as the default, ready to be edited. You need to change the date.

Type `12-01`

You can enter an **Ending Date** for the project if this is appropriate. The ledger also has a **Balance Forward** field for **Revenue** and **Expense**. These fields can be used to enter historical information — the amount of revenue and expense generated by the project before the records were converted to Simply Accounting. The balances are zero for Truman Tires because a new fiscal period is just beginning.

The next field shows the Status for the project.

Click the **Status field** or list arrow to see the status options:

The project may be Pending (not yet started), In Progress or ongoing, Cancelled or Completed. The two division projects at Truman Tires are In Progress or active.

Click **In Progress** from the Status drop-down list.

Click **Create Another** 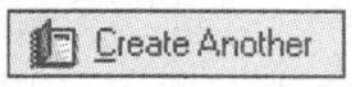 to save the new project.

Enter the **Service Division** project, using the steps described above for the Sales Division, **use Dec. 1, 2008** as the starting date and **select In Progress** as the Status.

Click **Save And Close**  to save the second project, close the ledger and return to the module window.

Click the **Projects icon** . Notice that Simply Accounting has created a listing for each project including the project name, its starting and ending dates and its status. **Close** the **Project window**.

Click the **Settings icon**  or **choose** the **Setup menu**, then **choose System Settings** and **click Settings**. **Click Project** if necessary to display the Settings window as shown here:

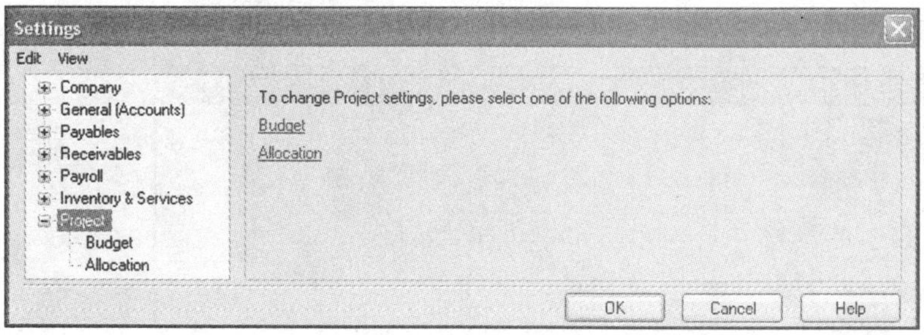

From the Home window, click the Setup tool . If the Project icon is not selected, choose Project from the Select Setup drop-down list and click Select. Or choose the Setup menu, then choose System Settings and click Settings. Click Project. If the Project icon is selected when you click the Setup tool, the Project Settings screen should open directly.

The Project Ledger has settings for budgeting and allocation. Budgeting is covered in Chapter 13. We need to view the setting for allocations.

Click **Allocation** either in the list under Project or in the list on the right:

NOTES

You can list projects by icon in the Project window by choosing the View menu and icon.

You can re-sort the project icons if they are out of order by choosing the Options menu and Re-sort Icons.

NOTES

If a Project module icon is selected, the Project tab will open directly. If no icon is selected, you will see the System Settings.

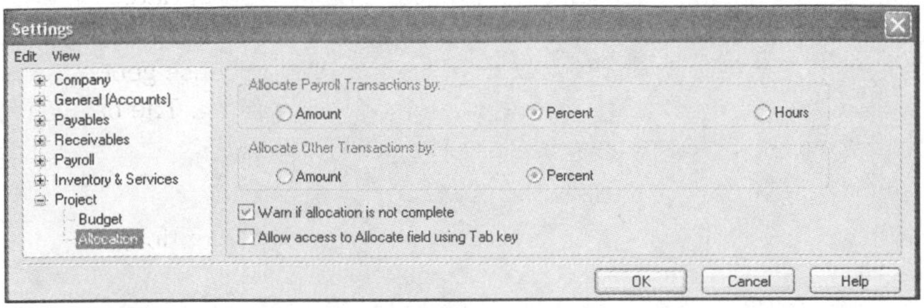

NOTES
You cannot change these settings in multi-user mode.

You can enter the allocation in different ways — by Amount, by Percent or by Hours. The option to Allocate By Amount requires you to enter the exact dollar amount for each project. Project work for payroll purposes is often recorded by time spent on the project. This is the third option for payroll allocations.

Simply Accounting includes a warning for incomplete allocations. It is easy to miss an allocation because you must complete the allocation procedure even if 100 percent of the costs are allocated to a single project, and you must allocate each account line in the journals. You will receive the warning if you try to post an entry that has not been fully allocated. If you are using projects, you should always turn on the warning. The warning should be selected by default.

NOTES
If you are not using the allocation feature, do not select the option to Allow Access To Allocate Using Tab Key so that the cursor will skip the unused Allo field.

If this option is not selected, click Warn If Allocation Is Not Complete. The remaining default settings, to allocate expenses by percentage, are correct.

You can also choose to access Allocation fields in journals with the tab key. Without this option, you must click the Allo field or tool to open the Allocation window. Using the tab key allows you to use the keyboard to enter the transaction and allocation. You can still click the field to move the cursor if you want.

Click **Allow Access To Allocate Field Using Tab Key**.

Click **OK** to save the allocation settings.

Close the **Project module** to restore the Home window.

Changing Project Names

The name of the Project Ledger can be changed to Department, Profit Centre, Division or something that is more appropriate for a business. The new name will replace Project in the Home window and on reports. We will change the ledger name to Division for Truman Tires' Sales and Service Departments.

NOTES
We are not using the name Department for Projects because Simply Accounting also has a feature called departmental accounting that is different from project allocation (see Chapter 18).

Choose the **Setup menu**, then **choose System Settings** and **click Names & Terminology**:

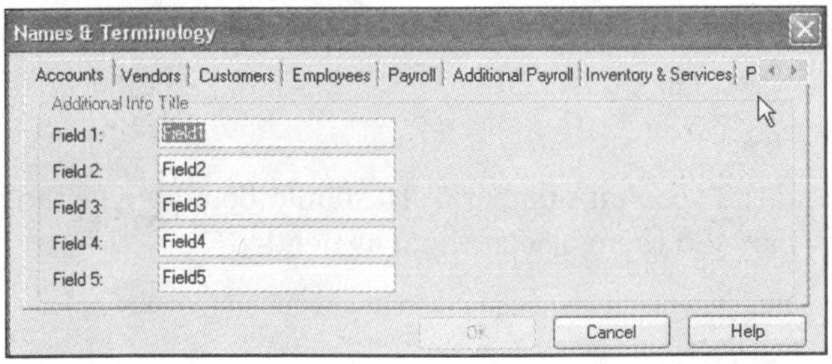

These input fields allow you to add your own user-defined fields for each ledger. The new fields will appear on the Additional Info tab screen in each ledger. The Accounts name fields are open first.

Click the **Project tab**. If necessary, scroll to the right to access the Project tab.

You will see the default names for the Project Ledger:

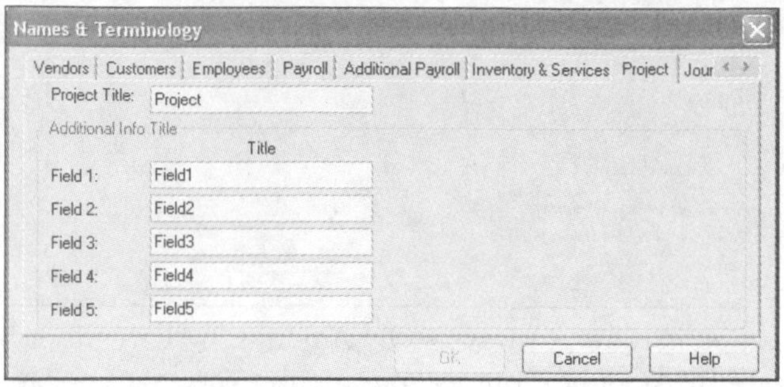

Press tab to move to the Project Title field.

Type `Division`

Click **OK** to save the name.

When you return to the Home window, Division 

replaces Project. All Project reports will have Division as the menu option and report name. The name can be changed at any time by repeating the steps above.

Entering Cost Allocations

NOTES

You can allow allocations for Balance Sheet accounts but we have not done so for Truman Tires.

Costs or expenses and revenues are allocated after the regular journal entry is completed but before it is posted. In a journal entry, whenever you use an account for which you have allowed project allocations in the General Ledger, the allocation option is available. For Truman Tires, all revenue and expense accounts allow project allocations.

Click the **Purchases icon** 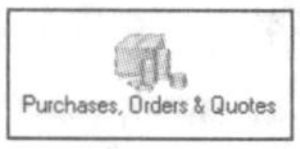

to open the Purchases Journal.

The journal has not changed with the setup of allocations, and we enter the purchase details the same way.

The first transaction does not involve the purchase of inventory items, so you will not use the inventory database to complete this transaction. Invoice is correct as the transaction type, and Pay Later is the correct payment method.

From the list of vendors,

Click **London Tool Rentals**.

Click the **Invoice field**.

Type `L-4441` **Press** tab **twice**.

The cursor moves to the Date field. Replace the default session date with the transaction date.

Type `dec 1`

The tax code GP and the account number 5110 should be added as the default. If they are not, you can add them or edit them as needed.

Enter a **description**.

Click the **Amount field** or press tab repeatedly to advance the cursor. **Enter** the **amount** of the invoice, excluding taxes.

Type `280` **Press** tab **twice** to reach the Allo column.

The journal now looks like a regular completed purchase transaction:

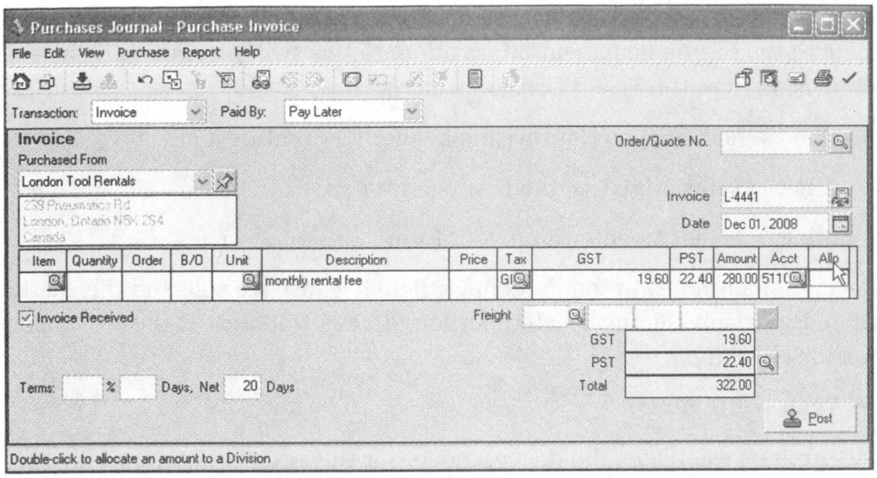

Notice that the Allocate tool is no longer dimmed. If the cursor has advanced to the next line of the invoice, the Allocate tool will be dimmed and unavailable.

Click the invoice line for the amount you want to allocate to activate the Allocate option. Only accounts that have selected the option to Allow Project Allocations will activate the Allocate tool.

Click the **Allocate tool**, or **press** *enter*, or **click** the **Allo column** beside the account or **choose** the **Purchase menu** and **click Allocate**.

NOTES

You can also press *ctrl* + *shift* + A to open the Division Allocation window.

You will see the Division Allocation window for the Purchases Journal:

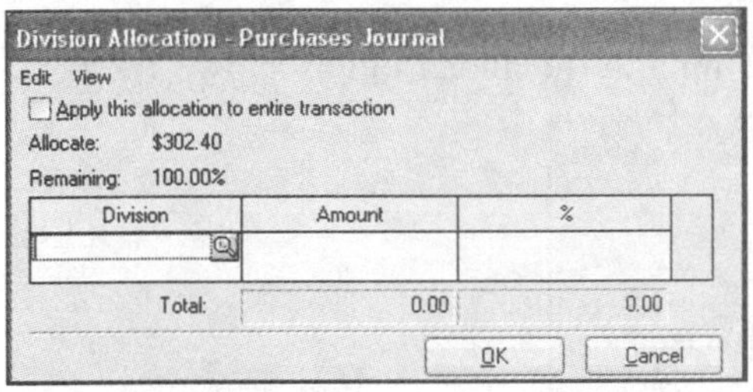

NOTES

Because we changed the project ledger name, Division appears in the screen and column headings in the allocation windows instead of Project.

The cursor is in the Division field. The full amount to be allocated, $302.40 (the expense amount plus PST), is shown at the top for reference together with the proportion remaining to be allocated, 100.00%. Amounts can be allocated by percentage or by actual amount. This choice is made in the Project Settings window shown on page 471 (choose the Setup menu, System Settings and then Settings and the Project or Division tab). The setting can be changed as needed. Truman Tires uses the Percentage allocation method as indicated in the Project Information.

NOTES

The GST amount is not allocated because it is not part of the expense.

You must complete the allocation process even if 100 percent of the revenue or expense is assigned to a single project or division. You must complete the allocation process for each account or invoice line on your input form.

Click the **Division List icon** to display the following list of Departments in alphabetic order:

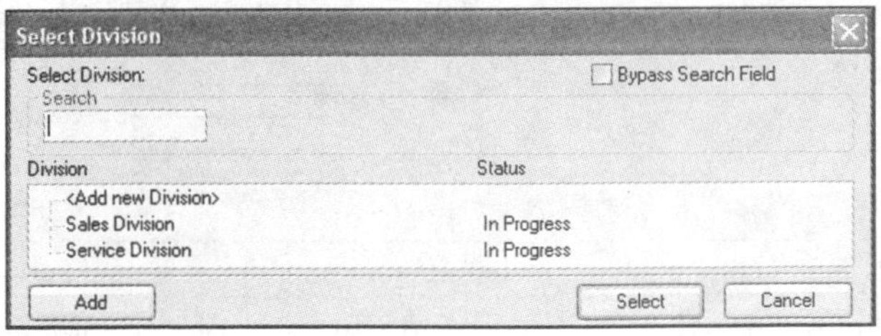

The first division is Sales, which incurs 20 percent of the total rental expense according to the source document information. Notice that you can add a new project/division from the Select Division window.

Choose Add to open the Division Ledger for creating a new project.

Click **Sales Division**, the first one we need.

Click **Select** to enter it on your form.

The cursor advances to the Percentage field because we selected this method of allocation. By default the unallocated portion (100%) is indicated in this field and it is selected for editing.

Type 20 **Press** (tab).

The program calculates the dollar amount for this project automatically based on the percentage entered. The percentage remaining at the top of the input form has been updated to 80.00%. The cursor moves to the next line in the Division field. Now you are ready to enter the amount for the remaining project, 80 percent. You need to repeat the steps above to allocate the remainder of the expense.

Press (enter).

Double click **Service Division**.

The cursor is in the Percentage field again, with 80.00 as the default amount because this is the unallocated percentage remaining. Since this amount is correct, we can accept it.

Press (tab) to enter it and complete the allocation as shown here:

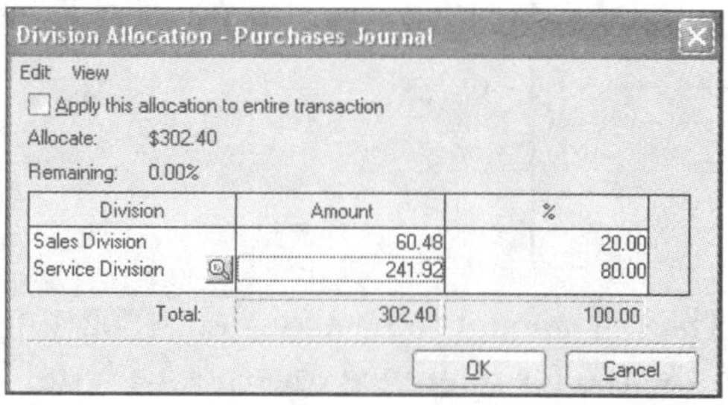

Click **OK** to return to the Purchases Journal.

Your form is now complete as shown, and you are ready to review your work:

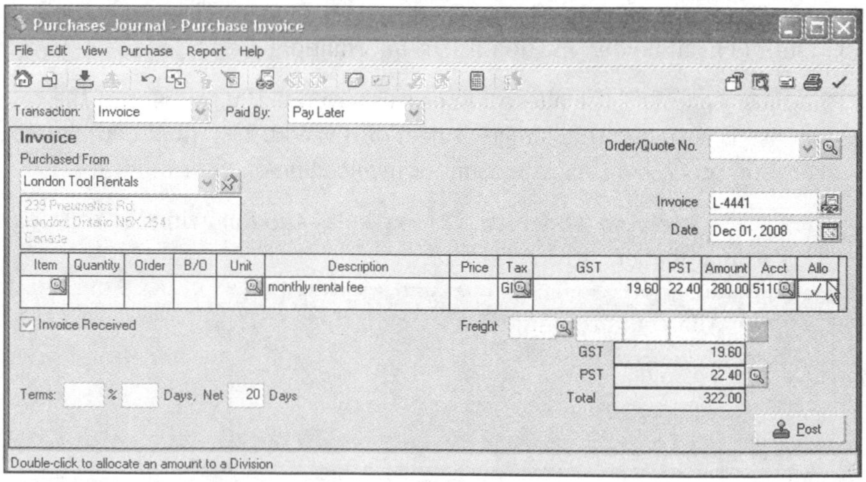

The journal appears unchanged, except for the ✓ in the Allo column indicating that the amount has been allocated.

Reviewing the Purchases Journal Allocation

As usual, you should review the journal entry before posting it.

Choose the **Report menu** and **click Display Purchases Journal Entry**:

Truman Tires

12/01/08 (J1)	Debits	Credits	Division
2670 GST Paid on Purchases	19.60	-	
5110 Tool Rentals	302.40	-	
- Sales Division			60.48
- Service Division			241.92
2200 Accounts Payable	-	322.00	
	322.00	322.00	

You may need to scroll to see all the information. Simply Accounting has automatically updated the *Accounts Payable* control account because the Payables and General ledgers are fully integrated. Notice also that the rental expense has been allocated to the two departments. Only the amount for the expense account *Tool Rentals* is allocated because the other accounts are Balance Sheet accounts that are not set up to allow allocations.

Close the **display** to return to the Purchases Journal input screen.

Click the **Store tool**. Accept the vendor name and **choose Monthly** as the frequency. **Click OK** to return to the journal.

To see the allocation again, click the Allocate tool when the cursor is on the relevant line or click the ✓ in the Allo column.

NOTES
When you store a transaction with allocations, the allocations are also stored with the other transaction details.

CORRECTING THE PURCHASES JOURNAL ENTRY ALLOCATION

Correct the Purchases Journal part of the entry as you would correct any other purchase invoice. Refer to page 125 if you need assistance.

If you have made an error in the allocation, **click** the **Allocate tool** ☑ to return to the Allocation window. **Click** the line for the **amount** being allocated to activate the Allocate tool if necessary. **Click** an **incorrect project** to highlight it. **Press** *enter* to access the Project list. **Click** the **correct project** and **click Select** to enter the change. **Click** an **incorrect percentage** and **type** the **correct information. Press** *tab* to save the correction. **Click OK** to return to the Journal window.

Posting

When you are certain that you have entered all the information correctly,

Click **Post** to save the entry.

If you have not allocated 100 percent of the amounts, you may see the warning:

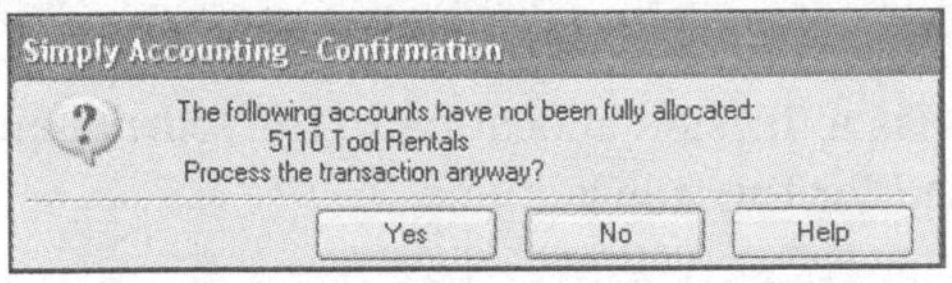
Simply Accounting - Confirmation
The following accounts have not been fully allocated:
5110 Tool Rentals
Process the transaction anyway?
Yes
No
Help

You will see a message like this one if you have not fully allocated a journal amount.

If you made an error, click No to return to the invoice in the Purchases Journal. Click the Allo column beside the account that is not fully allocated to return to the Allocation screen. Make the changes, click OK and then post.

If you do not want to allocate the full amount, or if the account that was not fully allocated was one that you cannot access the allocation procedure for, such as *Variance Costs*, you should click Yes to continue.

Close the **Purchases Journal** and **enter** the next **payment transaction**.

NOTES
Later in the chapter, we will see that cost variances are not allocated.
You may want to proceed with an incomplete allocation when part of the amount applies to none of the projects or it applies to an earlier time period before project recording was started.

Allocating Freight Expenses

When you purchase inventory items, the Allocate tool and menu option are not available because the asset accounts were not set up to allow allocations. However, the freight expense for these purchases can be allocated. The Freight fields have an Allocate button beside them for this purpose.

Enter the **purchase** from **Snowmaster Tire Company** in the usual way but **do not post** the transaction.

The Freight fields have an **Allocate button** to the right of them, indicated with the pointer in the following screen:

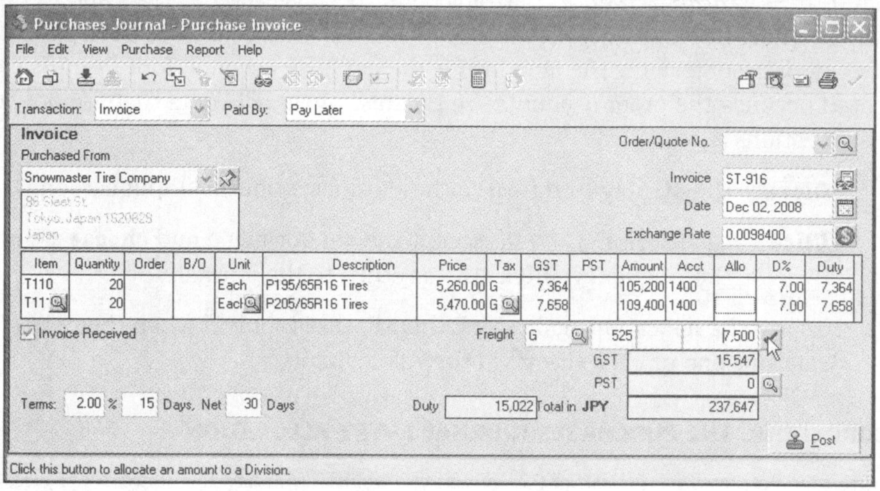

Click the **Allocate button** to the right of the Freight fields.

The Division Allocation screen opens. It is the same as the one we saw earlier. The Freight amount, ¥7 500, is entered as the amount to be allocated.

Choose the **Sales Division** and **accept 100%** as the allocation percentage.

Click **OK** to return to the journal. The journal has not changed in appearance.

Choose the **Report menu** and **click Display Purchases Journal Entry**:

Truman Tires

12/02/08 (J3)	Foreign Amt.		Debits	Credits	Division
1400 Winter Tires	¥229,622		2,259.48	-	
2670 GST Paid on Purchases	¥15,547		152.98	-	
5065 Freight Expense	¥7,500		73.80	-	
- Sales Division		¥7,500			73.80
2200 Accounts Payable	¥237,647		-	2,338.45	
2220 Import Duty Payable	¥15,022		-	147.81	
			2,486.26	2,486.26	

1 Japanese Yen equals 0.0098400 Canadian Dollars

Only the Freight Expense amount has a division allocation in the journal entry because it was the only amount allocated for the transaction.

Close the **Journal Entry** to return to the journal.

To correct the freight expense allocation, click the Allocate button beside the field to open the Division Allocation screen and make the needed changes.

Click **Post** to save the entry.

If you have not allocated the freight amount, you will see the warning about incomplete allocations on page 475.

Enter the next group of **transactions**.

NOTES

Freight is allocated by amount – the cursor advances to the Amount field on the Allocation screen after you select the Division. You cannot change this setting.

BASIC VERSION

In the Basic version, you will see foreign amounts in a column with the heading JPY Amount.

Allocating in the Sales Journal

Amounts for revenue accounts in the Sales Journal are allocated in the same way as amounts for expense accounts in the Purchases Journal. Each revenue amount in the journal must be allocated completely, but you can assign the same allocation percentages to all accounts in the journal rather than repeating the allocation entry for each invoice line. We will demonstrate this method by showing the steps involved in the Visa sale to Scinto on December 4.

Click the **Sales icon** (Sales, Orders & Quotes) to open the Sales Journal.

Enter **Bruno Scinto** in the Sold To field.

Press *tab* and **click Continue**.

Choose **Visa** as the method in the Paid By field.

Enter **Dec. 4** as the invoice date.

Choose **Tridon** as the salesperson in the Sold By field.

Click the **Use The Same Salesperson tool**.

Choose **T104** as the first inventory item for the sale.

Press *tab* to advance to the Quantity field.

Type 4

Press *tab* repeatedly to advance to the Allo field.

Click the **Allo field** to open the Division Allocation window.

As long as the cursor is on the invoice line you are allocating, the allocate function is available. Click the Allocate tool button or choose the Sales menu and click Allocate to open the Division Allocation screen.

Choose the **Sales Division** for 100% of the revenue amount.

The allocation screen has a check box for the option Apply This Allocation To Entire Transaction as shown:

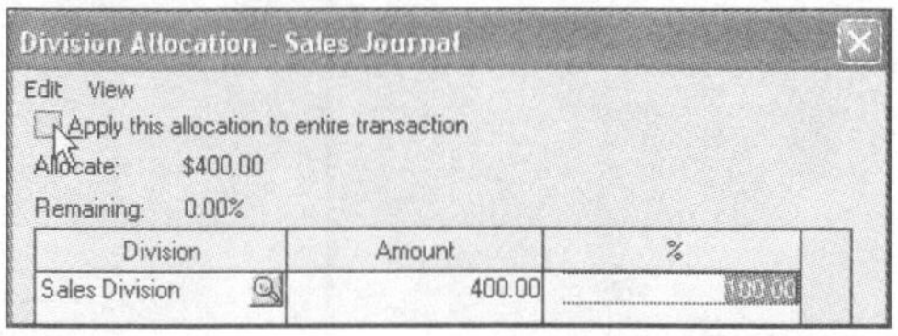

This option allows you to enter one allocation and let the program apply the same percentages for all other amounts automatically. Otherwise you will need to repeat the allocation procedure for each account in the journal.

Click **Apply This Allocation To Entire Transaction** to open the message about this selection:

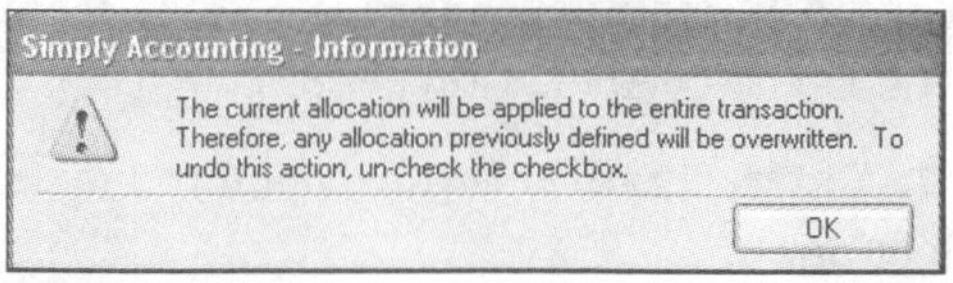

Simply Accounting - Information
The current allocation will be applied to the entire transaction. Therefore, any allocation previously defined will be overwritten. To undo this action, un-check the checkbox.
OK

Read the **message** and then **click OK** to return to the allocation screen.

If you do not want to continue with this selection, click the check box again.

> **NOTES**
> You can leave the Sales Journal open in the background while you complete transactions in other journals. The salesperson will remain selected until you change the session date. If you use this approach, ensure that you update the dates and payment methods or each sale.

> **NOTES**
> You can also press *ctrl* + *shift* + A to open the Division Allocation window.

The Division Allocation screen has changed as shown:

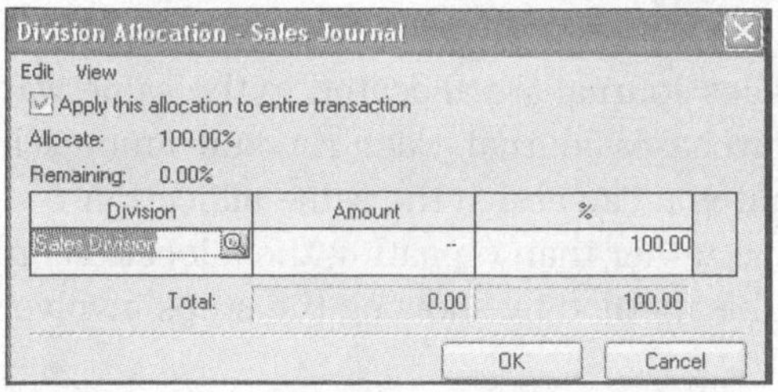

No amounts are entered at this time because the same percentages will be applied and the amounts will be different

Click **OK** to save the allocation and return to the journal.

Enter the **remaining inventory** and **service items** for the sale.

The ✓ is added to the Allo field automatically as you complete the invoice:

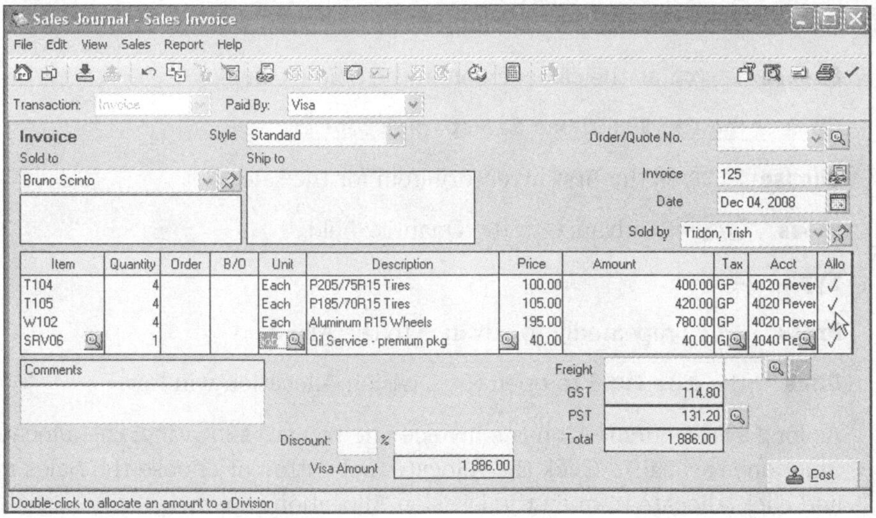

The invoice has been completely allocated, but the allocation is not correct, as you will see when you review the journal entry for the transaction:

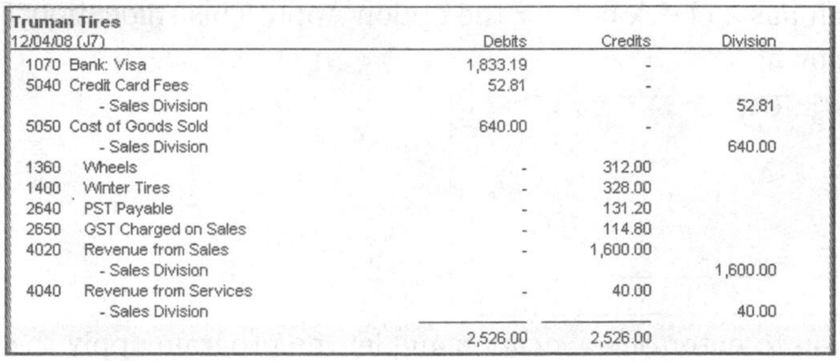

Truman Tires
12/04/08 (J7)

	Debits	Credits	Division
1070 Bank: Visa	1,833.19	-	
5040 Credit Card Fees	52.81	-	
- Sales Division			52.81
5050 Cost of Goods Sold	640.00	-	
- Sales Division			640.00
1360 Wheels	-	312.00	
1400 Winter Tires	-	328.00	
2640 PST Payable	-	131.20	
2650 GST Charged on Sales	-	114.80	
4020 Revenue from Sales	-	1,600.00	
- Sales Division			1,600.00
4040 Revenue from Services	-	40.00	
- Sales Division			40.00
	2,526.00	2,526.00	

The service revenue should not be allocated to Sales so we must change it.

Close the displayed **report** to return to the journal.

Click anywhere on the line for **item SRV06**.

Click the **Allo tool** ☑, **click** the **Allo field** or **choose** the **Sales menu** and **click Allocate** to open the Division Allocation screen.

Click **Apply This Allocation To Entire Transaction** to open the message about this change in selection:

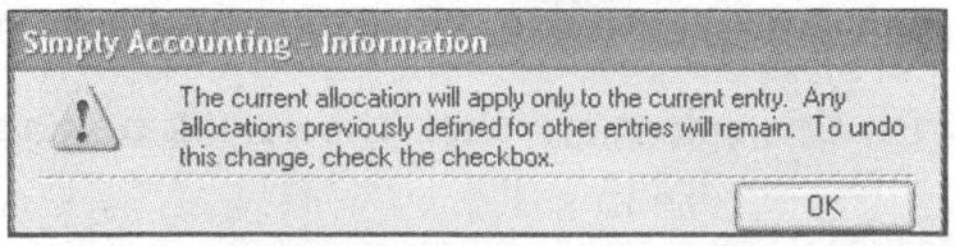

NOTES

You can allocate freight revenue amounts in the same way. Simply click the Allocate tool beside the Freight fields.

NOTES

You can also click or press *enter* in the Allo field, or press *ctrl* + *shift* + A for the selected item to open the Division Allocation screen.

We can change the allocation for this invoice line without changing any of the others.

Click **OK** to return to the Division Allocation screen. Sales Division is selected.

Press *enter* to open the list of departments.

Double click **Service Division** to add it the Division Allocation screen.

Click **OK** to save the change and return to the journal.

Choose the **Sales menu** and **click Display Sales Journal Entry**:

Truman Tires			
12/04/08 (J7)	Debits	Credits	Division
1070 Bank: Visa	1,833.19	-	
5040 Credit Card Fees	52.81	-	
- Sales Division			51.52
- Service Division			1.29
5050 Cost of Goods Sold	640.00	-	
- Sales Division			640.00
1360 Wheels	-	312.00	
1400 Winter Tires	-	328.00	
2640 PST Payable	-	131.20	
2650 GST Charged on Sales	-	114.80	
4020 Revenue from Sales	-	1,600.00	
- Sales Division			1,600.00
4040 Revenue from Services	-	40.00	
- Service Division			40.00
	2,526.00	2,526.00	

The allocation is now correct. We can post the entry.

Close the **Journal Entry** to return to the journal.

Click **Post** [Post] to save the entry.

Continue entering the **transactions**.

Creating Cost Variances

If inventory is sold to a customer when the inventory stock is too low to fill the sale completely, the levels in inventory fall below zero and the outstanding items are backordered. The estimated cost of goods for the sale is based on the average cost for the items in stock at the time of the sale. When the items are received, the price may have changed, and the items that are used to fill the rest of the customer's order will have a different cost price from that recorded. The difference is the cost variance and is assigned to the linked variance account for the inventory item. The amount of the variance shows in the journal entry for the purchase. Thus two conditions are required for a variance to occur — the inventory is oversold and the cost has changed.

Normally you do not have to do anything to record a cost variance because the program makes the calculations automatically and assigns the amount to the linked variance account for the inventory item.

After entering the purchase from Snowmaster Tire Company on Dec. 13, display the journal entry. It should match the one shown here:

Truman Tires					
12/13/08 (J25)	Foreign Amt.		Debits	Credits	Division
1400 Winter Tires	¥192,308		1,896.16	-	
2670 GST Paid on Purchases	¥13,181		129.96	-	
5055 Variance Costs	¥1,147		11.31	-	
5065 Freight Expense	¥7,500		73.95	-	
- Sales Division		¥7,500			73.95
2200 Accounts Payable	¥201,481		-	1,986.60	
2220 Import Duty Payable	¥12,656		-	124.78	
			2,111.38	2,111.38	
1 Japanese Yen equals 0.0098600 Canadian Dollars					

There was insufficient stock left for item T103 on Dec. 13 when the sale to Airport Taxi Service was recorded, so the average historic cost for eight tires, $304, was credited to *Cost of Goods Sold*. Only four tires were in stock at the time of the sale,

NOTES
The allocation for Credit Card Fees is automatically split in the correct proportion.

NOTES
When a purchase entry creates a variance and you have not set up the linked account for variances, you will be prompted to select or create a variance account.

NOTES
The calculated price for the four tires includes the import duty at the rate of 7 percent.

The 16 tires cost ¥61,920 (ST-1141 on page 461) plus duty for a total cost of ¥66,254.40. This amount is multiplied by the exchange rate of 0.00986 for a cost of $653.26 CAD.

with an average cost of $152. When the purchase of item T103 was recorded, the total cost for 16 tires was $653.26, or $163.31 for four. The difference, $11.31, between the new cost and the cost in the sales transaction is the cost variance.

When you post the transaction, you will see the following warning:

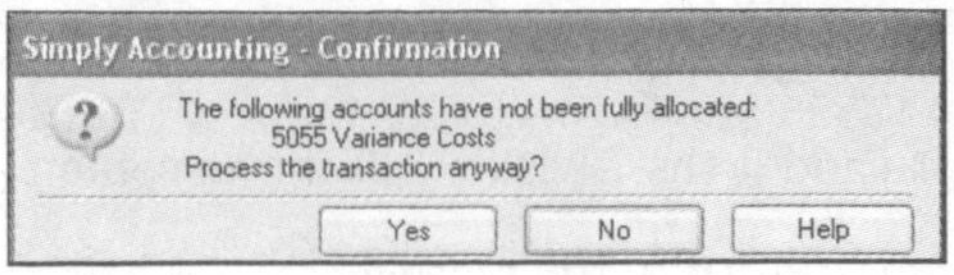

Variance costs cannot be allocated so you must accept the incomplete allocation.

Click **Yes** to continue posting the purchase.

Making Import Duty Remittances

Paying the import duty owing on imported merchandise is like paying other taxes. Normally duty must be paid before the package is released by Customs.

Open the **Payments Journal**. The cheque number and bank account are correct.

Choose **Make Other Payment** and **enter** the **date** of the cheque.

Choose **Receiver General** as the vendor.

Choose **2220 Import Duty Payable** as the account from the Selection list.

You should record the corresponding purchase invoice numbers in the journal as well. You can do this in the Description field if the entry is very long or in the Comment field if the entry is short.

Type Duty re ST916, ST114, SW876, SW1024

Press (tab) to move to the Amount field.

Type 448.36

Click the **Invoice/Ref. field** and **type** Memo 4 **Press** (tab).

Type Memo 4, Import duty remittance

Review the **journal entry**. **Close** the **display**. **Make corrections** if needed and then **post** the **transaction**.

Allocating in Other Journals

> **NOTES**
> The Paycheques Journal does not have an Allo column so you must use the tool or the menu approach.

Use the same principles outlined above to allocate revenues and expenses in the General Journal, Adjustments Journal or the Payroll journals to projects, departments or profit centres. You can change the setup to make allocations by dollar amounts or by percentage.

Once you have entered the journal information, the Allocate tool ☑ will be available. You can use it to enter the allocation information.

In the Paycheques Journal, click the Allo tool ☑.

To correct allocations, click ☑ to re-open the allocation screen.

In the setup for Payroll allocations, you can choose to allocate expenses according to the number of hours worked on each project.

In the Payroll Cheque Run Journal, use the Allo column for the employee who is selected from the list. You must allocate for one employee at a time. To begin the allocation, click the Allo column or choose the Payroll menu and click Allocate. You can also apply the same allocation to the entire transaction, just as we did in the Sales Journal.

NOTES
The Payroll Cheque Run Journal does not have an Allo tool so you must use the Allo column or the menu approach.

In the Payroll journals, the total payroll expense, not the net pay, is allocated. This includes employer contributions such as EI, CPP, WSIB/WCB and EHT. When you review the journal entry, you will see that all the payroll-related expenses are divided among the projects according to the percentages you entered. They are shown under the Project/Division column. You may have to scroll to see all the information.

Displaying Project/Division Reports

Displaying the Division List

Remember that in other data files, if the ledger name is unchanged, Project will appear instead of Division.

NOTES
You can display the Project Detail Report from the Project List.

Right-click the **Division icon** to select it.

Click the **Display tool** or **choose** the **Reports menu**, then **choose Lists** and **click Division** to see the options:

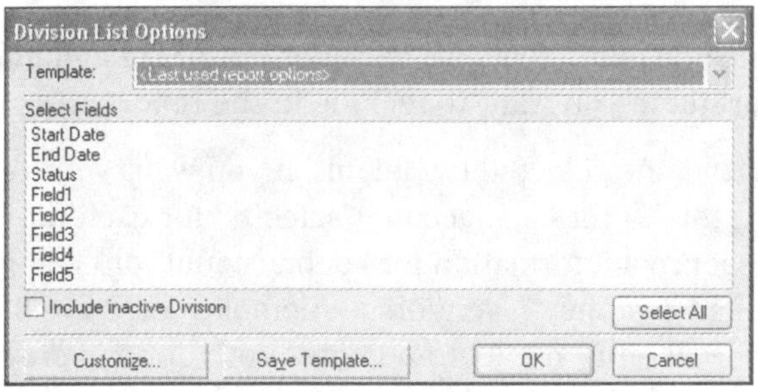

NOTES
Remember that if you have not changed the Project Ledger name, you will see Project instead of Division throughout the report menus and options.

Press and **hold** *ctrl* and **click** the **fields** you want to add to the report.

Click OK. Close the **display** when you have finished viewing the report.

Adding Project Details to Journal Reports

When you have entered project information in a journal, you can add the allocation details to any journal report. The Journal Report Options window will include a check box for division or project allocations as shown:

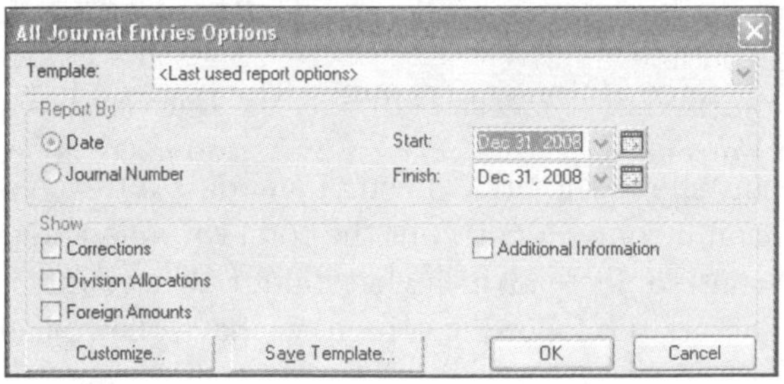

NOTES
The date list provided by the list arrow includes the earliest transaction date and the latest session date or latest transaction date. The earliest transaction date is a frequent choice for the starting date in reports.

Click Division Allocations to include project information in journal reports. By default, journal reports do not include project details.

Enter the **dates** for the report and **click OK. Close** the **display** when finished.

Displaying Division/Project Income Reports

The Project Income Report provides an income statement for each project with revenue, expenses and net income for each project you select for the report.

NOTES
You can drill down to the Project Detail Report from the Project Summary Report. You can drill down to the Project Ledger, Journal Report, General Ledger, Invoice Lookup, Customer or Vendor Aged or Employee reports (if applicable) from the Project Detail Report.

Choose the **Reports menu**, then **choose Division** and **click Income** to display the following Options window:

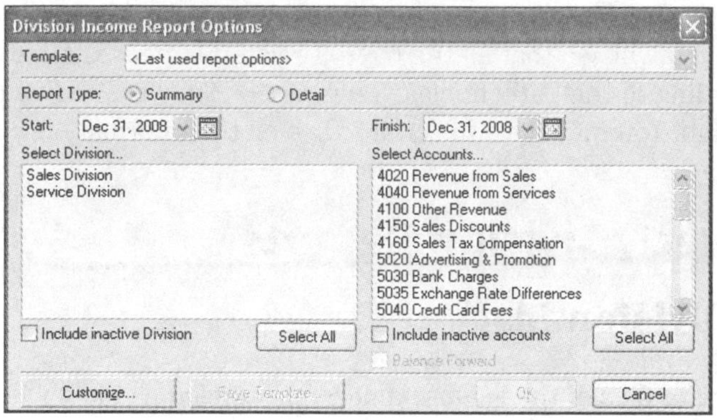

NOTES
You cannot customize the Project Income or the Project Allocation reports.

You can sort and filter project reports by date, comment, source, journal number and amount per transaction. As usual, the session date is the default.

Enter the **beginning date** for the report you want.

Enter the **ending date** for the report.

Click **Select All** to include all projects in the report, or **press** and **hold** ctrl and **click** the **projects** you want to include in the report.

Leave the Summary option, the one selected by default, if you want your report to show summary information (i.e., totals) for each account selected for each project. The Detail option provides complete journal information for each account for each project selected, including the names of all customers, vendors and employees, as well as the reference document number, journal entry number and date. Both options provide a calculation for revenue minus expense.

Next you should select the particular revenue or expense accounts you want in the report.

Click **Select All** or **press** and **hold** ctrl and **click** the **individual accounts** you want.

Click **OK** to display the report. **Close** the **display** when finished.

Displaying Division/Project Allocation Reports

When you allow allocation for Balance Sheet accounts, they are reported in the Division Allocation Report together with Income Statement accounts. The Division Income Report has only revenue and expense accounts.

The Division Allocation Report shows the breakdown of amounts for each project by account. It is similar to the Division Income Report, but the total revenue and expense and the net project income are omitted. Instead, a single total for all accounts is provided for each project. To generate the following screen, we have allowed allocation for all accounts.

Choose the **Reports menu**, then **choose Division** and **click Allocation** to display the Division Allocation Report Options window:

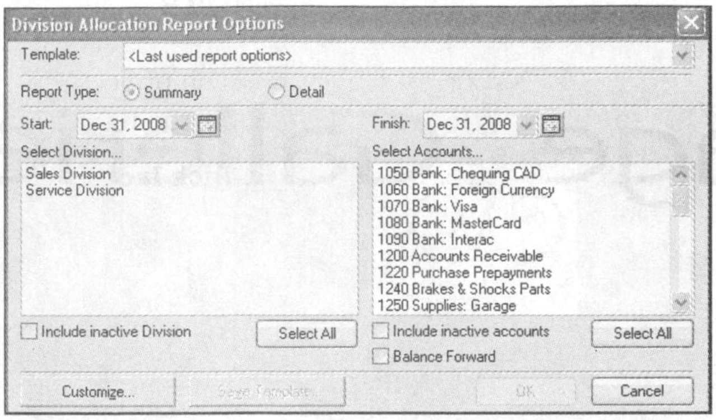

Enter the **start** and **end dates** for the report.

Click **Select All** to include all departments in the report, or **press** and **hold** ctrl and **click individual departments**.

Like the Income Report, the Summary option will show totals and the Detail option provides complete journal information for each account for each division.

After you have indicated which options you want, choose the accounts.

Click **Select All** or **press** and **hold** ctrl and **click** the **accounts** you want.

Click **OK** to display the report. **Close** the **display** when you have finished.

Displaying Division/Project Management Reports

There are management reports for the Project Ledger, just as there are for every other ledger in Simply Accounting.

Choose the **Reports menu**, then **choose Management Reports** and **click Division** to see the list of management reports:

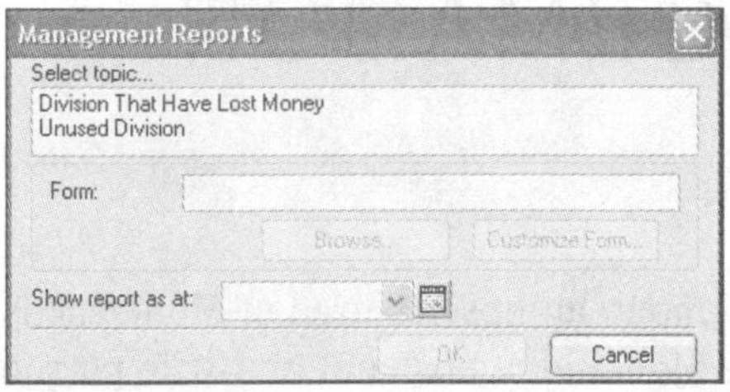

Click the **topic** for the report. **Click OK** to display the report. **Close** the **display** when you have finished.

Printing Reports

Display the **report** you want on the screen by following the instructions above. **Click** the **Print button** or **choose** the **File menu** and **click Print**. **Close** the **display**.

R E V I E W

The Student CD-ROM with Data Files includes Review Questions and Supplementary Cases for this chapter.

NOTES
To show this screen, we allowed allocations for the Balance Sheet accounts. Without this change, the Account list would include only the revenue and expense accounts.

NOTES
Drill-down reports from the Allocation Report are the same as the reports from the Project Income Report.

NOTES
The Service Division is operating at a loss according to the Management Report.

CHAPTER THIRTEEN

Village Galleries

OBJECTIVES

After completing this chapter, you should be able to

- ***turn on*** the budgeting feature in Simply Accounting
- ***determine*** budgeting periods and amounts
- ***allocate*** budget amounts to revenue and expense accounts
- ***enter*** transactions involving Quebec Sales Tax
- ***display*** and ***print*** income statements with budget comparisons
- ***graph*** budget reports
- ***analyze*** budget reports
- ***print***

COMPANY INFORMATION

Company Profile

NOTES
Village Galleries
509 Boul. Rouin
Montreal, Quebec H3F 5G5
Tel: (514) 529-6391
Fax: (514) 529-7622
Business No.: 236 412 540

Village Galleries, located in Outremont, an upscale area of Montreal, is owned and operated by Renée and Gilles Montand, a husband-and-wife partnership. The small family-run business recently hired one employee who will earn a commission on sales. She works in the store several days a week but the Montands maintain the regular operation of the business. Renée performs the accounting duties for the business. Other jobs are occasionally subcontracted.

The store, more like a furniture boutique, carries a limited range of high-quality inventory, selling to clients who are selective in their furniture and accessory preferences. Accessories and furniture for living rooms, bedrooms, dining rooms and kitchens comprise the major inventory items in the boutique. The brass furniture pieces are imported from Italy, and some items are high-quality reproductions of antiques made in small Quebec furniture factories by respected artisans. Most of the furniture is made of wood or wood frames covered with fine fabrics. The choice of wood includes mahogany, oak, cherry, ash and, of course, pine. Rich select woods of the highest quality are used to create solid wood pieces, but sometimes expensive veneers are used to complement the designs. In addition, the furniture boutique sells home accessories such as lamps, a small selection of handmade Persian and Oriental rugs made of wool and silk, mirrors and original framed numbered prints imported from Italy.

Most customers are local but, occasionally, customers from abroad who visit Montreal ask for furniture to be shipped to them. Delivery (shipping or freight) is charged on most orders and exported items. Preferred price list customers do not pay for delivery, and they receive discounted inventory prices. All account customers are entitled to a before-tax 2 percent discount if they settle their accounts within 10 days. After 30 days, interest charges accrue at the rate of 1.5 percent per month. Customer deposits from 20 to 25 percent of the total sale are required on all orders. Customers may pay by cheque, cash or credit card.

Some vendors with whom Village Galleries has accounts require deposits to accompany purchase orders, and some vendors offer after-tax purchase discounts for early payments. The store has a business credit card account with American Express.

The currency for all foreign transactions, the purchases from Italy and the sales to European customers, is the euro (€). Foreign prices for inventory are calculated from the exchange rate at the time of sale. No foreign prices are entered in the inventory ledger. Village Galleries pays import duties on the imported furniture but not on original art work such as the numbered prints.

Renée Montand used the following to set up the accounting files for Village Galleries in Simply Accounting:

- Chart of Accounts
- Post-Closing Trial Balance
- Vendor Information
- Customer Information
- Employee Information
- Inventory Information
- Accounting Procedures

CHART OF ACCOUNTS

VILLAGE GALLERIES

ASSETS

Current Assets
1060 Chequing Bank Account
1070 Visa Bank Account
1080 MasterCard Bank Account
1090 Bank Account - Euro
1100 Investment Portfolio
1150 Purchase Prepayments
1200 Accounts Receivable
1220 Office Supplies
1240 Furniture Supplies
1260 Prepaid Insurance

Inventory Assets
1320 Bedroom Furniture
1340 Home Accessories
1360 Kitchen & Dining Room Furniture
1380 Living Room Furniture

Fixed Assets
1420 Cash Register ▶
▶1440 Computer Equipment
1460 Equipment & Tools
1480 Gallery Fixtures
1500 Gallery

LIABILITIES

Current Liabilities
2200 Accounts Payable
2220 Prepaid Sales and Deposits
2250 Credit Card Payable
2260 Import Duty Payable
2330 Income Tax Payable
2350 QPP Payable
2360 Quebec Income Tax Payable
2370 QHSF Payable
2460 CSST Payable
2650 GST Charged on Sales
2670 GST Paid on Purchases
2800 Refundable QST Paid
2810 QST Charged on Sales ▶

▶Long Term Liabilities
2950 Mortgage Payable - Gallery

EQUITY

Owner's Equity
3560 Montand, Capital
3580 Montand, Drawings
3600 Current Earnings

REVENUE

4020 Revenue from Sales
4040 Sales Discount
4060 Freight Revenue
4100 Investment Revenue
4120 Interest Revenue

EXPENSE

Operating Expenses
5020 Advertising & Promotion
5030 Exchange Rate Differences
5040 Bank Charges
5050 Credit Card Fees ▶
▶5060 Cost of Goods Sold
5070 Variance Costs
5080 Furniture Supplies Used
5100 Damaged Inventory
5120 Purchase Discounts
5130 Freight Expense
5140 Delivery Expense
5160 Hydro Expense
5180 Insurance Expense
5190 Mortgage Interest Expense
5200 Office Supplies Used
5220 Telephone Expenses

Payroll Expenses
5300 Commissions
5330 CSST Expense
5340 QPP Expense
5350 QHSF Expense
5380 Subcontractor Fees

NOTES: The Chart of Accounts includes only postable accounts and Current Earnings. QPP (Quebec Pension Plan) replaces CPP in Quebec. QHSF (Quebec Health Services Fund) is an employer-funded provincial health and services tax program.
Linked payable and expense accounts for CPP and QPIP (Quebec Parental Insurance Plan) are also included because they are essential linked accounts but they are not used.

POST-CLOSING TRIAL BALANCE

VILLAGE GALLERIES

June 30, 2008

		Debits	Credits			Debits	Credits
1060	Chequing Bank Account	$ 51 897.25		▶ 1440	Computer Equipment	2 800.00	
1070	Visa Bank Account	5 445.00		1460	Equipment & Tools	1 500.00	
1080	MasterCard Bank Account	3 555.00		1480	Gallery Fixtures	1 000.00	
1090	Bank Account - Euro (€1 530)	2 100.00		1500	Gallery	150 000.00	
1100	Investment Portfolio	50 000.00		2200	Accounts Payable		$ 11 502.50
1200	Accounts Receivable	5 751.25		2250	Credit Card Payable		240.00
1220	Office Supplies	400.00		2260	Import Duty Payable		240.00
1240	Furniture Supplies	600.00		2650	GST Charged on Sales		1 680.00
1260	Prepaid Insurance	250.00		2670	GST Paid on Purchases	980.00	
1320	Bedroom Furniture	35 200.00		2800	Refundable QST Paid	90.00	
1340	Home Accessories	30 900.00		2810	QST Charged on Sales		1 926.00
1360	Kitchen & Dining Room Furniture	24 995.00		2950	Mortgage Payable - Gallery		145 000.00
1380	Living Room Furniture	41 925.00		3560	Montand, Capital		250 000.00
1420	Cash Register	1 200.00 ▶				$410 588.50	$410 588.50

VENDOR INFORMATION

VILLAGE GALLERIES

Vendor Name (Contact)	Address	Phone No. Fax No.	E-mail Web Site	Terms Tax ID
Domo Carvaggio (Arturo Dessini)	8 Via Artistes Forli, 47100 Italy	Tel: (39-0543) 457 882 Fax: (39-0543) 457 113	www.domocarvaggio.com	net 30
Énergie Québec (Marie Nuclaire)	5010 Ave. Atomique Montreal, Quebec H2B 6C9	Tel: (514) 782-6101	www.energie.quebec.ca	net 1
L'Ascension Mobiliers (Suzie LaChaise)	RR #2 Jonquière, Quebec G7S 4L2	Tel: (450) 821-1029 Fax: (450) 822-1927	suzie@lascension.com www.lascension.com	1/5, n/30 (after tax) 322 749 610
Montreal Persia Emporium (Perse Moquette)	40 Rue de Tapis Longueuil, Quebec J4K 2L7	Tel: (450) 288-4334 Fax: (450) 288-8201	moquette@MPE.com www.MPE.com	2/5, n/30 (after tax) 473 540 911
Normandin Meubles (Normand Armoire)	RR #3 Nicolet, Quebec J3T 1H5	Tel: (450) 371-7273 Fax: (450) 371-7229	na@normand.meubles.com www.normand.meubles.com	2/10, n/30 (after tax) 136 492 446
Papineau Delivery (Martin Camion)	56 Papineau Ave. Outremont, Quebec H1M 3B3	Tel: (514) 690-2810 Fax: (514) 691-7283	martin@papineau.com www.papineau.com	net 10 288 344 566
Receiver General for Canada	Sudbury Tax Services Office PO Box 20004 Sudbury, Ontario P3A 6B4	Tel 1: (800) 561-7761 Tel 2: (800) 959-2221	www.cra-arc.gc.ca	net 1
Staples (Hélène Magazinier)	777 Ave. de Bureau Montreal, Quebec H4K 1V5	Tel: (514) 759-3488 Fax: (514) 758- 3910	www.staples.com	net 15 128 634 772
Telébec (Robert Bavarde)	84 Rue Causerie Montreal, Quebec H3C 7S2	Tel: (514) 488-2355	www.bell.ca	net 1

NOTES: All vendor discounts are calculated on after-tax amounts.

OUTSTANDING VENDOR INVOICES

VILLAGE GALLERIES

Vendor Name	Terms	Date	Invoice	Amount CAD	Total
L'Ascension Mobiliers	1/5, n/30 (after tax)	June 29/08	LM-2114	$4 601.00	$4 601.00
Normandin Meubles	2/10, n/30 (after tax)	June 28/08	NM-192	$6 901.50	$6 901.50
			Grand Total		$11 502.50

CUSTOMER INFORMATION

VILLAGE GALLERIES

Customer Name (Contact)	Address	Phone No. Fax No.	E-mail Web Site	Terms Credit Limit
Caisse Metropolitain (Tomas Monaire)	50 Rue Berri Montreal, Quebec H1B 6F4	Tel: (514) 466-2991 Fax: (514) 468-1826	tmonaire@caissemetro.ca www.caissemetro.ca	2/10, n/30 $5 000
Cash Customers				cash or credit card
Deon Estates (Kaline Deon)	600 Rue St. Denis Montreal, Quebec H2K 7C9	Tel: (514) 729-8217 Fax: (514) 729-9283	kaline.deon@istar.com	2/10, n/30 $5 000
*St. Leonard's Homebuilders (Félice Charpentier)	31 Boul. St. Joseph Montreal, Quebec H4N 2M1	Tel: (514) 788-3645 Fax: (514) 787-7114	felice@stleonards.com www.stleonards.com	2/10, n/30 $10 000
*Westmount Primrose Condos (M.T. Sweets)	121 Rue Notre Dame Montreal, Quebec H3K 4G5	Tel: (514) 499-7117 Fax: (514) 498-2889	sweets@wpcondos.com www.wpcondos.com	2/10, n/30 $10 000

NOTES: All customer discounts are calculated on amounts before tax. Customers pay 1.5% interest on accounts over 30 days. Asterisk (*) indicates preferred price list customer.

OUTSTANDING CUSTOMER INVOICES

VILLAGE GALLERIES

Customer Name	Terms	Date	Invoice	Amount	Tax	Total
Deon Estates	2/10, n/30 (before tax)	June 24/08	168	$5 000	$751.25	$5 751.25

Employee Profile and TD1 Information

Lianne Décor started working for the boutique on July 1, 2008. Using her interior decorating and design skills, she visits homes for consultations to assess needs and suggest furniture from the store that matches the home style and customer taste. She is paid a commission of 20 percent of her monthly sales and takes four weeks of vacation each year. Décor is single and self-supporting. Her tax claim amounts are $10 419 federal and $10 200 provincial for basic and education amounts. She works for the store part time and supplements her sales commission with her independent business as an interior design consultant.

Other employee details:

SIN:	566 811 014	Address:	45 Rue Collage
Date of birth:	August 26, 1976		Montreal, Quebec
CSST (WCB) rate:	2.04		H2G 4R5
		Tel:	(514) 639-9202

NOTES

As an employer, Village Galleries makes contributions to the Quebec Health Services Fund equal to 2.7 percent of the total payroll amount for the provincial health care plan. This amount is entered in the Payroll Settings.

CSST (La Commission de la Santé et de la Sécurité au Travail) is the Workplace Compensation Board agency in Quebec.

Employer and employee deductions for the new Quebec Parental Insurance Plan are not required because Décor is not EI-insurable.

INVENTORY INFORMATION

VILLAGE GALLERIES

Code	Description	Unit	Min Qty	Selling Price Reg	Selling Price (Pref)	Qty on Hand	Total (Cost)	Duty (Taxes)
Bedroom Furniture: Total asset value $35 200 (Linked accounts: Asset 1320; Revenue 4020; COGS 5060; Variance 5070)								
BF-01	Armoire: dark oak	1-pc	0	$3 100	$3 000	2	$4 400	9.5%
BF-02	Armoire: light ash	1-pc	0	3 000	2 900	2	4 000	9.5%
BF-03	Bed: 3 piece oak	set	0	2 000	1 900	2	2 400	9.5%
BF-04	Bed: 5 piece light ash/oak	set	0	3 000	2 900	2	3 600	9.5%
BF-05	Bed: brass/silver	1-pc	0	1 800	1 700	3	3 300	8.0%
BF-06	Chest: cherry	1-pc	0	1 000	950	3	1 800	9.5%
BF-07	Dresser: cashmere, burl-maple	1-pc	0	1 600	1 500	5	4 500	9.5%
BF-08	Dresser: highboy - dark oak	1-pc	0	1 900	1 800	5	5 500	9.5%
BF-09	Wardrobe: light ash	1-pc	0	2 800	2 700	2	3 600	9.5%
BF-10	Wardrobe: pine	1-pc	0	1 750	1 650	2	2 100	9.5%
Home Accessories: Total asset value $30 900 (Linked accounts: Asset 1340; Revenue 4020; COGS 5060; Variance 5070)								
HA-01	Framed Art: prints 45 x 60cm	each	0	200	180	40	4 000	0.0%
HA-02	Framed Art: prints 75 x 100cm	each	0	300	270	30	4 500	0.0%
HA-03	Lamp: floor solid brass	1-pc	0	400	360	10	2 200	7.0%
HA-04	Lamp: table solid brass	1-pc	0	600	550	10	3 500	7.0%
HA-05	Mirror: oval dark oak	1-pc	0	500	450	5	1 500	9.5%
HA-06	Mirror: square ash/mahogany	1-pc	0	550	500	5	1 900	9.5%
HA-07	Rugs: Persian Isfahan 185 x 275cm	each	0	1 250	1 150	10	6 000	n/a
HA-08	Rugs: Persian Kashan 185 x 275cm	each	0	990	950	10	4 500	n/a
HA-09	Rugs: Persian Tabriz 90 x 160cm	each	0	650	600	10	2 800	n/a
Kitchen & Dining Room Furniture: Total asset value $24 995 (Linked accounts: Asset 1360; Revenue 4020; COGS 5060; Variance 5070)								
KD-01	Buffet: oak	1-pc	0	1 750	1 650	2	2 000	9.5%
KD-02	Buffet: cherry	1-pc	0	2 250	2 150	2	2 200	9.5%
KD-03	Chairs: 4 piece cherry	set	0	1 100	1 000	5	3 000	9.5%
KD-04	Chairs: 4 piece oak	set	0	975	950	5	2 375	9.5%
KD-05	China Cabinet: walnut	1-pc	0	2 100	2 000	2	2 100	9.5%
KD-06	China Cabinet: cherry	1-pc	0	850	800	2	800	9.5%
KD-07	Credenza: maple	1-pc	0	1 675	1 575	2	1 950	9.5%
KD-08	Extension Table: oak	1-pc	0	1 825	1 725	2	2 050	9.5%
KD-09	Huntboard: white pine	1-pc	0	725	650	2	850	9.5%
KD-10	Server: fruitwood	1-pc	0	980	950	2	1 000	9.5%
KD-11	Sideboard: cherry	1-pc	0	1 625	1 525	2	1 850	9.5%
KD-12	Table: brass with glass	1-pc	0	1 780	1 680	4	3 520	8.0%
KD-13	Table: ivory lacquer/pine	1-pc	0	625	550	4	1 300	9.5%
Living Room Furniture: Total asset value $41 925 (Linked accounts: Asset 1380; Revenue 4020; COGS 5060; Variance 5070)								
LR-01	Bookcase: oak/walnut solid	1-pc	0	1 150	1 050	3	1 950	9.5%
LR-02	Chair: various patterns cotton	1-pc	0	525	500	10	2 750	9.5%
LR-03	Cocktail Table: cherry	1-pc	0	925	850	5	2 375	9.5%
LR-04	Console Table: oak	1-pc	0	950	900	5	2 500	9.5%
LR-05	Curio Cabinet: walnut/oak	1-pc	0	1 450	1 350	3	2 400	9.5%
LR-06	Desk: mahogany	1-pc	0	1 840	1 740	5	4 400	9.5%
LR-07	End Table: brass with glass	1-pc	0	610	550	5	1 400	8.0%
LR-08	Lamp Table: ash/oak solid	1-pc	0	825	750	5	2 625	9.5%
LR-09	Loveseat: chenille	1-pc	0	1 325	1 225	5	3 625	9.5%
LR-10	Ottoman & Slipcover: grey leather	2-pc	0	380	350	5	1 000	9.5%
LR-11	Recliner & Ottoman: brown leather	2-pc set	0	1 020	950	5	3 100	9.5%
LR-12	Sectional Sofa: charcoal linen	3-pc	0	2 300	2 200	3	4 200	9.5%
LR-17	Settee: light ash	1-pc	0	850	800	3	1 650	9.5%
LR-18	Sofa & Slipcover: celadon	2-pc	0	1 475	1 375	5	4 375	9.5%
LR-19	Swivel Chair & Slipcover: cotton	2-pc	0	640	600	5	1 950	9.5%
LR-20	Wing Chair: pastel	1-pc	0	575	525	5	1 625	9.5%
Total Inventory Value							$133 020	

Accounting Procedures

The Goods and Services Tax (GST): Remittances

Village Galleries uses the regular method for remittance of the Goods and Services Tax. GST collected from customers is recorded as a liability in *GST Charged on Sales*. GST paid to vendors is recorded in *GST Paid on Purchases* as a decrease in the liability to Canada Revenue Agency. Montand files returns to the Receiver General for Canada by the last day of the month for the previous quarterly period, either requesting a refund or remitting the balance owing.

Quebec Sales Tax (QST)

Provincial sales tax (Quebec Sales Tax or QST) of 7.5 percent is applied to all cash and credit sales of goods and services in the province of Quebec. The Quebec Sales Tax is applied to the amount of the invoice with GST included (i.e., GST is taxable). This is often referred to as a "tax on a tax" or a "piggy-backed" tax. The defaults for this application are set so that the program will automatically calculate the QST on the amount with GST included. Accounting examples for sales taxes in different provinces are provided in Chapter 2.

QST owing (*QST Charged on Sales* less *Refundable QST Paid*) must be remitted quarterly to the ministre du Revenu du Québec.

Refundable and Non-refundable QST

Most business purchases qualify for refundable QST credits to reduce the QST owing in much the same way as the GST owing is calculated. Some exceptions are the QST on insurance and on some telecommunication services. The tax codes for GST and QST included in the ledgers for customers and vendors, therefore, include both refundable and non-refundable codes as follows:

G - GST @ 7%
GQ - GST @ 7%, QST @ 7.5%
Q - QST @ 7.5%, included, non-refundable

NOTES
In this chapter, insurance is the only item for which QST is not refundable. GST is not applied to insurance. The QST on all telecommunication services in this chapter is refundable.

Deposits on Custom Orders

When customers place a sales order for furniture, they pay an advance of 20 percent to 25 percent of the price. The deposit may be entered in the Receipts Journal or on the Sales Order form. The Accounts Receivable Ledger for the selected customer will be credited for the advance and *Chequing Bank Account* will be debited. When the work is complete, fill the sales order to make a Sales Journal entry for the full amount of the contract, including relevant taxes. When the customer settles the account, mark the invoice amount and the deposit (if you used the Receipts Journal) as paid. The balance in the Receipts Journal should then match the amount of the customer's cheque.

NOTES
Processing the advance in this way ensures that the advance will appear in the correct customer account in the Receivables Ledger. The manual approach, a General Journal entry that debits the bank account and credits Unearned Revenue, a liability account, does not show this link with the customer – the customer's ledger is updated separately.

Freight Expenses

When a business purchases inventory items, the cost of freight that cannot be directly allocated to a specific item of purchase must be charged to *Freight Expense*. This amount will be regarded as an expense and will not be part of the costs of any inventory asset account.

Printing Sales Invoices

If you want to print sales invoices through the program, complete the Sales Journal transaction as you would otherwise. Before posting the transaction, click Print or choose the File menu and then Print. Printing will begin immediately, so be sure you have selected the correct printer and forms before you begin. To e-mail an invoice, click the E-mail tool.

Foreign Purchases and Import Duty

Goods imported from Italy are subject to GST and to import duties at various rates. These taxes are collected at the time the goods are received and are usually paid directly to the Receiver General. To simplify the transactions in Simply Accounting, we have set up the foreign vendor record so that the vendor collects GST, just like vendors in Canada.

Import duties are handled separately in the program. Duty is calculated automatically because the rates are entered in the Inventory Ledger records. The amount is credited to the linked *Import Duty Payable* account instead of *Accounts Payable* so the duty is not added to the balance owing to the vendor. The linked asset account is debited.

On receiving the merchandise, the business writes a cheque to the Receiver General to pay the import duties on the purchase. This payment is just like any other tax remittance — enter the duty payable as a positive amount for a cash purchase from the Receiver General and choose *Import Duty Payable* as the account. The amount is the current General Ledger account balance.

WARNING!
The data file on the CD-ROM is missing the essential payroll linked accounts for QPIP. Replacement data files have been placed on the Web for downloading. Go to <www.pearsoned.ca/text/purbhoo2006>. Zipped files for both Basic and Pro versions are available.

Alternatively, you can add the missing accounts yourself. Refer to the note beside Memo 7 on page 496 for these instructions.

INSTRUCTIONS

1. **Set up** the **budget** for Village Galleries on July 1, 2008, using Simply Accounting. Detailed keystroke instructions to assist you begin on page 496 following the source documents.
2. **Enter** the **source documents** for July 2008 in Simply Accounting using the Chart of Accounts, Trial Balance, Vendor, Customer, Payroll and Inventory information provided.
3. **Print** the following **reports** and **graphs**. Instructions for budget reports and graphs begin on page 504.
   - Balance Sheet as at July 31
   - Journal Entries for all journals by date from July 1 to July 31
   - Inventory Sales Detail Report for Bedroom Furniture
   - Inventory Quantity Report for all items to check re-order requirements
   - Income Statement, Budget Report with Difference in Percentage for July 1 to July 31
   - Sales vs Budget graph for accounts 4020 and 4040
   - Expenses vs Budget graph for accounts 5060, 5120 and 5300

SOURCE DOCUMENTS

SESSION DATE – JULY 7, 2008

☐ **Memo #1** **Dated July 2/08**

From Owner: Pay import duties owing to the Receiver General on June 30. Issue cheque #125 for $240 in full payment of duty owing.

☐ **Sales Quote #71** **Dated July 2/08**

Delivery date July 14/08
To Caisse Metropolitain

1	HA-03	Lamp: floor solid brass	$ 400
1	HA-09	Rugs: Persian Tabriz 90 x 160cm	650
1	LR-01	Bookcase: oak/walnut solid	1 150
1	LR-12	Sectional Sofa: charcoal linen	2 300
		Delivery	100
		Goods and Services Tax	7.0%
		Quebec Sales Tax	7.5%

Terms: 2/10, n/30.

☐ **Memo #2** **Dated July 2/08**

From Owner: Convert sales quote #71 to sales order #71. All amounts, dates and terms are unchanged. Received cheque #922 for $1 000 as deposit #63 to accept sales order.

☐ **Purchase Quote #224** **Dated July 2/08**

Policy Start date July 5/08
From Quebecor Insurance Co. (use Quick Add), $3 600 for a one-year extension of business insurance policy. Terms: first two months' premium required as deposit on acceptance of quote. Balance is payable in 10 equal monthly payments. Enter 1 (one) as the quantity ordered and debit Prepaid Insurance.

☐ **Purchase Order #224** **Dated July 2/08**

Convert purchase quote #224 from Quebecor Insurance Co., $3 600 for a one-year extension of business insurance policy to a purchase order. Issued cheque #126 for $600 as deposit to accept the order.

☐ **Purchase Invoice #QI-7711** **Dated July 3/08**

From Quebecor Insurance Co., to fill purchase order #224, $3 600 for a one-year extension of business insurance policy. The premium balance is due in 10 equal monthly payments. Change the payment method to Pay Later.

☐ **Cash Receipt #43** **Dated July 3/08**

From Deon Estates, cheque #118 for $5 651.25 in payment of account including $100 discount for early payment. Reference invoice #168.

☐ **Cheque Copy #127** **Dated July 4/08**

To L'Ascension Mobiliers, $4 554.99 in payment of account including $46.01 discount for early payment. Reference invoice #LM-2114.

☐ **Cash Sales Invoice #170** **Dated July 4/08**

To Vasco Cardigos (use Full Add for the new Portuguese customer)

1	BF-02	Armoire: light ash	€2 201.03
1	HA-06	Mirror: square ash/mahogany	403.52
		Shipping	200.00
Invoice total			€2 804.55

Paid by Cheque #4322. The exchange rate is 1.3630.

☐ **Credit Card Purchase Invoice #A-1141** **Dated July 4/08**

From Antoine's Hardware Store (use Quick Add for the new vendor), $50 plus $3.50 GST and $4.01 QST for furniture wax and polish. Purchase invoice total $57.51 paid in full by Amex credit card.

NOTES

Prices for foreign transactions are taken from the exchange rate rather than from the Inventory Ledger records.

☐ Vasco Cardigos
Rua Mariella 36
1207 Lisbon, Portugal
Tel: (351-21) 347 6273
Terms: COD
Currency: EUR
Revenue account: 4020
Tax code: no tax

☐ **Credit Card Purchase Invoice #PD-211** **Dated July 5/08**

From Papineau Delivery, $180 plus $12.60 GST and $14.45 QST for contracted delivery of furniture. Purchase invoice total $207.05. Paid in full by Amex.

☐ **Interac Sales Invoice #171** **Dated July 6/08**

To Catherine Geneve (choose Cash Customers)

1	LR-04	Console Table: oak		$ 950.00
1	LR-05	Curio Cabinet: walnut/oak		1 450.00
		Delivery		100.00
		Goods and Services Tax	7.0%	175.00
		Quebec Sales Tax	7.5%	200.63
	Invoice total			$2 875.63

Paid by debit card #7695 4559 0062 0103.

☐ **Cheque Copy #128** **Dated July 7/08**

To Normandin Meubles, $6 763.47 in payment of account including $138.03 discount for early payment. Reference invoice #NM-192.

SESSION DATE – JULY 14, 2008

☐ **Memo #3** **Dated July 8/08**

From Owner: Adjust inventory for one HA-02 Framed Art Print dropped and damaged beyond repair. Charge to Damaged Inventory account.

☐ **MasterCard Sales Invoice #172** **Dated July 8/08**

To Pierre Boudin

1	HA-07	Rugs: Persian Isfahan 185 x 275cm		$1 250.00
1	KD-07	Credenza: maple		1 675.00
1	LR-02	Chair: various patterns cotton		525.00
		Delivery		100.00
		Goods and Services Tax	7.0%	248.50
		Quebec Sales Tax	7.5%	284.89
	Invoice total			$4 083.39

Paid by MasterCard #5450 5590 0620 1036.

☐ **Credit Card Purchase Invoice #S-34689** **Dated July 9/08**

From Staples, $150 plus $10.50 GST and $12.04 QST for sales invoice forms and other office supplies. Purchase invoice total $172.54 paid in full by Amex.

☐ **Credit Card Purchase Invoice #QA-197** **Dated July 10/08**

From Quik-Ads (use Quick Add), $200 plus $14.00 GST and $16.05 QST for promotional cards and flyers to advertise home design gallery. Purchase invoice total $230.05 paid in full by Amex credit card.

☐ **Cash Purchase Invoice #EQ-979764** **Dated July 13/08**

From Énergie Québec, $100 plus $7.00 GST and $8.03 QST for hydro service for one month. Purchase invoice total $115.03 paid in full by cheque #129.

☐ **Cash Sales Invoice #173** **Dated July 13/08**

To Marie Broussard

1	LR-18	Sofa & Slipcover: celadon		$1 475.00
		Goods and Services Tax	7.0%	103.25
		Quebec Sales Tax	7.5%	118.37
	Invoice total			$1 696.62

Received cheque #339 in full payment. Customer to arrange own delivery.

☐ **Visa Sales Invoice #174** **Dated July 14/08**

To Allysa Morel

1	KD-10	Server: fruitwood		$ 980.00
1	KD-12	Table: brass with glass		1 780.00
1	LR-09	Loveseat: chenille		1 325.00
		Goods and Services Tax	7.0%	285.95
		Quebec Sales Tax	7.5%	327.83
		Invoice total		$4 698.78

Paid by Visa #4185 4458 6712 8405.

☐ **Credit Card Purchase Invoice #QD-980** **Dated July 14/08**

From Quickie Delivery Service (use Quick Add), $50 plus $3.50 GST and $4.01 QST for emergency delivery of sofa to Marie Broussard. Purchase invoice total $57.51 paid in full by Amex.

☐ **Sales Invoice #175** **Dated July 14/08**

To Marie Broussard (use Quick Add), $50 plus $3.50 GST and $4.01 QST for delivery of sofa. Sales invoice total $57.51. Terms: net 10. (Credit Freight Revenue.)

☐ **Sales Invoice #176** **Dated July 14/08**

To Caisse Metropolitain, to fill sales order #71

1	HA-03	Lamp: floor solid brass	$ 400
1	HA-09	Rugs: Persian Tabriz 90 x 160cm	650
1	LR-01	Bookcase: oak/walnut solid	1 150
1	LR-12	Sectional Sofa: charcoal linen	2 300
		Delivery	100
		Goods and Services Tax	7.0%
		Quebec Sales Tax	7.5%

Terms: 2/10, n/30.

SESSION DATE – JULY 21, 2008

☐ **Credit Card Purchase Invoice #PD-274** **Dated July 15/08**

From Papineau Delivery, $300 plus $21 GST and $24.08 QST for contracted delivery of furniture. Purchase invoice total $345.08 paid in full by Amex.

☐ **Cash Purchase Invoice #T-55612** **Dated July 16/08**

From Telébec, $75 plus $5.25 GST and $6.02 QST for telephone service. Purchase invoice total $86.27 paid in full by cheque #130.

☐ **Purchase Invoice #MPE-664** **Dated July 17/08**

From Montreal Persia Emporium (Create new inventory)

2	HA-10	Rugs: Mashad 170 x 240cm	$1 000.00
2	HA-11	Rugs: Qum silk 80 x 150cm	1 600.00
		Goods and Services Tax	182.00
		Quebec Sales Tax	208.65
		Invoice total	$2 990.65

Terms: 2/5, n/30.

New inventory items

Number	Description	Unit	Min	Prices Reg.	(Pref.)
HA-10	Rugs: Mashad 170 x 240cm	1-pc	1	$ 800	($ 750)
HA-11	Rugs: Qum silk 80 x 150cm	1-pc	1	1 500	(1 400)

Linked Accounts: Asset 1340 Revenue 4020 Cost of Goods Sold 5060 Variance 5070

Taxes: GST exempt No PST exempt No Duty Rate Not applicable

☐ **Sales Order #72** **Dated July 17/08**

Delivery date July 20/08

From St. Leonard's Homebuilders (preferred customer)

1	BF-01	Armoire: dark oak	$3 000
1	BF-05	Bed: brass/silver	1 700
1	HA-08	Rugs: Persian Kashan 185 x 275cm	950
1	LR-09	Loveseat: chenille	1 225
		Goods and Services Tax	7.0%
		Quebec Sales Tax	7.5%

Terms: 2/10, n/30.

☐ **Memo #4** **Dated July 18/08**

From Owner: Adjust purchase invoice #MPE-664. Montreal Persia Emporium sent a revised invoice MPE-664A that included a freight charge of $50 plus $3.50 GST and $4.01 QST. New purchase invoice total $3 048.16.

☐ **MasterCard Sales Invoice #177** **Dated July 20/08**

To Jacques Altain

1	LR-06	Desk: mahogany		$1 840.00
1	LR-11	Recliner & Ottoman: brown leather		1 020.00
		Delivery		100.00
		Goods and Services Tax	7.0%	207.20
		Quebec Sales Tax	7.5%	237.55
	Invoice total			$3 404.75

Paid by MasterCard #5145 0559 0062 3612.

☐ **Sales Invoice #178** **Dated July 20/08**

To St. Leonard's Homebuilders, to fill sales order #72

1	BF-01	Armoire: dark oak	$3 000
1	BF-05	Bed: brass/silver	1 700
1	HA-08	Rugs: Persian Kashan 185 x 275cm	950
1	LR-09	Loveseat: chenille	1 225
		Goods and Services Tax	7.0%
		Quebec Sales Tax	7.5%

Terms: 2/10, n/30.

☐ **Credit Card Bill #AM-07020** **Dated July 20/08**

From American Express (Amex), $907.15 for new purchases before the billing date, July 14 plus $10.50 monthly fee. Total payment required to avoid interest charges is $917.65. Issue cheque #131 for $917.65 to pay Amex balance in full.

☐ **Cheque Copy #132** **Dated July 21/08**

To Montreal Persia Emporium, $2 987.20 in payment of account including $60.96 discount for early payment. Reference invoice #MPE-664A.

☐ **Interac Sales Invoice #179** **Dated July 21/08**

To Julie Marie Delpy

1	LR-20	Wing Chair: pastel		$375.00
		Goods and Services Tax	7.0%	26.25
		Quebec Sales Tax	7.5%	30.09
	Invoice total			$431.34

Paid by debit card #7855 5867 1284 0505.

Edit the selling price. The price was reduced because the chair legs were scratched. Enter "Final sale" as the Comment.

☐ **Cash Receipt #44** **Dated July 21/08**

From Caisse Metropolitain, cheque #967 for $4 199.16 in payment of account including $92 discount for early payment. Reference invoice #176 and deposit #63.

SESSION DATE – JULY 28, 2008

☐ **Sales Invoice #180** **Dated July 23/08**

To Westmount Primrose Condos (preferred customer)

1	LR-12	Sectional Sofa: charcoal linen	$2 200	
2	LR-19	Swivel Chairs & Slipcovers: cotton	600	each
		Goods and Services Tax	7.0%	
		Quebec Sales Tax	7.5%	

Terms: 2/10, n/30.

☐ **Visa Sales Invoice #181** **Dated July 27/08**

To Juliette Servais

1	KD-02 Buffet: cherry		$2 250.00
	Delivery		100.00
	Goods and Services Tax	7.0%	164.50
	Quebec Sales Tax	7.5%	188.59
	Invoice total		$2 703.09

Paid by Visa #4150 8671 2840 5052.

☐ **MasterCard Sales Invoice #182** **Dated July 28/08**

To Pierre Binoche

1	KD-08 Extension Table: oak		$1 825.00
	Delivery		100.00
	Goods and Services Tax	7.0%	134.75
	Quebec Sales Tax	7.5%	154.49
	Invoice total		$2 214.24

Paid by MasterCard #5555 8445 5900 6236.

☐ **Cash Receipt #45** **Dated July 28/08**

From Marie Broussard, cheque #357 for $57.51 in payment of account. Reference invoice #175.

SESSION DATE – JULY 31, 2008

☐ **Credit Card Purchase Invoice #PD-304** **Dated July 30/08**

From Papineau Delivery, $400 plus $28 GST and $32.10 QST for contracted delivery of furniture. Purchase invoice total $460.10 paid in full by Amex.

☐ **Bank Debit Memo #643177** **Dated July 30/08**

From Bank of Montreal, $30 for bank service charges for one month and $1 700 for mortgage payment including $1 525 interest and $175 principal.

☐ **Bank Credit Memo #46234** **Dated July 30/08**

From Bank of Montreal, $638 interest earned on investment securities deposited to chequing account.

☐ **Cash Receipt #46** **Dated July 30/08**

From St. Leonard's Homebuilders, cheque #3199 for $7 770.48 in payment of account including $137.50 discount for early payment. Reference invoice #178.

☐ **Memo #5** **Dated July 31/08**

From Owner: Issue cheque #133 for $300 to pay the premium for one month to Quebecor Insurance Co. Repeat the entry five times to prepare the remaining payments for the year as postdated cheques. Issue cheques #134 to 138, dated August 31, September 30, October 31, November 30 and December 31.

☐ **Memo #6** **Dated July 31/08**

From Owner: Make adjusting entries for July.

Office Supplies used	$75
Furniture Supplies used	50

☐ **Memo #7** **Dated July 31/08**

From Owner: Lianne Décor earned $5 200 in commissions on her share of sales in July. Issue cheque #139 to pay Décor's commissions.

☐ **Memo #8** **Dated July 31/08**

From Owner: Update all tax codes and tax code descriptions to apply the new GST tax rate at 6 percent.

☑ **Memo #9** **Dated July 31/08**

502 From Owner: Decrease all revenue and expense budget amounts by 10%.

☑ **Memo #10** **Dated July 31/08**

507 From Owner: Print all sales invoices for July.

WARNING!

If you see an error message about missing essential linked accounts, you will need to add linked accounts for QPIP. Although these accounts are not used, they are required by the program.

To add them,

- Click OK when you see the error message.
- Click the Payroll Taxes tab.
- Click the QPIP field in the Payables section.
- Type 2380 QPIP Payable.
- Press Tab and add the new account. This is a Subgroup account.
- Click the QPIP field in the Expenses section.
- Type 5360 QPIP Expense.
- Press Tab and add the new account. This is a Group account.
- Click OK to close the Linked Accounts screen and save the changes.
- Enter the payroll transaction.

KEYSTROKES

Setting Up Budgets

It is important for a business to gauge its performance against some standards. These standards can be provided through comparisons with other companies that are in the same kind of business or by comparing the same company over several time periods. It is common for a business to set goals for the future based on past performance. For example, there may be an expectation that profits will increase by 10 percent over the previous year or that expenses will be reduced because of the introduction of new cost-reduction methods. If a business waits until the end of the year to assess its progress toward its goals, it may be too late to make necessary corrections if things are not proceeding according to plan. Budgets offer a realistic financial plan for the future that can be used to assess performance.

Before analyzing a budget report, you must turn on the option and enter the budget amounts for the relevant accounts.

Turning on the Budgeting Feature

Open the **data files** for **Village Galleries**. Do not advance the session date until you have finished the budget setup.

Choose the **Setup menu**, then **choose System Settings** and **click Settings**.

Click **General** in the left-panel list.

You will display the following setup options for the General Ledger:

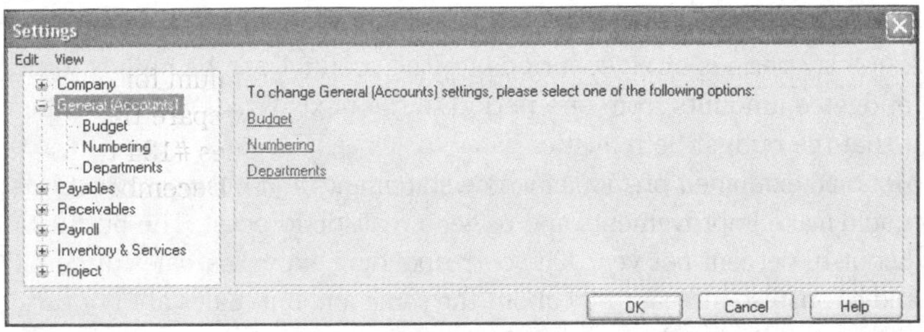

Click **Budget** to open the budgeting options:

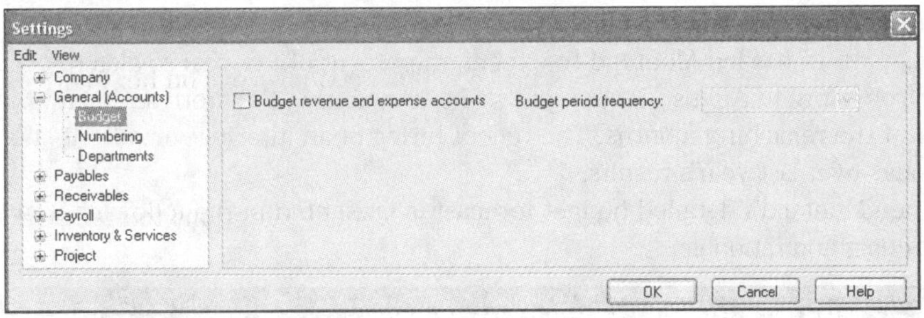

Click **Budget Revenue And Expense Accounts** to turn on the budgeting feature.

The first decision after choosing the budgeting feature involves a budget period. Whether a business chooses to budget amounts on a yearly, quarterly or monthly basis depends on the needs and nature of the business. Monthly budget reports will be appropriate if the business cycle of buying and selling is short but not appropriate if long-term projects are involved. The period chosen must provide meaningful feedback about performance. If the periods are too short, there may be insufficient information to judge performance; if the periods are too long, there may be no opportunity to correct problems because they will not be detected soon enough. Village Galleries will use monthly budget periods initially because the Montands want frequent progress reports.

Click the **Budget Period Frequency field** to see the period options:

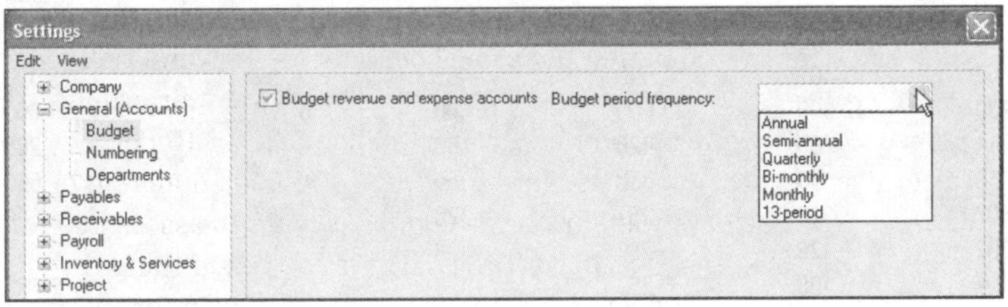

Click **Monthly**.

Click **OK** to return to the Home window and save the settings.

Setting a Budget

The next step is to enter the budget amounts for all expense and revenue accounts.

Budgets can be determined in several different ways. The most common methods are zero-based and incremental budgeting. With the zero-based method, a forecast is made for each revenue and expense account based on expectations about specific planned activities and expenditures. Each budget item must be justified. More commonly, last year's budgets and income statements are used as the starting point and a specific percentage change is included. Thus, a company might expect to improve its performance over last year by 5 percent, either by increasing sales or by decreasing

NOTES

You cannot activate the budget feature in multi-user mode, but you can add and change budget amounts.

expenses. Planned special events such as annual month-long sales, new customer drives, peak holiday periods or slow periods for the product can be built into the changes in budgeted amounts from one period to the next. Whatever method is used, it is important that the budget be realistic.

Renée Montand examined previous income statements and business practices to see where they could make improvements and to get a realistic forecast. The business has been growing by about 10 percent per year. The corresponding expenses, sales discounts, cost of goods sold and so on, also increased by about the same amount. Sales are not divided evenly throughout the 12-month period. Most customers purchase new furniture in the spring and summer, also the busiest home purchasing and moving seasons. Sales are slowest in the winter months and store sales are planned for those months.

This pattern has led Montand to expect 12 percent of the year's sales to occur each month from April to August, 10 percent in January during the store sales and 5 percent in each of the remaining months. The recent hiring of an interior consultant should also boost sales over last year's results.

Renée Montand's detailed budget forecast is presented in the following item-by-item budget chart and rationale:

MONTHLY BUDGET FORECAST FOR 2008

VILLAGE GALLERIES

Account	Jul–Aug	Sep–Dec	Jan	Feb–Mar	Apr–Jun	Total for 2008
REVENUE						
Revenue from Sales	$50 454	$21 023	$42 042	$21 023	$50 454	$420 450
Sales Discount	−504	−210	−420	−210	−504	−4 200
Freight Revenue	1 010	420	830	420	1 010	8 400
Investment Revenue	638	638	638	638	638	7 656
Interest Revenue	22	22	22	22	22	264
TOTAL REVENUE	$51 620	$21 893	$43 112	$21 893	$51 620	$432 570
EXPENSES						
Advertising & Promotion	$ 288	$ 120	$ 240	$ 120	$ 288	$ 2 400
Exchange Rate Differences	0	0	0	0	0	0
Bank Charges	29	12	23	12	29	240
Credit Card Fees	252	105	210	105	252	2 100
Cost of Goods Sold	30 720	12 800	25 600	12 800	30 720	256 000
Variance Costs	144	60	120	60	144	1 200
Furniture Supplies Used	50	50	50	50	50	600
Damaged Inventory	307	128	257	128	307	2 560
Purchase Discounts	−307	−128	−257	−128	−307	−2 560
Freight Expense	307	128	257	128	307	2 560
Delivery Expense	1 010	420	830	420	1 010	8 400
Hydro Expense	90	90	90	90	90	1 080
Insurance Expense	300	300	300	300	300	3 600
Mortgage Interest Expense	1 270	1 270	1 270	1 270	1 270	15 240
Office Supplies Used	65	65	65	65	65	780
Telephone Expenses	80	80	80	80	80	960
Commissions	3 000	1 250	2 500	1 250	3 000	25 000
CSST Expense	61	26	49	26	61	510
QPP Expense	125	52	103	52	125	1 040
QHSF Expense	144	60	120	60	144	1 200
Subcontractor Fees	600	250	500	250	600	5 000
TOTAL EXPENSES	$38 535	$17 138	$32 407	$17 138	$38 535	$327 910
NET INCOME	$13 085	$ 4 755	$10 705	$ 4 755	$13 085	$104 660

BUDGET RATIONALE FOR 2008

VILLAGE GALLERIES

Estimates used to create budget forecasts

Revenue from Sales: increase by 10% over previous year. January, 10% of annual sales; February and March 5%; April, May, June, July and August, 12%; September, October, November and December, 5% each

Sales Discount: expect about 1% of sales on average; most sales are not discounted

Freight Revenue: this has averaged around 2% of sales; most customers request delivery

Interest and Investment Revenue: constant monthly income; same as previous year

Cost of Goods Sold: 60% of net sales (based on markup)

Variance Costs: estimated from price variations in previous years

Damaged Inventory: 1% of Cost of Goods Sold

Purchase Discounts: average 1% of Cost of Goods Sold

Delivery: same amount as Freight Revenue

Freight Expense: average at about 1% of sales

Insurance and Mortgage Interest: same amount each month; small decrease from previous year

Furniture Supplies Used: for maintaining store inventory; constant amount each month

Commissions: estimate, will pay 20% of direct contributions to sales

EI, CPP and QPIP: these do not apply. Do not choose Budget This Account

QPP, WCB and QHSF: straight percentage of commissions (QPP replaces CPP for Quebec)

Subcontractors' Fees: estimated additional assistance needed for peak periods

Bank Charges & Credit Card Fees: increase over last year for increased credit card usage

Exchange Rate Differences: zero – these are expected to cancel each other over time

Other Expenses: constant each month; no change over last year

Entering Budget Amounts in the General Ledger

Click the **Search tool** in the Home window to open the Search window. Accounts is selected as the record type:

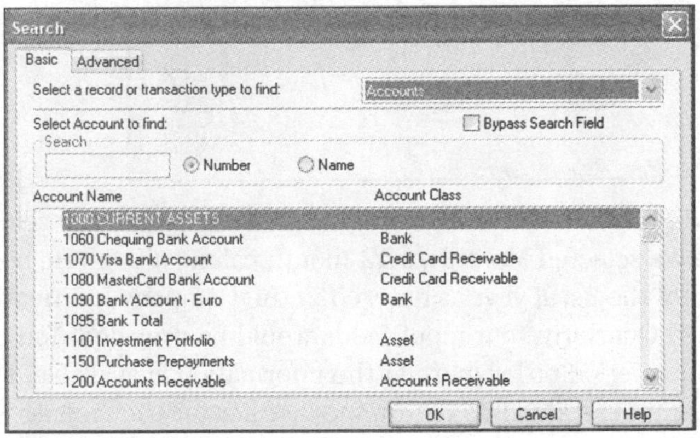

You can also click the Accounts icon in the Home window and then double click the account to open the ledger record.

Click the **Search field**.

Type 4 to advance the cursor and **scroll down** the list to see the 4000-level Revenue accounts.

Click **4020 Revenue from Sales** to highlight the first postable revenue account.

WARNING!

If you use the Search tool when a journal icon is selected, you will open the Search window for transactions.

NOTES

If the Accounts icon is selected, you will also open the Search window for accounts immediately when you click the Search tool.

If another ledger is selected (e.g., the Vendors icon) when you click the Search tool, the list of records for that ledger (e.g., vendors) will be displayed immediately.

Click **OK** to open the Account Ledger window as shown:

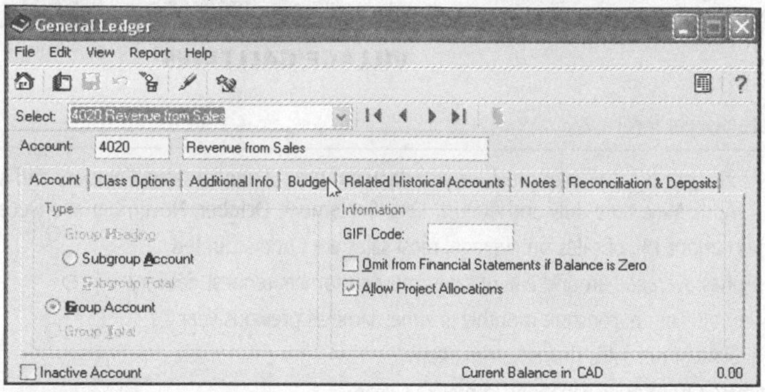

Because we turned on the Budgeting feature in the General Settings window, the Budget tab has been added. This tab will appear only for Income Statement accounts.

Click the **Budget tab** to open the budget activation window as shown:

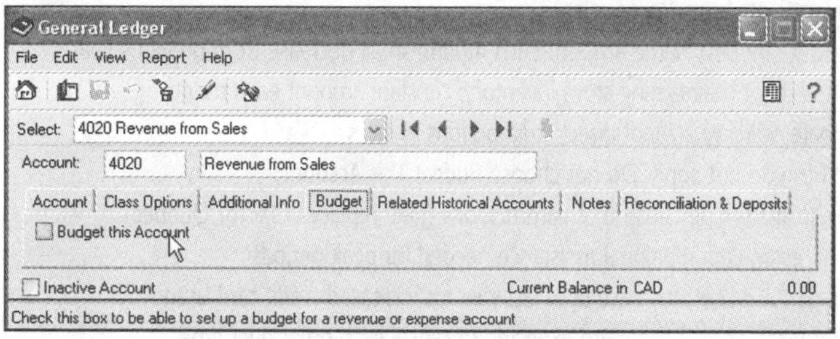

Click **Budget This Account** to open the Budget amount fields as shown:

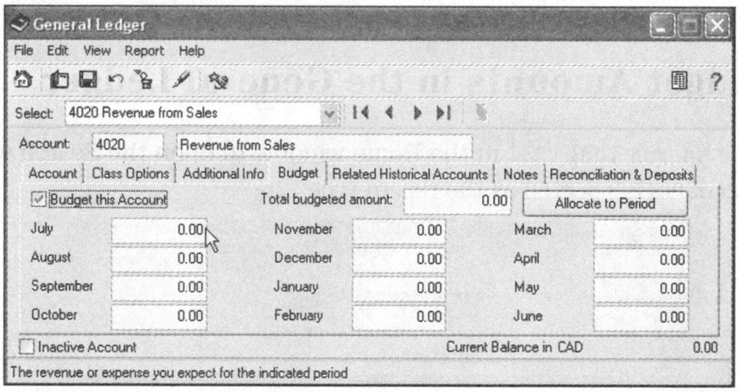

The budget periods displayed at this stage match the period frequency selected in the setup stage. Because we selected Monthly, a 12-month calendar is given, beginning with July, the first month of the fiscal year as entered in the Company Information window. If we had selected Quarterly, four input fields would be provided. You can enter the budget amounts for one period or for more, if the information is available. For Village Galleries, we will enter the amounts determined earlier for each month.

You can change the budget frequency at any time in the General Settings Budget option window. The program will reallocate the previously budgeted amounts proportionately for the new periods after warning you that this will be done and giving you a chance to confirm that you want to proceed.

Refer to the chart on page 498 for budget amounts.

For each revenue and expense, you may choose to add budget amounts or not. Of course, including budget details for all accounts will provide the most meaningful budget reports.

basic BASIC VERSION

The Notes and Related Historical Accounts tabs and the Refresh tool are not available in the Basic version.

NOTES

Budgeting applies only to the postable revenue and expense accounts on the Income Statement. Budget reports are Income Statement reports.

Click the **July field** to select the amount.

Type 50454 **Press** tab.

The cursor advances to the August field and highlights the entry for editing.

Enter the **amounts** for the **remaining 11 months** according to the budget forecast on page 498 by **typing** the **amount** and **pressing** tab to move to the next month.

You can use the **Copy** and **Paste** commands (Edit menu) to copy amounts from one field to another and save some data entry time.

The **Total Budgeted Amount** is updated continually as you enter amounts for each period. When you enter individual monthly amounts, use the Total Budgeted Amount to check your work. It should equal the budget amount for 12 months.

When you have entered the amounts for each month,

Click the **Next button** to advance to the next revenue account in the budget tab screen.

Enter **budget information** for the **remaining** revenue and expense **accounts** by following the steps outlined above. Use the amounts determined for each account in the chart on page 498.

Remember to enter **negative** budget amounts for accounts that decrease the total in a Group or Section (e.g., *Sales Discount*).

For some accounts, the budget amounts for each month are equal, and you can use a shortcut to enter the amounts. For example, for *4100 Investment Revenue*,

Click the **Total Budgeted Amount field**.

Type 7656 **Click Allocate To Period** to divide the amount evenly among all budget periods (638 is entered for each month, 7 656/12).

After entering the budget amounts for all accounts,

Close the **account's General Ledger window**.

Display or **print** the **Budget Report** to check your amounts (see page 504).

NOTES

Non-postable accounts, such as subtotals, headings and totals, do not have budget fields.

Do not enter budget amounts for CPP Expense and EI Expense. These accounts are not used by Village Galleries but they are required as essential linked accounts by the program.

NOTES

Because we accessed the ledger record using the Search tool, we bypassed the Accounts window. Closing the ledger record therefore returns you directly to the Home window.

Updating Budgets

Changing Budget Amounts

Budget amounts can be updated if needed based on feedback from earlier budget reports. They should not, of course, be changed without good reason.

If you discover that your budget forecasts are incorrect, you can update the amounts for each account individually by repeating the process described above for entering initial budget amounts. Or you can globally update all amounts by a fixed percentage. To update the amounts globally,

Choose the **Maintenance menu** in the Home window and **click Update Budget Amounts** to see the Update Budget window:

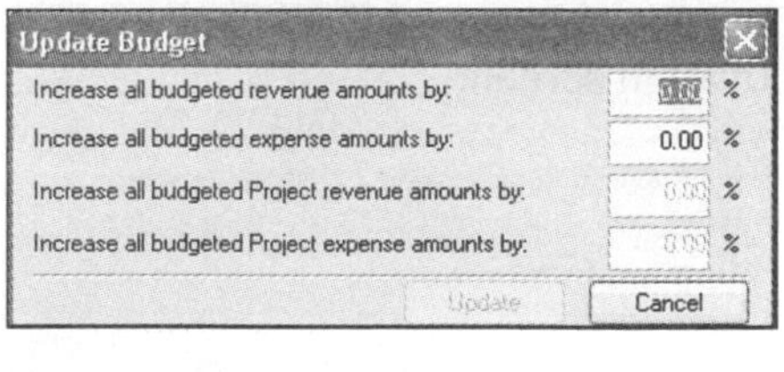

Type the percentage change that you want to apply, and type a negative number for decreases. Click Update to apply the change. The screen that follows asks you to confirm that you want to update the budget. Click Yes to apply the changes and return to the Home window.

You can change the budgets for revenue and expense accounts separately. You can change project revenue and expense amounts by a different percentage. When you review the account's budget information in the account ledger, you will see that the change has been applied.

Changing Budget Frequencies

You can also change the budget frequency in the General Ledger Settings screen. For example, to change the period from monthly to quarterly, choose the Setup menu, then choose System Settings and click Settings. Click the General tab. Then choose Quarterly from the Budget Period Frequency drop-down list and click OK.

NOTES

If you change the frequency to quarterly, the budget amount you entered for Revenue from Sales will become $105 112.50 each quarter ($420 450/12).

When you have a quarterly budget with different amounts for each quarter and you change the frequency to monthly, each month will have the same budget amount, the total for the four quarters divided by 12. You must edit the amounts if these are incorrect.

For example, a quarterly budget of $1 000, $3 000, $2 000 and $6 000 for the four quarters becomes $1 000 each month if the frequency is changed to monthly ($12 000/12).

Before applying the new budget settings, Simply Accounting generates the following warning each time you change a budget frequency:

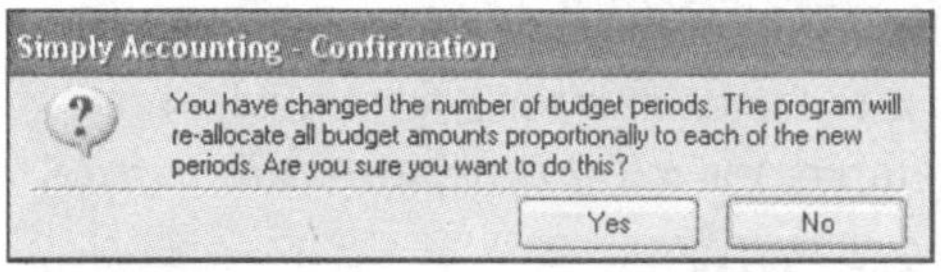

The statement warns that previous budget amounts will be reallocated evenly among the new number of periods. If you change a monthly budget to quarterly, each quarter will have the same budget amount.

Click **No** to cancel the change.

Adding Budget Amounts to Projects

If you are using project allocations, you can also enter budget amounts for each project. You must first turn on the budgeting feature and then choose a budget period or frequency. The following steps will illustrate this procedure.

Right-click the Project icon to select it and then click the Setup tool to open the Project Settings window:

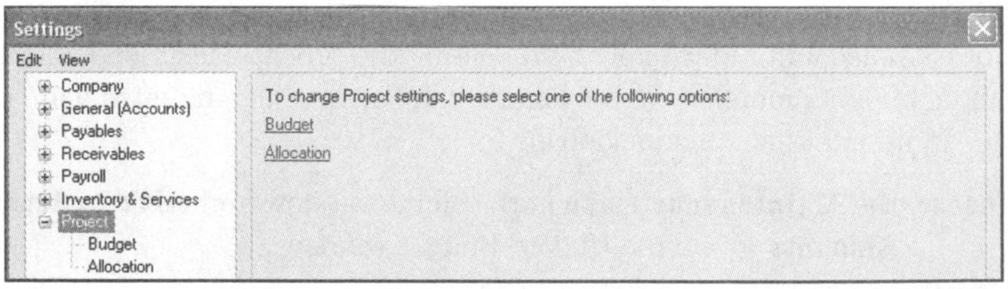

Click Budget to see the project activation screen:

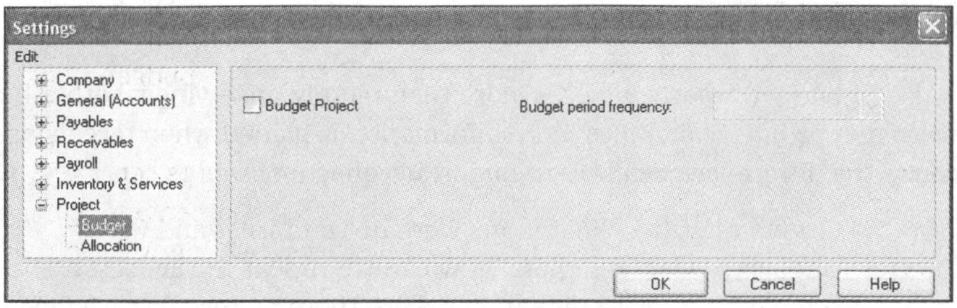

These options are like those for the General Ledger.

Click Budget Project.

Choose a frequency from the Budget Period Frequency drop-down list.

Click OK to save the settings.

Click the Project icon to open the Projects window.

Create the projects if you have not already done so.

The Project Ledger window includes a Budget tab as shown:

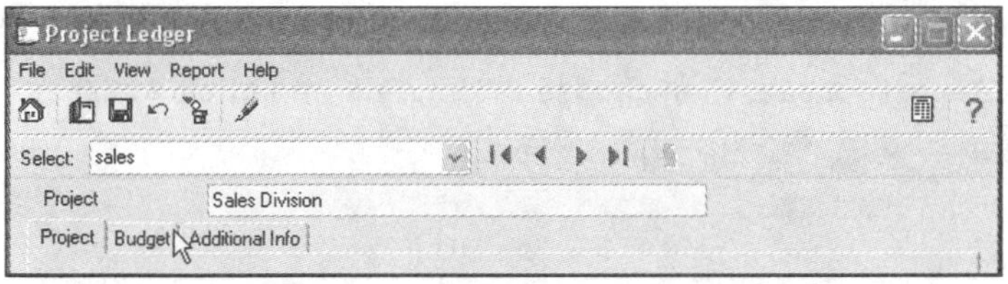

Click the Budget tab to open the budget activation window:

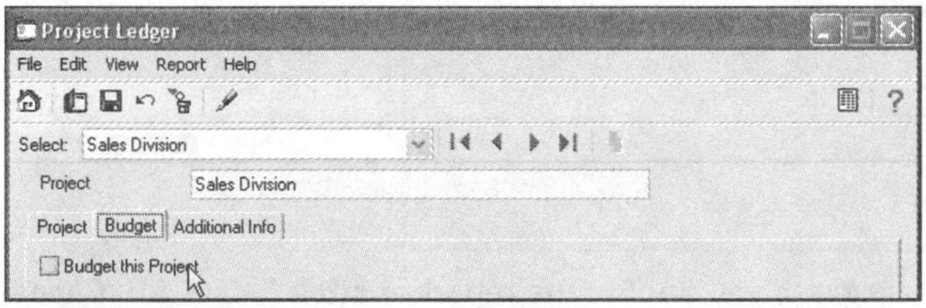

Click Budget This Project to open the budget amount fields. Quarterly periods have been selected for this illustration:

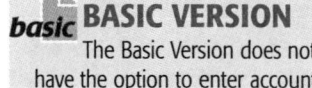

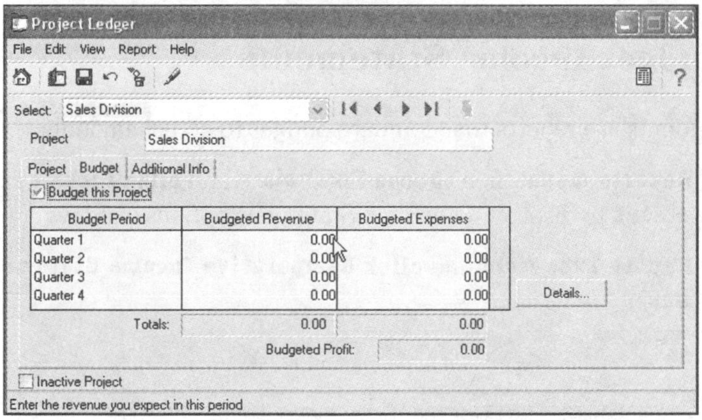

Enter the budgeted Revenue and Expense amounts for each period for this project. Open the ledger for the next project, and enter the budget amounts.

Close the ledger when finished and enter the allocations as usual in the journals. Project budget reports will be available.

NOTES

Click Details if you want to enter additional project budget amounts for individual accounts.

basic **BASIC VERSION**

The Basic Version does not have the option to enter account details.

Budget Reports

Effective use of budget reports involves more than merely observing whether budgeted targets were met or not. Sometimes more information is gained when targets are not met, because the differences can lead to important questions:

- Were the targets realistic? What items were not on target and why?
- If performance exceeds the targets, how can we repeat the success?
- If performance did not meet the targets, were there factors that we failed to anticipate?
- Should we revise future budgets based on the new information?

That is, the problem-solving cycle is set in motion. Even an Income Statement that is on target should be reviewed carefully. There may be room for improvement if the budget was a conservative estimate. Or, you may want to include new information that will affect future performance and was unknown when the budget was drawn up.

Displaying Budget Reports

NOTES
These reports are displayed from the Reports menu in the Home window.

NOTES
From the Budget Report, you can drill down to the General Ledger for the account so you can edit the budget amounts if necessary.
The Budget Report cannot be customized.

You can check the budget amounts you entered for accounts from the Budget Report.

Choose the **Reports menu**, then **choose Financials** and **click Budget**:

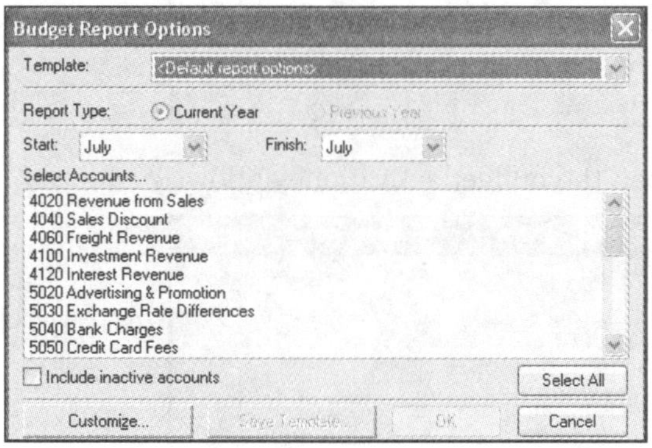

Select the **accounts** you want in the report or **click Select All**. **Choose** the **budget periods** and **click OK** to see the amounts.

Close the **display** when you have finished.

Displaying Budget Income Statements

Budget income statements are reports that compare budget to actual amounts.

Choose the **Reports menu**, then **choose Financials** and **click Income Statement** to display the Income Statement options window.

Click the **Report Type field** and **click Comparative Income Statement (2 Periods)**:

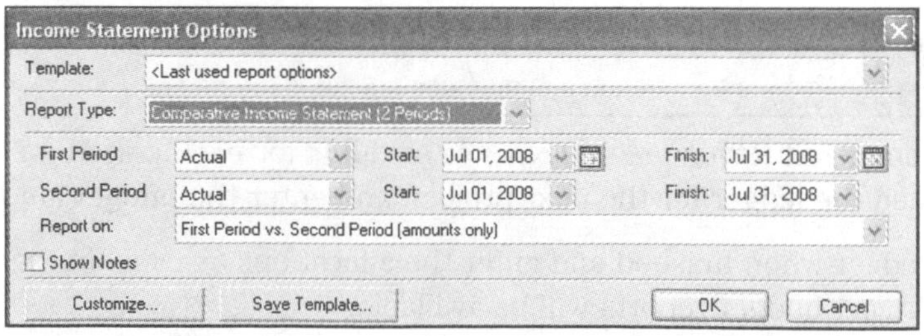

Click **Actual** in the Second Period field to see the budget-related option:

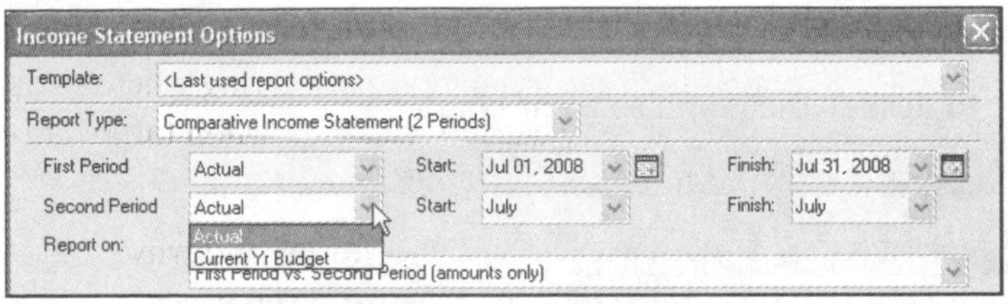

Click **Current Yr Budget** to change the option.

The **Report On** options are the same as the options for regular comparative income statements, but now the Second Period refers to budget amounts. Three types of reports are available. The first, **First Period Vs. Second Period (Amounts Only)**, lists the amounts that were budgeted for the revenue and expense accounts for the period indicated and the revenues and expenses actually obtained for the same period. The second, **First Period Vs. Second Period (Difference In Percentage)**, gives these two amounts as well as the percentage that the actual amount is above or below the budgeted amount. The third option, **First Period Vs. Second Period (Difference In Amounts)** provides budget and actual as base amounts, plus the difference between them as a dollar amount.

For the dollar difference and the percentage difference reports, a positive difference means that the budget was exceeded, a negative difference indicates that the results came in under budget. Remember that for revenues, a positive difference means results were better than expected, but for expenses, a positive difference means that results were poorer than expected (expenses were higher than budgeted). Cost of goods sold will increase directly with sales, so positive differences can mean either improved sales or higher costs, or both.

Click the **budget report** you want. **Close** the **display** when finished.

When you add budget details for projects, you can also create project budget reports. Choose the Reports menu, then choose Project and click Budget. Choose the Report Type, dates and projects and click OK.

To print budget reports,

Display the **report** you want to print. **Click** the **Print button** or **choose** the **File menu** in the report window and **click Print**. **Close** the **displayed report** when you have finished.

Graphing Budget Reports

When the Budgeting option is activated and set up, two budget-related graphs are added to the Graphs menu: Sales vs Budget and Expenses vs Budget.

Sales vs Budget Graphs

Choose the **Graphs menu** in the Home window and **click Sales Vs Budget** to display the set of revenue accounts:

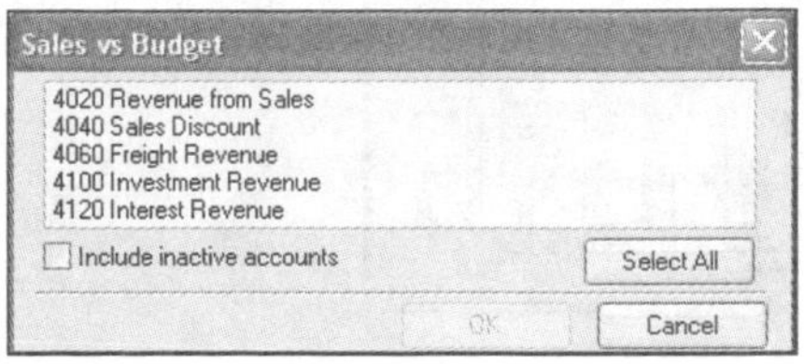

Press and **hold** ctrl and **click** the **accounts** you want to include in the graph or **click Select All**.

Click **OK** to display the graph as a bar chart:

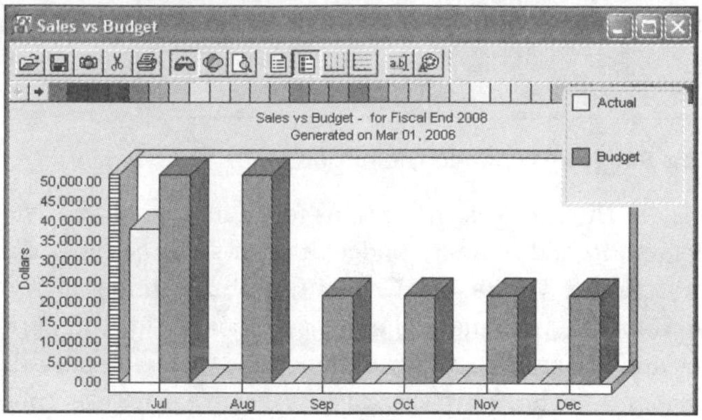

NOTES
Budget amounts are shown for the remaining months of the fiscal period but there are no actual amounts after July.

The options for displaying, editing, printing and copying budget graphs, and so on, are the same as those for other graphs.

The displayed graph includes all revenue accounts **before** the 10 percent budget decrease at the end of July. The amounts for the selected revenue accounts are added together in the single bar labelled Actual. The other bar represents the budgeted amount for the same accounts together. Revenue was much lower than expected, indicating a decline in performance.

Close the **displayed graph** when you have finished.

Expenses vs Budget Graphs

Choose the **Graphs menu** in the Home window and **click Expenses Vs Budget** to display the set of expense accounts:

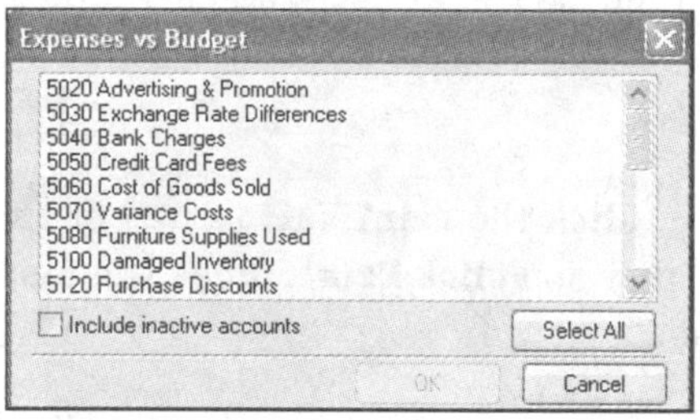

Press and **hold** ctrl and **click** the **accounts** you want to include in the graph or **click Select All**.

Click **OK** to display the bar chart:

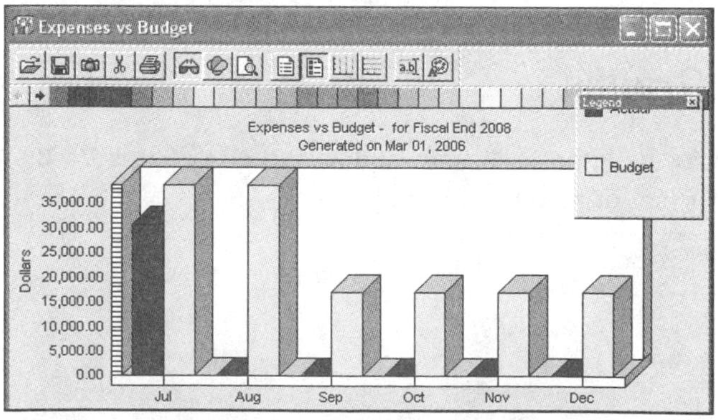

NOTES
Budget amounts are shown for the remaining months of the fiscal period but there are no actual amounts after July.

The displayed graph includes all expense accounts at the end of July, before changing the budget amounts. The amounts for the selected expense accounts are added together in the bar labelled Actual. The second bar represents the budgeted amount for the same accounts. The graph shows that expenses were also lower than expected, supporting the trend in the revenue graph for decreased sales because cost of goods sold, the largest expense, is directly proportional to sales. Net income for July was also significantly below the budget forecast.

Close the **displayed graph** when you have finished.

Printing in Batches

In addition to printing invoices, orders, quotes and cheques at the time of a transaction, you can print them in batches at the end of a period, such as the end of a business day. This batch printing makes it easier to share printers. Any of the forms that can be printed individually can be printed in batches. First you need to allow batch printing for the data file.

NOTES
To set up for printing in batches, you must work in single-user mode.

Choose the **Setup menu**, then **choose System Settings** and **click Settings**.

Click **Company** and then **click Forms** to open the Settings screen for Forms:

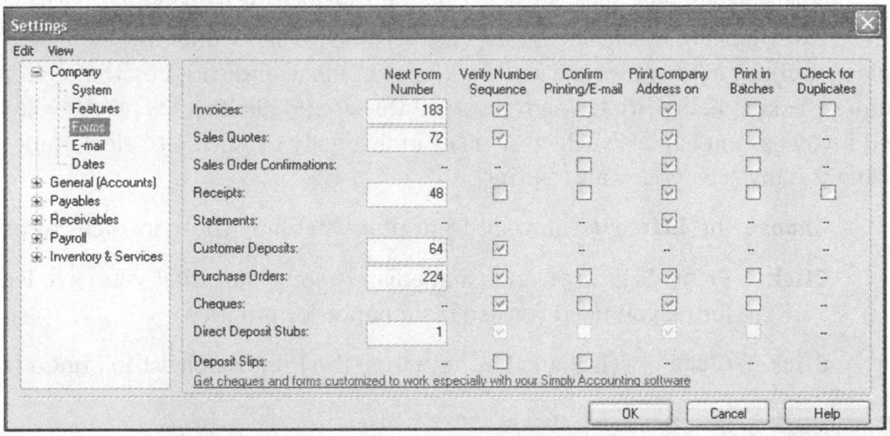

Click the **Print In Batches check box for Invoices**, the first form listed.

Click the **check box for the other forms** that you want to be able to print in batches.

Click **OK** to save the changes and see the following message:

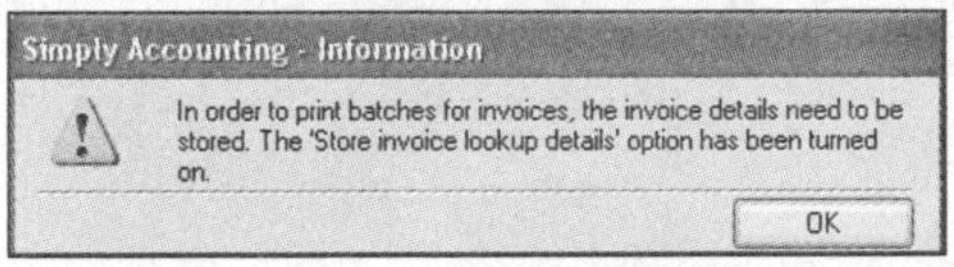

The message is a status check about storing invoice details. You must have this feature selected to print in batches.

Click **OK** to confirm and return to the Home window.

The Reports menu in the Home window has a Print Batches menu option added.

NOTES
Remember that you can customize the invoices before printing them.
You cannot preview the invoices from the Print Batches window.

Choose the **Reports menu** then **choose Print Batches** and **click Sales Invoices** to see the printing options:

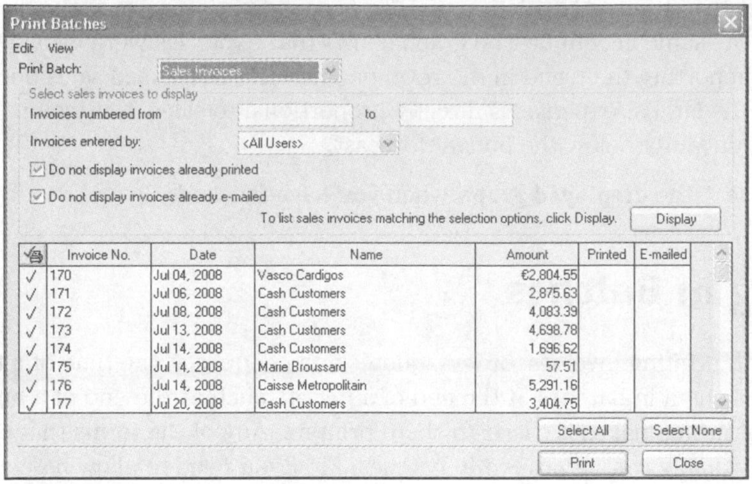

From this screen, you can choose other forms to print in batches. These are available from the **Print Batch** drop-down list. If some invoices have **Already** been **Printed** or **E-mailed**, you can remove them from the display by clicking the appropriate check boxes. You can choose a **range of Invoice Numbers** or a specific **User** as selection criteria. After making these selections, click **Display** to show only the requested invoices. Initially all invoices are selected for printing as indicated by the ✓ in the Print column. Clicking **Select None** will remove all the ✓ and clicking **Select All** will select all listed invoices. You can also select invoices individually by clicking Select None and then clicking the invoices you want to print.

Choose the **invoices** you want to print so that only those invoices have a ✓.

Click **Print**. Printing begins immediately so be sure that you have loaded the forms you need (or use plain paper for practice).

Click **Close** or select another form from the Print Batch list to print other forms.

REVIEW

The Student CD-ROM with Data Files includes Review Questions and Supplementary Cases for this chapter.

CHAPTER FOURTEEN

Tesses Tresses

OBJECTIVES

After completing this chapter, you should be able to

- ***prepare*** bank deposit slips
- ***print*** the Transaction Report for the bank account
- ***compare*** the bank statement with the Transaction Report
- ***turn on*** the account reconciliation feature
- ***create*** new accounts for reconciliation
- ***link*** the new reconciliation accounts
- ***set up*** the account reconciliation information
- ***reconcile*** the bank account statement with the General Ledger
- ***display*** and ***print*** account reconciliation reports
- ***clear*** paid invoices and ***remove*** accounts

COMPANY INFORMATION

Company Profile

NOTES
Tesses Tresses
55 Salon Rd.
Charlottetown
PEI C1A 6D3
Tel: (902) 729-6211
Fax: (902) 728-4821
Business No.: 136 422 374

Tesses Tresses, a hair salon in Charlottetown, Prince Edward Island, is a family business owned by Tess Dubois, her husband Ian and her daughter Felicia. All three had both professional and business management training to prepare them for running the salon. Together they provide a full range of hair care services to clients, most of whom return regularly. Unlike many salons where the price depends on the stylist and customer, Tesses Tresses charges one price for each service regardless of client gender or stylist. They also sell a limited range of high-quality hair care products.

The salon building that they own includes two apartments that are rented to students. These tenants provided postdated cheques for three months at the beginning of January.

Instead of hiring a maintenance, cleaning and laundry company to take care of the premises, the Dubois family share this responsibility to reduce expenses. Cleaning is required almost continually to meet hygiene standards for health and safety.

The salon's regular suppliers provide inventory products including those used in the salon for regular client services; office supplies; cleaning supplies for the salon; linens such as towels, capes, gowns; and hair dressing equipment. Vendor records are set up for all of these suppliers as well as for utility service companies and government agencies to which Tesses Tresses remits taxes. The salon pays GST on all purchases and PST on taxable goods and services except inventory.

Although most clients are one-time customers who pay by cash and credit card, some repeat customers have accounts and are entitled to a 2 percent discount if they pay within five days. Net payment is due in 15 days. The cash customers do not receive a discount. A record called Cash Customers is set up for the weekly summaries of cash and credit card sales. Customers pay both GST at 7 percent and PST at the rate of 10 percent on merchandise they buy from the salon and GST only on all services. The PST in Prince Edward Island is calculated on the base price of goods plus GST. The tax rates and codes are entered into customer and inventory records so the program automatically calculates taxes.

Tesses Tresses also provides hair styling services to local theatre companies, cutting and styling hair for cast members before performances, re-styling throughout the show for cast character changes and styling wigs. These evening commitments do not conflict with the usual daytime salon business hours. The theatre companies pay preferred prices at about 20 percent off regular prices in addition to the discount for early payment.

At the beginning of February, some unfilled purchase orders will provide the inventory for the additional purchases anticipated for Valentine's Day.

The accounting records for Tesses Tresses were converted to Simply Accounting at the beginning of January, and the transactions for January have been completed. The files are ready for January bank account transactions (deposits and account reconciliation) and February transactions. The current accounting records include:

- Chart of Accounts
- Trial Balance as at January 31, 2008
- Vendor Information
- Customer Information
- Inventory Information
- Accounting Procedures

CHART OF ACCOUNTS

TESSES TRESSES

ASSETS

1030 Undeposited Cash and Cheques
1060 Bank: Chequing Account
1080 Bank: Credit Cards
1200 Accounts Receivable
1240 Prepaid Insurance
1260 Prepaid Subscriptions
1300 Towels and Capes
1320 Office Supplies
1340 Washroom & Cleaning Supplies
1360 Salon Supplies
1420 Hair Care Products ▶
▶1520 Computer and Cash Register
1540 Furniture and Fixtures
1560 Salon Equipment
1580 Salon and Building

LIABILITIES

2100 Bank Loan
2150 Credit Card Payable
2200 Accounts Payable
2640 PST Payable
2750 GST Charged on Sales
2760 GST Paid on Purchases
2850 Mortgage Payable ▶

▶EQUITY

3100 TT Capital
3150 TT Drawings
3600 Net Income

REVENUE

4100 Revenue from Sales
4120 Revenue from Services
4140 Rental Income
4160 Sales Discounts
4200 Sales Tax Compensation
4220 Interest Revenue
4240 Other Revenue ▶

▶EXPENSE

5020 Advertising and Promotion
5040 Bank Charges
5060 Credit Card Fees
5080 Cost of Services
5180 Inventory Losses
5200 Cost of Goods Sold
5220 Purchase Discounts
5240 Insurance Expense
5260 Subscriptions Expense
5300 Supplies Used
5320 Utilities
5340 Interest Expense

NOTES: The Chart of Accounts includes only postable accounts and Net Income.

TRIAL BALANCE

TESSES TRESSES

January 31, 2008

		Debits	Credits			Debits	Credits
1030	Undeposited Cash and Cheques	$ 14 081.50		▶ 2750	GST Charged on Sales		1 578.36
1060	Bank: Chequing Account	33 076.16		2760	GST Paid on Purchases	255.22	
1080	Bank: Credit Cards	9 000.38		2850	Mortgage Payable		149 750.00
1200	Accounts Receivable	21.40		3100	TT Capital		101 749.00
1240	Prepaid Insurance	750.00		4100	Revenue from Sales		4 909.00
1260	Prepaid Subscriptions	270.00		4120	Revenue from Services		17 639.00
1300	Towels and Capes	530.00		4140	Rental Income		945.00
1320	Office Supplies	130.00		4160	Sales Discounts	52.52	
1340	Washroom & Cleaning Supplies	572.49		4200	Sales Tax Compensation		62.70
1360	Salon Supplies	329.50		5060	Credit Card Fees	327.44	
1420	Hair Care Products	1 886.50		5200	Cost of Goods Sold	2 145.00	
1520	Computer and Cash Register	4 200.00		5220	Purchase Discounts		63.33
1540	Furniture and Fixtures	7 600.00		5240	Insurance Expense	150.00	
1560	Salon Equipment	4 685.60		5260	Subscriptions Expense	30.00	
1580	Salon and Building	220 000.00		5300	Supplies Used	440.00	
2100	Bank Loan		$23 520.00	5320	Utilities	300.70	
2150	Credit Card Payable		82.39	5340	Interest Expense	1 370.00	
2200	Accounts Payable		1 380.30			$302 204.41	$302 204.41
2640	PST Payable		525.33 ▶				

VENDOR INFORMATION

TESSES TRESSES

Vendor Name (Contact)	Address	Phone No. Fax No.	E-mail Web Site	Terms Tax ID
Air Pro (Curly Locks)	390 Brows Lane Charlottetown, PE C1A 6M3	Tel: (902) 722-0217 Fax: (902) 723-8100	curly@airpro.com www.airpro.com	net 15 137 456 199
All U Need	Maypoint Plaza #64 Charlottetown, PE C1E 1E2	Tel: (902) 728-4314	www.alluneed.com	net 1 382 732 162
Atlantic Power Corp.	16 Lektrik Rd. Charlottetown, PE C1C 6G1	Tel: (902) 726-1615	www.apc.ca	net 1
Charlottetown City Treasurer	78 Fitzroy St. Charlottetown, PE C1A 1R5	Tel: (902) 725-9173	www.charlottetown.ca/fin	net 1
Eastern Tel (I.D. Caller)	36 Nassau St. Charlottetown, PE C1A 7V9	Tel: (902) 723-2355	www.bell.ca	net 1
Fine Brushes (Harry Bristle)	13 Ave. Costey Dorval, QC H9S 4C7	Tel: (514) 457-1826 Fax: (514) 457-1883	bristle@finebrushes.com www.finebrushes.com	net 20 188 462 457
Lookin' Good (N. Vayne)	18 Vivanle Cr. Summerside, PE C1N 6C4	Tel: (902) 829-4763 Fax: (902) 829-7392	vayne@lookingood.com www.lookingood.com	net 10 192 721 214
Pro-Line Inc. (Awl Fluff)	190 Rue Mutchmore Hull, QC J8Y 3S9	Tel: (819) 658-7227 Fax: (819) 658-7192	awl.fluff@proline.com www.proline.com	2/10, n/30 (after tax) 621 372 611
Provincial Treasurer	95 Rochford St., PO Box 2000 Charlottetown, PE C1A 7N8	Tel: (902) 368-4070 Fax: (902) 368-6164	www.gov.pe.ca/pt	net 1
Receiver General for Canada	Summerside Tax Centre Summerside, PE C1N 6L2	Tel: (902) 821-8186	www.cca-arc.gc.ca	net 1
Seaside Papers (Fyne Pulp)	40 Harbour View Dr. Charlottetown, PE C1A 7A8	Tel: (902) 720-1623 Fax: (902) 720-1639	pulp@seasidepapers.com www.seasidepapers.com	net 1 810 721 011

▶

Vendor Name (Contact)	Address	Phone No. Fax No.	E-mail Web Site	Terms Tax ID
Sharp Scissors (S. Cutter)	22 Bellevue Ave. Summerside, PE C1N 2C7	Tel: (902) 923-1995 Fax: (902) 923-1726	cutter@sharp.com www.sharp.com	net 10 138 221 100
Zines Inc. (Buetee Tipps)	344 Lepage Ave. Summerside, PE C1N 3E6	Tel: (902) 553- 6291 Fax: (902) 553-7155	tipps@zines.com www.zines.com	net 10 205 602 301

OUTSTANDING VENDOR INVOICES

TESSES TRESSES

Vendor Name	Terms	Date	Inv/Chq No.	Amount	Discount	Total
Fine Brushes	net 20	Dec. 20/07	FB-4321	$330.00		$330.00
		Jan. 09/08	CHQ 411	330.00		330.00
	net 20	Jan. 17/08	FB-6219	438.70		438.70
			Balance owing			$438.70
Pro-Line Inc.	2/10, n/30	Dec. 28/07	PL-1002	$ 945.00		$ 945.00
		Jan. 4/08	CHQ 410	926.10	$18.90	945.00
	2/10, n/30	Jan. 4/08	PL-1012	2 221.32		2 221.32
		Jan. 14/08	CHQ 413	2 176.89	44.43	2 221.32
Sharp Scissors	net 10	Jan. 24/08	SS-432	$941.60		$941.60
			Grand Total			$1 380.30

NOTES: Cash and Credit Card Purchases are not included in the chart of vendor invoices.

CUSTOMER INFORMATION

TESSES TRESSES

Customer Name (Contact)	Address	Phone No. Fax No.	E-mail Web Site	Terms Credit Limit
Atta Schule (tenant)		Tel: (902) 724-2996	atta.schule@undergrad.upei.ca	first of month
Brioche Bridal Party (Bonnie Brioche)	75 Marital Way Charlottetown, PE C1E 4A2	Tel: (902) 723-1194 Fax: (902) 726-1921	brioche@weddingbells.com	2/5, n/15 $1 000
Cash Customers				cash/credit card
Conn Seted	14 Hi Brow St. Charlottetown, PE C1E 3X1	Tel: (902) 723-0099	conn.seted@aol.com	net 15 $1 000
Irma Vannitee	77 Makeover Cr. Charlottetown, PE C1B 1J5	Tel: (902) 726-7715	irma.van@skindeep.com	2/5, n/15 $1 000
*On Stage Theatre Company (Marvelle Stage)	100 Marquee Blvd. Charlottetown, PE C1A 2M1	Tel: (902) 727-8201 Fax: (902) 727-0663	marvelle@onstage.com www.onstage.com	2/5, n/15 $2 000
Proud Family	98 Proud St. Charlottetown, PE C1B 3C1	Tel: (902) 721-1113	theprouds@shaw.ca	net 15 $1 000
Stu Dents (tenant)		Tel: (902) 724-7103	stu.dents@undergrad.upei.ca	first of month
*Twilight Theatre (Ona Roll)	55 Footlights Dr. Charlottetown, PE C1B 6V2	Tel: (902) 728-4661 Fax: (902) 724-1556	ona.roll@twilight.com www.twilight.com	2/5, n/15 $2 000

NOTES: All customer discounts are calculated on after-tax amounts.
* Indicates preferred customer.

OUTSTANDING CUSTOMER INVOICES

TESSES TRESSES

Customer Name	Terms	Date	Inv/Chq No.	Amount	Discount	Total
Atta Schule	rent payment	Jan. 2/08	CHQ 415			$395.00
	rent payment	Feb. 2/08	CHQ 416 (postdated rent payment)			395.00
Brioche Bridal Party	2/5, n/15	Jan. 9/08	468			$109.89
		Jan. 14/08	CHQ 911	$107.69	$2.20	109.89
Conn Seted	net 15	Jan. 24/08	477			$42.80
		Jan. 29/08	CHQ 238			42.80
Irma Vannitee	2/5, n/15	Dec. 28/07	452	$120.00		$120.00
		Jan. 2/08	CHQ 46	117.60	$2.40	120.00
	2/5, n/15	Jan. 2/08	464	93.41		93.41
		Jan. 7/08	CHQ 918	91.54	1.87	93.41
	2/5, n/15	Jan. 4/08	467	108.72		108.72
		Jan. 17/08	CHQ CC-61	108.72		108.72
	2/5, n/15	Jan. 16/08	471	62.60		62.60
		Jan. 20/08	CHQ 74	61.35	1.25	62.60
	2/5, n/15	Jan. 27/08	478	21.40		21.40
			Balance owing			$21.40
On Stage Theatre Company	2/5, n/15	Dec. 29/07	455	$250.00		$250.00
		Jan. 3/08	CHQ 382	245.00	$ 5.00	250.00
	2/5, n/15	Jan. 20/08	474	890.24		890.24
		Jan. 24/08	CHQ 474	872.44	17.80	890.24
	2/5, n/15	Jan. 28/08	479	890.24		890.24
		Jan. 31/08	CHQ 498	872.44	17.80	890.24
Stu Dents	rent payment	Jan. 2/08	CHQ 161			$550.00
	rent payment	Feb. 2/08	CHQ 162 (postdated rent payment)			550.00
Twilight Theatre	2/5, n/15	Dec. 28/07	453	$210.00		$210.00
		Jan. 2/08	CHQ 5121	205.80	$4.20	210.00
			Grand Total			$21.40

INVENTORY INFORMATION

TESSES TRESSES

Code	Description	Unit	Min Qty	Selling Price Reg	Selling Price (Pref)	Qty on Hand	Total (Cost)
Hair Products: Total asset value $1 886.50 (Asset account: 1420, Revenue account: 4100, Expense account: 5200)							
BRS1	Hair Brush: long hair	each	2	$21	($17)	14	$112.00
BRS2	Hair Brush: natural bristle	each	2	26	(22)	7	84.00
BRS3	Hair Brush: short hair	each	2	12	(10)	14	70.00
BRS4	Hair Brush: styling	each	2	18	(15)	16	128.00
CN1	Pro-Line Conditioner: reg 225 ml	bottle	5	15	(12)	30	180.00
CN2	Pro-Line Conditioner: treat 225 ml	bottle	5	18	(15)	8	64.00
CN3	Pro-Line Conditioner: deep 150 ml	bottle	3	25	(20)	20	220.00
CN4	Pro-Line Hot Oil Treatment 75 ml	tube	3	22	(18)	23	218.50
FRZ1	Pro-Line Defrizzer: cream 100 ml	jar	3	12	(10)	20	120.00
GEL1	Pro-Line Spray Gel: shaper 150 ml	can	5	21	(17)	18	162.00
GEL2	Pro-Line Mousse: gentle hold 100 ml	can	5	19	(16)	16	128.00
SHM1	Pro-Line Shampoo: regular 225 ml	bottle	5	15	(12)	25	150.00
SHM2	Pro-Line Shampoo: treated 225 ml	bottle	5	20	(16)	4	36.00
SPR1	Pro-Line Hair Spray: gentle 150 ml	can	5	14	(11)	21	126.00
SPR2	Pro-Line Hair Spray: xtra 150 ml	can	3	17	(14)	11	88.00

▶

Code	Description	Unit	Selling Price Reg	(Pref)	Tax PST	Tax GST
Salon Services (Revenue account: 4120, Expense account: 5080)						
SRV1	Colour	each	$ 45	($36)	No PST	Yes
SRV2	Conditioning Treatment	each	20	(16)	No PST	Yes
SRV3	Cut and Style	each	40	(32)	No PST	Yes
SRV4	Highlights: cap method	each	80	(64)	No PST	Yes
SRV5	Highlights: foil method	each	100	(80)	No PST	Yes
SRV6	Highlights: roots touchup	each	30	(24)	No PST	Yes
SRV7	Perm	each	80	(64)	No PST	Yes
SRV8	Wash and Style	each	20	(16)	No PST	Yes
SRV9	Wig Wash, Set and Style	each	30	(24)	No PST	Yes

NOTES: Brushes are purchased and sold individually. All other hair care products are purchased in cartons of 12 units and sold in individual units.

Accounting Procedures

Taxes

GST at 7 percent is charged on all goods and services sold by the salon. Tesses Tresses remits the GST owing — *GST Charged on Sales* less *GST Paid on Purchases* to the Receiver General by the last day of each month for the previous month.

PST at 10 percent for Prince Edward Island is charged on all inventory items sold by the salon. PST is calculated on the sale price plus the GST Charged (i.e., GST is taxable). Personal services, such as those provided by the salon, are exempt from PST. The inventory ledger records contain this information so that the correct taxes will be applied automatically. When PST is remitted, 3 percent of the PST collected is withheld as sales tax compensation, to an annual maximum compensation of $500.

Sales Summaries

Most salon sales are to one-time customers who do not have accounts. These sales are summarized weekly according to payment — by cash or by credit card — and entered for the customer named Cash Sales. By choosing Cash Sales as the customer for these sales, the default tax codes and terms should be correct.

Receipts and Bank Deposits

Cash and cheques received in payment are held for weekly deposits. Upon receipt, they are debited to the *Undeposited Cash and Cheques*.

NSF Cheques

If a cheque is deposited from an account that does not have enough money to cover it, the bank returns it to the depositor as NSF (non-sufficient funds). To record the NSF cheque, first reverse the receipt in the Receipts Journal. Turn on the option to Include Fully Paid Invoices and enter a negative payment amount. If a discount were taken for early payment, reverse this amount as well. Then enter a Sales Journal invoice for the amount of the handling charge. Refer to Chapter 6, page 181, if you need more help.

Cost of Supplies

NOTES
The store is liable for the PST on the cost of these transferred inventory items – the store sells the merchandise to itself at cost.

Instead of buying separate salon supplies for regular client services, Tesses Tresses uses its inventory stock of shampoos, conditioners, gels and so on. Inventory Adjustment entries are completed to make these transfers at cost from the inventory asset account to the supplies account.

INSTRUCTIONS

1. **Enter** the **deposit slips** and **set up** and **complete** the **account reconciliation** for January using the Chart of Accounts, Trial Balance, Vendor, Customer and Inventory information provided and using the keystrokes that start on page 528 as a guide. The journal transactions for January have been completed for you.
2. **Enter** the **source documents** for February including the account reconciliation.
3. **Print** the **reports** indicated on the chart below after completing your entries.

REPORTS

Lists
- [ ] Chart of Accounts
- [ ] Accounts
- [ ] Vendors
- [ ] Customers
- [ ] Inventory & Services

Journals
- [x] All Journals: from Feb. 1 to Feb. 28
- [ ] General
- [x] Account Reconciliation: from Jan. 1 to Feb. 28
- [x] Deposit Slips: from Jan. 1 to Feb. 28
- [ ] Purchases
- [ ] Payments
- [ ] Sales
- [ ] Receipts
- [ ] Item Assembly
- [ ] Adjustments

Financials
- [x] Comparative Balance Sheet dates: Feb. 1 and Feb. 28 with difference in percentage
- [x] Income Statement from Jan. 1 to Feb. 28
- [x] Trial Balance date: Feb. 28
- [x] General Ledger: for accounts 1060 and 1080 from Jan. 1 to Feb. 28
- [ ] Statement of Cash Flows
- [x] Cash Flow Projection Detail Report for account 1060 for 30 days
- [ ] Gross Margin Income Statement

Banking
- [x] Account Reconciliation Report Summary: for accounts 1060 and 1080 from Jan. 1 to Feb. 28
- [ ] Bank Transaction Report
- [ ] Account Reconciliation Transaction Report
- [x] Deposit Slips Detail Report for account 1060 from Jan. 1 to Feb. 28
- [ ] Cheque Log Report

Tax
- [ ] Report

Payables
- [ ] Vendor Aged
- [ ] Aged Overdue Payables
- [ ] Vendor Purchases
- [ ] Pending Purchase Orders

Receivables
- [ ] Customer Aged
- [ ] Aged Overdue Receivables
- [ ] Customer Sales
- [ ] Sales by Salesperson
- [ ] Pending Sales Orders
- [ ] Customer Statements

Inventory
- [ ] Inventory Synopsis
- [ ] Inventory Quantity
- [x] Inventory Statistics: all items and all details
- [ ] Inventory Sales
- [ ] Inventory Transaction
- [ ] Price Lists

Mailing Labels
- [ ] Labels

Management Reports
- [ ] Ledger

GRAPHS
- [ ] Payables by Aging Period
- [ ] Payables by Vendor
- [ ] Receivables by Aging Period
- [ ] Receivables by Customer
- [ ] Sales vs Receivables
- [ ] Receivables Due vs Payables Due
- [ ] Revenues by Account
- [ ] Expenses by Account
- [ ] Expenses and Net Profit as % of Revenue

SOURCE DOCUMENTS

SESSION DATE – JANUARY 31, 2008

☑ **Memo #7** **Dated Jan. 31/08**

528 Use the following charts to prepare deposit slips #1 to #5.

DEPOSIT SLIP # 1 **JANUARY 7, 2008**

Date	Cheque #	Name	Amount
Jan 2	46	Irma Vannitee	$ 117.60
Jan 2	5121	Twilight Theatre	205.80
Jan 2	161	Stu Dents	550.00
Jan 2	415	Atta Schule	395.00
Jan 3	382	On Stage Theatre Company	245.00
Jan 7	918	Irma Vannitee	91.54
		Total Cheques	$1 604.94
		Cash	$2 520.40
		(Consisting of 2 × $10; 50 × $20; 10 × $50; 10 × $100; Coin $0.40)	
		Total Deposit	$4 125.34

DEPOSIT SLIP # 2 **JANUARY 14, 2008**

Date	Cheque #	Name	Amount
Jan 9	61	Irma Vannitee	$106.55
Jan 14	206	Brioche Bridal Party	107.69
		Total Cheques	$214.24
		Cash	$1 840.95
		(Consisting of 4 × $10; 20 × $20; 8 × $50; 10 × $100; Coin $0.95)	
		Total Deposit	$2 055.19

DEPOSIT SLIP # 3 **JANUARY 21, 2008**

Date	Cheque #	Name	Amount
Jan 17	CC-61	Irma Vannitee	$108.72
Jan 20	74	Irma Vannitee	61.35
		Total Cheques	$170.07
		Cash	$1 891.66
		(Consisting of 8 × $5; 7 × $10; 14 × $20; 12× $50; 9 × $100; Coin $1.66)	
		Total Deposit	$2 061.73

DEPOSIT SLIP # 4 **JANUARY 28, 2008**

Date	Cheque #	Name	Amount
Jan 24	474	On Stage Theatre Company	$872.44
		Total Cheques	$872.44
		Cash	$1 693.71
		(Consisting of 12 × $5; 13 × $10; 20 × $20; 8 × $50; 7 × $100; Coin $3.71)	
		Total Deposit	$2 566.15

DEPOSIT SLIP # 5 **JANUARY 31, 2008**

Date	Cheque #	Name	Amount
Jan 29	238	Conn Seted	$ 42.80
Jan 31	498	On Stage Theatre Company	872.44
		Total Cheques	$915.24
		Cash	$2 357.85
		(Consisting of 13 × $5; 18 × $10; 18 × $20; 13 × $50; 11 × $100; Coin $2.85)	
		Total Deposit	$3 273.09

☑ **Memo #8** **Dated Jan. 31/08**

536 Set up account reconciliation for Bank: Chequing Account and Bank: Credit Cards.

☑ **Memo #9** **Dated Jan. 31/08**

539 Use the following bank statement to reconcile Bank: Chequing Account.

SAVERS TRUST

321 Queen St., Charlottetown, PE C1A 6D3 www.saverstrust.com

Tesses Tresses
55 Salon Road
Charlottetown, PE C1A 6D3

ACCOUNT STATEMENT
CHEQUING

Transit / Account No
0290 003 433 38-2

Statement period
Jan 1, 2008 to Jan 31, 2008

Date	Note #	Description	Deposits	Withdrawals	Balance
		Balance Fwd			37,148.00
2 Jan	1	Deposit	1,177.00		38,325.00
7 Jan		Cheque #410		926.10	37,398.90
7 Jan	2	Deposit	4,125.34		41,524.24
9 Jan		Cheque #411		330.00	41,194.24
14 Jan	2	Deposit	2,055.19		43,249.43
14 Jan		Cheque #412		203.30	43,046.13
14 Jan		Cheque #413		2,176.89	40,869.24
14 Jan		Transfer 0290 004 123 22-8	5,000.00		45,869.24
15 Jan		NSF Cheque #61		106.55	45,762.69
15 Jan	3	Service Charge – NSF cheque		30.00	45,732.69
17 Jan		Cheque #414		1,830.00	43,902.69
20 Jan		Cheque #415		117.70	43,784.99
21 Jan	2	Deposit	2,061.73		45,846.72
27 Jan		Cheque #416		431.00	45,415.72
27 Jan	5	Scheduled payment: loan		600.00	44,815.72
27 Jan	5	Scheduled payment: mortgage		1,500.00	43,315.72
28 Jan	2	Deposit	2,566.15		45,881.87
31 Jan	3	Service Charges		23.50	45,858.37
31 Jan	4	Interest	52.25		45,910.62
31 Jan		Closing balance			45,910.62

Total Deposits	# 7	$17,037.66
Total Withdrawals	# 12	$8,275.04

NOTES

These numbers correspond to the Note # column of the statement.

1 Deposit recorded in December
2 Deposit Slips: total amounts from deposit slips
3 Service charges
4 Interest received
5 Scheduled loan payments $2 100 (1 500 + 600)

☑ **Memo #10** **Dated Jan. 31/08**

550 Use the bank statement on the following page to reconcile Bank: Credit Cards. There is one outstanding prior transaction:
Sales invoice #457 dated Dec. 31, 2007 to Cash Sales for $230.

SAVERS TRUST

321 Queen St., Charlottetown, PE C1A 6D3 www.saverstrust.com

Tesses Tresses
55 Salon Road
Charlottetown, PE C1A 6D3

ACCOUNT STATEMENT
CREDIT CARD

Transit / Account No
0290 004 123 22-8

Statement period
Jan 1, 2008 to Jan 31, 2008

Date	Description	Deposits	Withdrawals	Balance
	Balance Fwd			1,970.00
2 Jan	Deposit	230.00		2,200.00
2 Jan	Deposit	2,306.48		4,506.48
9 Jan	Deposit	2,520.01		7,026.49
14 Jan	Transfer to 0290 003 433 38-2		5,000.00	2,026.49
16 Jan	Deposit	2,351.15		4,377.64
23 Jan	Deposit	2,213.92		6,591.56
30 Jan	Deposit	2,408.82		9,000.38
31 Jan	Service Charges		11.50	8,988.88
31 Jan	Interest	6.50		8,995.38
31 Jan	Closing balance			8,995.38

Total Deposits	# 7	$12,036.88
Total Withdrawals	# 2	$5,011.50

SESSION DATE – FEBRUARY 7, 2008

☐ **Cheque Copy #418** **Dated Feb. 2/08**

To Sharp Scissors, $941.60 in payment of account. Reference invoice #SS-432.

☐ **Sales Invoice #482** **Dated Feb. 2/08**

To Irma Vannitee

1	BRS1	Hair Brush: long hair	$21
1	CN2	Pro-Line Conditioner: treat 225 ml	18
1	SRV3	Cut and Style	40
1	SRV7	Perm	80
	GST		7%
	PST		10%

Terms: 2/5, n/15.

NOTES
Both PST and GST apply to the merchandise sold by the salon, while only GST applies to the salon services.

☐ **Purchase Invoice #PL-1988** **Dated Feb. 4/08**

From Pro-Line Inc., to fill purchase order #52

1	CN1	Pro-Line Conditioner: reg 225 ml	$ 72.00
1	CN2	Pro-Line Conditioner: treat 225 ml	96.00
1	CN3	Pro-Line Conditioner: deep 150 ml	132.00
1	CN4	Pro-Line Hot Oil Treatment 75 ml	114.00
1	FRZ1	Pro-Line Defrizzer: cream 100 ml	72.00
1	GEL1	Pro-Line Spray Gel: shaper 150 ml	108.00
1	GEL2	Pro-Line Mousse: gentle hold 100 ml	96.00
2	SHM1	Pro-Line Shampoo: regular 225 ml	144.00
1	SHM2	Pro-Line Shampoo: treated 225 ml	108.00
1	SPR1	Pro-Line Hair Spray: gentle 150 ml	72.00
1	SPR2	Pro-Line Hair Spray: xtra 150 ml	96.00
	GST	7%	77.70
	Invoice total		$1 187.70

Terms: 2/10, n/30.

NOTES
Remember that all these inventory items are purchased in units of dozens.

☐ **Sales Invoice #483** **Dated Feb. 4/08**

To Conn Seted

1	FRZ1	Pro-Line Defrizzer: cream 100 ml	$ 12
1	GEL1	Pro-Line Spray Gel: shaper 150 ml	21
1	SPR1	Pro-Line Hair Spray: gentle 150 ml	14
1	SRV1	Colour	45
1	SRV2	Conditioning Treatment	20
1	SRV3	Cut and Style	40
	GST		7%
	PST		10%

Terms: net 15.

☐ **Cash Purchase Invoice #CCT-8-2** **Dated Feb. 4/08**

From Charlottetown City Treasurer, $220 plus $15.40 GST for water and sewage treatment for three months. Purchase invoice total $235.40 paid by cheque #419 (Utilities account).

☐ **Sales Invoice #484** **Dated Feb. 5/08**

To Twilight Theatre to partially fill sales order #102

6	SRV3	Cut and Style	$32 each
18	SRV8	Wash and Style	16 each
	GST		7%

Terms: 2/5, n/15.

NOTES

Sales Invoice #484 provides services for four theatre performances for six cast members. The remainder of the order is filled later.

☐ **Cash Purchase Invoice CCT-299392** **Dated Feb. 6/08**

From Charlottetown City Treasurer, $4 800 for annual property tax assessment, payable in three equal instalments of $1 600. First instalment is due on receipt of invoice. Remaining two instalments are due May 6 and August 6. Issue cheques #420, 421 and 422 dated Feb. 6, May 6 and August 6 in payment of account. Create new Group account 5380 Property Taxes. Store as quarterly recurring entry and recall for postdated series.

☐ **Credit Card Sales Invoice #485** **Dated Feb. 6/08**

Sales Summary for credit card sales (to Cash Customers)

2	BRS2	Hair Brush: natural bristle	$ 26 each	$ 52.00
5	BRS4	Hair Brush: styling	18 each	90.00
5	CN1	Pro-Line Conditioner: reg 225 ml	15 /bottle	75.00
3	CN3	Pro-Line Conditioner: deep 150 ml	25 /bottle	75.00
3	FRZ1	Pro-Line Defrizzer: cream 100 ml	12 /jar	36.00
3	GEL1	Pro-Line Spray Gel: shaper 150 ml	21 /can	63.00
3	SHM2	Pro-Line Shampoo: treated 225 ml	20 /bottle	60.00
4	SPR2	Pro-Line Hair Spray: xtra 150 ml	17 /can	68.00
24	SRV3	Cut and Style	40 each	960.00
4	SRV5	Highlights: foil method	100 each	400.00
4	SRV7	Perm	80 each	320.00
5	SRV8	Wash and Style	20 each	100.00
	GST		7%	160.93
	PST		10%	55.54
	Invoice total paid by credit cards			$2 515.47

Deposited to credit card bank account.

☐ **Credit Card Purchase Invoice #AUN-344** **Dated Feb. 7/08**

From All U Need department store, $300 plus $21 GST and $32.10 PST for 100 white hand towels for use in the salon. Purchase invoice total $353.10 paid in full by credit card. Change the default account entry.

☐ **Cash Sales Invoice #486** **Dated Feb. 7/08**

Sales Summary for cash sales (to Cash Customers)

2	BRS1	Hair Brush: long hair	$21 each	$ 42.00
2	BRS4	Hair Brush: styling	18 each	36.00
4	CN2	Pro-Line Conditioner: treat 225 ml	18 /bottle	72.00
1	CN4	Pro-Line Hot Oil Treatment 75 ml	22 /tube	22.00
1	FRZ1	Pro-Line Defrizzer: cream 100 ml	12 /jar	12.00
3	GEL2	Pro-Line Mousse: gentle hold 100 ml	19 /can	57.00
5	SHM1	Pro-Line Shampoo: regular 225 ml	15 /bottle	75.00
3	SPR1	Pro-Line Hair Spray: gentle 150 ml	14 /can	42.00
1	SRV1	Colour	45 each	45.00
1	SRV2	Conditioning Treatment	20 each	20.00
16	SRV3	Cut and Style	40 each	640.00
1	SRV9	Wig Wash, Set and Style	30 each	30.00
	GST		7%	76.51
	PST		10%	38.29
	Invoice total paid by cash			$1 207.80

Deposited to Undeposited Cash and Cheques.

DEPOSIT SLIP # 6 **FEB. 7, 2008**

Date	Cheque #	Name	Amount
Feb 2	416	Atta Schule	$395.00
Feb 2	162	Stu Dents	550.00
		Total Cheques	$945.00
Feb 7		Cash	$1 207.80
		(Consisting of 1 × $5; 10 × $10; 5 × $20; 8 × $50; 6 × $100; Coin $2.80)	
		Total Deposit	$2 152.80

SESSION DATE – FEBRUARY 14, 2008

☐ **Cash Purchase Invoice #AP-63322** **Dated Feb. 8/08**

From Atlantic Power Corp., $220 plus $15.40 GST for hydro services for one month. Purchase invoice total $235.40 paid by cheque #423.

☐ **Sales Invoice #487** **Dated Feb. 8/08**

To Brioche Bridal Party to partially fill sales order #101

3	SRV3	Cut and Style	$40 each
	GST		7%

Terms: 2/5, n/15.

☐ **Sales Invoice #488** **Dated Feb. 9/08**

To Irma Vannitee

1	SRV8	Wash and Style	$20
	GST		7%

Terms: 2/5, n/15. Store as weekly recurring entry.

NOTES

Ignore the message about late payments for Vannitee because her cheque is on hand.

☐ **Credit Card Purchase Invoice #Z-6775** **Dated Feb. 10/08**

From Zines Inc., $110 plus $7.70 GST and $11.77 PST to renew subscriptions for one year to hair and fashion magazines. Purchase invoice total $129.47 paid in full by credit card (Prepaid Subscriptions account).

☐ **Cash Receipt #145** **Dated Feb. 10/08**

From Irma Vannitee, cheque #93 for $216.68 in payment of account including $0.43 discount for early payment. Reference sales invoices #478, 482 and 488.

☐ **Purchase Order #55** **Dated Feb. 10/08**

Delivery date Feb. 22/08
From Air Pro, $300 for two large hair dryers and $50 for two small hair dryers plus $24.50 GST and $37.45 PST. Purchase invoice total $411.95. Terms: net 15.

☐ **Purchase Invoice #FB-27731** **Dated Feb. 10/08**

From Fine Brushes, to fill purchase order #53

10	BRS1	Hair Brush: long hair	$ 80.00
20	BRS2	Hair Brush: natural bristle	240.00
10	BRS3	Hair Brush: short hair	50.00
20	BRS4	Hair Brush: styling	160.00
	GST	7%	37.10
Invoice total			$567.10

Terms: net 20.

☐ **Sales Invoice #489** **Dated Feb. 10/08**

To Proud Family

1	BRS2	Hair Brush: natural bristle	$ 26
1	BRS4	Hair Brush: styling	18
1	CN1	Pro-Line Conditioner: reg 225 ml	15
1	CN2	Pro-Line Conditioner: treat 225 ml	18
1	GEL2	Pro-Line Mousse: gentle hold 100 ml	19
1	SHM1	Pro-Line Shampoo: regular 225 ml	15
1	SHM2	Pro-Line Shampoo: treated 225 ml	20
3	SRV3	Cut and Style	40 each
1	SRV5	Highlights: foil method	100
1	SRV7	Perm	80
	GST		7%
	PST		10%

Terms: net 15.

☐ **Cheque Copy #424** **Dated Feb. 13/08**

To Pro-Line Inc., $1 163.95 in full payment of account including $23.75 discount for early payment. Reference invoice #PL-1988.

☐ **Credit Card Sales Invoice #490** **Dated Feb. 13/08**

Sales Summary for credit card sales (to Cash Customers)

4	BRS1	Hair Brush: long hair	$ 21 each	$ 84.00
8	BRS2	Hair Brush: natural bristle	26 each	208.00
3	BRS3	Hair Brush: short hair	12 each	36.00
6	BRS4	Hair Brush: styling	18 each	108.00
5	CN1	Pro-Line Conditioner: reg 225 ml	15 /bottle	75.00
4	CN3	Pro-Line Conditioner: deep 150 ml	25 /bottle	100.00
8	GEL2	Pro-Line Mousse: gentle hold 100 ml	19 /can	152.00
8	SHM1	Pro-Line Shampoo: regular 225 ml	15 /bottle	120.00
5	SPR2	Pro-Line Hair Spray: xtra 150 ml	17 /can	85.00
24	SRV3	Cut and Style	40 each	960.00
2	SRV4	Highlights: cap method	80 each	160.00
4	SRV5	Highlights: foil method	100 each	400.00
5	SRV6	Highlights: roots touchup	30 each	150.00
3	SRV7	Perm	80 each	240.00
4	SRV8	Wash and Style	20 each	80.00
	GST		7%	207.06
	PST		10%	103.59
Invoice total paid by credit cards				$3 268.65

Deposited to credit card bank account.

☐ **Purchase Order #56** **Dated Feb. 13/08**

Delivery date Feb. 21/08
From Pro-Line Inc.

1	CN2	Pro-Line Conditioner: treat 225 ml	$ 96.00
1	GEL1	Pro-Line Spray Gel: shaper 150 ml	108.00
1	GEL2	Pro-Line Mousse: gentle hold 100 ml	96.00
1	SHM1	Pro-Line Shampoo: regular 225 ml	72.00
2	SHM2	Pro-Line Shampoo: treated 225 ml	216.00
1	SPR1	Pro-Line Hair Spray: gentle 150 ml	72.00
1	SPR2	Pro-Line Hair Spray: xtra 150 ml	96.00
	GST	7%	52.92
Invoice total			$808.92

Terms: 2/10, n/30.

☐ **Purchase Invoice #SS-555** **Dated Feb. 14/08**

From Sharp Scissors, to fill purchase order #54, $600 plus $42.00 GST and $64.20 PST for professional high-grade stainless steel stylist scissors. Purchase invoice total $706.20. Terms: net 10.

☐ **Cash Sales Invoice #491** **Dated Feb. 14/08**

Sales Summary for cash sales (to Cash Customers)

8	BRS1	Hair Brush: long hair	$ 21 each	$ 168.00
6	BRS2	Hair Brush: natural bristle	26 each	156.00
5	CN2	Pro-Line Conditioner: treat 225 ml	18 /bottle	90.00
8	GEL1	Pro-Line Spray Gel: shaper 150 ml	21 /can	168.00
3	FRZ1	Pro-Line Defrizzer: cream 100 ml	12 /jar	36.00
5	SPR1	Pro-Line Hair Spray: gentle 150 ml	14 /can	70.00
4	SRV1	Colour	45 each	180.00
19	SRV3	Cut and Style	40 each	760.00
1	SRV5	Highlights: foil method	100 each	100.00
1	SRV6	Highlights: roots touchup	30 each	30.00
	GST		7%	123.06
	PST		10%	73.62
Invoice total paid by cash				$1 954.68

Deposited to Undeposited Cash and Cheques.

DEPOSIT SLIP # 7 **FEBRUARY 14, 2008**

Date	Cheque #	Name	Amount
Feb 10	93	Irma Vannitee	$216.68
		Total Cheques	$216.68
		Cash	$1 954.68
		(Consisting of 6 × $5; 2 × $10; 15 × $20; 12× $50; 10 × $100; Coin $4.68)	
		Total Deposit	$2 171.36

SESSION DATE – FEBRUARY 21, 2008

☐ **Sales Invoice #492** **Dated Feb. 16/08**

To Irma Vannitee

1	SRV8	Wash and Style	$20
	GST		7%

Terms: 2/5, n/15. Recall stored transaction.

☐ **Memo #11** **Dated Feb. 16/08**

From Owners: Transfer $10 000 from credit card account to chequing account.

☐ **Memo #12** **Dated Feb. 17/08**

From Owners: Pay GST owing to the Receiver General for the period ending January 31, 2008. Issue cheque #425 in payment.

☐ **Cash Purchase Invoice #ET-4588** **Dated Feb. 18/08**

From Eastern Tel, $110 plus $7.70 GST and $11.77 PST for telephone service. Purchase invoice total $129.47 paid in full by cheque #426.

☐ **Sales Quote #103** **Dated Feb. 19/08**

First performance date Mar. 1/08
To On Stage Theatre Company (for 12 theatre performances for three cast members) at preferred customer prices

3	SRV3	Cut and Style	$32 each
36	SRV8	Wash and Style	16 each
9	SRV9	Wig Wash, Set and Style	24 each
	GST		7%

Terms: 2/5, n/15.

☐ **Cash Receipt #146** **Dated Feb. 19/08**

From Conn Seted, cheque #269 for $167.67 in payment of account. Reference invoice #483.

☐ **Cash Receipt #147** **Dated Feb. 20/08**

From Twilight Theatre, cheque #5635 for $513.60 in payment of account. Reference invoice #484.

☐ **Credit Card Purchase Invoice #SP-399** **Dated Feb. 20/08**

From Seaside Papers, $200 plus $14.00 GST and $21.40 PST for office supplies for salon. Purchase invoice total $235.40 paid in full by credit card.

☐ **Credit Card Purchase Invoice #AUN-478** **Dated Feb. 20/08**

From All U Need department store, $90 plus $6.30 GST and $9.63 PST for cleaning supplies. Purchase invoice total $105.93 paid in full by credit card.

☐ **Purchase Invoice #AP-7111** **Dated Feb. 20/08**

From Air Pro, to fill purchase order #55, $350 plus $24.50 and $37.45 PST for two bonnet-style hair dryers and two hand-held hair dryers. Purchase invoice total $411.95. Terms: net 15.

☐ **Purchase Invoice #PL-3488** **Dated Feb. 20/08**

From Pro-Line Inc., to fill purchase order #56

1	CN2	Pro-Line Conditioner: treat 225 ml	$ 96.00
1	GEL1	Pro-Line Spray Gel: shaper 150 ml	108.00
1	GEL2	Pro-Line Mousse: gentle hold 100 ml	96.00
1	SHM1	Pro-Line Shampoo: regular 225 ml	72.00
2	SHM2	Pro-Line Shampoo: treated 225 ml	216.00
1	SPR1	Pro-Line Hair Spray: gentle 150 ml	72.00
1	SPR2	Pro-Line Hair Spray: xtra 150 ml	96.00
	GST	7%	52.92
Invoice total			$808.92

Terms: 2/10, n/30.

☐ **Cash Receipt #148** **Dated Feb. 20/08**

From Brioche Bridal Party, cheque #986 for $128.40 in payment of account. Reference invoice #487.

NOTES

You can use the Tax Report for GST for January to obtain the GST amounts for the remittance, or you can refer to the General Ledger Report for the two GST accounts.

☐ **Credit Card Sales Invoice #493** **Dated Feb. 20/08**

Sales Summary for credit card sales (to Cash Customers)

2	BRS2	Hair Brush: natural bristle	$26 each	$ 52.00
1	BRS3	Hair Brush: short hair	12 each	12.00
2	CN2	Pro-Line Conditioner: treat 225 ml	18 /bottle	36.00
1	CN4	Pro-Line Hot Oil Treatment 75 ml	22 /tube	22.00
3	GEL2	Pro-Line Mousse: gentle hold 100 ml	19 /can	57.00
1	FRZ1	Pro-Line Defrizzer: cream 100 ml	12 /jar	12.00
4	SHM2	Pro-Line Shampoo: treated 225 ml	20 /bottle	80.00
3	SPR2	Pro-Line Hair Spray: xtra 150 ml	17 /can	51.00
2	SRV1	Colour	45 each	90.00
16	SRV3	Cut and Style	40 each	640.00
1	SRV7	Perm	80 each	80.00
	GST		7%	79.24
	PST		10%	34.44
	Invoice total paid by credit cards			$1 245.68

Deposited to credit card bank account.

☐ **Purchase Order #57** **Dated Feb. 21/08**

Shipping date Mar. 3/08

From Lookin' Good, $400 plus $28.00 GST and $42.80 PST for 25 polyester and nylon water-resistant monogrammed capes for salon customer use. Purchase invoice total $470.80. Terms: net 10.

☐ **Cheque Copy #427** **Dated Feb. 21/08**

To Sharp Scissors, $706.20 in payment of account. Reference invoice #SS-555.

☐ **Cash Sales Invoice #494** **Dated Feb. 21/08**

Sales Summary for cash sales (to Cash Customers)

4	BRS2	Hair Brush: natural bristle	$26 each	$ 104.00
4	BRS4	Hair Brush: styling	18 each	72.00
2	CN3	Pro-Line Conditioner: deep 150 ml	25 /bottle	50.00
3	GEL1	Pro-Line Spray Gel: shaper 150 ml	21 /can	63.00
5	SHM1	Pro-Line Shampoo: regular 225 ml	15 /bottle	75.00
4	SPR1	Pro-Line Hair Spray: gentle 150 ml	14 /can	56.00
3	SRV1	Colour	45 each	135.00
22	SRV3	Cut and Style	40 each	880.00
10	SRV8	Wash and Style	20 each	200.00
6	SRV9	Wig Wash, Set and Style	30 each	180.00
	GST		7%	127.05
	PST		10%	44.94
	Invoice total paid by cash			$1 986.99

Deposited to Undeposited Cash and Cheques.

DEPOSIT SLIP # 8 **FEBRUARY 21, 2008**

Date	Cheque #	Name	Amount
Feb 19	269	Conn Seted	$ 167.67
Feb 20	5635	Twilight Theatre	513.60
Feb 20	986	Brioche Bridal Party	128.40
		Total Cheques	$809.67
		Cash	$1 986.99
		(Consisting of 17 × $5; 29 × $10; 28 × $20; 5 × $50; 8 × $100; Coin $1.99)	
		Total Deposit	$2 796.66

SESSION DATE – FEBRUARY 28, 2008

☐ **Sales Invoice #495** **Dated Feb. 23/08**

To Irma Vannitee

1	SRV8	Wash and Style	$20
	GST		7%

Terms: 2/5, n/15. Recall stored transaction.

☐ **Sales Invoice #496** **Dated Feb. 23/08**

To Brioche Bridal Party to fill remainder of sales order #101

5	SRV8	Wash and Style	$20 each
	GST		7%

Terms: 2/5, n/15.

☐ **Credit Card Bill Payment #2-08** **Dated Feb. 24/08**

From credit card company, $564.96 for purchases made before Feb. 11 and $24 annual card fee. Total payment due to avoid interest penalty $588.96. Issued cheque #428 for $588.96 in full payment.

☐ **Bank Debit Memo #983321** **Dated Feb. 25/08**

From Savers Trust Co., cheque #986 from Brioche Bridal Party was returned because of insufficient funds. The cheque amount, $128.40, and a service fee of $30 were deducted from the chequing account. Enter cash receipt #149 to reverse the receipt from Brioche Bridal Party and restore the balance owing. Reference invoice #487.

WARNING!
Remember to change the Deposit To account to Bank: Chequing Account.

NOTES
The NSF charge expense will be entered as part of the bank reconciliation at the end of the month.

☐ **Memo #13** **Dated Feb. 25/08**

Prepare sales invoice #497 for $30 to charge Brioche Bridal Party for the NSF fee. Credit Other Revenue. Terms: net 15. (Do not charge tax or allow discount.)

☐ **Sales Invoice #498** **Dated Feb. 25/08**

To Conn Seted

1	CN2	Pro-Line Conditioner: treat 225 ml	$18
1	SHM2	Pro-Line Shampoo: treated 225 ml	20
1	SRV6	Highlights: roots touchup	30
	GST		7%
	PST		10%

Terms: net 15.

☐ **Credit Card Sales Invoice #499** **Dated Feb. 27/08**

Sales Summary for credit card sales (to Cash Customers)

5	BRS4	Hair Brush: styling	$18 each	$ 90.00
3	CN1	Pro-Line Conditioner: reg 225 ml	15 /bottle	45.00
4	CN2	Pro-Line Conditioner: treat 225 ml	18 /bottle	72.00
4	GEL1	Pro-Line Spray Gel: shaper 150 ml	21 /can	84.00
1	FRZ1	Pro-Line Defrizzer: cream 100 ml	12 /jar	12.00
3	SHM1	Pro-Line Shampoo: regular 225 ml	15 /bottle	45.00
4	SPR1	Pro-Line Hair Spray: gentle 150 ml	14 /can	56.00
3	SRV1	Colour	45 each	135.00
23	SRV3	Cut and Style	40 each	920.00
8	SRV6	Highlights: roots touchup	30 each	240.00
2	SRV7	Perm	80 each	160.00
2	SRV8	Wash and Style	20 each	40.00
	GST		7%	132.93
	PST		10%	43.23
	Invoice total paid by credit cards			$2 075.16

Deposited to credit card bank account.

Sales Invoice #500 **Dated Feb. 27/08**

To Twilight Theatre to fill the remainder of sales order #102 (for five nights of theatre performances for four cast members) at preferred customer prices

4	SRV3	Cut and Style	$32 each
16	SRV8	Wash and Style	16 each
4	SRV9	Wig Wash, Set and Style	24 each
	GST		7%

Terms: 2/5, n/15.

Cash Receipt #150 **Dated Feb. 27/08**

From Brioche Bridal Party, certified cheque #RBC7333 for $158.40 in payment of account. Reference invoices #487 and 497 and bank debit memo #983321.

Cash Sales Invoice #501 **Dated Feb. 28/08**

Sales Summary for cash sales (to Cash Customers)

3	BRS2	Hair Brush: natural bristle	$ 26 each	$ 78.00
4	CN1	Pro-Line Conditioner: reg 225 ml	15 /bottle	60.00
2	CN2	Pro-Line Conditioner: treat 225 ml	18 /bottle	36.00
5	GEL1	Pro-Line Spray Gel: shaper 150 ml	21 /can	105.00
6	SHM2	Pro-Line Shampoo: treated 225 ml	20 /bottle	120.00
4	SPR2	Pro-Line Hair Spray: xtra 150 ml	17 /can	68.00
1	SRV1	Colour	45 each	45.00
21	SRV3	Cut and Style	40 each	840.00
5	SRV6	Highlights: roots touchup	30 each	150.00
1	SRV7	Perm	80 each	80.00
2	SRV8	Wash and Style	20 each	40.00
1	SRV9	Wig Wash, Set and Style	30 each	30.00
	GST		7%	115.64
	PST		10%	49.98
Invoice total paid by cash				$1 817.62

Deposited to Undeposited Cash and Cheques.

DEPOSIT SLIP # 9 **FEBRUARY 28, 2008**

Date	Cheque #	Name	Amount
Feb 27	RBC7333	Brioche Bridal Party	$158.40
		Total Cheques	$158.40
		Cash	$1 817.62
		(Consisting of 2 × $5; 22 × $10; 14 × $20; 12 × $50; 7 × $100; Coin $7.62)	
		Total Deposit	$1 976.02

Bank Debit Memo #10012 **Dated Feb. 28/08**

From Savers Trust Co. pre-authorized withdrawals

	Interest	Principal	Total
Mortgage	$1 240	$260	$1 500
Loan	115	485	600

Memo #14 **Dated Feb. 28/08**

Enter the adjustments for expired prepaid expenses. $150 of the prepaid insurance and $40 of the subscriptions have expired.

Memo #15 **Dated Feb. 28/08**

Enter adjustments for supplies used: Office Supplies	$ 60
Salon Supplies	285
Washroom & Cleaning Supplies	75

☐ **Memo #16** **Dated Feb. 28/08**

From Owners: The following items were transferred from inventory for use in the salon. Transfer all items at cost to Salon Supplies.

4	CN1	Pro-Line Conditioner: reg 225 ml
5	CN2	Pro-Line Conditioner: treat 225 ml
1	CN3	Pro-Line Conditioner: deep 150 ml
1	CN4	Pro-Line Hot Oil Treatment 75 ml
3	GEL1	Pro-Line Spray Gel: shaper 150 ml
1	GEL2	Pro-Line Mousse: gentle hold 100 ml
5	SHM1	Pro-Line Shampoo: regular 225 ml
6	SHM2	Pro-Line Shampoo: treated 225 ml
3	SPR1	Pro-Line Hair Spray: gentle 150 ml
1	SPR2	Pro-Line Hair Spray: xtra 150 ml

☐ **Memo #17** **Dated Feb. 28/08**

Edit the tax codes to change the rates and descriptions for the revised GST rate at 6 percent.

☐ **Memo #18** **Dated Feb. 28/08**

Use the following bank statements to reconcile the bank and credit card accounts for February.

SAVERS TRUST

321 Queen St., Charlottetown, PE C1A 6D3 www.saverstrust.com

Tesses Tresses
55 Salon Road
Charlottetown, PE C1A 6D3

ACCOUNT STATEMENT
CHEQUING

Transit / Account No
0290 003 433 38-2

Statement period
Feb 1, 2008 to Feb 28, 2008

Date	Deposit #	Description	Deposits	Withdrawals	Balance
		Balance Fwd			45,910.62
1 Feb	5	Deposit	3,273.09		49,183.71
2 Feb		Cheque #417		2,027.30	47,156.41
5 Feb		Cheque #418		941.60	46,214.81
5 Feb		Cheque #419		235.40	45,979.41
7 Feb	6	Deposit	2,152.80		48,132.21
8 Feb		Cheque #420		1,600.00	46,532.21
10 Feb		Cheque #423		235.40	46,296.81
14 Feb	7	Deposit	2,171.36		48,468.17
16 Feb		Cheque #424		1,163.95	47,304.22
18 Feb		Transfer funds from 004 123 22-8	10,000.00		57,304.22
19 Feb		Cheque #426		129.47	57,174.75
21 Feb	8	Deposit	2,796.66		59,971.41
21 Feb		Cheque #425		1,323.14	58,648.27
25 Feb		NSF Cheque #986		128.40	58,519.87
25 Feb		Service Charge - NSF cheque		30.00	58,489.87
26 Feb		Cheque #427		706.20	57,783.67
28 Feb		Scheduled loan payment		600.00	57,183.67
28 Feb		Scheduled mortgage payment		1,500.00	55,683.67
28 Feb		Service Charges - chequing acct		23.50	55,660.17
28 Feb		Interest	57.75		55,717.92
28 Feb		Closing balance			55,717.92

Total Deposits	# 6	$20,451.66
Total Withdrawals	# 14	$10,644.36

NOTES
Use the Inventory Adjustments Journal to transfer the inventory to the supplies account. Enter **negative** quantities and change the default Inventory Losses account to Salon Supplies for all items. Refer to Accounting Procedures, page 514.

NOTES
The data file **Bank\tess** has all the journal entries completed except the bank reconciliation for February. If you prefer, you can use this file to complete the bank reconciliation for February.

NOTES
You do not need to add linked accounts or prior transactions. Enter the statement ending balance and then mark journal entries as cleared (keystrokes on page 543) to complete the reconciliation.

Enter Feb 28 as the Statement End and Reconciliation dates.

There are four deposit slips for group deposits.

The loan and mortgage payments were entered together: 1 500 + 600 = 2 100

Remember to change the status of the NSF cheque from Brioche Bridal Party for $128.40 (in deposit slip #8) to NSF and the status of its reversing entry to Adjustment.

At the end of February, a cheque for $588.95 and one deposit for $1 976.02 are outstanding.

SAVERS TRUST

321 Queen St., Charlottetown, PE C1A 6D3 www.saverstrust.com

Tesses Tresses
55 Salon Road
Charlottetown, PE C1A 6D3

ACCOUNT STATEMENT
CREDIT CARD

Transit / Account No
0290 004 123 22-8

Statement period
Feb 1, 2008 to Feb 28, 2008

Date	Description	Deposits	Withdrawals	Balance
	Balance Fwd			8,995.38
6 Feb	Deposit	2,447.55		11,442.93
13 Feb	Deposit	3,180.40		14,623.33
18 Feb	Transfer funds to 003 433 38-2		10,000.00	4,623.33
20 Feb	Deposit	1,212.05		5,835.38
28 Feb	Service charges		11.50	5,823.88
28 Feb	Interest	8.25		5,832.13
28 Feb	Closing balance			5,832.13

Total Deposits	# 4	$6,848.25
Total Withdrawals	# 2	$10,011.50

NOTES
At the end of February, one deposit for $2 019.13 is outstanding.

☑ **Memo #19** **Dated Feb. 28/08**

552 Back up the data files. Clear journal entries and paid transactions that are no longer needed using January 31 as the date for clearing. Do not clear data for February.

WARNING!
Make a backup copy of your data files before you start. You cannot adjust deposit slips or account reconciliation after posting.

KEYSTROKES

Entering Bank Deposit Slips

Previously, we recorded receipts directly as deposits to the linked bank accounts. In this chapter, we show the procedure for recording receipts and deposits separately. The deposits for the cash and cheques received in January have not yet been recorded.

Open the files for **Tesses Tresses**. **Use January 31** as the session date.

Click the **General module heading** to open the General module window.

Deposits are made using the Deposit Slip Journal marked with the pointer:

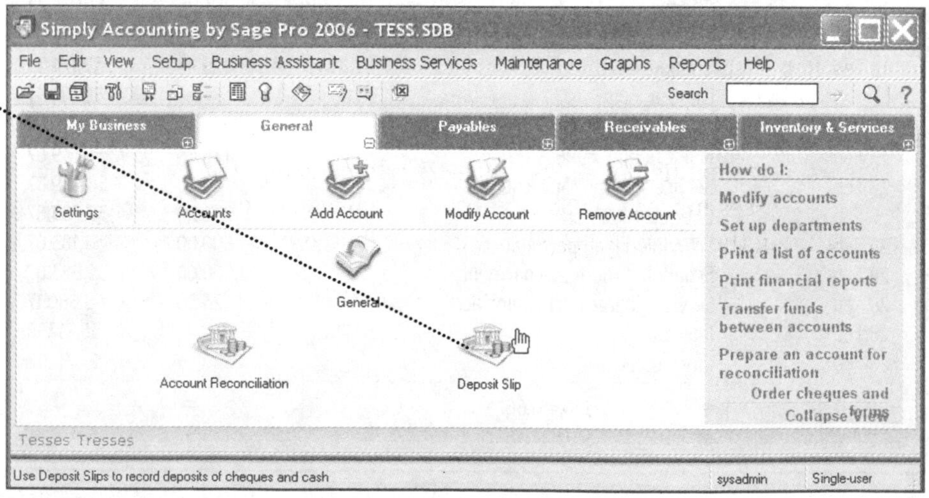

basic BASIC VERSION
The icon label is Deposit Slips.

Click the **Deposit Slip icon** to open the Reconciliation & Deposits journal:

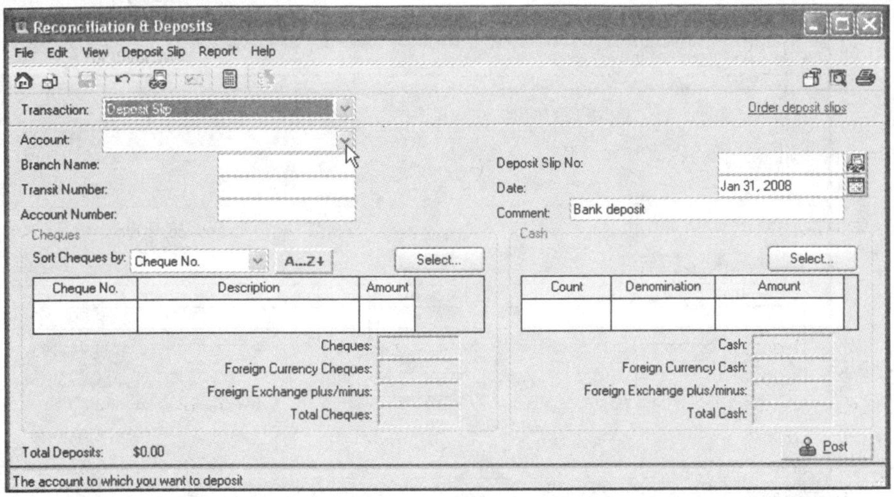

From the Home window, click the Reconciliation & Deposits icon  to open the journal and choose Deposit Slip from the Transaction drop-down list.

The journal is named Reconciliation & Deposits because both types of transactions are entered here. You can choose from the Transaction drop-down list to change the type. Deposit Slip is selected in the Transaction field because we selected this icon.

The deposit transaction has two parts: the Deposit To component that we see here and the Deposit From portion. All cash and cheques were debited to *Undeposited Cash and Cheques*, a Bank class clearing account that is the default account for all receipts. Now we need to transfer these receipts to the *Bank: Chequing Account* as deposits.

First we choose the bank account receiving the deposit.

Click the **Account list arrow** as shown:

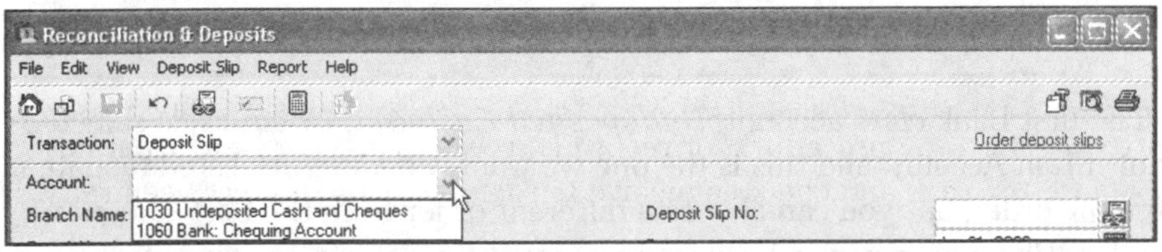

Both Bank class accounts are listed: *Undeposited Cash and Cheques* (the default linked Receivables bank account) and *Bank: Chequing Account*. We must select *Bank: Chequing Account*, the account that is receiving the deposit.

Click **Bank: Chequing Account**.

Click the **Deposit Slip No. field** so you can add the deposit slip number.

Type 1

The deposit slip number will be updated automatically from now on.

Tesses Tresses makes weekly deposits to the bank account of all cash and cheques received during the week. We need to enter the date of the first deposit.

Enter **January 7, 2008** in the Date field for the first deposit.

Next, we must select the outstanding cheques and cash that will be deposited. The Deposit Slip has cheques on the left and cash on the right. There are separate Select buttons for these two types of currency. We will add the cheques first by using the Select button in the centre of the journal, above the field for listing the cheques.

NOTES

Undeposited Cash and Cheques is set up as a Bank class account so that we can use it as the default linked principal bank account for the Receivables Ledger.

NOTES

When the bank account is set up for online reconciliation, the bank transit and account number are also required in the ledger record and will be added to the Deposit Slip Journal.

The deposit slip number may be entered automatically when you select the bank account.

The Select button we need is shown with the arrow pointer on it:

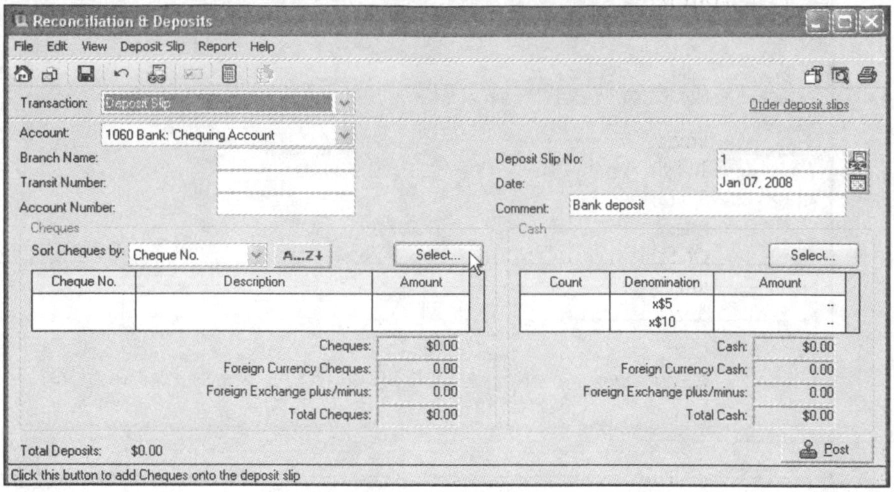

Click the **Select button** for Cheques to open the list of outstanding cheques:

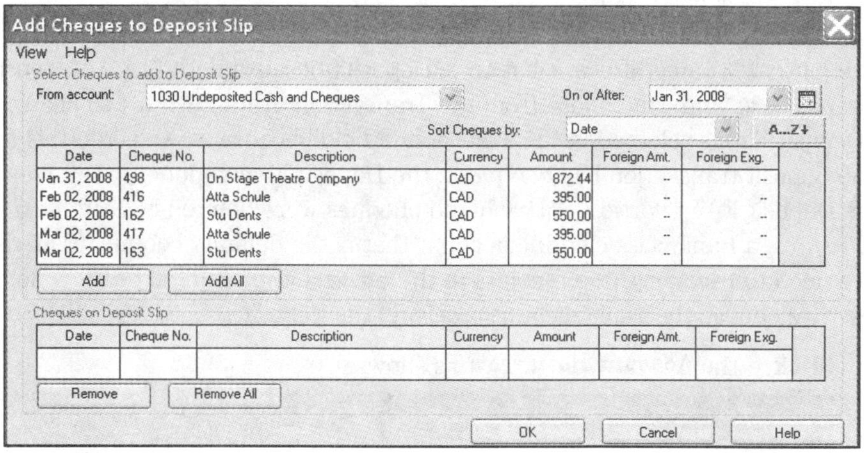

NOTES
Once the list is in descending order, the order button label changes to Z...A. Clicking this button again restores the list to ascending order.

The first Bank class account, *Undeposited Cash and Cheques*, is selected as the default From Account and this is the one we want. Cheques are listed by date in ascending order, but you can choose a different order from the Sort Cheques By drop-down list. Cheques may also be sorted by any of the column headings for the list of cheques (cheque number, currency, amount, description, foreign amount or foreign exchange amount). You can use the A...Z button to sort in descending order.

The session date, January 31, is entered in the On Or After date field, so only the cheques for January 31 and the postdated rent cheques are listed. We need to show all cheques that are dated on or after January 1, so this is the date we should enter.

NOTES
You can also choose Jan 1 from the On Or After date field drop-down list.

Click the **On Or After field Calendar icon** and **click Jan 1** as the date to list all the outstanding cheques:

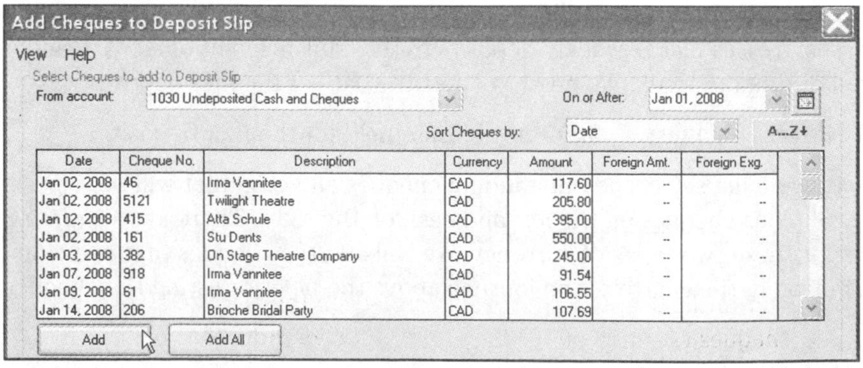

The next step is to select the cheques we want and add them to the deposit. Deposit slip # 1 from page 516 is repeated here for reference:

DEPOSIT SLIP # 1 **JANUARY 7, 2008**

Date	Cheque #	Name	Amount
Jan 2	46	Irma Vannitee	$ 117.60
Jan 2	5121	Twilight Theatre	205.80
Jan 2	161	Stu Dents	550.00
Jan 2	415	Atta Schule	395.00
Jan 3	382	On Stage Theatre Company	245.00
Jan 7	918	Irma Vannitee	91.54
		Total Cheques	$1 604.94
		Cash	$2 520.40
		(Consisting of 2 × $10; 50 × $20; 10 × $50; 10 × $100; Coin $0.40)	
		Total Deposit	$4 125.34

We should select the six cheques that are dated on or before January 7, cheques from Vannitee, Twilight Theatre, Stu Dents, Atta Schule and On Stage Theatre Company.

Click to select a single cheque. To select multiple cheques, press *ctrl* and click the next cheque to be selected and so on. To select several cheques in a row, click the first cheque you want, then press *shift* and click the last cheque you need.

Click **cheque number 46 from Irma Vannitee**, the first cheque on the list.

Click the **down scroll arrow** until you see cheque #918 from Vannitee.

Press *shift* and **click cheque number 918**.

All six cheques should now be selected. We should add them to the list of Cheques On Deposit Slip in the lower half of the form.

Click the **Add button** to place the selected cheques on the deposit slip:

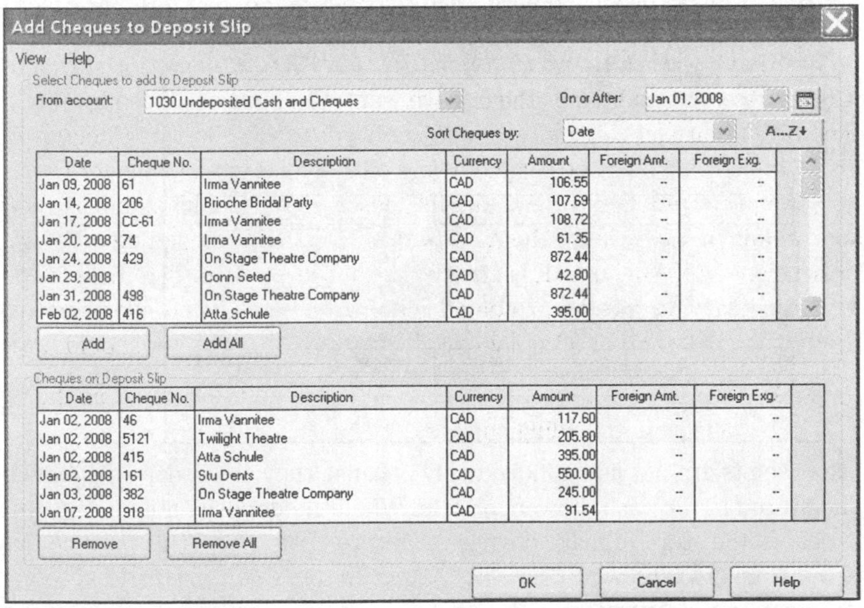

The six cheques we selected are now in the Cheques On Deposit Slip list.

You can also add the cheques one at a time. Click a cheque and then click the Add button to move the cheque. Then click the next cheque and click Add. Repeat until all the cheques you want are in the Cheques On Deposit Slip list. If all cheques should be deposited, you can click Add All.

To change a selection, click a cheque in the Cheques On Deposit Slip list and click Remove. To start again, click Remove All to clear the list.

Click **OK** to return to the updated Reconciliation & Deposits Journal:

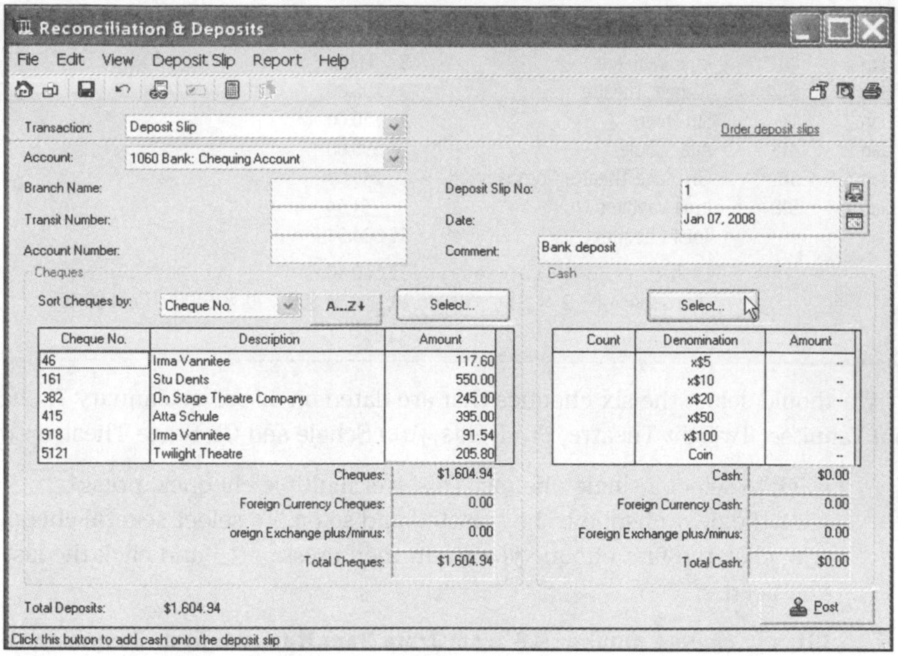

The total of the cheques should match the amount on the Deposit Slip source document. If it does not, click the Select button again to correct the cheque selection. If a cheque amount is incorrect, close the journal without saving the changes and correct the original receipt transaction.

The next step is to add the cash portion of the deposit. Tesses Tresses has one cash sale summary amount to deposit, $2 520.40.

Click the **Select button** for Cash to open the deposit form for cash:

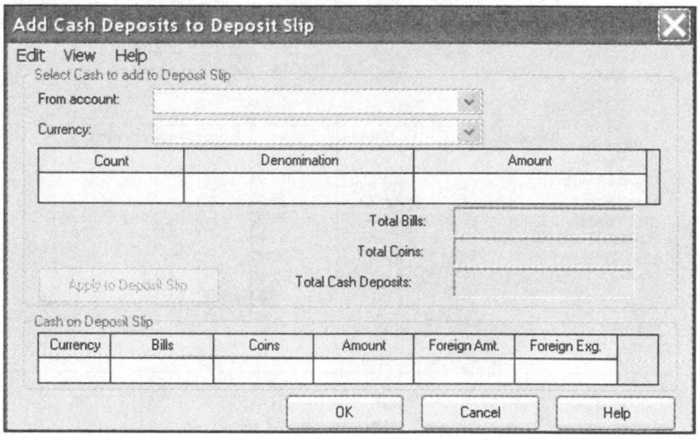

Cash receipts are not listed individually because they are usually combined in the store and stored in the cash drawers or safe. When the deposits are made, some cash may be held in the store to make change for future customers. This balance may be transferred from *Undeposited Cash and Cheques* to a *Cash on Hand* account by completing a General Journal transaction. Similarly, the denomination of notes and coins that are received from customers may not be the same as the ones that are deposited. To keep the exercise simple, we will deposit the full amount of cash received each week.

No account is selected by default so we first need to select the account that we are depositing from.

Choose Undeposited Cash and Cheques from the From Account drop-down list to modify the deposit form:

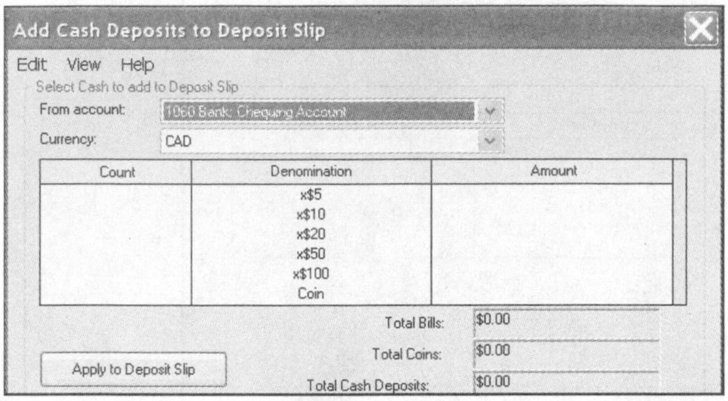

The Cash Deposit form is completed in the same way as a deposit slip at the bank. You enter the number of notes of each denomination or amount and the total amount of coins. Simply Accounting calculates and totals the amounts as soon as you enter the number of bills in the Count field. The $2 520.40 in deposited cash consists of 2 × $10; 50 × $20; 10 × $50; 10 × $100; and $0.40 in coins. There are no $5 notes.

Click the **Count field beside × $10** (on the second line).

Type 2 **Press** tab to enter $20 as the Amount.

Press tab **again** to move to the Count field for $20 notes.

Type 50

Press tab **twice** to advance to the Count field for $50 notes.

Type 10

Press tab **twice** to advance to the Count field for $100 notes.

Type 10

Press tab **twice** to advance to the Count field for coins.

NOTES

Instead of pressing tab twice, you can press ↓ to move the cursor to the next Count line on the form.

Instead of entering the count for each denomination, you can enter the amount and Simply Accounting will enter the corresponding count.

The amount for coins is entered as a total amount in the Amount field. You cannot type in the Count field.

Press tab to advance to the Amount field for coins.

Type .40 (You must enter the decimal.)

Press tab to update the total as shown:

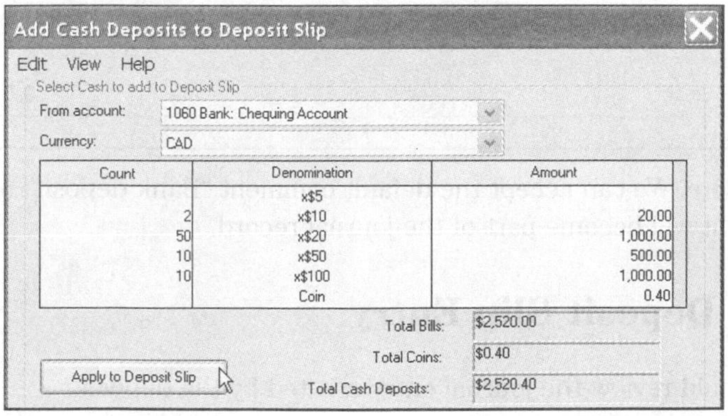

The total amounts for bills and coins remain separated, and the total deposit is calculated.

The next step is to apply the amount to the deposit slip.

Click the **Apply To Deposit Slip button** to update the form:

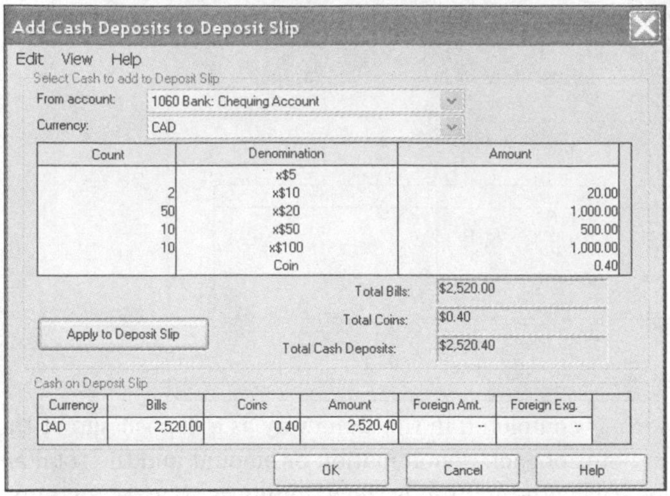

The total cash deposit amount is added to the Cash On Deposit Slip section. The currency for the amount is also included.

NOTES

Tesses Tresses does not have any foreign currency transactions.

To make changes, edit an amount in the Count field and press tab. Click Apply To Deposit Slip to update the Cash On Deposit Slip.

We are now ready to add this deposit information to the journal form.

Click **OK** to return to the Reconciliation & Deposits journal:

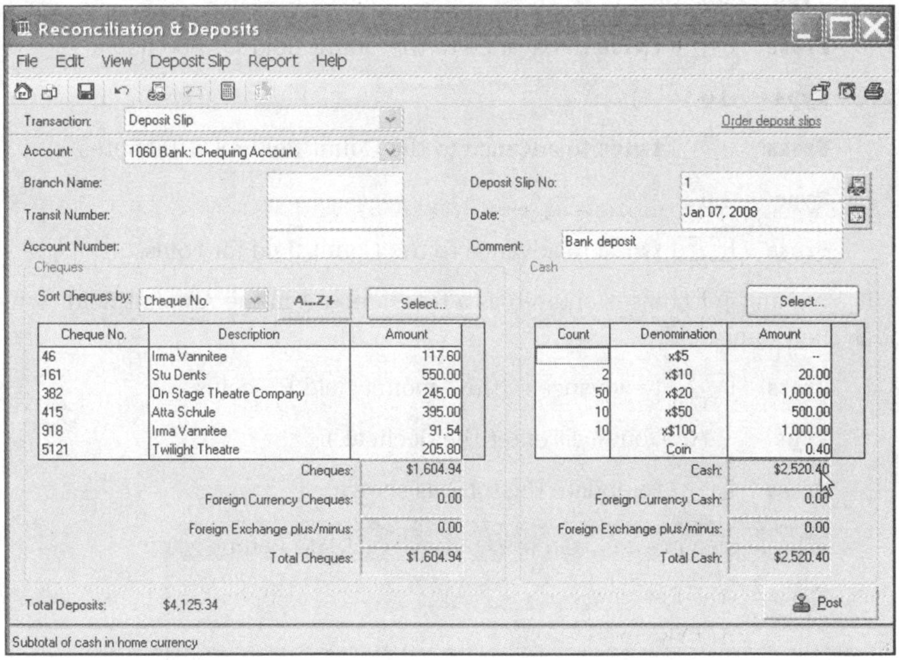

The form is complete. We can accept the default comment "Bank deposit" or change it. The comment will become part of the journal record.

Reviewing the Deposit Slip Entry

Before posting, we should review the journal entry created by the deposit.

Choose the **Report menu** and **click** **Display Deposit Slip Journal Entry**:

Deposit Slip Journal Entry Display

File Options Help

Tesses Tresses

01/07/08 (J54)	Debits	Credits
1060 Bank: Chequing Account Irma Vannitee	117.60	-
1060 Bank: Chequing Account Twilight Theatre	205.80	-
1060 Bank: Chequing Account Atta Schule	395.00	-
1060 Bank: Chequing Account Stu Dents	550.00	-
1060 Bank: Chequing Account On Stage Theatre Company	245.00	-
1060 Bank: Chequing Account Irma Vannitee	91.54	-
1060 Bank: Chequing Account CAD Cash Deposit From 1030	2,520.40	-
1030 Undeposited Cash and Cheques Irma Vannitee	-	117.60
1030 Undeposited Cash and Cheques Twilight Theatre	-	205.80
1030 Undeposited Cash and Cheques Atta Schule	-	395.00
1030 Undeposited Cash and Cheques Stu Dents	-	550.00
1030 Undeposited Cash and Cheques On Stage Theatre Company	-	245.00
1030 Undeposited Cash and Cheques Irma Vannitee	-	91.54
1030 Undeposited Cash and Cheques CAD Cash Deposit To 1060	-	2,520.40
	4,125.34	4,125.34

In the journal, each cheque and cash amount is listed separately. The payee for cheques is also included. Each deposit item is shown as a debit to the *Bank: Chequing Account* and a credit to *Undeposited Cash and Cheques*. This detailed reporting makes it easier to find mistakes if any have been made.

Close the **Journal Entry Display** to return to the journal.

Check your **work** and **make corrections** if necessary.

CORRECTING THE DEPOSIT SLIP JOURNAL ENTRY

To change the cheque part of the deposit, **click** the **Select button** for the Cheque part of the journal. To change a selection, **click** a **cheque** in the Cheques On Deposit Slip list and **click Remove**. To start again, **click Remove All** to clear the list. **Click Cancel** to close the Cash Deposits form and begin again.

If you need to make changes to the Cash part of the deposit, **click** the **Select button** on the Cash side of the Journal. **Click** the **incorrect amount** in the Count field and **type** the **correct amount. Press** tab to update the total. **Click Apply To Deposit Slip** to update the deposit amount that will be recorded. **Click Cancel** to close the Cash Deposits form and begin again.

WARNING!

You can look up deposit slips after posting them, but you cannot adjust them.

You should also preview and print the deposit slip before posting it.

Click the **Preview Simply Form tool** to open the deposit slip form preview window.

Click the **Print tool** to print the deposit slip.

Click **OK** to close the Preview window and return to the journal.

Click **Post** Post to save the transaction.

Enter the **remaining four deposits** for January. Remember to change the date for each deposit.

Close the **Reconciliation & Deposits Journal**.

You should return to the General module window. We are now ready to set up the bank accounts for reconciliation.

NOTES

To preview the deposit slip, you must choose Custom Simply Form in the Reports & Forms settings on the Deposit Slips screen.

Account Reconciliation

For any bank account, the timing of monthly statements is usually not perfectly matched with the accounting entries of the corresponding transactions. Usually some of the cheques written do not appear on the statement, and interest earned on the account or bank charges are not yet recorded because they may be unknown until receipt of the statement. Thus the balance of the bank statement usually does not match the General Ledger balance for the bank account. The process of identifying the differences to achieve a match is the process of account reconciliation.

You can apply account reconciliation to any Balance Sheet account for which you have regular statements, including credit card payable accounts. For each account you want to reconcile, you must complete the setup procedure.

The keystrokes that follow will set up account reconciliation for *Bank: Chequing Account* for Tesses Tresses.

Turning On the Account Reconciliation Feature

Before completing the reconciliation procedure, the General Ledger accounts that will be reconciled must be identified and modified. For the next stage, you will also need a report of all bank account transactions to compare with the bank statement. We will work from the General module window to modify the account.

Open the **General module window**. (Click the General heading.)

Click the **Modify Account icon** 

to open the Search window.

Click **1060 Bank: Chequing Account** and then **click OK** to open its ledger window:

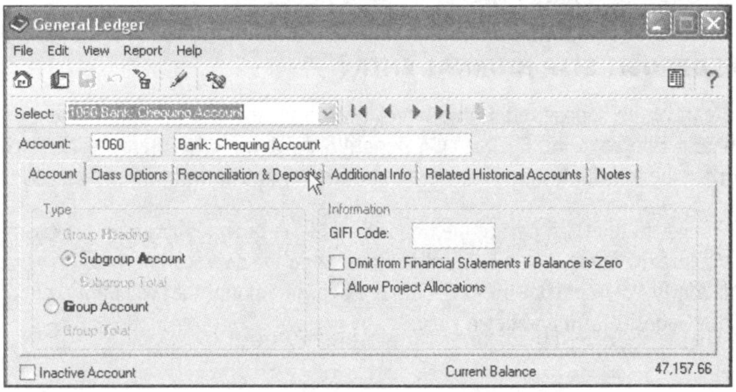

NOTES
Online bank reconciliation is explained in Appendix I. The Web site for this text is set up for online reconciliation so you can try this feature of the program.

All Balance Sheet accounts have a Reconciliation & Deposits tab. You can reconcile any account for which you have regular statements. Usually these are the bank accounts or credit card accounts.

Click the **Reconciliation & Deposits tab**:

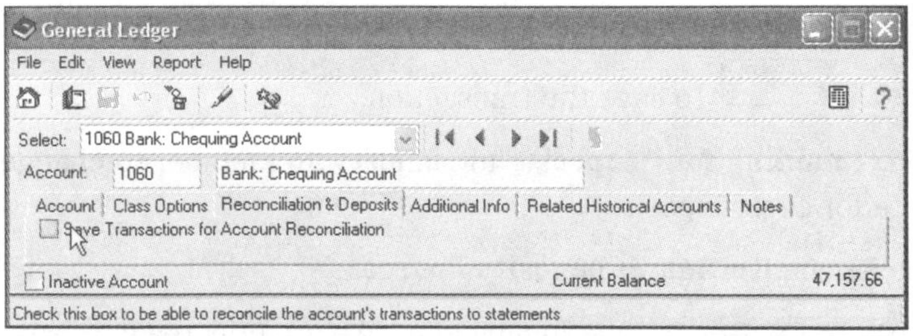

Click **Save Transactions For Account Reconciliation** to display the Set Up button shown in the following screen:

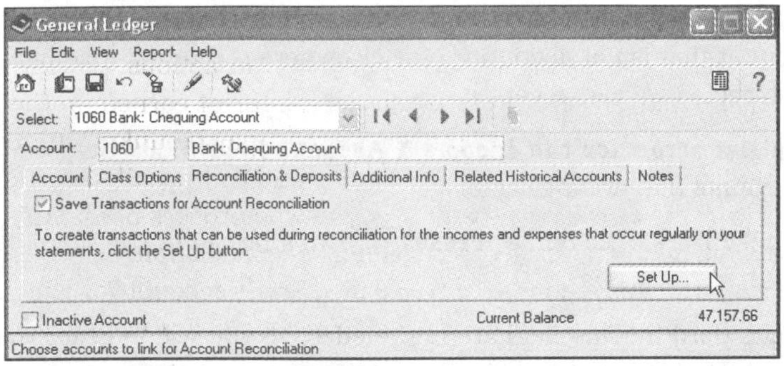

Naming and Linking Reconciliation Accounts

Most bank statements include monthly bank charges, loan or mortgage payments and interest on deposits. That is, there are usually some regular sources of income and expense. Normally the only source document for these bank account transactions is the bank statement. To use Simply Accounting's account reconciliation feature, you must first create the accounts that link to these regular bank account transactions. When you examine the January Bank Statement for Tesses Tresses on page 517, you can see that there is an interest deposit and a withdrawal for service charges. The salon already has accounts for both of these items. In addition, you will need an account to enter adjustments related to the reconciliation. The exact role of these accounts will become clearer as we proceed with the account reconciliation setup.

You can save your work and exit at any time. Any changes you have made will be saved and you can continue from where you left off when you are ready.

The next step is to name bank statement–related transactions and identify the appropriate General Ledger accounts that link to these transactions. Tesses Tresses has income (interest received) from bank deposits and expenses associated with the bank account, such as bank charges or interest paid on bank loans. A third account will be needed for adjustments — small discrepancies between the accounting entries and the bank statements, such as amounts entered incorrectly in journal transactions.

You can edit these names and accounts at any time, and you can add other sources of income or expense later if they are needed.

Click **Set Up** to display the following Linked Accounts screen:

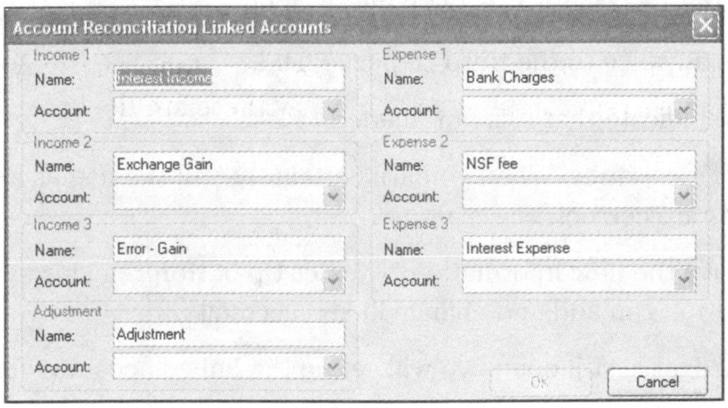

On this Account Reconciliation Linked Accounts form, you can identify up to three regular sources of income, three types of expenses and one adjustment account for each account you want to reconcile.

The name fields on this form cannot be left blank. You can leave the default names or enter "n/a" for not applicable if they are not needed.

The first Income Name field is highlighted, ready for editing. The only source of income for this account that is not accounted for elsewhere is interest income. This name is already entered so we can accept it.

Click the **list arrow for the Income 1 Account field** to list the revenue accounts that are available.

Click **4220 Interest Revenue**. **Press** tab to advance to the second Income field.

NOTES

You can enter n/a or leave the default names unchanged for the unused incomes and expenses.

This field and the third Income field are not needed, so you will indicate that they are not applicable.

Type n/a

Press tab **twice** to skip the Account field and advance to the third Income field. Indicate that it too is not applicable.

Leave the default name for adjustments unchanged.

Click the **Adjustment Account field**.

Either an expense or a revenue account can be used for adjustments. Tesses Tresses will create an expense account for this purpose.

Type 5050 **Press** tab. **Click Add** to start the Add An Account wizard.

Type Reconciliation Adjustments

Accept the **remaining defaults** and **click Finish** to add the account to the Linked Accounts form. **Press** tab to advance the cursor.

The first Expense 1 Name field is highlighted. The salon has one automatic bank account–related expense, bank charges. NSF fee, the second expense, is also used but we do not expect this to be a regular expense. These names are already entered as the default, so we can accept them. The same account is used for both expenses.

Click the **Account field list arrow for Expense 1** to display the list of expense accounts.

Select **5040 Bank Charges** for this expense account.

Click the **Account field list arrow for Expense 2** .

Select **5040 Bank Charges** for this expense account.

Press tab to advance to the third Expense field.

Type n/a to indicate that it is not needed.

Check your **work** carefully. When you are certain that all the names and accounts are correct,

Click **OK** to save the new information. The Set Up button remains available because you can add and change linked accounts.

While the General Ledger is still open, we will set up the linked accounts for the *Bank: Credit Cards*.

Click the **Next Account button**  to open the ledger we need.

Click the **Reconciliation & Deposits tab** if necessary.

Click **Save Transactions For Account Reconciliation**.

Click **Set Up**.

Choose **4220** as the linked account for Interest Income.

Choose **5050** as the linked account for Adjustment. **Press** tab.

Type Card Fees **Press** tab.

Choose **5060** as the linked account for Card Fees.

Click **OK** to save the reconciliation accounts.

Close the **Ledger window** to return to the General module window.

Reconciling the Bank Statement

Comparing the Bank Statement and Transaction Report

We are now ready to compare the Bank Transaction Report with the bank statement. The Bank Account Transaction Report will show all transactions for the account, similar to the General Ledger Report.

BASIC VERSION
Use the General Ledger Report for account 1060 for this step. (Choose the Reports Menu, Financials and General Ledger.) You will see the deposit slip total amounts instead of details in the General Ledger Report.

Choose the **Reports menu**, then **choose Banking** and **click Bank Account Transaction Report**:

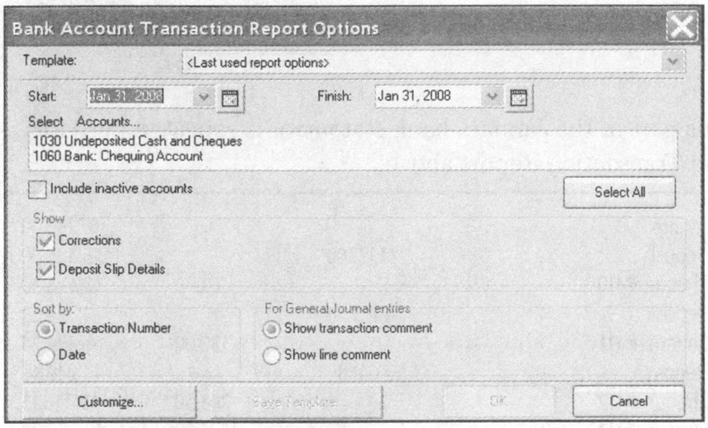

NOTES
You can also compare the General Ledger Report with the bank statement, but you will not have the option to show individual deposit items on the deposit slips.

Only bank class accounts are listed because the report is available only for bank accounts. The credit card bank account is not shown because it is classified as a Credit Card Receivable account. In order to reconcile the credit card account, you can display or print the General Ledger Report for the period covering the bank statement.

For bank account reports, you can include corrections and deposit slip details or omit them. By default both items are added to the report. Since it is easier to work from a report that most closely matches the bank statement, you should omit corrections for this step. The deposit slip details do not appear on the bank statement, but they can be viewed or omitted in the reconciliation journal. Because they can help us locate errors, we will include them at this stage.

You can also report by date or transaction number and include either transaction or line comments.

Click **1060 Bank: Chequing Account** to select the account.

Enter **Jan 1** in the Start date field.

In an ongoing business, include the date of the oldest outstanding item from your previous bank statement up to the date of the most recent statement.

Click **Corrections** to remove the ✓.

Click **OK** to view the report:

Bank Account Transaction Report

File Options Help

Tesses Tresses
Bank Account Transaction Report 01/01/08 to 01/31/08
Sorted by: Transaction Number

Date	Comment	Source #	JE#	Debits	Credits	Balance
1060	**Bank: Chequing Account**					38,325.00 Dr
01/04/08	Pro-Line Inc.	410	J15	-	926.10	37,398.90 Dr
01/09/08	Fine Brushes	411	J17	-	330.00	37,068.90 Dr
01/10/08	Atlantic Power Corp.: AP-5732...	412	J22	-	203.30	36,865.60 Dr
01/14/08	Pro-Line Inc.	413	J24	-	2,176.89	34,688.71 Dr
01/14/08	Transfer funds	Memo 1	J25	5,000.00	-	39,688.71 Dr
01/14/08	Receiver General for Canada: M...	414	J26	-	1,830.00	37,858.71 Dr
01/15/08	Irma Vannitee: Bank debit mem...	139	J27	-	106.55	37,752.16 Dr
01/18/08	Eastern Tel: ET-4003, telephon...	415	J34	-	117.70	37,634.46 Dr
01/24/08	Credit Card	416	J42	-	431.00	37,203.46 Dr
01/27/08	Savers Trust, mortgage & loan ...	DM-792218	J44	-	2,100.00	35,103.46 Dr
01/31/08	Provincial Treasurer: Memo 6, ...	417	J53	-	2,027.30	33,076.16 Dr
01/07/08	Bank deposit	1	J54	117.60	-	33,193.76 Dr
01/07/08	Bank deposit	1	J54	205.80	-	33,399.56 Dr
01/07/08	Bank deposit	1	J54	395.00	-	33,794.56 Dr
01/07/08	Bank deposit	1	J54	550.00	-	34,344.56 Dr
01/07/08	Bank deposit	1	J54	245.00	-	34,589.56 Dr
01/07/08	Bank deposit	1	J54	91.54	-	34,681.10 Dr
01/07/08	Bank deposit	1	J54	2,520.40	-	37,201.50 Dr
01/14/08	Bank deposit	2	J55	106.55	-	37,308.05 Dr
01/14/08	Bank deposit	2	J55	107.69	-	37,415.74 Dr
01/14/08	Bank deposit	2	J55	1,840.95	-	39,256.69 Dr
01/21/08	Bank deposit	3	J56	108.72	-	39,365.41 Dr
01/21/08	Bank deposit	3	J56	61.35	-	39,426.76 Dr
01/21/08	Bank deposit	3	J56	1,891.66	-	41,318.42 Dr
01/28/08	Bank deposit	4	J57	872.44	-	42,190.86 Dr
01/28/08	Bank deposit	4	J57	1,693.71	-	43,884.57 Dr
01/31/08	Bank deposit	5	J58	42.80	-	43,927.37 Dr
01/31/08	Bank deposit	5	J58	872.44	-	44,799.81 Dr
01/31/08	Bank deposit	5	J58	2,357.85	-	47,157.66 Dr
				19,081.50	10,248.84	

basic **BASIC VERSION**
Remember that the General Ledger Report will show the deposit slip total amounts instead of details.

The transactions part of the January bank statement is repeated here for comparison with the Transaction Report above:

Date	Note #	Balance Fwd			37,148.00
2 Jan	1	Deposit	1,177.00		38,325.00
7 Jan		Cheque #410		926.10	37,398.90
7 Jan	2	Deposit	4,125.34		41,524.24
9 Jan		Cheque #411		330.00	41,194.24
14 Jan	2	Deposit	2,055.19		43,249.43
14 Jan		Cheque #412		203.30	43,046.13
14 Jan		Cheque #413		2,176.89	40,869.24
14 Jan		Transfer 0290 004 123 22-8	5,000.00		45,869.24
15 Jan		NSF Cheque #61		106.55	45,762.69
15 Jan	3	Service Charge – NSF cheque		30.00	45,732.69
17 Jan		Cheque #414		1,830.00	43,902.69
20 Jan		Cheque #415		117.70	43,784.99
21 Jan	2	Deposit	2,061.73		45,846.72
27 Jan		Cheque #416		431.00	45,415.72
27 Jan	5	Scheduled payment: loan		600.00	44,815.72
27 Jan	5	Scheduled payment: mortgage		1,500.00	43,315.72
28 Jan	2	Deposit	2,566.15		45,881.87
31 Jan	3	Service Charges		23.50	45,858.37
31 Jan	4	Interest	52.25		45,910.62
31 Jan		Closing balance			45,910.62

NOTES
These numbers correspond to the Note # column of the statement.

1 Deposit recorded in December
2 Deposit Slips: total amounts from deposit slips
3 Service charges
4 Interest received
5 Scheduled loan payments $2 100 (1 500 + 600)

When you compare the statement with the Transaction Report, you will notice the following differences. (The numbers below correspond to the numbers in the margin notes and the statement's Note # column.)

1. One deposit on January 2 appears on the bank statement and not in the Bank Transaction Report because the deposit was entered late in December.
2. Four deposits on the bank statement were multiple deposits entered on deposit slips and do not match any single entry in the Bank Transaction Report.

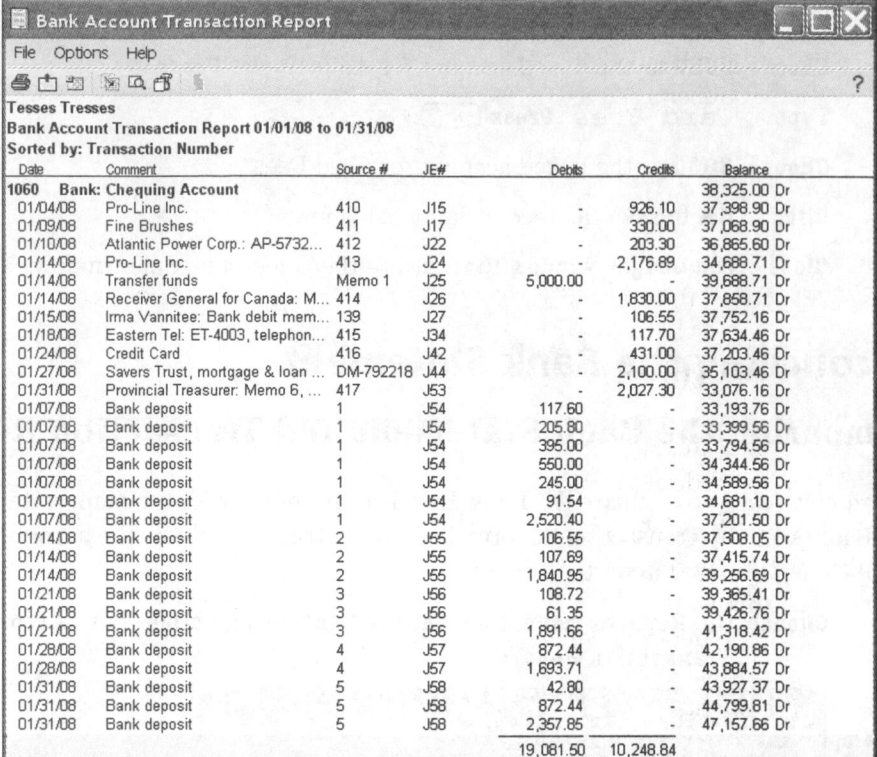

3 Monthly bank charges of $23.50 and NSF charges of $30.00 have not been recorded in the Bank Transaction Report.
4 Interest of $52.25 received on the deposit account does not appear in the Bank Transaction Report.
5 A single General Journal entry combined the loan and mortgage payments.

In addition,

- Deposit slip # 5 for $3 273.09 and cheque #417 for $2 027.30 in the Bank Transaction Report on January 31 are not listed on the bank statement.

All these items must be accounted for in order to have the bank statement match the bank balance in the account's General Ledger or on the Balance Sheet.

Reconciling the Account

After entering the linked accounts, you can begin the reconciliation. The account reconciliation procedure consists of the following steps to update the General Ledger.

1. Record the opening and ending balances from the bank statement for the account.
2. Add outstanding transactions from prior periods that were not resolved in the previous bank statement.
3. Identify all the deposits and withdrawals that have been processed by the bank.
4. Complete journal entries for any transactions for which the bank statement is the source document.

The result should be a match between the bank balances in the two statements. All these steps are completed in the Account Reconciliation Journal.

The General module window should still be open.

Click the **Account Reconciliation icon** shown with the hand pointer:

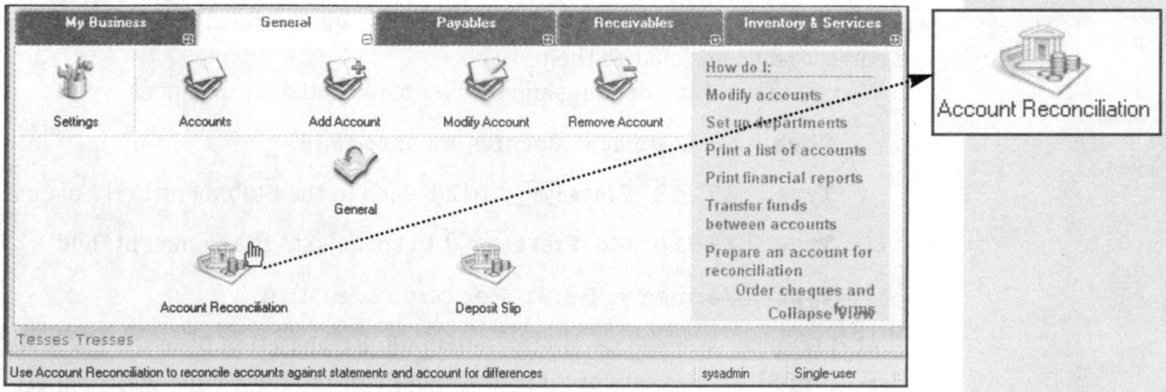

The Reconciliation Journal opens:

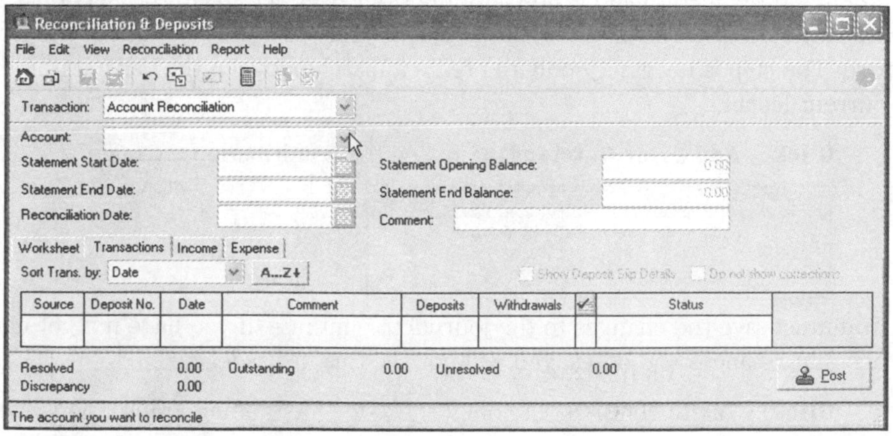

NOTES

There is no allocation option in the Account Reconciliation Journal but additional fields are available, as they are in the other journals.

From the Home window, click the Reconciliation & Deposits icon 

to open the journal. Choose Account Reconciliation from the Transaction drop-down list to change the type of transaction if necessary.

Click the **Account field list arrow** to display the available accounts for reconciliation. The list displays the bank and credit card accounts that we set up for account reconciliation.

Select **1060 Bank: Chequing Account** to display the reconciliation information for this bank account:

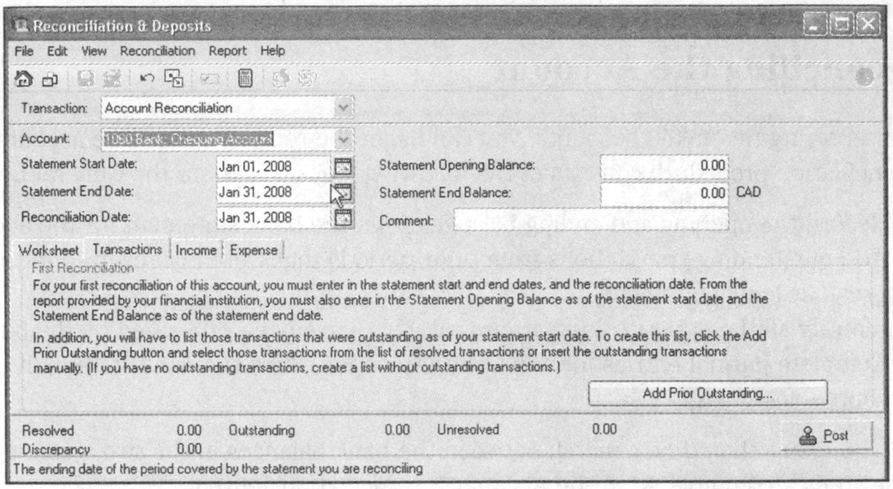

> **NOTES**
> Read the instructions on the screen before proceeding.

The account is entered in the Account field. The first transaction date is entered as the Statement Start Date and the session date is entered automatically in the Statement End Date field and the Reconciliation Date field. These dates will advance by one month when you have finished reconciling the bank account for the current month. The dates are correct so do not change them.

We need to add the opening and closing bank statement balances.

Click the **Statement Opening Balance field**.

Type `37148` **Press** *tab* to advance to the Statement End Balance field.

Type `45910.62` **Press** *tab* to advance to the Comment field.

Type `January Bank Reconciliation`

At this stage, we need to add the outstanding transaction from the previous period. A deposit of $1 177 appears on the bank statement but not in the ledger report. The deposit was made at the end of December, too late to be included in the December bank statement, so we need to add it now. Adding prior transactions in the Account Reconciliation Journal does not create a journal entry and does not affect the ledger balance. The step is necessary only to create a match between the bank statement and the current ledger.

> **WARNING!**
> The first time you complete a reconciliation for any account, you must complete this step (click Add Prior Outstanding) even if there are no outstanding prior transactions. If there are no prior transactions to add, click OK from the Add Outstanding Transactions screen.

Click **Add Prior Outstanding** to see the confirmation message:

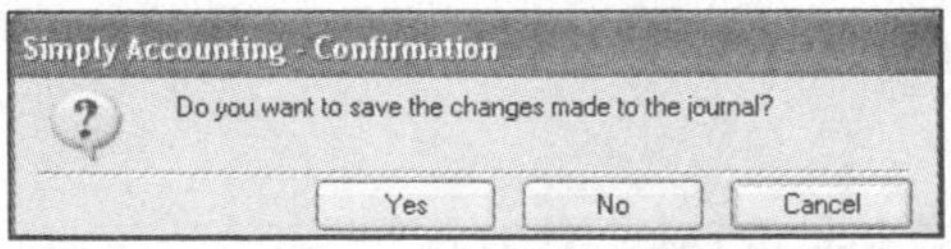

You must save the changes to the journal to continue. If you have not yet entered the account balances and dates, you will not see this message.

Click **Yes** to continue and open the Add Outstanding Transactions window:

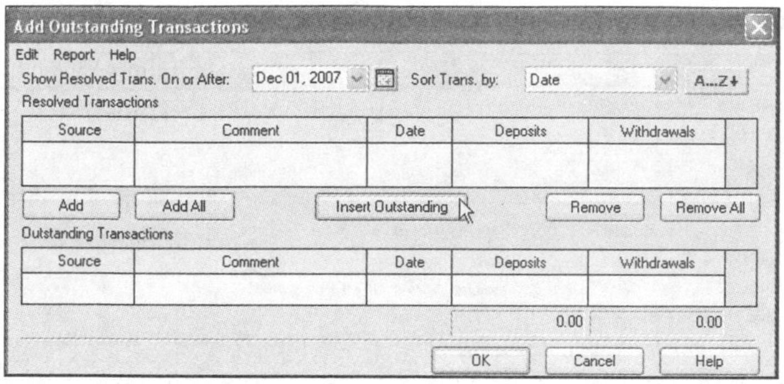

If there are no prior transactions that you need to insert, click OK at this stage to return to the journal.

If you have journal transactions that precede the bank statement starting date, they will appear in the upper portion of the screen, in the Resolved Transactions section. If they have been resolved, you can leave them there. If, however, some of them were outstanding, not included in the previous bank statement, you can add them to the lower Outstanding Transactions section by selecting them and choosing Add.

If we had entered February 1 as the statement starting date, all the January would appear in the Resolved Transactions section. We would then include them all as outstanding transactions by clicking Add All.

We need to add a transaction as outstanding. It preceded the first entry in Simply Accounting on January 1 so it will not be in the transactions list automatically. We can add these types of items directly to the Outstanding Transactions section.

Click **Insert Outstanding** to place the cursor in the Source field for Outstanding Transactions.

Type 5117 to enter the cheque number as the Source.

Press *tab* to move to the Comment field. We will enter the customer's name.

Type Twilight Theatre **Press** *tab* to move to the Date field.

December 31, 2007 is entered as the default date, the last date from the previous statement period. This date is correct so you do not need to change it. You can enter a different date if necessary.

Press *tab* to move to the Deposits column.

Type 1177 **Press** *tab*.

If there are other outstanding prior transactions, enter them in the same way.

If there are no prior transactions, click OK to return to the journal.

Click **OK** to return to the journal window.

WARNING!
You cannot access the Outstanding Transactions input fields until you choose Insert Outstanding.

Marking Journal Entries as Cleared

You are now ready to begin processing individual journal entries to indicate whether they have been cleared in this bank statement. That is, you must indicate whether the bank has processed the items and the amounts have been withdrawn from or deposited to the account.

The updated journal window now looks like the following:

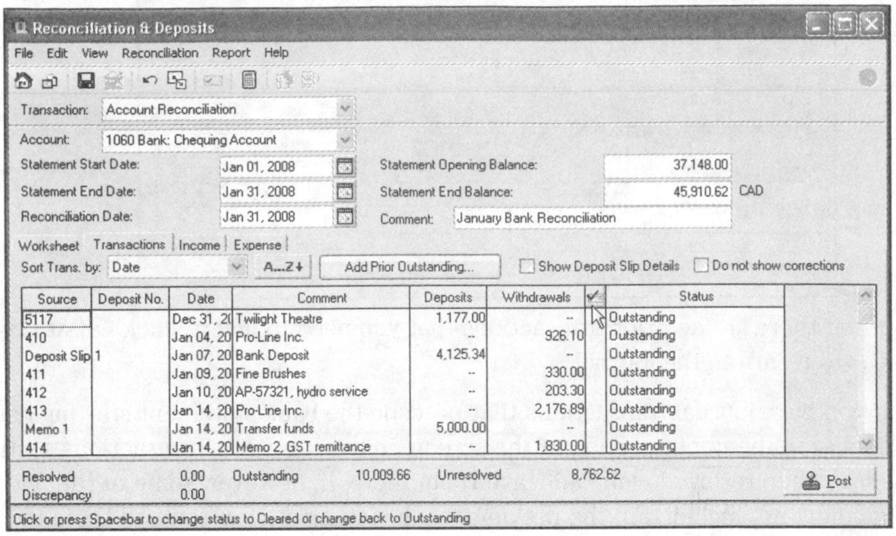

The Transactions tab is selected and all January bank account transactions are now listed, including the one we just added. The bottom section of the screen contains a summary of the transactions. Our goal is to reduce the unresolved amount to zero with no discrepancy.

The Statement End Balance should be correct because we entered it in the previous step. You can add or change it at this stage if necessary.

Group Deposits

Sometimes several cheques are deposited as a group, as they were by Tesses Tresses on the weekly deposit slips. Each of these group deposits can now be cleared as a group. If you have not completed the deposit slip journal entry, you can define a group deposit at this stage by entering the deposit slip number for each item in the Deposit No. field beside the Source. When you clear one item in the group, the others will be cleared at the same time.

> You may want to drag the lower frame of the journal window or maximize the journal window to include more transactions on your screen at the same time.

You are now ready to mark the transactions that have been cleared, that is, the ones that appear on the bank statement.

Click the ☑ column **for Cheque #5117** (click in the column), the first transaction on the list.

A checkmark appears in the Clear column ☑ and the Status has changed from Outstanding to Cleared. As you clear each item, the Resolved and Unresolved amounts are updated.

Clear the **remaining journal entries** that appear on the bank statement and scroll as necessary to display additional items.

Do not clear deposit slip #5 for $3 273.09 or the final cheque for $2 027.30.

If you mark an item as Cleared by mistake, click the ☑ column again to return the status to Outstanding.

Your transactions list appears as follows:

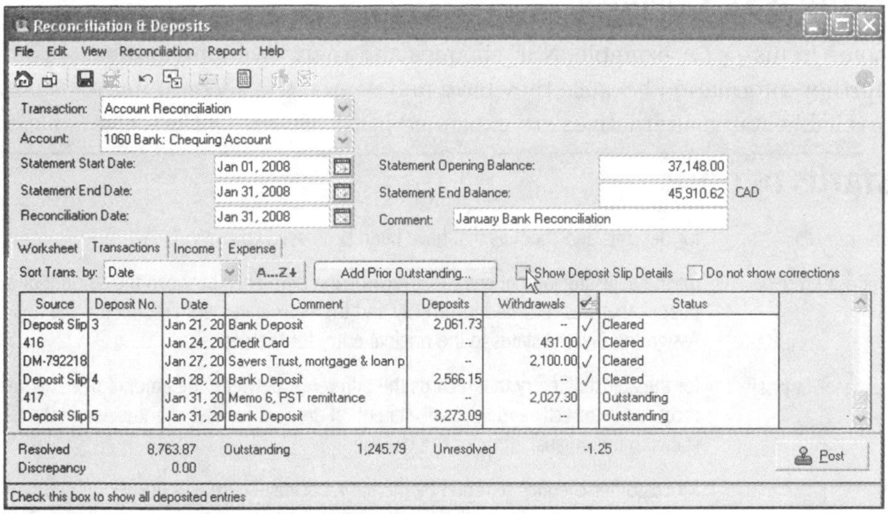

After clearing all transactions from the bank statement, the unresolved amount should be –1.25. This is the net difference for the three unmatched bank statement items: the NSF charge, the service charge and the interest. Journal entries for these items will be added later.

The next section describes the procedure for clearing transactions that are different in some way, like NSF cheques. By marking their status correctly, you will have a more accurate picture of your business transactions. Cheque #61 for $106.55 was returned as NSF and should be marked as such.

Showing Deposit Slip Details

The NSF cheque we need to mark was part of a group deposit (deposit slip #2), so it does not appear individually on the Transactions list. First we need to show the details of the deposit slips. Above the Transactions list is the **Show Deposit Slip Details** check box. This box is a toggle switch; you can hide the details when they are not required or show them if you need to change the status of a single item in the deposit group.

Click **Show Deposit Slip Details** to add a ✓.

Press the **down scroll arrow** until you see the items for deposit slip #2:

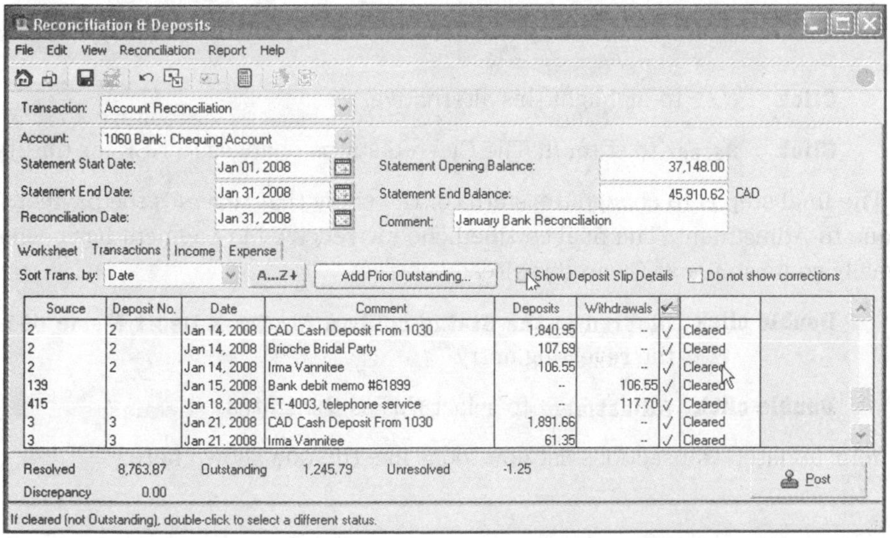

Notice that you can also hide or show correcting journal entries in the list of transactions by clicking Do Not Show Corrections. Removing incorrect and reversing entries can make the reconciliation easier by increasing the match with the statement.

Marking NSF Cheques

For some items — for example, NSF cheques and their reversing entries — you should add further information because they have not cleared the account in the usual way. The available status alternatives are explained in the Status Options chart that follows.

STATUS OPTIONS

Cleared (C)	for deposits and cheques that have been processed correctly.
Deposit Error (D)	for the adjusting journal entry that records the difference between the amount of a deposit that was recorded incorrectly and the bank statement amount for that deposit. Assign the Cleared status to the original entry for the deposit.
Payment Error (P)	for the adjusting entry that records the difference between the amount of a cheque recorded incorrectly and the bank statement amount for that cheque. Assign the Cleared status to the original entry for the cheque.
NSF (N)	for customer cheques returned by the bank because there was not enough money in the customer's account. Assign the Adjustment status to the adjusting entry that reverses the NSF cheque.
Reversed (R)	for cheques that are cancelled by posting a reversing transaction entry to the bank account or the Sales or Purchases journals, that is, journal entries that are corrected. Assign the Adjustment status to the reversing entry that cancels the cheque.
Void (V)	for cheques that are cancelled because of damage during printing. Assign the Adjustment status to the reversing entry that voids the cheque.
Adjustment (A)	for the adjusting or reversing entries that are made to cancel NSF, void or reversed cheques. (See the explanations for NSF, Void and Reversed above.)

To mark a cheque as NSF,

Click **Cleared** in the Status column for Irma Vannitee's cheque for $106.55 in deposit slip #2, the NSF cheque.

Press *enter* to display the alternatives for the Status of a journal entry:

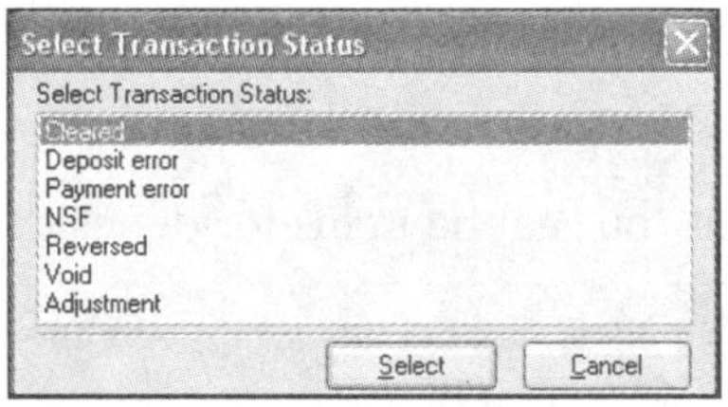

Click **NSF** to highlight this alternative.

Click **Select** to enter it. The Cleared status changes to NSF for this item.

The final step is to change the status of the entry that reverses the payment or NSF cheque to Adjustment. The final certified cheque received in payment has been cleared normally so its status as Cleared is already correct.

Double click **Cleared in the Status column for Bank Debit Memo #61899**, the reversing entry.

Double click **Adjustment** to select this as the status.

Your updated transactions list now looks like the one shown here:

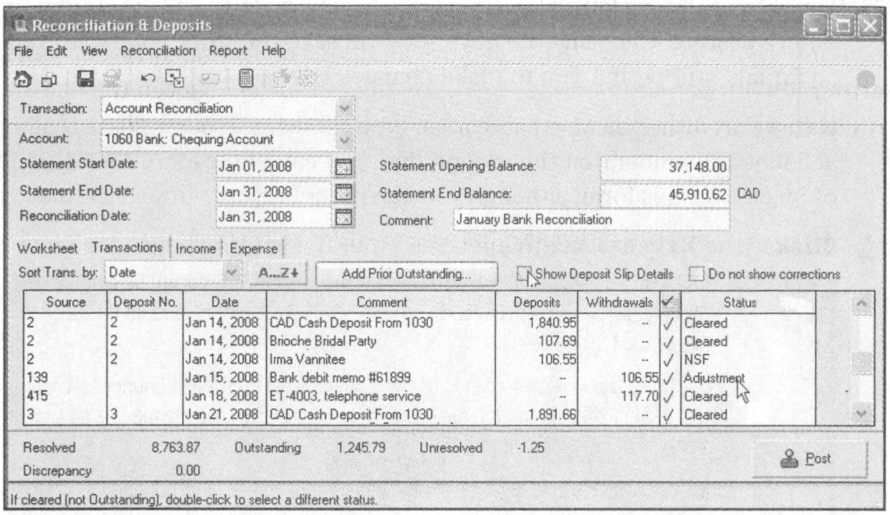

Click **Show Deposit Slip Details** to restore the summary version for deposits.

The resolved, unresolved and outstanding amounts, the net of deposit and withdrawal amounts, are continually updated as you work through the reconciliation procedure. If you display your journal entry from the Report menu at this stage, you will see a credit to *Bank: Chequing Account* and a debit to *Reconciliation Adjustments* for $1.25, the unresolved amount at this stage — the net amount of interest and all bank charges. The journal entries for these items will remove the unresolved amount.

Adding Account Statement Journal Entries

You are now ready to begin entering the journal information for income to this account.

Click the **Income tab**.

The Account Reconciliation Journal now includes journal entry fields as shown:

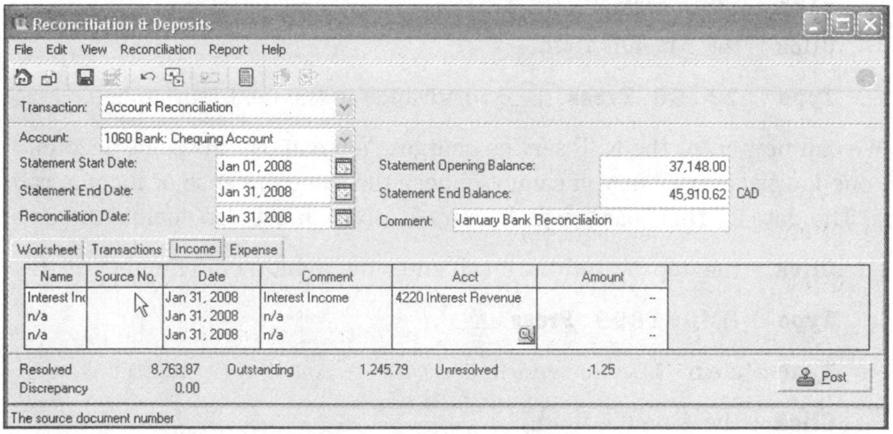

The first entry for Interest Income, the income source we named earlier, is partially completed with the correct default entries for date, comment and account. You can change any of these entries by editing the contents or selecting a different account.

Click the **Source No. field** to advance the cursor.

Type `Bk-Stmt`

Click the **Amount field**.

Type `52.25` **Press** tab. Notice that the unresolved amount — 53.50 — now matches the amount for the service fee plus the NSF charge.

You can edit these journal entries or transaction status entries at any time before posting. Choosing the Save tool will save the work you have completed so far and still permit you to make changes later.

If there are other income categories, type the name, source, date, comment, account and amount on the second line. You can enter more than three sources of income on this form, although you can predefine only three linked accounts.

Click the **Expense tab** to open the input fields for expense transactions:

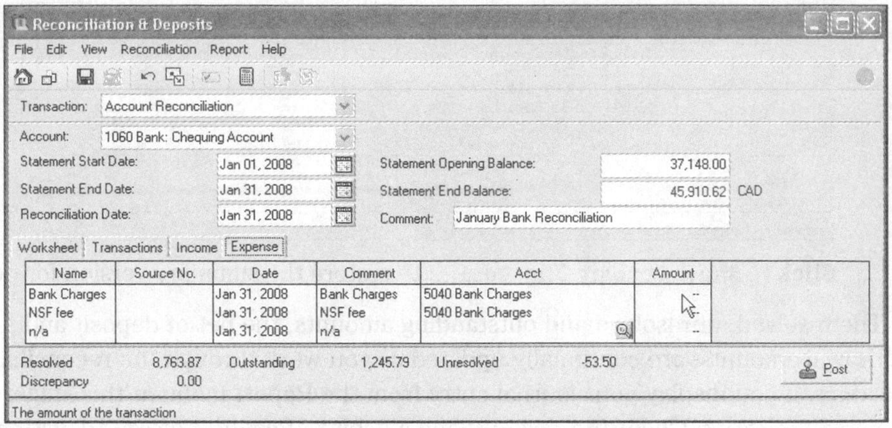

The expense transactions are also partially completed. We need to add the Source No. and the Amount. For the NSF fee, we need to change the date.

You can combine regular service charges with charges for other one-time or unusual services such as stopping a payment on a cheque or NSF fees. We have created a separate category for the NSF charge so that we can track this expense. The bank statement contains the amounts for the expenses.

Click the **Source No. field**. Duplicate source document codes are allowed in this journal.

Type Bk-Stmt

Click the **Amount field**.

Type 23.50 **Press** tab to advance to the next journal line.

We can now enter the NSF service charges. You can use the same account for more than one journal entry, but you cannot choose the same expense or income category twice. The date for this charge was January 15 so we must also change the default date.

Click the **Source field**. We will enter the debit memo number as the source.

Type DM#61899 **Press** tab.

Type Jan 15

Click the **Amount field**.

Type 30 **Press** tab.

If there are other expenses, enter the information in the same way.

At this stage, your unresolved amount should be zero if everything is reconciled. We will look at the Worksheet to see a summary of the changes we have made.

Click the **Worksheet tab**:

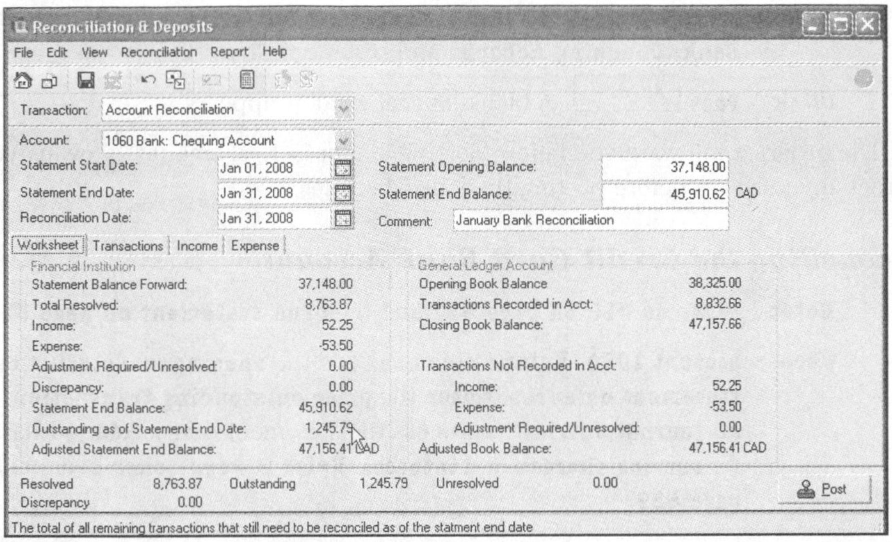

This summary shows the amounts for the bank statement and Simply Accounting records that have been entered to reconcile the differences. Both lists show the opening and closing balances and net total transaction amounts. The Account Reconciliation Journal transactions for income and expenses that were not recorded elsewhere are added to the General ledger balance, and outstanding amounts that were in the General Ledger but not on the bank statement are added to the Bank Statement balance. The result is a match between the two adjusted balance amounts.

You should also review the reconciliation journal entry before proceeding.

Choose the **Report menu** and **click Display Account Reconciliation Journal Entry**. Your journal entry should appear as follows:

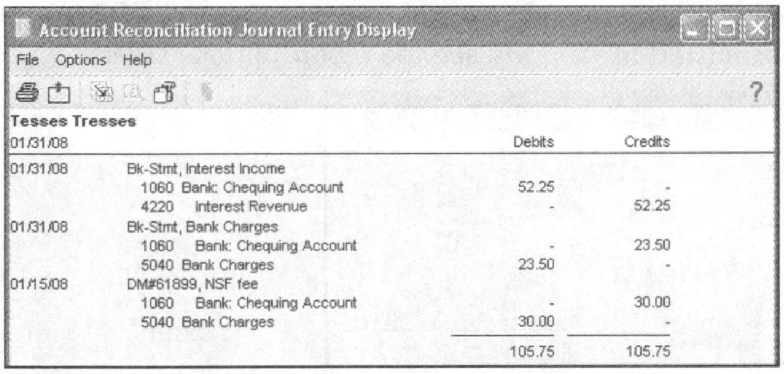

Account Reconciliation Journal Entry Display
File Options Help
Tesses Tresses
01/31/08 Debits Credits
01/31/08 Bk-Stmt, Interest Income
1060 Bank: Chequing Account 52.25 -
4220 Interest Revenue - 52.25
01/31/08 Bk-Stmt, Bank Charges
1060 Bank: Chequing Account - 23.50
5040 Bank Charges 23.50 -
01/15/08 DM#61899, NSF fee
1060 Bank: Chequing Account - 30.00
5040 Bank Charges 30.00 -
105.75 105.75

The income and expense journal entries are listed. In addition, an adjustment entry will be displayed if there is any unresolved amount.

Close the **Report window** when you have finished.

If the unreconciled amount is not zero, check your journal entries to see whether you have made an error. Click each option in the Display group to show your work for the corresponding part of the reconciliation procedure. Make corrections if necessary.

If you still have an unresolved amount, you can save the entry without posting and return later to try to determine whether you made a mistake or whether there was an error on the bank statement.

Any discrepancy or unresolved amount will be posted as an adjustment to the reconciliation adjustments expense account created earlier. This account should be used only for small amounts not significant enough to warrant a separate journal entry, such as differences from payroll tax rates in this text.

Click the **Save button** . **Click** to close the journal without posting.

WARNING!

You cannot adjust Account Reconciliation Journal entries, and correcting them after posting is quite difficult.

Do not post the Account Reconciliation Journal transaction until the unresolved amount is zero (or a small discrepancy that you can explain). You can click the Save button to save your work before posting, exit the journal and return later to find the error and make corrections.

Back up the **data file**. **Open** the **Account Reconciliation Journal**, **select 1060 Bank: Chequing Account** and resume your work.

Click **Post** [Post]. A blank journal window appears.

The program will warn you before posting an unresolved amount, allowing you to correct any mistakes before posting the journal entries.

Reconciling the Credit Card Bank Account

NOTES
There is one outstanding item from the previous month. There are no deposit slips.

Refer to **Memo #10 on page 517** and the **bank statement on page 518**.

Choose **account 1080**. **Enter** a **comment** and the **opening** and **closing bank statement balances**. **Enter** the **prior outstanding transaction**. **Clear all journal entries** to process the statement items. **Add** journal **entries** for **service charges** and **interest**. **Refer** to **keystrokes** beginning on **page 539**.

Displaying Account Reconciliation Reports

Account Reconciliation Journal

Right-click the **Account Reconciliation icon** [Account Reconciliation] in the General module window, or
the **Reconciliation & Deposits icon** [Reconciliation & Deposits] in the Home window.

Click [Display tool icon] (the Display tool) in the Home window.

Or, **choose** the **Reports menu**, **choose Journal Entries** and **click Account Reconciliation**. You will see the report options screen:

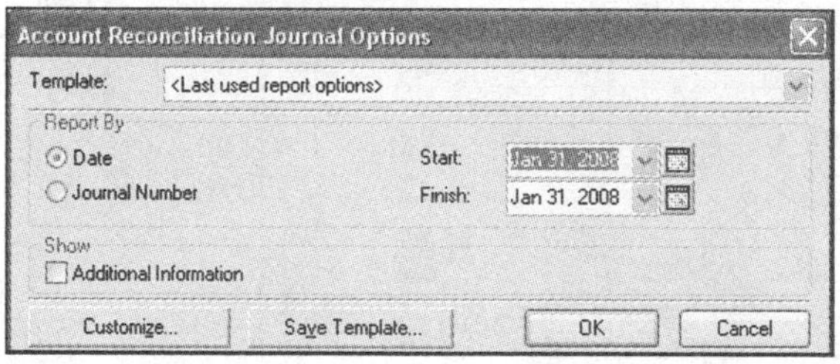

The journal can be prepared by journal entry numbers or by date. By default, the report uses posting dates. The usual journal report customizing, sorting and filtering options are available.

Enter the **starting** and **ending dates** or journal numbers for the report.

Click **OK**. **Close** the **display** when you have finished.

Deposit Slip Journal

basic BASIC VERSION
The icon label is Deposit Slips.

Right-click the **Deposit Slip icon** [Deposit Slip] in the General module window.

Click [Display tool icon] (the Display tool) in the Home window.

Or, **choose** the **Reports menu**, **choose Journal Entries** and **click Deposit Slips**. You will see the report options screen:

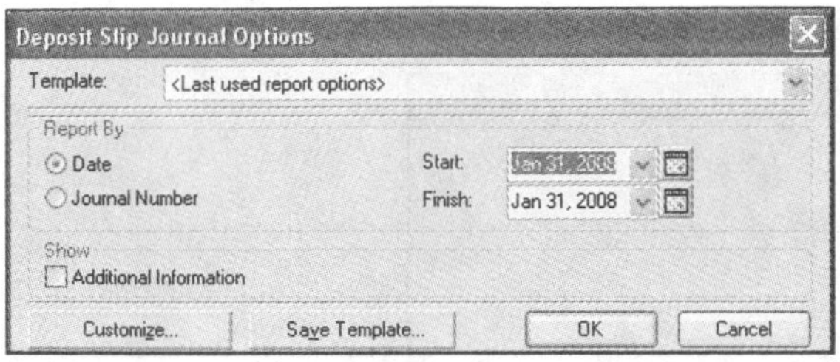

The journal can be prepared by journal entry numbers or by date. By default, the report uses posting dates. The usual journal report customizing, sorting and filtering options are available.

Enter the **starting** and **ending dates** or journal numbers for the report.

Click **OK**. **Close** the **display** when you have finished.

Account Reconciliation Report

NOTES
You can display Journal reports, Invoice Lookup, and Vendor or Customer Aged or Employee reports (if applicable) from the Account Reconciliation Detail Report.
The reconciliation reports cannot be customized.

Choose the **Reports menu**, then **choose Banking** and **click Account Reconciliation Report** to display the options:

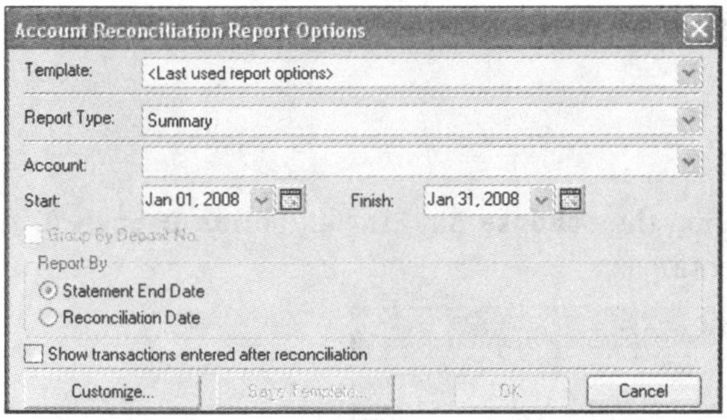

Type 1060 (to enter the bank account number in the Account field) or choose the account from the drop-down list for the Account field.

Enter the **start** and **end dates**. Usually these dates will coincide with the bank statement period.

From the Report Type drop-down list, choose the **Summary** Report to provide totals for each type of Status, totals for income and expense categories and outstanding amounts that will reconcile the bank statement with the General Ledger account balance.

Choose the **Detail** Report to list all journal entries with their status. You can group the Detail Report by Deposit Number.

Choose **Summary Report With Outstanding Transactions** to add the list of General Ledger transactions that have not been reported on bank statements.

Choose either the bank **Statement End Date** or the **Reconciliation Date** recorded in the journal for the report.

Click **OK**. **Close** the **displayed report** when you have finished.

Account Reconciliation Transaction Report

Choose the **Reports menu**, then **choose Banking** and **click Account Reconciliation Transaction Report**.

You will display the report options:

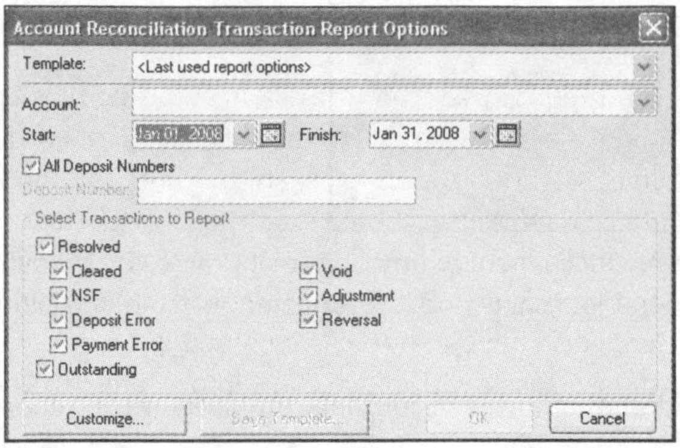

Choose the **account** for the report from the drop-down list.

Enter **Start** and **Finish** dates for the report.

Choose the **Status categories** to include in your reports. By default, all are included, so clicking a category will remove the ✓ from the check box and omit this category from your report.

Click **OK** and **close** the **displayed report** when you have finished.

Deposit Slip Report

NOTES
You can customize the Deposit Slip Report by selecting the columns to include but you cannot sort or filter the report.
You cannot drill down to other reports from the Deposit Slip Report.

Choose the **Reports menu**, then **choose Banking** and **click Deposit Slip Report** to display the options:

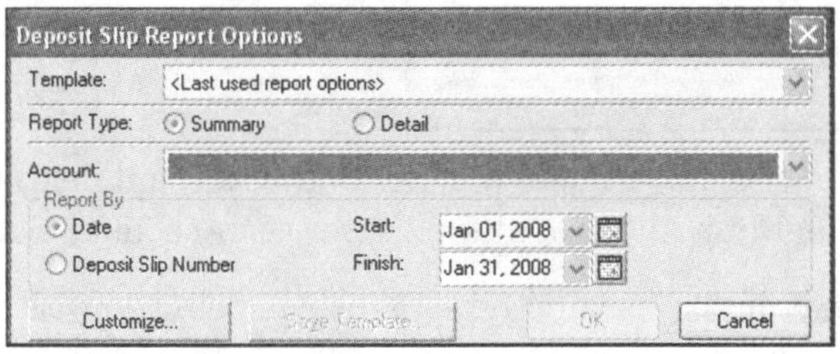

NOTES
The Cheque Log Report was covered in Chapter 5. Refer to page 151.

Choose the **account** for the report from the drop-down list.

You can display the report for a range of dates or deposit slip numbers. Choose the **Summary** option to see a list of totals for cash and cheques for each deposit slip. Choose **Detail** to see each item on each deposit slip and the totals.

Enter **Start** and **Finish** dates for the report.

Click **OK** and **close** the **displayed report** when you have finished.

Printing Account Reconciliation Reports

WARNING!
Back up the data files before proceeding and print all relevant available reports: journals, vendor and customer detail reports, inventory tracking reports and the other reports listed in the month-end checklist.
You may want to create a separate copy of the data file to practise clearing data. Use the File menu Save As command, enter a different file name and work with the new file that opens.

Display the **report** you want to print. **Click** [print icon] or **choose** the **File menu** and **click Print** to print the report. **Close** the **Report window** when finished.

End-of-Month Procedures

There are accounting activities that should be completed at the end of regular accounting periods. Earlier we used the checklists to review fiscal year-end accounting procedures. As we saw in Chapter 8, there are also checklists for the end of each business day and month. Normally a business will print all journal transactions at the end of each business day; statements and financial reports will be printed at the end of each month and all reports should be printed at the end of the fiscal period. T4s should be printed at the end of the calendar year.

Periodically, a business will clear old information from its accounting files to make space. In the manual system, it might store the details in archives or on microfiche to keep the current files manageable in size. Computerized systems should be similarly maintained by making backups of the data files and then clearing the information that is not required. These periodic procedures include clearing journal entries for prior periods, removing paid invoices from customer and vendor records and removing vendors and customers who no longer do business with the company.

Simply Accounting's checklists can assist with these routine procedures. You should be in the Home window.

Click the **Checklists button** or **choose** the **Business Assistant menu** and **click Checklists** to see the available lists.

Click **Month-End Procedures** to select it and then **click Modify**.

You will see the list of routines that should be completed at the end of a month:

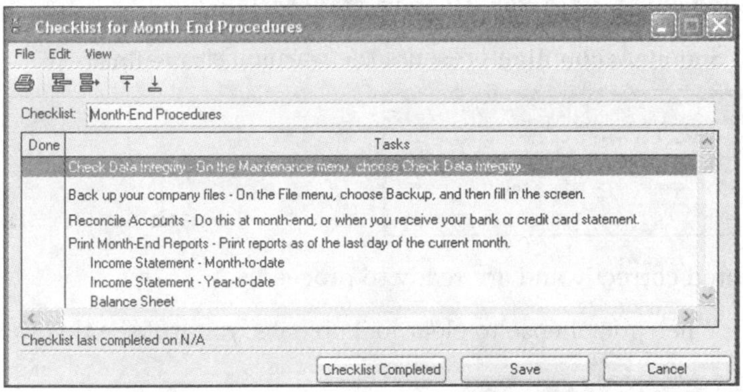

Read the task list. You have already completed some tasks on this list.

NOTES
Remember that you can print the task list for reference. Choose the File menu and click Print, click the Print tool or press ctrl + J to print the task list.

Click the **Done column beside** the two tasks that are completed — **Back Up** and **Reconcile Accounts**. We will complete the remaining tasks before marking them.

Click the **Home window** if part is showing or click the Simply Accounting button on the task bar to bring it to the front.

Choose the **Maintenance menu** and **click Check Data Integrity**.

If you do not see the message "Data OK" make a note of any data inconsistencies and return to your most recent backup copy of the file.

Click **OK** to close the Integrity Summary window.

Click the **Done column beside Check Data Integrity**.

Click **Save** to return to the main checklists window. A ✓ appears in the Task In Progress column beside Month-End Procedures.

Click **Close** to leave the checklists window and return to the Home window.

Clearing Paid Vendor Transactions

NOTES
You cannot clear data when you are working in multi-user mode.

Choose the **Maintenance menu**, then **choose Clear Data** and **Clear Paid Transactions** and **click Clear Paid Vendor Transactions**.

NOTES
If the Clear Data menu option is dimmed, close and then open the data file and try again.

The following vendor list will be displayed:

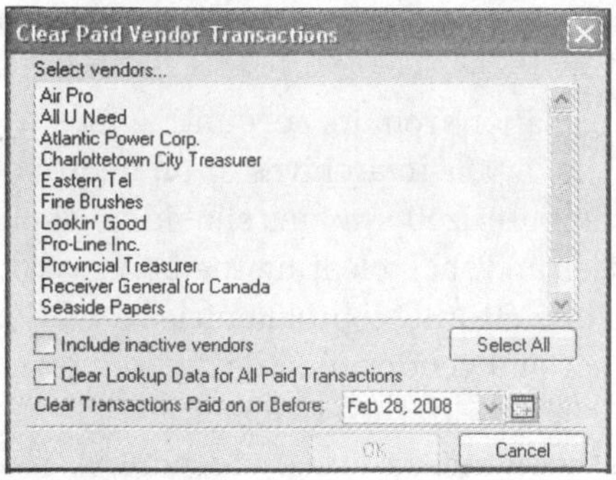

You can clear invoices for one or more vendors at the same time. Unpaid invoices are always retained.

Enter **Jan 31** as the last date for which you want to remove invoices.

Click **Select All**. (To select individual vendors, **press** *ctrl* and **click** their **names**.) We also have stored lookup details that we no longer need.

Click **Clear Lookup Data For All Paid Transactions**.

Click **OK**. Simply Accounting presents the warning shown here:

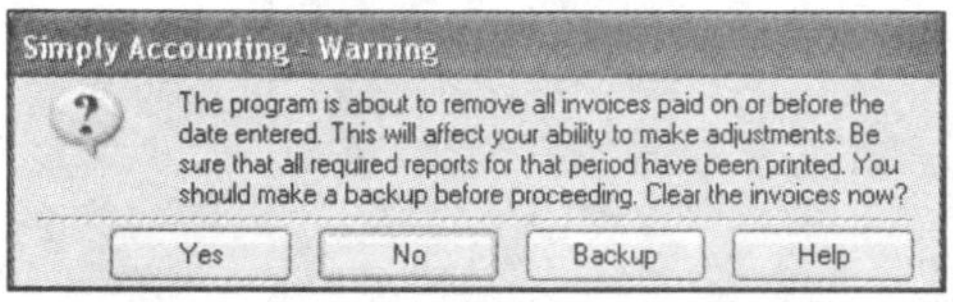

NOTES
After clearing data, display the relevant reports to see that the information has been cleared. You will be unable to look up and adjust posted invoices if you have removed lookup details for cleared paid transactions.

If you have selected correctly and are ready to proceed,

Click **Yes**. When you choose to clear lookup data, you will see this warning:

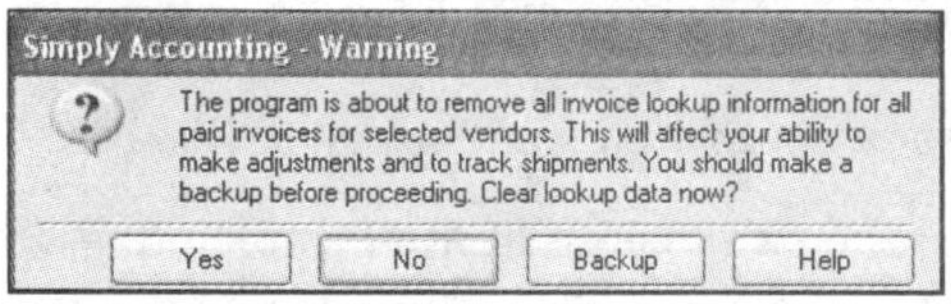

Again, if you are certain that you should continue,

Click **Yes**.

Clearing Paid Customer Transactions

Clearing customer invoices is similar to clearing vendor invoices.

Choose the **Maintenance menu**, then **choose** **Clear Data** and **Clear Paid Transactions** and **click** **Clear Paid Customer Transactions**:

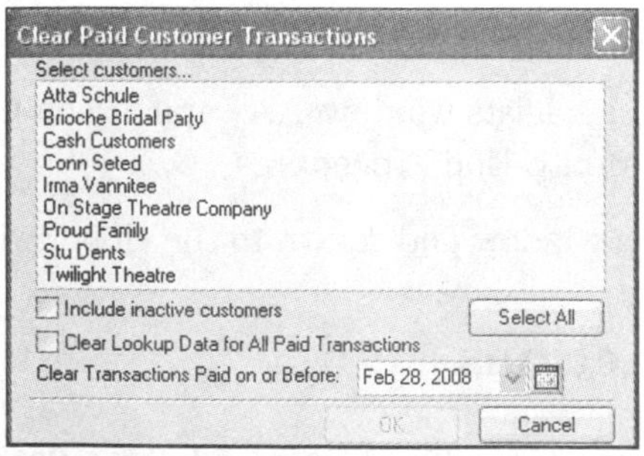

Enter **Jan 31** as the last date for which you want to remove invoices.

We will keep all transactions for February. We can clear the invoices and lookup data for Cash Customers and Atta Schule because these are not needed. You can clear paid invoices for all customers by clicking Select All.

Click **Atta Schule**. **Press** ctrl and **click Cash Customers**.

Click **Clear Lookup Data For All Paid Transactions**. **Click OK**.

The next warning is the same as the one we saw for removing vendor invoices. If you are ready, you should proceed.

Click **Yes**. Again, the additional warning for lookup data is shown. If you are certain that you want to continue,

Click **Yes** to return to the Home window. The requested information is removed.

Clearing Tax Reports

You should clear tax reports after filing the tax returns for the period covered by the return so that the next report will include only the current reporting period.

Choose the **Maintenance menu**, then **choose Clear Data** and **click Clear Tax Report** to display the options:

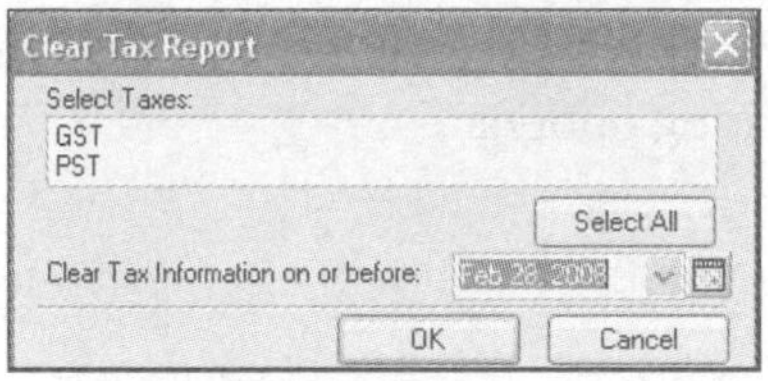

Select the tax or taxes you want to clear the reports for or click Select All. Then enter the date. Entries on and before the date you enter will be removed.

Click **OK** to see the familiar warning:

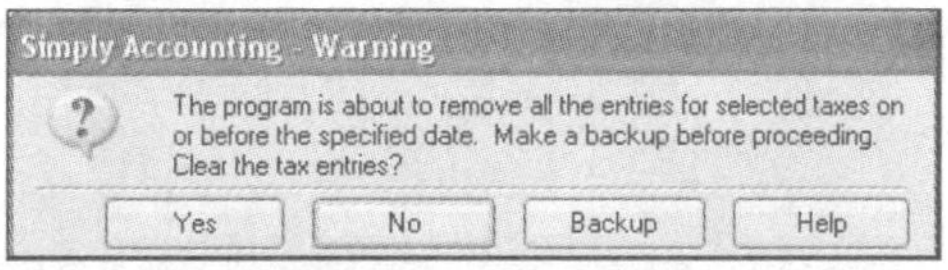

We do not want to remove any tax data because we have not submitted the returns.

Click **No** to cancel and return to the Home window.

Clearing Account Reconciliation Data

Choose the **Maintenance menu**, then **choose Clear Data** and **Clear Account Rec.** and **click Clear Account Rec. Data** to display the options:

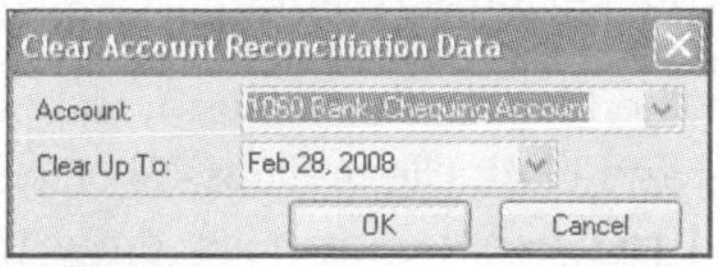

Select the account for which you want to remove the data. Then enter the date. Entries on and before the date you enter will be removed.

We do not want to remove the data at this time. If you choose to continue, you will see the familiar warning before any information is removed.

Click **Cancel** to return to the Home window.

Clearing Inventory Tracking Data

Choose the **Maintenance menu**, then **choose Clear Data** and **click Clear Inventory Tracking Data** to display the following dialogue box:

Enter **Jan 31** as the date. Entries on and before Jan 31 will be removed.

Click **OK**. Again, you see the warning before any data is removed.

If you are certain that you want to proceed,

Click **Yes** to delete the requested information and return to the Home window.

NOTES
If you choose to clear invoice lookup data for purchases or sales separately, you can choose to clear the data for one or more vendors (or customers) or for all of them.

Clearing Invoice Lookup Data

You can clear invoice lookup data for both purchase and sales invoices together in a single step or you can clear purchase and sales invoices in separate steps.

Choose the **Maintenance menu**, then **choose Clear Data** and **Clear Invoice Lookup Data** and **click Clear Purchase Invoice & Sales Invoice Lookup Data** to display the clearing options:

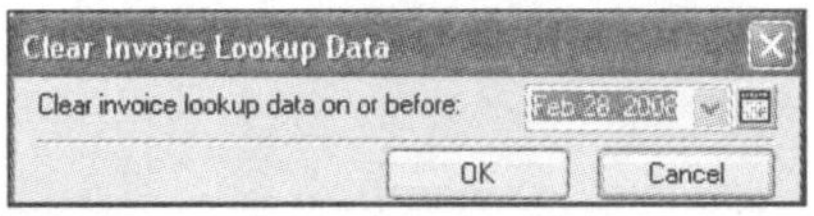

Enter **Jan 31** as the date. Entries on and before Jan 31 will be removed.

Click **OK**.

Once again, you see the warning before any data is removed. If you are certain that you want to proceed,

Click **Yes** to continue.

If you cleared the lookup data with the paid transactions, you will see an error message that there is no invoice lookup data to clear. Click OK to continue.

The requested information is deleted and you will return to the Home window.

If you want to clear only purchase invoice data, choose the Maintenance menu, then choose Clear Data and Clear Invoice Lookup Data and click Clear Purchase Invoice Lookup Data to display the list of vendors. Choose the vendors from which you want to clear the invoices, enter the data and click OK to see the familiar warning. Click Yes to continue with clearing the data.

To remove only sales invoice data, choose the Maintenance menu, then choose Clear Data and Clear Invoice Lookup Data and click Clear Sales Invoice Lookup Data. Select customers for which you want to clear the invoices, enter the date and click OK. Click Yes to continue with clearing the data.

Clearing Deposit Slip Lookup Data

Choose the **Maintenance menu**, then **choose Clear Data** and **click Clear Lookup Data For Deposit Slips** to display the options:

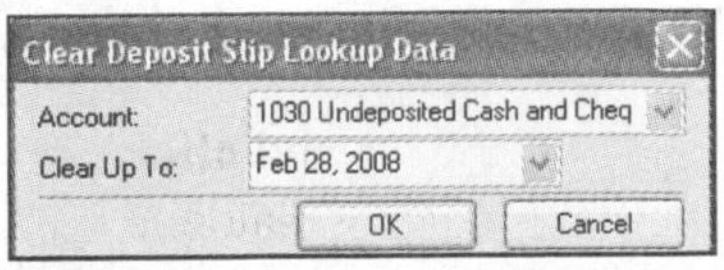

Select the account for which you want to remove the data. Then enter the date. Entries on and before the date you enter will be removed.

We do not want to remove the data at this time. If you choose to continue, you will see the familiar warning before any information is removed.

Click **Cancel** to return to the Home window.

Clearing Lookup Data for Other Payments

Lookup data for other payments are cleared separately from Purchases Journal invoices.

NOTES
From the Maintenance menu, Clear Data option, you can also clear lookup data for remittances, notes that you create in the Daily Business Manager, financial history and direct deposits. For each one, you can enter a date, after which all data will be retained, and you will be warned before any information is removed.

Choose the **Maintenance menu**, then **choose Clear Data** and **click Clear Lookup Data For Other Payments** to display the clearing options:

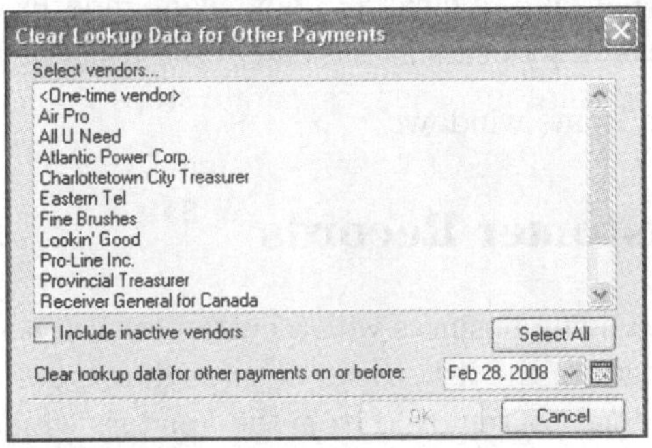

Choose the **vendors**. **Enter Jan 31** as the date for the data you want to remove.

Click **Select All** to select all vendors.

Click **OK**.

You will see the warning before any data is removed. If you want to proceed,

Click **Yes** to continue.

The requested information is deleted, and you will return to the Home window.

Automatically Clearing Data

Simply Accounting can also clear data automatically when you start a new fiscal period. Data may be retained for up to five years.

Choose the **Maintenance menu**, then **choose Clear Data** and **click Automatically Clear Data**.

The options screen shows the types of data you can clear automatically:

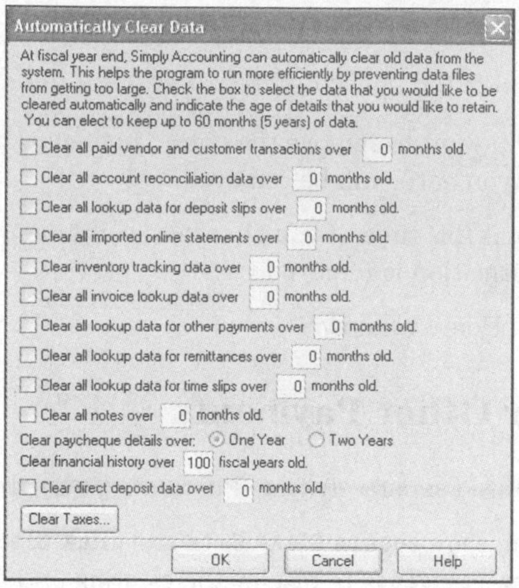
Automatically Clear Data
At fiscal year end, Simply Accounting can automatically clear old data from the system. This helps the program to run more efficiently by preventing data files from getting too large. Check the box to select the data that you would like to be cleared automatically and indicate the age of details that you would like to retain. You can elect to keep up to 60 months (5 years) of data.
Clear all paid vendor and customer transactions over 0 months old.
Clear all account reconciliation data over 0 months old.
Clear all lookup data for deposit slips over 0 months old.
Clear all imported online statements over 0 months old.
Clear inventory tracking data over 0 months old.
Clear all invoice lookup data over 0 months old.
Clear all lookup data for other payments over 0 months old.
Clear all lookup data for remittances over 0 months old.
Clear all lookup data for time slips over 0 months old.
Clear all notes over 0 months old.
Clear paycheque details over: One Year Two Years
Clear financial history over 100 fiscal years old.
Clear direct deposit data over 0 months old.
Clear Taxes...
OK
Cancel
Help

From this screen you can choose what data to clear and how many months of each type of data should be kept when the clearing occurs at the end of the fiscal period.

Click **Cancel** to return to the Home window.

Removing Vendor and Customer Records

Sometimes you know that you will not be doing business with a customer or vendor again. Removing their records reduces the length of the lists to scroll through for journal entries and saves on mailing costs. Vendors are removed from the Vendors window. Customers are removed from the Customers window. We will remove the customer (tenant) Stu Dents because he will be moving out of the apartment after March, the date of his final cheque. First we must clear all paid transactions.

Choose the **Maintenance menu**, then **choose Clear Data** and **Clear Paid Transactions** and **click Clear Paid Customer Transactions**.

Click **Stu Dents** on the customer list.

Enter **Jan. 31, 2008** as the date.

Click **OK**. When you see the warning,

Click **Yes** to confirm. **Click Yes** to confirm removing lookup data if asked.

Open the **Receivables module window** to open the Customers window.

Click the **Remove Customer icon** 
Remove Customer
to access the Search list:

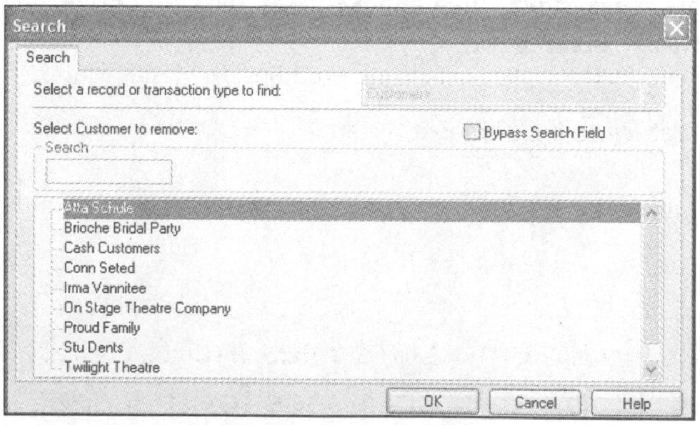
Search
Search
Select a record or transaction type to find:
Customers
Select Customer to remove:
Bypass Search Field
Search
Atta Schule
Brioche Bridal Party
Cash Customers
Conn Seted
Irma Vannitee
On Stage Theatre Company
Proud Family
Stu Dents
Twilight Theatre
OK
Cancel
Help

The option Remove Customer is selected in the Search window.

Click **Stu Dents** to highlight this customer. **Click OK**.

We have selected a customer for which the invoices have not been cleared. Simply Accounting will not permit you to remove a customer, or vendor, with uncleared transactions. You will see the following warning:

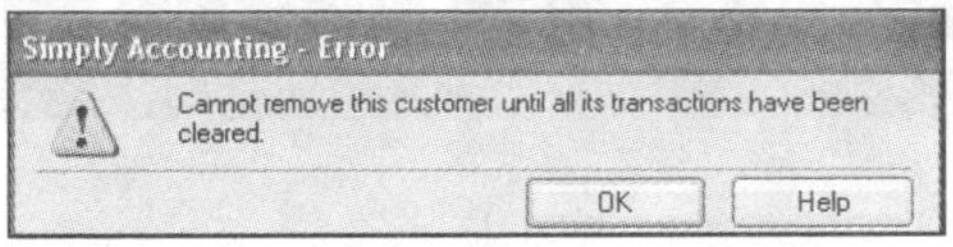

Click **OK** to return to the Receivables module window. Clear the details using March 2 as the date, and then remove the customer's record. If all transactions are cleared, you will see the familiar warning.

Check that you have selected the customer you want before continuing.

Click **Yes** if you have selected correctly.

Click Yes to continue if you see the message about removing lookup data. If you see the message that there is no lookup data, click OK to continue.

Close the **Receivables module window** to return to the Home window.

NOTES

There are postdated rent cheques for Stu Dents, so not all the paid transactions were cleared when January 31 was selected as the date.

You can select March 2 from the Date field drop-down list. (The latest transaction date is usually on the Date field drop-down lists.)

Completing the Month-End Checklist

We will now return to the month-end checklist by marking the remaining tasks as done. The tasks relating to budgeting do not apply so we can delete them from the list, thus customizing the list for Tesses Tresses.

Choose the **Business Assistant menu** and **click Checklists** to see the lists.

Double click **Month-End Procedures** to open this list.

You can also add tasks to customize the list even further. Just click on the list where you want to add a task, choose the Edit menu and click Insert Line (or click the Insert Line tool). Then type the task description.

NOTES

Refer to page 280 for more information on adding tasks to checklists.

Scroll down the **list** to the budget-related tasks.

Click **Check Your Budget** to select this line.

Click the **Remove Item tool**  or **choose** the **Edit menu** and **click Remove**.

Click **Yes** to confirm and select the next task. Remove it and the following one relating to budgets.

Click the **Done column** for the remaining tasks.

Click **Checklist Completed** to return to the opening Checklist window.

The session date appears as the Date Last Completed beside Month-End Procedures.

Click **Close** to return to the Home window.

REVIEW

The Student CD-ROM with Data Files includes Review Questions and Supplementary Cases for this chapter.

CHAPTER FIFTEEN

Flabuless Fitness

OBJECTIVES

After completing this chapter, you should be able to

- ***plan*** and ***design*** an accounting system for a small business
- ***prepare*** procedures for converting from a manual system
- ***understand*** the objectives of a computerized system
- ***create*** company files
- ***set up*** company accounts
- ***prepare*** files for foreign currency transactions and importing goods
- ***identify*** preferred customers for reduced prices
- ***enter*** preferred customer prices and import duty rates for inventory
- ***finish*** entering the accounting history for all modules
- ***insert*** new accounts, vendors, customers and employees as required
- ***export*** reports
- ***use*** spreadsheets for analyzing, planning and decision making
- ***enter*** transactions that result in inventory variances
- ***enter*** end-of-accounting-period adjustments
- ***perform*** end-of-accounting-period closing routines
- ***analyze*** and ***interpret*** case studies
- ***develop*** further group interpersonal skills
- ***develop*** further oral and written skills

INTRODUCTION

This application provides a complete accounting cycle for a merchandising business. It is a comprehensive application covering a three-month fiscal period. You will use Simply Accounting to convert a manual accounting system to a computerized accounting system and then enter transactions. The routines in this application are common to many small businesses, so they should be useful. The information in this chapter reflects the business realities in Ontario in 2006.

You may substitute information relevant to other provinces or the latest payroll and tax regulations wherever it is appropriate to do so. Rules for the application of the federal Goods and Services Tax (GST), provincial sales taxes and payroll may vary from one province to another.

Because of the length of the setup, instructions for working with the source documents are presented with those documents on page 636.

NOTES
Because of the length of the application, group work is encouraged in setting up error-free company files and completing the transactions.

COMPANY INFORMATION

Company Profile

Flabuless Fitness, in Hamilton, Ontario, sells a wide range of fitness equipment and accessories for home and light commercial use. Stephen Reeves, the owner, opened his business a few years ago after retiring as a professional athlete, gaining business experience with another store and completing some business courses. Reeves has three employees to assist with the work in the store. They also perform other duties. One employee does the accounting, one teaches yoga classes and one delivers equipment and provides personal training services to clients. Reeves works mostly outside the store, promoting the business.

NOTES
Flabuless Fitness
199 Warmup Rd., Unit 500
Hamilton, Ontario L8T 3B7
Tel 1: (905) 642-2348 (B-FIT)
Tel 2: (800) 448-2348 (B-FIT)
Fax: (905) 642-9100
Business No.: 245 138 121

Several of the equipment suppliers offer discounts to the store for early payment. Two suppliers are located in the United States. Accounts are also set up for other supplies and services that are provided locally. The store uses a credit card for some of these purchases.

Most customers are situated in the Hamilton region but Reeves has recently added two new customers in New York State. All account customers are given discounts for early payment and some preferred customers receive additional discounts. Individual customers usually pay by cash, debit or credit card and do not receive any discounts. Delivery is provided at a small charge and includes equipment setup and a brief demonstration on equipment use.

All items and services sold by the store are set up as inventory so that sales can be monitored. GST is charged on all sales and services, except to foreign customers. PST is charged on sales but not on services. The store pays GST and PST on all taxable purchases, but inventory purchased for resale in the store is exempt from PST.

The owner decided to use Simply Accounting for record keeping after a consultant prepared the report on the following pages. Reeves found an application called Hearth House in an older Simply Accounting textbook. It appeared similar in complexity and structure to Flabuless Fitness and even included complete instructions for creating the data files. Before converting the books for the store, he asked his assistant to work through this application for practice. Next she printed all the relevant business guide information and prepared the following reports to assist with the conversion on April 1, 2008:

- Income Statement
- Business Information
- Chart of Accounts
- Balance Sheet
- Post-Closing Trial Balance
- Vendor Information
- Customer Information
- Employee Information
- Inventory Information
- Accounting Procedures

MANAGER'S REPORT ON SIMPLY ACCOUNTING

PREPARED FOR FLABULESS FITNESS

1. Simply Accounting allows a business to process all source documents in a timely fashion. It can automatically prepare both single-period and comparative accounting reports for planning, decision making and controlling operations within the business.
2. The software eliminates some of the time-consuming manual clerical functions. For example, it can automatically prepare invoices, cheques and statements, and it can perform all the necessary mathematical calculations. Being freed from these chores, the accountant can extend her role to assume a much higher level of responsibility. For example, the accountant will have more time to spend analyzing reports with the owner and can work directly with the owner in making business decisions.
3. Simply Accounting can easily export reports to spreadsheets for further analysis, or link with the Internet, with other software programs and with vendors and customers for interactive data exchange. When combined with the graphing, account reconciliation and budgeting features, these reports permit the owner to analyze past trends and to make better predictions about the future behaviour of the business.
4. As the business grows, the manager can divide work more meaningfully among new accounting personnel. Since Simply Accounting provides subsidiary ledgers that are linked to control accounts in the General Ledger, it automatically coordinates accounting work performed by different individuals. Customizable window backgrounds can even accommodate mood changes of the different users.
5. Simply Accounting allows the owner to exercise business controls in a number of areas.

IN GENERAL

- Access to confidential accounting records and editing capability can be restricted to authorized personnel by using passwords.
- Mechanical errors can be virtually eliminated, since journal transactions with unequal debits and credits cannot be posted. Customer, vendor, employee, inventory and jobcost names appear in full on the journal entry input forms, making errors less likely.
- The ability to store recurring entries and look up posted invoices makes it possible to avoid errors in repeated information and to double check invoices in response to customer and vendor inquiries.
- Errors in General, Sales, Receipts, Purchases, Payments and Payroll Journal entries can be corrected as adjustments. The software automatically creates and posts the reversing entries.
- Simply Accounting provides an audit trail for all journals.
- Bank account, customer, vendor and inventory records can be set up to calculate many foreign currency transactions automatically, including import duties.
- Daily Business Manager lists and checklists provide reminders of upcoming discounts, recurring entries and routine tasks.
- Business guides, accounting advice and management reports and advice all provide helpful information for running the business.
- Simply Accounting provides a directory of customers, vendors and employees, and can create mailing labels for them.

GENERAL LEDGER

- The software provides a directory of accounts used by the business, including all linked accounts for the other ledgers in Simply Accounting.
- The information in these accounts can be used to prepare and analyze financial reports such as the Balance Sheet and Income Statement.

RECEIVABLES LEDGER

- Credit limit entries for each customer should reduce the losses from non-payment of accounts. Customers with poor payment histories can have their credit limits reduced or their credit purchase privileges removed.
- Preferred customers can be marked so that they automatically receive lower prices.
- Sales quote and order entries result in automatic Sales Journal entries when the quotes or orders are filled.
- Tax codes and accounts can be entered in the customer record so that they are automatically entered for sales when the customer is selected.
- Accounts receivable can be aged, and each customer's payment behaviour can be analyzed. This feature allows for the accurate calculation of provisions for bad debts.

PAYABLES LEDGER

- The information from the review of transactions with vendors and from the accounts payable aged analysis can be combined with detailed cash flow reports to make payment decisions. Simply Accounting helps to predict short-term cash needs in order to establish priorities for making payments and to schedule payments to vendors.
- The GST remittance or refund is calculated automatically because of the linked GST accounts in the Payables and Receivables ledgers.
- Simply Accounting purchase quote and order entries result in automatic Purchases Journal entries when quotes or orders are filled.
- The usual tax code and expense account for a vendor can be entered in the vendor record so that they are entered automatically for purchases when the vendor is selected.

PAYROLL LEDGER

- Simply Accounting maintains employee records with both personal and payment information for personnel files.
- Paycheques for several employees can be processed in a single entry with direct payroll deposit.
- Once records are set up, the program automatically withholds employee deductions including income tax, CPP (Canada Pension Plan) and EI (Employment Insurance) and is therefore less prone to error. Updated tax tables can be obtained from Sage Software, Inc.

▶

Manager's Report on Simply Accounting — Page 2

PAYROLL LEDGER CONTINUED

- Payroll summaries permit easy analysis of compulsory and optional payroll expenses and benefits, employee contributions and entitlements.
- Different kinds of income can be linked to different expense accounts. In addition, the wages for different employees can be linked to different expense accounts, again permitting better tracking of payroll expenses.
- Simply Accounting automatically links payroll with control accounts in the General Ledger. Remittance amounts are tracked and linked with the corresponding payroll authorities for monthly or quarterly remittance.

INVENTORY LEDGER

- The software provides an inventory summary or database of all inventory items.
- Services can be set up as inventory and tracked the same way as inventory items.
- Inventory reports flag items that need to be re-ordered, and the reports can be used to make purchase decisions.
- Import duty rates and different price list prices in home and foreign currencies can be set up in the ledger so they appear automatically in the journals.
- Inventory codes can be matched to the vendor and customer item codes so that common order forms are created automatically.
- The software calculates inventory variance costs when the items sold are out of stock and later purchased at different prices.
- Simply Accounting automatically updates inventory records when inventory is purchased, sold, transferred, lost, recovered or returned. It warns when you try to oversell inventory.
- Different units for stocking, selling and buying items can be saved for inventory items so that prices are automatically entered correctly for both sales and purchases. Reports can be prepared for any of the units on record.
- Inventory tracking reports can monitor sales and purchase activity on individual inventory items to see which ones are selling well and which are not. These reports can be used to determine optimum inventory buying patterns to reduce storage costs.

6. In summation, Simply Accounting provides an integrated management accounting information system.

INCOME STATEMENT

FLABULESS FITNESS

January 1 to March 31, 2008

Revenue			
4000	GENERAL REVENUE		
4020	Revenue from Sales	$78 450.00	
4040	Revenue from Services	8 335.00	
4060	Sales Discounts	–965.00	
4100	Net Sales		$85 820.00
4120	Exchange Rate Differences		–12.00
4150	Interest Revenue		1 980.00
4180	Sales Tax Compensation		248.00
4200	Freight Revenue		379.00
4390	TOTAL GENERAL REVENUE		$88 415.00
TOTAL REVENUE			$88 415.00
Expense			
5000	OPERATING EXPENSES		
5010	Advertising and Promotion		$ 530.00
5020	Bank Charges		128.00
5030	Credit Card Fees		1 480.00
5040	Damaged Inventory	$ 80.00	
5050	Cost of Goods Sold: Accessories	5 395.00	
5060	Cost of Goods Sold: Equipment	3 149.00	
5070	Cost Variance	64.00	
5080	Freight Expense	432.00	
5090	Purchase Discounts	–524.00	
5100	Purchases Returns & Allowances	–367.00	
5110	Net Cost of Goods Sold		8 229.00
5120	Depreciation: Cash Registers	300.00	
5130	Depreciation: Computer Equipment	150.00	
5140	Depreciation: Furniture & Fixtures	80.00	
5150	Depreciation: Retail Premises	2 440.00	
5160	Depreciation: Van	190.00	
5180	Net Depreciation		3 160.00
5190	Delivery Expense		63.00
5200	Hydro Expense		528.00
5210	Insurance Expense		1 200.00
5220	Interest on Loan		1 240.00
5230	Interest on Mortgage		5 600.00
5240	Maintenance of Premises		1 055.00
5250	Supplies Used		165.00
5260	Property Taxes		2 700.00
5270	Uncollectable Accounts Expense		500.00
5280	Telephone Expense		295.00
5285	Van Maintenance & Operating Expense		638.00
5290	TOTAL OPERATING EXPENSES		$27 511.00
5295	PAYROLL EXPENSES		
5300	Wages		8 295.20
5305	Salaries		22 800.00
5310	Commissions & Bonuses		284.80
5320	EI Expense		998.00
5330	CPP Expense		1 201.00
5340	WSIB Expense		379.00
5360	EHT Expense		309.00
5370	Gp Insurance Expense		105.00
5490	TOTAL PAYROLL EXPENSES		$34 372.00
TOTAL EXPENSE			$61 883.00
NET INCOME			$26 532.00

BUSINESS INFORMATION

FLABULESS FITNESS

COMPANY INFORMATION
Address 199 Warmup Rd., Unit 500
Hamilton, Ontario L8T 3B7
Tel 1 (905) 642-2348 (B-FIT)
Tel 2 (800) 448-2348 (B-FIT)
Fax (905) 642-9100
Industry Retail
Business No. 245 138 121
Business Province: Ontario

FISCAL DATES
Fiscal Start 04-01-2008
Earliest Transaction 04-01-2008
Fiscal End 06-30-2008

PRINTER: for __________

NAMES: EMPLOYEE
Field 1 Emergency Contact
Field 2 Contact Number

NAMES: PAYROLL
Income 1 Salary
Income 2 Commission
Income 3 No. Clients
Income 4 Bonus
Income 5 Tuition
Income 6 Travel Exp
Deduction 1 RRSP
Deduction 2 CSB Plan
User Expense 1 Gp Insurance
Entitlement 1 Vacation
Entitlement 2 Sick Leave
Entitlement 3 PersonalDays
Prov. Tax Not applicable

NAMES: TRANSACTIONS
Additional Field: Number

USER PREFERENCE SETUP CHANGES
Use Accounting Terms
Automatically save changes to records

USER PREFERENCE VIEW CHANGES
Daily Business Manager Turned off
Checklists Turned off

SYSTEM SETTINGS CHANGES
Warn if accounts not balanced
Backup Semi-monthly
Display a backup reminder

FORMS SETTINGS (NEXT NUMBER)
Sales Invoices No. 3000
Sales Quotes No. 41
Receipts No. 39
Customer Deposits No. 15
Purchase Orders No. 25
Direct Deposits No. 19

DATE FORMAT SETTINGS
Use Long Dates on the screen

GENERAL SETTINGS No changes

PAYABLES SETTINGS
Aging periods: 15, 30, 60 days
Discounts before tax: Yes

IMPORT DUTY
Track import duty
Linked account: 2220

RECEIVABLES SETTINGS
Aging periods: 10, 30, 60 days
Interest charges: 1.5% after 30 days
Statements include invoices for 31 days
Payment terms: 2/10, n/30
Discounts before tax: No
Use code GP for new customers

COMMENTS
On Sales Invoice Interest @ 1.5% per month charged on accounts over 30 days.

PAYROLL SETTINGS

Income	Type	Taxable	Vac. Pay
Regular	Income	Yes	Yes
Overtime 1	Income	Yes	Yes
Salary	Income	Yes	No
Commission	Income	Yes	No
Bonus	Income	Yes	No
No. Clients	Piece Rate	Yes	Yes
Tuition	Income	Yes	No
Travel Exp	Reimburse.	No	No

EI factor 1.4
EHT factor 0.98
WSIB rate 1.29

PAYROLL DEDUCTION SETTINGS
RRSP Before tax, after other deductions
CSB Plan After tax and other deductions

PAYROLL ENTITLEMENTS SETTINGS

Name	Track %	Max Days	Clear
Vacation	8.0%	25	No
Sick Leave	5.0%	15	No
PersonalDays	2.5%	5	No

PAYROLL REMITTANCE SETTINGS

Payroll Liability	Payroll Authority
EI, CPP, Income Tax	Receiver General
EHT, PST	Minister of Finance
WSIB	Workplace Safety & Insurance Board
Gp Insurance, RRSP	Ancaster Insurance
CSB	Mt. Hope Investment

INVENTORY SETTINGS
Profit evaluation by markup
Sort inventory by number
Allow inventory levels to go below zero
Foreign prices from inventory records

FOREIGN CURRENCY
USD United States Dollars
Tracking Account 4120
Exchange Rate on 04/01/08 1.1851

BANK ACCOUNT AND CLASS SETTINGS
Bank
1060 Bank: Hamilton Trust Chequing (CAD)
Next cheque no. 101
Next deposit no. 14
1080 Bank: Hamilton Trust Savings (CAD)
1140 Bank: USD Chequing (USD)
Next cheque no. 346
Cash
1030 Undeposited Cash and Cheques
Credit Card Receivable
1100 Bank: MasterCard
1120 Bank: Visa and Interac
Credit Card Payable
2250 Credit Card Payable

CREDIT CARD INFORMATION

Accept	Visa	MasterCard	Interac
Fee	2.5%	2.7%	0%
Expense	5030	5030	5030
Asset	1120	1100	1120

Use Visa
Payable 2250 Expense 5030

SALES TAXES

Tax	ID on forms	Track: Purch	Sales
GST	245 138 121	2670	2650
PST			2640

	Taxable?	Exempt?	Report?
GST	No	No	Yes
PST	No	No	Yes

Tax Codes:
G: GST, taxable, 7%, not included, refundable
GP: GST, taxable, 7%, not included, refundable
PST, taxable, 8% not included, not refundable
IN: GST, taxable, 7%, included, refundable
PST, taxable, 8%, included, not refundable

JOB CATEGORIES
Sales: employees are salespersons
All employees are in Sales category

CHART OF ACCOUNTS

FLABULESS FITNESS

ASSETS

1000 CURRENT ASSETS [H]
1010 Test Balance Account
1030 Undeposited Cash and Cheques [A]
1060 Bank: Hamilton Trust Chequing [A]
1080 Bank: Hamilton Trust Savings [A]
1100 Bank: MasterCard [A]
1120 Bank: Visa and Interac [A]
1140 Bank: USD Chequing [A]
1150 Net Bank [S]
1200 Accounts Receivable [A]
1210 Allowance for Doubtful Accounts [A]
1220 Advances Receivable [A]
1230 Interest Receivable [A]
1240 Net Receivables [S]
1250 Purchase Prepayments
1260 Office Supplies
1265 Linen Supplies
1270 Prepaid Advertising
1280 Prepaid Insurance
1300 TOTAL CURRENT ASSETS [T]

1500 INVENTORY ASSETS [H]
1520 Accessories
1540 Fitness Equipment
1580 TOTAL INVENTORY ASSETS [T]

1600 CENTRE & EQUIPMENT [H]
1610 Cash Registers [A]
1620 Accum Deprec: Cash Registers [A]
1630 Net Cash Registers [S]
1640 Computer Equipment [A]
1650 Accum Deprec: Computer Equipment [A]
1660 Net Computer Equipment [S]
1670 Furniture & Fixtures [A]
1680 Accum Deprec: Furniture & Fixtures [A]
1690 Net Furniture & Fixtures [S]
1700 Retail Premises [A]
1710 Accum Deprec: Retail Premises [A]
1720 Net Retail Premises [S]
1730 Van [A]
1740 Accum Deprec: Van [A]
1750 Net Van [S]
1890 TOTAL CENTRE & EQUIPMENT [T] ▶

▶LIABILITIES

2000 CURRENT LIABILITIES [H]
2100 Bank Loan
2200 Accounts Payable
2210 Prepaid Sales and Deposits
2220 Import Duty Payable
2250 Credit Card Payable
2300 Vacation Payable
2310 EI Payable [A]
2320 CPP Payable [A]
2330 Income Tax Payable [A]
2350 Receiver General Payable [S]
2380 EHT Payable
2400 RRSP Payable
2410 CSB Plan Payable
2420 Group Insurance Payable
2460 WSIB Payable
2500 Business Income Tax Payable
2640 PST Payable
2650 GST Charged on Sales [A]
2670 GST Paid on Purchases [A]
2750 GST Owing (Refund) [S]
2790 TOTAL CURRENT LIABILITIES [T]

2800 LONG TERM LIABILITIES [H]
2820 Mortgage Payable
2890 TOTAL LONG TERM LIABILITIES [T]

EQUITY

3000 OWNER'S EQUITY [H]
3560 S. Reeves, Capital
3600 Current Earnings [X]
3690 TOTAL OWNER'S EQUITY [T]

REVENUE

4000 GENERAL REVENUE [H]
4020 Revenue from Sales [A]
4040 Revenue from Services [A]
4060 Sales Discounts [A]
4100 Net Sales [S]
4120 Exchange Rate Differences
4150 Interest Revenue
4180 Sales Tax Compensation
4200 Freight Revenue
4390 TOTAL GENERAL REVENUE [T] ▶

▶EXPENSE

5000 OPERATING EXPENSES [H]
5010 Advertising and Promotion
5020 Bank Charges
5030 Credit Card Fees
5040 Damaged Inventory [A]
5050 Cost of Goods Sold: Accessories [A]
5060 Cost of Goods Sold: Equipment [A]
5065 Cost of Services [A]
5070 Cost Variance [A]
5080 Freight Expense [A]
5090 Purchase Discounts [A]
5100 Purchases Returns & Allowances [A]
5110 Net Cost of Goods Sold [S]
5120 Depreciation: Cash Registers [A]
5130 Depreciation: Computer Equipment [A]
5140 Depreciation: Furniture & Fixtures [A]
5150 Depreciation: Retail Premises [A]
5160 Depreciation: Van [A]
5180 Net Depreciation [S]
5190 Delivery Expense
5200 Hydro Expense
5210 Insurance Expense
5220 Interest on Loan
5230 Interest on Mortgage
5240 Maintenance of Premises
5250 Supplies Used
5260 Property Taxes
5270 Uncollectable Accounts Expense
5280 Telephone Expense
5285 Van Maintenance & Operating Expense
5290 TOTAL OPERATING EXPENSES [T]

5295 PAYROLL EXPENSES [H]
5300 Wages
5305 Salaries
5310 Commissions & Bonuses
5320 Travel Expenses
5330 EI Expense
5340 CPP Expense
5350 WSIB Expense
5360 EHT Expense
5370 Gp Insurance Expense
5380 Employee Benefits
5490 TOTAL PAYROLL EXPENSES [T]

NOTES: The Chart of Accounts includes all accounts and Net Income. Group account types are not marked. Other account types are marked as follows: [H] Heading, [A] subgroup Account, [S] Subgroup total, [T] Total, [X] Current Earnings.

BALANCE SHEET

FLABULESS FITNESS

March 31, 2008

Assets

1000	CURRENT ASSETS		
1060	Bank: Hamilton Trust Chequing	$ 77 988.00	
1080	Bank: Hamilton Trust Savings	108 250.00	
1100	Bank: MasterCard	3 975.00	
1120	Bank: Visa and Interac	4 650.00	
1140	Bank: USD (8 020 USD)	9 500.00	
1150	Net Bank		$204 363.00
1200	Accounts Receivable	17 250.00	
1210	Allowance for Doubtful Accounts	–800.00	
1220	Advances Receivable	100.00	
1230	Interest Receivable	420.00	
1250	Net Receivables		16 970.00
1260	Office Supplies		300.00
1265	Linen Supplies		450.00
1270	Prepaid Advertising		180.00
1280	Prepaid Insurance		4 800.00
1300	TOTAL CURRENT ASSETS		$227 063.00
1500	INVENTORY ASSETS		
1520	Accessories		15 280.00
1540	Fitness Equipment		78 616.00
1580	TOTAL INVENTORY ASSETS		$93 896.00
1600	CENTRE & EQUIPMENT		
1610	Cash Registers	5 000.00	
1620	Accum Deprec: Cash Registers	–1 000.00	
1630	Net Cash Registers		4 000.00
1640	Computer Equipment	3 000.00	
1650	Accum Deprec: Computer Equip	–1 000.00	
1660	Net Computer Equipment		2 000.00
1670	Furniture & Fixtures	2 000.00	
1680	Accum Deprec: Furn & Fixtures	–400.00	
1690	Net Furniture & Fixtures		1 600.00
1700	Retail Premises	200 000.00	
1710	Accum Deprec: Retail Premises	–5 000.00	
1720	Net Retail Premises		195 000.00
1730	Van	30 000.00	
1740	Accum Deprec: Van	–5 000.00	
1750	Net Van		25 000.00
1890	TOTAL CENTRE & EQUIPMENT		$227 600.00
	TOTAL ASSETS		$548 559.00 ▶

Liabilities

▶ 2000	CURRENT LIABILITIES		
2100	Bank Loan		$ 50 000.00
2200	Accounts Payable		17 120.00
2250	Credit Card Payable		220.00
2300	Vacation Payable		371.84
2310	EI Payable	$ 563.28	
2320	CPP Payable	824.77	
2330	Income Tax Payable	1 755.60	
2350	Receiver General Payable		3 143.65
2380	EHT Payable		320.50
2400	RRSP Payable		350.00
2410	CSB Plan Payable		350.00
2420	Group Insurance Payable		39.00
2460	WSIB Payable		392.51
2500	Business Income Tax Payable		3 600.00
2640	PST Payable		2 470.00
2650	GST Charged on Sales	2 940.00	
2670	GST Paid on Purchases	–1 260.00	
2750	GST Owing (Refund)		1 680.00
2790	TOTAL CURRENT LIABILITIES		$80 057.50
2800	LONG TERM LIABILITIES		
2820	Mortgage Payable		180 000.00
2890	TOTAL LONG TERM LIABILITIES		$180 000.00
	TOTAL LIABILITIES		$260 057.50

Equity

3000	OWNER'S EQUITY	
3560	S. Reeves, Capital	$261 969.50
3600	Current Earnings	26 532.00
3690	TOTAL OWNER'S EQUITY	$288 501.50
	TOTAL EQUITY	$288 501.50
	LIABILITIES AND EQUITY	$548 559.00

POST-CLOSING TRIAL BALANCE

FLABULESS FITNESS

March 31, 2008

		Debits	Credits
1060	Bank: Hamilton Trust Chequing	$ 77 988.00	
1080	Bank: Hamilton Trust Savings	108 250.00	
1100	Bank: MasterCard	3 975.00	
1120	Bank: Visa and Interac	4 650.00	
1140	Bank: USD Chequing (8 020 USD)	9 500.00	
1200	Accounts Receivable	17 250.00	
1210	Allowance for Doubtful Accounts		$ 800.00
1220	Advances Receivable	100.00	
1230	Interest Receivable	420.00	
1260	Office Supplies	300.00	
1265	Linen Supplies	450.00	
1270	Prepaid Advertising	180.00	
1280	Prepaid Insurance	4 800.00	
1520	Accessories	15 280.00	
1540	Fitness Equipment	78 616.00	
1610	Cash Registers	5 000.00	
1620	Accum Deprec: Cash Registers		1 000.00
1640	Computer Equipment	3 000.00	
1650	Accum Deprec: Computer Equipment		1 000.00
1670	Furniture & Fixtures	2 000.00	
1680	Accum Deprec: Furniture & Fixtures		400.00
1700	Retail Premises	200 000.00	
1710	Accum Deprec: Retail Premises		5 000.00 ▶
▶ 1730	Van	30 000.00	
1740	Accum Deprec: Van		5 000.00
2100	Bank Loan		50 000.00
2200	Accounts Payable		17 120.00
2250	Credit Card Payable		220.00
2300	Vacation Payable		371.84
2310	EI Payable		563.28
2320	CPP Payable		824.77
2330	Income Tax Payable		1 755.60
2380	EHT Payable		320.50
2400	RRSP Payable		350.00
2410	CSB Plan Payable		350.00
2420	Group Insurance Payable		39.00
2460	WSIB Payable		392.51
2500	Business Income Tax Payable		3 600.00
2640	PST Payable		2 470.00
2650	GST Charged on Sales		2 940.00
2670	GST Paid on Purchases	1 260.00	
2820	Mortgage Payable		180 000.00
3560	S. Reeves, Capital		288 501.50
		$563 019.00	$563 019.00

VENDOR INFORMATION

FLABULESS FITNESS

Vendor Name (Contact)	Address	Phone No. Fax No.	E-mail Web Site	Terms Tax ID	Expense Acct Tax Code
Ancaster Insurance (Feulle Cuvver)	718 Montgomery Dr. Ancaster, ON L9G 3H5	Tel: (905) 588-1773 Fax: (905) 588-1624	fc@ancaster.insur.ca www.ancaster.insur.ca	net 1	no tax (not exempt)
Bell Canada (Noel Coller)	100 James St. N. Hamilton, ON L8R 2K5	Tel: (905) 525-2355	www.bell.ca	net 1	5280 GP
City of Hamilton Treasurer (Budd Jett)	53 Main St. W. Hamilton, ON L8P 2Z3	Tel: (905) 461-0063 Fax: (905) 461-9204	www.hamilton.city.ca	net 1	5260 no tax (exempt)
Energy Source (Manny Watts)	91 NacNab St. Hamilton, ON L8R 2L9	Tel: (905) 463-2664	watts@energysource.ca www.energysource.ca	net 1	5200 G
Feelyte Gym Accessories (Stretch Theraband)	7 Onondaga Dr. Ancaster, ON L9G 4S5	Tel: (905) 588-3846 Fax: (905) 588-7126	stretch@feelyte.com www.feelyte.com	2/10, n/30 (before tax) 466 254 108	G
Footlink Corporation (Onna Treadmill)	39 Treadwell St. Oakville, ON L6M 3K9	Tel: (905) 777-8133 Fax: (905) 777-8109	onna@footlink.com www.footlink.com	1/15, n/30 (before tax) 274 309 481	G
Hamilton Spectator (Dawn Newsman)	15 Wentworth St. N. Hamilton, ON L8L 5T8	Tel: (905) 525-1800 Fax: (905) 525-1816	newsman@spectator.ca www.spectator.ca	net 10	1270 GP
Minister of Finance (N.O. Money)	631 Queenston Rd. Hamilton, ON L8K 6R5	Tel: (905) 462-5555	www.gov.on.ca/fin	net 1	no tax (exempt)
Mt. Hope Investment Corp. (P. Cuniary)	122 King St. W. Hamilton, ON L8P 4V2	Tel: (905) 462-3338 Fax: (905) 461-2116	pc@mt.hope.invest.ca www.mt.hope.invest.ca	net 15	2410 no tax (exempt)

▶

Vendor Name (Contact)	Address	Phone No. Fax No.	E-mail Web Site	Terms Tax ID	Expense Acct Tax Code
Prolife Exercisers Inc. (C. Glider) (USD vendor)	1500 Redmond Road Suite 100, Woodinville Washington 98072 USA	Tel: (509) 628-9163 Fax: (509) 629-7164	glider@prolife.ex.com www.prolife.ex.com	2/10, n/30 (before tax)	G
Receiver General for Canada	Sudbury Tax Services Office PO Box 20004 Sudbury, ON P3A 6B4	Tel 1: (800) 561-7761 Tel 2: (800) 959-2221	www.cra-arc.gc.ca	net 1	no tax (exempt)
Redux Home Gym Wholesalers (Bi Sepps) (USD vendor)	4900 Columbia St., #650 El Cerrito, California 94533 USA	Tel 1: (510) 525-4327 Tel 2: (800) 567-9152 Fax: (510) 526-1135	bisepps@redux.com www.redux.com	2/10, n/30 (after tax)	G
Scandia Weights Co. (B. Fitt)	82 Nordica Lane Hamilton, ON L8P 2G6	Tel: (905) 465-6247 Fax: (905) 466-3554	fitt@scandiawts.com www.scandiawts.com	net 30 372 640 813	G
Trufit Depot (Varry Shapely)	43 Paling Ave. Hamilton, ON L8H 5J5	Tel: (905) 529-7235 Fax: (905) 529-2995	shapely@trufitdepot.ca www.trufitdepot.ca	2/5, n/30 (before tax) 244 573 650	G
Waterdown Sunoco (Mick Annick)	101 Niska Dr. Waterdown, ON L0R 2H3	Tel: (905) 622-6181 Fax: (905) 622-4777	mick@goodforcars.com www.goodforcars.com	net 1	5285 IN
Westdale Office Supplies (Clip Papers)	26 Dalewood Ave. Hamilton, ON L8S 1Y7	Tel: (905) 528-8199 Fax: (905) 528-8221	papers@wos.com www.wos.com	net 30 259 491 820	1260 GP
Workplace Safety & Insurance Board (I.M. Hurt)	PO Box 2099 Hamilton, ON L8N 4C5	Tel: (800) 525-9100 Fax: (905) 523-1824	www.wsib.on.ca	net 1	2460 no tax (exempt)

NOTES: Year-to-date purchases and payments are not recorded because this is a new fiscal period.

OUTSTANDING VENDOR INVOICES

FLABULESS FITNESS

Vendor Name	Terms	Date	Inv/Chq No.	Amount	Tax	Total
Feelyte Gym Accessories	2/10, n/30 (before tax)	Mar. 30/08	FG-1611	$1 000	$70	$1 070
Footlink Corporation	1/15, n/30 (before tax)	Mar. 20/08	FC-618	$10 000	$700	$10 700
		Mar. 21/08	Chq 96	2 140		2 140
			Balance Owing			$8 560
Redux Home Gym Wholesalers	2/10, n/30 (after tax)	Mar. 28/08	R-914	$6 345 USD	@1.1805	$7 490 CAD
				Grand Total		$17 120

CUSTOMER INFORMATION

FLABULESS FITNESS

Customer Name (Contact)	Address	Phone No. Fax No.	E-mail Web Site	Terms Tax Code	Credit Limit
*Buffalo Health Clinic (Minnie Mussle)	75 Brawn Ave. Buffalo, New York 14202 USA	Tel: (716) 367-7346 Fax: (716) 367-8258	mmussle@buffalohealth.com www.buffalohealth.com Currency: USD	2/10, n/30 no tax	$12 000 ($10 500 USD)
*Chedoke Health Care (Wade Less)	13 Wellspring Dr. Hamilton, ON L8T 3B8	Tel: (905) 526-3344 Fax: (905) 525-1166	less@chedoke.healthcare.ca www.chedoke.healthcare.ca	2/10, n/30 GP	$12 000
Dundas Recreational Centre (X.S. Wayte)	190 Playtime Circle Dundas, ON L8C 2V8	Tel: (905) 466-5576 Fax: (905) 466-7284	xswayte@dundas.reccentre.ca www.dundas.reccentre.ca	2/10, n/30 GP	$12 000
Hamilton District Bd of Education (Nott Skinny)	10 James St. S. Hamilton, ON L8K 4G2	Tel: (905) 461-5997 Fax: (905) 461-6936	nskinny@hdsb.ca www.hdsb.ca	2/10, n/30 GP	$12 000

Customer Name (Contact)	Address	Phone No. Fax No.	E-mail Web Site	Terms Tax Code	Credit Limit
Lockport Gymnasium (B. Phatt)	62 Sweats St. Niagara Falls, New York 14301 USA	Tel: (716) 399-1489 Fax: (716) 399-2735	phatt@lockportgym.com www.lockportgym.com Currency: USD	2/10, n/30 no tax	$12 000 ($10 500 USD)
*McMaster University (Outov Shape)	Kinesiology Dept. McMaster University Hamilton, ON L8V 3M9	Tel 1: (905) 529-3000 Tel 2: (905) 529-3198 Fax: (905) 529- 3477	oshape@mcmasteru.ca www.mcmasteru.ca	2/10, n/30 GP	$12 000
*Mohawk College (Phat Nomore)	Physical Education Dept. Mohawk College Hamilton, ON L8F 7F2	Tel 1: (905) 622-9250 Tel 2: (905) 622-9238 Fax: (905) 622-9729	nomore@mohawkcoll.ca www.mohawkcoll.ca	2/10, n/30 GP	$12 000
*Stelco Health Club (Les Pound)	1 Stelco Rd. Hamilton, ON L8P 6N6	Tel: (905) 524-1000 Fax: (905) 524-1924	pound@stelco.health.com www.stelco.health.com	2/10, n/30 GP	$12 000
Stoney Creek Sports Arena (B. Thin)	93 Workout Rd. Stoney Creek, ON L7M 5C7	Tel: (905) 838-1800 Fax: (905) 838-1278	bthin@scsa.com www.scsa.com	2/10, n/30 GP	$12 000
Cash and Interac Customers				net 1	GP
MasterCard Sales (for MasterCard customers)				net 1	GP
Visa Sales (for Visa customers)				net 1	GP

NOTES: Preferred price list customers are marked with an asterisk (*). The Ship-to address is the same as the mailing address for all customers.

OUTSTANDING CUSTOMER INVOICES

FLABULESS FITNESS

Customer Name	Terms	Date	Inv/Chq No.	Amount	Total
Chedoke Health Care	2/10, n/30 (after tax)	Mar. 30/08	2199	$9 200	
		Mar. 30/08	Chq 488	2 300	
			Balance Owing		$6 900
Mohawk College	2/10, n/30 (after tax)	Mar. 26/08	2194	$5 750	$5 750
Stoney Creek Sports Arena	2/10, n/30 (after tax)	Mar. 23/08	2191	$4 600	$4 600
				Grand Total	$17 250

EMPLOYEE INFORMATION SHEET

FLABULESS FITNESS

Employee	George Schwinn	Nieve Prekor	Assumpta Kisangel
Position	Shipping/Trainer	Sales/Yoga Instructor	Sales/Accounting
Address	55 Carter St. Hamilton, ON L8B 2V7	2 Meditation Circle Hamilton, ON L8B 7C1	300 Track Rd. Hamilton, ON L9G 4K8
Telephone	(905) 426-1817	(905) 527-4412	(905) 688-5778
Social Insurance No.	532 548 625	783 455 611	488 655 333
Date of Birth (mm-dd-yy)	09/18/69	03/15/72	05/24/75
Date of Hire (mm-dd-yy)	01/06/03	02/15/00	08/25/03
Federal (Ontario) Tax Exemption - TD1			
Basic Personal	$9 039 (8 377)	$9 039 (8 377)	$9 039 (8 377)
Spousal	–	–	$7 675 (7 113)
Other	–	–	$3 933 (3 948)
Total Exemptions	$9 039 (8 377)	$9 039 (8 377)	$20 647 (19 438)
Additional Federal Tax	–	$50.00	–

Employee	George Schwinn	Nieve Prekor	Assumpta Kisangel
Employee Taxes			
Historical Income tax	$1 562.21	$2 392.08	$1 537.85
Historical EI	$217.54	$270.00	$248.96
Historical CPP	$375.20	$478.38	$438.16
Deduct EI; EI Factor	Yes; 1.4	Yes; 1.4	Yes; 1.4
Deduct CPP	Yes	Yes	Yes
Employee Income			
Advances: Historical Amount	$100.00	(use) ✓	(use) ✓
Benefits Per Period	$5.00	$12.00	$12.00
Benefits: Historical Amount	$35.00	$36.00	$36.00
Vacation Pay Owed	$371.84	(do not use)	(do not use)
Vacation Paid	$385.92	(do not use)	(do not use)
Regular Wage Rate (Hours per Period)	$16.00/hr (80 hours)	(do not use)	(do not use)
Regular Wages: Historical Amount	$8 960.00	(do not use)	(do not use)
Overtime 1 Wage Rate	$24.00/hr	(do not use)	(do not use)
Overtime 1 Wages: Historical Amount	$336.00	(do not use)	(do not use)
Salary (Hours Per Period)	(do not use)	$4 000.00 (150 Hours)	$3 600.00 (150 hours)
Salary: Historical Amount	(do not use)	$12 000.00	$10 800.00
Commission	(do not use)	(do not use)	(use) ✓ 2% (service revenue)
Commissions: Historical Amount	(do not use)	(do not use)	$284.80
No. Clients (piece rate)	$10	$10	$10
Bonus:	(use) ✓	(use) ✓	(use) ✓
Tuition: Historical Amount	(use) ✓	(use) ✓	$440
Travel Exp.: Historical Amount	(use) ✓	$120.00	(use) ✓
Pay Periods	26	12	12
Vacation Rate	6% retained	0% not retained	0% not retained
Record Wage Expenses in	Linked Accounts	Linked Accounts	Linked Accounts
Deductions			
RRSP (Historical Amount)	$50.00 ($350.00)	$100.00 ($300.00)	$100.00 ($300.00)
CSB Plan (Historical Amount)	$50.00 ($350.00)	$100.00 ($300.00)	$100.00 ($300.00)
WSIB and Other Expenses			
WSIB Rate	1.29	1.29	1.02
Group Insurance (Historical Amount)	$5.00 ($35.00)	$12.00 ($36.00)	$12.00 ($36.00)
Entitlements: Rate, Maximum Days, Clear? (Historical Amount)			
Vacation	–	8%, 25 days, No (15)	8%, 25 days, No (15)
Sick Leave	5%, 15 days, No (12)	5%, 15 days, No (10)	5%, 15 days, No (8)
Personal Days	2.5%, 5 days, No (4)	2.5%, 5 days, No (2)	2.5%, 5 days, No (3)
Direct Deposit			
Yes/No	Yes	Yes	Yes
Bank, Transit, Account No.	102, 89008, 2998187	102, 89008, 3829110	102, 89008, 2309982
Percent	100%	100%	100%
Additional Information			
Emergency Contact & Number	Adrian Ingles (905) 722-0301	Alex Prekor (905) 548-2973	Martha Kisangel (905) 688-5778
T4 and RL-1 Reporting			
EI Insurable Earnings	$9 681.92	$12 000.00	$10 800.00
Pensionable Earnings	$9 681.92	$12 000.00	$10 800.00
Withheld	$2 854.95	$3 740.46	$2 824.97
Net Pay	$6 926.97	$8 379.54	$8 699.83

Employee Profiles and TD1 Information

All Employees Flabuless Fitness pays group insurance premiums for all employees. They also are reimbursed for tuition fees when they successfully complete a university or college course. These benefits are both taxable. In addition, when they use their personal vehicles for company business, they are reimbursed for car expenses.

All employees are entitled to three weeks' vacation, ten days' sick leave and five personal days of leave per year. All three employees have sick leave and personal days that they can carry forward from the previous year. The two salaried employees take three weeks' vacation as paid time and the hourly employee receives 6 percent of his wages as vacation pay when he takes his vacation.

As an incentive to provide excellent customer service, all employees receive a quarterly bonus of $10 for every completed satisfactory customer survey.

George Schwinn is responsible for shipping, receiving, delivery and equipment setup for customers. He also works as the personal trainer in the store. He is single so he uses only the basic tax claim amount. Every two weeks his pay, at the rate of $16 per hour, is deposited to his account. For the hours beyond 40 hours in a week, he receives an overtime rate of $24 per hour. He is owed three months of vacation pay. He contributes to his RRSP and Canada Savings Bond plan through payroll deductions. He still owes $100 from an advance of $200 and will pay back $50 of the advance in each of the next two pay periods.

Nieve Prekor is the store manager and yoga instructor for Flabuless Fitness, and she assists with store sales. Her monthly salary of $4 000 is deposited directly into her bank account. Prekor is married with one child but uses the basic single claim amount because her husband is also employed. Her payroll deductions include additional federal income tax for other income and regular contributions to her Registered Retirement Savings Plan and Canada Savings Bonds.

Assumpta Kisangel does the accounting and manages the Payables, Receivables and Payroll in addition to sales in the store. Although she is single, she supports her infirm mother so she has the spousal equivalent claim and a caregiver amount in addition to the basic single claim amount. A commission of 2 percent of revenue from services supplements her monthly salary of $3 600 that is deposited directly into her bank account. She has RRSP and CSB contributions withheld from her paycheques.

INVENTORY INFORMATION

FLABULESS FITNESS

Code	Description	Min Stock	CAD Prices Reg	CAD Prices (Pref)	USD Prices Reg.	USD Prices (Pref)	Stock/Sell Unit	Buying Unit	Relationship	Qty on Hand	Total (Cost)
Accessories: Total asset value $15 280 (Linked Accounts: Asset 1520; Revenue 4020, COGS 5050, Variance 5070)											
A010	Body Fat Scale	2	$ 100	($ 90)	$ 85	($ 77)	unit	carton	12/carton	10	$ 400
A020	Dumbbells: Round pair	25	1.20	(1.10)	1.00	(0.90)	kg	100kg	100/100kg	400	250
A030	Dumbbells: Hexagonal pair	25	1.50	(1.40)	1.30	(1.20)	kg	100kg	100/100kg	400	300
A040	Dumbbells: 5kg set	5	15	(13)	13	(12)	set		same	25	150
A050	Dumbbells: 10kg set	5	25	(22)	21	(19)	set		same	25	250
A060	Dumbbells: 15kg set	5	40	(36)	34	(31)	set		same	25	400
A070	Glide Slidetrak	3	50	(45)	42	(38)	each		same	20	500
A080	Heart Rate Monitor	2	75	(68)	63	(57)	unit	box	12/box	10	300
A090	Power Blocks up to 100 kg	3	160	(144)	134	(121)	set		same	10	800
A100	Power Blocks up to 200 kg	3	300	(270)	260	(236)	set		same	10	1500

▶

Code	Description	Min Stock	CAD Reg	Prices (Pref)	USD Reg.	Prices (Pref)	Stock/Sell Unit	Buying Unit	Relationship	Qty on Hand	Total (Cost)
Accessories: Continued											
A110	Stability Balls	5	$ 10	($ 9)	$ 9	($ 8)	each		same	25	100
A120	Wavemaster	2	150	(135)	130	(119)	unit		same	10	750
A130	Weight Plates	25	1.20	(1.10)	1.00	(0.90)	kg	100kg	100/100kg	400	240
A140	Weights: Olympic 75 kg	5	150	(135)	132	(119)	set		same	20	1 500
A150	Weights: Olympic 100 kg	5	200	(180)	170	(151)	set		same	20	2 000
A160	Weights: Olympic 125 kg	5	250	(225)	210	(190)	set		same	20	$ 2 500
A170	Weights: Olympic 150 kg	5	300	(270)	260	(232)	set		same	20	3 000
A180	Workout Gloves: all sizes	5	10	(9)	9	(8)	pair	box	10/box	25	100
A190	Yoga Mats	3	30	(27)	26	(24)	unit	box	10/box	20	240
Equipment: Fitness: Total asset value $78 616 (Linked Accounts: Asset 1540; Revenue 4020, COGS 5060, Variance 5070)											
Elliptical Exercisers											
E010	Elliptical Exerciser: ME-100	2	1 100	(1 000)	925	(830)	unit		same	5	2 200
E020	Elliptical Exerciser: AE-200	2	1 700	(1 550)	1 430	(1 285)	unit		same	5	3 400
E030	Elliptical Exerciser: DE-300	2	2 000	(1 875)	1 680	(1 512)	unit		same	5	4 000
E040	Elliptical Exerciser: LE-400	2	2 200	(2 000)	1 850	(1 663)	unit		same	5	4 400
Exercise Bicycles											
E050	Bicycle: Calorie Counter CC-60	2	400	(360)	336	(302)	unit		same	10	1 600
E060	Bicycle: Dual Action DA-70	2	600	(540)	505	(455)	unit		same	10	2 400
E070	Bicycle: Recumbent R-80	2	750	(680)	630	(567)	unit		same	10	3 000
Exercise Equipment: Home Gyms											
E080	Home Gym: Basic HG-1400	2	1 000	(900)	840	(755)	set		same	5	$2 000
E090	Home Gym: Deluxe HG-1401	2	1 500	(1 400)	1 310	(1 180)	set		same	5	3 000
E100	Home Gym: Multi HG-1402	2	2 000	(1 875)	1 680	(1 512)	set		same	5	4 000
Riders, Walkers and Rowing Machines											
E110	Rider: Airwalker RA-900	3	300	(270)	265	(237)	unit		same	8	960
E120	Rider: Powerglider RP-1500	3	350	(315)	305	(275)	unit		same	8	1 120
E130	Rowing Machine: RM-1000	3	480	(435)	400	(360)	unit		same	8	1 536
Ski Exercisers											
E140	Ski Exerciser: Skitrek SE-680	3	400	(360)	335	(302)	unit		same	10	1 600
E150	Ski Exerciser: Linked SE-780	3	450	(410)	380	(340)	unit		same	10	1 800
E160	Ski Exerciser: Independent SE-880	3	600	(550)	505	(455)	unit		same	10	2 400
Stair Climbers											
E170	Stair Climber: Adjustable SC-A60	2	1 500	(1 375)	1 310	(1 180)	unit		same	5	3 000
E180	Stair Climber: Unlinked SC-U75	2	2 100	(1 925)	1 735	(1 560)	unit		same	5	4 200
Treadmills											
E190	Treadmill: Basic T-800B	3	1 200	(1 100)	1 000	(900)	unit		same	10	4 800
E200	Treadmill: Basic Plus T-910P	3	1 600	(1 450)	1 315	(1 180)	unit		same	10	6 400
E210	Treadmill: Deluxe T-1100D	3	2 400	(2 200)	2 015	(1 810)	unit		same	10	9 600
E220	Treadmill: Deluxe Plus T-1200P	3	2 800	(2 600)	2 360	(2 125)	unit		same	10	11 200
Services (Linked Accounts: Revenue 4040, COGS 5065)											
S010	Personal Trainer: 1 hour		75	(70)			hour		PST Tax Exempt		
S020	Personal Trainer: 1/2 day		200	(190)			1/2 day		PST Tax Exempt		
S030	Personal Trainer: full day		400	(380)			day		PST Tax Exempt		
S040	Yoga Instructor: 1 hour		100	(95)			hour		PST Tax Exempt		
S050	Yoga Instructor: 1/2 day		200	(190)			1/2 day		PST Tax Exempt		

NOTES: No duty is charged on items imported from the United States. The duty rate is 0%.
Stocking and selling units are the same for all items.
Buying units and the relationship to stocking units are entered only when these are different from the stocking/selling units.
"Same" is entered in the relationship column when the same unit is used for all measures.

Accounting Procedures

The Goods and Services Tax (GST)

GST at the rate of 7 percent is applied to all goods and services offered by Flabuless Fitness. Flabuless Fitness uses the regular method for remittance of the Goods and Services Tax. GST collected from customers is recorded as a liability in *GST Charged on Sales*. GST paid to vendors is recorded in *GST Paid on Purchases* as a decrease in liability to Canada Revenue Agency (CRA). These two postable accounts are added together in the subgroup total account *GST Owing (Refund)*. The balance of GST to be remitted or the request for a refund is sent to the Receiver General for Canada by the last day of the current month for the previous month.

Tax calculations will be correct only for customers and vendors for whom the tax exempt option was set as No. The GST Report available from the Reports menu will include transactions completed in the Sales, Purchases and General journals, but the opening historical balances will not be included. Therefore, the amounts shown in the GST Report may differ from the balances in the General Ledger GST accounts. You should use the General Ledger accounts to verify the balance owing (or refund due) and make adjustments to the report manually as necessary.

After the report is filed, clear the GST Report (choose the Maintenance menu, then Clear Data and click Clear Tax Report and select GST). Enter the last day of the previous month as the date for clearing. Always back up your files before clearing the GST Report.

Provincial Sales Tax (PST)

Provincial Sales Tax of 8 percent is applied to the sales of all goods but not services provided by Flabuless Fitness. It is applied to the amount of the sale without GST included and is not applied to freight. The PST collected must be remitted monthly to the Minister of Finance. Provincial Sales Taxes to be remitted must be set up as a liability owing to the vendor, Minister of Finance, in the Purchases Journal. The General Ledger balance for *PST Payable* for the last day of the previous month will provide the total owing. You may display or print this account for reference. A 5 percent sales tax compensation is earned if the remittance is made before the due date assigned to the business.

Business Income Tax

Flabuless Fitness pays income tax in quarterly instalments to the Receiver General based on its previous year's net income.

The Employer Health Tax (EHT)

The Employer Health Tax (EHT) is paid by all employers permanently established in Ontario to provide Ontario Health Insurance Plan (OHIP) coverage for all eligible Ontario residents. The EHT is based on the total annual remuneration paid to employees. Employers whose total payroll exceeds $400 000 must pay EHT. Although the payroll for Flabuless Fitness is less than this amount, we show the application of EHT so that you can learn how to set up the expense and make the remittances. In this application, EHT will be remitted quarterly. *EHT Payable* is set up as a liability owing to the vendor, Minister of Finance. The Remittance Payments Journal will provide you with the balance owing to the Minister of Finance when the liability is linked to this vendor.

Aging of Accounts

Flabuless Fitness uses aging periods that reflect the payment terms it provides to customers and receives from vendors. For customers, this will be 10, 30 and 60 days, and for vendors, 15, 30 and 60 days. Interest at 1.5 percent is charged on customer accounts that are not paid within 30 days. Regular customer statements show interest amounts, and invoices are then prepared to add the interest to the amount owing in the ledger record.

Discounts

Flabuless Fitness offers a 2 percent discount to regular account customers if they settle their accounts within 10 days. Full payment is requested within 30 days. These payment terms are set up as defaults. When the receipt is entered and the discount is still available, the program shows the amount of the discount and the net amount owing. No discounts are given on cash or credit card sales. Customer discounts are calculated on after-tax amounts.

Some customers receive preferred customer prices, approximately 10 percent below the regular prices. These customers are identified in the ledger records and the preferred prices are set up in the inventory ledger records.

NOTES
Daily Business Manager lists are helpful for making sure that you take advantage of available discounts.

Some vendors also offer discounts for early settlement of accounts. Again, when the terms are entered for the vendor and payment is made before the discount period expires, the program displays the discount as available and automatically calculates a net balance owing. Payment terms vary from vendor to vendor. Most vendor discounts are calculated on before-tax amounts but some are based on after-tax amounts.

Freight

When a business purchases inventory items, the cost of any freight that cannot be directly allocated to a specific item must be charged to *Freight Expense*. This amount will be regarded as a general expense rather than being charged to the costs of any inventory asset account. Customers also pay for delivery and setup. GST is charged on freight for both sales and purchases but there is no PST on freight. The tax code for all freight charges is code G.

Bank Deposits

Deposit slips are prepared weekly when cash and cheques are received. Receipts are debited to *Undeposited Cash and Cheques* and transferred weekly to *Bank: Hamilton Trust Chequing*.

Imported Inventory

NOTES
Although import duties are not charged on the items imported by Flabuless Fitness from the United States, we show the setup of import duties and set the rates at zero so that no tax will be charged.

Some inventory items are imported from the United States. The bank accounts, vendor records and inventory records are modified to accommodate the foreign currency transactions and import duties automatically.

Purchase Returns and Allowances

A business will sometimes return inventory items to vendors because of damage, poor quality or shipment of the wrong items. Usually a business records these returns after it receives a credit note from a vendor. The return of inventory is entered in the Purchases Journal as an inventory purchase:

- Select the item in the Item field and enter the quantity returned as a **negative** amount in the Quantity field. The program will automatically calculate a negative amount as a default in the Amount field. You cannot change the account number.
- Accept the default amount and enter other items returned to the vendor.

- When there are no further items, enter freight charges as a **negative** amount.
- Enter the appropriate tax code for each item returned and for freight.

The program will create a negative invoice to reduce the balance owing to the vendor and will reduce the applicable inventory asset accounts, the freight accounts, *GST Paid on Purchases* and the quantity of items in the Inventory Ledger database.

Purchase allowances for damaged merchandise that is not returned are entered as non-inventory negative purchase invoices. Enter the amount of the allowance as a **negative** amount in the Amount field and leave the tax fields blank (i.e., treat it as non-taxable). Enter *Purchases Returns and Allowances* in the Account field.

Sales Returns and Allowances

Sometimes customers will return inventory items. Usually a business records the return after it has issued a credit note. The return is entered in the Sales Journal as a negative inventory sale for the customer:

- Select the appropriate item in the Item field.
- Enter the quantity returned with a **negative** number in the Quantity field.
- The price of the item appears as a positive number in the Price field, and the Amount field is calculated automatically as a negative amount that should be correct. If it is not, you can change it.
- Enter the tax code for the sale and the account number for *Sales Returns & Allowances.*
- Enter freight charges, if there were any, as **negative** amounts with the appropriate tax code.

The program will create a negative invoice to reduce the balance owing by the customer, and *Cost of Goods Sold*, *GST Charged on Sales* and *PST Payable*. The applicable inventory asset accounts and the quantity of items in the Inventory Ledger database will be increased.

Sales allowances are entered as non-taxable, non-inventory negative sales invoices, creating a debit entry for *Sales Returns & Allowances* and a credit for *Accounts Receivable*. If the allowance is paid by cheque, enter the allowance in the Payments Journal as an Other Payment paid by cheque.

NOTES

The sales tax rules for credits, allowances and discounts are complex. They may be different for provincial and federal taxes and they may differ from one province to another. Adjusting General Journal entries may be required to adjust the amount of tax owing and calculate the tax remittance. We have chosen to leave out the tax component for transactions of this type. Refer to Chapter 2 for more information about sales taxes.

NSF Cheques

If a cheque is deposited from an account that does not have enough money to cover it, the bank returns it to the depositor as NSF (non-sufficient funds). If the cheque was in payment for a cash sale, you must process the NSF cheque through the Sales Journal because there was no Receipts Journal entry. Create a customer record if necessary and enter a positive amount for the amount of the cheque. Choose *Bank: Hamilton Trust Chequing* as the account. Choose Pay Later as the method of payment. If the customer is expected to pay the bank charges, enter these on the second invoice line as a positive amount and select the appropriate revenue account.

Adjustments for Bad Debt

Most businesses set up an allowance for doubtful accounts or bad debts, knowing that some customers will fail to pay. When the allowance is set up, a bad debts or uncollectable accounts expense account is debited. When a business is certain that a customer will not pay its account, the debt should be written off by crediting *Accounts Receivable* and debiting *Allowance for Doubtful Accounts*. When taxes apply, an extra step is required. Part of the original sales invoice was entered as a credit (increase) to *GST Charged on Sales* and to *PST Payable*. By entering the full amount and the tax code for taxes included, the GST and PST payable amounts will automatically be

NOTES

Allowance for Doubtful Accounts is a contra-asset account that normally has a credit balance. Therefore, a debit entry will reduce this credit balance.

reduced. In Simply Accounting, record the write-off of the debt in the Sales Journal using the following steps:

- Select the customer whose debt will not be paid.
- Enter a source document number to identify the transaction (e.g., memo).
- Enter a **negative** amount for the total unpaid invoice in the Amount field.
- Enter *Allowance for Doubtful Accounts* in the Account field.
- Enter the tax code **IN** (taxes included).

If the customer was also charged for the NSF fees, enter this information on the next invoice line:

- Enter a **negative** amount for the total NSF charge in the Amount field.
- Enter *Allowance for Doubtful Accounts* in the Account field.
- Enter the tax code **No tax**.

Review the transaction. *Accounts Receivable* is credited (reduced) by the full amount of the invoice to remove the balance owing by this customer. *Allowance for Doubtful Accounts* has been debited (reduced) by the amount of the invoice minus taxes. *GST Charged on Sales* and *PST Payable* have been debited for the tax portion of the invoice to reduce the tax liabilities.

After recording the write-off, "pay" both the original invoice and the write-off in the Receipts Journal. The balance will be zero and there will be no journal entry. This step removes the items from the journal for the customer so that you can clear the paid transactions and later remove the customer's record.

Manually you would complete the entry as follows:

1. Set up the Allowance for Bad Debts.

Date	Particulars	Debit	Credit
xx/xx	Uncollectable Accounts Expense	1 000.00	
	Allowance for Doubtful Accounts		1 000.00

2. Customer G. Bell declares bankruptcy. Write off outstanding balance, $230, including GST and PST.

Date	Particulars	Debit	Credit
xx/xx	Allowance for Doubtful Accounts	200.00	
	GST Charged on Sales	14.00	
	PST Payable	16.00	
	Accounts Receivable, G. Bell		230.00

Occasionally, a bad debt is recovered after it has been written off. When this occurs, the above procedure is reversed and the GST and PST liabilities must also be restored. The recovery is entered as a non-inventory sale in the Sales Journal using the following steps:

- Select the customer and enter the date and source document number.
- Type an appropriate comment such as "Debt recovered" as the Description.
- Enter a **positive** amount for the total invoice amount in the Amount field.
- Enter the tax code **IN** (taxes included).
- Enter *Allowance for Doubtful Accounts* in the Account field.

Review the transaction. You will see that *Accounts Receivable* has been debited for the full amount of the invoice. *Allowance for Doubtful Accounts* has been credited for the amount of the invoice minus taxes. *GST Charged on Sales* and *PST Payable* have been credited for the tax portion of the invoice to restore the tax liabilities.

As the final step, record the customer's payment in the Receipts Journal as you would record any other customer payment.

Remittances

The Receiver General for Canada:

- Monthly EI, CPP and income tax deductions withheld from employees must be paid by the 15th of each month for the previous month.
- Monthly GST owing or requests for refunds must be filed by the end of each month for the previous month.
- Business income tax is paid in quarterly instalments.

The Minister of Finance:

- Quarterly Employer Health Tax (EHT) deductions must be paid by the 15th of April, July, October and January for the previous quarter.
- Monthly Provincial Sales Taxes (PST) on revenue from sales must be paid by the 23rd of the month for the previous month. A 5 percent sales tax compensation is earned for prompt payment of PST.

Ancaster Insurance:

- Monthly Registered Retirement Savings Plan (RRSP) deductions withheld from employees must be paid by the 15th of the month for the previous month.
- Group insurance contributions paid by the employer must be paid by the 15th of the month for the previous month.

The Mt. Hope Investment Corporation:

- Monthly Canada Savings Bond Plan (CSB Plan) deductions withheld from employees must be paid by the 15th of the month for the previous month.

The Workplace Safety and Insurance Board:

- Quarterly Workplace Safety and Insurance Board (WSIB) assessment for employees must be paid by the 15th of the month for the previous quarter.

NOTES

In practice, a business would make these three federal tax remittances to different federal offices and the two provincial remittances to different provincial tax offices. Separate vendor accounts would be needed for each remittance. For this application, one vendor account and address has been used for the Receiver General and one for the Minister of Finance to reduce the length of the vendor list.

SPECIAL DATA FILES FOR FLABULESS FITNESS

Detailed keystroke instructions are included for you to set up the Flabuless Fitness application files. However, the Data CD also includes files for this application so that you can complete segments of the application rather than having to work through it entirely. Each file stands alone so you can work through any month at your discretion.

To Enter	For (Period Covered)	Use (File Name on Data CD)
Transactions:	April 1–April 30	setup\flab\flab-apr.sdb
Transactions:	May 1–May 31	setup\flab\flab-may.sdb
Transactions:	June 1–June 30	setup\flab\flab-jun.sdb

INSTRUCTIONS FOR SETUP

Set up the **company accounts** in Simply Accounting using the Business Information, Chart of Accounts, Balance Sheet, Income Statement, Post-Closing Trial Balance and Vendor, Customer, Employee and Inventory Information provided above for March 31, 2008. Instructions to assist you in setting up the company accounts follow. The setup of the Payroll and Inventory ledgers is given in detail. Abbreviated instructions are included for the remaining steps. Refer to the Toss for Tots and the Dorfmann Design applications if you need more detailed explanations.

KEYSTROKES FOR SETUP

Creating Company Files

We will create the company files from scratch. Once we create the files and define the defaults, we will add the accounts, define linked accounts for all ledgers, set up additional features, create vendor, customer, employee and inventory records and add historical data.

NOTES
You cannot complete the company setup in multi-user mode. Many of the settings options are dimmed and unavailable when you are working in multi-user mode.

Save your work and update your backup copy frequently as you work through the setup.

Start the **Simply Accounting program**. You should see the Select Company window.

Click **Create A New Company**.

Click **OK**. You will see the Setup wizard welcome screen.

Click **Next**.

Click **Express Setup** if necessary.

Click **Next** to skip the Business Partner screen.

Click **Create A New List Of Accounts From Scratch**.

Click **OK** to confirm your selection and return to the previous screen.

Click **Next**.

Choose **Retail** as the Industry for the business.

Click **Next**.

Choose **Ontario** as the Province of business.

Click **Next** to open the Company Name and Address screen. The default name (the template name) is selected for editing.

NOTES
Because we selected Ontario as the province, some defaults are added to the data file. Province fields are completed automatically in all the ledgers. WCB will be renamed WSIB.
The city and country will be added as defaults once we save the company information.

Type `Flabuless Fitness` (and your own name) **Press** *tab* to advance to the Street 1 address field.

Type `199 Warmup Rd.` **Press** *tab*.

Type `Unit 500` **Press** *tab*.

Type `Hamilton` **Skip** the province and province code. They are correct.

Click the Postal Code field.

Type `18t3b7` **Press** *tab*.

Type `Canada` **Press** *tab*.

Type `9056422348` **Press** *tab* to enter the first phone number.

Type `8004482348` **Press** *tab* to enter the second phone number.

Type `9056429100` to enter the fax number.

Check the **information** you have just entered and **correct** any **errors**.

Remember that you can edit this information later from the Setup menu, Company Information option. If you later change the province, you may have to change some linked settings.

Click **Next**.

Type flabless to replace the default entry for the file name.

Drag through **Tess** in the folder name field.

Type FLABLESS\

If you are using an alternative location for your company files, substitute the appropriate path, folder or drive in the example.

You can also type the complete path in the File Location field (e.g., Type c:\program files\winsim\data\flabless\).

Click **Next**.

Click **Yes** to confirm that you are creating a new folder and to open the company Dates window.

The cursor is in the Fiscal Year Start field, the date on which the business begins its fiscal year. Flabuless Fitness closes its books quarterly and is beginning a new quarter in April. To be certain that you have the correct year, you should type four digits for the year. Until we change the date format, they are displayed in the short form, but the order is still month/day/year.

Enter the **fiscal dates** as follows:

- Fiscal Start: April 1, 2008
- Earliest Transaction date: April 1, 2008
- Fiscal End: June 30, 2008

Click **Next** to see the list of Business Types.

Click **Sole Proprietorship** if necessary to make this selection.

Click **Next** to see the final express setup screen.

Click **Finish** to save the information.

(Close the reminder about payroll updates if it appears.) **Be patient**.

Close the **Help window** when it appears after a brief period.

Click **Collapse View** in the How Do I list to close the My Business tab window.

The program will automatically set up defaults for the session date and for the city, province and country fields for customers, vendors and employees based on the information you have just entered.

You will now see the Home window with the name Flabless at the top of the window and non-accounting term labels for the icons.

Preparing the System

The next step involves changing the defaults. Change the defaults to suit your own work environment if you have more than one printer or if you are using forms for cheques, invoices or statements. The keystroke instructions are given for computer-generated cheques, invoices and statements. Refer to the Business Information Chart on page 564 for the company default settings.

NOTES

Add your own name to the company name to personalize your data files.

NOTES

You can also select another folder by clicking Browse to open the folder path screen and then clicking the folder you want to use. Click OK to return to the Enter A File Name screen.

If the folder you want does not yet exist, click the folder you want to place the new folder in and click OK. Type FLABLESS\ at the end of the path in the Location field .

NOTES

Use the Backup feature frequently while setting up your files to update your backup copy.

Save your work frequently by choosing the Save command. You will also save your work by finishing your session properly. You may finish your session at any time while completing the setup.

Simply open the data file, accept the session date and continue from where you left off.

Changing Defaults

Correcting Company Information

Choose the **Setup menu**, then **choose System Settings** and **click Company Information**.

Click the **Business No. field**. **Type** `245 138 121`

Click **Browse**. **Choose** the **Setup\Logos folder** and **enter Flab.bmp** in the Company Logo file location field.

Make **corrections** to the remaining information if necessary.

Click **OK** to save the new information and return to the Home window.

Changing Default Names

Choose the **Setup menu**, then **choose System Settings** and **click Names & Terminology** to display the additional information screen for Accounts.

Flabuless Fitness keeps an emergency contact name and phone number for each employee in the personnel files. We will name these extra fields for the Payroll Ledger.

Click the **Employees tab** to open the additional fields for employee data:

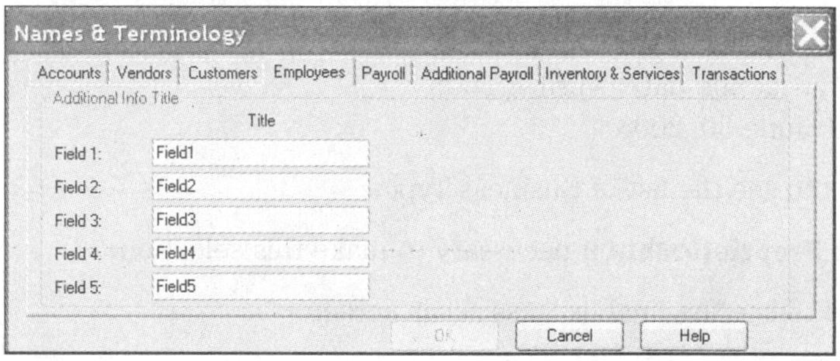

Double click **Field1**.

Type `Emergency Contact` **Press** *tab* to highlight the next field.

Type `Contact Number`

Click the **Payroll tab** to access the payroll income and deduction names:

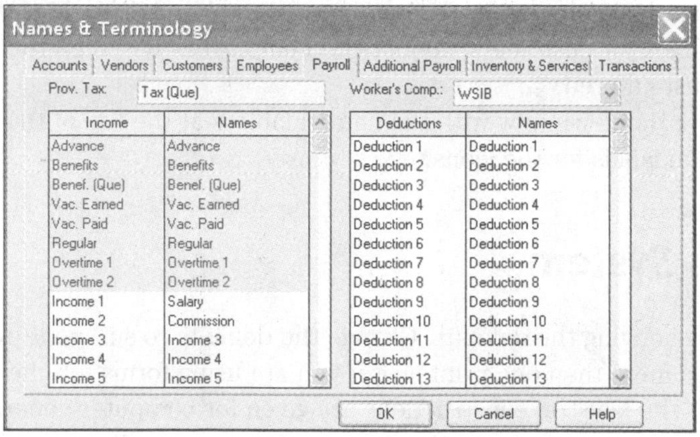

Many of the standard income types are mandatory and cannot be changed. These fields are shown in colour on a shaded background. Some of the other default names are also correct so you do not need to redefine them. You can leave Income 1 and Income 2, labelled "Salary" and "Commission," unchanged because Flabuless Fitness has two salaried employees and pays a sales commission to one employee. There is allowance for 20 different kinds of income in addition to the compulsory fields and 20 different payroll deductions. Each income and deduction label may have up to 12 characters.

The Prov. Tax field is used for Quebec payroll taxes. Since we will not choose Quebec as the employees' province of taxation, the program will automatically skip the related payroll fields. WSIB is entered as the name for WCB (Workers' Compensation Board) because we selected Ontario as the business province.

Flabuless Fitness uses the additional income fields for bonuses, piece rate pay and taxable benefits (tuition fee payments) so that these incomes can be identified by name on the paycheque. The piece rate pay is based on completed favourable client surveys for the employees. Travel expenses repaid directly to employees are also entered as income but they will not be taxed.

Flabuless also has two payroll deductions at this time: RRSP — the Registered Retirement Savings Plan; and CSB Plan — the Canada Savings Bond plan.

Click **Income 3 in the Names Column** to highlight the contents.

Type `No. Clients` **Press** tab to advance to the Income 4 field.

Type `Bonus` **Press** tab to advance to the Income 5 field.

Type `Tuition` **Press** tab to advance to the Income 6 field.

Type `Travel Exp.` **Press** tab to advance to the Income 7 field.

Press del to remove the entry. **Press** tab to select the next field.

Press del to remove the entry. **Press** tab to select the next field.

Delete the **remaining Income names** until they are all removed.

Press tab after deleting Income 20 to select Deduction 1 in the Deductions column.

Press tab again if necessary to select Deduction 1 in the Names column.

Type `RRSP` **Press** tab to advance to the second deduction Names field.

Type `CSB Plan` **Press** tab to highlight the next field.

Press del. You can delete the remaining Deduction fields because Flabuless Fitness does not have other payroll deductions.

Press tab to select the next field. **Delete** the **remaining deductions**.

Click the **Additional Payroll tab**:

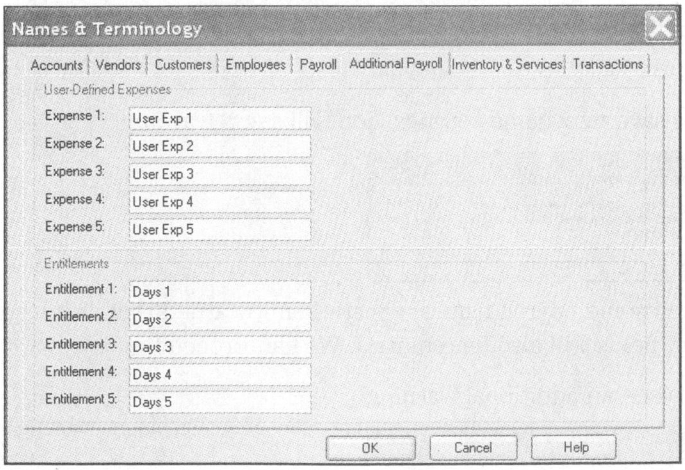

On this screen, we can name the additional payroll expenses for Flabuless, as well as the entitlements for employees. Flabuless has group insurance as a user-defined

WARNING!
If you later change the province in the Company Information screen, the WCB name entered does not change and you must enter the correction manually.

NOTES
For Lime Light Laundry, we used the generic Benefits field to enter all employee benefits.

NOTES
If clicking does not highlight the field contents, drag through an entry to select it. Double clicking will select only one word, either Income or 3.

NOTES
You can add names to any of these fields later if you need them.

expense and offers sick leave and personal leave days for all employees as well as vacation days for salaried employees.

A brief explanation of income (benefits) versus user-defined expenses is warranted. Group insurance is a taxable benefit for employees. It is also entered as a user-defined expense because the premiums are paid to a third party rather than to the employee. Tuition, the other taxable benefit, is paid to the employee through regular paycheques. Reimbursements may also be entered as income or as user-defined expenses. If we entered travel expenses as a user-defined expense, we would need to create a linked payable account and then issue a separate cheque to the employee to provide the reimbursement. Because we repay the expense on the payroll cheque, we defined it as a reimbursement — income that is not taxable.

> **NOTES**
> In Chapter 10, we created Travel Expenses as a user-defined expense and issued separate cheques to the employee for them.

Drag through **User Exp 1**, the Expense 1 field to highlight the contents.

Type `Gp Insurance` **Press** *tab* to highlight the next expense name.

Press *del*. **Press** *tab* to select the next field.

Delete the **remaining expenses**.

Drag through **Days 1**, the Entitlement 1 field to highlight the contents.

Type `Vacation` **Press** *tab* to highlight the next entitlement name.

Type `Sick Leave` **Press** *tab* to highlight the next entitlement name.

Type `PersonalDays` **Press** *tab* to highlight the next entitlement name.

Press *del*. **Press** *tab* to select the next field.

Press *del* to remove the final name.

> **NOTES**
> You can use up to 12 characters for User-Defined Expense and Entitlement names including spaces – that is why we omitted the space for the Personal Days entitlement name.

Click the **Transactions tab** (if necessary, click the scroll arrow):

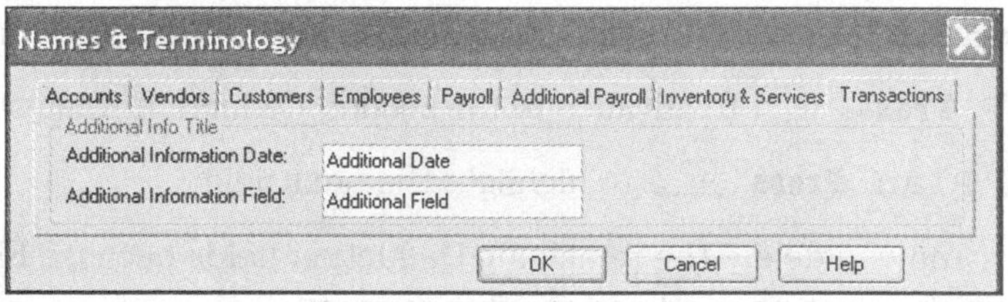

> **NOTES**
> After you choose to use accounting terms, the Transactions tab label will change to Journal Entries.

On this screen, you can define new names or labels for the additional fields in the journals. However, you must use the same names for all journals. We will therefore enter a generic label for the Additional Field.

Drag through **Additional Field**.

Type `Number`

Click **OK** to save new name settings. You will see a warning:

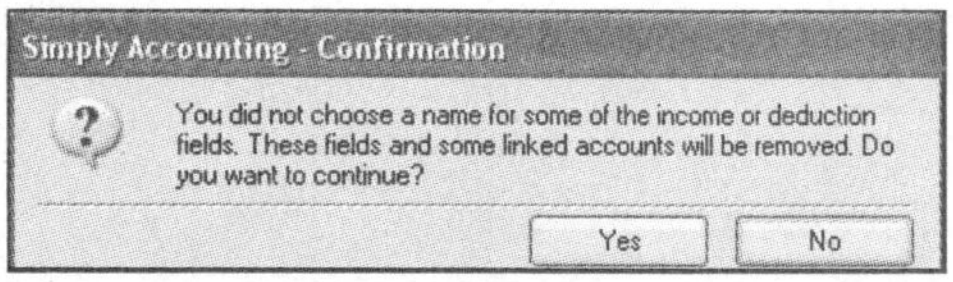

Because we deleted some payroll names, we are being warned that any accounts linked to these deleted fields will also be removed. We can proceed.

Click **Yes** to see an additional warning:

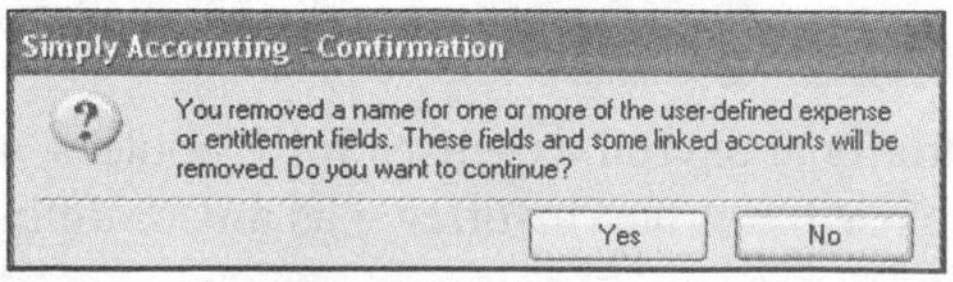

This time the message refers to the additional payroll names and we are again being warned that their linked accounts will also be removed. We can proceed.

Click **Yes** to return to the Home window.

You should now enter information about the printers you are using.

Changing Printer Settings

Reports and forms settings apply only to the data file that you are using. They must be set for each data file separately and the settings are saved with each file.

Choose the **Setup menu** and **click Reports & Forms**. The printer setting options for reports are given.

Choose the printer you will be using for reports. Change the margins if necessary. Choose fonts and type sizes for the report from the lists.

Click Setup to set the options for your particular printer if you need to change the paper size and location.

Click OK to save your settings and return to the previous Printer setting screen.

Each type of form — cheques, invoices and so on — has its own setup.

Click **Invoices** to see the settings for printing invoices:

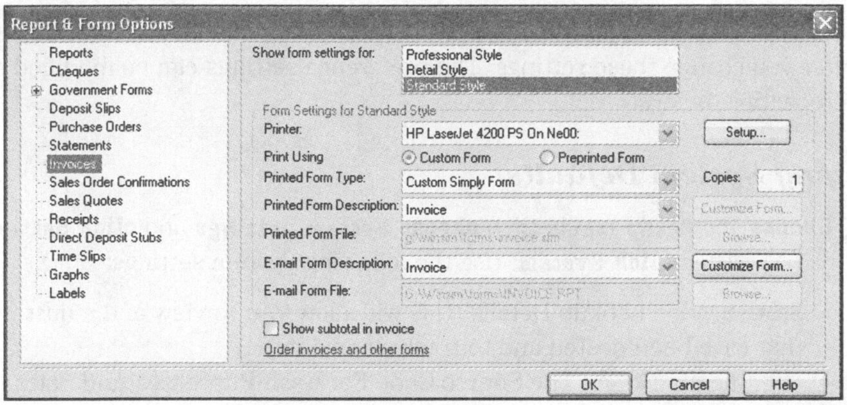

As you did for reports, select the printer, set the margins, font and type size to match the forms you are using. Preprinted forms were included as part of the program installation and are located in the Forms folder. You should Show Subtotals In Invoices.

For **E-mail Forms** you may want to choose generic forms such as Invoice and Purchase Order to avoid a file location error message from an incorrect file path in the Form File field. The file name field will be dimmed when you change the selection.

To preview invoices, you must select the **Custom Form** and **Custom Simply Form** options.

If you want to customize and preview the invoice form, choose **User-Defined Form** as the Printed Form Description.

To print labels, click Labels and enter the size of the labels and the number that are placed across the page.

To set the printer options for cheques or other forms, click the form you want and make the necessary changes.

Click **OK** to save the information when all the settings are correct and return to the Home window. You can change printer settings at any time.

WARNING!
Always check that the correct printer is selected before printing. Remember that you need to choose a printer for reports and for each form listed. The default may be incorrect if you have changed your computer setup after installing the program.
Printer settings and form selections may also be incorrect if you use a data file that was created on a different computer.

BASIC VERSION
The Basic version does not have a Time Slips entry.

NOTES
Your default locations and form selections may be different from the ones we show.

NOTES
Remember that to preview or customize invoices and statements, you must choose Custom Form and Custom Simply Form as the Printed Form Type. You cannot preview or customize the Crystal Reports forms.

NOTES
You can practise printing labels on plain paper.

Changing the User Preference Settings

You should make the following changes to the User Preferences from the Setup menu. Refer to Chapter 4, page 87, for assistance if necessary.

NOTES
Even if you are not using the Project and Time Slips ledgers, you do not need to hide them to finish the history because they have no linked accounts.

Choose the **Setup menu** and **click User Preferences** to open the Options tab screen.

Click **Use Accounting Terms**.

Click **Automatically Save Changes To Vendor....**

Click the **View tab**.

Click **After Changing Session Date** for **Daily Business Manager** and for **Checklists** to turn off this feature and remove the ✓.

WARNING!
Do not skip any ledger icon windows before completing the setup.

If you would like to hide the unused modules,

Click **Project** in the **Module column** to hide the module.

Click **Time & Billing** in the **Module column** to hide the module.

You may show the My Business Tab or hide it. If you want to hide it, click the My Business Tab heading and click Show My Business Tab to remove the ✓.

Click **OK** to save the settings and return to the Home window.

Notice that ledger and journal icons in the Home window have accounting term labels after you change these settings. The preference settings can be modified at any time by repeating these steps.

Changing System Defaults

Choose the **Setup menu**, then **choose System Settings** and **click Settings**. Then **click System**. Use the following System settings:

- Store Invoice Lookup Details (this will allow you to view and adjust invoices that have been posted and to track shipments)
- Use Cheque No. As The Source Code For Cash Purchases And Sales
- Do Not Allow Transactions Dated Before April 1, 2008
- Allow Transactions In The Future (Beyond The Session Date)
- Warn If Transactions Are More Than 7 Days In The Future
- Warn If Accounts Are Not Balanced When Entering A New Month
- Semi-monthly Backup Frequency
- Display a Backup Reminder When Closing This Company

NOTES
Remember that if you select a journal from the Select Setup list you will open the Linked Accounts window for that journal instead of the Settings window for the ledger.

Most of these settings are correct by default, and they can be modified at any time by returning to this screen.

Click OK at any time to save the settings and close the Settings window. To continue later, you can use the Setup tool to access Settings. If a ledger icon is selected in the Home window, click the Setup tool to display the Settings for that ledger. If no ledger icon is highlighted, click the Setup tool, select the ledger from the list and click Select to display the Settings for the ledger.

No changes are required for **Features settings** because quotes and orders are used by Flabuless Fitness.

Changing Default Settings for Forms

Click **Forms** to display the defaults.

Use the Forms options to set up the automatic numbering and printing of all cheques and invoices. They apply only to numerical invoices.

If you want to use automatic invoice numbering, type the next number from the source documents so the automatic numbering system can take over from the manual system. Using automatic numbering reduces the risk of typing and recording an incorrect invoice or cheque number even when you are not printing cheques and invoices through the program. For Flabuless Fitness, the next invoice is #3000.

Click 1 in the **Invoices Number field**.

Type 3000

Click the **Sales Quotes Number field**. **Type** 41

Click the **Receipts Number field**. **Type** 39

Click the **Customer Deposits Number field**. **Type** 15

Click the **Purchase Orders Number field**. **Type** 25

Click the **Direct Deposit Stubs Number field**. **Type** 19

Leave selected the option to verify number sequences for all forms so that the program will warn you if you skip or duplicate a number.

Click **Verify Number Sequence for Deposit Slips**.

Click a check box to add other features or to turn off an option once it is selected. The ✓ in the appropriate boxes indicates a feature is being used.

The option to Confirm Printing/E-mail will warn you to print before posting a transaction. When printing invoices, statements or cheques, you should include the company address, unless it is already printed on your forms.

If you print or e-mail invoices and cheques through the computer, you should turn on the option to Confirm Printing/E-mail.

We want to allow batch printing, printing several forms at once, after posting instead of one at a time while entering a transaction.

Click the **Print In Batches check box** for each form to add a ✓ to each box.

We should also check for duplicate numbers. This control is not selected by default.

Click the **Check For Duplicates check box for Invoices and Receipts**.

Changing Date Format Settings

Click **Dates**.

We want to use the long date form for all dates on the screen to verify that we are entering dates correctly. For the reports, you may use either the long or short form.

Click **Long Dates** as the setting for On The Screen, Use.

Changing General Ledger Defaults

No changes are required for General Ledger settings because budgeting is not used.

Changing Payables Defaults

Click **Payables** and then **click Options**. (The label is Vendors & Purchases if you use non-accounting terms.)

NOTES

Many invoices include the alpha or letter portion of the invoice number on the preprinted invoice form. You could then enter the next number from the numeric portion in the Invoices Number field. Alphanumeric invoice numbers, such as FF-399, cannot be increased automatically by the computer.

NOTES

If you hide the Time Slips module, the next number for time slips will not be included on the Forms tab screen. You can leave the field blank if you are not hiding the module.

You should change the intervals for the aging of accounts. Some vendors offer discounts for payment within 5, 10 or 15 days. Discounts from one-time vendors are calculated on before-tax amounts.

Set the **aging** intervals at **15**, **30** and **60** days.

Click **Calculate Discounts Before Tax For One-Time Vendors**.

We will set up the Duty option after we have entered accounts.

Changing Receivables Defaults

Click **Receivables** and then **click** **Options** to display the ledger's defaults. (The label is Customers & Sales if you use non-accounting terms.)

Flabuless Fitness prints the salesperson's name on all customer forms for the customer's reference in case a follow-up is required.

You can decide whether to charge interest on overdue accounts, how long to provide historical information about paid invoices on customer statements and enter payment terms and aging intervals.

Flabuless Fitness offers its account customers a 2 percent after-tax discount for 10 days; full payment is due in 30 days. Interest charges are 1.5 percent for accounts over 30 days. We will use the payment terms to set the aging intervals.

After we set up the sales taxes, we can enter a default tax code for new customers.

Enter **10**, **30** and **60** days as the **aging** periods.

Including paid invoices for 31 days is appropriate for the monthly statements.

Click **Interest Charges** to turn on the calculation.

Click the **% field** for **Interest Charges**.

Type `1.5` **Press** tab.

Type `30`

Click the **% field** of the **Early Payment Terms** section.

Type `2` **Press** tab.

Type `10` **Press** tab.

Type `30`

Click **Print Salesperson On Invoices Orders & Quotes**.

Changing Default Comments

Click **Comments**.

You may add a comment or notice to all your invoices, quotes and order confirmations. You could use this feature to include payment terms, a company motto or notice of an upcoming sale. Remember that you can change the default message any time you want. You can also edit it for a particular sale or quote when you are completing the invoice. The cursor is in the Sales Invoices field.

Type `Interest @ 1.5% per month on accounts over 30 days.`

Repeat this procedure to enter comments for the other forms.

Setting Defaults for Payroll

Use the Payroll Settings from the Business Information Chart on page 564 to complete this step.

Click **Payroll** to display the Payroll Ledger setting options:

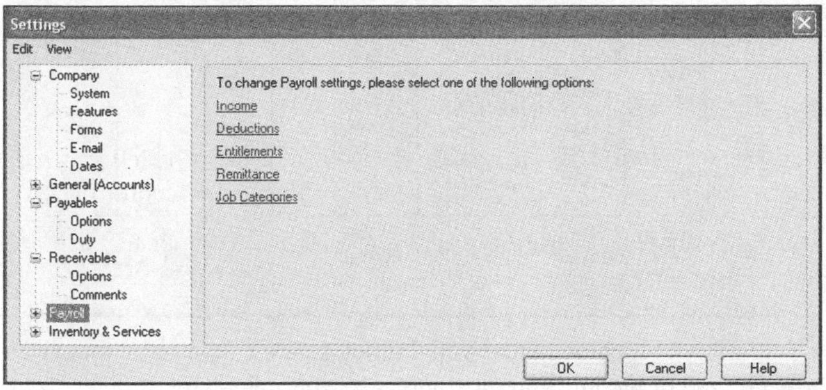

At this stage, we will change the settings for Income, Deductions and Entitlements. After creating vendor and employee records, we can change the Remittance and Job Category settings.

Click **Income**:

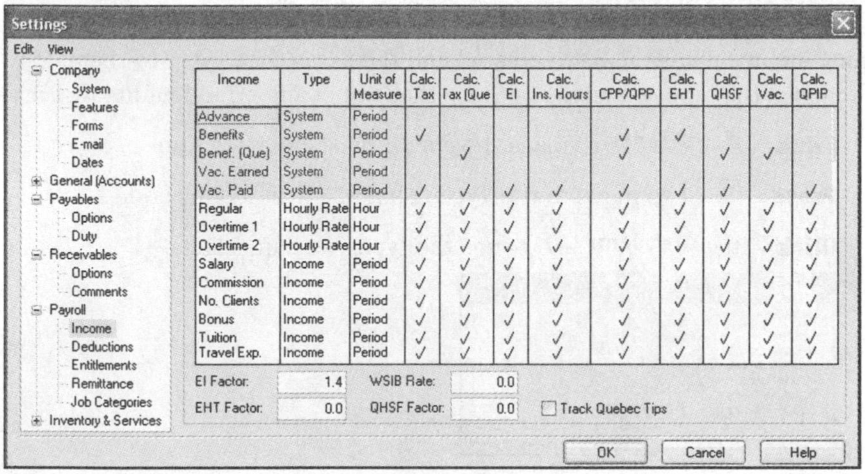

We will first modify this screen by deleting the columns that apply to Quebec so that only the columns we need are on-screen at the same time.

Point to the **right column heading margin for Calc. Tax (Que.)** until the pointer changes to a two-sided arrow ⇹.

Drag the **margin to the left** until the column is hidden.

Point to the **right column heading margin for Calc. QHSF** until the pointer changes to a two-sided arrow. **Drag** the **margin to the left** until the column is hidden.

Point to the **right column heading margin for Calc. QPIP** until the pointer changes to a two-sided arrow. **Drag** the **margin to the left**.

If necessary, drag the other margins to make the columns narrower.

NOTES

When you close and re-open the Payroll Settings screen, the hidden and resized columns will be restored.

QPIP (Quebec Parental Insurance Plan) provides parental leave benefits to EI insurable employees. Both employers and employees pay into the plan.

NOTES

If necessary, scroll to the right to see the column margin you need.

Your screen should now look like the following:

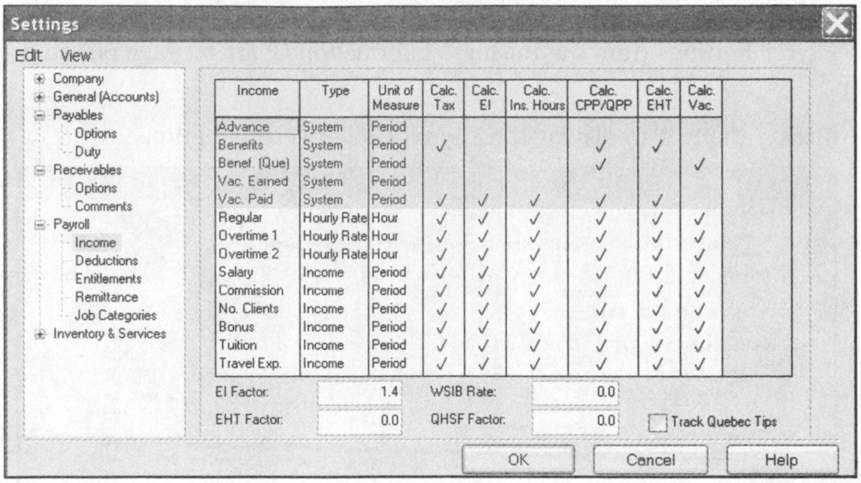

Income	Type	Unit of Measure	Calc. Tax	Calc. EI	Calc. Ins. Hours	Calc. CPP/QPP	Calc. EHT	Calc. Vac.
Advance	System	Period						
Benefits	System	Period	✓			✓	✓	
Benef. (Que)	System	Period				✓		✓
Vac. Earned	System	Period						
Vac. Paid	System	Period	✓	✓	✓	✓	✓	
Regular	Hourly Rate	Hour	✓	✓	✓	✓	✓	✓
Overtime 1	Hourly Rate	Hour	✓	✓	✓	✓	✓	✓
Overtime 2	Hourly Rate	Hour	✓	✓	✓	✓	✓	✓
Salary	Income	Period	✓	✓	✓	✓	✓	✓
Commission	Income	Period	✓	✓	✓	✓	✓	✓
No. Clients	Income	Period	✓	✓	✓	✓	✓	✓
Bonus	Income	Period	✓	✓	✓	✓	✓	✓
Tuition	Income	Period	✓	✓	✓	✓	✓	✓
Travel Exp.	Income	Period	✓	✓	✓	✓	✓	✓

Notice that only the income names you did not delete (page 581) appear on this screen. For each type of income you must indicate what taxes are applied and whether vacation pay is calculated on the income. Most of the information is correct. Regular and overtime hours are paid on an hourly basis while salary and commissions are paid at designated income amounts per period. All taxes apply to these types of income at Flabuless Fitness so these default settings are correct. Vacation pay, however, is calculated only on regular and overtime hourly wages so some of these checkmarks should be removed. In addition, we should designate the type of income for the remaining income names that we created and the taxes that apply to them. First we should choose the type of income because that will change the defaults that are applied.

Click **No. Clients** to place the cursor on the correct line.

Press *tab* to move to the Type column. A List icon is added.

Click the **List icon** to see the types we can select:

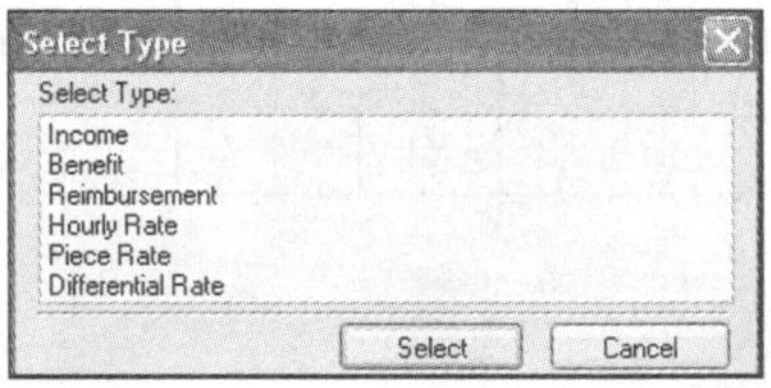

By default, all new income entries are assigned to the Income type. This assignment is correct for Bonus, the extra annual holiday payment. Tuition fee payment is a taxable benefit paid directly to the employee as income. The Benefit type is used for non-monetary items such as medical or life insurance premiums that the employer pays directly to a third party on behalf of the employee. The monetary value of the premiums is added as a benefit to the employee's gross wages to determine taxes but is not added to the net pay. The employee does not receive the actual dollar amount. If a benefit is added to net pay, it should be classified as an Income. Therefore, tuition is an Income.

Travel Expenses are **Reimbursements** and No. Clients is the name for the **Piece Rate** basis of paying bonuses. **Differential Rates** apply to different hourly rates paid at different times and are not used by Flabuless.

Click **Piece Rate** to select this type for No. Clients.

Click **Select** to add the Type to the Settings screen. **Press** *tab*.

The cursor advances to the Unit of Measure field and the entry has changed to Item. The amount paid to employees is based on the number of completed surveys. Notice that the Insurable Hours checkmark was removed when we changed the type.

NOTES

An alternative approach for tuition fees is to set them up as a user-defined expense, enter the amount in the Benefits field on the paycheque and then issue a cheque to the employee for the Tuition Payable amount.

In Lime Light Laundry, tuition was set up as a user-defined expense; the amount was paid directly to the college and entered as a benefit for the employee.

NOTES

Tuition is defined as an "Income" rather than a benefit because it is paid directly to the employee. It is not a reimbursement because it is taxable.

Type Surveys

Click **Travel Exp** to select this income line. **Press** (tab).

Click the **List icon** to see the types we can select.

Double click **Reimbursement** to enter this type on the Settings screen. All taxes are removed because this type of payment is not taxable.

We need to make some other modifications. Insurable Hours, the number of work hours, is used to determine eligibility for Employment Insurance benefits. Regular, overtime and salary paid hours are entered but commissions, bonuses and benefits are not. No work time can be reasonably attached to commissions and bonuses so they are not counted. The checkmarks for them should be removed.

Click **Commission** to select this income line.

Press (tab) **repeatedly** until the cursor is in the **Calc. Ins. Hours field**.

Click to remove the ✓, or **press** the **space bar**.

Press (↓) **twice** to place the cursor in the **Calc. Ins. Hours field for Bonus**.

Click to remove the ✓, or **press** the **space bar**.

Press (↓) to place the cursor in the **Calc. Ins. Hours field for Tuition**.

Click to remove the ✓, or **press** the **space bar**.

We still need to modify the entries for vacation pay. In Ontario, vacation pay is calculated on all performance-based wages. This includes the regular wages, overtime wages and piece rate pay. We need to remove the remaining ✓. The ✓ for Travel Exp has already been removed. Salaried workers receive paid time off rather than a percentage of their wages as vacation pay. We do not need to remove the ✓ for Overtime 2. If it is used later, vacation pay will be calculated on it as well.

Click **Salary** in the Income column.

Press (tab) **repeatedly** until the cursor is in the **Calc. Vac. column**.

Click to remove the ✓, or **press** the **space bar**.

Press (↓) to place the cursor in the **Calc. Vac. field for Commission**.

Click to remove the ✓, or **press** the **space bar**.

Press (↓) to place the cursor in the **Calc. Vac. field for No. Clients**.

Press (↓) to place the cursor in the **Calc. Vac. field for Bonus**.

Click to remove the ✓, or **press** the **space bar**.

Press (↓) to place the cursor in the **Calc. Vac. field for Tuition**.

Click to remove the ✓, or **press** the **space bar**.

The next group of fields refers to the rate at which employer tax obligations are calculated. The factor for Employment Insurance (**EI Factor**) is correct at 1.4. The employer's contribution is set at 1.4 times the employee's contribution. In the next field, you can set the employer's rate for **WSIB** (Workplace Safety and Insurance Board) premiums. On this screen, you can enter 1.29, the rate that applies to the majority of employees. You can modify rates for individual employees in the ledger records.

The next field, **EHT Factor**, shows the percentage of payroll costs that the employer contributes to the provincial health plan. The rate is based on the total payroll costs per year; the percentage for Flabuless Fitness is 0.98 percent.

NOTES

Vacation pay is calculated on all wages. This calculation includes the piece rate pay – number of client evaluations – because it is a performance-based wage or income. Bonuses are not based on measurable performance; therefore, vacation pay is not applied to these amounts or to the other benefits.

The regulations governing vacation pay are set provincially.

NOTES

EHT in Ontario applies if the total payroll is greater than $400 000. We show the entry of the EHT rates so that you can learn how to change the settings.

WSIB is the name for WCB in Ontario.

QHSF was used for Village Galleries.

The **QHSF Factor** (Quebec Health Services Fund) and the option to **track tips** apply to payroll in Quebec, so we do not need to enter them. QHSF is similar to EHT.

Click the **WSIB Rate field**.

Type 1.29

Press *tab* to advance to the EHT Factor field.

Type .98

We do not need to change the Quebec tax settings. They will not be applied when we select Ontario as the province for employees. The completed Settings screen is shown below:

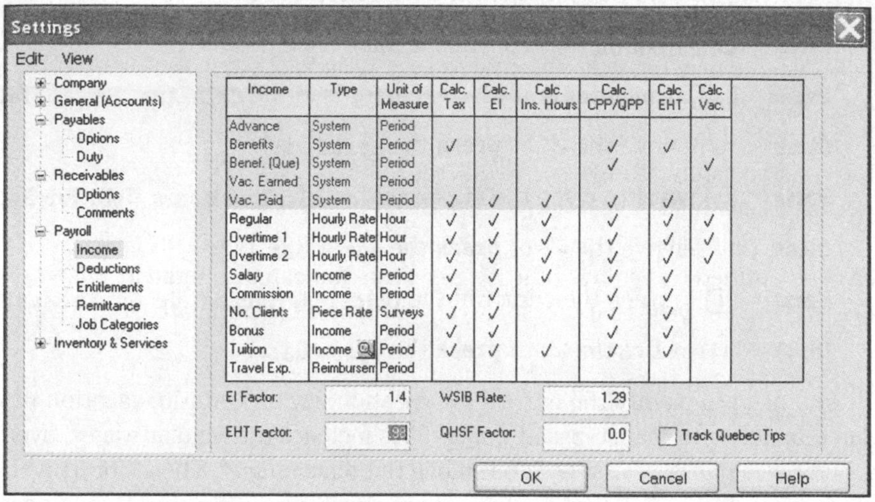

Click **Deductions** under Payroll:

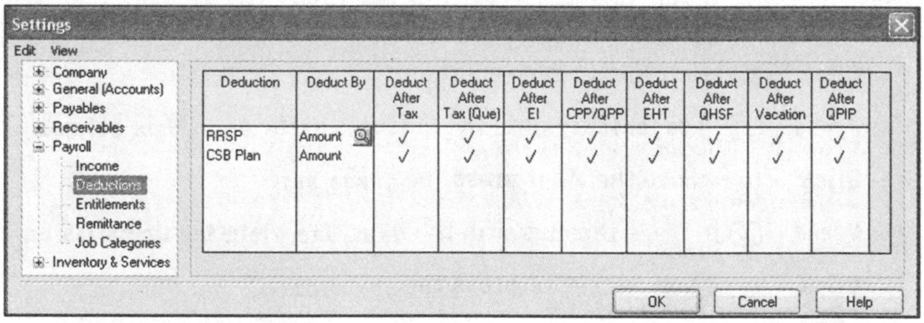

NOTES

You can modify this screen as we modified the Entitlements Settings screen so that only the columns we need are on-screen. You can remove the Deduct After Tax (Que.), QHSF Calc and Deduct After QPIP columns.

Only the two deduction names you entered earlier appear on this screen. You can calculate deductions as a percentage of the gross pay or as a fixed amount. Some deductions, like union dues, are usually calculated as a percentage of income. The Amount settings are correct for Flabuless Fitness.

All deductions are set by default to be calculated after all taxes (Deduct After Tax is checked). For CSB Plan, this is correct — it is subtracted from income after income tax and other payroll taxes have been deducted. However, RRSP contributions qualify as tax deductions and will be subtracted from gross income before income tax is calculated, but not before EI, CPP and so on, so you must change this setting.

Click the **Deduct After Tax check box** for RRSP to remove the ✓ and change the setting to before tax.

The remaining settings are correct. RRSP is deducted after the other payroll taxes and vacation pay because these deductions are based on gross wages.

Click **Entitlements** under Payroll:

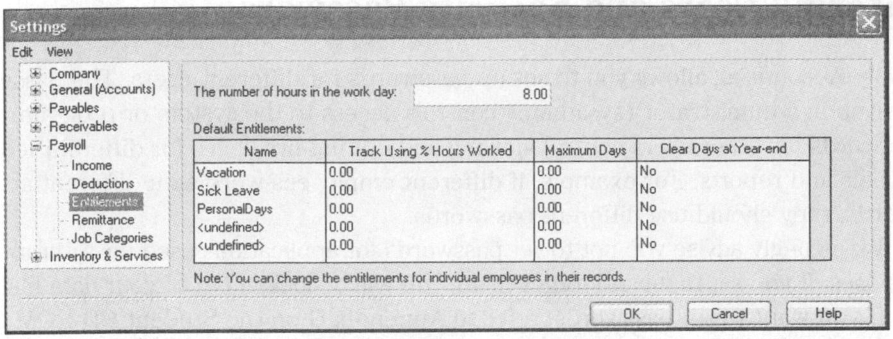

On this screen you can enter the rules for entitlements that apply to all or most employees. When we enter the rules here, they will be added to each employee's record. You can change entitlement amounts for individual employees in their ledger records.

Entitlements may be given directly or may be linked to the number of hours worked. For example, usually employees are not entitled to take vacation time until they have worked for a certain period of time. Or they may not be allowed to take paid sick leave immediately after being hired. You can use the **Track Using % Hours Worked** to determine how quickly vacation or sick days accumulate. For example, 5 percent of hours worked yields about one day per month. Thus, you would enter 5 percent if the employee is entitled to 12 days of leave per year. You can also indicate the **Maximum** number of **Days** per year that an employee can take or accumulate. And finally, you must indicate whether the days unused are **cleared at the end of a year** or can be carried forward. If the days earned, but not used, at the end of a year are carried forward, then the Maximum will still place a limit on the number of days available. The number of days is based on an eight-hour day but you can change this entry.

Flabuless Fitness gives salaried workers three weeks of vacation (8 percent) and allows a maximum of 25 days. Sick leave at 10 days per year is earned at the rate of 5 percent to the maximum of 15 days. Personal leave days (5 days) accrue at the rate of 2.5 percent for a maximum of 5 days per year. None are cleared at the end of the year.

Flabuless Fitness allows two of the three weeks of vacation time and five of the ten days of sick leave to be carried over to the following year. Personal leave days cannot be carried forward — the maximum is the same as the yearly allotment.

Click the **Track Using % Hours Worked field for Vacation**.

Type 8 **Press** tab to advance to the Maximum Days field.

Type 25 **Press** tab.

Click the **Track Using % Hours Worked field for Sick Leave**.

Type 5 **Press** tab to advance to the Maximum Days field.

Type 15 **Press** tab.

Click the **Track Using % Hours Worked field for PersonalDays**.

Type 2.5 **Press** tab to advance to the Maximum Days field.

Type 5 **Press** tab.

We will modify inventory settings after adding currency information. We will add Payroll Remittance Settings after adding vendors.

We have hidden the Project module so the settings options for it are also hidden. To see the Project module options, refer to page 470. Time and Billing, introduced in Chapter 17, has no settings options.

Click **OK** to save the Settings changes and return to the Home window.

NOTES

Inventory Settings options change when you add currency information, so we will delay these settings until we have added the foreign currency details (page 594). We will also add Payroll Remittance Settings later because these involve linked accounts and vendors.

Entering Users and Security Passwords

Simply Accounting allows you to set up passwords for different users. The password for the system administrator (sysadmin) controls access to the system or program. Passwords for other users control viewing and editing privileges for different ledgers, journals and reports. For example, if different employees work with different accounting records, they should use different passwords.

We strongly advise you not to set passwords for applications used for tutorial purposes. If you set them and forget them, you will be locked out of your data files.

If you want to set passwords, refer to Appendix G on the Student CD-ROM and your Simply Accounting manuals before you begin.

Preparing the Ledgers

NOTES
Remember that you can save your work and finish your session at any time. This will give you an opportunity to read the next section.

The third stage in setting up an accounting system involves preparing each ledger for operation. This stage involves

1. organizing all accounting reports and records (this step has been completed)
2. creating new accounts
3. identifying linked accounts for all ledgers
4. activating additional features and entering their linked accounts
5. inserting vendor, customer, employee and inventory information
6. entering historical startup information
7. printing reports to check the accuracy of your records

Creating New Accounts

The next step is to create the accounts, including the non-postable accounts. Remember to enter the correct type of account. For postable accounts you should also indicate whether you want to omit accounts with zero balances from financial statements. You need to refer to the company Chart of Accounts, Balance Sheet and Income Statement, page 563 and pages 565–566, to complete this step.

Current Earnings is the only pre-defined account, and you do not need to edit it.

Refer to Format of Financial Statements (page 91) for a review of these topics if needed. Refer to the instructions in the Toss for Tots application, page 99, if you need help with creating accounts.

Click the **Accounts icon** to open the Accounts window.

Maximize the Accounts window.

If the accounts are not displayed by name or by type, you should change the view. Click the Display By Type tool or choose the View menu and click Type.

NOTES
You can also press ctrl + N to open a New Account ledger window and create a new account.

Click the **Create tool** in the Accounts window or **choose** the **File menu** and **click Create**.

Drag the Ledger window so that both the Accounts window and Ledger window are visible. This will make it easier to monitor your progress.

Type the **account number**. **Press** tab and **type** the **account name**.

Click the correct **account type**. Remember subgroup accounts (A) must be followed by a subgroup total (S).

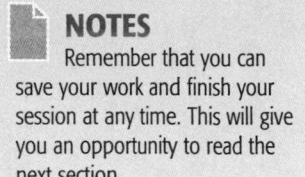

Click **Omit From Financial Statements If Balance Is Zero** to select this option.

Allow Project Allocations will be selected by default for all postable revenue and expense accounts so you do not need to change this option.

You will enter the account balances in the next stage.

When all the information is correct, you must save your account.

Click **Create Another** [Create Another] to save the new account and advance to a blank ledger account window.

Create the **other accounts** by repeating these procedures.

Select **Operating Expense** as the Account Class (Class Options tab) for all Expense accounts. (See margin notes.)

Close the **General Ledger window** when you have entered all the accounts on page 565, or when you want to end your session.

After entering all the accounts, you should check for mistakes in account number, name, type, order and account class (for expense accounts).

Display or **print** your updated **Chart of Accounts** at this stage to check for accuracy of account names and numbers.

Click [✓] or **choose** the **Edit menu** and **click** **Check The Validity Of Accounts** to check for errors in account sequence such as missing subgroup totals, headings or totals. The first error is reported.

Correct the **error** and **check** the **validity** again. Repeat this step until the accounts are in logical order.

Close the **Accounts window** to return to the Home window.

NOTES

After creating all expense accounts, open the ledger for 5010 and click the Class Options tab. Choose Operating Expense from the Account Class drop-down list. Click the Next Account tool. The Class Options tab remains selected. Continue changing the class for the remaining postable expense accounts.

You can also make these changes when you change the account class for bank and credit card accounts (page 594).

WARNING!

It is important to have the accounts in logical order at this stage. You will be unable to display some reports when the accounts are not in logical order, so you will not be able to check some of your work. You cannot finish the history either if accounts are not in logical order.

Entering Historical Account Balances

The opening historical balances for Flabuless Fitness can be found in the Post-Closing Trial Balance dated March 31, 2008 (page 567). All Income Statement accounts have zero balances because the books were closed at the end of the first quarter. Headings, totals and subgroup totals (i.e., the non-postable accounts) do not have balances. Remember to put any forced balance amounts into the *Test Balance Account*.

Open the account information window for **1060 Bank: Hamilton Trust Chequing**, the first account requiring a balance.

Click the **Opening Balance field**.

Type the **balance**.

Correct the **information** if necessary by repeating the above steps.

Click the **Next button** [▶] to advance to the next ledger account window.

Enter **negative numbers for accounts that decrease the total** in a group or section (e.g., *Allowance for Doubtful Accounts*, *Accum Deprec*, *GST Paid on Purchases*). These account balances are indicated with a minus sign (–) in the Balance Sheet.

Repeat the above **procedures** to **enter** the **balances** for the remaining accounts in the Post-Closing Trial Balance on page 567. *Test Balance Account* should have a zero balance.

NOTES

For account 1140 Bank: USD Chequing, enter $9 500, the balance in Canadian dollars. The USD balance will be added after we set up currencies.

NOTES
Remember that you can finish your session any time. To continue, just open the file, accept the session date and start again from where you left off.

basic BASIC VERSION
The Basic version allows only one foreign currency. Choose United States Dollars from the Foreign Currency drop-down list. Enter Apr 1 in the date column and press tab. Enter 1.185 as the rate for that date.

NOTES
Refer to the chart on page 564 for currency details and to page 309 for a review if you need more assistance.
You can create the new linked account from the currency setup window if needed.

NOTES
Refer to the chart on page 564 for bank information and to page 311 for review of Bank class accounts.

NOTES
We must define 1030 Undeposited Cash and Cheques as a Bank or Cash class account so that we can enter it as the linked bank account for Receivables. Cash is the most appropriate selection.
Both Bank and Cash class accounts are available in the Deposit To field for cash sales and receipts.

Close the **Ledger window** and then the **Accounts window** to return to the Home window.

Display or **print** your **Trial Balance** after entering all account balances to check the account balances.

Adding a Foreign Currency

Flabuless Fitness purchases some inventory items from vendors in the United States and must set up the company files to allow transactions in USD, United States dollars. We will set up the foreign currency now because we need this information for bank account and vendor settings.

Choose the **Setup menu**, then **choose System Settings** and **click Currencies** to open the Currency Information screen.

Click **Allow Transactions In A Foreign Currency**.

Next you must enter the linked account to track exchange rate differences and rounding differences that result from working with only two decimal places for amounts.

Choose **4120 Exchange Rate Differences** from the drop-down list account.

Click the **Foreign Currency List icon**.

Choose **United States Dollars** from the list.

Click **Select** to return to the currency setup screen and add the currency.

Click the **Exchange Rate tab**.

Click the **Date column**.

Type `apr 1` **Press** tab to advance to the Exchange Rate field.

Type `1.185`

Click **Display A Reminder If The Exchange Rate Is One Day Old** to turn on the warning.

Click **OK** to return to the Home window. You are now ready to add all the bank account details.

Defining Bank and Credit Card Class Accounts

Defining bank accounts involves changing the account class to Bank and indicating the currency for the accounts and the cheque and deposit number sequences. If you use online banking, you must also enter the bank name, account numbers and Web site. We must also change the class for *Undeposited Cash and Cheques* to either Bank or Cash to use it as the linked account for receipts. Cash is the appropriate selection. Remember that the bank account class changes must be saved before we can enter the next cheque numbers. Changes are saved automatically when we open the next ledger record.

We must also define the account class for the credit card asset and the credit card payable accounts. We will make all these changes before continuing the setup.

Click the **Accounts icon** 

to open the Accounts window.

Double click **1030 Undeposited Cash and Cheques** to open the ledger.

Click the **Class Options tab**.

Choose **Bank** from the drop-down list of account classes.

Click the **Next Account button** ▶ to open the ledger for account **1060**.

Choose **Bank** from the list of account classes. CAD is the correct currency.

Click the **Next Deposit Number field**.

Type 14

Click the **Next Account button** ▶.

Choose **Bank** as the account class for *1080 Bank: Hamilton Trust Savings.*

Click **Chequing** (Account Type field). **Click Savings** from the list.

Click the **Next Account button** ▶ to **open** the ledger for **1100 Bank: MasterCard**.

Choose **Credit Card Receivable** as the account class.

Click the **Next Account button** ▶ to **open** the ledger for **1120 Bank: Visa and Interac**.

Choose **Credit Card Receivable** as the account class.

Click the **Next Account button** ▶ to **open** the ledger for **1140 Bank: USD Chequing**.

Choose **Bank** as the account class.

Choose **USD** from the Currency field list.

Click the **Select Account list arrow**. Simply Accounting shows a warning:

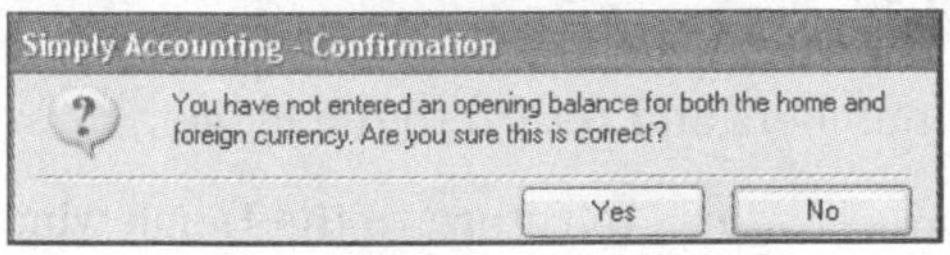

We entered a balance for the foreign account only in Canadian dollars because only one balance field was available at the time. We can now add the USD balance.

Click **No** to return to the Ledger window because we need to enter the opening balance in the second currency.

Click the **Account tab** to access the Opening Balance field. There are now two balance fields, one for each currency.

Click the **Opening Balance In USD field**. **Type** 8020

Click the **Select Account list arrow** again.

Click **2250 Credit Card Payable** to open its ledger screen.

Click the **Class Options tab**.

Choose **Credit Card Payable** as the account class. Credit Card Receivable is not available as a class option for the liability account.

If you have not yet changed the account class for expense accounts,

Click the **Select Account list arrow** again and **choose 5010 Advertising and Promotion**.

Select **Operating Expense** as the account class.

Click the **Next Account button** ▶. **Select Operating Expense** as the account class for the remaining postable expense accounts.

We can now enter the cheque number sequence for the two chequing accounts.

NOTES

To open the ledger for Credit Card Payable, you can click the Next Account button repeatedly or choose the account from the Select Account list arrow.

Click the **Select Account list arrow** again and choose **1060 Bank: Hamilton Trust Chequing**. The Class Options tab screen should still be open.

Click **Change The Next Cheque Number** to open the Reports & Forms window with account 1060 selected in the panel on the left:

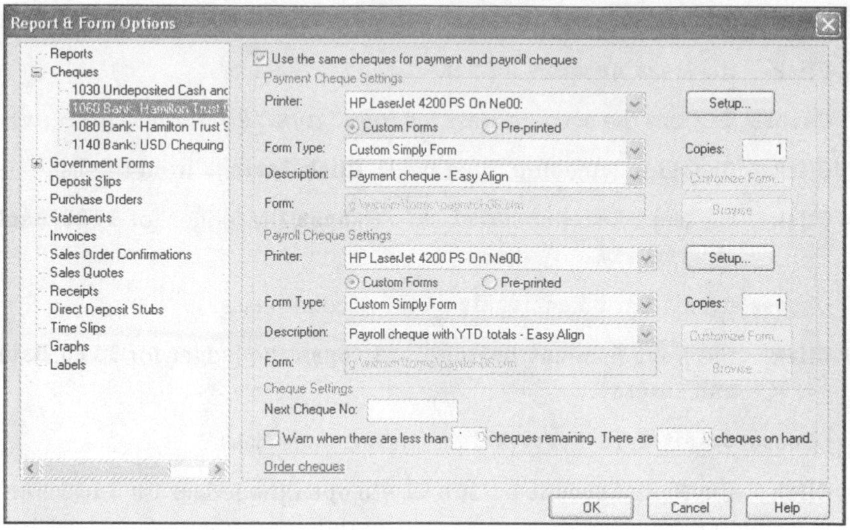

NOTES
Remember that if a cheque is printed in error, an appropriate entry or comment should be recorded to explain the discarded cheque or the missing number.

Click the **Next Cheque No. field** in the Cheque Settings section.

Type `101`

Click **1140 Bank: USD Chequing** in the panel on the left.

Click the **Next Cheque No. field**. **Type** `346`

Click **OK** to save the cheque numbers and return to the ledger.

Close the **Ledger** and **Accounts windows** to return to the Home window.

Setting Defaults for Inventory & Services

Choose the **Setup menu**, then **choose System Settings** and **Settings** and **click Inventory & Services** to see the options for this ledger:

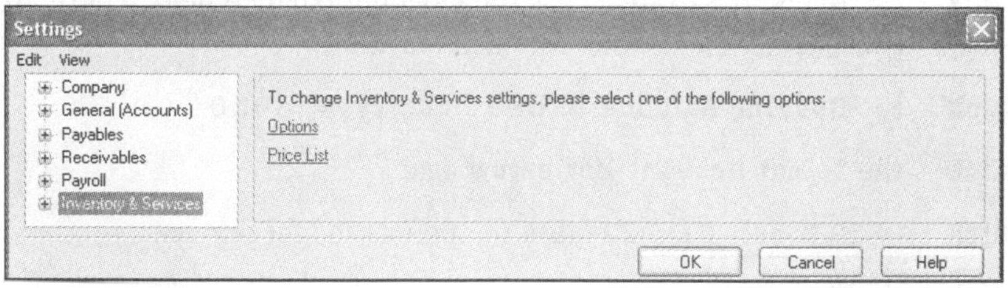

basic BASIC VERSION
The Price List option is not available in the Basic version.

We will enter the Inventory Options now; later we will examine Price List options.

NOTES
Price List settings are used to update inventory prices globally so we must create the inventory items before using this feature.

Click **Options**:

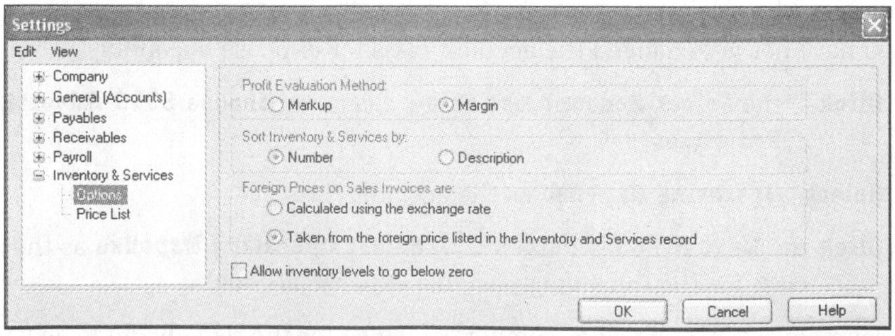

Profits may be calculated on the basis of margin or markup. You can change the setting at any time, so you can prepare reports using both evaluation methods. The formulas for profit evaluation by Margin and Markup are as follows:

Margin = (Selling Price – Cost Price) x 100%/Selling Price

Markup = (Selling Price – Cost Price) x 100%/Cost Price

Flabuless Fitness uses the markup method of evaluating the profit on inventory sales so we need to change the default setting.

Click **Markup** to change the calculation method.

If you choose to sort Inventory Ledger items by description, the product name field will appear before the product number in the Inventory Ledger input forms, and inventory selection lists will be sorted alphabetically by name. When item numbers are not used, sorting by description will make it easier to find the item you want.

Because we added a foreign currency, the option to take foreign prices for sales from the Inventory Ledger or from the exchange rate is added. The default setting to use the foreign price in the Inventory Ledger Record is correct, so we do not have to change the Inventory settings after adding the currency. With this pricing option, you can switch pricing methods for individual items. If you choose the exchange rate method, you cannot choose different methods for different items.

The final option is to Allow Inventory Levels To Go Below Zero. Flabuless Fitness will choose this option to permit customer sales for inventory that is backordered.

Click **Allow Inventory Levels To Go Below Zero** to select the option.

Click **OK** to return to the Home window.

Defining Linked Accounts

Linked accounts are General Ledger accounts that are affected by entries in other journals. For example, recording an inventory purchase will update the Inventory Ledger, several General Ledger accounts and the balance owing to the vendor. Refer to page 313 for a review of linked accounts. Refer to page 93 for a review of the Current Earnings Account. Linked accounts are also needed for other features.

WARNING!

Simply Accounting will not allow you to remove an account while it is being used as a linked account. When you try to remove an account, click OK in the Warning window to return to the Accounts window. First, turn the linking function off by deleting the account in the Linked Accounts window. Then remove the account in the Accounts window. You cannot remove an account if it has a balance or if journal entries have been posted to it.

Identifying General Linked Accounts

The *Current Earnings* capital account records the changes in net income resulting from sales and expenses. At the end of the fiscal period, the net income, the balance from *Current Earnings*, is transferred to the Retained Earnings capital account — *S. Reeves, Capital* is the Retained Earnings account for Flabuless Fitness — and income and expense accounts are reset to zero to prepare for the new fiscal period.

The General Ledger has two linked accounts. Both must be capital accounts.

You should be in the Home window.

GENERAL LINKED ACCOUNTS

Retained Earnings	3560	S. Reeves, Capital
Current Earnings	3600	Current Earnings

Right-click the **General Journal icon** to select it.

Click the **Setup tool** or **choose** the **Setup menu**, then **choose** **System Settings** and **Linked Accounts**. The **General tab** screen opens.

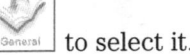

> **NOTES**
> You can create new accounts from any Linked Accounts screen by typing a new account number in the Account field and pressing *tab* to start the Add An Account wizard.

If a journal icon is selected in the Home window, clicking the Setup tool will display the Linked Accounts window for the corresponding ledger.

If no icon is highlighted, click the Setup tool and click General — the journal from the drop-down list — and click Select to display the ledger's linked accounts.

Type the **account number** or **select** the **account** from the drop-down list.

Identifying Linked Accounts for the Payables Ledger

> **NOTES**
> To add the Payables Ledger linked accounts from the Home window, right-click the Purchases or the Payments Journal icon in the Home window to select it.
> Click the Setup tool or choose the Setup menu, then choose System Settings and Linked Accounts and click the Payables tab.

Flabuless Fitness uses *Bank: Hamilton Trust Chequing* as its principal linked bank account for the subsidiary Payables and Payroll ledgers — for all home currency cheque transactions.

PAYABLES		
Bank Account to use for Canadian Dollars	1060	Bank: Hamilton Trust Chequing
Bank Account to use for United States Dollars	1140	Bank: USD Chequing
Accounts Payable	2200	Accounts Payable
Freight Expense	5080	Freight Expense
Purchase Discount	5090	Purchase Discounts
Prepayments and Prepaid Orders	1250	Purchase Prepayments

Click the **Payables tab**.

Type the **account number** or **select** the **account** from the drop-down list for the bank accounts and then for the remaining Payables accounts.

Receivables Linked Accounts

> **NOTES**
> To add the Receivables Ledger linked accounts from the Home window, right-click the Sales or the Receipts Journal icon in the Home window to select it.
> Click the Setup tool or choose the Setup menu, then choose System Settings and Linked Accounts and click the Receivables tab.

The following accounts are required as linked accounts for the Receivables Ledger.

RECEIVABLES LINKED ACCOUNTS		
Bank Account to use for Canadian Dollars	1030	Undeposited Cash and Cheques
Bank Account to use for United States Dollars	1140	Bank: USD Chequing
Accounts Receivable	1200	Accounts Receivable
Freight Revenue	4200	Freight Revenue
Sales Discount	4060	Sales Discounts
Deposits and Prepaid Orders	2210	Prepaid Sales and Deposits

Cheques and cash receipts are held in the *Undeposited Cash and Cheques* account and then deposited weekly to the *Bank: Hamilton Trust Chequing* account. Therefore, the default bank account for receipts is *Undeposited Cash and Cheques*.

Click the **Receivables tab**.

Type the **account number** or **select** the **account** for all Receivables accounts. Start with the bank accounts.

Identifying the Payroll Linked Accounts

There are many linked accounts for payroll because each type of income, tax, deduction and expense that is used must be linked to a General Ledger account. The following linked accounts are used by Flabuless Fitness for the Payroll Ledger.

PAYROLL LINKED ACCOUNTS

Principal Bank 1060 Bank: Hamilton Trust Chequing

INCOME

Vacation Owed	2300 Vacation Payable	Advances	1220 Advances Receivable
Vac. Earned	5300 Wages	Commission	5310 Commissions & Bonuses
Regular	5300 Wages	No. Clients	5310 Commissions & Bonuses
Overtime 1	5300 Wages	Bonus	5310 Commissions & Bonuses
Overtime 2	Not used	Tuition	5380 Employee Benefits
Salary	5305 Salaries	Travel Exp.	5320 Travel Expenses

DEDUCTIONS

RRSP	2400 RRSP Payable	CSB Plan	2410 CSB Plan Payable

TAXES

Payables

				NOT USED
EI	2310 EI Payable	EHT	2380 EHT Payable	Tax (Que.)
CPP	2320 CPP Payable	WSIB	2460 WSIB Payable	QPP
Tax	2330 Income Tax Payable			QHSF
				QPIP

Expenses

				NOT USED
EI	5330 EI Expense	WSIB	5350 WSIB Expense	QPP
CPP	5340 CPP Expense	EHT	5360 EHT Expense	QHSF
				QPIP

USER-DEFINED EXPENSES

Payables: Gp Insurance	2420	Group Insurance Payable
Expenses: Gp Insurance	5370	Gp Insurance Expense

Click the **Payroll Income tab** to display the Linked Accounts for Income:

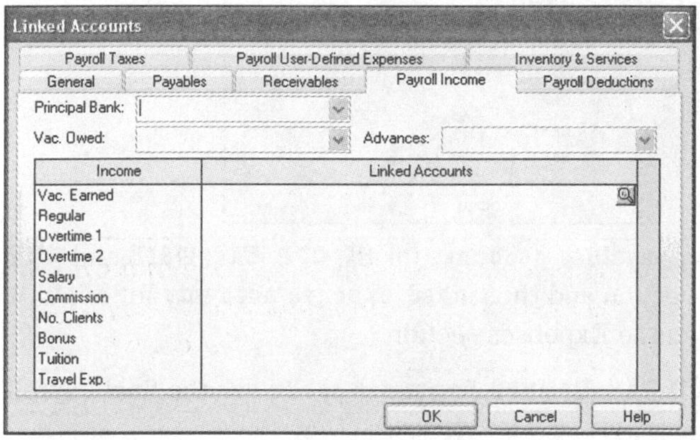

The linked accounts for all types of income appear together on this first tab screen. You must identify a wage account for each type of employee payment used by the company, even if the same account is used for all of them. Once the Payroll bank account is identified as the same one used for Payables, the program will apply a single sequence of cheque numbers for all cheques prepared from the Payables and Payroll journals.

If you can use an account for more than one link, the account will be available in the drop-down list. Otherwise, once an account is selected as a linked account, it is removed from the list.

Type the **account number** or **select** the **account** from the drop-down list.

Press *tab* to advance to the next linked account field.

Choose **1060 Bank: Hamilton Trust Chequing** for the Principal Bank field.

Choose **2300 Vacation Payable** for the Vacation field.

NOTES

To add the Payroll Ledger linked accounts from the Home window, right-click the Paycheques or the Payroll Cheque Run Journal icon in the Home window to select it.

If another Home window icon is already highlighted, you can use the appropriate arrow keys to select the Paycheques icon.

Click the Setup tool or choose the Setup menu, then choose System Settings and Linked Accounts and click the Payroll Income tab.

If no Home window icon is selected, you can use the Setup tool icon pop-up list, choose Payroll and click Select.

NOTES

The deleted income and deduction names do not appear on the screens for linked accounts.

NOTES

You can add accounts from the Linked Accounts windows. Type a new number, press *enter* and choose to add the account.

Choose **1220 Advances Receivable** for the Advances field.

Choose **5300 Wages** for Vacation Earned, Regular and Overtime 1.

Choose **5310 Commissions & Bonuses** for Commission, No. Clients and Bonus.

Choose **5380 Employee Benefits** for Tuition.

Choose **5320 Travel Expenses** for Travel Exp.

Click the **Payroll Deductions tab** to see the next set of Payroll accounts:

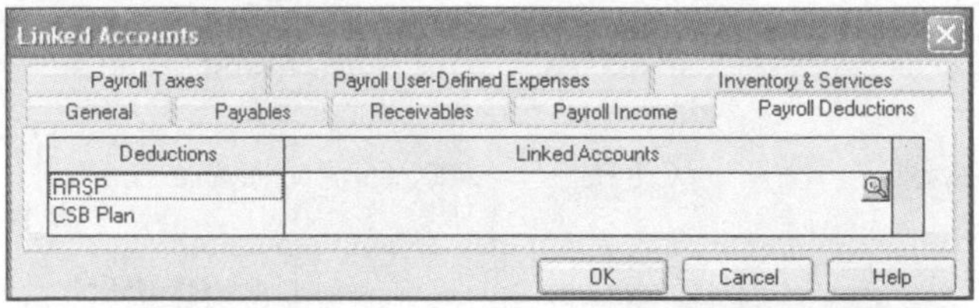

The names here are the ones you entered in the Names & Terminology window from the Setup menu. If you deleted a name, it will not appear here.

Enter the **linked** payable **accounts** for **RRSP** and **CSB Plan** from the chart on page 599.

Click the **Payroll Taxes tab** to see the next set of Payroll linked accounts:

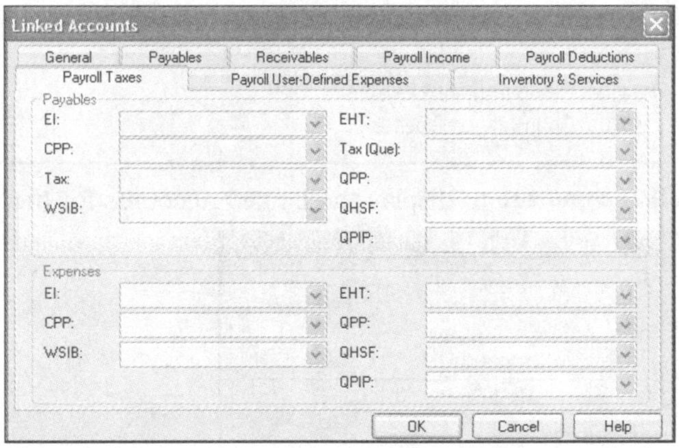

Enter the **linked payables accounts** for **EI**, **CPP**, **Tax**, **WSIB** and **EHT** in the Payables section and the **linked expense accounts** for **EI**, **CPP**, **WSIB** and **EHT** in the Expenses section.

Click the **Payroll User-Defined Expenses tab** to see the final Payroll accounts:

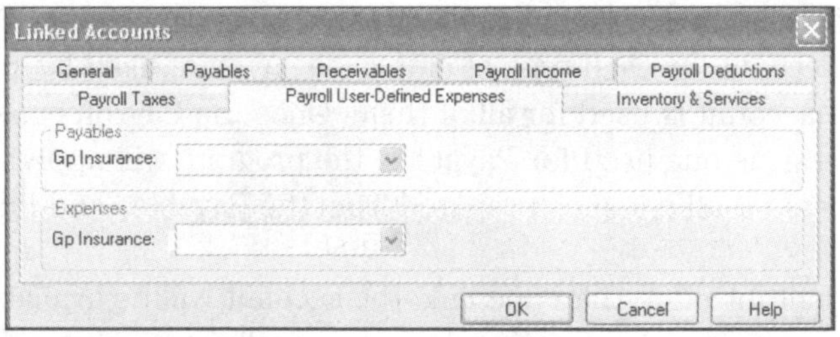

Enter the **linked** payable **accounts** for **Gp Insurance Payable** and **Gp Insurance Expense** from the chart on page 599.

Check the **linked** payroll **accounts** against the chart on page 599 before proceeding. **Click** the **tabs** to see different linked account screens.

Inventory Items Linked Accounts

Flabuless Fitness currently uses only one linked account for inventory, the one for inventory adjustments or damaged merchandise. The linked accounts for the Inventory Ledger are listed here:

INVENTORY	
Item Assembly Costs	Not used
Adjustment Write-off	5040 Damaged Inventory

Click the **Inventory & Services tab** to open the Inventory Linked Accounts window:

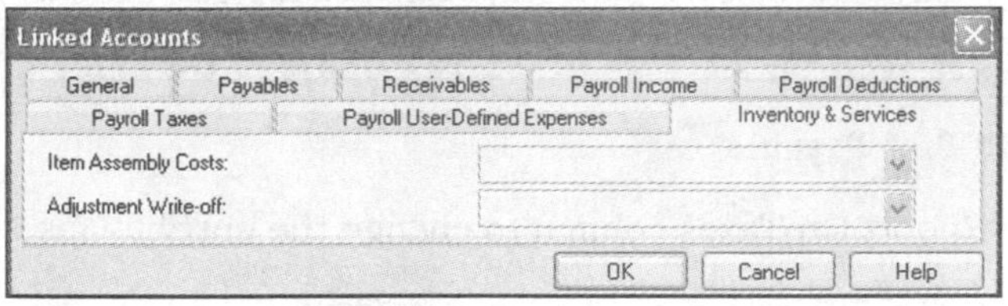

Type the **account number** or **select** the **account** from the drop-down list.

Choose **5040 Damaged Inventory** as the Adjustment Write-off linked account.

Click **OK** to save the new linked accounts.

Click **Yes** to accept the account class change for account 3560.

Click **Yes** to accept the account class change for *Accounts Payable*.

Click **Yes** to accept the account class change for *Accounts Receivable* and return to the Home window.

NOTES
To add the Inventory and Services Ledger linked accounts from the Home window, right-click the Item Assembly or the Inventory Adjustments Journal icon in the Home window to select it.

Click the Setup tool or choose the Setup menu, then choose System Settings and Linked Accounts and click the Inventory & Services tab.

WARNING!
Check your work carefully. Although you can change the designated linked accounts at any time, journal entries will be posted incorrectly if you do not have the correct linked accounts.

Setting Up Sales Taxes

Flabuless Fitness charges and pays GST and PST so we need to set up default codes for these two taxes. The business wants to generate reports on both taxes.

Choose the **Setup menu**, then **choose System Settings** and **click Sales Taxes** to access the Sales Tax Information screen:

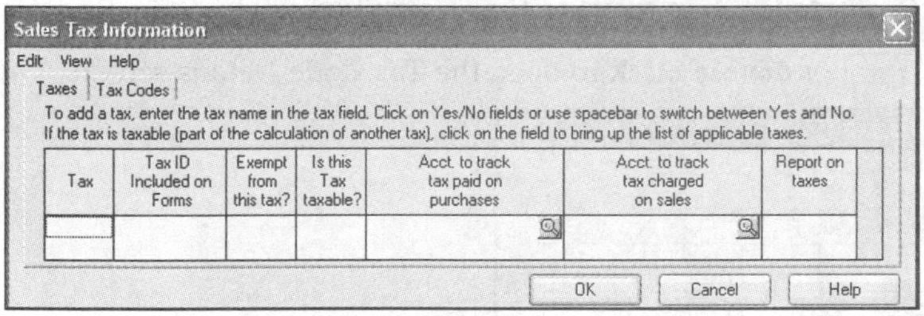

The cursor is in the Tax field on the Taxes tab screen where you should enter the name of the tax. We will enter the information for GST first.

Type GST **Press** *tab* to advance to the Tax ID field where we enter the business number.

Type 245 138 121 **Press** *tab* to advance to the **Exempt From This Tax?** column.

Flabuless Fitness is not tax exempt for GST so the default, No, is correct. GST is not taxable in Ontario (no other tax is charged on GST as it is in PEI and Quebec).

Click , the **List icon for Acct To Track Tax Paid On Purchases**.

NOTES
Refer to the chart on page 564 for sales tax information. Refer to page 317 for a review of sales taxes if you need further assistance.

NOTES
For PEI in the Tesses Tresses application, and for Quebec in the Village Galleries application, we entered Yes for GST for Is This Tax Taxable? because PST is charged on GST in those provinces. (GST is taxable.) When you click Yes in the Is This Tax Taxable? column for GST, a list of taxes opens, and you can select the taxes that are to be charged on GST.

Choose **2670 GST Paid on Purchases**. The cursor advances to the field for the Account To Track Taxes Charged On Sales.

Choose **2650 GST Charged on Sales** from the List icon list of accounts. The cursor advances to the Report On Taxes field.

Click **No** to change the default entry to Yes.

Press *tab* so you can enter the information for PST.

Type PST

NOTES

Flabuless Fitness is exempt from PST on purchases of inventory items for sale in the store. These exemptions are handled through the vendor tax codes.

Flabuless Fitness is not exempt for PST, the ID number is not required, PST is not taxable and the tax is not refundable so PST paid on purchases is not tracked.

Click , the **List icon for Acct To Track Tax Charged On Sales**.

Double click **2640 PST Payable**.

Click **No** in the Report On Taxes column to change the entry to Yes.

Entering Tax Codes

Click the **Tax Codes tab** to open the next information screen:

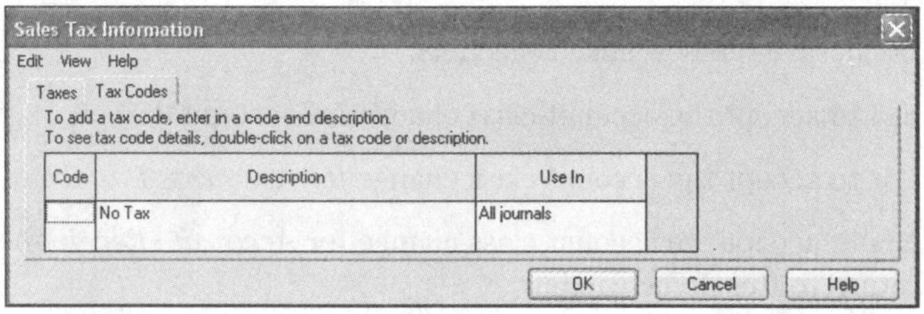

A single code, No Tax, is created as a default.

We need to create tax codes for sales and purchases when GST alone is charged and when both PST and GST apply. There are currently no situations where Flabuless Fitness charges or pays only PST but there are purchases with both taxes included so we need a code for this situation as well (e.g., gasoline is priced with all taxes included).

Click the **Code column** below the blank on the first line.

Type G **Press** *tab* to move to the Description field.

Press *enter* or **double click** to open the Tax Code Details screen:

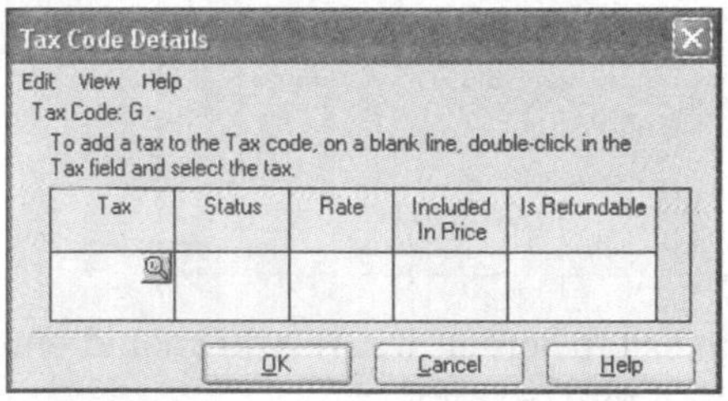

Click the **Tax field List icon** to see the list of taxes entered:

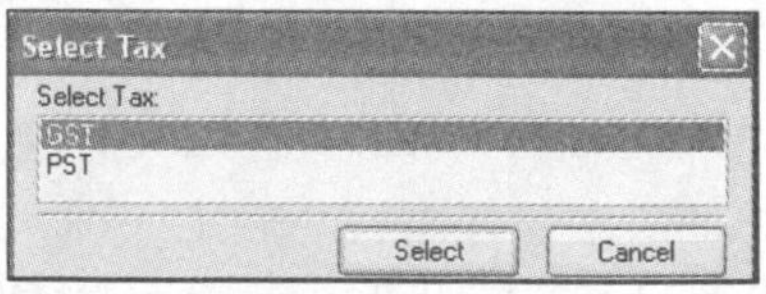

Both taxes from the Taxes tab screen appear on the list.

Click **Select** because GST is already selected and return to the Details.

Defaults are entered for the remaining fields. The **Status** is **Taxable** and the tax is **not included** — these are correct — tax is calculated and charged and is not included in the price.

Click the **Rate field**.

Type 7

Click **No** in the Is Refundable column to change the entry to Yes.

Click **OK** to return to the Tax Codes screen for additional codes.

The description GST @ 7% appears beside the code G and the tax is used in all journals. You can edit the description if you want. If the tax were not refundable, non-refundable would be added to the description automatically. We are ready to enter the second code, to apply both GST and PST.

Press tab **twice** to advance to the next line in the Code column.

Type GP **Press** tab to move to the Description field.

Press enter to open the Tax Code Details screen.

Click the **Tax field List icon**. **Click** **Select** because GST is already selected and return to the Details.

Again, the defaults — **Status (Taxable)** and **not included** — are correct.

Click the **Rate field**. **Type** 7

Click **No** in the Is Refundable column to change the entry to Yes.

Press tab to return to the Tax field again.

Press enter and then **press** enter again to select PST.

Click the **Rate field**. **Type** 8

PST is taxable, not refundable, not included in the price and the tax is used in all journals so the remaining defaults are correct.

Click **OK** to return to the Tax Codes tab screen. The description GST @ 7%; PST @ 8%, non-refundable has been added.

Press tab **twice** to advance to the next line in the Code column, below GP.

Type IN **Press** tab to move to the Description field.

Press enter or **double click** to open the Tax Code Details screen.

Click the **Tax field List icon** to see the list of taxes.

Click **Select** to enter GST, the selected tax, and return to the Details.

The tax Status for GST is Taxable and this is correct.

Click the **Rate field**. **Type** 7

Click **No** in the Included In Price column to change the entry to Yes.

Click **No** in the Is Refundable column to change the entry to Yes.

Press tab to return to the Tax field again. PST at 8% is taxable, included in the price and not refundable.

Press enter and **click** **Select** to add PST.

Click the **Rate field**. **Type** 8

Click **No** in the Included In Price column to change the entry to Yes.

Click **OK** to return to the Tax Codes tab screen.

No description appears beside the code IN so we must add it. The cursor is in the Description field beside IN.

Type `GST @ 7%, included; PST @ 8%, included`

Click **OK** to save the settings and return to the Home window.

Entering a Default Customer Tax Code

The default tax code will be selected when we enter the customer records.

Right-click the **Customers icon** and **click** the **Setup tool**.

Click **Options**.

Click the **Tax Code For New Customers field** to see the list of tax codes.

Click **GP GST @ 7%; PST @ 8%, non-refundable**.

Leave the **Settings window open** for the next step.

Setting Up Import Duties

Although most goods imported from the United States are not subject to tariffs or import duties because of NAFTA (the North American Free Trade Agreement), you should know how to set up this feature. We will set up the program to charge duty but set the rates at zero so that no duty will be applied on purchases. You must activate the Duty option before creating vendor records so that you can indicate in the vendor records those vendors that supply goods on which duty is charged. Without these two steps, the duty fields in the Purchases Journal will be unavailable.

A Payables account is linked to import duties for the liability to the Receiver General.

Click **Payables** and then **click Duty** to access the settings we need:

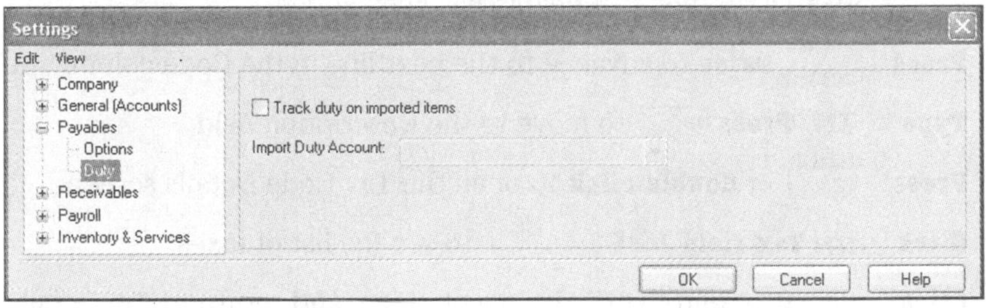

Click **Track Duty On Imported Items** to use the feature.

Click **2220 Import Duty Payable** from the Import Duty Account drop-down list.

Click **OK** to return to the Home window.

NOTES
Refer to the chart on page 564 for credit card details. To review credit card setup, refer to page 320 for additional information.

Setting Up Credit Cards

Flabuless Fitness accepts Visa and MasterCard credit card payments from customers as well as debit cards (Interac). The store also uses a Visa card to pay for some purchases. Setting up credit cards includes naming them, identifying the linked accounts and entering fees associated with the cards.

You should be in the Home window.

Choose the **Setup menu**, then **choose System Settings** and **click Credit Cards** to see the Credit Card Information screen. The cursor is in the Credit Card Name field for Credit Cards Accepted.

Type Visa **Press** tab to advance to the Discount Fee % field.

Type 2.5 **Press** tab to advance to the Expense Account field.

Press enter to see the list of accounts available for linking.

Double click **5030** to choose and enter the account. The cursor advances to the Asset Account field.

Press enter to see the list of accounts available for linking.

Double click **1120** to choose and add the credit card bank account.

Enter **MasterCard** as the name, **2.7** as the fee, **5030** as the Expense account and **1100** as the Asset account for the second credit card.

Enter **Interac** as the name, **0** as the %, **5030** as the Expense account and **1120** as the Asset account to set up the debit card.

Click the **Credit Cards Used tab** to open the screen for the cards that the business uses. Flabuless Fitness uses a Visa card.

Click the **Credit Card Name field**.

Type Visa **Press** tab to move to the Payable Account field.

Press enter to see the list of available accounts.

Double click **2250** to add the account and move to the Expense Account field.

Press enter to see the account list.

Double click **5030**.

Click **OK** to save the information.

NOTES
You must choose a Credit Card Receivable or Bank class account as the Asset Account for cards accepted.

WARNING!
Although accounts in other classes appear on the Select Account list, selecting them will generate an error message when you save the entries.

NOTES
You must choose a Credit Card Payable or Bank class account as the Payable Account for cards used.

Preparing the Payables Ledger

Use Flabuless Fitness's Vendor Information on pages 567–568 to create the vendor records and add the outstanding historical invoices. If any information is missing for a vendor, leave that field blank.

NOTES
For a review of the Payables Ledger setup, refer to page 322.

Entering Vendor Accounts

Click the **Vendors icon** in the Home window to open the Vendors window.

Click the **Create button** or **choose** the **File menu** and **click Create** or **press** ctrl + **N**. The Vendor field is highlighted in the Payables Ledger window, ready for you to enter information.

Enter the vendor's **name**. On the Address tab screen, enter the **contact**, **address**, **phone**, **fax** and **tax ID** numbers, and the **e-mail** and **Web site** addresses from pages 567–568.

Click the **Options tab**.

NOTES
We do not provide default expense accounts for vendors if more than one account is linked to the vendor. For example, Ancaster Insurance is linked to Prepaid Insurance, RRSP Payable and Group Insurance Payable. The Receiver General is linked to both GST accounts and to the income tax-related payables accounts.

Vendors who supply inventory items also have no default account because inventory purchases have account numbers entered automatically.

Enter the **discounts**, if there are any, in the Terms fields, and the number of days in which the net amount is due. **Click Calculate Discounts Before Tax** if the discounts are before tax. Otherwise, leave the box unchecked.

You can print the contact on cheques if this is appropriate for the vendor.

Enter the **default expense account** for the vendor if there is one.

Click the **Taxes tab** to open the tax information screen for the vendor.

Click the **Tax Code field list arrow** to see the codes:

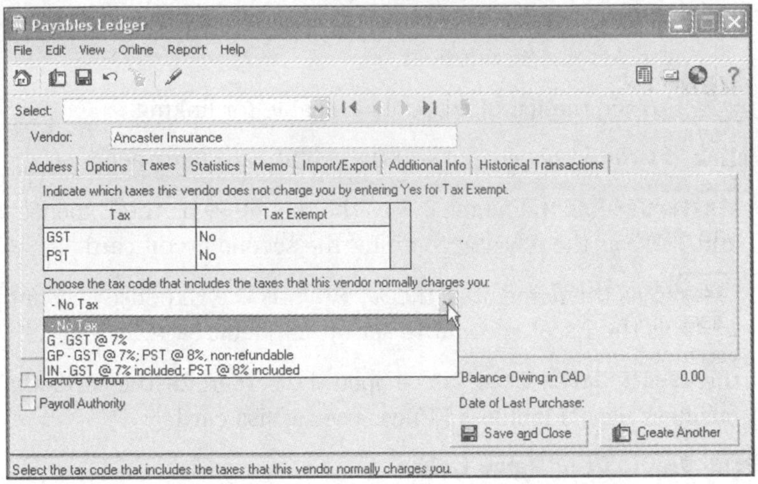

NOTES
Leaving the code as No Tax and leaving the exempt status set at No will permit you to charge taxes if needed. PST is applied to insurance in Ontario.
If taxes are not calculated correctly for a vendor or customer, check that the Ledger entries for Tax Exempt are No.

The Taxes screen is shown above for the first vendor that you enter, Ancaster Insurance. The selection No Tax is correct for Ancaster Insurance because some transactions are taxable and others are not.

Click **No** in the Tax Exempt column for GST to change the setting to Yes.

Do not change the tax exempt setting for PST because PST is charged on insurance in Ontario.

It is not necessary to change Tax Exempt entries. Leaving the setting at No will make all tax codes available for a vendor. As long as the tax code in the journal is correct, taxes will be calculated correctly. You can change the tax settings at any time.

Correct any **errors** by returning to the field with the mistake, highlighting the errors and entering the correct information.

Enter **historical transactions** using the keystroke instructions in the following section if the vendor has historical transactions.

Click **Create Another** 

to save the record and open a blank Payables Ledger window.

Click the **Address tab** to begin entering the next vendor record.

NOTES
Feelyte Gym Accessories is the first vendor with historical invoices.

Entering Historical Vendor Transactions

The chart on page 568 provides the information you need to complete this stage.

Click the **Historical Transactions tab**.

Click **Save Now**.

Click **Invoices**.

Enter the **Invoice Number**, **Date**, **Pre-Tax Amount** and **Tax** for the first invoice. The default terms should be correct.

Press tab to advance to the next field after entering each piece of information.

When all the information is entered correctly, you must save your vendor invoice.

Click **Record** to save the invoice and to display another blank invoice for this vendor.

Repeat these steps to **enter other invoices** for this vendor.

Click **Close** to return to the Payables Ledger when you have recorded all outstanding invoices for the vendor.

Historical Payments

Click **Payments**.

Click the **Number field**.

Enter the **cheque number** for the first payment.

Press tab and **enter** the **payment date** for the first payment. Skip the Discount fields because discounts are taken only when the early payment is a full payment.

Click the **Amount Paid column** (on the line for the invoice being paid).

Enter the **payment amount**.

Press tab to advance to the next invoice if there is one. Delete any amounts or discounts that are not included in the payment.

Click **Record** to save the information and to display an updated statement for this vendor.

Repeat these steps to **enter other payments** to this vendor.

When you have recorded all outstanding payments for a vendor,

Click **Close** to return to the Payables Ledger for the vendor. Notice that the payments you have just entered have been added to the Balance field.

Click the **Create tool** to display a new blank Payables Ledger screen.

Click the **Address tab**.

Repeat these procedures to **enter** the **remaining vendors** and their **historical transactions**.

Identifying Foreign Vendors

In order to identify Prolife Exercisers Inc. and Redux Home Gym Wholesalers as foreign vendors, the Options tab screen requires additional information.

NOTES
The historical invoices and payments will be entered on the Statistics tab screen as Last Year's Purchases and Payments because we are starting a new fiscal period.

NOTES
Footlink Corporation is the only vendor with historical payments.

WARNING!
If you save an incorrect invoice amount, you must pay the invoice, clear paid invoices for the vendor (Home window, Maintenance menu), reset the payments for the year to zero (vendor's ledger, Statistics tab) and re-enter the outstanding invoices. Refer to page 339.

The Options tab fields for Prolife Exercisers Inc. are shown here:

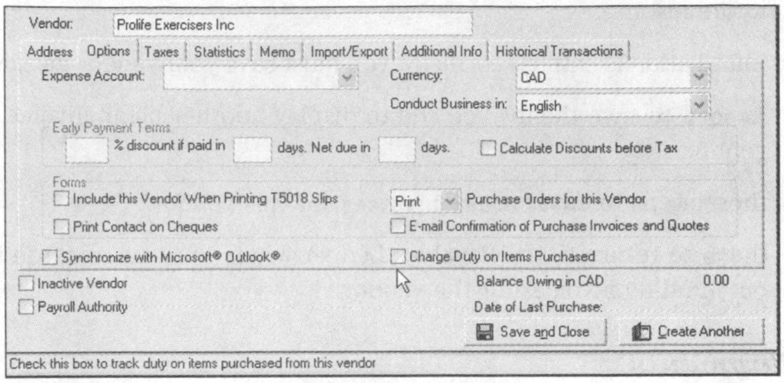

Enter **2**% in **10** days, net **30** days as the Early Payment Terms for the vendor.

Click **Calculate Discounts Before Tax**.

Click the **Currency field list arrow**.

Click **USD**.

Click **Charge Duty On Items Purchased**.

You must change this Duty setting to access the duty fields in the Purchases Journal for this vendor.

You cannot enter a default expense account for inventory purchases because the account is selected automatically by the program from the Inventory Ledger record. You do not need to enter any details on the Statistics, Memo and Import/Export tab screens. The Balance Owing will be entered automatically by the program once you have entered historical invoices.

Click the **Taxes tab** and **choose code G** for the foreign vendor.

Correct any **errors** by returning to the field with the mistake, highlighting the errors and entering the correct information.

Click the **Historical Transactions tab** and **click Save Now** if the vendor has historical transactions. (Proceed to the next keystroke section.)

Click **Create Another** 

to save the record and open a blank Payables Ledger window.

Click the **Address tab** to begin entering the next vendor record.

WARNING!

You cannot change a vendor's currency after adding historical transactions. You will need to pay the invoices, clear paid transactions and then remove the vendor record.

You cannot access the duty fields in the Purchases Journal unless Charge Duty On Items Purchased is checked in the vendor's ledger.

Invoices for Foreign Vendors

Click **Invoices** on the Historical Transactions tab screen.

The Historical Invoices input screen for foreign vendors has additional fields for the second currency information, as shown here for Redux Home Gym Wholesalers:

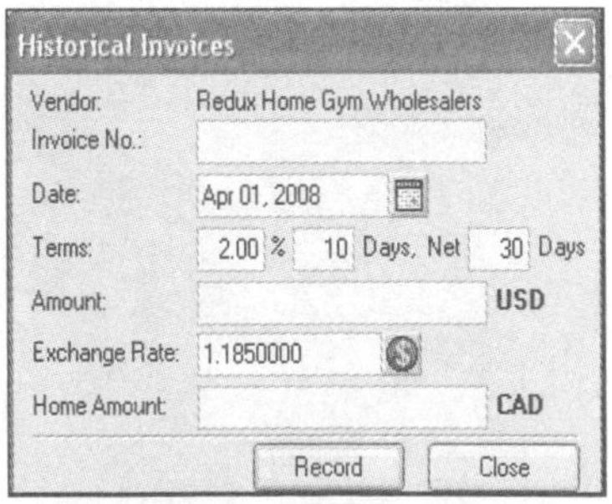

You can edit the payment terms for individual invoices if needed.

Because Redux discounts are calculated after taxes, there are no separate fields for pretax and tax invoice amounts.

Enter **R-914** as the **Invoice Number** and **Mar 28** as the invoice **Date**.

Press tab to see the Exchange Rate screen.

Click **Cancel**. We will enter the amounts in both currencies and allow the program to calculate the exchange rate.

WARNING!
You must enter this information in the correct order for the exchange rate calculation to be made correctly.

Click the **Amount field for USD**.

Type 6345

Click the **Home Amount field for CAD**.

Type 7490 **Press** tab.

The exchange rate is determined automatically from these two amounts.

Click **Record**.

When you have recorded all outstanding invoices for a vendor,

Click **Close** to save the invoice and return to the Historical Transactions tab screen.

The invoices you entered have been added to the Balance fields. Balances are displayed in both currencies. Continue by entering historical payments to this vendor if there are any, or proceed to enter the next vendor.

Click the **Create tool**. **Click** the **Address tab**. **Enter** the **remaining vendors**.

Click **Save and Close** Save and Close after adding the last vendor and then **close** the **Vendors window**.

Display or **print** the **Vendor List** and the **Vendor Aged Detail Report**, including terms and historical differences, to check the accuracy of your work.

Preparing the Receivables Ledger

Use Flabuless Fitness's Customer Information on pages 568–569 to create the customer records and add the outstanding historical invoices. Revenue accounts are added from the inventory records so they are not needed in the customers' records. If any information is missing for a customer, leave that field blank.

NOTES
For a review of the Receivables Ledger setup, refer to page 331.

Entering Customer Accounts

Click the **Customers icon** Customers in the Home window to open the Customers window.

Click the **Create button** Create or **choose** the **File menu** and then **click** **Create**. The Customer field in the Receivables Ledger window is highlighted, ready for you to enter information.

Enter the customer's **name**. On the Address tab screen, enter the **contact**, **address**, **phone** and **fax numbers**, and the **e-mail** and **Web site addresses** according to pages 568–569.

You can edit the default payment terms for individual customers or for individual historical invoices if necessary.

Click the **Ship-To Address tab**.

Click **Same As Mailing Address** to have the same address apply to both fields on invoices, orders and quotes.

Click the **Options tab**.

Most entries on the Options tab screen are correct. Terms are entered from the default Receivables settings. Customer statements should be printed. Buffalo Health Clinic and Lockport Gymnasium are USD customers. All other customers are Canadian and use the Home currency (CAD).

NOTES
The preferred customers are:
Buffalo Health Clinic
Chedoke Health Care
McMaster University
Mohawk College
Stelco Health Club

Choose **USD** from the Currency list for Buffalo Health Clinic (and for Lockport Gymnasium).

Choose **Preferred** from the Price List field list for **Buffalo Health Clinic** and for other preferred customers (the ones marked with * in the customer information chart) to change the price list for these customers.

WARNING!
Do not forget to remove the discount for cash and credit card customer sales. Changing the ledger records will make the sales invoice terms correct automatically.

Change the payment **terms** to **net 1** for **Cash and Interac**, **Visa** and **MasterCard customers**.

Click the **Taxes tab**. For most customers, the default code GP is correct.

Buffalo Health Clinic and Lockport Gymnasium, the foreign currency customers, do not pay taxes.

Select **tax code No Tax** from the drop down list for the US customers.

Click the **Statistics tab**.

Enter the **credit limit** in both currencies in the Credit Limit fields.

This is the amount that the customer can purchase on account before payments are required. If the customer goes beyond the credit limit, the program will issue a warning before posting an invoice.

The balance owing will be included automatically once you have provided the outstanding invoice information. If the customer has outstanding transactions, proceed to the next section on historical information. Otherwise,

Click **Create Another** 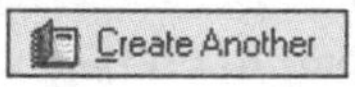

to save the information and advance to the next new Receivables Ledger input screen.

Click the **Address tab**.

Entering Historical Customer Information

WARNING!
If you save an incorrect invoice amount, you must pay the incorrect invoice, clear paid transactions for the customer, then re-enter the customer's outstanding invoices. Refer to page 339.

The chart on page 569 provides the information you need to complete this stage.

Click the **Historical Transactions tab**.

Click **Save Now**.

Click **Invoices**.

Enter the **invoice number**, **date** and **amount** for the first invoice. The default terms should be correct.

Press *tab* to advance to the next field after entering each piece of information.

When all the information is entered correctly, you must save the customer invoice.

Click **Record** to save the information and to display another blank invoice for this customer.

Repeat these procedures to **enter** the **remaining invoices** for the customer, if there are any.

When you have recorded all outstanding invoices for a customer,

Click **Close** to return to the Receivables Ledger window for the customer.

The invoices you entered have been added to the Balance field. Continue by entering payments received from this customer, if there are any, or proceed to enter the next customer.

Click **Payments**.

Click the **Number field**.

Enter the **cheque number** for the first payment.

Press tab and **enter** the **payment date** for the first payment. Again, discounts apply only to full payments made before the due dates, so you can skip the Discount fields.

Click the **Amount Paid column** (on the line for the invoice being paid).

Enter the **payment amount**.

Press tab to advance to the next amount if other invoices are being paid. Delete any amounts or discounts that are not included in the payment.

Click **Record** to save the information and to display an updated statement for this customer.

Repeat these procedures to **enter** the **remaining payments** from the customer.

When you have recorded all outstanding receipts from a customer,

Click **Close** to return to the Receivables Ledger window for the customer.

The payments you entered have been added to the customer's Balance field.

Click **Create tool** to open another new Receivables Ledger input screen.

Click the **Address tab** to prepare for entering other customers. After entering all customer records and historical data,

Click **Save and Close** Save and Close (or ☒) after adding the last customer. **Close** the **Customers window** to return to the Home window.

Display or **print** the **Customer List** and the **Customer Aged Detail Report**, including terms and historical differences, to check your work.

WARNING!
Remember not to include any discounts taken in the historical payments.

Preparing the Payroll Ledger

Use the Flabuless Fitness Employee Information Sheet, Employee Profiles and Additional Payroll Information on pages 569–571 to create the employee records and add historical information.

We will enter the information for Flabuless Fitness employee George Schwinn.

Click the **Employees icon** Employees in the Home window.

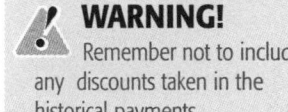

The Employees icon window opens:

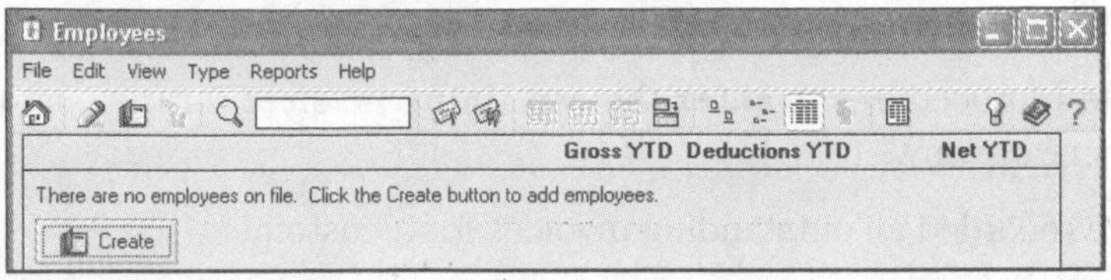

The Employees icon window is blank because no employees are on file at this stage.

Click the **Create button** Create or **choose** the **File menu** and **click Create**.

Entering Personal Details for Employees

The following Payroll Ledger new employee information form will open at the Personal information tab screen so you can begin to enter the employee record:

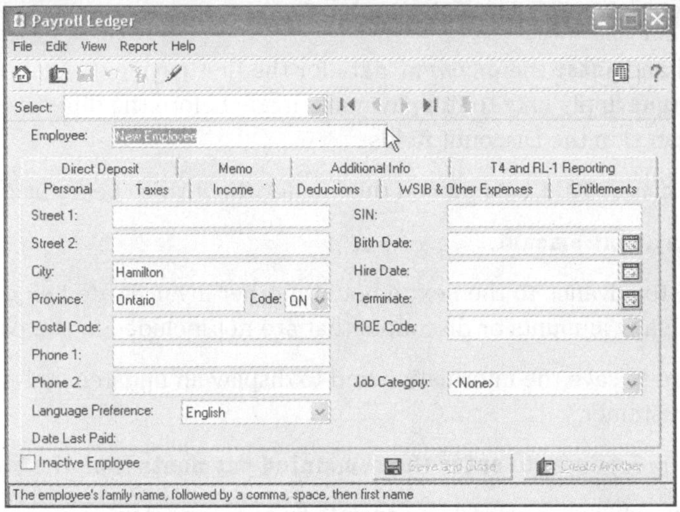

If you skip the Employees icon window in the Setup menu, User Preferences, View tab screen you will see the Payroll Ledger window immediately when you click the Employees icon.

The Payroll Ledger has a large number of tabs for the different kinds of payroll information. The Employee field is highlighted, ready for you to enter information. By entering the surname first, your employee lists will be in correct alphabetic order.

Type `Schwinn, George` **Press** *tab*.

The cursor advances to the Street 1 field.

Type `55 Carter St.`

The default city, province and province code, those for the store, are correct.

Click the **Postal Code field**.

Type `l8b2v7` **Press** *tab*.

The program corrects the postal code format and advances the cursor to the Phone 1 field.

> **NOTES**
> The program will allow you to omit the Social Insurance Number but you must enter the employee's birth date.

Type `9054261817`

The default **Language Preference** is correctly set as English.

Click the **Social Insurance Number (SIN) field**. The program corrects the telephone number format. You must use a valid SIN.

Type `532548625` **Press** *tab*.

The cursor advances to the Birth Date field. Enter the month, day and year using any accepted date format.

Type 9-18-69 **Press** *tab* **twice**.

The cursor moves to the Hire Date field, which should contain the date when the employee began working for Flabuless Fitness.

Type 1-6-03

The next two fields will be used when the employee leaves the job — the date of termination and the reason for leaving that you can select from the drop-down list. The final option designates employees as active or inactive. All employees at Flabuless Fitness are active, so the default selection is correct.

Job Categories are used to identify salespersons who can be linked to specific sales so that their sales revenue is tracked and used to calculate commissions. The employee's Job Category can be selected here if categories are already set up, or you can place employees in categories when you create the categories. We will create categories later and assign employees to them at that stage.

When you use Simply Accounting to pay employees, the Date Last Paid will be entered automatically by the program.

The remaining details for the employee are entered on the other tab screens.

NOTES

The termination date and reason for leaving a job will determine the employee's eligibility to collect Employment Insurance.

Entering Employee Tax Information

Click the **Taxes tab** to advance to the next set of employee details:

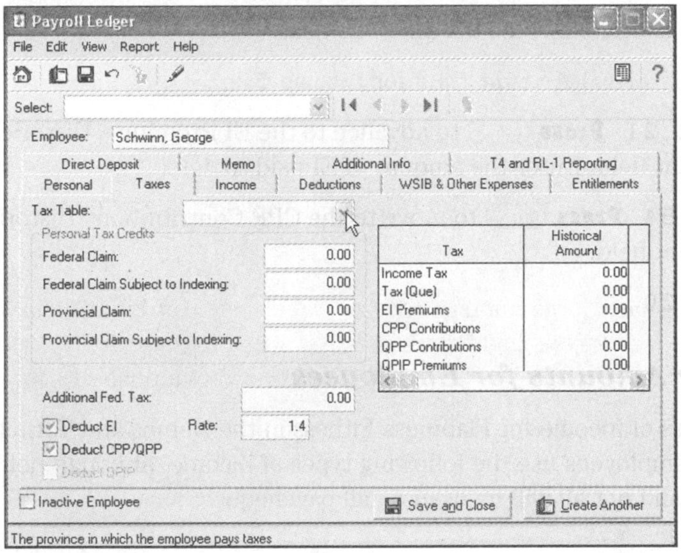

This screen allows you to enter income tax–related information for an employee, including the historical amounts for the year to date.

Click the **Tax Table list arrow**. A list of provinces and territories appears on the screen.

Click **Ontario**, the province of taxation for Flabuless Fitness for income tax purposes.

Press *tab* to advance to the **Federal Claim** field, which holds the total claim for personal tax credits.

Type 9039 **Press** *tab* to advance to the **Federal Claim Subject To Indexing**. This is the amount of personal claim minus pension and tuition/education exemption amounts.

NOTES

For all Flabuless Fitness employees, the total federal and provincial claim amounts are subject to indexing. Governments raise these claim amounts based on inflation and budget decisions.

Type 9039 **Press** (tab) to advance to the Provincial Claim field.

Since 2001, provincial personal income taxes have not been linked to the rates for federal income taxes so separate **provincial claim** amounts are needed.

Type 8377 **Press** (tab).

Type 8377 **Press** (tab) to enter the Provincial Claim Amount Subject To Indexing.

The cursor advances to the **Additional Federal Tax** field.

If an employee has chosen to have additional federal income tax deducted from each paycheque, you can enter the amount of the deduction in the **Additional Fed. Tax** field. Employees might make this choice if they receive regular additional income from which no tax is deducted. By making this choice, they avoid paying a large amount of tax at the end of the year and possible interest penalties. Prekor is the only employee with other income who chooses to have additional taxes withheld.

For **Prekor**, click the Additional Fed. Tax field and type 50.

If an employee is insurable by EI, you must leave the box for **Deduct EI** checked. The default EI contribution factor, 1.4, for Flabuless Fitness is correct. We entered it in the Payroll Income Settings window (page 587).

All employees at Flabuless make CPP contributions so this check box should remain selected. Employees under 18 or over 70 years of age do not contribute to CPP so checking the option for these employees will ensure that CPP is not deducted from their paycheques.

We will enter the historical income tax amounts next.

Click the **Historical Amount field** for **Income Tax**.

Type 1562.21 **Press** (tab) to advance to the EI Premiums Historical Amount field. Enter the amount of EI paid to date.

Type 217.54 **Press** (tab) to move to the CPP Contributions Historical Amount field.

Type 375.20

NOTES
The program skips the Quebec tax fields because Ontario was selected as the province of taxation.

Entering Income Amounts for Employees

We defined all the types of income for Flabuless Fitness in the Names and Terminology setup (page 580). All employees use the following types of income, although not all will have regular amounts and not all will be used on all paycheques:

- Advances
- Benefits
- No. Clients
- Bonus
- Tuition
- Travel Exp.

For Schwinn the following incomes are also used: Vacation (Vac) Owed, Vacation (Vac) Paid, Regular and Overtime 1.

For Kisangel and Prekor the following incomes are used: Salary and Commission. Because Quebec is not selected as the province of taxation, Benefits (Que) is not preselected. Advance, Benefits and Vacation checkmarks cannot be removed.

All the details you need to complete the Income tab chart are on page 570.

Click the **Income tab** to open the next screen of employee details:

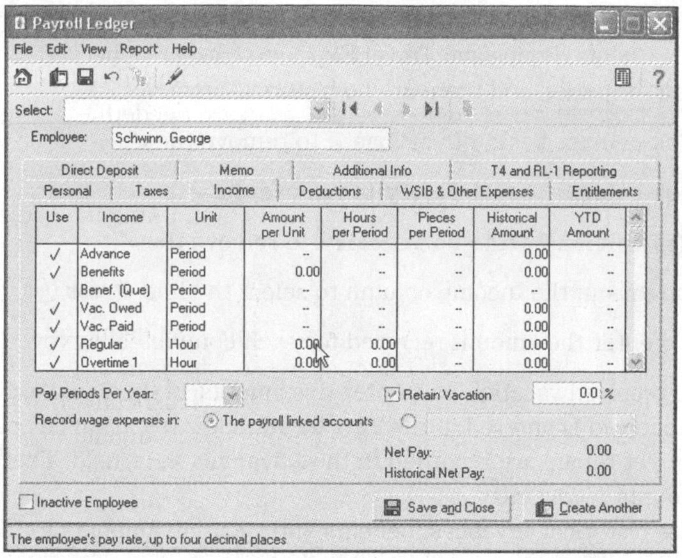

On the Income chart you can indicate the types of income that each employee receives (the **Use** column), the usual rate of pay for that type of income (**Amount Per Unit**), the usual number of hours worked (**Hours Per Period**), the usual number of pieces for a piece rate pay base (**Pieces Per Period**) and the amounts received this year before the earliest transaction date or the date used for the first paycheque (**Historical Amount**). The **Year-To-Date (YTD) Amount** is added automatically by the program based on the historical amounts you enter and the paycheques entered in the program.

Checkmarks should be entered in the Use column so that the fields are available in the payroll journals, even if they will not be used on all paycheques.

Click **Regular** in the Income column to select the line.

Press *tab* to advance to the Amount Per Unit field where we need to enter the regular hourly wage rate.

Type 16

Press *tab* to advance the Hours Per Period field.

The usual number of work hours in the bi-weekly pay period is 80. You can change the default amount in the Payroll journals. Salaried workers normally work 150 hours each month.

Type 80 **Press** *tab* to advance to the Historical Amount field.

Historical income and deduction amounts for the year to date are necessary so that taxes and deductions can be calculated correctly and T4 statements will be accurate.

Type 8960 **Press** *tab*.

The amount is entered automatically in the YTD column and the cursor advances to the Use column for Overtime 1.

Press *tab* **twice** so you can enter the overtime hourly rate.

Type 24

Press *tab* **twice** to advance to the Historical Amount field. There is no regular number of overtime hours.

Type 336

The next three income types do not apply to Schwinn so they should not be checked. The next income that applies is No. Clients, the piece rate method of pay. There is no

NOTES
In the chart on page 570, the incomes that are used by an employee have ✓ (use) or an amount in the employee's column.

NOTES
Checkmarks are added by default for all incomes, deductions and expenses that have linked accounts entered for them.

WARNING!
Do not click the Use column beside Regular as that will remove the checkmark.

NOTES
Pressing the space bar when you are in the Use column will also add a ✓ or remove one if it is there.

Pressing ↓ will move you to the next line in the same column.

historical amount, but we need to enter the rate or amount per unit (survey). The remaining incomes (No. Clients, Bonus and Travel Exp.) are correctly checked. There is no fixed amount per unit or period and there are no historical amounts.

Click the **Use column beside Overtime 2** to remove the ✓.

Click the **Use column beside Salary** to remove the ✓.

Click the **Use column beside Commission** to remove the ✓.

Click **No. Clients** in the Income column to select the line. **Press** tab.

Type 10 to enter the amount received for each completed survey.

If employees have received vacation pay, enter this amount in the **Vac. Paid** field. Vacation pay not yet received is entered in the **Vac. Owed** field. Any advances paid to the employees and not yet repaid are recorded in the **Advances Paid** field. There is no record of advance amounts recovered.

We need to add the historical advances, benefits and vacation amounts for Schwinn. Schwinn has $100 in advances not yet repaid, and he has not used all the vacation pay he has earned this year.

Click the **Historical Amount column beside Advance** to move the cursor.

Type 100

Press tab to move to the Amount Per Period column for Benefits. The group insurance premiums paid by the employer are employee benefits.

Type 5 **Press** tab to move to the Historical Amount for Benefits.

Type 35 **Press** tab to advance to the Historical Amount for Vac. Owed.

Type 371.84 **Press** tab to advance to the Historical Vac. Paid Amount.

Type 385.92

For **Prekor**, click the Use column for Regular, Overtime 1, Overtime 2 and Commission to remove the ✓. Enter the monthly salary and press tab. Enter 150 as the number of hours worked in the pay period. Press tab and enter the historical amount. For No. Clients, enter 10 as the amount per unit. For Travel Exp., enter 120 as the historical amount. You cannot remove the ✓ for Vac. Owed and Vac. Paid, even if they are not used.

For **Kisangel**, repeat these steps but leave Commission checked and enter the historical amount. For Tuition, enter 440 as the historical amount.

Pay Periods Per Year refers to the number of times the employee is paid, or the pay cycle. Schwinn is paid every two weeks, 26 times per year.

Click the **list arrow** beside the field **for Pay Periods Per Year**.

Click **26**.

Retaining Vacation pay is normal for full-time hourly paid employees. Part-time and casual workers often receive their vacation pay with each paycheque because their work schedule is irregular. You will turn the option to retain vacation off when an employee receives the vacation pay, either when taking a vacation or when leaving the company. If the employee is salaried and does not receive vacation pay, the option should also be turned off (see page 382). For Schwinn, or any employee who receives vacation pay, leave the option to Retain Vacation checked and type the vacation pay rate in the % field.

Double click the % **field beside Retain Vacation**.

WARNING!
Enter employee historical payroll details carefully. You will be unable to edit these fields after finishing the history or after making Payroll Journal entries for the employee.

They must also be correct because they are used to create T4s for tax reporting.

WARNING!
The totals for all employees for advances paid and vacation pay owing must match the corresponding General Ledger account balances before you can finish entering the history.

NOTES
Remember that commissions must be calculated manually and entered in the Payroll journals. The Commission field in the Payroll Ledger allows only a fixed amount, not a percentage of sales, as the entry.

NOTES
Employees may be paid yearly (1), semi-annually (2), monthly for 10 months (10), monthly (12), every four weeks (13), every two weeks for a 10-month year (22), twice a month (24), every two weeks (26) or weekly (52).

Type 6

For **Prekor** and **Kisangel**, click Retain Vacation to remove the ✓.

Employee wages may be linked to the default expense account or to another account. Wage expenses for all Flabuless Fitness employees are linked to the default accounts entered on page 599.

Entering Default Payroll Deduction Amounts

Click the **Deductions tab** to open the screen for payroll deductions:

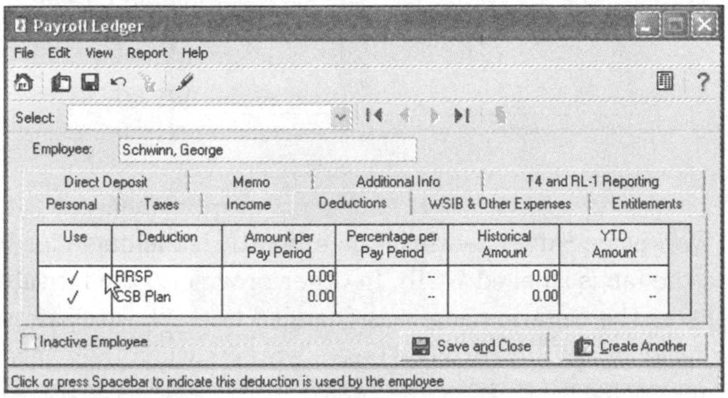

On this screen, you can indicate which deductions apply to the employee, the amount normally deducted and the historical amount — the amount deducted to date this year. Both deductions are correctly selected in the Use column.

By entering deductions here, they will be included automatically on the Payroll Journal input forms. Otherwise, you must enter them manually in the Journal for each pay period. Since all three employees have chosen to participate in these plans, you can enter the information here so that the deductions are made automatically. You should make permanent changes by editing the employee ledger record.

If you choose to calculate deductions as a percentage of gross pay in the Payroll Settings, the Percentage Per Pay Period fields will be available.

For one-time changes, you can edit deduction amounts in the Paycheques Journal on the Deductions tab screen. You cannot edit deduction amounts in the Payroll Cheque Run Journal.

Click **RRSP** in the Deduction column to select the line.

Press (tab). You should enter the amount that is withheld in each pay period.

Type 50 **Press** (tab) to advance the cursor to the Historical Amount field.

Type 350 **Press** (tab) to advance the cursor to the Use column for CSB Plan.

Press (tab). Enter the amount that is to be withheld in each pay period.

Type 50 **Press** (tab) to advance the cursor to the Historical Amount field.

Type 350 **Press** (tab) to update the YTD Amount.

The remaining deductions are not used by Flabuless Fitness. The names were deleted so they do not appear on the chart.

Entering WSIB and Other Expenses

Click the **WSIB & Other Expenses tab**.

NOTES

When you select a specific account, all payroll expenses for that employee will be linked to the same account – the one you identify in this field. If you want to use different accounts for different wage expenses, you must use the linked accounts.

The user-defined expenses we created in the Additional Payroll Names screen (page 581) and the default WSIB rate (page 589) are entered on this next screen:

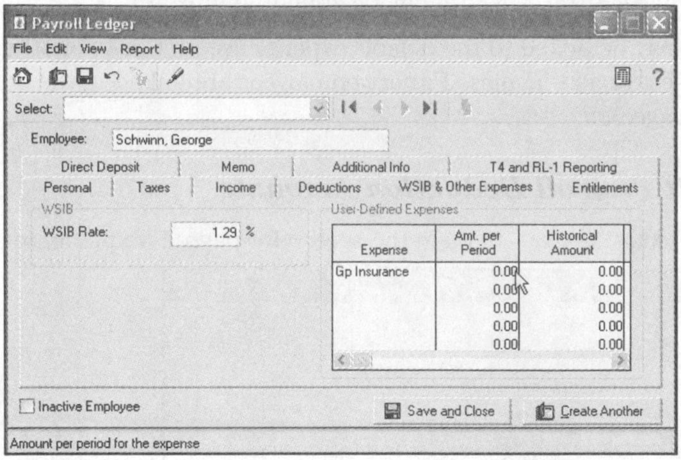

In Ontario, WSIB (Workplace Safety and Insurance Board) is the name for Worker's Compensation Board so the tab is labelled WSIB. In other provinces, the tab label will be WCB & Other Expenses. The Ontario name was changed to emphasize safety rather than compensation for accidents. WSIB (or WCB) pays workers when they have been injured on the job and are unable to work.

The default WSIB rate is entered from our setup information, but you can enter a different rate for an individual employee in this field. The rate is correct for Schwinn.

For **Kisangel**, enter 1.02 as the WSIB rate.

Other user-defined expenses are also added on this screen. Flabuless Fitness has only group insurance as a user-defined expense.

Click the **Gp Insurance Amt Per Period**. Enter the amount that the employer contributes in each pay period.

Type 5 **Press** tab to advance to the Historical Amount field.

Type 35

The remaining expenses are not used by Flabuless Fitness.

NOTES

If employees take days before the sufficient number of hours worked have been accrued, the program will warn you. Then you can allow the entry for entitlements or not. This entry is similar to allowing customers to exceed their credit limits.

Entering Employee Entitlements

We entered the default rates and amounts for entitlements as Payroll Settings, but they can be modified in the ledger records for individual employees.

We must also enter the historical information for entitlements. This historical number will include any days carried forward from the previous periods. The number of days accrued cannot be greater than the maximum number of days defined for the entitlement for an employee. The number of Net Days Accrued, the amount unused and available for carrying forward, is updated automatically from the historical information and current payroll journal entries.

Click the **Entitlements tab**:

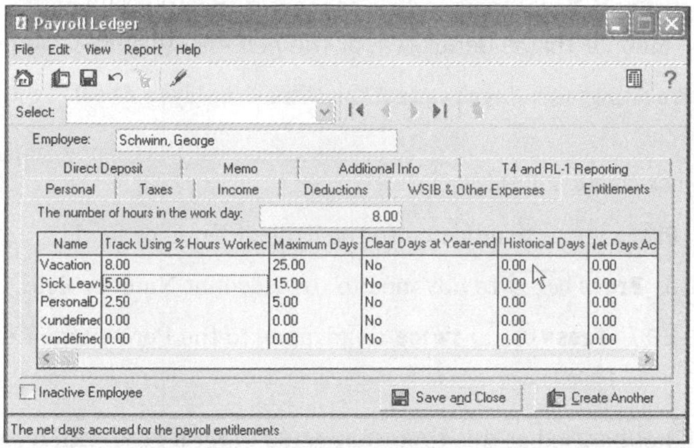

You cannot enter information directly in the Net Days Accrued fields on the Entitlements tab screen.

Schwinn receives vacation pay instead of paid time off so the vacation entitlements details should be removed. The defaults for sick leave and personal days are correct.

Click the **Track Using % Hours Worked field for Vacation**.

Press *del* to remove the entry.

Press *tab* to advance to the Maximum Days field.

Press *del* to remove the entry.

Click the **Historical Days field for Sick Leave**.

Type 12

Press ↓ to advance to the Historical Days field for PersonalDays. The number of days is added to the Net Days Accrued.

Type 4 **Press** *tab* to enter the amount.

For Kisangel and Prekor, the default entries for tracking and maximum days are correct, but you must enter the Historical Days for each entitlement.

Entering Direct Deposit Information

Click the **Direct Deposit tab:**

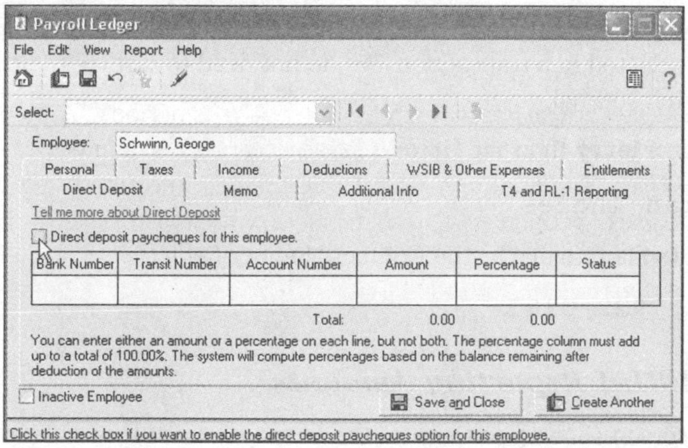

All three employees have elected to have their paycheques deposited directly to their bank accounts. On this screen, we need to enter the bank account details. For each employee who has elected the Direct Deposit option, you must turn on the selection in the Direct Deposit Paycheques For This Employee check box. Then you

NOTES

All banks in Canada are assigned a three-digit bank number and each branch has a unique five-digit transit number. Account numbers may vary from five to twelve digits.

NOTES

The paycheque deposit may be split among more than one bank account by entering different percentages for the accounts.

To delete bank account details, change the status to Inactive and then delete the bank information.

must add the three-digit **Bank Number**, five-digit **Transit Number**, the bank Account Number and finally the amount that is deposited, or the percentage of the cheque.

Click the **Direct Deposit Paycheques For This Employee check box** to add a ✓.

Click the **Bank Number field.**

Type 102 **Press** tab to advance to the Transit Number field.

Type 89008 **Press** tab to advance to the Account Number field.

Type 2998187 **Press** tab **twice** to advance to the Percentage field.

Type 100

The Memo tab will not be used at this time. You could enter a note with a reminder date to appear in the Daily Business Manager, for example, a reminder to issue vacation paycheques on a specific date or to recover advances.

Entering Additional Information

Flabuless Fitness has chosen to enter the name and phone number of the person to be contacted in case of an emergency involving the employee at work.

Click the **Additional Info tab** to access the fields we added for the ledger when we entered Names:

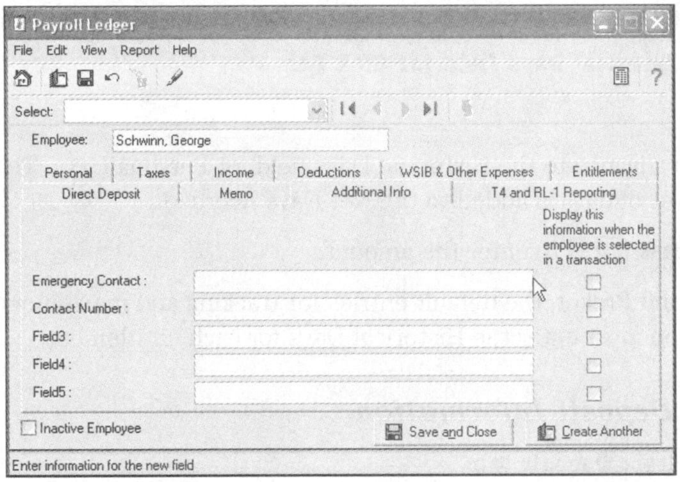

NOTES
Additional information for other ledgers may also be displayed or hidden in journal transactions.

NOTES
The Contact Number field is not predefined as a telephone number so its format will not be corrected automatically by the program.

You can indicate whether you want to display any of the additional information when the employee is selected in a transaction. We do not need to display the contact information in the Payroll Journal.

Click the **Emergency Contact field.**

Type Adrian Ingles

Press tab **twice** to move to the Contact Number field.

Type (905) 722-0301

Entering T4 and RL-1 Reporting Amounts

The next information screen allows you to enter the year-to-date EI insurable and pensionable earnings. By adding the historical amounts, the T4 slips prepared for income taxes at the end of the year and the record of employment termination reports will also be correct.

Because there are yearly maximum amounts for CPP and EI contributions, these historical details are also needed. Totals for optional deductions are also retained in the employee record.

Click the **T4 and RL-1 Reporting tab** to open the next screen we need to complete:

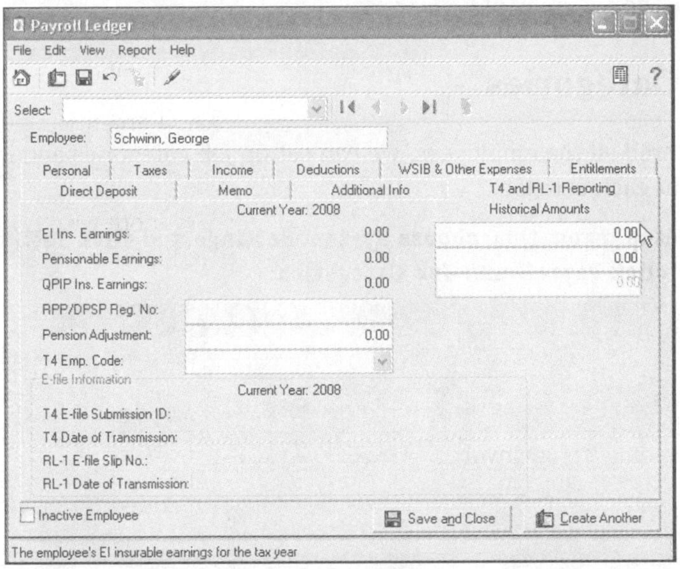

In the **Historical EI Ins. Earnings** field, you should enter the total earned income received to date that is EI insurable. The program will update this total every time you make payroll entries until the maximum salary on which EI is calculated has been reached. At that time, no further EI premiums will be deducted.

Pensionable Earnings are also tracked by the program. This amount determines the total income that is eligible for Canada Pension Plan. The Pension Adjustment amount is used when the employee has a workplace pension program that will affect the allowable contributions for personal registered pension plans and will be linked with the Canada Pension Plan. Workplace pension income is reduced when the employee also has income from the Canada Pension Plan. Since Flabuless Fitness has no company pension plan, the Pension Adjustment amount is zero.

The T4 Employee Code applies to a small number of job types that have special income tax rules.

Click the **Historical Amounts field for EI Ins. Earnings**.

Type 9681.92

Click the **Historical Amounts field for Pensionable Earnings field**.

Type 9681.92

Correct any employee information **errors** by returning to the field with the error. **Highlight** the **error** and **enter** the **correct information**. **Click each tab** in turn so that you can check all the information.

When all the information is entered correctly, you must save the employee record.

Click **Create Another** 

to save the record and to open a new blank employee information form.

Click the **Personal tab** so that you can enter address information.

Repeat these procedures to **enter** other employee **records**.

NOTES

The EI Insurable amount is the total of gross wages, including overtime wages and vacation pay.

NOTES

We will not use the remaining tax information fields for Flabuless Fitness. Flabuless Fitness does not have a company pension plan with regular payroll deductions so there is no plan registration number. The Pension Adjustment amount is used when an employee contributes to a company pension plan and these payments reduce the amount the employee can contribute to a private registered pension plan. The company pension plan payments also affect the CPP amount received at retirement, but not CPP premiums.

Click **Save And Close** [Save and Close] after entering the last record to save the record and close the Payroll Ledger.

Close the **Employees window** to return to the Home window.

Display or **print** the **Employee List** and the **Employee Summary Report** to check the accuracy of your work.

Entering Job Categories

Now that we have entered all the employees, we can set up job categories and indicate which employees are in each category.

Choose the **Setup menu**, then **choose System Settings** and **click Settings.** Then **click Payroll** and **Job Categories**:

BASIC VERSION
The column for Submit Time Slips is not available in the Basic version. It applies to Time and Billing, a Pro feature.

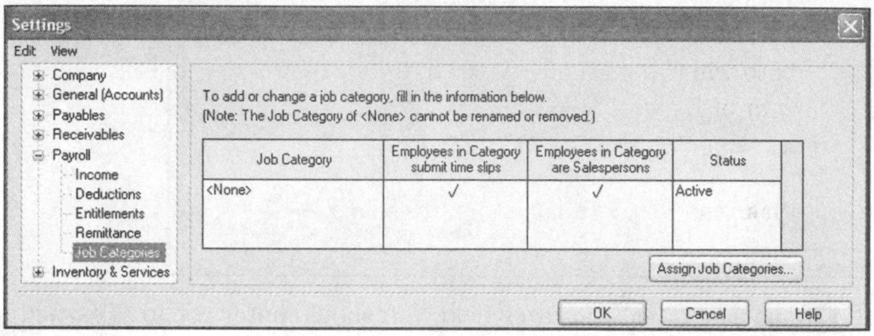

On the Job Category tab screen, you enter the names of the categories and indicate whether the employees in each category submit time slips and whether they are salespersons. Categories may be active or inactive. We need a new category called Sales.

Notice that if you do not create categories, the employees in the default selection <None> are salespersons so they can be selected in the Sales Journal.

Click the **Job Category field below <None>**.

Type `Sales` **Press** *tab* to add checkmarks to the next two columns and set the status to Active.

Click **Assign Job Categories** to change the screen:

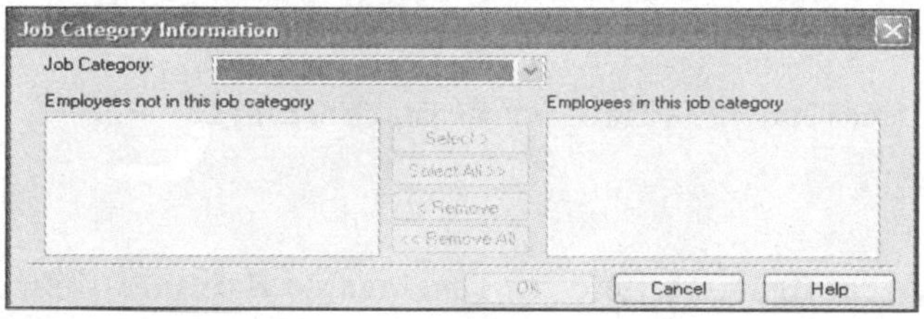

No information appears yet because no category is selected.

Choose **Sales** from the drop-down Job Category list.

Notice that <None> is one of the category list choices. The screen is updated with employee names. Initially all are Employees Not In This Job Category as shown:

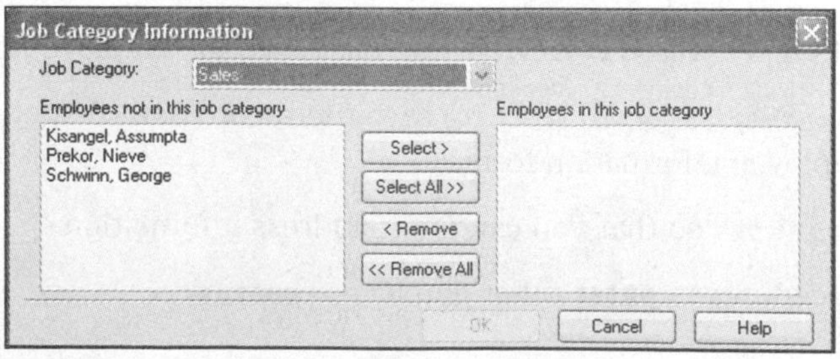

You can add employee names to the category by choosing an employee and clicking **Select** or by choosing **Select All**. Once employees are in a category (the column on the right), you can remove them by selecting an employee and clicking **Remove** or clicking **Remove All** to move all names at the same time.

Click **Select All** to place all employees in the Sales category.

Click **OK** to save the information and return to the Home window.

Setting Up Payroll Remittances

Because we have entered all payroll settings and all vendors, we can set up the payroll remittances information. This process has three steps: identifying the vendors who receive payroll remittance amounts, linking the vendors to the taxes or deductions they receive, and entering opening dates and balances. First we should designate the payroll authorities. Refer to the chart on page 564 for the Payroll remittance settings.

The vendors to which we remit payroll taxes or other deductions are: Ancaster Insurance, Minister of Finance, Mt. Hope Investment Corp., Receiver General for Canada and Workplace Safety & Insurance Board.

Right-click the **Vendors icon** 

to select it.

Click the **Search tool**  to open the Search window for vendors:

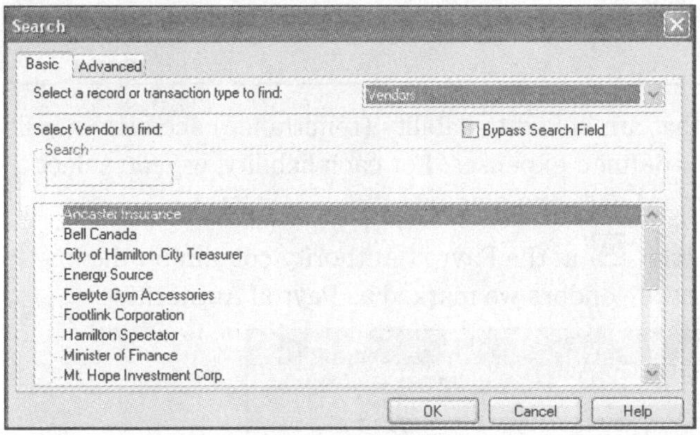

Click **Ancaster Insurance** and then **click OK** to open the vendor's record:

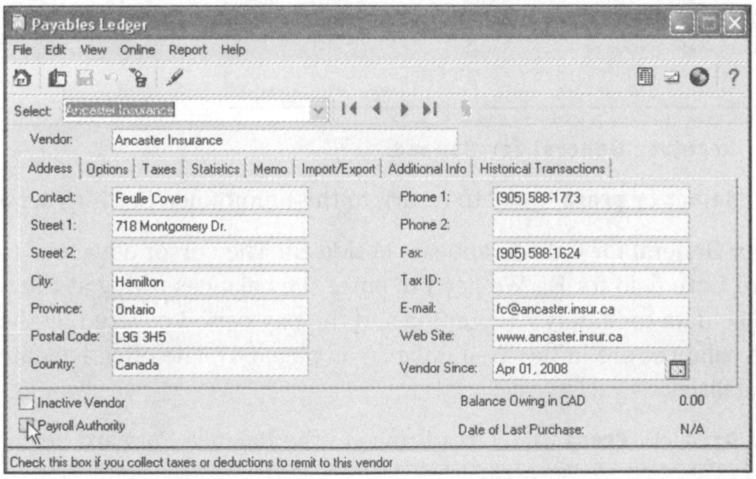

Click **Payroll Authority** to add the ✓ and change the vendor's payroll status.

Click the **Next Vendor tool**  **repeatedly** to access the record for the Minister of Finance, the next payroll authority.

Or, you can

Click the **Select list arrow** and **click Minister of Finance**.

Click **Payroll Authority** to add the ✓ and change the vendor's payroll status.

Repeat these **steps** for the remaining payroll authorities: **Mt. Hope Investment Corp.**, **Receiver General for Canada** and **Workplace Safety & Insurance Board**.

Close the **Payables Ledger window** to return to the Home window.

Choose the **Setup menu**, then **choose System Settings** and **click Settings** to open the Settings screen.

Click **Payroll** to display the payroll settings options.

Click **Remittance** to open the screen we need:

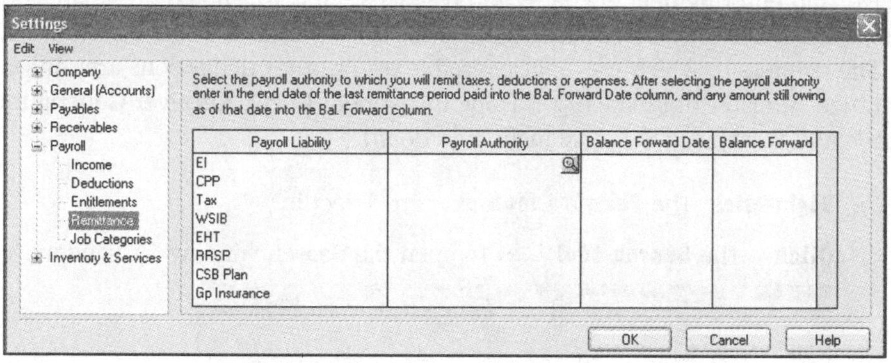

NOTES

You can also double click the vendor's name to add it to the Settings screen.

If you type the first few letters of the name and then press *tab*, the Select Vendor list will have the vendor you need selected. Press *enter* to add the name to the Settings screen.

All the payroll items that are linked to liability (remittance) accounts are listed: taxes, deductions and user-defined expenses. For each liability, we can select a vendor and enter the balance forward date and amount.

Click the **List icon** in the Payroll Authority column on the line for EI to see the list of vendors we marked as Payroll Authorities:

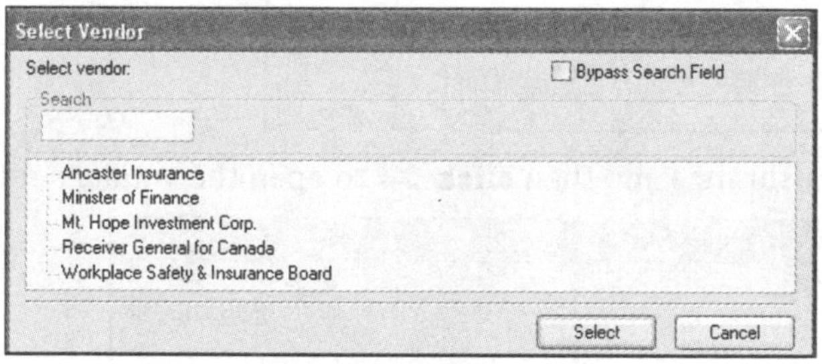

Click **Receiver General for Canada**.

Click **Select** or **press** *enter* to return to the Remittance Settings screen.

The Receiver General for Canada appears beside EI. The cursor advances to the Balance Forward Date field for EI. We need to enter the balances owing at the time we are converting the data to Simply Accounting and the pay period covered by those amounts. These balances are in the Trial Balance on page 567 The effective date is April 1 for all liabilities.

NOTES

Refer to the Company Information on page 564 and the Trial Balance on page 567 to complete the remittance setup.

Type `Apr 1` **Press** *tab* to advance to the Balance Forward field.

Type `563.28` **Press** *tab* to advance to the Payroll Authority field for CPP.

Enter the remaining **Payroll Authorities**, **dates** and **balances**.

Click **OK** to save the settings.

Preparing the Inventory Ledger

Use the Flabuless Fitness Inventory Information and chart on pages 571–572 to record details about the inventory items on hand.

Entering Inventory Records

The following keystrokes will enter the information for Flabuless Fitness's first inventory item, Body Fat Scale.

Click the **Inventory & Services icon** [Inventory & Services] in the Home window. Again, with no inventory items on file, the icon window is empty.

Click the **Create button** [Create] or **choose** the **File menu** and **click Create**.

You will display the Inventory Ledger for new inventory items:

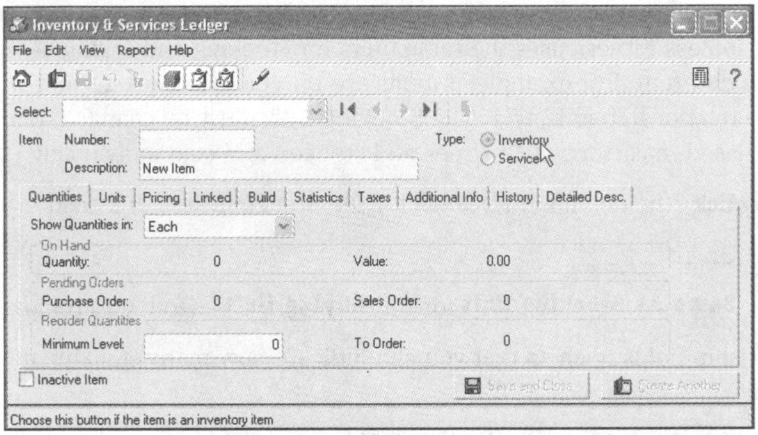

If you skip the Inventory icon window (View menu, User Preferences), you will see this Inventory Ledger immediately when you click the Inventory icon.

The cursor is in the Item Number field. Use this field for the code or number for the first item. When you sort inventory by description, the two item fields shown here will be reversed — the Description field will appear first.

Type `A010` **Press** *tab* to advance to the Item Description field, the field for the name of the inventory item.

Type `Body Fat Scale`

The Type is set correctly for this item as Inventory rather than Service.

The Show Quantities In field allows you to select the units displayed in the ledger. If you have entered different units for stocking, selling and buying, these will be available from the drop-down list. The Quantity On Hand and Value fields are updated by the program as are the Purchase Orders and Sales Orders Pending.

Click the **Minimum Level field**. Here you should enter the minimum stock level or re-order point for this inventory item.

Type `2`

basic BASIC VERSION
The Inventory & Services icon in the Basic version does not include the clock part of the image.

basic BASIC VERSION
There isn't a Build tab in the Basic version, and only two show icons will be included in the tool bar. The Show Activities tool applies only to Pro features, and the Refresh tool is used in the multi-user option in Pro.

WARNING!
Enter inventory details very carefully. You cannot remove an inventory record or change the Type if there is a quantity on hand. You must edit the History fields to reduce the quantity and value to zero. Then remove the item and re-enter all the details correctly.

To change the Type, close the ledger to save the changes in the history. When you open the ledger again, you may edit the Type.

WARNING!
You must enter the unit relationship information before entering the history for inventory so that purchase prices and average costs will be calculated correctly.

Click the **Units tab** to see the next information screen:

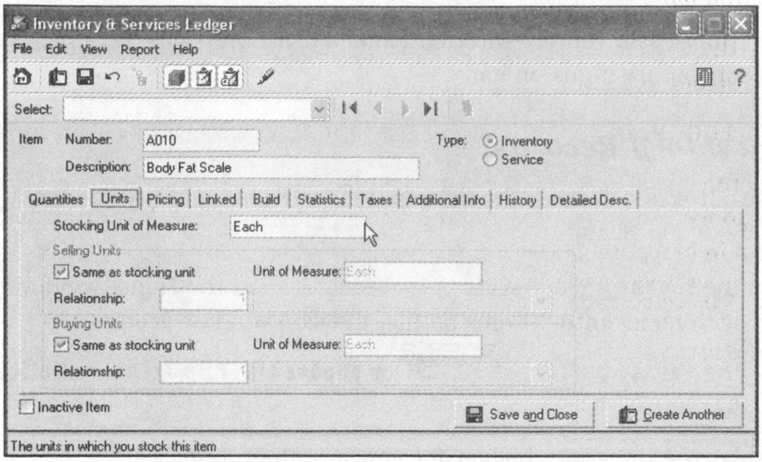

You can enter different units for items when the units for buying, stocking and selling differ. Flabuless Fitness uses the same units for stocking and selling but some buying units are different. For example, if items are purchased in dozens and stocked individually, the relationship is 12 to 1. The Stocking Unit must be changed. Body Fat Scales are purchased in cartons of 12 scales and stocked and sold individually (unit).

Double click the default entry **Each** for the Stocking Unit Of Measure.

Type `Unit`

Click **Same As Stocking Unit** for the **Buying Units** section to remove the ✓.

The relationship fields open so that you can indicate how many stocking units are in each buying unit.

Press *tab* to advance to the Unit Of Measure field.

Type `Carton` **Press** *tab* to advance to the Relationship field.

Type `12` **Press** *tab*.

Check that the entry is 12 Unit Per Carton. If it is not, click the drop-down list and choose this relationship.

Click the **Pricing tab** to open the next group of inventory record fields:

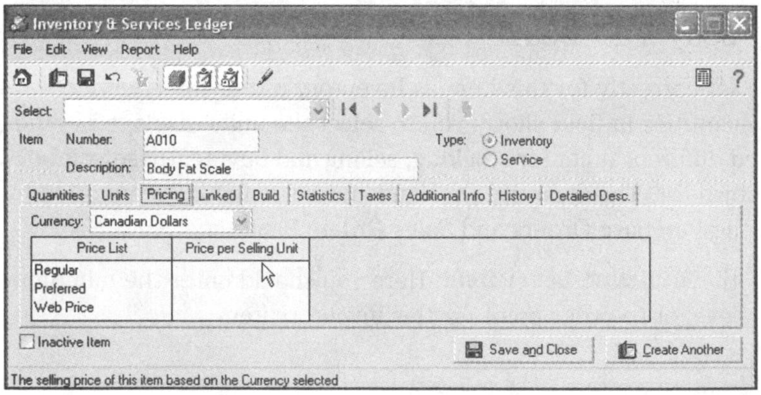

NOTES
To see the Inventory Ledger Settings, refer to page 596. You cannot change these settings while the Inventory Ledger is open.

The Currency field and foreign price fields are available only if you indicated that inventory prices should be taken from the Inventory Ledger and not calculated using the exchange rate. The pricing option appears on the Inventory Settings screen only after you enter foreign currency information. That is why we added currency information first. Taking prices from the Ledger is the default setting.

On the Pricing tab screen, you can enter regular and preferred prices in the currencies that you have set up. The home currency (Canadian Dollars) is selected first.

Click the **Regular Price Per Selling Unit field**. Here you should enter the selling price for this inventory item.

Type 100 **Press** (tab) to advance to the Preferred Selling Price field.

The regular price is also entered as the default Preferred and Web Price. We do not have Web sales so we can accept the default entry for Web prices. Preferred selling prices are shown in brackets in the Inventory Information chart on pages 571–572.

Type 90 to replace the default entry.

Choose United States Dollars from the Currency list to open USD price fields:

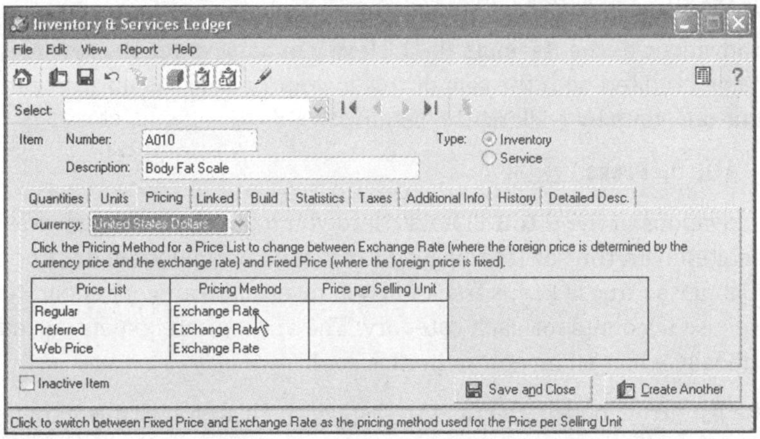

The pricing method is entered separately for each price. You can choose either Exchange Rate or Fixed Price for Regular and Preferred prices.

Click Exchange Rate beside Regular to change the entry to Fixed Price.

Press (tab) to advance to the Regular Price Per Selling Unit field.

Type 85 **Press** (tab) to advance to the Pricing Method field.

Click Exchange Rate to change the entry to Fixed Price.

Press (tab) to advance to the Preferred Price Per Selling Unit field.

Type 77 **Press** (tab).

Click the **Linked tab** to open the linked accounts screen for the item:

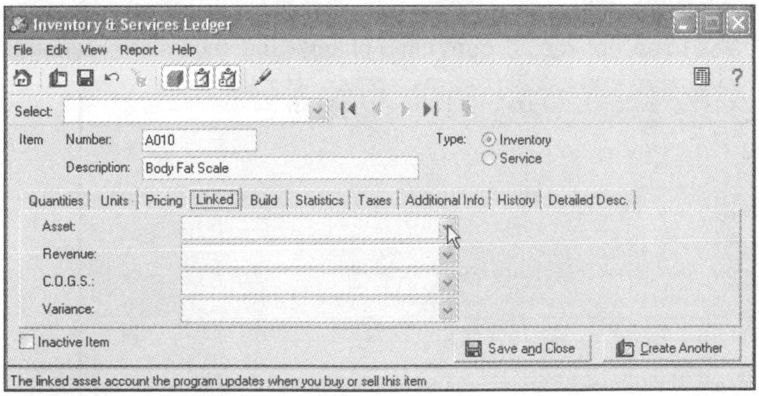

Click the **Asset field list arrow**.

Here you must enter the **asset** account associated with the sale or purchase of this inventory item. Refer to the Chart of Accounts on page 565 and the Inventory chart on

NOTES

The Web Price must be fixed. It cannot be based on exchange rates.

NOTES

If you add a new account at this stage, you can include an Opening Balance using the Add An Account wizard. Because the history is not finished, the Opening Balance field is added to the wizard.

pages 571–572 to find the account number for the inventory asset category Accessories. All available asset accounts are in the displayed list.

Enter the account by clicking the list arrow and choosing from the drop-down account list, or

Type 1520 **Press** *tab*.

The program asks you to confirm the account class change for account 1520:

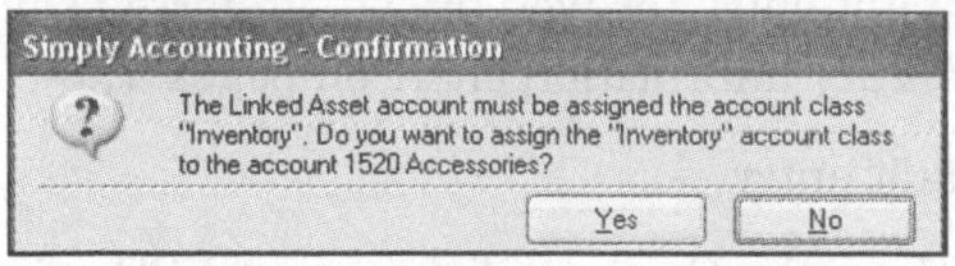

Click **Yes** to accept the change.

The cursor advances to the **Revenue** field. Here you must enter the revenue account that will be credited with the sale of this inventory item. Again, you can display the list of revenue accounts by clicking the list arrow. Or,

Type 4020 **Press** *tab*.

The cursor advances to the **C.O.G.S.** field. Here you must enter the expense account to be debited with the sale of this inventory item, normally the *Cost of Goods Sold* account. Flabuless Fitness keeps track of each inventory category separately and has different expense accounts for each category. The appropriate expense account is updated automatically when an inventory item is sold.

Click the list arrow beside the field to display the list of available expense accounts. Or,

Type 5050 **Press** *tab* to advance to the Variance field.

Click **Yes** to accept the account class change.

NOTES

If you did not change the account class for expense accounts, you will not see the message about account class changes for 5050 and 5070. However, if all expense accounts are designated as Cost of Goods Sold accounts, you cannot produce an accurate Gross Margin Income Statement.

Simply Accounting uses the **Variance** linked account when sales are made of items that are not in stock. If there is a difference between the historical average cost of goods remaining in stock and the actual cost when the new merchandise is received, the price difference is charged to the variance expense account at the time of the purchase. If you have not indicated a variance account, the program will ask you to identify one when you are entering the purchase.

Type 5070 or click the list arrow and choose the account.

Click the **Build tab**.

Click **Yes** to accept the account class change and access the Statistics screen:

BASIC VERSION

The Build tab screen is not included in the Basic version. Click the Statistics tab as the next step.

NOTES

As soon as you click the next tab, you will be prompted to change the account class for the variance linked account.

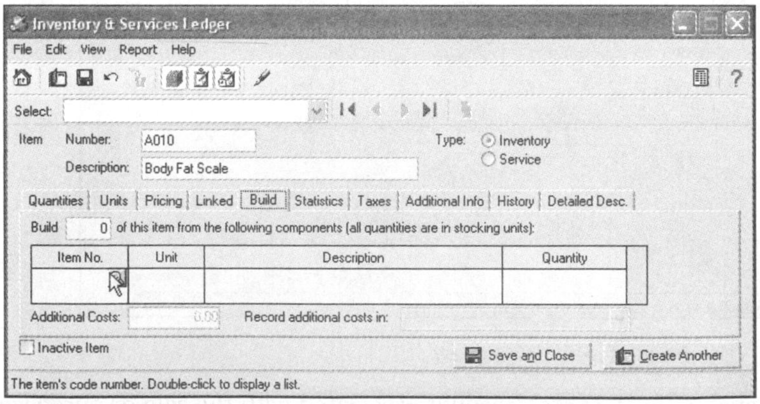

The Build feature is available in Pro but not in the Basic version of Simply Accounting. You can use this screen to define how this item is made or built from other

inventory items. Then, in the journal, you can build the item by choosing it from the available list and entering the number of units you want to build. This screen holds the components portion of the Item Assembly Journal.

Click the **Statistics tab** to open the next tab information screen:

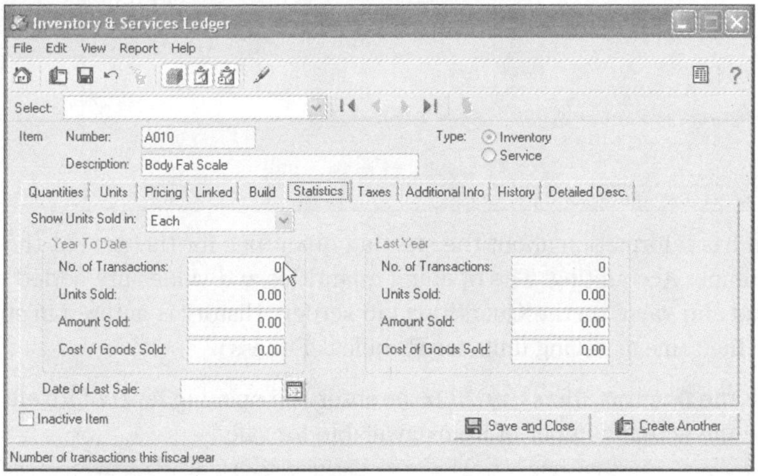

On this screen, you can enter historical information about the sale of the product. It would then be added to the inventory tracking information for reports.

The first activity field, the Date Of Last Sale, refers to the last date on which the item was sold. The next two sections contain information for the Year To Date and the previous year. Since Flabuless Fitness has not kept this information, you can skip these fields. Refer to the description of new inventory items on page 425 in the Adrienne Aesthetics application for a more detailed description of these historical fields.

Click the **Taxes tab** to input the sales taxes relating to the inventory item:

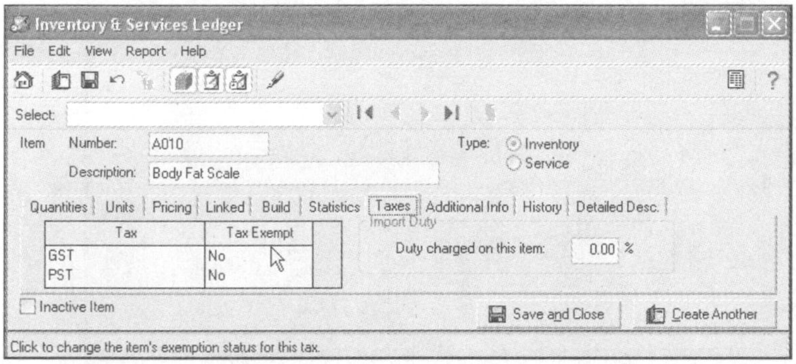

You can indicate whether the item is taxable for all the taxes you set up, provincial and federal sales taxes in this case. Both PST and GST are charged on sales of all inventory items so the default entry No for **Tax Exempt** is correct.

For service items, you must change the PST entry to Yes because PST is not charged on services offered by Flabuless Fitness.

Duty is also entered on this screen. You must activate the duty tracking option before the duty rate field becomes available. Since no duty is charged on the imported inventory, you can leave the duty rate at 0%.

We have not added fields to the ledger record as we did for Payroll so we can skip the **Additional Info** screen.

The next step is to add the opening historical balances for the inventory items.

NOTES

To open the Duty fields in the Purchases Journal, you must activate tracking of duty information and indicate in the vendor record that duty is charged on purchases from the vendor. Rates entered in the Inventory Ledger records will appear automatically in the Purchases Journal for those items. Duty rates can also be entered in the journal if you have not entered them in the ledger records.

Click the **History tab**:

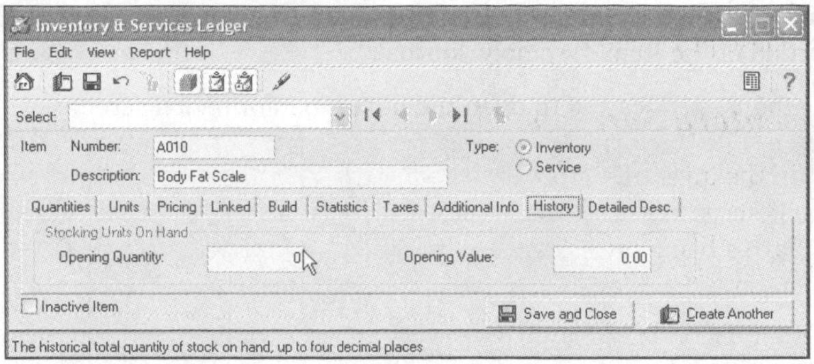

This screen has information about the starting quantities for the item at the time of conversion to Simply Accounting. The opening quantities and values are added to the quantity on hand and value on the Quantities tab screen. History is entered in stocking unit quantities (the same as selling units for Flabuless Fitness).

WARNING!
The total opening value amounts for all items in an asset group must match the General Ledger asset account balance before you can finish entering the history.

Click the **Opening Quantity field** to enter the opening level of inventory — the actual number of items available for sale.

Type 10 **Press** tab.

The cursor advances to the Opening Value field, where you should enter the actual total cost of the inventory on hand.

Type 400

The remaining tab allows you to enter further descriptive information.

Click the **Detailed Desc. tab**:

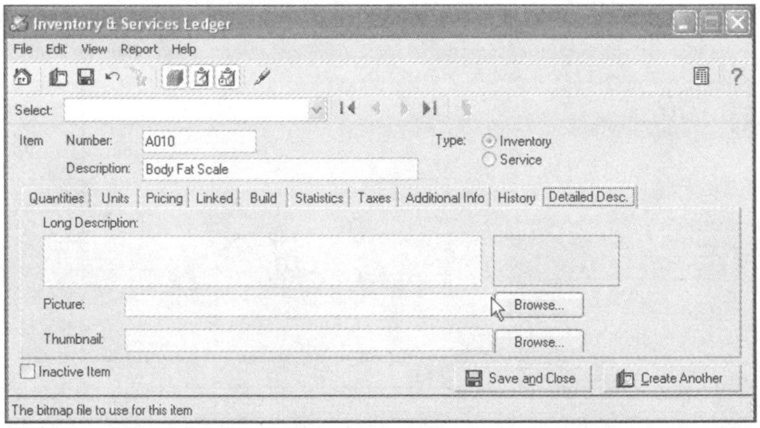

This optional information provides a detailed description of the inventory item (about 500 characters) as well as a picture in image file format.

NOTES
If you add a .bmp format picture file, you will see the picture in the box beside the Long Description field. Other file formats may be used, but the pictures will not be displayed.

NOTES
We have not provided picture files for the remaining inventory items.

Type the detailed item description in the Long Description text box.

Click **Browse** beside Picture. **Click** the **Up One Level tool** . **Double click** **Setup** and then **Logos** and **scale.bmp** to add the file name and picture.

Correct any **errors** by returning to the field with the mistake. **Highlight** the **error** and **enter** the **correct information**. **Click** the different **tabs** to see all the information that you entered.

When all the information is entered correctly, you must save your inventory record.

Click **Create Another** 

to save the record and advance to a new input screen.

Click the **Quantities tab** to prepare for entering the next item.

Repeat these procedures to **enter other** inventory **records**.

Entering Inventory Services

The final items on the inventory chart are services that Flabuless Fitness provides. Entering service items is similar to entering inventory, but there are fewer details.

You should have a blank Inventory & Services Ledger window open at the Quantities tab screen.

Click **Service** to change the Type in the upper right section of the screen.

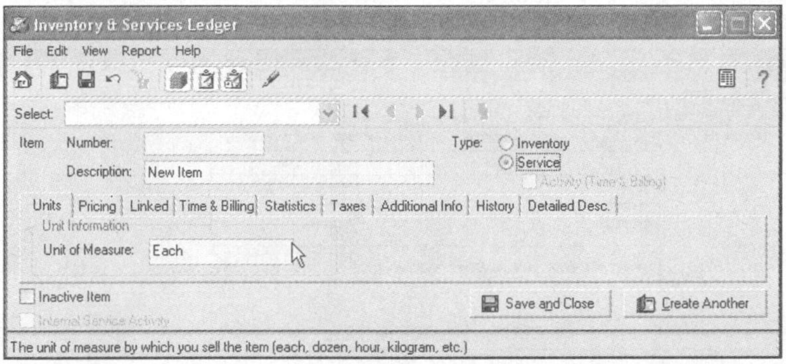

There are fewer tabs and fields for services because some item details do not apply. The Unit Of Measure and Selling Price have the same meaning for services as they do for inventory items. Because service items are not kept in stock or purchased, only the selling unit is applicable, there is no minimum quantity and the History tab fields are removed. Flabuless Fitness' services are not exported so you do not need to enter foreign prices. Only expense and revenue accounts are linked for services. The other two linked account fields do not apply and are removed for services. Remember to use *Revenue from Services* and *Cost of Services* as the linked accounts for inventory services.

basic BASIC VERSION

The Time & Billing tab screen is used to set up Time & Billing, a feature that is not available in the Basic version. The Activity setting and Internal Customer also apply to the Time & Billing feature.

Enter the **Item Number** and **Description** and the **Unit Of Measure**.

Click the **Pricing tab** and add **Regular** and **Preferred prices** in Canadian dollars.

Click the **Linked tab**. **Enter** the linked accounts for **Revenue (4040)** and **Expense (5065)**. Accept the account class change.

NOTES

In Ontario, some services, such as repairs to tangible property – cars, machinery, etc. – are PST taxable. Personal services are generally not taxed with PST in Ontario.

Most services in Canada are subject to GST. Some services are subject to Provincial Sales Taxes but others are not. These rules also vary from one province to another. Therefore, you should indicate in the Ledger record whether the service is exempt from the tax. By indicating in the Ledger that the service is exempt, PST will not be calculated on sales of the services. All services offered by Flabuless Fitness are exempt from PST so you should change the Tax Exempt setting in the Taxes tab screen to Yes for PST.

Click the **Taxes tab**.

Click **No** to change the entry to Yes in the Tax Exempt column for PST.

Click **Create Another** [Create Another].

Click the **Units tab**. **Repeat** these procedures to **enter other service records**.

Click **Save And Close** [Save and Close] after entering the last service record.

Close **Inventory & Services window** to return to the Home window.

NOTES

The tax code in the Sales Journal for services may show as GP, the code for the customer. However, as we have seen in earlier applications, the tax calculations will be correct if the service record information is correct.

Display or **print** the **Inventory List**, **Synopsis**, **Quantity** and **Price Lists** reports to check them for accuracy.

Creating and Updating Inventory Price Lists

basic BASIC VERSION
You cannot create additional price lists or update them globally in the Basic version.

The Pro version allows you to define additional price lists and to update prices in a single step on one screen. This feature is available as one of the settings for the Inventory Ledger. If prices are raised by a fixed percentage for one or more items or services, you can make the price changes globally. You can also set the prices in one list relative to the prices in another list indicating the percentage increase or decrease.

Choose the Setup menu, then choose System Settings and Settings. Click Inventory and then click Price List to see the Price List Settings:

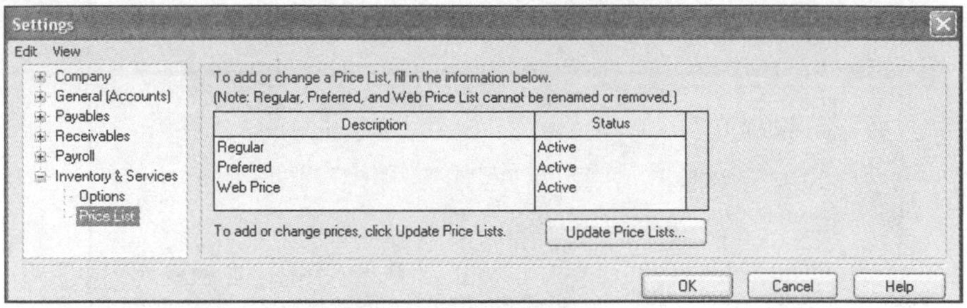

At this stage, you can define new price lists. You cannot modify the three predefined price list names.

Type the new price list names below Web Price in the Description column.

Click Update Price Lists:

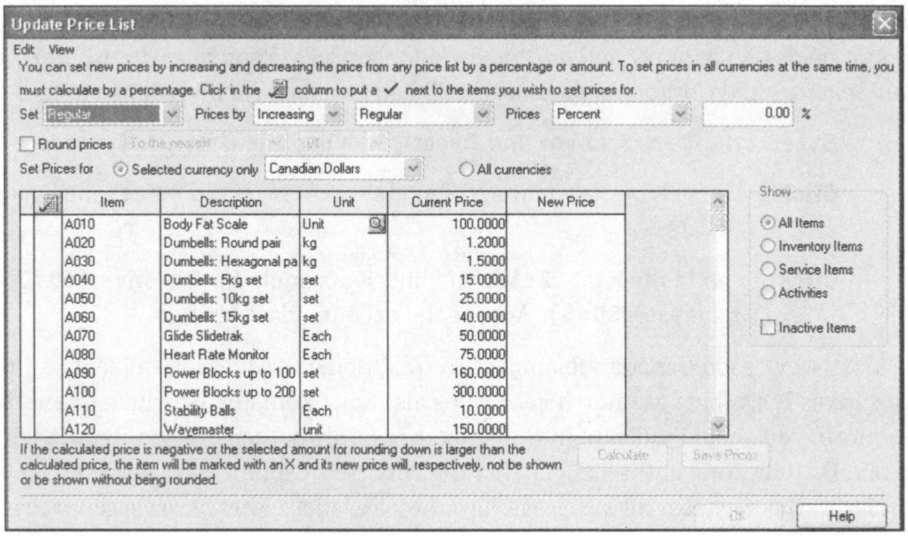

The inventory list opens. You can display the list of all items, only inventory items, only service items or only activities (for use with the time and billing feature).

You can select the items whose prices you want to update globally. You can set the prices in one list relative to another list by increasing or decreasing the reference prices by a fixed percentage. Then you can round off the prices to the nearest unit — ranging from 0.0001 dollar to 1 000 dollars. You can make the price changes for one currency or for all currencies at the same time. You can also enter or edit individual prices in the new price column so you can also use this list to enter price changes manually for all inventory items on a single screen, without opening each ledger record separately.

Choose the list you want to display and work with (All Items, Inventory Items, Service Items or Activities). The default is to display all items.

Click the Select Item column to add a checkmark and choose an item for global updating.

Select the unit you are modifying if you have different units for stocking and selling.

Choose the price list you want to change from the Set drop-down list.

Choose Increasing or Decreasing from the Prices By drop-down list to indicate the direction of the change.

Choose the price list that serves as the reference point for the increase from the next Prices drop-down list.

Choose Percent or Amount to indicate how you want to change prices.

Enter the percentage or amount by which prices should change.

Click Round Prices if you want to work with even amounts.

Choose the direction for rounding off the price, up to the nearest, down to the nearest or to the nearest.

Choose the nearest unit you want to round to from the drop-down list.

Click Calculate if you are modifying list items by a specific percentage or amount.

Edit individual prices in the New Price column if necessary.

Click Save Prices when you have modified all the prices you want. The new prices move to the Current Price column.

Click OK to close the Settings window and return to the Home window.

Finishing the History

The last stage in setting up the accounting system involves finishing the history for each ledger. Before proceeding, you should check the data integrity (Home window, Maintenance menu) to see whether there are any out-of-balance ledgers that will prevent you from proceeding. Correct these errors and then make a backup copy of the files.

WARNING!
Before you finish entering the history, make a backup copy of Flabuless Fitness company files. This is necessary if you find later that you need to correct some of the historical information. Remember, once you finish entering the history, you cannot add information for any period before the earliest transaction date.

Making a Backup of the Company Files

With the Flabuless Fitness files open, use the File menu Backup command to create a backup. You may also want to create a complete working copy of the not-finished files.

Choose the **File menu** and **click Save A Copy**.

Choose the **data folder you want** for the not-finished version of the data file. If you are using a different location for your files, substitute the file name and path for your setup.

Click the **New Folder tool** to create a new folder.

Type NF-FLAB to rename the folder.

Double click **NF-FLAB** to **open** the new folder.

Double click the **File name field**.

Type `nf-flab`

Click **Save** to create a copy of all the files for Flabuless Fitness.

The "NF" designates files as not finished to distinguish them from the ones you will work with to enter journal transactions. You will return to your working copy of the file so you can finish the history.

Changing the History Status of Ledgers to Finished

NOTES
If modules are hidden and then later unhidden, they will appear with the open history quill pen icon. When you later view these modules and choose the History menu, open or unfinished modules will be listed individually so you can set them as finished one at a time.

Refer to page 102 and page 339 for assistance with finishing the history and correcting history errors.

Choose the **History menu** and **click Finish Entering History**.

If your amounts, account types and linked accounts are correct, you will see the warning about this step not being reversible and advising you to back up the file first.

Click **Proceed** when there are no errors and you have backed up your files.

If you have made errors, you will not see the warning message. Instead you will see a list of errors.

Click **Print** so that you can refer to the list for making corrections.

Click **OK** to return to the Home window. **Make** the **corrections**, then **try again**.

NOTES
Project and Time and Billing do not have not-finished (open history) symbols.

Click **Proceed**.

The Flabuless Fitness files are now ready for you to enter transactions. Notice that all the Home window icons appear without the open history icons.

Only unhidden modules are set as finished. For Flabuless Fitness, all not-finished symbols are removed. All the ledgers are ready for transactions.

Congratulations on reaching this stage! This is a good time to take a break.

Finish your **session**. This will give you an opportunity to read the next section and the instructions before starting the source document transactions.

Exporting Reports

NOTES
Integration with other software is described further in Appendix H on the Student CD-ROM.

Simply Accounting allows you to export reports to a specified drive and path. The files created by the program may then be used by spreadsheet or wordprocessing programs.

Exporting files will allow you to perform additional calculations and interpret data for reporting purposes. This process of integrating Simply Accounting files with other software is an important step in making the accounting process meaningful.

The following keystrokes will export the opening Balance Sheet for Flabuless Fitness to a Lotus Version 2 file.

NOTES
Depending on your previous export selection, your default format and folder may be different from the ones we show here.

Display the **Balance Sheet** or the report you want to export.

Click the **Export Report tool** or **choose** the **File menu** and **click Export** to display the following screen:

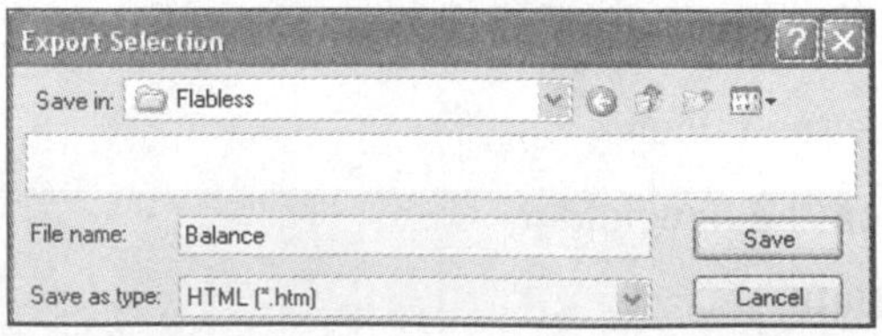

Click the **Save As Type list arrow** to see the types of files you can create:

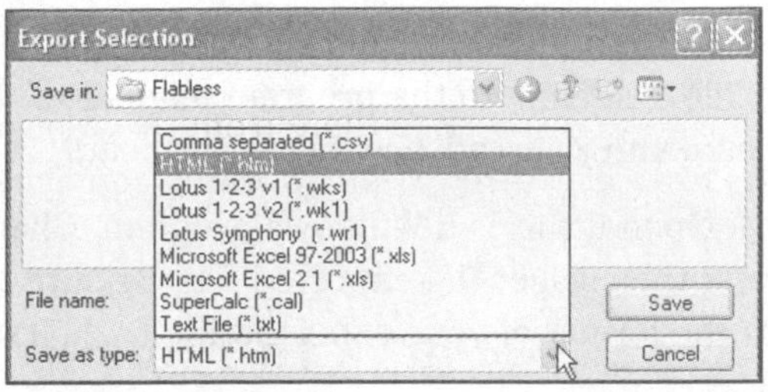

File formats available for export purposes include HTML for Web pages, Text for a wordprocessing format file, Lotus 1-2-3 Versions 1 and 2, Lotus Symphony, Microsoft Excel Versions 97–2003 and 2.1, Supercalc and Comma separated.

Click **Lotus 1-2-3 v2** as the type for the Balance Sheet in the Save As Type field. Use the field list arrow to display the file type options if needed.

Choose the **location** for your exported file. By default your working folder is selected, or the folder you used for the previous exported report.

Click the **list arrow** for the **Save In field** to access the drive and folder you want.

For example, click 3½ Floppy (A:) from the Save In field list to select Drive A. (Be sure that you have a formatted disk in Drive A.) Then double click the folder you want to use to store your file or create a new folder.

Accept the default **file name**, or **type** the **name** you want for your file. The program assigns an extension to the file name so that Lotus will recognize the new file as a Lotus file.

Click **Save**.

To create an Excel spreadsheet, click Microsoft Excel 97–2003 (or 2.1 if your version is older than Excel 97). To generate a file that you can use with word-processing software, click Text.

Using Simply Files and Reports with Other Software

Any Simply Accounting report that you have on display can be opened as a Microsoft Excel spreadsheet. Formulas for totals, and so on, are retained and you can then use the spreadsheet file immediately.

Display the **Simply Accounting report** you want to use in Excel.

Click the **Open In Excel tool** or **choose** the **File menu** and **click Open In Excel** to see the file name window:

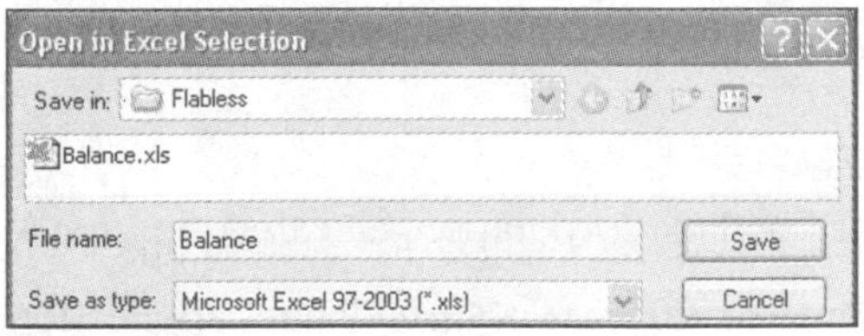

Choose a **location** for your spreadsheet data file.

Click **Save** to open the spreadsheet. Your Simply Accounting data file will remain open. (Save the Excel file if you want to work with it later.)

Close the **Excel file** when finished.

basic **BASIC VERSION**
The Open In Excel option is not available. Instead, you should export the file using an Excel file type and then open the file with Excel.

You can now work with a report that you have exported.

Finish the session using Simply Accounting. Start the software program you want to use with the exported file, referring to the program manuals if necessary. When the blank document or spreadsheet screen appears,

Choose the File menu and click Open if this is a Windows program. Change folders if necessary to locate and then select the exported file. Be sure that the selected file type also matches the format of your exported file (e.g., .txt for a text file, or .xls for Excel).

Some spreadsheet programs can open and convert a file that was saved in the format of a different program. For example, Microsoft Excel can open (or save) text files or Lotus 1-2-3 files. Simply choose the alternative file type in your Open File (or Save File) window. Click OK. Your exported file should replace the blank document screen.

Once you have exported a financial statement as a text file, you can include it in a written report prepared with any wordprocessing program. You can then use the features of the wordprocessing software to enhance the appearance of the statement using format styles that are consistent with the remainder of the report. If you have exported a spreadsheet file, you can use the spreadsheet program to perform additional calculations. Then you can save the modified report as a text file or copy the cells you want to be incorporated in a wordprocessing report. We used exported spreadsheets to create the bank statements for this text.

NOTES
The bank statements for Chapter 14 and for Chapter 15, Case 6 in Appendix E on the Student CD-ROM, were created by exporting the General Ledger reports to a spreadsheet, modifying the data and then copying the results to a wordprocessing file.

When working with a spreadsheet program such as Lotus 1-2-3 or Microsoft Excel, you can use the calculation capabilities of the spreadsheet program to make comparisons between statements from different financial periods. You might also want to use the charting or graphing features to prepare presentation materials.

Exporting reports offers advantages over re-creating the statements. Not only do you save the time of retyping, but you also ensure greater accuracy by avoiding errors made while retyping the numbers and accounts.

SOURCE DOCUMENT INSTRUCTIONS

Instructions for April

NOTES
You can use the data file setup\flab\flab-apr to complete the transactions for April.

1. **Enter** the **transactions** for April using all the information provided.
2. **Print** the following **reports**:
   a. Journal Entries (All Journals) for April, including foreign amounts, corrections and additional transaction details
   b. Customer Aged Detail Report for all customers for April
   c. General Ledger account reports for
      - Bank: Hamilton Trust Chequing
      - Revenue from Sales
      - Sales Returns and Allowances
   d. Vendor Purchases Summary for Footlink Corporation, all categories, for April
3. **Export** the **Balance Sheet** as at April 30, 2008, to a spreadsheet application. **Calculate** the following **key ratios** in your spreadsheet and compare them with the ratios in the Daily Business Manager Business Performance indicators:

   a. current ratio b. quick ratio
4. **Set up** a **budget** for use in May and June and **enter amounts** based on expenses and revenues for April and for the first quarter.

Instructions for May

1. **Enter** the **transactions** for May using all the information provided.
2. **Print** the following **reports**:
   a. Journal Entries (All Journals) for May, including foreign amounts, corrections and additional transaction details
   b. Vendor Aged Detail Report for all vendors for May
   c. Employee Summary Report for all employees for the pay period ending May 31, 2008
   d. Inventory Synopsis Report (observe and report items that have not sold well over the two-month period)
   e. Customer Sales Summary (all customers, items and categories) for May
3. **Export** the **Comparative Balance Sheet** for April 30 and May 31, 2008, to a spreadsheet application. You will use these at the end of the quarter for three-month comparisons.
4. **Compare** May's **performance against** April's budget **forecast**.

NOTES
You can use the data file setup\flab\flab-may to complete the transactions for May. This file does not include budget amounts.

Instructions for June

1. **Enter** the **transactions** for June using all the information provided.
2. **Print** the following **reports**:
   a. Journal Entries (All Journals) for June, including foreign amounts, corrections and additional transaction details
   b. Trial Balance, Balance Sheet and Income Statement on June 30
   c. Inventory Activity Report for Fitness Equipment (All Journals) for June
   d. Bank Transaction Report for all bank accounts from April 1 to June 30
3. **Export** the **Balance Sheet** and **Income Statement** to a spreadsheet application. Combine the Balance Sheet with the comparative one for April and May. **Compare** first- and second-quarter figures, item by item, to assess the performance of Flabuless Fitness.
4. **Make** a **backup copy** of your data files. **Advance** the **session date** to July 1, 2008.
5. **Print** the **Trial Balance**, **Balance Sheet** and **Income Statement** for July 1. **Compare** the end of June and the first of July **statements** and note the changes that result from Simply Accounting closing the books for the new fiscal period.

NOTES
You can use the data file setup\flab\flab-jun to complete the transactions for June. This file does not include budget amounts.

basic **BASIC VERSION**
Print the General Ledger Report for the bank accounts instead of the Bank Transaction Report.

WARNING!
Chapter 15, Case 6 in Appendix E on the Student CD-ROM, has the data you need to complete the bank account reconciliation for Flabuless Fitness. You must use the data files for June 30 to complete the reconciliation, so make sure that you make a backup copy before you advance the session date to the new fiscal year.

SOURCE DOCUMENTS

SESSION DATE – APRIL 15, 2008

☐ **Cash Receipt #39** **Dated April 1, 2008**

From Stoney Creek Sports Arena, cheque #147 for $4 508 in payment on account including $92 discount for early payment. Reference invoice #2191.

NOTES
Remember that receipts are deposited to Undeposited Cash and Cheques. This should be the default account.

NOTES
Remember that PST is not charged on Freight in Ontario so you need to change the tax code for Freight to G.

NOTES
If you want, you can enter Kisangel as the salesperson for all sales that include service revenue. Then you can use the Sales By Salesperson Report to determine her commission.

☐ **Sales Order #41-DRC** **Dated April 2, 2008**

Shipping date April 6, 2008
To Dundas Recreation Centre

2	A080	Heart Rate Monitor	$ 75/ unit
40	A130	Weight Plates	1.20/ kg
1	E020	Elliptical Exerciser: AE-200	1 700/ unit
1	E040	Elliptical Exerciser: LE-400	2 200/ unit
2	E140	Ski Exerciser: Skitrek SE-680	400/ unit
1	E190	Treadmill: Basic T-800B	1 200/ unit
5	S010	Personal Trainer: 1 hour	75/ hour
2	S040	Yoga Instructor: 1 hour	100/ hour
		Freight (tax code G)	50
		GST	7%
		PST	8%

Terms: 2/10, n/30.
Received cheque #96 for $1 000 as down payment (deposit #15) to confirm sales order.

☐ **Cheque Copy #101** **Dated April 3, 2008**

To Footlink Corporation, $8 460 in payment of account including $100 discount for early payment. Reference invoice #FC-618.

☐ **Purchase Order #25** **Dated April 3, 2008**

Shipping date April 8, 2008
From Footlink Corporation

2	E190	Treadmill: Basic T-800B	$ 960.00
2	E200	Treadmill: Basic Plus T-910P	1 280.00
		Freight	40.00
		GST	159.60
		Total	$2 439.60

Terms: 1/15, n/30.

☐ **Cash Receipt #40** **Dated April 4, 2008**

From Mohawk College, cheque #73 for $5 635 in payment of account including $115 discount for early payment. Reference invoice #2194.

☐ **Cheque Copy #346** **Dated April 5, 2008**

To Redux Home Gym Wholesalers, $6 218.10 USD in payment of account including $126.90 discount for early payment. Reference invoice #R-914. The exchange rate is 1.181.

☐ **Sales Invoice #3000** **Dated April 5, 2008**

To Dundas Recreational Centre, to fill sales order #41-DRC

2	A080	Heart Rate Monitor	$ 75/ unit
40	A130	Weight Plates	1.20/ kg
1	E020	Elliptical Exerciser: AE-200	1 700/ unit
1	E040	Elliptical Exerciser: LE-400	2 200/ unit
2	E140	Ski Exerciser: Skitrek SE-680	400/ unit
1	E190	Treadmill: Basic T-800B	1 200/ unit
5	S010	Personal Trainer: 1 hour	75/ hour
2	S040	Yoga Instructor: 1 hour	100/ hour
		Freight	50
		GST	7%
		PST	8%

Terms: 2/10, n/30.

☐ **Credit Card Purchase Invoice #HS-114** **Dated April 6, 2008**

From Hamilton Spectator, $500 plus $35 GST and $40 PST for prepaid advertisement to run over the next 12 weeks. Purchase invoice total $575 paid in full by Visa.

☐ **Credit Card Purchase Invoice #W-1149** **Dated April 6, 2008**

From Westdale Office Supplies, $150 plus $10.50 GST and $12.00 PST for stationery and other office supplies for store. Purchase invoice total $172.50 paid in full by Visa.

☐ **Purchase Invoice #FC-691** **Dated April 6, 2008**

From Footlink Corporation, to fill purchase order #25

2	E190	Treadmill: Basic T-800B	$ 960.00
2	E200	Treadmill: Basic Plus T-910P	1 280.00
	Freight		40.00
	GST		159.60
	Total		$2 439.60

Terms: 1/15, n/30.

☐ **Deposit Slip #14** **Dated April 7, 2008**

Prepare deposit slip for all receipts for April 1 to April 7 to deposit the funds to Bank: Hamilton Trust Chequing from Undeposited Cash and Cheques. The total deposit for the three cheques is $11 143.

NOTES

All deposits are made to Bank: Hamilton Trust Chequing from Undeposited Cheques and Cash.

☐ **Memo #4-1** **Dated April 8, 2008**

Re: Damaged Inventory

Two (2) stability balls, item A110, were torn and damaged beyond repair. Adjust the inventory to recognize the loss.

☐ **Cheque Copy #102** **Dated April 9, 2008**

To Feelyte Gym Accessories, $1 050 in payment of account including $20 discount for early payment. Reference invoice #FG-1611.

☐ **Memo #4-2** **Dated April 9, 2008**

From Visa, received monthly credit card statement for $240 including $220 for purchases up to and including April 3 and $20 annual renewal fee. Submitted cheque #103 for $240 in full payment of the balance owing.

☐ **Cash Receipt #41** **Dated April 9, 2008**

From Chedoke Health Care, cheque #472 for $6 716 in payment of account including $184 discount for early payment. Reference invoice #2199.

☐ **Sales Invoice #3001** **Dated April 12, 2008**

To Hamilton District Bd of Education

8	A070	Glide Slidetrak	$ 50 each
5	A110	Stability Balls	10 each
1	E030	Elliptical Exerciser: DE-300	2 000/ unit
1	E060	Bicycle: Dual Action DA-70	600/ unit
2	E070	Bicycle: Recumbent R-80	750/ unit
	Freight		50
	GST		7%
	PST		8%

Terms: 2/10, n/30.

☐ **Credit Card Purchase Invoice #WS-6112** **Dated April 14, 2008**

From Waterdown Sunoco, $92 including GST and PST for gasoline purchase for delivery vehicle. Invoice paid in full by Visa. (Use tax code IN.)

NOTES
Use Memo 4-3A and Memo 4-3B as the invoice numbers for the sales tax remittances.

NOTES
Enter Memo 4-4A, Memo 4-4B, and so on, in the Additional Information field as the reference numbers for the payroll remittances.

You cannot enter a date earlier than April 1 in the Pay Ending date field.

Memo #4-3 **Dated April 14, 2008**

☐ Record GST for March as a liability to the Receiver General for Canada. Issue cheque #104 in full payment.

☐ Record PST Payable for March as a liability to the Minister of Finance. Remember to collect 5% of the amount owing as the sales tax compensation. Issue cheque #105 in full payment.

Memo #4-4 **Dated April 14, 2008**

Payroll Remittances: Use April 1 as the End of Remitting Period date to make the following payroll remittances in the Payments Journal.

☐ Record EI, CPP and Income Tax Payable up to April 1 as a liability to the Receiver General for Canada. Issue cheque #106 in full payment.

☐ Record EHT Payable up to April 1 as a liability to the Minister of Finance. Issue cheque #107 in full payment.

☐ Record RRSP Payable up to April 1 as a liability to Ancaster Insurance. Issue cheque #108 in full payment.

☐ Record CSB Payable up to April 1 as a liability to Mt. Hope Investment Corporation. Issue cheque #109 in full payment.

☐ Record Group Insurance Payable up to April 1 as a liability to Ancaster Insurance. Issue cheque #110 in full payment.

☐ Record WSIB Payable up to April 1 as a liability to Workplace Safety and Insurance Board. Issue cheque #111 in full payment.

☐ **Credit Card Sales Invoice #3002** **Dated April 14, 2008**

To MasterCard customers (sales summary)

30	A020	Dumbbells: Round pair	$ 1.20/ kg	$ 36.00
2	A050	Dumbbells: 10kg set	25/ set	50.00
2	A060	Dumbbells: 15kg set	40/ set	80.00
2	A090	Power Blocks up to 100 kg	160/ set	320.00
1	A150	Weights: Olympic 100 kg	200/ set	200.00
1	A190	Yoga Mats	30/ unit	30.00
1	E170	Stair Climber: Adjustable SC-A60	1 500/ unit	1 500.00
5	S010	Personal Trainer: 1 hour	75/ hour	375.00
1	S040	Yoga Instructor: 1 hour	100/ hour	100.00
1	S050	Yoga Instructor: 1/2 day	200/ 1/2 day	200.00
	GST		7%	202.37
	PST		8%	177.28
	Total paid by MasterCard			$3 270.65

☐ **Credit Card Sales Invoice #3003** **Dated April 14, 2008**

To Visa customers (sales summary)

1	A010	Body Fat Scale	$ 100/ unit	$ 100.00
5	A040	Dumbbells: 5kg set	15/ set	75.00
1	A100	Power Blocks up to 200 kg	300/ set	300.00
5	A110	Stability Balls	10 each	50.00
40	A130	Weight Plates	1.20/ kg	48.00
1	A160	Weights: Olympic 125 kg	250/ set	250.00
3	A180	Workout Gloves: all sizes	10/ pair	30.00
2	E130	Rowing Machine: RM-1000	480/ unit	960.00
1	E210	Treadmill: Deluxe T-1100D	2 400/ unit	2 400.00
1	S020	Personal Trainer: 1/2 day	200/ 1/2 day	200.00
1	S030	Personal Trainer: full day	400/ day	400.00
1	S050	Yoga Instructor: 1/2 day	200/ 1/2 day	200.00
	GST		7%	350.91
	PST		8%	337.04
	Total paid by Visa			$5 700.95

☐ **Deposit Slip #15** **Dated April 14, 2008**

Prepare deposit slip for all receipts for April 8 to April 14 to deposit the funds. One cheque for $6 716 is being deposited.

☐ **Employee Time Summary Sheet #14** **Dated April 14, 2008**

For the Pay Period ending April 14, 2008
George Schwinn worked 80 regular hours and 2 hours of overtime in the period. Recover $50 advance. Issue payroll deposit slip DD19.

☐ **Cash Receipt #42** **Dated April 15, 2008**

From Dundas Recreational Centre, cheque #195 for $6 527.82 in payment of account including $153.63 discount for early payment. Reference invoice #3000 and deposit #15.

SESSION DATE – APRIL 30, 2008

☐ **Purchase Order #26** **Dated April 18, 2008**

Shipping date April 23, 2008
From Prolife Exercisers Inc.

1	E020	Elliptical Exerciser: AE-200	$ 550.00	USD
1	E030	Elliptical Exerciser: DE-300	670.00	USD
1	E040	Elliptical Exerciser: LE-400	740.00	USD
	Freight		110.00	USD
	GST		144.90	USD
	Total		$2 214.90	USD

Terms: 2/10, n/30. The exchange rate is 1.179.

NOTES
Edit the default purchase cost entered in the Amount field.

☐ **Cash Purchase Invoice #ES-64329** **Dated April 21, 2008**

From Energy Source, $120 plus $8.40 GST paid for hydro service. Purchase invoice total $128.40. Terms: cash on receipt of invoice. Issue cheque #112 in full payment.

☐ **Cash Purchase Invoice #BC-59113** **Dated April 21, 2008**

From Bell Canada, $80 plus $5.60 GST paid and $6.40 PST for monthly phone service. Purchase invoice total $92. Terms: cash on receipt of invoice. Issue cheque #113 in full payment.

☐ **Cheque Copy #114** **Dated April 21, 2008**

To Footlink Corporation, $2 416.80 in payment of account including $22.80 discount for early payment. Reference invoice #FC-691.

☐ **Deposit Slip #16** **Dated April 22, 2008**

Prepare deposit slip for all receipts for April 15 to April 22 to deposit the funds. The total deposit for the single cheque is $6 527.82.

☐ **Sales Invoice #3004** **Dated April 22, 2008**

To Stelco Health Club (preferred customer)

1	A140	Weights: Olympic 75 kg	$ 135/ set
1	E030	Elliptical Exerciser: DE-300	1 875/ unit
1	E070	Bicycle: Recumbent R-80	680/ unit
1	E140	Ski Exerciser: Skitrek SE-680	360/ unit
1	E190	Treadmill: Basic T-800B	1 100/ unit
	GST		7%
	PST		8%

Terms: 2/10, n/30.

NOTES
Use H-2008-2 and H-2008-3 as the Invoice numbers for the postdated payments for property taxes.

☐ **Cash Purchase Invoice #H-2008-1** **Dated April 23, 2008**

From City of Hamilton Treasurer, $900 in full payment of first instalment of quarterly property tax assessment (paid in three monthly instalments). Terms: EOM. Issued cheque #115 in full payment. Store as monthly recurring entry. Recall the stored transaction to issue cheques #116 and #117 as postdated cheques for the next two instalments, dated May 23 and June 23.

☐ **Purchase Invoice #PE-364** **Dated April 23, 2008**

From Prolife Exercisers Inc. to fill purchase order #26

1	E020	Elliptical Exerciser: AE-200	$ 550.00	USD
1	E030	Elliptical Exerciser: DE-300	670.00	USD
1	E040	Elliptical Exerciser: LE-400	740.00	USD
	Freight		110.00	USD
	GST		144.90	USD
	Total		$2 214.90	USD

Terms: 2/10, n/30. The exchange rate is 1.177.

☐ **Employee Time Summary Sheet #15** **Dated April 28, 2008**

For the Pay Period ending April 28, 2008

George Schwinn worked 80 regular hours and 4 hours of overtime. Recover $50 advance. Issue payroll deposit slip DD20.

☐ **Credit Card Sales Invoice #3005** **Dated April 28, 2008**

To MasterCard customers (sales summary)

1	A010	Body Fat Scale	$ 100/ unit	$ 100.00
2	A040	Dumbbells: 5kg set	15/ set	30.00
1	A050	Dumbbells: 10kg set	25/ set	25.00
1	A060	Dumbbells: 15kg set	40/ set	40.00
5	A110	Stability Balls	10 each	50.00
1	A160	Weights: Olympic 125 kg	250/ set	250.00
4	A190	Yoga Mats	30/ unit	120.00
1	E020	Elliptical Exerciser: AE-200	1 700/ unit	1 700.00
1	E200	Treadmill: Basic Plus T-910P	1 600/ unit	1 600.00
10	S010	Personal Trainer: 1 hour	75/ hour	750.00
1	S030	Personal Trainer: full day	400/ day	400.00
1	S040	Yoga Instructor: 1 hour	100/ hour	100.00
	GST		7%	361.55
	PST		8%	313.20
	Total paid by MasterCard			$5 839.75

☐ **Credit Card Sales Invoice #3006** **Dated April 28, 2008**

To Visa customers (sales summary)

20	A020	Dumbbells: Round pair	$ 1.20/ kg	$ 24.00
20	A030	Dumbbells: Hexagonal pair	1.50/ kg	30.00
2	A080	Heart Rate Monitor	75 each	150.00
3	A090	Power Blocks up to 100 kg	160/ set	480.00
1	A100	Power Blocks up to 200 kg	300/ set	300.00
2	A180	Workout Gloves: all sizes	10/ pair	20.00
1	E060	Bicycle: Dual Action DA-70	600/ unit	600.00
1	E190	Treadmill: Basic T-800B	1 200/ unit	1 200.00
1	E220	Treadmill: Deluxe Plus T-1200P	2 800/ unit	2 800.00
1	S020	Personal Trainer: 1/2 day	200/ 1/2 day	200.00
2	S050	Yoga Instructor: 1/2 day	200/ 1/2 day	400.00
	GST		7%	434.28
	PST		8%	448.32
	Total paid by Visa			$7 086.60

☐ **Sales Invoice #3007** **Dated April 28, 2008**

To Stoney Creek Sports Arena

1	A120	Wavemaster	$ 150/ unit
40	A130	Weight Plates	1.20/ kg
1	E110	Rider: Airwalker RA-900	300/ unit
1	E200	Treadmill: Basic Plus T-910P	1 600/ unit
	Freight		30
	GST		7%
	PST		8%

Terms: 2/10, n/30.

☐ **Cash Purchase Invoice #DMC-55** **Dated April 28, 2008**

From Dundurn Maintenance Co. (use Full Add), $300 plus $21 GST paid for cleaning and maintenance of premises. Terms: cash on receipt. Issue cheque #118 in payment. The company bills monthly for their services so store the entry as a monthly recurring transaction.

NOTES

☐ Dundurn Maintenance Co.
(contact Vak Kume)
890 Dundurn St. N.
Hamilton, ON L8G 2P9
Tel: (905) 529-4187
Fax: (905) 529-3116
Terms: net 1
Tax code: G
Expense account: 5240

☐ **Credit Invoice #8** **Dated April 28, 2008**

To Stelco Health Club, $50 allowance for scratched treadmill unit. Reference invoice #3004. There is no tax on the allowance. Enter a negative amount. Create new Subgroup Account 4070 Returns and Allowances. Change the customer terms to net 60; there is no discount. Delete or change the comment.

☐ **Credit Card Purchase Invoice #WS-6533** **Dated April 28, 2008**

From Waterdown Sunoco, $69 including GST and PST for gasoline (tax code IN) and $40 plus $2.80 GST and $3.20 PST for oil change (tax code GP). Purchase invoice total $115 charged to Visa account.

NOTES

Enter the two items purchased from Waterdown Sunoco on separate lines because you need different tax codes for them.

☐ **Cheque Copy #347** **Dated April 30, 2008**

To Prolife Exercisers Inc., $2 173.50 USD in payment of account including $41.40 discount taken for early payment. Reference invoice #PE-364. The exchange rate is 1.1810.

☐ **Memo #4-5** **Dated April 30, 2008**

Transfer $5 000 USD to cover the cheque to Prolife Exercisers. Transfer money to Bank: USD Chequing from 1100 Bank: MasterCard.

☐ **Memo #4-6** **Dated April 30, 2008**

Transfer $12 000 CAD to Bank: Hamilton Trust Savings from 1120 Bank: Visa and Interac.

☐ **Memo #4-7** **Dated April 30, 2008**

Prepare the payroll for the two salaried employees, Nieve Prekor and Assumpta Kisangel. Add 2 percent of revenue from services for April as a commission to Kisangel's salary. Issue payroll deposit slips DD21 and DD22.

NOTES

You must calculate the amount of the commission manually and then enter the amount in the journal.

Use the Revenue from Services amount in the Income Statement for the month of April to calculate the commission.

☐ **Bank Debit Memo #91431** **Dated April 30, 2008**

From Hamilton Trust, authorized withdrawals were made from the chequing account on our behalf for the following:

Bank service charges	$ 35
Mortgage interest payment	1 880
Mortgage principal reduction	120
Bank loan interest payment	420
Bank loan principal reduction	480

SESSION DATE – MAY 15, 2008

☐ **Cash Receipt #43** **Dated May 1, 2008**

From Stelco Health Club, cheque #434 for $4 627.05 in payment of account including $95.45 discount for early payment. Reference sales invoice #3004 and credit invoice #8.

☐ **Sales Invoice #3008** **Dated May 1, 2008**

To McMaster University (preferred customer)

1	E030	Elliptical Exerciser: DE-300	$1 875/ unit
1	E070	Bicycle: Recumbent R-80	680/ unit
1	E080	Home Gym: Basic HG-1400	900/ set
1	E190	Treadmill: Basic T-800B	1 100/ unit
1	E210	Treadmill: Deluxe T-1100D	2 200/ unit
		Freight	40
		GST	7%
		PST	8%

Terms: 2/10, n/30.

NOTES

Remember to check the prices and edit them when they have changed.

☐ **Purchase Order #27** **Dated May 2, 2008**

Delivery date May 7, 2008

From Prolife Exercisers

2	E020	Elliptical Exerciser: AE-200	$1 100.00 USD
2	E030	Elliptical Exerciser: DE-300	1 340.00 USD
2	E040	Elliptical Exerciser: LE-400	1 480.00 USD
		Freight	180.00 USD
		GST	287.00 USD
		Invoice total	$4 387.00 USD

Terms: 2/10, n/30. The exchange rate is 1.1790.

☐ **Purchase Order #28** **Dated May 2, 2008**

Delivery date May 10, 2008

From Footlink Corporation

2	E190	Treadmill: Basic T-800B	$ 960.00
2	E200	Treadmill: Basic Plus T-910P	1 280.00
2	E210	Treadmill: Deluxe T-1100D	1 920.00
2	E220	Treadmill: Deluxe Plus T-1200P	2 240.00
		Freight	50.00
		GST	451.50
		Invoice total	$6 901.50

Terms: 1/15, n/30.

NOTES

Refer to pages 601–604 for assistance with adding tax codes.

☐ **Memo #5-1** **Dated May 3, 2008**

Create new tax code P for purchases that charge only PST at 8%. The status is taxable and PST is not included and not refundable.

NOTES

Use Prepaid Insurance account and tax code P for the insurance purchase.

If the Tax Exempt setting for PST is set at Yes in the Vendor's Ledger, you will be unable to add PST to the purchase invoice.

☐ **Cash Purchase Invoice #AI-6921** **Dated May 3, 2008**

From Ancaster Insurance, $2 400 plus $192 PST for six months of insurance coverage. Invoice total $2 592. Issued cheque #119 in payment.

☐ **Purchase Order #29** **Dated May 4, 2008**

Delivery date May 14, 2008

From Redux Home Gym Wholesalers

2	E080	Home Gym: Basic HG-1400	$820.00 USD
		GST	57.40 USD
		Invoice total	$877.40 USD

Terms: 2/10, n/30. Free delivery. The exchange rate is 1.17905.

☐ **Purchase Order #30** **Dated May 4, 2008**

Delivery date May 12, 2008
From Feelyte Gym Accessories

10	A040	Dumbbells: 5kg set	$ 60.00
10	A070	Glide Slidetrak	250.00
5	A090	Power Blocks up to 100 kg	400.00
15	A110	Stability Balls	60.00
1	A190	Yoga Mats (1 box of 10 mats)	120.00
	GST		62.30
	Invoice total		$952.30

Terms: 2/10, n/30.

☐ **Cash Receipt #44** **Dated May 5, 2008**

From Stoney Creek Sports Arena, cheque #198 for $2 395.90 in payment of account, including $48.90 discount for early payment. Reference invoice #3007.

☐ **Deposit Slip #17** **Dated May 5, 2008**

Prepare deposit slip for all receipts for April 29 to May 5 to deposit the funds. The total deposit for the two cheques is $7 022.95.

☐ **Memo #5-2** **Dated May 5, 2008**

Adjust the selling prices for item E080 (Home Gym: Basic HG-1400) to reflect the cost increase for the next delivery. Change the prices in the Inventory Ledger. The new selling prices are

Regular Canadian dollar price	$1 100 CAD
Preferred Canadian dollar price	1 000 CAD
Regular United States dollar price	950 USD
Preferred United States dollar price	860 USD

☐ **Purchase Invoice #PE-2014** **Dated May 7, 2008**

From Prolife Exercisers, to fill purchase order #27

2	E020	Elliptical Exerciser: AE-200	$1 100.00 USD
2	E030	Elliptical Exerciser: DE-300	1 340.00 USD
2	E040	Elliptical Exerciser: LE-400	1 480.00 USD
	Freight		180.00 USD
	GST		287.00 USD
	Invoice total		$4 387.00 USD

Terms: 2/10, n/30. The exchange rate is 1.1805.

☐ **Cash Receipt #45** **Dated May 9, 2008**

From McMaster University, cheque #1257 for $7 654.83 in payment of account, including $156.22 discount for early payment. Reference invoice #3008.

☐ **Credit Card Purchase Invoice #WS-6914** **Dated May 10, 2008**

From Waterdown Sunoco, $69 including GST and PST for gasoline. Purchase invoice total $69 charged to Visa account.

☐ **Purchase Invoice #FC-768** **Dated May 10, 2008**

From Footlink Corporation, to fill purchase order #28

2	E190	Treadmill: Basic T-800B	$ 960.00
2	E200	Treadmill: Basic Plus T-910P	1 280.00
2	E210	Treadmill: Deluxe T-1100D	1 920.00
2	E220	Treadmill: Deluxe Plus T-1200P	2 240.00
	Freight		50.00
	GST		451.50
	Invoice total		$6 901.50

Terms: 1/15, n/30.

☐ **Purchase Invoice #FG-1804** **Dated May 12, 2008**

From Feelyte Gym Accessories, to fill purchase order #30

10	A040	Dumbbells: 5kg set	$ 60.00
10	A070	Glide Slidetrak	250.00
5	A090	Power Blocks up to 100 kg	400.00
15	A110	Stability Balls	60.00
1	A190	Yoga Mats (1 box of 10 mats)	120.00
	GST		62.30
	Invoice total		$952.30

Terms: 2/10, n/30.

☐ **Sales Order #5-1-MC** **Dated May 12, 2008**

Delivery date May 14, 2008
From Mohawk College (preferred customer)

40	A130	Weight Plates	$ 1.10/ kg
1	A170	Weights: Olympic 150 kg	270/ set
1	E050	Bicycle: Calorie Counter CC-60	360/ unit
1	E060	Bicycle: Dual Action DA-70	540/ unit
1	E090	Home Gym: Deluxe HG-1401	1 400/ set
1	E110	Rider: Airwalker RA-900	270/ unit
1	E120	Rider: Powerglider RP-1500	315/ unit
	Freight		30
	GST		7%
	PST		8%

Terms: 2/10, n/30.

☐ **Credit Card Sales Invoice #3009** **Dated May 12, 2008**

To MasterCard customers (sales summary)

1	A010	Body Fat Scale	$ 100/ unit	$ 100.00
10	A030	Dumbbells: Hexagonal pair	1.50/ kg	15.00
1	A050	Dumbbells: 10kg set	25/ set	25.00
1	A090	Power Blocks up to 100 kg	160/ set	160.00
5	A110	Stability Balls	10 each	50.00
1	E180	Stair Climber: Unlinked SC-U75	2 100/ unit	2 100.00
10	S010	Personal Trainer: 1 hour	75/ hour	750.00
1	S030	Personal Trainer: full day	400/ day	400.00
	GST		7%	252.00
	PST		8%	196.00
	Total paid by MasterCard			$4 048.00

☐ **Credit Card Sales Invoice #3010** **Dated May 12, 2008**

To Visa customers (sales summary)

20	A020	Dumbbells: Round pair	$1.20/ kg	$ 24.00
4	A040	Dumbbells: 5kg set	15/ set	60.00
1	A060	Dumbbells: 15kg set	40/ set	40.00
4	A070	Glide Slidetrak	50 each	200.00
2	A080	Heart Rate Monitor	75/ unit	150.00
1	A090	Power Blocks up to 100 kg	160/ set	160.00
1	A100	Power Blocks up to 200 kg	300/ set	300.00
1	A150	Weights: Olympic 100 kg	200/ set	200.00
2	A180	Workout Gloves: all sizes	10/ pair	20.00
3	A190	Yoga Mats	30/ unit	90.00
1	E160	Ski Exerciser: Independent SE-880	600/ unit	600.00
1	S020	Personal Trainer: 1/2 day	200/ 1/2 day	200.00
	GST		7%	143.08
	PST		8%	147.52
	Total paid by Visa			$2 334.60

☐ **Memo #5-3** **Dated May 12, 2008**

From Visa, received monthly credit card statement for $954.50 for purchases up to and including May 3. Submitted cheque #120 for $954.50 in full payment.

☐ **Deposit Slip #18** **Dated May 12, 2008**

Prepare deposit slip for all receipts for May 6 to May 12 to deposit the funds. The total deposit for the single cheque is $7 654.83.

☐ **Employee Time Summary Sheet #16** **Dated May 12, 2008**

For the Pay Period ending May 12, 2008
George Schwinn worked 80 regular hours in the period. He will receive $200 as an advance and have $50 recovered from each of the following four paycheques. Issue payroll deposit slip DD23.

☐ **Purchase Invoice #R-1031** **Dated May 13, 2008**

From Redux Home Gym Wholesalers, to fill purchase order #29

2	E080	Home Gym: Basic HG-1400	$820.00	USD
	GST		57.40	USD
	Invoice total		$877.40	USD

Terms: 2/10, n/30. Free delivery. The exchange rate is 1.1820.

☐ **Cash Receipt #46** **Dated May 13, 2008**

From Mohawk College, cheque #284 for $1 000 as down payment (deposit #16) in acceptance of sales order #5-1-MC.

Memo #5-4 **Dated May 14, 2008**

☐ Record GST for April as a liability to the Receiver General for Canada. Issue cheque #121 in full payment. Clear the GST Report up to April 30.

☐ Record PST Payable for April as a liability to the Minister of Finance. Remember to collect 5% of the amount owing as the sales tax compensation. Issue cheque #122 in full payment. Clear the PST Report up to April 30.

NOTES
Enter Memo 5-4A and Memo 5-4B as the reference numbers for the tax remittances.

Memo #5-5 **Dated May 14, 2008**

Payroll Remittances: Make the following remittances for the period ending April 30. Choose Pay Remittance for payroll remittances.

☐ Record EI, CPP and Income Tax Payable for April as a liability to the Receiver General for Canada. Issue cheque #123 in full payment.

☐ Record RRSP Payable as a liability to Ancaster Insurance. Issue cheque #124 in full payment.

☐ Record CSB Payable as a liability to Mt. Hope Investment Corporation. Issue cheque #125 in full payment.

☐ Record Group Insurance Payable for April as a liability to Ancaster Insurance. Issue cheque #126 in full payment.

NOTES
Enter Memo 5-5A, Memo 5-5B, and so on, in the Additional Information field as the reference numbers for the payroll remittances.

☐ **Memo #5-6** **Dated May 15, 2008**

Create new inventory item:

Item:	E105 Home Gym: Free Weight HG-1403
Selling price:	$2 200 /set Regular ($2 000 Preferred) CAD
Foreign currency price:	$1 850 Regular ($1 680 Preferred) USD
Minimum level:	1
Linked accounts:	
Asset	1540 Fitness Equipment
Revenue	4020 Revenue from Sales
Expense	5060 Cost of Goods Sold: Equipment
Variance	5070 Cost Variance

☐ **Purchase Invoice #R-1047** **Dated May 15, 2008**

From Redux Home Gym Wholesalers, new inventory item purchase

2	E105	Home Gym: Free Weight HG-1403	$2 200.00	USD
	GST		154.00	USD
	Invoice total		$2 354.00	USD

Terms: 2/10, n/30. Free delivery. The exchange rate is 1.1825.

☐ **Cheque Copy #348** **Dated May 15, 2008**

To Prolife Exercisers, $4 305 USD in payment of account including $82 discount for early payment. Reference invoice #PE-2014. The exchange rate is 1.1825.

☐ **Sales Invoice #3011** **Dated May 15, 2008**

To Mohawk College, to fill sales order #5-1-MC

40	A130	Weight Plates	$ 1.10/ kg
1	A170	Weights: Olympic 150 kg	270/ set
1	E050	Bicycle: Calorie Counter CC-60	360/ unit
1	E060	Bicycle: Dual Action DA-70	540/ unit
1	E090	Home Gym: Deluxe HG-1401	1 400/ set
1	E110	Rider: Airwalker RA-900	270/ unit
1	E120	Rider: Powerglider RP-1500	315/ unit
	Freight		30
	GST		7%
	PST		8%

Terms: 2/10, n/30.

SESSION DATE – MAY 31, 2008

☐ **Cheque Copy #127** **Dated May 18, 2008**

To Footlink Corporation, $6 837 in payment of account including $64.50 discount for early payment. Reference invoice #FC-768.

☐ **Deposit Slip #19** **Dated May 19, 2008**

Prepare deposit slip for the single cheque for $1 000 for May 13 to May 19.

☐ **Cash Purchase Invoice #ES-79123** **Dated May 20, 2008**

From Energy Source, $125 plus $8.75 GST paid for hydro service. Purchase invoice total $133.75. Terms: cash on receipt of invoice. Issue cheque #128 in full payment.

☐ **Cash Purchase Invoice #BC-71222** **Dated May 20, 2008**

From Bell Canada, $80 plus $5.60 GST paid and $6.40 PST for monthly phone service. Purchase invoice total $92. Terms: cash on receipt of invoice. Issue cheque #129 in full payment.

☐ **Cheque Copy #130** **Dated May 21, 2008**

To Feelyte Gym Accessories, $934.50 in payment of account including $17.80 discount for early payment. Reference invoice #FG-1804.

☐ **Credit Card Purchase Invoice #M-1034** **Dated May 22, 2008**

From Mountview Delivery (use Quick Add for the new vendor), $80 plus $5.60 GST paid for delivery services. Invoice total $85.60. Full amount paid by Visa. Enter tax code G in the Purchases Journal.

☐ **Cheque Copy #349** **Dated May 22, 2008**

To Redux Home Gym Wholesalers, $3 166.77 USD in payment of account including $64.63 discount for early payment. Reference invoices #R-1031 and #R-1047. The exchange rate is 1.1785.

☐ **Memo #5-7** **Dated May 22, 2008**

Transfer $4 000 USD to cover the cheque to Redux. Transfer money to Bank: USD Chequing from 1100 Bank: MasterCard.

☐ **Sales Invoice #3012** **Dated May 22, 2008**

To Chedoke Health Care (preferred customer)

1	E010	Elliptical Exerciser: ME-100	$1 000/ unit
1	E130	Rowing Machine: RM-1000	435/ unit
1	E150	Ski Exerciser: Linked SE-780	410/ unit
3	S040	Yoga Instructor: 1 hour	95/ hour
2	S050	Yoga Instructor: 1/2 day	190/ 1/2 day
	Freight		30
	GST		7%
	PST		8%

Terms: 2/10, n/30.

☐ **Cash Receipt #47** **Dated May 22, 2008**

From Mohawk College, cheque #391 for $2 633.28 in payment of account including $74.15 discount for early payment. Reference invoice #3011 and deposit #16.

☐ **Memo #5-8** **Dated May 24, 2008**

Add Charitable Donations as a payroll deduction. Flabuless Fitness will match employee donations so a user-defined expense is also needed.

Create new Group accounts
- 2430 Charitable Donations - Employee
- 2440 Charitable Donations - Employer
- 5390 Charitable Donations Expense

Add Donations as new name (Setup, System Settings, Names)
- for Deduction 3 on Payroll tab screen
- for User-Defined Expense on Additional Payroll tab screen.

Add new payroll linked accounts
- 2430 for Donations (Payroll Deductions tab)
- 2440 for Donations (Payroll User-Defined Expenses tab, Payables)
- 5390 for Donations (Payroll User-Defined Expenses tab, Expenses)

Change Deduction Settings
- Deduct Donations After Tax, EI, CPP, EHT And Vacation Pay
- Deduct Donations By Amount

Enter amounts in Payroll Ledger for Deductions and WSIB & Other Expenses
- Kisangel: Check Use for the deduction; enter $20 for both amounts
- Prekor: Check Use for the deduction; enter $25 for both amounts

NOTES

To add deductions, refer to
page 580 for names
page 590 for payroll deductions settings
page 598 for linked accounts
page 617 for entering the deduction and WSIB & other expense amounts.

☐ **Debit Card Sales Invoice #3013** **Dated May 24, 2008**

To Bruno Scinto (cash and Interac customer)

1	A080	Heart Rate Monitor		$ 75.00
1	A190	Yoga Mats		30.00
1	E170	Stair Climber: Adjustable SC-A60		1 500.00
1	E220	Treadmill: Deluxe Plus T-1200P		2 800.00
	GST		7%	308.35
	PST		8%	352.40
	Invoice total paid in full			$5 065.75

Debit Card #5919 7599 7543 7777. Amount deposited to Visa and Interac account.

☐ **Cash Receipt #48** **Dated May 26, 2008**

From Chedoke Health Care, cheque #532 for $2 808.09 in payment of account including $57.31 discount for early payment. Reference invoice #3012.

☐ **Deposit Slip #20** **Dated May 26, 2008**

Prepare deposit slip for all receipts for May 20 to May 26 to deposit the funds. The total deposit for two cheques is $5 441.37.

☐ **Employee Time Summary Sheet #17** **Dated May 26, 2008**

For the Pay Period ending May 26, 2008
George Schwinn worked 80 regular hours in the period and 2 hours of overtime. Recover $50 advanced and issue payroll deposit slip DD24.

☐ **Credit Card Sales Invoice #3014** **Dated May 26, 2008**

To MasterCard customers (sales summary)

1	A010	Body Fat Scale	$ 100/ unit	$ 100.00
20	A020	Dumbbells: Round pair	1.20/ kg	24.00
20	A030	Dumbbells: Hexagonal pair	1.50/ kg	30.00
4	A040	Dumbbells: 5kg set	15/ set	60.00
10	A110	Stability Balls	10 each	100.00
80	A130	Weight Plates	1.20/ kg	96.00
1	A190	Yoga Mats	30/ unit	30.00
1	E020	Elliptical Exerciser: AE-200	1 700/ unit	1 700.00
1	E050	Bicycle: Calorie Counter CC-60	400/ unit	400.00
1	E080	Home Gym: Basic HG-1400	1 100/ set	1 100.00
1	E190	Treadmill: Basic T-800B	1 200/ unit	1 200.00
10	S010	Personal Trainer: 1 hour	75/ hour	750.00
1	S030	Personal Trainer: full day	400/ day	400.00
1	S040	Yoga Instructor: 1 hour	100/ hour	100.00
	GST		7%	426.30
	PST		8%	387.20
	Total paid by MasterCard			$6 903.50

☐ **Credit Card Sales Invoice #3015** **Dated May 26, 2008**

To Visa customers (sales summary)

1	A050	Dumbbells: 10kg set	$ 25/ set	$ 25.00
1	A060	Dumbbells: 15kg set	40/ set	40.00
4	A070	Glide Slidetrak	50 each	200.00
1	A080	Heart Rate Monitor	75/ unit	75.00
2	A090	Power Blocks up to 100 kg	160/ set	320.00
1	A100	Power Blocks up to 200 kg	300/ set	300.00
1	A120	Wavemaster	150/ unit	150.00
1	A150	Weights: Olympic 100 kg	200/ set	200.00
2	A180	Workout Gloves: all sizes	10/ pair	20.00
1	E040	Elliptical Exerciser: LE-400	2 200/ unit	2 200.00
1	E060	Bicycle: Dual Action DA-70	600/ unit	600.00
1	E100	Home Gym: Multi HG-1402	2 000/ set	2 000.00
1	E110	Rider: Airwalker RA-900	300/ unit	300.00
1	E200	Treadmill: Basic Plus T-910P	1 600/ unit	1 600.00
1	S020	Personal Trainer: 1/2 day	200/ 1/2 day	200.00
2	S050	Yoga Instructor: 1/2 day	200/ 1/2 day	400.00
	GST		7%	604.10
	PST		8%	642.40
	Total paid by Visa			$9 876.50

☐ **Cash Purchase Invoice #DMC-68** **Dated May 28, 2008**

From Dundurn Maintenance Co., $300 plus $21 GST paid for cleaning and maintenance of premises. Terms: cash on receipt. Issue cheque #131 in payment. Recall stored transaction.

☐ **Credit Card Purchase Invoice #WS-7823** **Dated May 30, 2008**

From Waterdown Sunoco, $115, including GST and PST, for gasoline and $40 plus $2.80 GST and $3.20 PST for tire repairs. Purchase invoice total $161 paid in full by Visa. (Remember to change the tax code for the tire repairs.)

☐ **Memo #5-9** **Dated May 31, 2008**

Prepare the payroll for Nieve Prekor and Assumpta Kisangel, the salaried employees. Kisangel took one day personal leave. Add 2 percent of service revenue for May as a commission to Kisangel's salary. Issue payroll deposit slips DD25 and DD26.

☐ **Memo #5-10** **Dated May 31, 2008**

Print customer statements. Prepare invoice #3016 to charge Hamilton District Bd of Education $79.29 interest — 1.5% of the overdue amount. Terms: net 15.

NOTES

Remember that if you want to preview the customer statement, you must choose Custom Simply Form as the Form Type in the Reports and Forms settings on the Statements tab.

☐ **Bank Debit Memo #96241** **Dated May 31, 2008**

From Hamilton Trust, authorized withdrawals were made from the chequing account on our behalf for the following:

Bank service charges	$ 35
Mortgage interest payment	1 870
Mortgage principal reduction	130
Bank loan interest payment	400
Bank loan principal reduction	500

SESSION DATE – JUNE 15, 2008

☐ **Purchase Order #31** **Dated June 2, 2008**

Delivery date June 7, 2008
From Footlink Corporation

2	E190	Treadmill: Basic T-800B	$ 960.00
	Freight		30.00
	GST		69.30
	Invoice total		$1 059.30

Terms: 1/15, n/30.

☐ **Purchase Order #32** **Dated June 3, 2008**

Delivery date June 8, 2008
From Prolife Exercisers

2	E020	Elliptical Exerciser: AE-200	$1 100.00 USD
2	E030	Elliptical Exerciser: DE-300	1 340.00 USD
	Freight		120.00 USD
	GST		179.20 USD
	Invoice total		$2 739.20 USD

Terms: 2/10, n/30. The exchange rate is 1.1788.

☐ **Purchase Order #33** **Dated June 3, 2008**

Delivery date June 15, 2008
From Feelyte Gym Accessories

1	A080	Heart Rate Monitor (1 carton of 12)	$360.00
20	A110	Stability Balls	80.00
2	A180	Workout Gloves: all sizes (2 boxes of 10)	80.00
	GST		36.40
	Invoice total		$556.40

Terms: 2/10, n/30.

NOTES

Taxes are not charged on freight for foreign customers.

☐ **Sales Invoice #3017** **Dated June 3, 2008**

To Buffalo Health Clinic, New York (preferred USD customer)

1	E210	Treadmill: Deluxe T-1100D	$1 810/ unit USD
1	E220	Treadmill: Deluxe Plus T-1200P	2 125/ unit USD
		Freight	60 USD

Terms: 2/10, n/30. The exchange rate is 1.1788.

☐ **Sales Invoice #3018** **Dated June 5, 2008**

To Hamilton District Bd of Education

60	A130	Weight Plates	$ 1.20/ kg
1	E020	Elliptical Exerciser: AE-200	1 700/ unit
1	E030	Elliptical Exerciser: DE-300	2 000/ unit
1	E050	Bicycle: Calorie Counter CC-60	400/ unit
1	E130	Rowing Machine: RM-1000	480/ unit
1	E150	Ski Exerciser: Linked SE-780	450/ unit
		Freight	30
		GST	7%
		PST	8%

Terms: 2/10, n/30.

☐ **Purchase Invoice #TD-1127** **Dated June 5, 2008**

From Trufit Depot

2	E110	Rider: Airwalker RA-900	$240.00
2	E130	Rowing Machine: RM-1000	384.00
		GST	43.68
		Invoice total	$667.68

Terms: 2/5, n/30. Free delivery.

☐ **Purchase Invoice #FC-861** **Dated June 7, 2008**

From Footlink Corporation, to fill purchase order #31

2	E190	Treadmill: Basic T-800B	$ 960.00
		Freight	30.00
		GST	69.30
		Invoice total	$1 059.30

Terms: 1/15, n/30.

☐ **Purchase Invoice #PE-2079** **Dated June 8, 2008**

From Prolife Exercisers, to fill purchase order #32

2	E020	Elliptical Exerciser: AE-200	$1 100.00	USD
2	E030	Elliptical Exerciser: DE-300	1 340.00	USD
		Freight	120.00	USD
		GST	179.20	USD
		Invoice total	$2 739.20	USD

Terms: 2/10, n/30. The exchange rate is 1.1815.

☐ **Employee Time Summary Sheet #18** **Dated June 9, 2008**

For the Pay Period ending June 9, 2008

George Schwinn worked 80 regular hours in the period (no overtime) and took one day of sick leave. Recover $50 advanced and issue payroll deposit slip DD27.

☐ **Cheque Copy #132** **Dated June 9, 2008**

To Trufit Depot, $655.20 in payment of account including $12.48 discount for early payment. Reference invoice #TD-1127.

☐ **Cash Receipt #49** **Dated June 9, 2008**

From Hamilton District Bd of Education, cheque #1431 for $11 146.70 in payment of account including $117.99 discount for early payment. Reference invoices #3001, #3016 and #3018.

☐ **Memo #6-1** **Dated June 9, 2008**

From Visa, received monthly credit card statement for $315.60 for purchases made before June 3, 2008. Submitted cheque #133 for $315.60 in full payment of the balance owing.

☐ **Credit Card Sales Invoice #3019** **Dated June 9, 2008**

To MasterCard customers (sales summary)

1	A010	Body Fat Scale	$ 100/ unit	$ 100.00
20	A020	Dumbbells: Round pair	1.20/ kg	24.00
4	A070	Glide Slidetrak	50 each	200.00
5	A110	Stability Balls	10 each	50.00
1	A150	Weights: Olympic 100 kg	200/ set	200.00
1	A160	Weights: Olympic 125 kg	250/ set	250.00
1	A180	Workout Gloves: all sizes	10/ pair	10.00
2	A190	Yoga Mats	30/ unit	60.00
1	E110	Rider: Airwalker RA-900	300/ unit	300.00
1	E120	Rider: Powerglider RP-1500	350/ unit	350.00
5	S010	Personal Trainer: 1 hour	75/ hour	375.00
1	S030	Personal Trainer: full day	400/ day	400.00
	GST		7%	162.33
	PST		8%	123.52
	Total paid by MasterCard			$2 604.85

☐ **Credit Card Sales Invoice #3020** **Dated June 9, 2008**

To Visa customers (sales summary)

10	A030	Dumbbells: Hexagonal pair	$1.50/ kg	$ 15.00
4	A040	Dumbbells: 5kg set	15/ set	60.00
1	A050	Dumbbells: 10kg set	25/ set	25.00
1	A060	Dumbbells: 15kg set	40/ set	40.00
2	A080	Heart Rate Monitor	75/ unit	150.00
2	A090	Power Blocks up to 100 kg	160/ set	320.00
1	A100	Power Blocks up to 200 kg	300/ set	300.00
1	A120	Wavemaster	150/ unit	150.00
1	A140	Weights: Olympic 75 kg	150/ set	150.00
1	A170	Weights: Olympic 150 kg	300/ set	300.00
1	E170	Stair Climber: Adjustable SC-A60	1 500/ unit	1 500.00
1	E190	Treadmill: Basic T-800B	1 200/ unit	1 200.00
5	S010	Personal Trainer: 1 hour	75/ hour	375.00
1	S020	Personal Trainer: 1/2 day	200/ 1/2 day	200.00
3	S040	Yoga Instructor: 1 hour	100/ hour	300.00
2	S050	Yoga Instructor: 1/2 day	200/ 1/2 day	400.00
	GST		7%	383.95
	PST		8%	336.80
	Total paid by Visa			$6 205.75

☐ **Deposit Slip #21** **Dated June 9, 2008**

Prepare deposit slip for the single cheque for $11 146.70 being deposited.

☐ **Memo #6-2** **Dated June 14, 2008**

Record GST for May as a liability to the Receiver General for Canada. Issue cheque #134 in full payment. Clear the GST Report up to May 31.

NOTES

Enter Memo 5-4A and Memo 5-4B as the reference numbers for the tax remittances.

☐ Record PST Payable for May as a liability to the Minister of Finance. Remember to collect 5% of the amount owing as the sales tax compensation. Issue cheque #135 in full payment. Clear the PST Report up to May 31.

Memo #6-3 **Dated June 14, 2008**

Payroll Remittances: Make the following payroll remittances for the pay period ending May 31 in the Payments Journal.

☐ Record EI, CPP and Income Tax Payable for May as a liability to the Receiver General for Canada. Issue cheque #136 in full payment.

☐ Record RRSP Payable as a liability to Ancaster Insurance. Issue cheque #137 in full payment.

☐ Record CSB Payable as a liability to Mt. Hope Investment Corporation. Issue cheque #138 in full payment.

☐ Record Group Insurance Payable for May as a liability to Ancaster Insurance. Issue cheque #139 in full payment.

☐ Record Charitable Donations payable for May as a liability to Canadian Cancer Society. Create a new vendor record and select Payroll Authority for the vendor. Choose the new vendor in the Payroll Remittance Settings screen for both Donations entries. Include employee and employer contributions in remittance. Issue cheque #140 in full payment.

NOTES
Enter Memo 6-3A, Memo 6-3B, and so on, in the Additional Information field as the reference numbers for the payroll remittances.

NOTES
You cannot create the new vendor from the Pay Remittance form in the Payments Journal.
Refer to page 623 for setting up payroll authorities and remittances.

☐ **Purchase Invoice #FG-2187** **Dated June 15, 2008**

From Feelyte Gym Accessories to fill purchase order #33

1	A080	Heart Rate Monitor (1 carton of 12)	$360.00
20	A110	Stability Balls	80.00
2	A180	Workout Gloves: all sizes (2 boxes of 10)	80.00
		GST	36.40
		Invoice total	$556.40

Terms: 2/10, n/30.

☐ **Cheque Copy #350** **Dated June 15, 2008**

To Prolife Exercisers, $2 688 USD in payment of account including $51.20 discount for early payment. Reference invoice #PE-2079. The exchange rate is 1.1825.

NOTES
The next deposit, from Buffalo Health Clinic, will cover the bank overdraught.

☐ **Cash Receipt #50** **Dated June 15, 2008**

From Buffalo Health Clinic, cheque #638 for $3 995 USD in payment of account. Reference invoice #3017. The exchange rate is 1.1825.

SESSION DATE – JUNE 30, 2008

☐ **Sales Invoice #3021** **Dated June 16, 2008**

To Stelco Health Club (preferred customer)

40	A130	Weight Plates	$ 1.10/ kg
1	E080	Home Gym: Basic HG-1400	1 000/ set
1	E100	Home Gym: Multi HG-1402	1 875/ set
1	E105	Home Gym: Free Weight HG-1403	2 000/ set
		Freight	30
		GST	7%
		PST	8%

Terms: 2/10, n/30.

☐ **Memo #6-4** **Dated June 16, 2008**

Transfer $25 000 from the Visa bank account and $10 000 from the MasterCard bank account to the savings account.

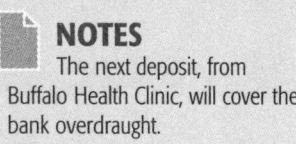

☐ **Memo #6-5** **Dated June 18, 2008**

Pay $5 000 to the Receiver General for Canada for quarterly instalment of business income tax. Issue cheque #141. Create new Group account 5550 Business Income Tax Expense. (Hint: Remember Business Income Tax Payable.)

☐ **Memo #6-6** **Dated June 18, 2008**

Create appropriate new Heading and Total accounts around the new Group account 5550 to restore the logical order of accounts.

☐ **Cash Purchase Invoice #BC-86344** **Dated June 19, 2008**

From Bell Canada, $100 plus $7 GST paid and $8 PST for monthly phone service. Purchase invoice total $115. Terms: cash on receipt of invoice. Issue cheque #142 in full payment.

☐ **Cash Purchase Invoice #ES-89886** **Dated June 19, 2008**

From Energy Source, $120 plus $8.40 GST paid for hydro service. Purchase invoice total $128.40. Terms: cash on receipt of invoice. Issue cheque #143 in full payment.

☐ **Cheque Copy #144** **Dated June 20, 2008**

To Footlink Corporation, $1 049.40 in payment of account including $9.90 discount for early payment. Reference invoice #FC-861.

☐ **Cash Sales Invoice #3022** **Dated June 20, 2008**

To Jim Ratter (choose Continue)

1	A010	Body Fat Scale		$100.00
	GST		7%	7.00
	PST		8%	8.00
	Invoice total			$115.00

Received cheque #16 in full payment.

☐ **Cheque Copy #145** **Dated June 23, 2008**

To Feelyte Gym Accessories, $546 in payment of account including $10.40 discount for early payment. Reference invoice #FG-2187.

☐ **Credit Card Sales Invoice #3023** **Dated June 23, 2008**

To MasterCard customers (sales summary)

20	A020	Dumbbells: Round pair	$ 1.20/ kg	$ 24.00
3	A070	Glide Slidetrak	50 each	150.00
2	A090	Power Blocks up to 100 kg	160/ set	320.00
1	A140	Weights: Olympic 75 kg	150/ set	150.00
1	A170	Weights: Olympic 150 kg	300/ set	300.00
2	A180	Workout Gloves: all sizes	10/ pair	20.00
1	E060	Bicycle: Dual Action DA-70	600/ unit	600.00
1	E090	Home Gym: Deluxe HG-1401	1 500/ set	1 500.00
1	E140	Ski Exerciser: Skitrek SE-680	400/ unit	400.00
10	S010	Personal Trainer: 1 hour	75/ hour	750.00
1	S030	Personal Trainer: full day	400/ day	400.00
	GST		7%	322.98
	PST		8%	277.12
	Total paid by MasterCard			$5 214.10

☐ **Cash Receipt #51** **Dated June 23, 2008**

From Stelco Health Club, cheque #499 for $5 575.17 in payment of account including $113.78 discount for early payment. Reference invoice #3021.

☐ **Deposit Slip #22** **Dated June 23, 2008**

Prepare deposit slip for two cheques totalling $5 690.17 to deposit funds.

☐ **Credit Card Sales Invoice #3024** **Dated June 23, 2008**

To Visa customers (sales summary)

20	A030	Dumbbells: Hexagonal pair	$ 1.50/ kg	$ 30.00
3	A040	Dumbbells: 5kg set	15/ set	45.00
1	A050	Dumbbells: 10kg set	25/ set	25.00
1	A060	Dumbbells: 15kg set	40/ set	40.00
2	A080	Heart Rate Monitor	75/ unit	150.00
1	A100	Power Blocks up to 200 kg	300/ set	300.00
5	A110	Stability Balls	10 each	50.00
1	A150	Weights: Olympic 100 kg	200/ set	200.00
2	A190	Yoga Mats	30/ unit	60.00
1	E070	Bicycle: Recumbent R-80	750/ unit	750.00
1	E110	Rider: Airwalker RA-900	300/ unit	300.00
1	E170	Stair Climber: Adjustable SC-A60	1 500/ unit	1 500.00
1	S020	Personal Trainer: 1/2 day	200/ 1/2 day	200.00
3	S040	Yoga Instructor: 1 hour	100/ hour	300.00
2	S050	Yoga Instructor: 1/2 day	200/ 1/2 day	400.00
	GST		7%	304.50
	PST		8%	276.00
	Total paid by Visa			$4 930.50

☐ **Employee Time Summary Sheet #19** **Dated June 23, 2008**

For the Pay Period ending June 23, 2008
George Schwinn worked 80 regular and 2 overtime hours in the period and took 1 day of sick leave. Recover $50 advanced and issue payroll deposit slip DD28.

Issue a cheque to George Schwinn for vacation pay. George will be going on vacation for two weeks. A contract has been arranged with a local delivery company to complete deliveries during this period. Issue cheque #146.

NOTES
Remember to remove all wage amounts, deductions and user-defined expense amounts for the vacation paycheque.

☐ **Memo #6-7** **Dated June 24, 2008**

Received Bank Debit Memo #99142 from Hamilton Trust. Cheque #16 from Jim Ratter for $115 was returned as NSF.
Prepare a sales invoice to charge Ratter (use Quick Add) for the sales amount and add $20 in service charges for the cost of processing the cheque. Create new Group account 4220 Other Revenue. Terms: net 30.

NOTES
For the Ratter invoice, credit chequing account for $115, credit Other Revenue for $20, debit Accounts Receivable for $135.

☐ **Purchase Order #34** **Dated June 24, 2008**

Delivery date July 1, 2008
From Scandia Weights Co.

1	A130	Weight Plates (1 order of 100 kg)	$ 60.00
3	A140	Weights: Olympic 75 kg	225.00
3	A150	Weights: Olympic 100 kg	300.00
3	A160	Weights: Olympic 125 kg	375.00
3	A170	Weights: Olympic 150 kg	450.00
	GST		98.70
	Purchase invoice total		$1 508.70

Terms: net 30.

☐ **Sales Invoice #3025** **Dated June 25, 2008**

To Lockport Gymnasium, New York

1	E010	Elliptical Exerciser: ME-100	$ 925/ unit USD
1	E040	Elliptical Exerciser: LE-400	1 850/ unit USD
1	E180	Stair Climber: Unlinked SC-U75	1 735/ unit USD
1	E190	Treadmill: Basic T-800B	1 000/ unit USD
	Freight		60 USD

Terms: 2/10, n/30. The exchange rate is 1.1800.

☐ **Memo #6-8** **Dated June 26, 2008**

Write off Jim Ratter's account because attempts to locate him were unsuccessful. The outstanding amount is considered a bad debt. Improved screening of customers who pay by cheque will be implemented immediately.

☐ **Cash Purchase Invoice #DMC-89** **Dated June 28, 2008**

From Dundurn Maintenance Co., $300 plus $21 GST paid for cleaning and maintenance of premises. Terms: cash on receipt. Issue cheque #147 in payment. Recall stored transaction.

☐ **Credit Card Purchase Invoice #WS-9855** **Dated June 30, 2008**

From Waterdown Sunoco, $98 including GST and PST paid for gasoline. Purchase invoice total $98 paid in full by Visa.

☐ **Credit Card Sales Invoice #3026** **Dated June 30, 2008**

To MasterCard customers (sales summary)

1	A040	Dumbbells: 5kg set	$ 15/ set	$ 15.00
5	A110	Stability Balls	10 each	50.00
1	E050	Bicycle: Calorie Counter CC-60	400/ unit	400.00
1	E130	Rowing Machine: RM-1000	480/ unit	480.00
1	S020	Personal Trainer: 1/2 day	200/ 1/2 day	200.00
2	S040	Yoga Instructor: 1 hour	100/ hour	200.00
	GST		7%	94.15
	PST		8%	75.60
	Total paid by MasterCard			$1 514.75

☐ **Credit Card Sales Invoice #3027** **Dated June 30, 2008**

To Visa customers (sales summary)

1	A070	Glide Slidetrak	$ 50 each	$ 50.00
20	A130	Weight Plates	1.20/ kg	24.00
1	E060	Bicycle: Dual Action DA-70	600/ unit	600.00
5	S010	Personal Trainer: 1 hour	75/ hour	375.00
1	S030	Personal Trainer: full day	400/ day	400.00
1	S050	Yoga Instructor: 1/2 day	200/ 1/2 day	200.00
	GST		7%	115.43
	PST		8%	53.92
	Total paid by Visa			$1 818.35

☐ **Memo #6-9** **Dated June 30, 2008**

Prepare the payroll for Nieve Prekor and Assumpta Kisangel, the salaried employees. Add 2 percent of service revenue for June as a commission to Kisangel's salary. Issue payroll deposit slips DD29 and DD30.

Prepare separate payroll deposit slips to pay all employees for completed surveys and quarterly bonuses. Withhold 10 percent income tax. (See margin notes.)

Kisangel	$300 bonus, 20 completed client surveys, $50 income tax
Prekor	$250 bonus, 28 completed client surveys, $53 income tax
Schwinn	$250 bonus, 26 completed client surveys, $51 income tax

☐ **Bank Credit Memo #7642** **Dated June 30, 2008**

From Hamilton Trust, semi-annual interest was deposited to bank accounts. $155 was deposited to chequing account and $815 to the savings account. Remember interest receivable balance $420.

NOTES

Use tax code IN for $115, the sale portion of the bad debt. Use No Tax as the code for the $20 handling charge. Remember to "pay" the account. Refer to Accounting Procedures, page 575.

NOTES

Use the Payroll Journal to enter the piece rate pay and bonuses.

- Click Enter Taxes Manually so that you can edit the income tax amounts.
- On the Income tab screen, remove all hours, wage, salary and benefit amounts. Do not remove Vacation Accrued for Schwinn.
- On the remaining tab screens, remove entitlement hours and deduction and user-defined expense amounts.
- Click the Taxes tab.
- Click Recalculate Taxes.
- Enter the income tax amount. Do not change the EI or CPP amounts.
- Click Enter Taxes Automatically after creating the bonus cheques.

☐ **Bank Debit Memo #143661** **Dated June 30, 2008**

From Hamilton Trust, authorized withdrawals were made from the chequing account on our behalf for the following:

Bank service charges	$ 35
Mortgage interest payment	1 850
Mortgage principal reduction	150
Bank loan interest payment	380
Bank loan principal reduction	520

☐ **Memo #6-10** **Dated June 30, 2008**

Prepare quarterly adjusting entries for depreciation on fixed assets using the following amounts:

Cash Registers	$ 300
Computer Equipment	150
Furniture & Fixtures	80
Retail Premises	2 450
Van	1 875

☐ **Memo #6-11** **Dated June 30, 2008**

Increase the allowance for doubtful accounts by $500 in preparation for the next fiscal period.

☐ **Memo #6-12** **Dated June 30, 2008**

Prepare adjusting entries for the following:

Office Supplies used	$ 290
Linen Supplies used	120
Prepaid Insurance expired	2 016
Prepaid Advertising expired	620
Payroll Liabilities accrued for Schwinn	680

Create a new Group liability account Accrued Payroll 2260.

☐ **Memo #6-13** **Dated June 30, 2008**

Edit the tax codes (rates and descriptions) to apply the reduction in the GST rate to 6 percent.

REVIEW

The Student CD-ROM with Data Files includes Review Questions and Supplementary Cases for this chapter including bank reconciliation and online banking.

CHAPTER SIXTEEN

Stratford Country Inn

OBJECTIVES

After completing this chapter, you should be able to

- ***plan*** and ***design*** an accounting system for a small business
- ***prepare*** a conversion procedure from manual records
- ***understand*** the objectives of a computerized accounting system
- ***create*** company files
- ***set up*** company accounts
- ***finish*** entering historical data to prepare for journal entries
- ***enter*** accounting transactions from realistic source documents
- ***display*** and ***print*** reports
- ***analyze*** and ***interpret*** case studies
- ***develop*** further group interpersonal skills
- ***develop*** further oral and written skills

COMPANY INFORMATION

Company Profile

NOTES
Stratford Country Inn
100 Festival Road
Stratford, Ontario
N5A 3G2
Tel 1: (519) 222-6066
Tel 2: (888) 272-6000
Fax: (519) 272-7960
Business No.: 767 698 321

Stratford Country Inn is situated in Ontario just outside the Stratford city limits, close to Stratford Festival Theatres. The Inn has room for approximately 50 people, with additional cots available for families who want to share rooms. In addition to the theatre, which attracts most of the guests, the Inn has facilities for rowing and canoeing on the small lake area near the Thames River, and a forested area nearby is used for lovely summer walks or cross-country skiing in winter. Boxed lunches and dinners are provided for picnics on the waterfront before theatre events or for afternoons in the woods or on the lake. Thus, many guests stay for several days at a time, and weekly rates are offered.

For an additional cost, a private consultant will pamper the guests with aromatherapy sessions. The consultant pays a rental fee to the Inn for use of her studio.

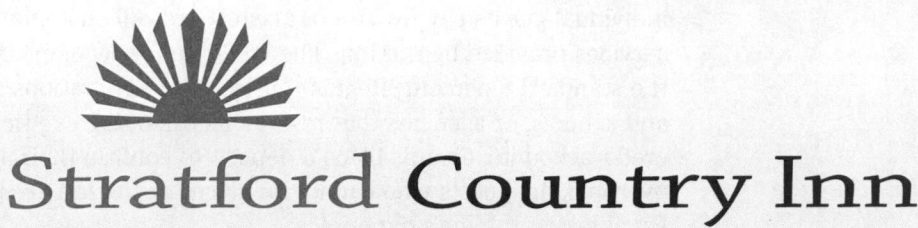

Customers come from near and far, and even a few American theatre groups have become regular visitors. The Inn prepares invoices and accepts payments in United States dollars for US accounts. For the American groups, an agency books group tours for a fixed price that includes theatre tickets and accommodation. Most individual guests pay by Visa or MasterCard. All customers pay GST and PST on the services provided by the Inn. The PST rate for accommodation is 5 percent instead of the standard 8 percent. Regular customers, corporations such as colleges, universities and schools, or agencies that reserve blocks of theatre tickets and accommodation have credit accounts. Groups place a deposit to confirm their accommodation. In the event of overbooking, guests who cannot be placed at the Inn are put up at a nearby Bed & Breakfast at the Inn's expense.

The grounds of the Inn include conference rooms for discussions and debates about theatre performances and related topics. Buses take guests to the theatre and return them to the Inn on a scheduled basis. Meals can be included for those who want an all-inclusive package. The Inn's dining room serves all full accommodation guests and also caters to the public and to guests who choose not to take a full meal package.

The owner, manager and desk attendant look after the front office. Five additional staff cater to all the other needs of the guests.

Accounts Payables have been set up for food supplies, a maintenance contract (a cleaning crew vacuums the Inn), maintenance and repairs (electrical and carpentry work), linen supplies for kitchen and guest rooms, and laundry services for towels and bedding.

By June 30, the Inn was ready to convert its accounting records to Simply Accounting and had gathered the following reports to make the conversion:

- Chart of Accounts
- Post-Closing Trial Balance
- Vendor Information
- Customer Information
- Employee Information and Profiles

CHART OF ACCOUNTS

STRATFORD COUNTRY INN

ASSETS
Bank: Stratford Trust CAD Chequing
Bank: Stratford Trust USD Chequing
Bank: Credit Card
Accounts Receivable
Advances Receivable
Purchase Prepayments
Prepaid Advertising
Prepaid Insurance
Food Inventory
Linens & Towels
Blankets & Bedding
Supplies: Computer
Supplies: Office
Supplies: Dining Room
Supplies: Washroom
Computer Equipment
Accum Deprec: Computers
Furniture & Fixtures ▶
▶Accum Deprec: Furn & Fix
Vehicle
Accum Deprec: Vehicle
Country Inn & Dining Room
Accum Deprec: Inn & Dining Room
Grounds & Property

LIABILITIES
Bank Loan
Accounts Payable
Prepaid Sales and Deposits
Credit Card Payable
Vacation Payable
EI Payable
CPP Payable
Income Tax Payable
EHT Payable
Group Insurance Payable
Tuition Fees Payable
WSIB Payable ▶
▶PST Payable
GST Charged on Services
GST Paid on Purchases
Mortgage Payable

EQUITY
E. Prospero, Capital
Current Earnings

REVENUE
Revenue from Inn
Revenue from Dining Room
Rental Fees
Sales Tax Compensation
Other Revenue
Exchange Rate Differences

EXPENSE
Advertising & Promotion
Bank Charges and Card Fees
COGS: Food ▶
▶Depreciation: Computers
Depreciation: Furn & Fix
Depreciation: Vehicle
Depreciation: Inn & Dining Room
Purchase Discounts
Interest Expense: Loan
Interest Expense: Mortgage
Hydro Expenses
Maintenance & Repairs
Overflow Accommodation
Telephone Expense
Vehicle Expenses
Wages: Management
Wages: General
Wages: Dining Room
EI Expense
CPP Expense
WSIB Expense
EHT Expense
Tuition Fees Expense

NOTES: Use appropriate account numbers and add subgroup totals, headings and totals to organize your Chart of Accounts as necessary. Remember to add a test balance account for the setup.

POST-CLOSING TRIAL BALANCE

STRATFORD COUNTRY INN

June 30, 2008

	Debits	Credits
Bank: Stratford Trust CAD Chequing	$34 000	
Bank: Stratford Trust USD Chequing (2 400 USD)	3 000	
Bank: Credit Card	12 000	
Accounts Receivable (deposit)		$ 1 000
Advances Receivable	250	
Prepaid Advertising	50	
Prepaid Insurance	400	
Food Inventory	1 650	
Linens & Towels	2 000	
Blankets & Bedding	3 000	
Supplies: Computer	400	
Supplies: Office	500	
Supplies: Dining Room	800	
Supplies: Washroom	250	
Computer Equipment	4 000	
Accum Deprec: Computers		1 200
Furniture & Fixtures	38 000	
Accum Deprec: Furn & Fix		4 200
Vehicle	50 000 ▶	
▶ Accum Deprec: Vehicle		10 000
Country Inn & Dining Room	400 000	
Accum Deprec: Inn & Dining Room		20 000
Grounds & Property	200 000	
Bank Loan		25 000
Accounts Payable		7 852
Credit Card Payable		395
Vacation Payable		4 946
EI Payable		1 092
CPP Payable		1 759
Income Tax Payable		3 109
EHT Payable		577
Group Insurance Payable		330
WSIB Payable		1 310
PST Payable		3 200
GST Charged on Services		3 080
GST Paid on Purchases	700	
Mortgage Payable		300 000
E. Prospero, Capital		361 950
	$751 000	$751 000

VENDOR INFORMATION

STRATFORD COUNTRY INN

Vendor Name (Contact)	Address	Phone No. Fax No.	E-mail Web Site	Terms Tax ID
Avon Maintenance Services (Ken Sparkles)	66 Kleen Road Stratford, Ontario N5A 3C3	Tel: (519) 272-4611 Fax: (519) 272-4813	www.avonservices.com	net 30 631 393 461
Bard's Linen & Towels (Jason Bard)	21 Venice Street Stratford, Ontario N5A 4L2	Tel: (519) 271-2273 Fax: (519) 271-9333	bard@bards.com www.bards.com	2/10, n/30 after tax 763 271 673
Bell Canada (Bea Heard)	30 Whisper Road Stratford, Ontario N5A 4N3	Tel: (519) 273-2355	bheard@bell.ca www.bell.ca	net 1 634 345 373
Minister of Finance (Payroll Authority for EHT)	PO Box 3000, Stn A Toronto, Ontario M5C 1M2		www.gov.on.ca/fin	net 1
Perth County Hydro (Wynd Mills)	66 Power Road Stratford, Ontario N5A 4P4	Tel: (519) 272-6121	www.perthenergy.com	net 1 721 431 214
Receiver General for Canada (Payroll Authority)	PO Box 20002, Stn A Sudbury, Ontario P3A 5C3	Tel: (800) 959-5525	www.cra-arc.gc.ca	net 1
Stratford Service Centre (A.L.L. Ledfree)	33 MacBeth Avenue Stratford, Ontario N5A 4T2	Tel: (519) 271-6679 Fax: (519) 276-8822	ledfree@ssc.com www.ssc.com	net 1 634 214 211
Tavistock Laundry Services (Martin Tavistock)	19 Merchant Road Stratford, Ontario N5A 4C3	Tel: (519) 271-7479 Fax: (519) 271-7888	www.tavistock.com	net 30 639 271 343
Tempest Food Wholesalers (Vita Minns)	35 Henry Avenue Stratford, Ontario N5A 3N6	Tel: (519) 272-4464 Fax: (519) 272-4600	vita@tempest.com www.tempest.com	net 30 673 421 936
Travellers' Life (Payroll Authority for group insurance)				
Workplace Safety & Insurance Board (Payroll Authority for WCB)				
Zephyr Advertising Services (Tom DeZiner)	32 Portia Blvd. Stratford, Ontario N5A 4T2	Tel: (519) 271-6066 Fax: (519) 271-6067	tom@westwinds.com www.westwinds.com	net 1 391 213 919

OUTSTANDING VENDOR INVOICES

STRATFORD COUNTRY INN

Vendor Name	Terms	Date	Inv/Chq No.	Amount	Total
Avon Maintenance Services	net 30	June 7/08	AM-68	$535	
	net 30	June 14/08	AM-85	535	
	net 30	June 21/08	AM-101	535	
	net 30	June 28/08	AM-127	535	
			Balance owing		$2 140
Tavistock Laundry Services	net 30	June 8/08	TL-693	$856	
	net 30	June 22/08	TL-742	856	
			Balance owing		$1 712
Tempest Food Wholesalers	net 30	June 23/08	TF-113	$2 000	
	net 30	June 30/08	TF-183	2 000	
			Balance owing		$4 000
			Grand Total		$7 852

CUSTOMER INFORMATION

STRATFORD COUNTRY INN

Customer Name (Contact)	Address	Phone No. Fax No.	E-mail Web Site	Terms Credit Limit
Festival Club of Rosedale (Jane Birken)	3 Rosedale Valley Rd. Toronto, Ontario M5G 3T4	Tel: (416) 482-6343	janebir@conundrum.com	net 5 $6 000
Hamlet Holiday Agency (Ron Doleman)	60 Tibault Avenue Stratford, Ontario N5A 3K3	Tel 1: (519) 272-6461 Tel 2: (800) 777-7777	rdoleman@hamlet.com www.hamlet.com	net 5 $6 000
Metro Arts Appreciation Group (R. Downey)	4400 Yonge St. North York, Ontario M6L 3T4	Tel: (416) 923-8142	RDowney@artnet.com www.artnet.com	net 5 $6 000
NY Friends of Shakespeare (J. Monte)	33, 16th Avenue Buffalo, NY 13002	Tel 1: (716) 755-4992 Tel 2: (888) 755-5000	monte@aol.com	net 5 $4 000 (USD)
Waterloo University Literary Club (T. Fornello)	88 College Rd. Waterloo, Ontario N2A 3F6	Tel: (519) 431-6343	fornello4@uwo.ca	net 5 $6 000

OUTSTANDING CUSTOMER INVOICES

STRATFORD COUNTRY INN

Customer Name	Terms	Date	Inv/Chq No.	Total
Hamlet Holiday Agency	net 30	June 30/08	Deposit #40 (Chq 317; enter a negative invoice)	$1 000

EMPLOYEE INFORMATION SHEET

STRATFORD COUNTRY INN

	Owen Othello	Clara Claudius	Mary MacBeth	Hedy Horatio	Juliet Jones	Shelley Shylock	Bud Romeo
Position	Manager	Clerk	Cook	Waiter	Concierge	Waiter	Service
Social Insurance No.	691 113 724	873 863 211	284 682 556	294 654 421	177 162 930	891 263 634	254 685 829
Address	38 Falstaff St. Stratford, ON N5A 3T3	147 King Henry St. Mary's, ON N4X 1B2	3 Bard Cr. Stratford, ON N5A 6Z8	17 Elizabeth St. Stratford, ON N5A 4Z1	5 Capella Cres. Stratford, ON N5A 5M1	29 Avon St. Stratford, ON N5A 5N5	42 Hosteller St. New Hamburg, ON N0B 2G0
Telephone	(519) 272-2191	(519) 373-6495	(519) 277-1338	(519) 278-5343	(519) 273-9122	(519) 273-5335	(519) 381-3738
Date of Birth (mm-dd-yy)	6-29-71	4-21-64	8-3-69	12-3-76	1-25-70	3-12-80	5-27-69
Date of Hire (mm-dd-yy)	3-1-98	5-2-91	6-1-01	6-1-03	1-1-02	1-1-06	12-16-00
Federal (Ontario) Tax Exemption - TD1							
Basic Personal	$9 039 (8 377)	$9 039 (8 377)	$9 039 (8 377)	$9 039 (8 377)	$9 039 (8 377)	$9 039 (8 377)	$9 039 (8 377)
Spouse	–	–	$7 675 (7 113)	–	$7 675 (7 113)	–	$7 675 (7 113)
Other	$4 240 (4 420)	–	–	$2 410 (2 530)	$7 933 (7 948)	$8 140 (8 548)	–
Total Exemptions	$13 279 (12 797)	$9 039 (8 377)	$16 714 (15 490)	$11 449 (10 907)	$24 647 (23 438)	$17 179 (16 925)	$16 714 (15 490)
Additional Federal Tax	–	–	–	$50.00	–	$50.00	–
Employee Taxes							
Historical Income tax	$4 110.12	$2 796.42	$3 029.01	$2 655.52	$3 345.44	$1 013.86	$1 499.66
Historical EI	$501.60	$376.20	$513.51	$329.55	$468.16	$176.36	$325.85
Historical CPP	$989.34	$721.44	$1 014.83	$621.80	$917.87	$294.49	$613.90
Employee Income							
Advances: Historical	–	–	–	$100.00	–	–	$150.00
Benefits: Historical	$2 800.00	–	–	–	–	$2 470.00	–
Vacation Pay Owed	–	–	$1 400.57	$898.85	$1 276.85	$480.96	$888.77
Regular Wage Rate	–	–	$22.00/hr.	$14.00/hr.	$20.00/hr.	$12.00/hr.	$14.00/hr.
No. Hours Per Period	160	160	80	80	80	80	80
Wages: Historical	—	–	$22 880.00	$14 560.00	$20 800.00	$7 872.00	$14 560.00
Overtime 1 Wage Rate	–	–	$33.00/hr	$21.00/hr	$30.00/hr	$18.00/hr	$21.00/hr
Overtime 1: Historical	–	–	$462.00	$420.00	$480.00	$144.00	$252.00
Regular Salary	$3 800/mo.	$2 850/mo.	–	–	–	–	–
Salary: Historical	$22 800.00	$17 100.00	–	–	–	–	–
Commission	1% (Sales–Returns)	–	–	–	–	–	–
Pay Periods	12	12	26	26	26	26	26
Vacation Rate	4 weeks	4 weeks	6% retained	6% retained	6% retained	6% retained	6% retained
Wage Account	Management	General	Dining Room	Dining Room	General	Dining Room	General
Deductions							
Group Insurance	$30.00	$60.00	$30.00	$15.00	$30.00	$15.00	$30.00
Insurance: Historical	$180.00	$360.00	$390.00	$195.00	$390.00	$195.00	$390.00
WSIB and User-Defined Expenses							
WSIB Rate	2.55	2.55	1.70	1.70	2.55	1.70	2.55
Tuition: Historical	$2 800.00	–	–	$1 450.00	–	$2 470.00	–
Entitlements (Rate, Maximum Days, Clear, Days Accrued)							
Vacation	8%, 30, No, 20	8%, 30, No, 20	–	–	–	–	–
Sick Leave	5%, 15, No, 9	5%, 15, No, 7	5%, 15, No, 8	5%, 15, No, 9	5%, 15, No, 10	5%, 15, No, 3	5%, 15, No, 8
T4 and RL-1 Reporting							
EI Insurable Earnings	$22 800.00	$17 100.00	$23 342.00	$14 980.00	$21 280.00	$8 016.00	$14 812.00
Pensionable Earnings	$22 800.00	$17 100.00	$23 342.00	$14 980.00	$21 280.00	$8 016.00	$14 812.00
Withheld	$5 781.06	$4 254.06	$4 947.35	$3 801.87	$5 121.47	$1 679.71	$2 829.41
Net Pay	$17 018.94	$12 845.94	$18 394.65	$11 278.13	$16 158.53	$6 336.29	$12 132.59

Payroll Information

NOTES

Enter entitlements as Payroll Settings and edit records for each employee as needed.

Tuition is a user-defined payroll expense and taxable benefit. The benefits for Othello, Horatio and Shylock have already been paid, so only historical amounts are entered.

Remember that WSIB is the name for WCB in Ontario.

General Payroll Information E. Prospero, the owner, has arranged group insurance for his employees, and all employees have elected to join the plan. As entitlements, all staff may take 10 days' sick leave per year, and the vacation allowances are quite generous for the industry — four weeks of paid vacation for salaried staff after three years of service and 6 percent for all hourly paid employees. As an additional benefit, employees are reimbursed for their tuition fees on completion of eligible courses. Salaried employees are paid monthly, and hourly employees are paid every two weeks. All employees are eligible for EI and pay CPP; the EI factor is 1.4. The Inn pays 0.98 percent of payroll for EHT, the provincial health tax. WSIB rates vary for different types of work performed by the employees of the Inn.

Wage expenses for the manager, the dining room staff and the remaining general employees are tracked separately in three different payroll expense accounts.

Employee Profiles and TD1 Information

NOTES

Enter the total federal and provincial amounts as claim amounts for each employee. Enter the full claim amounts as the amount subject to indexing.

E. Prospero owns the Inn and oversees all activities. Together with family members, he fills in where needed. He does not collect a salary and is not recorded as an employee.

Owen Othello is the salaried manager for the Inn. He welcomes guests, instructs other employees and discusses issues, problems and plans with the owner. He is single and studies part time in an MBA program. One night a week he commutes to Toronto. An education allowance — $120 per month federal and $135 provincial — and $2 800 for tuition increase his basic tax claim amounts. Othello is the salesperson for all sales, and beginning in July, he will receive a commission of 1 percent of sales.

Clara Claudius has been with the Inn the longest and works as the desk attendant. Although her primary job is reservations clerk, she also performs the accounting for the Inn. She too is salaried. Because her husband is also fully employed, she uses only the basic single tax claim amounts. They have two young children as dependants.

Mary MacBeth works as the cook in the dining room. As a single parent with dependent children she is allowed to use the eligible dependant claim as the spousal equivalent for tax purposes. She is paid at an hourly rate of $22 per hour for the first 40 hours each week and $33 per hour after that.

Hedy Horatio divides her time between waiting tables and helping the cook for her pay at the rate of $14 per hour plus $21 per hour for overtime hours. She studies part time at Conestoga College in the chef training program. The $1 450 tuition fee and the education tax claims — $120 per month federal and $135 provincial — supplement her basic single claim.

Juliet Jones deals with requests from guests, working as the concierge and arranging for room service. She lives with and cares for her father and therefore has the eligible dependant claim plus a caregiver claim. She also has additional deductions transferred from her father ($4 000 federal and provincial) to supplement her basic single claim. Her hourly wage rate is $20 for the first 40 hours in the week and $30 for additional hours.

Shelley Shylock waits tables in the dining room at the Inn. During the summer and festival months, she works full time for the Inn at the rate of $12 per hour and $18 for hours beyond the first 40 each week. She works part time until summer while she is a full-time student at the University of Waterloo. The education deduction of $400 ($451 provincial) per month plus tuition fees at $4 940 supplement her tax claim amounts.

Bud Romeo takes care of room service requests and also handles the baggage for the guests. He is married with two dependent children, so he has the spousal claim amount in addition to the basic single amount. He too is paid hourly at the rate of $14 per hour and $21 per hour for the time beyond 40 hours per week.

INSTRUCTIONS

1. Use all the information presented in this application to set up the company accounts for Stratford Country Inn in Simply Accounting using the following steps:
   a. Create company files in a new data folder for storing the company records.
   b. Enter the company information, starting a new fiscal period on July 1, 2008, and finishing the period on September 30, 2008.
   c. Enter names and printer information.
   d. Prepare the settings by changing the default settings as necessary.
   e. Organize the Balance Sheet and Income Statement accounts.
   f. Create accounts to correspond to your Balance Sheet and Income Statement.
   g. Set up currency information for the USD transactions. The exchange rate on June 30 is 1.250.
   h. Change the bank account class and set up the cheque sequence.
   i. Enter linked accounts for the ledgers and credit cards. The fee is 2.75%.
   j. Enter sales tax information and create tax codes for GST @ 7%, refundable; PST @ 8% for regular transactions and PST @ 5% for accommodation. On some items, GST alone is charged and on others PST is charged alone. GST is also sometimes charged with PST at 5% and sometimes with PST at 8%.
   k. Enter customer, vendor and employee information.
   l. Enter historical balances in all ledgers.
   m. Create two Job Categories: Sales (employees are salespersons) and Other (employees in this category are not salespersons). Assign Othello to Sales and all other employees to the Other category.
   n. Set up Payroll Authorities and Payroll Remittances. Add the balance forward amounts from the Trial Balance as at July 1, 2008.
   o. Back up your files.
   p. Finish entering the history for all ledgers and finish your session.
2. Using the information provided, enter the source documents using Simply Accounting.
3. After you have completed your entries, print the following reports:
   a. Journal Entries (All Journals) from July 1 to July 31, 2008
   b. Vendor Aged Detail Report for all vendors on July 31, 2008
   c. Customer Aged Detail Report for all customers on July 31, 2008
   d. Employee Summary (all employees) for the pay period ending July 31, 2008
   e. Income Statement for the period ending July 31, 2008

WARNING!
Save your work and make backups frequently.

WARNING!
Remember to use a test balance account to check the trial balance before finishing the history for the General Ledger. Print the appropriate reports to check your work as you enter the company data.

NOTES
Set up two taxes, GST and PST. GST is refundable and PST is not refundable.
Then create tax codes for:
GST only
PST only at 8%
GST with PST at 5%
GST with PST at 8%

SOURCE DOCUMENTS

Create new accounts or vendor and customer records as needed for the source documents that follow.

NOTES
PST is paid on purchases at the rate of 8%.

☐

Telephone: (519) 271-BARD (2273)
Fax: (519) 271-9333

Bard's Linen & Towels

Website: www.bards.com
E-mail: bard@bards.com

Invoice: BLT-64
Date: July 1, 2008

Sold to: Stratford Country Inn
100 Festival Road
Stratford, ON
N5A 3G2

STOCK NO.	QTY.	DESCRIPTION	PRICE	AMOUNT
1601	20	Satin Sheets	35.00	700.00
1801	100	Bath Towels	10.00	1000.00
2802	100	Face Cloths	3.00	300.00

CUSTOMER COPY	Terms on Account: 2/10, N/30			GROSS	2000.00
Method of payment:	On Account	C.O.D.	Credit Card	GST 7%	140.00
GST #763 271 673	✓			PST 8%	160.00
				TOTAL	2300.00

☐

AVON Maintenance Services
66 Kleen Road, Stratford, ON N5A 3C3
Telephone (519) 272-4611
Fax: (519) 272-4813
www.avonservices.com

Invoice: AM-148
Date: July 5, 2008
Sold to: Stratford Country Inn
100 Festival Road
Stratford, ON
N5A 3G2
Phone: (519) 222-6066

Code	Service Description	Price
KX-55	Vacuum Premises Floor Polishing Washroom Cleaning Maintenance and repairs Recurring weekly billing	500.00

Signature: E Prosper	Terms: Net 30 days	GST	35.00
	GST #631 393 461	Amount owing	535.00

☐

100 Festival Road, Stratford, ON N5A 3G2
Tel.: (519) 222-6066 1-888-272-6000
Fax.: (519) 272-7960

Stratford Country Inn

No: 701

Date 0 5 0 7 2 0 0 8
D D M M Y Y Y Y

Pay to the order of Avon Maintenance Services $ 2,140.00

Two Thousand One Hundred Forty 00 /100 **Dollars**

STRATFORD TRUST
80 Sterling Avenue
Stratford, ON N5A 3G3

Treasurer

392451 22 701

Re: Invoices AM-68, 85, 101, 127 $ 2,140.00 **No: 701**

July 5, 2008

☐

100 Festival Road, Stratford, ON N5A 3G2
Tel.: (519) 222-6066 1-888-272-6000
Fax.: (519) 272-7960
prospero@stratfordinns.com

Stratford Country Inn

The comfort of Home www. stratfordinns.com

No: 701

GUEST STATEMENT

To: Hamlet Holiday Agency,
60 Tibault Avenue,
Stratford, ON
N5A 3K3

Check in: July 1/08

Check out: July 6/08

Room(s)

Date	Transaction	Daily Rate	Price	
July 6/08	Accommodation and Room Services		2600	00
	Restaurant Services		400	00
	contractual prices			
GST # 767 698 321				

Signature:	**Terms:** Net 5 days	**GST**	210	00
	Clerk CC / **Payment Method:** CASH ☐ CHEQUE ☐ ON ACCOUNT ☑	**PST 1**	130	00
		PST 2	32	00
		BALANCE	$3372	00

NOTES

PST1 is the tax at 5% on room accommodation and PST2 is the tax at 8% on restaurant services.

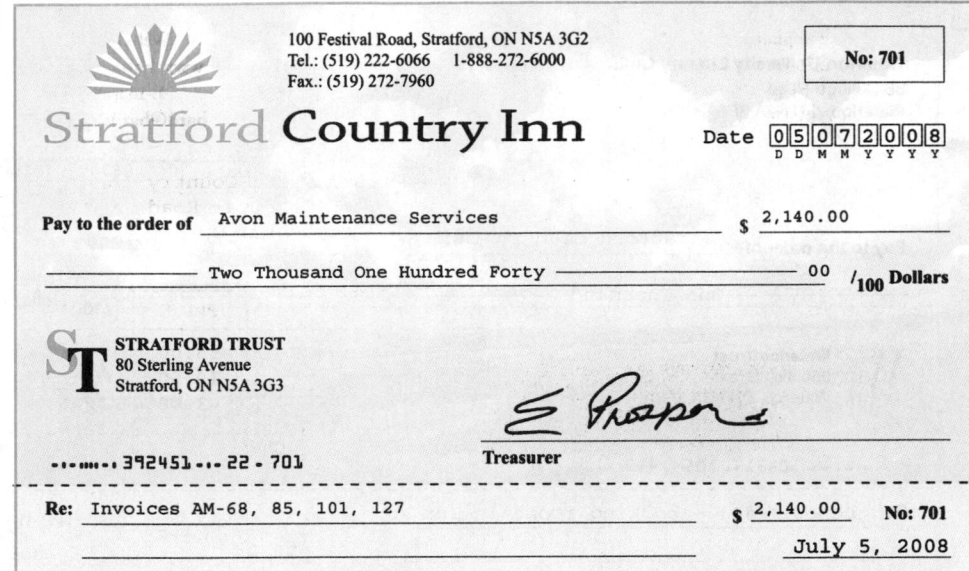

☐

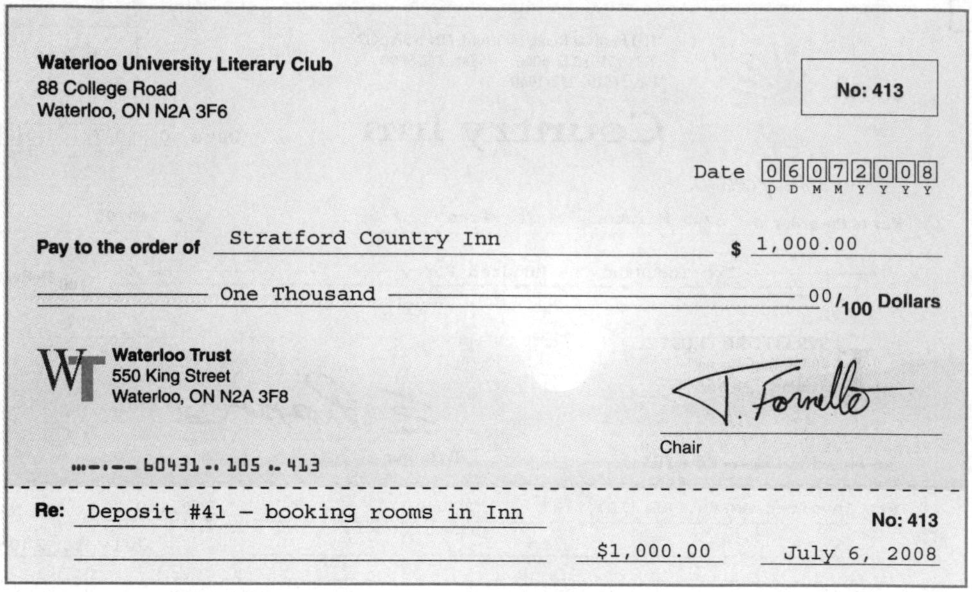
Waterloo University Literary Club
88 College Road
Waterloo, ON N2A 3F6

No: 413

Date 0 6 0 7 2 0 0 8
D D M M Y Y Y Y

Pay to the order of Stratford Country Inn $ 1,000.00

One Thousand 00/100 Dollars

WT Waterloo Trust
550 King Street
Waterloo, ON N2A 3F8

Chair

⑈⑆ 60431 ⑆ 105 ⑈ 413

Re: Deposit #41 – booking rooms in Inn

No: 413

$1,000.00 July 6, 2008

☐

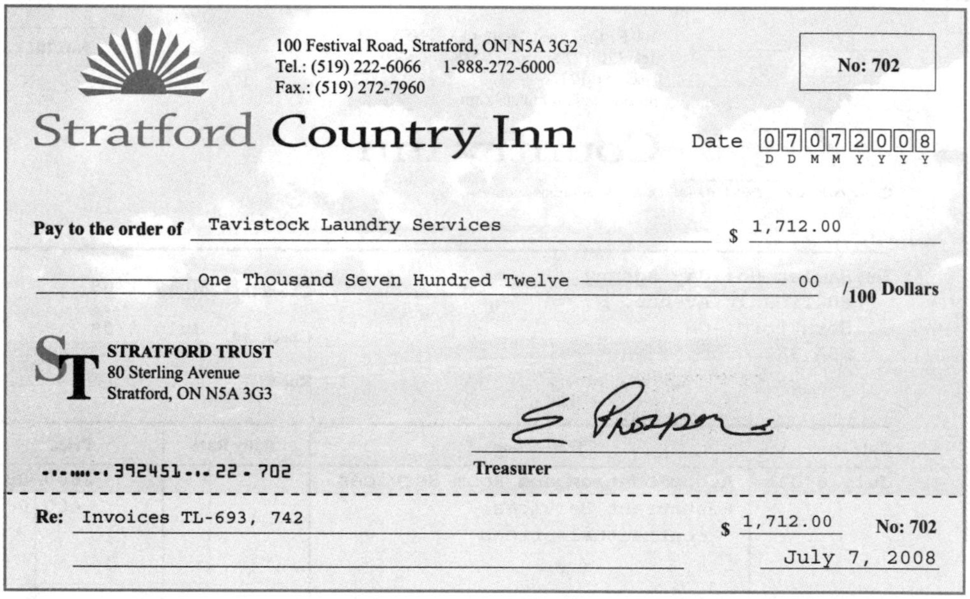
100 Festival Road, Stratford, ON N5A 3G2
Tel.: (519) 222-6066 1-888-272-6000
Fax.: (519) 272-7960

Stratford Country Inn

No: 702

Date 0 7 0 7 2 0 0 8
D D M M Y Y Y Y

Pay to the order of Tavistock Laundry Services $ 1,712.00

One Thousand Seven Hundred Twelve 00 /100 Dollars

ST STRATFORD TRUST
80 Sterling Avenue
Stratford, ON N5A 3G3

Treasurer

⑈⑆ 392451 ⑆ 22 ⑈ 702

Re: Invoices TL-693, 742 $ 1,712.00 No: 702

July 7, 2008

☐

100 Festival Road, Stratford, ON N5A 3G2
Tel.: (519) 222-6066 1-888-272-6000
Fax.: (519) 272-7960
prospero@stratfordinns.com

Stratford Country Inn
The comfort of Home
www. stratfordinns.com

VISA **No: 27 V**

SALES SUMMARY STATEMENT

Week July 7, 2008

Accommodation ☑

Restaurant ☑

Transaction	Amount	
Accommodation and Room Services	3,000	00
Restaurant Services	1,000	00
Goods and Services Tax	280	00
Provincial Sales Tax 1	150	00
Provincial Sales Tax 2	80	00
VISA Receipts	4,510	00

GST # 767 698 321

Approved: E Prospero

☐

100 Festival Road, Stratford, ON N5A 3G2
Tel.: (519) 222-6066 1-888-272-6000
Fax.: (519) 272-7960
prospero@stratfordinns.com

Stratford Country Inn
The comfort of Home
www. stratfordinns.com

CASH **No: 27 C**

SALES SUMMARY STATEMENT

Week July 7, 2008

Accommodation ☑

Restaurant ☑

Transaction	Amount	
Accommodation and Room Services	2,250	00
Restaurant Services	750	00
Goods and Services Tax	210	00
Provincial Sales Tax 1	112	50
Provincial Sales Tax 2	60	00
Amount deposited in bank	3,382	50

GST # 767 698 321

Approved: E Prospero

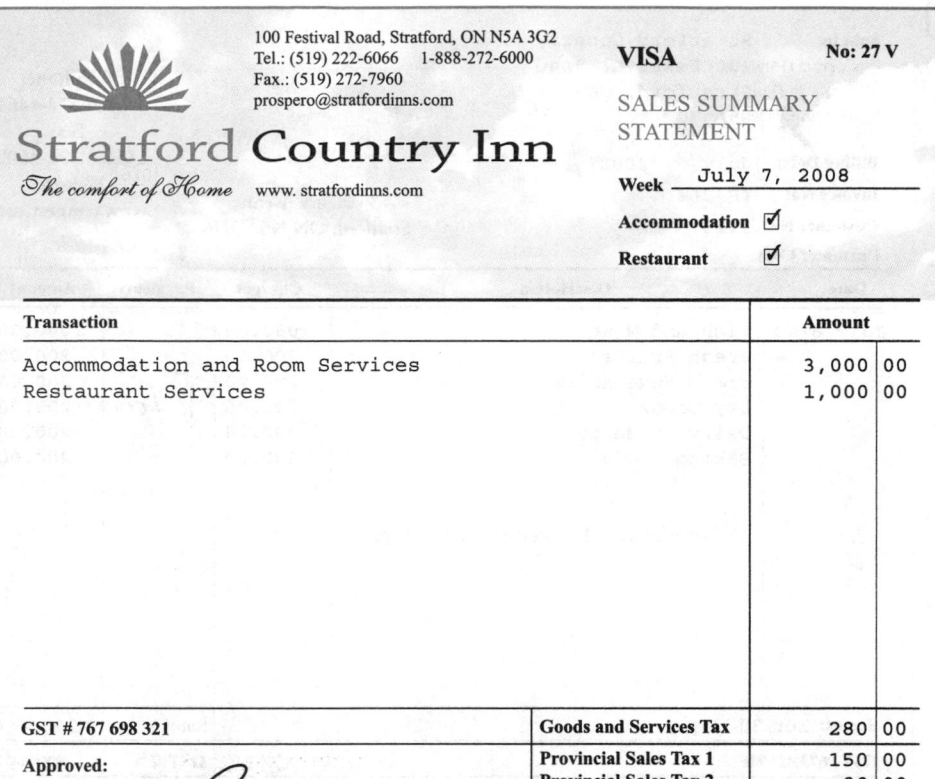

Sold to: Stratford Country Inn
100 Festival Road
Stratford, ON
N5A 3G2

Billing Date: July 8, 2008
Invoice No: TF-284
Customer No.: 3423
Customer Copy

TEMPEST Fine Wholesalers
35 Henry Avenue
Stratford, ON N5A 3N6

Telephone: (519) 272-4464
Fax: (519) 272-4600
Website: www.tempest.com

Date	Description	Charges	Payments	Amount
July 8/08	Fish and Meats	1000.00		1000.00
	Fresh Fruits	200.00		200.00
	Fresh Vegetables	200.00		200.00
	Dry Goods	200.00		200.00
	Dairy Products	200.00		200.00
	Baking Goods	200.00		200.00
	Recurring bi-weekly billing			

Terms: Net 30 days		**Subtotal**	2000.00
GST #673 421 936		**GST 7%**	exempt
Signature: E Proper		**PST 8%**	exempt
Overdue accounts are subject to 16% interest per year		**Owing**	2000.00

Invoice No: TL-798
Date: July 8, 2008
Customer: Stratford Country Inn
100 Festival Road
Stratford, ON
N5A 3G2

Phone: (519) 222-6066

TAVISTOCK LAUNDRY Services
19 Merchant Road
Stratford, ON
N5A 4C3

Phone: (519) 271-7479
Fax: (519) 271-7888
www.tavistock.com

GST #639 271 343

Code	Description	Price	Amount
C-11	10 Loads Sheets	40.00	400.00
C-14	5 Loads Pillow Covers	20.00	100.00
C-20	15 Loads Towels	20.00	300.00
	Recurring bi-weekly billing		

Overdue accounts are subject to a 2% interest penalty per month	**Sub-total**	800.00
Terms: Net 30 days	**GST**	56.00
Signature: E Proper	**Total**	856.00

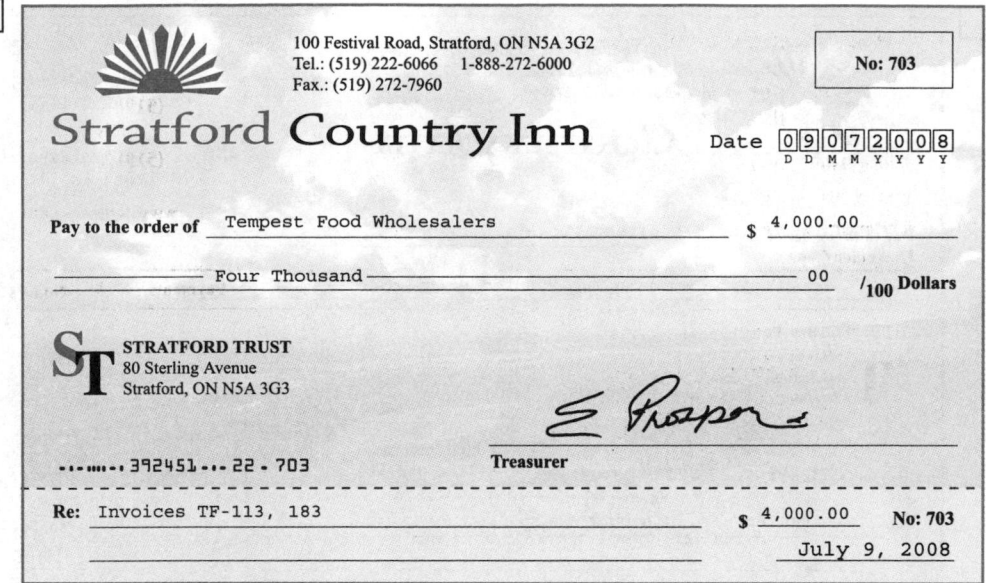

100 Festival Road, Stratford, ON N5A 3G2
Tel.: (519) 222-6066 1-888-272-6000
Fax.: (519) 272-7960

No: 703

Stratford Country Inn

Date 09072008
D D M M Y Y Y Y

Pay to the order of Tempest Food Wholesalers $ 4,000.00

——————— Four Thousand ——————————————— 00 /100 **Dollars**

STRATFORD TRUST
80 Sterling Avenue
Stratford, ON N5A 3G3

E Prosper

..·...···· 392451 ··· 22 · 703 **Treasurer**

- -

Re: Invoices TF-113, 183 $ 4,000.00 No: 703
 July 9, 2008

Hamlet Holiday Agency
60 Tibault Avenue,
STRATFORD, ON N5A 3K3

No: 349

Date 10072008
D D M M Y Y Y Y

Pay to the order of Stratford Country Inn $ 2,372.00

————— Two thousand, three hundred & seventy-two ——— 00 /100 **Dollars**

Scotia Bank
44 Welland Avenue
STRATFORD, ON N5A 3F6

Ron Doleman
Treasurer

···−·−− 64299 −·· 168 ·· 349

- -

Re: Deposit #40 (Cheque #317) No: 349
 Invoice #701 $2,372.00 July 10, 2008

☐

100 Festival Road, Stratford, ON N5A 3G2
Tel.: (519) 222-6066   1-888-272-6000
Fax.: (519) 272-7960

No: 704

Stratford Country Inn

Date 1 0 0 7 2 0 0 8
D D M M Y Y Y Y

Pay to the order of Bard's Linen & Towels $ 2,254.00

Two Thousand Two Hundred Fifty-four 00 /100 **Dollars**

STRATFORD TRUST
80 Sterling Avenue
Stratford, ON N5A 3G3

E Prospor

Treasurer

•••••• 392451 ••• 22 • 704

Re: Invoices BLT-64, Discount taken $46.00 $ 2,254.00   **No: 704**

July 10, 2008

☐

STRATFORD SERVICE CENTRE
33 MacBeth Avenue
Stratford, ON N5A 4T2
Tel: (519) 271-6679
Fax: (519) 276-8822
www.ssc.com

Date: July 11, 2008   **Invoice:** 1143

Customer: Stratford Country Inn
100 Festival Road
Stratford, ON
N5A 3G2

Phone: (519) 222-6066

GST #634 214 211

Code	Description	Price	Amount
M-114	Lube, Oil and Filter	40.00	40.00
XF-1	Fuel	120.00	120.00
		Sub-total	160.00
		GST	11.20
		PST	12.80
		Owing	184.00

APPROVAL
EP

CUSTOMER COPY

Cash	VISA	On Account
	✓	

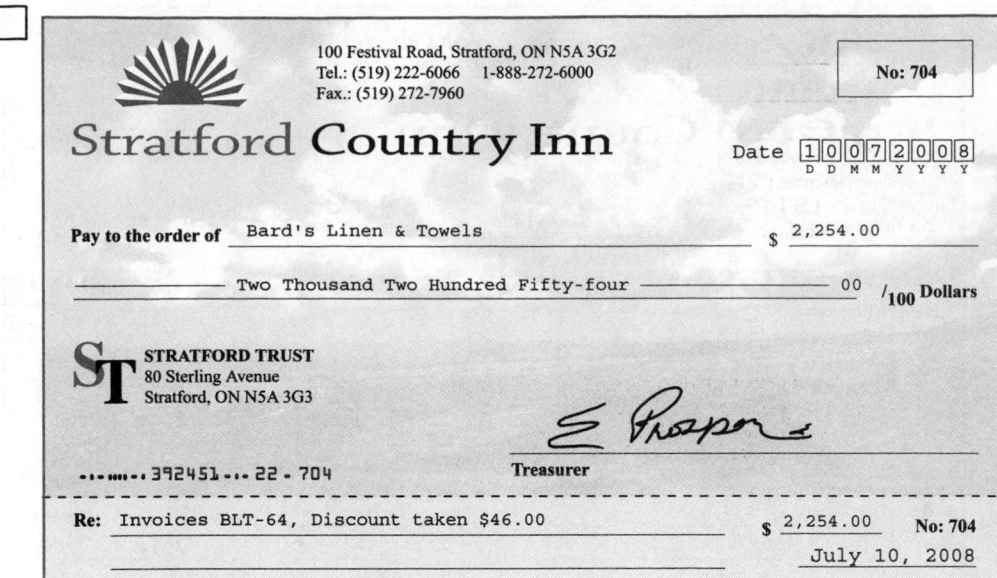

AVON Maintenance Services
66 Kleen Road, Stratford, ON N5A 3C3
Telephone (519) 272-4611
Fax: (519) 272-4813
www.avonservices.com

Invoice No: AM-168
Date: July 12, 2008
Sold to: Stratford Country Inn
100 Festival Road
Stratford, ON
N5A 3G2
Phone: (519) 222-6066

Code	Service Description	Price
KX-55	Vacuum Premises Floor Polishing Washroom Cleaning Maintenance and repairs Recurring weekly billing	500.00

Signature: E Prospero

Terms: Net 30 days	**GST**	35.00
GST #631 393 461	**Amount owing**	535.00

100 Festival Road, Stratford, ON N5A 3G2
Tel.: (519) 222-6066 1-888-272-6000
Fax.: (519) 272-7960

Stratford Country Inn

No: 705

Date 1 2 0 7 2 0 0 8
D D M M Y Y Y Y

Pay to the order of Minister of Finance $ 3,040.00

Three Thousand Forty 00 /100 **Dollars**

STRATFORD TRUST
80 Sterling Avenue
Stratford, ON N5A 3G3

E Prospero
Treasurer

--- 392451 --- 22 - 705

Re: PST $3,200 less 5% sales tax commission earned for early payment ($160) $ 3,040.00 **No: 705**
July 12, 2008

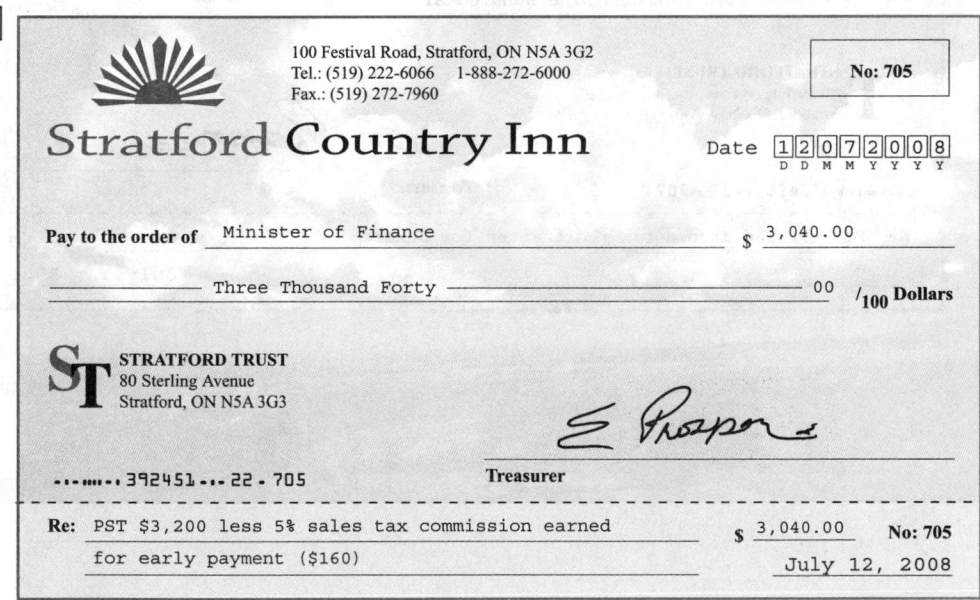

☐

100 Festival Road, Stratford, ON N5A 3G2
Tel.: (519) 222-6066 1-888-272-6000
Fax.: (519) 272-7960

Stratford Country Inn

No: 706

Date 1 2 0 7 2 0 0 8 (D D M M Y Y Y Y)

Pay to the order of The Receiver General for Canada $ 2,380.00

Two Thousand Three Hundred Eighty 00/100 Dollars

STRATFORD TRUST
80 Sterling Avenue
Stratford, ON N5A 3G3

E Prosper
Treasurer

392451 22 - 706

Re: GST Remittance for June $ 2,380.00 No: 706

July 12, 2008

☐

100 Festival Road, Stratford, ON N5A 3G2
Tel.: (519) 222-6066 1-888-272-6000
Fax.: (519) 272-7960

Stratford Country Inn

No: 707

Date 1 2 0 7 2 0 0 8 (D D M M Y Y Y Y)

Pay to the order of The Receiver General for Canada $ 5,960.00

Five Thousand Nine Hundred Sixty 00/100 Dollars

STRATFORD TRUST
80 Sterling Avenue
Stratford, ON N5A 3G3

E Prosper
Treasurer

392451 22 - 707

Re: EI, CPP and Income tax remittances for June $ 5,960.00 No: 707

July 12, 2008

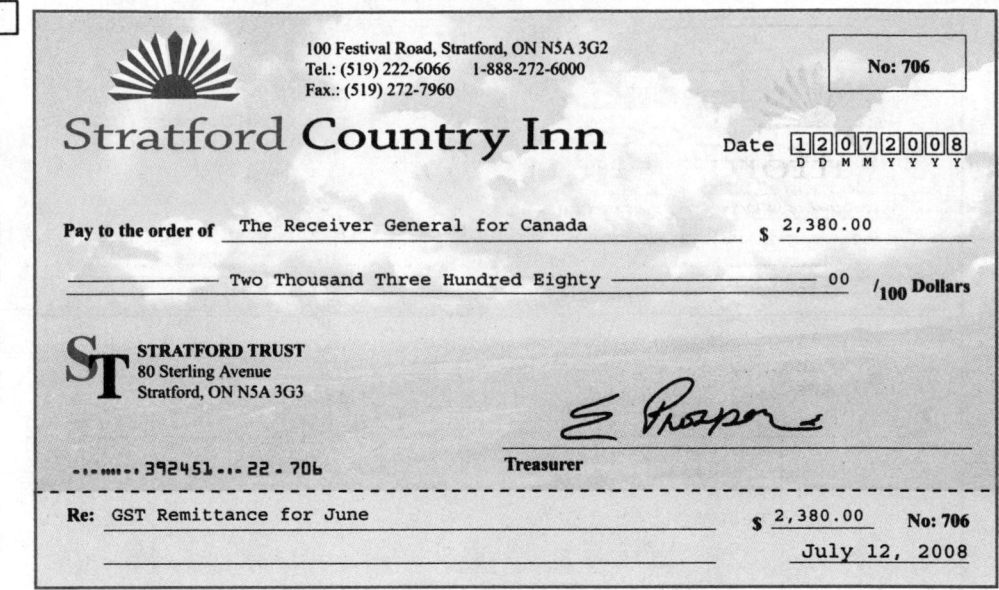

☐

100 Festival Road, Stratford, ON N5A 3G2
Tel.: (519) 222-6066 1-888-272-6000
Fax.: (519) 272-7960
prospero@stratfordinns.com

No: 702

Stratford Country Inn

The comfort of Home www. stratfordinns.com

GUEST STATEMENT

To: Waterloo University
Literary Club,
88 College Road,
Waterloo, ON
N2A 3F6

Check in: July 7/08
Check out: July 13/08
Room(s) 6

Date	Transaction	Daily Rate	Price
July 13/08	Accommodation and Room Services		2900 00
	Restaurant Services		500 00
	contractual prices		

GST # 767 698 321

Signature:	Terms: Net 5 days	GST	238 00
T. Fornello	Clerk: CC; Payment Method: CASH ☐ CHEQUE ☐ ON ACCOUNT ☑	PST 1	145 00
		PST 2	40 00
		BALANCE	$3823 00

☐

NY Friends of Shakespeare
33, 16th Avenue,
Buffalo, NY 13002

No: 137

Date 13072008
D D M M Y Y Y Y

Pay to the order of Stratford Country Inn $ 1,000.00 (USD)

One thousand 00/100 Dollars

CB Chase Bank
4, 12th Avenue
Buffalo, NY 13002

J.Monte

⑈–⑆–– 93937 –⑆ 301 ⑆– 137

Re: Deposit #42 – booking rooms in Inn. United States Currency. Currency Exchange 1.1815 $1,000.00 (USD) July 13, 2008

No: 137

100 Festival Road, Stratford, ON N5A 3G2
Tel.: (519) 222-6066 1-888-272-6000
Fax.: (519) 272-7960
prospero@stratfordinns.com

Stratford Country Inn

The comfort of Home

www. stratfordinns.com

CASH

No: 28 C

SALES SUMMARY STATEMENT

Week July 14, 2008

Accommodation ☑

Restaurant ☑

Transaction	Amount	
Accommodation and Room Services	2,100	00
Restaurant Services	700	00
GST # 767 698 321 — **Goods and Services Tax**	196	00
Approved: — **Provincial Sales Tax 1**	105	00
Provincial Sales Tax 2	56	00
Amount deposited in bank	3,157	00

100 Festival Road, Stratford, ON N5A 3G2
Tel.: (519) 222-6066 1-888-272-6000
Fax.: (519) 272-7960
prospero@stratfordinns.com

Stratford Country Inn

The comfort of Home

www. stratfordinns.com

VISA

No: 28 V

SALES SUMMARY STATEMENT

Week July 14, 2008

Accommodation ☑

Restaurant ☑

Transaction	Amount	
Accommodation and Room Services	3,150	00
Restaurant Services	1,050	00
GST # 767 698 321 — **Goods and Services Tax**	294	00
Approved: — **Provincial Sales Tax 1**	157	50
Provincial Sales Tax 2	84	00
VISA Receipts	4,735	50

☐

100 Festival Road, Stratford, ON N5A 3G2
Tel.: (519) 222-6066 1-888-272-6000
Fax.: (519) 272-7960
prospero@stratford.com

ET27

Stratford Country Inn

The comfort of Home www. stratfordinns.com

EMPLOYEE TIME SUMMARY SHEET

Pay period ending: July 14, 2008

Name of Employee	Regular hours	Overtime hours	Sick days
☐ Horatio, Hedy	80	0	0
☐ Jones, Juliet	80	0	1
☐ MacBeth, Mary	80	2	0
☐ Romeo, Bud	80	2	0
☐ Shylock, Shelley	80	2	0

Memo: Issue cheques #708 to #712
Recover $100 advance from Horatio and Romeo

☐

Waterloo University Literary Club
88 College Road
Waterloo, ON N2A 3F6

No: 479

Date 17072008
D D M M Y Y Y Y

Pay to the order of Stratford Country Inn **$** 2,823.00

Two Thousand Eight Hundred & Twenty-three —— 00 /100 **Dollars**

Waterloo Trust
550 King Street
Waterloo, ON N2A 3F8

T. Fornello
Chair

⑈—⑆— 60431 ⑆ 105 ⑆ 479

Re: Deposit #41 (Cheque #413) **No: 479**
Invoice #702 $2,823.00 July 17, 2008

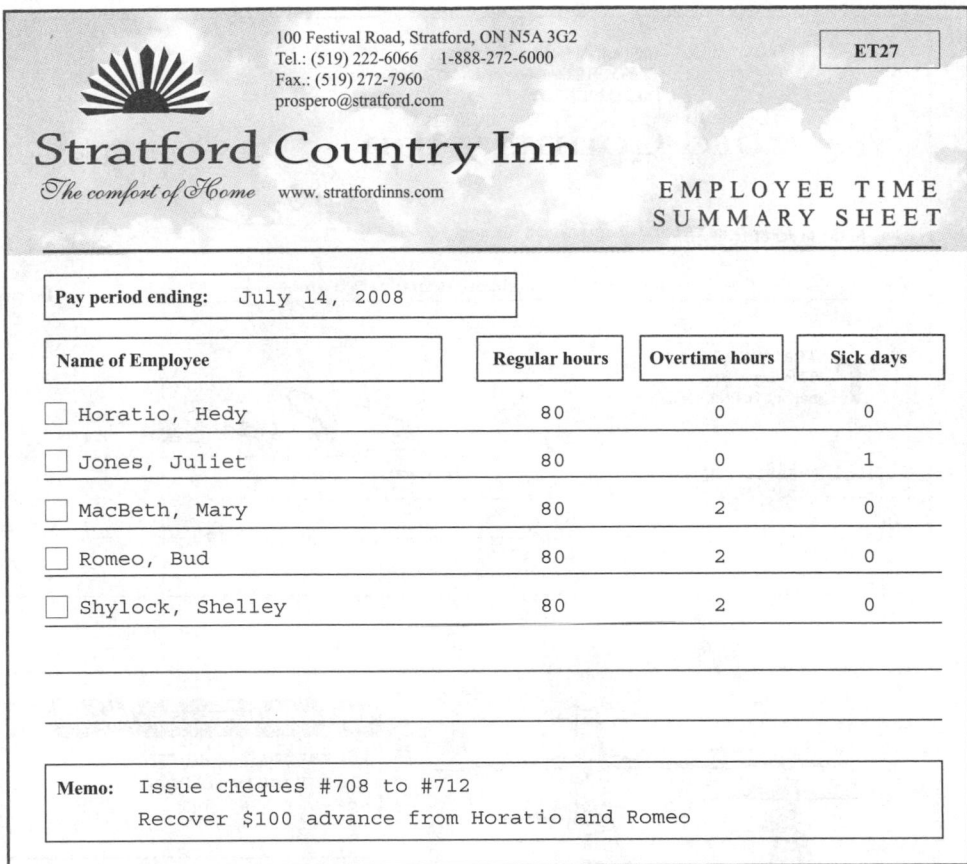

☐

100 Festival Road, Stratford, ON N5A 3G2
Tel.: (519) 222-6066 1-888-272-6000
Fax.: (519) 272-7960

Stratford Country Inn

No: 713

Date 18072008
D D M M Y Y Y Y

Pay to the order of Hartford Insurance Group $ 2,592.00

Two Thousand Five Hundred Ninety-two 00/100 Dollars

STRATFORD TRUST
80 Sterling Avenue
Stratford, ON N5A 3G3

E Prospero
Treasurer

•••m••392451•••22-713

Re: Renewal of Insurance policy for 2 years $ 2,592.00 No: 713
$2,400. PST Paid $192. Total $2,592. July 18, 2008

☐

PERTH COUNTY HYDRO
66 Power Road, Stratford,
Ontario N5A 4P4
www.perthenergy.com

Customer Care:
272-6121

CUSTOMER NAME / SERVICE ADDRESS
Stratford Country Inn
100 Festival Road
Stratford, ON
N5A 3G2

Date: July 18, 2008
Account No: 3921 462 513
Invoice No: 37232

Months	Reading	Description		Net Amount
1	86527	Commercial Consumption		300.00
1		Flat Rate Charge — Water Heaters		60.00
1		Rental of Equipment		40.00
		Total Current Charges		400.00
		Previous Charges	385.20	
		Total Payments, Thank You	385.20	
		Balance Forward		0.00
		Adjustments		0.00

Average Daily KWh Consumption		GST #721 431 214	Due Date	GST 7%	28.00
Same Period Last Year	This Bill	After due date, a 1.5% monthly late payment interest charge will apply.	July 25/08		
269	258		Pay This Amount	TOTAL	428.00

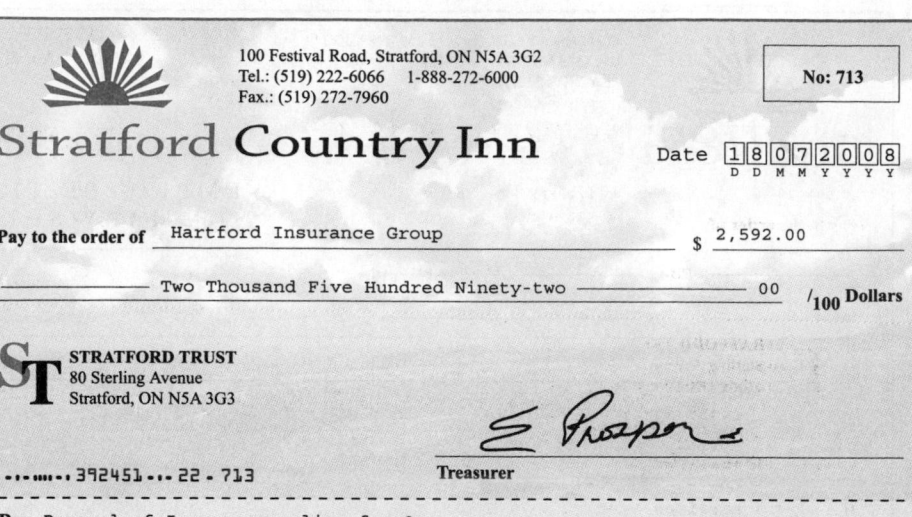

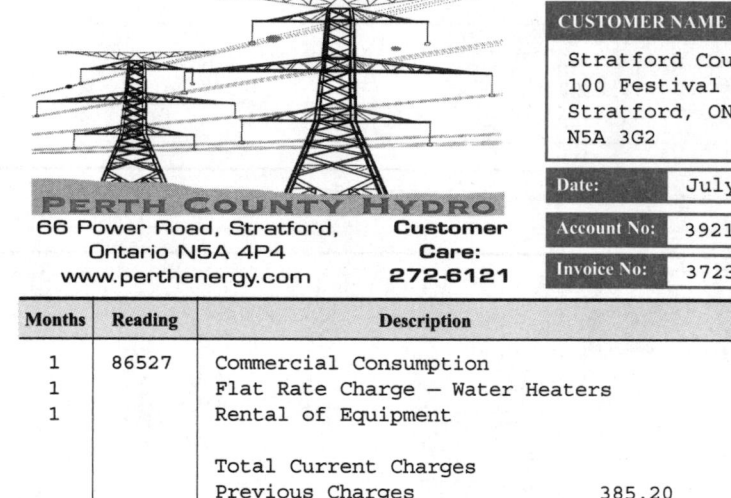

☐

100 Festival Road, Stratford, ON N5A 3G2
Tel.: (519) 222-6066 1-888-272-6000
Fax.: (519) 272-7960

Stratford Country Inn

No: 714

Date 18072008
D D M M Y Y Y Y

Pay to the order of Perth County Hydro $ 428.00

Four Hundred Twenty-eight 00 /100 **Dollars**

STRATFORD TRUST
80 Sterling Avenue
Stratford, ON N5A 3G3

E Prosper
Treasurer

••••••• 392451 ••• 22 •

Re: Hydro services $400. GST Paid $28. Purchase Invoice total $428. Reference Invoice 37232. $ 428.00 **No: 714** July 18, 2008

☐

Bell

30 Whisper Road
Stratford, ON
N5A 4N3

www.bell.ca

Account Inquiries: 273-BELL (2355)

Account Number
519-222-6066

Account Address
Stratford Country Inn
100 Festival Road
Stratford, ON
N5A 3G2

July 18, 2008

ACCOUNT SUMMARY

Current Charges	
Monthly Services (June 12 to July 12)	240.00
Equipment Rentals	50.00
Chargeable Messages	30.00
GST 634 345 373	22.40
PST	25.60
Total Current Charges	368.00
Previous Charges	
Amount of Last Bill	323.00
Payment Received June 19 – Thank You	323.00
Adjustments	0.00
Balance Forward	0.00

Invoice: BC-66431	PLEASE PAY THIS AMOUNT UPON RECEIPT ⇨	$368.00

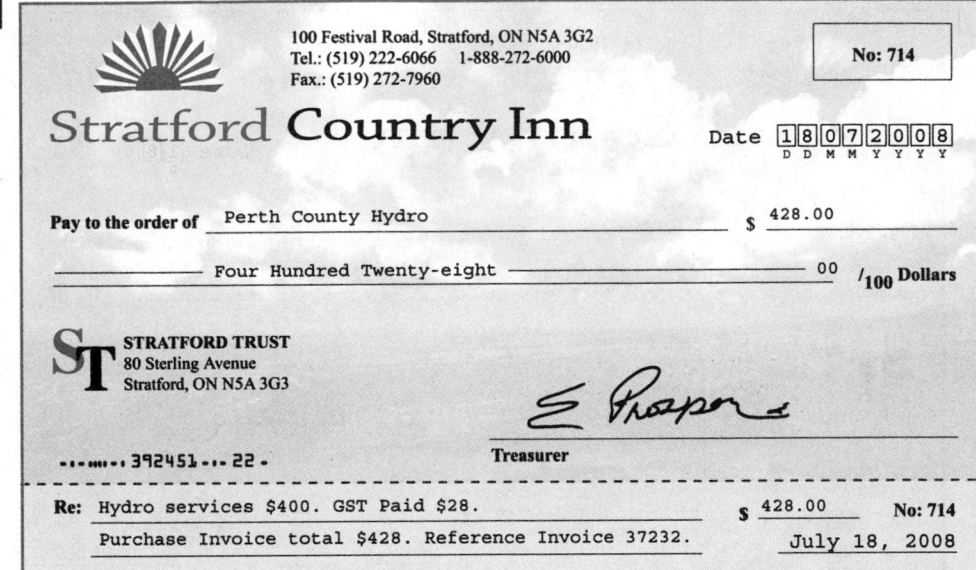

100 Festival Road, Stratford, ON N5A 3G2
Tel.: (519) 222-6066 1-888-272-6000
Fax.: (519) 272-7960

Stratford Country Inn

No: 715

Date 1 8 0 7 2 0 0 8
D D M M Y Y Y Y

Pay to the order of Bell Canada $ 368.00

Three Hundred Sixty-eight 00 /100 **Dollars**

STRATFORD TRUST
80 Sterling Avenue
Stratford, ON N5A 3G3

E Prosper

Treasurer

392451 22 - 715

Re: Telephone services $320. GST Paid $22.40, PST Paid $25.60. Purchase Invoice $368. Reference Invoice #BC-66431. $ 368.00 **No: 715** July 18, 2008

AVON Maintenance Services
66 Kleen Road, Stratford, ON N5A 3C3
Telephone (519) 272-4611
Fax: (519) 272-4813
www.avonservices.com

Invoice No: AM-184
Date: July 19, 2008
Sold to: Stratford Country Inn
100 Festival Road
Stratford, ON
N5A 3G2
Phone: (519) 222-6066

Code	Service Description	Price
KX-55	Vacuum Premises * Floor Polishing Washroom Cleaning Maintenance and repairs Recurring weekly billing * new price as described in our previous notice	550.00

Signature: E Prosper

Terms: Net 30 days		**GST**	38.50
GST #631 393 461		**Amount owing**	588.50

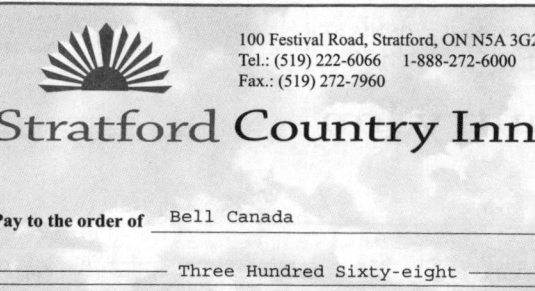

100 Festival Road, Stratford, ON N5A 3G2
Tel.: (519) 222-6066 1-888-272-6000
Fax.: (519) 272-7960
prospero@stratfordinns.com

No: 703

Stratford Country Inn

The comfort of Home www. stratfordinns.com

GUEST STATEMENT

To: NY Friends of Shakespeare,
33, 16th Avenue,
Buffalo, NY
13002

Check in: July 14/08
Check out: July 20/08
Room(s) 8

Date	Transaction	Daily Rate		Price	
July 20/08	Accommodation and Room Services			2600	00
	Restaurant Services			400	00
	contractual prices				
	All amounts billed in United States currency Exchange rate: 1.1895 CAD				
GST # 767 698 321					

Signature:	Terms: Net 5 days		GST	210	00
J.Monte	Clerk CC	Payment Method: CASH ☐ CHEQUE ☐ ON ACCOUNT ☑	PST 1	130	00
			PST 2	32	00
			BALANCE	$3372	00

Festival Club of Rosedale
3 Rosedale Valley Rd.
Toronto, Ontario
M5G 3T4

No: 61

Date 20072008
D D M M Y Y Y Y

Pay to the order of Stratford Country Inn $ 1,000.00

One Thousand 00 /100 **Dollars**

Royal Bank
56 Bloor Street
Toronto, ON M5N 3G7

Jane Birker
Chairperson

⑈--- 34298 -⑆021-⑆ 061

Re: Deposit #43 – booking rooms in Inn

No: 61

$1,000.00 July 20, 2008

☐

Metro Arts Appreciation Group
4400 Yonge Street,
North York, ON
M6L 3T4

No: 79

Date 2 0 0 7 2 0 0 8
D D M M Y Y Y Y

Pay to the order of Stratford Country Inn $ 1,000.00

One Thousand 00 /100 **Dollars**

CIBC **CIBC**
4800 Yonge Street
North York, ON M6L 3T4

R. Downey

⑈--- 396421⑆214⑈079

Re: Deposit #44 – booking rooms in Inn **No: 79**

$1,000.00 July 20, 2008

☐

ST **STRATFORD TRUST**
80 Sterling Avenue
Stratford, ON N5A 3G3

VISA

Statement Period (M D Y)	Account Number	Account Enquiries	Daily Interest Rate	Annual Interest Rate
From 06/15/08 To 07/15/08	4512 6221 1384 6201	1-800-272-VISA	.05068%	18.5%

Trans. Date	Post Date	Particulars	Amount	Bus. Exp.
06 13	06 16	Stratford Service Centre, Stratford, ON	85.00	EP
06 18	06 21	Office Supplies Unlimited, Stratford, ON	88.00	EP
06 25	06 27	Stratford Service Centre, Stratford, ON	133.00	EP
06 28	06 30	Bullrich Dept. Store #32, Stratford, ON	113.00	EP
06 28	06 30	Bullrich Dept. Store #32, Stratford, ON	-24.00	EP
07 11	07 13	Stratford Service Centre, Stratford, ON	184.00	EP
06 20	06 20	Payment – Thank You	-422.00	EP

Balance $579 paid in Full
by cheque # 716
E Prosper
July 21/08

Credit Limit	Opening Balance	Total Credits	Total Debits	Your New Balance
8500.00	422.00	446.00	603.00	579.00

Available Credit	Payment Due Date (Month Day Year)	Overlimit or Past Due	Current Due	Minimum Payment	Payment Amount
7921.00	07/24/08		57.90	57.90	579.00

☐

100 Festival Road, Stratford, ON N5A 3G2
Tel.: (519) 222-6066 1-888-272-6000
Fax.: (519) 272-7960
prospero@stratfordinns.com

Stratford Country Inn

The comfort of Home

www. stratfordinns.com

VISA

No: 29 V

SALES SUMMARY STATEMENT

Week July 21, 2008

Accommodation ☑

Restaurant ☑

Transaction	Amount	
Accommodation and Room Services	2,700	00
Restaurant Services	900	00
GST # 767 698 321 — **Goods and Services Tax**	252	00
Approved: — **Provincial Sales Tax 1**	135	00
Provincial Sales Tax 2	72	00
VISA Receipts	4,059	00

E Prospero

☐

100 Festival Road, Stratford, ON N5A 3G2
Tel.: (519) 222-6066 1-888-272-6000
Fax.: (519) 272-7960
prospero@stratfordinns.com

Stratford Country Inn

The comfort of Home

www. stratfordinns.com

CASH

No: 29 C

SALES SUMMARY STATEMENT

Week July 21, 2008

Accommodation ☑

Restaurant ☑

Transaction	Amount	
Accommodation and Room Services	2,550	00
Restaurant Services	850	00
GST # 767 698 321 — **Goods and Services Tax**	238	00
Approved: — **Provincial Sales Tax 1**	127	50
Provincial Sales Tax 2	68	00
Amount deposited in bank	3,833	50

E Prospero

☐

Sold to: Stratford Country Inn
100 Festival Road
Stratford, ON
N5A 3G2

TEMPEST Food Wholesalers
35 Henry Avenue
Stratford, ON N5A 3N6

Telephone: (519) 272-4464
Fax: (519) 272-4600
Website: www.tempest.com

Billing Date: July 22, 2008
Invoice No: TF-344
Customer No.: 3423
Customer Copy

Date	Description	Charges	Payments	Amount
July 22 /08	Fish and Meats	1000.00		1000.00
	Fresh Fruits	200.00		200.00
	Fresh Vegetables	200.00		200.00
	Dry Goods	200.00		200.00
	Dairy Products	200.00		200.00
	Baking Goods	200.00		200.00
	Recurring bi-weekly billing			

Terms: Net 30 days	**Subtotal**	2000.00
GST #673 421 936	**GST 7%**	exempt
Signature: E Prospor	**PST 8%**	exempt
Overdue accounts are subject to 16% interest per year	**Owing**	2000.00

☐

Invoice No: TL-841
Date: July 22, 2008
Customer: Stratford Country Inn
100 Festival Road
Stratford, ON
N5A 3G2

Phone: (519) 222-6066

TAVISTOCK LAUNDRY Services
19 Merchant Road
Stratford, ON
N5A 4C3

Phone: (519) 271-7479
Fax: (519) 271-7888
www.tavistock.com

GST #639 271 343

Code	Description	Price	Amount
C-11	10 Loads Sheets *	45.00	450.00
C-14	5 Loads Pillow Covers	20.00	100.00
C-20	15 Loads Towels	20.00	300.00
	Recurring bi-weekly billing * new prices		

Overdue accounts are subject to a 2% interest penalty per month	**Sub-total**	850.00
Terms: Net 30 days	**GST**	59.50
Signature: E Prospor	**Total**	909.50

Zephyr Advertising Services
32 Portia Blvd.,
Stratford, ON
N5A 4T2

Telephone (519) 271-6066
Fax (519) 271-6067
www.westwinds.com
orders: contact tom@westwinds.com

Stratford Country Inn
100 Festival Road
Stratford, ON
N5A 3G2

ZA - 6998

Date	Description	Charges	Amount
July 23, 2008	Brochures & Flyers	100.00	100.00
		GST	7.00
		PST	8.00
GST # 391 213 919	**Terms:** Cash on Receipt	**Total**	115.00

100 Festival Road, Stratford, ON N5A 3G2
Tel.: (519) 222-6066 1-888-272-6000
Fax.: (519) 272-7960

Stratford Country Inn

No: 717

Date 23072008 (DDMMYYYY)

Pay to the order of Zephyr Advertising Services $ 115.00

One Hundred Fifteen 00 /100 **Dollars**

STRATFORD TRUST
80 Sterling Avenue
Stratford, ON N5A 3G3

392451 22 717

Treasurer

Re: Advertising brochures and flyers, $100. GST Paid $7. PST Paid $8. Purchase Invoice $115. Ref. # ZA-6998

$ 115.00 **No: 717**

July 23, 2008

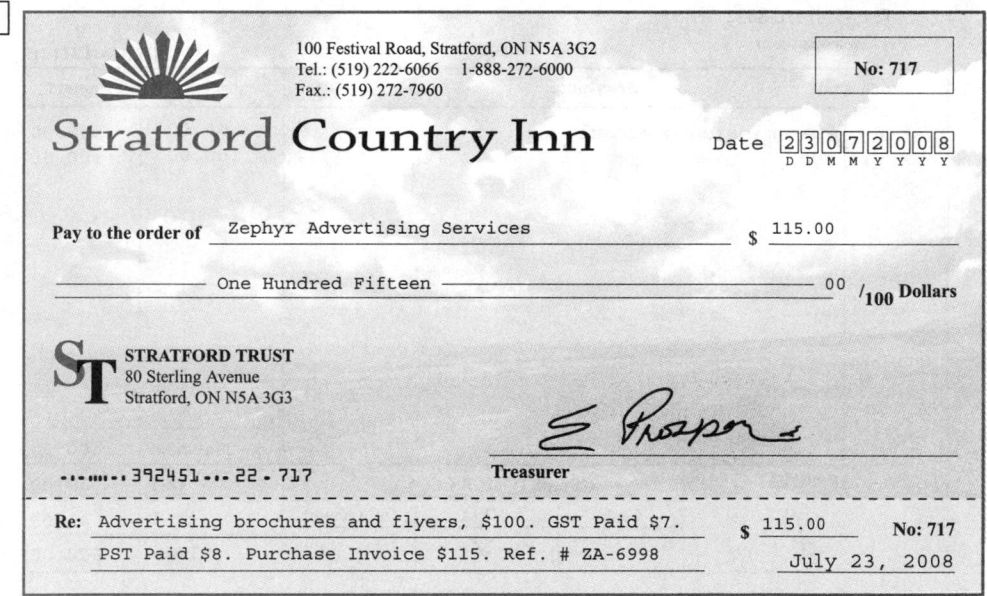

☐

NY Friends of Shakespeare
33, 16th Avenue,
Buffalo, NY 13002

No: 181

Date 2 4 0 7 2 0 0 8
D D M M Y Y Y Y

Pay to the order of Stratford Country Inn **$** 2,372.00 (USD)

——— Two Thousand, three hundred seventy-two ——— 00/100 **Dollars**

CB **Chase Bank**
4, 12th Avenue
Buffalo, NY 13002

J.Monte

⑈—⑆—— 93937 ⑆ 301 ⑈ 181

Re: Deposit #42 – (Cheque #137) Invoice #703.
U.S. Currency. Currency Exchange 1.181 Cdn. $2,372.00(USD)

No: 181
July 24, 2008

☐

STRATFORD SERVICE CENTRE
33 MacBeth Avenue
Stratford, ON N5A 4T2
Tel: (519) 271-6679
Fax: (519) 276-8822
www.ssc.com

Date: July 25, 2008 **Invoice:** 1207

Customer: Stratford Country Inn
100 Festival Road
Stratford, ON
N5A 3G2

Phone: (519) 222-6066

GST #634 214 211

Code	Description	Price	Amount
R-69	Transmission–overhaul	500.00	500.00
XF-1	Fuel	100.00	100.00
		Sub-total	600.00
		GST	42.00
		PST	48.00
		Owing	690.00

APPROVAL	CUSTOMER COPY		
	Cash	**VISA**	**On Account**
EP		✓	

☐

AVON Maintenance Services
66 Kleen Road, Stratford, ON N5A 3C3
Telephone (519) 272-4611
Fax: (519) 272-4813
www.avonservices.com

Invoice: AM-208
Date: July 26, 2008
Sold to: Stratford Country Inn
100 Festival Road
Stratford, ON
N5A 3G2
Phone: (519) 222-6066

Code	Service Description	Price
KX-55	Vacuum Premises Floor Polishing Washroom Cleaning Maintenance and repairs Recurring weekly billing	550.00

Signature:	Terms: Net 30 days	GST	38.50
E Prospero	GST #631 393 461	Amount owing	588.50

☐

100 Festival Road, Stratford, ON N5A 3G2
Tel.: (519) 222-6066 1-888-272-6000
Fax.: (519) 272-7960
prospero@stratfordinns.com

No: 704

Stratford Country Inn
The comfort of Home
www. stratfordinns.com

GUEST STATEMENT

To: Metro Arts Appreciation Group,
4400 Yonge Street,
North York, ON
M6L 3T4

Check in: July 21/08
Check out: July 26/08
Room(s) 5

Date	Transaction	Daily Rate	Price
July 26/08	Accommodation and Room Services Restaurant Services contractual prices		2200 00 200 00
GST # 767 698 321			

Signature:	Terms: Net 5 days		GST	168 00
R. Downey	Clerk CC	Payment Method: CASH ☐ CHEQUE ☐ ON ACCOUNT ☑	PST 1 PST 2	110 00 16 00
			BALANCE	$2694 00

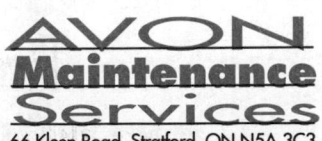

Hamlet Holiday Agency
60 Tibault Avenue,
STRATFORD, ON N5A 3K3

No: 393

Date 27072008
D D M M Y Y Y Y

Pay to the order of Stratford Country Inn **$** 1,000.00

One thousand 00/100 **Dollars**

Scotia Bank
44 Welland Avenue
STRATFORD, ON N5A 3F6

Treasurer

⑈—⑆—— 64299 ⑆ 168 ⑆ 393

Re: Deposit #45 — booking rooms in Inn **No: 393**

$1,000.00 July 27, 2008

100 Festival Road, Stratford, ON N5A 3G2
Tel.: (519) 222-6066 1-888-272-6000
Fax.: (519) 272-7960
prospero@stratfordinns.com

Stratford Country Inn
The comfort of Home
www. stratfordinns.com

VISA

No: 30 V

SALES SUMMARY STATEMENT

Week July 28, 2008

Accommodation ☑

Restaurant ☑

Transaction	**Amount**	
Accommodation and Room Services	2,400	00
Restaurant Services	800	00
GST # 767 698 321 — **Goods and Services Tax**	224	00
Approved: — **Provincial Sales Tax 1**	120	00
Provincial Sales Tax 2	64	00
VISA Receipts	3,608	00

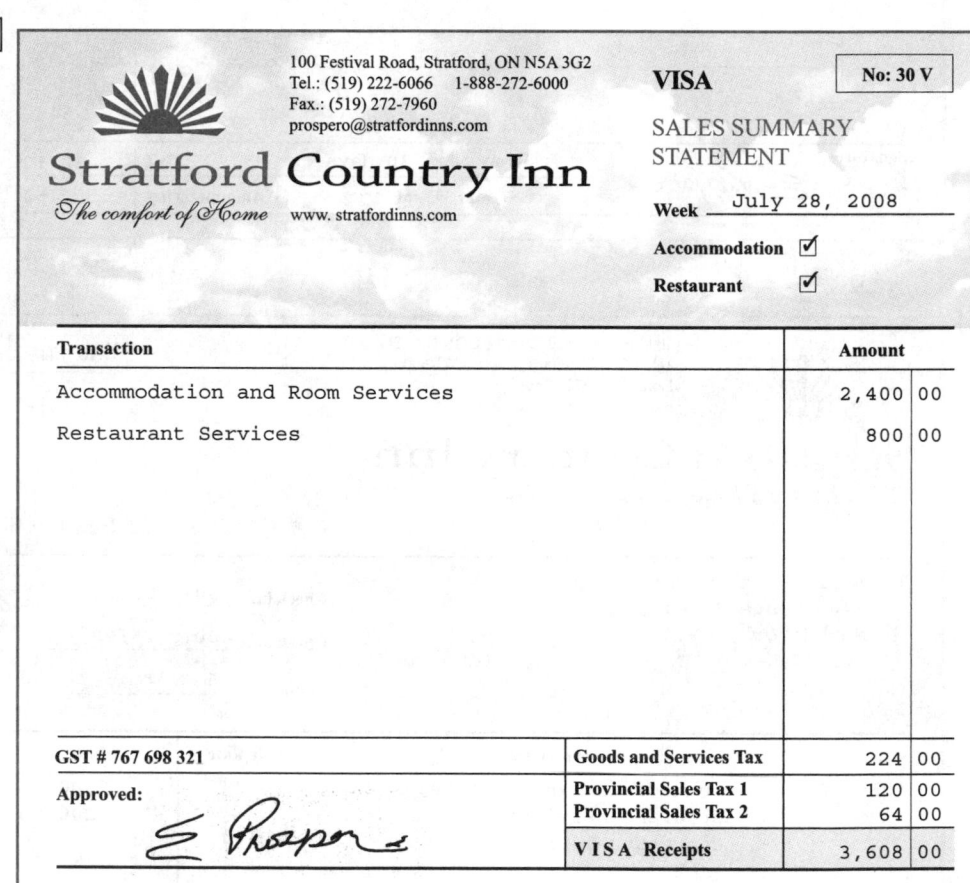

100 Festival Road, Stratford, ON N5A 3G2
Tel.: (519) 222-6066 1-888-272-6000
Fax.: (519) 272-7960
prospero@stratfordinns.com

Stratford Country Inn
The comfort of Home
www. stratfordinns.com

No: 30 C

CASH
SALES SUMMARY STATEMENT

Week July 28, 2008

Accommodation ☑
Restaurant ☑

Transaction	Amount	
Accommodation and Room Services	2,100	00
Restaurant Services	700	00
Goods and Services Tax	196	00
Provincial Sales Tax 1	105	00
Provincial Sales Tax 2	56	00
Amount deposited in bank	3,157	00

GST # 767 698 321

Approved: E Prospero

100 Festival Road, Stratford, ON N5A 3G2
Tel.: (519) 222-6066 1-888-272-6000
Fax.: (519) 272-7960
prospero@stratford.com

Stratford Country Inn
The comfort of Home
www. stratfordinns.com

ET28

EMPLOYEE TIME SUMMARY SHEET

Pay period ending: July 28, 2008

Name of Employee	Regular hours	Overtime hours	Sick days
☐ Horatio, Hedy	80	2	0
☐ Jones, Juliet	76	4	0
☐ MacBeth, Mary	80	0	0
☐ Romeo, Bud	80	0	1
☐ Shylock, Shelley	80	2	0

Memo: Issue cheques #718 to #722
Recover $50 advance from Romeo

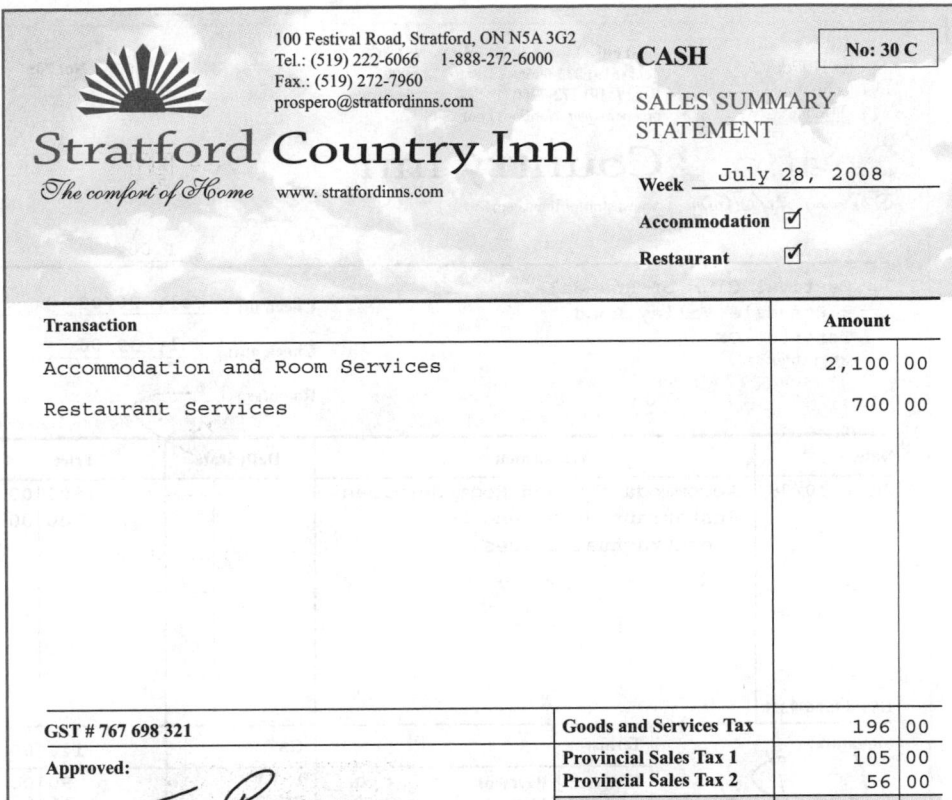

100 Festival Road, Stratford, ON N5A 3G2
Tel.: (519) 222-6066 1-888-272-6000
Fax.: (519) 272-7960
prospero@stratfordinns.com

No: 705

Stratford Country Inn

The comfort of Home www. stratfordinns.com

GUEST STATEMENT

To: Festival Club of Rosedale,
3 Rosedale Valley Road,
Toronto, ON
M5G 3T4

Check in: July 26/08

Check out: July 30/08

Room(s) 6

Date	Transaction	Daily Rate	Price
July 30/08	Accommodation and Room Services		1800 00
	Restaurant Services		200 00
	contractual prices		

GST # 767 698 321

Signature: Jane Birker	**Terms:**		**GST**	140 00
	Clerk CC	**Payment Method:** CASH ☐ CHEQUE ☐ ON ACCOUNT ☑	**PST 1**	90 00
			PST 2	16 00
			BALANCE	$2246 00

100 Festival Road, Stratford, ON N5A 3G2
Tel.: (519) 222-6066 1-888-272-6000
Fax.: (519) 272-7960
prospero@stratfordinns.com

CASH

SALES SUMMARY
STATEMENT

No: 31 C

Stratford Country Inn

The comfort of Home www. stratfordinns.com

Week July 31, 2008

Accommodation ☑

Restaurant ☑

Transaction	Amount
Accommodation and Room Services	1,125 00
Restaurant Services	375 00

GST # 767 698 321	**Goods and Services Tax**	105 00
Approved: E Prospero	**Provincial Sales Tax 1**	56 25
	Provincial Sales Tax 2	30 00
	Amount deposited in bank	1,691 25

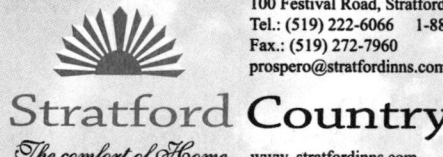

100 Festival Road, Stratford, ON N5A 3G2
Tel.: (519) 222-6066 1-888-272-6000
Fax.: (519) 272-7960
prospero@stratfordinns.com

Stratford Country Inn
The comfort of Home www. stratfordinns.com

MEMO

From: the owner's desk
To: Clara Claudius
July 31, 2008

1. a) Pay Owen Othello, manager, salary and sales commission for one month. Issue cheque #723.
   b) Pay Clara Claudius, desk attendant, salary for one month. Issue cheque #724.
2. Prepare adjusting entries for the following:
   a) Food Inventory on hand $1395
   b) Write off $200 of Prepaid Insurance
   c) Write off $50 of Prepaid Advertising
   d) Depreciation on assets:
      Country Inn & Dining Rooom $600
      Computers $100
      Furniture & Fixtures $600
      Vehicles $800
3. Pay quarterly balances owing as at July 1
   a) To Minister of Finance (EHT)
   b) Workplace Safety and Insurance Board (WSIB)
   c) Travellers' Life (Group Insurance)
   Issue cheques # 725, 726, 727

REVIEW

The Student CD-ROM with Data Files includes a comprehensive supplementary case for this chapter.

Part 3
Advanced Pro Features

CHAPTER SEVENTEEN

Flabuless Fitness

OBJECTIVES

After completing this chapter, you should be able to

- ***set up*** inventory service activities for time and billing
- ***enter*** employee time slips
- ***import*** activity summaries to prepare employee paycheques
- ***import*** activity summaries to prepare customer invoices
- ***display*** and ***print*** time and billing reports
- ***set up*** additional currencies
- ***build*** new inventory from Inventory Ledger record details
- ***show*** related accounts for multiple fiscal periods
- ***display*** and ***print*** reports for multi-period financial reports

basic BASIC VERSION
You will be unable to complete this chapter if you are using the Basic version.

COMPANY INFORMATION

Time and Billing Profile

Flabuless Fitness will modify its service inventory to invoice customers according to the time spent on various activities. The Time and Billing module of the Pro version is designed for this purpose. After modifying the service records to price the services according to the time spent providing them, the company can track the work performed by each employee for each customer.

Additionally, new vendors in countries outside of North America will sell inventory to the company. Even with the extra shipping charges, the new prices are very competitive. No duty is charged on imported gym and exercise equipment.

In July, Flabuless Fitness will begin to provide repair service for the equipment it sells. Repair work is billed in three ways: regular repairs are billed at an hourly rate; equipment that is under warranty is repaired at no charge; and repairs for customers with service contracts are charged at a flat rate for each service call regardless of the time required to complete the repairs.

A fourth employee, Yvonne Tinker, has been hired to assist Schwinn with the repairs and maintenance of exercise equipment. Tinker is also trained as a yoga instructor and can provide service as a personal trainer.

The company's fiscal period will be reduced to one month and customer invoice summaries will be used to reduce the number of source documents that you enter in this application.

SOURCE DOCUMENTS

SESSION DATE – JULY 1, 2008

☑ **Memo #7-1** **Dated July 1, 2008**

703 Change the company fiscal dates. The new fiscal end is July 31, 2008.
Change account number for 1150 Net Bank to 1190 to accommodate the new bank account for foreign currency transactions.

☐ **Memo #7-2** **Dated July 1, 2008**

Prepare an adjusting entry to reverse the year-end adjustment for $680 for accrued payroll. (Debit Accrued Payroll and credit Wages.)

NOTES

The wage expense credit entry that reverses the accrued payroll ensures that the correct amount from this pay period will be assigned to the previous year, adhering to the principle of recording expenses in the period in which they were incurred.

☑ **Memo #7-3** **Dated July 1, 2008**

704 Add euro as a foreign currency to prepare for purchases from a new vendor in Germany. The linked account for exchange rate differences is 4120 and the exchange rate on July 1 is 1.370.
Create new Subgroup account 1150 Bank: Euro Chequing. 1150 is a Bank class account and the next cheque number is 101.
Add 1150, the new bank account, as the linked account for Payables and Receivables bank transactions in euros.

☑ **Memo #7-4** **Dated July 1, 2008**

706 Create new inventory service records to add services and include Time & Billing information:

Item	Description	Selling Price Reg	(Pref)	Unit	Related to Time?	Billable?	Billing Basis	Rate
S060	Repair Service	$ 80	($75)	Hour	Yes	billable	billable time	
S070	Contract Repairs	100	(90)	Service Call	No	billable	flat fee	1 call × price
S100	Warranty Repairs	0	(0)	Service Call	No	non-billable		

Linked accounts: Revenue: 4050 Revenue from Repairs (new Subgroup account)
Expense: 5065 Cost of Services
Taxes: Charge GST and PST on repair service work.

☑ **Memo #7-5** **Dated July 1, 2008**

710 Edit the remaining service inventory records to add Time & Billing information and change the Canadian dollar prices.

Item	Selling Price Reg	(Pref)	Unit	Related to Time?	Relation	Billable?	Billing Basis
S010	$ 75	($ 70)	hour	yes		billable	billable time
S020	210	(195)	1/2 day	yes	3 hours/ 1/2 day	billable	billable time
S030	420	(385)	day	yes	7 hours/ day	billable	billable time
S040	100	(95)	hour	yes		billable	billable time
S050	210	(195)	1/2 day	yes	3 hours/ 1/2 day	billable	billable time

NOTES

The full TD1 claim amounts are subject to indexing.

Refer to pages 611–621 if you need assistance with entering the new employee. There is no historical information for the new employee.

Tinker will not receive the group insurance benefit or the piece rate pay (No. Clients) or Bonus initially. They will be apply after she finishes her probationary work period.

☐ **Memo #7-6** **Dated July 1, 2008**

Create an employee record for Yvonne Tinker, new employee. Yvonne will work exclusively on customer jobs (activities) billed on the basis of time. She will be paid for the hours worked but her minimum pay will be for 20 hours per week.
Address: 499 Toolkit Dr., Hamilton, ON L7F 2P9
Telephone: (905) 458-7192
SIN: 420 011 009
Birthdate: 06-23-79
Date of Hire: 07-01-08
Tax Table: Ontario
TD1 Federal (Provincial) Claim Amounts: $9 039 ($8 377)
Regular Wage Rate: $16/hour for 20 hours (minimum hours in paycheque)
Overtime Wage Rate: $24/hour
Do not use Salary and Commission
Pay Period: Weekly (52 per year)
Vacation: 4% Retained
Record Wage Expenses in: Payroll linked accounts
WSIB Rate: 1.29
Entitlements: Sick leave at 5%, with 15 days as the maximum
Personal leave at 2.5% with 5 days as the maximum
Delete the Vacation entitlement entry
Direct Deposit: 100% of paycheque to bank #102, transit #89008, account #341002

☐ **Cash Receipt #53** **Dated July 1, 2008**

From Lockport Gymnasium, cheque #1628 for $5458.60 USD in full payment of account including $114.40 discount for early payment. Reference sales invoice #3025. The exchange rate is 1.186.

SESSION DATE – JULY 14, 2008

✓ **TIME SLIP #1** **DATED JULY 7, 2008**

712 For George Schwinn

Customer	Item	Actual Time	Billable Time	Billable Amount	Payroll Time
McMaster University	S010	2 hours	1.5 hours	$105.00	2 hours
McMaster University	S070	2 hours	2 hours	90.00	2 hours
Mohawk College	S020	4 hours	4 hours	260.00	4 hours
Mohawk College	S060	2 hours	2 hours	150.00	2 hours
Mohawk College	S100	2 hours	-	-	2 hours

NOTES

Remember to enter 330 for 3.5 hours. You cannot enter decimals in the Time Slips Journal.

☐ **TIME SLIP #2** **DATED JULY 7, 2008**

For Yvonne Tinker

Customer	Item	Actual Time	Billable Time	Billable Amount	Payroll Time
McMaster University	S050	7 hours	6 hours	$390.00	7 hours
McMaster University	S060	4 hours	3.5 hours	262.50	4 hours
Chedoke Health Care	S020	4 hours	3 hours	195.00	4 hours
Chedoke Health Care	S060	6 hours	5 hours	375.00	6 hours
Chedoke Health Care	S100	2 hours	-	-	2 hours

✓ **Employee Time Summary Sheet #20** **Dated July 7, 2008**

716 For the Pay Period ending July 7, 2008
Use time slips to prepare the paycheque for Yvonne Tinker. Issue deposit slip #34. George Schwinn worked 80 regular hours in the period and 2 hours of overtime. Recover $50 advanced and issue deposit slip #35.

☑ **Sales Invoice #3028** **Dated July 7, 2008**

718 To McMaster University: Complete sales invoice for $847.50 plus GST and PST from time slip activities. Include all activities to date. Sales invoice total $926.55. Terms: 2/10, n/30.

☐ **Sales Invoice #3029** **Dated July 7, 2008**

To Mohawk College: Complete sales invoice for $410 plus GST and PST from time slip activities. Include all activities to date. Sales invoice total $446.60. Terms: 2/10, n/30.

☐ **Sales Invoice #3030** **Dated July 7, 2008**

To Chedoke Health Care: Complete sales invoice for $570 plus GST and PST from time slip activities. Include all activities to date. Sales invoice total $634.20. Terms: 2/10, n/30.

☑ **Memo #7-5** **Dated July 7, 2008**

720 Create a new inventory record for a promotional fitness package that bundles together several popular fitness accessories. Create new Asset account: 1510 Promotions when prompted.

Item: AP100 Promotional Fitness Package
Unit: package
Minimum: 0
Linked accounts: Asset 1510 Promotions Revenue 4020 COGS 5050

Currency	Regular Selling Price	Preferred Selling Price
CAD	$210	$200
USD	$175	$165
EUR	€150	€140

Tax exempt: GST No PST No
Build Components: use 1 of each A010 Body Fat Scale
A030 Dumbbells: Hexagonal pair
A040 Dumbbells: 5kg set
A080 Heart Rate Monitor
A110 Stability Balls
A180 Workout Gloves: all sizes
A190 Yoga Mats

☑ **Memo #7-6** **Dated July 7, 2008**

722 Build two packages of the new item Promotional Fitness Package.

☐ **Purchase Invoice #ABS-7597** **Dated July 7, 2008**

From ABS International (use Full Add for new foreign vendor)

5	E050	Bicycle: Calorie Counter CC-60	€ 560.00
5	E060	Bicycle: Dual Action DA-70	860.00
5	E070	Bicycle: Recumbent R-80	1 080.00
		Freight	100.00
		GST	156.00
		Purchase invoice total	€2 756.00

The duty rate for these items is 0%.
Terms: net 30.
The exchange rate is 1.383.
Change the default amounts.

☐ **Memo #7-7** **Dated July 10, 2008**

From Visa, received monthly credit card statement for $98 for purchases made before July 2, 2008. Submitted cheque #148 for $98 in full payment of the balance owing.

NOTES
The GST rate has been changed to 6 percent in this chapter.

NOTES
ABS International
☐ (contact Steele Bunns)
Schumacher Str. 96
55123 Mainz, Germany
Tel: (49-6131) 468 913
Fax: (49-6131) 468 248
Currency: EUR
Terms: net 30
Tax code: G

NOTES

The GST amounts are adjusted automatically for the GST rate change from 7 percent when the purchase order was entered to 6 percent when it is filled.

☐ **Purchase Invoice #SW-1775** **Dated July 10, 2008**

From Scandia Weights Inc. to fill purchase order #34

1	A130	Weight Plates (1 order of 100 kg)	$ 60.00
3	A140	Weights: Olympic 75 kg	225.00
3	A150	Weights: Olympic 100 kg	300.00
3	A160	Weights: Olympic 125 kg	375.00
3	A170	Weights: Olympic 150 kg	450.00
		GST	84.60
		Purchase invoice total	$1 494.60

Terms: net 30.

☐ **Sales Invoice #3031** **Dated July 10, 2008**

To Stoney Creek Sports Arena

50	A030	Dumbbells: Hexagonal pair	$ 1.50/ kg
2	E160	Ski Exerciser: Independent SE-880	600/ unit
2	E210	Treadmill: Deluxe T-1100D	2 400/ unit
		Freight (tax code G)	75
		GST	6%
		PST	8%

Terms: 2/10, n/30.

Memo #7-8 **Dated July 14, 2008**

Remittances: Use the June 30 balances to make the following remittances in the Payments Journal. (See margin notes.)

☐ Record GST for June as a liability to the Receiver General for Canada. Issue cheque #149 in full payment. Clear the GST Report up to June 30.

☐ Record PST Payable for June as a liability to the Minister of Finance. Remember to collect 5% of the amount owing as the sales tax compensation. Issue cheque #150 in full payment. Clear the PST Report up to June 30.

☐ Record EI, CPP and Income Tax Payable for June as a liability to the Receiver General for Canada. Issue cheque #151 in full payment.

☐ Record EHT Payable for the quarter as a liability to the Minister of Finance. Issue cheque #152 in full payment.

☐ Record RRSP Payable as a liability to Ancaster Insurance. Issue cheque #153 in full payment.

☐ Record CSB Payable as a liability to Mt. Hope Investment Corporation. Issue cheque #154 in full payment.

☐ Record Group Insurance Payable for June as a liability to Ancaster Insurance. Issue cheque #155 in full payment.

☐ Record Charitable Donations Payable for June as a liability to Canadian Cancer Society. Include both employer and employee contributions. Issue cheque #156 in full payment.

NOTES

Choose Previous Year in the report options window to make the June 30 balances available for sales tax amounts.

Choose Make Other Payment to remit the sales taxes.

Choose Pay Remittance to remit payroll taxes and deductions.

You must use July 1 as the End Of Remitting Period Date for the payroll remittances or, if you change the System Settings to allow transactions before July 1, you can enter June 30.

☐ **Sales Order #7-1 DRC** **Dated July 14, 2008**

Delivery date July 24, 2008

From Dundas Recreational Centre, to replace old gym equipment

3	E020	Elliptical Exerciser: AE-200	$1 700/ unit
3	E030	Elliptical Exerciser: DE-300	2 000/ unit
3	E040	Elliptical Exerciser: LE-400	2 200/ unit
5	E050	Bicycle: Calorie Counter CC-60	400/ unit
5	E060	Bicycle: Dual Action DA-70	600/ unit
5	E070	Bicycle: Recumbent R-80	750/ unit
2	E080	Home Gym: Basic HG-1400	1 100/ set
		GST	6%
		PST	8%

Terms: 2/10, n/30.

SESSION DATE – JULY 31, 2008

☐ **Cash Receipt #54** **Dated July 16, 2008**

From Stoney Creek Sports Arena, cheque #314 for $6 864.90 in payment of account including $140.10 discount for early payment. Reference sales invoice #3031.

☐ **Cash Receipt #55** **Dated July 16, 2008**

From Dundas Recreational Centre, cheque #438 for $6 000 as down payment (deposit #17) in acceptance of sales order #7-1 DRC.

☐ **Cash Purchase Invoice #BC-00124** **Dated July 20, 2008**

From Bell Canada, $110 plus GST and PST for monthly phone service. Purchase invoice total $125.40. Terms: cash on receipt of invoice. Issue cheque #157 in full payment.

☐ **Cash Purchase Invoice #ES-93215** **Dated July 20, 2008**

From Energy Source, $130 plus GST for hydro service. Purchase invoice total $137.80. Terms: cash on receipt of invoice. Issue cheque #158 in full payment.

☐ **TIME SLIP #3** **DATED JULY 21, 2008**

For George Schwinn

Customer	Item	Actual Time	Billable Time	Billable Amount	Payroll Time
Dundas Recreational Centre	S020	4 hours	3 hours	$210.00	4 hours
Dundas Recreational Centre	S070	1 hour	1 hour	100.00	1 hour
McMaster University	S060	3 hours	3 hours	225.00	3 hours
McMaster University	S100	2 hours	–	–	2 hours
Stoney Creek Sports Arena	S020	4.5 hours	4 hours	280.00	4.5 hours
Stoney Creek Sports Arena	S060	2 hours	2 hours	160.00	2 hours
Stoney Creek Sports Arena	S100	2 hours	–	–	2 hours

NOTES

Remember to enter 430 for 4.5 hours.

☐ **TIME SLIP #4** **DATED JULY 21, 2008**

For Yvonne Tinker

Customer	Item	Actual Time	Billable Time	Billable Amount	Payroll Time
Mohawk College	S030	16 hours	14 hours	$770.00	16 hours
Mohawk College	S050	6 hours	6 hours	390.00	6 hours
Mohawk College	S060	3 hours	3 hours	225.00	3 hours
Mohawk College	S100	6 hours	–	–	6 hours
Stelco Health Club	S020	6 hours	6 hours	390.00	6 hours
Stelco Health Club	S060	8 hours	7.5 hours	562.50	8 hours

☐ **Employee Time Summary Sheet #21** **Dated July 21, 2008**

For the Pay Period ending July 21, 2008

Edit the employee record for Yvonne Tinker. Tinker will be paid every two weeks (26 pay periods per year) and her minimum number of hours will be 40. If her contract hours from time slips are less than 40 hours, she will be paid for 40 hours. Use time slips to prepare the bi-weekly paycheque for Yvonne Tinker for the actual number of hours worked. Issue deposit slip #36.

George Schwinn worked 80 regular hours in the period and 4 hours of overtime. Issue deposit slip #37 in payment. (Add time from time slips but choose Yes to use regular hours when prompted.)

NOTES

Pay Periods are entered on the Income tab of the Employee Ledger record.

Use the Paycheques Journal for the payroll transactions so that you can enter the correct cheque and period ending dates. You cannot change the cheque date in the Payroll Cheque Run Journal.

☐ **Deposit Slip #23** **Dated July 21, 2008**

Prepare deposit slip for $12 864.90 for two cheques received in previous week.

☐ **Sales Invoice #3032** **Dated July 21, 2008**

To Dundas Recreational Centre: Complete sales invoice for $310 plus GST and PST from time slip activities. Include all activities to date. Sales invoice total $336.60. Terms: 2/10, n/30.

☐ **Sales Invoice #3033** **Dated July 21, 2008**

To McMaster University: Complete sales invoice for $225 plus GST and PST from time slip activities. Include all activities to date. Sales invoice total $256.50. Terms: 2/10, n/30.

☐ **Sales Invoice #3034** **Dated July 21, 2008**

To Stoney Creek Sports Arena: Complete sales invoice for $440 plus GST and PST from time slip activities. Include all activities to date. Sales invoice total $479.20. Terms: 2/10, n/30.

☐ **Sales Invoice #3035** **Dated July 21, 2008**

To Mohawk College: Complete sales invoice for $1 385 plus GST and PST from time slip activities. Include all activities to date. Sales invoice total $1 486.10. Terms: 2/10, n/30.

☐ **Sales Invoice #3036** **Dated July 21, 2008**

To Stelco Health Club: Complete sales invoice for $952.50 plus GST and PST from time slip activities. Include all activities to date. Sales invoice total $1 054.65. Terms: 2/10, n/30.

☐ **Credit Card Purchase Invoice #WS-12331** **Dated July 24, 2008**

From Waterdown Sunoco, $125 including GST and PST paid for gasoline and $380 plus GST and PST for vehicle repairs. Purchase invoice total $558.20 paid in full by Visa. Use Tax code IN for the gasoline purchase and tax code GP for the repairs.

☐ **Sales Invoice #3037** **Dated July 24, 2008**

To Dundas Recreational Centre to fill sales order #7-1 DRC

3	E020	Elliptical Exerciser: AE-200	$1 700/ unit
3	E030	Elliptical Exerciser: DE-300	2 000/ unit
3	E040	Elliptical Exerciser: LE-400	2 200/ unit
5	E050	Bicycle: Calorie Counter CC-60	400/ unit
5	E060	Bicycle: Dual Action DA-70	600/ unit
5	E070	Bicycle: Recumbent R-80	750/ unit
2	E080	Home Gym: Basic HG-1400	1 100/ set
	GST		6%
	PST		8%

Terms: 2/10, n/30. Allow customer to exceed credit limit.

☐ **TIME SLIP #5** **DATED JULY 31, 2008**

For George Schwinn

Customer	Item	Actual Time	Billable Time	Billable Amount	Payroll Time
McMaster University	S010	4 hours	4 hours	$280.00	4 hours
McMaster University	S070	2 hours	2 hours	90.00	2 hours
Stelco Health Club	S020	4 hours	4 hours	260.00	4 hours
Stelco Health Club	S060	2.5 hours	2.5 hours	187.50	2.5 hours
Mohawk College	S060	3.5 hours	3.5 hours	262.50	3.5 hours
Mohawk College	S100	2 hours	–	–	2 hours

NOTES

Remember to enter 230 for 2.5 hours and 330 for 3.5 hours.

☐ **TIME SLIP #6** **DATED JULY 31, 2008**

For Yvonne Tinker

Customer	Item	Actual Time	Billable Time	Billable Amount	Payroll Time
Dundas Recreational Centre	S010	14 hours	13 hours	$975.00	14 hours
Dundas Recreational Centre	S070	2 hours	2 hours	100.00	2 hours
Mohawk College	S020	10 hours	9 hours	585.00	10 hours
Stelco Health Club	S040	9 hours	8 hours	760.00	9 hours
Stelco Health Club	S100	6 hours	–	–	6 hours

☐ **Sales Invoice #3038** **Dated July 31, 2008**

To McMaster University: Complete sales invoice for $370 plus GST and PST from time slip activities. Include all activities to date. Sales invoice total $399.40. Terms: 2/10, n/30.

☐ **Sales Invoice #3039** **Dated July 31, 2008**

To Mohawk College: Complete sales invoice for $847.50 plus GST and PST from time slip activities. Include all activities to date. Sales invoice total $919.35. Terms: 2/10, n/30.

☐ **Sales Invoice #3040** **Dated July 31, 2008**

To Stelco Health Club: Complete sales invoice for $1 207.50 plus GST and PST from time slip activities. Include all activities to date. Sales invoice total $1 294.95. Terms: 2/10, n/30.

☐ **Sales Invoice #3041** **Dated July 31, 2008**

To Dundas Recreational Centre: Complete sales invoice for $1 075 plus GST and PST from time slip activities. Include all activities to date. Sales invoice total $1 147.50. Terms: 2/10, n/30.

☐ **Bank Debit Memo #143661** **Dated July 31, 2008**

From Hamilton Trust, authorized withdrawals were made from the chequing account on our behalf for the following:

Bank service charges	$ 35
Mortgage interest payment	1 850
Mortgage principal reduction	150
Bank loan interest payment	380
Bank loan principal reduction	520

☐ **Debit Card Sales Invoice #3042** **Dated July 31, 2008**

To Interac customers (sales summary)

1	A010	Body Fat Scale	$100/ unit	$ 100.00
6	A110	Stability Balls	10 each	60.00
2	A180	Workout Gloves: all sizes	10/ pair	20.00
1	A190	Yoga Mats	30/ unit	30.00
1	E110	Rider: Airwalker RA-900	300/ unit	300.00
2	S010	Personal Trainer: 1 hour	75/ hour	150.00
1	S040	Yoga Instructor: 1 hour	100/ hour	100.00
1	S050	Yoga Instructor: 1/2 day	210/ 1/2 day	210.00
	GST		6%	58.20
	PST		8%	40.80
	Total paid by Interac			$1 069.00

☐ **Credit Card Sales Invoice #3043** **Dated July 31, 2008**

To Visa customers (sales summary)

1	A010	Body Fat Scale	$ 100/ unit	$ 100.00
10	A020	Dumbbells: Round pair	1.20/ kg	12.00
2	A180	Workout Gloves: all sizes	10/ pair	20.00
2	A190	Yoga Mats	30/ unit	60.00
1	E110	Rider: Airwalker RA-900	300/ unit	300.00
1	E220	Treadmill: Deluxe Plus T-1200P	2 800/ unit	2 800.00
2	S010	Personal Trainer: 1 hour	75/ hour	150.00
2	S030	Personal Trainer: full day	420/ day	840.00
6	S040	Yoga Instructor: 1 hour	100/ hour	600.00
1	S050	Yoga Instructor: 1/2 day	210/ 1/2 day	210.00
4	S060	Repair Service	80/ hour	320.00
	GST		6%	324.72
	PST		8%	288.96
	Total paid by Visa			$6 025.68

☐ **Credit Card Sales Invoice #3044** **Dated July 31, 2008**

To MasterCard customers (sales summary)

30	A030	Dumbbells: Hexagonal pair	$ 1.50/ kg	$ 45.00
1	A100	Power Blocks up to 200 kg	300/ set	300.00
5	A110	Stability Balls	10 each	50.00
10	A130	Weight Plates	1.20/ kg	12.00
1	A150	Weights: Olympic 100 kg	200/ set	200.00
1	AP100	Promotional Fitness Package	210/ package	210.00
1	E120	Rider: Powerglider RP-1500	350/ unit	350.00
1	E130	Rowing Machine: RM-1000	480/ unit	480.00
1	E150	Ski Exerciser: Linked SE-780	450/ unit	450.00
1	E200	Treadmill: Basic Plus T-910P	1 600/ unit	1 600.00
5	S010	Personal Trainer: 1 hour	75/ hour	375.00
1	S020	Personal Trainer: 1/2 day	210/ 1/2 day	210.00
1	S030	Personal Trainer: full day	420/ day	420.00
8	S040	Yoga Instructor: 1 hour	100/ hour	800.00
4	S050	Yoga Instructor: 1/2 day	210/ 1/2 day	840.00
6	S060	Repair Service	80/ hour	480.00
	GST		6%	409.32
	PST		8%	334.16
	Total paid by MasterCard			$7 565.48

☐ **Memo #7-9** **Dated July 31, 2008**

Prepare the payroll for Nieve Prekor and Assumpta Kisangel, the salaried employees. Add 2 percent of service revenue for July as a commission to Kisangel's salary. Issue deposit slips #38 and #39.

☐ **Memo #7-10** **Dated July 31, 2008**

Interest earned but not yet received for bank accounts for July is $295.

☐ **Memo #7-11** **Dated July 31, 2008**

Prepare month-end adjusting entries for depreciation on fixed assets using the following amounts:

Cash registers	$100
Computer equipment	50
Furniture & fixtures	25
Retail premises	810
Van	625

☐ **Memo #7-12** **Dated July 31, 2008**

Prepare end-of-period adjusting entries for the following:

Office Supplies used	$ 100
Linen Supplies used	60
Prepaid Insurance expired	812
Prepaid Advertising expired	100
Payroll Liabilities accrued	1 540

✓ **Memo #7-13** **Dated July 31, 2008**

729 Print all financial reports for the fiscal period.
Back up the data files.
Start a new fiscal year. Do not clear old data.
Change the fiscal end to August 31, 2008.

KEYSTROKES

Modifying Company Information

Changing Fiscal Dates

Open the **data files** for **Flabuless Fitness** from the Time folder (Time\flab-time.sdb).

Accept July 1, 2008 as the session date.

Choose the **Setup menu**, then **choose System Settings** and **click Company Information** to access the fields for fiscal dates:

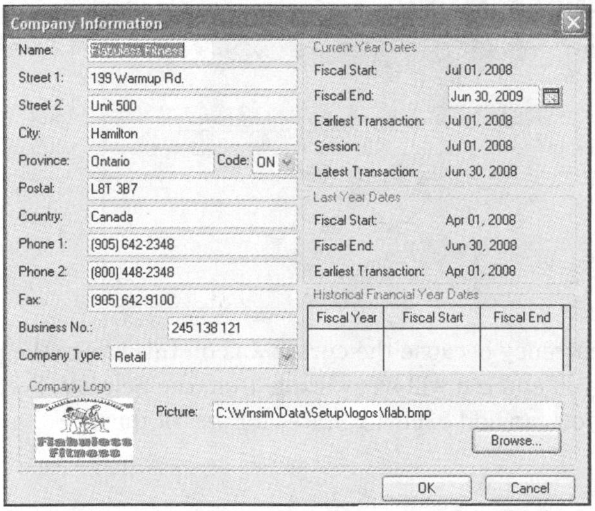

Most fiscal dates cannot be changed. Only the fiscal end can be edited. After starting a new fiscal period, the fiscal end is updated to one year past the new fiscal start because this period is most commonly used. Flabuless, however, closed its books quarterly in the past and will now use a one-month fiscal period.

Drag through June 30 2009 in the Fiscal End field.

Type 07-31-2008

Click OK to save the change and return to the Home window.

NOTES
Use the data file Time\flab-time to complete the transactions in this chapter.

Adding a Foreign Currency

The Pro version of Simply Accounting allows more than one foreign currency. Setting up additional currencies is similar to adding the first one. We will add euro as the second foreign currency because a new vendor in Germany will supply some inventory items.

Choose the **Setup menu**, then **choose System Settings** and **click Currencies** to open the Currency Information window:

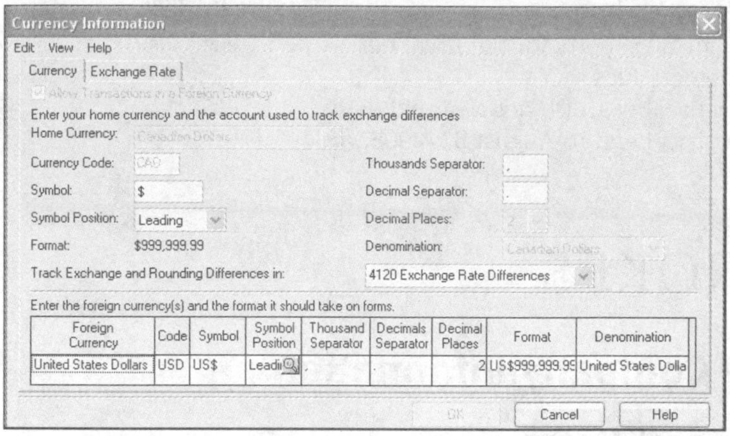

The currency added previously and its linked account are entered. You can select a different linked account, but you must use the same linked account for all currencies.

Click the **Foreign Currency column** below United States Dollars. **Click** the **List icon**  to see the currency selection list.

Click **Euro** and then **click Select** to return to the Currency window.

Click the **Exchange Rate tab**:

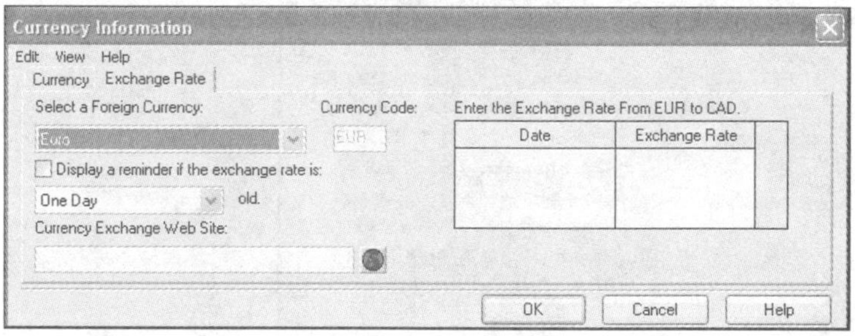

Euro is selected as the currency because the cursor was on this line in the previous screen. All other currencies you entered will be available from the Select A Foreign Currency drop-down list so you can add exchange rates for any of them.

Click the **Date column**.

Type Jul 1 **Press** *tab* to move to the Exchange Rate column.

Type 1.3805

Click **Display A Reminder If The Exchange Rate Is**.

Click **OK** to return to the Home window.

NOTES

If you choose United States Dollars from the Select A Foreign Currency list, you will see a list of all the dates and exchange rates you have already used.

Adding a Foreign Bank Account

Before using the currency in transactions, we need to create a new bank account for euro transactions.

Click the **Accounts icon** 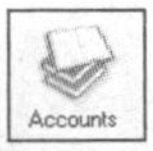

to open the Accounts window.

Change the account **number for 1150** Net Bank, the bank Subtotal account, to 1190 if you have not already done so.

Click the **Create tool**  to open a new ledger window and **add** the new account **1150 Bank: Euro Chequing**.

Click **Subgroup Account** to change the Type if necessary.

Click the **Class Options tab**.

Choose **Bank** from the Account Class drop-down list.

Click the **Currency list arrow** to see the options:

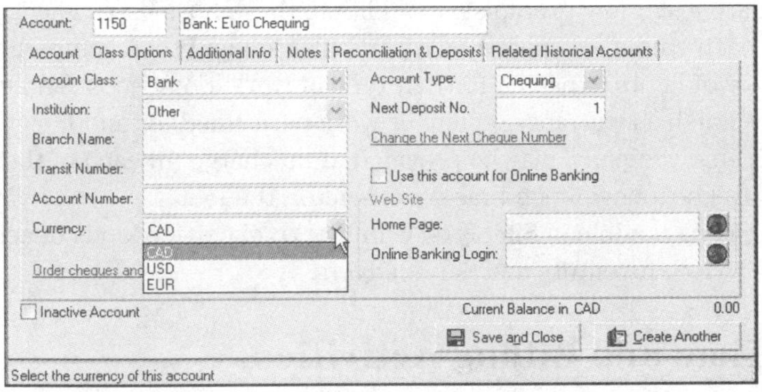

Click **EUR**. We must save the account before adding the cheque number.

Click the **Save tool** .

Click **Change The Next Cheque Number** to open the Reports & Forms settings.

Click the **Next Cheque Number field**.

Type 101 **Click OK** to save the number and return to the ledger window.

Close the **Ledger window** and then **close** the **Accounts windows**.

Adding Linked Bank Accounts

We need to identify the new account as the linked account for euro transactions.

Choose the **Setup menu**, then **choose System Settings** and **Linked Accounts** and **click** the **Payables tab**:

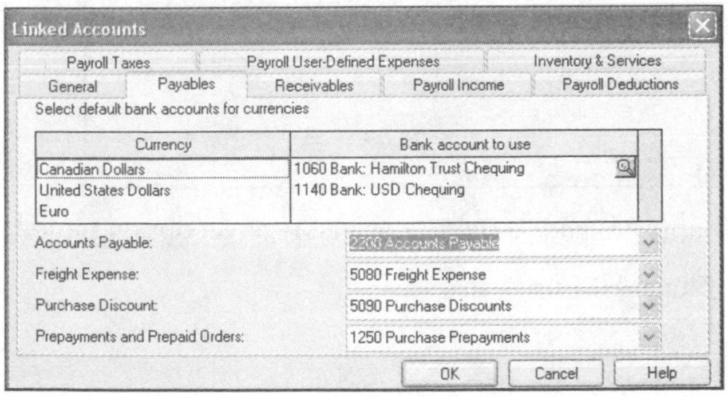

Click the **Bank Account To Use column** beside Euro.

Click the **List icon**. Notice that only the Canadian and Euro bank accounts can be selected as the Euro currency bank account.

Double click **1150**.

Click the **Receivables tab**.

Click the **Bank Account To Use column** beside Euro.

Type `1150` **Press** tab.

Click **OK** to save the account information.

Time and Billing

Many businesses that provide services use time as the basis for billing customers. Law firms, consulting businesses and service businesses that complete repair and maintenance work are just a few examples. In addition, these businesses may keep track of how much time each employee spends on a particular job and then compare this with the standard number of hours expected for that type of work. Some jobs can be billed at a flat rate and some, such as warranty repairs or work performed for another department of the same company, may be provided at no charge. In each of these cases, it is still important to know how much time was spent on the job.

The Time and Billing module in Simply Accounting tracks these kinds of activities by integrating the Payroll, Inventory and Sales ledgers.

Setting Up Time and Billing Activities

Before recording the services provided by employees to customers, that is, filling in time slips, we must modify the inventory records so that we can apply time and billing. First we will create the new services.

NOTES
Or press ctrl + N to open a new record for inventory.

Click the **Inventory & Services icon** to open the icon window.

Click the **Create tool** to open a new record for inventory.

Type `S060` **Press** tab.

Type `Repair Service`

Click **Service** as the Type of item to modify the form for service items:

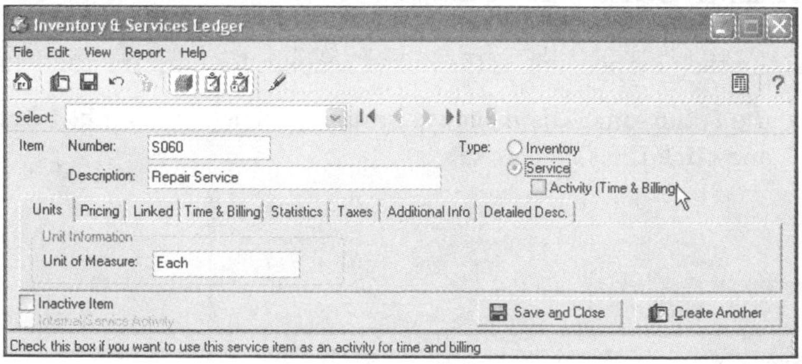

The Units tab window appears and Activity is available as an option under Service.

Click **Activity (Time & Billing)** to add a ✓.

This selection will open the fields related to time and billing on the Time & Billing tab. The Units information is now dimmed. We will enter units on the Time & Billing tab screen, as indicated by the message on the screen. The Internal Service Activity option becomes available because this also applies to the Time & Billing module.

Click the **Pricing tab** to open the Canadian dollar (home currency) price list.

Click the **Regular Price Per Selling Unit field**.

Type `80` **Press** *tab* to advance to the Preferred Selling Price field.

Type `75`

Click the **Linked tab**.

Click the **Revenue account field**. We will add the new account.

Type `4050` **Press** *tab* and **click Add** when asked if you want to create the account. The Add An Account wizard opens with the account number already entered.

Press *tab* to advance to the account Name field.

Type `Revenue from Repairs`

Click **Next three times** to accept the defaults until you see the **Subgroup And Group Accounts** screen.

Click **Yes** because this account is a Subgroup account.

Accept the **remaining defaults** to finish creating the account.

Click the **Expense field** and **type** `5065`

Click the **Time & Billing tab** to see the next group of fields to be set up:

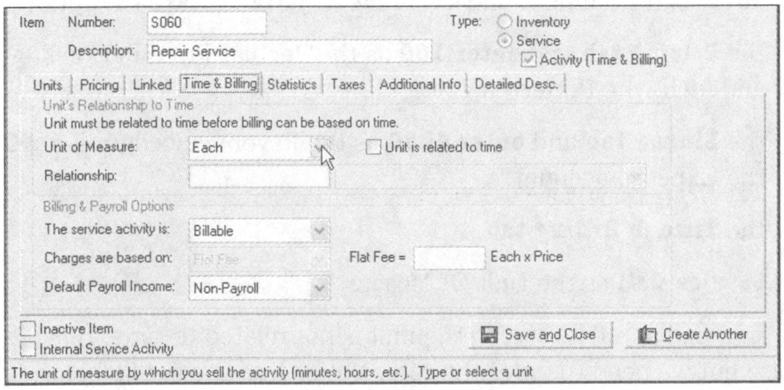

This screen has all the details that relate to the Time & Billing module. On this screen we must define the unit that the price is based on, indicate whether the unit is based on time and then add the relationship between the time and the unit of measure.

Click the **list arrow beside Each** in the Unit Of Measure field.

Click **Hour**.

This Unit is automatically recognized as related to time, and the Relationship fields are now dimmed because we have already indicated a time unit. The next group of fields defines the billing options. Billable is selected as the default for the service activity and this is correct. The other options are that an activity is Non-Billable or that there is No Charge for the activity. Charges for the service can be based on a Flat Fee or on Billable Time. Repair work is based on billable time.

Click **Flat Fee** in the Charges Are Based On field or its list arrow.

NOTES
Businesses often track the number of hours of service provided internally to other departments in the company as a way of monitoring internal efficiency or tracking departmental costs. They may monitor the time even if there is no charge for the service to the other department.

NOTES
Foreign prices do not apply to services because they are not exported.

WARNING!
If you do not change the account type to Subgroup Account at this stage, the accounts will not be in logical order, and you will be unable to display some reports. You should correct the account type in the General Ledger to restore the logical account order.

Click **Billable Time** to change the entry.

> **NOTES**
> A service activity may be non-payroll if salaried workers or managers complete the activity because these individuals are not paid on the basis of hours worked.

The next option allows the time worked on the activity to be credited directly to an employee's paycheque. You can choose whether the time should be charged to the default payroll income account or to overtime. The non-payroll option may be selected if the work is completed by salaried employees. All services offered by Flabuless Fitness are provided by the regular employees at the regular hourly wage rate.

Click **Non-Payroll** in the Default Payroll Income field or its list arrow.

Click **Regular** to complete the Time & Billing tab screen as shown here:

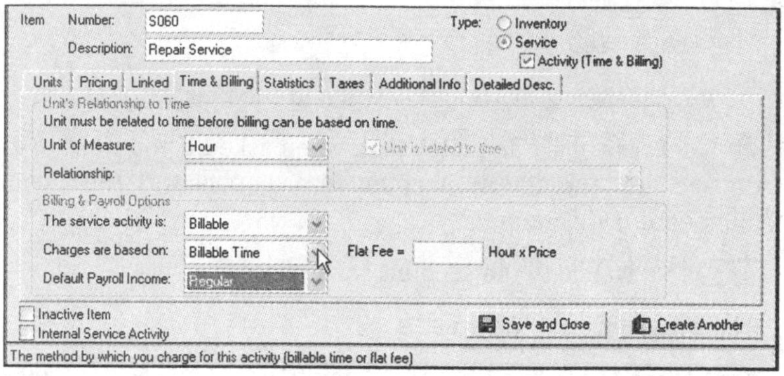

Click the **Taxes tab**. The defaults are correct. Both GST and PST are charged, so the service is not tax exempt for either tax.

Click **Create Another** [Create Another] to save the record.

You are now ready to enter the next service. Service and Activity (Time & Billing) remain selected from the previous entry and are correct.

Enter **S070** as the Number and **Contract Repairs** as the Description.

Click the **Pricing tab** and **enter 100** as the Regular Price Per Selling Unit and **90** as the Preferred Price.

Click the **Linked tab** and **enter 4050** as the Revenue account and **5065** as the Expense account.

Click the **Time & Billing tab**.

Enter **Service Call** as the Unit Of Measure.

The service is priced at a flat rate, so the unit is not related to time. Billable is also the correct choice but we need to enter the rate. Notice that the field label is Flat Fee = ___ Service Call x Price. This means that we must enter a number, not a price. The price will be calculated as the number of service calls made multiplied by the price that is taken from the Pricing tab fields.

The flat rate for this service is one times the price; each service call is priced at $100, or $90 for preferred customers.

Click the **field beside Flat Fee =**.

Type 1

Choose **Regular** as the Default Payroll Income category.

The default tax information is correct. Both GST and PST apply, so the record is complete. Your Time & Billing screen should look like the one shown here:

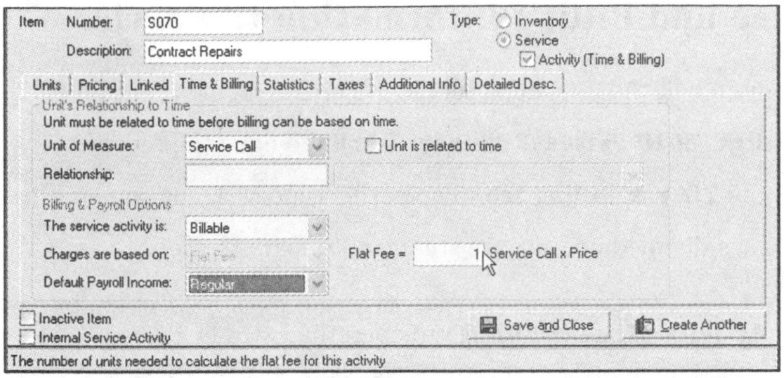

Click **Create Another** [Create Another] to save the record.

The final service is provided at no charge to customers but it is entered as an inventory item so that the time spent on warranty repairs can be monitored. The price will be entered as zero.

Enter **S100** as the Number and **Warranty Repairs** as the Description.

Click the **Pricing tab**. The zero entries are correct.

Click the **Linked tab** and **enter 4050** as the Revenue account and **5065** as the Expense account.

Click the **Time & Billing tab**.

Enter **Service Call** as the Unit Of Measure.

The service call for warranty work is not related to time because there is no charge for this service. We must indicate that the work is not billable.

Click the **list arrow beside Billable**.

Click **Non-Billable** to change the entry.

Choose **Regular** as the Default Payroll Income category to complete the record:

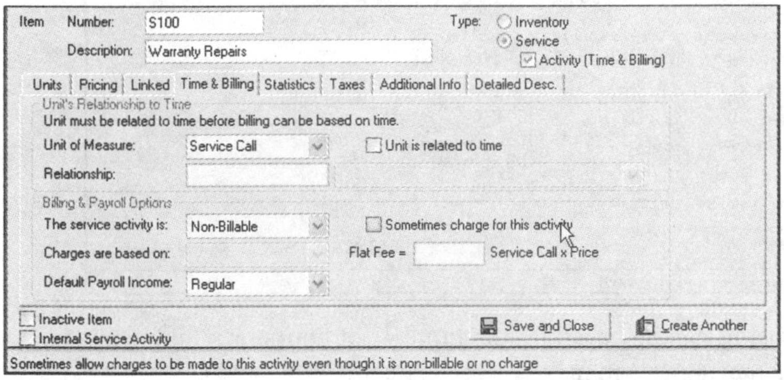

Another option for services that are normally not billed is to **sometimes charge**. When you choose the No Charge or Non-Billable options, this category becomes available. The pricing options are the same as for billable activities. You can relate the unit to time and enter the number of hours or minutes per unit, or enter a flat fee for the exceptional price. Prices are taken from Price fields on the Pricing tab screen.

Click **Save and Close** [Save and Close] to save the record and return to the Inventory & Services window.

NOTES

Even though no revenue is generated from this service, the linked accounts are required by the program to complete the record.

NOTES

Employees are paid at their usual wage rate for completing warranty work, even though the customer does not pay.

Adding Time and Billing Information to Services

You are now ready to edit the remaining service records to apply time and billing.

Double click S010 Personal Trainer: 1 hour to open the record.

Click the **Time & Billing tab** to open the Time & Billing screen.

All the fields are dimmed because we still need to mark the service as an Activity for time and billing.

Click **Activity (Time & Billing)** to open the extra fields.

Most of the selections are correct. Hour is selected as the Unit, the service is Billable and charges are based on Billable Time. You need to select the payroll income.

Choose Regular as the Default Payroll Income category.

The next service, **S020 Personal Trainer: 1/2 day**, requires additional information to indicate how many hours are in the 1/2 day. The service will still be billed at an hourly rate, but the rate is lower when a longer time period is purchased.

Click the **Next Item tool** to open the record for **S020**.

Click **Activity (Time & Billing)**.

Click **Unit Is Related To Time** to add a ✓ and open the relationship fields.

Each one-half day is based on three billable hours of activity, so the relationship is entered as 3 hours per 1/2 day.

Click the **first Relationship field**.

Type 3

Click the **list arrow beside the second Relationship field** to see the list:

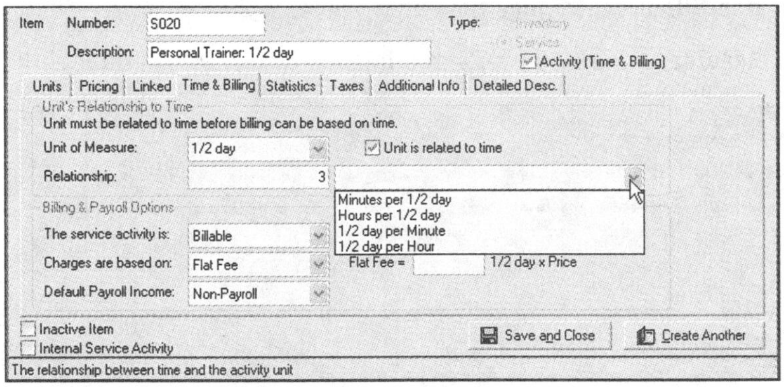

The relationship can be based on the number of hours or minutes per unit, or the number of units per hour or minute.

Click **Hours Per 1/2 Day**.

The next option is correct — the activity is Billable. However, it is charged on the basis of time, not at a flat rate so we need to change the entry for Charges Are Based On.

Click **Flat Fee** in the Charges Are Based On field or its list arrow.

Click **Billable Time** and then **choose Regular** as the Default Payroll Income category to complete the record changes.

Click the **Next Item tool** to open the record for **S030**.

Click **Activity (Time & Billing)**.

Click **Unit Is Related To Time** to add a ✓ and open the relationship fields.

Each full day is based on seven billable hours of activity, so the relationship is entered as 7 hours per day.

Enter **7** in the first Relationship field.

Choose **Hours Per Day** from the second Relationship field list.

Click **Flat Fee** in the Charges Are Based On field or its list arrow..

Click **Billable Time** and **choose Regular** as the Default Payroll Income category to complete the record changes.

Click the **Next Item tool** [▸] to open the record for **S040**.

Click **Activity (Time & Billing)**.

Again, because Hour is the unit, most of the default details are correct.

Choose **Regular** as the Default Payroll Income category.

Click the **Next Item tool** [▸] to open the record for **S050**.

Click **Activity (Time & Billing)**.

Click **Unit Is Related To Time**.

Each 1/2 day is based on three billable hours of activity, so the relationship is entered as 3 hours per 1/2 day.

Click the **first Relationship field**.

Type `3`

Click the **list arrow beside the second Relationship field**.

Click **Hours Per 1/2 Day**.

Click **Flat Fee** in the Charges Are Based On field or its list arrow.

Click **Billable Time** and **choose Regular** as the Default Payroll Income category to complete the record changes.

We will now edit the prices for these services. The prices for S010 and S040 are correct.

Click the **Pricing tab**.

Click **200** in the **Regular Price Per Selling Unit field**.

Type `210` **Press** (tab) to advance to the Preferred Price field.

Type `195`

Click the **Previous Item tool** [◂] **twice** to go to the record for **S030 Personal Trainer: full day**.

Click the **Regular Price field**.

Type `420` **Press** (tab) to advance to the Preferred Price field.

Type `385`

Click the **Previous Item tool** [◂] to open the record for **S020 Personal Trainer: 1/2 day**.

Click the **Regular Price field**.

Type `210` **Press** (tab) to advance to the Preferred Price field.

Type 195

Close the **Inventory Ledger window**.

Close the **Inventory & Services window** to return to the Home window.

Enter the **new employee record** and the **cash receipt**.

Preparing Time Slips

After setting up the service records to mark the activities and enter the billing information, you can track the amount of time that each employee works for each customer at each activity by completing Time Slips.

Time and billing information is entered in the Time Slips Journal as indicated below:

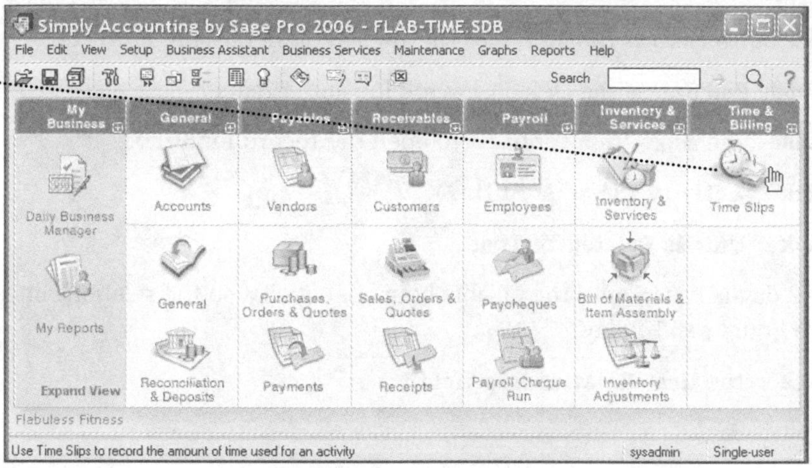

Click the **Time Slips icon** to open the Time Slips Journal:

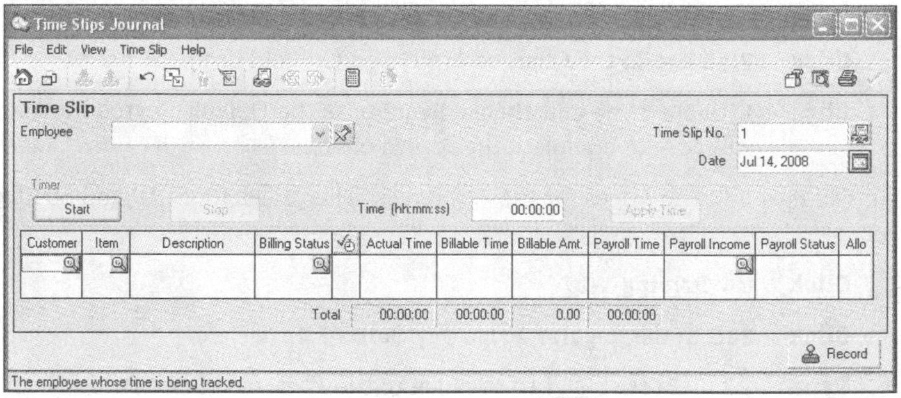

NOTES
Remember that you can maximize the window, scroll to see additional information or change the width of the columns by dragging.

All the tool icons in this window are the same as those found in other journals. Also, as in other journals, employees can be selected from a drop-down list and List icons are available for many of the fields.

Many features in other journals are also available for time slips. You can access these options from the tool buttons as you do in other journals, or you can use the Time Slip menu. For example,

- Click the Store tool  and enter a name and frequency to store the time slip as a recurring transaction.
- Click the Look Up Time Slip tool  to look up a time slip just as you look up purchases or sales invoices.
- Click the Adjust Time Slip tool  to adjust a time slip after recording. You cannot adjust a time slip for selecting the wrong employee.

The Time Slips number is updated automatically by the program. Its starting number is taken from the Forms Settings, just like the next number for other forms. If the Time & Billing module is not hidden, the Next Number field for Time Slips is included in the Forms tab Settings screen. The number is correct.

The first time slip is for Schwinn. His first job was completed for McMaster University, a preferred customer.

Click the **Employee list arrow** and **choose George Schwinn**.

Enter **July 7** as the date for the Time Slip.

Click the **Customer field List icon** and **select McMaster University**.

Click the **Item field List icon** to see the Select Activity list:

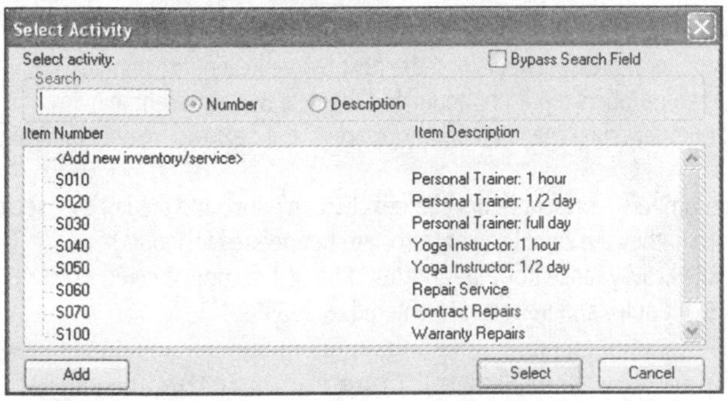

All services for which you selected Activity as the type of Service and added time and billing details will be on this list. Other services and inventory will not be included.

Double click **S010 Personal Trainer: 1 hour** to add it to the journal.

The Item and Description fields are the usual ones for inventory and service transactions. The next field is completed from the Time & Billing tab details in the ledger record. Usually the defaults are correct. The **Billing Status** field has a List icon and a selection list. Activities may be Billable, Non-Billable or provided at No Charge. You can change the default entry if needed.

If an activity is billable, you can use the **Timer** in this window to track the time worked on the activity. A checkmark in the **Stopwatch column** indicates that you can use the timer. If there is no checkmark, clicking will add it. Clicking will also remove the checkmark once it is there. Some businesses track all time spent for a customer. For example, if a customer phoned for advice, and telephone advice was a billable activity, you could start the timer at the beginning of the phone call and then stop at the end to have an accurate measure of the duration of the call.

To use the timer, click the Stopwatch column for the customer and activity if the ✓ is not already there. Click the Start button. The counter will keep time in seconds until you click Stop. Then you can use this measurement as the actual time for the activity by clicking Apply Time.

Time is entered as the number of hours, minutes and seconds. The simplest way to explain the format for entering time is with a few examples, and the best way to learn is by entering different numbers to see how the program records them in the journal.

NOTES

Notice that decimals are not allowed for the time entries. You must enter the hours, minutes and seconds as whole numbers.

The following chart summarizes the examples and outlines some of the rules:

EXAMPLES OF TIME ENTRIES IN THE TIME SLIPS JOURNAL

Entering This Number	Records This Time
1 or 01 or 100 or 10000	1 hour
001 or 0001 or 000100	1 minute
00001 or 000001	1 second
130 or 0130 or 013000	1.5 hours (1 hour and 30 minutes)
0110 or 110 or 11000	1 hour and 10 minutes
1030 or 103000	10 hours and 30 minutes
11515 or 011515	1 hour, 15 minutes and 15 seconds
995959	99 hours, 59 minutes and 59 seconds

RULES FOR ENTERING TIME IN THE TIME SLIPS JOURNAL

- A one- or two-digit number is always interpreted as the number of hours (zero minutes, zero seconds).
- For a three-digit entry, the first number represents hours and the next two represent the minutes.
- For a four-digit number, the first two numbers represent hours and the next two represent minutes.
- For a five-digit number, the first number represents the number of hours, the next two, minutes and the final two, seconds.
- For a six-digit entry, the first two numbers represent hours, the next two, minutes, and the last two, seconds.
- You can omit seconds and minutes if they are zero. Leading zeros are not needed for hours.
- The times allowed on a line for one activity range from the shortest time of 1 second, entered as 000001 or 00001, to the longest, 99 hours, 59 minutes and 59 seconds, entered as 995959.

NOTES

An employee may be paid for the actual number of hours, the billable number of hours or some other time agreed on between the employee and the employer. For example, the pay may be limited to a maximum number of hours for a specific job to encourage efficient work habits.

There are three columns for time: the **Actual Time** spent at the activity; the **Billable Time** or amount of time that the customer pays for; and the **Payroll Time** or hours the employee is paid for. Sometimes the customer is billed for fewer hours than the job actually required. For example, if an estimate has been given and the work is much more complex than anticipated, a business will usually not bill the customer for the full amount in the interest of good customer relations. At other times, the customer may be charged for more time than the activity requires. For example, a job may have a minimum time component, such as one hour of labour. Most companies will want to keep track of all times so that they can revise their prices to reflect their true costs.

Schwinn spent two hours completing the first job (actual time); the customer will pay for 1.5 hours of work (billable time); and Schwinn will be paid for two hours of work for this job (payroll time).

Click the **Actual Time field**.

Type 2 **Press** *tab*. Your journal now looks like the one below:

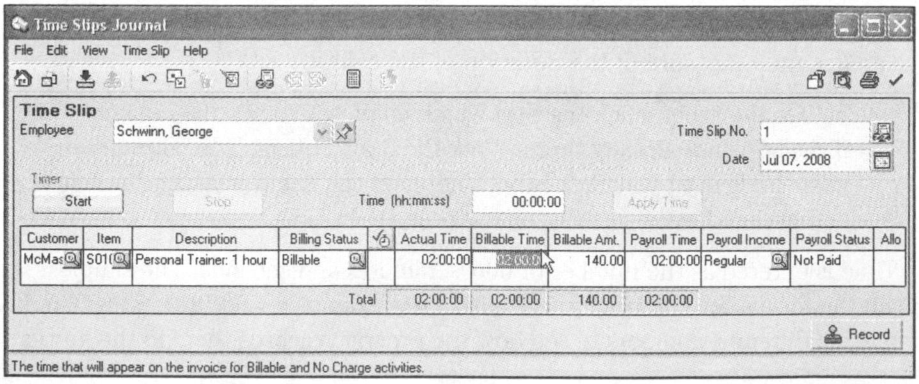

The program enters the actual time as the billable time and the payroll time. The price (**Billable Amt.**) is the billable time multiplied by the price from the ledger for that time unit, 2 hours multiplied by the preferred hourly rate of $70. Notice that the **Payroll Status** is Not Paid. You can edit the billable time, the billable amount, the payroll time and payroll income category for individual activities. We need to change the billable time to 1.5 hours, 1 hour and 30 minutes. The billable time is already selected.

Type 130 **Press** (tab) to update the billable amount.

Click the **Customer list icon** and **select McMaster University** for the second activity.

Click the **Item list icon** and **select S070 Contract Repairs**.

Click the **Actual Time column**.

Type 2 **Press** (tab).

This time the flat rate is entered and you cannot edit the billable time. However, you can edit the billable amount. The next activity is for another customer.

Click the **Customer list icon** . **Select Mohawk College**.

Click the **Item list icon** and **select S020 Personal Trainer: 1/2 day**.

Click the **Actual Time column**.

Type 4 **Press** (tab).

For this ledger record, recall that we entered 3 hours as the usual number of hours in the 1/2 day of activity and the hourly rate was determined as the Preferred Selling Price divided by the usual number of hours — $195 divided by 3 or $65. Thus the amount for 4 hours is 4 x $65 or $260.

Click the **Customer list icon** and **select Mohawk College** for the fourth activity.

Click the **Item list icon** and **select S060 Repair Service**.

Click the **Actual Time column**.

Type 2 **Press** (tab).

Repair service work is billed at a straight hourly rate so the amount is the billable time multiplied by the hourly rate for the preferred customer.

Click the **Customer list icon** and **select Mohawk College** for the final activity.

Click the **Item list icon** and **select S100 Warranty Repairs**.

Click the **Actual Time column**.

Type 2 **Press** (tab).

No amount is entered because the activity is non-billable, but the hours are added to the employee's payroll time. The journal is complete and should look like the one below:

Customer	Item	Description	Billing Status	✓	Actual Time	Billable Time	Billable Amt.	Payroll Time	Payroll Income		Payroll Status	Allo
McMaster	S010	Personal Trainer: 1 hour	Billable		02:00:00	01:30:00	105.00	02:00:00	Regular		Not Paid	
McMaster	S070	Contract Repairs	Billable (Flat F		02:00:00	02:00:00	90.00	02:00:00	Regular		Not Paid	
Mohawk C	S020	Personal Trainer: 1/2 day	Billable		04:00:00	04:00:00	260.00	04:00:00	Regular		Not Paid	
Mohawk C	S060	Repair Service	Billable		02:00:00	02:00:00	150.00	02:00:00	Regular		Not Paid	
Mohaw	S10(	Warranty Repairs	Non Billable		02:00:00	02:00:00		02:00:00	Regular		Not Paid	
			Total		12:00:00	11:30:00	605.00	12:00:00				

Time Slips Journal

File Edit View Time Slip Help

Time Slip
Employee Schwinn, George Time Slip No. 1
Date Jul 07, 2008

Timer
Start Stop Time (hh:mm:ss) 00:00:00 Apply Time

Record

Indicates whether the employee has been paid for this activity

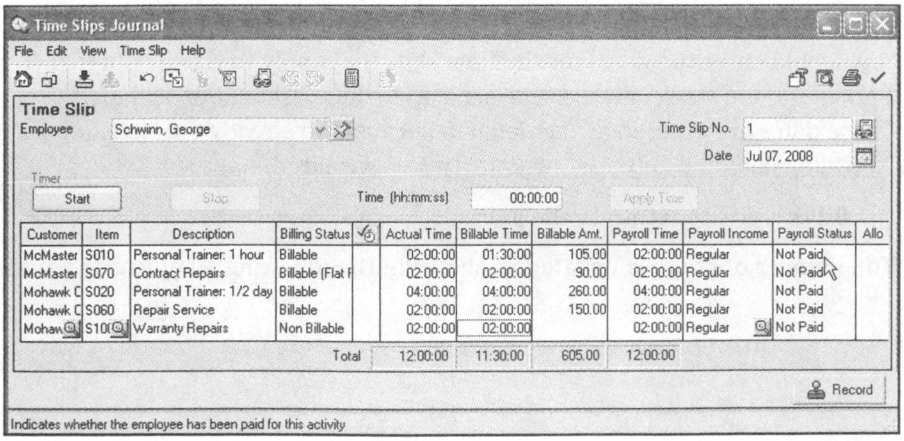

WARNING!
There is no journal entry to review the time slip so check it carefully.
You can adjust the time slip if you find an error after you record it.
If you selected the wrong employee, edit the time slip by deleting all time entries. The program will remove the time slip from the system but the time slip number cannot be used again.

Check the **time slip** carefully before recording and **correct mistakes**.

Click the **Record button** [Record] to save the entry.

Complete **Time Slip #2** and then **close** the **Time Slips Journal**.

Paying Employees from Time Slips

When activities are set up in the Inventory and Services Ledger, and time slips are entered for employees, Simply Accounting tracks the hours worked so you can use the summary of these time slips to prepare paycheques.

We will use this method to prepare the paycheque for the new employee, Yvonne Tinker, because her primary responsibility is for work on these activities.

NOTES
You can also add time slips information in the Payroll Cheque Run Journal by selecting the employee and then clicking the Add Time tool button or choosing the menu item. However, the cheque date in the Payroll Cheque Run cannot be changed. It must match the session date.

Click the **Paycheques icon** [Paycheques] to open the Payroll Journal.

Enter **July 7** as the Date and the Period Ending date.

Choose **Tinker** from the Employee list and **press** (tab) to enter her default information as shown below:

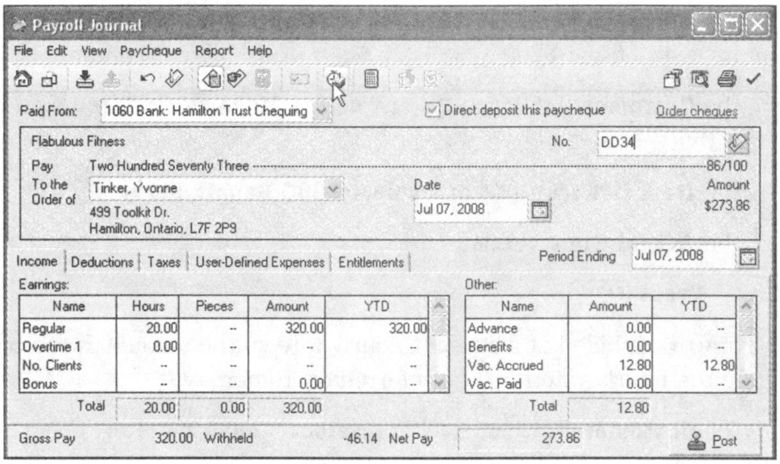

Click the **Add Time From Time Slips tool** or **choose** the **Paycheque menu** and **click** **Add Time From Time Slips**.

The Payroll Hour Selection screen opens:

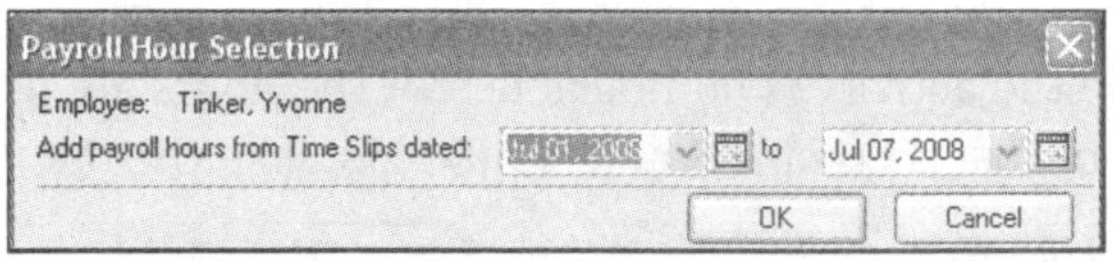

You should enter the dates for the time slips that apply to this pay period. Tinker has worked for one week and the time slips up to July 7 should be included.

These dates are entered as the defaults because we already entered July 7 as the period ending date and July 1 is the date Tinker was hired.

Click **OK** to return to the journal.

The number of hours is updated as shown in the following completed journal entry:

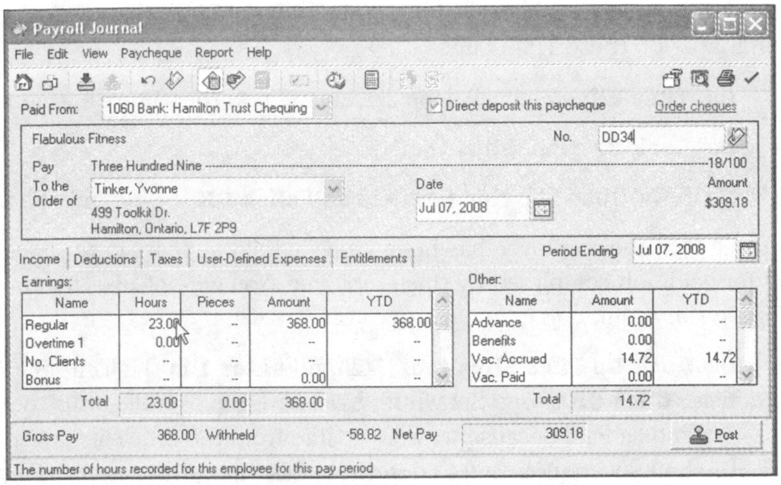

You can edit the number of hours as usual if necessary, and you can add advances or other deductions if they are appropriate.

Review the **journal entry** and, when you are certain that it is correct,

Click **Post** to save the transaction. **Click Yes** to continue.

Choose **Schwinn** from the Employee list and press *tab* to enter his default payroll information.

Click the **Add Time From Time Slips tool** or **choose** the **Paycheque menu** and **click Add Time From Time Slips** to open the Payroll Hour Selection screen:

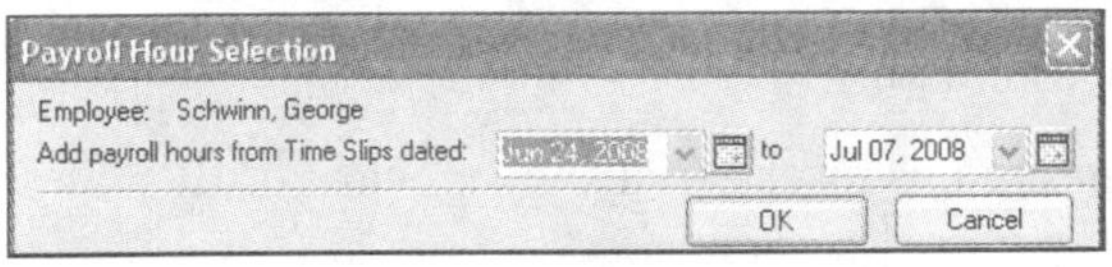

Again, the time slip period matches the pay period for the employee.

Click **OK** to see the warning:

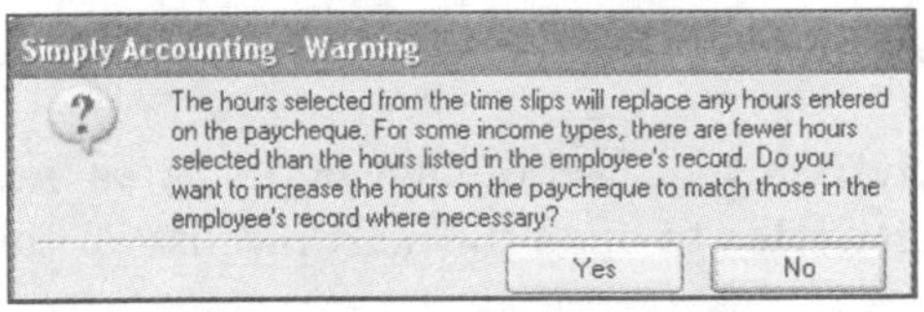

For Schwinn, the hours worked exceed the hours on his time slip for the various customer jobs because he also performs other duties at the store. You have the option of accepting the Time Slip information or increasing the hours to match the default in the employee records. For Schwinn, the Payroll Ledger entry is the correct one.

Click **Yes** to increase the number of hours and return to the journal. The number of Regular hours remains unchanged at 80 hours.

Click the **Overtime1 field** and add the overtime hours by **typing** 2.

Click the **Advance field** and **accept** the **default** because only $50 remains to be repaid.

Review the **journal entry** and make corrections if necessary.

Click **Post**. **Click Yes** to continue and save the transaction.

Close the **Payroll Journal**.

WARNING!

You must complete the step of adding time from the time slips. If you do not, the payroll status for these activities will continue to show as Not Paid and the employee could be incorrectly paid a second time for the same work.

> **NOTES**
> When you use the Time Slip number to look up the time slip, the Previous and Next tools will not be available.
> You can click Browse in the Search lookup window to list all the time slips and then select one as we did in other journals.

The program will update the Payroll Hours Selection dates for the next paycheque, and the Payroll Status on these Time Slips.

Click the **Time Slips Journal icon** to open the Time Slips Journal.

Click the **Look Up Time Slips tool**.

Type 2 in the Time Slip Number field and **click OK** to see Tinker's time slip.

You should see that the employee has been paid — Paid appears in the Payroll Status column for each job completed by this employee. You cannot use this time slip information for payroll again.

Click the **Look Up Time Slips tool** and **enter 1** in the Time Slip Number field. **Click OK** to see Schwinn's time slip. His payroll status too is marked as Paid because we added time from the time slips, even though the hours were not used to determine his pay.

Close the **Time Slips Journal**.

Preparing Sales Invoices from Time Slips

When sales invoices are prepared for mailing to the customers, the activities from the time slips can be added directly to the invoices without re-entering each activity.

Click the **Sales icon** to open the Sales Journal.

Choose McMaster University as the customer. Invoice and Pay Later are correct.

Enter July 7 as the invoice date.

Time slip activities may be entered using the tool shown below or the Sales menu option:

Click the **Add Time Slip Activities tool** or **choose** the **Sales menu** and **click Add Time Slip Activities** to open the activities list for this customer:

> **NOTES**
> If necessary, scroll or change the column width to see all the columns.

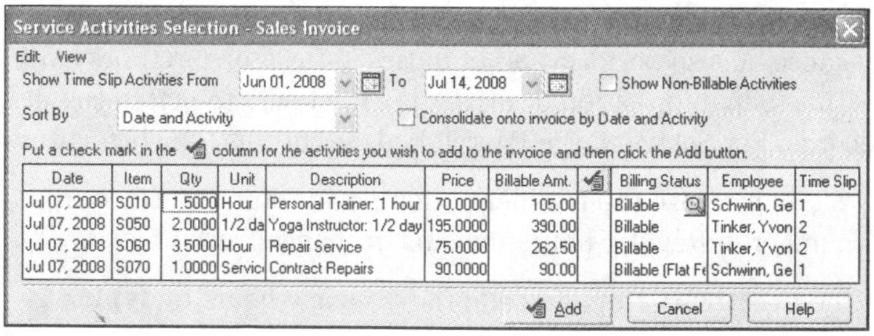

Services provided to the customer by all employees will be listed, and you can also include Non-Billable Activities by clicking its check box. You may need to scroll to see the information in all the columns. You can Sort the list By Date And Activity, the default, By Employee And Activity or By Activity. You can also Consolidate the list By Date And Activity, combining the amounts for each activity on the same date. You can select all the activities for the invoice, or omit some if they are incomplete, or if they come after the billing date. All activities should be included in the invoice for McMaster University.

Click the **Add Activity column** for the first activity, S010. Only activities with a ✓ in this column are added to the sales invoice.

Click the **Add Activity column** for the remaining activities.

Click the **Add button** Add to return to the Sales Journal.

The activities are now added to the journal so the transaction is complete as shown:

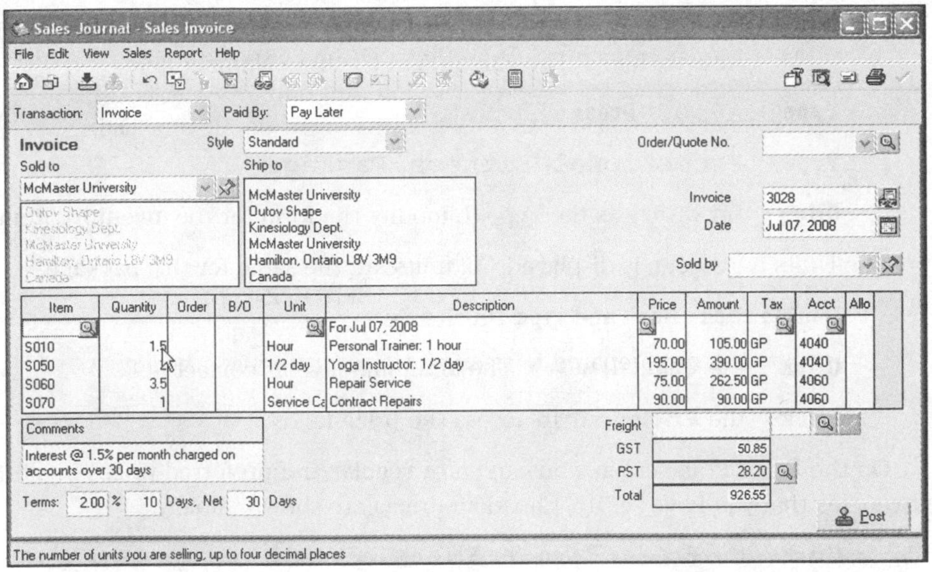

Notice that the Quantity refers to the units in the ledger — for S050, the customer pays for two one-half day units of three hours each and for S070, the quantity for the flat-rate service call is one. You can add other regular services or inventory to the sales invoice if they were sold to the same customer; you do not need to create a separate invoice for them.

You should review the journal entry before posting it.

Choose the **Report menu** and **click Display Sales Journal Entry**:

Flabuless Fitness

07/07/08 (J5)	Debits	Credits	Project
1200 Accounts Receivable	926.55	-	
2640 PST Payable	-	28.20	
2650 GST Charged on Sales	-	50.85	
4040 Revenue from Services	-	495.00	
4060 Revenue from Repairs	-	352.50	
	926.55	926.55	

The journal entry is the same as any other sales journal entry. The tax amounts are correct because the Service Ledger records include tax information. PST is charged on repairs but not on the other services. GST is charged on all services provided by Flabuless Fitness.

Close the **report** when you have finished viewing it.

Make **corrections** if necessary.

To correct the activities, click to return to the Service Activities Selection list. Previously selected activities are shown as Invoiced in the Billing Status column. Clicking the Add Activity column will remove the ✓ and restore the status to billable so you can select a different group of activities.

Click **Post** Post to save the journal entry.

Enter the next **two sales invoices** by adding items from the time slips.

NOTES

Clicking the Add Activity column heading will select all the activities in the list at once. Then you can click one to deselect it if you need to.

NOTES

If the information in the Time Slip was incorrect, close the Sales Journal without posting the invoice and adjust the Time Slip. Then re-enter the sales invoice.

Building New Inventory

Instead of assembling inventory using the Item Assembly method, you can set up the inventory assembly components as part of the ledger record and then use this information to build an item using the Bill of Materials method. We will create the new inventory Promotional Fitness Package, including the items or materials that make up the package.

Click the **Inventory & Services icon** to open the icon window.

Click the **Create tool** to open the Inventory Ledger for new Service Activity items. The cursor is in the Item Number field.

Type AP100 **Press** tab.

Type Promotional Fitness Package

Click **Inventory** as the Type to modify the form for the inventory item.

The Units tab screen is displayed. All units are the same for this package.

Double click **Each** and **type** Package

Click the **Quantities tab**. The Minimum level is correct at 0.

Click the **Pricing tab** to access the price fields.

On the Pricing tab screen, you can enter regular and preferred prices in all the currencies that you have set up. Canadian prices are shown initially.

Click the **Regular Price Per Selling Unit field**.

Type 210 **Press** tab to advance to the Preferred Price field.

Type 200

Choose **United States Dollars** from the Currency list.

Foreign prices for Flabuless Fitness are fixed so we need to change the default setting. Clicking the entry will change the setting.

Click **Exchange Rate** beside Regular to change the setting to Fixed Price.

Press tab to advance to the Regular Selling Price for United States Dollars.

Type 175 **Press** tab to advance to the Preferred Pricing Method.

Click **Exchange Rate** to change the setting to Fixed Price. **Press** tab.

Type 165

Choose **Euro** from the currency list.

Click **Exchange Rate** beside Regular to change the setting to Fixed Price.

Press tab to advance to the Regular Price for Euro.

Type 150 **Press** tab to advance to the Preferred Pricing Method.

Click **Exchange Rate** to change the setting. **Press** tab.

Type 140

Click the **Linked tab** to open the linked accounts screen.

Click the **Asset field**.

Type 1510 **Press** tab. We need to add the account.

Click **Add** and **press** `tab` to advance to the account field.

Type `Promotions`

Accept the remaining **defaults** for the account and the account class change.

Press `tab` to advance to the Revenue account field.

Type `4020` **Press** `tab` to advance to the COGS account field.

Type `5050`

The variance linked account is not needed for this item.

Click the **Taxes tab** to see the sales taxes relating to the inventory.

The default entry No for Tax Exempt is correct — both PST and GST are charged on the sale of this item. Duty is not charged on this item because it is not purchased.

Click the **Build tab** to see the information screen that we need for entering the assembly or building components for inventory items:

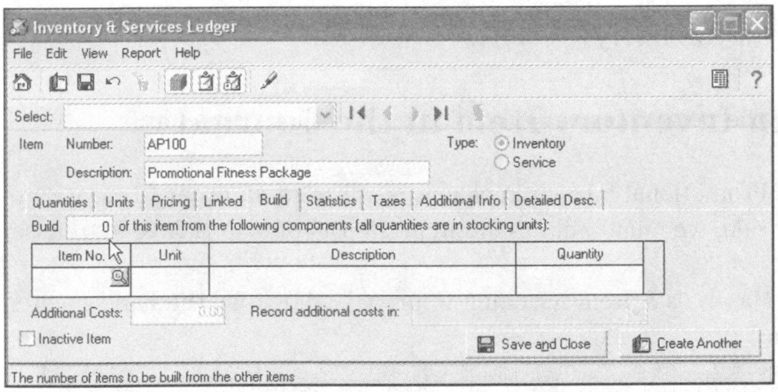

On this screen, we enter the relationship between the new inventory and its components, that is, how many new items we are building and how many of each input item this number of units requires. This is very similar to the Item Assembly Journal, except that we are only defining the building process at this stage. The actual building or assembly still takes place in the journal. One package is created from the set of accessories and one unit of each accessory is used — we build one package at a time.

The components are listed here again for easy reference:

A010 Body Fat Scale
A030 Dumbbells: Hexagonal pair
A040 Dumbbells: 5kg set
A080 Heart Rate Monitor
A110 Stability Balls
A180 Workout Gloves: all sizes
A190 Yoga Mats

Click the **Build field** to enter the actual number of packages being assembled from the set of components.

Type `1` **Press** `tab` to advance to the Item No. field.

Click the **List icon** and **select A010 Body Fat Scale** to enter the first item.

The cursor advances to the Quantity field after entering the unit and description. Here you need to enter the number of Body Fat Scales included in each Promotional Fitness Package. We are defining the unit relationship between the assembled item and its components. One of each component item is used to make the package.

Type `1` **Press** `tab` to advance to the second Item No. line.

Enter the **remaining components** and **enter 1** as the quantity for each.

The Additional Costs and its linked account field (Record Additional Costs In) became available once we entered the number of units to build. These fields have the same meaning as they do in the Item Assembly Journal. However, in the Pro version, costs are entered in the ledger record and separate assembly linked accounts can be defined for each item. There are no additional costs associated with creating the package so we should leave these fields blank.

Click the **Quantities tab**. The quantity on hand remains at zero until we build the item in the journal.

Correct any **errors** by returning to the field with the mistake. **Highlight** the **error** and **enter** the **correct information**. **Click** the different **tabs** to see all the information that you entered.

When all the information is entered correctly, you must save the record.

Click **Save And Close** [Save and Close] to save the record.

Close the **Inventory & Services window**.

basic **BASIC VERSION**
In the Basic version, there is one linked Item Assembly Costs account for the ledger, and it is entered on the Inventory Linked Accounts screen. In the Pro version, you can enter a different linked assembly costs account for each item you build.

Building an Inventory Item in the Journal

The quantity of Promotional Fitness Packages is still zero. In order to create stock of the package for sale, we must build the item in the Bill of Materials & Item Assembly Journal.

The Bill Of Materials & Item Assembly Journal is shown by the hand pointer in the following screen:

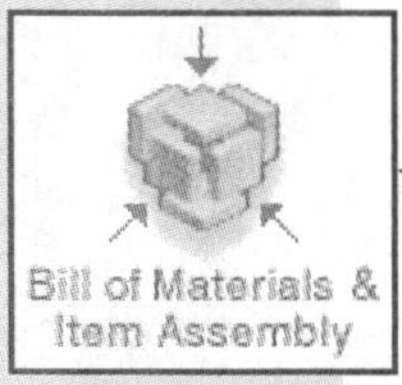

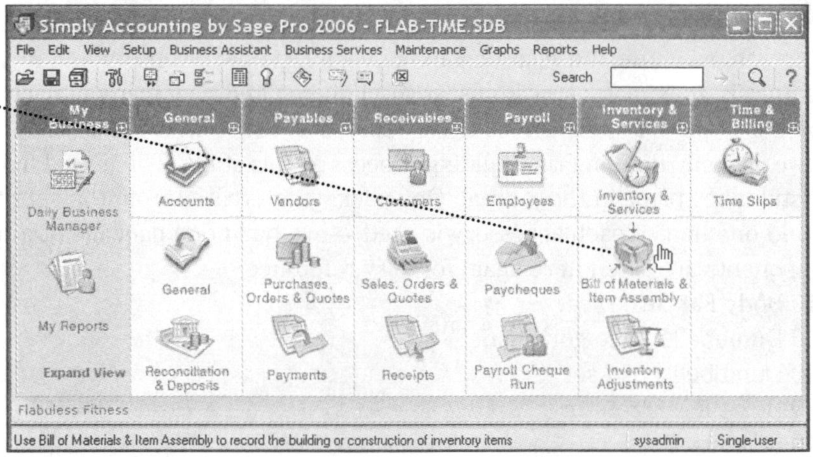

Click the **Bill Of Materials & Item Assembly icon** to open the journal:

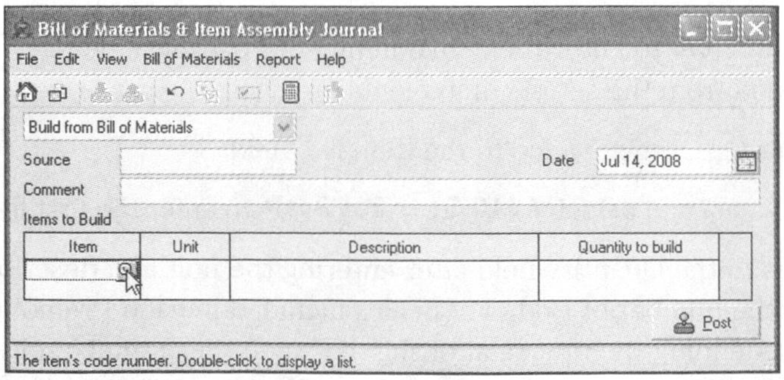

NOTES
Build From Bill Of Materials will be the default journal if this is the first time you are opening this journal.

The journal opens with the Build screen that you used most recently. If that was Build From Item Assembly, you must change the setting. In the Pro version, you can assemble new inventory items either by using the Item Assembly method that we used in previous applications, or the Bill of Materials method that follows.

Click **Build From Bill Of Materials** (or **Build From Item Assembly**) to access the drop-down list of options:

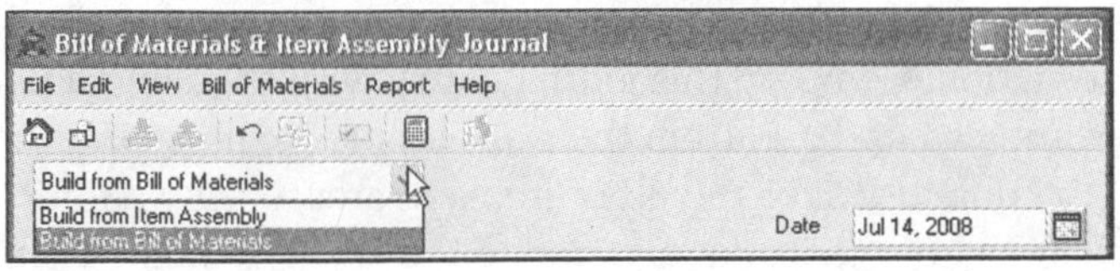

Click **Build From Bill Of Materials** to change the transaction type if necessary.

The journal resembles half of the Item Assembly Journal screen in the Basic version or the Build From Item Assembly screen in the Pro version, but without costs.

NOTES
The additional costs and the components information are taken from the ledger record – the Build tab screen details. Item cost, as usual, is the average cost for each component.

Click the **Source field**.

Type Memo 7-6 **Press** tab to advance to the Date field.

Type 7-7 **Press** tab **twice** to advance to the Comment field.

Type Create promotional packages **Press** tab. The cursor moves to the Item field.

Click the **List icon** to open the selection list:

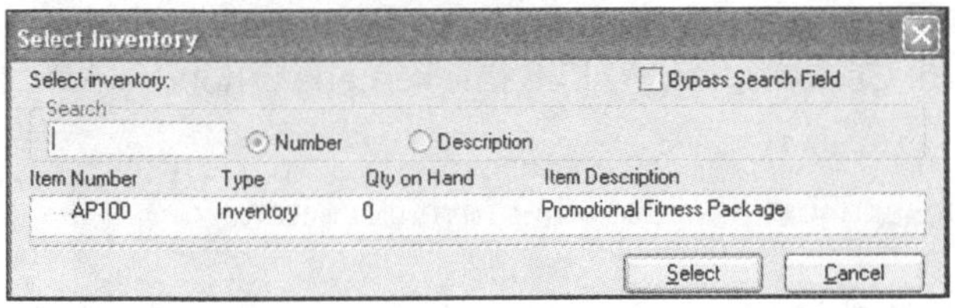

All the items for which you have added build information will be listed on this screen. Because we have entered these details only for the Promotional Fitness Package, it is the only one listed.

Double click **AP100** to add it to the journal.

NOTES
The default quantity is taken from the ledger record's Build tab screen, where we entered that we build one item at a time.

The unit and description are added for the package and the default quantity is 1. The quantity is selected so we can change it. We are creating two packages.

Type 2 to complete the journal entry as shown:

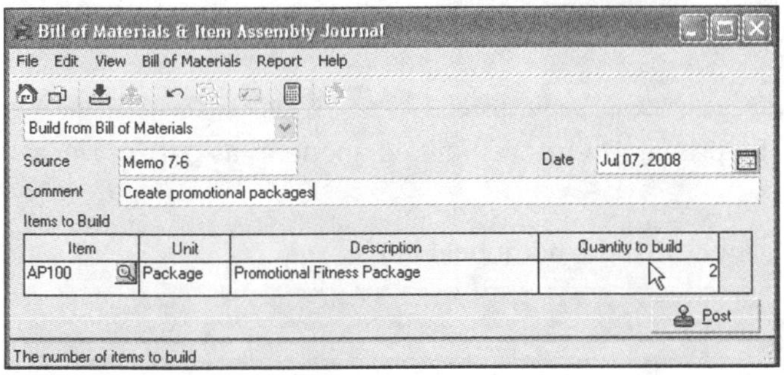

If you have other items to build, you can continue by choosing the items and entering a quantity for each of them.

Review your **work** before posting the transaction.

Choose the **Report menu** and **click Display Bill Of Materials & Item Assembly Journal**.

NOTES

When you link the same asset account to the assembled item and its components, you will see the message that no journal entry results from the transaction. However, all inventory quantities are updated by the transaction.

You will display the journal transaction:

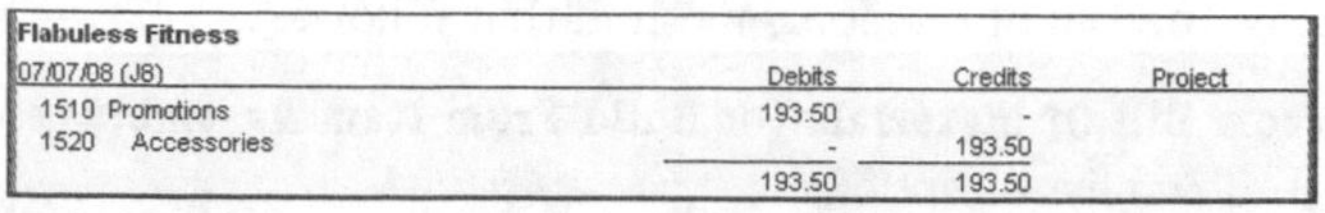

Flabuless Fitness

07/07/08 (J8)	Debits	Credits	Project
1510 Promotions	193.50	-	
1520 Accessories	-	193.50	
	193.50	193.50	

The asset account balances have been updated by the transaction, just as they are in an Item Assembly transaction. Compare this journal entry with the one on page 430. The inventory quantities are also updated from the transaction — the quantity of packages increases and the quantities for the other items decrease. Any additional costs would be credited to the linked cost account and debited to the assembled item asset account.

Close the **journal display** and **make corrections** if necessary.

If there is not enough inventory of any item in stock to complete the build, you will see an error message asking you to reduce the quantity to build:

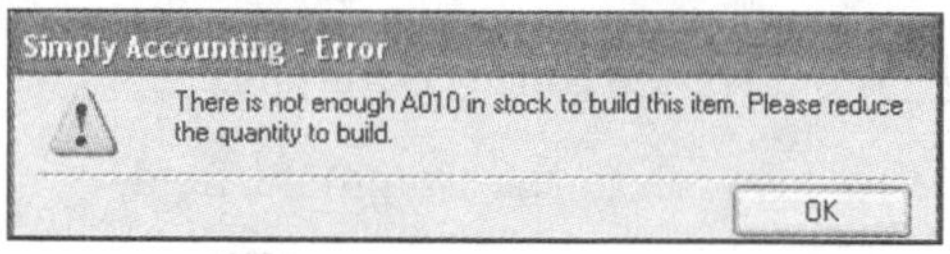

Click OK and reduce the number of units you are building.

Click **Post** Post to save the entry.

Click the Item list icon to see that the number of promotional packages has been changed to two. Click Cancel to close this screen without making a selection.

You can now sell the package just like any other inventory item.

Multiple Levels of Build

You can use a built item just like any other single inventory item. The process is the same when you are selling the item or using it as a component to build other inventory.

Nested building components are common in construction work. When you use a built item as a component for a second-stage build, you select it on the Build tab screen just like other inventory. When you are building the new second-stage item in the Bill of Materials Journal, the built component may be out of stock. In this case, Simply Accounting provides the following message:

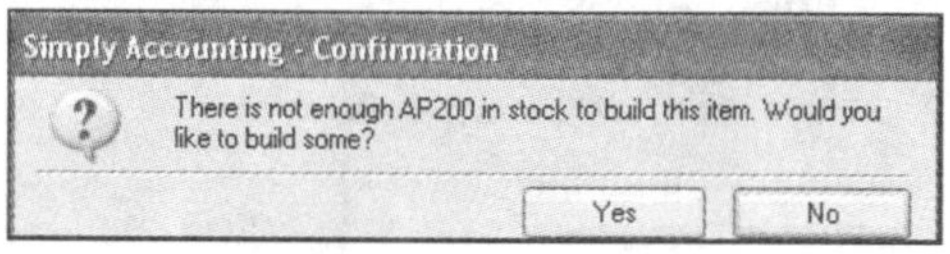

You can now build the primary item, the built component, as part of the same journal transaction.

NOTES

If there are further layers of building nested in a transaction, Simply Accounting will offer the chance to build the necessary components at each stage in the same way to complete the initial transaction.

Click Yes to continue with the additional build:

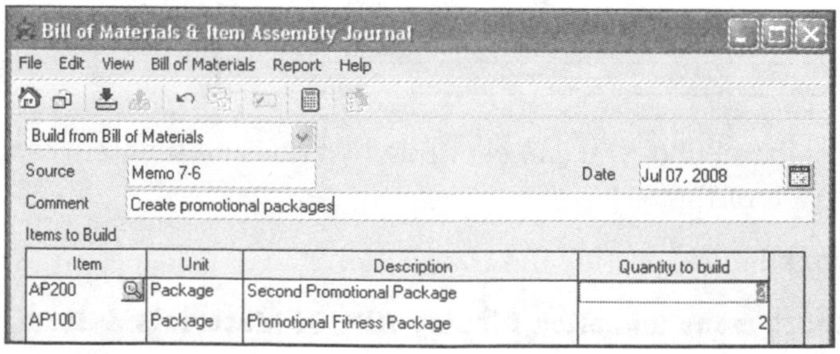

Simply Accounting will add the out-of-stock item to the Bill of Materials Journal as the first item to build. The number of units built will be that required to complete the secondary build.

Close the **journal**.

Displaying Time and Billing Reports

The various Time and Billing reports provide different ways of organizing the same information. You can view the reports by customer, by employee and by activity. You must be in the Home window to see Time and Billing reports.

Billing Time by Customer Report

Time and Billing reports by customer show the time and billed amounts organized by customer.

Choose the **Reports menu**, then **choose Time & Billing** and **Billing** and **click Time By Customer** to open the report options screen:

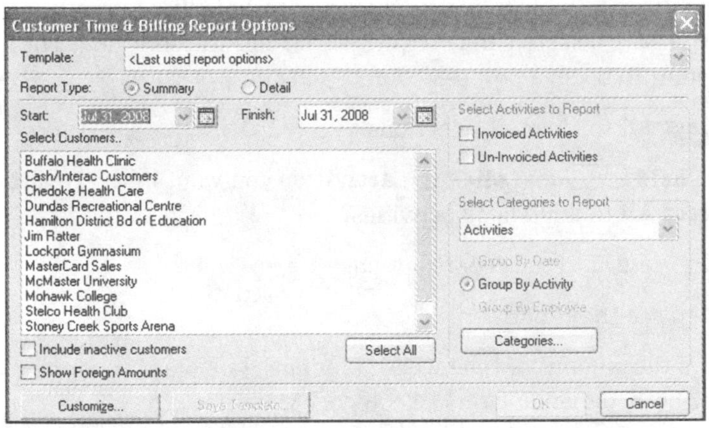

Summary and Detail reports are available. **Detail** reports include a report line for each activity or employee on each time slip while the **Summary** reports show only the totals for each selected category (activity or employee). You can select one or more customers for inclusion in the report. The reports will include columns for several billing details — actual time spent on activities, non-billable time, no-charge time, billable time, billable percentage (the proportion of the total time worked for which the customer was charged) and billable amounts. In addition, if you changed the prices for any of the services, the report will show these changes as amounts written down or up and as percentages of the billable amounts. In the report, the invoiced amounts will then be different from the billable amounts. The effective billable percentage shows the relation between the invoiced amount and the billable amount. You can customize the report by selecting the columns to include. The report details can also be grouped — by date, by activity or by employee.

You can include **invoiced activities** (bills have been sent) or **uninvoiced activities** (the bills have not been created and sent) or both.

The next decision for the report relates to the **categories** you want to include. You can report on the time spent according to the **activities** performed for the customer, or according to the **employee** who completed the work or both. In all cases, the categories are shown for each customer you selected.

Enter **Start** and **Finish dates** for the report.

NOTES
Sorting and filtering are not available for Time and Billing reports.

Choose the **customers** for the report. **Press** and **hold** ctrl and **click** the **customer names** or **click Select All** to include all customers.

Choose the **invoicing details** for the report. **Click** a **detail** to remove a ✓ or to add it.

Click the **Select Categories To Report list arrow** to select activities or employees or both.

Click the **Categories button** to open the secondary selection list.

If you choose Activity, you will see the list of activities:

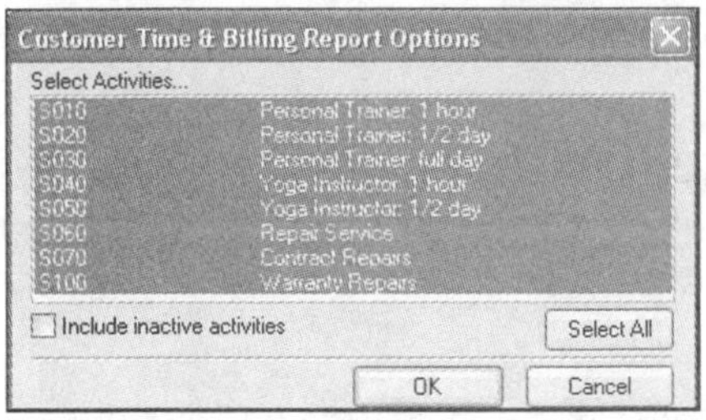

If you choose Employees as the category, you must select from the employee list. If you choose both Activity and Employees, you must choose from lists for both.

Initially, all activities are selected and clicking will change the selection. The selection acts like a toggle switch. To begin a new selection of activities,

Click **Select All** to clear all selections.

Press and **hold** ctrl and **click** the **activities** you want in the report or **click Select All** to include all activities.

Click **OK** to return to the report options screen.

Click **OK** to see the report.

The report shows the amount of time worked for each customer according to the activity, employee or both, depending on the category you selected.

Close the **report** when you have finished.

Billing Time by Employee and Activity Reports

The other two Time and Billing reports are similar to the Time By Customer Report, except that they organize the amounts by employee or by activity. The first options screen for the **Time By Employee Report** will show the Employee list, and the second selection screen will list the customers, the activities or both, depending on the category you choose. The Time by Employee Report shows the time and billed amounts for each employee for each customer, each activity or both, depending on the categories you choose.

Similarly, the first options screen for the **Time By Activity Report** will show the Activity list, and the second selection screen will list the customers, the employees or both, depending on the category you choose. The Time by Activity Report shows the time and the billed amounts for each activity for each customer or by each employee or both, depending on the category you choose.

Other report options are the same as they are for the Time by Customer Report, and both reports are available as a Summary or a Detail report.

Payroll Time Sheet Reports

The Time Sheet Report provides a summary of the hours of each income category that is involved on the time sheets. The number of hours of non-payroll, regular payroll and overtime for each employee can be included.

Choose the **Reports menu**, then **choose Time & Billing** and **Payroll** and **click Time Sheet** to access the Report Options window:

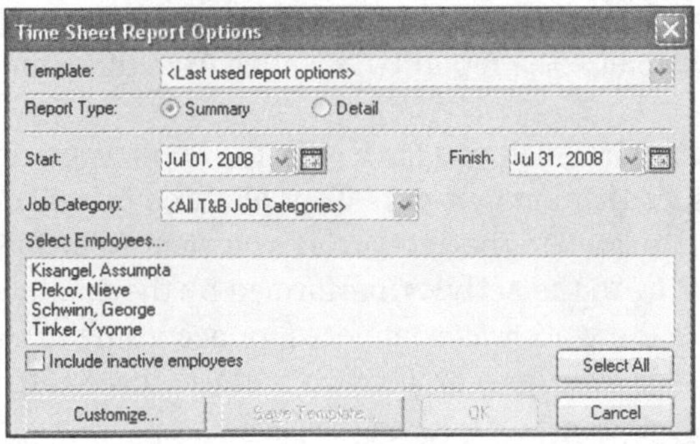

The **Summary** Report will provide the total number of hours in each payroll category for each employee selected for each time period during the report interval. The **Detail** Report will show the number of hours in each payroll category for each time sheet.

You can customize the report by selecting columns for the payroll category. Non-payroll, Regular and Overtime 1 columns — the payroll category in the ledger record for the activity — may be selected.

Enter **Start** and **Finish dates** for the report.

Choose the **employees** for the report. **Press** and **hold** ctrl and **click** the **employee names** or **click Select All** to include all employees.

Click **OK** to display the report.

Close the **report** when you have finished.

Payroll Time by Employee Reports

The remaining Payroll Time reports provide information about the cost effectiveness of the service activities by comparing the labour costs with the income generated — the amount billed to the customer. Employee productivity is also measured by examining the actual hours, billable hours, wages paid and invoiced amounts.

Choose the **Reports menu**, then **choose Time & Billing** and **Payroll** and **click Time By Employee** to see the report options:

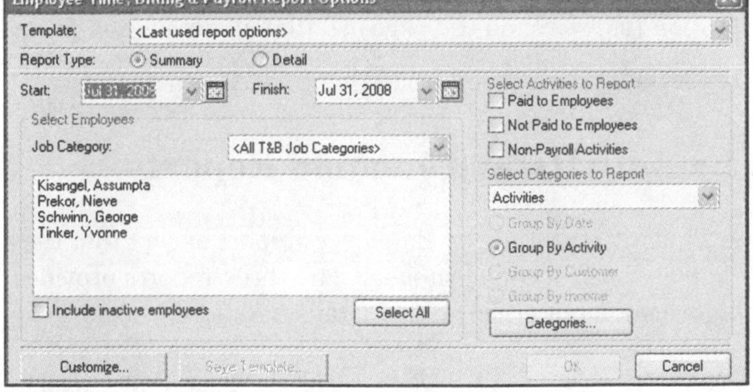

NOTES

A good way to understand activity reports is to prepare a very complete report. For example, select the Detail Report, choose all employees, click all Details and Activities and choose Activities and Customers as the categories for the report. Then choose all service activities from the next list. Print the report. Choose Redo Report (click the tool or choose from the Options menu in the report). Compare this report with the Summary Report for the same details and categories.

Summary and Detail reports are available. **Detail** reports include a report line for each time sheet entry while the **Summary** reports show only the totals for each selected category. You can select one or more employees for inclusion in the report. The reports will include several time and billing **details** — actual time spent on activities, payroll time, payroll percentage (payroll time as a proportion of actual time), billable time, billable percentage (the proportion of the total time worked for which the customer was charged), billable amounts, the actual payroll expense and the productivity ratio (the billable amount compared to the payroll expense) can be included. The effective productivity ratio percentage shows the relation between the invoiced amount and the payroll expense amount. You can customize the report by selecting from these time and billing details.

The report can include **activities** for which you have **paid** the employees, activities that have **not yet been paid**, activities that are **non-payroll** or all three payroll details.

The next decision for the report relates to the **categories** you want to include. You can report on the time spent according to the **activity** performed by the employee, according to the **customer** for whom the work was completed, or according to the **income** (that is, regular, non-payroll or overtime) or any two of these three categories. In all cases, the categories are shown for each employee you selected.

You can also group report details — select from date, activity, customer or income.

Enter **Start** and **Finish dates** for the report.

Choose the **employees** for the report. **Press** and **hold** ctrl and **click** the **employee names** or **click Select All** to include all employees.

Choose the **payroll details**. **Click** a **detail** to add or to remove a ✓.

Choose the **categories** for the report from the drop-down list.

Click the **Categories button** to open the secondary selection list.

If you select the Activities category, you will see the complete list of all services defined as activities in the ledger:

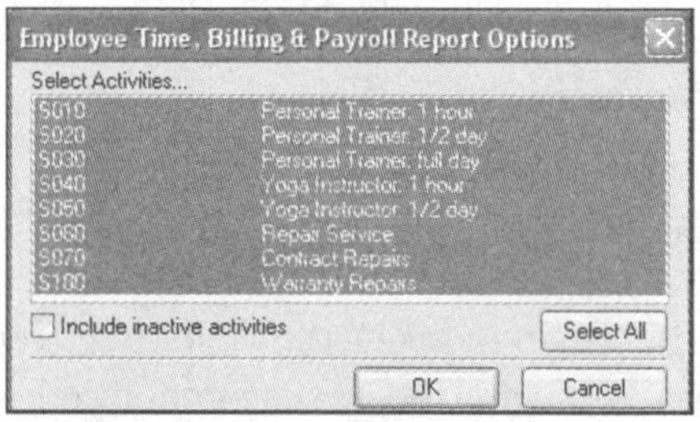

NOTES

If you select Customers or Income as the category, you will see selection lists for each category. If you selected two categories, you can choose from selection lists for both categories.

Choose the **activities** for the report. **Press** and **hold** ctrl and **click** the **activity names** or **click Select All** to include all activities.

Click **OK** to return to the report options screen.

Click **OK** to see the report. By default the report will print in landscape orientation (sideways on the page) so that all details can fit on a line.

Close the **report** when you have finished.

Payroll Time by Activity and Income Reports

These two reports are similar to the Time by Employee Report except that they organize amounts by activity or by income category. The three reports provide essentially the same information but organize the details in different ways.

The first options screen for the **Time by Activity Report** will show the Activity list, and the second selection screen will list the customers, employees, incomes or any two of these that you select, depending on the category you choose. The Time by Activity Report shows the same details as the Time by Employee Report but lists them for each activity for each customer, each employee, each income or any two of these, depending on the categories you choose.

Similarly, the first options screen for the **Time by Income Report** will show the income list, and the second selection screen will list the customers, the employees, activities or any two of these three, depending on the category you choose. The Time by Income Report shows the same details as the Time by Employee Report but lists them for each activity for each customer, by each employee, each activity or any two of these, depending on the category you choose.

Other report options are the same as they are for the Time by Employee Report, and both reports are available as a Summary or a Detail report.

Multiple Fiscal Periods and Reports

After you have accumulated two fiscal periods of financial data, you can produce historical reports for these additional periods. Data for the current and previous years are always available, unless you have cleared the information.

Print the **financial reports** for July (Income Statement, Balance Sheet, Trial Balance, Vendor and Customer Aged reports, Employee Summary Report and Inventory Synopsis and Quantity reports).

Prepare a **list** of inventory items that should be ordered.

Choose the **Maintenance menu** and **click Start New Year** to begin a new fiscal year.

Choose Yes when asked if you want to Back Up Your Data Files Before Beginning The New Fiscal Year and follow the backup instructions.

Choose No when asked if you want to clear the old data.

The Update Locking Date screen opens with the Do Not Allow Transactions Dated Before field.

Enter 08/01/08 as the new date. **Click OK** to update the earliest transaction.

Choose the **Setup menu**, then **choose System Settings** and **click Company Information** to see the new fiscal dates:

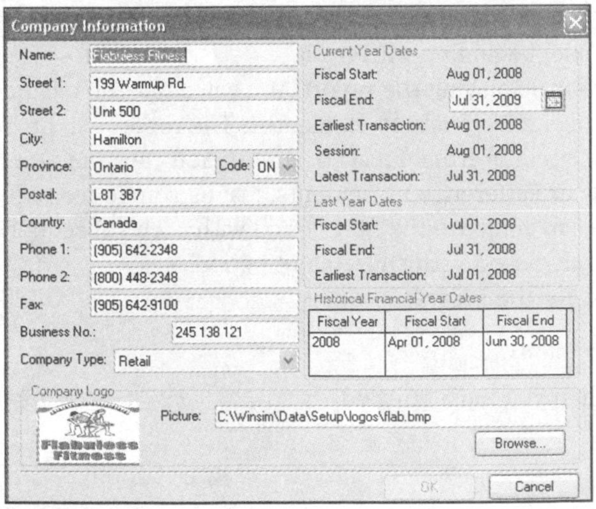

Notice that the first fiscal period, April 1 to June 30, 2008, is now listed in the section for Historical Financial Year Dates.

Drag through the **Fiscal End date**.

Type 08-31-08

Click **OK** to save the change and return to the Home window.

Multi-period Financial Reports

Multiple period reports are available for the Balance Sheet, Income Statement and Trial Balance. All are accessed from the Reports menu under Financials as shown in the following screen:

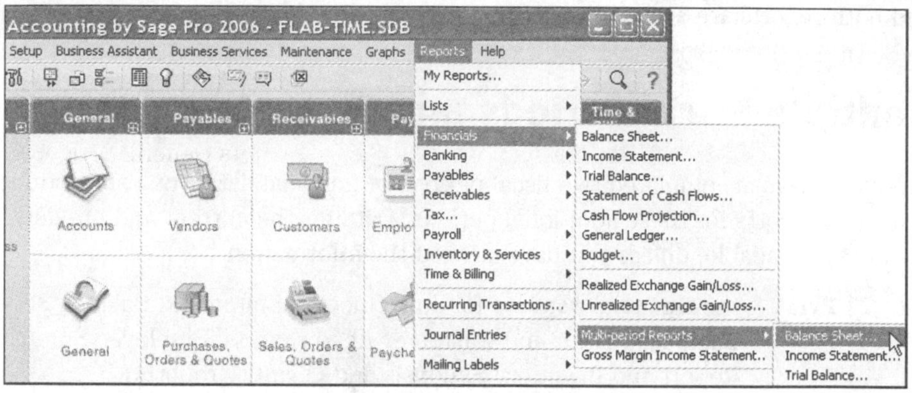

Choose the **Reports menu**, then **choose Financials** and **Multi-Period Reports** and **click Balance Sheet** to see the report options:

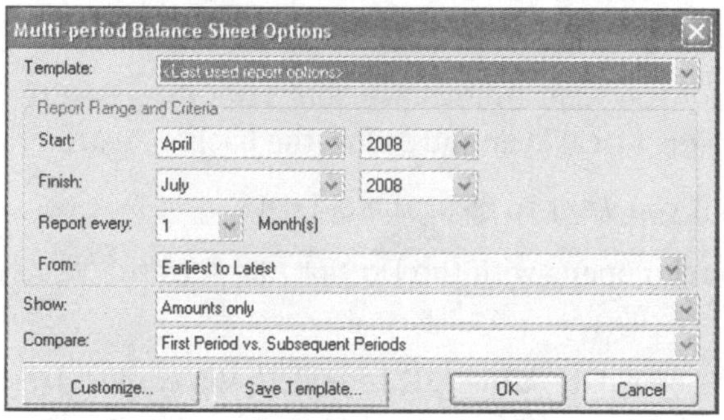

NOTES

Dates before the previous fiscal period that are eligible for the report will show in the Historical Financial Year Dates section of the Company Information screen (see page 729).

The Start and Finish dates apply only to the periods before the current fiscal period, including those before the previous period. The previous period is available in the regular financial reports.

Monthly reports are available, beginning with April.

There are several options for displaying the report. You can show the balances for each month for any interval ranging from one to 12 months. The report can be ordered from the earliest period to the latest or from latest to earliest. You can show Amounts Only, Difference In Percentage or Difference In Amounts, just as you do for regular comparative reports. And you can compare the first period with each subsequent period, or you can compare each period with subsequent periods.

After choosing the options for the report,

Click **OK** to see the report.

Close the **report** when you have finished.

The **Income Statement** and **Trial Balance** are available for the same periods as the Balance Sheet. You can select them from the same menu and choose from the same report options. To see these reports,

Choose the **Reports menu**, **Financials**, **Multi-Period Reports**, and **click Income Statement** or **Trial Balance**.

Choose the **report options** and **click OK**.

Close the **report** when you have finished.

Related Historical Accounts

Because we have advanced to the next (third) fiscal period, we can see the list of related accounts. You can see and edit the related historical accounts in the General Ledger record for the account in the Related Historical Accounts tab screen.

Click the **Accounts icon**.

Double click the **account** you want to see to open its General Ledger record.

Click the **Related Historical Accounts tab** to see the accounts used in previous periods.

If an account currently being used has a different name and number than the account used for the same purpose in a previous period, you can link them.

Each account shows itself as the related historical account if it has been used for more than two fiscal periods. Each account can be related to only one account. Therefore, if it is already related to itself, you cannot select it again. Instead, you can link a new account to the old one.

Open the record for the previously used account. Then select the new account from the account selection list in the Related Historical Accounts tab.

Close the **Ledger window** and then **close** the **Accounts window**.

If you have used different accounts for the same purpose over the periods and you have related them, you can add the related accounts to the Account List. To see the report of related account numbers,

Choose the **Reports menu**, then **choose Lists** and **click Accounts**.

Click **Related Historical Accounts** and then **click OK** to see the report.

The report will list all General Ledger accounts with the current information and the accounts that were used for those same purposes in previous fiscal periods — the information that is stored in the General Ledger Related Historical Accounts tab fields.

Close the **report** when you have finished.

Close the **Home window** to exit the Simply Accounting program.

CHAPTER EIGHTEEN

Flabuless Fitness

OBJECTIVES

After completing this chapter, you should be able to

- ***activate*** departmental accounting
- ***create*** departments
- ***add*** departments to accounts, vendors and customers
- ***add*** departments in journal entries
- ***display*** and ***print*** department reports

DEPARTMENTAL ACCOUNTING

Departmental accounting is similar to working with projects, but departments are more powerful and can provide more information than projects. Most companies are divided into departments such as sales, marketing, service, finance, human resources and manufacturing. And most companies want to track the costs and performance of these departments separately. Setting up the departments in Simply Accounting permits more detailed analysis.

Rather than operating as projects that work only through journal entries, departments are connected to all ledgers and journals. Individual departments can be associated with individual accounts, vendors and customers. You can also choose the department for an account in journal entries.

Each account may be used by only one department or by more than one department. For example, automotive parts in a car dealership will be used by the service department but not by the human resources or sales departments. Other accounts, such as a bank account, may be connected to all departments. Similarly, individual vendors, such as a car-parts supplier, may be linked to a specific department while others, such as utility providers, are linked to all departments. Customers, too, may be connected to specific departments. When you set up these connections, the departmental links are added to journal entries automatically, and you can generate detailed reports with departmental information.

Departmental account balances are generated when you add departmental information to journal entries. If the accounts start with zero balances when you create the departments, all account balances will be divided among the various departments. You cannot allocate the opening account balances to departments. Therefore, ideally, you will add departmental information when you create company files so that you can have departmental information for all accounts. You can also choose to use departments only for income statement accounts and start using departments at the beginning of a fiscal period when these accounts have zero balances.

Setting Up Departments

The following example uses the Flabuless Fitness data file at the beginning of April, the start of a new fiscal period. If you want to practise setting up departments, you can use the data file **Depart\Flab-dept.sdb**. We will add two departments, Sales and Service.

Open **Depart\Flab-dept.sdb** from the Data folder.

Accept **April 1** as the session date.

Creating Departments

Before using departmental accounting, you must activate this feature and create the departments you want for the company. The feature is not turned on by default, and you can add departments to an existing Simply Accounting data file. The feature is turned on from the Setup menu.

WARNING!
You cannot remove departments once you add them and use them. You should work with a separate backup copy of the data file for this exercise.

Choose the **Setup menu**, then **choose** **System Settings** and **Settings**. **Click** **General (Accounts)** to access the General Ledger settings list:

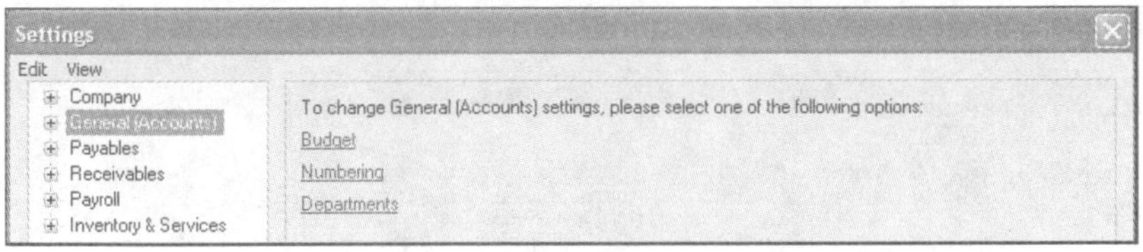

Click **Departments** to access the Department Settings window:

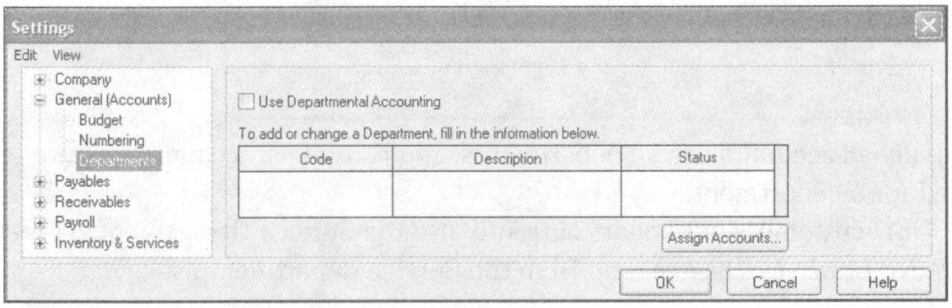

Click **Use Departmental Accounting** to see the warning:

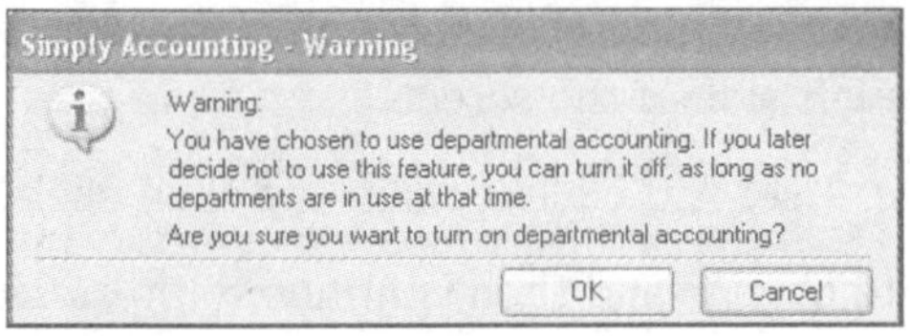

Adding departments is not a reversible step, unless the departments have not yet been used.

Click Cancel if you are not working with a separate copy of the data file, and make a backup first.

Click **OK** to return to the Departments Settings screen.

For each department you want, you must assign a four-digit code and a name.

Click the **Code field**.

NOTES
The Department Code must be a four-digit number. No letters or other characters are allowed.

Type 0100 **Press** tab to advance to the Description field. The Status is automatically set as Active.

Type Sales

If a department is not used, you can change its status to Inactive by clicking Active.

Click the **Code field** on the next line.

Type 0200 **Press** tab to advance to the Description field.

Type Service

Click the **Assign Accounts button** to open the next screen:

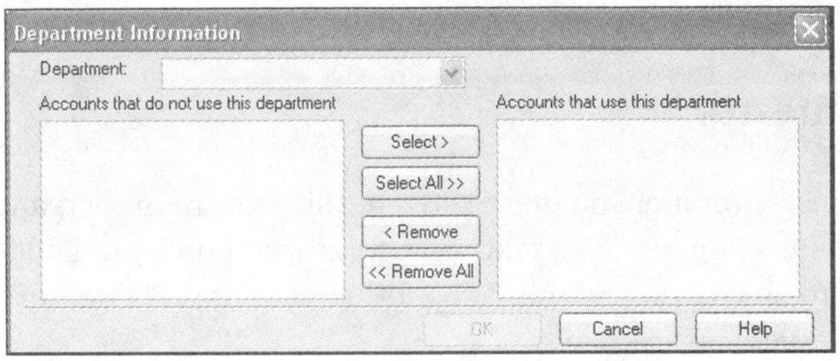

From this screen, you can indicate which accounts use the departments. First we must select a department from the drop-down list in the Department field.

Choose **Service** as the Department from the Department list:

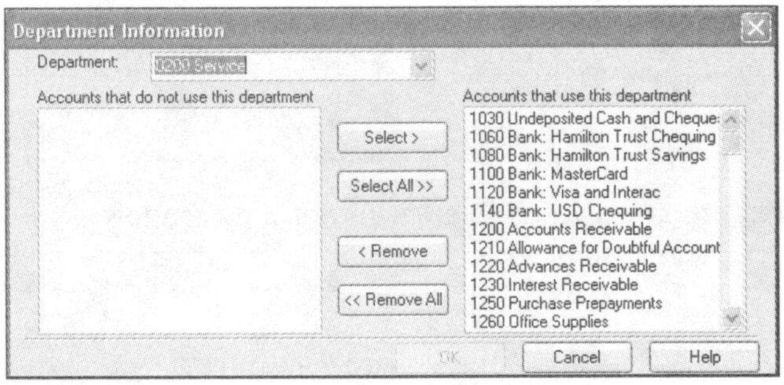

Initially all accounts use all departments. You can select accounts that are to be removed for a department.

No USD customers or vendors currently use the Service Department. Therefore we can remove *Bank: USD Chequing* from the Service department list.

Click **1140 Bank: USD Chequing** to select the account.

Click **Remove**. The account moves to the list of Accounts That Do Not Use This Department on the left side of the screen.

To move the account back to the "Use" list, click it again and then click Select.

Click an account that you want to change and then continue to press ctrl and click the next account until all the accounts you want are included.

Click the Remove button to shift the selected accounts to the other column.

Click Remove All to shift all the accounts to the "Do Not Use" column.

If only a few accounts use a department, it is easier to place them all on the "Do Not Use" side and then move the few to the "Use" side.

Reverse this procedure to move an account from the "Do Not Use" to the "Use" side. Click the account on the "Do Not Use" side and then click the Select button.

Click **OK** to return to the Settings window. **Click OK** to return to the Home window.

Adding Departments to Vendor Records

If some vendors are connected with only one department, you can add this information to the vendor record. If a vendor is used by more than one department, you should not add a department to the record.

Prolife Exercisers sells inventory to the store for sale so it is connected only with the Sales Department.

Click the **Vendors icon** 

and then **double click Prolife Exercisers** to open the record at the Address tab screen.

A Department field is added to the screen.

Click the **Department list arrow** to see the drop-down list of departments:

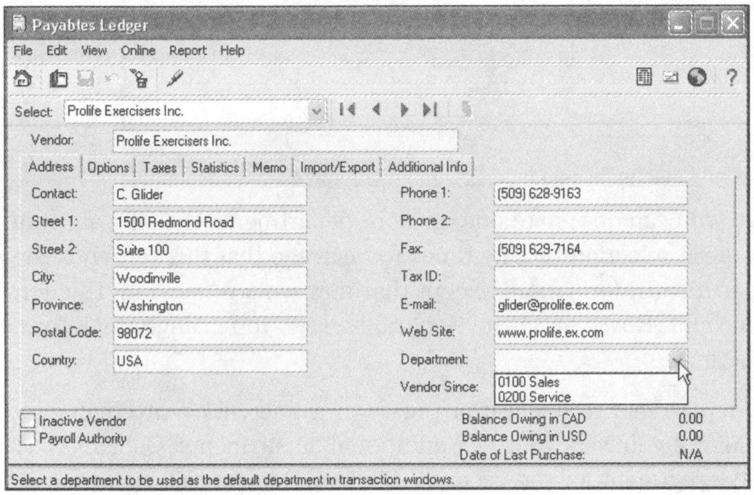

Click **Sales** to select the department.

Repeat these steps for any other vendors that are used exclusively by one department.

Close the **ledger record** and the **Vendors window** when you have finished.

Adding Departments to Customer Records

If a customer is connected exclusively with one department, you can add the department to the customer record, just as you do for vendors. For example, US customers do not use any of the services offered by Flabuless Fitness, so you can choose the Sales Department for all US customers.

Open the Customers window and then open the customer record. The Department field has been added to the Address tab screen.

Click the Department field list arrow to see the departments and click the one you want.

Repeat this procedure for other customers.

Close the customer record and the Customers window to return to the Home window.

Adding Departments to Accounts

Instead of adding department information to accounts from the Department Information window, you can modify the account ledger record from the Accounts window.

Click the **Accounts icon** and then **double click 1060 Bank: Hamilton Trust Chequing** to open the General Ledger.

A new tab, Departments, has been added to the ledger record.

Click the **Departments tab** to open the new screen:

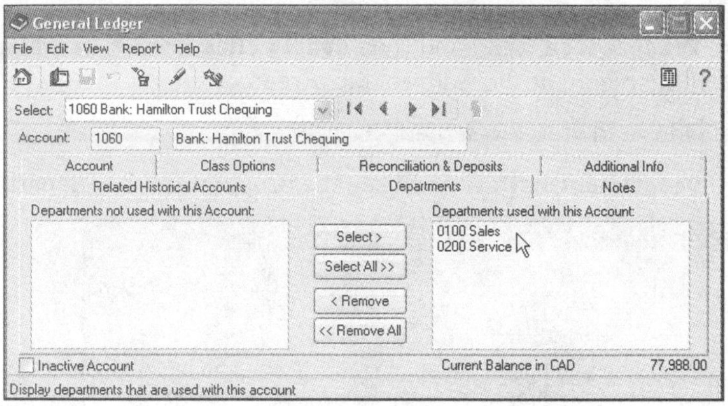

At this stage, you can designate one or more departments that the account uses. You can modify these selections at any time. You can see that this screen is the same as the one for Department Information, except that now we are "moving" the department instead of the account. However, in the General Ledger, you change the information for one account at a time.

Click a department to select it or press *ctrl* and click more than one department if you want to select additional departments. Clicking Select will add the department for the account. Clicking Remove will remove a selected department for the account and place it on the "Not Used" side. Remove All and Select All will move all departments at once to the other side.

For the two inventory accounts, 1520 and 1540, select Sales as the only department used by the account.

Open the **Ledger record for 1140 Bank USD Chequing** and **click** the **Departments tab**.

Notice that Service is located on the left side under the Departments Not Used With This Account because we moved it earlier. Sales is still listed on the right side under Departments Used With This Account.

Close the **Ledger window** and then **close** the **Accounts window**.

Adding Departments to Journal Entries

When you are entering transactions and have set up departments, you can choose a department from any Account field that allows you to select an account.

Click the **Purchases icon** 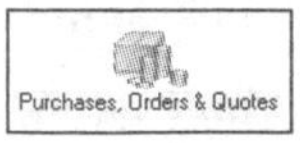

and **choose Prolife Exercisers** as the Vendor.

Click the **Account field List icon** to see the modified Select Account list.

Each account has a ⊞ icon added to it to indicate additional information is available. When you click the ⊞, all departments used by that account will be listed so you can select a department for the transaction.

Click the ⊞ **icon** beside **1060 Bank: Hamilton Trust Chequing**.

Click the ⊞ **icon** beside **1140 Bank: USD Chequing**.

The modified list now shows the departments connected with the two accounts as shown here:

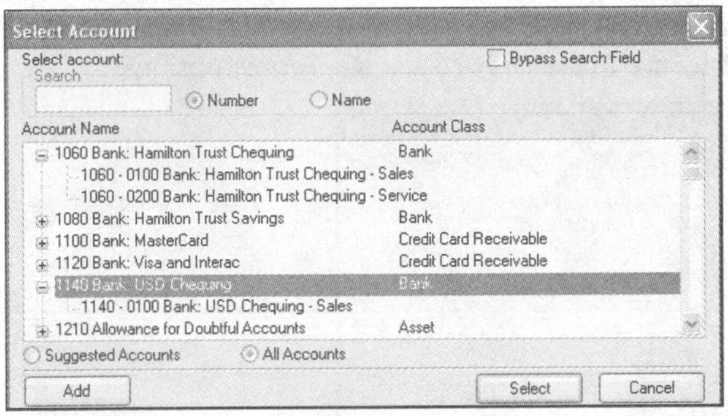

Bank: Hamilton Trust Chequing has both departments available for a journal transaction, and *Bank: USD Chequing* has only the Sales Department available because we removed the Service Department for that account.

When you purchase inventory, the account field is not available, so you cannot designate the department for the inventory asset account.

You can select only one department for each transaction line. You must make a department selection for each account shown in the journal, even if the account is used with only one department and you have selected that department in the ledger.

If you need to split a purchase or sale between two departments, you should split the amount over two invoice lines and choose the appropriate department for each invoice line.

If you select a department for a vendor, and make no other department selections in the journal, the amounts for *Accounts Payable*, *GST Paid on Purchases* and *Freight Expense* — all the linked accounts for the journal — will be connected to the department for the vendor.

The following journal entry display was created after selecting the Sales department for the vendor, Prolife Exercisers, and for the *Fitness Equipment* account.

Flabuless Fitness				
04/01/08 (J1)		Foreign Amt.	Debits	Credits
1540	Fitness Equipment	US$400.00	474.04	-
2670 - 0100	GST Paid on Purchases - Sales	US$35.00	41.48	-
5080 - 0100	Freight Expense - Sales	US$100.00	118.51	-
2200 - 0100	Accounts Payable - Sales	US$535.00	-	634.03
			634.03	634.03

Account department information is not added automatically because you can choose more than one department for use with each account. Because you can choose only one department for vendors or customers, this information can be added to the journal entry automatically. Payments to this vendor will also show the department for *Accounts Payable* and *Purchase Discounts* amounts automatically. However, the asset account that appears in the journal has no department connected to it because we did not (were unable to) access the Select Account screen for it.

Similarly, when you connect a customer to one department, linked accounts for sales and receipts — *Accounts Receivable*, *GST Charged on Sales*, *PST Payable*, *Freight Revenue* and *Sales Discounts* — will show the department connection automatically.

Department Reports

Many of the standard Simply Accounting reports can have department information added to them. In addition, the primary financial statements, the Balance Sheet, Income Statement and Trial Balance are available as departmental reports.

Displaying Departmental Income Statements

If you want Income Statement information for each department, you should prepare the Departmental Income Statement.

Choose the **Reports menu**, then **choose Financials** and **Departmental Reports** and **click Income Statement** to see the report options:

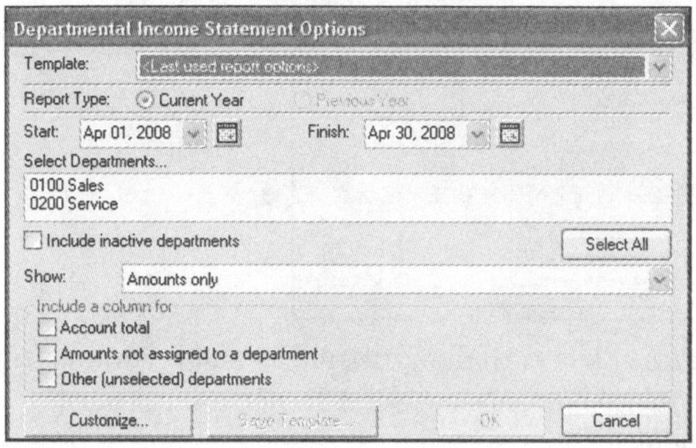

You can report on one or more departments or all departments. The departments are shown as column headings, so you have a complete Income Statement for each department you selected.

Reports can include **Amounts** only or each amount as a **Percentage Of The Total**. You can also add **extra columns** for the total amount for each account, for amounts not assigned to any department and for the total amount for other departments not included in the report.

Choose the **departments** you want to include.

Choose the **Amounts** or **Percentage** option.

Choose the **additional columns** you want and **click OK**.

Close the **display** when you have finished.

Departmental Balance Sheet and Trial Balance Reports

The Departmental Balance Sheet and Departmental Trial Balance are also available from the Departmental Reports menu option under Financials.

For both reports, select the departments to include in the report and choose whether you want to include amounts that are not assigned to a department. You can show amounts only or add the percentage of the total amount in your reports. In other respects, these reports are like the standard non-departmental reports.

Adding Departments to Other Reports

Many other reports allow departmental details to be added after you set up and use departments. **Journal reports** automatically include the department number with the account numbers if you have added that information to the journal transaction.

The **Balance Sheet**, **Income Statement**, **Trial Balance** and **General Ledger** all have a **Show Departments** check box added. Project reports also have this option.

Access the **report options** in the usual way from the Reports menu.

The Show Departments option is shown in the following Balance Sheet Options window:

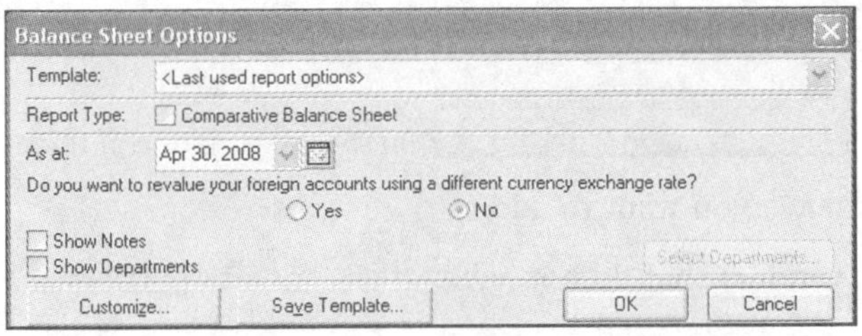

Click **Show Departments** to have the details added to the report.

Click the **Select Departments button** to open the department list:

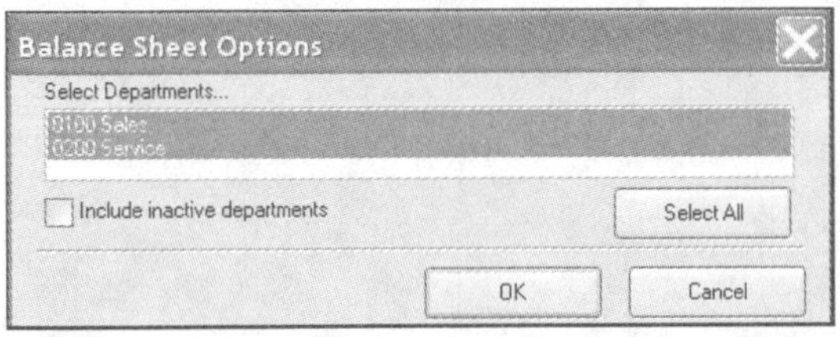

Select the **departments** you want to add to the report.

Click **OK** to return to the initial Balance Sheet Options window.

Choose other **report options** in the usual way and **click OK** to see the report.

Close the **display** when you have finished.

Department information can also be added to customer and vendor reports. The Vendor Aged and Aged Overdue reports and the Pending Purchase Order Report allow you to group the vendors by department for the report. The Customer Aged and Aged Overdue reports and the Pending Sales Order Report have the same option for grouping customers by department.

The following Vendor Aged Report Options screen shows this option:

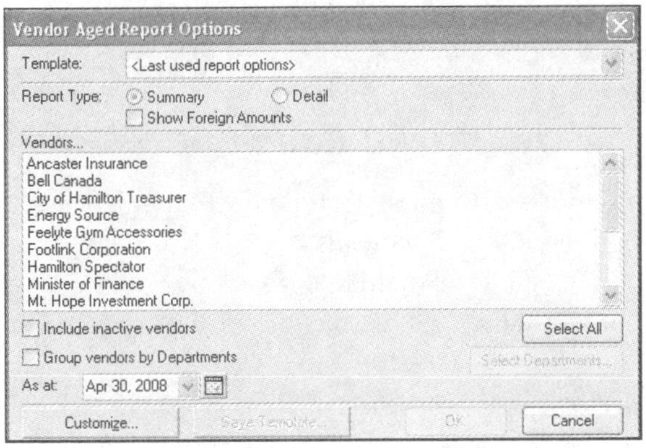

Click **Group Vendors By Departments** to select the option.

Click the **Select Departments button** to open the department list:

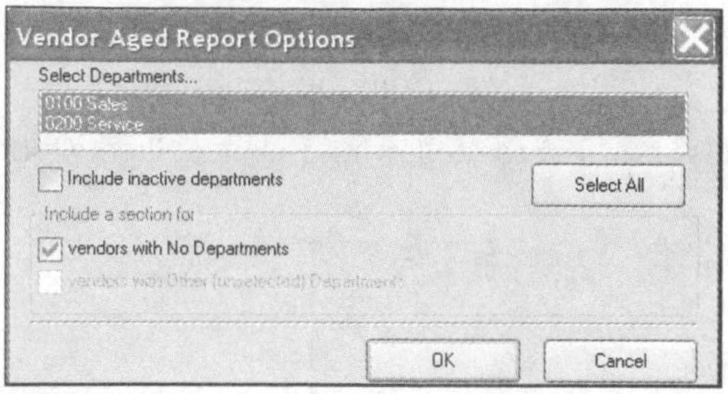

Select the **departments** you want to add to the report.

You can include or omit vendors that do not have an assigned department.

Click **OK** to return to the Vendor Aged Report Options screen.

Choose other **report options** in the usual way.

Click **OK** to see the report.

Close the **display** when you have finished.

Part 4
Appendices

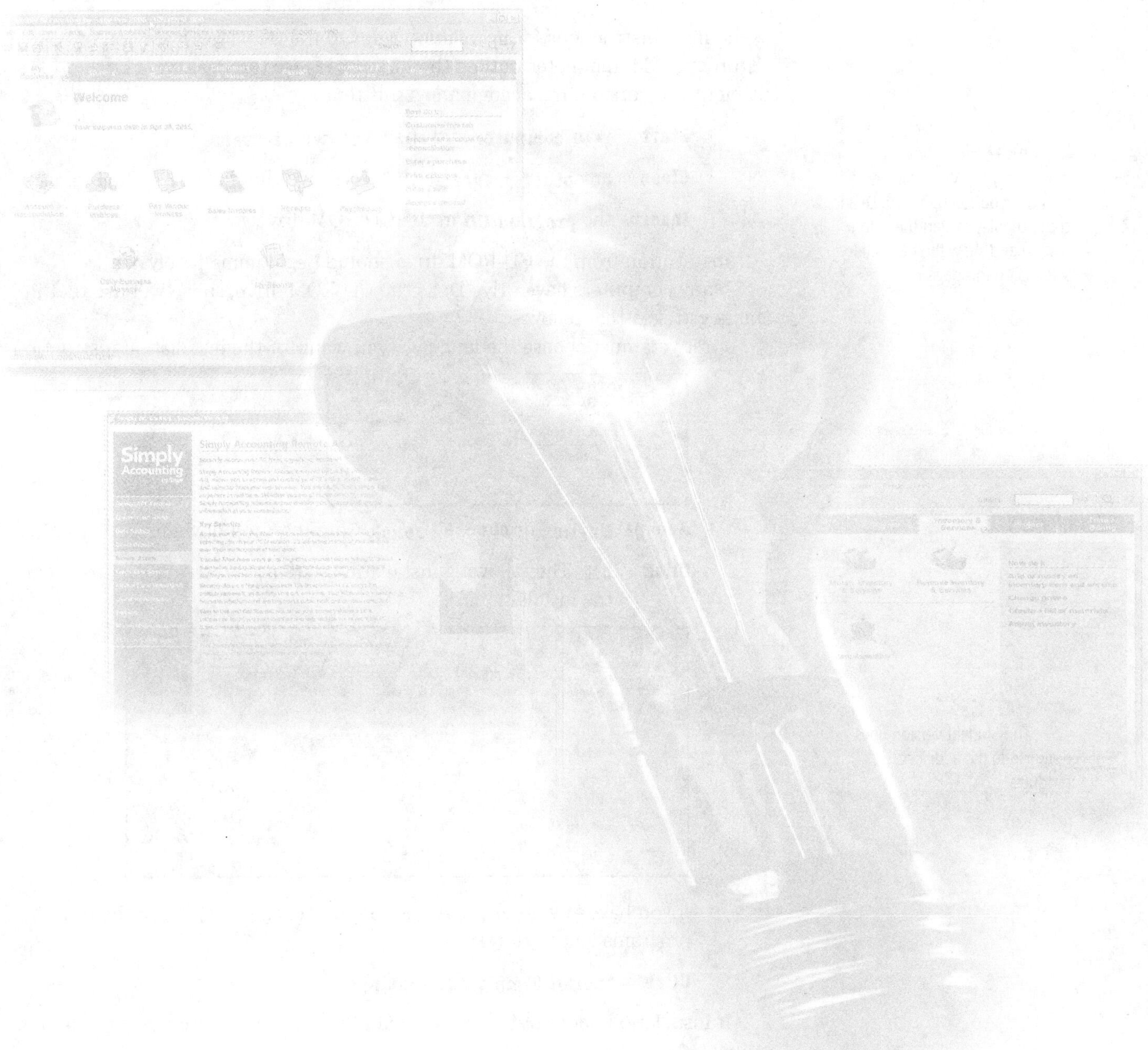

APPENDIX A

Installing Simply Accounting

The main instructions for installation refer to the regular Pro version of the program. Margin notes outline the differences for the Basic version and for the Student Pro version that accompanies this text.

Start your **computer** and the **Windows program**.

Close any **other programs** that you have running before beginning.

Insert the **program CD** in the CD-ROM drive.

> **NOTES**
> From the My Computer window, you can right-click D: and click Autoplay to start the autorun feature and show the Installation screens on this page.

Installation from the CD-ROM drive should begin immediately.

Many computers have drive D: as the CD-ROM drive, so we will use that in the keystrokes that follow.

First you must choose the language you want for the installation instructions:

Accept English or **choose French** from the drop-down list.

Click OK. The following installation options screen appears to begin the installation:

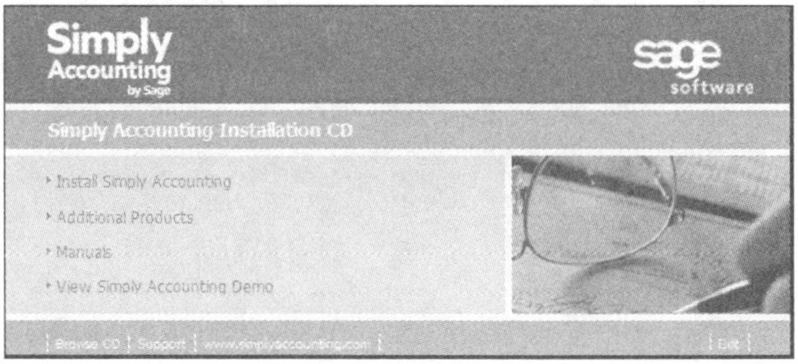

> **NOTES**
> The Student version does not include the additional products.

If you have any other programs running, click (Exit), close the other programs and start again.

Click Install Simply Accounting.

If installation does not begin immediately, follow the instructions in the box on page A-3.

IF INSTALLATION DOES NOT BEGIN IMMEDIATELY

You can install the program from the Windows opening screen or from the desktop. Many computers have drive D: as the CD-ROM drive, so we will use that drive in the keystrokes that follow.

Double click the **My Computer icon** 

. **Double click** the **Control Panel icon** 

or **name** 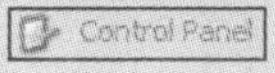

to see the components that are installed on your computer.

If you are using the icon view for the My Computer window, you will see the Control Panel icon. If you are viewing by list or by detail, you will see the name with a small icon.

Or, **click Start** on the task bar, **choose Settings** and **click Control Panel.**

Double click the **Add Or Remove Programs icon** 

.

Click the **Add New Programs icon** 

on the left side of the window.

The installation may begin immediately at this stage. If it does not,

Click the **CD Or Floppy button** to proceed. Insert the CD if you have not already done so.

Click Next to continue. Windows will search for the installation program.

Click Browse. The CD drive window should open with the Simply Accounting installation CD and the setup program shown. If it does not, locate the CD from the Browse window.

Double click the Simply folder to open it. The installation may begin at this stage. If not,

Click Setup (or **Setup.exe**).

Click Open to open the Run Installation Program window.

Click Finish to begin the installation.

Or, you can start from the Run menu. **Choose Start** and then **click Run. Type d:\Simply\setup** in the Open field and **click OK**. (For drive D:, substitute the drive letter for your CD-ROM drive.)

NOTES
The instructions in the shaded box beside this note will begin the installation of the Simply Accounting Program directly and bypass the CD Installation screens on the previous page.

Wait for the Setup Language selection screen to appear:

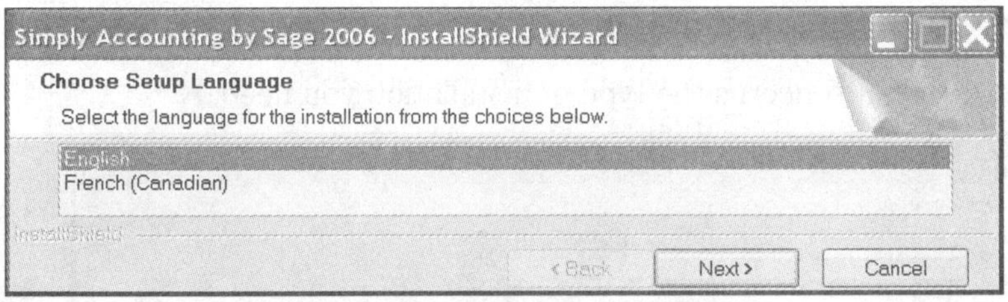

Click your **language preference** and **click Next**.

When the InstallShield setup window closes, the Welcome screen appears. You must enter the serial number exactly as it appears on the program package or CD case before you can continue.

The cursor is in the Serial Number field ready for you to enter the number:

NOTES
The serial number is printed on the Simply Accounting program CD package.

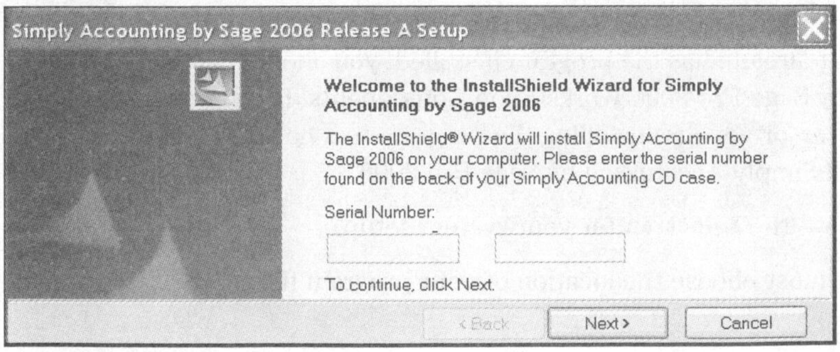

WARNING!
The serial number is case sensitive. You must type it exactly as it appears on the program case.

Type your **Serial Number** in the space provided.

Click **Next** to advance to the license agreement:

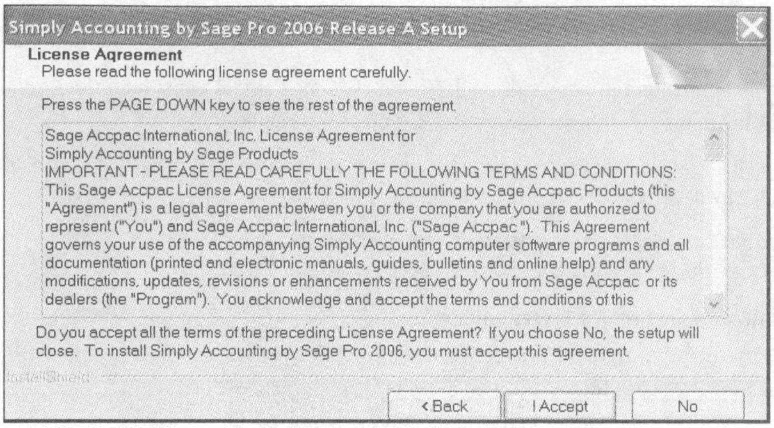
Simply Accounting by Sage Pro 2006 Release A Setup
License Agreement
Please read the following license agreement carefully.
Press the PAGE DOWN key to see the rest of the agreement.
Sage Accpac International, Inc. License Agreement for
Simply Accounting by Sage Products
IMPORTANT - PLEASE READ CAREFULLY THE FOLLOWING TERMS AND CONDITIONS:
This Sage Accpac License Agreement for Simply Accounting by Sage Accpac Products (this "Agreement") is a legal agreement between you or the company that you are authorized to represent ("You") and Sage Accpac International, Inc. ("Sage Accpac"). This Agreement governs your use of the accompanying Simply Accounting computer software programs and all documentation (printed and electronic manuals, guides, bulletins and online help) and any modifications, updates, revisions or enhancements received by You from Sage Accpac or its dealers (the "Program"). You acknowledge and accept the terms and conditions of this
Do you accept all the terms of the preceding License Agreement? If you choose No, the setup will close. To install Simply Accounting by Sage Pro 2006, you must accept this agreement.
InstallShield
< Back
I Accept
No

NOTES
In the Student version, you will not see this screen. You will enter the key code to register and activate the program later when you start the program.

Read the **agreement**, and if you accept the agreement, **click I Accept** to begin installing the program.

The next screen prompts you to enter your name and your company name:

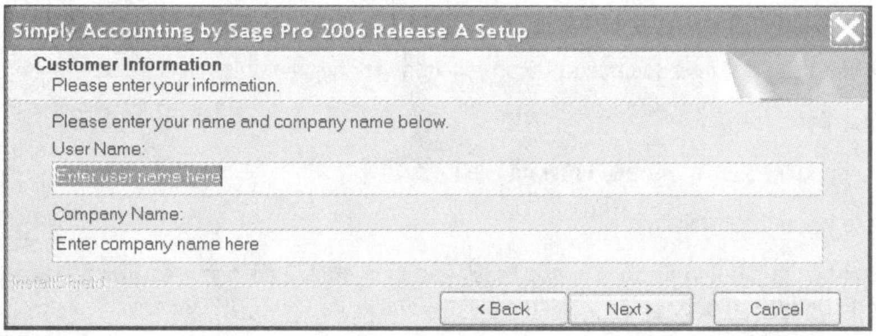
Simply Accounting by Sage Pro 2006 Release A Setup
Customer Information
Please enter your information.
Please enter your name and company name below.
User Name:
Enter user name here
Company Name:
Enter company name here
InstallShield
< Back
Next >
Cancel

Enter the **required information**. **Press** *tab* to advance to the next field.

Click **Next**.

Your next decision concerns the type of installation you need:

NOTES
You will not see this screen for Pro single-user versions or for the Student version.

BASIC VERSION
You will not see this screen when you install the Basic version because it applies to multi-user setups.

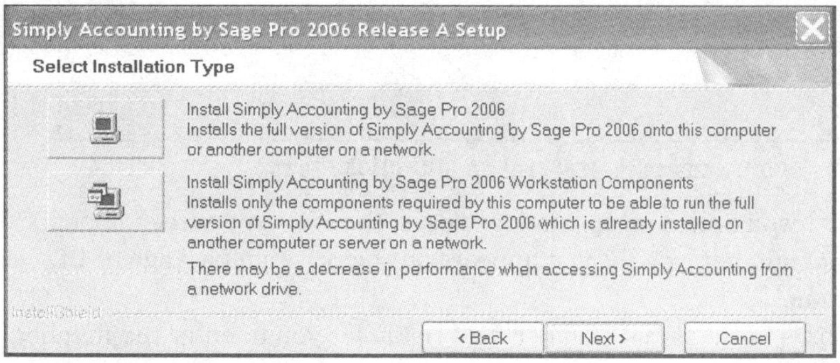
Simply Accounting by Sage Pro 2006 Release A Setup
Select Installation Type
Install Simply Accounting by Sage Pro 2006
Installs the full version of Simply Accounting by Sage Pro 2006 onto this computer or another computer on a network.
Install Simply Accounting by Sage Pro 2006 Workstation Components
Installs only the components required by this computer to be able to run the full version of Simply Accounting by Sage Pro 2006 which is already installed on another computer or server on a network.
There may be a decrease in performance when accessing Simply Accounting from a network drive.
InstallShield
< Back
Next >
Cancel

If you are working on a network and your computer is connected to a host computer that already has the program installed, you should choose Install Simply Accounting by Sage Pro 2006 Workstation Components. If you are working on a stand-alone computer, or you are installing the program to a network server, you would choose Install Simply Accounting by Sage Pro 2006.

Make the **selection** for your system setup.

Now you must choose the location of your program files:

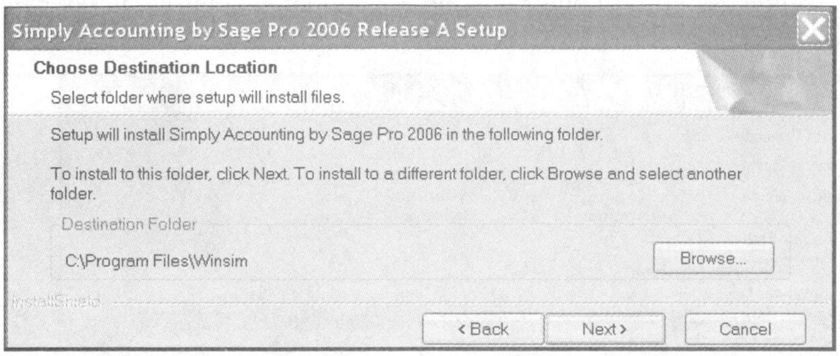

NOTES
If you want to keep earlier versions of the program that are already installed, you must change the default location and program name.

You can accept the default location, C:\Program Files\Winsim.

To choose another folder, click Browse and choose an existing folder from the pop-up window, or type an alternative location in the Browse window. Click OK.

Click **Next** to continue and select the program components to install:

NOTES
This screen is not shown for the Student version installation.

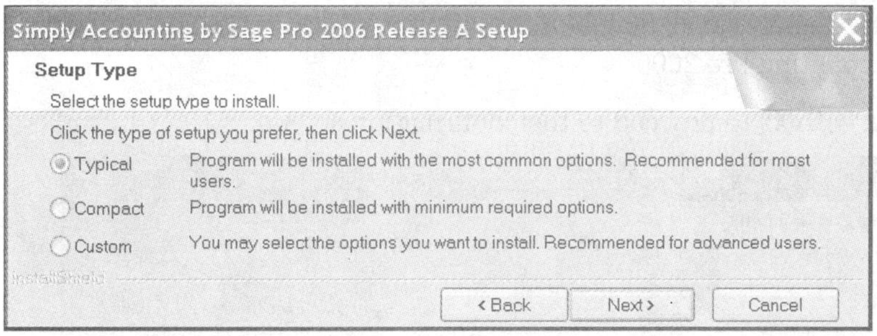

Accept the Typical installation option to include all the program elements.

Click **Next**.

If you are updating an earlier version of Simply Accounting, you may see a message advising you that the new program will overwrite any changes you have added to customize your program. If you choose No, you should copy your customized forms to another folder before continuing with the installation. Click Yes if you do not want to keep the modifications.

Simply Accounting Pro is now available for handheld computers so you must indicate whether you are using the program on a handheld computer:

***basic* BASIC VERSION**
The Basic version is not available for handheld computers.

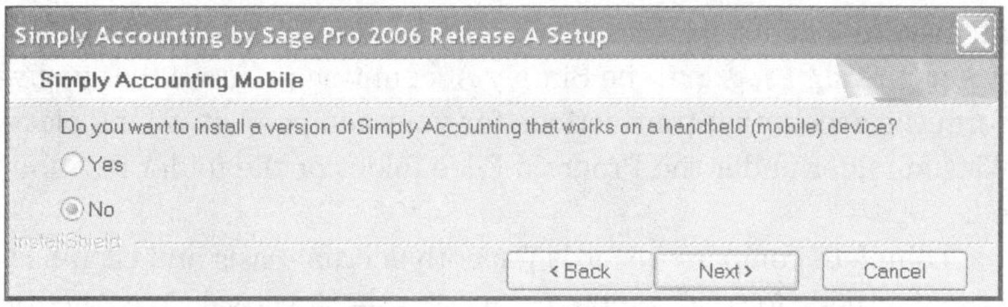

NOTES
The Student version cannot be used with handheld computers.

Make the **selection** for your system setup.

The next screen asks you to enter a name for Simply Accounting in your Programs folder:

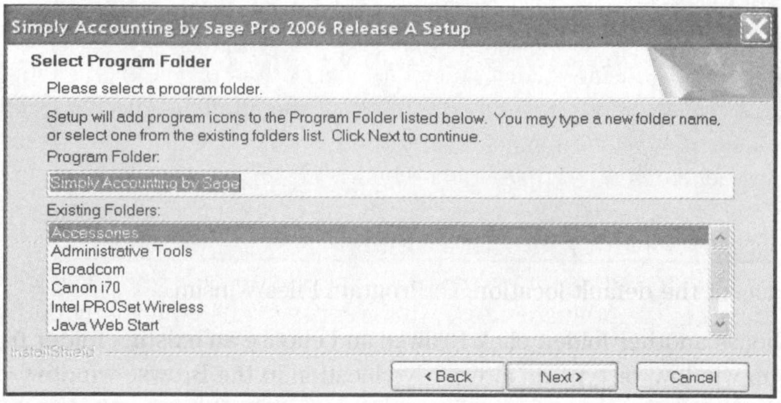

basic BASIC VERSION

The program folder name will be Simply Accounting by Sage.

The name you enter here will be the name that appears on the Programs list. You can accept the default name, Simply Accounting by Sage, or type a different name such as Simply Accounting Pro 2006.

Click **Next** to proceed to the confirmation screen:

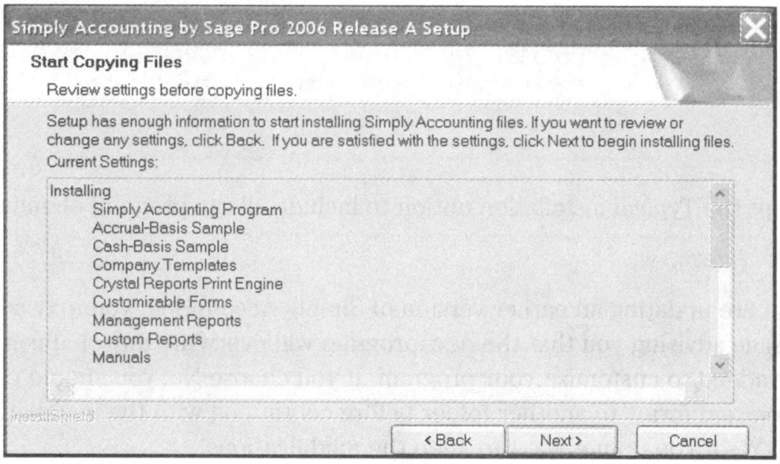

To omit any of these components, click Back to return to the previous screens and choose the Custom installation option.

By default, all components are selected for installation as follows:

- **Simply Accounting Program**: the Simply Accounting program that you will need to perform the accounting transactions for your company. It will be placed in the main Winsim folder under the Program Files folder or the folder location you selected.
- **Samples**: complete company records for both accrual-basis and cash-basis accounting methods for two sample companies — Universal Construction and Universal Crustacean Farm. They will be placed in the folder under Winsim called Samdata if you install them.
- **Templates**: predefined charts of accounts and settings for a large number of business types. These files will be stored in a folder under Winsim called Template. Two starter files with only charts of accounts also appear in this folder.
- **Crystal Reports Print Engine**, **Forms** and **Management Reports**: a variety of commonly used business forms and reports that you can customize to suit your own business needs and the program to access and print them. They will be placed in a folder under Winsim called Forms.

- **Customizable Forms and Custom Reports**: a variety of MS Office documents designed for integrated use with Simply Accounting. They are placed in a Reports folder under Winsim.
- **New Business Guide**: a number of checklists showing the steps to follow in setting up a new business, customized for a variety of business types in different provinces. These guides include addresses, phone numbers and Web addresses that you can contact for further information.
- **Manuals**: documentation that will help you learn the program.
- **Add-in for Microsoft Outlook**: a program link that connects your data with MS Outlook. This is a Pro feature not available in Basic.
- **Upgrade Utility**: a program to convert accounting records that were created using DOS versions of the program into a Windows version of Simply Accounting. Data files in older Windows versions of the program are updated automatically.

BASIC VERSION
basic You will not see the MS Outlook Add-in message in the Basic version.

Click **Next**.

Wait until the program prompts you with the Microsoft Outlook message:

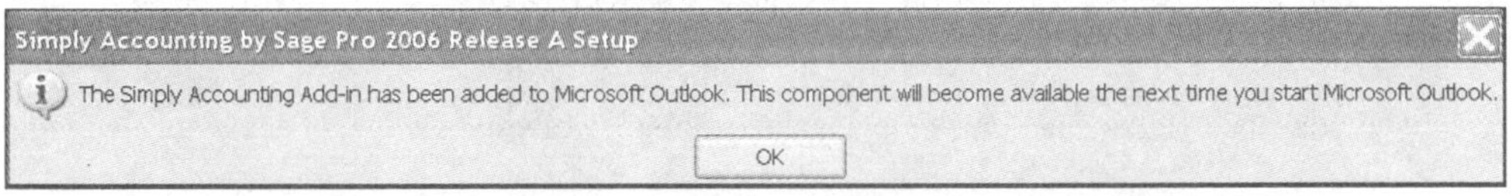

Simply Accounting will coordinate with your Microsoft Outlook program database.

Click **OK** to continue.

You can choose to place a shortcut on your desktop to open the program.

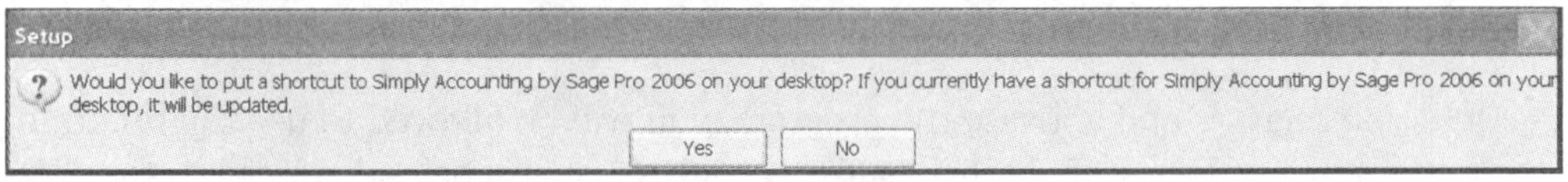

Click **Yes** when prompted to add the desktop shortcut.

The Install program creates the folders for all the components described above. There is an additional folder, **Winsim\Data**, that is empty initially. We will use this folder to store the data files for the applications in the workbook.

In addition, the installation procedure adds names in the Programs list for the Simply Accounting program, for Custom Reports, for the Upgrade program if it is installed and for the New Business Guide.

If you have previously installed versions of the software, you may be asked whether you want to replace individual program files. You can choose to replace them all or decide on an individual basis.

If shared programs that are part of the installation procedure are encountered, you may be asked whether you want to replace them or not. You should not replace individual programs that are more recent than the one you are installing.

The next option is to view the ReadMe file, or start the program or both:

We will start the program immediately so we can register and activate the program.

Click **Yes, I Want To Start Simply Accounting**.

Click **Finish** to complete the installation and open the ReadMe screen.

Registering and Activating Simply Accounting

NOTES
The Student version must also be registered and activated. Go to the Web site listed on the registration screen to get the key codes. You will not need a Payroll ID. The Web site for registering the Student version is different from the one for the standard program.

WARNING!
Wait for the Setup window to close after you close the ReadMe window. This may take a while.

Read the **information** about recent changes to the program that may not yet be documented elsewhere.

Close the **ReadMe screen** to see the Registration message:

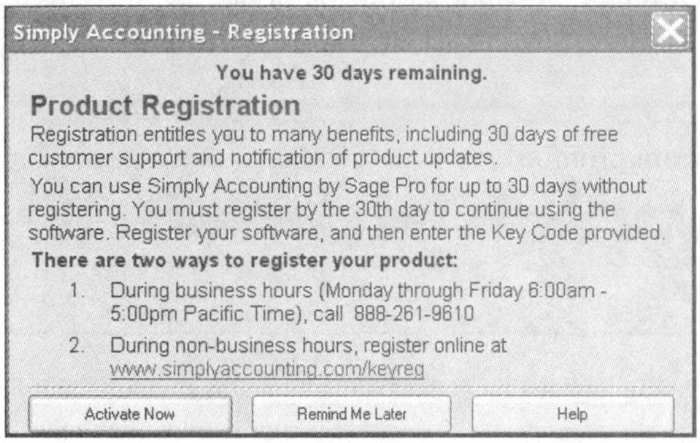

If you choose Remind Me Later, choose the Help menu and click Enter Key Code to see the screen shown above. This reminder message will also appear each time you start the program.

Until you register and activate the program, you will be allowed to use the program a limited number of times. If you have already registered and have the activation codes, skip the next step.

WARNING!
The Company Name must match the name you use to register the program with Sage.
Enter all numbers exactly as they are given to you, including spaces and punctuation. The Key Code is also case sensitive so be sure to type uppercase letters when required.

Have your product serial number ready for the registration. You can register online or by telephone. The telephone number is provided. To register online, start your Internet connection. Enter the Web address given on the registration information screen or double click the Web address on this screen. Follow the instructions provided. Print a copy of the codes screen for reference.

When you register, you will provide the Serial Number from the program package or CD and receive a Client ID number, a Key Code number and a payroll ID number. These numbers will be linked to the serial number you provided and cannot be used for a different copy of the program.

Click **Activate Now** to start the activation procedure:

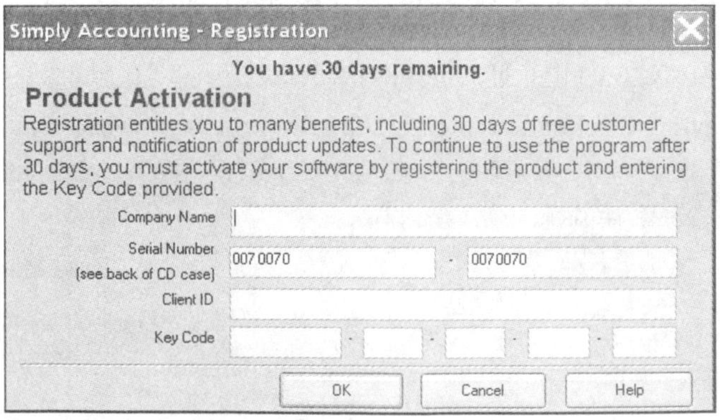

Enter your **Company Name** and the **Client ID** and **Key Code** provided by Sage Software for the program you have registered.

Enter all numbers exactly as they are given to you, including spaces and punctuation. The Key Code is also case sensitive so be sure to type uppercase letters when required.

If you make a mistake, the program will warn you and you can re-enter the information.

Click **OK** to continue to Simply Accounting's Welcome screen:

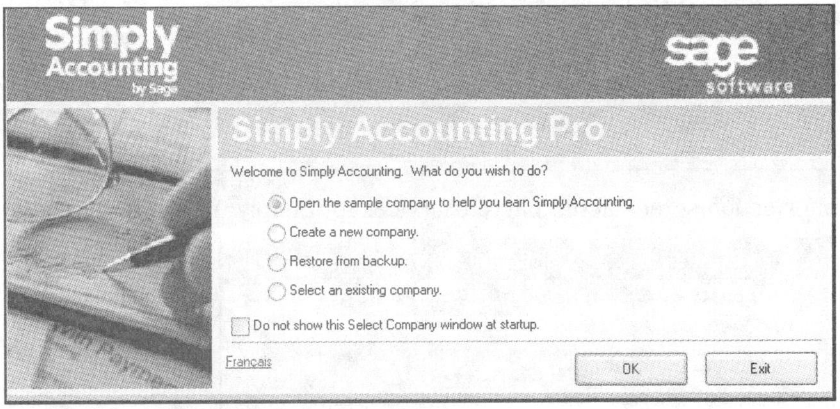

Click **Open Sample Company**.

You can choose accrual- or cash-basis accounting for the sample data set.

Click **Accrual-Basis** to continue to the Session Date window:

Click **OK** to accept the default session date.

Now you may see a message about automatic program updates:

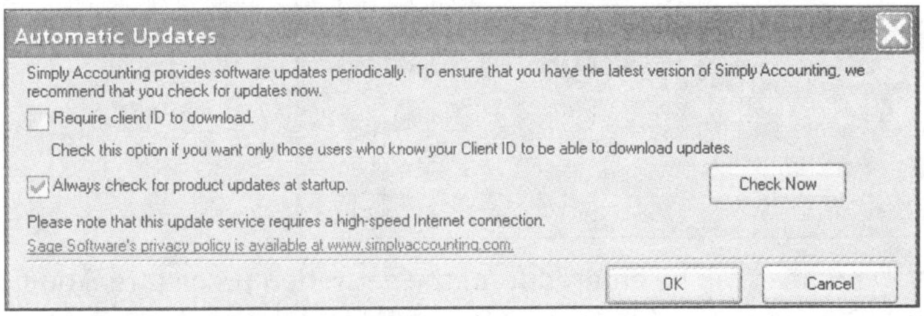

You can also download updates automatically or periodically when needed. If you are working with the data files in this text, you should not update the program beyond the version we use, which is Release B. Therefore, you should turn off the automatic update option.

Click **Always Check For Product Updates At Startup** to remove the ✓ and turn off the automatic update option.

Click **OK** to open the sample company data file at Daily Business Manager.

Close the **Daily Business Manager window** to access the Home window.

STUDENT VERSION

In the Student version, you will not see the message about updates. The first time you use the program, you will receive a message about the limits of the Student version. You will be able to use the program 300 times and access any single company data file 50 times.

NOTES

If you have not activated the program yet, you can activate the program from the Help menu. Choose Enter Key Code from the Help menu to open the You Have XX Days Remaining screen shown on page A-8.

WARNING!

If you download program updates, you may download a later version than the one we use and your payroll amounts may be different from the ones we show. If you are installing Release A, you should use the Update program provided on the Student CD-ROM to update your program to Release B to match the version we use.

Unlocking the Payroll Features

We will unlock and activate the payroll module before proceeding. You will not need to unlock payroll in the Student version of the program.

Choose the **Help menu** and **click Unlock Auto Payroll** as shown:

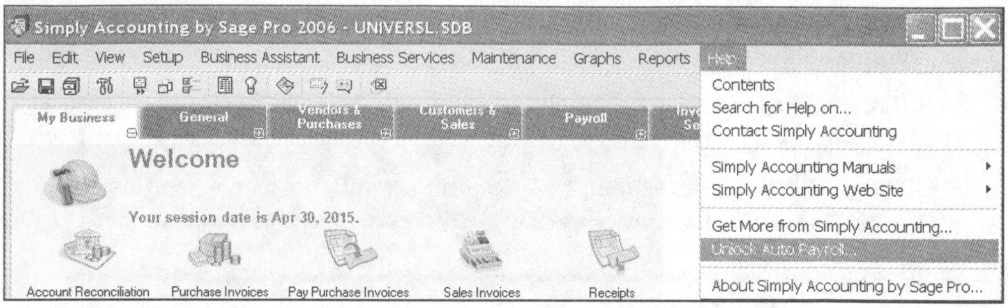

An information screen about payroll services for Simply Accounting opens:

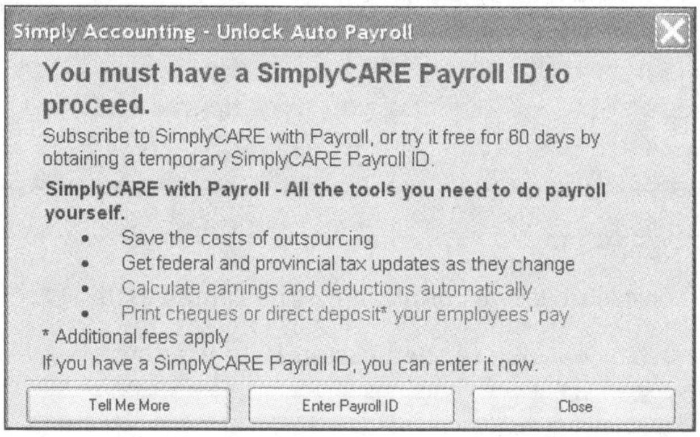

This screen advises you that you need a Payroll ID and subscription to the Simply Accounting Payroll Plan — a fee-based service — to use the payroll features in the program. To learn more about the payroll plan or to subscribe, click Tell Me More.

Click **Enter Payroll ID**:

WARNING! The Payroll ID number is also case sensitive, so be careful to use uppercase letters when required.

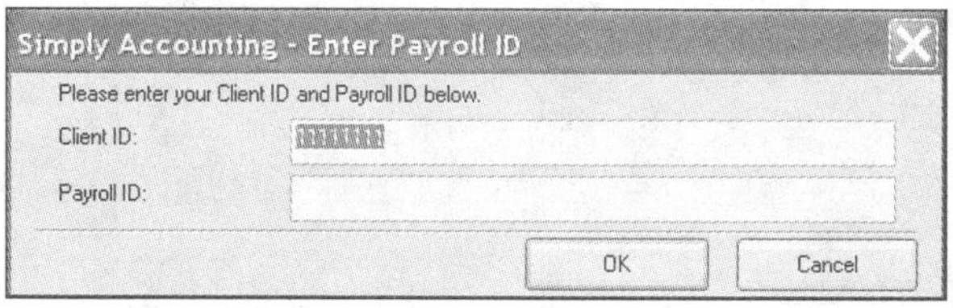

Your client ID number will be entered from the activation procedure. You must enter the Payroll ID number provided when you registered the program.

Click the **Payroll ID field** and type the number provided, exactly as it is given to you.

If the activation is successful, you will see the following message

WARNING! Do not remove the program CD before clicking Exit on the opening Simply Accounting Installation screen (see the illustration on page A-2).

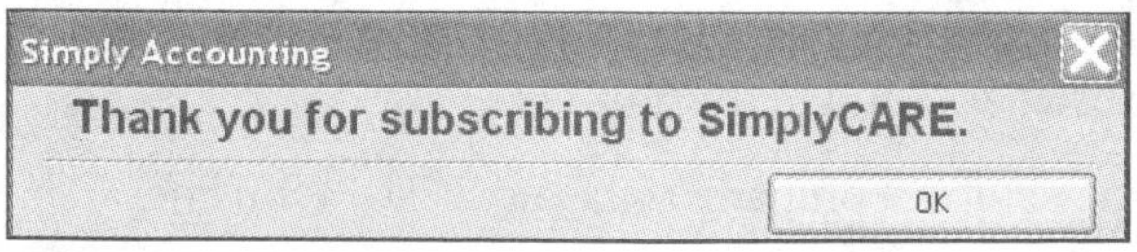

Click **OK** to continue.

You can now use all features of the program.

Click [X] to close the Simply Accounting Home window.

You will see the option to make a backup copy of the data file:

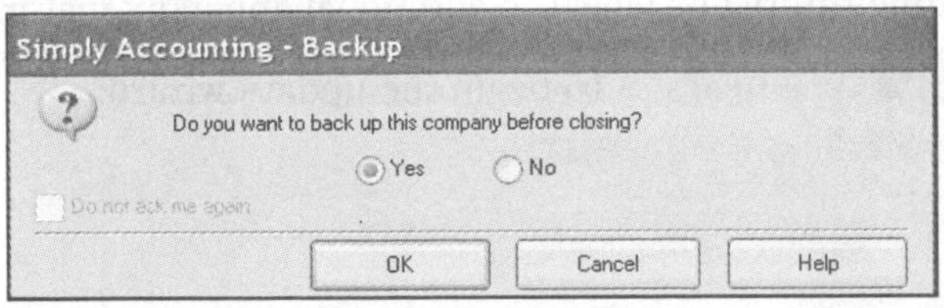

Normally you would choose to back up the data but you do not need to make a copy of the sample file.

Click **No**.

Click **Exit** to close the Simply Accounting installation screen unless you want to install other programs or documents.

Click ☒ to close the Control Panel window if it is open.

Updating Simply Accounting to Release B

WARNING!
If you download the upgrade from the Web site later, you may upgrade to a later release and the payroll tax tables will no longer match the ones used to create the data files for the text.

The Student version of Simply Accounting included with the text is a Release A version. Before using the data files on the Student CD-ROM, you must upgrade this program to Release B. You will be unable to access the files with Release A. When you are accessing a file that has been converted to a later version or release of the program, or has been converted to the Premium version, you will see the following message:

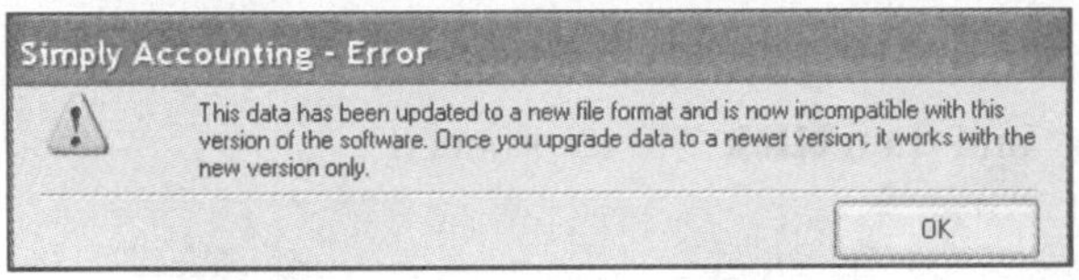

Click **OK**.

Sage Software Company has given us permission to include the update program on the Student CD-ROM so that you can upgrade to the version we use for the text. The update program will locate the Simply Accounting program you installed and run the update installation wizard. This single program will update either the Basic or the Pro versions of the program.

Insert the **Student CD-ROM** into your Disk Drive:

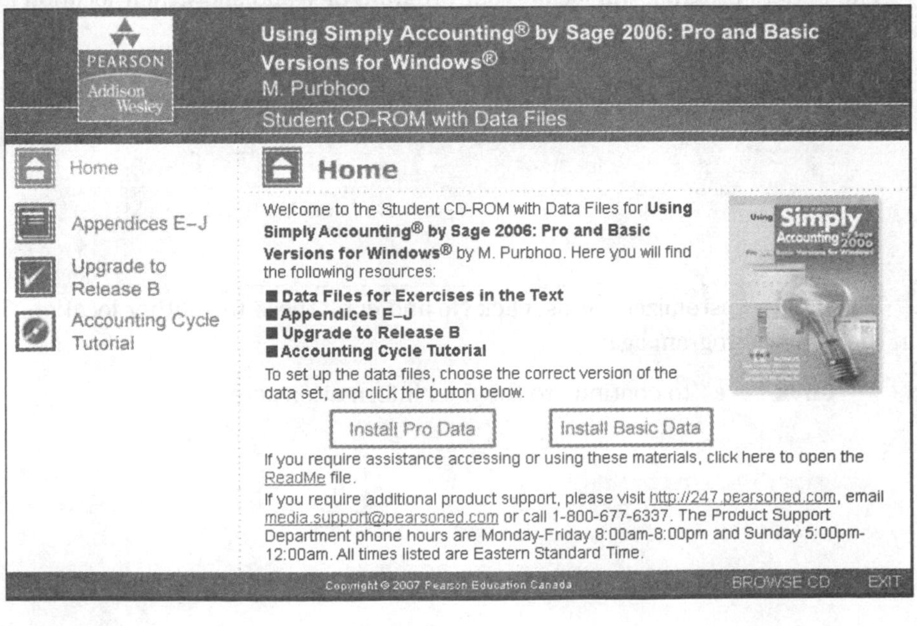

You should see the CD Home window with the options to install data files, update your program, run the accounting tutorial or view the additional appendix material.

Click **Update Program To Release B** to begin the update wizard:

Click **Next** to open the License Agreement screen:

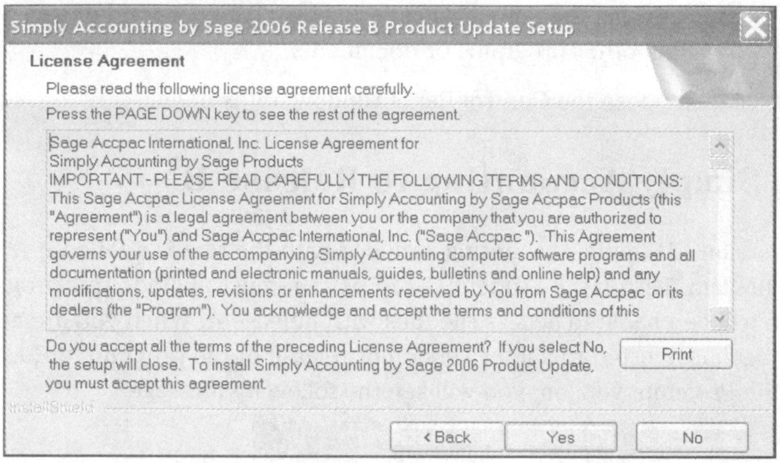

Read the **agreement** and then **click Yes** to proceed:

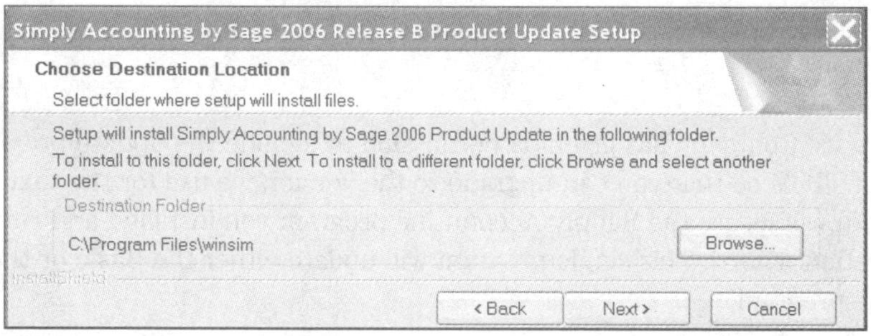

The update program will locate your program files and show their location as the destination for the update.

Click **Next** to see the warning about overwriting existing files:

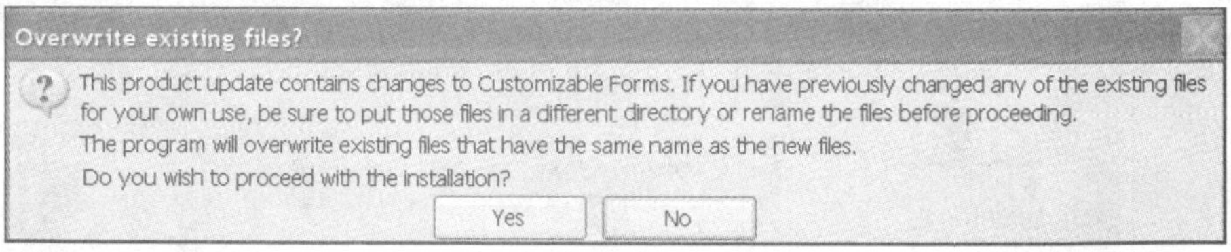

Overwrite existing files?
This product update contains changes to Customizable Forms. If you have previously changed any of the existing files for your own use, be sure to put those files in a different directory or rename the files before proceeding.
The program will overwrite existing files that have the same name as the new files.
Do you wish to proceed with the installation?
Yes
No

If you have customized forms, click No and copy these to another location. Then run the update program again.

Click **Yes** to continue to the final information screen:

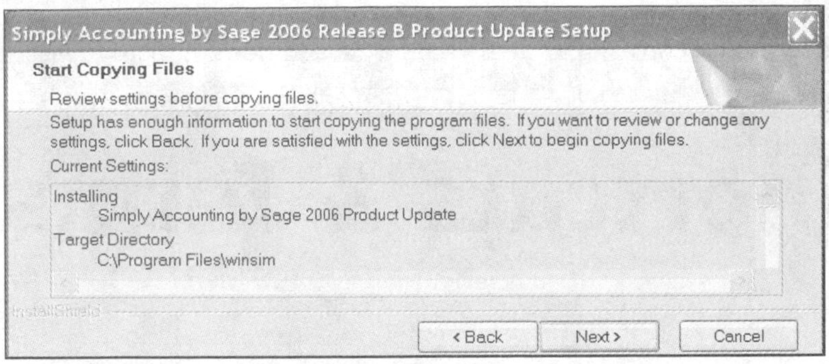

Click **Next** to continue, unless you still need to back up customized forms.

The program update will begin. When it has finished, you will see the confirmation:

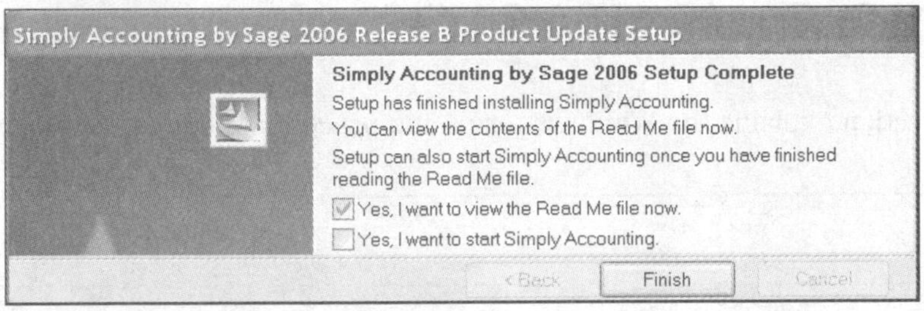

At this stage, you can start the Simply Accounting program, view the ReadMe files or exit.

Click **Finish** to open the ReadMe file.

Close the **ReadMe file** after reading the information.

Your program is now ready to use with the data files for this text.

APPENDIX B

Windows Basics, Shortcuts & Terms

WINDOWS BASICS

This section explains the Windows terms and procedures commonly used in the text.

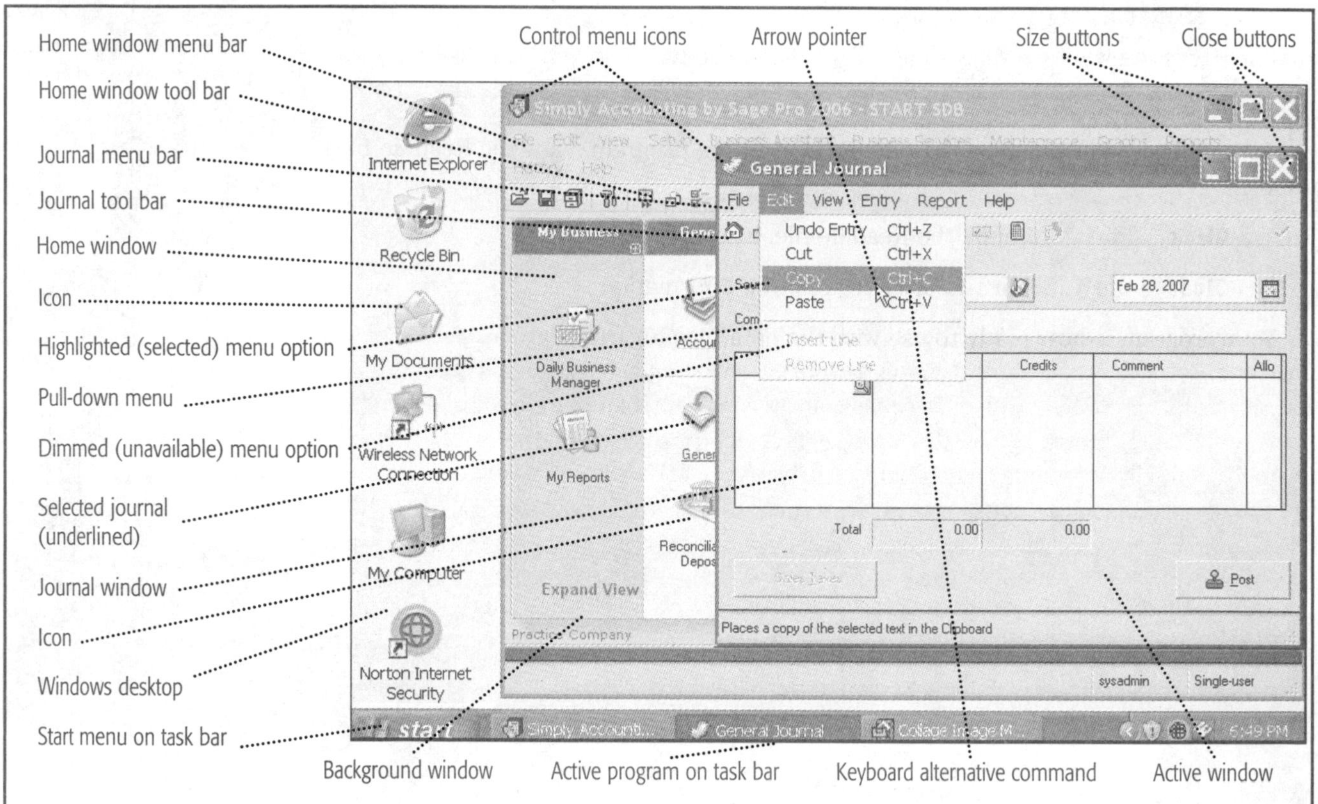

In the illustration above, the Simply Accounting program is open on the Windows XP desktop. The General Journal is open and active with the Home window in the background. The Journal's Edit menu is pulled down and Copy is selected.

The **mouse** is used to move the cursor. When you move the mouse, an **arrow** or **pointer** moves to indicate the cursor placement. If you **click** (press) the left mouse button, the cursor will move to the location of the arrow (if this is a legitimate place for the cursor to be at the time). That is, you use the mouse to **click** (point to and click) a screen location, item on a list, command or icon.

The arrow or pointer changes shape depending on what actions you may perform. When you are moving the mouse, it appears as an arrow or hand pointer.

When you are in a field that can accept text, it appears as a long **I-shaped bar**. Clicking will change it to an insertion point — a flashing vertical line in a text field. When the computer is processing information and you are unable to perform any action, you will see an **hourglass**. This is your signal to wait.

Dragging refers to the method of moving the mouse while holding the left button down. As you drag through the options in a menu, each one will be successively highlighted or darkened. Dragging through text will highlight it. Point to the beginning of the text to be highlighted. Then click and hold the mouse button down while moving through the entire area that you want to highlight. Release the mouse button at the end of the area you want to highlight. You can highlight a single character or the entire contents of a field. The text will remain highlighted and can be edited by typing new text. Delete text by pressing the Backspace key or del. Clicking a different location will remove the highlighting.

To **double click** means to press the left mouse button twice quickly. This action can be used as a shortcut for opening and closing windows. Double clicking an icon or file name will open it. Double clicking the Control icon will close the window. The Simply Accounting files are set up to open journals and windows with a single click instead of a double click.

The **active window** is the one that you are currently working in. If you click an area outside the active window that is part of a background window, that window will move to the foreground. To return to a previous window, click any part of it that is showing. If the window you need is completely hidden, you can restore it by clicking its button on the task bar. Click to reduce an active window to a task bar button.

An **icon** is a picture form of your program, file name or item. **Buttons** are icons or commands surrounded by a box frame. In Simply Accounting, clicking the Home window tool button will bring the Home window to the front and make it active.

The **menu bar** is the line of options at the top of each window. Each menu contains one or more commands or selections (the **pull-down menu**) and can be accessed by clicking the menu name. Each window has different menu selections, and the options in the pull-down menu may differ. To choose an option from the menu, click the menu name and then click the option you want in order to **select** (**highlight**) it. If an option is dimmed, you will be unable to highlight or select it.

Some menus are **cascading menus**. When the menu option you want has an arrow, ▸, it has a second level of menu choices. To select from a cascading menu, click the menu bar name and point to the first-level menu option. When the next level of the menu appears, click the selection that you need.

You can **select multiple items** from a screen or list. Click the first item to select it. Then press and hold ctrl while you click each of the other items you want to select. The items previously selected will remain selected. If the items are in a list and you want to select several items in a row, click the first item and then press and hold shift while clicking the last item that you want to include. All the items between the two will also be selected. To change your selection, click somewhere else.

The **Control Menu icon** is situated in the upper left-hand corner of each window. The icon looks different for different programs and windows. It has its own pull-down menu, including the Close and Size commands. To close windows, you can double click this icon, choose Close from its pull-down menu or click the **Close button** in the upper right-hand corner of the window.

Size buttons are located in the upper right-hand corner of the window. Use them to make a window larger (**Maximize** to full screen size) or to reduce the window to a task bar button (**Minimize**). If the window is full screen size or smaller than usual, restore it to its normal size with the (**Restore**) button.

You can also change the size of a window by dragging. Point to a side. When the pointer changes to a two-sided arrow, drag the window frame to its new size.

NOTES

Often a program will include dialogue boxes that look like windows but do not have menu bars. Usually they require you to make a choice, such as answering a question, before you can proceed. You cannot make a dialogue box into a background window; you must click one of the options such as Yes, No, OK, Proceed, Cancel and so on to continue. Closing the dialogue box without making a choice is like choosing Cancel.

When a window contains more information than can fit on the screen at one time, the window will contain **scroll arrows** (▼, ▶, ▲, or ◀) in any corner or direction next to the hidden information (bottom or right sides of the window). Click the arrow and hold the mouse button down to scroll the screen in the direction of the arrow you are on.

Input fields containing data may have a **drop-down** or **pop-up list** from which to select. A **list arrow** beside the field ▼ indicates that a list is available. When you click the arrow, the list appears. Click an item on the list to add it to the input field directly.

SHORTCUTS

Using the Keyboard Instead of a Mouse

All Windows software applications are designed to be used with a mouse. However, there may be times when you prefer to use keyboard commands to work with a program because it is faster. There are also times when you need to know the alternatives to using a mouse, as when the mouse itself is inoperative. It is not necessary to memorize all the keyboard commands. A few basic principles will help you to understand how they work, and over time you will use the ones that help you to work most efficiently. Some commands are common to more than one Windows software program. For example, ctrl + C (press and hold the Control key while you press C) is commonly used as the copy command and ctrl + V as the paste command. Any selected text or image will be copied or pasted when you use these commands.

The menu bar and the menu choices can be accessed by pressing alt. The first menu bar item will be highlighted. Use arrow keys, ↑ and ↓, to move up and down through the pull-down menu choices of a highlighted menu item or ← and → to go back and forth to other menu items. Some menu choices have direct keyboard alternatives or shortcuts. If the menu item has an underlined letter, pressing alt together with the underlined letter will access that option directly. For example, alt + F (press alt, and while holding down alt, press F) accesses the File pull-down menu. Then pressing O (the underlined letter for Open) will give you the dialogue box for opening a new file. Some tool buttons in Simply Accounting have a direct keyboard command, and some menu choices also have a shortcut keyboard command. When available, these direct keystrokes are given with the button name or to the right of a menu choice. For example, alt + f4 is the shortcut for closing the active window or exiting from the Simply Accounting program when the Home window is the active window.

To cancel the menu display, press esc.

In the Simply Accounting Home window, you can use the arrow keys to move among the ledger and journal icons. Press alt, alt and → to highlight the first icon (either the Daily Business Manager or the Accounts icon), and then use the arrow keys to change selections. Each icon is highlighted or selected as you reach it and deselected as you move to another icon.

To choose or open a highlighted or selected item, press enter.

When input fields are displayed in a Simply Accounting window, you can move to the next field by pressing tab or to a previous field by pressing shift and tab together. The tab key is used frequently in this workbook as a quick way to accept input, advance the cursor to the next field and highlight field contents to prepare for immediate editing. Using the mouse while you input information requires you to remove your hands from the keyboard, while the tab key does not.

A summary of keyboard shortcuts used in Simply Accounting follows:

SUMMARY OF KEYBOARD SHORTCUTS

Shortcut	Resulting Action
ctrl + A	Adjust, begin the Adjust a Posted Entry function.
ctrl + B	Bring the Home window to the front.
ctrl + C	Copy the selected text.
ctrl + E	Look up the Previously Posted Invoice (from a journal lookup window).
ctrl + F	Search, begin the search function.
ctrl + J	Display the journal entry report.
ctrl + K	Track shipment from a previously posted invoice lookup screen.
ctrl + L	Look up a previously posted transaction from the lookup window.
ctrl + N	Look up the next posted Invoice (from a journal lookup window).
ctrl + N	Open a new record window (from a ledger icon or ledger record window).
ctrl + P	Print, open the print dialogue box.
ctrl + R	Recall a stored journal entry (from a journal window when an entry is stored).
ctrl + R	Remove the account record, or remove the quote or order (from ledger, quote or order window).
ctrl + S	Access the Save As function from the Home window (Home window, File menu) to save the data file under a new name. Keep the new file open.
ctrl + S	Save changes to a record; keep the ledger window open (from any ledger window).
ctrl + T	Store the current journal entry (open the Store dialogue box).
ctrl + V	Paste the selected text at the cursor position.
ctrl + X	Cut (delete) the selected text.
ctrl + Z	Undo the most recent change.
alt + C	Create another record; saves the record you are creating and opens a new record form to create another new record.
alt + N	Save and close; save the new record and close the ledger.
alt + P	Post the journal entry or record the order or quote.
alt + f4	Close the active window (if it has a close button). Closes the program if the Home window is active.
alt + the underlined character on a button	Select the button's action. An alternative to clicking the button and pressing enter.
alt	Access the first item on the menu bar.
alt + alt	Select the first icon in the Home window.
tab	Advance the cursor to the next field.
shift + tab	Move the cursor to the previous field.
Click	Move the cursor or select an item or entry.
shift + Click	Select all the items between the first item clicked and the last one.
ctrl + Click	Select this item in addition to ones previously selected.
enter	Choose the selected item or action.
Double click	Select an entire word or field contents. In fields with lists, open the selection list.
→	Move right to the next icon to select it or to the the next character in text.
←	Move left to the next icon to select it or to the the next character in text.
↓	Move down to the next icon or entry in a list to select it.
↑	Move up to the previous icon or entry in a list to select it.

ACCOUNTING VS. NON-ACCOUNTING TERMS

We have used accounting terms in this workbook because they are familiar to students of accounting, and because we needed to provide a consistent language for the book. The most frequently used non-accounting terms are included here for reference and comparison, in case you want to leave the non-accounting terms selected (Home window, Setup menu, User Preferences and Options tab screen).

SUMMARY OF EQUIVALENT TERMS

MAJOR TERMS	ACCOUNTING TERMS	NON-ACCOUNTING TERMS
	General Journal	Miscellaneous Transactions
	Journal Entries	Transaction Details
	Payables	Vendors & Purchases
	Receivables	Customers & Sales
	Post	Process

DETAILED LIST: LOCATION	ACCOUNTING TERMS	NON-ACCOUNTING TERMS
Home window icon	General (Journal)	Miscellaneous Transactions
Setup menu, System Settings – Settings screen	Payables	Vendors & Purchases
	Receivables	Customers & Sales
Setup menu, System Settings – Linked Accounts, tab headings	Payables	Vendors & Purchases
	Receivables	Customers & Sales
Setup menu, User Preferences, View tab – Modules	Payables	Vendors & Purchases
	Receivables	Customers & Sales
Graphs menu	Payables	Unpaid Purchases
	Receivables	Unpaid Sales
Reports menu – Financials	General Ledger	Transactions by Account
Reports menu	Payables	Vendors & Purchases
	Receivables	Customers & Sales
Reports menu	Journal Entries – General	Transaction Details – Miscellaneous
Reports menu – Management Reports	Payables	Vendors & Purchases
	Receivables	Customers & Sales
All Icon window menus	Type	Transactions
Accounts window – menu	Type – General	Transactions – Miscellaneous Transactions
Accounts ledger window	General Ledger	Chart of Accounts Records
Vendors ledger window	Payables Ledger	Vendor Records
Customers ledger window	Receivables Ledger	Customer Records
All journals (button and menu)	Post	Process

APPENDIX C

Correcting Errors after Posting

We all make mistakes. This appendix outlines briefly the procedures you need to follow for those rare occasions when you have posted a journal entry incorrectly and you cannot use the Adjust Journal Entry feature.

Obviously, you should try to detect errors before posting. Reviewing the journal entry should become routine practice. The software has built in a number of safeguards that help you avoid mistakes. For example, outstanding invoices cannot be overpaid and employee wages and payroll deductions are calculated automatically. Furthermore, names of accounts, customers, vendors, employees and inventory items appear in full, so that you may check your journal information easily.

Before making a reversing entry, consider the consequences of not correcting the error. For example, misspelled customer names may not be desirable, but they will not influence the financial statements. After making the correction in the ledger, the newly printed statement will be correct (the journal will retain the original spelling). Sometimes, however, the mistake is more serious. Financial statements will be incorrect if amounts or accounts are wrong. Payroll tax deductions will be incorrect if the wage amount is incorrect. GST and PST remittances may be incorrect as a result of incorrect tax codes or sales or purchase amounts. Discounts will be incorrectly calculated if an invoice or payment date is incorrect. Some errors also originate from outside sources. For example, purchase items may be incorrectly priced by the vendor.

For audit purposes, prepare a memo explaining the error and the correction procedure. A complete reversing entry is often the simplest way to make the corrections for a straightforward audit trail. With Simply Accounting's recall and lookup features, a reversing entry is made easier because you can see an exact copy of the original incorrect entry. With invoice lookup turned on, you can automatically reverse and correct Sales and Purchases journal entries by adjusting the original entry. Choose Adjust Invoice from the pull-down menu under Sale or Purchase, or click the Adjust Invoice tool in the journal (pages 185 and 138, respectively). General Journal and Payroll entries can be reversed and corrected in the journal by choosing Adjust Entry or Cheque menu item, or by clicking the appropriate Adjust tool (pages 43 and 368, respectively). Payments and receipts can be similarly adjusted by choosing the Adjust A Payment or Adjust A Receipt tool, or by choosing Adjust from the Payment or Receipt menu (see pages 145 and 183). Under all circumstances, Generally Accepted Accounting Principles should be followed.

Reversing entries in all journals have several common elements. In each case, you should use an appropriate source number that identifies the entry as reversing (e.g., add ADJ or REV to the original source number). You should use the original posting date and add a comment. Make the reversing entry as illustrated on the following pages. Display the journal entry, review it carefully and, when you are certain it is correct, post it. Next, you must enter the correct version of the transaction as a new journal entry with an appropriate identifying source number (e.g., add COR to the original source number).

You cannot adjust a posted invoice if you selected the wrong customer, vendor or employee. In these cases, you must complete a reversing entry.

Reversing entries are presented for each journal. Only the transaction portion of each screen is shown because the remaining parts of the journal screen do not change. The original and the reversing entry screens and most of the corresponding journal displays are included. Explanatory notes appear beside each set of entries.

GENERAL JOURNAL

Use the same accounts and amounts in the reversing entry as in the original entry.

Accounts that were debited should be credited and accounts that were credited originally should be debited.

Click the Sales Taxes button if you used this screen. Choose the tax code and, if necessary, enter the Amount Subject To Tax with a minus sign.

Repeat the allocation using the original percentages.

The General Journal display is not shown because it basically looks the same as the journal input form.

You can use the Adjust Entry feature instead. See page 43.

GENERAL JOURNAL: Original Entry

Account	Debits	Credits	Comment	Allo
1240 A/R - Stoney Plain Plaza	1,605.00	--	Marble work: terms: net 30	
4150 Revenue from Repairs	--	1,500.00	Repair marble fountain	
2650 GST Charged on Sales	--	105.00	GST collected @ 7%	
Total	1,605.00	1,605.00		

Reversing Entry

Account	Debits	Credits	Comment	Allo
4150 Revenue from Repairs	1,500.00	--	reversing Repair revenue entr	
2650 GST Charged on Sales	105.00	--	reversing GST collected	
1240 A/R - Stoney Plain Plaza	--	1,605.00	reversing Marble work: terms:	
Total	1,605.00	1,605.00		

PURCHASES JOURNAL

The only change you must make is that positive amounts in the original entry become negative amounts in the reversing entry (place a minus sign before the amount in the Amount field).

Similarly, negative amounts, such as for GST Paid in GST remittances, must be changed to positive amounts (remove the minus sign).

If freight was charged, enter the amount of freight with a minus sign.

Use the same accounts and amounts in the reversing entry as in the original entry. Tax amounts change automatically.

Repeat the allocation with the original percentages.

If you have invoice lookup turned on, you can use the Adjust Invoice option instead (page 138).

Remember to "pay" the incorrect and reversing invoices to remove them from the Payments Journal and later clear them.

PURCHASES JOURNAL (NON-INVENTORY): Original Entry

Item	Quantity	Order	B/O	Unit	Description	Price	Tax	GST	PST	Amount	Acct	Allo
					printing promotional material		GI	42.00	48.00	600.00	511(	✓

☑ Invoice Received

Freight

Terms: % Days, Net 20 Days

GST 42.00

PST 48.00

Total 690.00

12/28/08 (J72)		Debits	Credits	Division
2670	GST Paid on Purchases	42.00	-	
5110	Tool Rentals	648.00	-	
	- Sales Division			388.80
	- Service Division			259.20
2200	Accounts Payable	-	690.00	
		690.00	690.00	

Reversing Entry

Item	Quantity	Order	B/O	Unit	Description	Price	Tax	GST	PST	Amount	Acct	Allo
					printing promotional material		GP	-42.00	-48.00	-600.00	5110	✓

☑ Invoice Received Freight

Terms: % Days, Net 20 Days

GST -42.00
PST -48.00
Total -690.00

12/28/08 (J73)	Debits	Credits	Division
2200 Accounts Payable	690.00	-	
2670 GST Paid on Purchases	-	42.00	
5110 Tool Rentals	-	648.00	
- Sales Division			-388.80
- Service Division			-259.20
	690.00	690.00	

PAYMENTS JOURNAL – OTHER PAYMENTS: Original Entry

Acct	Description	Amount	Tax	GST	PST	Allo
5150 Telephone Expense	telephone service	180.00	GP	12.60	14.40	✓

Tax 27.00
Total 207.00

12/28/08 (J74)	Debits	Credits	Division
2670 GST Paid on Purchases	12.60	-	
5150 Telephone Expense	194.40	-	
- Service Division			155.52
- Sales Division			38.88
1050 Bank: Chequing CAD	-	207.00	
	207.00	207.00	

Reversing Entry

Acct	Description	Amount	Tax	GST	PST	Allo
5150 Telephone Expense	telephone service	-180.00	GP	-12.60	-14.40	✓

Tax -27.00
Total -207.00

12/29/08 (J75)	Debits	Credits	Division
1050 Bank: Chequing CAD	207.00	-	
2670 GST Paid on Purchases	-	12.60	
5150 Telephone Expense	-	194.40	
- Service Division			-155.52
- Sales Division			-38.88
	207.00	207.00	

PAYROLL REMITTANCES

Simply Accounting - Confirmation

Adjustment amounts will adjust the amount owing for remittances and create a transaction that will affect the account balances in linked payroll accounts.

If your payroll accounts prior to this adjustment already have the correct balances, you will need to reverse the transaction created by the adjustment by making a miscellaneous transaction (general journal) entry.

Do you want to continue?

Yes No

OTHER PAYMENTS

The only change you must make is that positive amounts in the original entry become negative amounts in the reversing entry (place a minus sign before the amount in the Amount field).

Similarly, negative amounts, such as for GST Paid in GST remittances, must be changed to positive amounts (remove the minus sign).

Use the same accounts and amounts in the reversing entry as in the original entry. Tax amounts change automatically.

Repeat the allocation with the original percentages.

If you have invoice lookup turned on, you can use the Adjust Invoice option instead (page 140).

PAYROLL REMITTANCES

Payroll remittance entries cannot be reversed. You must make corrections in the Adjustments column of the Remittance Journal if incorrect amounts were remitted. When you enter an amount in the Adjustments column, the program warns you with the message shown here.

Positive remittance adjustment amounts create expense account entries – they do not affect the payable amounts in the ledger. You must make additional General Journal adjusting entries so that the final ledger amounts are correct.

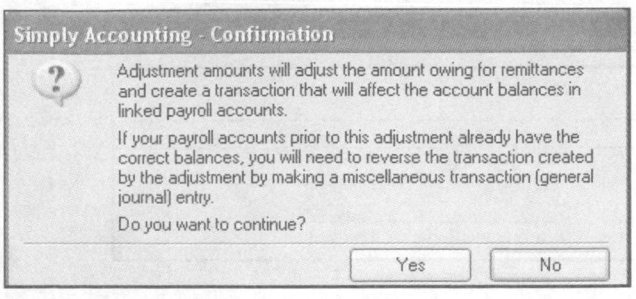

PAYMENTS

Click the Include Fully Paid Invoices tool button.

The only change you must make is that positive amounts in the original entry become negative amounts in the reversing entry.

In the Payment Amt. field, click the invoice line for the payment being reversed.

Type a minus sign and the amount.

If a discount was taken, type the discount amount with a minus sign in the Disc. Taken field.

This will restore the original balance owing for the invoice. Refer to page 181.

If you have already cleared the paid invoice, prepare a new Purchases Journal entry for the amount of the payment (non-taxable) to restore the balance owing. Enter a positive amount in the Amount field for the amount of the cheque and the Bank account in the Account field. On the next line, enter the discount amount (positive) with the Purchase Discounts account in the Account field. This will debit the Bank and Purchase Discounts accounts and credit Accounts Payable.

You can also use the Adjust Payment tool. (See page 145.)

CREDIT CARD PAYMENTS

Enter the same amounts as in the original entry.

Add a minus sign to the Additional Fees And Interest amount and to the Payment Amount in the reversing entry.

PAYMENTS: Original Entry

Invoice/Pre-pmt.	Original Amt.	Amt. Owing	Disc. Available	Disc. Taken	Payment Amt.
MT-1894	856.00	856.00	17.12	17.12	838.88
				Total	838.88

12/29/08 (J76)	Debits	Credits	Division
2200 Accounts Payable	856.00	-	
1050 Bank: Chequing CAD	-	838.88	
5130 Purchase Discounts	-	17.12	
	856.00	856.00	

Reversing Entry

Invoice/Pre-pmt.	Original Amt.	Amt. Owing	Disc. Available	Disc. Taken	Payment Amt.
MT-1521	811.06	0.00	0.00		
MT-1894	856.00	0.00	0.00	-17.12	-838.88
				Total	-838.88

12/31/08 (J77)	Debits	Credits	Division
1050 Bank: Chequing CAD	838.88	-	
5130 Purchase Discounts	17.12	-	
2200 Accounts Payable	-	856.00	
	856.00	856.00	

CREDIT CARD PAYMENTS: Original Entry

Credit Card Payable Account Balance:	1,107.45
Additional Fees and Interest:	120.00
Payment Amount:	1,120.00

12/23/08 (J79)	Debits	Credits	Division
2250 Credit Card Payable	1,000.00	-	
5040 Credit Card Fees	120.00	-	
1050 Bank: Chequing CAD	-	1,120.00	
	1,120.00	1,120.00	

Reversing Entry

Credit Card Payable Account Balance:	107.45
Additional Fees and Interest:	-120.00
Payment Amount:	-1,120.00

12/24/08 (J80)	Debits	Credits	Division
1050 Bank: Chequing CAD	1,120.00	-	
2250 Credit Card Payable	-	1,000.00	
5040 Credit Card Fees	-	120.00	
	1,120.00	1,120.00	

INVENTORY PURCHASES: Original Entry

Item	Quantity	Order	B/O	Unit	Description	Price	Tax	GST	PST	Amount	Acct	Allo
WN01	4			dozen	Chrome Wheel Nuts	48.00	G	13.44		192.00	1380	
WN03	4			dozen	Nickel/Chrome Wheel Nuts	57.00	G	15.96		228.00	1380	

☑ Invoice Received

Freight G 1.40 20.00 ✓

GST 30.80

PST 0.00

Terms: 2.00 % 10 Days, Net 30 Days

Total 470.80

12/24/08 (J81)	Debits	Credits	Division
1380 Wheel Nuts & Locks	420.00	-	
2670 GST Paid on Purchases	30.80	-	
5065 Freight Expense	20.00	-	
- Sales Division			20.00
2200 Accounts Payable	-	470.80	
	470.80	470.80	

Reversing Entry

Item	Quantity	Order	B/O	Unit	Description	Price	Tax	GST	PST	Amount	Acct	Allo
WN01	-4			dozen	Chrome Wheel Nuts	48.00	G	-13.44		-192.00	1380	
WN	-4			zen	Nickel/Chrome Wheel Nuts	57.00	G	-15.96		-228.00	1380	

☑ Invoice Received

Freight G -1.40 -20.00 ✓

GST -30.80

PST 0.00

Terms: 2.00 % 10 Days, Net 30 Days

Total -470.80

12/27/08 (J82)	Debits	Credits	Division
2200 Accounts Payable	470.80	-	
1380 Wheel Nuts & Locks	-	420.00	
2670 GST Paid on Purchases	-	30.80	
5065 Freight Expense	-	20.00	
- Sales Division			-20.00
	470.80	470.80	

SALES JOURNAL (INVENTORY AND NON-INVENTORY): Original Entry

Item	Quantity	Order	B/O	Unit	Description	Price	Amount	Tax	Acct	Allo
T105	8			Each	P185/70R15 Tires	105.00	840.00	GP	4020 Rever	✓
					repairs		240.00	GP	4040 Rever	✓

Comments

Freight 40.00 G ✓

GST 78.40

PST 86.40

Terms: 2.00 % 10 Days, Net 30 Days

Total 1,284.80

12/27/08 (J83)	Debits	Credits	Division
1200 Accounts Receivable	1,284.80	-	
5050 Cost of Goods Sold	336.00	-	
- Sales Division			336.00
1400 Winter Tires	-	336.00	
2640 PST Payable	-	86.40	
2650 GST Charged on Sales	-	78.40	
4020 Revenue from Sales	-	840.00	
- Sales Division			840.00
4040 Revenue from Services	-	240.00	
- Service Division			240.00
4180 Freight Revenue	-	40.00	
- Sales Division			40.00
	1,620.80	1,620.80	

INVENTORY PURCHASES

Change positive quantities in the original entry to negative ones in the reversing entry (place a minus sign before the quantity in the Quantity field).

Similarly, change negative quantities, such as for returns, to positive ones (remove the minus sign).

Add a minus sign to the freight amount if freight is charged.

Use the same accounts and amounts in the reversing entry as in the original entry. Tax amounts are corrected automatically.

Repeat the allocation using the original percentages.

If you have invoice lookup turned on, you can use the Adjust Invoice option instead (page 138).

Remember to "pay" the incorrect and reversing invoices to remove them from the Payments Journal and later clear them.

SALES JOURNAL

For inventory sales, change positive quantities in the original entry to negative ones in the reversing entry (place a minus sign before the quantity in the Quantity field). Similarly, change negative quantities, such as for returns, to positive ones (remove the minus sign).

For non-inventory sales, change positive amounts in the original entry to negative amounts in the reversing entry (place a minus sign before the amount in the Amount column).

Add a minus sign to the freight amount if freight is charged. Add the salesperson.

Use the same accounts and amounts in the reversing entry as in the original entry.

Repeat the allocation using the original percentages.

If invoice lookup is turned on, you can use the Adjust Invoice option instead (page 185).

Remember to "pay" the incorrect and reversing invoices to remove them from the Receipts Journal and later clear them.

Reversing Entry

Item	Quantity	Order	B/O	Unit	Description	Price	Amount	Tax	Acct	Allo
T105	-8			Each	P185/70R15 Tires	105.00	-840.00	GP	4020 Rever	✓
					repairs		-240.00	P	4040 Re	✓

Comments			
	Freight	-40.00 G	✓
	GST	-78.40	
	PST	-86.40	
Terms: 2.00 % 10 Days, Net 30 Days	Total	-1,284.80	

12/28/08 (J84)	Debits	Credits	Division
1400 Winter Tires	336.00	-	
2640 PST Payable	86.40	-	
2650 GST Charged on Sales	78.40	-	
4020 Revenue from Sales	840.00	-	
- Sales Division			-840.00
4040 Revenue from Services	240.00	-	
- Service Division			-240.00
4180 Freight Revenue	40.00	-	
- Sales Division			-40.00
1200 Accounts Receivable	-	1,284.80	
5050 Cost of Goods Sold	-	336.00	
- Sales Division			-336.00
	1,620.80	1,620.80	

DEPOSITS
You cannot enter a negative amount in the Deposit field so you must "pay" the deposit.

Click the Payment Amount field for the Deposit line and press ⌨ tab. Deposit amounts are shown in red under the heading Deposits.

DEPOSITS or PREPAYMENTS: Original Entry

Invoice/Deposit	Original Amt.	Amt. Owing	Disc. Available	Disc. Taken	Payment Amt.
138-A	5,865.00	4,845.00	0.00		

Deposit Reference No. 14	Deposit Amount	1,100.00
	Total	1,100.00

12/27/08 (J85)	Debits	Credits	Division
1050 Bank: Chequing CAD	1,100.00	-	
2150 Prepaid Sales and Deposits	-	1,100.00	
	1,100.00	1,100.00	

Reversing Entry

Invoice/Deposit	Original Amt.	Amt. Owing	Disc. Available	Disc. Taken	Payment Amt.
138-A	5,865.00	4,845.00	0.00		
Deposits 14	1,100.00	1,100.00			1,100.00

Deposit Reference No. REV-Dep14	Deposit Amount	0.00
	Total	-1,100.00

12/27/08 (J86)	Debits	Credits	Division
2150 Prepaid Sales and Deposits	1,100.00	-	
1050 Bank: Chequing CAD	-	1,100.00	
	1,100.00	1,100.00	

NOTES
When you post the transaction, you will be asked to confirm that you want to make the payment to the customer.

Click Yes to continue.

Simply Accounting - Confirmation

? The total of the deposits being used is more than the total of the invoices being paid. This means that you are about to give the difference back to the customer in cash. Do you want to continue?

Yes No

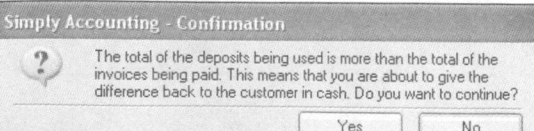

RECEIPTS WITH DEPOSITS: Original Entry

Invoice/Deposit	Original Amt.	Amt. Owing	Disc. Available	Disc. Taken	Payment Amt.
138-A	5,865.00	4,845.00	117.30	117.30	4,727.70
Deposits					
15	1,100.00	1,100.00			1,100.00

Deposit Reference No. 16 — Deposit Amount 0.00 — Total 3,627.70

12/22/08 (J88)	Debits	Credits	Division
1050 Bank: Chequing CAD	3,627.70	-	
2150 Prepaid Sales and Deposits	1,100.00	-	
4150 Sales Discounts	117.30	-	
1200 Accounts Receivable	-	4,845.00	
	4,845.00	4,845.00	

Reversing Entry

Invoice/Deposit	Original Amt.	Amt. Owing	Disc. Available	Disc. Taken	Payment Amt.
116	1,380.00	0.00	0.00		
138-A	5,865.00	0.00	0.00	-117.30	-4,727.70
Deposits					
14	1,100.00	0.00			-1,100.00

Deposit Reference No. 16 — Deposit Amount 0.00 — Total -3,627.70

12/22/08 (J89)	Debits	Credits	Division
1200 Accounts Receivable	4,845.00	-	
1050 Bank: Chequing CAD	-	3,627.70	
2150 Prepaid Sales and Deposits	-	1,100.00	
4150 Sales Discounts	-	117.30	
	4,845.00	4,845.00	

PAYROLL JOURNAL: Original Entry

Income | Deductions | Taxes | User-Defined Expenses | Entitlements — Period Ending Jun 30, 2008

Earnings:

Name	Hours	Pieces	Amount	YTD
Regular	80.00	--	1,280.00	17,920.00
Overtime 1	4.00	--	96.00	672.00
No. Clients	--	10.00	100.00	360.00
Bonus	--	--	100.00	350.00
Tuition	--	--	0.00	--
Total	84.00	10.00	1,576.00	

Other:

Name	Amount	YTD
Advance	100.00	150.00
Benefits	5.00	70.00
Vac. Accrued	88.56	104.16
Vac. Paid	0.00	1,232.96
Travel Exp.	100.00	100.00
Total	293.56	

Gross Pay 1,581.00 Withheld -463.32 Net Pay 1,312.68 Post

Income | Deductions | Taxes | User-Defined Expenses | Entitlements

Deductions:

Name	Amount	YTD
RRSP	50.00	700.00
CSB Plan	50.00	700.00

Income | Deductions | Taxes | User-Defined Expenses | Entitlements

EI	29.47	QPIP
CPP/QPP	71.60	
Tax	262.25	
Prov. Tax		

Income | Deductions | Taxes | User-Defined Expenses | Entitlements

	Amount per pay period
Gp Insurance	5.00
Donations	

Income | Deductions | Taxes | User-Defined Expenses | Entitlements

The number of hours worked in this pay period: 80.00

	Days Earned	Days Released
Vacation		
Sick Leave	0.50	1.00
PersonalDays		

RECEIPTS

Click the Include Fully Paid Invoices tool.

Change positive amounts in the original entry to negative amounts in the reversing entry.

In the Payment Amt. field, click the invoice or deposit line for the payment being reversed.

Type a minus sign and the amount for invoices and deposits.

If a discount was taken, type the discount amount with a minus sign in the Disc. Taken field.

This will restore the original balance owing for the invoice. Refer to page 181.

If you have already cleared the invoice, make a new Sales Journal entry for the payment amount (non-taxable) to restore the balance owing. Enter both the cheque and discount amounts as positive amounts to credit Bank and Sales Discounts.

You can also use the Adjust Receipt tool (see page 183).

PAYROLL JOURNAL

Redo the original incorrect entry but DO NOT POST IT!

Click the Enter Taxes Manually tool to open all the deduction fields for editing.

Type a minus sign in front of the number of hours (regular and overtime) or in front of the Salary and Commission amounts. Press tab to update the amounts, including vacation pay (i.e., change them to negative amounts).

For the Advance field, change the sign for the amount. Advances should have a minus sign in the reversing entry and advances recovered should be positive amounts.

Click the Deductions tab and edit each deduction amount by typing a minus sign in front of it. ▶

PAYROLL JOURNAL CONTINUED

▶ Click the Taxes tab. Check the amounts for CPP, EI and Tax with the original journal entry because these amounts may be incorrect (the employee may have reached the maximum contribution since the original entry, or may have entered a different tax bracket). Change the amounts to match the original entry if necessary. The Employee Detail Report will provide the amounts entered for each paycheque.

Click the User-Defined Expenses tab. Change the original positive amounts to negative by adding a minus sign.

Click the Entitlements tab. You cannot enter a negative number for days released so you must edit the number of days earned. Click the number in the Days Earned field for the entitlements taken. Add back the number of days released from the original entry. For example, change 0.5 to 1.5 if 1 day was taken.

Repeat the allocation with the original percentages.

Remember to click the Calculate Taxes Automatically button before you make the correct payroll entry.

The year-to-date balances will be restored.

You can use the Adjust Cheque option instead to reverse and correct the Payroll Journal entry (see page 368).

06/30/08 (J143)	Debits	Credits	Project
1220 Advances Receivable	100.00	-	
5300 Wages	1,464.56	-	
5310 Commissions & Bonuses	200.00	-	
5320 Travel Expenses	100.00	-	
5330 EI Expense	41.26	-	
5340 CPP Expense	71.60	-	
5350 WSIB Expense	20.39	-	
5360 EHT Expense	15.49	-	
5370 Gp Insurance Expense	5.00	-	
1060 Bank: Hamilton Trust Chequing	-	1,312.68	
2300 Vacation Payable	-	88.56	
2310 EI Payable	-	70.73	
2320 CPP Payable	-	143.20	
2330 Income Tax Payable	-	262.25	
2380 EHT Payable	-	15.49	
2400 RRSP Payable	-	50.00	
2410 CSB Plan Payable	-	50.00	
2420 Gp Insurance Payable	-	5.00	
2460 WSIB Payable	-	20.39	
	2,018.30	2,018.30	

Reversing Entry

Income | Deductions | Taxes | User-Defined Expenses | Entitlements — Period Ending: Jun 30, 2008

Earnings:

Name	Hours	Pieces	Amount	YTD
Regular	-80.00	--	-1,280.00	15,360.00
Overtime 1	-4.00	--	-96.00	480.00
No. Clients	--	-10.00	-100.00	160.00
Bonus	--	--	-100.00	150.00
Tuition	--	--	0.00	--
Total	-84.00	-10.00	-1,576.00	

Other:

Name	Amount	YTD
Advance	-100.00	50.00
Benefits	-5.00	65.00
Vac. Accrued	-88.56	15.60
Vac. Paid	0.00	1,232.96
Travel Exp.	-100.00	--
Total	-293.56	

Gross Pay -1,581.00 Withheld 463.32 Net Pay -1,312.68 Post

Income | Deductions | Taxes | User-Defined Expenses | Entitlements

Deductions:

Name	Amount	YTD
RRSP	-50.00	600.00
CSB Plan	-50.00	600.00

Income | Deductions | Taxes | User-Defined Expenses | Entitlements

EI	-29.47	QPIP
CPP/QPP	-71.60	
Tax	-262.25	
Prov. Tax		

Income | Deductions | Taxes | User-Defined Expenses | Entitlements

	Amount per pay period
Gp Insurance	-5.00
Donations	

Income | Deductions | Taxes | User-Defined Expenses | Entitlements

The number of hours worked in this pay period: -80.00

	Days Earned	Days Released
Vacation		
Sick Leave	1.00	
PersonalDays		

06/30/08 (J150)	Debits	Credits	Project
1060 Bank: Hamilton Trust Chequing	1,312.68	-	
2300 Vacation Payable	88.56	-	
2310 EI Payable	70.73	-	
2320 CPP Payable	143.20	-	
2330 Income Tax Payable	262.25	-	
2380 EHT Payable	15.49	-	
2400 RRSP Payable	50.00	-	
2410 CSB Plan Payable	50.00	-	
2420 Gp Insurance Payable	5.00	-	
2460 WSIB Payable	20.39	-	
1220 Advances Receivable	-	100.00	
5300 Wages	-	1,464.56	
5310 Commissions & Bonuses	-	200.00	
5320 Travel Expenses	-	100.00	
5330 EI Expense	-	41.26	
5340 CPP Expense	-	71.60	
5350 WSIB Expense	-	20.39	
5360 EHT Expense	-	15.49	
5370 Gp Insurance Expense	-	5.00	
	2,018.30	2,018.30	

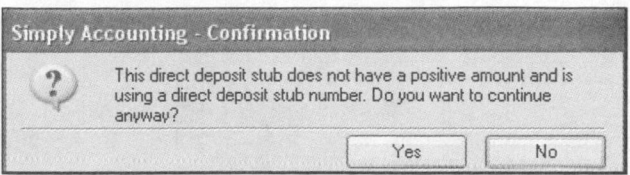

Simply Accounting - Confirmation

This direct deposit stub does not have a positive amount and is using a direct deposit stub number. Do you want to continue anyway?

Yes | No

NOTES

When you are reversing a direct deposit entry, you must confirm that a negative amount is entered as the net deposit.

Click Yes to continue.

ITEM ASSEMBLY JOURNAL: Original Entry

Assembly Components

Item	Qty	Unit	Description	Unit Cost	Amount
T105	8	Each	P185/70R15 Tires	40.00	320.00
W106	8	Each	Chrome-Steel R15 Wheels	35.00	280.00
WN03	2	pkg	Nickel/Chrome Wheel Nuts	5.00	10.00

Additional Costs 100.00

Total 710.00

Assembled Items

Item	Qty	Unit	Description	Unit Cost	Amount
LC1	2	contract	Lovely U Inventory	355.00	710.00

Total 710.00

12/28/08 (J89)	Debits	Credits	Division
1440 Reserved Inventory for Workorders	710.00	-	
1360 Wheels	-	280.00	
1380 Wheel Nuts & Locks	-	10.00	
1400 Winter Tires	-	320.00	
5045 Assembly Costs	-	100.00	
	710.00	710.00	

ITEM ASSEMBLY JOURNAL

Re-enter the assembly as you did originally.

Type a minus sign in front of each quantity in the Qty field in both the Assembly Components and Assembled Items sections.

Also type a minus sign in front of the amount for Additional Costs.

Reversing Entry

Assembly Components

Item	Qty	Unit	Description	Unit Cost	Amount
T105	-8	Each	P185/70R15 Tires	40.00	-320.00
W106	-8	Each	Chrome-Steel R15 Wheels	35.00	-280.00
WN03	-2	pkg	Nickel/Chrome Wheel Nuts	5.00	-10.00

Additional Costs -100.00

Total -710.00

Assembled Items

Item	Qty	Unit	Description	Unit Cost	Amount
LC1	-2	contract	Lovely U Inventory	355.00	-710.00

Total -710.00

12/28/08 (J90)	Debits	Credits	Division
1360 Wheels	280.00	-	
1380 Wheel Nuts & Locks	10.00	-	
1400 Winter Tires	320.00	-	
5045 Assembly Costs	100.00	-	
1440 Reserved Inventory for Workorders	-	710.00	
	710.00	710.00	

BILL OF MATERIALS JOURNAL

Change the sign for the quantity in the Quantity To Build field (positive to negative or negative to positive).

Notice that the journal entries are exactly the same as those for the Item Assembly Journal transactions.

BILL OF MATERIALS JOURNAL: Original Entry

Items to Build

Item	Unit	Description	Quantity to build
PM1	contract	Reserved Inventory	2

12/29/08 (J91)	Debits	Credits	Division
1440 Reserved Inventory for Workorders	1,076.00	-	
1360 Wheels	-	576.00	
1380 Wheel Nuts & Locks	-	8.00	
1400 Winter Tires	-	272.00	
5045 Assembly Costs	-	220.00	
	1,076.00	1,076.00	

Reversing Entry

Items to Build

Item	Unit	Description	Quantity to build
PM1	contract	Reserved Inventory	-2

12/29/08 (J92)	Debits	Credits	Division
1360 Wheels	576.00	-	
1380 Wheel Nuts & Locks	8.00	-	
1400 Winter Tires	272.00	-	
5045 Assembly Costs	220.00	-	
1440 Reserved Inventory for Workorders	-	1,076.00	
	1,076.00	1,076.00	

ADJUSTMENTS JOURNAL

Change the sign for the quantity in the Qty field (positive to negative or negative to positive).

Repeat the allocation using the original percentages.

ADJUSTMENTS JOURNAL: Original Entry

Item	Qty	Unit	Description	Unit Cost	Amount	Acct	Allo
T105	-2	Each	P185/70R15 Tires	41.00	-82.00	5100 Invent	✓
				Total	-82.00		

12/30/08 (J93)	Debits	Credits	Division
5100 Inventory Losses	82.00	-	
- Sales Division			82.00
1400 Winter Tires	-	82.00	
	82.00	82.00	

Reversing Entry

Item	Qty	Unit	Description	Unit Cost	Amount	Acct	Allo
T105	2	Each	P185/70R15 Tires	41.00	82.00	5100 Invent	✓
				Total	82.00		

12/30/08 (J94)	Debits	Credits	Division
1400 Winter Tires	82.00	-	
5100 Inventory Losses	-	82.00	
- Sales Division			-82.00
	82.00	82.00	

APPENDIX D

Working in Multi-user Mode

WORKING IN MULTI-USER MODE

The Pro version is available in multi- and single-user versions. The Student Pro and Basic versions are both single-user versions of the program.

In multi-user mode, several people can access and work with a data file at the same time. Some features and functions are not available in multi-user mode. These restrictions are described in the text whenever they apply. Access to some aspects of the program may be restricted to the system administrator (sysadmin).

Accessing Data Files

The Pro version allows several users to access the data files at the same time, with or without passwords. When no users and passwords are set up for a data file, access to the file is the same for multi- and single-user mode. The data file opens in single-user mode. Once the data file is open, you can switch to multi-user mode from the File menu.

If you try to open a data file that is currently used by another user in single-user mode, you will see the following error message:

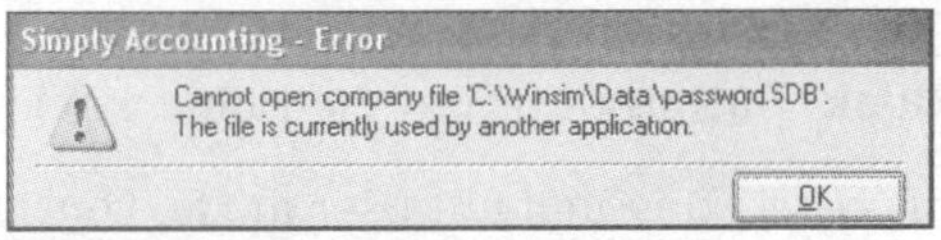

Click **OK** to close the message.

Only one person at a time can work with a data file in single-user mode so you must switch the status of the open file to multi-user.

Choose the **File menu** and **click Switch To Multi-User Mode**.

If you have not entered users, the Add Users wizard will begin (see the instructions in Appendix G, page A-75 on the Student CD-ROM). Otherwise, you will see the following warning:

WARNING! Be sure to finish working with the open journals and ledgers before closing all the open windows.

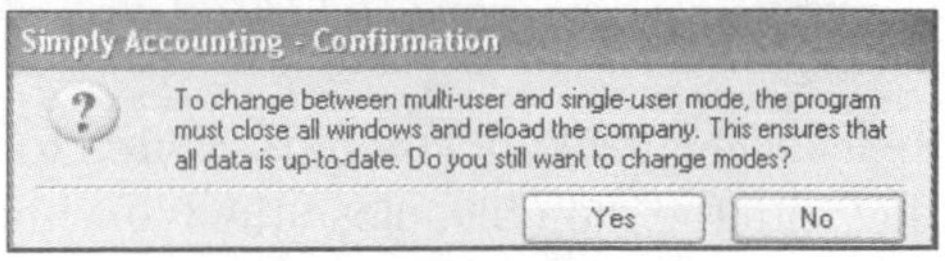

Click **Yes** to proceed.

No changes are apparent in the Home window, but some menu options are dimmed because they are not available in multi-user mode. All Refresh tools in the ledger and journal windows will be available and no longer dimmed.

If users and passwords have been set up for the program, you will see the following screen when you open the data file:

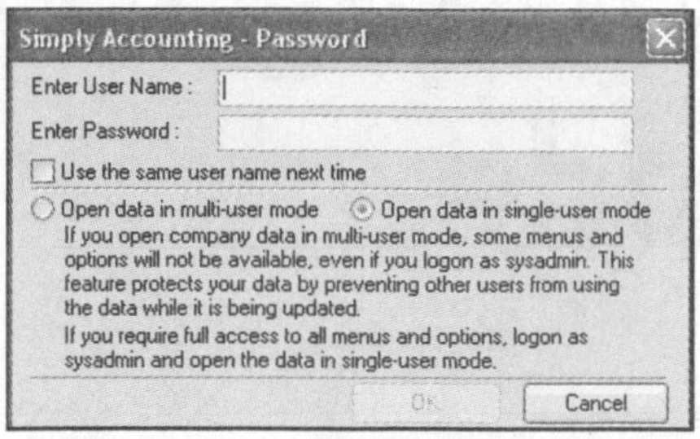

Enter your user name and password; choose whether you want to work in single-user or multi-user mode and then click OK. Passwords are case-sensitive. That is, you must type the password in upper- or lower-case letters, exactly as the password was created initially. For more information on passwords, refer to Appendix G on the Student CD-ROM.

If another user is already working with the data file when you try to access it in single-user mode, you will see the following warning:

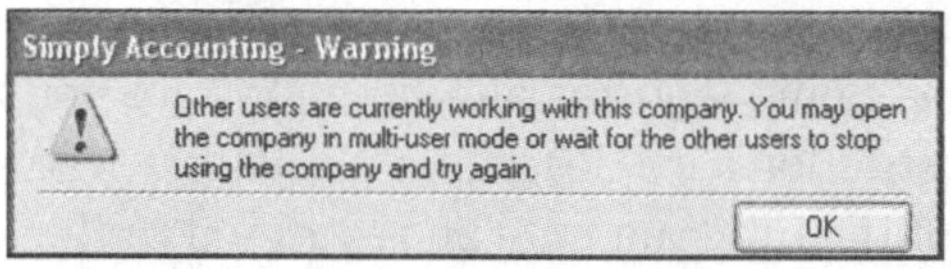

You must open the data file in multi-user mode, wait until the other users have finished or, if only one person is using the file, switch that user's file to single-user mode.

Click **OK** to return to the Select Company window.

To switch to single-user mode at any time:

Choose the **File menu** and **click Switch To Single-User Mode**.

If other users are currently using the file, you will see the following warning:

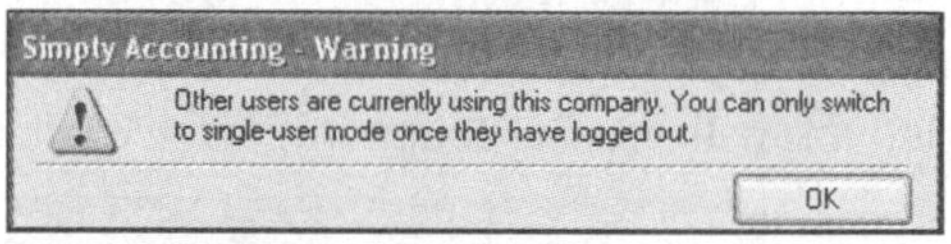

Click **OK** to return to the Home window.

If you are working in multi-user mode, your user name and "Multi-user" will appear in the status bar as shown:

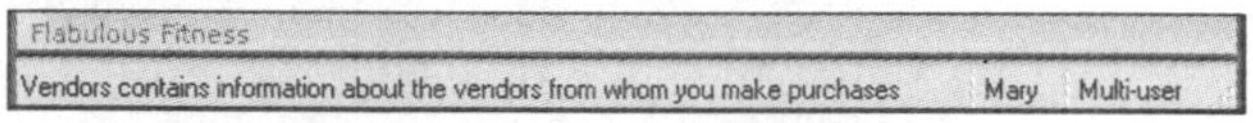

When you close a data file in multi-user mode, you will see the following closing message about backups:

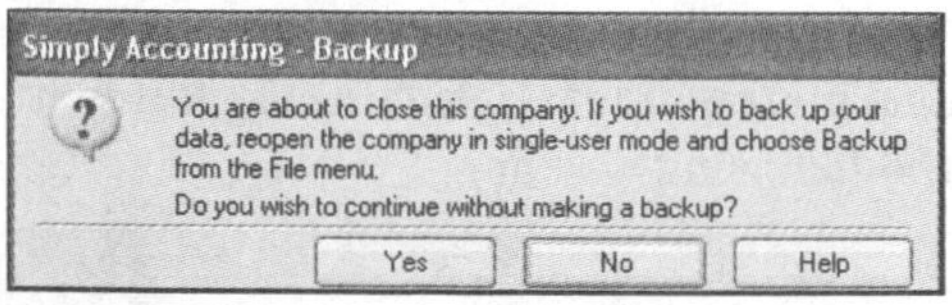

Before making a backup, you must switch to single-user mode. If other users are still working with the data file, close the file without making a backup.

Click **Yes** to close the file.

Refreshing Data in Multi-User Mode

In multi-user mode, different users can work with and modify the same data file at the same time. Therefore, the program allows you to automatically refresh the data set with changes made by other users or to refresh the data set only when the Refresh option is selected. All ledger, journal and report windows include Refresh tools that allow you to update the data periodically. If you want the program to update the data continually, you can change this preference setting for individual users.

Choose the **File menu**, then **choose User Preferences** and **click Settings**:

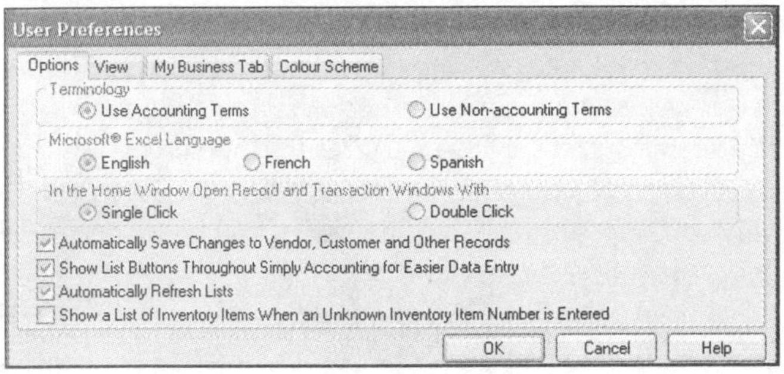

NOTES
The Automatically Refresh Lists setting does not apply to all users. It is set by individual users.

Click **Automatically Refresh Lists** and **click OK** to save the change.

Refresh Tools

All journals have the **Refresh Lists** tool in the tool bar. This tool applies to the multi-user mode — different users use, access and modify the company data files simultaneously. Clicking the Refresh Lists tool ensures that you use the most recent version of the data set — the one that exists after all changes from all users have been applied.

All report windows include the **Refresh Report** tool icon. In multi-user mode, the journal entry number is omitted from the journal display (different users may be creating journal entries at the same time so the number is not known for certain until after posting).

The **Refresh Invoices** tool in the Payments and Receipts journals ensures that the list of outstanding invoices for a vendor or customer is the current one, after applying the changes made by other users.

The **Refresh Data** tool in the icon windows looks the same as the Refresh Report icon and serves the same purpose, updating accounts (vendors, customers, employees or inventory) with changes made by other users. It appears just before the Select A Report tool in all ledger icon windows. The icon is dimmed in single-user mode and when you are creating a new ledger record.

In ledger windows, the **Refresh Record tool** updates the ledger record with changes made by other users. The tool is located on the Select account line in the ledger and looks the same as the Refresh Report tool.

INDEX

PAGES A33–A110 ON STUDENT CD-ROM

A33–A62 in Appendix E
A63–A68 in Appendix F
A69–A78 in Appendix G
A79–A92 in Appendix H
A93–A98 in Appendix I
A99–A110 in Appendix J

PAGES A33–A110 ON STUDENT CD-ROM
A33–A62 in Appendix E
A63–A68 in Appendix F
A69–A78 in Appendix G
A79–A92 in Appendix H
A93–A98 in Appendix I
A99–A110 in Appendix J

PAGES A33–A110 ON STUDENT CD-ROM
A33–A62 in Appendix E
A63–A68 in Appendix F
A69–A78 in Appendix G
A79–A92 in Appendix H
A93–A98 in Appendix I
A99–A110 in Appendix J

PAGES A33–A110 ON STUDENT CD-ROM
A33–A62 in Appendix E
A63–A68 in Appendix F
A69–A78 in Appendix G
A79–A92 in Appendix H
A93–A98 in Appendix I
A99–A110 in Appendix J

PAGES A33–A110 ON STUDENT CD-ROM

A33–A62 in Appendix E
A63–A68 in Appendix F
A69–A78 in Appendix G
A79–A92 in Appendix H
A93–A98 in Appendix I
A99–A110 in Appendix J

PAGES A33–A110 ON STUDENT CD-ROM
A33–A62 in Appendix E
A63–A68 in Appendix F
A69–A78 in Appendix G
A79–A92 in Appendix H
A93–A98 in Appendix I
A99–A110 in Appendix J

PAGES A33–A110 ON STUDENT CD-ROM
A33–A62 in Appendix E
A63–A68 in Appendix F
A69–A78 in Appendix G
A79–A92 in Appendix H
A93–A98 in Appendix I
A99–A110 in Appendix J

"AS IS" LICENCE AGREEMENT AND LIMITED WARRANTY